The Blackwell Encyclopedia of Sociology

Volume II

C

Edited by

George Ritzer

Blackwell
Publishing

BLACKWELL PUBLISHING
350 Main Street, Malden, MA 02148-5020, USA
9600 Garsington Road, Oxford OX4 2DQ, UK
550 Swanston Street, Carlton, Victoria 3053, Australia

First published 2007 by Blackwell Publishing Ltd

1   2007

Library of Congress Cataloging-in-Publication Data

Blackwell encyclopedia of sociology, the / edited by George Ritzer.
    p. cm.
Includes bibliographical references and index.
ISBN 1-4051-2433-4 (hardback : alk. paper) 1. Sociology—Encyclopedias. I. Ritzer, George.

HM425.B53 2007
301.03—dc22

                                                    2006004167

ISBN-13: 978-1-4051-2433-1 (hardback : alk. paper)

A catalogue record for this title is available from the British Library.

Set in 9.5/11pt Ehrhardt
by Spi Publisher Services, Pondicherry, India
Printed in Singapore
by COS Printers Pte Ltd

For further information on
Blackwell Publishing, visit our website:
www.blackwellpublishing.com

Contents

capital: economic, cultural, and social

Paul M. de Graaf

The distinction between economic, cultural, and social capital has proven to be useful to explain the way in which parents pass their status on to their children, and to explain why there is individual variation in the status attainment process. One of the core questions in the sociology of social stratification is how status is attained within a given society, and how the determinants of status attainment vary over historical periods and over societies. An important part of the status attainment model, as developed by Blau and Duncan (1967), consists of the effects the family of origin have on offspring status. The key notion of the working of the different types of capital is that educational attainment, occupational achievement, and income attainment are affected by the resources an individual has at his or her disposal. Note that many sociologists in the field of social stratification do not use the word *capital*, but refer to economic, cultural, and social *resources*. Whereas the distinction between economic, cultural, and social resources has been developed to explain the effects of the family of origin on educational and occupational attainment, it has proven to be fruitful in other realms of the status attainment process as well.

Economic resources refer to an individual's income and wealth. In the status attainment process an individual can take advantage of the economic resources of his or her parents. An individual's financial or material position is important both with respect to intergenerational transfers and with respect to career advancement. In the first place, economic resources play an important role in the process of educational attainment, especially when the cost of education is high. Second, the intergenerational transmission of occupational status can be directly governed by a family's economic resources, especially by the transmission of the ownership of a business and by financial support. Third, intragenerational (career) mobility can be facilitated by the economic resources to which an individual has access.

The term cultural capital comes from Bourdieu (1973). Cultural capital, or cultural resources, refers to cultural distinctions between status groups, which are based on differences in education, occupation, and wealth. Children of the higher-status groups have access to cultural capital, which consists of appropriate manners, good taste, proper use of language, and respect for formal culture. Through family socialization the values of the formal culture and receptivity to the beaux arts (classical music, theater, painting, sculpture, and literature) are inculcated. This receptivity is taken for granted in the higher forms of secondary education and in tertiary education (DiMaggio 1982). Bourdieu's theory of cultural reproduction was formulated to explain the relationship between parents' social position and their offspring's educational attainment. The theory of cultural reproduction argues that pupils who are familiar with formal culture are favored and profit more from education than other children. It is possible to elaborate on the value of cultural capital by arguing that it does not only affect educational careers, but is also productive in the labor market, especially to be selected in high-prestige professions.

Social capital refers to the resources one has access to through one's network: family members, neighbors, friends, acquaintances, and colleagues (Lin 1982). It is important to note that the size of the network itself is not decisive. Social capital is dependent on (1) the amount of resources available in the network, and (2) the willingness of the network member to share these resources. In other words, social capital is a combination of the number of people who can be expected to provide support and the resources those people have at their disposal. The resources available through the network consist of the members' economic, cultural, and social resources. The mechanism behind the impact of social capital is in the fact that an individual's social network can lead to direct support and access to information. Social capital has proven to be a major predictor in educational and (especially) occupational careers. Social capital can be received from one's parents, but most of it is built up during one's career and by the association with other people, such as in voluntary organizations or in one's neighborhood, or via friends and acquaintances.

The value of economic, cultural, and social capital may vary between societies and over historical periods. Bourdieu's main hypothesis is that cultural capital has replaced economic capital as the main type of parental resource which explains the intergenerational transmission of educational opportunities (Bourdieu 1973; de Graaf 1986). There are several reasons why parental financial resources do not matter much in modern society. First, the direct costs of education have decreased considerably, especially in the European welfare states. Compulsory education is almost free of cost, and tertiary education is inexpensive. Second, the indirect (opportunity) costs of education, like forgone income and extended financial dependency on parents, have decreased as well, especially because the rising returns of education have made the investment worthwhile. Third, due the great increase in affluence during the second half of the twentieth century, the costs of education have become much easier to bear. Fourth, decreasing fertility adds to the declining importance of financial resources in the parental home. Functionalist approaches to social inequality argue that talent has become the main determinant of educational attainment, and that a system of meritocracy has become prevalent. Since talent (intelligence)

is partly hereditary, some reproduction of inequality from one generation to the next is unavoidable. However, conflict sociology (Collins 1971; Bourdieu 1973) argues that privileged parents have found a new way to secure their offspring's social position by using their cultural capital. The basic mechanism behind this is that the children of parents with high levels of cultural capital do not object to extending their educational careers, whereas children of lower classes prefer to leave education at younger ages. It is important to note however that this strategy has not been overall a successful one, given that empirical evidence has shown that the association between social origins and educational attainment has decreased in western society. Apparently, the total impact of all parental resources combined has decreased.

SEE ALSO: Bourdieu, Pierre; Cultural Capital; Cultural Capital in Schools; Distinction; Educational and Occupational Attainment; Life Chances and Resources; Stratification, Distinction and; Stratification: Functional and Conflict Theories

REFERENCES AND SUGGESTED READINGS

Blau, P. M. & Duncan, O. D. (1967) *The American Occupational Structure*. Wiley, New York.
Bourdieu, P. (1973) Cultural Reproduction and Social Reproduction. In: Brown, R. (Ed.), *Knowledge, Education and Cultural Changes*. Tavistock, London, pp. 71–112.
Collins, R. (1971) Functional and Conflict Theories of Educational Stratification. *American Sociological Review* 36: 1002–19.
de Graaf, P. M. (1986) The Impact of Financial and Cultural Resources on Educational Attainment in the Netherlands. *Sociology of Education* 59: 237–46.
DiMaggio, P. (1982) Cultural Capital and School Success: The Impact of Status Culture Participation on the Grades of US High School Students. *American Sociological Review* 47: 189–201.
Lin, N. (1982) Social Resources and Instrumental Action. In: Marsden, P. V. & Lin, N. (Eds.), *Social Structure and Network Analysis*. Sage, Beverly Hills, pp. 131–45.

capital punishment

Ray Paternoster

The first recorded execution on American soil was of Captain George Kendall, put to death in 1608 by firing squad. Since that time, there have been more than 15,000 known executions. About one-third of executions in the United States have occurred since 1930. Figure 1 shows the number of executions that have taken place in the US from 1930 until the end of 2003. One important thing to note in this figure is that the frequency with which the death penalty has been used has varied substantially over time. There were between 150 and 200 executions per year in the US during the 1930s, but then there occurred a long-term decline. There were no executions at all during the ten-year period from 1967 to 1977 because state and federal courts were deciding whether the death penalty was constitutional. After 1976 there was a fairly consistent but slow increase in the number of executions up to a peak of 98 executions in 1999. There are two points to keep in mind about this, however. First, although the frequency of the death penalty has increased since 1976, the number of executions is nowhere near what it had been from the 1930s to the 1950s. Second, although the frequency of the use of the death penalty had begun an upward trend in 1976, the peak of this increase occurred in 1999. From 1999 to 2003 there has been another decline in the frequency of executions, with only 65 occurring in 2003.

Another important characteristic of the death penalty is the fact that it has always been a relatively rare criminal sanction. No matter what time period is chosen, the number of executions is a relatively small proportion of the total number of potentially capital crimes. As only one example, in the year 2000 there were approximately 15,000 murders committed in the United States and only 85 executions.

Although not every state has executed someone over the time period 1930–2003, most states did have the death penalty on their books. However, the different states have used capital punishment with varying degrees of regularity. Figure 2 shows the percentage of executions in four regions of the United States during two different time periods. This figure clearly illustrates that the vast majority of executions in the United States have taken place in Southern states. This is true during the period 1930–67, when approximately 60 percent of all executions occurred in Southern states, but is even more true today, when over 80 percent of the executions since 1977 have taken place in Southern states.

One of the things we have learned thus far about the death penalty is that it could have been used far more frequently than it has. Another indication of our complicated attitude about the death penalty is that historically we have tried to impose it in the least painful manner. Before 1930, the most frequent method of carrying out the death penalty was by hanging. Death by hanging was supposed to be a quick and painless death. Unfortunately, hanging someone was not technically easy to do and there were many "botched" executions

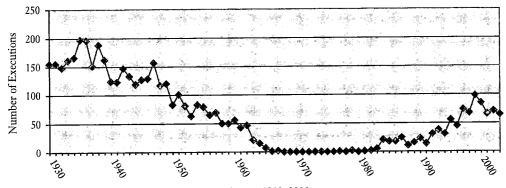

Figure 1   Number of executions in the United States, 1930–2003

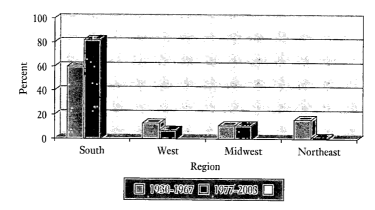

Figure 2   Percentage of executions by region of the United States

where the condemned were slowly choked to death. The frequency of botched hangings encouraged the search for more humane ways to impose the death penalty. Late in the 1800s, New York State devised the electric chair, which promised a quick and painless death through the application of a massive dose of electricity. For most of the period 1930–67 the majority of the executions in the US were carried out by electrocution, while a few states continued with hanging, and others experimented with lethal gas and death by firing squad. Death by electrocution never seemed to fulfill its promise of providing a painless way to put someone to death. In many cases the first surge of electricity did not cause either death or a loss of consciousness and the condemned seemed to experience a great deal of suffering. In other instances flames broke out on the condemned's body during the course of the electrocution. In the late 1970s there was a movement among death penalty states to devise alternatives to the electric chair and the gas chamber. In 1977, Oklahoma became the first state to adopt the use of lethal injection as its method of imposing the death penalty. Other states soon followed and since that time about 80 percent of all executions have been carried out by lethal injection.

There is one final and controversial feature about the death penalty in the United States to be addressed. From the very beginning the claim has been made by critics of the death penalty that capital punishment has been imposed in a racially discriminatory manner. During the period 1930–67 about 90 percent of the executions for rape involved a black offender and the vast majority of these offenses had a white victim. Since then there have been numerous empirical studies of the imposition of the death penalty and the majority of these seem to suggest that non-white offenders who kill white victims are at a substantially higher risk of being sentenced to death. This issue was raised before the United States Supreme Court in the case of *McCleskey* v. *Kemp* in 1987. In that case the Court held that the statistical evidence did not support the conclusion that the state of Georgia acted with intentional discrimination in its administration of the death penalty. It left open the possibility, however, that evidence of racial discrimination could more successfully be presented before state legislatures. What is clear is that the death penalty will continue to be around for many years in the United States and that there will always be controversies surrounding it.

THE DEATH PENALTY IN OTHER COUNTRIES

The United States is, of course, not the only country in the world that uses capital punishment, but it is in odd company. Figure 3 shows

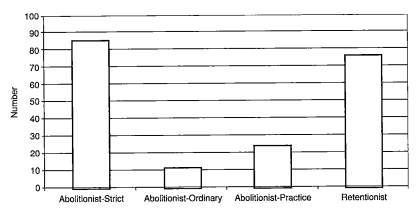

Figure 3 Number of countries that have abolished the death penalty in some form or have retained it (2005).
Source: Amnesty International, www.amnesty.org.

the number of countries in the world that have abolished the death penalty for all crimes (abolitionist-strict), those that have abandoned it for ordinary crimes but not for a few strictly specified extraordinary crimes such as treason (abolitionist-ordinary), those that have abolished the death penalty in practice in that, although they continue to maintain the death penalty by law, they have not executed an offender in ten years or more (abolitionist-practice), and those countries that retain the death penalty (retention). There are approximately as many strictly abolitionist countries (86) as there are retentionist (76), but far more countries have abolished the death penalty in some form than have retained it for ordinary criminal offenses like murder. Moreover, not all countries that have retained the death

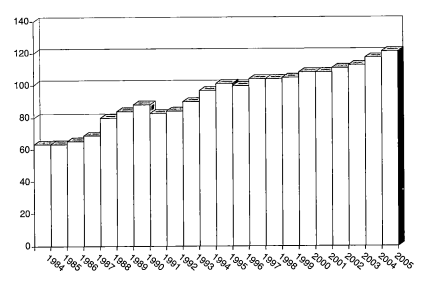

Figure 4 Number of countries that have abolished the death penalty by law or in practice.
Source: Death Penalty Information Center, www.deathpenaltyinfo.org.

penalty impose it with the same frequency. Amnesty International has estimated that there were approximately 4,000 executions world-wide in 2004, occurring in 25 different countries (www.amnesty.org). About 97 percent of those 4,000 executions took place in only four countries (China, Iran, Vietnam, and the United States), with about 85 percent occurring in China alone (some 3,400 executions).

It is probably not true that the world has abandoned the death penalty. It is, however, fair to say that western democratic countries have turned away from capital punishment and that there is likely a worldwide trend away from it. The list of strictly abolitionist countries includes Belgium, Denmark, France, Germany, Ireland, Italy, the Netherlands, Norway, Spain, Sweden, Switzerland, and the United Kingdom, countries that the United States would likely consider its democratic "peers." In addition to the number of countries that have abolished the death penalty, therefore, it is also important to look at which countries have rejected it, and which continue to use it. As mentioned, abolitionist countries include the most advanced industrialized countries with democratic governments and excellent records on protecting human rights. Retentionist countries are more likely to include non-democratic countries with a history of human rights abuses.

Evidence that the world community as a whole may be moving away from the death penalty can be seen in Figure 4, which indicates that the number of abolitionist countries has increased steadily over the past 20 years, and in fact has nearly doubled.

SEE ALSO: Criminal Justice System; Law, Criminal; Race and the Criminal Justice System

REFERENCES AND SUGGESTED READINGS

Baldus, D. C., Woodworth, G. G., & Pulaski, C. A., Jr. (1990) *Equal Justice and the Death Penalty.* Northeastern University Press, Boston.
Banner, S. (2002) *The Death Penalty: An American History.* Harvard University Press, Cambridge, MA.
Paternoster, R. (1991) *Capital Punishment in America.* Lexington Books, New York.

capital, secondary circuit of

Ray Hutchison

For Marx, the second circuit of capital is the sphere of unproductive labor, where commodities are sold and money capital is created. David Harvey used the second circuit of capital to explain urban growth under capitalism, while Henri Lefebvre used the same ideas to study the production of space in capitalist society.

Marx's political economy describes two spheres of social activity: a substructure of productive activity where commodities are created for sale, and a superstructure of circulation for the buying and selling of monies and credits and of commodities themselves. The circulation of capital is specified as $M - C \ldots P \ldots C' - M'$ where M is money and credit, C is commodities, C' is the increased amount of commodities created by the productivity of labor (P), and M' is the increased monetary value from the sale of the output. In the first $M - C$ phase money capital is used to purchase commodities that will be consumed productively (to create surplus value) or consumed unproductively; in the second $C' - M'$ phase profits from the sale of commodities are transformed into money capital. The two phases in the circulation of capital are independent of one another and are distinct from the production process itself.

The circulation of capital is a continuous process in which money is exchanged to purchase commodities (labor power, raw materials, machinery) that are used to produce a new commodity that is sold to produce a profit (surplus value). Profits may be reinvested (to purchase additional labor power, materials, and machinery) to create even greater surplus value. This is the first circuit of capital. But surplus profit and surplus labor must be absorbed, and this process takes place in the second circuit of capital. Marx described the second circuit of capital as investment in the various infrastructures required for production: factory buildings and housing for workers, transportation for raw materials and finished products, and the like. There is a fundamental opposition between the two: while the first circuit of capital is productive (it is capable of producing surplus value), the second circuit of capital is not productive (it does not generate surplus value). Marx understood that as the mode of production and the process of capital accumulation changed over time, the content and form of these relations would also change.

The second circuit of capital has influenced recent social theory in significant ways. The circulation of capital requires the reproduction of labor power. This process, referred to as social reproduction, occurs in schools, hospitals, and individual households, all of which are situated in the second circuit of capital. Similarly, capital must also have access to raw materials found in nature, and as ecosystems have been depleted, the reproduction of nature becomes necessary for the continued expansion of capital.

In Lefebvre's work on *La Revolucion urbain* (1970), the second circuit of capital refers to land and the advanced capitalist relations of production (involving finance, construction, government) that govern the production of land: "*Real estate*, as they call it, plays the role of a second sector of a parallel circuit to that of industrial production." The construction of housing, the development of space, speculation in land, the formation of capital markets, and the like constitute a fundamental force of social development. In a significant break with orthodox Marxism, Lefebvre notes that real estate speculation may become a source of capital formation and an independent source of surplus value. Capitalism imposes its form of abstract space everywhere, resulting in a built environment within which everyday life is lived – an environment that has been organized to facilitate the production of surplus capital. Lefebvre's account of capital accumulation and the production of urban space through the second circuit of capital was influential in the development of the new urban sociology in Europe in the 1980s, and continues to influence work in the new urban sociology in the US at present.

The second circuit of capital occupies a critical space in David Harvey's model of urban growth under capitalism. The continued expansion of capitalism requires that surplus capital and surplus labor generated in the first circuit of capital must be channeled into other uses. A portion of this surplus flows into the second circuit, including investments in (and the labor power required to produce) housing, transportation, and the built environment more

generally. These investments represent a new form of fixed capital (they require large, lumpy investments that are subject to some degree of risk, particularly as capital flows from the first circuit may result in the overproduction of housing, retail space, and the like) and they require a tertiary circuit of education, finance, government, science, and technology to manage and control the activities of the second circuit and to increase surplus value in the first sector. The result is a dynamic model that links investment cycles to housing markets, commercial and retail construction, and the like, to the production, appropriation, and concentration of economic surplus: the flow of capital into the second circuit of capital creates urban forms that facilitate capital accumulation.

The second circuit of capital has had a marked influence on the development of social theory and, in particular, urban sociological theory. The analysis of space has moved beyond the spatiality of geography to important encounters with Lefebvre's notions of abstract space, formal space, representational space, etc. Harvey's work renewed interest in the Marxist analysis of urban society. New applications of the second circuit of capital will need to take into account changes in the circulation of capital resulting from the restructuring of capitalism in the new global economy: as Marx foresaw, investments in science and technology have annihilated space and time, moving investment out of the second circuit of capital (where urban infrastructures, land-based transportation, etc. are increasingly less relevant for the reproduction of capital) into new and as yet unexplored circuits of capital.

SEE ALSO: Capitalism; Lefebvre, Henri; Marx, Karl; Space; Urban Space

REFERENCES AND SUGGESTED READINGS

Harvey, D. (1985) *The Urbanization of Capital.* Oxford University Press, Oxford.

Lefebvre, H. (1970) *La Revolucion urbaine.* Gallimard, Paris.

Marx, K. (n.d.). *Capital*, Vol. 3. Progress Publishers, Moscow.

Marx, K. (1973) *Grundrisse.* Vintage, New York.

capitalism

Jacques Delacroix

Capital is anything of value, such as money, put to work to produce revenue. Capitalism is the organizing principle of any society that relies on market forces and private parties, as opposed to tradition or to government action, to put wealth to work on a systematic basis (rather than incidentally or intermittently).

The discipline of sociology began largely as a critical commentary on capitalism. The emergence of modern, society-wide capitalism in Western Europe in the late eighteenth century was accompanied by deep social transformations, including a dramatic rise in urban, and therefore highly visible, poverty. (The rise of capitalism is inseparable from the Industrial Revolution.) These upheavals triggered a general intellectual malaise and generated both the social and intellectual movement of socialism and the academic discipline of sociology. Perhaps because of the circumstances of its birth, sociology has always cast a pessimistic look at capitalism (Feagin 2001). Accordingly, sociologists tend to ignore Adam Smith, the moral philosopher (1723–90) who first laid out the links between capitalism and prosperity.

The founders of sociology, including Georg Simmel (1858–1918) and Émile Durkheim (1858–1917), generally viewed capitalism as a central object of their inquiry. Two nineteenth-century thinkers in particular exercised a lasting influence on American sociology's study of capitalism: Karl Marx (1818–83), a German philosopher and socialist revolutionary working mostly in Great Britain, whose main book is even entitled *Capital*, and the German economic historian and sociologist Max Weber (1864–1920).

THE CRITICAL MARXIST LOOK AT CAPITALISM

Scholars favorable to capitalism rarely use the word "capitalism," preferring to refer to the "market" and "market forces." Consequently, the influence of Marx and of his followers, critics, and opponents of capitalism may well dominate the literate public's understanding of the phenomenon.

The social thought of Marxism has influenced sociology both indirectly and directly. It is possible to speculate that the pressure of the Marxist critique of capitalism has prompted sociologists (including many not identified with Marxism) to pay close attention to social and economic inequalities. Stratification research has been very productive over the years, providing many innovative causal descriptions of important features of contemporary capitalist societies (see, e.g., Renzulli et al. 2000).

More directly, Marxist thought has prompted a large number of cross-national studies of economic development, under the headings of "dependency theory" and "world-system theory," seamlessly followed by "globalization studies." This sociological research track is based partly on the paradoxical argument that the expansion of capitalism worldwide, from its historical center in Europe and North America (correctly predicted by Marx and Engels in 1848), impedes or somehow distorts the development of poor countries (see Firebaugh 1996).

In fact, international statistics demonstrate that between 1980 and 2001 conventionally defined economic growth in the less developed countries occurred more slowly (+3.22 percent per year, on average) than in the United States (+3.44), but considerably faster than in the European Union (+2.6). Tangible indicators of human welfare also show that social improvement accompanies the expansion of capitalism in most of the less developed world. Thus, the following poor countries increased by more than ten percentage points their population with access to clean water between 1990 and 2000: Ecuador, El Salvador, Guatemala, Paraguay, Nepal, the Central African Republic, Ghana, Kenya, Mali, Tanzania (by 30 points). India, Pakistan, and Vietnam together brought clean water to an additional 200 million people during the decade. The life expectancy of the average Costa Rican in 2003 was 10 percent higher than the life expectancy of the average European in 1955–8 (all data for this paragraph from the World Bank's *World Development Indicators 2003*; Kuznets' 1964 *Postwar Economic Growth*). A 2002 World Bank study concludes that the poor countries with the slowest economic growth between 1980 and 2000 were those *least* touched by globalization, that is, those least affected by the latest expansion of capitalism.

Sociologists of economic development also commonly concern themselves with inequality between and within countries. Unfortunately, they seldom specify whether they refer to the poor becoming poorer or to a situation where some become richer faster than others. (The latter is a logical inevitability in the presence of any growth because there is no likelihood that all sociologically recognizable entities will benefit at exactly the same rate.) However, this imprecision may not matter because the same 2002 World Bank study indicates that "globalization" (greater integration in capitalist networks of trade and investment) does *not* increase inequality between countries *or* within countries.

CAPITALISM, COMMUNISM, AND SOCIALISM

Slippery terminology obscures our understanding of capitalism and of its possible alternatives. Since the end of the nineteenth century, and even more since World War II, many political parties and some countries have called themselves "socialist" or "communist" while some communist countries called themselves something else. In addition, several "socialist" countries exhibited no trace of socialism, in any form. In all cases, these terms signal hostility toward capitalism. At any time, a "communist country" was simply a country under the political control of a communist party. The United Nations used to designate such countries by the neutral and more accurate term "centrally planned economies." This designation indicates a massive attempt to replace market forces with government planning of the economy and the control of capital by a self-perpetuating political elite. Those countries also restricted private ownership of productive property to varying degrees.

From the end of World War II to the early 1990s, the Soviet Union (accompanied by its reluctant satellite states in Eastern Europe) and China, both under the control of communist parties, positioned themselves as political and military rivals to the United States and to the western European countries. As a part of this

rivalry, those countries' elites announced that they were, each in their own way, building new societies not relying on market forces. They proclaimed that their economic growth would soon outpace that of capitalist countries and, ultimately, "bury" capitalism. For brief periods, their economies did grow faster than capitalist economies. The race ended abruptly in the early 1990s with the collapse of the Soviet Union and the rejection of communist parties in the satellites.

The Communist Party of China (later followed by that of Vietnam) had earlier begun to abandon anti-market policies while retaining a monopoly on political power. In the early 2000s, communist Vietnam had become a favorite of multinational firms. In 2004, the communist economic alternative to capitalism was represented only by impoverished Cuba and by North Korea, a country raked by frequent famines.

THE WEBERIAN TRADITION

The strong influence of Max Weber on American sociology is somewhat surprising because it stems mostly from one short book, *The Protestant Ethic and the Spirit of Capitalism*, published in 1905, which constitutes a minor and peripheral part of his monumental production. The first part of Weber's endeavor consisted in precisely defining various historical forms of capitalism and in outlining social conditions that constrained earlier and geographically diverse manifestations of capitalism. In particular, Weber joined Marx and Engels in stating that there cannot be real capitalism unless much of the workforce is legally free. However, some academics have argued against this viewpoint (Steinberg 2003), or offered empirical demonstrations to the contrary, including showing that American southern slavery was quite compatible with capitalism (Fogel & Engerman 1974). In spite of any historical restrictions, there have always been instances of capitalist enterprise because someone always purchases goods to sell them for higher prices in other places or at another time.

Weber's work reminds us that money, or any other form of income, is not invariably put to work, or "invested." When it is invested, it is not always by private parties because government appropriates much income in the form of taxes. Historically, money was rarely invested, for several reasons. First, many societies existed barely above the subsistence level and therefore had little to invest. Second, when and where subsistence levels have been exceeded, people, from the Pacific Northwest Kwiakiutl Indians to Beverly Hill stars, have often expanded income to acquire prestige, or power, or both: Louis XIV of France built a sumptuous palace where he gave lavish parties in order to domesticate his sometimes-rebellious aristocracy as well as to awe his neighbor kings. Money can also be used directly to buy friends in high and low places.

Thirdly, money can be kept for a rainy day, under the mattress, buried beneath the apple tree, or even dangling as jewelry from women's ears, as has been the case in India for hundreds of years. Such practices used to be encouraged until recently by general insecurity and by the scarcity of opportunities for ordinary people to invest.

In *The Protestant Ethic* Weber also constructed a historical argument implying that the Protestant Reformation – a specifically European phenomenon – laid the attitudinal groundwork for the genesis of the modern, western capitalism he had previously defined. A short article, "The Protestant Sects and the Spirit of Capitalism" (1946), additionally sketched the role of trust in entrepreneurship. Many other Weber writings tangentially relevant to his study of capitalism are periodically collected in English and published under different titles.

Taught in more or less distorted form in innumerable college sociology and business classes, the idea that capitalism requires a particular collective attitudinal predisposition has captured the American popular imagination. It is frequently mentioned as historical fact throughout the American mass media. However, empirical verifications of arguments derived from Weber's thesis and conducted according to ordinary, contemporary sociological methods have been scarce. Following Samuelsson (1993 [1957]), Delacroix and Nielsen (2001) submitted one common interpretation of the Protestant ethic thesis to several simple empirical historical tests. They concluded that it was unlikely that the putative linkage between Protestantism, on the one hand, and early industrial

capitalism, on the other, ever existed. Nevertheless, the scholarly exegesis of Weber's work on capitalism has produced an abundant American sociological literature imbued with lasting passion as well as interesting sociohistorical studies.

VARIANTS OF CAPITALISM

The wealthiest countries are unmistakably capitalist countries, except for a handful of small petroleum-rich states. Since all wealthy capitalist countries possess representative institutions, control over their governments tends to switch back and forth. In many of these, at various times, political parties that persist in calling themselves "socialist" are in power. All such parties have abandoned the project of ever replacing capitalism with some other socioeconomic arrangement. However, the label still matters a little because socialist parties often implement distinctive policies. To complicate matters further, parties that don't call themselves socialist may implement similar policies.

As a rough approximation, socialist party administrations favor government-imposed income redistribution, some in the form of generous welfare benefits, the providing of social services by government rather than by the market or by other private initiative, strong and pervasive rather than light-handed government regulation of economic activities, and a great deal of job security. Last but not least, the extension of leisure time at most levels of society often follows the accession of socialist parties to power. Not surprisingly, these features that together define "welfare capitalism" require high taxes. As another approximation, since World War II, the US and Japan have kept closer to pure market policies while the European countries and, to a lesser extent, Canada and Australia tended toward welfare capitalism.

Socialist parties' policy distinctiveness is a matter of degree rather than categorical. In 2001, government expenditures amounted to about 57 percent of GDP in Sweden, a country known for its lavish social programs; they were 42 percent in Canada, and still 35 percent in the US (*OECD Observer 2003*). The government's share of the economy is growing everywhere. The socioeconomic policies of wealthy capitalist countries are thus composed from the same menu, with different emphases, irrespective of what party or coalition is in power. Formerly, a fair degree of government ownership of large business enterprises and of those considered strategically situated, such as banks and public utilities companies, was also associated with socialist party rule. However, the movement toward privatization is very advanced and appears irreversible. Significantly, in the spring of 2004, one of the last holdouts, the French Socialist Party (then out of power), gave its passive assent to a financial maneuver that privatized Air France, the very visible and highly symbolic national airline.

CAPITALISM, GROWTH, AND FLEXIBILITY

Different fiscal and social policies have thus proven compatible with the maintenance of capitalism although they are not equally conducive to economic growth. The American economy, denounced by many European critics as too capitalistic, has, for the past 20 years, grown considerably faster than its European counterparts, which were often guided by socialist parties. In 2001, Puerto Rico's real per capita income reached the same level as that of European Union member Portugal. In 2004, the GDP per capita of a poor southern American state such as Arkansas was just about on par with that of Germany. It may be that the immobilization of capital in government structures and services, as well as leisure time, are more difficult to transform into investment and growth than is consumption of goods by private parties.

Welfare capitalism also appears to lack flexibility. For the period 1998–2001 (determined by data availability), unemployment of more than one year affected four German workers in one hundred but fewer than two American workers in *one thousand*. Moreover, socialist governments are more likely to limit competition, deliberately or inadvertently through invasive regulations. (In France, retailers are allowed to hold discount sales only twice a year, on dates decreed by the central government in Paris.) In addition, the remaining government-controlled business entities may compete less

vigorously than their wholly private counterparts. Competition stimulates technical and organizational innovation (Kogut & Zander 2000) while weeding out poor performers at a fast clip. Both innovation and the elimination of inferior performers improve productivity and, therefore, economic growth. Yet, Japan, a rich capitalist country with a weak socialist party, saw its economy stagnate for the better part of the 1990s. Yet, the western European countries, with their strong welfare proclivities, have forged ahead with the construction of the European Union, an entity rooted in two basic tenets of capitalism: that free trade and freedom of investment promote economic growth.

CAPITALISM AS IT REALLY IS

The actual workings of capitalism at the beginning of the twenty-first century reflect closely the object neither of Marx's nor of Weber's inquiry, nor again that of many of their followers within the sociological discipline. Capitalism is both more hemmed in by government regulation and encompasses many more active participants than the former anticipated and, it seems, than the latter still expect.

In wealthy societies, private economic actors operate within a largely government-managed financial context. Government entities (central banks) determine the availability of credit with or without legal mandate because they have become by far the largest economic players thanks to their power of taxation. The value of the main national currencies is partly decided by frequent negotiations between the governments of the richest countries. In addition, the full coercive power of the nation-state is brought to bear without cease on private economic players. Governments of capitalist countries implement numerous regulations the violation of which results in outright punishment, including fines and prison terms. In the European Union, as in the US, permanent regulatory commissions (such as the US Federal Trade Commission) wield quasi-judicial influence over business conduct. Elsewhere, as in Japan, cultural norms allow government bureaucracies to exercise significant and often arbitrary power over whole industries.

CAPITALISM, THE WORKING CLASS, AND STOCK OWNERSHIP

Although real stock exchanges have been in existence at least since the late eighteenth century, neither Marx nor Weber seems to have grasped fully the importance of these institutions. Contemporary sociologists have also not given them the attention they deserve.

Stock companies have proved effective to put ordinary people's money to work, for three reasons. First, stocks can usually be purchased in small units: a 21-year-old American saving his beer money for six months can acquire a significant portfolio through a mutual fund company. Second, stocks allow small investors to distribute their risk prudently: even a personal investment of as little as $1,000 (less than 1/30 of American GDP per capita in 2004) can be apportioned between as many as ten different companies in ten different industries, possibly even in ten different countries. Third, the modern corporate form, existing in all advanced capitalist countries, insures that the small investor cannot legally lose more money than he has invested in a particular company. The minimization of risk inherent in wide investment spread and in limited liability nevertheless allows for large gains: $1,000 of Intel stock in 1978 (the price of a small moped then) would have grown to $350,000 (the price of a good house in the American Midwest) in 2004.

The implementation of modern communication technology in stock exchange and other financial operations, allowing simultaneously large numbers of anonymous transactions, has given major flexibility to this approach to putting money to work. It's not clear whether these developments will mostly serve the interests of small investors directly, or through non-profit organizations such as pension funds (some of which boast of assets larger than the national incomes of many countries). Alternatively, technological progress may favor anew large corporations effectively controlled by professional managers rather than by their shareholders, an issue of considerable sociological importance.

Marx (with Engels in 1848, and again in *Capital*) expected, and some of the sociologists his work inspired still anticipate, capitalism's self-destruction. The corresponding scenario involves two mutually reinforcing processes. First, the industrial working class, with no ownership stake in productive property, would increase massively in number by absorbing other social groups while sinking into deeper and deeper poverty (Burawoy et al. 2004; Robinson 2004). Second, the ownership of productive property would become concentrated in ever fewer hands.

In reality, the blue-collar class has *shrunk* to about 20 percent of the labor force in rich countries. Counting generously, it was only 22 percent of the American workforce in 2002, that is, probably more than in 1848, but significantly less than in 1980 (28 percent). This shrinkage occurred while the value of manufacturing production in the same countries kept rising year by year, increasing by 50 percent in real dollars in the US in the last decade of the twentieth century. Nearly everyone in capitalist countries, including the industrial working class, has many more possessions, of much better quality, than his or her parents, as well as more leisure time; most attend school longer. People also live longer: American life expectancy increased by a mean 6.5 years between 1970 and 2001, with black women benefiting the most. (All figures in this paragraph from the *Statistical Abstract of the United States* 2002 and 2003.)

In the meantime, the ownership of the means of production has become very *dispersed* rather than concentrated: more than half of American families held stocks in the early 2000s. However, this very multiplication of the number of shareholders, added to their geographical dispersion, and to the fast transfer of stocks from owner to owner, has forced a deep separation between the actual management of capitalist enterprises and their legal ownership. This, in turn, poses recurrent problems with respect to honest governance and social responsibility, problems offering fertile ground for future sociological research.

SEE ALSO: Base and Superstructure; Bourgeoisie and Proletariat; Capitalism, Social Institutions of; Class Consciousness; Communism; Durkheim, Émile; Engels, Friedrich; Industrial Revolution; Marx, Karl; Marxism and Sociology; Simmel, Georg; Smith, Adam; Socialism; Weber, Max

REFERENCES AND SUGGESTED READINGS

Burawoy, M., Gamson, W., Ryan, C., Pfohl, S., Vaughan, D., Derber, C., & Schor, J. (2004) Public Sociologies: A Symposium from Boston College. *Social Problems* 51: 103–30.

Delacroix, J. & Nielsen, F. (2001) The Beloved Myth: Protestantism and the Rise of Industrial Capitalism in Nineteenth-Century Europe. *Social Forces* 80–2: 509–53.

Feagin, J. R. (2001) Social Justice and Sociology: Agenda for the Twenty-First Century. *American Journal of Sociology* 66: 1–20.

Firebaugh, G. (1996) Does Foreign Capital Harm Poor Nations? New Estimates Based on Dixon and Boswell's Measures of Capital Penetration. *American Journal of Sociology* 102: 563–75.

Fogel, R. W. & Engerman, S. L. (1974) *Time on the Cross: The Economics of Negro Slavery*. Little, Brown, Boston.

Kogut, B. & Zander, U. (2000) Did Socialism Fail to Innovate? A Natural Experiment of the Two Zeiss Companies. *American Sociological Review* 65–2: 169–90.

Renzulli, L. A., Aldrich, H., & Moody, J. (2000) Family Matters: Gender, Networks and Entrepreneurial Outcomes. *Social Forces* 79: 523–46.

Robinson, W. I. (2004) *A Theory of Global Capitalism: Production, Class and State in a Transnational World*. Johns Hopkins University Press, Baltimore.

Samuelsson, K. (1993 [1957]) *Religion and Economic Action: The Protestant Ethic, the Rise of Capitalism, and the Abuse of Scholarship*. University of Toronto Press, Toronto.

Steinberg, M. W. (2003) Capitalist Development, the Labor Process, and the Law. *American Journal of Sociology* 109: 445–95.

Wilenski, H. L. (2002) *Rich Democracies: Political Economy, Public Policy and Performance*. University of California Press, Berkeley, CA.

World Bank (2002) *Globalization, Growth, and Poverty: Building an Inclusive World Economy*. World Bank and Oxford University Press, Washington and New York.

capitalism, social institutions of

Pursey P. M. A. R. Heugens

The concept of capitalism refers to the idea that societies should allow economic actors to rationally organize the social and financial capital at their disposal in pursuit of perpetually renewed profits (Weber 1989: 17ff). The particular organizational forms with which actors have chosen to organize economic transactions vary considerably, but an oft-used classification distinguishes between formal organizations, markets for the exchange of commodities and capital goods, and organization–market "hybrids" like interorganizational networks and alliances. As these organizational forms represent the core engines of production and exchange of consumer and capital goods in capitalist societies, these three discrete structural alternatives are typically referred to as the economic institutions of capitalism (Williamson 1985).

But though economic institutions are necessary ingredients of capitalist societies, they are not in and of themselves sufficient conditions to support the maintenance of a capitalist system of production. The success of economic institutions is wholly contingent on the presence of a number of fundamental background conditions, notably (1) some form of social peace, (2) individual freedom, (3) transferable property rights, and (4) enforceable contracts. These four characteristics are upheld by a separately distinguishable set of institutions: the social institutions of capitalism (Heugens et al. 2004). The latter may be defined as a set of public or private arrangements for the regulation and enforcement of exchange transactions between two or more autonomous capitalist actors.

Before a given capitalist actor can produce products or deliver services, it must be put in a context in which some form of social peace has been achieved (Roe 2003). Although the pursuit of profit by force and coercion – piracy, banditry – has never been eradicated from human societies, these types of activities are governed by their own laws and should not be put in the same analytical category as activities oriented towards the extraction of profit from peaceful exchange (Weber 1989). In fact, such parasitic ways of rent extraction are largely detrimental to the capitalist enterprise because they negatively affect its value-generating potential. Firms and factories that fail to deliver services or produce products because of internal strife or external struggle are simply less valuable than those running smoothly (Roe 2003). In fact, if capitalist actors anticipate too much trouble to begin with, new economic institutions of capitalism may not come into being in the first place. Hence, all wealthy capitalist societies are characterized by efficacious social institutions that, regardless of their shape or form, have succeeded in diminishing potential conflict and promoting the conditions that support cooperation.

Furthermore, any economic system built on the voluntary exchange of goods and services must also provide social institutions guaranteeing at least some actors the individual freedom to engage in exchange agreements and co-dictate their terms. Needless to say, capitalist societies have a far from perfect track record with respect to promoting the freedom of all individuals. Present-day capitalist states like the UK, the US, France, Portugal, and the Netherlands were once able to juxtapose capitalist enterprise and a system of slave labor. Moreover, critical management scholars also see contemporary labor–management relations between capitalist employers and nominally free workers as colored by domination, and organizations as coercive institutions. Nevertheless, for the capitalist system to work, at least some classes of actors – usually managers or entrepreneurs – must enjoy the institutionally guaranteed freedom to engage in economic exchanges.

To facilitate the conclusion of transactions in the marketplace, it is moreover necessary that bundles of property rights be attached to physical commodities or services, and that these rights may be exchanged without much friction in the form of transaction costs (Demsetz 1967). Property rights are societal instruments, which help internalize externalities such as the harms and benefits associated with capitalist production. They also help make capitalist exchange processes more predictable. The owner of a bundle of property rights may rightfully expect fellow capitalist actors not to interfere with these prespecified rights and allow them to be exercised in certain mutually agreed-upon ways. Capitalist societies thus have a profound need for social institutions that install private property rights and facilitate their frictionless transfer.

Finally, from a capitalist exchange perspective it is necessary that there are instruments available in the form of contracts that facilitate the making of mutual promises about future exchanges, and that these instruments are enforceable such that the promises they record are usually kept (Macneil 1980). The nature of the capitalist production process means that the future cannot always be foreseen, that reciprocation in economic exchange transactions is not always direct, and that private information about the competence and effort levels of exchange partners is not always symmetrical. To accommodate the myriad problems associated with these conditions, intended exchange transactions must be recorded in instruments that are designed for that specific purpose, and appropriate social institutions must be in place to uphold these instruments in the face of potential deception and defection (van Oosterhout et al. 2006).

Whether any of the social institutions of capitalism referenced above should be classified as public or private depends on their position vis-à-vis the relationships they govern, as well as on the nature of the sanctions they rely on to regulate and enforce capitalist exchange (Elster 1989a). Private institutions typically arise within long-lasting exchange relationships between two or more capitalist actors, and serve to make those relationships self-enforcing and self-policing. The sanctions that private institutions employ ultimately derive their disciplining potential from the threat of terminating the relationship or expelling a member from the larger group, thus keeping the sanctioned party from the future benefits that would have accrued to it if it had remained in the relationship. Public institutions, on the other hand, are positioned external to the exchange relationship. They typically exist in the form of a separate entity with some form of authority to police and enforce the exchange relationships over which it presides. Because of their independent status, they are also often called third-party enforcement mechanisms. The sanctions they employ range from relatively subtle measures like taxes and reprimands to largely coercive measures like fines and imprisonment. Capitalist actors tend to rely on private institutions whenever possible, because they are faster in terms of execution than public institutions, cheaper to operate, and considerably less "transaction-rupturing" (Williamson 1979).

Nevertheless, not all four of the background conditions necessary to operate and maintain a capitalist system of production can always be provided by such intrinsically more efficient private institutions. Social peace and individual freedom have a strong public goods character. Everyone benefits when these conditions are in place, but no single actor can produce them by individual means or even has the incentive to contribute to their advancement. Under such conditions, the rational pursuit of private objectives by self-interested individuals may produce collectively disastrous outcomes (Elster 1989b). Individuals have every incentive to exploit the social peace by making an easy living as brigands and highwaymen. The condition of individual freedom is also easily eroded when certain individuals use organized force to subject others and exploit them as serfs or slaves. The classical way out of the dilemma of the provision of public goods is the abdication of individual authority to some form of Hobbesian Leviathan – a public institution. This is the terrain of classical social contract theory (Heugens et al. 2004). This body of work suggests that individuals may jointly agree on certain collective limitations to their natural rights and freedoms, in return for long-run stability (social peace) and greater security and actually getting to enjoy the rights they do retain (e.g., certain forms of individual freedom). In all modern capitalist societies these collective limitations have taken the form of the state. This quintessential social institution of capitalism represents a Pareto optimal solution in that all its citizens benefit from the collective behavioral constraints – laws, covenants, social norms – it provides to overcome problems of collective action.

The state is a versatile creature in that it not only provides for social peace and individual freedom, but also creates and delivers transferable property rights and enforceable contracts. But states are public institutions, and as such are often criticized for being slow, inefficient, and breeding the bureaucratic personality. Fortunately, whereas state bureaucracy and public sector governmentality probably represent the only feasible solutions to the problem of providing social peace and individual freedom, private institutional alternatives are available for the provision of transferable property rights and enforceable contracts. These institutions include (but are certainly not limited to) kinship ties, clans, and more intangible enforcement mechanisms like trust and reputation.

All of these institutions are private in the sense that they are either synonymous with long-term relationships between formally independent actors (the former two) or clearly derive from them (the latter two). Since property rights are essentially social conventions pertaining to (1) which individuals are entitled to certain goods and commodities and (2) what they get to do with these, extended families and clans are perfectly capable of providing equivalent solutions to legally recognized property rights. By erecting and policing clear social norms pertaining to the distribution of wealth over kin and clan members, these private institutions effectively circumvent any resort to public institutions and may even fill the voids in case the latter are absent or deficient in a given setting (Khanna & Palepu 2000). One important boundary constraint in this respect is of course that these norms often cannot be used to govern transactions between kin and clan members on the one hand and outsiders on the other.

Private social institutions of capitalism also exist for the enforcement of contracts. In addition to the kin and clan-related mechanisms discussed above, trust and reputation represent two additional institutions that can secure this necessary background condition for capitalist exchange. The added benefit of the latter two mechanisms is that they can also emerge in long-term exchange relationships between two or more parties that are not affiliated by clan or kinship ties. The sanctions on which these two mechanisms draw can be divided into dyadic and third-party sanctions. The former derive their disciplining potential from the fear of a potential contract breaker to forgo the future benefits associated with continuing the dyadic relationship, including the utility this party derives from being trusted or enjoying a good reputation. The latter derive their power from the potential offender's fear of being excluded from the benefits of present and future transactions with third parties that could potentially observe the breach of a contract, which again include not only the economic value of those relationships but also the trust and esteem contained in them (Brennan & Pettit 2004). The private character of the social institutions of capitalism discussed here not only guarantees their relative differential efficiency as compared with public institutions, but also the speed with which they may be applied and their relationship leading to salvaging rather than rupturing effects.

SEE ALSO: Bureaucracy and Public Sector Governmentality; Bureaucratic Personality; Capitalism; Labor–Management Relations; Organizations as Coercive Institutions

REFERENCES AND SUGGESTED READINGS

Brennan, G. & Pettit, P. (2004) *The Economy of Esteem: An Essay on Civil and Political Society.* Oxford University Press, Oxford.
Demsetz, H. (1967) Toward a Theory of Property Rights. *American Economic Review* 57(2): 347–59.
Elster, J. (1989a) *Nuts and Bolts for the Social Sciences.* Cambridge University Press, Cambridge.
Elster, J. (1989b) *The Cement of Society: A Study of Social Order.* Cambridge University Press, Cambridge.
Heugens, P. P. M. A. R., van Oosterhout, J., & Vromen, J. J. (2004) *The Social Institutions of Capitalism: Evolution and Design of Social Contracts.* Edward Elgar, Cheltenham.
Khanna, T. & Palepu (2000) Is Group Affiliation Profitable in Emerging Markets? An Analysis of Diversified Indian Business Groups. *Journal of Finance* 55(2): 661–75.
Macneil, I. R. (1980) *The New Social Contract: An Inquiry into Modern Contractual Relations.* Yale University Press, New Haven.
Roe, M. J. (2003) *Political Determinants of Corporate Governance: Political Context, Corporate Impact.* Oxford University Press, Oxford.
Van Oosterhout, J., Heugens, P. P. M. A. R., & Kaptein, S. P. (2006) The Internal Morality of Contracting: Advancing the Contractualist Endeavor in Business Ethics. *Academy of Management Review* 31(4).
Weber, M. (1989 [1930]) *The Protestant Ethic and the Spirit of Capitalism.* Unwin Hyman, London.
Williamson, O. E. (1979) Transaction-Cost Economics: The Governance of Contractual Relations. *Journal of Law and Economics* 22: 233–61.
Williamson, O. E. (1985) *The Economic Institutions of Capitalism.* Free Press, New York.

captive mind

Syed Farid Alatas

The concept of the captive mind was originated by the Malaysian sociologist Syed Hussein Alatas and was developed to conceptualize the nature of scholarship in the developing world, particularly in relation to western dominance in the social sciences and humanities. The captive mind is defined as an "uncritical and imitative mind dominated by an external source, whose thinking is deflected from an independent perspective" (Alatas 1974: 692). The external source is western social science and humanities and the uncritical imitation that influences all the constituents of scientific activity such as problem selection, conceptualization, analysis, generalization, description, explanation, and interpretation (Alatas 1972: 11). Among the characteristics of the captive mind are the inability to be creative and raise original problems, the inability to devise original analytical methods, and alienation from the main issues of indigenous society. The captive mind is trained almost entirely in the western sciences, reads the works of western authors, and is taught predominantly by western teachers, whether in the West itself or through their works available in local centers of education. Mental captivity is also found in the suggestion of solutions and policies. Furthermore, it reveals itself at the levels of theoretical as well as empirical work.

Alatas elaborated the concept in two papers published in the early 1970s (Alatas 1972, 1974) but had raised the problem in the 1950s referring to the "wholesale importation of ideas from the Western world to eastern societies" without due consideration of their sociohistorical context, as a fundamental problem of colonialism (Alatas 1956). He had also suggested that the mode of thinking of colonized peoples paralleled political and economic imperialism. Hence the expression academic imperialism (Alatas 1969, 2000), the context within which the captive mind appears.

While the phenomenon of the captive mind is important, discourse on the concept as developed by Alatas has been limited to citations in works of scholars sympathetic to the type of critique undertaken by him. There have been no systematic expositions or rebuttals of the concept and it seems to be largely ignored, particularly in western social science establishments (interview with Syed Hussein Alatas, August 29, 2004).

Since the latter part of the nineteenth century, scholars in the non-western areas such as India, Southeast Asia, and the Middle East, noting that the humanities and social sciences originate in the West, raised the issue of the relevance of these fields of knowledge to the needs and problems of their own societies. From the 1950s onwards there was a strong recognition of the academic dependence of the third world on the West as far as the social sciences were concerned. This dependence was seen in terms of both the structures of academic dependency and the ideas derived from alien settings and whose relevance is in question. The former can be gauged from the relative availability of first world funding for research, the prestige attached to publishing in American and British journals, the high premium placed on a western university education, the design of curricula and adoption of textbooks in non-western universities, as well as several other indicators (Altbach 1977; Weeks 1990; S. F. Alatas 2003). The latter problem of dependence on ideas can be illustrated by a survey of concepts and theories that are in vogue across a range of disciplines in the developing world. The captive mind exists within this context of dependency.

The discourse on the captive mind belongs to that genre of social science literature that consciously addresses various problems relating to the state of the social sciences in the third world. These problems can be subsumed under concepts and movements such as the critique of colonialism, academic imperialism, decolonization (of knowledge), critical pedagogy, deschooling, academic dependency, Orientalism, Eurocentrism, and the captive mind.

Alatas begins his conceptualization of the captive mind with a parallel idea, the demonstration effect, developed by James Duesenberry in connection with consumer behavior. According to the idea of the demonstration effect, rising income would result in higher levels of consumption as consumers attempt to match the consumption patterns of those whose lifestyles they wish to imitate (Duesenberry 1949). Alatas suggests that the thinking of third world social scientists can be understood in terms of the demonstration effect. According to this interpretation, the consumption of social science knowledge from the West arises from the belief in the superiority of such knowledge. Among the traits of this consumption that parallel the economic demonstration effect are: (1) the frequency of contact with western knowledge; (2) the weakening or erosion of local or indigenous knowledge; (3) the prestige attached to imported knowledge; and (4) that such consumption is not necessarily rational and utilitarian (Alatas 1972: 10–11).

Alatas provides illustrations of the workings of the captive mind from development studies. The dangerous consequences of the captive mind lie in the weaknesses of the thought pattern in, for example, development studies in the West which are being imitated elsewhere. These cover various areas of scientific activity such as abstraction, generalization, conceptualization, problem-setting, explanation, and the understanding and mastery of data (Alatas 1972: 12). For instance, in the area of abstraction and generalization, Alatas discusses the work of Tinbergen (1967) on development planning as being marred by general and abstract propositions that are redundant (Alatas 1972: 12–13). In another illustration, this time from the work of Kuznets, Alatas criticizes some of the propositions for being so general that they lack any utility for meaningful analysis. This problem could have been avoided had the work attempted to derive propositions and conclusions directly from historical and comparative data (Alatas 1972: 14). Another problem in development studies discussed by Alatas is that of erroneous judgment as a result of unfamiliarity with data or ignorance of the context. The example given is Hagen's view that digging with the Southeast Asian hoe is an "awkward process," but the spade, which is a better instrument, can only be of limited use in low-income societies to the extent that shoes are not widely used (Hagen 1962: 31–2, cited in Alatas 1972: 15). Alatas suggests that Hagen did not comprehend the function of the hoe in its proper context. In the Southeast Asian context, the hoe is actually the more efficient instrument because of terrace cultivation on mountain slopes. Hagen's failure to judge the efficiency and utility of the hoe by reference to its context is a violation of an important anthropological principle (Alatas 1972: 15).

It is problems such as these in development studies as well as the social sciences in general that are imitated and assimilated by the captive mind and result in ill-conceived development plans. Dominated by western thought in a mimetic and uncritical way, the captive mind lacks creativity and the ability to raise original problems, is characterized by a fragmented outlook, is alienated from both major societal issues and its own national tradition, and is a consequence of western dominance over the rest of the world (Alatas 1974: 691). The problem of the captive mind is unique to the non-western world. While uncreative, imitative, fragmented, and alienated minds are to be found in the West as well, the context in which these occur is not the same. Alatas argues that the counterpart of the captive mind does not exist in the West because in the West we do not find people who are trained in non-western sciences, in non-western universities, trained by non-western professors, and assigned works of non-western scholars in non-western languages (Alatas 1974: 692). The captive mind is a phenomenon peculiar to the developing world in that the uncritical and imitative thought exists in the context of the domination by an external civilization, the West (Alatas 1976).

The logical consequence of the awareness of the problem of the captive mind is the development of an autonomous social science tradition that would function to eliminate or restrict the intellectual demonstration effect or the captive mind (Alatas 1972: 20). An autonomous social science tradition is defined as one which independently raises problems, creates concepts, and creatively applies methodologies without being intellectually dominated by another tradition (Alatas 2002: 151). This does not mean that there are no influences from other traditions or that there is no learning involved from other traditions. Translating the notion of autonomous social science into practice involves the following aspects (Alatas 1972: 20–1): (1) restricting the development of the captive mind by encouraging a process of selective and independent assimilation of knowledge from the West; (2) setting higher

scientific and intellectual standards by comparing local and regional social sciences with their counterparts in developed countries; (3) encouraging interest in comparative studies in the training of social scientists; (4) creating awareness in government and among the elite in the development of an autonomous social science tradition; (5) obtaining the support of those foreign scholars sympathetic to the idea; (6) attacking faulty development planning and the abuse of social science thought that arises from the workings of the captive mind with reference to concrete local targets; and (7) awakening the consciousness of social scientists regarding their intellectual servitude.

SEE ALSO: Colonialism (Neocolonialism); Decolonization; Dependency and World-Systems Theories; Eurocentrism; Uneven Development

REFERENCES AND SUGGESTED READINGS

Alatas, S. F. (2003) Academic Dependency and the Global Division of Labour in the Social Sciences. *Current Sociology* 51(6): 599–613.

Alatas, S. H. (1956) Some Fundamental Problems of Colonialism. *Eastern World* (November), London.

Alatas, S. H. (1969) Academic Imperialism. Lecture delivered to the History Society, University of Singapore, September 26.

Alatas, S. H. (1972) The Captive Mind in Development Studies. *International Social Science Journal* 24(1): 9–25.

Alatas, S. H. (1974) The Captive Mind and Creative Development. *International Social Science Journal* 26(4): 691–700.

Alatas, S. H. (1976) Intellectual Captivity and the Developing Societies. Paper presented at the 30th International Congress of Human Sciences in Asia and North Africa, Mexico, August 3–8.

Alatas, S. H. (2000) Intellectual Imperialism: Definition, Traits and Problems. *Southeast Asian Journal of Social Science* 28(1): 23–45.

Alatas, S. H. (2002) The Development of an Autonomous Social Science Tradition in Asia: Problems and Prospects. *Asian Journal of Social Science* 30 (1): 150–7.

Altbach, P. G. (1977) Servitude of the Mind? Education, Dependency, and Neocolonialism. *Teachers College Record* 79(2): 187–204.

Amin, S. (1989) *Eurocentrism*. Zed Books, London.

Duesenberry, J. S. (1949) *Income, Saving, and the Theory of Consumer Behavior*. Harvard University Press, Cambridge, MA.

Garreau, F. H. (1985) The Multinational Version of Social Science with Emphasis upon the Discipline of Sociology. *Current Sociology* 33(3): 1–169.

Hagen, E. E. (1962) *On the Theory of Social Change*. Dorsey Press, Homewood, IL.

Said, E. (1979) *Orientalism*. Vintage, New York.

Said, E. (1993) *Culture and Imperialism*. Chatto & Windus, London.

Tinbergen, J. (1967) *Development Planning*. Weidenfeld & Nicolson, London.

Wallerstein, I. (1996) Eurocentrism and Its Avatars: The Dilemmas of Social Science. Paper presented at the East Asian Regional Colloquium on The Future of Sociology in East Asia, jointly organized by the Korean Sociological Association and the International Sociological Association, November 22–3.

Weeks, P. (1990) Post-Colonial Challenges to Grand Theory. *Human Organization* 49(3): 236–44.

caregiving

Patricia Drentea

Caregiving is the act of providing unpaid assistance and support to family members or acquaintances who have physical, psychological, or developmental needs. Caring for others generally takes on three forms: instrumental, emotional, and informational caring. Instrumental help includes activities such as shopping for someone who is disabled or cleaning for an elderly parent. Caregiving also involves a great deal of emotional support, which may include listening, counseling, and companionship. Finally, part of caring for others may be informational in nature, such as learning how to alter the living environment of someone in the first stages of dementia.

Sociologists generally limit their discussion of caregiving to unpaid workers. Caregivers are typically family members, friends, and neighbors. Sometimes caregiving is done by those affiliated with religious institutions. While caregiving of all types is also done by paid workers such as nurses, social workers, and counselors, this is paid work, and thus is not in the same category. Caregiving rarely refers to the daily care that parents provide for their children, because this is classified as parenting; however, caring for an adult disabled daughter would be considered caregiving because it is outside of the norm of expectations for older adults.

Recently, sociologists have begun to use the term carework rather than caregiving. Carework is considered more accurate to describe a relationship that is not always voluntary and freely given. The word caregiving stems from gerontological work, where a service ethic is presumed to motivate the caregiver. Sociologists have chosen the word carework to highlight the inequality in who generally cares for others. They note that families, and particularly women within families, provide care. Additionally, with few affordable market-based options in carework, those with more money have better options to decline caregiving, thus further showing the inequality of who cares for whom. Finally, the social supports issued by welfare states are not always stable and dependent, resulting in contextual or geopolitical differences in who "chooses" to caregive (Harrington et al. 2000).

Caregiving is measured by ascertaining what type of care is provided and how many hours are spent caring for others over a typical day, week, month, or year. The constellation of factors important to consider in caregiving research is the relationship with the care recipient, and the levels of care needed and provided. The personal demands on the caregiver are also typically measured, such as family and work status, and physical impairment of the caregiver (Pavalko & Woodbury 2000). The amount of social support available to the caregiver is important, as are the contexts in which the caregiver and care recipient live. Socioeconomic status, sex, race and ethnicity, and age of both caregiver and care recipient are integral to understanding the level of stress created by the caregiving relationship (Aneshensel et al. 1995). It is often wise to study caregiving within a certain disease cluster or category, such as caring for the elderly with several functional limitations, or caring for someone with HIV/AIDS, since each cluster will bring about specific issues surrounding the context of the problem.

Much research focuses on caregiver burden, which examines the level of stress and burnout associated with caregiving. Other research, however, highlights positive aspects of caregiving, in which caregivers have reported the meaning and fulfillment that caring for someone has brought to their lives. Researchers also try to assess the context in which the caregiving relationship takes place, and many have designed interventions to support the caregivers. Respite care, often provided by for-profit businesses, allows caregivers to have a break and take care of their own needs while someone else cares for their loved one on a short-term basis.

Most caregiving is done informally by family members. This informal, unpaid service saves the government billions of dollars each year (Arno et al. 1999); however, it may cost employers in lost days of work when caregivers must handle emergencies. It also results in lost wages for employees who must provide care rather than engage in paid work.

Caregiving is one of the most studied areas in social gerontology (George 1990). Additional research, however, will be increasingly useful as the population ages. First of all, we must continue to monitor the amount of care provided by others, as we expect it to increase while the baby boom ages. Second, we must continue to assess the effect caregiving has on the economy, in terms of lost wages, lost employee hours, and saving the government/welfare state from providing the care. The context of caregiving should continually be studied to assess under which conditions caring for others is most stressful versus most enjoyable. Interventions and more respite care should follow for the most stressful of situations (with studies of *when* caregivers are willing to use respite care). Monitoring what delays nursing home placement is important to scholars and policymakers. We know little about those receiving care: when possible, interviewing care recipients would greatly increase our understanding of this complex, often emotional relationship. More research could also be done on racial and ethnic variations in caregiving, and when men provide care. Finally, social scientists should strive to get their work on caregiving into the hands of policymakers, as this is one of the most common "second careers" of most adults at some point in their lives.

SEE ALSO: Aging and Health Policy; Aging and Social Policy; Carework; Elder Care; Emotion Work; Ethic of Care; Gender, Aging and; Gender, Work, and Family; Healthy Life Expectancy; Social Support; Stress and Health

REFERENCES AND SUGGESTED READINGS

Aneshensel, C. S., Pearlin, L. I., Mullan, J. T., Zarit, S. H., & Whitlatch, C. J. (1995) *Profiles in Caregiving: The Unexpected Career*. Academic Press, San Diego.

Arno, P. S., Levine, C., & Memmott, M. M. (1999) The Economic Value of Informal Caregiving. *Health Affairs* 18: 182–8.

George, L. (1990) Caregiver Stress Studies: There Really Is More To Learn. *Gerontologist* 30: 580–1.

Harrington, M., Herd, P., & Michele, M. (2000) Introduction: The Right To – Or Not To – Care. In: Harrington, M. (Ed.), *Care Work: Gender, Class, and the Welfare State*. Routledge, New York, pp. 1–4.

Pavalko, E. K. & Woodbury, S. (2000) Social Roles as Process: Caregiving Careers and Women's Health. *Journal of Health and Social Behavior* 41: 91–105.

carework

Joya Misra

Carework refers, simply, to the work of caring for others, including unpaid care for family members and friends, as well as paid care for others. Caring work includes taking care of children, the elderly, the sick, and the disabled, as well as doing domestic work such as cleaning and cooking. As reproductive labor, carework is necessary to the continuation of every society. By deploying the term "carework," scholars and advocates emphasize the importance of recognizing that care is not simply a natural and uncomplicated response to those in need, but actually hard physical, mental, and emotional work, which is often unequally distributed through society (Meyer 2000). Because care tends to be economically devalued, many scholars who study carework emphasize the skill required for care, and the importance of valuing care.

The scholarship on carework addresses several key issues. Understanding the balance in care provision among families, states, and markets is a central concern. There are significant issues about the relationship between family provision of care and market provision of care (paid versus unpaid care). The state plays its own role, in terms of providing care, supporting care, and encouraging care. Many carework scholars call for the state to play a larger role in care provision, both to eliminate gendered expectations for care provision within families and to subsidize provision due to the expense of and demand for high-quality care. These issues of family, state, and market have played out within the feminist welfare state literature for decades, and have become more integrated with carework scholarship that focuses more specifically on the experiences of the provision of care (Meyer 2000; Daly 2001).

Scholarship on carework also highlights the tensions between paid versus unpaid care. The commodification of care is viewed with significant suspicion, in part due to concerns that paid care provides less emotional nurturing. Indeed, the rationalization of carework can lead to a greater respect and reward by making visible the skills and hard work involved in carework. Yet the emotional and nurturing aspects of carework are important both to the care recipient and to paid and unpaid careworkers (Foner 1994). For paid carework, a focus on efficiency and billable hours may have extremely detrimental effects. This tension simply exists because society devalues the worth of nurturance and love. Although the commodification of care changes the nature of care, the result need not be a loss in quality. While unpaid family care may be of very high quality, elder abuse and child abuse happen within families as well as in paid-care settings, and professionals can at times provide better care, particularly for the disabled and sick. Paid care should also not be seen as replacing unpaid care; unpaid care often continues alongside paid care. Paid and unpaid caregivers may work together, and may need to negotiate successful strategies for sharing care (Abel & Nelson 1990; Ungerson 1997).

Another tension exists between care quality and costs for care. Care improves significantly with lower ratios of careworkers to recipients. For example, a person caring for two parents with dementia may face greater stress than a person caring for only one parent. Similarly, a nursing home center with a 3:1 ratio of nurses to care recipients will allow higher-quality care than one with a 10:1 ratio of nurses to care recipients. Yet, costs increase when care is provided in this manner. As a result, lower quality of care is often necessary, which may create higher levels of burnout for careworkers as well as poor outcomes for care recipients. Yet, most families simply do not have the time or money to provide what may be the highest-quality care, and must make difficult choices.

Care may also be experienced by unpaid careworkers as both a burden and a right. Unpaid carework takes place in a larger context, which includes enduring ideologies about the gendered nature of carework, unstable social support for care, and limited market-based options for care (Meyer 2000; Daly 2001). Many unpaid careworkers, due to a lack of options, must juggle work, care, and other responsibilities, and may feel pushed into providing care. Yet, the provision of care can also be seen as a right. Those with the least resources and autonomy (e.g., lesbian or gay partners, immigrant domestic workers, or women under US welfare reform) do not have the same ability to *choose* care; when their family members need care, they may be relatively powerless to help. The social context plays an important role in structuring and limiting choices about care. Care is a profound and central experience in many people's lives; it is critical to analyze the experience of care with more subtlety, recognizing that care may be empowering as well as oppressive – and may be both at the same time.

Finally, as all of these points suggest, inequalities provide a key approach for analyzing carework. Carework clearly reinforces gender inequality, but also inequalities of race, ethnicity, class, sexuality, ability, and nation. For example, in the United States, race and gender systems have historically devalued the care racial and ethnic minority women provide for their own families, while appropriating this care for white families. At its most basic, research on carework investigates differences in carework based on social location, and seeks to show how different social locations are linked through care provision.

SEE ALSO: Caregiving; Elder Care; Emotion Work; Ethic of Care; Inequality/Stratification, Gender; International Gender Division of Labor; Welfare State

REFERENCES AND SUGGESTED READINGS

Abel, E. K. & Nelson, M. K. (1990) *Circles of Care: Work and Identity in Women's Lives*. State University of New York Press, Albany.
Cancian, F. & Oliker, S. (2000) *Gender and Caring*. Pine Forge Press, Thousand Oaks, CA.
Daly, M. (Ed.) (2001) *Carework: The Quest for Security*. International Labor Office, Geneva.
Folbre, N. (2001) *The Invisible Heart: Economics and Family Values*. New Press, New York.
Foner, N. (1994) *The Caregiving Dilemma: Work in the American Nursing Home*. University of California Press, Berkeley.
Meyer, M. H. (Ed.) (2000) *Carework: Gender, Class, and the Welfare State*. Routledge, New York.
Ungerson, C. (1997) Social Politics and the Commodification of Care. *Social Politics* 4(3): 362–81.

caste: inequalities past and present

Rita Jalali

Societies all over the world are socially stratified but they vary in the ways in which inequality is structured. To categorize different forms of stratification systems sociologists most frequently examine the way resources such as wealth, power, and prestige are acquired in society. In some societies, such valued resources are acquired on the basis of achievement or merit. In others, these resources are accorded to individuals on the basis of ascribed, not achieved, characteristics. One is born into them or inherits them, regardless of individual abilities or skills. A person's position is unalterable during his or her lifetime. The idea of

ascribed and achieved status is used to contrast caste systems with class systems. In class systems one's opportunities in life, at least in theory, are determined by one's actions, allowing a degree of individual mobility that is not possible in caste systems. In caste systems a person's social position is determined by birth, and social intercourse outside one's caste is prohibited.

Caste systems are to be found among the Hindus in India. Examples of caste-like systems, where groups are ranked and closed, and where one's position is fixed for life, can also be found in other non-Hindu societies such as Japan, during the Tokugawa period, and South Africa, during the era of apartheid.

The term "caste" itself is often used to denote large-scale kinship groups that are hierarchically organized within a rigid system of stratification. Early Hindu literary classics describe a society divided into four *varnas*: *Brahman* (poet-priest), *Kshatriya* (warrior-chief), *Vaishya* (trader), and *Shudra* (menial, servant). The *varnas* formed ranked categories characterized by differential access to spiritual and material privileges. They excluded the Untouchables, who were despised because they engaged in occupations that were considered unclean and polluting.

This hierarchical system persisted throughout the Hindu subcontinent for millennia. The basis of caste ranking was the sacred concept of purity and pollution. Brahmans were considered ritually pure because they were engaged in priestly duties. Untouchables were regarded as impure since they were employed in manual labor and with ritually polluting objects. Usually those who had high ritual status also had economic and political power. Relations between castes were generally regulated by beliefs about pollution. Thus, intermarriage between castes was not allowed; there were strict rules about the kind of food and drink one could accept and from what castes; and there were restrictions on approaching and visiting members of another caste. Violations of these rules entailed purification rites and sometimes expulsion from the caste.

How did such a stratification system achieve legitimacy? Traditional Hindu religious beliefs about *samsara* (reincarnation) and *karma* (quality of actions) provided the justification for the operation of this hierarchical society. A person's actions in previous lives determined his or her social ranking in this life. Those who were born in a Brahman family must have performed good deeds in their earlier lives. Being born a Shudra or an Untouchable was punishment for the sinful acts committed in previous lives. The *varna* scheme refers only to broad categories of society, for in reality the small endogamous group or subcaste (*jati*) forms the unit of social organization. In each linguistic area there are about 2,000 such sub-castes. The status of the subcaste, its cultural traditions, and its numerical strength vary from one region to another, often from village to village. Some *jatis* contain millions of persons and others a few hundred.

Field studies of local caste structures in India revealed that there was some mobility within the caste system. Castes were often able to change their ritual position after they had acquired economic and political power. Upward mobility occurred for an entire caste, not for an individual or a family. However, those at the top and bottom of the hierarchy – the Brahmans and the Untouchables – maintained their high and low status.

The Indian social structure was profoundly affected by British colonialism. Western ideas, the legal system, English educational institutions, and new economic activities brought greater mobility and new opportunities to even the low castes, but those that derived the most benefits were the upper castes, the Brahmans. After the country became independent in 1947, the Indian leaders enacted legislative and legal measures to create a more egalitarian society. A new constitution was adopted, which abolished untouchability and prohibited discrimination in public places. In addition, special benefits were provided for those who had suffered most from the caste system. Places were reserved for Untouchables in higher educational institutions, government services, and in the lower houses of the central and state legislatures.

What progress has the country made toward improving the lives of the Untouchables, who now form 16 percent of the population? Has the traditional caste system disintegrated? The movement from a traditional to a modern economy, together with India's democratic electoral system, has had a significant impact on the institution of caste. An urban middle class has formed whose members are drawn from various caste groups. Divisions based on income, education, and occupation have become more important than caste cleavages for social and economic purposes. In rural areas, the dominant castes are no longer from the higher castes but belong to the middle and lower peasant castes.

The structural and cultural changes are most prominent among the upper socioeconomic strata in urban areas whose members share a common lifestyle. For those who live in rural areas (nearly 72 percent) caste factors are an integral part of their daily lives. In many parts of the country *Dalits* (the term means oppressed and is preferred by the members of the Untouchable community rather than the government-assigned label, Scheduled Castes) are not allowed inside temples and cannot use village water wells. In rural and urban areas, marriages are generally arranged between persons of the same caste. With the support of government scholarships and reservation benefits, a small proportion of Dalits has managed to gain entry into the middle class – as schoolteachers, clerks, bank tellers, typists, and government officials. Reservation of seats in the legislature has made the political arena somewhat more accessible. The recent rise of a Dalit political party, the Bahujan Samaj Party, is evidence that Dalits are finally gaining some political power. They are particularly strong in the northern regions of the country. In the 2004 national elections, they captured 19 seats (and 5.33 percent of the votes) in the parliament. The majority of Dalits, however, remain landless agricultural laborers, powerless, desperately poor, and illiterate. Poverty rates among them remain much higher than for other castes. As in the past, rural and urban areas in India will continue to witness inter-caste conflicts. Yet, what is significant is that, like ethnic conflicts elsewhere between groups, these conflicts have more to do with control over political and economic resources and less over caste beliefs and values.

SEE ALSO: Affirmative Action; Conflict (Racial/Ethnic); Racial Hierarchy; Stratification, Race/Ethnicity and

REFERENCES AND SUGGESTED
READINGS

Berreman, G. (1981) *Caste and Other Inequities*. Manohar, Delhi.
Beteille, A. (1992) *The Backward Classes in Contemporary India*. Oxford University Press, Delhi.
Dumont, L. (1970) *Homo Hierarchicus*. University of Chicago Press, Chicago.
Galanter, M. (1984) *Competing Equalities: Law and the Backward Classes in India*. University of California Press, Berkeley.
Jaffrelot, C. (2003) *India's Silent Revolution: The Rise of the Lower Castes in North India*. Hurst, London.
Jalali, R. (1993) Preferential Policies and the Movement of the Disadvantaged: The Case of the Scheduled Castes in India. *Ethnic and Racial Studies* 16(1): 95–120.
Mendelsohn, O. & Vicziany, M. (1998) *The Untouchables: Subordination, Poverty and the State in Modern India*. Cambridge University Press, New York.
Srinivas, M. N. (1987) *The Dominant Caste and Other Essays*. Oxford University Press, Delhi.

Castoriadis, Cornelius (1922–97)

Phillip Ablett

Cornelius Castoriadis was a Greco-French philosopher, economist, psychoanalyst, social theorist, and post-Marxist revolutionary. Born in Constantinople (Istanbul) in 1922, Castoriadis grew up in Greece amid dictatorship, invasions, and civil war. Educated in philosophy, law, and politics at the University of Athens, Castoriadis fought the Nazis as part of the communist, and later Trotskyist, resistance. In 1945 Castoriadis went to study in Paris, where in 1948 he cofounded the libertarian socialist group and journal *Socialisme ou Barbarie* (1949–67), many of whose ideas influenced the 1968 worker–student uprising. He was unable to obtain French citizenship until 1970 and led a revolutionary's double life by working professionally as a senior OECD economist. As the journal's preeminent theoretician, Castoriadis initiated a series of thoroughgoing internal critiques of the Marxist tradition. Against statist definitions of socialism as nationalization, Castoriadis advocated workers' self-management, which he expanded into a project of human autonomy. After 1970, Castoriadis retrained as a psychoanalyst and became director of studies at the Écoles des Hautes Études.

Castoriadis's mature work, exemplified in *The Imaginary Institution of Society* (1975) and numerous essays, presents an original, interdisciplinary critique of contemporary capitalist societies, in the course of which he formulates an alternative to both foundationalist social science and poststructural relativism. The interdisciplinary and "extra-academic" character of most of Castoriadis's writing has contributed to its slow reception in sociology, despite sympathetic appraisals from Habermas, Heller, and Bauman. His work, however, has much to offer sociology's interpretive, action perspectives and publicly engaged critical theory. Like the latter, Castoriadis sees theory as a necessary but partial moment in our sociohistorical *doing*. Accordingly, his sociological ideas are inextricably tied to rethinking ways in which social action might institute human freedom and justice.

Philosophically, Castoriadis builds his social theory upon ontology. Against the dominant traditions of western thought, he posits a basic indeterminacy in social and natural reality. This challenges the exhaustive knowledge claims of objectivist determinism (what Castoriadis calls "identitarian-ensemblistic" or "ensidic" logic): the idea that reality consists solely of a rationally or empirically bounded set of determinate objects. For Castoriadis, objects related through chains of inevitable cause and effect represent just one determinate layer of being. There remains an indeterminate layer, which in the social world is revealed in the human capacity for creative imagination, both at the personal (*radical imaginary*) and collective (*social imaginary*) levels.

Imagination is not simply the illusory, but rather the capacity to see things otherwise, "provide new responses to the '*same*' situations or create new situations" (Castoriadis 1987 [1975]: 44). Consequently, Castoriadis conceives of social institutions as the creations of the social imaginary in action. The social imaginary for Castoriadis is an unstable "*magma*" of cultural meanings (transcending reason or empirical reality) that give a society its broadest self-definition. Society (the sociohistorical) is, therefore, an open-ended dialectic between the already created array of symbolically mediated institutions and the creating of new ones; it is "the union *and* the tension of instituting society and of instituted society, of history made and of history in the making" (Castoriadis 1987 [1975]: 108). In this light, institutions cannot be "explained" by reference to causes and functions but require an elucidation of the significations that animate and transform them.

Society as an imaginary creation does not represent in itself a reflexive or democratic accomplishment for Castoriadis. Since the rise of "civilization" in ancient Mesopotamia, most societies have been characterized by heteronomy (i.e., "rule of the other"), in which the imaginary of the dominant group is instituted as natural or divinely sanctioned. Autonomy or self-determination, however, remains historically possible for both the individual and society.

Social autonomy means a society being able to self-consciously institute and revise its own laws with the maximum participation of all of its members. It begins whenever a subordinate group starts to question the dominant imaginary that construes its subordination as inevitable and seeks equal participation. Castoriadis characterizes as revolutionary praxis this exceptional form of deliberate social self-creation, which simultaneously recognizes the autonomy of the other. His examples include the ancient Greek democracies, medieval Italian communes, the English Civil War, the American and French Revolutions, workers' councils, and contemporary social movements where direct democracy is sought against elite rule. Castoriadis counterposes these instances of praxis to the currently dominant imaginary of neoliberalism, where people surrender their agency to "representative" democracy (which he calls "liberal oligarchy") and market despotism. He does this not to prove that democracy is inevitable but to remind us that societies have imagined and can pursue such paths.

By attesting to the power of imagination in social life, Castoriadis's work is a robust reproach to pronouncements that history ended with the triumph of global capitalism. It is also an invitation to imagine something new and better.

SEE ALSO: Action Research; Critical Theory/ Frankfurt School; Democracy; Marxism and Sociology; Neoliberalism; Praxis; Revolutions

REFERENCES AND SUGGESTED READINGS

Bauman, Z. (1994) Morality Without Ethics. *Theory, Culture, and Society* 11(4).
Castoriadis, C. (1987 [1975]) *The Imaginary Institution of Society.* Trans. K. Blamey. Polity Press, Cambridge; MIT, Boston.
Castoriadis, C. (1997a) *The Castoriadis Reader.* Ed. and Trans. D. A. Curtis. Blackwell, Oxford.
Castoriadis, C. (1997b) *World in Fragments.* Ed. and Trans. D. A. Curtis. Stanford University Press, Stanford.
Curtis, D. A. (1992) Cornelius Castoriadis. In: Beilharz, P. (Ed.), *Social Theory: A Guide to Central Thinkers.* Allen & Unwin, Sydney.
Heller, A. (1991) With Castoriadis to Aristotle; From Aristotle to Kant; From Kant to Us. In: Heller, A. & Feher, F. (Eds.), *The Grandeur and Twilight of Radical Universalism.* Transaction, New Brunswick, NJ.
Joas, H. (1989) Institutionalization as a Creative Process: The Sociological Importance of Cornelius Castoriadis's Political Philosophy. *American Journal of Sociology* 94(5).

Catholicism

Émile Poulat

Catholicism, along with Orthodoxy and Protestantism, is one of Christianity's three principal branches and statistically the most important. Today's use of the term is a recent, secularized means of referring to the Catholic Church, whose head is the pope and whose headquarters are in the Vatican City in Rome.

The word Catholicism is a latecomer in the long history of the church, a word whose history has yet to be written. It is scarcely more than four centuries old in the French language, where it seems to have been born amid the sixteenth-century wars of religion as a counterpart to the Protestantism of the Calvinists. The schism between German Lutherans (the Church of the Augsburg Confession) and

Catholics – only recently healed after lengthy ecumenical dialogue – has no exact parallel in the relations between the Catholic and Orthodox Churches: the orthodoxy Constantinople claims for itself is not opposed to any putative Roman heresy, but to the iconoclasts over whom it triumphed in the ninth century.

Relations between confessions are inflected with language difficulties about which no unanimity exists and which are open to multiple interpretations. "Church" is a theological concept that each confession develops in its own way. Doctrinal differences have led to the establishment of separate churches whose ecclesiological peculiarities limit and undermine ecumenical dialogue. In contemporary Catholic usage the word Church is regarded as the result of contamination or degradation and reflects vacillation and uncertainty. Formerly, "Holy Church" referred to the only true Church, mother of all and universal teacher. Today, reference to the Roman Catholic Church or the Anglican Church, for example, indicates the existence or absence of a linkage to the See of Peter (*cathedra Petri*), a nuance current in the Anglican tradition and more generally in the English-speaking world.

By invoking its divine institution the universal Catholic Church affirms itself to be independent of any earthly power and sovereign in its own order. This exceptional prerogative of which it is the sole beneficiary is recognized at the international level. The Catholic Church is a society with no national frontiers but with a place among the nations, possessing a territorial base of its own (Vatican City) and legally embodied by its supreme organ of governance, the Holy See (called such by the UN), where ambassadors are accredited from around 164 nations with whom it has diplomatic relations. Thus, while Catholicism is a religion in the modern sense of the word, it is also more than that, making it of great sociological interest.

Statistics about the demography and membership of religions need to be interpreted cautiously. The last research dates from 1982, with forward projections to the year 2000 (Barrett 1982). For Catholicism, however, such statistics can be updated by means of the *Annuario pontificio* and the *Annuaire statistique de l'Église*. The number of adherents is thus estimated at about a thousand million, distributed among close to 3,000 major territories, of which 2,700 are dioceses with the full exercise of episcopal authority, and some 400,000 parishes. This framework is supported by 4,500 bishops, assisted by 265,000 diocesan priests (called secular clergy), 2,000,000 religious priests (of which 125,000 are priests called "regular" because they live under a rule, *regimen*), 80,000 nuns, 26,000 permanent deacons, 80,000 lay missionaries, and 2,500,000 catechists.

Two subsets can be distinguished from this vast collectivity. The first were once called mission territories, entrusted to vicariates or apostolic prefects working with missionary orders and congregations and foreign resources. These once had considerable territorial significance. The second were once very local: the churches of the oriental rites that were united to Rome, whose special autonomy has always been recognized by virtue of their nonderivative origins. Decolonization has accelerated somewhat the establishment of such fully operative churches, and while missionary activity has not ceased, it has undergone profound transformation. Migration has also led to the multiplication of dioceses of the oriental rites in western countries (e.g., 75 percent of Arabs living in the US are Christian), while the Latin Christians of the East have declined to the point of atrophy.

As one would expect, such a culturally diverse communion is not only spiritual in nature, but also a consciously hierarchical and strongly centralized organization that rests on extensive legal, administrative, and financial resources. Over the centuries the Catholic Church has been closely associated with the political life of Europe, as well as Latin America. For millennia, religion was a public matter and its laws were also those of society. The two orders of temporal and spiritual authority possessed respectively civil and ecclesiastical power, but their exact relationship and the question of which had authority over the other – the pope or the sovereign – was debated endlessly and often bitterly. Today, confessional states are now the exception rather than the rule. The separation of church and state and the principle of secular government have more or less succeeded the principle of Catholicity.

It is no longer religion that is public, but each person's *freedom* of religion (i.e., freedom of conscience and worship). Religion itself, it is held, is a private matter. However, the privatization of the church is not an inevitable outcome of freedom of conscience and the religious neutrality of the state. The church does not cease its active presence in public life, nor does the nature of that presence cease to be transformed or to take new directions.

The history of the Catholic Church from the end of the nineteenth century is the history of its difficult and necessary conversion to this new order of society, which provides the conditions for its very existence. The singularity of the Catholic Church – its strength and its weakness – is really its deep dislike of *any* regime and for the modern invention of the separation of church and state. What the church teaches and what it does always refer to an ideal of *integration*, although the words necessary for expressing this ideal are freighted with the old opposition between the church and the world.

The "conversation" this entails between church and state is supervised on the church's side by the papacy. The papacy consists of the current pope himself, plus the historical institution for which he assumes responsibility and the continuity of which he represents. The Holy See is at one and the same time the Roman pontiff, the central government of the universal church (over which he exercises "the supreme and full power of jurisdiction"), and the legal personification of the Catholic communion. The activity of the Holy See is exercised above all by a traditional but periodically reformed organization, the Roman curia. Since 1967 it has had at its head a secretary of state who serves as the leader of the government and who directs the policy of the church in its relations with states. He oversees the work of 9 congregations, which constitute as many ministries but whose heads remain directly responsible to the pope. Their names clearly indicate the tasks for which they are responsible:

1 Doctrine of the Faith (the old Holy Office, successor to the Inquisition), under which is an International Theological Commission and a Biblical Commission

2 Oriental Churches
3 Divine Liturgy and Discipline of the Sacraments
4 Causes of Saints (procedures for beatification and canonization)
5 Bishops
6 Missions (previously called the Congregation for the Propagation of the Faith and today called the Congregation for the Evangelization of Peoples)
7 Clergy
8 Institutes of Consecrated Life (vowed religious)
9 Catholic Education (seminaries and Catholic schools and universities)

In addition to these congregations, three tribunals exist under archaic names: (1) the Apostolic Signature, which judges appeals and administrative disputes; (2) the Roman Rota, for cases of marriage litigation; and (3) the Sacred Penitentiary, for matters of conscience that are private or reserved to the pope. Then there are offices or bureaus, among them the Prefecture of Economic Affairs (accounts office) and the Administration of the Patrimony of the Holy See.

Among various permanent commissions, there are pontifical councils established after the Second Vatican Council in 1962–5 (Unity of Christians, Interreligious Dialogue, for the Laity, for Culture, Pastoral Council of Migrants, Family, Health, Charitable Works, etc.). To these entities of government are added institutions responsible for administering the cultural patrimony of the Holy See and making it accessible to the public: the Vatican Library, the Vatican Archives, and the Vatican Museum. Only 3,500 active permanent staff (with a thousand retired) are employed in this administration – not many, given the task and the size of the budget, the balancing of which has become a problem.

"The Vatican" is partly mythic (a kind of shorthand), but also a reality of international law, defined by the Lateran Accords (1929) between the Holy See and Italy. It is a miniature state of 44 hectares: testimony to a distant historical past (the Papal States) and endowed with a system and government of its own (bureaus of work and places of service), but above all a territorial basis for the independence of the Holy See.

The papacy is often considered one of the last absolute monarchies, but this is inappropriate. If the power of the pope is supreme and complete, it is neither absolute nor solitary, but vicarious and collegial. This relativization did not prevent its growth from the end of the nineteenth century, nor block the reestablishment of episcopal collegiality at the Second Vatican Council. This takes effect at several levels: in a unique way on the occasion of a council; periodically by the holding of synods (11 from 1967 to 2005, to which are added an extraordinary session and 8 special sessions); and regularly in national or regional episcopal conferences. Compared to these, the particular council of the pope that the Sacred College of Cardinals comprises (120 below the age of 80 years) seems a lighter and more mobile structure. Its major responsibility is to elect a successor at the death of the pope.

The Holy See is not supranational: it is not a state among states while participating in their organizations as an "observer," and the Vatican citizenship that its officers enjoy is in addition to that of their national origin. The Catholic Church thinks of itself as being transnational: state boundaries are accommodated and respected, but without thereby discriminating among the faithful. As for the latter, they voluntarily give an international form to their national activities. Thus, since 1951, there has been a Conference of International Catholic Organizations (OIC) comprising 36 member organizations, 4 associated ones, and 4 invited, most of which have NGO consultative status at the UN and its specialized agencies, such as UNESCO.

If the diocese and the parish have been the ordinary structures of the church for a thousand years, the importance of other structures should not be neglected: the ancient, strongly controlled network of orders, congregations, and other institutes of religious life; the teaching sector (seminaries and Catholic schools and universities); the periodical and book publishing sector; hospital care and charities, complemented by missionary cooperation and economic development; and the immense movement of the lay apostolate, long identified – narrowly – as Catholic Action, but the forms

and orientations of which vary considerably by country and era.

Tensions can arise between the two aspects of these intertwining activities: an internal aspect turned toward spirituality and sometimes tempted to ignore "the world," and an external aspect turned toward the apostolate and evangelization, engaged in the world to the point of losing its Christian identity – hence, it is possible to go from "dechristianization" to "deconfessionalization." This was the great adventure of the Catholic Social Movement, born in Western Europe around 1870, from which arose Christian labor unions and political parties of Christian inspiration. If these were not or are no longer specifically Catholic, a study of Catholic organization cannot pass over them in silence, for they speak to the church's capacity to maintain a presence.

Globally, the Catholic Church is an immense mosaic of cultures, traversing all the social classes, speaking all the languages. At the center of this Catholicity there exists a relatively small bureaucracy which no official of any country would judge sufficiently large. Political scientists would do well to examine this phenomenon more closely. They would discover that the principle of episcopal collegiality involves decentralization and subsidiarity, associating strict control at all levels with features of voluntary association. In itself this fundamental principle cannot guarantee functionality – historians and sociologists have known that for a long time. Nevertheless, despite all the difficulties it experiences and the struggles it encounters, the Catholic Church continues.

SEE ALSO: Christianity; Church; Religion; Religion, Sociology of

REFERENCES AND SUGGESTED READINGS

Barrett, D. B. (Ed.) (1982) *World Christian Encyclopedia: A Comparative Study of Churches and Religions in the Modern World.* Oxford University Press, Oxford.

Cuneo, M. W. (1987) *Conservative Catholicism in North America: Pro-Life Activism and the Pursuit of the Sacred.* Pro Mundi Vita, Brussels.

Grabiel, K. & Kaufmann, F.-X. (Eds.) (1980) *Zur Soziologie des Katolizismus* (Toward the Sociology of Catholicism). Matthias-Grünwald, Mainz.

Hebaugh, H. R. (Ed.) (1991) *Religion and Social Order: Vatican II and US Catholicism*. JAI Press, Greenwich, CT.

Hornsby-Smith, M. (1991) *Roman Catholic Beliefs in England: Contemporary Catholicism and Transformations of Religious Authority*. Cambridge University Press, Cambridge.

McSweeney, B. (1987) *Roman Catholicism: The Search for Relevance*. Blackwell, Oxford.

O'Toole, R. (Ed.) (1989) *Sociological Studies in Roman Catholicism: Historical and Contemporary Perspectives*. Edwin Mellen, Lewiston, NY.

Poulat, E. (1965) *Catholicisme, démocratie et socialisme* (Catholicism, Democracy, and Socialism). Casterman, Paris.

Poulat, E. (1969) *Intégrisme et catholicisme intégral* (Fundamentalism and Integral Catholicism). Casterman, Paris.

Poulat, E. (1986) *L'Église c'est un monde. L'Ecclésiosphère* (The Church is a World: The Ecclesiosphere). Éditions du Cerf, Paris.

Vaillancourt, J. G. (1980) *Papal Power: A Study of Vatican Control over Lay Catholic Elites*. University of California Press, Berkeley.

caudillismo

Sergio Tamayo

Etymologically, *caudillo* comes from the latino term *capitellus* or *caput*, which means head. A political system or political regime based on *caudillaje* is named *caudillismo* and is under the mandate of a *caudillo* (political leader). *Caudillo* means the boss or leader of an army at war. However, political and military leaders who lead emancipation or popular movements are also designated with the same word. Different authors have analyzed *caudillismo* from two main orientations: as a social movement or institutional regime, and as a reflection of the action of a leader or *caudillo*. It has been a phenomenon associated mainly with Latin American politics. Nevertheless, various movements or regimes have been recognized by the name of their *caudillo* (e.g., Peronism in Argentina, Cardenism in Mexico, Cesarism in Rome, Bonapartism in France, Bismarckism in Germany, Franquism in Spain, *Duce* to Mussolini, *Führer* to Hitler, etc.).

The main issue in this characterization is not the fact that the *caudillo* or leader maintain a rightist or leftist ideology, nor that they consider themselves, at the same time, fascist, nationalist, populist, democratic, revolutionary, or authoritarian. The personal characteristics of leadership and the social-historical context are transcendental. There are also other social types that have been associated with the notion of *caudillo*, such as the social bandit, *cacique*, the mafias, the revolutionary *caudillo*, the charismatic leader of masses, and the political boss.

Caudillismo is related to historical periods, movements, and political regimes. These moments are characterized by being political transitions led by charismatic leaders. It is important to stress in these phenomena the structural similarities as well as the reproduced figure of the *caudillo*.

The term *caudillismo* has been established mainly in Latin America to identify the period of independence (1810–25) and the post-independence stage that continued with the making of nation-states in the nineteenth century. Though not all the Latin American countries went through similar transitions, it is possible to observe historical components that permitted the presence of *caudillismo*. A significant aspect is the change in economic model when Spain left its American colonies. In the case of Argentina and Chile, the decline of the colonial system implied the flourishing of an exporting oligarchy linked to English capitalism. The development of the economy was based on exportation, which provoked the fragmentation of the artisan industry still linked to colonial forms of organization: a clash between exporting sectors and groups of artisans and of incipient manufacturers. The confrontation was between the rural provinces and centralism in the cities. In Mexico, Peru, and Bolivia the economic crisis registered a sharp reduction in fiscal income. The dispersion of power benefited the formation of weak and disaggregated national governments. In both cases *caudillismo* appeared due to the power vacuum generated by the disintegration of the colonial system and the need to reunite the population around a national project.

Sarmiento's novel *Facundo* shows us these political conditions in Argentina. The right of property was agrarian: large estates or haciendas in the case of Mexico, the landscape of the pampa, the rudimentary exploitation of work, and violence as a way of life. He describes the farmland in its dogmatic, isolationist, Catholic tradition. The *gaucho* was both a social subject and a *caudillo*. The *caudillo* was shown as a tyrant leader. The antagonism was mirrored against the city, the center of rationalism, order, and democracy.

Although in appearance the emergence of the *caudillo* can express these contradictions between the country and the city, *caudillismo* according to Frank (1970) represents the existence of antagonistic groups that seek to position themselves in the same capitalist system. In Argentina, for example, the allies of the English interests that supported the politics of exportation were placed against the nationalists who represented the interests of the provinces, the artisan production in traditional manufacturing. The *caudillo* was a result of these tensions. He was capable of canalizing social conflicts. The *caudillo* became a hinge that articulated the old colonial model with the new capitalist market.

The study of *caudillismo* in Latin America has looked for generalities and parallelisms with other times. The work of Krauze (1997, 1999a, 1999b) is particularly relevant because of his characterization of the Mexican *caudillos*. The nineteenth-century *caudillo* was made by the independent and liberal leaders who built the Mexican nation. The biographies of power dominated the period of the 1910 Mexican Revolution. The revolt can be explained by the function of charismatic leaders, who were viewed by their followers as secular saints. Brading (1980) also refers to the origin of the Mexican Revolution as a struggle between regional *caciques* worried only about their own interests and dominance over their people. In the case of Mexico, the *caciques* were different in the North and in the South of the country. Those in the North received financing from the local governments that opposed the dictatorship of Porfirio Diaz. Those in the South were helped by popular uprisings. The process continued a transformation from the local *caciques* to regional *caudillos*, from a local vision to one supported by the popular movement. These changes ended in a new national synthesis: presidentialism. The role of the *caudillo* permitted a type of institutionalization of national power.

Caudillismo, especially that which was seen in the first decades of the nineteenth century in Latin America, is connected to the Bonapartism experienced in France after the *coup d'état* of Louis Bonaparte in December 1851. Bonapartism was possible partly due to the fact that it permitted equilibrium between the contending parties in an unresolved struggle. The charismatic and despotic political leader embodied the government with the objective of bringing discipline and order. With this strategy, the head of state was placed above the conflict, limiting the contenders in any political participation. The measures of industrialization made the workers as well as the bourgeoisie benefit from the intervention of the state. The leader professed himself savior of the working class when parliament was abolished. And the bourgeoisie permitted it because in its place order and stability were imposed. With heroic national wars Bonaparte put a stop to the interests of the working class. The internal struggle became static. Bonaparte moderated the conflicts and repressed social explosion. That is why the state moved towards its automatization. Bonapartism is a phenomenon that can always appear when society is shaken by destructive conflicts with no way out. It is the inevitable outcome of situations of anarchy and chaos.

Bonapartism has also been associated with Cesarism. Cesarism reveals elements similar to those in the political leadership in Latin America. Originally, Cesarism was defined as that regime established in ancient Rome by Cayo Julius Cesar. It represented a solid power that came from the interests of the groups in battle, supported by strong ties to the army. The term Cesarism has also been used to define the French governments that arose from both Bonapartes. Gramsci (1975) refers to Cesarism as a situation in which a strong leader is present. The Cesarist, he says, arises from a setting in which conflicting social forces are more or less equal. If they continue in this manner the struggle leads to mutual destruction. Cesarism as well as Bonapartism expresses arbitrated solutions, conferred by a great personality, the political leader. The Cesarist is the heroic figure of the charismatic boss. In this sense, Cesarism and Bonapartism have also been associated with phenomena such as fascism and Bismarckism.

This kind of political leadership operates in transitions toward the making of industrial, urban, and modern societies. In such a mutation, political forces do not find themselves sufficiently developed. The reinforcement of the state is necessary by means of a charismatic figure who protects the interests of the nation and exercises a mediating function between different antagonisms.

Other regimes or movements of the masses in which the role of the political or charismatic leader is relevant are recognized as populism and neopopulism. Latin American populism is sustained by a broad social mobilization under the precept of the integration of the popular classes. Populism refuses class struggle. The government emphasizes industrialization pushed by an interventionist state, a mixed economy, a nationalist ideology, and a strongly personalized driving force. In this way there is supremacy of the Will of the People and a direct relationship between the people and the charismatic leadership. The leader interprets the spirit of the people. In the same manner, populism emerges not only because of tensions between subdeveloped countries and colonizing countries, but also between subdeveloped regions and the fairly industrialized centers within the same countries. To many authors, this is a constant source of tension between metropolis and province. In any case, a society in crisis is presented as a division between the "traditional" and the "modern" sectors. In such conflictive and social-tension situations, the masses are subordinated to the charismatic leader. The leader represents the state that, at the same time, is the expression of the people and of national history.

Juan Dominguez Perón has turned into the prototype of the charismatic leader, with a government at the same time populist and personalized. He was a leader driven by a broad popular movement. Other populisms have been identified with the chiefs of Latin American states (e.g., Lazaro Cárdenas in Mexico and

Belaúnde Terry in Peru). Political parties have identified themselves as populists when they boost social political movements of nationalist inspiration, such as the Peruvian APRA (*Alianza Popular Revolucionaria Americana*) and the Mexican PRI (*Partido de la Revolución Institucional*). In the case of Mexico, the PRI led the influence and the orientations of the *caciques* and rearticulated political patronage. New post-revolutionary *caciques* were formed, but they were based on different political loyalties. This association between populism, political leadership, and Bonapartism has led some authors to claim that the Mexican regime is strongly presidential and therefore Bonapartist. Recently, a few scholars have defined certain Latin American regimes as variants of populism and neopopulism. Chávez in Venezuela and Fujimori in Peru are the best examples for conceptualizing neopopulism. Salinas of Mexico and Menem from Argentina are also included. Neopopulism is defined as a regime that promotes social and economic modernization along with the exercise of authoritarian and personalized power (sometimes dictatorial). Neopopulism is characterized by strong executives and the fragility of institutions, which promotes hyper-presidentialism.

In some cases political leadership is sustained by marginal classes, as in the case of Fujimori, without forgetting the interests of enterprises and industries. In other cases, like that of Chávez, neopopulism confronts elites and generates certain benefits for marginal sectors, but at the same time it leads to growing political polarization. In all such situations the system of political parties and legislative institutions is weak and the opposition loses its credibility.

The political movements and regimes that have been identified with a strong leadership are various, but they all share two historical characteristics: (1) a weakness of the social forces in conflict during transitional periods, in a process of modernization or the formation of a nation-state; (2) the emergence of a charismatic leader who puts himself above the conflict and solves it. These situations are inserted into the context of civil wars or national independence processes in which the strong leadership can reflect different realms and scales: in local, regional, or national events; in gangs, movements, or regimes. Depending on these realms and scales, we can refer to manifestations such as social bandits, leaders, mafias, *caudillos*, mass leaders, or political bosses. Nevertheless, the constant characteristic of the *caudillo* is charisma.

Charisma, according to Weber, is a particular form of power because of its link to a certain type of domination. The authority of the *caudillo* leader is based on a natural talent involving the capacity to fascinate, which they possess to an exceptional degree. It is not enough to have the power of attraction: the gift must serve to announce or realize a mission that can be religious, political, military, or social. The charismatic leader is not an isolated character but needs followers – those who recognize the gift of the leader and recognize themselves in him. The legitimacy of the actions of the *caudillo* rests upon the recognition of his particular *don*, which reaches such a degree of acceptance that it justifies the obedience of his followers. The charismatic person achieves his power because he is converted into a spokesperson for their security, hope, and salvation. In Christianity a charismatic leader is one who possesses an extraordinary faculty to make miracles happen or to formulate prophecies that become real. He is a leader who can emerge victorious in conditions of extreme inferiority. Charisma can be expressed in revolutionary, conservative, or resistance movements.

Thus the *caudillo*, the boss, the social bandit, the Cesarist, the Bonapartist, or the populist are all charismatic leaders. There are many examples of the social bandit or *bandolero* (e.g., Robin Hood). Hobsbawm (1965) regards the social bandit as a man who is not considered to be a criminal. He believes in the justice of his actions, which are directed mainly against the rich and based on the customs and traditions of the local community. The bandit is righteous to the people and criminal to the state. The case of the bandit Heraclio Bernal in Mexico illustrates the charisma superimposed by his followers and the defects incorporated by his detractors. According to his followers, Heraclio was tall and attractive, intelligent, friendly, chivalrous, generous, dashing, and without fear. They claimed that he challenged the authorities because he was imprisoned for crimes he did not commit. His accusers claimed that he was lawless, socially worthless, ignorant, deviant, cruel, and uncivilized; they described him as scrawny and small. The relationship between bandit-followers is based on loyalty, prestige, and the authority of the bandit, characteristic of a political leadership. Admiration for the bandit is reproduced in his vision of the future and of justice for the suffering.

The *cacique* is a local boss, only worried about his own interests. He maintains power over his towns and regions. But the *cacique* can be the first step in the conversion into a *caudillo* because he has used coercion on those close to him to obtain loyalty; he also rewards them with privileges to maintain unity. The interest of the *cacique* is to subdue a limited territory to his influence and to establish alliances with the central power to maintain his dominance. The *cacique* turns into a *caudillo* when his worries and interests go beyond the regional and he adheres to a social cause, such as a political movement or a social or revolutionary struggle.

Guzmán (1995) points out the characteristics of *caudillos* in different periods. In discussing Mexican President Porfirio Díaz (1876–1910) he emphasizes his physical qualities: a leader who shone with embroideries and medals; virile and potent because of his slim and robust height, wide shoulders, and severe figure. Krauze summarizes the charisma of the Independence *caudillos* Miguel Hidalgo and José María Morelos y Pavón. The first was a priest influenced by Creole patriotism, a professional gambler of a spendthrift and disorderly disposition. The mass of his followers were also disorganized, unreliable, and amorphous. Although he did not have an alternative political project, Hidalgo could be bloody with his enemies. Morelos was also a priest, more dedicated to spiritual service and helping the helpless. He organized, trained, and uniformed his followers. He was unrelenting, but not bloody; he was moved by political and military objectives. The ideal of equality was given more importance by Morelos, as well as the task of building an independent nation.

During the Mexican Revolution the *caudillo* Emiliano Zapata was followed by thousands of farmers without land. The elite considered him a bandit and a leader of thieves. To his supporters, Zapata was a charismatic leader. The *caudillo* is synonymous with *leader*. The leader is the fundamental element in the treatment of social movements. Smelser (1995) discusses the characteristics of leaders of collective action and highlights their charismatic qualities. They unify the mobilization and express the feelings of the people. They use myths to motivate action and to create awareness in their followers. They lead the movement and can lead rebellions, but the character of the leader is permeated by democratic or authoritarian practices. A leader with authoritarian practices – frequently seen in the social urban movements in Latin America – can be considered a "local leader," as claimed by Nuñez (1990), who points out that neighborhood leaders are those who organize people. They also become the intermediaries between society and government. The leader or urban *cacique* imposes himself on a territorial group. The population accepts him through a mixture of fear, prestige, and necessity. The power of the leader is created by the access he has to certain resources, added to his charismatic qualities, forms of expression, and giving of orders; it is reinforced by the violence used by his most loyal supporters against dissidents within the movement. He also works as a community leader. He holds a great deal of autonomy with respect to the masses and the authorities.

For Stewart et al. (1989), a leader makes decisions and acts as the image of the movement. He must have three attributes: charisma, prophecy, and pragmatism. His authority and power are therefore based on the consistency of his character (charisma). He possesses the truth that only he can reveal (prophecy) and he is a practical man in his decisions to reach the goals and obtain the wishes of the group (pragmatism). The leader becomes a *caudillo* of the masses.

SEE ALSO: Charisma; Leadership; Populism

REFERENCES AND SUGGESTED READINGS

Frank, A. G. (1970) *Capitalismo y subdesarrollo en América Latina*. Siglo XXI, Mexico City.
Gramsci, A. (1975) *Notas sobre Maquiavelo, sobre política y sobre el estado moderno*. Juan Pablos, Mexico City.
Guzmán, M. L. (1995) *Caudillos y otros extremos*. Universidad Nacional Autónoma de México, Mexico City.
Hobsbawm, E. J. (1965) *Primitive Rebels: Studies in Archaic Forms of Social Movement in the 19th and 20th Centuries*. W. W. Norton, New York.
Krauze, E. (1997). *Biografía del poder (1910–1940)*. Fábula Tusquets Editores, Mexico City.
Krauze, E. (1999a) *Caudillos Culturales en la Revolución Mexicana*. Tusquets Editores, Mexico City.
Krauze, E. (1999b) *Siglo de Caudillos. Biografía política de México (1810–1910)*. Fábula Tusquets Editores, Mexico City.
Nuñez, O. (1990) *Innovaciones democrático-culturales del movimiento urbano-popular*. Universidad Autónoma Metropolitana, Mexico City.
Smelser, N. J. (1995) *Teoría del comportamiento colectivo*. Fondo de Cultura Económica, Mexico City.
Stewart, C., Smith, C., & Denton, R. (1989) *Persuasion and Social Movements*. Waveland Press, Prospect Heights, IL.
Weber, M. (1978) *Economy and Society*. University of California Press, Berkeley.

celebrity and celetoid

Chris Rojek

Celebrity is the assignment of honorific or sensational status to an individual through the agency of mass communication. An important distinction in the field is between *ascribed* and *achieved* forms of celebrity. The former refers to the assignment of status on the basis of genealogy. For example, in Britain Prince William and Prince Harry possess ascribed celebrity on the basis of their bloodline. In the US the children of presidents, such as Chelsea Clinton and Jenna and Barbara Bush, fall into the same category. Ascribed celebrities tend to predominate in the power hierarchy of traditional societies in which rule is organized around monarchical or charismatic leaders. Achieved celebrity refers to the attribution of honorific or scandalous status by virtue of the accomplishments of an individual. This type of celebrity is common in modern societies attached to legal–rational forms of legitimacy. Within celebrity culture there are institutionalized categories of sports stars, pop idols, artists, film stars, and politicians into which achieved celebrities can be positioned. Generally speaking, the transition from traditional to modern society involves the eclipse of ascribed celebrity and its replacement by the achieved form.

There have been a variety of attempts to explain the rise of celebrity culture. Subjectivist accounts focus on the unique, God-given talents of individuals and the expansion of the global mass media in accelerating and broadening data exchange. This position concentrates on the singularity of the celebrity. For example, it holds that no one can rival Jennifer Lopez as the ideal of contemporary female beauty, Tom Cruise as the all-round action hero, or Picasso as the greatest twentieth-century artist. Subjectivist accounts rest upon strong interpretations and for this reason are often controversial. Because they prioritize the irreplaceable singularity of the celebrity they marginalize the role of cultural intermediaries (managers, promoters, publicists, impression management personnel) in creating the public face of the celebrity for mass consumption. In societies based around fully developed mass communications, celebrities are typically socially constructed rather than naturally produced. Today, few achieved celebrities wake up to find themselves famous overnight as Lord Byron allegedly did after the publication of *Childe Harold* in 1812. Rather, they require their image to be fashioned and mediated to mass consumers.

Structuralist accounts of celebrity place more emphasis on the role of cultural intermediaries and manipulation in the construction of celebrities. Generally, the main purpose behind constructing the public face of achieved celebrity is pecuniary gain. One of the strongest examples of the structuralist approach is Adorno and Horkheimer's culture industry thesis, which presents popular culture as the calculated expression on multinationals based in the entertainment industry. Marcuse's later theory of one-dimensional society follows the same line of argument. Structuralist accounts prioritize relations of production over relations of consumption. While audiences and fans can bend and inflect the constructions of the culture industry, they are ultimately depicted as secondary actors. The primary player is the culture industry, which orchestrates consumer demand

for the consumption of achieved celebrity through its control of advertising, marketing, and other branches of mass persuasion.

The structuralist approach is subject to three main criticisms. First, it tends to neutralize the accomplishments of the celebrity in favor of an explanation which focuses on the pronouncement and manipulation of celebrity. As a result, issues of talent and skill are oddly ignored. Second, it undervalues the power of audiences and fans to counteract the pronouncements and manipulations of the culture industry. In consumer culture the relationship between production and consumption is more one of hegemony than domination. Third, structuralist accounts tend to be too glib about the function of celebrity. Achieved celebrity certainly makes use of techniques of manipulation as a means of persuasion, but it does not follow that this practice necessarily eventuates in the subordination and enslavement of the consumer. Achieved celebrities can perform an emancipatory function in raising consciousness, building a sense of belonging, and expediting distributive justice.

Poststructuralist approaches to celebrity employ the motif of intertextuality to explain the appeal of celebrity and the rise of celebrity culture. Intertextuality proceeds on the basis that meaning is always an effect of the interplay between agents and texts. The method developed in poststructuralist philosophy as a way of destabilizing phonocentric or logocentric readings of meaning which assume the notion of transcendental presence. For example, Richard Dyer explores celebrity as the constant interplay and negotiation between cultural intermediaries, achieved celebrities, and audiences. Unlike structuralist approaches that tend to assume a prime-mover in the construction of celebrity (usually, the culture industry), poststructuralist approaches emphasize shifting power alliances and a continuous process of exchange and negotiation.

However, in privileging the role of textuality and discourse in the construction of celebrity, poststructuralist approaches produce a curiously disembodied account of celebrity. The glamor and sensuality of celebrity are missing. Similarly, these accounts are usually based upon weak comparative and historical perspectives, which means that they have difficulties in explaining or predicting change in genres of celebrity.

Without doubt the expansion of mass communications has been the principal factor in the enlargement of celebrity culture. Globalization and the disembedding of populations have created a new role of cultural adhesion for celebrities. Their presence in everyday life may be largely at the level of virtual reality. Nonetheless, one can argue that they anchor exchange and interaction by providing foci of continuity, glamor, and sensuality. As organized religion has declined, the culture of achieved celebrity has emerged to offer new narratives of belonging and recognition. The lifestyles of the rich and famous may even perform the function of late-modern parables in which audiences gain insights and support into lifestyle management issues. By the same token, the proliferation of celebrity culture has created divisions and sectarianism. Celebrities are certainly often efficient in manipulating public opinion and for this reason the employment of celebrities in the advertising industry has become a more prominent feature of commodity culture.

A *celetoid* is an individual who achieves concentrated media attention for an intense but brief time span and then fades from collective memory. The concept arose from the analysis of celebrity and the emergence of achieved celebrity culture. Celetoids are the product of the age of the mass media and especially checkbook journalism. One recent example that is familiar globally is Monica Lewinsky, who was at the center of sexual allegations involving President Bill Clinton in his second term of office. For a relatively short time, Lewinsky was the focal point of mass media attention, featuring in newspaper stories, TV documentaries, and talk shows. Her involvement with Clinton produced a lucrative book deal and other media spin offs. However, as media interest subsided, collective interest in and memory of Lewinsky receded. Other examples of celetoids are one-hit wonders, have-a-go-heroes, reality TV contestants, and medical phenomena such as octuplets, Siamese twins, and so on.

In the age of electronic mass communications the celetoid can be regarded as embodying the carnivalesque tradition identified by

Mikhail Bakhtin in which the categories – especially the hierarchy of formal order – are subject to parody, ridicule, or more restrained forms of contest. However, the celetoid is also a powerful weapon in the ratings wars in which agents of the media exaggerate or create scandals and sensationalism in pursuit of high sales.

SEE ALSO: Celebrity Culture; Consumption; Culture Industries; Media Literacy; Music and Media; Popular Culture; Popular Culture Icons

REFERENCES AND SUGGESTED READINGS

Braudy, L. (1997) *The Frenzy of Reknown*. Random House, New York.
Bruce, S. (1990) *Pray TV*. Routledge, London.
Elliott, A. (1999) *The Mourning of John Lennon*. University of California, Berkeley.
Rojek, C. (2001) *Celebrity*. Reaktion, London.
Turner, G. (2004) *Celebrity and Culture*. Sage, London

celebrity culture

Ellis Cashmore

Celebrity culture is characterized by a pervasive preoccupation with famous persons and an extravagant value attached to the lives of public figures whose actual accomplishments may be limited, but whose visibility is extensive. It became a feature of social life, especially in the developed world, during the late 1980s/early 1990s and extended into the twenty-first century, assisted by a global media which promoted, lauded, sometimes abominated, and occasionally annihilated figures, principally from entertainment and sports.

Celebrity culture defined thought and conduct, style and manner. It affected and was affected by not just fans but entire populations whose lives had been shaped by the shift from manufacturing to service societies and the corresponding shift from consumer to aspirational consumer.

While some have argued that there have been acclaimed and illustrious characters of considerable renown since the days of the Macedonian king Alexander the Great in the third century BCE, and perhaps before, the distinguishing features of contemporary celebrity culture are: the prodigious number of famous individuals whose fame is predicated less on achievement and more on the attention of the media; the ubiquity of their representation; and the immoderate esteem afforded them by a wide constituency of consumers.

A further distinguishing peculiarity of celebrity culture was the shift of emphasis from achievement-based fame to media-driven renown. This was captured in the contrived verb *to celebrify*, which, while never formally defined, might be interpreted to mean "to exalt; praise widely; make famous; invest common or inferior person or thing with great importance."

In his *Illusions of Immortality*, David Giles (2000: 25) submits that: "The ultimate modern celebrity is the member of the public who becomes famous solely through media involvement." While the "ultimate" celebrity's rise might be attributable "solely" to the media, celebrities typically performed some deed, however modest, to attract initial attention. That deed might involve an appearance on a reality television show, a criminal action, or an inept showing at a major sports event. In other words, conduct that would hardly be regarded as commendable and deserving of recognition in earlier eras, perhaps as recently as the 1980s.

During the late 1980s and early 1990s, however, conceptions of merit were rendered indeterminate and figures who traditionally earned distinction and drew praise for their efforts vied with more prosaic characters whose achievements were often uncertain. This heralded what we might call the Age of the Celebrity, in which idolatrous followings accrued to what seemed literally worthless individuals. In fact, they were not worthless, worth being an equivalent value of merit conferred on someone or something by a population. Whether the neophyte celebs actually deserved reverence is a less interesting question to a sociologist than the reasons why so many believed they deserved it. A participant in a reality television show, a contestant in a quiz show, a hitherto unknown bank clerk featured in an advertising

campaign: these were the types of characters who ascended from obscurity to public visibility and, in some cases, veneration. They became estimable without seeming to do anything.

What they *did* do was appear; their images were relayed to millions via television and Internet sites; newspapers recorded their exploits; magazines recounted their thoughts. "Media involvement," to repeat Giles's term, was the key to their deeds: they involved themselves with the media.

Various accounts purported to explain the zeal with which consumers pursued celebrities, who, by the late 1990s, were assigned an unofficial alphanumeric rating, members of the A-list afforded most prestige. Most arguments suggested that being a fan – and that probably included anyone who was aware of celebrities, i.e., all but recluses, hermits, and ascetics – sought and discovered a sense of empowerment. Though rarely interrogated, empowerment (at least in the context of celebrity culture) meant a fortification of confidence, especially in controlling one's own life, and perhaps claiming one's rights.

THE LEADERSHIP VACUUM AND THE GLOBALIZED MEDIA

While it appeared to pop out of a vacuum at the end of the 1980s, there were three conditions under which celebrity culture came into being. The first is a widespread loss of faith and confidence in established forms of leadership. In times of national crisis, we are forced to place our faith in traditional leaders. Engaged in war or under siege, people look to their politicians, generals, and church leaders. These were active people, who based their reputations on what they said and did.

In the absence of crises, our commitment became less secure and we had no need to trust them anymore. In his *Big League, Big Time*, Len Sherman (1998) argues that, while celebrities might not have been obvious replacements, they were functional equivalents of leaders: people who represented, influenced, perhaps inspired and commanded our attention, if not respect. In addition, they possessed a kind of exemplary authority. As such, they became what Sherman describes as "the most watched, admired, privileged, and imitated people."

The next condition was the time-space compression. The globalization of the media introduced the capacity to transmit large volumes of information – news, entertainment, and advertising – around the world, not just quickly, but instantly. Satellites, or transponders, were the instruments of the media's global expansion. By wrapping the world in an invisible network of communications, satellite broadcasters were able to bounce information off satellites and send them literally anywhere. Satellite television companies recognized no national boundaries. This effectively meant that virtually everyone on earth was part of one huge market.

Rupert Murdoch, perhaps more than any other media figure, exploited the opportunities offered by the satellite technology pioneered in the 1960s, and the deregulation and privatization of the television industry in the 1980s and early 1990s. In February 1989, Murdoch's European satellite started beaming programs via satellite through his Sky network. By the end of the 1990s, his various channels reached 66 percent of the world's population.

The problem with having so many channels is content: what do you fill them with? MTV supplied a clue. To keep so much of the world glued to the screen, television networks needed a formula. Televised programming detached itself from fixed content and began firing off in the direction of entertainment, for which we should read *amusement* – something that occupies us agreeably, diverting our minds from matters that might prompt introspection, analysis, or reflection. This is not to suggest that drama that provokes contemplation and critical examination cannot be entertaining too, nor even that the narratives of soaps or cartoons are not open to critical reading. And it certainly does not underestimate the viewers' speedy acquisition of skills for screening and skimming information. But, for the most part, entertainment does not prompt us to modify ourselves in any way.

Light entertainment, to use a more indicative term, became a staple of a formula that demanded only a modest level of attention from viewers. Music+movies+sport. Asked to respond to this in the 1990s, an informed person might have said: people will soon get sick of it; they will feel bombarded, under siege, overwhelmed by too much entertainment. This did not prove to be the case.

Of course, the communications revolution did not end with television and the proliferation of multimedia brought a further layer of information conduits, notably the Internet.

THE NEW TRANSPARENCY

The third condition concerned the relationship between performers and the newly emergent media. Even before it was called showbusiness, the entertainment industry furnished individual artists who drew acclaim and were used as selling points. From nineteenth-century minstrel shows, through ragtime, the British music halls, silent film, radio, and, of course, theater, popular entertainment forms invariably provided a showcase for figures who distinguished themselves from their contemporaries. The Hollywood star system, beginning in the 1940s, was able to exploit this as no other industry ever had, operating a smooth-functioning, factory-like production line in which "stars" were treated much as commodities. Their use value was in generating box office sales.

While the concept of producing stars rather than waiting for them to emerge stayed largely intact until the mid-1980s, the newly abundant media both offered different opportunities and demanded a different kind of engagement with artists. Madonna, perhaps more than any other entertainer, realized this.

After the success of her fourth album, *Like a Prayer*, in 1989, Madonna appears to have seen the future: the days when people got to be famous and stayed that way through just making movies, hit records, or writing bestsellers were approaching an end. The most important feature of the coming age was visibility: doing was less important than just being in the public gaze. With so many channels of communication being filled up with all manner of entertainment, there was bound to be an overflow of entertainers, most of whom would make little impression on the public consciousness. The ones who did were those who would not just make themselves visible but transparent – there was no contradiction.

Madonna not only epitomized this, she also helped it materialize. She seems to have struck a bargain with the media. It was something like: "I will tell you more, show you more about me than any other rock or movie star in history; I will disclose my personal secrets, share my fears, joys, sorrows, what makes me happy or sad, angry or gratified; I will be more candid and unrestricted in my interviews than any other entertainer. In other words, I'll be completely see-through. In return, I want coverage like no other: I want to be omnipresent, ubiquitous, and pervasive – I want to be everywhere, all the time." It was an intriguing quid pro quo; almost as if new rules of engagement with the media had been formulated. The age of celebrity began.

As the 1980s turned to the 1990s, Madonna was, as she wanted to be, everywhere. This was surely the meaning of Blonde Ambition, the title of her 1991 tour. The following year, she bared herself in her book *Sex*, accompanied by the album *Erotica*. Being famous was no longer sufficient: it was necessary to make consumers privy to as many aspects of a celebrity's life as permissible.

The beauty of the age of celebrity, though, was that the consumers were not hapless chumps: they were educated in the arts of celeb-production by the very channels that presented them. Put another way, they didn't just look at the pictures: they were able readers. They did most of the work. This is the thesis of Joshua Gamson's study *Claims to Fame*, which portrays fans as knowing and savvy participants in the celebrity production process: "The position audiences embrace includes the roles of simultaneous voyeurs of and performers in commercial culture" (1994: 137).

All the celebs did was make themselves available. Madonna was the first celebrity to render her manufacture completely transparent. Unabashed about revealing to her fandom evidence of the elaborate and monstrously expensive publicity and marketing that went into her videos, CDs, stage acts, and, indeed, herself, Madonna laid open her promotional props, at the same time exposing her utterly contrived persona changes.

CONSUMPTION AND COMMODIFICATION

Writers such as Graeme Turner (2004) and Helga Dittmar et al. (1995) have pointed out the ways in which celebrities, perhaps inadvertently, promote aspirational consumption by becoming ambulant advertisements. In this sense, celebrity culture is perfectly consonant with commodification – the process whereby everything, including public figures, can be converted into an article of trade to be exchanged in the marketplace.

Consumer culture was originally built on the avarice, envy, and possessiveness that flourished in the post-war years. Robert K. Merton's classic study "Social Structure and Anomie" had concluded that desire drives us toward appropriation: we want to possess the things we see dangled in front of us by advertising. The advertising industry had sensed that people didn't buy products just because they needed them: the needs had to be encouraged. Desire worked much better. If someone desires something, the second they procured it, the desire is gone. So, the trick was to keep pumping up new desires: as soon as consumers upgraded the fridge, they needed to start thinking about a new car. As soon as they got the car, they started thinking about a new house. "The accelerator of consumer demand," as Zygmunt Bauman calls it, is pressed hard down as new offers keep appearing on the road ahead.

In his article "Consuming Life," Bauman (2001: 16) argues that one of the triumphs of the consumer culture is in liberating the pleasure principle from the perimeter fence beyond which pleasure seekers once could venture only at their peril. "Consumer society has achieved a previously unimaginable feat: it reconciled the reality and pleasure principles by putting, so to speak, the thief in charge of the treasure box," he concludes.

In other words: consumers still want to possess commodity goods, but they allow themselves the indulgence of whimsically wishing for things that they know are out of reach. However, that does not stop consumers wishing to be like any number of other celebrities who actually possess not only the coveted goods but also a congruent lifestyle. Consumers do not just want the attainable: they wish for the unattainable. What once seemed totally irrational now appears completely logical. Human desire has been transformed.

Shopping is now considered glamorous, not utilitarian. The consumer is encouraged to declare her worth by spending money on items that will help her look like, play like, or in some other way be like someone else. That someone else is the celebrity, or more likely, celebrities with whom she feels or wants to feel an attachment. In this sense, the consumer's enterprise is as much to express a sense of bonding or even identity with the celebrity as acquiring new possessions.

Celebrity culture is a phenomenon that is simultaneously well known and recondite. Many are fascinated by celebrities without actually understanding why they are fascinated. Everyone is aware of celebrity culture while remaining ignorant of when, where, and why it came into being. Maintaining this paradox is arguably the greatest triumph of celebrity culture.

SEE ALSO: Celebrity and Celetoid; Fans and Fan Culture; Popular Culture; Popular Culture Icons

REFERENCES AND SUGGESTED READINGS

Bauman, Z. (2001) Consuming Life. *Journal of Consumer Culture* 1(1).

Dittmar, H., Beattie, J., & Friese, S. (1995) Gender Identity and Material Symbols: Objects and Decision Considerations in Impulse Purchases. *Journal of Economic Psychology* 15: 391–511.

Gamson, J. (1994) *Claims to Fame: Celebrity in Contemporary America*. University of California Press, Berkeley.

Giles, D. (2000) *Illusions of Immortality: A Psychology of Fame and Celebrity*. Macmillan, London.

Merton, R. K. (1969) Social Structure and Anomie. Reprinted in: Cressey, D. R. & Ward, D. A. (Eds.), *Delinquency, Crime and Social Process*. Harper & Row, New York.

Sherman, L. (1998) *Big League, Big Time: The Birth of the Arizona Diamondbacks, the Billion-Dollar Business of Sports, and the Power of the Media in America*. Pocket Books, New York.

Turner, G. (2004) *Understanding Celebrity*. Sage, London.

Waters, M. (2001) *Globalization*, 2nd edn. Routledge, New York.

censorship

Matt Hills

Censorship has generally been of interest to social theorists when considered as a matter of state control over "free speech" and/or mass-mediated content. This governmental censorship has tended to focus on notions of protecting "vulnerable" (young/lower-class/female) audiences from representations of sex, violence, and criminality which, it is assumed, may deprave, corrupt, or desensitize them (Dewe Mathews 1994).

Media–sociological work on censorship (e.g., Barker & Petley 2001) argues that it has worked to support the ideological power of hegemonic blocs, tending to repress expression which does not fall into normative cultural categories, as well as especially restricting popular rather than "literary" culture. "Educated," middle-class audiences for elite culture are not as likely to be represented as "vulnerable" as audiences for popular film and television. In the US, the cinema Production Code of 1930 infamously detailed exactly what could not be shown in classical Hollywood film: sexual relations between heterosexual characters were elided; morally bad characters were depicted as never triumphing thanks to their crimes; and homosexual relationships could not be shown nor even strongly implied (Jacobs 1991; Berenstein 1996).

As well as restricting popular culture through codes of conduct for producers or industry self-regulation, censorship can also be said to act productively (Kuhn 1988). Though it has historically produced gaps and absences in pop culture, it has also shaped texts and genres, especially by favoring moral messages such as "crime will be punished."

Censorship debates have been recurrently linked to moral panics surrounding new media technologies. One of these was the UK's "video nasties" panic in the 1980s (Critcher 2003), when the new media technology of video recording was felt to have undermined media regulation by making "adult" horror texts depicting violence and gore available to "children." More recently, the Internet has occasioned similar outcries, with the availability of online pornography supposedly threatening state and industry regulation of such imagery.

Despite the focus on state and media industry censorship, the term can be addressed sociologically in a variety of other ways. For example, Hill (1997) analyzes subjective "self-censorship," whereby media audiences, as social agents, reflexively monitor their own media consumption, seeking to avoid specific types of imagery. Hills (2005) argues that censorship practices underpin certain fan-cultural distinctions, as genre fans construct their communal self-identity against both governmental censors and "mainstream" audiences.

SEE ALSO: Fans and Fan Culture; Film; Genre; Media, Regulation of; Moral Panics

REFERENCES AND SUGGESTED READINGS

Barker, M. & Petley, J. (Eds.) (2001) *Ill Effects: The Media/Violence Debate*, 2nd edn. Routledge, London.
Berenstein, R. (1996) *Attack of the Leading Ladies*. Columbia University Press, New York.
Critcher, C. (2003) *Moral Panics and the Media*. Open University Press, Buckingham.
Dewe Mathews, T. (1994) *Censored*. Chatto & Windus, London.
Hill, A. (1997) *Shocking Entertainment: Viewer Response to Violent Movies*. University of Luton Press, Luton.
Hills, M. (2005) *The Pleasures of Horror*. Continuum, New York.
Jacobs, L. (1991) *The Wages of Sin*. University of Wisconsin Press, Madison.
Kuhn, A. (1988) *Cinema, Censorship and Sexuality, 1909–1925*. Routledge, London.

central business district

Michael Indergaard

The central business district (CBD) is the downtown of the American city, which in the early twentieth century possessed two sorts of centrality: first, it was usually at or near the city's geographical center and, second, it hosted its most important economic functions. The term

emerged as business districts were developing in outlying areas, but downtowns, with their skyscrapers, mammoth department stores, and movie palaces, remained dominant. However, after downtowns peaked in importance in the 1920s, policy debates and sociological discussions increasingly focused on (1) problems related to their decline and (2) organized attempts to bolster or reestablish their centrality.

Like the term downtown, the idea of a CBD was uniquely American, reflecting a sharp separation between place of work and place of residence that distinguished US cities from those in Europe. In the 1920s CBDs were dense concentrations of businesses that were largely depopulated, but visited on a daily basis by a majority of the city's residents who came to work, shop, or seek amusement. It was commonly thought that their standing was confirmed, rather than challenged, by the decentralization of population and business. This notion was theoretically affirmed by Ernest Burgess, one of the founders of the Chicago School of Sociology, who proposed that as the city grew it expanded radially from the CBD in a series of concentric zones or rings. Fusing notions from human ecology and neoclassical economics, Burgess depicted the CBD as a crucible of competition that improved efficiencies in land use across the city; only intensive users that could exploit its central location (e.g., department stores, banks, central offices) could afford to pay its high prices while others were dispatched to search out the places that best fit their respective needs and abilities to pay. Thus, he concluded that the CBD naturally remained the center of economic, political, and cultural life.

The concentric zone thesis inspired several decades of research, but by the 1930s downtowns were beset with falling property values and tax revenues, decaying residential areas, and unrelenting traffic congestion. Subsequently, real estate interests and their allies repeatedly mobilized to revitalize CBDs. Their argument that the central city needed to be made more attractive so as to draw capital and middle-class residents back spawned notions such as urban redevelopment and urban renewal, and influenced federal policies for over three decades. These efforts disrupted many minority neighborhoods, but had limited success in revitalizing CBDs, which were buffeted by the extension of freeways, suburbanization, racial tension, and industrial decline. In the 1970s, the federal government left cities on their own, while market thinkers proposed that their fortunes depended on their ability to compete for capital; some suggested that it was natural that CBDs were declining in importance. Against the naturalism of market thinkers (and human ecology) a critical approach (urban political economy) emerged, stressing that the city was a built environment shaped by economic and political power. Critical scholars linked the changing fortunes of CBDs to investment cycles and showed that centrality was accompanied by social exclusion and hierarchy. In the 1980s, they focused on growth coalitions wherein city officials and various interests joined to boost property values and how gentrification fed off of, and reinforced, the centrality of downtowns.

In the 1990s, scholars drew attention to new forms of centrality in CBDs related to the growing economic importance of globalization and culture. Global city theorists proposed that the diverse resource base of some major cities, along with their positioning vis-à-vis communication networks and corporate headquarters, allowed them to assume several central functions in the global economy: to exercise command and control over decentralized production systems and to serve as sites for new dominant sectors, namely, finance and producer services, and for related innovations and markets. Their centrality involves their standing vis-à-vis global networks: their CBDs are less connected to, and provide few benefits for, other areas and social segments within their own region. Another body of work focused on issues related to the roles cities play in the symbolic economy: a new focus on organizing consumption, including publicly subsidized construction of large entertainment projects (e.g., professional sports stadiums, festival malls) that aim to bring the middle class to the CBD as visitors; the role of artists in altering property images and values; and the rising importance of creative workers – a less conventional middle-class segment drawn to the city's distinctive lifestyles and employment opportunities.

Identifying the boundaries and essential features of CBDs has become ever more problematic as the production of centrality is increasingly wedded to flows of images and finance capital. During the 1990s, areas on the margins of CBDs gained instant centrality through linking up with Internet infrastructures, startups, and financing networks. It is unclear how resilient this sort of centrality will prove to be. Concentrations of creative firms can exploit advantages of face-to-face interaction to make new applications of digital technology. But technology also facilitates further decentralization – an option made newly attractive by the threat that terrorism poses to symbols of global centrality.

SEE ALSO: Chicago School; Ecological Models of Urban Form: Concentric Zone Model, the Sector Model, and the Multiple Nuclei Model; Global/World Cities; Megalopolis; Metropolis; Metropolitan Statistical Area; Park, Robert E. and Burgess, Ernest W.; Urban; Urban Renewal and Redevelopment; Urbanization

REFERENCES AND SUGGESTED
READINGS

Burgess, E. W. (1924) The Growth of the City: An Introduction to a Research Project. *Publications of the American Sociological Society* 18: 85–97.
Fogelson, R. M. (2001) *Downtown: Its Rise and Fall, 1880–1950.* Yale University Press, New Haven.
Gotham, K. F. (2001) Urban Redevelopment, Past and Present. In: Gotham, K. F. (Ed.), *Critical Perspectives on Urban Redevelopment*, vol. 6. Elsevier, London, pp. 1–31.
Harvey, D. (1973) *Social Justice and the City.* Johns Hopkins University Press, Baltimore.
Sassen, S. (1991) *The Global City: New York, London, Tokyo.* Princeton University Press, Princeton.
Zukin, S. (1991) *Landscapes of Power: From Detroit to Disney World.* University of California Press, Berkeley.

Certeau, Michel de (1925–86)

Ian Buchanan

Born in 1925 in Chambéry, France, Michel de Certeau obtained degrees in classics and philosophy at the universities of Grenoble,

Lyon, and Paris. Joining the Society of Jesus in 1950, he was ordained in 1956. He completed a doctorate on the mystical writings of Jean-Joseph Surin at the Sorbonne in 1960 and taught in Paris and San Diego. He died of stomach cancer in 1986.

Certeau's career can be divided into three stages. The first was largely concerned with traditional religious history; then, after "the Events of May" (1968), his work took a very different turn, becoming both contemporary and sociocultural; then, after a highly productive decade writing about contemporary issues, Certeau's thoughts returned to the history of religion and he produced what would be his last book, a two-volume history of seventeenth-century mysticism in Europe.

The first stage of Certeau's career culminated in a profound retheorization of history, the fruit of which is to be seen in *L'écriture de l'histoire* (*The Writing of History*), first published in 1975. Greatly influenced by Lacanian psychoanalysis, Certeau argued that history is a machine for calming the anxiety most westerners feel in the face of death. It works by raising the specter of death within a memorial framework that gives the appearance that we will live forever after all. Ultimately, Certeau's project was an attempt to understand "the historiographic operation" itself, which he described as a threefold relation between a *place*, an analytic *procedure*, and the construction of a *text*.

The second stage of Certeau's career began abruptly in May 1968 when the streets of Paris erupted in a paroxysm of student and blue-collar protest. The essays written on the run in these heady days (*The Capture of Speech*) are of lasting interest to social theorists for the way they begin to theorize everyday forms of resistance. Certeau was given an opportunity to expand on these preliminary investigations in the early 1970s when he was given a large research grant to study French culture on a broad scale. Pierre Mayol and Luce Giard were brought on board to assist, contributing two ethnographic studies on "living" (Mayol) and "cooking" (Giard). The legacy of this work is the two volumes of *The Practice of Everyday Life* (a third was planned, but never completed). Certeau completed a project on migrants (*Culture in the Plural*), also government

funded (the OECD). In terms of their uptake in sociology, Certeau's most important and influential concepts come from this period: strategy and tactics, place and space.

Both strategy and tactics are determined as *calculations*. In his early thinking on the subject, Certeau toyed with the idea of connecting the notions of strategy and tactics to modal logic and game theory, but this was never brought to fruition. The essential difference between strategy and tactics is the way they relate to the variables that everyday life inevitably throws at us all. Strategy works to limit the sheer number of variables that can effect it by creating some kind of protected zone, a place, in which the environment can be rendered predictable if not properly tame. Tactics, by contrast, is the approach one takes to everyday life when one is unable to take measures against its variables. Tactics refers to the set of practices that strategy has not been able to domesticate. They are not in themselves subversive, but they function symbolically as daily proof of the partiality of strategic control.

The transition point between the second and third stage of his career is Certeau's unfinished project on the anthropology of belief. He started it while working at the University of California San Diego, a position he held from 1978 to 1984, but set it aside after completing only three essays to work on what turned out to be his last work, *The Mystic Fable*. These essays concern the way the forerunners to modern anthropology – Montaigne (*Heterologies*), Léry (*The Writing of History*), and Lafitau ("Writing vs. Time") – encountered the manifold differences of the New World as alterity and turned that alterity into a means of authorizing their own discourse about the Old World. Certeau described this discourse as heterological, which strictly speaking means discourse of the other. But since he died before formulating either a specific thesis or a particular method, we can only speculate on what he actually intended by the term. It is clear, however, that he meant "other" to be understood as a complex interweaving of its theological and psychoanalytic trajectories.

Certeau began to work in earnest on his mysticism project, which culminates the third and final stage of his career, when he returned to France after nearly a decade in California. This project revisits the topic with which

Certeau's career began, but as with his critique of historiography, its aim was not merely to add yet another catalogue of curiosities to an already well-stocked cabinet. Rather, he wanted to understand the logic of mysticism, to try to understand it for itself as its own peculiar kind of discourse. In this respect, as he explains in the opening pages of the first volume of *The Mystic Fable*, his aim can best be grasped as the attempt to revive (literally, make live again) the lost discourse known as mystics, which, like physics, metaphysics, ethics, and so on, was once a discipline in its own right. But since in contrast to these other discourses mystics has in fact vanished, Certeau also had to account for its subsequent disappearance. He argued that mystics exhausted itself because its project of trying to resurrect the word of God in an era that no longer knew its God simply could not be sustained. Mystics could, through its bold linguistic experiments, occasionally evoke the essential mystery of God, but it could not convert that into an enduring presence.

SEE ALSO: Everyday Life; Lefebvre, Henri; Practice

REFERENCES AND SUGGESTED READINGS

Ahearne, J. (1995) *Michel de Certeau: Interpretation and its Other*. Polity, Cambridge.

Buchanan, I. (2000) *Michel de Certeau: Cultural Theorist*. Sage, London.

Buchanan, I. (2002) *De Certeau in the Plural*. Duke University Press, Durham, NC.

Certeau, M. de (1980). Writing vs. Time: History and Anthropology in the Works of Lafitau. Trans. J. Hovde. *Yale French Studies* 59: 37–64.

Certeau, M. de (1984) *The Practice of Everyday Life*. Trans. S. Rendall. University of California Press, Berkeley.

Certeau, M. de (1986) *Heterologies: Discourse on the Other*. Trans. B. Massumi. University of Minnesota Press, Minneapolis.

Certeau, M. de (1988 [1975]) *The Writing of History*. Trans. T. Conley. Columbia University Press, New York.

Certeau, M. de (1992) *The Mystic Fable*. Trans. M. B. Smith. Chicago University Press, Chicago.

Certeau, M. de (1997a) *The Capture of Speech and Other Political Writings*. Trans. T. Conley. University of Minnesota Press, Minneapolis.

Certeau, M. de (1997b) *Culture in the Plural*. Trans. T. Conley. University of Minnesota Press, Minneapolis.

Certeau, M. de, Giard, L., & Mayol, P. (1998) *The Practice of Everyday Life*. Vol. 2: *Living and Cooking*. Trans. T. J. Tomasik. University of Minnesota Press, Minneapolis.

Dosse, F. (2002a) *Michel de Certeau, le marcheur blessé*. La Découverte, Paris.

Dosse, F. (Ed.) (2002b) *Michel de Certeau, chemins d'histoire*. Éditions Complexe, Paris.

chance and probability

Stephen Turner

Chance is an informal concept, sometimes meaning probability, sometimes meaning randomness. Probability is a formal mathematical concept expressed in its most simple form as dependent probability, which is a number between 0 and 1 that represents the likelihood that, for example, a person with one property will have another property. Thus, the probability of a live birth being female is a dependent probability in which the two properties are live birth and female. Probabilities may also be assigned to beliefs. In this case, known as subjective probability, the number represents the strength with which we believe another belief to be true. This is the kind of probability that one employs in making a bet with a friend about whether or not something is true.

It is commonly asserted that social processes are probabilistic and that causal relations in social sciences are probabilistic. This usually means that the causal relationships or processes in question are not deterministic. It is something of a paradox that despite this widespread belief, there are few theories and only a few models that employ formal notions of probability. However, only very infrequently can numerical dependent probabilities be assigned to non-deterministic processes or causal relations. Typically, the relations are not only non-deterministic, but are subject to a large number of additional causal influences which are themselves non-deterministic.

Why is this the case? The problem, as John Stuart Mill saw 150 years ago, is complexity and entanglement. The social processes we are interested in are typically influenced by a large number of variables and cannot be isolated from these influences and identified and estimated. Consequently, we also cannot estimate their interactions. Thus, it is impossible to obtain precise knowledge of the causal relationships that interest us, and which we believe to be fundamentally probabilistic. Moreover, constructing theories or models with multiple probabilities is mathematically difficult. Thus, probabilities generally play very little formal role in sociological theories. Because actually identifying probabilities and deriving predictions from them is so difficult, alternative methods are used.

Our normal substitute for knowledge of the actual mechanisms is the causal model. Causal models are not based on probabilistic relations between inputs and outputs, but instead use a particular kind of simplification, which uses non-probabilistic linear relations, which are known or assumed to be false as representations of the unknown underlying processes, but which are easy to formulate mathematically. These are treated as representing actual causal processes with a determinable degree of "error." Error here is understood as the difference between the outcomes that would be predicted if the simplifications were true and the actual outcomes. Some philosophers and statisticians, such as Clark Glymour, have argued that this is the only kind of causal knowledge available to the social scientist, and that consequently the usual way of formulating the theoretical aspirations of social science, by comparing it to physics (which does use probabilities to represent basic causal processes), is misguided.

The terms used in standard statistical discussion, notably "error," despite the fact that they are enshrined in statistical usage, are confusing and potentially misleading in this context. The term error is correctly applied to such cases as errors of observation (e.g., in the distribution or curve of errors that multiple observers make when they are identifying the position of a star through a telescope). The application to the social sciences is confusing because the numerical phenomena to which it is typically applied in social sciences are not errors of observation, but rather the distribution of observed values

that result from actual non-deterministic, entangled, causal processes, and would appear whether or not there was any error of observation at all.

The source of the usage is historical. The standard method of modeling causal relations in the social sciences originated with Karl Pearson, who invented correlation and regression analysis. The method involved measuring the degree to which knowledge of the value of one variable enabled the value of the second variable to be predicted. This was done by identifying the (deterministic, linear) equation, graphically represented as a line, which had the least error as a representation of the relationship. A close relationship with relatively little variation or "error" around this line produced a high correlation, while a relationship in which there was more variation produced a low correlation. This notion of variation used the mathematics of error and calculated variation in terms of least squared deviations from regression lines.

Although this error-based notion of probability as variation is the basis of standard causal models of the kind used in sociology, there are alternatives. Some forms of modeling employ the notion of dependent probability and attempt to measure the goodness of fit of such models with data. Subjective probabilities, or probabilities of belief, are employed in Bayesian statistics in which new data are understood to improve probabilistic estimates or estimates of variation.

SEE ALSO: Fact, Theory, and Hypothesis: Including the History of the Scientific Fact; Statistics

REFERENCES AND SUGGESTED READINGS

Freedman, D. A. (2005) *Statistical Models: Theory and Practice*. Cambridge University Press, New York.
Humphreys, P. (1992 [1989]) *The Chances of Explanation: Causal Explanation in the Social, Medical, and Physical Sciences*. Princeton University Press, Princeton.
Glymour, C. (1983) Social Science and Social Physics. *American Behavioral Scientist* 28(2): 126–34.

change management

Patrick Dawson

A key aim of change management is to manage processes towards a future that, even when anticipated and planned for, can never be fully foreseen. It is a paradox that continues to generate considerable debate and conceptual and definitional confusion.

DEFINING CHANGE MANAGEMENT

There are many different definitions of change management. Simple definitions tend to stress the process of planning, controlling, and managing company change, whereas the more elaborate definitions detail the various cultural and structural elements of change as well as the need to overcome forces of resistance. The term is commonly used to refer to the process of managing a shift from some current state of operation toward some future state. This movement may be either in the form of a proactive strategy or in response to unforeseen changes in internal operations or external business market conditions. Change management is therefore about managing the process of *changing*. Whether this process involves extensive planning or is an unplanned response to unexpected forces will influence how the process is managed. Some commentators, for example, seek to identify best-practice guidelines on how best to manage planned change through drawing on company experience and building on research findings. Improving our abilities to manage change is a reasonable aim, yet the large majority of major change efforts still fail to achieve their stated objectives. It is the unpredictability of change, the complex and messy processes of changing, that makes this a fascinating area and one in which there will never be any sure-fire guidelines on how to make change succeed.

So how should we define change management? Change management is the control and coordination of processes in the transition to new forms of working arrangements and ways of operating. In managing change there is an intention to orchestrate or steer these processes toward some preferred or predefined outcome.

MAIN ELEMENTS AND TYPES OF CHANGE MANAGEMENT

Change management centers around planning and directing, monitoring and evaluating, and correcting and adapting change processes. The degree of manageability of these three elements of direction, appraisal, and regulation will be influenced by the scale and type of change. Change may take the form of fine-tuning operating practices through small developmental activities or it may involve a major reconfiguration of structures. Change may be in response to an unanticipated change in business market conditions or as part of a planned proactive strategy to reconceptualize business. If we combine the scale of change with whether change is in response to the unexpected or part of a planned strategy, then we can differentiate four ideal types. First, *reactive small-scale change* initiatives that seek to accommodate and adapt to unforeseen changes in, for example, local business market conditions. Second, *developmental proactive change* programs that seek to gradually improve on current ways of doing things over a planned period of time. Third, *proactive large-scale change* initiatives that seek to reinvent and renew company business. Fourth, *reactive large-scale change*; for example, the unanticipated need to respond to a change in business or world events that necessitates a major repositioning of a company.

As well as the dimensions of the scale and depth of change, and whether change is reactive or proactive, we can also consider a number of other elements: for example, the essential nature and content of the change (whether new technology or management technique), timeframes of change (whether change is to occur quickly or over a protracted period of time), the triggers to change (whether internal or external), and the effects of change on employee attitudes and perceptions. Internal drivers for change include structural and administrative elements, changes in the nature of products and the delivery of services, technology, and initiatives aimed at the human side of enterprise, whereas external drivers include changes in business market activity, world events, legislation, trade regulations, and advances in technology.

428 change management

HUMAN RESPONSES TO CHANGE MANAGEMENT

If people perceive change as being required in order to ensure business survival and maintain jobs then they are more likely to support change. However, if change is seen by employees as an attempt by management simply to tighten workplace controls in their search for greater levels of productivity in order to raise company profits or their own career profiles, then people are likely to resist change.

Human responses to change vary according to individual and group perceptions and the context within which change is taking place. For some people, change may form a routine part of their daily business activities. For example, they may be working in a highly dynamic business context where change is constant and as such forms part of the culture of the workplace. Within this context, employees may expect certain patterns of change and concerns may be raised over failure to sustain change (change is the norm rather than the exception). Alternatively, people working in an established large public organization may view change less as an ongoing driving dynamic and more as a disruption to daily activities and established ways of working. In this context, change occurs on an irregular basis and is not part of the culture of the organization. Today, the pervasiveness of company change has resulted in a myriad of change initiatives, often in the form of multiple and overlapping programs rather than single change projects, in which employees may become cynical of repeated announcements of the need to change. A lowering of status, disruption to social arrangements, change in job tasks, the threat of unemployment, and change fatigue can all cause people to resist company change initiatives. Their response to a minor change in work tasks to accommodate an ICT systems upgrade will differ to their response to a fundamental shift in the way things are done and organized. It is the manageability of large-scale transitions and transformational change initiatives (also referred to as "first-order change") that has drawn the greatest attention among academic researchers, the media, and the business community, as it is these changes that generally involve large investments in time and

money, are highly disruptive to employees, are often viewed as critical to business survival, and may raise issues of job security and employment.

THE CHANGING WORLD OF WORK: OLD WINE IN NEW BOTTLES

Interest in change is nothing new, as economic, social, legislative, technological, political, and business market forces continue to trigger processes of change in organizations. With the emergence of a new form of factory organization following the industrial revolution, the rise and fall of the textile industry, the mass manufacture of automobiles in the twentieth century, and the shifting fortunes of electronic and telecommunications companies in the twenty-first century, change management remains a central activity for companies that wish to remain in business. Early concerns centered on how to structure an efficient form of organization. For example, in the late nineteenth and early twentieth centuries, principles and concepts of organizations and their functioning were developed independently by a number of organization theorists: Henri Fayol, normally associated with administrative theory (an old term, which in the past has been used to refer to the principles of management); Max Weber, who focused his analysis on the emergence of the bureaucratic phenomenon; and Frederick Taylor, who formulated his principles of scientific management.

DIVISION OF LABOR UNDER NEW FACTORY REGIMES

Frederick Taylor advocated the close scrutiny of the way workers worked in order to identify the most efficient way of performing tasks. His time and motion studies were used to collect detailed data on the physical movements and characteristics of employees, the type of material and tools used in their work, and the time taken for them to complete tasks. From the scientific study of work he argued that it would be possible to redesign work processes to improve output while simultaneously ensuring that workers worked to their full capacity. For Taylor, the "variability" of labor is a recurrent managerial problem that needs to be tackled in the redesign of work that enables greater predictability and control in the transformation of a worker's capacity to work into actual work. His theory of change management is based on the assumption that there is one best way to structure an organization (a formalized structure to achieve specific goals) and that people are economic beings (workers are primarily motivated by monetary rewards).

WORK AS A COMPLEX SOCIAL SYSTEM: PEOPLE AND CHANGE

The human and social side to industry was highlighted in the famous set of studies carried out at the Western Electric Company, Hawthorne Works in Chicago. Their studies found how continuous improvements in employee performance could not simply be accounted for by more favorable conditions of work, but involved the effects of human associations on individual and group feelings of self-worth. Three major findings from these studies were that employees' physical capacities are generally less important than workgroup norms; employee decision-making typically reflects workgroup norms; and informal workgroup leaders have a key role in the motivation of staff and the maintenance of group objectives. By drawing attention to the social organization of work, these studies stimulated interest in the potential development and implementation of "ways of working" that would increase the motivation and efficiency of employees.

MECHANIZATION AND SOCIO-TECHNICAL SYSTEMS THEORY

In Britain, the Tavistock Institute of Human Relations was established in London in the late 1940s and was concerned with discovering ways of simultaneously improving worker satisfaction and employee productivity. Research on the mechanization of coal mining (assembly-line cutting, known as the longwall method) demonstrated the importance of social and community relations (rather than simply the psychology of individual needs). They concluded that there is a need to reconcile human

needs with technical efficiency, and in this case, they proposed a composite method that supported semi-autonomous workgroups. Socio-technical systems (STS) theory thereby evolved, maintaining that change initiatives that focus on either the purely technical or social aspects of work are likely to have limited "success," in producing a situation where the whole is sub-optimized for developments in one dimension.

STRATEGIES AND STRUCTURES: CONTINGENCIES OF CHANGE

Up until the 1960s the focus had mainly been on the internal characteristics of organizations and their operation, rather than on business context. Researchers were aware of the importance of external factors (noted in both the Hawthorne studies and the Durham coal-mining studies), but it was the emergence of contingency theory that brought this to the fore. Their basic theoretical tenet is that, while there is no one best way of organizing, it is possible to identify the most appropriate organizational form to fit the context in which a business has to operate. The factors that are deemed to be of primary significance include either single variables, such as technology or the environment, or a range of variables, such as in the ambitious study by the Aston group that examined the relationship between contextual factors and structural variables. Essentially, contingency theorists reject the search for a universal model (a one-best-way approach) and set out to develop useful generalizations about appropriate strategies and structures under different typical conditions.

NEW MANAGEMENT TECHNIQUES AND THE RISE OF THE ELECTRONIC ORGANIZATION

In the 1980s and 1990s, with the success of Japanese industry, attention turned to new methods of organizing and working, particularly within the engine of economic growth for the twentieth century, the automotive industry. Western manufacturing supremacy was being called into question by Japan, which had embraced the importance of quality management and employed new manufacturing methods such as Just-In-Time (JIT) management. Throughout the 1990s, organizations embarked on a plethora of change initiatives through a whole range of new production and service concepts that were often combined with developments in new technology. Since the turn of the century, attention continues to focus on developments in communication and information technologies and how these are "revolutionizing" our home and work lives. Debates on the effects of new forms of electronic business, jobs, and employment patterns in the so-called "e-age" combine with issues of globalization, cultural and political change, and the implications of the emergence of new industrial economies such as China.

COMPETING PERSPECTIVES AND THE IDEOLOGY OF CHANGE MANAGEMENT

There are a number of competing perspectives on change management and these often reflect the ideological positioning of the protagonists and/or their methodological preferences for conducting research. The positivistic tradition of contingency theorists, for example, has resulted in the design of certain types of studies to identify best strategies for managing change given certain prevailing circumstances. These snapshot studies (typically, quantitative) contrast with the more longitudinal qualitative studies that seek to study change over time. Ideologically, debates over whether change management is ultimately tied up with controlling and exploiting labor in the pursuit of company profits, or whether change management is essentially about improving the lot of workers and employees' experience of work, remain at the hub of many contemporary studies. Two worth reviewing here are the planned organizational development (OD) approach and the processual perspective.

ORGANIZATIONAL DEVELOPMENT: PLANNING FOR CHANGE

The three general steps identified by Kurt Lewin for successful change comprise *unfreezing*, *changing*, and *refreezing*. Unfreezing is the stage in which there is a recognized need for change and action is taken to unfreeze existing attitudes and behavior. This preparatory stage is deemed essential to the generation of employee support and the minimization of employee resistance. Lewin found that in order to minimize worker resistance, employees should be actively encouraged to participate in the process of planning proposed change programs. Managing change through reducing the forces that prevent change, rather than through increasing the forces which are pushing for change, is central to Lewin's approach and his technique of force-field analysis. He maintained that within any social system there are driving and restraining forces which serve to maintain the status quo, and that organizations generally exist in a temporary state of balance (quasi-stationary equilibrium) which is not conducive to change. Consequently, to bring about change you need either to increase the strength of the driving forces or decrease the strength of the resisting forces.

For OD specialists, change management centers on providing data to unfreeze the system through reducing the restraining forces rather than increasing the driving forces. Once an imbalance has been created then the system can be altered and a new set of driving and restraining forces put into place. A planned change program is implemented and only when the desired state has been achieved will the change agent set about "refreezing" the organization. The new state of balance is then appraised and where appropriate methods of positive reinforcement are used to ensure employees "internalize" attitudes and behaviors consistent with new work regimes. The values underpinning this approach are that individuals should be treated with respect and dignity, that hierarchical control mechanisms are not effective, that problems and conflicts should be confronted and reconciled, and that people affected by change should be involved in its implementation.

PROCESSUALISTS AND LONGITUDINAL RESEARCH ON CHANGE MANAGEMENT

Apart from these two perspectives, a more pluralist political process view has been promoted by a group of researchers known as processualists. Andrew Pettigrew's book *The Awakening Giant: Continuity and Change in ICI* (1985) powerfully demonstrates the limitations of theories that view change either as a single event or as a discrete series of episodes that can be decontextualized. In a comparative analysis of five cases of strategic change, the study illustrates how change as a continuous incremental process (evolutionary) can be interspersed with radical periods of change (revolutionary).

This foundational work of Pettigew has been widely referenced in the change management literature and the processual perspective is further developed in the work of Patrick Dawson. The three main factors that are seen to shape change processes comprise the politics, the context, and the substance of change. This perspective is concerned with the voices of employees at all levels within an organization, and with the political arenas in which decisions are made, histories re-created, and strategies rationalized. In this approach, change management is not simply about how managers manage change, but about how individuals and groups seek to make sense of their change experience. It is also concerned with understanding change through taking into account the enabling and constraining characteristics of change, as well as the scale and type of change (substance); and the conditions under which change is taking place in relation to external elements (e.g., business market environment) and internal elements (including the history and culture of an organization).

ONGOING DEBATES, FUTURE CONCERNS, AND EMERGING ISSUES

For those who view conflict and political process as an essential element of organizations in which a range of different individuals and groups compete, power is central and yet the divisions are not characterized as a dichotomy between management and workers (a criticism leveled at early labor process theories). Although many labor process theorists do take a far more sophisticated position than the one

characterized here, the essential element of the need to control workers under capitalist modes of production remains a central tenet. For those in the organizational development camp, conflicts are to be reconciled with democracy being key through a process of employee participation. Between these three characterizations lies a host of other positions and frameworks (for example, we could contrast a technical-bureaucratic with a cultural perspective, or a postmodern approach with a modernist position), and increasingly (if somewhat ironically) the sociological analysis of change management innovations is being more widely researched within business schools than sociology departments.

Current sociological thinking is moving towards a concern with a world of dualities in which the complexity and dynamics of process are recognized. The dualities of change and continuity, innovation and convention, centralization and decentralization, and organizing and strategizing question neat sequential models or simple continua that contrast and compare two dimensions. In the search for a division between dual factors, past studies have focused on definitional and conceptual issues in drawing boundaries to clarify the domain in question. In the case of change management, the possibility of managing change to improve industrial democracy and enhance employees' experience of work has been contrasted with studies that view change management as ultimately caught up with the exploitation of labor in the capitalist pursuit of ever-greater profits. Increasingly, many of these simple divisions are being called into question, highlighting the need for more detailed sociological studies of change management that are able to critique and inform such debates.

SEE ALSO: Knowledge Management; Organizational Learning; Strategic Decisions

REFERENCES AND SUGGESTED READINGS

Burnes, B. (2000) *Managing Change*, 3rd edn. Pitman, London.

Dawson, P. (2003) *Understanding Organizational Change*. Sage, London.

chaos

Leslie Wasson

Chaos theory emerged over the past several decades in the physical sciences as an explanatory framework for processes that appeared disorderly, such as turbulence or weather patterns, but which had complex mathematical models behind their seeming randomness. Complexity theory developed as an offshoot of chaos theory. It seeks to explain, among other things, the diversification of biological systems using a parsimonious set of predictors.

Social science has a history of applying theoretical findings from the physical sciences. However, theories which are highly predictive for disciplines such as chemistry or physics fall short of explanation for the diverse phenomena and larger standard error margins of human behavior. The apparent promise of chaos or complexity theories for sociology is their tolerance for ambiguity, uncertainty, or unpredictability, and their assertion that apparent disorder in human behavior may in fact be orderly at a higher level than we are measuring (Lee 2002).

However intriguing the theoretical or methodological possibilities may appear, at the time of this writing few sociological studies have been published that successfully apply chaos or complexity mathematics to empirical research results. Journal articles more frequently use concepts and models of chaos or complexity as metaphors, and they may fail to distinguish between the two theories. One example would be Weigel and Murray's (2000) article on stability and change in relationships. They suggest that the more dynamic and flexible modeling potential of chaos theory might provide additional explanatory power for studies of intimacy.

A few books and edited collections were published in the middle to late 1990s to explore the potential applications of chaos and complexity theories to the study of human behavior (Eve et al. 1997; Kiel & Elliott 1997; Byrne 1998) and to elucidate some of their methodological implications (Brown 1995).

Promising sociological research directions may also be found in the incorporation of fuzzy set theory to social science research methods (Ragin 2000; Ragin & Pennings 2005; Smithson 2005). "Fuzzification," according to its originator Lotfi Zadeh (1965, 1973, 1975), is a methodology used to generalize a specific theory from a crisp (discrete) to a continuous (fuzzy) form. Individual members of a fuzzy set may or may not have full membership in the discrete sense, but may be assigned a value indicating their degree of possible membership. For an empirical research example, readers might examine recent work on social movements (Amenta et al. 2005).

SEE ALSO: Knowledge, Sociology of; Kuhn, Thomas and Scientific Paradigms; Mathematical Sociology; Science and Culture; Science, Social Construction of; Scientific Knowledge, Sociology of

REFERENCES AND SUGGESTED READINGS

Amenta, E., Caren, N., & Olasky, S. J. (2005) Age for Leisure? Political Mediation and the Impact of the Pension Movement on US Old-Age Policy. *American Sociological Review* 70, 3 (June): 516–38.

Brown, C. (1995) *Chaos and Catastrophe Theories.* Sage, London.

Byrne, D. S. (1998) *Complexity Theory and the Social Sciences.* Routledge, London.

Eve, R. A., Horsfall, S., & Lee, M. E. (Eds.) (1997) *Chaos, Complexity, and Sociology: Myths, Models, and Theories.* Sage, London.

Kiel, L. D. & Elliott, E. W. (Eds.) (1997) *Chaos Theory in the Social Sciences: Foundations and Applications.* University of Michigan Press, Ann Arbor.

Lee, R. E. (2002) Imagining the Future: Constructing Social Knowledge After "Complexity Studies." *International Review of Sociology* 12, 2 (July): 333–41.

Ragin, C. C. (2000) *Fuzzy Set Social Science.* University of Chicago Press, Chicago.

Ragin, C. C. & Pennings, P. (2005) Fuzzy Sets and Social Research. *Sociological Methods and Research* 33, 4 (May): 423–30.

Smithson, M. (2005) Fuzzy Set Inclusion: Linking Fuzzy Set Methods With Mainstream Techniques. *Sociological Methods and Research* 33, 4 (May): 431–61.

Weigel, D. & Murray, C. I. (2000) The Paradox of Stability and Change in Relationships: What Does Chaos Theory Offer for the Study of Romantic

Relationships? *Journal of Social and Personal Relationships* 17, 3 (June): 425–49.

Zadeh, L. (1965) Fuzzy Sets. *Information and Control* 8: 338–53.

Zadeh, L. (1973) Outline of a New Approach to the Analysis of Complex Systems. IEEE Transactions on Systems. *Man and Cyb.* 3.

Zadeh, L. (1975) The Calculus of Fuzzy Restrictions. In: Zadeh, L. A. et. al. (Eds.), *Fuzzy Sets and Applications to Cognitive and Decision-Making Processes.* Academic Press, New York, pp. 1–39.

charisma

Stephen Hunt

The term "charisma" is one of the most enduring conceptions in the annals of sociology. Its origin, meaning "gift," as derived from the Greek, is close to Max Weber's understanding of the term which has subsequently passed into common vocabularies. The notion of charisma can be seen as one of Weber's core typologies, one related to the underlying basis of authority. Weber, in such works as *The Religion of China* (1951), speaks of charismatic leadership not only in terms of group cohesion but also in terms of education (pp. 30, 190), virtue of dynasty (pp. 198f., 119f., 135) – the belief in the transfer of extraordinary endowments of religious, political, or military descendants – and as hereditary (pp. 140, 141, 164). Weber also uses the term "gentile charisma" with reference to such families (pp. 35, 167, 264). In a sociological sense, charisma refers to the qualities of those who possess, or are believed to possess, powers of leadership either as a virtue of exceptional personality or derived from some unusual inspiration such as a magical, divine, or diabolical source, powers not possessed by the ordinary person (Weber 1947). Since Weber's notion of charisma is closely related to the sacred, it has parallels in Durkheim's *mana* – a dynamic which may be socially disruptive and seems to be inherent in certain objects or persons in tribal societies, as evidenced in the *orenda* among some North American tribes and *maga* in ancient Persia.

In his section on religion in *Economy and Society* (1978), translated and published separately as the *Sociology of Religion* (1965), Weber begins his analysis by examining what he considers to be the most elementary forms of religious belief and behavior. In tribal collectives, he observes, religious orientation is largely motivated by the desire to survive the immediate problems of everyday life through magical and manipulative means. Magic begins to develop into religion when charisma is attributed less to the objects themselves than to something behind the object which determines power – in other words, to a spirit, soul demon, or some similar conception. Once charisma is located outside the material world, the way is open for ethical demands of God(s).

Weber believed that all the great oriental religions were largely the product of intellectual speculation on the part of relatively privileged strata. Even more significant, however, have been intellectuals derived from relatively less privileged groups, especially those who, for one reason or another, stood outside the traditional class structure. The latter have tended to establish highly ethical and radical religious conceptions which Weber saw as marking a profound impact upon the development of the societies in which they emerged, in contrast to the rather conservative and elitist religious intellectualism of privileged strata. To one degree or another, these individuals also displayed charismatic qualities.

Charisma issues an evocation, and those who respond do so with conviction. Thus every charismatic leader invariably subscribes to the proposition, "It is written … but I say unto you …!". Charisma is thus unusual, spontaneous, and creative in a fundamentally sociological sense. It may be inherent or acquired. When acquired by a human being, it is usually the result of undergoing some extraordinary experience or involvement in practices which are extraordinary. It may, for example, be acquired through rigorous ascetic practices or time spent in mystical contemplation or through altered states of mind typified by trance or possession by spirits. Since charisma represents the extraordinary, the non-routine aspects of life and reality, it is something which can transcend established ideas and established order. It thus tends to be radical and revolutionary and opposed to tradition.

Charisma is a source of instability and innovation and therefore constitutes a dynamic element in social change. The concept of a cultural breakthrough was essential to Weber's understanding of the process of social transformation. At each "turning point" in a society's development, he argued, there are two possible directions in which it could advance. If it were to proceed in one direction, the society would undergo profound transformation in the established order, but, if it were to take the other, the existing order would be reinforced. The breakthrough juncture in social change is associated with the idea of charisma and prophets representing the prototypes of leaders with such qualities. Charismatic leadership is, in Weber's account, the source which precipitates it. Thus pure charisma is alien to the established institutions of society and prevailing economic arrangements in particular.

Three points have to be considered in association with the concept of charisma in relationship to social change. The first is the role of the individual who initially conceives and initiates the breakthrough and challenges the legitimacy of the established system. Secondly, a good deal of emotional fervor surrounds charismatic leadership which, according to Weber, may border on the pathological. Thirdly, charisma is *relative* and restricted to time and place. The charismatic leader will only succeed if the level of commitment to the new ideas enjoys a level of social receptivity. In other words, a charismatic leader can emerge only if the total situation is one that is conducive to change. Visionaries may be present all the time, but they will be only remote voices on the margins of society unless conditions within a given society are such that people will respond emotionally in support of their ideas.

The charismatic prophet was, for Weber, one of the most important figures in religious history. The prophet is the agent of religious change and of the development of new and more complete solutions to the problem of salvation. His or her message is one which is accepted out of regard for the personal qualities and gifts of the charismatic leader. Prophecy is fundamentally founded not upon reason or intellectual analysis but upon insight and revelation. In contrast to the prophet, the priest stands for tradition, established authority, and conservatism. The latter is a full-time professional attached to a cult and its ceremonies and often administering divine grace as part of an established religious tradition.

Charismatic authority is considered legitimate because it is based on the magnetic, compelling personal style of leadership. By contrast, bureaucratic authority is considered legitimate because it is founded on abstract rules. Traditional authority is rendered legitimate since it rests on precedence. Charismatic leadership and legal-rational systems of domination stand at opposite poles. Of all these forms of authority, charismatic leadership is the least stable. Such leaders are unpredictable, their lifestyles chaotic, their moods labile, and their commands often unfathomable. Moreover, the authority of charismatic leaders depends entirely on the support of their followers. If the followers lose faith, the leader is left with no power of command. For this reason the charismatic leader's position is precarious.

Charisma, as Wilson notes, is perhaps the most extreme claim to legitimacy, but it relies on faith and total trust. The image of the charismatic leader depends on a mythology of origins; on the incidents of portents and signs; on exceptional experiences; on his having had the opportunity to assimilate past wisdom; on hearsay stories of stamina, energy, untutored insight, and untrained exceptional abilities. Above all, he must be above normal human failings and beyond the need of such therapeutic or miraculous powers as he is supposed to possess and which he applies to others. With such an image, the charismatic leader is always at risk. He may not suffer ill health, nor yet, in any ordinary way, indulge in the pleasures of the senses (Wilson 1990: 234).

In principle, followers have a duty to acknowledge the leader's charismatic quality, so if they are hesitant or doubtful it is a failing on their part, and one the leader may come to resent (Bendix & Roth 1971: 175). Lacking the shelter of a bureaucratic office or the sanctity of tradition, the charismatic leader must be ready to perform miracles to satisfy the followers' craving for proof of his charismatic endowment, and to keep them motivated in the face of persecution by the authorities and mockery by unbelievers. It is therefore a misconception to think that charismatic leaders simply issue commands which followers automatically obey. Leaders may initially meet resistance or may face demands that they are unable or unwilling to satisfy.

Despite apparent freedom, the charismatic leader lacks institutional support: if the followers lose faith, his authority simply evaporates. The possibility of defection and betrayal is therefore inherent in charismatically led movements. Paradoxically, a charismatic leader can come to feel trapped by his or her own followers, who may demand miracles or this-worldly success which the leader simply cannot deliver or regard as irrelevant to the mission. As Wilson observes, a charismatic leader may capitalize on the claims made for him: he need never explain himself, indeed, there is some advantage in his inexplicability and unpredictability. His followers will rationalize his idiosyncrasies and aberrations. Nonetheless, outsiders may seize on just these vulnerabilities to discredit charismatic claims (Wilson 1990: 234).

Wilson also refers to "charismatic deflation," by which he means that at some time the sect or comparable constituency will experience a pattern of scrutiny of their claims and the charismatic claims of their founders or early leaders: leaders are cut down to human size, and their weaknesses and ambition, their *amour-propre*, are regularly exposed. And this not only by rivals and outsiders: there may occur reinterpretations among some brought up in the faith, and religious movements in which past leadership has been charismatically legitimated are thus likely to be undergoing particular strain. Movements which trace their origins to seekers or collective leadership have less trouble on this score. For others, once equivocation occurs, what was once a source of strength becomes an embarrassing handicap. The greater the past reliance, moreover, the greater the present disabilities (Wilson 1990: 115).

For Weber, charismatic leadership tends to become routinized. The first phase of a religious movement passes fairly quickly. Charismatic phenomena are unstable and temporary and can prolong their existence only by becoming routinized – that is, by transformation into institutionalized structure. After this event, the followers must make a new adjustment if the group is to be maintained. The life of a charismatic band of disciples is arduous. Typically, the followers wish to continue the original religious experience under new conditions,

and this means that eventually they must experience a crisis of succession.

If the authority of charismatic leaders is precarious during their own lifetime, the survival of the charismatic movement after the leader dies is a crisis since something of his charisma dies too. Weber suggests that the way the crisis is met is of crucial importance, for the authority relations that are established at that historical moment will shape the nature of the religious institutions that will follow. In particular, the question of succession is problematic since it cannot be filled by traditional or legal-bureaucratic authority and can unleash a succession crisis. Other means must be deployed for succession and they are typically ritualized and rich in symbolism, involving such elements as consulting oracles, praying for divine guidance, and commencing initiation ceremonies.

Weber distinguished three ways in which charisma can be passed on. Firstly, the transmission of charisma can be based on symbolically charged criteria which guarantee the outcome. Secondly, the leader may designate his or her successor, sometimes making an unpredictable choice. Thirdly, the leader's close disciples may designate the successor. Whatever the method of selection, the duty of the faithful is to acclaim a new leader, who governs by right. Generally, an authoritative institution is built up to fill the place of the founder after his death. Typically, this phase of the religion's life cycle transforms the movement from an extraordinary, tradition-breaking experience to an organized, socially acceptable institution that fits in comfortably with the established order. This developmental process has three different aspects. Firstly, the cult, or patterns of worship, becomes ritualized. Secondly, the ideas and beliefs become more rational. Thirdly, the religious community becomes rationally organized, with well-defined roles and responsibilities.

Routinization is frequently associated with the development of the priestly role – mediators between man and God(s). By incorporating authority in established offices the clergy protect their position from what are considered inauthentic charismatic outpourings. This means, in effect, that what has come to be called the "routinization of charisma" actually involves the *containment* of charisma. Thus, a movement that begins as a dramatic break with tradition becomes in time an established orthodoxy, neatly meshing and compromising with other social institutions. Routinization for Weber meant that charisma could become part of everyday life. Nonetheless, as Wallis (1984: 86–118) notes, routinization may be countered by an attempt to restore the charisma which set the movement off in the first place. It may thus remain latent as a resource on which revivalists can draw. For instance, the claim of charismatic renewal within mainstream Christian denominations is to restore to the faithful the gifts of the Holy Spirit (the charismata) that were given to the apostles at the first Pentecost.

Sectarian developments have provided fertile ground for a study of charisma. Wilson observes that by no means all Christian sects begin under charismatic leadership, but a good number have, or have had, powerful inspirational leadership to warrant a comparative exercise respecting the implications of charisma for the development of religious sects (1990: 110–12). Charismatic leadership has also been a major theme in the exploration of new religious movements. In movements with such a leadership, great effort is devoted to what Barker (1995) calls "charismatization": socializing people to recognize and orientate toward charismatic authority. As with the Unification Church, charismatization is achieved through the accumulation of elements, many of them apparently minor but many tending in the same direction, to render charismatic claims plausible.

The all-pervading charismatic authority has frequently proved to be a license for exemption from external moral restraint allowing the charismatic leader to indulge in sexual, financial, or violent excess (Anthony & Robbins 1997). Indeed, Barker (1984: 137) sees the charismatic leader's claim to divine authority and monopoly of decision-making as potentially threatening signs to the well-being of members of new religious movements. At other times leaders may actively seek to enhance their charisma when, as in the case of sociology, outside persecution threatens the movement (Wallis 1984). By contrast, such movements may bring a democratization of charisma, as with the Christian charismatic movement in relation to the "gifts of the spirit" (Poloma 1989).

Charisma is particularly precarious in the modern world. Wilson points out that at least since the time of Hobbes, the idea has been widely held that no man stands much above another, however forcefully his image may be projected. As information and communication have improved, following widespread literacy, rational-empirical argumentation, and scientific method, the claims to exceptional charisma have become more difficult to sustain and a less acceptable legitimation of leadership. The modern mind is cynical, seeking rationally based explanations for individual differences and solutions for social problems. Democracy, too, formally assumes that one person is the equal of another, and this democratic current even affects charisma itself (Wilson 1990: 110–11). Moreover, as Fenn (2003: 466–7) establishes, it is difficult to sustain charisma in terms of the secular religious groupings as a source of inspiration and authority in the context of the nation-state, which claims a greater authority and loyalty and has itself a form of charismatic endowment. This may be exemplified by the violent confrontations between the authoritarian theocratic organization of the Mormon Church under the leadership of a charismatic prophet and its clash with secular powers and the spirit of modern democracy.

Wilson (1990: 234) regards the public's readiness to see charisma deflated as the simple counterpoise of unbelief to the commitment of a movement's votaries. This readiness has undoubtedly grown in modern society, in which charismatic manifestations are increasingly confined to the fringes, in which there is dependence on systems and not on persons, in which objectively tested routine procedures and forward planning are relied upon rather than the exceptional competences of individuals. The charismatic becomes the bizarre: few individuals believe that social problems can be solved even by the collective will, let alone by the supposed extraordinary willpower of one gifted and divinely inspired individual. The charismatic leader thus easily becomes the object of ridicule.

SEE ALSO: Buddhism; Bureaucratic Personality; Charisma, Routinization of; Charismatic Movement; Christianity; Durkheim, Émile and Social Change; Islam; New Religious

Movements; Religion, Sociology of; Sect; Weber, Max

REFERENCES AND SUGGESTED READINGS

Anthony, R. & Robbins, T. (1997) Religious Total-ism, Exemplary Dualism, and the Waco Tragedy. In: Robbins, T. & Palmer, S. (Eds.), *Millennium, Messiahs, and Mayhem: Contemporary Apocalyptic Movements*. Routledge, New York, pp. 261–84.

Barker, E. (1984) *The Making of a Moonie: Brain-washing or Choice?* Blackwell, Oxford.

Barker, E. (1995) *New Religious Movements: A Prac-tical Introduction*. HMSO, London.

Bendix, R. & Roth, G. (1971) *Scholarship and Parti-sanship: Essays on Max Weber*. University of Cali-fornia Press, Berkeley.

Fenn, R. (2003) Editorial Commentary. Religion and the Secular; the Sacred and the Profane: The Scope of the Argument. In: *Blackwell Companion to Sociology of Religion*. Blackwell, Malden, MA, pp. 3–22.

Poloma, M. (1989) *The Assemblies of God at the Cross-roads*. University of Tennessee Press, Knoxville.

Wallis, R. (1984) *The Elementary Forms of Religious Life*. Routledge & Kegan Paul, London.

Weber, M. (1947) *Theory of Social Action*. Trans. A. M. Henderson & T. Parsons. Ed. T. Parsons. Oxford University Press, New York, pp. 358–9.

Weber, M. (1951) *The Religion of China*. Trans. and Ed. H. H. Gerth. Introduction C. K. Yang. Free Press, Glencoe, IL.

Weber, M. (1965) *Sociology of Religion*. Methuen, London.

Weber, M. (1978) *Economy and Society: An Outline of Interpretive Sociology*. Ed. G. Roth & C. Wittich. University of California Press, Berkeley.

Wilson, B. (1990) *The Social Dimensions of Sectarian-ism: Sects and New Religious Movements in Con-temporary Society*. Clarendon Press, Oxford.

charisma, routinization of

Ray Gordon

Weber (1978: 241) notes that those attributed charismatic authority are considered "extraor-dinary and endowed with supernatural, super-human, or at least specifically exceptional powers or qualities ... regarded as divine in origin or as exemplary, and on the basis of them [qualities] the individual concerned is treated as a leader." In this sense, the social relationships directly involved with charismatic authority are strictly personal and irrational in character. Weber points out, however, that if these relationships are not to remain a transi-tory phenomenon, they and the charismatic authority they are involved with "cannot remain stable; they will become either tradi-tionalized or rationalized, or a combination of both" (p. 246). What Weber means is that, over time, either a bureaucracy vested with rational legal authority will supersede the char-ismatic leader or institutionalized structures will incorporate the charismatic impetus. This rationalization or institutionalization process is what Weber refers to as the routinization of charisma.

Weber discusses a number of social forces that contribute to the routinization of charisma. He argues that it is only in the initial stages of a charismatic leader's reign that members of his or her community will live on the basis of "faith and enthusiasm, on gifts, booty, or sporadic acquisition" (p. 249). In contrast to the irrational and sporadic nature of charisma, the community's members have interests in continuing their lives in a way that offers them security and stability on an everyday basis. To highlight his point, Weber refers to the pro-blem of appointing a successor to the charis-matic leader once he or she disappears. How this succession problem is met has direct impact on the character of the subsequent lea-der–subordinate relationships involved. The original basis of recruitment may be charisma; however, the appointed leader will also need to satisfy established norms. These norms may include training and tests of eligibility and/or heredity. Weber adds that the anti-economic character of charisma will also be altered because the leader must have some form of fiscal organization to provide for the needs of his or her community; this fiscal organization "becomes transformed into one of the everyday authorities, the patrimonial form, especially in the estate-types or bureaucratic variant" (p. 251). In short, the fiscal organization acquires a differential power imbued with its own traditions, norms, and interests, which the charismatic leader will need to be both materially and ideally satisfied.

Weber's routinization of charisma is an illustration of how social structures constrain the agentic capacity of individuals. Since Weber's work, numerous writers have discussed the interplay between agency and structure. Parsons (1937) and Goffman (1961), albeit from different perspectives, researched the effect of social institutions on the behavior of specific social groups. Later, building on Berger and Luckmann's (1966) social constructionist perspective, institutional theorists such as Meyer and Rowan (1977) as well as DiMaggio and Powell (1983) argued that modern societies consist of institutional rules that, over time, become rationalized myths that are widely believed but never tested: they originate and are sustained through public opinion, the education system, laws, and other institutional forms (see Clegg et al. 2005: 53). From a more abstract perspective, Giddens (1984) argued that structures are not something external to social actors but are rules and resources produced and reproduced by actors in their practices. In more recent times, theorists such as Clegg (1989), Haugaard (1997) and Flyvbjerg (1998, 2002), drawing on the work of Weber, Foucault, and others, use a theory of power to illustrate how the relationship between agency and structure is more fluid and discursive in nature; they show how the practices of individuals are both constrained and enabled by the understanding these individuals have of the knowledge that underpins their social system: knowledge that has been constituted by the disciplined adherence to rules, norms, and hidden sociocultural codes of order.

Returning to Weber's link between charisma and leadership, charismatic leadership resurfaced during the 1980s and 1990s under the guise of the "transformational leadership" thesis. The thesis attracted significant interest and still constitutes much of the work being done in the field today. However, apart from an indirect approach adopted by those writers who address transactional leadership (Bass & Avolio 1990), little if any of the transformational leadership literature addresses what Weber had to say about the routinization of charisma. Rather than seeing charismatic leadership as an irrational phenomenon, the vast majority of transformational leadership theorists appear to adopt a normative approach that assumes rationality on behalf of the leader: irrationality and the routinization process are simply not considered because they do not fit the theoretical framework. With Weber's work in mind, one can argue that the routinization of charisma and its effects on transformational leadership is one area that requires further scrutiny.

SEE ALSO: Authority and Conformity; Charisma; Charismatic Movement; Institutionalism; Structure and Agency; Weber, Max

REFERENCES AND SUGGESTED READINGS

Bass, B. M. & Avolio, B. (1990) The Implications of Transactional and Transformational Leadership for Individual Team, and Organizational Development. *Research and Organizational Change and Development* 4: 231–72.

Berger, P. & Luckmann, T. (1966) *The Social Construction of Reality*. Doubleday, New York.

Clegg, S. R. (1989) *Frameworks of Power*. Sage, London.

Clegg, S. R., Kornberger, M., & Pitsis, T. (2005) *Managing and Organization: An Introduction to Theory and Practice*. Sage, London.

Dimaggio, P. J. & Powell, W. W. (1983) The Iron Cage Revisited: Institutional Isomorphism and Collective Rationality in Organizational Fields. *American Sociological Review* 48(2): 127–71.

Flyvbjerg, B. (1998) *Rationality and Power: Democracy in Practice*. University of Chicago Press, Chicago.

Flyvbjerg, B. (2002) *Making Social Science Matter: Why Social Inquiry Fails and How It Can Succeed Again*. Cambridge University Press, Cambridge.

Giddens, A. (1984) *The Constitution of Society*. Polity Press, Cambridge.

Goffman, E. (1961) *Asylums*. Penguin, London.

Haugaard, M. (1997) *The Constitution of Power: A Theoretical Analysis of Power, Knowledge and Structure*. Cambridge University Press, Cambridge.

Meyer, J. & Rowan, B. (1977) Institutionalized Organizations: Formal Structure as Myth and Ceremony. *American Journal of Sociology* 83: 340–63.

Parsons, T. (1937) *The Structure of Social Action*. McGraw Hill, New York.

Weber, M. (1978 [1914]) *Economy and Society*, Vol. 1: *An Outline of Interpretive Sociology*. Ed. G. Roth & C. Wiltich. University of California Press, Berkeley.

charismatic movement

Paul Freston

Movements usually referred to as "charismatic" developed within Protestant and Catholic Christianity from the mid-twentieth century, and especially the 1960s. Protestant versions are sometimes called "neo-Pentecostalism" and the Catholic movement was initially styled "Catholic Pentecostal," highlighting connections with the broader Pentecostal movement. Charismatic Christianity is usually considered to include: (1) renewal movements within established denominations; (2) independent charismatic churches and new denominations; and (3) charismatic parachurch organizations. The number of charismatics has steadily risen worldwide, and in 2000 probably represented some 10 percent of the world's Christian population.

While there is diversity among charismatics, all stress the importance and current availability of various "charismata" or "gifts of the Holy Spirit" mentioned in the New Testament, especially glossolalia ("speaking in tongues"), prophecy, healing, and other "supernatural" gifts. Often this is framed in terms of a definite experience known as "baptism in the Holy Spirit," as well as a desire to renew ecclesiastical institutions by recapturing the vibrancy of the early church.

The charismatic movement is related phenomenologically to the Pentecostal movement of early twentieth-century Protestantism. There are, however, important differences. While classical Pentecostalism was typically of the poor and dispossessed, charismatic Christianity began and largely continues within middle-class and professional circles. Related to this are its more restrained tone and concern with therapy and self-fulfillment; charismatics tend to be more world-affirming and distant from Pentecostalism's world-denying "holiness" roots. Other differences are theological (charismatics put less stress on glossolalia as a sign of Spirit-baptism) and ecclesiastical (they do not join classical Pentecostal denominations but remain in mainline churches or form independent groups). As the phenomenon has spread worldwide, the extreme social inequality in many countries has created a yawning cultural gap

between Pentecostals and charismatics. Nevertheless, within Protestant circles the latter have often influenced the former in recent decades.

The origins of the charismatic renewal, traditionally dated to the 1960s, are often explained in terms of the developed West: as a reaction to the bureaucratization of church life and the numerical decline of the churches; as an experiential affirmation of Christian spirituality in the face of secularization and rationalization; as a search for community in the impersonality of urban late modernity marked by social and geographical mobility. It has thus been characterized as simultaneously anti-modern (in its "fundamentalistic" biblical literalism and moral traditionalism), modern (in its grassroots ecumenism in the face of religion's marginalization), and postmodern (in its hedonistic individualism, buttressing of economic goals by "spiritual" reinforcements, and use of metonymy).

But other authors have stressed that charismatic Christianity is a global culture characterized not by unilateral diffusion from the West but by parallel developments and complex flows. It is global because experiential and iconic, predominantly urban and heavily involved in high-tech media use; its informal networks transcend national and cultural boundaries. It is everywhere recognizable by its expressive worship and its cultivation of the immanence of God and the contemporaneity of the miraculous. Many (but not all) of the "waves" through which it has gone (driven by the desire for fresh experiences) have also been diffused widely. But these waves (together with the tendency to controversial authoritarian forms of church government) have only accentuated the divisiveness of the movement, aided by the inherent instability of its experiential theology.

Large swathes of the charismatic world have adopted a dualistic form of "spiritual warfare" doctrine, in which the reality and ubiquity of evil spiritual forces are confronted by prayer. The public behavior of many charismatics has been influenced by belief in "territorial spirits," which hold demonic control of geographical regions or sectors of social life. Also controversial is the "health and wealth" gospel especially popular in North America, much of Africa, and parts of Asia (but less so in Europe). Teaching that Christ's atonement includes the removal not just of sin but also of sickness and poverty, the power of God is viewed as a force that can be tapped by "faith." Of North American provenance, its global diffusion is, however, complex and "glocalized."

The myth of origins of the Protestant charismatic movement locates the beginnings in the US Episcopalian Church in 1960; an Episcopal priest's experience of "baptism in the Spirit" reached major news magazines. But this version is parochial and says more about the ability to publicize developments than about global reality. Charismatic movements had existed before (e.g., among black Anglicans in South Africa from the 1940s; in the Reformed Church in France; among Brazilian Baptists in the 1950s). While American influence was undoubtedly great (especially through popular books), the global charismatic movement is not an American "product."

In the developed anglophone world, the pattern of development was, firstly, of attempts to influence the mainline Protestant denominations and form ecumenical charismatic networks. By the late 1970s, this was eclipsed by new independent ministries, often influenced by "Restorationist" teaching that the "new wine" of charismatic experience required the "new wineskins" of New Testament patterns of church organization, centered around "apostolic" leadership and authoritarian "shepherding" relationships. This would herald a final revival before the return of Christ. What were effectively new denominations emerged (such as New Frontiers and Ichthus in the United Kingdom). But as Restorationism aged, it moderated its tone and began to have an enduring cultural impact on other sectors of the church.

Perhaps the greatest impact in the 1980s was from John Wimber's Vineyard movement. Starting in California, it emphasized "power evangelism," linking proclamation of the gospel to manifestation of spiritual gifts. This involved "mapping" the spiritual terrain and "power encounters" with the supernatural. This self-styled "third wave" (after the original Pentecostal and charismatic "waves") had great impact also on classical Pentecostal and conservative evangelical circles. One result was the "Marches for Jesus," popular in many countries from the late 1980s, inspired by the idea of "territorial spirits" as a theory both of

evangelism and of charismatics' role in society. The "discerning" of territorial spirits often follows a politically conservative line, but in some Brazilian and African cases has been adapted to "third worldist" concerns.

It was also in the 1980s that the "Word of Faith" or prosperity gospel became popular, especially in the United States, Africa, and parts of Latin America and Asia. Leading global exponents included the American Kenneth Hagin, the Korean Yonggi Cho, the Nigerian Benson Idahosa, and the Argentinian Héctor Giménez.

With the growth of charismatic megachurches, an emphasis on small groups known as "cells" developed, as a way both of maintaining cohesion and community and of gaining the supposed advantages of small and socially homogeneous groups in attracting converts. This trend is often interpreted as a recognition that religion is increasingly deinstitutionalized, and as an absorption of consumerist strategies of predictability and control.

Another major influence of the 1990s was the "Toronto Blessing." This phenomenon involved outbursts of uncontrollable laughter or convulsive body movements and animal utterances. Interpreted as being "slain in the Spirit," the phenomenon dominated the life of many charismatic churches for several years and was understood as preparation for revival. It provoked mass pilgrimages to the Toronto church which publicized it globally, but other charismatics rejected it. In fact, similar phenomena had occurred elsewhere beforehand (especially in Argentina) but without the capacity to globalize them.

The late 1990s saw the growing popularity of Alpha, an introductory course in Christianity aimed at bridging the ever-widening gulf with secular culture. Based on a premise of hidden religiosity in individualistic forms which the church needs to tap into, it quickly spread to some 75 countries and transcended the charismatic milieu.

By 2000, charismatic Protestantism in the developed West was often regarded as one of the few sectors of church growth. But much of this comes from recycling Christians rather than conversion of the unchurched. The charismatic movement represents largely a redirection of western Christianity in terms of style, emphases, and organizational forms.

In some parts of the world, however, the movement flourishes in a context of general church growth. A major focus has been West Africa; since the 1980s, large churches in Ghana and Nigeria have become a focus for younger, educated urbanites, and their leaders are significant players on the global charismatic stage. In South Africa, white charismatic leaders started influential multiracial (but mainly white-led) churches in the 1980s, matched since the end of apartheid by similar black churches influenced by West African models.

In Brazil, which has the world's second-largest community of practicing Protestants, all the historical Protestant denominations suffered charismatic splits by the 1970s, but recent Protestant expansion in the middle class has been mainly due to new charismatic "communities." Considerable female leadership is characteristic, as is the integration of pastoral and entrepreneurial activities. Rather than the "Toronto Blessing," Brazil has had its own equivalents (such as gold teeth fillings in believers' mouths).

Some Latin American charismatics have been very influential worldwide, especially Argentinian evangelists as well as the Colombian church leader César Castellanos, responsible for the "G-12" adaptation of the "cell" method, a major charismatic influence since the late 1990s. In Guatemala, two (controversial) charismatic Protestants have become president.

Charismaticism represents a new stage in the inculturation of Protestantism in Latin America. The penetration of the youth culture, the assimilation of musical rhythms, the adoption of secular communication styles, the reinterpretation of spiritual warfare in terms of local religious rivalries, the acceptance of social categories and symbols of prestige once placed under taboo – all point to charismatic Christianity in the third world as both a global culture, with multiple foreign influences, and a creative local adaptation.

The charismatic movement has also been extremely important within Catholicism. Its "myth of origins" talks of an American university location in 1967 (and of a basically university ambience for its first years), and of Protestant charismatic influence on the originators. It also claims to be a child of the Second

Vatican Council. Certainly, without Vatican II the absorption of such a "Protestant" phenomenon would have been unlikely, and the Council also prepared the way by its liturgical changes and greater emphasis on the Bible and lay initiative.

Known initially as "Catholic Pentecostalism," the Catholic Charismatic Renewal (CCR) had become international by the mid-1970s, with the patronage of Cardinal Suenens of Belgium and the blessing of Pope Paul VI. By 1990 it had become effectively global with the encouragement of Pope John Paul II, who appreciated its politics, its activism for traditional sexual mores, and its contribution to parish renewal.

By the year 2000 the CCR had declined in the US but had expanded worldwide, involving (to some degree) about 10 percent of all Catholics. Latin America was the hub, and secondarily the third world in general. The CCR now has a bureaucratic organization. Having started as a lay movement, it still has considerable lay leadership, but clerical influence has strengthened. Since 1993, the central organ, the International Catholic Charismatic Renewal Services, has had papal recognition. Below it, the CCR is organized at the continental, country, diocesan, and parochial levels.

Unlike the Protestant movement, the CCR adapts the "baptism in the Holy Spirit" to Catholic sacramental theology and emphasizes the eucharist and (increasingly) the Virgin Mary. But there is some variety within the CCR globally (in clerical roles, in the relative emphasis on particular gifts, etc.). In part, this is because the CCR spread not only through missionary priests but also through separate local initiatives which later became incorporated into the CCR. An example of the latter is the controversial Archbishop Milingo of Zambia, whose version was strongly oriented to an African understanding of healing.

One of the largest movements within the CCR is El Shaddai in the Philippines, led by a layman and said to have 7 million members. Another large CCR is Brazil's. Started in 1969 by American Jesuits and initially very middle class, the movement achieved (somewhat reluctant) episcopal recognition in the 1990s as a way to combat Pentecostalism. Since then, it has become very visible in the media and politics (largely in a fairly conservative direction). The hierarchy has warned against exorcism and a "magical" mindset in general, and has demanded loyalty to papal teaching and Marian devotion (the clearest distinguishing mark from Protestant charismatics). In the late 1990s, the CCR gained extra visibility through the "singing-priest" Marcelo Rossi, whose "aerobics of the Lord" attracted multitudes to his masses.

In the context of growing religious pluralism in Brazil, the CCR extended its reach amongst the lower classes and by 2000 involved some 8 million people, although it remained disproportionately strong amongst middle-class women, many of whom found an outlet for leadership. The CCR has embraced bureaucratic organization and advanced technology. It consolidates a "Catholicism of choice" in the new competitive religious field, rather than a "Catholicism of birth." In addition, it is often interpreted in Brazil as a strategy to limit the influence of liberation theology. However, other studies point to the internal diversity of the movement and the anti-institutional and oppositional potential in its direct contact with the sacred and its legitimation of lay (and female) leadership.

With regard to the future of charismatic Christianity (Protestant and Catholic), some authors see it as condemned to incessant splintering and on the verge of becoming a spent force. Neither in its size nor in its nature does it contain anything that might significantly challenge trends to secularization. Notwithstanding its supernaturalism, it fits in well with the secular world of late capitalism and merely rearranges the percentages within a declining Christian world. Other authors see it as one of the forms of religion likely to do best in the twenty-first century, with its combination of subjectivism and community discipline. In between, while avoiding the (oft-repeated) predictions of decline (especially when viewed from a global perspective), one can also recognize its sociological limitations (e.g., to reverse secularization in the West, or to prevent the erosion of Catholic allegiance in Latin America).

SEE ALSO: Charisma; New Religious Movements; Religious Cults

REFERENCES AND SUGGESTED READINGS

Anderson, A. (2002) *An Introduction to Pentecostalism.* Cambridge University Press, Cambridge, ch. 8.

Burgess, S. & van der Maas, E. (Eds.) (2002) *The New International Dictionary of Pentecostal and Charismatic Movements.* Zondervan, Grand Rapids.

Coleman, S. (2000) *The Globalization of Charismatic Christianity.* Cambridge University Press, Cambridge.

Csordas, T. (2002) *Language, Charisma and Creativity: Ritual Life in the Catholic Charismatic Renewal.* Palgrave Macmillan, New York.

Hunt, S., Hamilton, M., & Walter, T. (Eds.) (1997) *Charismatic Christianity: Sociological Perspectives.* Macmillan, Basingstoke.

Poewe, K. (Ed.) (1994) *Charismatic Christianity as a Global Culture.* University of South Carolina Press, Columbia.

Chicago School

Ray Hutchison

The Chicago School of Urban Sociology refers to work of faculty and graduate students at the University of Chicago during the period 1915–35. This small group of scholars (the full-time faculty in the department of sociology never numbered more than 6 persons) developed a new sociological theory and research methodology in a conscious effort to create a science of society using the city of Chicago as a social laboratory. The Chicago School continues to define the contours of urban sociology, most clearly in the contributions of urban ecology and applied research within the urban environment.

The University of Chicago was founded in 1890 as a research university modeled after Johns Hopkins University and Clark University. The Chicago School of the period discussed here is represented by three generations of faculty. The first group included Albion Small (founder of the department), W. I. Thomas, Charles R. Henderson, Graham Taylor, and George E. Vincent. The second generation included Small, Thomas, Ernest Burgess, Ellsworth Faris, and Robert Park. It was this group that trained the graduate students responsible for the classic studies of the Chicago School. The third generation included Park, Burgess, Louis Wirth, and William Ogburn. This group of faculty would remain intact until the time Park retired from the university in 1934.

While it is common to date the origin of urban sociology at Chicago with Park's arrival in 1914 and his subsequent work with Burgess, the idea of the city as a laboratory for social research came much earlier. Henderson applied for funds for a systematic study of the city in the first decade, and Thomas began his research on *The Polish Peasant in Europe and the United States* in 1908. An early (1902) description of the graduate program in the *American Journal of Sociology* stated:

> The city of Chicago is one of the most complete social laboratories in the world. While the elements of sociology may be studied in smaller communities ... the most serious problems of modern society are presented by the great cities, and must be studied as they are encountered in concrete form in large populations. No city in the world presents a wider variety of typical social problems than Chicago.

The sociology faculty pioneered empirical research using a variety of qualitative and quantitative methods in an effort to develop a science of sociology. Park formulated a new theoretical model based upon his observation that the city was more than a geographic phenomenon; the basic concepts of human ecology were borrowed from the natural sciences. Competition and segregation led to formation of *natural areas*, each with a separate and distinct *moral order*. The city was "a mosaic of little worlds that touch but do not interpenetrate." Burgess's model for the growth of the city showed a central business district surrounded by the zone in transition, the zone of workingmen's homes, the residential zone, and the commuter zone (see Fig. 1). Roderick McKenzie expanded the basic model of human ecology in his later study of the metropolitan community.

The research and publication program of the Chicago School was carried out under the auspices of a Local Community Research

Committee, an interdisciplinary group comprised of faculty and graduate students from sociology, political science (Charles Merriam), and anthropology (Robert Redfield). Support came from the Laura Spellman Rockefeller Memorial (more than $600,000 from 1924 to 1934). Graduate students under the guidance of Park and Burgess mapped local community areas and studied the spatial organization of juvenile delinquency, family disorganization, and cultural life in the city. The research program produced a diverse array of studies broadly organized around the themes of urban institutions (the hotel, taxi dance hall), social disorganization (juvenile delinquency, the homeless man), and natural areas themselves. Among the notable Chicago School studies are Frederick Thrasher, *The Gang* (1926); Louis Wirth, *The Ghetto* (1928); Harvey W. Zorbaugh, *The Gold Coast and the Slum* (1929); Clifford S. Shaw, *The Jackroller* (1930); E. Franklin Frazier, *The Negro Family in Chicago* (1932); Paul G. Cressey, *The Taxi-Dance Hall* (1932); Walter C. Reckless, *Vice in Chicago* (1933); and E. Franklin Frazier, *The Negro Family in Chicago* (1932).

The Chicago School dominated urban sociology and sociology more generally in the first half of the twentieth century. By 1950 some 200 students had completed graduate study at Chicago. Many were instrumental in establishing graduate programs in sociology across the country, and more than half of the presidents of the American Sociological Association were faculty or students at Chicago. The *American Journal of Sociology*, started by Small in 1895, was the official journal of the American Sociological Association from 1906 to 1935. The dominance of the Chicago School also generated antagonism, and a "minor rebellion" at the annual conference in 1935 would result in the founding of a new journal, the *American Sociological Review*, and marks the decline of influence of the Chicago department

There were early critiques of the Chicago School, including Missa Alihạn's 1938 critique of the determinism inherent in Park's human ecology (Park wrote that "on the whole" the criticisms were correct). Maurice Davie (in 1938) reanalyzed data from Clifford Shaw's *Delinquency Areas* (1929) and showed that

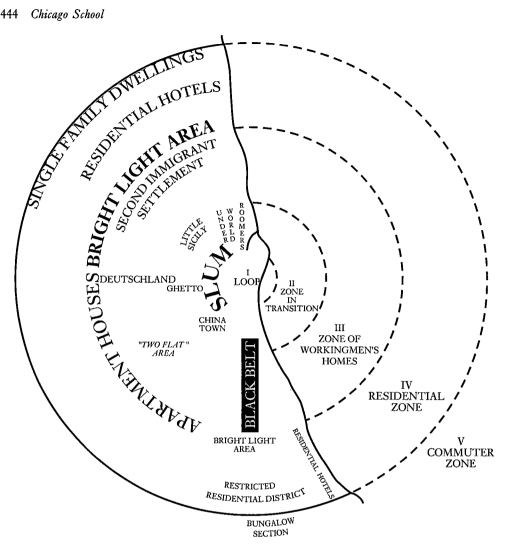

Figure 1   Burgess's model of urban growth

delinquency was associated with areas of physical deterioration and high immigrant populations and not in the concentric zone model used in the Chicago studies. Burgess's concentric zones were soon replaced by a variety of models showing multiple-nuclei and eventually the decentralized, poly-centered city. Still, urban ecology remains the dominant model and method among urban sociologists at present.

Recent attention has focused on the role of women in the development of the Chicago School. Deegan (1986) argued that the contribution of women was marginalized by Park and other male faculty. Jane Addams's Hull-House had conducted early community studies. Edith Abbott was a part-time instructor in the department, and Addams had been offered a part-time position. Many of the Chicago faculty were involved with Hull-House and other social reform movements; Graham Taylor was one of the early members of the department. Burgess would later note that systematic urban research at Chicago started with the Hull-House studies begun by Abbot and Sophonsia Breckenridge in 1908. Although many of the graduate students would use the settlement houses to assist their research, efforts to distinguish themselves from social reform and the emerging field of social work may explain a reluctance to connect the Chicago School with these earlier studies.

The influence of the early work of the Chicago School may be seen in some later studies, notably St. Clair Drake and Horace Cayton's *Black Metropolis* (1945) and in several community studies directed by Morris Janowitz in the 1970s. William Julius Wilson's work on poverty neighborhoods in 1980–95 once again made use of the city as a social laboratory, including a sustained program of training for graduate students, but Wilson would leave for Harvard before this research agenda was completed. The Chicago School of Urban Sociology has not had lasting influence in the work of the department.

In addition to urban sociology, there are claims to various other Chicago Schools in ethnic studies, crime and delinquency, symbolic interaction, and other fields. The Chicago School of Urban Sociology does not usually include G. H. Mead or W. Lloyd Warner, both of whom were important figures in the department in the 1930s (Mead) and 1940s (Warner). Louis Wirth noted that the Chicago School included many different theoretical models and perspectives and included methodologies ranging from personal documents and ethnography to quantitative analysis. Park felt that Thomas's work formed the foundation for the department, but wrote that he was not aware that he was creating a "school" or a "doctrine." The Chicago School label developed in large measure from critiques by scholars from other universities. Recent work in urban geography has argued that while Chicago was the model for urban theory of the twentieth century, Los Angeles is the model for urban theory of the future. It should be noted that the Los Angeles School (a title coined by the authors themselves, in contrast to the Chicago School) is more appropriately urban studies, rather than urban sociology.

SEE ALSO: Addams, Jane; American Sociological Association; Park, Robert E. and Burgess, Ernest W.; Robert E. Park, Ernest W. Burgess, and Urban Social Research

REFERENCES AND SUGGESTED READINGS

Abbott, A. (1999) *Department and Discipline: Chicago Sociology at One Hundred.* University of Chicago Press, Chicago.

Becker, H. S. (n.d.) *The Chicago School, So-Called.* Online. www.home.earthlink.net/~hsbecker/chicago.html.

Blumer, M. (1984) *The Chicago School of Sociology: Institutionalization, Diversity, and the Rise of Sociological Research.* University of Chicago Press, Chicago.

Deegan, M. J. (1986) *Jane Addams and the Men of the Chicago School, 1892–1918.* Transaction Books, New Brunswick, NJ.

Faris, R. E. L. (1970) *Chicago Sociology, 1920–32.* University of Chicago Press, Chicago.

Kurtz, L. R. (1984) *Evaluating Chicago Sociology: A Guide to the Literature, with an Annotated Bibliography.* University of Chicago Press, Chicago.

Matthews, F. H. (1977) *Quest for an American Sociology: Robert E. Park and the Chicago School.* McGill-Queen's University Press, Montreal.

Short, J. F. (Ed.) (1971) *The Social Fabric of the Metropolis: Contributions of the Chicago School of Urban Sociology.* University of Chicago Press, Chicago.

The University and the City: A Centennial View of the University of Chicago: The Urban Laboratory. Online. www.lib.uchicago.edu/projects/centcat/centcats/city/citych3_01.html.

Chicago School: social change

Andrew Abbott

Like most schools of thought, the Chicago School was not a unified and single-minded orthodoxy. Although the idea of social change was essential to virtually all the Chicago writers, they defined it in various ways and then used those resulting concepts in quite varying places in their work. It was only William Fielding Ogburn who foregrounded the phrase itself in his writings. But for W. I. Thomas on the one hand and Robert Park and Ernest Burgess on the other, change was, if possible, even more central than it was for Ogburn. Yet, in the long run, both sociologists and popular literature have chosen to accept Ogburn's sense of social change as society-wide upheaval and transformation (indeed, this is now the lay sense of the phrase). But that current meaning should not lead us to read the Chicago works teleologically. (For the standard account of the Chicago School in English, see Bulmer 1984; for more recent revisionist accounts with relatively current bibliographies, see Abbott 1999; Chapoulie 2001.)

The Chicago writers all worked within traditions for which the notion of perpetual change was axiomatic. Historicism came with department founder Albion Small. Pragmatism was embodied in faculty colleagues John Dewey and George Herbert Mead. The department's reformists – Charles Henderson, George Vincent, and W. I. Thomas, as well as Small (and Mead, who was in the philosophy department) – were all tied to Hull-House and other Chicago institutions interested in changing society for the better. It is then little surprising that nearly all the writers of the classical era of the Chicago School (i.e., these men and their students, writing through the period 1915–35) took for granted the notion that social life is first and foremost a free process rather than a regular motion within a fixed structure. This notion of the social as processual, along with its correlate that all social facts have particular locations, was indeed the philosophical foundation of the Chicago School.

But these ideas expressed themselves differently in different writers. There were three basic versions of social change in the writings of the Chicagoans. The most familiar is William Fielding Ogburn's conception of social change as the sum total of societal-wide trends. Ogburn's most far-reaching statement is found in the two-volume 1933 report on *Recent Social Trends*. The social survey tradition reached its apogee in this "survey" of the whole nation, done by a Hoover-appointed committee of which Ogburn was both a member and director of research. The volumes begin with a summary, followed by 29 chapters by experts discussing topics ranging from population and natural resources to education, attitudes, labor, consumption, arts, religion, and taxation. The report's introduction sets out a view of social change that Ogburn was to repeat and elaborate

throughout his career. Society consisted of a number of divided areas of social organization (Ogburn was never clear about whether these were institutions or functions or simply complexes of social organization). But not all parts of our organization are changing at the same speed or at the same time. Some are rapidly moving forward and others are lagging (note the implicit assumption of progress). Although he argued that the order of these changes could vary – sometimes social developments might precede mechanical developments, and sometimes vice versa – in general, Ogburn argued that scientific and mechanical inventions led the process. These led to changes in those parts of economic and social organization close to technology – factories, labor, and so on – and then onward to changes in the family, government, schools, and so on. At the end came changes in values and norms. This was the argument that became enshrined as "cultural lag."

Ogburn's conception of social change was thus one that aggregated across the social world. Trends and time graphs of trends pervade his work. Because of this level of aggregation, the focus on particularity and location characteristic of the other Chicagoans disappeared. Also, Ogburn's strong positivism led him to pay more attention to things that were easier to measure. It is thus hardly surprising that inventions (already "measured" by patents) would come first in his account of aggregate change and that beliefs and values – notoriously difficult to measure and ultimately capturable only in the aggregate change of summed survey responses over time – would come last. All the same, Ogburn's work was almost obsessively processualist. Indeed, his insistence on the pervasiveness of broad social change led him to downplay great events and great men, rather as did his contemporaries of the Annales School in France. The table of contents of the *Recent Social Trends* volumes indeed makes no mention of the tumultuous events of 1929 to 1933, although of course they are discussed in the individual articles.

For Robert Park, Ernest Burgess, and the ecologists, on the other hand, social change was not a term of art. Like Ogburn, they too were processualists – social theorists whose fundamental axioms rested not on structure and organization but on story and trajectory.

But unlike him, they chose their underlying metaphor from plant ecology, with its passive cycle of contact, interaction, invasion, conflict, accommodation, and assimilation. In human ecologies, this might be punctuated by collective behavior (runaway events) and tamed by social control (which referred mostly to what we would today call symbolic or cultural systems). Theories of and examples of these processes took up the vast majority of the 1921 Park and Burgess textbook of sociology, *Introduction to the Science of Sociology*. But whereas progress was the most important implicit model of change in Ogburn, neither progress nor indeed directed change of any sort was important in the Park and Burgess view. Process was simply process.

In addition, unlike Ogburn with his division of the social world into abstract complexes of social organization or institutions, Park, Burgess, and their students tended to divide the world into types of people (racial, ethnic, religious, occupational, and age groups) doing types of activities (suicide, divorce, ganging, striking, whoring, delinquency, movie-going, etc.) in particular places (central business district vs. outlying zones, on ecological boundaries vs. in the core of natural areas, in "belts" that crossed zonal boundaries, etc.). Where Ogburn had many charts of trends, they had many maps of activities. Whereas social change lost in them the direction Ogburn had given it, it gained a location (social and geographic) that he ignored.

For Park himself the core change concept was the natural history. By this, Park meant something like typical sequence of events. Most of his students undertook natural histories of their topics: of gangs (Thrasher), of revolutions (Edwards), of churches (Kincheloe), of taxidance halls (Cressey), and so on. At the individual level, this concept of a typical sequence of events was often called the life cycle. It is illustrated in Cressey's 1932 "life cycle of the taxi dancer," Mowrer's 1927 "behavior sequences in family disorganization," and in many individual life histories – Shaw's two book-length biographies of delinquents, Mowrer's "Diary of Miriam Donaven," and so on. These concepts of typical sequence were never theorized by the Chicago School, but they certainly pervaded its writing.

This notion of patterns of change across the life course came less from Park and Burgess than from the monumental example of Thomas and Znaniecki in the *Polish Peasant* (1918–21) and from Thomas's continuing production of individual, social psychological studies. One of the five original *Polish Peasant* volumes was a single life history. Moreover, the theoretical scheme sketched in the famous "Methodological Note" with which the series opens is based on the notion of a life pattern organized by attitudes.

Thomas's is thus the third major conception of social change in the Chicago School proper (chronologically it was the first; it is taken third here because it is the least familiar today). Although Thomas's theorizing could be obscure, he had a firm sense that change and dynamism – not stability – were the natural state of society. (His collaborator Znaniecki would make this explicit in responding to Herbert Blumer's critique of *The Polish Peasant* in 1938.) Thomas's three concepts for theorizing this constant flux were social organization, social disorganization, and social reorganization. These received careful but not always consistent definition in the "Methodological Note." They all involved the mutual adjustment of individual attitudes with social values, an adjustment occurring within a context where large social forces were threatening and transforming the social foundations of social values even while the steady flow of events across the life course presented challenges to the personal organization of attitudes. Social organization (along with its correlative, individual organization) denoted the situation in which the social values and personal attitudes mutually determined a dynamically stable accommodation of individual and society. Social (and correlatively individual) disorganization denoted the situation in which they did not. Social reorganization referred to the reestablishment of the individual/society accommodation, a reestablishment which Thomas sometimes attributed to the leadership of individuals and sometimes to changes in social values.

The triad of organization, disorganization, and reorganization appears throughout the writings of the Chicago PhDs of the 1920s and 1930s, chiefly in studies of suicide, divorce, crime, delinquency, ganging, and other "social problems." In these writings (and particularly in later readings of them), the subtleties of Thomas's conceptualizations were usually lost. The three terms simply became a list describing the perpetual and mutually disturbing fluctuation of group values and individual attitudes so familiar in the reformist literature. Although for Thomas the terms had lacked normative content, their deployment in the context of social problems and reformism led by a kind of contagion to a much more normative understanding of "organization." This gradual redefinition destroyed the original utility of the triad of terms as a processual and nonnormative alterative to the clearly normative term "social structure" favored by the rising structural-functionalists of the late 1930s.

The Chicago School was thus completely organized around the notion of social change. Indeed, they took change as the natural state of social life. Their analysis of change ranged from the trends of Ogburn to the typical sequences and patterns of Park and Burgess and the organization and reorganization of Thomas. Only the Ogburn view would survive the eclipse of Chicago thinking by the structural-functional school. Parsons's teleological evolutionism could only admit the kind of directed, progressive change that was implicit in Ogburn's thinking. The perpetual flux of Thomas as well as the located but often random contact and competition processes of Park and Burgess would become an esoteric subtext in American sociology until the concept of conflictual change took center stage again in the 1970s.

SEE ALSO: Chicago School; Mead, George Herbert; Park, Robert and Burgess, Ernest W.; Parsons, Talcott; Pragmatism; Social Change; Structural Functional Theory; Znaniecki, Florian

REFERENCES AND SUGGESTED READINGS

Abbott, A. (1999) *Department and Discipline*. University of Chicago Press, Chicago.
Bulmer, R. (1984) *The Chicago School of Sociology*. University of Chicago Press, Chicago.
Chapoulie, J.-M. (2001) *La Tradition sociologique de Chicago*. Editions du Seuil, Paris.
Ogburn, W. F. (President's Research Committee on Recent Social Trends) (1933) *Recent Social Trends*, 2. Vols. McGraw-Hill, New York.
Park, R. E. & Burgess, E. W. (1921) *Introduction to the Science of Sociology*. University of Chicago Press, Chicago.
Thomas, W. I. & Znaniecki, F. (1918–21) *The Polish Peasant in Europe and America*, 5 Vols. University of Chicago Press, Chicago; Badger, Boston.

child abuse

Karen Polonko

Throughout the world, literally hundreds of millions of children are victims of abuse, neglect, and exploitation. Restricting our focus to the US, over 3 million children are reported to official agencies for severe maltreatment in any given year (English 1998). While approximately 15 percent of children have been reported to agencies for maltreatment, surveys indicate that this figure grossly underestimates the true extent of the problem, as over a third of adults in the US report having experienced physical, sexual, emotional abuse and/or neglect as a child.

How child abuse is defined has enormous implications for the safety and well-being of children and reflects existing cultural, political, and structural inequalities. Narrowly defining child maltreatment, as we do in the US, as only the extremes of abuse with demonstrable injuries, not only results in artificially low estimates of child maltreatment, but also limits the government's ability to intervene on behalf of children, affords abusing parents the greatest protection, and places children in the greatest danger.

As summarized by the World Health Organization (2002: 59), "Child abuse or maltreatment constitutes all forms of physical and/or emotional ill-treatment, sexual abuse, neglect or negligent treatment or commercial or other exploitation, resulting in actual or potential harm to the child's health, survival, development, or dignity in the context of a relationship of responsibility, trust, or power."

Child physical abuse involves a parent or caretaker intentionally inflicting physical pain on the child and can range, for example, from shaking, dragging, or spanking a child to the extremes of kicking, punching, or beating. Child sexual abuse involves a caretaker using a child for sexual gratification and can range from noncontact abuse (proposition, exhibition) to the extremes of actual penetration, to commercial sexual exploitation. Child emotional abuse involves inflicting psychological pain on the child. This includes, for example, yelling at, ridiculing, degrading, or humiliating a child; communicating that the child is flawed or unlovable; threatening a child or a child's loved one; exposure to domestic violence.

Child neglect involves a caretaker's failure to provide for the child's basic needs. This includes physical neglect (adequate shelter, food, clothing), medical neglect (adequate health care), cognitive or educational neglect (intellectual stimulation, involvement in child's schooling), supervision neglect (monitoring the child's whereabouts, involvement in child's activities), and emotional neglect (providing emotional responsiveness, support, and affection). Prenatal neglect and abuse (failure to obtain proper care and/or substance abuse during pregnancy) constitutes yet another category of maltreatment.

CONSEQUENCES OF CHILD ABUSE AND NEGLECT

The consequences of child maltreatment are considerable, not only for the child, but also for society. Some consequences for the child are greater for one type of maltreatment than another. For example, child neglect is most strongly associated with the child having a lower IQ and lower educational achievement; child physical abuse with the child engaging in violence as a teen and adult; and, child emotional abuse with subsequent psychopathology. However, all forms of maltreatment are associated with adverse effects for children and the adults they become. Child physical and emotional abuse and neglect all increase the likelihood that the child will subsequently:

- Be cognitively impaired (e.g., lower IQ and cognitive development; lower grades and educational achievement).

- Have impaired moral reasoning (e.g., less empathy, less compliance, and less developed conscience).
- Engage in violence and crime (e.g., more likely to engage in juvenile delinquency, nonviolent crime, and violent criminal behavior as a teenager and adult).
- Be violent in relationships (e.g., more likely to assault their siblings and other children, and later to abuse their spouse, child, and elderly parents).

In addition, all types of child maltreatment, physical and emotional abuse and neglect, and sexual abuse increase the likelihood that the child will subsequently:

- Have mental health problems as a child, teenager, and adult (e.g., higher rates of depression, anxiety, anger, anti-social personality disorder, eating disorder, etc.).
- Become a substance abuser of both legal and illegal substances as a teenager and adult.
- Become pregnant as a teenager and engage in risky sexual behavior (e.g., engage in earlier first intercourse, higher rates of STDs, more partners, and teenage pregnancy).
- Have poor health when older (e.g., higher rates of cancer, heart disease, chronic lung disease, irritable bowel syndrome, liver diseases, etc.).

Aside from the obvious, reasons why the effects of child abuse and neglect are so profound and long-lasting include the neurological changes in the child's brain that result from maltreatment; the modeling effects of seriously inadequate parenting; the adoption of a belief system about self, others, and the world as malevolent; and the defense mechanisms that maltreated children must develop to cope with their terror, despair, and hopelessness.

CAUSES OF CHILD ABUSE AND NEGLECT: CHARACTERISTICS OF PARENTS

Many of the parents who abuse and neglect their children were themselves maltreated as children. In addition, having been maltreated as a child also increases the likelihood that one will suffer other outcomes such as lower IQ and educational attainment, more mental health problems, substance abuse, and teen pregnancy – each of which, in turn, independently increases the risk of maltreating one's child. In other words, many of the consequences of having been abused and neglected as a child are also the causes of growing up to maltreat one's own child, laying the foundation for a cycle of abuse and neglect across generations. For example, parents who abuse or neglect their children are more likely to:

- Have been maltreated as a child.
- Have mental health problems, including parent depression.
- Have a violent marriage.
- Be a substance abuser.
- Be a teenage mother.
- Have lower levels of education and to be chronically poor.

In addition to the above, parents who abuse or neglect their children are also more likely to:

- Have serious parenting deficits (e.g., have unrealistic expectations for their children).
- Use harsh and aggressive parenting with their children (i.e., high levels of emotional abuse).
- Have low levels of parental involvement and supervision, give their children low levels of attention and affection (i.e., high levels of physical and emotional neglect).
- Frequently use corporal punishment on their children (i.e., high levels of physical abuse).
- Have less play materials or any cognitively stimulating materials in the home for their children (i.e., high levels of neglect).

The first set of factors points to the cycle of child abuse and neglect. The second set of factors indicates that engaging in low or "culturally acceptable" levels of harsh parenting, corporal punishment, and neglect significantly increases the likelihood that parents will proceed to more severely abuse and/or neglect their children. Moreover, at least in the area of physical violence, more frequent corporal punishment has the *same* adverse consequences

as physical abuse, from lower IQ to more violent behavior, mental health problems, and risky sexual behavior, except to lesser degrees.

CHILD ABUSE AND THE LARGER COMMUNITY AND SOCIETY

Child maltreatment is associated with substantial costs to society. The World Health Organization (2002: 70) estimated that the total financial cost of child maltreatment in the US was $12.4 billion, which includes, for example, the costs of services to families of maltreated children, the loss of the contributions of victims, and related costs of the criminal justice and health care system. In addition, it is important to acknowledge the ways in which the larger community and society fail children, neglecting them (e.g., high levels of child poverty, poor-quality schools, lack of neighborhood monitoring of children) and abusing them (exposure to high levels of violence and crime, legal support for children as property).

Intervention and prevention must address the larger context of child abuse, including for example:

- The degree to which the government and corporations support policies that benefit children (e.g., providing quality childcare for every child).
- The degree to which children are economically provided for by encouraging gender equality in the labor force, enforcing fathers' child support payments, and having a strong social welfare system which provides for all children.
- The provision of sex education, on-site availability of contraceptives, and parenting classes in high school designed to help teens, and ultimately all parents, postpone childbearing until they are mentally and financially able to raise a child without maltreatment.
- The level of help provided to maltreated children and survivors.
- The extent of protection for children provided by the law, agencies, and the criminal justice system.
- The degree to which children are viewed as the property of parents as opposed to the responsibility of the entire community.

- The level of support for extending human rights to children.

In these and other ways, a society can move toward protecting rather than forsaking its children.

SEE ALSO: Childhood; Rape/Sexual Assault as Crime; Victimization; Violent Crime

REFERENCES AND SUGGESTED READINGS

Adams, J. A. & East, P. L. (1999) Past Physical Abuse is Significantly Correlated with Pregnancy as an Adolescent. *Journal of Pediatric and Adolescent Gynecology* 12: 133–8.
Briere, J. (1992) *Child Abuse Trauma: Theory and Treatment of the Lasting Effects*. Sage, Newbury Park, CA.
Child Trauma Academy (2003) Child Trauma Academy version of chapter first published in Osofsky, J. (Ed.) (1997) *Children, Youth and Violence: The Search for Solutions*. Guilford Press, New York, pp. 124–48.
Dong, M., Anda, R., Felitti, V., Dube, S., Williamson, D., Thompson, T., Loo, C., & Giles, W. (2004) The Interrelatedness of Multiple Forms of Childhood Abuse, Neglect and Household Dysfunction. *Child Abuse and Neglect* 28: 771–84.
English, D. J. (1998) The Extent and Consequences of Child Maltreatment. *The Future of Children* 8(1): 39–53.
Felitti, V. J., Anda, R. F., Nordenberg, D., Williamson, D. F., Spitz, A. M., Edwards, V., Koss, M., & Marks, J. S. (1998) Relationship of Childhood Abuse and Household Dysfunction to Many of the Leading Causes of Death in Adults. *American Journal of Preventive Medicine* 14(4): 245–58.
Hildyard, K. L. & Wolfe, D. A. (2002) Child Neglect: Developmental Issues and Outcomes. *Child Abuse and Neglect* 26: 679–95.
McLoyd, V. C. (1998) Socioeconomic Disadvantage and Child Development. *American Psychologist* 53(2): 185–204.
Myers, J., Berliner, L., Briere, J., Hendrix, C. T., Jenny, C., & Reid, T. A. (Eds.) (2002) *The APSAC Handbook on Child Maltreatment*, 2nd edn. Sage, Thousand Oaks, CA.
Perry, B. D. (1997) Incubated in Terror: Neurodevelopmental Factors in the "Cycle Of Violence." Online. www.childtrauma.org/CTAMATERIALS/incubated.asp.
Scher, C. D., Forde, D. R., McQuaid, J. R., & Stein, M. B. (2004) Prevalence and Demographic Correlates of Childhood Maltreatment in an Adult Community Sample. *Child Abuse and Neglect* 28: 167–80.
Small, S. & Luster, T. (1994) Adolescent Sexual Activity: An Ecological, Risk-Factor Approach. *Journal of Marriage and the Family* 56(1): 181–92.
Straus, M. A. (2001) *Beating the Devil Out of Them: Corporal Punishment in American Families and Its Effects on Children*, 2nd edn. Transaction Publishers, New Brunswick, NJ.
UNICEF (2005) *Facts on Children*. Online. www.unicef.org/media/media_9482.html.
World Health Organization (2002) *World Report on Health and Violence*. WHO, Geneva. Online. www.who.int/violence_injury__prevention/violence/world_report/en/full_en.pdf.

child custody and child support

Janet Walker

Since the 1960s, growing proportions of children worldwide have been experiencing their parents' separation at an increasingly early age. Parental separation entails a series of transitions and family reorganizations, including changes in parenting arrangements, residence, family relationships, and standard of living, that influence children's development and adjustment over time. All pose risks for children.

When parents separate, a number of important decisions have to be taken. These relate to:

- where children will live and with whom – usually referred to as child custody, child physical custody, or child residence;
- who will make decisions about the children's day-to-day care and their overall upbringing in areas like education, religious affiliation, and health – sometimes referred to as child legal custody;
- what arrangements will be made for the non-custodial or non-resident parent to stay involved in the children's lives – known as child contact, access, or visitation;
- how property and assets will be divided;
- whether financial transfers between the ex-spouses will continue – called spousal support/maintenance;

- how sufficient financial provision will be ensured for the proper maintenance and care of the children – usually called child support.

These decisions are critical factors in promoting healthy child development and reducing the risk of difficulties enduring into adulthood. Changing approaches to child custody and child support reflect a mix of tradition, prevailing cultural values about childrearing, expectations about family life, and sensitivities surrounding state intervention in intensely private family matters.

There is a growing tendency to encourage parents to make decisions and agree arrangements for their children informally between themselves, often called "private ordering," rather than rely on legal remedies and the courts. But reaching agreement can be fraught with difficulty given the emotional, relational, and practical issues surrounding parental separation and parenting across two households. When parents cannot agree, they normally turn to the courts to resolve their disputes, and so the search for less adversarial, more conciliatory approaches to decision-making, which minimize tensions and conflicts for parents and children alike, has intensified. Concerns have been expressed not only about the increasing number of children experiencing family breakup, but also about the potentially detrimental consequences for their well-being and development. Research indicates that increased mental health problems for children are related to stresses such as parental instability, interparental conflict, loss of time with parents, and economic decline (Amato 2000). Governments in countries with high divorce rates, such as the US, Canada, Australia, and the UK, struggle to find the correct balance between respecting the privacy of family life and protecting vulnerable children who grow up in increasingly complex and shifting family structures.

Such dilemmas are comparatively new. Until the mid-nineteenth century, when parents separated fathers had an absolute right of control over their children and the mother had access only at the father's discretion. Attitudes began to change when awareness of the importance of maternal love and care began to emerge. In 1839, the Child Custody Act in England made it possible for the court to transfer legal custody of children under the age of 7 to the mother and made provision for visitation rights, in the belief that children should be brought up enjoying the affection of both parents. This "tender years" doctrine continued to influence the determination of child custody throughout most of the twentieth century. Mothers were usually regarded as the best parent to provide psychological, emotional, and physical care. Moreover, the classical economic model of the western household, involving a breadwinner husband and a homemaker wife, reinforced the belief that mothers should be granted custody of children after divorce and that fathers should provide the necessary financial support and play a role in the upbringing of their children through regular access.

Since the 1960s, this traditional gendered division of responsibilities has been steadily eroded. Mothers have gained much greater financial independence through increased participation in the workforce and fathers have devoted more time to childcare activities. The appropriate determination of both child custody and child support has been thrown into question and simple gendered solutions no longer appear appropriate. Although the ultimate test is that the child's best interests have primacy when parents separate, keeping both parents involved, emotionally and financially, in their children's lives has become a policy imperative. Either the mother or the father having sole custody of the children is increasingly viewed as the least desirable option. The focus is on encouraging joint parental responsibility so that children spend time with both parents, although the links between parenting time and shared parental responsibility are likely to be complex and, as yet, are not well understood.

In some countries, terminology has changed to reflect this shift. The 1989 Children Act in England and Wales, a landmark piece of legislation, emphasized that the primary responsibility for the care and upbringing of children rests with both parents. The notion of one parent having "custody" of a child was abandoned because it implied a kind of ownership which could exclude the other parent. Instead parents are referred to as the resident parent (with whom the child lives most of the time) and the non-resident parent (who has contact with the child but does not provide the primary residence). Residence orders, determining where a child should live, do not assign custodial status to either parent. In 1995, Australia adopted similar terminology, and in 2004 New Zealand also followed this trend. Whatever terms are used, however, arrangements for children continue to arouse strong emotions in and conflict between parents.

When courts have to be the final arbiter of arrangements for children, judges often turn to mental health professionals and social workers to help them make better-informed and more effective decisions about what would be in a child's best interests. In the US, child custody evaluations have become a burgeoning field of practice, and concerns have been expressed about overreliance on the recommendations they contain. Tippins and Wittman (2005) have argued that custody evaluations can have a profound impact on the direction a child's life will take after judicial disposition and that the best-interest standard is a legal and sociomoral concept rather than one capable of scientific assessment. Given that many custody recommendations lack an adequate empirical foundation and tend to be influenced by current trends, Tippins and Wittman suggest that they hold significant potential to harm rather than protect a child.

In Canada, by 2000 joint physical custody was awarded for 37 percent of children whose custody was part of the final divorce decree (Juby et al. 2005). While there is some evidence that children living in shared care/joint custody arrangements seem to be better adjusted than those in sole custody situations (Bauserman 2002), the parents who manage to share care may well differ in important ways such as having higher levels of education and financial resources. Nevertheless, disentangling the emotional ties associated with the marital relationship while reformulating parental ties represents a hugely demanding and difficult transition for parents, and making joint parental responsibility a reality is no easy task (Walker et al. 2004). Sole custody is a more straightforward option to implement, although it typically results in significant dissatisfaction among non-custodial parents who experience their parental role as episodic rather than continuous. Mothers may well regard it as a fairer reflection of the allocation of parenting tasks prior to separation, however, since in the majority of households it is they who undertake most of the childcare. Certainly, parents who agree their own arrangements tend to continue previous allocations of responsibility. It is still the norm for children to live mainly with mothers despite growing demands by fathers' groups for legal presumptions of equal parenting time. Research into the benefits for children of equal parenting time or dual residence is extremely limited, however, and in France it is ruled out as being against the best interests of children. More longitudinal research is needed to establish what kinds of parenting arrangements may be in each child's best interests, in view of the complexities and changes associated with post-separation family relationships and obligations. Nevertheless, existing research indicates that the factors having the greatest impact on children after parental separation are quality of family relationships, notably those between children and each parent, continuity of parental care, and financial stability (Amato & Gilbreth 1999). How to ensure that fathers stay committed and involved when they are not the resident parent remains a key challenge. Requiring them to pay child support is one mechanism.

Lone-parent families have always been the most economically vulnerable, and for over 100 years attempts have been made to recover money from fathers who no longer live with their children. Collecting payments has presented huge challenges and large numbers of mothers become dependent on social welfare assistance. Many of the current policies have grown out of concerns not only about the lower living standards of lone parents, but also about the numbers of parents dependent on welfare, the low amounts of child support paid by non-custodial parents, and the difficulties of enforcing payments through the courts. Child support policy straddles many technical domains, including estimating the costs of bringing up children, which are undoubtedly higher in separated households, the interaction between income support and taxation policy, and the complexities associated with dividing assets between parents and making post-separation financial settlements. These calculations are complicated further by varying perceptions of what mothers and fathers regard as fair and just. Residence and contact arrangements are highly variable and liable to change as children grow up and when stepfamilies are formed, making it hard for policies relating to child support to stay simple, transparent, and appropriate.

Governments have attempted to enforce parental responsibility through a variety of child support regimes, which seek to be fair in light of the complex personal circumstances of most separated families, to advance the well-being of children, to ensure cooperation and compliance, and to reduce the cost of lone parenting to the public purse. Achieving these diverse agendas is problematic and there have been some serious failures. Child support policy has become the locus for negotiating the limits of public and private responsibility for children. Whereas governments in England, Canada, and Australia have developed and imposed arm's-length, formulaic determinations rarely regarded as fair by fathers or mothers, the trend in continental Europe has been toward creating enabling structures and procedures which encourage parental cooperation in working out realistic child support arrangements, which may ensure higher compliance rates.

Although courts have long maintained that child support and child contact are independent obligations, they are inevitably closely associated in the minds of parents (Bradshaw & Skinner 2000). Most of the evidence suggests a generally positive relationship between paying child support and having contact with children. Proposals to link the amount of child support paid to the amount of parenting time are contentious, however. Fathers rarely question their parental obligation to contribute financially to the care of their children, but calculations relating to child support and modes of collecting and enforcing payments need to be facilitated through an increased understanding of the emotional turmoil that accompanies parental separation, and the inevitably changed and changing nature of the relationship non-residential parents have with their children. Facilitating contact and involvement between non-resident/non-custodial parents and their children when it is in children's best interests to do so may be critical in ensuring that financial support is forthcoming. Child support is not just about

money, and more research is needed to understand non-compliance and the complex interrelationships between child residence, contact, perceptions of fairness, and financial transfers.

Child support and child contact remain two of the most complex and controversial aspects of family policy because they require delicate balances to be struck between the competing needs of children, resident parents, non-resident parents, and the state (Smyth & Weston 2005). Moreover, they are primarily adult issues, but hearing the voice of the child is an increasingly important aspect of decision-making relating to arrangements which involve children. Young people are very concerned with issues of fairness and an enduring sense of family despite the breakdown of their parents' relationship. Although shared parenting may better meet the needs of children and young people than traditional custodial arrangements, and more closely reflect their perceptions of what is fair in terms of contact and child support (Parkinson et al. 2005), achieving it remains a major challenge.

SEE ALSO: Children and Divorce; Divorce; Family Demography; Family Structure; Life Course and Family; Lone-Parent Families; Non-Resident Parents; Stepfamilies

REFERENCES AND SUGGESTED READINGS

Amato, P. R. (2000) The Consequences of Divorce for Adults and Children. *Journal of Marriage and the Family* 62(4): 1269–87.
Amato, P. R. & Gilbreth, J. G. (1999) Non-Resident Fathers and Children's Well-Being: A Meta-Analysis. *Journal of Marriage and the Family* 61: 557–73.
Bauserman, R. (2002) Child Adjustment in Joint-Custody versus Sole-Custody Arrangements: A Meta-Analytic Review. *Journal of Family Psychology* 16: 91–102.
Bradshaw, J. & Skinner, C. (2000) Child Support: The British Fiasco. *Focus* 21(1): 80–6.
Corden, A. (2001) Comparing Child Maintenance Systems: Conceptual and Methodological Issues. *International Journal of Social Research Methodology* 4(4): 287–300.
Juby, H., Le Bourdais, C., & Marcel-Gratton, N. (2005) Sharing Roles, Sharing Custody? Couples'

Characteristics and Children's Living Arrangements at Separation. *Journal of Marriage and the Family* 67(1): 157–72.

Parkinson, P., Cashmore, J., & Single, J. (2005) Adolescents' Views of the Fairness of Parenting and Financial Arrangements after Separation. *Family Court Review* 43(3): 429–44.

Smyth, B. & Weston, R. (2005) *A Snapshot of Contemporary Attitudes to Child Support*. Research Report No. 13, Australian Institute of Family Studies.

Tippins, T. M. & Wittman, J. P. (2005) Empirical and Ethical Problems with Custody Recommendations: A Call for Clinical Humility and Judicial Vigilance. *Family Court Review* 43(2): 193–222.

Walker, J., McCarthy, P., Stark, C., & Laing, K. (2004) *Picking Up the Pieces: Marriage and Divorce Two Years After Information Provision*. Department for Constitutional Affairs, London.

child labor

Virginia Morrow

Child labor refers to a form of child work. Child labor was first conceptualized as a social problem during industrialization in nineteenth-century Britain, and the reasons were related to the need for cheap unskilled factory labor, and new moral concerns about childhood (Cunningham 1996). It is usually assumed that children in contemporary industrialized or post-industrial societies do not work, and that child labor is a "problem" in developing or majority world countries, but many children are "economically active" in some way, and accordingly there are many definitions of child labor. Economists Rodgers and Standing (1981) produced a typology of child activities and differentiate between the following categories of child work: domestic work; non-domestic, non-monetary work; tied or bonded labor; wage labor; and marginal economic activities.

Definitions of the terms "child" and "labor" and "child labor" are contested, and the topic is hotly debated. The category "child" (following the UN Convention on the Rights of the Child) includes "all those under the age of 18," but in many societies and cultures the distinction between childhood and adulthood is not made according to age, but according to stage in the life course. Western ideas about "work" and "labor" equate "work" with paid employment in the formal labor market, but social anthropologists have argued that work has many meanings, and can be broadly understood as the performance of necessary tasks and the production of necessary values (Wallman 1979). The International Labor Organization, a UN organization that promotes "decent work," combining workers' (represented by Trades Unions), employers', and governmental organizations, has over the years defined child labor as:

- Labor performed by a child who is under the minimum age specified in national legislation for that kind of work; and
- Labor that jeopardizes the physical, mental, or moral well-being of a child, known as hazardous work (Minimum Age Convention, No. 138, 1973); and
- Unconditional "worst" forms of child labor, internationally defined as slavery, trafficking, debt bondage and other forms of forced labor, forced recruitment for use in armed conflict, prostitution and pornography, and illicit activities (Worst Forms of Child Labor Convention No. 182 (1999) (ILO 2004).

Convention 182 reiterates the forms of work that are already prohibited for both children and adults in human rights treaties, and unconditionally prohibits all work for children under the age of 12.

In most countries, national legislation restricts the formal employment of children, but it is not effective in many circumstances, and needs to be seen in the context of poverty and underdevelopment, and the provision of acceptable alternative activities for children, especially high-quality education services which do not exist in most countries, and tend to be limited to "elementary education" for 5 years only.

Child labor is generally not well researched, and numbers of child laborers are usually estimated or are broad guesstimates. The extent of official data on labor-force participation of children is very limited even in developed countries, where it is often based indirectly on recorded violations of child labor legislation, or (rarely and not officially) on health and safety data of accidents at work, rather than direct national statistics about the nature and extent of child employment. Many forms of child labor are not reported, or are under-reported, and governments are under no obligation and have no incentives to collect such data.

Approaches to the study of child labor evolved during the twentieth century, and four dominant overlapping perspectives have been identified (Myers 2001; Ennew et al. 2005). The labor market perspective initially dominated European interventions and arose through concern from trade unions, employer associations, government departments, and philanthropic organizations during the early part of the twentieth century. It involved the construction of child labor as a "problem," not least competing with adult employment, requiring abolition through the extension of compulsory education and enforcement of labor legislation. This approach expanded gradually internationally and remains the dominant model.

The human capital perspective views child labor resulting from economic underdevelopment, and childhood as preparation for adulthood, seeing children as potential economic producers, thus requiring skills and literacy to be developed through intensive education. This approach emphasizes the benefits of "investing in children."

The social responsibility perspective sees child labor as arising from social inequalities, and defines children's work as exploitative, alienating, or oppressive work that excludes children from protection, and depicts child labor as a collective moral responsibility. This approach has generated innovative non-formal education programs in developing countries, such as street education and work–school arrangements.

The children-centered perspective takes into account the effects of labor on children's well-being and individual/social development and also balances these with the advantages of work from children's perspectives. Recently, this view has become linked with notions of children's rights and the UN Convention on the Rights of the Child (1989), which set standards for freedom from exploitation at work (Article 32), but also for participation (Article 12), which guarantees children's rights to participate in decisions concerning them. This view sees children as active social agents who have capabilities and responsibilities, rather than as passive victims or blank slates upon whom culture is inscribed.

Within European sociology there is growing awareness among researchers that children's perspectives on why they work give a different, more complex picture (Liebel 2004) and in some developing countries groups of working children have organized themselves and emphasize the right to decent work for children. However, the views of these groups are generally excluded from the debates at policy level about child labor, in which powerful vested interests continue to operate.

SEE ALSO: Child Abuse; Childhood; Human Rights; Industrial Revolution; Marx, Karl

REFERENCES AND SUGGESTED READINGS

Cunningham, H. (1996) Combating Child Labor: The British Experience. In: Cunningham, H. & Viazzo, P. P. (Eds.), *Child Labor in Historical Perspective: 1880–1985: Case Studies from Europe, Japan and Colombia.* UNICEF/ICDC, Florence.

Ennew, J., Myers, W. E., & Plateau, D. P. (2005) Defining Child Labor As If Human Rights Really Matter. In: Weston, B. H. (Ed.), *Child Labor and Human Rights: Making Children Matter.* Lynne Rienner, Boulder.

International Labor Organization (ILO) (2004) *Child Labour: A Textbook for University Students.* ILO/IPEC, Geneva.

Liebel, M. (2004) A Will of Their Own. In: *Cross-Cultural Perspectives on Working Children.* Zed Books, London.

Myers, W. E. (2001) Valuing Diverse Approached to Child Labour. In: Lieten, K. & White, B. (Eds.), *Child Labour: Policy Options.* Aksant Publishers, Amsterdam.

Rodgers, G. & Standing, G. (Eds.) (1981) *Child Work, Poverty and Underdevelopment.* International Labor Organization, Geneva.

Wallman, S. (Ed.) (1979) *Anthropology of Work.* Academic Press, London.

childcare

Julia Brannen

Childcare is a term which typically is applied to adults taking responsibility for younger children and looking after them on a daily basis in the private sphere of families and the home. In societies where women and men are employed outside the home, their under-school-age children may be cared for by kin or their care may be commodified, in which case care is provided through private markets, through quasi-markets (childminding), or by the state. In the latter case, in western societies which have strong welfare states, childcare is provided in the public sphere for all children as a right as part of the social rights of citizenship (Leira 2002). In residual welfare states, the state and institutions step in only when children are deemed to be at risk or vulnerable because of abuse, neglect, or loss of both parents.

DEVELOPMENTS IN THE CONCEPT OF CARE

No contribution to this topic is complete without a brief exploration of the concept of care. Care is a multifaceted concept which over 20 years has undergone a number of theoretical developments. Until the 1970s care was theoretically subsumed within discussions of the "natural" role of mothers. In the 1970s, feminists argued that care such as childcare constitutes work and is a burden upon those who do an inordinate amount of it (traditionally women). Care has since been elaborated as a concept which has a relational ontology and belongs to the moral realm in which the self can only exist with and through others, and vice versa (Gilligan 1988; Tronto 1993; Sevenhuijsen 1998). In this conceptualization, care is not an automatic obligation associated with a particular role but a situated practice in which all people must interpret questions concerning an "ethic of care" – what is "the right thing to do," when to care, and how much care in relation to a variety of conditions (Finch & Mason 1993). To give care is thus not a top-down moral obligation but negotiated with others and with the self, involving both receivers and givers of care. Care is also a disposition: it involves values of attentiveness, responsibility, competence, and responsiveness. It is a social process with a number of associated phases: caring about; caring for; taking care of; and being responsive to care.

CHILDCARE IN THE PRIVATE SPHERE

Children's care in the private sphere has received a good deal of attention over the past 30 years as women's position in society has changed and gender equality has increased. Until the 1970s, childrearing, as it was then conceptualized, was predominantly the province of psychology and was assumed to take place exclusively within the family. Childcare was bracketed with motherhood; mothers were assumed to be the only carers of importance for children.

By the end of the 1970s, Bronfenbrenner (1979) had located the "individual developing child" within a hierarchy of social settings. Childcare as a concept began to be further elaborated in feminists' theoretical challenges to the dominant psychological paradigm of the "developing individual." The care of children, they argued, in falling disproportionately upon women was a cornerstone of their oppression and precluded women from positions of power in the public sphere. However, children's care also offered women a sense of power and gave meaning to their lives, albeit this was often turned against women's interests. Its significance was moreover underpinned by fantasies connected with women's own childhoods (Chodorow & Contratto 1982), while women's practices were normalized by the discourses of experts (e.g., Urwin 1985 with respect to young children).

Not surprisingly, fathers have remained very much as background figures in childcare, especially in the care of young children. How far their invisibility results from the concept of childcare is worthy of some consideration, in respect of both researchers' and informants' interpretations. For what fathers do with and for their children is likely to be shaped not only by what passes for care in a particular historical and social milieu but also by hegemonic notions of masculinity.

Much of the childcare research has been conducted on mothers with younger children so that childcare has been narrowly interpreted in relation to fulfilling the needs of small children relating to their material, social, and emotional requirements and their health and well-being (Ribbens 1994). How far the concept stretches to encompass many of the other aspects of parenting as children enter school and remain materially dependent for longer as education is extended is doubtful. Indeed, much of what may be conceptualized as childcare in terms of looking after children's interests sits unsatisfactorily within the concept, namely, the considerable amount of consumption involved in bringing up children and the support that parents give children -- with homework, preparing them for the world of work, and myriad other activities. Parents are pivotal figures mediating the household and the public world. However, this activity is often captured in other concepts such as health care and home–school relations.

CHILDCARE IN THE PRIVATE/PUBLIC SPHERE

Childcare is increasingly conceptualized at the interface between the public and private spheres. Work–family studies are a growing field of research which examine how mothers (and fathers) negotiate this interface with implications for the childcare they use and the childcare they do themselves. Studies show how childcare choices are shaped, for example, by labor and childcare markets, social class, ethnicity, lone parenthood, and time. In relation to time, Hochschild (1997) shows how mothers are increasingly driven by the "Taylorization" of family life and a consequent lack of time while, in the workplace, they are subject to work intensification and feelings of job insecurity, making it difficult for mothers to take up family-friendly policies. Thus in these studies, childcare per se becomes less central as the focus shifts to the work–family strategies of parents, employers, and public policy.

Childcare is commodified in a variety of contexts. For example, in Britain public policy concerning childcare provision has been a backwater. Before the increase in the employment of mothers of young children that began in the late

1980s, the term "childcare" suggested rather uninspiring and unpromising connotations (Riley 1983, cited in Brennan 1998: 3). The British concept – spelt "childcare" and also "child care" – has no direct reciprocal meaning in other public policy contexts (Moss 2003).

There are two major policy areas concerning childcare. The first policy meaning (usually signified by two words) concerns the role of the state when it intervenes to protect children or when children are defined as being "in need." Here childcare is often underpinned by assumptions of maternalism as being the "best" form of care for children and is (increasingly in the UK) carried out by foster carers and (less often in the UK) in institutional settings.

Childcare (one word) refers to the way children are looked after when parents are in paid work. In the US and the UK, the care of young children has historically been a sphere in which public policy has not intervened to any great extent compared with many European countries. In the former countries, it has typically been dominated by ideas of maternalism (Brannen & Moss 2003). Care by family members and childminding (family day care) have been commonplace and continue to be so. The childcare workforce is typically low qualified and low paid.

Childcare, in both policy senses, takes on a different meaning in other countries, notably Scandinavia and some other European countries, where it refers to the fields of theory and practice concerning children. Here the educational content of childcare is more prominent and the concept of "pedagogy" is used to refer to the whole child (body, mind, and feelings). Pedagogy also involves an ethic of care (see above) that develops between pedagogues and children in their "care." Thus relationships between carers and children take on forms different from mother–child relationships and are less governed by neoliberal economics (many childcare providers in the UK and the US are businesses) and by concerns of risk aversion (keeping children safe as being the central priority for children's care).

The commodification of childcare also occurs in the context of globalization. In the US, home-based childcare workers are increasingly recruited from poor developing countries, leading to a drain on the resources of the source countries (Hochschild 2000). Moreover, the women concerned often employ other women in their countries of origin to care for their children in their absence. This practice highlights the issue of power between those who delegate care to others and those who work in the growing childcare workforce. Thus care relationships may not only contribute to love, responsibility, and attentiveness but also bring about inequalities and exploitation.

In this conceptual frame of childcare as relational, it is important to suggest that children are not just recipients of childcare. This is a crucial issue for future research in the field to explore. For children need to be seen as active partners in their care. Similarly, there is a need to examine childcare services as spaces in which children participate together and with adult carers, creating milieux that are qualitatively different from the home and which offer children many challenges and opportunities.

SEE ALSO: Caregiving; Carework; Child Custody and Child Support; Childhood; Divisions of Household Labor; Divorce; Ethic of Care; Fatherhood; Motherhood

REFERENCES AND SUGGESTED READINGS

Brannen, J. & Moss, P. (Eds.) (2003) *Rethinking Children's Care*. Open University Press, Buckingham.

Brennan, D. (1998) *The Politics of Australian Child Care*. Cambridge University Press, Cambridge.

Bronfenbrenner, U. (1979) *The Ecology of Human Development*. Harvard University Press, Cambridge, MA.

Chodorow, N. & Contratto, N. (1982) The Fantasy of the Perfect Mother. In: Thorne, B. & Yalom, M. (Eds.), *Rethinking the Family: Some Feminist Questions*. Longman, New York.

Finch, J. & Mason, J. (1993) *Negotiating Family Responsibilities*. Routledge, London.

Gilligan, C. J. (1988) Remapping the Moral Domain: New Images of Self in Relationship. In: Gilligan, C. J., Ward, V., & Taylor, J. M., with Bardige, B. (Eds.), *Mapping the Moral Domain: A Contribution of Women's Thinking to Psychological Theory and Education*. Harvard University Press, Cambridge, MA.

Hochschild, A. (1997) *The Time Bind: When Work Becomes Home and Home Becomes Work*. Metropolitan Books, New York.

Hochschild, A. (2000) Global Care Chains and Emotional Surplus Value. In: Hutton, W. & Giddens, A. (Eds.), *On the Edge: Living with Global Capitalism*. Jonathan Cape, New York.

Leira, A. (2002) Care, Actors, Relationships, Contexts. In: Hobson, B., Lewis, J., & Siim, B. (Eds.), *Contested Concepts in Gender and Social Politics*. Edward Elgar, Cheltenham.

Moss, P. (2003) Getting Beyond Childcare: Reflections on Recent Policy and Future Possibilities. In: Brannen, J. & Moss, P. (Eds.), *Rethinking Children's Care*. Open University Press, Buckingham.

Ribbens, J. (1994) *Mothers and Their Children: A Feminist Sociology of Childrearing*. Sage, London.

Sevenhuijsen, S. (1998) *Citizenship and the Ethics of Care: Feminist Considerations on Justice*. Routledge, London.

Tronto, J. (1993) *Moral Boundaries: A Political Argument for the Ethics of Care*. Routledge, London.

Urwin, C. (1985) Constructing Motherhood: The Persuasion of Normal Development. In: Steedman, C., Urwin, C., & Walkerdine, V. (Eds.), *Language, Gender and Childhood*. Routledge & Kegan Paul, London.

childhood

Sally McNamee

What is now known as the "new paradigm" of the sociology of childhood grew out of a rejection of traditional sociological and psychological theories of childhood. Children in earlier sociological accounts were subsumed into accounts of the family or the school – in other words, into the major sites of socialization. Children were, therefore, most visible when they were being socialized. Socialization, which is sociology's explanation for how children become members of society, parallels developmental psychology, in that children progress from incompetent to competent adulthood through the process of acculturation or socialization. In both socialization theory and developmental psychology there was no view of children as active social agents; rather, children were seen (if they were seen at all) as passive recipients of socialization. In addition, both socialization theory and developmental psychology fail to see the child as existing in the present – instead, the focus is on what children *become*.

ialization theory ignores children's role in socializing both themselves and others. In fact, it fails to take account of the child as a competent social actor. What was missing from sociology, then, was an account of the socially constructed nature of childhood which focused on children as social actors rather than passive "becomings."

The historian Philippe Ariès noted that childhood as a concept has not always existed in the same way. In *Centuries of Childhood* (1962 [1960]) Ariès discusses the development of the *idea* of childhood through reference to diaries, paintings, and other such historical documents and traces the changes in attitudes to children from those based, for example, on indifference, to coddling (the child as a plaything), to the seventeenth-century development of psychological interest and "moral solicitude." Ariès's work shows us the child as part of society in medieval times. Childhood at that time did not exist as a separate concept.

The childhoods described by Ariès are very different from the modern, particularly western, conception of childhood to which we subscribe. In the western view, childhood is a time of innocence and children are in need of protection from adult society, not expected to join it. In order to see some of the anomalies around childhood in contemporary western society, we have only to think of the ages by which children are – and are not – allowed to do certain things. For example, in the UK, children can work (in certain jobs) at the age of 14. They attain the legal age of responsibility at 10 years old, but cannot vote until the age of 18.

Of course, as well as differing over time, or historically, what "childhood" is also differs across cultures – a modern western childhood looks very different from that experienced by children in other cultures. For example, the work of Samantha Punch shows that children in rural Bolivia are, from the age of 5 years old, expected to work. This work might be collecting firewood or bringing water, or milking animals. Punch shows us the ways in which children contribute to family life and feel a sense of pride in so doing. A cross-cultural view of childhood allows us to see one of the central tenets of the "new paradigm" very clearly – that of children as competent social actors. Many children in the developing world

(and some children in the West) work and/or care for families – and in some cases combine these activities with attending school. If "childhood" was indeed a time of innocence and if children were all in need of protection, then how is it that children in other cultures lead such competent (one might almost say "adult") lives? Of course, many commentators would see this as being an intrinsically bad thing – and this is not arguing against that view, merely pointing out that age is no barrier to living a competent social life.

Those working within the "new paradigm" began the task of de- and re-constructing childhood in the 1980s. Of particular note in the UK is the work of Allison James, Chris Jenks, and Alan Prout. Collectively and separately, they have authored many texts which have stimulated and led the debate around childhood. In Europe, the work of Qvortrup and others working on the "childhood as a social phenomenon" project contributed to the debate (see Qvortrup et al. 1994), and in the US Sharon Stephens's (1995) work has also been of importance. James, Jenks, and Prout's (1998) work provides the social study of childhood with a paradigm which is able to draw together different disciplines and which can locate a conceptual space for theories of childhood. The new social study of childhood, then, moves away from a conception of childhood as an age-bound developmental process and from a view of children as passive recipients of socialization toward seeing childhood as a time of competence and agency. The central tenets of the "new paradigm" as set out by James and Prout (1997) are as follows:

- Childhood is to be understood as a social construction.
- Childhood as a variable of social analysis cannot be separated from other variables such as class, gender, or ethnicity.
- Childhood, and children's social relationships, are worthy of study in their own right.
- Ethnography is a methodology which has a particular role to play in the new sociology of childhood.
- Childhood sociology engages in and responds to the process of reconstructing childhood in society.

Under the rubric of the "new paradigm" many aspects of children's everyday social lives have been studied over the last 10 to 20 years. These include, but are not restricted to, the study of children and time, children and schooling, children and leisure, children and health, street children, working children, and so on. In fact, children in almost every social setting have been studied by those working in the new social study of childhood. Childhood is now theorized, not as a universal concept, but as being fragmented by variables such as gender, disability, and class.

There have in the past been concerns that research with children and young people is problematic in terms of the difficulties involved in gathering meanings from children, a result of an expressed fear that children are unable to clearly articulate their own social worlds. This concern has largely been dispelled by the volume of good social research which has been successfully carried out with children. Good research with children is important not only to understand and document their social lives but also in terms of the development of social policy. Children's voices from research are now beginning to be incorporated in policy for children. In the main, the majority of studies using the "children as social actors" approach discussed here have used the ethnographic technique, as called for by James and Prout (1997). However, within the broadly qualitative methods used to study children and childhood, a variety of tools have been used, and this reflects the interdisciplinary background of childhood studies: although called the "new sociology" of childhood, it is actually an interdisciplinary field of study. Researchers working within this area include geographers, psychologists, historians, sociologists, and anthropologists. Geographers, for instance, may use mapping and photography as methods, while historians would use documents. Some researchers currently use more quantitative methods, such as questionnaire surveys, which can elicit data that can be just as valid as ethnographic material. As with any research, the methods chosen to investigate reflect the standpoint of the researcher, the questions asked, and the tools used. It is possible to trace a movement over the last 20 years from research "on" children, which saw children as objects, to research "with"

children, which sees them more as subjects. More recently, there is a movement which has children as researchers, designing and carrying out their own research.

Childhood as a concept has been examined and children's social lives made visible from many angles. In order to do this, children were metaphorically removed from the home and the school where previously they were hidden – and yet, paradoxically, at the same time were more truly present than in any other site. Future directions for the social study of childhood may involve returning the child to the home, the family, and the school. In the same way that early feminism had to deconstruct gender in order to make the oppression of women in patriarchal society visible, childhood sociologists have liberated childhood from the oppression of adult society. Now that there appears to be an acceptance of the child as a competent social actor in mainstream social science disciplines, perhaps now is the time to retheorize childhood as part of society rather than removed from it.

SEE ALSO: Childcare; Childhood Sexuality; Developmental Stages; Ethnography; Socialization; Youth/Adolescence

REFERENCES AND SUGGESTED READINGS

Ariès, P. (1962 [1960]) *Centuries of Childhood*. Jonathan Cape, London.

Goddard, J., McNamee, S., James, A., & James, A. L. (Eds.) (2004) *The Politics of Childhood*. Palgrave, London.

James, A. & Prout, A. (Eds.) (1997) *Constructing and Reconstructing Childhood: Contemporary Issues in the Sociological Study of Childhood*, 2nd edn. Falmer, London.

James, A., Jenks, C., & Prout, A. (1998) *Theorizing Childhood*. Polity, Cambridge.

Jenks, C. (1996) *Childhood*. Routledge, London.

Punch, S. (2004) Negotiating Autonomy: Children's Use of Time and Space in Rural Bolivia. In: Lewis, V. et al. (Eds.), *The Reality of Research with Children and Young People*. Sage/Open University Press, London.

Qvortrup, J. et al. (1994) *Childhood Matters*. Avebury, Aldershot.

Stephens, S. (Ed.) (1995) *Children and the Politics of Culture*. Princeton University Press, Princeton.

UNICEF website, www.unicef.org/crc/crc.htm.

Waksler, F. C. (1991) Beyond Socialization. In: Waksler, F. C. (Ed.), *Studying the Social Worlds of Children*. Falmer, London.

childhood sexuality

Karen Corteen

Children and sexuality are in their own right particularly sensitive areas. Bringing the two together is to end a dominant and ideological taboo (Jackson 1982). Consequently, within America and the UK the area of childhood sexuality is research arid, and the established literature is predominantly undertheorized and uncritical (Plummer 1991; Weis 2005). Childhood sexuality is a sensitive and controversial area and this is particularly the case when the issue of children's sexuality challenges heterosexual norms and highlights the rights of all children to make informed choices about their own bodies, sexual desires, practices, and identity (Levine 2002; Corteen 2003a). Evidently, it deals with issues that are both personal and private as well as public and political. The issue of childhood sexuality when approached holistically is concerned with children's lives and experiences, their physical health and their emotional well-being. Thus, it is more than a theoretical and analytical endeavor. Discussions around and constructions of childhood sexualities, whether they are underpinned by a scientific developmental approach or a sociological approach, can result in the validation or invalidation, the sanctioning or condemnation of sexual desires, practices, and identities. The subject is socially, politically, ideologically, and academically awash with commonsensical ideologies regarding children, childhood, sexuality, and childhood sexuality.

Despite the obsession with adolescent (hetero)sexual behavior and fears concerning pedophilia and child sexual abuse within American and British cultures (Plummer 1991; Levine 2002), research concerned with childhood sexuality is sparse. Such scarcity derives from a reluctance to undertake research in this area, together with practical and ethical methodological considerations and societal ideologies and taboos which restrict investigation. Researching the area of childhood sexualities is empirically problematic and this situation is produced and compounded by ideologies concerned with the protection of "childhood innocence" and prohibitive conventions which prevail in relation to "childhood eroticism, and childhood sexual expression and learning" (Weis 2005: 1). Traditionally and contemporarily in America and the UK the limited literature and research focused on childhood sexuality have been viewed through the lens of childhood development. Yet, while Freud's theory of psychosexual stages has been a major influence in many quarters in various parts of the world, his discussion of the sexual character of children's development has not been embraced. Plummer (1991) notes that the Freudian stance has been used to justify both the repression and the liberation of child sexuality, including childhood sexuality. Notwithstanding, the framework of development presumes that a child's capacity to make sense of and to make appropriate decisions regarding sex and sexuality via adult guidance is predicated on biological development. The child's "sexual development passes through a series of stages of competence on the way to a 'maturity' in adult life" (Plummer 1991: 244). Due to the theoretical framework being employed, the conceptualization of these stages will vary. Nonetheless, developmental theories have and continue to have significant influence regarding the way in which childhood sexualities are imagined and responded to. For example, there are "academic models of development which are established which can serve to homogenize and standardize children's sexuality" (ibid.). However, contemporary approaches within social science have problematized this presumption through a contextualization of childhood sexualities in relation to external individual and structural influences.

The issue of childhood sexualities is inextricably connected to the construction of "childhood," "childhood innocence," sexuality, protection, the separateness of children, and the adult–child relation. Although the immaturity of children is a biological fact, there are variations across time and space in the manner in which such immaturity is understood and managed (Hendrick 1997).

Definitions of childhood and conceptions of childhood sexuality are primarily the product of the society from which they emerge (Plummer 1991; Corteen 2003a).

In addition, while sexual desire, practice, and identity are connected to biological and physiological influences, they are not determined by them (Jackson 1982; Plummer 1991). They are not biological givens, but are socially constructed and mediated by society. This can be evidenced in cross-cultural studies and research findings regarding the onset, types, and frequency of predominantly heterosexual activity, rates of underage and premarital conceptions, and use of contraception. The development of children's "sexual script" is a complex process of constant negotiation and "the child cannot *not* do it" (Plummer 1991: 238). "Such scripting is highly variable and context bound" (ibid.); however, cross-culturally both historically and contemporarily heterosexuality is rarely acknowledged as a sexual practice, category, or identity. Yet, in the discursive production of sexuality, heterosexuality is constructed and represented as the normal, natural, and desirable sexuality. Sexual minorities are subsequently produced as unnatural, abnormal, and undesirable. In debates surrounding childhood sexuality, minority sexualities such as bisexuals, intersexuals, transvestites, transgendered, and transsexual individuals are predominantly excluded, while lesbians and gay men are marginalized and disqualified. This process also operates through formal and informal rules and expectations regarding sexual behavior and gender representation.

The laws, conventions, and ideologies which govern sexuality are learnt. Official and popular discourses underpin the conceptualization of "children," "childhood innocence," "sex," and sexuality. In so doing they inform the reproduction of childhood (hetero)sexuality. Children learn to assess the costs and benefits of particular sexual behaviors and sexualities through the law, the family and other state institutions, and through civil society. The production and management of childhood sexualities entail a complex interrelationship between individuals and institutions. Adults and children internalize, police, regulate, and punish themselves and others with regard to sexual desire, practice, and identity. Children are not just acted upon; they are agentic subjects and to some extent they engage in these processes. This can be evidenced in children's own gender and sexual performances and name-calling and bullying related to gender and sexual representations. Regarding childhood sexualities, in order to "fit in" and to avoid violence and punishment, children must attempt to engage in compulsory and repetitive gender performances which demonstrate their heterosexuality while simultaneously distancing themselves from "non-heterosexualities." This is particularly detrimental to the emotional and physical well being of young minority sexualities.

A "progress model" of "childhood" is rooted in an idealist conceptualization of history (Goldson 1997) which perceives the construction of childhood and institutional intervention into the lives of children, including concerns regarding their sexual development, as being in the best interest of the child. In so doing, state surveillance, regulation, and management of children are considered to be predicated on benevolent, philanthropic, and altruistic social reformism, humanitarianism, and enlightenment. Such intervention is legitimated through welfarist and protectionist discourses.

However, a more critical approach contextualizes such interventions and concerns within the determining contexts of age, adultism, the imperatives of social control, and the capitalist patriarchal ordering of society. Critical theorists recognize the historical and cross-cultural differences in the meanings and experiences of childhood, together with the identification of childhood as a social institution (Holt, in Archard 1993) which is neither natural nor universal (Jackson 1982). While there remains a continual renegotiation and revision of definitions of childhood, childhood is a structural concept and a determining context. In the naturalization of "childhood" and "childhood innocence" the structural dimensions of the adult–child relation and the construction of childhood are absent.

The conceptualization of childhood and childhood sexuality, academically, politically and popularly, continues to be informed and facilitated by a biologically deterministic conceptualization of naturalness. Subsequently, historically and contemporarily children are conceptualized as on a biologically determined path of development, the final stage being that of adulthood. The period of physical and emotional development is herein constructed around dependency, innocence, and protection.

Prior to the fifteenth century, childhood was not a distinct phase in a person's life. In the west from the fifteenth century onwards childhood began to emerge as a distinct phase of life and the gradual removal of children from the everyday life of adults can be evidenced. This was facilitated by the conceptualization of children as special and in need of protection. The construction of children as different to adults and subsequent concerns regarding children and childhood innocence gathered strength during the sixteenth and seventeenth centuries. Within western society in particular, the universalization of childhood and the "concern over and surveillance of the sexual, emotional, social and physiological immaturity and lack of autonomy of those defined within childhood" increased during the development and consolidation of capitalism (Evans 1994: 3). Historically, the concern with and the production of the "modern child," "childhood innocence," and child sexuality can be traced to the beginning of the nineteenth century (Hendrick 1997). Pivotal to the construction of the "modern child" was the development of compulsory education for all children. Compulsory schooling "demanded a state of innocence" (ibid.). In America and in the UK ignorance was (and continues to be) equated with innocence (Goldman & Goldman 1982; Jackson 1982; Levine 2002; Corteen 2003a). "Childhood innocence" together with children's assumed natural and normal heterosexuality required protection from external and internal influences "en route to adulthood" (Evans 1994).

According to Weeks (1989), the "conceptualization of the separateness of children went hand in hand with the socially felt need to protect their purity and innocence." This can be evidenced in the changing attitudes towards and the treatment of children with regard to sex and sexual matters. Jackson (1982: 27) asserts "the anxiety and controversy surrounding the issue of children and sex must be seen in the context of the 'prolongation of childhood.'"

Foucault (1979: 105) maintained that the discursive deployment of the "pedagogization of sex" during this time, due to concerns and campaigns regarding the health of the nation, entailed the sexualization and subsequently the problematization of children. During this period infantile masturbation in particular became a "subject of obsessive concern" with the masturbator situated as perpetrator, "the archetypal image of the sexual deviant" (Weeks 1989: 4). Subsequently, children became pivotal to the anxieties embedded in medico-legal discourse, which underpinned health interventions against "dangerous sexualities" (Mort 1987). Middle-class values were imposed on the "morally degenerate" and "vice-ridden" poor as child protection was directed downwards and administered by those in authority.

Child (hetero)sexuality was constructed as "precious, active ... ever present" (Foucault 1979: 28) and therefore had to be managed. This was especially the case regarding adolescents, as adolescence was (and still is) affiliated with biological and physiological growth during puberty. External pubescent physical changes were demarcated as signifiers of children's awareness of, and capacity to understand, sexual matters. The management of child (hetero)sexuality was and continues to be established as the preserve of adults (Plummer 1991; Levine 2002; Weis 2005). Armed with the remit of surveying, analyzing, and classifying children and their sexual desires and practice, various "experts" were established. Children were paradoxically constructed as asexual and yet saturated with (hetero)sexual potential; they were preliminary (hetero)sexual beings, yet imbued with (hetero)sexual potential. Children were innocent, yet capable of being corrupted and corrupting others (Gittins 1998; Wies 2005). They were seen as in danger from their own emerging desires and/or at risk of corruption by others. In the containment of child sexuality the heterosexual presumption can be evidenced. For example, in many societies this can be seen in the architectural and physical organization of schools designed to separate boys and girls through the layout of desks, changing rooms, and in boarding school dormitories and rules for monitoring bedtime. Indeed, it has been documented that the first experience of heterosexual penetrative intercourse demarcates sexual maturity (Corteen 2003b).

The taboo of children and sex (Jackson 1982) impacted on childrearing practices. Children were denied independent access to knowledge regarding sex and sexual matters. Subsequently, standards of modesty and decency and rules governing sexual matters were taught to children. Regulation, management, and control of children's sexuality operated on a number of levels. It entailed the incitement of discourses as well as discursive silences. Thus, it comprised both repression and production (Foucault 1979). The "restrictive economy" resulted in the disappearance of the longstanding "freedom" and openness of language between children and adults concerning sex. There was a gradual stifling of "the boisterous laughter that had accompanied the precocious sexuality of children for so long – and in all social classes" (ibid.: 27). Simultaneously, there was also a proliferation of discourses centering on sex and in particular on children and sex. Thus, children's sexualities are not so much repressed as produced (Plummer 1991).

The western ideology of "childhood innocence" forged during the development and consolidation of capitalism remains powerful and pervasive. "Childhood innocence" continues to be a major signifier regarding the distinction of children from adults. Indeed "innocence" still constitutes the "defining characteristic of the 'child'" (Gittins 1998: 7). In America and in the UK the taboo of children and sex remains firmly entrenched and sexual matters and sex itself persist literally, as well as socially, politically, and legally, "for adults only." Various rules, conventions, and laws are in place to position sex as the preserve of adults. Sexuality, and children and sex in particular, continue to be controversial, evocative, and provocative subjects. Whenever such issues arise they are met with public scandal and moral crusades; battle lines are drawn between conservative and liberal camps.

Socially, politically, and legislatively, protectionist and welfarist discourses prevail concerning the protection of pre(hetero)sexual children and childhood innocence together with the natural trajectory of heterosexuality. Contemporary research has demonstrated that children are presumed to be heterosexual unless there are explicit signifiers to suggest otherwise. Therefore, although heterosexuality is contested and changing, and while it is not experienced or occupied in a homogeneous manner, it has not

relinquished its hold. Childhood (hetero)sexuality is to be protected and nurtured. In particular children are to be guarded against and steered away from sexual desires, practices, and identities which deviate from the heterosexual norm. This is also the case regarding age and intergenerational sexualities (Plummer 1991). In the West, increased tolerance of sexual minorities such as lesbians and gay men can be discerned, but tolerance is far short of full acceptance. Subsequently, with regard to children there is no positive advocacy of "homosexuality" and lesbianism or other sexual minorities with regard to the dissemination of knowledge.

In western representations of childhood, children are protected by adults and it is the responsibility of adults (primarily parents and carers) to act in the best interests of the child and to attend to their needs (Goldson 1997). This welfarist and protectionist understanding and representation of childhood and the adult–child relation underpins commonsense thinking. However, this conceptualization is lacking. It lacks an understanding of childhood as a surveyed, regulated, and disciplined period of life. So while there clearly are important considerations regarding child protection generally and child protection specifically regarding sex and sexuality, it is fundamental to recognize and acknowledge that the emphasis on welfare and protection can result in marginalization, exclusion, and oppression on the grounds of age. Children are "objects of both care and control" and therefore it is important to distinguish between "what society does *to* them" and "what society does *for* them" (Goldson 1997: 27). This is particularly the case regarding childhood sexualities. The "sexual politics of fear" which results in censoring information about sexual matters from children is not protection but is indeed "harmful to children" (Levine 2002: xxi). What is potentially harmful to children is unplanned conceptions, sexually transmitted infections, and damaging sexual experiences, including sexual violence. The "means of [children's] self-defense" against the perils of sex are "knowledge and courage as well as rights and respect, political and sexual citizenship" (ibid.: 238).

Children are very aware of sex and sexuality and can understand and express sexual feelings and emotions prior to puberty (Goldman & Goldman 1982; Plummer 1991; Levine 2002). However, adults consistently underestimate children's awareness and understanding regarding sexual matters. Children are also surrounded by confused and confusing messages regarding their own sexuality and sex and sexuality generally. Further, some children will have been subjected to sexual abuse. In a vacuum of limited, partial, and distorted knowledge, children have to come to terms with and negotiate their sexual development, physically and emotionally. This constitutes a "politics of denial" wherein children are "systematically and institutionally ... denied access to information and knowledge concerning their physical and sexual development and its broader social and cultural context" (Goldman & Goldman 1982: 77). Contemporary research illustrates that the information children in America and the UK receive regarding childhood sexualities, sex, and sexualities generally is limited and partial and does not reflect their material realities. In the UK the official knowledge they receive concerning sexuality is driven by a health-oriented "damage limitation" model (Corteen 2003a) and in America "the embrace of abstinence appears nearly unanimous" (Levine 2002: 92). This is particularly evident in the official schooling of sexualities which is underpinned by welfare protectionism and authoritarian surveillance, regulation, and discipline (Corteen 2003a). The information children receive is not primarily concerned with the needs, concerns, rights, and lives of children, but the needs and concerns of states and particular sexual, economic, and political social orders. In the institutionalized dissemination of knowledge regarding sexual matters children are not taught about pleasure or the complexities and matrix of sex, sexualities, and relationships. Further, the "language of sexual intimacy, the fluidity of sexuality, and the creativity of human sexual responses" (Sears 1992: 13) are demonized and rendered out of bounds. Arguably, there is a failure to equip both heterosexual children and sexual minority children with an appropriate knowledge and understanding of sexualities which reflect their lives. Put on a continuum the result is that at the softer end children may be ill-informed, misinformed, and confused. At the sharp end

children are marginalized, disqualified, and discriminated against. Such prejudice has the potential to do real damage, up to and including self-harm and suicide (Corteen 2003a). Research shows that this is especially the case for young lesbians and gay men. Arguably, ignorance does not equate with innocence; ignorance potentially makes all children vulnerable and unequipped to deal with sexual matters (Levine 2002; Corteen 2003a).

When approaching childhood sexualities the controversial and sensitive nature of the issue must be understood. Further, it is important to acknowledge the predominant liberal, domesticating hegemonic approaches to childhood sexualities and the need to counter this with a more radical and democratic approach derived in commitment to children's rights (Corteen 2003a). Resistance to dominant conceptualizations and constructions of childhood (hetero) sexuality must also be acknowledged, as there are oppositional desires, practices, and identities, including among children themselves.

SEE ALSO: Childhood; Compulsory Heterosexuality; Pedophilia; Sex Education; Sexual Politics; Sexuality

REFERENCES AND SUGGESTED READINGS

Archard, D. (1993) *Children's Rights and Childhood*. Routledge, London.

Corteen, K. (2003a) *The Sexual Ordering of Society: A Critical Analysis of Secondary School Sex and Relationship Education*. PhD thesis. Lancaster University.

Corteen, K. (2003b) Beyond (Hetero)Sexual Consent. In: Cowling, M. & Reynolds, P. (Eds.), *Making Sense of Sexual Consent*. Ashgate, Aldershot.

Evans, D. (1994) Fallen Angels? The Material Construction Children as Sexual Citizens. *International Journal of Children's Rights* 2: 1–33.

Foucault, M. (1979) *The History of Sexuality*, Vol. 1: *An Introduction*. Trans. R. Hurley. Penguin, London.

Gittins, D. (1998) *The Child in Question*. Macmillan, London.

Goldman, R. & Goldman, J. (1982) *Children's Sexual Thinking*. Routledge & Kegan Paul, London.

Goldson, B. (1997) "Childhood": An Introduction to Historical and Theoretical Analyses. In: Scraton, P. (Ed.), *"Childhood" in "Crisis"?* UCL Press, London.

Hendrick, H. (1997) Constructions and Reconstructions of British Childhood: An Interpretative Survey, 1800 to the Present. In: Jones, A. & Prout, A. (Eds.), *Constructing and Reconstructing Childhood: Contemporary Issues in the Sociological Study of Childhood*. Falmer Press, London.

Jackson, S. (1982) *Childhood and Sexuality*. Blackwell, Oxford.

Levine, J. (2002) *Harmful to Minors*. Thunder Mouth Press, New York.

Mort, S. (1987) *Dangerous Sexualities: Medico-Moral Politics in England Since 1830*. Routledge & Kegan Paul, London.

Plummer, K. (1991) Understanding Childhood Sexualities. In: Sanfort, T., Brongersma, E., & van Naerssen, A. (Eds.), *Male Intergenerational Intimacy: Historical, Socio-Psychological, and Legal Perspectives*. Harrington Park Press, New York.

Sears, J. T. (1992) Dilemmas and Possibilities of Sexuality Education: Reproducing the Body Politic. In: Sears, J. T. (Ed)., *Sexuality and the Curriculum: The Politics and Practices of Sexuality Education*. New York Teachers College, Columbia University, New York.

Weis, D. L. (2005) Childhood Sexuality. Online. www.2.rz.hu-berlin.de/sexology/GESUND/ARCHIV/IES/USA08.HTM.

children and divorce

Mark A. Fine

The issue of how children are affected by parental divorce has arguably evoked as much controversy as has any other topic in the social sciences. The controversy reflects the importance and timeliness of the topic – in the beginning of the twenty-first century, Census Bureau data indicate that at least 50 to 60 percent of children in the United States will spend some period of time before they reach 18 in a home in which divorce has occurred (Harvey & Fine 2004). One-third or more of the children in the United States will live in a stepfamily by the time they reach 18 (Coleman et al. 2000). Similar rates have been found in other western countries (Barber & Demo 2006). Further, when children experience the divorce of their parents, they become approximately twice as likely to divorce themselves as adults (Amato 2000).

This debate has recently extended into the popular press, with the publication of two books by prominent scholars: Wallerstein et al. (2000) and Hetherington and Kelly (2002). These two sets of researchers reached quite different conclusions regarding the effects of divorce on children. Wallerstein and her colleagues concluded that as many as 50 percent of the young people in their sample became worried, underachieving, self-deprecating, and sometimes angry because of their parents' divorces. By contrast, Hetherington and colleagues found that there was initial turmoil in the lives of children of divorce, but that there were few meaningful long-term differences between these children and their peers from first-marriage families. These differences in findings and interpretations are substantive and show that scholars often reach conflicting conclusions regarding the extent to which divorce negatively affects children (Fine & Demo 2000).

MAJOR DIMENSIONS OF THE TOPIC

A synthesis of the literature by Emery (1999) is helpful in making sense of these seemingly contradictory conclusions regarding the effects of divorce on children. Emery suggested that there are five "facts" related to children and divorce: (1) divorce is very stressful for children; (2) divorce increases the risk of psychological problems; (3) despite the increased risk, most children whose parents divorce function as well as do children from first-marriage families; (4) children whose parents divorce report considerable pain, unhappy memories, and continued distress; and (5) children's post-divorce adjustment is strongly influenced by post-divorce family life, particularly the quality of the child's relationships with the parents, the nature and extent of interparental conflict, and the family's socioeconomic status.

According to Emery, some researchers, particularly Wallerstein, tend to emphasize the fourth point (i.e., that children experience pain following divorce) without adequately considering the others, whereas others tend to minimize the distress and pain experienced by these children and young adults and, instead, emphasize the other facts. Emery's synthesis is particularly helpful because it acknowledges that there is some "truth" to each of the varying sets of conclusions. Below, each of Emery's divorce-related "facts" is briefly reviewed.

Divorce is stressful for children. As noted by Emery (2004), divorce brings a wide variety of changes into the lives of most children, including transitions in residence and school, a decrease in economic well-being, and changes in the quality and closeness of parent–child relationships. Virtually all children of divorce experience some of these changes, and change, even if positive in nature, is inherently stressful.

Divorce increases the risk of psychological problems. Divorce has been identified as being related to children's and adolescents' social, emotional, behavioral, and academic problems. For example, compared to children from first-marriage families, children whose parents divorce are twice as likely to see a mental health professional, up to twice as likely to have behavior problems, twice as likely to drop out of high school before graduation, and are 25–50 percent more likely to be clinically depressed (Emery 2004). Meta-analyses have consistently reported that, on average, parental divorce has a small, but statistically significant, negative impact on the well-being of children in the United States (Amato 2000). Rodgers and Pryor's (1998) review of research conducted in the United Kingdom, Australia, and New Zealand supported this conclusion.

These negative effects are most common around the period of the divorce and many children and families recover from the initial distress and resume normal functioning within a few years (Emery 1999; Hetherington & Kelly 2002). However, many adolescents whose parents divorce remain disadvantaged years after the divorce relative to their peers in first-marriage families (Simons & Associates 1996; Hetherington & Kelly 2002).

Most children of divorce function as well as children from first-marriage families. The data discussed earlier with respect to risk also speak to the resilience of children of divorce. Even if 20 percent of children whose parents divorced exhibit clinically significant behavior problems, 80 percent do not. Even though this risk is greater than among children from first-marriage families (10 percent), the fact remains that the vast majority of children whose parents divorce function within clinically normal limits, just as is the case for children from first-marriage families.

Divorce is painful. Wallerstein and Lewis (1998) reported on a 25-year longitudinal study of a non-randomly selected sample of 131 children and adolescents from 80 California families that had experienced separation and divorce. Their participants' earliest memories of their parents' divorces were abandonment, terror, and loneliness. Adolescence was marked by early sexual activity and experimentation with drugs or alcohol. The respondents' early adulthood also was marked by fewer resources for college funding, fears of intimacy, and strained relationships with their parents, particularly their fathers.

Wallerstein et al.'s (2000) analysis revealed considerable flux in their participants' relationship lives after their parents divorced. These individuals spent much of their early adulthood negotiating relationships. Many were not married, nor interested in becoming married. Many did not want children. Wallerstein and colleagues reported that many of their respondents were very afraid of being abandoned.

Reflecting a recent trend toward asking individuals to tell stories about their experiences, Harvey and Fine (2004) described the narrative accounts that college students constructed about how divorce had impacted them. Harvey and Fine found considerable variability in both the tone of the stories and the reactions to divorce; however, a consistent theme was that many of the individuals, when describing the divorce, reported considerable pain, unhappy memories, and distress, supporting Wallerstein and colleagues' conclusions about the post-divorce pain and sadness.

Children's post-divorce adjustment is influenced by post-divorce (and even pre-divorce) family life. The quality of children's adjustment following divorce can be predicted as strongly (or more strongly) by family processes occurring after (and before) the divorce than by the actual divorce itself (Fine 2000). For example, research has suggested that children's adjustment is facilitated to the extent that their parents engage in relatively little conflict with each other, that they do not experience a loss in financial well-being, that their parents are psychologically adjusted, and that they are adequately parented by the parental figures in their lives (Barber & Demo 2006).

Another line of evidence that supports the importance of family processes on child adjustment comes from Amato and Booth's (1997) longitudinal research on families that have not yet experienced divorce. They found that poor marriages (defined by the participants as involving consistently high levels of conflict and distancing) harmed children in multiple ways, including problematic relations with parents; greater difficulty in dating (fewer dates, more problems); lower marital quality among those who later married; and relatively high rates of dissolution of close relationships. Children from divorced families showed similar patterns, although the effects were not as strong as those related to parents' low marital quality. Amato and Booth's study suggests the possibility that family processes (in this case, marital quality) may be more salient for children's development than is the actual change in family structure (e.g., from a first-marriage to a divorced family).

CHANGES OVER TIME IN THE TOPIC AND ITS TREATMENT

A change in how divorce among children has been studied is that there has been an increase in the amount of qualitative research that has been conducted. Qualitative research examines, often through intensive interviews of a relatively small sample of individuals, the meanings that participants attach to their divorce-related experiences and can identify issues, patterns, and trends that may go undiscovered with the more traditional quantitative type of research. The Harvey and Fine (2004) collection of college students' narratives regarding their experience with their parents' divorce is an example of this research trend.

A second change is the manner in which societal institutions have attempted to help children cope more effectively with their parents' divorce. The most popular intervention in this area has become parenting education courses for divorcing parents (Blaisure & Geasler 2006). These courses attempt to help children by educating their parents about how to sensitively guide their children through the divorce process and by teaching them how not to put their children in the middle of their ongoing disputes. This type of intervention has become mandated for divorcing parents in many jurisdictions in the United States and in some other western countries. The increasing popularity of parent education for divorcing parents has occurred primarily because this approach has considerable intuitive appeal and because most participants report being satisfied with the intervention; there are few studies that have directly supported their effectiveness.

CURRENT EMPHASES IN RESEARCH AND THEORY

In terms of research, current emphases include: (1) more longitudinal work that tracks changes in family processes and child adjustment over time; (2) more "within-family" studies, meaning that investigators examine variation within divorced families rather than only comparing them to children and families from first-marriage families; (3) more attention to family processes, such as ex-spouse conflict and parenting styles, rather than solely focusing on family structure (i.e., divorced vs. intact); and (4) more focus on family processes that occurred before the divorce as possible contributors to children's adjustment.

Theoretically, a number of new orientations have been utilized in recent years to study divorce and its consequences for children. First and foremost, there have been efforts to identify conceptual sets of variables that might mediate the small, but reliable, effects of divorce on children. These sets of variables can roughly be categorized as pertaining to the child (e.g., the child's temperament, with children having "easier" temperaments reacting more positively to divorce), the parent (e.g., parents who are less depressed have children with fewer divorce-related problems), the parent–child dyad (e.g., parents who have higher-quality relationships with their children before the divorce and who place appropriate limits on their children's behavior have children with fewer behavior problems), the interparental relationship (e.g., parents who are able to resolve their conflicts successfully tend to have better-adjusted children), and the family as a unit (e.g., post-divorce families with more consistent routines have better-adjusted children). These developments reflect attempts to explain theoretically *why* divorce has effects on children and, in a broader context, to explore how individual, dyadic, and family *processes* work in conjunction with changes in children's family *structure* to contribute to children's development.

A second theoretical development is that there has been more attention to genetic and biological contributions to divorce. For example, some individuals may have a biological predisposition to have certain characteristics (e.g., neuroticism) that make them prone to divorce (Booth et al. 2000). If there is such a biological predisposition to divorce, it may be genetically transmitted to offspring, explaining why offspring of divorce are themselves more likely to divorce. With respect to children, recent efforts to examine how children's behavior is at least partially biologically determined have important implications for understanding the consequences of divorce on children. It seems logical that children's temperament, which is thought to be genetically determined, influences how they react to major stressors, such as divorce. Most conceptualizations of children's adjustment to divorce have understandably focused on environmental factors, but more attention needs to be given to possible genetic and biological factors.

METHODOLOGICAL ISSUES

There are several methodological issues that pose challenges for researchers of children and divorce. First, the research designs that we are ethically and practically able to use make it very difficult to draw causal inferences that divorce causes certain deficits in child outcomes. When differences are found between children from divorced and first-marriage (or any other family types) families, it is not possible to determine if divorce caused the differences noted, or if there were some other, unmeasured differences between the groups that caused the observed differences. The lack of random assignment to groups poses a challenge to the internal validity of the research designs. For example, children from divorced families have been found to be more likely to drop out before graduating from high school than are children in first-marriage

families. However, we cannot determine if divorce is responsible for this group difference, or if other variables are responsible (e.g., lower socioeconomic status, less parental supervision and monitoring).

Second, it is difficult to acquire representative samples that allow us to draw conclusions regarding the effects that divorce has on children in the general population. It is quite difficult to obtain a sample that is randomly chosen from the population of children and families who have experienced divorce. Most studies have used small-scale samples of those in mental health treatment (clinical samples) or non-random samples of people who volunteer to participate in the study. Even with the use of such techniques as obtaining names from divorce court records or random digit dialing, it is challenging to find samples that allow generalization to the population of interest. The few large-scale studies that have utilized random samples thus take on even more importance because they allow us to draw inferences about children in general and how they react to divorce.

A third methodological challenge is to disentangle the effects of pre-divorce factors from post-divorce ones. Evidence is mounting that some of the child problems observed following the divorce actually began before the divorce (see Cherlin et al. 1991; Amato & Booth 1997). Children, couples, and families are not randomly assigned to divorce versus continually married conditions, and it appears that couples and families that function less positively are more inclined to experience a parental divorce than are well-functioning families. Thus, some of the child adjustment difficulties that have been attributed to divorce may be more accurately attributed to these pre-divorce (and/or biological) factors. The methodological challenge inherent in identifying pre-divorce factors is that longitudinal studies with large samples must be conducted, which are time-consuming and expensive.

FUTURE DIRECTIONS IN RESEARCH, THEORY, AND METHODOLOGY

Researchers will likely continue the trend of studying children's development before, during, and after they experience stressors like divorce. There may be less direct attention to *divorce* per se and more attention to how child, parent, parent–child, interparental, and family factors act individually and in combination to determine how well children cope with major changes in their life.

The increased focus on the multitude of factors that affect children as they develop calls for both qualitative and quantitative research advances. Qualitatively, more investigators will use such methods as in-depth interviewing, participant observation, and narrative account-making to gain a richer description of how divorce is experienced. Most of these studies will include only those children who have experienced divorce. Quantitatively, there will be more nationally representative longitudinal studies of children and their families that will allow us to track child development over time, as well as how their development is affected by such stressors as divorce. Many of these studies will fruitfully compare children from a variety of different types of families (e.g., divorced vs. first marriage).

SEE ALSO: Child Custody and Child Support; Divorce; Family Diversity; Lone-Parent Families; Non-Resident Parents; Stepfamilies

REFERENCES AND SUGGESTED READINGS

Amato, P. R. (2000) The Consequences of Divorce for Adults and Children. *Journal of Marriage and the Family* 62: 1269–87.
Amato, P. R. (2001) Children of Divorce in the 1990s: An Update of the Amato and Keith(1991) Meta-Analysis. *Journal of Family Psychology* 15: 355–70.
Amato, P. R. & Booth, A. (1997) *A Generation at Risk: Growing Up in an Era of Family Upheaval.* Harvard University Press, Cambridge, MA.
Barber, B. L. & Demo, D. H. (2006) The Kids are Alright (At Least Most of Them): Links Between Divorce and Dissolution and Child Well-Being. In: Fine, M. A. & Harvey, J. H. (Eds.), *Handbook of Divorce and Relationship Dissolution.* Erlbaum, Mahwah, NJ.
Blaisure, K. & Geasler, M. (2006) Educational Interventions for Separating and Divorcing Parents and Their Children. In: Fine, M. A. & Harvey, J. H. (Eds.), *Handbook of Divorce and Relationship Dissolution.* Erlbaum, Mahwah, NJ.

Booth, A., Carter, K., & Granger, D. A. (2000) Biosocial Perspectives on the Family. *Journal of Marriage and the Family* 62: 1018–34.
Cherlin, A., Furstenberg, F., Chase-Lansdale, P., Kiernan, K., Robins, P., Morrison, D., & Teitler, J. (1991) Longitudinal Studies of Effects of Divorce on Children in Great Britain and the United States. *Science* 252: 1386–9.
Coleman, M., Ganong, L., & Fine, M. (2000) Reinvestigating Remarriage: Another Decade of Progress. *Journal of Marriage and the Family* 62: 1288–307.
Emery, R. E. (1999) *Marriage, Divorce, and Children's Adjustment.* Sage, Thousand Oaks, CA.
Emery, R. E. (2004) *The Truth About Children of Divorce: Dealing with the Emotions So You and Your Children Can Thrive.* Viking Penguin, London.
Fine, M. A. (2000) Divorce and Single Parenting. In: Hendrick, C. & Hendrick, S. S. (Eds.), *Sourcebook of Close Relationships.* Sage, Newbury Park, CA, pp. 139–52.
Fine, M. A. & Demo, D. H. (2000) Divorce: Societal Ill or Normative Transition? In: Milardo, R. M. & Duck, S. (Eds.), *Families as Relationships.* Wiley, New York, pp. 135–56.
Harvey, J. H. & Fine, M. A. (2004) *Children of Divorce: Stories of Loss and Growth.* Erlbaum, Mahwah, NJ.
Hetherington, E. M. & Kelly, J. (2002) *For Better or for Worse: Divorce Reconsidered.* Norton, New York.
Rodgers, B. & Pryor, J. (1998) *Divorce and Separation: The Outcomes for Children.* Rowntree Foundation, York.
Simons, R. L. & Associates (1996) *Understanding Differences Between Divorced and Intact Families.* Sage, Thousand Oaks, CA.
Wallerstein, J. S. & Lewis, J. (1998) The Long-Term Impact of Divorce on Children: A First Report from a 25-Year Study. *Family and Conciliation Courts Review* 36: 368–83.
Wallerstein, J. S., Lewis, J. M., & Blakeslee, S. (2000) *The Unexpected Legacy of Divorce: A 25-Year Landmark Study.* Hyperion, New York.

chonaikai

Yasushi Suzuki

Chonaikai refers to the neighborhood associations in modern Japanese cities. Although the name varies from city to city, with some called "self-governing" associations, *chonaikai* seems to be the most common name. A *chonaikai* is principally composed of *all* households in a neighborhood, with sizes varying from about ten to more than a thousand households. They perform comprehensive functions including anti-crime activities, traffic safety campaigns, fire and disaster prevention, sanitation, promoting mutual friendships, culture and leisure activities, mutual aid, transmitting information from city hall, and representing neighborhoods to local governments.

The origins of *chonaikai* also vary from neighborhood to neighborhood. Some date back to feudal villages and the neighborhood units of feudal cities from before the Meiji Restoration of 1868. After the national government enacted the new law governing the cities, towns, and villages in 1888, some of the older villages and neighborhood units of the feudal ward systems became administrative wards supervised by local governments (Akimoto 1990; Nakata 1993). Yet they were not exactly the same as the *chonaikai* defined above, because their membership was limited to wealthy landlords. Others were organized spontaneously in the first wave of urbanization beginning in the 1920s. The rise of self-employed merchants and factory owners and the influx of migrants from rural areas prompted the organization of *chonaikai* and similar associations in urban neighborhoods (Nakamura 1990; Tanaka 1990; Tamano 1993). In 1940, the Interior Ministry issued Ordinance No. 17, ordering all such organizations to standardize as *chonaikai* and *burakukai* – the rural counterpart of the neighborhood association – in order to mobilize all of the nation's people for World War II. Thus, the *chonaikai* were reorganized legally as local units of the totalitarian regime. After the war, the General Headquarters of the occupying Allied Forces identified the *chonaikai* as organizations for cooperating with militarism and abolished them in 1947. The *chonaikai* nevertheless persisted eventually as "voluntary" associations. Almost all of the earlier *chonaikai* had been rebuilt by 1952, when the occupation ended. Local governments acknowledged their existence, at least in practice, often appointing their leaders as part-time officials. Since then, the *chonaikai* have developed an ambiguous character. They are private,

non-juridical associations of residents, on the one hand, and de facto representatives of their neighborhoods on the other. Most urban residents in Japan are organized in *chonaikai* or similar neighborhood associations. In the second wave of urbanization in the 1960s, they flourished in the newly developing urban and suburban areas. There were more than 270,000 such associations in 1980 (Iwasaki 1989: 7). Even in the central districts of Tokyo, *chonaikai* persist and play many significant roles.

Sociological accounts of the *chonaikai* in Japan differ in their characterizations. Some identify the *chonaikai* as a distinctive Japanese "cultural pattern." Others characterize them as the local agents of public administrations. Still others emphasize that they are self-governing neighborhood organizations.

The "cultural pattern" thesis arose in discussions about the prospects of modernization and urbanization in Japanese society. Modernization theorists expected functionally undifferentiated local groups such as *chonaikai* to be replaced by special interest groups, but the *chonaikai*, as mentioned, were reestablished in the 1950s. As urbanization accelerated, some sociologists questioned whether "urbanism as a way of life" would develop in Japan or not (Ohmi 1958). Although massification seemed to be the dominant trend, the persistence of *chonaikai* as local groups appeared to be a significant exception. While most sociologists considered them to be remnants of feudal society and therefore expected them to disappear, the culturalists countered that they would not disappear because they were rooted in Japan's cultural pattern. Although they indeed persist, it is doubtful that the culturalist "explanation" provides a sufficient answer to the question of why they persist. Are they still the same as the local groups of feudal society? Is the organization of associations based on neighborhoods an invariable pattern across Japan? Is it unique to Japan? The principle of organizing *all* of the households in a neighborhood did not appear before the 1920s, which indicates that it is a "modern" principle that only appeared in the early stages of urbanization (Nakamura 1990; Tamano 1993). Furthermore, some analysts reported the existence of similar associations in the Philippines (Ohtsubo

& Masatoshi 1986), Indonesia (Yoshihara 2000), Thailand (Kaewmanotham et al. 2000), South Korea (Torigoe 1994; Noh 2000), Hong Kong (Yoshihara 2000), and the People's Republic of China (Kuroda 2000). Some of these associations may have been transplanted from Japan during the period of military occupation in the 1940s, such as the RT/RW in Indonesia (Yoshihara 2000), the Kaifong association in Hong Kong (Yoshihara 2000), and Bansanghoi in South Korea (Torigoe 1994; Noh 2000), but others seem to be indigenous. One should not forget again that these associations were reorganized, or newly organized, in the process of modernization. These are not exactly the same as *chonaikai*, but it is easy to see that characteristics such as the membership policy for organizing all households and the comprehensive functions they perform are very similar to the *chonaikai* in Japan.

Those who claimed that *chonaikai* is a local agent of the public administration emphasized that the functions performed by *chonaikai* complemented those of the fire department, the police office, and other bureaus of the municipality. More important, however, is the historical fact that the *chonaikai*'s predecessors were founded when the national government reorganized the old villages as administrative wards in 1888, and that they were reorganized again under the militarist regime in 1940 (Akimoto 1990). Together with the functions they perform, these facts imply that the *chonaikai* is principally a local agent of the state bureaucracy. Its leaders were initially recruited from the ranks of the honored landlords of the late nineteenth-century towns, and they gradually gave way to small merchants and factory owners, or the "old middle class," at the turn of the century. Even today, this group typically comprises the more active membership of the *chonaikai* and tends to use it as a base for the conservative political machine (Okuda 1964; Akimoto 1990; Tamano 1993; see also Bestor 1989). From the local agent perspective, the *chonaikai* are bodies of grassroots conservatism, whether characterized as "premodern" or not. From this perspective, as the new middle-class residents took part in local communities, the dominance and effectiveness of the *chonaikai* would decline. Yet some critics reported that

in some housing developments the new middle-class suburbanites involved themselves in *chonaikai,* so they assumed a more liberal character (Nakamura 1965). Another critic suggested that there is tension between the politically conservative *chonaikai* and municipal administration (Bestor 1989).

Finally, some scholars argue that *chonaikai* are not simply local groups but self-governing associations of residents. They are thus something like a municipality of the neighborhood (Yasuda 1977), or an association for the collective management of the area (Nakata 1993). As territorial associations, the membership policy and comprehensive functions performed, including cooperation with the local government, are easy to understand. They might thus be rooted in the self-governing tradition of Japanese community, but have not been properly treated by the government. Some scholars view this tradition as democratic (Iwasaki 1989); others see it as a historical development from the dominance of the honored landlords to the collective management of all the residents of the local area (Nakata 1993). Whether these interpretations are correct or not, the *chonaikai* have often contributed to improving local life and have effectively derived policy interventions from local governments (Iwasaki 1989). Many case studies since the 1970s have reported that some *chonaikai* have been involved in urban planning for community-based redevelopments in inner industrial areas; others have succeeded in preserving the residential environment of middle-class suburbs. Nevertheless, what kind of and whose interest the *chonaikai* represents should be carefully investigated in each case.

In sum, it seems clear that the *chonaikai* has characteristics of both a self-governing association and a local agent of public administration. It is also clear that this form of neighborhood association in Japan has a distinct history. Yet, similar associations are also found in other East and Southeast Asian countries. Such associations were organized in the contexts of military mobilization, the local administration of the development dictatorship, or the empowerment and development devices for slum dwellers. Comparative analyses are required to develop an understanding of the nature of the various organizational forms of neighborhood associations in different contexts. Such analyses may reveal the same complexities as those surrounding the *chonaikai* in Japan. However, the fundamental issue in all cases seems to be how to answer two questions: how the ruling structure of the state bureaucracy incorporates the neighborhood associations in order to foster support for administrative power and to monitor the local area and the residents effectively; and how people work their way into the administrative structure so as to empower themselves by taking part in the self-governing activities. The neighborhood associations of Japan provide a good example for studying dialectics of social power based on localities.

SEE ALSO: Culture, Organizations and; Culture, the State and; Local Residents' Movements; Organizations, Voluntary; Urban Community Studies; Urbanism/Urban Culture; Urbanization

REFERENCES AND SUGGESTED READINGS

Akimoto, R. (1990) *Chonaikai* as an Intermediate Group. In: Kurasawa, S. & Akimoto, R. (Eds.), *Chonaikai and Local Groups*. Minerva, Kyoto, pp. 129–57.

Bestor, T. C. (1989) *Neighborhood Tokyo*. Stanford University Press, Stanford.

Iwasaki, N. (Ed.) (1989) *The Study of Chonaikai*. Ochanomizu, Tokyo.

Kaewmanotham, M., Makita, M., & Fujii, W. (2000) Thailand. In: Nakata, M. (Ed.), *Neighborhood Associations in the World*. Jichitaikenkyu-sya, Tokyo.

Kuroda, Y. (2000) China. In: Nakata, M. (Ed.), *Neighborhood Associations in the World*. Jichitaikenkyu-sya, Tokyo.

Nakamura, H. (1965) Urban Chonaikai Reexamined. *Municipal Problems* 56(5): 69–81.

Nakamura, H. (1990) Chonaikai as a Cultural Pattern. In: Kurasawa, S. & Akimoto, R. (Eds.), *Chonaikai and Local Groups*. Minerva, Kyoto, pp. 62–108.

Nakata, M. (1993) *Sociology of Collective Management of the Local Area*. Toshindo, Tokyo.

Noh, B. (2000) South Korea. In: Nakata, M. (Ed.), *Neighborhood Associations in the World*. Jichitaikenkyu-sya, Tokyo.

Ohmi, T. (1958) Urban Local Groups. *Social Science Review* 3(1): 181–230.

Ohtsubo, S. & Masatoshi, I. (1986) Review in the Research on Barangay about Philippine Coup d'État. *Bulletin: Faculty of Sociology, Toyko University* 24(1): 43–64 and 24(2): 195–236.

Okuda, M. (1964) Urban Neighborhood Association Led by the Old Middle Class. *Japanese Sociological Review* 55: 9–14.

Tamano, K. (1993) *Urbanization and the Formation of Chonaikai in Modern Japan*. Kojinsya, Tokyo.

Tanaka, S. (1990) History of *Chonaikai* and its Analytical Points. In: Kurasawa, S. & Akimoto, R. (Eds.), *Chonaikai and Local Groups*. Minerva, Kyoto, pp. 27–60.

Torigoe, H. (1994) *The Study of Neighborhood Associations*. Minerva, Kyoto.

Yasuda, S. (1977) On Chonaikai: Research Notes on Japanese Society (5). *Contemporary Sociology* 7: 173–83.

Yoshihara, N. (2000) *Neighborhood Associations in Asian Societies*. Ochanomizu, Tokyo.

Christianity

Lluís Oviedo

As a basic description, Christianity is the religious faith grounded on the life and teachings of Jesus of Nazareth. Beyond this point, the scholarly understanding of that concept has been the object of much discussion in modern times, particularly in the realm of the social sciences. In an attempt to put some order into the social, religious, historical, and ideological reality that corresponds to the term "Christianity," a synthetic account may be offered, covering its history and the main dimensions.

Christianity was, at its inception, a religious movement of messianic-apocalyptic character, born from the preaching and destiny of Jesus, deemed by his disciples to be "the Christ" (Messiah or Redeemer), in the context of the anxieties and expectations of the Jewish religious milieu of the first century. The experiences of his followers after the death of their master and, particularly, their purported encounter with him as a resurrected person triggered the first expansion of this movement, which was perceived at the time as just another apocalyptic sect within Judaism.

Gradually, the Christian teaching reached ever more people outside the Jewish boundaries. It finally appeared as a new religious faith oriented to a broader public inside the Roman Empire, and achieved stability as a more institutional and salvific religion. The new faith expanded despite the persecutions suffered throughout the first three centuries of its existence, and finally acquired the status of the official religion of the empire. During that time, the new religion struggled to better define its own beliefs, among many contrasting interpretations, in order to organize its aggregations at all levels, and to discipline its followers.

All of this endeavor in pursuit of order was unable to prevent successive splits among different groups and ideological orientations, the most remarkable being the schism between the eastern and western branches of the church during the Middle Ages, followed by the various Reformations of the sixteenth century.

Over the centuries, Christianity has shown a particular ability to adapt to the changing social and cultural conditions within which it finds itself. It was nurtured by the waning classical paradigm of Greco-Roman society, later adapted to the new structures of feudalism in the traumatic early medieval period, and flowered during the High Middle Ages, when the faith, supported by the church, was a central element of the social and cultural configuration of society. Modern times have raised new challenges for Christianity, now impelled to search for a new balance within highly pluralistic societies and (in the western world) a less religious cultural milieu. Christianity, however, has always suffered from considerable stress caused by a polarization between two tendencies, one centripetal, seeking the establishment of a common realm, a unity that is not only religious but also cultural and political, and the other centrifugal, as some historians have shown, which is the ability of a religion to render self-conscious and empower the identity of different peoples and social entities, nourishing their own self-affirmation and providing the space for a more pluralistic society (Brown 1996).

At the present, Christianity is acknowledged as a "global faith" that numbers, according to the latest estimates, around 2 billion nominal members, spread through nearly the entire world, which assumes a multiplicity of confessional forms, Catholicism being the largest (around 1 billion members).

SOCIOLOGICAL DIMENSIONS OF CHRISTIANITY

Christianity is basically a faith, canonically established and regulated through a system of "dogmas" or "mandatory beliefs" concerning the understanding of God and the way he saves or benefits humans. A significant feature of this faith has been its ability to engage with reason since its first appearance within Greco-Roman classical culture. Indeed, for some authors, the cognitive form of the Christian religion is the synthesis between a positive, revealed religion of Semitic origin and the rational framework provided by ancient Greek philosophy. However, this synthetic encounter has not always been peaceful and is far from simple, and sometimes contrasts blatantly with the dogmatic – i. e., not open to rational enquiry – nature of its principles. It would seem that this cognitive framework is rather based on a permanent tension and dialectic between faith and reason, a tension that continually arises in the ongoing struggle to cope with new standards of rationality in the long history of Christianity. The permanent struggle with reason has been deemed a sign of vitality for a religion called to actualize permanently its core beliefs through innovation and dialogue. Furthermore, a symptom of the "rational incompleteness" of Christian faith is the irresolvable dialectic between its apophatic and cataphatic aspects – mysterious/ mystic and affirmative/rational. As a result, the Christian faith experiences a polarization of cognitive expressions, along the dualistic schema, which distinguishes faith as an experience of the mystery or the limits of human intelligence and faith as a way of understanding and deepening human knowledge. Even if the first seems to give rise to a "religion of mystics" and the second to a "religion of intellectuals," Christianity has kept both ways as legitimate expressions of the same faith.

Christianity has a plurality of religious practices along its confessional lines. The tension arises this time between a more sacramental-communitarian trend and a more introspective-personal one. Most mainline Christian communities express their faith through a double ritual schema: the public reading and comment (preaching) of the canonical scriptures (the Bible) and the celebration of sacraments or rituals of mediation of divine force (grace). The second way of religious expression is through personal prayer, which has multiple expressions. A good deal of Christianity looks for a complementarity and balance of both dimensions, the ritual and the spiritual, but the achievement of balance varies among different Christian confessions and even within the same confession, allowing for different spiritual traditions.

Since its first days, Christian faith has been seen as a religion presided over by a quite strict moral code, struggling with an environment of more lax standards. However, Christianity has adapted its moral code to several different cultures, and has shown a certain degree of flexibility in the process. In this respect, a moral tension has been kept alive, among successive apocalyptic waves, reform movements, and the permanence of groups of "religious virtuosi," more prone to strictness and to stress the difference between Christian fellowship and a worldly way of life. Christian morality has tended to be more communitarian, emphasizing engagement for others or "love of neighbor." These ethics of mutual dependence and responsibility, however, are grounded on a strong call to self-awareness and the personal divine call to mission. It seems that only with this sense of individuality and personal freedom before God and his norms is it able to provide for a moral schema of social responsibility.

Christianity has been from its very beginning organized in communities of hierarchical structure, which constitute the "church." The term is applied to all Christian people – at least those belonging to the same confession – and, in a more limited fashion, to any community of believers led by a pastor or priest that gathers periodically for ritual, instruction, and exchange, and offers different services to the community at large. The communitarian emphasis is not taken for granted in any part of this large religious spectrum. Indeed, some forms of Christianity have adopted a more individualistic stance. Conversely, church activity has evolved in many areas into a kind of "agency" providing rituals and other services to a broad public, changing significantly its meaning and becoming less personal. A second organizational trait concerns the balance between "church" – as institution – and

"sect." Christianity has lived the normal process, typified by every religious movement, of evolution from a more sectarian reality to a more institutional, open form: the "church." It is not easy to know how long the process lasted, even if it appears that quite early Christianity took on an institutional, less apocalyptically oriented, form. Thus, a dual schema has persisted within the Christian organization, predominantly as an institutional church but leaving room for sectarian expressions, which historically harbored minorities of greater religious intensity. At the moment Christianity has a multiplicity of organizational forms, ranging between both extremes of the spectrum: church, denominations, cults, and sects.

Also in this case a plural panorama is noted, as Christianity has developed many models of relationship with its social environment. Many scholars, from inside and outside the Christian field, have tried to objectify this plurality, which ranges from the extreme of total integration and cooperation to the opposite, of distinction and sharp contrast. This configuration has given rise to several political systems as well (Niebuhr 1951). Even if historically Christian churches have tried to "Christianize" their respective societies, raising moral standards, promoting their own agenda, or implementing "Christian policies," more frequently they have looked for accommodation within the social conditions of their context, adapting to successive changes. This, however, does not exclude moments of confrontation and resistance, or of unrest and social criticism, very often nourished by apocalyptic expectations. Yet, almost always, these tendencies have been those of the minority, and have represented only factions of a particular intensity, searching for social change or inspired by radical interpretations of biblical texts. Mainline Christianity has adopted a more "realistic stance" in its relationship with constituted powers, often serving even as a legitimizing agency, and has reacted only when the conditions for its survival have been threatened. In this respect, it is difficult to conclude whether Christian faith favors any kind of political or social agenda, as some authors have suggested. A kind of flexibility presides over its influence, which perhaps is to be seen at a different level: that of providing moral commitment and ideological empowerment to any cause deemed worthy of fighting for.

CHRISTIANITY AS A SOCIOLOGICAL QUESTION

The sociological understanding of Christianity has dealt with several problems, which sometimes have challenged, and still do, the scientific enterprise. A very short list would include: the historic question on the origins and rise of Christian faith, the paradoxical relationship between Christian religion and modernity, and the enigma of secularization or the possible end of religion.

(1) From a sociological point of view, Christian origins seem to offer a "case study" on the "probability of the improbable," to use Luhmann's expression. The rational reasons which might explain the success of a religious movement fail in this respect. Almost everything conspired for the failure of this project: the disastrous end of its founder, the persecutions suffered from the beginning by his followers, the hostile environment encountered among Jews and pagans. Modern times have seen several attempts to rationalize the rise of Christianity and to supply an answer to the question of its unexpected success. Liberal understandings of biblical criticism have pointed to the eschatological strength of the new religion, able to convey the anxieties of a segment of the population at that time. Marxism has shown the ability of that faith to inspire an expectation of fulfillment for masses living in the midst of miserable conditions. Nietzsche has denounced the Christian maneuver of inverting values in order to satisfy the resentment of the weakest. The list may be enriched with many other kinds of arguments. Recently, more sophisticated sociological analysis has endeavored to decipher some of the clues of Christianity's success, in a close alliance with insights offered by modern biblical scholarship. It seems, according to this point of view, that the growth rate, through conversion, in early Christianity is not much higher than that observed in other processes of religious conversion (Stark 1996). Class, gender, and social structure are some of

the factors contributing to the positive trend, and engagement with the needy, especially in times of crisis, convinced ever greater numbers of people of the advantages – rationally speaking – inherent in such a religion. It must be said, however, that aside from the fruitful engagement of biblical studies with sociology, the explanations provided by a more rational stance do not exclude, or, for that matter, require the presence of what can be called the "religious factor" or some measure of "religious capital."

(2) The problematic relationship between Christianity and modern society has been shown, perhaps better than anybody else, by Max Weber. In *The Protestant Ethic and the Spirit of Capitalism* (1906) and later works, the German sociologist struggled with the foundational role of this faith as a necessary element for the configuration of the modern western world, social differentiation, and the development of science. Weber was concerned with the historical data which showed the lack of modern forms outside of the Christian matrix, and researched the positive role played by Protestant ethics and subsequent strictness in the development of capitalist societies, even if the causal relationship was minimized as a mere "elective affinity." The relationship could be broadened, as Christianity is discovered as a factor of greater rationalization in diverse fields, theoretical and practical, anticipating a modern trend. Furthermore, Christianity is perceived as a key driver in the rationalization process, either in the theoretical or in the practical dimension, and as contributing to modern development. For Weber, the dialectics between Christianity and modernity are, nevertheless, more complex. Modernity may be seen as a result of mature Christian expression, but at the same time as a factor resulting in religious crisis. Indeed, the faith that helped give birth to the modern world later suffers the pressure of modern differentiation and disenchantment (*Entzauberung*), which deprives it of its ideological and practical basis. In a further step, Weber has conjoined religious crisis and personal disruptions brought on by the lack of a framework where certain values and sensitivities find their support. Other sociologists have tried to better understand this complex

relationship, which very often appears as para-doxical: it seems that modern society can go on neither with nor without Christian faith. Func-tional analysis has demonstrated the needed contribution of this religion for social processes in advanced societies. That "function" may be construed in many ways, from the classically attributed or acknowledged capacity of social integration and moral enforcement to the more abstract views of Luhmann: the "management of contingency," the "semantic openness that allows evolution," and the "blocking of reflex-ivity" needed to avoid an unmanageable num-ber of paradoxes (Luhmann 1977, 2000). At the same time, sociologists may be concerned with the negative effects that may unleash an "excess of religious faith," undermining the proper functioning of a society intended as a system. There is currently a lack of empirical proof regarding the possibility of a modern society without – at least some measure of – Christian religious presence.

(3) The last observations point to the third question: "secularization" as a dynamic affect-ing the essence of Christian faith, threatening its existence and giving rise to dark expecta-tions. Even if the discussion around the so-called "secularization thesis" remains active, some agreement has been reached on the study pertaining to the Christian origins of the secu-larization process, intended as a byproduct of modernization. Many see the secularization question as a "Christian question," i.e., as a problem arising from the constituency of the Christian faith, which has conceded great autonomy in many spheres of action and long acknowledged the special dignity of rational inquiry. In that sense Christianity creates the conditions for the possibility of its own histor-ical demise, as social differentiation makes that faith more dispensable and scientific progress seems to make it more irrelevant. In other words, it would seem that the Christian faith may be more vulnerable to practical dissolution than others, being too prone to accommodation to social realities, which in the end leave no space for religious affirmation. The question refers to the Weberian perception of a kind of "social incompleteness" which requires in some ways the presence of the religious element that helped to implement such a society. Thus, the more a society becomes secularized, the more it

needs a Christian reference. The situation is perceived as very problematic, from both a theoretical and empirical point of view: first, because, as Löwith (1949) has demonstrated, many ideas and values of modernity are the outcome of a secularized process of Christian ideas and values, and no one knows if these values can survive completely outside of a reli-gious matrix; second, because the survival of a society without religion is still an open ques-tion, and a greater question is posed as to whether "modern social configuration" might find a firmer foundation by means of other secular or religious forms once the "Christian capital" has been exhausted.

CHRISTIAN FAITH AND SOCIOLOGY: AN OPEN QUESTION

At a deeper level, Christianity may be seen as a kind of "competing instance" with social science, and sociology as a renewed attempt to accomplish the enlightened tendency to "reli-gion's *Aufhebung*," or its suppression and repla-cement by rational means. Since August Comte, sociological endeavor has been sus-pected of presupposing the dissolution of reli-gion, and the sociological understanding of society has been perceived as being incompati-ble with the religious one. This applies parti-cularly to western Christianity, because it has kept its own "theory of society," its own view of the goals, limits, and means of social action, which have been challenged by a more enligh-tened or rational program (Hervieu-Léger 1986). Recent theological approaches have radi-calized the perceived tension and denounced the aporetic character of the attempt to provide a secular program for social development, because of the violent and nihilistic basis of such a voluntaristic enterprise (Milbank 1990). The relationship between sociology and Chris-tianity has been marked by conflict and signed by warfare until very recently. As any other social science, sociology has been suspected of applying a "reductive stance" to Christian realities, hiding any element which could not be completely rationalized. The suspicion has at times reached empirical sociology, deemed as unable to "observe" what is, by definition, an inside and mysterious unobservable reality.

This, however, is only a part of the story. There is yet a tradition of collaboration between Christian faith and social studies. Surely there is no other religion so able to integrate and to make good use of sociological research, as this faith has, more often than not, accepted the challenge of rational inquiry, even when applied to itself. Furthermore, it is important to consider the fact of the existence of sociologists working often for church agencies and, more interestingly, recent trends in sociological research which have stressed a less reductive approach and a disposition to acknowledge a place, even a "rational weight," to the "religious factor," though they may apply an economic method for better understanding it (Iannaccone 1998; Stark & Finke 2000).

SEE ALSO: Belief; Catholicism; Church; Denomination; Luhmann, Niklas; Protestantism; Religion; Religion, Sociology of; Sect; Secularization; Televangelism; Theology; Weber, Max

REFERENCES AND SUGGESTED READINGS

Brown, P. R. L. (1996) *The Rise of Western Christendom: Triumph and Diversity, AD 200–1000*. Blackwell, Oxford.
Hervieu-Léger, D. (1986) *Vers un nouveau christianisme? Introduction à la sociologie du christianisme occidental*. Cerf, Paris.
Iannaccone, L. R. (1998) Introduction to the Economics of Religion. *Journal of Economic Literature* 36: 1465–96.
Löwith, K. (1949) *Meaning in History*. University of Chicago Press, Chicago.
Luhmann, N. (1977) *Funktion der Religion*. Suhrkamp, Frankfurt am Main.
Luhmann, N. (2000) *Die Religion der Gesellschaft*. Suhrkamp, Frankfurt am Main.
Milbank, J. (1990) *Theology and Social Theory*. Blackwell, Oxford.
Niebuhr, H. R. (1951) *Christ and Culture*. Harper & Row, New York.
Stark, R. (1996) *The Rise of Christianity: A Sociologist Reconsiders History*. Princeton University Press, Princeton.
Stark, R. & Finke, R. (2000) *Acts of Faith: Explaining the Human Side of Religion*. University of California Press, Berkeley.
Weber, M. (1958 [1906]) *The Protestant Ethic and the Spirit of Capitalism*. Charles Scribner's Sons, New York.

chronic illness and disability

Kathy Charmaz

Chronic illness lasts. A chronic illness has a lengthy duration, uncertain outcome, and unpredictable episodes, often with intrusive symptoms and intermittent or progressive disability. Having a chronic illness poses life problems such as following a medical regimen, managing ordinary responsibilities, and experiencing stigma and discrimination. A disease, in contrast, may remain silent for years without eliciting a diagnosis or causing noticeable symptoms and life disruptions. Experiencing chronic illness makes disease real. Sociological definitions of chronic illness start with the experience of disruption and impairment. Social definitions of disability start from the lack of societal accommodation to certain individuals' needs, thereby disadvantaging them and discriminating against them. Such definitions of disability tend to presuppose that the people involved have static, visible conditions with predictable and sustained needs.

Chronic illness and disability emerged as fields of sociological inquiry in early ethnographic studies such as Julius Roth's *Timetables: Structuring the Passage of Time in Hospital Treatment and Other Careers* (1963), Erving Goffman's *Stigma: Notes on the Management of Spoiled Identity* (1963), and Fred Davis's *Passage Through Crisis: Polio Victims and Their Families* (1963). These sociologists' depiction of patients' actions and interactions with professionals contrasted with Talcott Parsons's (1953) theoretical concept of the sick role. Parsons's concept assumed recovery from illness; impartial, active physicians; direct medical intervention; and reciprocal roles with passive patients whose temporary exemption from normal adult responsibilities allowed them to follow their physicians' advice and to concentrate on recovery.

Parsons's concept of the sick role fit neither the treatment goals for chronic illness and disability nor their corresponding treatment roles. Illness continues, disability persists. Hence, physicians treat symptoms rather than causes, attempt to minimize complications, and rely on patients and their caregivers for information, but monitoring and managing occur at home. Studies of chronic illness and disability further reveal the limits of the sick role and its accompanying acute care model because individuals intermittently need a range of auxiliary health services as well as continuing social and community services.

Patients' conditions become part of their lives rather than a time-out apart from them. Despite institutional, interactional, and physical or mental constraints, studies of chronic illness show that actors have agency. Roth's *Timetables* (1963) and Goffman's *Asylums* (1961) depict patients as active, creative individuals who adapt to their situations but, moreover, adapt these situations, when possible.

Researchers began to study illness and disability as problematic in their own right instead of solely as a health indicator or status variable. From that point, sociologists have taken the experience of illness and disability as research topics to understand their consequences for self, identity, and social life. Their studies start from the perspective of adults and account for their experiences in sociological terms without the implied judgments of psychological interpretations.

The fields of chronic illness and disability share certain origins, although disability studies also has structural roots. The early attention to the organization and goals of rehabilitation to understand disability has continued. The emergence of the disability rights movement strengthened the structural roots of disabilities studies. Researchers and disability rights activists joined to produce a strong emphasis on social justice and activism in disabilities studies. As an exemplar of early activism, the 1960s Independent Living Movement made autonomy a major goal and won rights for people with severe disabilities to leave institutions and to live unsupervised in their communities. The Independent Living Movement relied, however, on the individual responsibility of persons with disabilities to organize and manage their care; the movement did not address how larger structural barriers impeded their efforts. Since then, disability studies adopted an explicit social model based on assumptions that *society*

disables people with defined impairments by failing to accommodate to them.

The fields of chronic illness and disability provide an important corrective to the extensive literature in medical sociology that focuses on doctor–patient relationships. For people with chronic illnesses and disabilities, the doctor–patient relationship represents a small – albeit consequential – part of their illness experience. Ordinarily, they are people, not patients.

Studies about managing chronic illness assumed the significance of maintaining personal control and demonstrated ways that people achieved and maintained it. They reorganize their homes, schedules, activities, and relationships and manage actual and potential stigma. These studies also show how people normalized the adaptations they made to live with an illness. Yet the onset of illness and many disabilities in adult life constitutes a "biographical disruption" (Bury 1982) that raises existential questions and spurs a reconstruction of self, as well as a reorganization of daily life. Charmaz (1991) furthers studying reconstruction of self and experienced time. From having long stretches of empty time to needing extraordinary amounts of time to handle ordinary tasks, existential meanings shift and change during a chronic illness. Health and social crises that puncture routine existence become long-remembered turning points. Experiencing chronic illness magnifies turning points in adult life and often minimizes the time between them. For committed partners, the meanings and consequences of these biographical processes become shared and result in collaborative work to manage illness and disability.

Studies of chronic illness reveal the empirical significance of the body and thus encourage theorizing to begin at this basic level, rather than from texts and extant theories. These studies have also spawned a nascent sociology of suffering. When people define illness as disrupting their lives, they reveal taken-for-granted assumptions that their expectations have gone awry. Boundaries have been broken and trust in their bodies has been shattered. Questions of "why me?" follow. Under these conditions, experiencing chronic illness calls for a search for explanation and understanding. The turmoil and troubles of lifelong poverty may, however, lead to accepting and normalizing chronic distress and impairment.

Disabilities studies moved its discourse from stigma, personal tragedy, and victimization to societal structures that separated people with disabilities and discriminated against them. From this perspective, assuming that impairment causes disability erroneously grants fundamental significance to medical definitions and interventions and thus obscures other forms of oppression, such as those inherent in power arrangements with their concrete expression in environmental barriers. Therefore, disability studies also challenge the concept of medicalization because it overstates the significance of physicians and understates that of global economic and power structures.

The place of personal narratives as scholarship remains debated. Do they provide insight into reconstructing coherence or proclaim self-indulgence? Several personal narratives by social scientists have exerted considerable influence. Irving K. Zola's *Missing Pieces: A Chronicle of Living with a Disability* (1982) found a ready audience among people in the disabled community because he learned to integrate his disability into his life after years of trying to overcome it. Arthur Frank's *At the Will of the Body* (1991) describes how having cancer and enduring pain separated him from ordinary worlds and from those closest to him. His story conveys the experience of suffering, recounts tales of loss and transcendence, inspires hope, and challenges commodification and dehumanization in medical care. Robert Murphy's *The Body Silent* (1987) chronicles his progressive paralysis as a benign tumor in his spinal column made him quadriplegic. Murphy saw himself as damaged, dependent, and deficient: defective. Like many people with chronic illnesses and disabilities, he believed his disability symbolized atonement for some prior wrong. Some members of the disabled community revere the book for its honesty, while others revile its reaffirmation of demeaning images of disability. Although Murphy's book records a dark descent, such books reveal the quest to make sense of an existential journey and of the self that emerges from it.

The fields of chronic illness and disability have become more distinct over time.

Sociological studies of people with chronic illness primarily remained social psychological, while disability studies grew more structural and interdisciplinary with foundational contributions by historians and political scientists. Structural disability theorists soon asked how ideological views, power politics, and economic practices shaped how societies constructed definitions of disability and impairment.

A constructionist perspective has informed both fields, but their usual starting points differ. Studies of chronic illness document how features of society influence individuals' experience and how they respond to the difficulties they face. David Locker's (1983) interview study of people with arthritis bridges chronic illness and disability. He observes that people's resources and strategies for managing life alter their definitions of impairment, disability, and disadvantage, which render constructions of disability less static than ordinarily presumed. Given their explicit commitment to social justice, however, some disability theorists and researchers disdain social psychological studies of chronic illness with their inductive methods, analytic emphases, and focus on individuals. Disability scholars have engaged the politics of welfare and subsequent meanings of dependency, disadvantage, and difference to a greater extent than researchers in chronic illness. These theorists apply current structural approaches in novel, although deterministic, ways; however, they have not generated new theories.

In contrast, major empirical studies of chronic illness have advanced theoretical conceptions in interpretive sociologies, including symbolic interactionism and narrative analysis. These studies move the theoretical discourse beyond roles – whether treated as patient roles, impaired roles, or rehabilitation roles – and into fresh analyses of situated actions, negotiated meanings, reconstruction of self, identity goals, definitions of duration, temporal benchmarks, time perspective, and narrative reconstruction.

Despite the theoretical directions suggested by major studies, however, most empirical studies of chronic illness do not advance theory but do further understanding of specific research problems, of research participants and their worlds, and of studied interactions and processes. Critical discussions of the theoretical implications of studies in this field have, however, produced cutting-edge analyses of the limits of positivism, postmodernism, and structuralism and subsequently altered views of the impaired body and biomedicine.

After some years of becoming distinctive areas, important areas of convergence between chronic illness and disability are evident. These areas include (1) inevitable disabilities among aging populations, (2) the later life incidence of chronic illness in people with lifelong disabilities, (3) the subsequent narrowing or collapsing of stable plateaus among people with disabilities, (4) the growing recognition of invisible disabilities and contested, disabling illnesses, (5) the disabling effects of medical and surgical treatment of illness, (6) structural inequities that differentially affect people with chronic illnesses or disabilities, and (7) critical efforts to situate theorizing illness and impaired bodies within their structural realities. These points of convergence may raise anew issues of suffering, loss, stigma, uncertainty, and reconstruction of self and identity at the individual level and economic divisions, power prerogatives, and the institutionalization of disadvantage and discrimination at the societal level.

A strong tradition of qualitative research has continued in studies of chronic illness, whereas disability studies draws on a wide range of methods. Throughout qualitative studies of chronic illness and disability, researchers have relied more on what people say during interviews and less on what they do and say in their own settings. Researchers tend to reify their participants' stories as though they reproduce reality without considering the taken-for-granted assumptions and practices on which those stories rest. We have given insufficient attention to silences and their meanings, although many people's struggles with chronic illness and disability occur in silence. Silences are crucial for learning what lies between statements and taken-for-granted actions. Understanding how people become silenced and when suffering leads to silence would deepen our knowledge of chronic illness and disability. Suffering fills silent spaces and may remain unacknowledged – in research participants' stories and in researchers' narratives. Yet new imperatives to bring the body into research and

theorizing necessitate gaining a more nuanced understanding of suffering.

The future of disability studies portends continuing its interdisciplinary traditions, critical stance, and activist agenda with critiques of developments in social policy and medical care. Disability activists and scholars challenge current practices and potential trends that reduce disabled populations, such as using prenatal diagnosis of genetic diseases for abortion decisions and legalizing assisted suicide. They raise theoretical and ethical questions about biological determinism, the value of life, and whose lives have value. Gary Albrecht's (1992) book suggests many potential directions for disability studies that remain untapped. For example, he notes that work in health clubs and sports medicine sells prevention and maintenance. With the commodification of fitness and function among older populations, disability studies may also move toward critical analyses of health promotion and maintenance.

In both fields, the effects of capitalism on technical advances, availability and distribution of supplies and services, and personal and professional relationships will outline individual experiences and fuel research on structure and experience and the connections between them. Future insights and arguments in these fields about visibility, temporality, identity, responsibility, and reciprocity portend illuminating what it means to be human and what it takes to create a caring society.

SEE ALSO: Body and Society; Disability as a Social Problem; Illness Experience; Medical Sociology; Sick Role; Symbolic Interaction

REFERENCES AND SUGGESTED READINGS

Albrecht, G. (1992) *The Disability Business: Rehabilitation in America*. Sage, Newbury Park, CA.
Bury, M. (1982) Chronic Illness as Biographical Disruption. *Sociology of Health and Illness* 4: 167–82.
Charmaz, K. (1991) *Good Days, Bad Days: The Self in Chronic Illness and Time*. Rutgers University Press, New Brunswick, NJ.
Charmaz, K. (1995) Body, Identity, and Self: Adapting to Impairment. *Sociological Quarterly* 36: 657–80.

Charmaz, K. (2002) Stories and Silences: Disclosures and Self in Chronic Illness. *Qualitative Inquiry* 8: 302–28.

Corbin, J. M. & Strauss, A. (1988) *Unending Work and Care: Managing Chronic Illness at Home.* Jossey-Bass, San Francisco.

Cornwall, J. (1984) *Hard-Earned Lives: Accounts of Health and Illness from East London.* Tavistock, London.

Goffman, E. (1961) *Asylums.* Doubleday, Garden City, NY.

Locker, D. (1983) *Disability and Disadvantage: The Consequences of Chronic Illness.* Tavistock, London.

Parsons, T. (1953) *The Social System.* Free Press, Glencoe, IL.

Scambler, G. (2002) *Health and Social Change: A Critical Theory.* Open University Press, Buckingham.

Shakespeare, T. (Ed.) (1998) *The Disability Reader: Social Science Perspectives.* Cassell, London.

Strauss, A. L., Corbin, J., Fagerhaugh, S., Glaser, B. G., Maines, D., Suczek, B., & Wiener, C. L. (1984) *Chronic Illness and the Quality of Life,* 2nd edn. Mosby, St. Louis.

Williams, S. (1999) Is Anybody There? Critical Realism, Chronic Illness and the Disability Debate. *Sociology of Health and Illness* 21: 797–820.

Williams, S. (2003) *Medicine and the Body.* Sage, London.

church

Luca Diotallevi

Sociology, especially in its classic works, provides analytic perspectives for understanding specific ecclesiastic religious phenomena (i.e., churches and church-oriented religions). But long before the birth of sociology – in its contemporary empirical version – modern philosophy, both Continental and Atlantic, was deeply engaged with the ecclesiological question (Olivetti 1992). This philosophical attention attributed special theoretical relevance to observation of certain socio-religious phenomena. This was particularly true in the classical era of the philosophy of religion – in the specifically modern meaning of the term – especially from Hume and Kant through Hegel. This emerged in the attempt to consider and

represent the tension between philosophical ecclesiology and theory of society (a tension that implies themes such as secularization, the relationship between church and state, the relationship between religion and morality, and the process of social differentiation and its limits). Thus the ecclesiological question, as a close relationship between the empirical and the theoretical sphere, plays a crucial role for that aspect of the crisis of ontotheological metaphysics known as philosophy of religion, regardless of the various solutions proposed by individual scholars. An exemplary case is *Religion* as the epilogue to Kant's transcendental program. Kant deals with the need to think and represent the church, but also with the contradiction of the more general assumptions this line of thought leads to. Another example is the classical (especially romantic and idealistic) theme of the opposition of *invisible* and *visible* church.

This theoretical and cultural context was an important part of the terrain where contemporary sociology started to appear in the mid-nineteenth century, first as sociology of religion. This implied that the new discipline would pay special attention to the definition of "church" and remain devoted to this specific question. This turned out to be only partly true, and even then only sporadically.

CLASSIC AUTHORS

Weber (1963) and Troeltsch (1960) first defined church as a specific kind of religious organization which enforces its decisions by means of psychic coercion realized through managing religious benefits. As opposed to a sect, a church has a more hierarchical and more bureaucratic organizational structure, is larger, offers a way of belonging which is generally universal and therefore exploits territorial boundaries, has a generally lower level of intensity of participation, has a culture, a degree and a form of differentiation which is less radically opposed to those of the social context in which it operates, and suffers from greater inertia and resistance to change and innovation (Wilson 1997; Wuthnow 1988). This comparison shows how the concept of church, as opposed to that of sect, is multidimensional. There is a plurality of roots (theological, sociological, etc.) to that opposition, but also a potential instability, with a risk of explosion when social forces (especially social differentiation) reduce the correlation among these dimensions. This orientation, right from the start, thus conceived of a church in terms of its greater complexity and articulation compared to a sect (Guizzardi & Pace 1987). Careful bibliographical analysis by Beckford (1973, 1984) shows that even today the prevailing sociological conceptions of church can be traced to the positions outlined in the works of Weber and Troeltsch. Even in the past two decades, attempts to define church more carefully in conceptual terms have usually been oriented towards this tradition. This is true for the new paradigm of rational choice theory applied to the analysis of socioreligious phenomena: church and sect are assumed to be theoretically distinct kinds of religious organization. The new theory is used to express the two concepts and their formal and operational opposition (Iannaccone 1988: 242; Stark & Bainbridge 1996: 124).

Over time, the sociological idea of church as a specific kind of religious organization has encountered problems and limits. At the general level, a first critical trend was identified by Kaufmann (1974): empirical studies began to focus on topics related to individual religious experience or behavior, or related to basic and therefore small-sized religious groups, but ignored broader religious organizations. Whether this is the cause or effect (or both) of the guiding characteristics of this first analytic perspective is now less important than the growing risk that – on this basis – the sociology of religion will lose its ability to examine more complex religious phenomena.

Among these limits, there were the effects of the various disciplinary contributions in defining the church/sect opposition, or at least its *vulgata* (Swatos 1975, 1976). In other cases, the difficulties in applying the church/sect conceptual scheme could be attributed to the specific socioreligious context in relation to which that opposition was elaborated. It was much less complex than later socioreligious contexts. In any case, there is no reason to suppose that the church vs. sect scheme was more appealing for its useful simplicity than for any real

analytic power at the time of its first and classic elaboration.

Even the best analytic systems cannot predict how social situations will change. This does not mean, however, that eventual conceptual redefinitions forced by social changes cannot refer back to previous analytical systems and start from there (Swatos 1976: 142; Guizzardi & Pace 1987). During the twentieth century, Niebuhr (1975), with his work on the social roots of the process of denominalization of American Christianity, provided one of the best-known examples of overcoming and integrating the church/sect scheme as a means of accounting for the dramatic transformations which had taken place in religious organizations and institutions. Niebuhr, in presenting the reasons for his research and in describing its first results, interprets these social transformations in terms of degrees and forms of social differentiation, and in terms of degrees and forms of "internal" religious complexity (Niebuhr 1975: 283). And these are nothing but the exact same questions already noted at the onset of theoretical and cultural debate over the ecclesiological issue.

Later, the influence of the work of Luckmann (1967) – especially a very simplified interpretation of his ideas, in agreement with the orthodoxy of secularist ideology – may have helped to spread the opinion that the crisis of this approach to the analysis of religious organizations, especially those that were larger and/or more ecclesiastical, was actually proof of the incompatibility between modern organizational principles and spiritual or religious phenomena and experiences. Beckford himself, although he proposed a moratorium on using the church/sect conceptual couplet, justified his proposal for very different reasons. Beckford (1984) argued as follows: the growing difficulty in understanding large institutionalized religions such as churches is strongly and primarily related to the challenge in understanding the great transformations (above all, differentiations) inside religious realities, and between these realities and the social context. For example, it is no longer possible to assume, a priori, that churches rather than sects are capable of greater adaptation to today's social contexts (see Wuthnow 1988: 495).

It appears that Kaufmann's (1974) appeal had not been sufficiently accepted. Nonetheless, although it is increasingly difficult to understand ecclesiastical realities simply as particular forms of religious organization, important contributions to the sociology of religion can still emerge from organizational studies and from the sophisticated tools of this discipline (Di Maggio 1998). This has been shown particularly in the case of Catholicism (and therefore of a church), where it is increasingly clear that a vast number of organizations are working, both generalist and specialist. In sum, could a church of such internal complexity, operating in such a differentiated context as advanced modern society, still be studied as an organization, and, as if that were not enough, as a *single* organization?

It is precisely this situation that allows for the possibility of a radically different analytic perspective. This change lies in a sort of break in the requested moratorium. The proposal radicalizes, rather than abandons, the organizational approach to all collective religious phenomena, historical churches included. The possibility is considered by several scholars, using very different conceptual and theoretical means. For the most part, these texts share a double refusal: a refusal to reduce sociology of religion to a sociology of individual religiosity (whether "diffused," "implicit," or other) and a refusal to assume large-scale religious realities as a starting point for doing research.

These options are shared by many scholars, even when they share little else. They are very clear, for example, in the work by Chaves, who takes the Weberian idea of religious organization as one of his starting points and traces its consequences (which, in many empirical and theoretical works, have been shown to be quite interesting). Thus, the heart of his analysis is the minimum religious organization, the congregation in the American case, as the reality where two structures meet: the religious authority structure and religious agencies. What is important here is that this analytic strategy radically eliminates any concept of church. From this point of view "church sociology" would appear to be nothing but a trap (Chaves 1993).

This conclusion clearly reveals one of the possibilities for managing the difficulties created by the great internal and external complexity inherent in sociological analysis of such religious realities as churches. It is worth underscoring a couple of corollaries to this. First, the sociology of religion could benefit from distancing itself not just from the concept of church, but also from those of religion and secularization. This would allow for a more detailed view of phenomena previously considered to fall into these categories. Second, a corollary which is perhaps an axiom: here once again there is a recognition of the need to concentrate on the phenomena of social differentiation, and above all to "de-Parsonsify its current theory (Chaves 1994).

Right from the start of sociology there has been at least one other way to understand the church conceptually, although it has not been as widespread as the one above. Durkheim (1965) defines church as a community whose fellows are connected to each other through shared representations of the sacred and of its relationships and distinctions with the profane, and resulting in identical practices expressing these shared representations. This means that "church" must cover not only institutional phenomena, but also organizational phenomena. Once again, even if in a different way, there is the necessity of coping with complexity and social differentiation implied by the church question: complexity of social phenomena, organizations and institutions, and beliefs and behaviors, from religion to social environments. Durkheim considered differentiation as a positive phenomenon up to a certain point, after which it becomes dangerous. Further, he assigns religion (more precisely, church) a key role in managing and containing the process through which social differentiation increases social complexity.

Durkheim inspired sociological thought and imagination, while the attempt to operationalize his concepts and formalize his theories has met with difficulty and has not always succeeded. This was also the case for his sociology of religion and his concept of church. However, there are echoes or at least apparent analogies with that sociological concept of church in later sociological research. Talcott Parsons (1951), for example, treats churches as the greatest expression of the institutionalization of beliefs, thereby ensuring them a significant active role within and for the social system (Moberg 1984). It is easy to imagine how the ongoing social differentiation of both social functions and social "levels" (Luhmann 1985b) created problems for trust in the empirical usefulness of such a concept of church.

CONTEMPORARY SOCIOLOGY

The ecclesiological question appears as both a theoretical and an empirical question. It is characterized by the need to account for (and the difficulty of so doing) very high degrees of complexity and for the equally high degrees and multiple forms of differentiation. It entails the double requirement of not ignoring the organizational dimension and not reducing church to that dimension. In addition, the ecclesiological question as addressed from a sociological perspective is made more difficult by the requirement for empirically operative concepts.

As seen by Chaves and others, a solution to such difficulties can be found that excludes, among other things, the usefulness itself of any concept of church. Yet it is also possible to find the opposite approach in the sociological literature: conceptual proposals concerning church elaborated within an analytic paradigm that accounts for the level of complexity and the level and forms of differentiation characteristic of advanced modern societies.

Few proposals satisfy these criteria, and they differ greatly. One, however, stands out: that offered by Luhmann (1977, 1985a, 2000) and already used by other scholars (even if Luhmann's disciples are not always aware of this). The paradigm proposed by Luhmann on the basis of system theory is noteworthy for the radical way in which it focuses attention on questions of social complexity, contingency, and functional differentiation, especially that phase in which the main characteristic is the differentiation of society by functions (the phase coinciding with advanced modernization). In the domain of social systems, in reciprocal system/environment relationships with personal systems (both processes independently reducing either internal or external complexity), Luhmannian categories distinguish between three types of social systems: interaction, organization, and society (the last one by means of an increasing

functional differentiation tends to become global society: *Weltgesellschaft*). These social systems consist of communicative events. The very high level of social complexity, as well as the extreme contingency of each communicative event, depends on the degree reached, and on the form taken, by the social differentiation processes. The growth in differentiation between functions leads to a noticeable increase – tendentially radicalizing – of the differentiation between interactions, organizations, and society, with all three in a system/environment relationship with the others. With regard to Chaves's suggestion, Luhmann does not include a transcendental catalog of social functions or functional societal subsystems; this reveals just how far his theory of social differentiation is from that of Parsons.

The assumptions and solutions offered by Luhmann obviously have to be discussed, but they clearly provide a sociological paradigm that addresses the theoretical background of the ecclesiological question. The fact that Luhmann identifies a possibility for religion in such a social scenario is particularly relevant here. In fact, the process of social constitution of the meaning and the phenomenon of communication implies two problems in particular (Luhmann 1985a). The first is the reduction of indeterminate or indeterminable complexity to determined or determinable complexity. The second and connected problem is that of the deparadoxalization of the social system's self-reference. These problems have hitherto been resolved by social performances ensured by religious traditions. There is no reason to believe, however, that this means that religions are not constantly exposed to competition concerning this social function from potential functional equivalents – competition where the outcome is always unpredictable.

Luhmann's (1977: 56) analysis of religion elaborates and uses a concept of church. Church is religiously specialized communication. Church is more or less analogous to money in the economic subsystem, law in the political subsystem, scientific truth in the scientific subsystem, etc. In the course of the process of functional social differentiation, each subsystem (politics, economy, religion, science, etc.) manages three types of relations: with other subsystems (*Leistungen*), with the society system (*Funktion*), and with itself (*Reflexion*).

Religious communication, or church, is the *Funktion* of the religious subsystem. From the religious subsystem, as from any other functionally specialized societal subsystem, one can observe the differentiation of functions within society. "Secularization" is then the religious mode for understanding the phenomenon of functional differentiation: understanding a relative reduction in influence and – simultaneously – a relative increase in the independence of the religious subsystem from other functional subsystems. This mode has an equivalent in each of the other functional subsystems.

The nexus between the ecclesiological question and that of social differentiation is once again apparent; in this case, however, it takes the form of a potentially direct and not inverse correlation. In fact, the more society is functionally differentiated, the better the conditions become for a clear manifestation of religious phenomena with specifically ecclesial traits. Obviously, religious traditions may or may not exploit these social conditions.

The concept of church (or religious communication) also appears to have a characteristic which distinguishes it from some forms of specialized social communication, even as it links it to others. Religious communication is governed by a code (transcendence/immanence), but does not have its own medium (Luhmann 1977: 72; 2000 187). In short, Luhmann's sociological perspective allows for a concept of church more or less comparable to those of specialized communication through law, money, scientific truth, or other media.

We have to consider two objections to Luhmann's idea of church, in order to clarify some aspects of the question. Especially in a global society, and with religion as its equally global specialized subsystem, the use of the term "church," derived from a particular religious tradition, can raise suspicions that such a general phenomenon (religious communication) is not encompassed by the term (church). This objection obviously cannot be addressed with extra-sociological responses, such as those offered by a certain Christian theology through demonstration of ecclesiology with an important ecumenical and interreligious dimension, or by historical research stressing the decisive role played by the Christian tradition in the development of a global religious system (Beyer

1998). On the contrary, it may be useful to turn back to an empirically useful distinction, such as that between money and currencies, according to which it is possible therefore to use the term "church" in this case as both analogy and in more precise terms. This leads us to address a second group of critics.

If the process of functional differentiation tends to radicalize the differentiation between social "levels" or types of social systems (interaction, organization, society), it is also clear how church (societal religious communication) is not a type of religious organization (a great difference appears between this concept of church and that of religion at a societal level used by authors like Karel Dobbelaere, who adopt completely different paradigms such as those distinguishing between micro, meso and macrosocial levels). Nonetheless, once the contents of the concept of church are delimited, it would be a serious cognitive oversight not to prepare conceptual instruments that allow us to identify and distinguish ecclesiastical and non-ecclesiastical religious organizations, as well as individual "church oriented religiosity" and other kinds of religiosity.

Luhmann's proposal is particularly useful because it allows for the rather analytical consideration of the relationship between organizations and society. The more society and its subsystems become unorganizable through advanced modernization, the more organizations have achieved a previously unthinkable importance. Organizations, in fact, can influence societal communication (and vice versa). This naturally holds true for religion (Luhmann 1977: 272; 2000: 226), starting with the phenomenon of governance of communicative codes – through "religious dogmatics" (Luhmann 1977: 72). This is the ground for distinguishing between organization as more or less able to influence the governing of religious communication, and therefore between church (*Kirche*) and ecclesiastical organization (*Amtskirche*) with such an ability.

Returning to the first objection (why call societal religious communication "church"?), the way in which the term "church" is used can be appreciated, both to give a name to the concept of specialized religious communication in general (according to an analogy) and a name to those phenomena of religious communication where the main influence in codification is that of organizations active within the Christian religious tradition (where "church" is a religious currency or just a kind of money). One can also imagine a religious communication regulated according to Christian schemas which influence (or fail to influence) religious organizations, religious interactions, and forms of religiosity, inside or outside Christian religious tradition. For example, the study of Christian liturgy lends itself to a delineation of the advantages of such a set of distinctions and concepts. The study of Christian theology and the scope of its influence can also be mentioned in this regard.

PERSPECTIVES

Luhmann's concept of church (or religious communication) has begun to be used implicitly and explicitly and produced results. First of all, this understanding of the degrees of differentiation between functions and between types of social systems provides the basis for that concept of church, and can help to reduce the occasionally paralyzing emphasis placed on intuitions such as the well-known "believing without belonging" (Beckford 1984; Davie 1990). In broader Luhmannian sociological theory, this (like the unorganizability of the church) is one of the effects of the religious variant of the differentiation between organizations and society, and therefore between religious organizations and societal religion (as well as between religion and religiosity). This does not exclude and actually stresses the current potentialities of ecclesiastical organizations in terms of recruitment and participation. The realization of participative potentialities related to ecclesiastical (and non-ecclesiastical) religious organizations in an advanced modern society cannot be measured and assessed through a comparison with situations marked by lower degrees of social differentiation. A similar benefit in utilizing the Luhmannian approach to church and religion is its answer to the proposal to abandon the concept of secularization (Chaves 1994) because of the presumed lack of analogy between religion and other subsystems in terms of managing and representing functional differentiation. Beyer (1994) has

fully demonstrated the advantages of using this conceptual approach for the recognition and the study of the process of religious globalization and the formation of the global religious system.

It has also been shown how in this perspective it is possible to find analytic indications useful for overcoming the "puzzle" emerging in the debate between the new and the old paradigm, such as that in the Italian case (Diotallevi 2001, 2002). If, as the new paradigm suggests, there are insufficient reasons to assume a necessary correlation between social modernization and decline of organized religion, it is difficult to explain the case of Italy, an apparently efficient religious monopoly (and yet a "church religion" monopoly working within a social context of advanced modernization, and therefore contrary also to the old paradigm's predictions). Yet, thanks to the use of Luhmann's perspective, it is possible to capture the degree of internal diversification of religious supply that certain church polities and policies have allowed to develop. This understanding, however, is possible once it is clear that within a single ecclesiastic religious tradition many religious firms may operate: once it is clear that a church is not necessarily a religious organization, through the recognition that this church may "have" many religious organizations.

SEE ALSO: Catholicism; Denomination; Durkheim, Émile; Organizations, Tradition and; Organizations, Voluntary; Orthodoxy; Protestantism; Religion; Sect; Secularization; Social Movement Organizations; Strategic Management (Organizations); Weber, Max

REFERENCES AND SUGGESTED READINGS

Beckford, J. A. (1973) Religious Organization. *Current Sociology* 21(2).
Beckford, J. A. (1984) Religious Organization: A Survey of Some Recent Publications. *Archives des sciences sociales des religions* 57(1): 83–102.
Beckford, J. A. (1991) *Religion and Advanced Industrial Society*. Unwin Hyman, London.
Beyer, P. (1994) *Religion and Globalization*. Sage, London.
Beyer, P. (1998) The Religious System of Global Society: A Sociological Look at Contemporary Religion and Religions. *Numen* 45: 1–29.

Chaves, M. (1993) Denominations as Dual Structures: An Organizational Analysis. *Sociology of Religion* 54(2): 147–69.

Chaves, M. (1994) Secularization as Declining Religious Authority. *Social Forces* 749–74.

Davie, G. (1990) Believing Without Belonging. *Social Compass* 37: 455–69.

Di Maggio, P. (1998) The Relevance of Organization Theory to the Study of Religion. In: Demerath, N. J., III (Ed.), *Sacred Companies*. Oxford University Press, New York, pp. 7–23.

Diotallevi, L. (2001) *Il Rompicapo della Secolarizzazione Italiana*. Rubbettino, Soveria Mannelli.

Diotallevi, L. (2002) Italian Case and American Theories: Refining Secularization Paradigm. *Sociology of Religion* 63(2): 137–56.

Durkheim, E. (1965) *The Elementary Forms of Religious Life*. Free Press, New York.

Guizzardi, G. & Pace, E. (1987) La chiesa e le altre organizzazioni religiose. In: De Masi, D. & Bonzanini, A. (Eds.), *Trattato di Sociologia del Lavoro e dell'Organizzazione*. Angeli, Milan, pp. 493–532.

Iannaccone, L. R. (1988). A Formal Model of Church and Sect. *American Journal of Sociology* (suppl. 94): 241–68.

Kaufmann, F.-X. (1974). Religion et bureaucratie. Le problème de l'organisation religieuse. *Social Compass* 21(1): 101–7.

Luckmann, T. (1967) *The Invisible Religion*. Macmillan, New York.

Luhmann, N. (1977) *Funktion der Religion*. Suhrkamp, Frankfurt am Main.

Luhmann, N. (1985a) Society, Meaning, Religion – Based on Self-Reference. *Sociological Analysis* 46: 5–20.

Luhmann, N. (Ed.) (1985b) *Soziale Differenzierung. Zur Geschichte einer Idee*. Westdeutscher, Opladen.

Luhmann, N. (2000) *Die Religion der Gesellschaft*. Suhrkamp, Frankfurt am Main.

Moberg, D. O. (1984) *The Church as a Social Institution: The Sociology of American Religion*. Backer, Grand Rapids, MI.

Niebuhr, R. H. (1975) *The Social Sources of Denominationalism*. New American Library, New York.

Olivetti, M. M. (1992) *Analogia del soggetto*. Laterza, Roma-Bari.

Parsons, T. (1951) *The Social System*. Free Press, New York.

Stark, R. & Bainbridge, W. S. (1996) *A Theory of Religion*. Rutgers University Press, New Brunswick.

Swatos, W. H., Jr. (1975). Monopolism, Pluralism, Acceptance, and Rejection: An Integrated Model for Church–Sect Theory. *Review of Religious Research* 16(3): 174–85.

Swatos, W. H., Jr. (1976). Weber or Troeltsch? Methodology, Syndrome, and the Development of Church–Sect Theory. *Journal for the Scientific Study of Religion* 15(2): 129–44.

Troeltsch, E. (1960) *The Social Teaching of the Christian Churches*. Harper & Row, New York.

Weber, M. (1963) *The Sociology of Religion*. Beacon Press, Boston.

Weber, M. (1978) *Economy and Society*. University of California Press, Los Angeles.

Wilson, B. R. (1997) Religiosa, organizzazione. In: *Enciclopedia delle Scienze Sociali*, Vol. 7. Istituto della Enciclopedia Italiana "G. Treccani."

Wuthnow, R. J. (1988) Sociology of Religion. In: Smelser, N. J. (Ed.), *Handbook of Sociology*. Sage, Beverly Hills, pp. 473–510.

citations and scientific indexing

Yuri Jack Gómez-Morales

A classic analytical distinction between a citation and a reference reads: "if paper R contains a bibliographic footnote using and describing paper C, then R contains a reference to C, and C has a citation from R." According to this, citation and referencing are relations among published texts. But whereas referencing is an intratextual relation between a written word, statement, description, or even an entire argument and a bibliographic reference, citation is an extratextual relation between a complete piece of scientific literature, namely a book or a journal article (just to mention classic forms), and many other pieces of literature of a latter publication date. A reader can easily see a reference by inspecting a text; after all, referencing is a technical standard for editing publishable texts. But a reader cannot see citation directly. Whereas referencing, when it happens, takes place within a singular piece of edited and published material, citation, when it happens, is something that takes place across a section of published literature and it becomes visible for a reader, so to speak, as long as some kind of bibliographic control of that literature can be exerted. This is the purpose that a citation index accomplishes. A citation index is a form to organize and display a body of bibliographical references. These references are collected from reference lists of journal articles, books, and so on, and then organized alphabetically by author. Once this list is ready, under each of the entries one finds the record of published works that have cited them at some point.

A citation index is one of several tools developed throughout centuries of printing for controlling the literature bibliographically. In fact, among the first textual devices functioning as indexes, the Roman Catholic *Index Librorum Prohibitorum* (Rome, 1559) constitutes a good example of the double-sided nature of this textual technology that is at once social and textual. Journals, too, since their very inception in seventeenth-century Europe were used as bibliographical control tools for a growing mass of published material until a whole range of secondary serials (abstracting and indexing services) was launched toward the end of the nineteenth century. However, the bibliographical control of scientific literature through citation indexing was a twentieth-century achievement in which developments in both journal editorial standards (Bazerman 1984) and computing technology concurred in the making of scientific indexing through citation an empirical possibility (Garfield 1955). In contrast with the Roman *Index*, which served the purpose of catching what the Catholic Church considered as heretical texts, authors, and distribution networks during an age of religious turmoil, an index to scientific literature serves to identify significant scientific contributions, significant scientific authors, and relevant sociocognitive and sociotechnical networks. And it is because of this that when a citation index for science became a technical reality and a prosperous commercial enterprise in the realm of information retrieval by 1964 (Garfield 1979), further implications were immediately sought for the sociology of science and for science policymaking and management, where the notion of citation and its associated technical procedure of indexing have been consequential.

As an information retrieval tool, citation indexing of scientific literature has empowered scientists by providing them with means and search criteria for taking hold over an increasingly growing mass of scientific literature, and thus has become instrumental for scientific research. As a methodological operationalization within sociology it contributed substantially to the advancement of the empirical investigations on the normative structure of science. And yet, further considerations on the notion of referencing as a rhetorical resource (Gilbert 1977; Latour & Fabbri 1977; Woolgar 1988), on the one hand, and citation as part of the credibility cycle in science (Latour & Woolgar 1979), on the other, opened up new theoretical avenues for exploring sciences as social phenomena. As for science policy and management concerns, citation indexing of scientific literature, used as an evaluative tool often leading to research resource allocation, has proved to be a widespread practice and certainly an effective mechanism of social control, whether one likes it or not. This revolutionary technique for indexing scientific literature pushed forward quantitatively oriented studies on the history of science as well. Indeed, in conjunction with several other notions such as scientific productivity and scientific growth, citation (and cocitation) analysis allowed the construction of the scientific literature itself as a knowledge-object deserving systematic investigation by scientometrics.

For the main purposes concerning us here, some sociologists used citation and scientific indexing at first as a means for developing analytic methods, based on observable patterns traceable in the literature, for studying the actual operation of norms and values responsible for the emergence of science as a social institution in modern societies, and therefore deserving of sociological examination. The interpretation of citation as an expression of an institutionalized pattern of conduct (acknowledging the sources on which one's work has been built) in science was set down by Merton and Zuckerman in a classic paper on the issue (Zuckerman & Merton 1973) and presented in context later in Merton's episodic memoirs (Merton 1977). When a scientific author references someone else's work in his or her own paper, this author is at least acknowledging authorship (a property right) to someone else. As is immediately obvious, in order to be granted with intellectual property rights over a piece of literature, a scientist must become an author in the first place; science is published knowledge. Thus, Zuckerman and Merton conceived of publication in science as an ingenious procedure for socially granting intellectual property in science, and at the same time contributing to advancing certified knowledge by making it public. If publication grants a basis for claiming intellectual right, it is through citation that this right is socially enjoyed, though not being cited is like being the owner of a useless result from a cognitive point of view. The idea that the more a paper or book is cited, the more impact it has had within a field of studies, and the greater its influence in the community, led some sociologists to conclude that social standing and mobility within the scientific community depend, to a great extent, on the quality of a scientist's work, as this quality can be ascertained objectively through citation counting. On this ground, the use of citation counting as an evaluative tool among science policymakers and science managers became widespread. However, it is important to notice that normative sociologists' interest in scientific quality was related to a more far-reaching research agenda on the institutionalization of science. Functionalists used citation measurements not for the sake of measuring and ranking people, institutions, and countries but as empirical evidence supporting an explanation of social stratification in science as a result of an operating structure of institutionalized norms and internalized values.

The idea of citation counting as an objective measurement of scientific quality as well as the attempts at writing a "scientific history" of science, or drawing maps of knowledge using citation and co-citation analysis, has been as controversial as it has been fruitful (Edge 1977). The citation debate opened new avenues for studying science in which emphasis is placed on the mirror image of citation: referencing. Normative uses of citations assume that cognitive and technical standards for research performance and for evaluating scientific results are shared by participants. However, when focusing on scientific practice as it actually takes place in laboratory settings, some sociologists found that those standards were outcomes of social negotiation among participants and therefore context-dependent (Mulkay

1991 [1976]). In this light, semiotic-minded analyses of scientific texts were undertaken to substantiate the view according to which scientists' claims of objectivity with regard to the facts presented in their published papers are actually constructed in the text, and referencing is one among several other "stylistic" resources for doing so (Woolgar 1988). The study of scientific writing showed that the use of references might be understood as a rhetorical resource used in scientific papers whose aim is to persuade readers on different matters. These studies have shown a consistent "style" in scientific writing that starts by portraying a reported result as a genuine novelty. This is often achieved by reviewing the current state of the art in the introductory section of a paper where referencing is used profusely. In the material and methods section of the paper, referencing serves also the purpose of stating that adequate and authoritative techniques were employed. Very often, too, scientific authors typically show, usually in a concluding section, how their findings illuminate or solve problems reported in current literature, also referenced in the paper, as a means to substantiate the importance of the new published result (Woolgar 1988). A paper's reference list, then, provides rhetorical force for its arguments by appealing to a persuasive community made out of references that partially set the context of reading for the audience. Thus, by using references, scientists manage to assemble a network which is at once social and technical, a network that may be adequately deployed to support the facticity of a particular statement, or to deny or undermine the facticity of someone else's statement. Thus the intended audience of a paper is made up of those who are collectively of the opinion that the referenced papers on the list deserve a citation (Gilbert 1977), and those who have been persuaded of this or who find it useful for the advancement of their particular claims (Latour & Woolgar 1979). The more citations a paper receives over time has nothing to do with its objective quality. Citation counting provides only secondary evidence of the success of a particular scientist, research team, or laboratory in advancing their interests which, in the last analysis, can be reduced to remaining well positioned within a continuous cycle of credibility-gaining as a means for actually being able to do more science and starting the cycle once more.

Almost without exception, studies concerned with one of the several varieties of citation analysis have been of an empirical nature and based on the counting of the number of citations. However, despite the several warnings that the citation debate arose on the inadvisability of employing citation data without a sound theoretical underpinning, little progress has been made toward the formulation of a "theory of citation." Lately, though (Leydesdorff 1998), a reflexive view on citation states that the quest for a theory of citation presumes that citations themselves should be explained. The moment one starts to count citations to a published work, one is assuming that this tally tells us something about the cited text, about its position in a host of networks: semantic networks, networks of journals, institutional networks (Wouters 1998). If citation analysis is just a tool for explaining, for example, the growth of science, a "theory of citation" cannot be more than a methodological reflection designed to improve the accuracy of this measurement, merely a technical issue (Woolgar 1991). But when one raises questions such as whether citations indicate "impact," "influence," or "quality," one is in need of a clear definition of these concepts with reference to units of analysis. The reflexive lesson to be learned from the citation debate is that the functions of citations are expected to be different when different contexts or different levels of aggregation are studied, as suggested in the above competing sociological interpretations of citation. Citation analysis is based on a theoretical reflection of scientific practices that have been shaped historically, but the historical, philosophical, and/or sociological positions taken by citation analysts, however, have usually remained implicit. Understanding citation in terms of interacting networks of authors and texts over time enables the possibility of a new theory of citation as a "dynamic operation that allows for reduction of complexity in various contexts at the same time. The dynamic perspective of selections operating upon selections in other networks accounts for the character of citations as statistical indicators, for their specificity and for their multi-contextuality" (Leydesdorff 1998).

SEE ALSO: Matthew Effect; Scientific Norms/Counternorms; Scientific Productivity; Scientometrics

REFERENCES AND SUGGESTED READINGS

Bazerman, C. (1984). Modern Evolution of Experimental Report in Physics: Spectroscopy Articles in *Physical Review*, 1893–1980. *Social Studies of Science* 14: 163–96.

Edge, D. (1977) Why I Am Not a Co-Citationist. In: *Essays of an Information Scientist (1977–1978)*, Vol. 3. ISI Press, Philadelphia, pp. 240–6.

Garfield, E. (1955) Citation Index for Science. *Science* 122: 108–11.

Garfield, E. (1979) *Citation Index: Its Theory and Application in Science, Technology, and Humanities*. Wiley, New York.

Garfield, E., Merton, R. K., Malin, M. V., & Small, H. G. (1978) Citation Data as Science Indicators. In: Elkana, Y., Lederberg, J., Merton, R. K., Thackray, A., & Zuckerman, H. A. (Eds.), *Toward a Metric of Science: The Advent of Science Indicators*. Wiley, New York, pp. 179–207.

Gilbert, G. N. (1977) Referencing as Persuasion. *Social Studies of Science* 7: 113–22.

Latour, B. & Fabbri, P. (1977) La rhétorique de la science: pouvoir et devoir dans un article de la science exacte. *Actes de la Recherche en Sciences Sociales* 13: 81–95.

Latour, B. & Woolgar, S. W. (1979) *Laboratory Life: The Construction of Scientific Facts*. Sage, Beverly Hills.

Leydesdorff, L. (1998) Theories of Citation? *Scientometrics* 43: 5–25.

Merton, R. K. (1977) The Sociology of Science: An Episodic Memoir. In: Merton, R. K. & Gaston, J. (Eds.), *The Sociology of Science in Europe*. Southern Illinois University Press, Feffer and Simons, Carbondale and London, pp. 3–141.

Mulkay, M. J. (1991 [1976]) Norms and Ideology. In: *Sociology of Science: A Sociological Pilgrimage*. Open University Press, Milton Keynes, pp. 62–78.

Woolgar, S. W. (1988) *Science: The Very Idea*. Ellis Horwood, Chichester.

Woolgar, S. W. (1991) Beyond the Citation Debate: Towards a Sociology of Measurement Technologies and Their Use in Science Policy. *Science and Public Policy* 18: 319–26.

Wouters, P. (1998) The Signs of Science. *Sciento-metrics* 41: 225–41.

Zuckerman, H. A. & Merton, R. K. (1973) Institu-tionalized Patterns of Evaluation in Science. In: Storer, N. W. (Ed.), *The Sociology of Science: Theoretical and Empirical Investigations*. University of Chicago Press, Chicago, pp. 460–96.

cities in Europe

Patrick Le Galès

The European city concept derives from Max Weber and historians of the Middle Ages. In "The City," Weber characterizes the med-ieval western city – in modern language, wes-tern European city – as having the following features: a fortification, a market, and a spe-cifically urban economy of consumption, exchange, and production; a court of law and the ability to ordain a set of rules and laws; rules relating to landed property (since cities were not subject to the taxes and constraints of feudalism); and a structure based on associa-tions (of guilds) and – at least partial – political autonomy, expressed in particular through the existence of an administrative body and the participation of the burghers in local govern-ment. This combination of political autonomy, religious culture, specifically urban economy, and differentiated social structure, all sur-rounded by a wall, made the western city an original sociological category and a structuring element in the Europe of the Middle Ages between 1000 and 1500. This golden age of urban Europe reached its high point at the end of the Middle Ages, when feudal structures were gradually fading, but before the states had established their domination everywhere (Tilly 1990).

The "western city" model elaborated by Weber defines an original set of analytical per-spectives to analyze cities from a sociological perspective. Firstly, the "western city" is char-acterized as an ideal type by contrast to the Oriental city in particular. There is no general theory of urbanization and convergence of cities here, but rather the analysis of differences and complex causal mechanisms. Comparison over time and between regions of the world allows Weber to characterize a particular social struc-ture and its evolution over time.

Secondly, the European city is analyzed as a political actor. Weber analyzes the mechanisms of aggregation and representation of interest and culture that bring together local social groups, associations, organized interests, pri-vate firms, and urban governments and also the competition between different powers such as bishops, lords, burghers, and sometimes the state, between the great families, or between cities themselves, i.e., in political and institu-tional terms. Indeed, the power of the burghers led to the creation of the communes. A com-mune was characterized by its own political rights, by autonomous courts and economic policy, and less frequently by international pol-icy and a military force.

Thirdly, the western European city is ana-lyzed as an original social structure dominated by a new social class, the burghers. The city is conceived as an integrated local society and as a complex social formation, sometimes a local society. Bagnasco stresses the fact that Weber analyzed cities as a group, equipped with an administrative apparatus and with a leader, reg-ulating the economy. The creation of the city as collective actor came about through the forma-tion of confederacies of burghers – a bourgeoi-sie as collective actor, which can take different forms.

The Europe of cities was not just the Europe of early capitalism and of merchants but also that of intellectuals, universities, and culture that launched the Renaissance. The medieval European city was the crucible of European societies, in which new cultural and political models developed by contrast and opposition to the principles of feudal societies. The city gave rise to new social relations and cultural and organizational innovations, which were furthered by interactions between the various populations living within it. The conditions of the city promoted mechanisms for learning a collective way of life, for innovation and spread-ing innovation, rapid accumulation, transforma-tion of behaviors, interplay of competition and cooperation, and processes of social differentia-tion engendered by proximity. But medieval

European cities were progressively integrated within nation-states. The founding fathers of sociology were taken by the strength of the Industrial Revolution and the making of modern national societies. European cities were no longer original social structures but were absorbed in the making of national societies. Therefore, urban sociologists, Georg Simmel and his analysis of the metropolis, sociologists at the University of Chicago, or later writers in the Marxist political economy tradition did not follow that line of analysis. Instead they concentrated on both the rapid rise of industrial cities and the modern metropolis defined by contrast to the western city ideal type.

CITIES IN EUROPE: A DISTINCTIVE FEATURE OF EUROPEAN SOCIETIES

Cities in Europe include industrial cities of the nineteenth century, a small number of large metropolises, and a stable bulk of medium-sized cities.

Over the twentieth century, the issue of the city in Europe was not an important one. Analysis of European societies, including cities, was exclusively focused upon the nation-state framework. Differences of language, social structure, and culture were reinforced by the strengthening of the nation-state and wars. This increased both differentiation between European societies and integration within each national society, i.e., the dual movement in which borders are strengthened and the inside is differentiated from the outside, while an internal order is organized and a national society gradually homogenizes despite international relations. Social relations, classes, and politics were defined not in urban terms but in national terms. These elements of national societies have been more or less in place since the late nineteenth century in most European countries. Cities were therefore analyzed within national categories as, for example, Swedish, Italian, or Dutch cities.

Urban sociologists were interested in the convergence of cities as industrial cities, or as modern metropolises with differentiated neighborhood and ever-expanding suburbs. In the nineteenth century, the city became the site of

capitalist industrial development. Concentration in great metropolises and large industrial areas lent a different dynamic to cities, changing them both socially and physically (Hohenberg & Hollen Lees 1985). Outside Great Britain, the greatest impact of industrialization was in creating the industrial cities of the German Ruhr, Wallonia, and Upper Silesia in Prussia, with a lesser effect on the ports and industrial areas of Scandinavia, Holland, and France. The impact of the Industrial Revolution was much more limited in Southern Europe (with the exception of Bilbao and the Asturias), and it was not until the end of the century that the impact of industrialization was seen in the northwest triangle of Italy (Turin, Genoa, Milan) and in Barcelona, Bilbao, Oporto, and Lisbon. As industrialization developed, it benefited the major cities that already existed.

By contrast, the rise in the nineteenth century of the modern metropolises of London, Berlin, Paris, and Vienna was associated with the making of nation-states and their empires. Capital cities benefited from the consolidation of states, the shift of political life onto the national level, and their capacity for control, as well as from industrial development and colonization. They absorbed a large part of the flow of migration, thus providing sizable reserves of labor. They were the first beneficiaries of the transport revolution, from tramways to road and rail networks. As university cities and cultural centers, they were the focus of unrest and the sites of the political and social revolts that punctuated the nineteenth century. The great metropolis became the site of consumption, of department stores and wide avenues, of hyperstimulation that changed the urban cultural experience. This led also to physical transformation with the ever-increasing diffusion of urbanization around those large metropolises, hence the rise of suburbs, either working-class suburbs such as the red belt in Paris, or bourgeois suburbs where the middle classes abandoned the center of English cities. The rise of the large metropolis then became an American phenomenon: New York and Chicago, and later Los Angeles, gradually replaced European cities in the urban imagination of the modernist metropolis.

EUROPEAN CITIES IN THE EUROPEAN
UNION

The issue of cities of Europe and of European
cities experienced a resurgence in the 1980s, for
two reasons. Firstly, the growing field of comparative empirical urban research stressed the
growth and dynamism of middle-size cities all
over Europe. They were even booming in some
cases, such as in France or Scandinavia. Secondly, it was related to the question of European societies that emerged because of the
acceleration of the political project of European
integration and increased interdependence
between national societies, the rise of globalization, and the tensions within national societies.
Searching for common ground to define European societies in comparison with the US or
Japan, scholars such as Therborn (1985) identified European cities as a major distinctive
feature of European societies. Following Therborn's insights and building upon the work of
historians, Bagnasco and Le Galès (2000; Le
Galès 2002) developed the Weberian perspective to portray European cities as a particular
type of social structure within the urban world.
By contrast, a great deal of the urban sociological research of the 1990s was once again
examining convergence patterns between cities
throughout the world, either the rise of "global
cities" or the complete urbanization of the
world following the Los Angeles model. However, empirical research in Europe showed
different results.

Contemporary European cities are characterized by the following features. They are part of
an old urban system, consituted in the Middle
Ages, which has remained more or less stable –
meta-stability – over time. The industrial period appeared as a parenthesis in the making of
urban Europe; it had a massive impact only in
Britain and Germany. This long-term stability
is also visible: most cities are organized around
the center, main squares, monuments, and
buildings of power; in part the physical form
of the center has kept its organization and
symbolic meaning over time. Setting aside
London, Paris, the Randstad, and the Rhine/
Ruhr region, Western Europe is made up
mainly of medium-sized cities with populations
between 200,000 and 2 million. Even if one
takes into account the larger metropolitan area,

most European metropolitan areas are medium-
sized by contrast to the US and Japan, where
large metropolises dominate the urban map.
The form of the city, the existence of public
spaces, and the mix of social groups all suggest
the idea of a continuing sense of "urbanity"
characterizing European cities (Zijderveld
1998). Despite sprawl, the resistance of the
old city centers epitomizes their peculiarity.
One can take the example of public collective
transport together with pedestrian areas and
cycle paths to demonstrate the strength of the
idea of the European city.

Beyond this long-term stability, and by sharp
contrast to the literature on the urban crisis in
the US and the UK or the rise of global cities,
medium-sized European cities have enjoyed
considerable economic and often demographic
growth and dynamism since the early 1980s
(but not everywhere; growth has been less in
Southern Europe in particular).

In order to explain this dynamism of medium-sized European cities – with the notable
exception of the UK – several points need to be
noted. Firstly, European cities are characterized
by a mix of public services and private firms,
including a robust body of middle-class and
lower-middle-class public sector workers (about
a third of the jobs on average), who constitute
a firm pillar of the social structure. They are
organized in trade unions and political parties,
and support public investment in cities.

A second point worth mentioning is the fact
that European cities, although they are gaining
more autonomy, are still structured and organized within European states – in particular,
welfare states. According to OECD figures,
Western European state taxes represent over
45 percent of annual GDP, in contrast to 32
percent in the US. This huge gap then translates into jobs in social services, education, and
so on, which are crucially concentrated in
cities. The social structure of medium-sized
European cities is therefore a major element
of continuous political support for investment
in urban amenities, services, and utilities.
Moreover, because of the ongoing decentralization trend in most European countries, except
in the UK, an average of about 60 percent of
public investment is now controlled by local
authorities in Europe and more importantly
in cities, hence there is a constant flow of

investment in collective services in the cities, in particular in schools, hospitals, social services, housing, planning, transport, culture, and so on.

Thirdly, European cities are becoming more European, in the sense that the institutionalization of the European Union (EU) is creating rules, norms, procedures, repertoires, and public policies that have an impact on most, if not all, cities. The EU also is a powerful agent of legitimation. By designing urban public policies and agreeing (under the influence of city interests) to mention the idea of "a Europe of cities" as one of the components of the EU, it is giving a boost to cities to act and behave as actors within EU governance. Now part of an increasing number of transnational networks, European cities are being recognized as such.

Fourthly, the economy is becoming more urban and, beyond global cities, medium-sized regional capitals – usually well equipped in research centers, universities, and diversified economic sectors – have benefited in terms of job growth. Last but not least, the continuing representation of the city as a whole, as well as the increased legitimacy of political elites in sustaining and reinventing the idea of European cities, has helped the making of modes of governance of European cities.

EUROPEAN CITIES AS INCOMPLETE LOCAL SOCIETIES AND POLITICAL ACTORS?

Beyond the relevance of the category "European cities" (for a debate see Kazepov 2004), the updated Weberian perspective on studying cities suggests going beyond the fluidity of day-to-day interactions and encounters on the one hand and determinist globalization trends on the other (Marcuse & Van Kempen 2000). Cities may be more or less structured in their economic and cultural exchanges and their different actors may be related to each other in the same local context with long-term strategies, investing their resources in a coordinated way and adding to the riches of the social capital. In this case, the urban society appears as well structured and visible, and one can detect forms of (relative) integration. If not, the city reveals itself as less structured and as such no

longer a significant subject for study: somewhere where decisions are made externally by separate actors. This analysis suggests looking at the interplay and conflicts of social groups, interests, and institutions, and the way in which regulations have been put in place through conflicts and the logics of integration. Cities do not develop solely according to interactions and contingencies: groups, actors, and organizations oppose one another, enter into conflict, coordinate, produce representations in order to institutionalize collective forms of action, implement policies, structure inequalities, and defend their interests. This perspective on cities highlights the informal economy, the dynamism of localized family relations, the interplay of associations, reciprocity, culture and ways of life, the density of localized horizontal relations, and local social formations (Kazepov 2004).

European cities are not immune to common pressures in terms of immigration, rising inequalities, suburban sprawl, or network fragmentation. However, European cities remain strong within metropolitan areas in the making, governance issues are now more visible within European cities, as are the interdependence and interrelation between different actors and organizations – all things that used to be represented and made visible on the national and European scene. This new-found visibility of interdependence gives opportunities to social and political actors to be involved in modes of urban governance or, by contrast, to increase the fragmentation and dislocation of European cities. European cities have not (yet?) been dislocated and they have considerable resources on which to draw in adapting to or resisting the new frame of constraints and opportunities.

SEE ALSO: Consumption, Urban/City as Consumerspace; Global/World Cities; Metropolis; Urbanization; Weber, Max

REFERENCES AND SUGGESTED READINGS

Bagnasco, A. & Le Galès, P. (Eds.) (2000) *Cities in Contemporary Europe*. Cambridge, Cambridge University Press.

Crouch, C. (1999) *Social Changes in Western Europe*. Oxford, Oxford University Press.

Hohenberg, P. & Hollen Lees, L. (1985) *The Making of Urban Europe*. Harvard, Harvard University Press.

Kazepov, Y. (Ed.) (2004) *Cities of Europe: Changing Context, Local Arrangements, and the Challenge to Urban Cohesion*. Blackwell, Oxford.

Le Galès, P. (2002) *European Cities, Social Conflicts, and Governance*. Oxford, Oxford University Press.

Marcuse, P. & Van Kempen, M. (Eds.) (2000) *Globalizing Cities: A New Spatial Order?* Oxford, Blackwell.

Pirenne, H. (1956) *Medieval Cities: Their Origins and the Revival of Trade*. Doubleday Anchor, Garden City, NY.

Therborn, G. (1985) *European Modernity and Beyond*. Sage, London.

Tilly, C. (1990) *Coercion, Capital, and European States, AD 990–1990*. Oxford, Blackwell.

Tilly, C. & Blockmans, W. (Eds.) (1994) *Cities and the Rise of States in Europe*. Westview Press, Boulder, CO.

Weber, M. (1978) *Economy and Society*. University of California Press, Berkeley.

Zijderveld, A. C. (1998) *A Theory of Urbanity*. Transaction, New Brunswick, NJ.

citizenship

Jack Barbalet

Citizenship refers to membership in a political community organized as a territorial or national state. The nature and content of citizenship varies with the form of state. Citizenship in the classic Greek *polis*, for instance, provided membership to a political elite, whereas modern liberal democratic citizenship provides opportunity to vote once every 3 or 4 years in a political election cycle. Sociological theories, however, recognize that citizenship has more than a mere political dimension.

Types of citizenship can be characterized in terms of two distinct axes or dimensions, one being *access* to citizenship status and the other being the *quality* of the rights and duties that attach to citizenship. Rules of access to citizenship separate citizens from non-citizens. Two alternative legal possibilities include *jus sanguinis* or citizenship by descent and *jus soli* or citizenship by birthplace. Which of these operates can have large consequences for persons

who have moved across national boundaries either through the internationalization of economic activity and labor markets or the transformation of political units, both of which have relocated significant numbers of people transnationally over the last century.

Under conditions of *jus sanguinis* it is not sufficient to be born in a country to have access to its citizenship. To be a German or a Japanese citizen, for instance, it is not sufficient to be born in Germany or Japan. In these cases citizenship is based on descent or appropriate ethnic-cultural qualities and birth in its territory has no bearing on access to citizenship, even for second- and third-generation settlers. The range of possibilities under *jus soli* arrangements, on the other hand, is broader. American and Australian citizenship, for instance, can be acquired by virtue of being born in those countries. French citizenship, on the other hand, is attributed to a person born in France if at least one parent was also born in France (or a French colony or territory prior to independence). The legal requirements of acquisition of citizenship by naturalization are also quite variable between nation-states.

The second axis of citizenship, which is that of quality, refers to what is provided by formal membership of a political community once it is attained. The quality of citizenship comprises the rights and duties that are available to persons as citizens. The rights and duties of citizenship include not only those of political participation but also those that relate to legal and social capacities. Marshall (1950), for instance, distinguishes civil, political, and social citizenship.

The civil component of citizenship, according to Marshall, consists of those rights and duties that derive from legal institutions and especially courts of law. Civil rights include equal treatment before the law, rights of contract and property, and freedom from constraint by the state. Political rights are typically understood as rights of participation in the nation's political processes and especially the right to vote and stand for election. The social rights of citizenship are described by Marshall as rights to a basic level of material well-being through state provision independently of a person's market capacities. Other writers have added to these three sets of rights, as when Janoski (1998), for instance, includes participation rights along with civil, political, and social rights. Accounts of the quality of citizenship have also been supplemented by reflection on recent social movements, which lead to consideration of rights associated with gender, ethnic, and green citizenship, to which we shall return.

The analytic distinction between different rights of citizenship in Marshall's account is also a historical narrative of the development of citizenship and, within that development, of the relationship between citizenship and social class. Also, this historic developmental account of citizenship says something important about its institutional basis. Marshall's distinction between civil, political, and social rights operates in the context of an account of the incremental development of citizenship in England from the eighteenth century. At this time legal innovations functioned to oppose and undermine the remnants of feudal privilege that had persisted in English law. In that sense the advent of civil rights of citizenship was progressive. At the same time, civil rights encouraged market relations that gained strength during the eighteenth century, and they therefore harmonized economic and social inequalities characteristic of the class system. By the mid-nineteenth century the industrialization that grew out of the market economy produced a working-class movement that, among other things, laid claim to political membership in the states within which they lived and worked. The resulting parliamentary reform led to political rights becoming rights of citizenship rather than an adjunct to the privilege of property ownership. Here arises an element of antagonism between citizenship and the class system because, through political citizenship, organized electors without economic power can potentially influence market forces through the political process. This antagonism become more pronounced in the twentieth century, according to Marshall, because through social citizenship, won by working-class voters, there arises participation as a right in a material culture that was previously the preserve of those who enjoyed class advantage.

Unlike a number of philosophical accounts of rights and citizenship that operate in terms of moral or ethical categories, Marshall's

sociological account underscores rights institutionally. This therefore avoids the problem of inappropriate historical judgments that are based on the values the writer takes to the situation they treat rather than those that emerge out of it directly. Marshall understands citizenship rights to exist in terms of the institutions that are pertinent to them. Civil rights are based on the courts of law, political rights on representative institutions, and social rights on the social services of the welfare state, including public education. Without the appropriate institutions, the corresponding rights have no basis. This approach does not deny aspirations for particular rights. In fact, such aspirations to as yet unachieved or denied rights in reality have the practical task of institution building to secure and sustain those rights. The virtue of this approach, then, is that it encourages an understanding of the history and practice of citizenship through a grasp of the development and role of institutions.

Citizenship is generally treated in terms of the rights that are available to citizens and denied to non-citizens, but there are also duties of citizenship and the relationship between rights and duties in citizenship has drawn interest from sociological writers (Janowitz 1980; Janoski 1998). Citizenship duties or obligations arguably have a role in the maintenance of social order and integration, but for most writers this aspect of citizenship remains secondary to the importance of citizenship in providing otherwise unobtainable capacities to persons through the rights of citizenship. One difficulty with the notion of obligation is that it is not co-terminous with the concept and practice of rights: it is erroneous to assume that to each right there is a corresponding obligation. This is because, as we have seen, citizenship rights are institutionally bounded and the relevant institutions require an organizational form; obligations or duties, on the other hand, operate as imperatives for citizens and as exhortations for compliance are morally, politically, and ideologically bounded. The disarticulation of rights and obligations is further evident in the fact that many obligations exacted by the nation-state are not confined to citizens but also embrace non-citizens, including the obligations of taxation, conformity to the law, exercise of social tolerance, and so on.

Marshall's influential account of citizenship has a social, political, and intellectual context that no longer obtains, and the changes that have occurred since the time his account was written lead to necessary modifications in the understanding of citizenship it provided. The full-employment policies of the immediate post-World War II period in all western societies meant that social citizenship could be fiscally supported by a large and growing workforce. Structural economic and demographic changes since that time have meant that the financial basis of the social services required for social citizenship are no longer as secure as they were. When unemployment was typically "frictional" – associated with moving from one job to another – then high levels of unemployment benefits did not impose a strain on state financial support for social citizenship. When unemployment becomes "structural" and long term, and the non-working sector of the population is extended further through increasing numbers of aged persons coupled with a declining birth rate, then the social services can draw on only a diminishing tax base and funding for social rights of citizenship can no longer be taken for granted.

Marshall's assumption of a full-employment economy is coupled with another, namely that the basic social unit is the family, comprising a male breadwinner and a dependent female spouse and children. This, too, can no longer be assumed, which also has consequences for consideration of citizenship. Since the 1970s in all western economies erosion of the share of real national income going to wage and salary earners has been so severe that earnings of male breadwinners are insufficient to maintain a traditional family. At the same time there has been a massive increase in the workforce of women with dependent children. The economic decomposition of the traditional family means that the individual and not the family is the basic social unit. Marshall's citizen was sexually neutral because uniformly male. The labor-force significance of economically independent females means that the citizen is now undeniably sexed. Sexually distinct perspectives on citizenship rights are now unavoidable.

There are a number of issues of "green" citizenship that Marshall and his generation did not face, associated with a now unacceptable assumption of unlimited resources. Once it is accepted that natural resources are inherently limited two tenets of green citizenship arise. First, in a world of non-renewable resources the community of citizens must include an intergenerational membership such that the rights of as yet unborn citizens feature in present calculations of distributive well-being. Second, as some writers have argued (Turner 1986), an ecological perspective on citizenship means that natural objects such as land, trees, and animals must be accorded citizenship rights. Given the difficulties of claiming and enforcing such rights this concern might be translated to issues concerning new duties or responsibilities of citizenship. In any event it has to be acknowledged that the environment upon which national well-being depends is not confined to national boundaries. The radioactivity released by the Chernobyl disaster in 1986 spread across Western Europe. Green citizenship raises questions of transnational citizenship.

A further development that has affected issues of citizenship is the changing composition of national communities, through migration, from culturally homogeneous populations to mosaics of national, ethnic, religious, and racial diversity. These changes pose problems of integration and social segmentation. From the migrant's point of view this is the issue of access to the rights of citizenship, a problem classically treated by Parsons (1969) in his discussion of the citizenship consequences of internal migration and racial diversity in the US. Today, the question of access to rights by outsiders is associated with the broader questions of the increasing internationalization of national economies and displacement of persons through war and national decomposition and the consequent movement of large numbers of people across national boundaries. This raises questions concerning the impact of international organizations on national citizenship rights. Indeed, in Western Europe today there are in effect different levels of citizenship participation insofar as non-national residents may have civil and social rights and even certain political rights by virtue of the laws of their host countries that operate in terms of EU-sponsored human rights protocols and other transnational directives.

SEE ALSO: Capitalism; Democracy; Markets; Migration and the Labor Force; Sexual Citizenship; Welfare State

REFERENCES AND SUGGESTED READINGS

Barbalet, J. M. (1989) *Citizenship: Rights, Struggle and Class Inequality*. University of Minnesota Press, Indianapolis.

Brubaker, R. (1992) *Citizenship and Nationhood in France and Germany*. Harvard University Press, Cambridge, MA.

Janoski, T. (1998) *Citizenship and Civil Society: A Framework of Rights and Obligations in Liberal, Traditional and Social Democratic Regimes*. Cambridge University Press, New York.

Janowitz, M. (1980) Observations on the Sociology of Citizenship: Obligations and Rights. *Social Forces* 59(1): 1–24.

Marshall, T. H. (1950) *Citizenship and Social Class*. Cambridge University Press, Cambridge.

Parsons, T. (1969) Full Citizenship for the American Negro? In: *Politics and Social Structure*. Free Press, New York, pp. 252–91.

Turner, B. S. (1986) *Citizenship and Capitalism: The Debate over Reformism*. Allen & Unwin, London.

Vogel, U. & Moran, M. (1991) *The Frontiers of Citizenship*. St. Martin's Press, New York.

city

Alan Bairner

Cities were a feature of all the great ancient civilizations. Relatively small by modern standards, they nevertheless facilitated a far more diverse range of activities than was possible in other forms of human settlement. The city and the urban way of life that accompanies it, however, inasmuch as they have interested sociologists, are of more recent origin and are closely linked to the rise of industrialism.

In the nineteenth century the city and urbanism began to exert a powerful fascination upon social theorists and sociologists. Marx and Engels saw the rise of the city as an integral part of human development and they recognized, as did Weber, that differing cultural and historical conditions lead to different types of cities. In addition, however, they argued that the human condition experienced in cities is the product of economic structure. Engels went so far as to examine the human condition of the working class in nineteenth-century Manchester in what has come to be seen as a pioneering exercise in social inquiry.

Tönnies drew an unfavorable contrast between the social bonds that are experienced in rural societies (*Gemeinschaft*) with the much weaker ties that are common to towns and cities (*Gesellschaft*). This pessimistic view of life in the city was shared by Simmel, who regarded the unique characteristic of the modern city as the intensification of nervous stimuli contrasting with the slower, more habitual and even quality of rural existence. Durkheim, on the other hand, while acknowledging that city life brings with it impersonality, alienation, and the potential for conflict, also believed that the organic solidarity that emerges in the city can be the basis of a deeper form of social cohesion than that of mechanical solidarity found in pre-urban societies.

The industrial age made urban centers increasingly attractive to immigrants: both internal, from the rural hinterland, and external, from other parts of the world. As a consequence, all modern industrial societies became heavily urbanized and since the second half of the twentieth century the global process has also become an increasing element in the social transformation of developing countries.

In this period, cities have become the centers of economic, industrial, and political power. But how have they impacted on social life? Opinions vary today just as they did among the classical sociological thinkers of the nineteenth and early twentieth centuries. For some, cities are dynamic, full of creative energy and offering a previously unknown range of diverse opportunities. For others though, they are infernal places, characterized by violence, crime, corruption, and ill health. More realistically, they are a blend of the attributes that are indicated at both ends of this spectrum of opinion. What is undeniable, however, is that they are unequal and divided social spaces that have continued throughout the twentieth and into the twenty-first centuries to be the objects of sociological analysis and research.

The study of cities has involved focusing on the built environment, on the social life or urban people, and on the relationship between the two. A hugely significant work in this respect was *The Death and Life of Great American Cities* written in 1961 by Jane Jacobs. However, the origins of urban sociology can be traced to the work of the Chicago School in the 1920s and 1930s and in particular to Robert E. Park, Ernest Burgess, and Louis Wirth. Park was the founder of an ecological approach which likened cities to biological organisms. Many subsequent studies of cities have been influenced by this approach despite the fact that its emphasis on the natural development of the city ignores the importance of economic and political decisions about planning.

Wirth was responsible for introducing the idea of urbanism as a way of life. Extending the concerns of earlier social thinkers, he argued that in cities people may live in close proximity but they do not truly know each other. Weak social bonds, a more frenetic pace of life, and the centrality of competition rather than cooperation characterize their lives. Wirth's views on the impersonal nature of modern urban life were highly influential. It has often been suggested, however, that both he and Park were overly influenced by their experiences of North American cities. Indeed, even in the US at the time they were writing, although arguably less so today, it was possible to find close-knit communities resembling villages which helped to preserve ethnic difference even in huge ethnically diverse cities such as Chicago itself and New York.

There is no doubt, however, that the idea of life in the city as being a distinctive form of human existence has continued to figure in sociological debate. Indeed, this concern has intensified with the emergence of what is generally known as the post-industrial city. Since it was previously thought that the modern city and industrialism are inextricably linked, the idea of a city with very little industrial activity has proved difficult to understand.

More recent major contributors to the sociological understanding of the city include Henri Lefebvre, David Harvey, and Manuel Castells. Like Simmel, Lefebvre was interested in the relationship between the social space of the city and the mental life of its citizens. In addition, he sought to demonstrate the extent to which urbanization in and of itself has come to replace

industrialization as the key determinant of capitalist accumulation. For Harvey and Castells, however, the city remains a product of industrial capitalism rather than its major driving force. More specifically, according to Harvey, industrial capitalism continually restructures space and, for that reason, urbanism has been an important product – arguably the most visible product – of industrialization. For Castells, the spatial form of the city is bound up with the overall mechanism of its development. That is to say, unlike the Chicago School, he does not regard the city solely as a distinct location, but also as an integral part of the entire process of collective consumption. In such ways has the sociological debate moved from seeing cities as natural spatial processes to socially and physically constructed features of the social and economic systems of power. In so doing, however, this intensely theoretical contemporary debate has tended to inspire far less empirical research than was generated by the Chicago School.

That said, theoretical considerations alone have undeniably underpinned numerous emerging concerns within the overall study of the city. These include suburbanization, inner-city decay, urban conflict, urban renewal (including gentrification and civic boosterism), and spatially identifiable inequalities. Sharon Zukin, for example, has powerfully demonstrated the ways in which access to "public" spaces in modern cities is increasingly controlled. Studies have also taken into account the relationship between globalization and the city, including the emergence of what are described as global cities, the rapid growth of cities in the developing world, and the city as the agent of consumer capitalism.

SEE ALSO: Arcades; Built Environment; Chicago School; Cities in Europe; City Planning/Urban Design; Gentrification; Lefebvre, Henri; Park, Robert E. and Burgess, Ernest W.; Simmel, Georg; Urbanism/Urban Culture

REFERENCES AND SUGGESTED READINGS

Castells, M. (1977) *The Urban Question: A Marxist Approach.* Edward Arnold, London.
Engels, F. (1892) *The Condition of the Working Class in England in 1844.* Allen & Unwin, London.

Hannerz, U. (1980) *Exploring the City: Inquiries Toward an Urban Anthropology*. Columbia University Press, New York.

Harvey, D. (1973) *Social Justice and the City*. Edward Arnold, London.

Jacobs, J. (1992 [1961]) *The Death and Life of Great American Cities*. Vintage Books, New York.

Lefebvre, H. (2003) *The Urban Revolution*. University of Minnesota Press, Minneapolis.

Reiss, A. J., Jr. (Ed.) (1964) *Louis Wirth on Cities and Social Life*. University of Chicago Press, Chicago.

Short, J. F., Jr. (Ed.) (1971) *The Social Fabric of the Metropolis: Contributions of the Chicago School of Urban Sociology*. University of Chicago Press, Chicago.

Zukin, S. (1995) *The Cultures of Cities*. Blackwell, Oxford.

city planning/urban design

Regina M. Bures

City planning encompasses the policies and processes that influence the development of towns, cities, and regions. While planning occurred in early cities, it was not until the early twentieth century that city (urban) planning emerged as a distinct discipline. In response to the rapid growth of cities that accompanied industrialization, early urban sociologists sought to address the social issues that emerged. Early planning initiatives were related to the conservation movement and sought to address the physical and social ills that had arisen in the industrial cities. By the late twentieth century, most city governments housed a planning board or agency.

Social structures and processes shape the spatial form of the city. Because city planning can shape the spatial form of cities, it also has an impact on the social life of cities. A number of dimensions of this reciprocal relationship between planning and the social environment are of interest to sociologists. These include: the relationship between the physical nature of the city and social relations in the city; the influence of cultural and social divisions on the planning process; the effect of planning on the distribution of groups and resources in cities; and the role of planning in creating and maintaining social divisions.

Addressing the impact of the physical nature of the city on social relations was the goal of the early planning movement. Plans for utopian communities, such as Robert Owen's New Harmony, sought solutions to the social problems of the industrial cities. In his seminal book *Garden Cities of Tomorrow* (1902), Ebenezer Howard's self-contained, decentralized garden cities with their surrounding greenbelts were the antithesis to the industrial towns of the time. More recently, the focus has been on creating green space in existing cities.

The desire for aesthetically appealing cities fueled the popularity of the City Beautiful Movement. This trend emerged following the Chicago Columbian World Expedition of 1893 with its neoclassically designed White City. The City Beautiful Movement, which had a strong influence on the design of public buildings and spaces in the United States, however overlooked the issue of housing and did little to improve the immediate environs for poorer city residents.

This disconnect reflects the extent to which different cultural and social groups may influence the planning process. While groups with more resources may favor large-scale planning, residents with fewer resources may desire better housing or city services. In a market economy, individuals with more resources will pay more for better housing and services. Developers will offer better housing, shopping, and other amenities if they are able to make a profit. The strength of a city's culture or sense of place will affect the impact of capital on development and planning.

The potential for conflicting interests between social groups in the planning process can be illustrated by looking at the social consequences of using gentrification as a redevelopment tool. Gentrification can be an important element of urban redevelopment plans by helping communities maintain coherent identities and architectural integrity. Yet gentrification may also lead to the displacement of existing communities. Minorities and less affluent residents may be displaced by rising rents and property values.

The causes and consequences of city planning fall under two sociological perspectives: the ecological perspective, which overlaps significantly with neoclassical economic theory, describes the effects of planning and development in terms of housing supply and the preferences of specific groups.

Development within cities is shaped by the combination of social, political, and economic factors that are unique to that city. Sociologists are also concerned with the effect of planning on the distribution of groups and resources in cities. The perspective most often associated with this is human ecology (Chicago School), which emphasizes the spatial distribution of groups within cities and draws heavily from neoclassical economics. On the other hand, the political economy perspective sees development as a process shaped primarily by political and economic forces. As an applied political economy perspective, the Los Angeles School of urban sociology uses the fragmented social and spatial landscape of Los Angeles to illustrate the characteristics of the new postmodern city (see Dear 2002).

Both of these perspectives are useful for understanding the consequences of urban planning and development processes. But to fully understand these consequences, one must consider the interplay between the physical and social environment of the city. As plans are enacted and development occurs, changes in the physical environment will affect the social environment as well.

The impacts of urban planning on the social environment evolve over time. Two key issues in urban redevelopment debates, neighborhood succession and involuntary dislocation, follow from the ecological and political economy perspectives. The changing ecology of communities leads to neighborhood succession, while changes in the political economy of an area may result in the dislocation of residents.

Planning often plays a role in creating and maintaining social divisions. Planning determines the land use and transportation patterns that shape the community life of cities. There is a distinct spatial dimension here. Social divisions manifest themselves in space as segregation, the physical separation of members of one racial, ethnic, social, or economic group from members of another group.

In the United States, local governments control zoning which can restrict access to and the use of land; however, individuals and market forces shape the development of new land. The type and density of housing in a neighborhood will predispose it to specific social groups. Neighborhoods organize life chances in the same sense as do the more familiar dimensions of class and caste.

Also of interest to sociologists are cross-national and historical comparisons of urban policies and planning strategies. Such studies examine changes over time in planning and planning outcomes. Often these offer examples of different types of governmental interactions. For example, in the United States much more emphasis is placed on private development. On the other hand, government control over land and use of public transportation are greater in European cities.

Current emphasis in sociological research and theory on urban planning builds on these themes in a number of ways. These include solutions to housing inequality, urban sprawl, and the impact of the created environment on social relations. Each of these topics incorporates an explicit awareness of the spatial dimension, reflecting a common theme of the relationship between the planned and social environments.

Housing costs and neighborhood status are closely related. At the same time, many city residents with lower incomes have a difficult time finding affordable housing. A number of factors come into play: market factors, institutional factors, and individual preferences.

Market factors such as accessibility, rents, and "best use" determine urban land use and structure. When the concern is maintaining property values, institutional mechanisms such as zoning and homeowners' associations seek to maintain homogeneity within neighborhoods.

To address the issues of density and urban sprawl, there is a focus on planning strategies to contain sprawl. Planning strategies for minimizing sprawl include smart growth policies, growth boundaries, and New Urbanist communities. Smart growth policies seek to shape city growth in a manner that limits sprawl. As an example of smart growth policies, growth boundaries set limits to development, often specifying conservation buffers to protect open land.

A second strategy for addressing sprawl was pioneered by the architects Andres Duany and Elizabeth Peter-Zyberk. Their "New Urbanism" principles were grounded in the belief that the spatial design of a neighborhood can influence the development of community: communities built using the principles of the New Urbanism that communities should be walkable and include both residential and commercial elements. New Urbanist communities are more like small towns than suburban developments. The limitation of this planning style is that it assumes that physical features of neighborhoods that are associated with traditional neighborhoods, such as front porches, will increase street-level activity and interaction among residents.

A number of recent studies have examined the relationship between the social and the created environment, focusing specifically on the diversity of the created environment. In the absence of a historical culture or sense of place, planning offers a market-oriented model of community. Analysis of the social consequences of development and redevelopment processes can illustrate the limitations of such created environments.

The planning process shapes the city, but the city's physical, political, and economic environments shape the planning process. As sociologists study the urban environment they often focus on the social and historical components, and the spatial components are often overlooked. The nature of the give-and-take relationship between the social environment of the city and the urban planning process means that there are abundant opportunities to study the impact of planning processes and policies on the social environment of our cities.

Modern computing technology and the increased interest in using mapping techniques to complement other social science methods have made it much easier for urban scholars to study the consequences of planning decisions at both the neighborhood and city levels. Understanding urban processes at multiple levels is important with the awareness that social processes at the individual level cannot

be accurately inferred from aggregate data and individual-level processes (ecological fallacy). While qualitative approaches often unpack the meaning and social significance of places, quantitative studies are used to better understand the social context in which planning decisions are made as well as their social implications.

To understand the developmental patterns within a city, it is useful to examine its historical patterns of land use and the degree to which these patterns have changed. The social environment is both time and context dependent. Thus, an approach to urban development that includes both socially and spatially conscious methods is most appropriate. Current efforts in sociology include the integration of spatial perspectives into theory and methodology into the discipline.

Perhaps the biggest limitation of planning is that the planning process is so often divorced from the social environments that it will affect. Groups with little economic or political power are often overlooked in the planning process. While change is an important part of the urban environment, we need to consider more innovative approaches to maintaining community and social environment while preserving the physical environment. As we learn more about the relationship between maintaining communities and restoring communities, urban sociologists and planners should seek to balance the social, political, and economic dimensions of cities.

SEE ALSO: Chicago School; Gentrification; Growth Machine; Levittown; Mumford, Lewis; New Urbanism; Park, Robert E. and Burgess, Ernest W.; Urban Ecology; Urban Renewal and Redevelopment

REFERENCES AND SUGGESTED READINGS

Dear, M. (2002) Los Angeles and the Chicago School: Invitation to a Debate. *City and Community* 1(1): 5–32.
Fainstein, S. S. (2000) New Directions in Planning Theory. *Urban Affairs Review* 35(4): 451–78.
Jacobs, J. (1961) *The Death and Life of Great American Cities*. Vintage, New York.

civil minimum

Yasushi Suzuki

According to Japanese political scientist Keiichi Matsushita, "civil minimum" is a minimum standard for living in urban society that should be assured by municipalities. It comprises social security, social overhead capital, and public health. Civil minimum is based on the right to life, and should be considered as the postulate of urban policies, decided through democratic procedures including citizen participation, and indicated by numerical goals. It may vary from municipality to municipality, but it should exceed the "national minimum."

The civil minimum was initially proposed in the late 1960s. The rapid economic growth of the time brought about massive immigration from rural to urban areas, and the national and local governments were required to develop urban infrastructures as soon as possible. However, the governments prioritized economic growth, preferentially investing in industrial infrastructures rather than public facilities and services for urban residents. As a result, problems such as air and water pollution, fetid odors, traffic congestion, and the deficiency of urban facilities such as fire stations, parks, schools, sanitation systems, hospitals, welfare institutions, and others became major issues of urban politics. In the early 1970s, coalitions of reformists including the Social Democratic and the Communist parties raised these issues and won elections for mayors and governors in some major cities and prefectures. The new reformist administrations set agendas based on the idea of a civil minimum. For example, the Tokyo Metropolitan Government, where economist Ryokichi Minobe was elected governor in 1967, formulated a mid-term plan for achieving the civil minimum quickly (1968), then developed social indicators for Tokyo (1973a), and published a long-term *Plan for Tokyo Metropolis with Plaza and Blue Sky* (1973b), in which "Plaza" signaled the principle of citizens' involvement and "Blue Sky" symbolized an ideal urban environment. The series of plans adopted by the Minobe administration embodied the idea of civil minimum. Although the minimum standards

for various areas were not easy to determine (Tokyo Metropolitan Government 1972), the idea of a civil minimum was adopted by about one-third of Japanese municipalities by the mid-1970s. Its impact on the local administrative structures was profound, since Japanese local governments have been supervised, and effectively ruled, by the national government for a long time.

Although the reformist administrations suffered from fiscal crises during the economic depression following the oil crises and were politically defeated in the late 1970s, the "civil minimum" standards were largely satisfied during the asset-inflated "bubble" economy in the late 1980s. Recently, in connection with the national reform of the local administration system in 2000, the civil minimum has been reinterpreted as criteria for local governments to provide public services under the principle of "subsidiarity" applied to the relationships between local and national governments, and social indicators have been considered as benchmarks that measure the specific goals and performances of public services (Matsushita 2003).

Thus, the term "civil minimum" has become well established in Japanese political and administrative language. It signifies a seminal idea on the principles of municipal policies and has contributed to facilitating the decentralization of the local administration system in Japan.

SEE ALSO: Environment and Urbanization; Human Rights; Local Residents' Movements; *Seikatsu/Seikatsusha*; Social Policy, Welfare State; Urban Policy

REFERENCES AND SUGGESTED READINGS

Matsushita, K. (1973) Civil Minimum and Urban Policy. *Contemporary Urban Policy X: Civil Minimum.* Iwanami-syoten, Tokyo, pp. 3–28.
Matsushita, K. (2003) *Civil Minimum Reconsidered: Benchmarks and Manifests.* Booklet of Saturday Lecturers on Local Self-Government, No. 92. Kojin-no-tomo sya, Tokyo.
Tokyo Metropolitan Government (1968) *Mid-Term Plan for Tokyo Metropolis: How to Achieve the Civil Minimum.* Tokyo.

Tokyo Metropolitan Government (1972) *Developing Social Wellbeing Indicators for Tokyo Metropolis by Using the Two-Criteria Method*. Tokyo.

Tokyo Metropolitan Government (1973a) *Tokyo Social Trends*. Tokyo.

Tokyo Metropolitan Government (1973b) *Plan for Tokyo Metropolis with Plaza and Blue Sky*. Tokyo.

civil religion

David Yamane

Civil religion refers to the cultural beliefs, practices, and symbols that relate a nation to the ultimate conditions of its existence. The idea of civil religion can be traced to the French philosopher Jean-Jacques Rousseau's *On the Social Contract* (1762). Writing in the wake of the Protestant–Catholic religious wars, Rousseau maintained the need for "social sentiments" outside of organized religion "without which a man cannot be a good citizen or faithful subject." The broader question motivating Rousseau concerned political legitimation without religious establishment.

Although he does not use the term, Durkheim's work in *The Elementary Forms of Religious Life* (1912) was clearly influenced by his countryman's concern for shared symbols and the obligations they articulate. Recognizing that "the former gods are growing old or dying," Durkheim sought a more modern basis for the renewal of the collective sentiments societies need if they are to stay together. He found that basis in the "hours of creative effervescence during which new ideals will once again spring forth and new formulas emerge to guide humanity for a time." Civil religious ideals arise from national civil religious rituals.

Robert Bellah's 1967 *Daedalus* essay "Civil Religion in America" brought the concept and its Rousseauian-Durkheimian concern into contemporary sociology. Bellah argued that civil religion exists alongside and is (crucially) distinct from church religion. It is actually a religious "dimension" of society, characteristic of the American republic since its founding.

Civil religion is "an understanding of the American experience in the light of ultimate and universal reality," and can be found in presidential inaugural addresses from Washington to Kennedy, sacred texts (the Declaration of Independence) and places (Gettysburg), and community rituals (Memorial Day parades). It is especially evident in times of trial for the nation like the Revolution and Civil War.

Like Rousseau and Durkheim, Bellah saw legitimation as a problem faced by every nation, and civil religion as one solution – under the right social conditions. Bellah argued in *Varieties of Civil Religion* (1980) that in premodern societies the solution consisted either in a fusion of the religious and political realms (in the archaic period) or a differentiation but not separation (in the historic and early modern periods). Civil religion proper comes into existence only in the modern period when church and state are separated as well as structurally differentiated. That is, a civil religion that is differentiated from both church and state is only possible in a modern society.

Its structural position relative to both church and state allows civil religion to act not only as a source of legitimation, but also of prophetic judgment. "Without an awareness that our nation stands under higher judgment," Bellah wrote in 1967, "the tradition of the civil religion would be dangerous indeed." By 1975, Bellah declared in *The Broken Covenant* that American civil religion was "an empty and broken shell" because it had failed to inspire citizens and lost its critical edge. Much of this nuance was lost on critics of Bellah and of the concept of civil religion, who often accused him of promoting idolatrous worship of the state, so much so that Bellah himself did not use the term in *Habits of the Heart* (1985) or thereafter, despite the substantive continuity from his earlier to his later work.

Although Bellah's concern was primarily normative, his essay stimulated considerable definitional and historical debates about American civil religion, as well as some empirical research. Systematizing and operationalizing civil religion in a way that Bellah's original essay did not, Wimberly (1976) found evidence for the existence of civil religion as a dimension of American society distinct from politics and organized religion. Some research also tested the concept of civil religion cross-nationally, finding unique constellations of legitimating myths and symbols in Israel, Italy, Japan, Mexico, Poland, and Sri Lanka.

Before a consensus could emerge on the meaning and reality of civil religion, however, the concept lost favor among sociologists. By 1989, James Mathisen was asking "Whatever happened to civil religion?" In fact, in Mathisen's (1989) account, interest in civil religion peaked just a decade after Bellah's essay was published. Part of what happened was the emergence of religious nationalism and fundamentalism worldwide. This highlighted the divisive aspects of religious politics and politicized religion over and against the potentially integrative effect of civil religion. Examining the American situation after the rise of the New Christian Right, Wuthnow (1988) found not a single civil religion, but two civil religions – one conservative, one liberal – in dispute and therefore incapable of creating a unifying collective consciousness. Shortly thereafter, Hunter dramatically captured this situation in the title of his 1991 book, *Culture Wars*.

By the 1990s, other concepts began to compete in the arena once dominated by civil religion, most notably "public religion" and concern with the role of religion in civil society. Where civil religion was principally treated as a cultural phenomenon, this recent work has been much more focused on institutions (e.g., Jose Casanova's 1994 *Public Religions in the Modern World*) and social movements (e.g., Richard Wood's 2002 *Faith in Action*). Even Bellah and his colleagues in *The Good Society* (1991) turned their attention to the institutional dimension of "the public church."

Whether or not future research and reflection is conducted in the name of "civil religion," the fundamental religio-political problem of legitimation remains. Sociologists in the future, therefore, will continue to grapple with the question to which civil religion is one answer, hopefully standing on the shoulders of Rousseau, Durkheim, and Bellah as they do so.

SEE ALSO: Durkheim, Émile; Religion; Religion, Sociology of

REFERENCES AND SUGGESTED READINGS

Gehrig, G. (1981) *American Civil Religion: An Assessment*. Society for the Scientific Study of Religion, Storrs, CT.

Hammond, P. E. (1976) The Sociology of American Civil Religion. *Sociological Analysis* 37: 169–82.

Mathisen, J. A. (1989) Twenty Years After Bellah: Whatever Happened to American Civil Religion? *Sociological Analysis* 50: 129–47.

Richey, R. E. & Jones, D. E. (Eds.) (1974) *American Civil Religion*. Harper & Row, New York.

Wimberly, R. C. (1976) Testing the Civil Religion Hypothesis. *Sociological Analysis* 37: 341–52.

Wuthnow, R. (1988) *The Restructuring of American Religion*. Princeton University Press, Princeton.

Civil Rights Movement

Aldon Morris

Just 50 years ago African Americans were a severely oppressed group. They did not enjoy many of the basic citizenship rights guaranteed by the US Constitution. This was especially true of the American South, where large numbers of black Americans resided. In fact, state laws explicitly denied many of these rights and prevailing social customs disregarded them altogether.

In the South black people were controlled by an oppressive social system known as the Jim Crow regime. Under Jim Crow, blacks were denied the franchise, barred from interacting with whites in public spaces, and were trapped at the bottom of the economic order, where they were relegated to the poorest paying and least desirable jobs. This inequality was buttressed by the ideology that blacks were genetically and culturally inferior and thus deserved their wretched place in the social order. This racial inequality and ideology was thoroughly entrenched in the fabric of American society because it had reigned supreme for two and a half centuries of slavery and the Jim Crow era that was established after the brief Reconstruction period that ended in the late nineteenth century. This oppressive system was backed by state laws and white violence utilized by white supremacist groups such as the Ku Klux Klan. It was condoned by the US Supreme Court, which declared in the 1896 *Plessey* v. *Ferguson* ruling that racial segregation did not violate the Constitution so long as separate facilities for blacks were equal to those of whites. Yet the most cursory examination of race relations made it glaringly clear that this premise was false.

As a result, there could be no denying that blacks were legally and socially stripped of the basic rights promised in a society that represented itself as the world's leading democracy. By the 1950s, blacks faced the dilemma that had dogged them for centuries: how could they wage a successful struggle to overthrow their oppression without being fatally crushed by a superior enemy? This question is the basic one that all oppressed people have had to address in their quest to attain freedom and justice.

The social movement is the vehicle available to oppressed people to overthrow oppression. A social movement is an organized collective effort by large numbers of people for the purpose of generating the social power required to initiate social change. The hallmark of the social movement is the use of unruly tactics and strategies to generate the power needed to usher in change despite resistance. The social disruption created by movements is essential to change precisely because conventional methods – lobbying, voting, legal action, and the like – are either unavailable or ineffective for oppressed people who are not constituents of established polities. While conventional methods are often used by social movements, they must be coupled with disruptive tactics to be effective. In short, effective social movements specialize in disruptive tactics because they undermine social order. Social disruption enables social movement leaders to demand change in exchange for the cessation of unruly protest, thus making it possible for social order to be reestablished.

THE RISE OF THE MODERN CIVIL RIGHTS MOVEMENT

The modern Civil Rights Movement that became a major social force in the mid-1950s was the means by which African Americans and

their supporters overthrew the Jim Crow regime. It is erroneous to assume that African Americans did not begin to fight for the overthrow of racial inequality until the 1950s. Indeed, the historic black freedom struggle began on the slave ships in the seventeenth century and continued throughout the slave and Jim Crow periods. This struggle intensified especially during and following World War II. This period gave rise to mass marches and protest rallies that demanded full equality for blacks in the military and the larger society. The labor and civil rights leader A. Philip Randolph explicitly called for nonviolent mass action by blacks modeled after the Gandhi movement to overthrow British rule. Powerful social movements that generate change have long histories usually rooted in prior struggles, protest organizations, leaders and politically conscious members of the oppressed masses who have participated in or been influenced by previous struggles. Thus, like other major movements, the Civil Rights Movement did not spring from thin air, but was rooted in a long history of struggle.

The modern Civil Rights Movement came of age in 1955 during the year-long Montgomery bus boycott organized by local black leaders and led by Martin Luther King, Jr., who would become the charismatic leader of the national Civil Rights Movement. In Montgomery, as in cities throughout the South, the black community was a victim of the racially segregated Jim Crow regime. All aspects of race relations in Montgomery were circumscribed by racial segregation, including the local buses, where blacks had to ride in the Jim Crow section located in the rear of the bus. On December 1, Rosa Parks was arrested for refusing to relinquish her seat to a white rider, thus violating Alabama segregation laws. Local black leaders organized a boycott of the buses that resulted in victory after an entire year of protest. This struggle became the model for the Civil Rights Movement that would occupy the world stage for over a decade.

The Montgomery bus boycott became an exemplary model for the larger Civil Rights Movement for several reasons. First, it was highly visible because it lasted a year and resulted in victory when the Supreme Court ruled that bus segregation in Montgomery was unconstitutional. Second, it championed nonviolent direct action as the unruly method of protest that could be effective because such peaceful and legal protest could not easily be crushed by white violence and resistance. Third, it revealed that an entire black community could be organized into a disciplined struggle. Prior to this movement, there were divisions and conflicts in Montgomery's black community. The boycott community solved this problem by forming a new protest organization – Montgomery Improvement Association – that combined all the political and voluntary organizations into one "organization of organizations" that mobilized and sustained the movement. Fourth, it demonstrated that the black church could be utilized as the movement's institutional and cultural framework to produce mobilization and solidarity through frequent mass meetings. Fifth, it proved that blacks themselves were capable of raising the bulk of the funds needed to finance the movement. Sixth, the Montgomery struggle catapulted Martin Luther King, Jr. into the charismatic leadership of the movement. His eloquent oratory and dedication attracted media attention, thus providing national and international visibility to the struggles by African Americans to overthrow the Jim Grow regime.

Similar protest movements in other Southern cities were organized within months of the Montgomery bus boycott. They embraced the same organizational, cultural, and tactical characteristics as the Montgomery movement. Within a short time, Dr. King, Ella Baker, Bayard Rustin, and other leaders of the local movements organized the Southern Christian leadership Conference (SCLC), the purpose of which was to organize and coordinate protest movements throughout the South to overthrow racial inequality. The National Association for the Advancement of Colored People (NAACP) (which had been formed in 1910 with similar goals) became active in the emerging movement. Because the NAACP championed the legal method, it addressed many of the legal issues and court challenges associated with protest. The Congress of Racial Equality (CORE), organized in 1942 to initiate nonviolent protest against racial segregation, also became active in the Civil Rights Movement by initiating protest. Despite tensions and rivalries, these

national organizations and the plethora of new local protest organizations constituted the infrastructure of the modern Civil Rights Movement. From this base, the new movement launched its attack on the Jim Crow regime.

The Civil Rights Movement encountered serious opposition from the Jim Crow regime and the white privileges it protected had no intention of passing into history without a fight. The white opposition responded to protest with mass arrests, racially motivated laws to stall the movement, economic reprisals, and strategic white violence designed to frighten participants into submission. In fact, the white opposition organized counter-movements designed to undermine civil rights protests and to bolster the racial status quo. Thus, the protest activities and the opposition it spun set the stage for dramatic confrontations that became the hallmark of the modern Civil Rights Movement. This tug of war between these two forces alerted the nation and the world to the magnitude of racism existing in the bosom of American democracy.

By 1960 the modern movement involved significant numbers of young blacks, but it was an adult-driven phenomenon. This changed significantly in the spring of 1960s when black college students began organizing sit-ins at racially segregated lunch counters. These sit-ins spread so rapidly across the South that they became known as the student sit-in movement. These student-led protests drew thousands of young people into the Civil Rights Movement and it mobilized thousands of adults who rallied to their support. Many of the sit-ins successfully desegregated lunch counters.

The leaders of the sit-ins, supported by Ella Baker of SCLC, decided they needed to become an organized and independent wing of the Civil Rights Movement. Following the sit-ins they organized a new protest organization, the Student Nonviolent Coordinating Committee (SNCC). The SNCC represented a dynamic force in the movement, for it involved young people full of idealism, relative freedom from economic pressures, and the absence of rigid time constraints. Thus, the SNCC joined the SCLC and CORE as the activist wing of the movement. In their efforts they were supported by the NAACP and the National Urban League. The young people of the SNCC inspired and ignited another force – white students largely of elite backgrounds from the North – who joined with them to overthrow Jim Crow and seek the realization of a robust democracy. Significant numbers of these students joined the sit-in movement and subsequent protests, adding to the strength of the Civil Rights Movements.

The Civil Rights Movement matured into a major social force during the 1960s. Its tactical repertoire of social disruption expanded and was increasingly deployed with razor-like precision to generate the political leverage needed to convince the economic and political rulers of the Jim Crow regime that it was in their interests to dismantle legally enforced racial segregation. Boycotts, mass marches, mass arrests, sit-ins, freedom rides, attempts to register at all-white schools, lawsuits, and other unruly tactics created economic and political chaos. The opposition used bombings, billy clubs, high-pressure water hoses, and attack dogs to try to put out the political fire created by the movement. These vicious attacks on peaceful demonstrators occurred as television cameras and satellites recorded the carnage for the world to witness. The brutal confrontations in the streets also put pressure on the federal government and courts to support the goals of the movement because of their unwillingness to appear to support open tyranny against black citizens while the world watched and examined how the leading democracy would respond to injustice while being gripped by a Cold War with the Soviet Union to determine which nation would emerge as the reigning superpower.

ACCOMPLISHMENTS

In a decade (1955–65) the formal Jim Crow regime was overthrown. In 1964 the federal government issued the 1964 Civil Rights Act, which barred discrimination based on race, sex, religion, or national identity. This Act snatched crucial power from the regime because in effect it reversed the 1896 *Plessey* v. *Ferguson* ruling by declaring that racial segregation had no place in America. This historic Act was a direct response to the 1963 Birmingham confrontation led by King and the thousands of protests it generated throughout the nation. Yet the dying regime still had life because the 1964 Civil

Rights Act did not seize the franchise for millions of Southern blacks. It was the 1965 Selma, Alabama protest and its march to Montgomery which served as both the symbolic capital of the Confederacy and the birthplace of the modern Civil Rights Movement that led to the franchise for Southern African Americans. These protests were massive and so was the brutal opposition, who responded by murdering several protesters while beating and tear-gassing hundreds more. As a result, President Lyndon Johnson worked for a federal Act that would land the vote in the hands of the descendants of slaves. In 1965 Johnson signed the Voting Rights Bill, thus making the franchise available to all eligible American citizens.

EXTERNAL OPPORTUNITIES

Movements are fought by those seeking change. Without such heroic struggles, oppression and injustice would be far more prevalent than it is today. Yet certain realities outside the protest group can affect the mobilization and the outcomes of social movements. This was true for the Civil Rights Movement. By the 1950s record numbers of blacks had migrated from the rural South to the urban cities of the North and South. Urban black communities developed stronger institutions, leaders, and economic resources than had been possible in the South. Thus, because of this urban migration, blacks possessed the economic and institutional resources that could sustain a protracted struggle. Additionally, by the late 1950s televisions and satellites made it possible for protest groups to dramatize their grievances to national and international audiences, thereby garnering their sympathy and support. Finally, the Civil Rights Movement gained additional strength because of the Cold War environment following World War II. It was a period in which the Soviet Union and the US struggled for world supremacy and each courted the colored nations of Africa and Asia who were attaining independence from European colonialism. The dramatic and brutal confrontations in American streets caused by protest severely hampered America's foreign policy aimed at attracting the support of the world's colored people. As a result, the executive branch of the government as well as the federal courts shifted toward supporting civil rights for blacks so that America could realize its global aspirations. The marriage of protest and these external developments combined to make the Civil Rights Movement a powerful social force.

POLITICAL AND SCHOLARLY OUTCOMES

The Civil Rights Movement became a national and international model for social change. It did so because of its exemplary organization, pioneering innovative tactics, cultural creativity, and success. This movement succeeded in revealing that oppressed people can play a crucial role in determining their fate. It taught that social movements are capable of generating the political leverage required for oppressed people to confront power holders and demand change and to do so effectively. In America it was not long before students, women, environmentalists, anti-war activists, gays and lesbians, farm workers, the disabled, and many other groups launched their own movements by drawing on the model, inspiration, and lessons learned from the Civil Rights Movement. This was also true in other parts of the world. For example, the anti-apartheid movement of South Africa, China's Pro-Democracy movement, Poland's Solidarity movement, and many others in Europe also drew lessons and inspiration from the American Civil Rights Movement. Its anthem "We Shall Overcome" has been adopted by numerous movements globally. The political impact of the Civil Rights Movement continues to be felt around the world.

The Civil Rights Movement has had a scholarly impact as well. Prior to this movement the dominant view among scholars was that movements were spontaneous, unorganized, non-rational, and highly emotional. They were viewed as exotic phenomena, usually disappearing before accomplishing significant goals. This scholarly consensus did not fit the basic characteristics and outcomes of the Civil Rights Movement. Rather than being spontaneous, that movement was anchored in longstanding institutions and cultural traditions of the black community. Indeed, organizational activity lay at the core of the movement. Because this movement resulted from a high degree of organizing, it could not be conceptualized as an unorganized enterprise. It was characterized by careful planning and strategic thinking and therefore could not be accurately described as driven by emotion. Because of its duration and the real goals it achieved, the movement evolved as an explicit political development that pursued unconventional avenues to achieve its goals. Partly as a response to this groundbreaking movement, scholars have fashioned a new view of social movements where organization, strategic thinking, cultural traditions, and political encounters figure heavily as explanatory factors in their analyses.

It is clear that racial inequality still exists in America and this is especially true from an economic standpoint. Thus, the Civil Rights Movement did not accomplish all of its goals, despite the fact that it changed American race relations substantially by overthrowing formal Jim Crow. Worldwide inequality is still a stark reality. The Civil Rights Movement proved that such inequalities can be attacked through social movements. Such movements are the vehicles by which the voice of the oppressed can make a difference.

SEE ALSO: Accommodation; *Brown v. Board of Education*; Charismatic Movement; Collective Action; Color Line; Direct Action; Labor Movement; Social Movements; Social Movements, Political Consequences of

REFERENCES AND SUGGESTED READINGS

Bartley, N. V. (1969) *The Rise of Massive Resistance.* Louisiana State University Press, Baton Rouge.
Branch, T. (1988) *Parting the Waters: America in the King Years, 1954–1963.* Simon & Schuster, New York.
Carson, C. (1981) *In Struggle: SNCC and the Black Awakening of the 1960s.* Harvard University Press, Cambridge, MA.
Evans, S. (1979) *Personal Politics: The Roots of Women's Liberation in the Civil Rights Movement and the New Left.* Vintage Books, New York.
Gamson, W. (1975) *The Strategy of Social Protest.* Dorsey Press, Homewood, IL.

Garrow, D. (1978) *Protest at Selma: Martin Luther King Jr. and the Voting Rights Act of 1965*. Yale University Press, New Haven, CT.

Gitlin, T. (1980) *The Whole World is Watching: Mass Media in the Making and Unmaking of the New Left*. University of California Press, Berkeley.

McAdam, D. (1982) *Political Process and the Development of Black Insurgency 1930–1970*. University of Chicago Press, Chicago.

Moody, A. (1968) *Coming of Age in Mississippi*. Laurel/Dell, New York.

Morris, A. D. (1984) *The Origins of the Civil Rights Movement: Black Communities Organizing for Change*. Free Press, New York.

Morris, A. D. & Staggenborg, S. (2005) Leadership in Social Movements. In: Snow, D. A., Soule, S. A., & Kriesi, H. (Eds.), *The Blackwell Companion to Social Movements*. Blackwell, Oxford.

Payne, C. (1995) *I've Got the Light of Freedom: The Organizing Tradition and the Mississippi Freedom Struggle*. University of California Press, Berkeley.

Piven, F. F. & Cloward, R. A. (1977) *Poor People's Movements: Why They Succeed, How They Fail*. Vintage, New York.

civil society

Larry Ray

Civil society is often understood as a defense against excessive state power and atomized individualism, which otherwise threatens to create conditions for authoritarianism. The term can be traced to Roman juridical concepts (*ius civile*), but its contemporary use to describe contractual relations, the rise of public opinion, representative government, civic freedoms, plurality, and "civility" first appeared in seventeenth and eighteenth-century political philosophy. Thomas Hobbes's theory of the sovereign state (Leviathan) was premised on the existence of two branches of society – political and civil – tied by a "social contract" between subjects and the state. Surrender of sovereignty to the state protected society from the war of all against all. Although the political system was the dominant part, the civil and political were mutually sustaining systems, in which private activity, while governed by sovereign laws, was otherwise bound only by conscience and the rules of civic association. Disputing Hobbes's negative

views of human nature, John Locke further enhanced the status of civil society as a space of association, contract, and property regulated by the law. When, for Locke, subjects entered a commonwealth of property they contracted authority to the state for their self-protection, but they did so conditionally, and political rule is answerable to law derived from natural rights that inhere in civil society.

In subsequent theories civil society became an autonomous sphere separate from and possibly opposed to the state. Based on limited networks of aristocratic men and an emerging public–private dichotomy, the model of free association and debate was often that of the coffee house in which public activity actually took place in small and exclusive social circles. Civil society theories were concerned to defend the idea of a space for public debate and private association at a time when such liberal principles were not widely shared. For Adam Ferguson (1966), the development of civil society reflected the progress of humanity from simple, clan-based militaristic societies to complex commercial ones. However, this process of social differentiation and loss of community threatened increased conflict and weakened the social fabric. Civil society has the potential to establish a new order requiring dispersal of power and office, the rule of law, and liberal (i.e., tolerant) sentiments, which secure people and property "without requiring obligation to friends and cabals." An important implication here is that civil society does not refer to just *any* kind of informal or private social relations, which exist in all societies, but to morally guided relations that make possible anonymous social exchanges and thereby facilitate social integration.

The classical tradition of civil society theory formulated a concept closely associated with liberal market values and community involvement. This idea links the Scottish moralists (e.g., Ferguson), Tocqueville, Durkheim, and contemporary writers such as Robert Putnam (1993). Active, voluntary, and informal groups and networks make for more stable democracy and protect against incursion by the state. Civil society thus has a recursive property – it protects against state incursion while strengthening the (liberal democratic) state. Conversely, the

flicts in commercial society and the demands of

society and the demands of

absence of civil society is both an explanation and reinforcement of authoritarianism.

However, an implicit tension between conflicts in commercial society and the demands of social peace was highlighted by Hegel, for whom civil society was divided between ethical life (*Sittlichkeit*) and egotistical self-interest. Objective Spirit achieves self-knowledge through differentiation into discrete spheres, which form a totality of the family (socialization towards moral autonomy), civil society (production, distribution, and consumption), and the state. Hegel's view of civil society anticipated Marx's critique of class polarization as "the conflict between vast wealth and vast poverty ... turns into the utmost dismemberment of will, inner rebellion and hatred" (Hegel 1967: 151). This will be overcome if the constitutional-legal state (*Rechtsstaat*) synthesizes ethical life with the public domain of civil society. But Marx dismissed civil society simply as the equivalent of bourgeois society, an arena of conflict, class oppression, and illusory emancipation. The proletarian victory would substitute for the old civil society a classless association in which there would be neither political power nor the antagonisms of civil society (Marx 1978).

Gramsci reintroduced the concept into Marxism in the 1920s when − attempting to combat economic reductionism − he defined civil society as a sphere of cultural struggle against bourgeois hegemony. This formulation was influential among Eurocommunist parties in the 1970s and 1980s, although ironically a significant revival of the concept came in the anti-communist revolutions of 1989. Here a central idea was to identify diverse social spaces for public discussion, local initiatives, and voluntary citizens' associations that were neither narrowly merged with the market nor adjuncts of the state. Arato (1991) described the revolutions of 1989 as "self-limiting," in that they eschewed central control of power and utopian visions of the future. Active citizens would replace communist power with self-managed civil societies and permanently open democracy. In the event many commentators view post-communist civil societies with disappointment, in the face of cultures of distrust, the habit of informal dealings, and the

strengthening of particularistic visions and elements (Misztal 2000).

Alongside and possibly supplanting national state–civil society relations, some suggest that there is a global civil society made up of international non-governmental organizations, transnational social movements, and digitally mediated social networks (Norris 2001). Although this idea has been influential, there is a conflict between the goal of creating transnational cosmopolitan values and the unregulated growth of world markets brought by global neoliberalism that has resulted in heightened levels of social inequality, which neither states nor international organizations have the capacity to address. Global political and corporate institutions are not (yet?) embedded within constraining networks of a global civil society and there is a risk here of an excessively elastic and insufficiently complex concept.

SEE ALSO: Democracy; Gramsci, Antonio; Individualism; Marx, Karl; Public Sphere; Transnational Movements

REFERENCES AND SUGGESTED READINGS

Arato, A. (1991) Social Theory, Civil Society and the Transformation of Authoritarian Socialism. In: Féher, F. & Arato, A. (Eds.), *The Crisis in Eastern Europe*. Transaction Books, New Brunswick, NJ, pp. 1–26.
Ferguson, A. (1966 [1767]) *An Essay on the History of Civil Society*. Edinburgh University Press, Edinburgh.
Hegel, G. W. F. (1967 [1821]) *Philosophy of Right*. Oxford University Press, Oxford.
Marx, K. (1978 [1847]) *The Poverty of Philosophy*. Foreign Languages Press, Peking.
Misztal, B. (2000) *Informality*. Routledge, London.
Norris, P. (2001) *Digital Divide − Civic Engagement, Information Poverty, and the Internet Worldwide*. Cambridge University Press, Cambridge.
Putnam, R. D. (1993) *Making Democracy Work: Civic Traditions in Modern Italy*. Princeton University Press, Princeton.
Ray, L. J. (2004) Civil Society and the Public Sphere. In: Nash, K. & Scott, A. (Eds.), *The Blackwell Companion to Political Sociology*. Blackwell, Oxford.

civilization and economy

Roberta Garner and Larry Garner

"The economy" is a social institution that is constructed and reproduced through human action, as human beings collectively produce their conditions of survival and well-being. In sociological perspective, "the economy" is not reified as a thing or mechanism apart from human actions, interaction, and relationships.

This definition of the economy guides sociological analysis of relationships between economic institutions and civilization – culture, ideology, art, law, religion, and prevailing forms of thought, feeling, and discourse.

THE INTEGRATION OF ECONOMY AND CULTURE

One sociological distinction is that between non-market societies and market societies as two broad categories of civilization. In the former, economic activities are embedded in cultural, social, and political institutions and limited by them. In market societies, the economy is clearly differentiated from such cultural, social, and political institutions, while at the same time it has powerful effects on them, creating a distinct form of civilization.

In *non-market societies*, market institutions are secondary or absent, and production and distribution are primarily embedded in kinship and/or hierarchical power relationships among status groups. Economic activities are limited or "hedged in" by norms of institutions in which they are embedded.

In early human societies, and still today in smaller societies, economic activities are inextricably linked with kinship, and roles associated with economic activities are kinship and gender roles (as suggested by the derivation of "economy" from Greek *oikos*, "household").

Societies of surplus extraction and redistribution emerged from kinship-based economies in the regions that produced "civilizations" in the traditional sense of the term – stratified, state-level societies. As subsistence activities became more productive and a surplus became available, ruling groups appropriated this surplus and used it not only to enrich themselves but also to build armies, organize large projects, and construct elite cultural and religious institutions. Kinship-based economic activities persisted at the local, micro level, but at the macro level civilizations became stratified. Slavery, tribute collection, and feudal serfdom are examples of stratification systems associated with surplus appropriation. These types of articulation can be seen, for instance, in classical antiquity, ancient China and India, MesoAmerican civilizations, African kingdoms, and European and Japanese feudalism. In these civilizations, production and distribution were closely tied to differential power between groups such as lords and serfs, slaveowners and slaves, tribute collectors and tribute bearers. In many instances, stratified groups (clans, castes, and distinct ethnic groups) were defined by ascribed characteristics, stable membership, and differentiated honor as well as power differences. These unequal groups were status groups, quite different from economically defined classes in market society. While many of these civilizations included market exchanges, the market remained a secondary or supplementary form of organizing distribution and had only a limited impact on production decisions; it was highly circumscribed by traditional rules, roles, and obligations.

Another type of society is comprised of *market societies* in which "the economy" is clearly differentiated from other social institutions. In market societies, decisions about production and distribution are linked to exchanges between buyers and sellers of products and services. These commodified, market relationships have a strong impact on non-economic institutions, relationships, norms, and culture. They shape a civilization organized around profit and commodification, as well as constant, rapid flux in social relationships, technology, and the human impact on the natural environment.

The modern era, after the European Middle Ages, saw the rise of market or capitalist societies in which markets became the major institutional form of economic activity. Production was increasingly for markets, not for household use nor for powerholders capable of extracting and redistributing goods. Market exchange for profit became the driving force of economic activity and accrued to private firms and individuals that owned productive property. Labor power was not organized through coercion as in slavery, corvée, and tribute collection, nor was it mobilized by traditional obligations; instead, it became a commodity traded in labor markets. Market institutions were closely linked with rational calculation and monetized or commodified relationships among individuals and groups. Status groups and traditional forms of authority declined in importance. Class inequality based on economic standing and market position replaced status group distinctions as the dominant form of social differentiation. Legal systems shifted toward juridical equality of individuals, at the same time that individuals' economic positions were highly unequal.

In the twentieth century there were attempts, most notably in the Soviet Union and China, to establish command or planned economies in which political institutions and decision-making in a centralized state organized production and distribution in lieu of market mechanisms. These forms of society not only are structurally different, but also constitute different civilizations, distinct in their culture and the values, discourses, ideas, and consciousness shared by their members. In the words of sociologist C. Wright Mills (1959), there are differences in the "varieties of men and women that prevail in this society." In this respect, one can identify a general link between economy and civilization.

CLASSICAL THEORY: ANALYZING THE EMERGENCE OF CAPITALIST CIVILIZATION

The systematic analysis of the relationship between "economy" and "civilization" began with the Enlightenment and the rise of modern nation-states interested in increasing their wealth and power by specific economic policies. The merits of mercantile and *laissez-faire* models of development intrigued theorists of this period, culminating in Adam Smith's thesis that self-regulating markets were the best way to enhance the wealth of nations. But even Smith warned of the deleterious social effects of the division of labor and specialization of skill: monotonous labor routines dull the

workers' senses and alienate workers from their work.

Almost 75 years later, Karl Marx and Friedrich Engels (1948 [1848]) provided a detailed, comprehensive, and critical look at the historical sequence of modes of production, each characterized by distinct economic activities, technical knowledge, and class relationships. Technology and economy are not conceptualized as reified "determining forces" but are themselves created in the context of interactions among human beings. In all historical societies, these interactions are patterned as class relationships. Corresponding to each mode of production are compatible political and ideological institutions that function to reproduce the class relationships associated with production. Each type of society constituted by a mode of production plus political and ideological institutions is a distinct social formation.

For Marx and Engels, there was an evolutionary sequence of social formations from primitive communism (no classes, no state, no literate culture), to slave societies and despotic kingdoms, and then, in some regions such as Western Europe and Japan, to feudal societies based on serfdom. Capitalism emerged from class struggles within feudal society. The capitalist ruling class, the bourgeoisie, oversaw an organization of social and economic life in which "the cash nexus" dominated all forms of social interaction. Marx and Engels envisioned the overthrow of capitalism by its exploited masses and the creation of a future society in which social relations and activities would no longer be driven by the logic of commercialization. In communist societies, class inequalities and the state would disappear, and thanks to a very high level of economic production and technical knowledge, human beings would be liberated from the division of labor and fixed economic roles. These fixed roles would be replaced by pleasurable activities in fluid accord with individual talents and changing dispositions (1970 [1845–6]).

Each social formation is characterized by ideas, values, discourses, art forms, ways of thinking, and ways of interacting – in short, a compact civilization – which mesh with the economic base. In the case of capitalism, we find commodification of human relationships, rapid social change, emergence of global

516 civilization and economy

culture, disintegration of traditional forms of authority, and an ideology of freedom and individualism.

The complex Marxist model, with its evolutionary sequence, dialectic of agency and structure, and emphasis on the strong but never reified role of the mode of production in shaping the civilization as a whole, has left an indelible mark on subsequent analysis of the relationships between economy and culture. Later theorists were often in "a debate with Marx's ghost" (Zeitlin 1997).

Three great classical sociologists of the beginning of the twentieth century – Max Weber, Georg Simmel, and Émile Durkheim – also focused on the role of economic activity in society. Like Marx and Engels, they show a deep ambivalence about the effects of capitalism on civilization, decrying its oppressive monetization of human relationships, yet recognizing that it swept away superstition, magical beliefs, caste-like status inequalities, and feudal oppression.

For Durkheim, even more than for Marx and Engels, "the economy" is not a separate reified structure but inextricably linked with the overall social order. He emphasized, for example, that capitalism's exchange relationships, in which each party at all times seeks to maximize gain, would be altogether socially unstable without a non-contractual base of contracts – the shared norm or value of the inviolability of contract. Like Marx and Engels, Durkheim was interested in the changing forms of the division of labor; he linked them to changing forms of social control and social cohesion, noting that as the division of labor became more complex, the normative order and collective conscience became less harsh, punitive, and undifferentiated. An advanced, complex division of labor, itself arising due to the material force of greater social density, can create a higher type of social cohesion. In advanced market societies, organic solidarity based on differentiation of functions and mutual dependency can replace mechanical solidarity, based on similarity and conformity. The resulting civilization is potentially a higher, more complex form in which diversity, individuation, and moral autonomy are more respected and highly developed, but in this evolution, there is always the risk of anomie,

a pathological loosening of normative regulation, as well as the disintegration of social bonds (Durkheim 1964 [1893]).

Georg Simmel, deeply influenced by Friedrich Nietzsche's attack on modern civilization, offered a critique of the money economy. Like Marx and Engels, he saw capitalism engendering a civilization in which money takes on a life of its own, infusing all aspects of social, cultural, and psychological life, and accentuating the individual's alienation from self and others. He concurred with Durkheim that capitalist civilization is characterized by feelings of limitlessness, especially limitless wants. In the money economy, social relationships are subordinated to exchange value and the impersonal calculation of monetary gain. Capitalist civilization produces social types that reflect the abstractness of money, its detachment from use value and specific experience. Among these types are the miser and the spendthrift, who appear to be opposites yet are linked in their exclusive focus on the potentiality of money. Simmel also pointed out that when individuals leave rural communities and enter the urban money economy, they experience a kind of liberation: they enjoy greater personal autonomy (concomitant with the anonymity afforded by the city) and the stimulating, enlightening effect of living in an ever changing milieu (1971 [1903]; 1978 [1907]).

Max Weber, influenced by both Marx and Engels and Nietzsche, brought a new perspective to analysis of economy and civilization. Without rejecting the Marxist interest in effects of the mode of production on culture, he also gave weight to economic consequences of non-economic beliefs and activities. In *The Protestant Ethic and the Spirit of Capitalism* (1958 [1904–5]), he asserts that Protestant beliefs and values were preconditions of capitalist accumulation. It was the culture and beliefs of the Protestant Reformation – the sense of calling, asceticism, and predestinarian faith – that unintentionally encouraged the behaviors underlying capitalist accumulation in Western Europe. This analysis is part of an even larger perspective on economy and civilization: his argument that the moral demands articulated by the Hebrew prophets set in motion a cultural transformation in the West toward a disenchanted understanding of the world, suppression of magical belief, and insistence on self-aware action. This transformation makes possible both modern capitalism and the modern ascendancy of instrumental reason – the rationality of means that accompanies both capitalism and bureaucracy. The conception of the omnipotent God of the Hebrew Bible, emphasized anew in the Protestant Reformation, actually creates an ever growing space of rational action. In western belief, the multitude of weak, immanent, spirit beings that are tolerant of human transgressions and can be compelled by magic gave way to a single, intolerant, transcendent, and demanding God who holds people morally accountable and forces them into constant monitoring of their own actions (Weber 1952; Zeitlin 1997).

To summarize, the classical theorists had highly ambivalent views of capitalism and rationalization, seeing in it both the development of culture beyond magical and mystical views of the world, and the source of intense alienation and new forms of exploitation, now legitimated in the name of reason, accumulation, and efficiency.

TWENTIETH-CENTURY THOUGHT: CAPITALISM AND CIVILIZATION

A series of twentieth-century social theorists returned to these themes, adding new elements and reinterpreting theories in light of changes in the global economy itself.

Karl Polanyi's contribution was to insist that over the course of history the market was not the primary economic institution in most societies and that not all societies are market societies. Reciprocity and redistribution, rather than exchange, are the basic relationships of production and distribution in many societies. The extreme marketization and monetization of life in capitalist societies is a recent phenomenon in human history. It has a corrosive effect on the social fabric and reduces human beings to a "factor of production." Polanyi (2001) developed these influential views on market and non-market societies in an analysis of the transition of western European societies into market societies in the early modern period.

The world-systems school is interested not only in the transition from precapitalist to capitalist civilization in the West, but also in the expansion of capitalism into the rest of the globe. Influenced both directly by Marxist thought and by the French Annales School of historiography (emphasizing the material basis of culture and the analysis of change over long periods), Immanuel Wallerstein (1974) develops a broad historical perspective on the emergence of a global capitalist social formation. The capitalist world system emerged during European expansion after 1450, with devastating consequences for all other cultures and civilizations. The global capitalist system is composed of three levels, a core of industrialized, developed capitalist nations (basically Western Europe, North America, and Japan), a semi-periphery of partially industrialized nations (Eastern Europe, the Southern Cone of Latin America, parts of East Asia), and a periphery of underdeveloped nations and (in the past) colonized regions. As capitalist culture penetrates the periphery and semi-periphery, local cultures and traditions are transformed by commodity relations and globalized media. Nationalist and fundamentalist movements in the periphery are responses to the disintegrative effects of western capitalism on traditional civilizations (Wallerstein 2003).

While both Polanyi and world-systems theory examined the relationship between non-market and market civilizations, other theorists provided insights into key characteristics of capitalism as a civilization with a distinctive culture. In the period between the world wars, the Frankfurt School pioneered the analysis of the relationship between capitalism, which the scholars tended to analyze in Marxist terms, and culture, art, and individual social psychological characteristics, to which they brought Freudian, Hegelian, and even surrealist concepts. Walter Benjamin (1996 [1968]) suggests that the work of art loses its "aura," its unique and sacred quality, under conditions of capitalist commodity production and mechanical reproduction in industries such as film, music recording, and photography. Commodified, fragmented, subjected to industrial assembly processes, and disseminated to the masses, the work of art ceases to be a cultural treasure. For Benjamin, this is not a loss but a dramatic delegitimation of icons of bourgeois culture, a radical undermining of authority that has revolutionary potential.

Other Frankfurt School theorists, most notably Theodor Adorno (2001), were less optimistic about cultural forms under capitalism,
seeing them all – even jazz, for instance – as
instruments of domination. This theme has
reappeared in contemporary work on capitalism
and culture, for example in Thomas Frank's
The Conquest of Cool (1997), an essay about
the enormous recuperative power of capitalist
culture which is able to capture, incorporate,
commodify, and thus nullify every effort at
rebellion.

THE CIVILIZATION OF CAPITALISM IN THE INFORMATION AGE

In the last decades of the twentieth century, the
hegemonic expansion of capitalist civilization
accelerated as the global political economy
shifted under the impact of neoliberal policies
and structural adjustment programs. Globalization, with speeded-up transnational flows of
capital, media, and migrants, weakened local
and national cultural institutions and broadened cultural horizons. With globalization
came extension of values and behaviors that
had previously been found in developed market
societies, such as standardization, commodification, the discourse of efficiency, rapid technological change, and the triumph of the "bottom
line" and instrumental reason. Marx and
Engels's phrase, "all that is solid melts into
air," presciently sums up this rapid penetration
of globalized, commodified culture into regions
and communities where non-market relationships had persisted into the twentieth century.

Manuel Castells (1996), in a massive work on
informational capitalism, emphasizes the links
between new technologies of production, specifically information technologies, on the one
hand, and new global forms of culture in the
network society, including the formation of
oppositional identities and collective actions
against corporate globalization, on the other.
Informationalism is a major change within the
framework of globalized capitalism that can be
seen as constituting a civilization distinctly different from industrial capitalism.

Other theorists emphasized the growing reign
of instrumental reason and its penetration into
all areas of life. This view of the civilization
of our era was already expressed by Jürgen
Habermas (1984) and Herbert Marcuse (1992)
during the decades of transition from industrial
capitalism to globalized, information-era capitalism. The triumph of instrumental reason was
analyzed more recently and accessibly in George
Ritzer's (2000) McDonaldization thesis, which
argues that the giant fast food corporation is now
the paradigm of culture and social relationships,
governed by efficiency, calculability, predictability, and technological control.

Fredric Jameson (1992) suggests that there
are some genuinely new forms of culture –
postmodern culture – associated with advanced
capitalism. He proposes a concept, "the cultural dominant," to express the impersonal
mechanism whereby the economic forms of
our age shape culture through an invisible and
unintentional process, not through conscious
molding by the bourgeoisie but through unconscious penetration of all culture by the logic of
advanced capitalism – architecture, visual arts,
"style" and design in fashion and consumer
products, writing, movies, and so on. High
and low culture, mass culture and elite culture
– all are produced as commodities in the market. Cultural products take on the logic of
advanced capitalism: its ephemeral quality; the
devaluation of the past which is reduced to
"nostalgia" or "retro"; the mediated and shallow
nature of experience which is expressed through
shifting surface intensities. In order to illustrate
this shift within capitalist culture, Jameson contrasts Van Gogh's painting of peasant shoes that
express struggle, labor, and class inequality to
Andy Warhol's shiny, empty, decontextualized
Diamond Dust Shoes. Advanced capitalism as
a civilization replicates the central features of
the market economy – commodification, rapid
change, evanescence – but in new, heightened
forms that seem difficult to challenge by older
types of class struggle.

Richard Sennett (1998) develops a similar
theme with respect to social character, the
forms of relationships and worldviews that
emerge with flexible capitalism. He argues that
character has been corroded by extreme flexibility in economic production, accompanied by
globalization, new technologies, and concentration of economic power. The "varieties of
men and women" generated in the culture of
flexible capitalism experience their world as

fragmented, dislocated, unpredictable, and disconnected from both the individual and the collective past.

SEE ALSO: Capitalism; Commodities, Commodity Fetishism, and Commodification; Consumption, Mass Consumption, and Consumer Culture; Culture, Economy and; Culture Industries; Globalization, Culture and; Ideology, Economy and; McDonaldization; Markets; Social Embeddedness of Economic Action

REFERENCES AND SUGGESTED READINGS

Adorno, T. (2001) *Culture Industry*. Routledge, New York.

Benjamin, W. (1996 [1968]) The Work of Art in the Age of Mechanical Reproduction. In: *Illuminations*. Harcourt Brace, New York.

Castells, M. (1996) *The Information Age*. Blackwell, Oxford.

Durkheim, É. (1964 [1893]) *The Division of Labor in Society*. Free Press, New York.

Frank, T. (1997) *The Conquest of Cool: Business Culture, Counterculture, and the Rise of Consumerism*. University of Chicago Press, Chicago.

Habermas, J. (1984, 1987) *The Theory of Communicative Action*, 2 vols. Beacon Press, Boston.

Jameson, F. (1992) *Postmodernism, or, the Cultural Logic of Late Capitalism*. Duke University Press, Durham, NC.

Marcuse, H. (1992) *One Dimensional Man: Studies in Ideology of Advanced Industrial Society*. Beacon Press, Boston.

Marx, K. & Engels, F. (1948 [1848]) *Manifesto of the Communist Party*. International Publishers, New York.

Marx, K. & Engels, F. (1970 [1845–6]) *The German Ideology*. International Publishers, New York.

Mills, C. W. (1959) *The Sociological Imagination*. Oxford University Press, New York.

Polanyi, K. (2001) *The Great Transformation: The Political and Economic Origins of Our Time*. Beacon Press, Boston.

Ritzer, G. (2000) *The McDonaldization of Society*. Pine Forge Press, Thousand Oaks, CA.

Sennett, R. (1998) *The Corrosion of Character*. W. W. Norton, New York.

Simmel, G. (1971 [1903]) The Metropolis and Mental Life. In: Levine, D. (Ed.), *Georg Simmel*. University of Chicago Press, Chicago.

Simmel, G. (1978 [1907]) *The Philosophy of Money*. Ed. and Trans. T. Bottomore & D. Frisby. Routledge & Kegan Paul, London.

Wallerstein, I. (1974) *The Modern World System*. Academic Press, New York.

Wallerstein, I. (2003) *The Decline of American Power: The US in a Chaotic World*. W. W. Norton, New York.

Weber, M. (1952) *Ancient Judaism*. Free Press, Glencoe, IL.

Weber, M. (1958 [1904–5]) *The Protestant Ethic and the Spirit of Capitalism*. Scribner, New York.

Zeitlin, I. (1997) *Ideology and the Development of Sociological Theory*, 6th edn. Prentice-Hall, Upper Saddle River, NJ.

civilizations

S. N. Eisenstadt

The approach to the civilizational dimension in sociological analysis presented here is based on a shift in the comparative analysis of institutions which took place in the early 1970s. This was essentially a move from a strong emphasis on structural differentiation, as well as to some extent on ecological factors as the major criteria according to which societies have to be compared – an emphasis to be found in many of the evolutionary approaches of the 1950s and 1960s – to a perspective which stresses the interweaving of structural aspects of social life with its regulatory and interpretive context. The central analytical core of the concept of civilization as presented here – in contrast to such social formations as political regimes, different forms of political economy or collectivities like "tribes," ethnic groups, or nations, and from religion or cultural traditions – is the combination of ontological or cosmological visions, of visions of transmundane and mundane reality, with the definition, construction, and regulation of the major arenas of social life and interaction.

The central core of civilizations is the symbolic and institutional interrelation between the formulation, promulgation, articulation, and continuous reinterpretation of the basic ontological visions prevalent in a society, its basic ideological premises and core symbols on the one hand, and on the other the definition, structuration, and regulation of the major arenas of institutional life, of the political arena, of authority and its accountability, of the economy, of family life, social stratification, and of the construction of collective identities.

The impact of such ontological visions and premises on institutional formation is effected through various processes of social interaction and control that develop in a society. Such processes of control – and the opposition to them – are not limited to the exercise of power in the "narrow" political sense; as even sophisticated Marxists have stressed, they involve not only class relations or "modes of production." Rather, they are activated by major elites and influentials in a society.

The structure of such elite groups is closely related, on the one hand, to the basic cultural orientations prevalent in a society; that is, different types of elite groups bear different types of orientation or visions. On the other hand, and in connection with the types of cultural orientations and their respective transformation into basic premises of the social order, these elite groups tend to exercise different modes of control over the allocation of basic resources in the society.

The very implementation or institutionalization of such premises and the concomitant formation of institutional patterns through processes of control, symbolic and organizational alike, also generate tendencies to protest, conflict, and change effectively the activities of secondary elite groups who attempt to mobilize various groups and resources to change aspects of the social order as it was shaped by coalitions of ruling elite groups. Although potentialities for conflict and change are inherent in all human societies, their concrete development – their intensity and the concrete directions of change and transformation they engender – vary greatly among different societies and civilizations according to the specific constellations within them of the factors analyzed earlier.

In most societies in the long history of humankind such combinations of ontological visions and of definition, structuration, and regulation of institutional areas were embedded in the concrete institutional organizations and collectivities without being the object of specific institutional formations or bearers thereof, and with but very weak – if any – distinct collective identity or consciousness. A full development of the distinct ideological and institutional civilizational dimensions – and of

some awareness of their distinctiveness – occurred only in some very specific historical settings, namely, the so-called axial civilizations – even if some very important steps in that direction can be identified in some archaic civilizations such as the ancient Egyptian, Assyrian, or Mesoamerican ones, and especially in what may be called proto-axial ones, such as in the Iranian-Zoroastrian one (Eisenstadt 1982a, 1986; Breuer 1994).

AXIAL AGE CIVILIZATIONS

By axial age civilizations (to use Karl Jaspers's nomenclature) we mean those civilizations that crystallized during the half-millennium from 500 BCE to the first century of the Christian era, within which new types of ontological visions, conceptions of a basic tension between the transcendental and mundane orders, emerged and were institutionalized in many parts of the world. Examples of this process of crystallization include ancient Israel, followed by Second-Commonwealth Judaism and Christianity; Ancient Greece; possibly Zoroastrianism in Iran; early imperial China; Hinduism and Buddhism; and, beyond the axial age proper, Islam. It was through the emergence of the axial civilizations that civilizations crystallized as distinct entities and an explicit consciousness thereof developed (Schluchter 1985, 1989; Weber 1970–1).

The crystallization of these civilizations constitutes a series of some of the greatest revolutionary breakthroughs in human history, which have shaped the contours of human history in the last two to three millennia. The central aspect of these revolutionary breakthroughs was the emergence and institutionalization of new basic ontological metaphysical conceptions of a chasm between the transcendental and mundane orders. The development and institutionalization of these ontological conceptions entailed the perception of the given mundane order as incomplete, inferior – often as evil or polluted – and as in need of reconstruction to be effected according to the basic transcendental ontological conceptions prevalent in these societies (i.e., in line with the conception of bridging the chasm between the transcendental and the mundane orders, according to the precepts of a higher ethical or metaphysical order or vision). In all these civilizations it gave rise to attempts to reconstruct the mundane world, from the human personality to the sociopolitical and economic order, according to the appropriate "higher" transcendental vision.

One of the most important manifestations of such attempts was a strong tendency – manifest in all these civilizations – to construct a societal center or centers to serve as the major autonomous and symbolically distinct embodiments of respective ontological visions, and therefore as the major loci of the charismatic dimension of human existence. But at the same time the "givenness" of the center (or centers) could not necessarily be taken for granted. The construction and characteristics of the center tended to become central issues under the gaze of the increasing reflexivity that was developing in these civilizations. The political dimension of such reflexivity was rooted in the transformed conceptions of the political arena and of the accountability of rulers. The political order as one of the central loci of the "lower" mundane order had to be reconstituted according to the precepts of the transcendental visions. It was the rulers who were usually held responsible and accountable for organizing the political order according to such precepts.

At the same time the nature of the rulers became greatly transformed. The king-god, the embodiment of the cosmic and earthly order alike, disappeared, and a secular ruler appeared (even if he often retained strong sacral attributes). He was in principle accountable to some higher order. Thus, there emerged a new conception of the accountability of rulers and community to a higher authority: God, Divine Law, and the like. Accordingly, the possibility of calling a ruler to judgment appeared. A striking case of such developments occurred in ancient Israel, with elaborations of the ancient Israeli Judaic religion. More secular versions of such accountability, with a stronger emphasis on the community and its laws, appeared on the northern shores of the eastern Mediterranean, in ancient Greece, and in the Chinese conception of the Mandate of Heaven. In varying forms the idea of accountability appeared in all axial age civilizations.

Of special importance from the point of view of this analysis is the fact that one of the major manifestations of the attempts to reconstitute the social order in these civilizations was the development of a strong tendency to define certain collectivities and institutional arenas as most appropriate for the implementation of their respective transcendental visions. The most important development of this sort was the construction of "cultural" or "religious" – indeed, of civilizational – collectivities as distinct from "ethnic" or "political" ones. A crucial component of the construction of such civilizational collectivities was the development of specific collective "civilizational" consciousness or identity as distinct from purely religious, political, or "ethnic" ones. Such civilizational collectivities or frameworks usually comprised many different political and ethnic groups, while at the same time continually impinging on and interacting with these units, which became subcurrents within the broader civilization frameworks, but which could also cut across such different frameworks.

AUTONOMOUS ELITES AS BEARERS OF CIVILIZATIONAL VISIONS

In the axial age civilizations, the development and institutionalization of this new ontological conception was closely connected with the emergence of a new social element, of a new type of elite, of carriers of models of cultural and social order. These were often autonomous intellectuals, such as the ancient Israelite prophets and priests and later on the Jewish sages, the Greek philosophers and sophists, the Chinese literati, the Hindu Brahmins, the Buddhist Sangha, and the Islamic Ulema, which were of crucial importance in the constitution of the new "civilizational" collectivities and the concomitant patterns of collective identity.

The new type of elites that arose with the processes of institutionalization of such transcendental visions differed greatly from the ritual, magical, and sacral specialist in the pre-axial age civilizations. They were recruited and legitimized according to autonomous criteria, and were organized in autonomous settings distinct from those of the basic ascriptive political units of the society. They acquired a conscious, potentially countrywide and also trans-country status of their own. They also tended to become potentially independent of other categories of elites, social groups, and sectors.

At the same time there took place a far-reaching transformation of other elites, such as political elites, or the articulators of the solidarity of different collectivities. All these elites tended to develop claims to an autonomous place in the construction of the cultural and social order. Moreover, each of these elites was more or less heterogeneous, and within each of them as well as within the broader sectors of the society there developed a multiplicity of secondary elites and influentials, often carrying different conceptions of the cultural and social order – and frequently competing strongly with each other, especially over the production and control of symbols and media of communication. These new groups became transformed into relatively autonomous partners in the major ruling coalitions. They also constituted the most active elements in the movements of protest and processes of change that developed in these societies and which evinced some very distinct characteristics at both the symbolic and organizational levels (Eisenstadt 1982b).

First, there was a growing symbolic articulation and ideologization of the perennial themes of protest which are to be found in any human society, such as rebellion against the constraints of division of labor, authority, and hierarchy, and of the structuring of the time dimension, the quest for solidarity and equality, and for overcoming human mortality.

Second, utopian orientations were incorporated into the rituals of rebellion and the double image of society. It was this incorporation that generated alternative conceptions of social order and new ways of bridging the distance between the existing and the "true" resolution of the transcendental tension.

Third, new types of protest movements appeared. The most important were intellectual heterodoxies, sects, or movements which upheld different conceptions of the resolution of the tension between the transcendental and the mundane order, and of the proper way to institutionalize such conceptions. Since then, continuous confrontation between orthodoxy on the one hand, and schism and heterodoxy on the other, and the accompanying development of strong antinomian tendencies, has been a crucial component in the history of humankind.

Concomitantly, there developed the possibility of the development of autonomous political movements and ideologies – with their own symbolisms – usually oriented against existing political and sometimes also religious centers. Protest movements made important organizational changes in their confrontation – especially the growing possibility of structural and ideological links between different protest movements and foci of conflict. These links could be effected by different coalitions of different secondary elites, above all by coalition. The new dynamics of civilization transformed group conflicts into potential class and ideological conflicts, cult conflicts into struggles between the orthodox and the heterodox. Conflicts between tribes and societies could become missionary crusades. The zeal for reorganization, informed by the distinctive transcendental vision of each civilization, made the entire world at least potentially subject to cultural-political reconstruction.

EXPANSION OF AXIAL CIVILIZATIONS

With the institutionalization of axial civilizations, a new type of intersocietal and intercivilizational world history or histories emerged. Within all these civilizations there developed, in close connection with the tendencies to reconstruct the world, a certain propensity to expansion, in which ideological, religious impulses were combined with political and to some extent economic ones. To be sure, political and economic interconnections have existed between different societies throughout human history. Some conceptions of a universal or world kingdom emerged in many post-axial civilizations, as in the case of Genghis Khan, and many cultural interconnections developed between them, but only with the institutionalization of axial civilizations did a more distinctive ideological and reflexive mode of expansion with potentially strong semi-missionary orientations develop. Such expansion could be geographically concomitant with that of religion, but these two processes were not necessarily identical. This mode of expansion also gave rise to greater awareness of civilizational frameworks or collectivities encompassing many different societies, and of collective consciousness and identities, which usually encompassed different political or ethnic groups.

The expansion of axial civilizations entailed their continuous encounter with non-axial or pre-axial ones. In the encounter of axial with non-axial it was usually the axial side that emerged victorious, without however necessarily obliterating many of the symbolic and institutional features of the latter. These were often incorporated in the former, transforming them and often leading to their attenuation. Japan has been the most important continuous case of an encounter of non-axial with axial civilization, in which the former absorbed the latter and led to the de-axialization of many of its components (Eisenstadt 1995).

MULTIPLICITY OF AXIAL CIVILIZATIONS AND WORLD HISTORIES

The general tendency to reconstruct the world, with all its symbolic-ideological and institutional repercussions, and to continual expansion, was common to all the post-axial age civilizations. But their concrete implementation, of course, varied greatly. No one homogeneous world history emerged, nor were the different types of civilizations similar or convergent. Rather, there emerged a multiplicity of different, divergent, yet continuously mutually impinging world civilizations, each attempting to reconstruct the world in its own mode, according to its basic premises, and either to absorb the others or consciously to segregate itself from them.

Two sets of conditions were of special importance in shaping the different modes of institutional creativity and of expansion of these civilizations. One such set consists of variations or differences in the basic cultural orientations prevalent in them. The other is the concrete structure of the social arenas in which these institutional tendencies can be played out.

Among the different cultural orientations the most important have been differences in the very definition of the tension between the transcendental and mundane orders and the modes of

resolving this tension. There is the distinction between the definition of this tension in relatively secular terms (as in Confucianism and classical Chinese belief systems and, in a somewhat different way, in the Greek and Roman worlds) and those cases in which the tension was conceived in terms of a religious hiatus (as in the great monotheistic religions and Hinduism and Buddhism).

A second distinction, within the latter context, is that between the monotheistic religions in which there was a concept of God standing outside the Universe and potentially guiding it, and those systems, like Hinduism and Buddhism, in which the transcendental, cosmic system was conceived as impersonal and in a state of continuous existential tension with the mundane system.

A third major distinction refers to the focus of the resolution of the transcendental tensions, or in Weberian – basically Christian – terms, of salvation. Here the distinction is between purely this-worldly, purely other-worldly, and mixed this- and other-worldly conceptions of salvation.

A second set of cultural orientations which influenced the expansion of the various axial civilizations had to do with access to their centers and major manifestations of the sacred, and the extent to which this was open to all members of the community or was mediated by specific institutions. Further differences related to the way in which relations between cosmic and social order, the civilizational collectivities, and the major primordial ascriptive collectivities were conceived – there may be a total disjunction between these levels, or they may be mutually relevant and each can serve as a referent of the other without being totally embedded in it.

The concrete working out of all such tendencies depends on the second set of conditions – the arenas for the concretization of these broad institutional tendencies. These conditions included, first, the respective concrete economic political-ecological settings, whether they were small or great societies, or whether they were societies with continuous compact boundaries or with cross-cutting and flexible ones. Second was the specific historical experience of these civilizations, including encounters with other societies, especially in terms of mutual penetration, conquest, or colonization. It is the interplay between the different constellations of the cultural orientations analyzed above, their carriers, and their respective visions of restructuring of the world and the concrete arenas and historical conditions in which such visions could be concretized, that has shaped the institutional contours and dynamics of the different axial age civilizations, and the subsequent courses of world histories.

INTERNAL TRANSFORMATION OF THE AXIAL CIVILIZATION

One of the most important aspects of the dynamics of axial civilizations was the development of an internal transformative capacity which sometimes culminated in secondary breakthroughs. Examples include Second Temple Judaism and Christianity, later followed by Islam, but also Bhuddism and to a lesser extent Neo-Confucianism, all of which developed out of heterodox potentialities inherent in the respective "original" axial civilization.

The most dramatic transformation from within one of the axial civilizations has probably been the emergence of modernity as a distinct new civilization, which promulgated a distinct cultural and institutional program, a distinct mode of interpretation of the world, of a social *imaginaire* (Castoriadis 1987), which first crystallized in Western Europe and then expanded to most other parts of the world, giving continual rise to the development of multiple, continually changing modernities.

The cultural and political program of modernity as it crystallized in Europe constituted in many ways a sectarian and heterodox breakthrough in the West and Central European Christian axial civilization. Strong sectarian heterodox visions had been a permanent component in the dynamics of these civilizations, but with some partial exceptions, especially among some Islamic sects, they did not give rise to radical transformation of the political arena, its premises, and symbols. Such transformation took place in the realm of European-Christian civilizations through the transformation of these sectarian visions through the Reformation and later the Great Revolutions, in which there developed a very strong empha-

sis on the bringing together of the City of God and the City of Man (Eisenstadt 1999). It was in these revolutions that such sectarian activities were taken out from marginal or segregated sectors of society and became interwoven not only with rebellions, popular uprisings, and movements of protest, but also with the political struggle at the center and were transposed into general political movements with aspirations to control the center. Themes and symbols of protest became a basic component of the core social and political symbolism.

The religious (more specifically, sectarian) roots of modernity, and especially of the tensions between totalistic Jacobin and pluralistic orientations which developed initially in Europe, could – in the course of European expansion – find a very strong resonance in the utopian sectarian traditions of other axial civilizations. The religious roots of the modern political program also help to explain the specific modern characteristics of what have often been portrayed as the most anti-modern type of contemporary movements: the various fundamentalist movements. Contrary to the view which sees them as traditionalistic, they constitute a new type of modern Jacobin movements, which reconstruct tradition as a modern, totalistic ideology (Eisenstadt 1999).

CULTURAL AND POLITICAL PROGRAM OF MODERNITY

The cultural and political program of modernity, as it crystallized first in Western Europe from around the seventeenth century, was rooted in the distinctive premises of the European civilization and European historical experience and bore their imprints, but at the same time it was presented and was perceived as being of universal validity and relevance. This program of modernity entailed a major shift in the conception of human agency and of its autonomy, and of its place in the flow of time. It entailed a very strong component of reflexivity and uncertainty about the basic ontological and cosmological premises, as well as about the bases of social and political order of authority prevalent in society – far beyond the reflexivity that developed in the axial civilizations – a reflexivity which was shared even by the most radical critics of this program, who in principle denied the legitimacy of such reflexivity. The reflexivity that developed in the modern cultural program came to question the very givenness of such visions and of the institutional patterns related to them. It gave rise to the awareness of the existence of a multiplicity of such visions and patterns and of the possibility that such visions and conceptions can indeed be contested, thus creating a situation in which specific patterns of legitimation lost their markers of certainty (Lefort 1988). Closely related was the development of a conception of the future as open to various possibilities which can be realized by autonomous human agency, or by the inexorable march of history. This program entailed a very strong emphasis on autonomous participation of members of society in the constitution of social and political order and its constitution; on autonomous access of the major social sectors; indeed, of all members of the society to these orders and their centers.

Central to this cultural program was the emphasis on the growing autonomy of man and woman, but in the first foundations of the program, certainly of the emancipation from the fetters of traditional political and cultural authority and the continuous expansion of the realm of personal and institutional freedom and activity, such autonomy entailed other dimensions: first, reflexivity and exploration; second, active construction, mastery of nature, possibly including human nature and of society.

Out of the conjunctions of these different conceptions there developed, within this modern cultural program, the belief in the possibility of active formation, by conscious human activity rooted in critical reflection, of central aspects of social, cultural, and natural orders.

In connection with these orientations there took place far-reaching transformations of symbolism and structure of modern political centers as compared with their predecessors in Europe or with the centers of other civilizations. The crux of this transformation was first the charismatization of the political centers as the bearers of the transcendental vision promulgated by the cultural program of modernity; second was the development of continual tendencies to permeation of the peripheries by the centers and of the impingement of the peripheries on the centers, of the concomitant blurring of the distinctions between center and periphery; and third was the combination of such charismatization with the incorporation of themes and symbols of protest which were central components of the modern transcendental visions as basic and legitimate components of the premises of these centers. It was indeed the incorporation of themes of protest into the center which heralded the radical transformation of various sectarian utopian visions into central components of the political and cultural program.

This program entailed also a very distinctive mode of the construction of the boundaries of collectivities and collective identities. Such identities were continually constructed and continually problematized in a reflexive way and it constituted a focus of continual struggles.

CRYSTALLIZATION AND EXPANSIONS OF MODERNITY

The new and distinctive civilization of modernity crystallized out of the conjunction of these cultural orientations with the development of capitalism through its successive market, commercial, and industrial phases, as well as the formation of a new political order and state system, together with the military and imperialist expansion inherent in the whole pattern.

The crystallization of early and later modernities and their expansion were not peaceful developments. Contrary to optimistic visions of progress, they were closely interwoven with wars and genocides; repression and exclusion were permanent components of modern social structures. Wars and genocide were not, of course, new in the history of humankind. But they were radically transformed through their interweaving with the basic cultural program of modernity; with its initial institutionalization in the nation-states, which became the main frame of reference for citizenship and collective identity. This interaction was of course intensified by the technologies of communication and of war, constituting a continual component of the crystallization of the modern European state system and of European expansion beyond Europe.

Military, political, and economic expansion were not of course new in the history of humankind, especially not in the history of the "great" civilizations. What was new was first that the great technological advances and the dynamics of modern economic and political forces made this expansion, the changes and developments triggered by it, and their impact on the societies to which it expanded, much more intensive. The result was a tendency – new and practically unique in the history of humankind – towards the development of universal, worldwide institutional, cultural, and ideological frameworks and systems. All of these frameworks were multi-centered and heterogeneous, each generating its own dynamics and undergoing continual changes in constant relations to the others. The interrelations among them have never been "static" or unchanging, and the dynamics of these international frameworks or settings gave rise to continuous changes in these societies. The dynamics of these frameworks and systems – and the different countries within them – were closely interwoven with the specific cultural programs of modernity as it crystallized first in Europe.

At the same time, the crystallization of the first modernity and its later developments were continually interwoven with internal conflicts and confrontations, rooted in the contradictions attendant on the development of the capitalist systems and, in the political arena, with the growing demands for democratization. These conflicts accelerated with the continual overall and colonial expansion of modernity, an expansion which has also greatly contributed to the self-conception of European and western civilizations as superior to others.

Of special importance in this context was the relative place of the non-western societies in the various economic, political, and ideological international systems. Non-western constellations differ greatly from western ones and not only because western societies were the "originators" of this new civilization. More importantly, the expansion of the world systems, especially insofar as it took place through colonization and imperialist expansion – gave western powers a hegemonic place within them. But it was in the nature of these international systems that they generated a dynamics which gave rise both to political and ideological challenges to existing hegemonies, as well as to continual shifts in the loci of hegemony within Europe, from Europe to the US, then also to Japan and East Asia.

But it was not only the economic, military-political, and ideological expansion of the civilization of modernity from the West throughout the world that was important in this process. Of no lesser – possibly even of greater – importance was the fact that this expansion has given rise to continual confrontation between the cultural and institutional premises of western modernity, and those of other civilizations – those of other axial civilizations as well as non-axial ones, the most important of which has of course been Japan. True enough, many of the basic premises and symbols of western modernity and its institutions – representative, legal, and administrative – seem to have been accepted within these civilizations, but at the same time far-reaching transformations and challenges have taken place and new problems have arisen.

It was out of the continual interaction between the development of these economic, technological, political, and cultural processes and the attempt to institutionalize the cultural and political program of modernity with its tensions and contradictions that the concrete institutional and cultural patterns of different modern societies crystallized.

CONTINUALLY CHANGING MULTIPLE MODERNITIES

The concrete contours of the different cultural and institutional patterns of modernity, and of the distinct programs of modernity as they crystallized in different societies, were continually changing. They were continually changing first of all because of the internal dynamics of the technological, economic, political, and cultural arenas as they developed in different societies and expanded beyond them. Second, they were changing because of the continual confrontations between premises enunciated or promulgated by respective centers and the elites and the concrete developments, conflicts, and displacements attendant on the institutionalization of these premises. Third, they were continually changing through the political struggles and confrontation between different states, between different centers of political and economic power that played a constitutive role in the formation of European modernity, and later through the conflict-ridden expansion of European, American, and Japanese modernity. Such confrontations had already developed within Europe with the crystallization of the modern European state system and became further intensified with the crystallization of "world systems" from the sixteenth or seventeenth centuries on.

Fourth, they were continually changing because of the shifting hegemonies in the major international systems that developed in the wake of ongoing changes in the economic, political, technological, and cultural arenas, and in the centers thereof. Fifth, the institutional and cultural contours of modernities were continually changing due to the very contradictions and antinomies inherent in the cultural program of modernity and to the potentialities inherent in its openness and reflexivity, and due to the continual promulgation by different social actors (especially social movements) of varying interpretations of the major themes of this program and of the basic premises, narratives, and myths of the civilizational visions.

Accordingly, new questionings and reinterpretations of different dimensions of modernity develop continuously within modern societies – and competing cultural agendas have emerged in all of them. All these attested to the growing diversification of the visions and understandings of modernity, of the basic cultural orientations of different sectors of modern societies, far beyond the homogeneous and hegemonic paradigms of modernity that were prevalent in the 1950s. The fundamentalist and the new communal-national movements are one of the most recent episodes in the unfolding of the potentialities and antinomies of modernity.

Thus, while the spread or expansion of modernity has indeed taken place throughout most of the world, it did not give rise to just one civilization, one pattern of ideological and institutional response, but to at least several basic versions which in turn are subject to further variations.

Multiple modernities, made up of all the components mentioned above, developed around the basic antinomies and tensions of the modern civilizational program from the very beginning of the institutionalization of modern regimes in Europe. With the expansion of modern civilizations beyond the West, in some ways already as a result of the European conquest of the Americas, and with the dynamics of the continually developing international frameworks or settings, several new crucial elements have become central in the constitution of modern societies.

The preceding considerations about the multiple programs of modernity do not of course negate the obvious fact that in many central aspects of their institutional structure – be it in occupational and industrial structure, in the structure of education or of cities, in political institutions – very strong convergences have developed in different modern societies. These convergences have indeed generated common problems, but the modes of coping with these problems (i.e., the institutional dynamics attendant on the development of these problems) differed greatly between these civilizations.

Such developments may indeed give rise also to highly confrontational stances – especially with regard to the West, but the positions in question are formulated in continually changing modern idioms, and they may entail an ongoing transformation of these indications and of the cultural programs of modernity. While this diversity has certainly undermined the old hegemonies, it was at the same time closely and often paradoxically connected with the development of new multiple common reference points and networks, and with the globalization of cultural networks and channels of communication far beyond what existed before.

AGENCY, STRUCTURE, AND CULTURE FROM A CIVILIZATIONAL PERSPECTIVE

Civilizational analysis, as presented above, has some bearing on central problems of sociological analysis, above all the problems of agency and social structure, as well as culture and social structure (Eisenstadt 1995). Here we can only outline a few themes and issues to be explored.

Theories which treat social structure and agency as distinct, ontological realities cannot explain certain crucial aspects of human activity, social interaction, and cultural creativity. In particular, many aspects of institutional formations and dynamics, such as the structure of the centers or the construction of boundaries of collectivities and modes of political protest, cannot be explained entirely in terms of the "natural," autonomous tendencies of these spheres of activity in terms of some inherent cultural belief or traditions, in terms of the rational, ability-oriented consideration of the actors and not in terms of some inherent cultural belief, predisposition, or tradition. As against these approaches the civilizational perspective highlights interconnections among the three levels (i.e., between human activity, social interaction, and human creativity). Civilizational theory is not committed to extreme culturological explanations. But it argues that central dimensions of "culture" are of great importance in shaping institutional formations and patterns of behavior, even if they always operate through specific social processes and institutional frameworks. The crystallization of such central aspects of social interaction, institutional formations, and cultural creativity is best understood in terms of the processes through which symbolic and organizational aspects or dimensions of human activity are interwoven. Such social processes do not shape directly the concrete behavior of different individuals. Rather, they shape the frameworks within which such behavior is undertaken, the institutional ground rules – the "rules of the game" – within which the rational, utilitarian considerations (although not only they) may play an important role. Thus, culture and social structure are best analyzed as components of social action and interaction and of human creativity, as constitutive of each other and of the social and cultural orders.

These considerations bear also on the explanation of social change. Such changes are not caused naturally by the basic ontologies of any civilization, or by structural forces or patterns of social interaction in themselves, but rather by the continuous interaction between them – an interaction in which contingency plays a very important role. Historical changes and the constructions of new institutional formations presuppose processes of learning and accommodation, as well as different types of decision-making by individuals placed in appropriate arenas of action, responding to a great variety of historical events and drawing on a range of interpretive frameworks. Similar contingent forces, however, can have different impacts in different civilizations – even civilizations sharing many concrete institutional or political-ecological settings – because of the differences in their premises.

Thus, any concrete pattern of change is to be understood as the combination of historical contingency, structure, and culture understood as compiling the basic premises of social interaction and the reservoir of models, themes, and tropes that are prevalent in a particular society. At the same time, the rise of new forms of social organization and activity entails new interpretations of the basic tenets of cosmological visions and institutional premises, which greatly transform many of a civilization's antecedent tenets and institutions. The most dramatic of such changes are relatively rare in history; as argued above, the two outstanding cases are the emergence of axial civilizations and the transition to modernity.

It is appropriate to conclude with a brief comment on the problem succinctly posed in Marx's famous statement: "Men make their own history, but they do not make it under circumstances chosen by themselves, but under circumstances directly encountered, given, and transmitted from the past." While we may expect that this basic problem will never be fully resolved and will continue to pose a challenge to social and historical analysis, the preceding discussion may help to advance our understanding of some aspects. The structures and frameworks of activity and interaction are created by human action and interaction, but no human action or interaction can become actualized except through such frameworks and structures.

The civilizational perspective adds three main points to this very general thesis. First, the radical indeterminacy of all these frameworks – the absence of any natural or rational, evolutionary or revolutionary, foundation for uniform development – provides an opening for cultural and institutional variety. Second, the most fundamental and far-reaching cultural patterns which develop within such broad frameworks co-determine the various dimensions of social life, and the long-term combinations of cultural and structural formations give rise to distinctive civilizational complexes. Third, the creative indeterminacy that is at the root of civilizational pluralism may reappear within a given civilizational framework and find expression in dissent, heterodoxy, and critical questioning, as well as in innovative patterns of cultural and institutional production. A comparative approach to the study of civilizational dynamics will need to take all these aspects into account.

SEE ALSO: Culture; Divison of Labor; Empire; Modernity; Political Sociology; Religion; Religion, Sociology of; Revolutions, Sociology of; Social Change: The Contributions of S. N. Eisenstadt; Weber, Max

REFERENCES AND SUGGESTED READINGS

Aron, R. (1993) Remarques sur la gnose léniniste. In *Machiavel et les tyrannies modernes*. Editions de Fallois, Paris, pp. 405–21.
Breuer, S. (1994) Kulturen der Achsenzeit. Leistung und Grenzen eines Geschichtsphilosophischen Konzepts. *Saeculum* 45: 1–33.
Castoriadis, C. (1987) *The Imaginary Constitution of Society*. Polity Press, Cambridge.
Eisenstadt, S. N. (1982a) The Axial Age: The Emergence of Transcendental Visions and Rise of Clerics. *European Journal of Sociology* 23(2): 294–314.
Eisenstadt, S. N. (1982b) Heterodoxies and Dynamics of Civilizations. *Diogenes* 120: 3–25.
Eisenstadt, S. N. (Ed.) (1986) *The Origins and Diversity of Axial Age Civilizations*. State University of New York Press, Albany.
Eisenstadt, S. N. (1995) *Power, Trust and Meaning*. University of Chicago Press, Chicago.
Eisenstadt, S. N. (1996) *Japanese Civilization: A Comparative View*. University of Chicago Press, Chicago.
Eisenstadt, S. N. (1998) Comparative Studies and Sociological Theory. *American Sociologist* 29(1): 38–58.
Eisenstadt, S. N. (1999) *Fundamentalism, Sectarianism and Revolution: The Jacobin Dimension of Modernity*. Cambridge University Press, Cambridge.
Lefort, C. (1988) *Democracy and Political Theory*. University of Minnesota Press, Minneapolis.
Schluchter, W. (1985) *The Rise of Western Rationalism: Max Weber's Developmental History*, 2nd edn. University of California Press, Berkeley.
Schluchter, W. (1989) *Rationalism, Religion and Domination: A Weberian Perspective*. University of California Press, Berkeley.
Weber, M. (1970–1) *Gesammelte Aufsätze zur Religionsociologie*, 3 vols. Mohr, Tübingen.

civilizing process

Robert van Krieken

The concept of the civilizing process arises from a particular approach to the idea of "civilization," a word which first appeared in French and English in the eighteenth century, although there were earlier precursors. The understanding of "civilization" on which the conception of it being a *process* rests needs to be distinguished from other possible approaches. "Civilization" can be used in the *plural* to refer to particular assemblies of social, cultural, moral, political, institutional, and economic forms, to the historical emergence of civilizations and the interrelationships between them. Febvre referred to this as the ethnographic sense of the word, verging on being interchangeable with "culture," but with an added material and institutional dimension.

"Civilization" can also be used as a singular noun, referring to anchoring of social power and authority in rational and impersonal rules and structures, and to the existence of processes of rational cultivation, refinement, education, or formation of otherwise unreasonable human beings as a crucial element of a peaceful and productive civil society. This is generally what is meant when "civilization" is opposed to "barbarism," although at other times it is opposed to "culture," which is seen as representing the realm of values, norms, intellectual creativity, and spirituality. This meaning has also frequently been allied with Christianity, colonialism, and progress, as well as (since the end of World War II) the forms of social, political, cultural, and economic life found in the US (Beard & Beard 1962).

Underpinning the idea of the civilizing process, however, is a conception of "civilization" as a verb, aiming at an understanding of those social and political conditions, practices, strategies, and figurations which have produced changing conceptions and experiences of civility. In this approach there is a concern to link the analysis of social, cultural, political and economic structures, processes and lines of development to the analysis of changing forms of habitus, of subjective and intersubjective forms and relationships. The concept is used most precisely and in the greatest depth by the German sociologist Norbert Elias and his followers, but it also usefully captures a cluster of developments examined by a variety of other social theorists who have observed and analyzed the emergence of a specifically modern disciplined character, mode of conduct, or habitus along similar lines. Foucault and Weber, for example, agree that one can trace a developmental trend towards increasing self-discipline, a regularization and routinization of the psyche, so that one's inner "economy of the soul" coordinates with the outer economy of an increasingly bureaucratized, rationalized, and individualized social world. Their work converges on the notion that there has been "societalization of the self," a transition in European history from a social order based on external constraint to one increasingly dependent on the internalization of constraint (van Krieken 1990a, 1990b).

Elias's particular approach to the civilizing process aimed to counter the understanding of civilization as a "state," which was somehow a stable and natural characteristic of a particular people or nation, by showing (1) that what is experienced as "civilization" is founded on a particular psychic structure or habitus which had changed over time, and (2) that it can only be understood in connection with changes in the structure and form of broader social relationships. His account of "the civilizing process" can be understood as an "archeology" of the modes and norms of conduct that are today simply assumed to be natural and self-evident, revealing their history and their intimate linkages with broader social, political, and economic developments.

In *The Civilizing Process*, first published in 1939, Elias (2000) examined successive editions of a variety of etiquette manuals, showing that the standards applied to violence, sexual behavior, bodily functions, eating habits, table manners, and forms of speech became gradually more sophisticated, with an increasing threshold of shame, embarrassment, and repugnance. Gradually, more and more aspects of human behavior become regarded as "distasteful" and "removed behind the scenes of social life," including the infliction of physical violence and pain on other human beings. The institutional nucleus of this development was the emergence of "court society," the organization of the lives of the European upper classes around courts and their associated, ever-changing codes of conduct.

The social process of "courtization" which underpinned the transformation of feudal society subjected first knights and warriors, and then ever-expanding circles of the population, to an increasing demand that expressions of violence be regulated, that emotions and impulses be subjected to ever-increasing self-reflection and surveillance, and placed ever more firmly in the service of the long-term requirements of complex networks of social interaction imposing increasingly ambivalent expectations. In court society we see the beginnings of a form of mutual and self-observation which Elias referred to as a "psychological" form of perception, and which is now analyzed in terms of reflexive self-awareness.

The restraint imposed by such differentiated, complex networks of social relations became increasingly internalized, and less dependent on its maintenance by external social institutions, underpinning the development of what Freud recognized as the super-ego. Freud (1930) had earlier argued for the idea of a historical "process of cultural development" or "civilization," and stressed the importance of an accurate understanding of how human dispositions were subjected to cultural transformation. These transformations are to be understood in the context of developments in the structuring of social relations, including the development of a money economy and urbanization, but for Elias the two most important ones were (1) the process of state formation with its monopolization of the means of violence, and (2) the gradual differentiation of society, the increasing range, diversity, and interdependence of competing social positions and functions composing European societies.

The increasing monopolization of the means of violence associated with state formation created a pressure towards other means of exercising power in competitive social relations, so that social success and distinction is increasingly dependent on "continuous reflection, foresight, and calculation, self-control, precise and articulate regulation of one's own affects, knowledge of the whole terrain, human and non-human, in which one acts" (Elias 2000: 398). The increasing density of European societies, produced by a combination of population growth and urbanization, and the ever-larger circles of people that any single individual would be interdependent with, no matter how fleetingly, also facilitated the "rationalization" of human conduct, its placement at the service of long-term goals, and the increasing internalization of social constraint, eventually making a highly regulated mode of conduct effectively "second nature."

Important as driving forces behind the civilizing process are *competition* and the opportunities for advantage offered by being *distinctive* in the realm of manners and morals. Continuing competition between various social groups has generated both the willingness to submit to the demands of etiquette and the increasing subjection of people's bodies, emotions, and desires to stringent controls and ever-more demanding forms of self-discipline. Competition has also driven the spread of the civilizing process, first to the higher bourgeois strata, in their attempts to enter court society, and then in turn to the strata below them.

An important development in the understanding of the civilizing process, which arose from Elias's (1996) more specific engagement with a sociological understanding of the Holocaust, as well as evolving from the critical debates around the earlier accounts of the civilizing process, has been the emergence of more detailed explorations of the extent to which it can be regarded as unlinear, the ways in which it can reverse its direction under particular circumstances, and how it can also be accompanied simultaneously by processes of *de*civili-Fletcher 1997). There is also increasing examination of the issue of contradictions and conflicts within civilizing processes, and the question of "civilized barbarism," whether the infliction of violence should be seen simply as having been "reduced," or as changed in form, such as from physical to symbolic violence. The monopolization of physical force by the state,

through the military and the police, cuts in two directions and has, as Elias (1996) put it, a "Janus-faced character," because such monopolies of force can then be all the more effectively wielded by powerful groups within any given nation-state, such as under the Nazi regime. The formation of any inclusive social bonds is at the same time unavoidably exclusionary in relation to those seen as lying outside the community, village, nation, state, or "people," or lower down the social scale, and more recently this idea has informed analyses of genocide and other types of "civilized barbarism."

The concept is an important element of research and theory in a number of social scientific fields. Social and historical studies of the self, identity, emotions, and the body draw on the idea of the civilizing process to help explain the emergence of socially and historically specific psychological dispositions, modes of conduct, and moral orientations. The sociology of sport looks at the role of sport in the civilizing process, as an arena of "controlled decontrolling" of interpersonal violence and strong emotions, substituting sporting matches for war. Social histories of crime and punishment show both that the incidence of violent crime has decreased over the centuries, and that tolerance for the "spectacle of suffering" also gradually declined, although these is also debate around an apparent decivilizing trend towards greater levels of incarceration and greater intensity of punishment. Studies of genocide and the conduct of war refer to the debates around the civilizing process to explain both how mass killings take place and how the practices of professional soldiers continue to change over time. Sociological studies of organizations are making increasing use of the concept to analyze the ways in which organizational forms have developed over time and to understand key elements of organizational subjectivity. Discussions of international relations and globalization also make use of Elias's account of the underlying mechanisms of state formation and the monopolization of violence to explain current developments in relations between nation-states and the global movements of people as migrants and refugees.

The methodological and theoretical problems associated with the idea of the civilizing process include whether there has been too much emphasis placed on it as a largely unplanned process, and not enough attention paid to it as the aim and outcome of the consciously planned projects of particular social groups and agencies, as a civilizing *mission* or *offensive*. This is of particular relevance to the role of the concept of civilization in colonialism. Elias's own account of the civilizing process in Western Europe paid only slight attention to religion and religious institutions, and his focus was primarily on the intrastate civilizing process, leaving open the analysis of interstate civilizing processes.

There are also a cluster of concerns which together can be called the "anthropological critique." Anthropologists (Goody 2002) have raised doubts about the extent to which the behavior of people both in earlier historical periods and in other cultural contexts differed from people in western societies today, drawing attention to those features of human relations in all cultural and historical contexts which produce roughly similar forms of behavior. Medieval villagers and members of tribal societies were and are subjected to considerably more restraint than inhabitants of a modern industrial city, and that what is interpreted as the result of a lesser degree of internalized self-constraint can equally be understood as *produced* by particular social and cultural expectations. Very similar regimes of managing emotions and impulses in the service of longer-term ends can arise in the absence of the centralization of political power in the state, which is at the core of Elias's explanation of the European civilizing process.

Although Elias set out to analyze the social conditions underpinning European's perception of themselves as being civilized, much of the research working with the concept of the civilizing process can be seen to take on that self-perception as its own, slipping back into the normative understanding of civilization as equated with progress and improvement. At this point the opposition of civilization to culture reemerges, along with the power dynamics built into the civilizing process, highlighting the ways in which it can be experienced as an essentially colonizing process.

The themes which will dominate future discussion of the civilizing process include extending the analysis of civilizing processes beyond the advanced industrial societies, understanding decivilizing processes and contradictions within the civilizing process, particularly in relation to genocide and other continuing forms of organized violence, the nature of contemporary civilizing processes and the emotional and moral dimensions of current social change, and the regulation of crime and organizational corruption, as well as the analysis of legal institutions and legal change more broadly, the application of the concept to international relations between states, especially in arenas such as human rights and cosmopolitanism in world politics, as well as to the broader analysis of globalization.

SEE ALSO: Body and Cultural Sociology; Civil Society; Civilizations; Disciplinary Society; Distinction; Elias, Norbert; Figurational Sociology and the Sociology of Sport; Foucault, Michel; Freud, Sigmund; Genocide; Habitus/Field; Holocaust; Weber, Max

REFERENCES AND SUGGESTED READINGS

Beard, C. A. & Beard, M. R. (1962) *The American Spirit: A Study of the Idea of Civilization in the United States*. Collier, New York.

Elias, N. (1996) *The Germans: Studies of Power Struggles and the Development of Habitus in the 19th and 20th Centuries*. Polity Press, Cambridge.

Elias, N. (2000) *The Civilizing Process: Sociogenetic and Psychogenetic Investigations*, rev. edn. Blackwell, Oxford.

Febvre, L. (1998 [1930]) Civilization: Evolution of a Word and a Group of Ideas. In: Rundell, J. & Mennell, S. (Eds.), *Classical Readings in Culture and Civilization*. Routledge, London, pp. 160–90.

Fletcher, J. (1997) *Violence and Civilization*. Polity Press, Cambridge.

Freud, S. (1930) *Civilization and its Discontents*. Hogarth Press, London.

Goody, J. (2002) Elias and the Anthropological Tradition. *Anthropological Theory* 2 (4): 401–12.

Linklater, A. (2004) Norbert Elias, The Civilizing Process and the Sociology of International Relations. *International Politics* 41 (1): 3–35.

Loyal, S. & Quilley, S. (Eds.) (2004) *The Sociology of Norbert Elias*. Cambridge University Press, Cambridge.

Mennell, S. (1992) *Norbert Elias: An Introduction*. Blackwell, Oxford.

Pagden, A. (2000) "Stoicism, Cosmopolitanism, and the Legacy of European Imperialism." *Constellations* 7 (1): 3–22.

Starobinski, J. (1993) The Word "Civilization." In: *Blessings in Disguise; or, The Morality of Evil.* Harvard University Press, Cambridge, MA, pp. 1–35.

van Krieken, R. (1990a) The Organization of the Soul: Elias and Foucault on Discipline and the Self. *Archives Européennes de Sociologie* 31 (2): 353–71.

van Krieken, R. (1990b) Social Discipline and State Formation: Weber and Oestreich on the Historical Sociology of Subjectivity. *Amsterdams Sociologisch Tijdschrift* 17 (1): 3–28.

van Krieken, R. (1998) *Norbert Elias.* Routledge, London.

class

Lois A. Vitt

Class refers to a stratification system that divides a society into a hierarchy of social positions. It is also a particular social position within a class stratification system: lower class, working class, middle class, upper class, or other such class designations. It is a method of social ranking that involves money, power, culture, taste, identity, access, and exclusion. Conceptualizations of class belong not only to sociology, but also to the popular press, the marketplace, the political process, and to those who perceive themselves as being located within a particular class position. People who do perceive class distinctions are "class conscious" and may feel the impact of class in powerful ways. Others barely notice it or refuse to concede its existence despite living with its effects. To some people, class connotes differing economic circumstances, lifestyles, and tastes; to others it is about social status, esteem, and respect.

New students of sociology will quickly encounter the concept of class. They will become familiar with the writings of Marx and Weber and other prominent social theorists who have contrasted, debated, explained, and elaborated the works of these foundational figures over the past century. They will be introduced to the research methods and applications that have alternatively advanced and constrained class studies, especially in the US. They will also find that the topic of class is both ideologically and emotionally charged, and that its usage in academic as well as interpersonal settings can be fraught with controversy and strong sentiment.

During and after the years of the "Red scare" following World War I and the era of McCarthyism in the 1950s, fear of communism and anything "Marxian" contributed greatly to individual and academic tension over the topics of class and class conflict in the US. American anxiety stemming from these periods served to strengthen the widespread creed that America is a "classless society," a land of opportunity for everyone who is willing to work hard and strive for economic and material achievement through personal effort. With emphasis on enterprise and the freedom to succeed, the stage was set early on for an American-style social stratification system that differed from those that had evolved over time in the Old World. Henry Chistman, a missionary touring the colonies in the nineteenth century, wrote: "American[s] can never flourish on leased lands. They have too much enterprise to work for others or remain tenants."

Divergent class perspectives in the literature capture differences in the historical development of class systems in Europe and the US. Egalitarianism, in its American meaning, pertains to equality of opportunity and respect, not of result or condition, and reflects the absence of inherited feudal structures, monarchies, and aristocracies. It indicates an achievement-oriented system and a history of political democracy prior to industrialization that remains unreceptive to European-style class consciousness. While European social theory was concerned with the role of economic classes (and class conflict) in industrial society, most American sociologists concentrated instead on studies of social mobility, analyses of the occupational structure, and subjective perceptions about occupational prestige. To soften the Marxist model of class, social class was transformed into a continuous gradation of social class positions based on prestige rankings through which individuals could evolve as a consequence of personal effort. The new class model, adapted from Weber's "status" theories, was extended and elaborated by sociologists seeking to understand the "American form" of social stratification.

Formal definitions of objective social class and subjective social class appear in the sociological literature. *Objective* social class is defined by Hoult (1974) as "social class in terms of objective criteria decided upon by the sociologist, for example, income, occupation, and education. The criteria chosen by the sociologist are usually based on observations and studies of how the people in the community view the system of stratification." Hoult defines *subjective* "Social class in terms of how people place themselves within the society. People may be asked what social classes exist in their community and then asked to place themselves within one of these classes, or they may be asked to rate themselves within a system of classes presented by the investigator."

In both European and American settings today, class is used in a wide range of descriptive and explanatory contexts. Depending upon context, various concepts of class are employed as well. Together with other authors in *Approaches to Class Analysis*, Wright (2005) portrays class concepts through a variety of theoretical prisms for the purpose of clarifying alternative traditions. Definitions, concepts, and elaborations of class, however, are fundamentally shaped by the questions they seek to answer.

A primary task has been to seek answers about (or to try to prevent) the social cleavages and conflicts that can impact and change the course of history. Others use class to locate and explore the objective or subjective identity and lived experiences of individuals and families in contemporary society. Questions within these research traditions may be related, such as when class location is used to reveal and explain the culture, interests, or antagonisms of different classes. Sociologists also use class distinctions to measure social mobility from one generation to another and within and between societies, or to explain variances on any number of lifestyle, preference, voting, and other social and economic measures.

All class research approaches, whether designed to probe for conflicting class interests, to measure social mobility, or to test for variances, are descended from overarching theoretical class frameworks. They are rooted in the writings of Marx, followed by refinements and rebuttals in the works of Weber and numerous other social thinkers across many disciplines. Although many use the term social class after Plato, concepts of class (and social class) received little attention until Marx made it central to his theory of social conflict and to the role that classes play in social movements and social change.

For Marx, class division and conflict between classes exist in all societies. Industrial society consists mainly of two conflicting classes: the bourgeoisie, owners of the means of production (the resources – land, factories, capital, and equipment – needed for the production and distribution of material goods); and the proletariat, who work for the owners of productive property. The owning class controls key economic, political, and ideological institutions, placing it inevitably in opposition to non-owners as it seeks to protect its power and economic interests. "Class struggle" is the contest between opposing classes and it is through the dynamic forces that result from class awareness of conflicting interests that societal change is generated.

Marx himself seems never to have attempted to state in any precise and definitive way just what he meant by class, although four classes that are characteristic of a capitalist society have emerged from Marxist literature: (1) the capitalist class (the bourgeoisie); (2) a class of professionals, merchants, and independent craftsmen (the petty bourgeois); (3) the working class (the proletariat) ; and (4) a class whose members for a variety of reasons cannot work (the lumpenproletariat). In well-developed capitalist economies the working class constitutes the majority of the population. The capitalist class owns most of society's assets and holds most of the economic and political power. In between capitalists and workers is a class that consists of professionals, merchants, shopkeepers, craftsmen, and other independent proprietors. Like capitalists, they own their own means of production and hire workers to assist them. They often contribute much of the labor required for creating or selling their goods and/or services and therefore can be their own "workers." Sometimes members of this class identify their interests with capitalists, while on other occasions their interests are in line with those of the working class.

Marx believed that all productive (capitalist) systems must eventually give way to more advanced social systems wherein workers will control the means of production and in which there will be no classes. His analysis was concerned primarily with the structure and dynamics of capitalist industrial societies against which he predicted workers would eventually revolt. Revolution did occur in Eastern Europe (although the resulting communist system ultimately failed), but a workers' revolution did not materialize in the West. Marx did not foresee that as industrial capitalism thrived in the West, the fundamental objective of workers became a larger share of the economic pie, not a change in the system itself. Further problems with Marxian theory occurred in the changing class structure itself. While Marx called for a growing contraposition of the two major opposing classes, the polarization of owners and workers did not occur. Instead, the middle class grew and both the working and middle classes accommodated to, even embraced, the capitalist system. Although not accurate in some predictions, the Marxian view of society is nevertheless valuable to understanding class, class antagonisms, conflicting interests, and social stratification in human societies.

Weber's concepts and contributions to stratification theory expanded and refined Marxian understandings of advanced industrial society. Like Marx, Weber believed that economic stratification produces social classes: "We may speak of a class when (1) a number of people have in common a specific causal component of their life chances, insofar as (2) this component is represented exclusively by economic interests in the possession of goods and opportunities for income, and (3) is represented under the conditions of the commodity or labor markets." But Weber suggested that classes could form in any market situation, and he argued that other forms of social stratification could occur independently of economics. Weber's was a three-dimensional model of stratification consisting of (1) *social classes* that are objectively formed social groupings having an economic base; (2) *parties* which are associations that arise through actions oriented toward the acquisition of social power; and (3) *status* groups delineated in terms of social estimations of honor or esteem.

For Weber, classes are aggregates of individuals who share similar "life chances" in their education and work and in their ability to purchase material goods and services. Life chances experienced within social classes are based upon the degree of *control* exercised over particular markets: money and credit, property, manufacturing, and various learned skills that earn income in the workforce. Dominant classes achieve a tight monopoly on some lucrative markets; less dominant classes get only partial market participation (Collins 1985).

In Weberian terms a class is more than a population segment that shares a particular economic position relative to the means of production. Classes reflect "communities of interest" and social prestige as well as economic position. Class members share lifestyles, preferences, and outlooks as a consequence of socialization, educational credentials, and the prestige of occupational and other power positions they hold, which also serve to cloak the economic class interests that lie beneath. This status ideology eases the way for class members to monopolize and maintain the prestige, power, and financial gain of higher socioeconomic positions, as only persons who seem like "the right kind" are allowed into preferred positions (Collins 1985).

The social class structures of several American communities (and cities) were identified in classic studies from the late 1930s through the late 1960s. In 1941 W. Lloyd Warner and his associates, on the basis of his research in a New England community, conceptualized classes as groups of people, judged as superior or inferior in prestige and acceptability to the classes below or above them. Coleman and Neugarten, for their 1950s study of social class in Kansas City, built on this research, but converted class to status groupings in order to test the symbols of social status such as neighborhood, social clubs, homes, churches, educational attainment, and occupations. Weber's dimensions of class were disaggregated into "socioeconomic variables" that included income, education, and occupation. Attention was shifted away from purely economic interests to include subjective differences among individuals and families in neighborhoods and communities. The results of these studies were in line with Weber's conception of status groups delineated in terms of social estimations of subjective status. They also showed a highly developed awareness of social ranking based upon status symbols – homes, neighborhoods, social clubs – and the relative social status of the individuals and families who owned or otherwise enjoyed them.

Community studies "demonstrated" that a continuum exists among occupations ranked primarily by prestige. The top and bottom status groups were seen as small in size and were defined in extreme terms as the richest and the poorest people. This description left the rest as one large middle class, a perception similar to class images that persist in the US today. Is the US a "classless society?" In such a society, social classes are ill-defined, blurred, and overlapping. There is little or no consciousness of class divisions and there are no subcultures based on social class. Some policymakers, journalists, and others use concepts or dimensions of status, alone or in some combination, to describe the categories of a basically classless system. The resulting social separations that consign most Americans to the "middle" are frequently either blurred or arbitrarily drawn. Vanneman and Cannon (1987) describe this all-too-common practice: "Class sorts out positions in society along a many-runged ladder of economic success and social prestige; in this continuous image, classes are merely relative rankings along the ladder: upper class, lower class, upper-middle class, 'the Toyota set,' 'the BMW set,' 'Brahmins,' and the dregs 'from the other side of the tracks.'"

By contrast, a true class society is characterized by population segments having distinctive attitudes, values, and other cultural qualities and forming subcultures within the larger societal culture as a whole. The perception that one belongs to a given social class – whether higher or lower in relative ranking – involves familiarity with certain manners and customs, similar lifestyles, access to (or exclusion from) sources of privilege, knowledge, income, wealth, and feelings of community with other members of the same class. Personal interests may or may not depend upon the position and attainments of the social class as a whole, since relations between and among social classes are complicated by race, gender, age, and ethnicity,

and changing workplace and regulatory issues as well.

A theoretical case in point concerns the emergence of a much more complex work environment in the twenty-first century, simultaneously calling for broad (and deeper) sociological understanding of the impact of global enterprise on human collectivities at home and abroad, and a rethinking of the effects of financial interests that are more diffusely held, more complex, and more competitively focused than in the past. To address the new workplace complexity, Wright (2005) recognizes (1) that class analyses of actual societies today require identifying ways in which different class relations may be combined, and (2) that simple, one-dimensional property rights are no longer valid, but instead are actually complex bundles of rights and powers subject to government restrictions, union representation on boards of directors, employee stock ownership, and delegations of power to managers, and other rights and powers that are being "decomposed and redistributed." Such redistribution of rights and powers moves class relations away from simple, abstract forms of polarized relations.

Recent studies, the popular press, and public discourse argue that the US is not a classless society and that class is a powerful force in American life. Class differences and the obvious movement of families up and down the economic ladder present a contradictory but compelling picture of stagnating mobility, emerging elites, and the lived experience of social class cultures, particularly those involving the intersections of race and gender. Despite controversy and disagreement among some social scientists that the era of class is over, it appears that interest in the concept of class, far from being over, is actually on the rise.

Ironically, the operation of class in the US is becoming more apparent as globalization serves to illuminate increasingly unequal distribution of income, wealth, and personal power at home. Responsibility for job and income security, health insurance and health care, education, and retirement security has been shifting steadily for some time from government and business interests to working Americans. Over the last two decades the income gap between wealthy Americans (who own investments and enjoy federal tax breaks) and those at the middle and bottom of the pay scale has widened. Wages are stagnant, the middle class is shouldering a larger tax burden, and prices for health care, housing, tuition, gasoline, and food have soared.

In US popular culture and political conversation, class is often referred to as the "haves and have-nots." What is really meant is "rich" and "poor," but class is about more than money. The emotional and practical difficulties of transcending class boundaries have been well documented by sociologists and others in both classic and recent literature. America still celebrates the idea that there is opportunity to move up from humble beginnings to achieve greatness, and for some fortunate Americans this scenario may still be true. For those who follow social policy trends, however, there are ominous signs that all but a privileged few may be losing hard-won economic gains and that a permanent underclass may be hardening.

At a time when retirement income is on the horizon for pre-retirees, employers are trimming or cutting entirely previously promised pension and health care benefits. At a time when a college degree matters more than ever, success in obtaining an education is being linked to class position and to the finances required to make up for previous public support of higher education. At a time of extraordinary advances in medicine, class differences in health and lifespan are wide and appear to be widening (Scott & Leonhardt 2005). There is far less actual upward mobility than once believed and far more downward sliding than is being acknowledged. Most problematic of all may be the prospective loss of the pervasive ideology that social class boundaries in America merely exist to be overcome. The stage seems set for renewed serious interest by sociologists in the realities of social class in America today.

SEE ALSO: Class Conflict; Class Consciousness; Class, Status, and Power; Marx, Karl; Stratification and Inequality, Theories of; Weber, Max

REFERENCES AND SUGGESTED READINGS

Coleman, R. P. & Neugarten, B. L. (1971) *Social Status in the City*. Jossey-Bass, San Francisco.
Collins, R. (1985) *Three Sociological Traditions*. Oxford University Press, New York.
Correspondents of the *New York Times* (2005) *Class Matters*. New York Times, New York.
Gerth, H. H. & Mills, C. M. (1946) *Max Weber: Essays in Sociology*. Oxford Universtiy Press, Oxford.
Hoult, T. F. (1974) *Dictionary of Modern Sociology*. Littlefield, Adams, Totowa, NJ.
Lipset, S. M. (1996) *American Exceptionalism: A Double-Edged Sword*. W. W. Norton, New York.
Marger, M. N. (2002) *Social Inequality: Patterns and Processes*, 2nd edn. McGraw Hill, Boston.
Scott, J. & Leonhardt, D. (2005) Shadowy Lines That Still Divide. In: Correspondents of the *New York Times, Class Matters*. New York Times, New York.
Vanneman, R. D. & Cannon, L. W. (1987) *The American Perception of Class*. Temple University Press, Philadelphia.
Vitt, L. A. (1993) *Homeownership, Well Being, Class and Politics: Perceptions of American Homeowners and Renters*. Institute for Socio-Financial Studies, Washington, DC.
Warner, W. L., Meeker, M. L., & Eells, K. (1949) *Social Class in America*. Science Research Associates, Chicago.
Weber, M. (1982) The Distribution of Power: Class, Status, Party. In: *Classes, Power, and Conflict*. University of California Press, Berkeley.
Wright, E. O. (2005) Foundations of a Neo-Marxist Class Analysis. In: Wright, E. O. (Ed.), *Approaches to Class Analysis*. Cambridge University Press, Cambridge.

class conflict

Stephen Hunt

Marx famously stated "the history of all societies up to the present is the history of the class struggle." In his interpretation, the term class is used to refer to the main strata in all stratified society as constituted by a social group whose members share the same relationship to the forces of production. This was evident, according to Marx, in western societies which developed through the epochs of primitive communism, ancient society, feudal society, and industrial capitalism. Primitive communism, based on a communal mode of production and distribution, typified by a subsistence economy, represents the only example of a classless society. From then on, all societies are divided into essentially two major classes that are in an antagonistic relationship: masters and slaves in ancient society, lords and serfs under feudalism, and bourgeoisie and proletariat under the capitalist order. During each historical epoch the labor power required for production was supplied by the majority subject class. While, for Marx, class conflict arises in the exploitative situation evoked by the relationship to the forces of production, it is also evident through the development of such forces by an emerging class. The superiority of the capitalist forces of production, by way of illustration, led to a rapid transformation of the social structure, but only after the revolutionary triumph of the emergent class over the feudal order.

In terms of class conflict, or potential class conflict, Marx distinguished between a "class in itself" and a "class for itself." The former comprises a social grouping whose constituents share the same relationship to the forces of production. However, for Marx, a social grouping only fully becomes a class when it forms a "class for itself." At this stage, its members have achieved class consciousness and solidarity – a full awareness of their true situation of exploitation and oppression. Members of a class subsequently develop a common identity, recognize their shared interest, and unite, so creating class cohesion and ultimately taking recourse to revolutionary violence.

Much of Marx's work was concerned with class conflict in capitalist industrial society. Class antagonisms could not be resolved within its structure. Thus, the contradictions inherent in capitalism and its accompanying sociopolitical structures would bring class conflict to its ultimate realization. As capitalism develops, the workforce is concentrated in large factories where production becomes a social enterprise and thus illuminates the exploitation of the proletariat and its shared grievances. The increasing use of machinery would result in a homogeneous class since such technology brings a leveling process of deskilling, enhancing a sense of common experience and engendering an increasing sense of alienation.

Marx believed that the class struggle that would overthrow the capitalist order would ensure that private property would be replaced by communally owned property, though industrial manufacture would remain as the basic

modus operandi of production in the new society, communally owned but at a higher level of technological development. Since history is one of the class struggle, history would eventually come to an end. The socialist society that would replace capitalism would contain no dialectical contradictions, while, in effect, the working class would abolish itself.

Among those who systematically addressed Marx's theory of class conflict was Max Weber. Weber agreed with many of the fundamental aspects of Marxian thought, particularly in viewing the economy as the crucial source of stratification. In contrast to Marx, however, Weber added to the economic dimension of stratification two other dimensions: prestige and power. Property differences generated "classes"; prestige differences forged "status groupings"; and power differences brought factions or political blocs ("parties"). Whereas Marx assumed that members of any one economic class could develop class consciousness and become united in a shared interest and purpose, Weber regarded this as unlikely. Rather, class consciousness would evolve only when it is obvious to all constituents that the interests of antagonistic groups are incompatible and that conflict would ensue. In fact, Weber says quite explicitly that economic classes do not normally constitute communities, whereas status groups – united on the subjective basis of common degrees of social prestige – are more likely to do so. Moreover, there may be a discrepancy between one's status and one's class. Weber also identified an intimate relationship between classes, status groups, and parties. He held that parties may form on the basis of similar "class" interests or similar "status" or both, yet this was rare and class conflict in the form of revolutionary process was improbable (Gerth & Mills 1958: 194).

Since Weber, critics of Marx's theory of class conflict have focused on various aspects of his work. Two examples may be cited here. Dahrendorf (1959) argued that, contrary to Marx's prediction, the manual working class was becoming increasingly heterogeneous. Dahrendorf saw this as resulting from changes in industrial technology leading to differences in skill, economic and status rewards, and interests within the ranks of the manual workers that undermined collective class consciousness and hence negated class conflict. Another approach was to question Marx's thesis that the proletariat was a particularly revolutionary class. In her key work, Skocpol (1979) identifies, instead, the peasant class as *the* ingredient for successful social revolutions. This she concludes from her comparative study of the revolutionary outcomes in feudal France, Russia, and China. Skocpol also identifies the state as a determinant in whether class conflict ultimately results in a revolution process. As a relatively autonomous system of institutions, the state must be weakened by external pressures in the global order and internally by the loss of coercive structures before the revolutionary process can be brought to fruition.

SEE ALSO: Bourgeoisie and Proletariat; Class Consciousness; Class, Perceptions of; Conflict Theory; False Consciousness; Marx, Karl; Weber, Max

REFERENCES AND SUGGESTED READINGS

Darendorf, R. (1959) *Class and Class Conflict in Industrial Society*. Routledge & Kegan Paul, London.

Gerth, H. & Mills, C. W. (Eds). (1958) *From Max Weber*. Oxford University Press, New York.

Marx, K. & Engels, F. (1977 [1848]) The Communist Manifesto. In: McLellan, D. (Ed.), *Karl Marx: Selected Writings*. Oxford University Press, Oxford, pp. 221–46.

Skocpol, T. (1979) *States and Revolutions*. Cambridge University Press, Cambridge.

class consciousness

Wendy Bottero

Deriving from Marxist class analysis, "class consciousness" refers to a developing process in which those sharing common objective economic relations (a "class-in-itself") become aware of their shared class interests and work together to achieve common class aims, acting as a self-conscious social grouping (a "class-for-itself"). In the classic Marxist formulation, class position leads to class consciousness, which in turn leads to class action. Karl Marx identified within society an underlying economic "base" which determines the social and political "superstructure," arguing that the revolutionary class consciousness of the working class will emerge as the result of economic developments that make the conditions of class inequality increasingly clear and transparent.

Marx did not think that it was simply shared class interests that generated a self-conscious social class. He argued, for example, that small-holding peasants formed a collective class only in the sense that "potatoes in a sack form a sack of potatoes" because, despite sharing similar conditions of existence, the peasant mode of production isolated peasants from one another rather than forging social relations between them; so to the extent that "the identity of their interests begets no community, no national bond and no political organization among them, they do not form a class" (Marx & Engels 1969: 478–9). It is only under specific conditions that a "class-in-itself" transforms into a "class-for-itself," with a series of economic transformations helping members to become aware of their shared interests and to act in a concerted way to achieve common goals.

In Marx's model, working-class consciousness will result from the intensely competitive nature of capitalism, which simplifies the class structure, resulting in society "splitting up into two great hostile camps, into two great classes, directly facing each other: Bourgeoisie and Proletariat" (Marx & Engels 1998 [1848]: 3). The capitalist pursuit of profit eliminates skill divisions amongst the working class, with all workers reduced to unskilled labor. The proletariat are homogenized, and concentrated together in larger and larger working units. A polarized gap develops between an increasingly large working class, trapped in shared conditions of miserable poverty, working alongside each other in large factories, and a tiny group of capitalists, running a handful of enormous monopolistic enterprises. Intense competition between capitalists, and the "boom and bust" economy that results, force down wages and make the livelihood of the working class increasingly insecure. All these factors combine to make the working class a solidaristic, self-aware, class-for-itself.

One key problem with Marx's model is that class polarization and pauperization have not occurred in capitalist societies as he predicted, with rising affluence and the expansion of middle-order groups complicating, not simplifying, the class structure. Similarly, class consciousness when it has emerged has done so in a limited, intermittent, and generally non-revolutionary fashion (more often described as "trade union consciousness"). This has led to revisions of the original Marxist model, with suggestions that the working class are characterized by *false consciousness*: the notion that ideological beliefs act as a smokescreen, obscuring the exploitative conditions of the working class and blurring their commonality, thus preventing them from realizing and acting upon their shared class interests.

A more radical set of criticisms sees the empirical failure of revolutionary class consciousness as a symptom of a more serious theoretical weakness within Marxist class analysis, in particular casting doubt on Marx's *economic* account of the formation of social consciousness and social groupings. It is pointed out that Marx's acknowledgment that class solidarity does not inevitably arise out of shared class interests raises the serious question of just how class consciousness and solidarity *do* emerge, and what processes operate to sustain them. The apparent lack of a straightforward connection between class location and class consciousness has been characterized as the "weakest link in the chain" of Marxist class theory (Lockwood 1988).

In an alternative formulation of the class consciousness question, by Max Weber, classes are not communities but only "possible, and frequent, bases for social action" (1978 [1910]: 927). Unlike Marx's model (in which class position *will* lead to class consciousness and action, given certain tendencies in economic relations), Weber (1978 [1910]: 302–3) argued that there is no necessary logic by which economic class categories with distinct life chances will result in classes as social groupings or lead to class struggle or revolution. For Weber, economic location (and its associated life chances) is only one factor amongst many affecting our social consciousness and identity. So we cannot predict that *class* consciousness (or action) will emerge from a common class situation, as this

is only one possible contingency. This is partly because Weber believed social classes were internally differentiated (by skill and property differences) and so were always a potentially unstable basis of commonality, but also because he believed there were other bases of social consciousness – status and party affiliations – which cross-cut economic interests and potentially undermine the formation of "class" consciousness. Much subsequent class analysis has adopted a neo-Weberian stance, rejecting the idea that political action follows directly from class position, and instead arguing that class position creates only "potential interests," as just one source of influence sitting alongside – and competing with – many other structural influences on identity and action (Goldthorpe & Marshall 1992: 383–4).

In neo-Weberian terms, the task of class analysis is to investigate the *degree* to which objective class situation influences subjective consciousness, social identities, and political action. This is a considerable retrenchment from earlier accounts, which made stronger theoretical claims about the links between economic and social behavior, and this retrenchment has itself been taken by some critics as a sign of the theoretical exhaustion of class theory (Pahl 1993). Moreover, Savage, reviewing the evidence of the relation between class position and social attitudes and beliefs, concludes that most studies have found severe limits to class consciousness. Although people can, and do, identify in class terms, this identification is often fleeting and does not seem to be a major source of group belonging. Savage concludes that people's social attitudes are "too ambivalent to be seen as part of a consistent class-related world view," with class location shaping only some of their views in "highly mediated and complex ways" (2000: 40).

In recent times, the issue of class consciousness has been reformulated as the problem of class identities. It is no longer the absence of revolutionary consciousness that is addressed, but rather the apparent failure of class to explain variation in social attitudes, beliefs, and identities. For critics alleging the "death of class," the absence of class consciousness – in the form of clear-cut class identities – has been taken as evidence of the declining significance of class in late modern or postmodern societies.

Pakulski and Waters (1996: 90) claim that "class" was most salient when it occurred in close-knit communities based on single industries (such as mining or steel towns), where the domination of one class by another was highly visible and shared class interests could be easily recognized. However, with the rise of service economies and more flexible and fragmented labor markets, such communities have disappeared. With affluence and highly differentiated consumption patterns, it is argued that societies have become individualized and fragmented, and so the prospects for material inequality giving rise to class communities, solidarity, consciousness, or political action have receded. Beck (1992: 131), for example, argues that people in the same class now exhibit quite different lifestyles, so that knowing an individual's class position is no longer a useful guide to that person's outlook, social and political ideas, family life, or personal identity.

Whilst this claim is contested, conventional neo-Weberian class analysis has become increasingly cautious about the extent to which class relations generate class identities (Goldthorpe & Marshall 1992; Hout et al. 1996). The neo-Weberian emphasis has been on how class continues to shape *objective life chances*, which, it has been argued, has tended to neglect the issue of *subjective beliefs* and *identities*. Critics argue that neo-Weberian class analysis has marginalized the cultural and subjective aspects of class at the same time that cultural identity has become of ever greater importance in the social sciences more generally (Savage 2000: 1).

A later generation of class theorists, influenced by Pierre Bourdieu (1984), do focus on issues of cultural identity but argue that the starting point for class analysis should be the *weakness* of class consciousness (Savage 2000: 34). The focus of "culturalist" class analysis is on how specific cultural practices are bound up with the reproduction of hierarchy. Such accounts draw inspiration from Bourdieu's research on how "class" inequalities are reproduced through the hierarchically differentiated nature of tastes and dispositions. In Bourdieu's account, everyday tastes in things ranging from the types of food and clothing we like to our preferences in music, art, decoration, gardening, or sports, and even our intellectual attitudes, act as both a reflection and reinforcement of

"class" differences, but "class" is interpreted very broadly in terms of location within an economic and cultural space. "Taste," for Bourdieu, reflects internalized class dispositions which are shaped by the people and social conditions around us. However, Bourdieu argues that these class dispositions and tastes are largely *unconscious* and *pre-reflective* since, he suggests, the impact of social location on social perception and behavior typically occurs in implicit, taken-for-granted ways. The emphasis here is not on the development (or not) of class consciousness, but rather on the classed nature of particular social and cultural practices. People do not have to explicitly recognize class issues, or identify with discrete class groupings, for class processes to operate. Class cultures are viewed as modes of differentiation rather than as types of collectivity, and "class" processes operate through individualized distinction rather than in social groupings.

For a later generation of class theorists this helps tackle the paradox that class remains structurally important in shaping people's lives but that this does not translate into consciously "claimed" cultural identities. Work on class "dispositions" suggests much more implicit and unself-conscious "class identities," but still argues that "class" continues to shape people's social identity; so that even if collective class consciousness dies out, class remains important as a "social filter" for socially "placing" ourselves and others (Reay 1997: 226). Such models explicitly downgrade the importance of reflexive or self-aware forms of class consciousness, and reflect the considerable shift in thinking that has occurred in class analysis since Marx's time. Rather than the classic Marxist model of "class-in-itself" giving rise to "class-for-itself" in which inequality triggered consciousness and action, this new model sets out a reverse process, in which explicit class identification and awareness may dissolve, but class dispositions remain implicitly encoded as a form of identity through (largely unconscious) class-differentiated tastes and practices.

SEE ALSO: Bourgeoisie and Proletariat; Bourdieu, Pierre; Capitalism; Class, Perceptions of; Class Conflict; Class, Status, and Power; Distinction; False Consciousness; Marx, Karl; Weber, Max

REFERENCES AND SUGGESTED READINGS

Beck, U. (1992) *Risk Society.* Sage, London.

Bourdieu, P. (1984) *Distinction: A Social Critique of the Judgment of Taste.* Harvard University Press, Cambridge, MA.

Goldthorpe, J. & Marshall, G. (1992) The Promising Future of Class Analysis. *Sociology* 26(3): 381–400.

Hout, M., Brooks, C., & Manza, J. (1996) The Persistence of Classes in Post-Industrial Societies. In: Lee, D. & Turner, B. (Eds.), *Conflicts About Class.* Longman, Harlow.

Lockwood, D. (1988) The Weakest Link in the Chain. In: Rose, D. (Ed.), *Social Stratification and Economic Change.* Hutchinson, London.

Marx, K. & Engels, F. (1969) *Selected Works*, Vol. 1. Progress Publishers, Moscow.

Marx, K. & Engels, F. (1998 [1848]) *The Communist Manifesto.* Monthly Review Press, New York.

Pahl, R. (1993) Does Class Analysis Without Class Theory Have A Future? *Sociology* 27: 253–8.

Pakulski, J. & Waters, M. (1996) *The Death of Class.* Sage, London.

Reay, D. (1997) Feminist Theory, Habitus, and Social Class: Disrupting Notions of Classlessness. *Women's Studies International Forum* 20(2): 225–33.

Savage, M. (2000) *Class Analysis and Social Transformation.* Open University Press, Buckingham.

Weber, M. (1978 [1910]) *Economy and Society: An Outline of Interpretive Sociology.* Ed. G. Roth & C. Wittich. University of California Press, Berkeley.

class and crime

Roland Chilton and Ruth Triplett

There is a longstanding controversy over the importance of social class in the production of criminal conduct. Some argue that there is a strong relationship between social class and crime while others say there is little or no relationship. This controversy is often an argument over the definition and measurement of crime, and the meaning of class.

Although official definitions of crime are legislative, in practice crime is defined by administrative policies and enforcement practices. Those who study crime and delinquency also define crime. The definition of crime was greatly expanded when criminologists began asking people to report their own illegal or improper behavior. In some of the early self-report studies, so much behavior was defined as delinquent that almost any child could be said to have committed a delinquent act. At the other extreme, some criminologists have suggested that conduct such as economic exploitation and racial discrimination are criminal even when the conduct does not violate existing law.

Researchers differ as well on how they measure crime. Some measures of crime are based on official counts of crime – reports of offenses or offenders produced by police, court, or correctional agencies. These efforts create information on offenses, victims, and offenders. Official data cover activities that are illegal and considered serious enough to warrant recognition by the criminal justice system. A different set of crime measures is created when interviews or questionnaires are used to ask people about crimes they have committed. The measures of crime used in such studies vary widely. The acts presented range from very minor offenses, or offenses that are illegal only for children, to very serious offenses.

In addition to issues of the definition and measurement of crime, disagreements about the meaning and measurement of social class make it difficult to conclude whether class is linked to crime. We can say in a general way that those who own a great deal of property and have high incomes are rich or upper class; those who own little or nothing and have low incomes are poor or lower class. Beyond this general notion the issue is quickly complicated. No commonly accepted set of classes exists.

RESEARCH ON CLASS AND CRIME

For the first half of the twentieth century, the question of the link between class and crime was examined in three basic ways. First, investigators looked at the impact of economic conditions on crime rates, asking if crime increases with economic downturns. A basic assumption in this approach was that poor economic conditions are harder on the poor than the middle class and that this produces increased crime.

A second approach examined the social class of prisoners or others formally identified as offenders. Generally, convicts were and are poor. In a third approach, crime rates for specific geographical areas were compared with a set of social and economic characteristics of the areas. These studies asked if areas with indications of high poverty rates and low social class were also areas with high crime rates. In general the answers to these questions were yes. All three of these approaches probably influenced the development of theories either attempting to explain the reasons for the class–crime relationship or assuming such a relationship.

However, in the 1940s and 1950s there was a shift in focus in criminology. The first aspect of the shift came when Edwin Sutherland introduced the notion of "white-collar crime" to call attention to offenses committed by high-status people in conjunction with their occupations. A second shift in focus came about when some criminologists fixed their attention on young people and on middle-class delinquency. Researchers concluded that there was a great deal of unreported criminal and delinquent conduct committed by middle-class teenagers. And that, with some exceptions, the relationship between class and crime was weak or nonexistent.

In trying to reconcile the conflicting results of a number of individual-level confessional studies with those comparing area characteristics with area crime rates, some questioned the accuracy, representativeness, and scope of the surveys. Others played down or ignored the problems presented by the survey approach and concluded that the impact of social class on crime was a myth (Tittle et al. 1978).

In 1979, John Braithwaite published a careful review of a large number of area and confessional studies and a balanced discussion of the advantages and limitations of each. After reviewing studies carried out through the mid-1970s, he concluded that lower-class children and adults commit the types of crime handled by the police at higher rates than middle-class children and adults. On the "myth" of the class–crime relationship, he warns us to "be wary of reviews that pretend to be exhaustive but are in fact selective" (p. 63).

Studies since the 1970s have continued to focus both on the geographical distribution of crime and the relationship of an individual's class membership to crime. They have also continued to differ in their findings. Studies of the geographical distribution of crime generally continued to reinforce earlier findings that official delinquency rates for small urban areas were linked to indicators of poverty and disadvantage (Chilton 1964). In 1991 Patterson reviewed 22 studies of poverty and crime published from 1976 to 1986 and found that, although some of the studies did not find a relationship between class and crime, most of the studies showed positive effects of poverty on crime.

Analyses of the relationship between class and crime at the individual level, however, were less supportive of a relationship. Some researchers using reports of individuals suggested that while social origin might play a minor role in explaining juvenile criminality, the effect of the individual's own social position is important for adult criminality (Thornberry & Farnworth 1982). Others suggested that the correlations between self-reported delinquency and social class are weak and should be weak in part because of the offenses used and in part because traits associated with high and low social class scores are related to different kinds of crime.

Responding to the general absence of studies on the impact of social class on adult crime, Dunaway and his colleagues used three different measures of social class to analyze the responses of an adult sample for a single city – an "underclass" measure, a gradational measure of class based on income and education, and respondents' business ownership and position as employers or employees. In addition, they used two measures of crime, the total number of offenses reported when respondents were asked to check one or more offenses from a list of 50 that they might have committed over the preceding year and a violent crime scale.

They found that what one could conclude about class and crime depended on the measures of class and crime used. For example, when the full set of offenses was used to measure crime, only income was inversely related to crime. Using the violence subset as a measure of crime, they reported an inverse relationship between crime and some of their social class measures.

What measure of crime and class is used may well explain, in part, why studies of geographical areas find a stronger relationship of class to crime than do individual studies. Another possible explanation of the conflicting results is the distinctly different locations of the people and situations studied. Studies of geographical location are usually carried out for urban areas, Metropolitan Statistical Areas, urban counties, cities, or census tracts. Individual studies have frequently been carried out in small towns and areas with very small minority populations. These studies have often been unable to tap both the high and the low ends of the social class distribution. Nowhere is this clearer than in the way the two approaches deal with race. One classic self-report study dropped all black respondents from the analysis. The area studies include minority populations in the crime counts and in the population counts.

The relationship of race to crime is important in any understanding of the class–crime relationship. US public health statistics on homicide as a cause of death indicate that this is a leading cause of death for black males. In addition, the Federal Bureau of Investigation's Supplementary Homicide Reports (SHR) suggest that black offenders are responsible for most homicides with black victims. More importantly, black males have been over-represented in both the victimization figures and the offender figures for over 35 years.

The traditional response to this situation is to say that high homicide-offending rates for black males are a function of social class. Peterson and Krivo (1993) analyzed homicide victimization rates for 125 US cities and found that black homicides were linked to racial segregation. Parker and McCall's city-level analysis of interracial and intraracial homicide provides another indication of the probable utility of race-specific data. Using race-specific independent variables for about 100 US cities, they conclude that economic deprivation affects the intraracial homicide rates for whites and blacks. In addition, in a study that used arrest counts to create race-specific offense rates, Ousey (1999) reported a large gap between black and white homicide rates. The black rates were five times as high as the white rates. Although he found that measures of poverty and deprivation had an impact on both black and white homicide rates, he found that the effects of these variables were stronger for whites than for blacks. He suggests that extensive and long-term disadvantage may have produced cultural and normative adaptations that have created this gap in the rates. The patterns of homicide rates by race suggest that the rates are probably linked to exclusion and segregation – economic, racial, and ethnic – but especially to the separation and isolation of large segments of the urban population based on income and assets. This separation is frequently based on race or ethnicity but it is increasingly linked to a combination of racial separatism and poverty.

As John Hagan (1992) has suggested, the relationship between class and crime may be class- and crime-specific. It is also probably race- and gender-specific. He is probably also right in his assertion that not only does class have an impact on crime, but also some kinds of crime, or at least some responses to crime, have an impact on the social class of some offenders. This is why he is right in his assessment that "the simple omission of class from the study of crime would impoverish criminology."

SEE ALSO: Criminology; Criminology: Research Methods; Measuring Crime; Race and Crime; Sex and Crime

REFERENCES AND SUGGESTED READINGS

Braithwaite, J. (1979) *Inequality, Crime, and Public Policy*. Routledge & Kegan Paul, London.
Chilton, R. (1964) Delinquency Area Research in Baltimore, Detroit, and Indianapolis. *American Sociological Review* 29: 71–83.
Dunaway, R. G., Cullen, F. T., Burton, V. S., Jr., & Evans, T. D. (2000) The Myth of Social Class and Crime Revisited: An Examination of Class and Adult Criminality. *Criminology* 38: 589–632.
Hagan, J. (1992) The Poverty of a Classless Criminology: The American Society of Criminology 1991 Presidential Address. *Criminology* 30: 1–19.
Nye, F. I. & Short, J. F. (1957) Scaling Delinquent Behavior. *American Sociological Review* 22: 326–31.
Ousey, G. C. (1999) Homicide, Structural Factors, and the Racial Invariance Assumption. *Criminology* 37: 405–26.
Peterson, R. D. & Krivo, L. J. (1993) Racial Segregation and Black Urban Homicide. *Social Forces* 71: 1001–26.

Sampson, R. J. (1987) Urban Black Violence: The Effect of Male Joblessness and Family Disruption. *American Journal of Sociology* 93: 348–82.

Thornberry, T. P. & Farnworth, M. (1982) Social Correlates of Criminal Involvement: Further Evidence on the Relationship Between Social Status and Criminal Behavior. *American Sociological Review* 47: 505–18.

Tittle, C. R., Villemez, W. A., & Smith, D. A. (1978) The Myth of Social Class and Criminality: An Empirical Assessment of the Empirical Evidence. *American Sociological Review* 43: 643–56.

Wright, B. R. E. et al. (1999) Reconsidering the Relationship Between SES and Delinquency: Causation But Not Correlation. *Criminology* 37: 175–94.

class, perceptions of

Wendy Bottero

How people perceive class inequality is not just a question of class consciousness but also entails the issue of consciousness of class (and inequality), of class as social description and social identity (Cannadine 1998: 23). When people describe their unequal worlds, they are often engaged in making claims about the relative worth of different groups and the fairness (or otherwise) of social arrangements. All accounts of hierarchy contain "images of inequality," social pictures which classify and grade the members of society. These are politically loaded descriptions, and the images individuals draw partly depend on their social location and the agendas that they are pursuing.

Historians of social imagery argue that the language of social description is fluid and ambiguous, with frequent mixing of models. Ossowski (1963) sees "class" imagery as metaphorical, enabling people to draw on shared understandings, but with a very wide range of possible meanings. The ambiguity of such terms gives them their appeal – rather than identifying an objective social structure or precise social group, the language(s) of "class," "us and them," and so on reflect the shifting politics for which they are used. Images of inequality are not a reflection of reality but an "intervention" within it (Crossick 1991: 152).

Subjective perceptions of inequality have been used to construct "maps" of the objective social hierarchy. One early example (Warner 1949) used community rankings. Noticing that people in a community continually referred to the reputation of their neighbors, Warner aggregated these perceptions into "social class" rankings of the entire community. This method (aggregating subjective evaluations of rank) rests on the assumption that perceptions of status straightforwardly reflect the stratification structure. Yet Warner's own research found that such perceptions vary systematically by status.

A related approach is used to construct prestige scales, mapping the stratification structure by looking at the general reputation of occupational categories. A sample of individuals ranks or rates a list of occupations, and the results are aggregated into a status scale. In support of this it is claimed that there is considerable consensus over such rankings, with rich and poor, educated and uneducated, young and old, all – it is argued – having the same perceptions of the prestige hierarchy, with little variation in their relative ratings (Treiman 1994: 209). This similarity is taken as evidence of a consensus about the worth of occupations, supporting functionalist claims of shared values about social rewards. Such conclusions are contested, however. Critics argue that considerable popular disagreement over occupational rankings is minimized by the methods of prestige studies (Pawson 1989). There is also controversy about what prestige scales measure. For critics, prestige ratings simply assess the various objective attributes (skill, income, etc.) that make jobs more or less advantaged. If so, then differential rankings of occupations are statements of fact rather than any indication of moral approval for varying rewards. But if prestige ratings are simply "error-prone estimates" (Featherman & Hauser 1976) of the objective socioeconomic characteristics of jobs, it may make more sense to measure socioeconomic position directly (Goldthorpe & Hope 1972).

Critics also argue that attempts to map stratification through the subjective perceptions of the population rest on a false assumption "that a single structure pervades the social consciousness" (Coxon & Davies 1986: 13). Unlike sociologists, "people on the street" are less interested in, or aware of, the "big picture" of an overall status continuum, because they instead focus on the relative rankings of the people and social roles that immediately concern them (Coxon & Davies 1986: 40). Whilst individuals may be concerned with distinctions and differences in the occupations that they encounter on a daily basis (at work, through friends and family), the differences between occupations that they rarely encounter, or simply hear about in the abstract, may not mean much to them. Prestige rankings may be an artifact of the sociological exercise rather than a deep-seated feature of the social consciousness.

Many commentators suggest that perceptions of inequality depend on social location *within* a structure of inequality. The classic statement, by Lockwood, argues that people's perceptions of the "larger society" vary according to how they experience inequality in the "smaller societies in which they live out their daily lives" (1975: 16). However, subsequent research reveals that people's images of inequality are not so clear-cut, with different views "wheeled on" in different situations (Savage 2000: 27). Cannadine (1998) argues that different models are often used to describe the same social structures by the same speaker, with slippage occurring within accounts. The model used partly depends on what point the speaker is trying to make.

Just as images of inequality are never simple descriptions of social structure, so we cannot just "read off" an individual's social imagery from his or her social position. In a six-nation study of subjective class identification, Kelley and Evans (1995: 166) found that a "middling" self-image was held by those at all levels of the objective stratification hierarchy. Their conclusion was, in almost all societies, very few people identify with the top or bottom classes, with most people subjectively identifying with the middle classes. Despite big differences in people's social position, most people located themselves as "average" or "middling" in the social order. This does not mean that hierarchical social location has no effect on images of the social order, however. Kelley and Evans argue that claims to being "middling" are related to the hierarchical nature of general social networks, because "reference-group forces" constrain people's subjective perceptions to a restricted range

of the class hierarchy. "Reference-group forces" refers to the way in which people assess their own class position in relation to the education, occupations, authority, and income of the people who immediately surround them. Because such social relations are themselves hierarchically sorted, this leads to a distorted perception of the class hierarchy, as "even very high status people see many others above themselves, and very low status people see others even lower" (Evans et al. 1992: 465).

Because we tend to see our own social milieu as "typical" and "middling," high-status people tend to exaggerate the size of the higher classes and minimize the size of the lower classes, resulting in a relatively egalitarian image of society, whilst low-status people exaggerate the size of the lower classes, resulting in a more elitist image (Evans et al. 1992: 477). This means that public debates over issues of equality and the politicization of images of society are likely to emerge from, and affect, unequally located groups differently.

SEE ALSO: Class; Class Consciousness; Class, Status, and Power; Stratification and Inequality, Theories of

REFERENCES AND SUGGESTED READINGS

Cannadine, D. (1998) *Class in Britain*. Yale University Press, London.

Coxon, A. & Davies, P. (1986) *Images of Social Stratification*. Sage, London.

Crossick, G. (1991) From Gentlemen to the Residuum: Languages of Social Description in Victorian Britain. In: Corfield, P. J. (Ed.), *Language, History, and Class*. Blackwell, Oxford.

Evans, M. D. R., Kelley, J., & Kolosi, T. (1992) Images of Class: Public Perceptions in Hungary and Australia. *American Sociological Review* 57: 461–82.

Featherman, D. & Hauser, R. (1976) Prestige or Socioeconomic Scales in the Study of Occupational Achievement. *Sociological Methods and Research* 4(4): 403–5.

Goldthorpe, J. & Hope, K. (1972) Occupational Grading and Occupational Prestige. In: Hope, K. (Ed.), *The Analysis of Social Mobility*. Clarendon Press, Oxford.

Kelley, J. & Evans, M. D. R. (1995) Class and Class Conflict in Six Western Nations. *American Sociological Review* 60: 157–78.

Lockwood, D. (1975) Sources of Variation in Working-Class Images of Society. In: Bulmer, M. (Ed.), *Working-Class Images of Society*. Routledge & Kegan Paul, London.

Ossowski, S. (1963) *Class Structure in the Social Consciousness*. Routledge & Kegan Paul, London.

Pawson, R. (1989) *A Measure for Measures*. Routledge, London.

Savage, M. (2000) *Class Analysis and Social Transformation.* Open University Press, Buckingham.

Treiman, D. (1994) Occupational Prestige in Comparative Perspective. In: Grusky, D. (Ed.), *Social Stratification*. Westview, Boulder, CO.

Warner, W. L. (1949) *Social Class in America.* Harper & Row, New York.

class, status, and power

Wout Ultee

Class, Status, and Power is the title of an edited collection by Reinhard Bendix and Seymour Martin Lipset. The first edition was published in 1953, and after several reprints a thoroughly revised edition appeared in 1966. "Class, status, and power" is also an apt name for the research program that dominated the sociology of stratification in the first decades after World War II. This program denied the existence, in all times and in every society, of one fundamental dimension of stratification and viewed societal stratification as three-dimensional, with the task of sociological research being to determine in concrete cases the interplay of class, status, and power and its consequences for the extent to which societies change or are stable.

Taking the lead from a statement by Weber (1968 [1922]), the program of class, status, and power wished to overcome unproductive oppositions between various theoretical paradigms. This hope seemed to be dashed around the mid-1960s by an upsurge in Marxist and neo-Marxist theorizing in sociology, but since the 1980s a neo-Weberian approach has had the upper hand. The aim of the program of class, status, and power was to move beyond detailed descriptions of particular contemporary societies, especially the United States, to historical and comparative studies of various aspects of stratification. In this respect the program was

successful. The study of stratification flourishes in all nations with research universities, and comparisons of aspects of stratification in a large number of societies are the order of the day. However, the program of class, status, and power suffered from theoretical incoherences. One was admitted by Bendix and Lipset in a footnote to the 1966 introduction: classes and status groups are themselves aggregations of power. By the term power they in effect referred to political power. Indeed, Weber had maintained that classes, status groups, and parties are phenomena of the power relationships within a society.

Ultimately, the yield of the program of class, status, and (political) power remained limited because it did not specify strong hypotheses about how the three pinpointed dimensions of stratification interact in various types of societies and how this affects societal stability or change. Dahrendorf (1979) admitted as much in a correction of Dahrendorf (1957). His old propositions like "the radicalness of structure change co-varies with the intensity of class conflict" do not say enough about either the substance of conflict or the direction of change. He added that the notion of life chances goes some way toward remedying this deficiency, indicating what a more fruitful program of research looks like.

Perhaps the oldest theories of societal stratification are those of scholars like Plato and Machiavelli, but also of twentieth-century thinkers like Pareto and Mosca. These theories have as a starting point a quite visible phenomenon within most societies: their population consists of a small number of official rulers and numerous persons who are being ruled. To the extent that rulers are wise, cunning, or whatever, societies are stable. Some theories of political power assert an inevitable decline in these respects among the persons ruling a society; other theories of political power maintain that the circulation of elites fails to result in important societal changes. According to the program of class, status, and power, this view of society is limited: political power is but one of three dimensions of stratification.

According to another unidimensional theory of societal stratification, the fundamental dimension of this phenomenon is the relationship between the members of a society and its means of subsistence. Whatever the rulers of a society do, they rarely procure their own food and the inhabitants of a society in some way or another make a living. According to Scottish moral philosophers of the eighteenth century such as Ferguson, Millar, and Smith, hunting was one mode of subsistence, herding another, cultivating the earth a third, and division of labor and commerce others. Each had particular rules of ownership with respect to territories for hunting, pastures for grazing herds, fields for cultivating grain, and tools for producing tradable goods. In the nineteenth century, Marx (cf. Jordan 1971) proposed that the history of human societies was that of a struggle between classes, be they freemen and slaves in ancient societies, lords and serfs under medieval feudalism, or capital owners and wage-laborers in contemporary societies with private ownership and free markets for capital and labor. Unemployment was the scourge of laborers, and the next economic downturn would be accompanied by more unemployment than the previous one.

The starting point of a third unidimensional theory of social stratification is that every society contains notions about the degree to which individual activities are valuable to society at large, and about the standard of living appropriate for persons differing in occupation, as well as the respect due to them. Widespread in each society too are ideas about how persons ought to be recruited to these more and less valuable positions. These hypotheses most clearly were stated by Durkheim (1960 [1897]). Since the shared ideas refer to the esteem bestowed on persons of a certain category, these groupings have been called status groups. Durkheim added that ideas about legitimate rewards are not immutable, and that they change with the general level of living and with the moral ideas current within a society. Ideas about legitimate recruitment change too; at one time the title a person received at birth was the almost exclusive principle of recruitment, but in Durkheim's France only inequalities resulting from the inheritance of wealth, merit, and innate capacities were considered just.

The program of class, status, and power attempted to unite these unidimensional theories into one general theory. It did so by

recognizing that the dimensions cannot always be reduced to one and the same dimension. As to political power, it was held that the power of the persons commanding a society's state does not rest only upon violence, threats to life, and weapons. These persons seek to establish themselves more or less successfully as legitimate rulers, turning their rule of might into a rule of right. Although a society's laws protect the economically dominant classes and a society's courts are run by persons connected to them, in a state with laws and courts, decisions by judges do not always favor the participant who is economically dominant. The economically dominant class comprises more persons than the participant in court, and it is in their interest that laws, precisely because they are slanted toward them, are upheld – even though in some cases decisions go against the economically dominant participant appearing in court. Also, since ideas have a logic of their own, the ruling ideas of a society are never fully the ideas of its ruling class.

According to the program of class, status, and power, in pre-industrial societies persons who attain political power often afterwards amass economic power, and in this way prolong their rule. This tells against an idea of the theory that class is the fundamental dimension of stratification: according to this notion, political power would follow economic power. Political parties in industrial societies do not always seek to improve the living conditions of one specific economic class. In some countries parties mainly aim to conquer the state and to dispense its spoils – jobs, tax receipts, and all kinds of legal privileges – to its leaders and followers, making them brokerage parties. Also, some parties are ideological. They proclaim a worldview, often part of some religion but sometimes too of a secular system of thought, and reject any governmental policy that does not square with this.

As to the unidimensional theory that notions about legitimate status are fundamental to societal stratification, it should be said that according to Durkheim in France during the nineteenth century, guilds had been abolished and church and state separated, with the state leaving the economy to the free interplay of labor and capital. Under such conditions, so the hypothesis runs, notions about what is just *de jure* simply are not realized *de facto*. Also, it will be clear that by allowing for changes in notions about legitimate reward and recruitment, Durkheim to some extent did away with the assumption of shared ideas. Changes in the collective conscience cannot be so hard and fast that from one day to another a particular general agreement is replaced by a vastly different consensus. In contrast, theories taking class as the prime dimension of stratification hold that consensus rarely is present, and to the extent that it is, consensus is imposed by the economically dominant class. How this class did so was unclear, and Marxist theories of religion remained underdeveloped. Expanding the notion that religions promise the oppressed salvation in life after death, Weber held that persons privileged in property, honor, and political power have a need to assure themselves that these actual privileges are legitimate, and that some religions cater to this need.

Although the program of class, status, and power pointed toward various findings that are difficult to square with this or that unidimensional theory of societal stratification, it did not provide much guidance for making progress. It offered case studies, but whether they turned into exemplars is another matter. According to a study by Wolfgang Eberhard adduced in the first edition of *Class, Status, and Power*, inherently unstable notions about what is valuable to society become more widespread by an intertwining of political and economic power, making this society more stable. This happened in agrarian China through the strategies of families with a branch of bureaucrats and another one of landlords. If such meshing does not obtain, struggles will be more violent.

Lenski (1954) surmised that persons with inconsistent positions on various dimensions of stratification are more likely to get involved in movements aimed at societal change. Lenski regarded these inconsistencies, say high in education but low in occupation, as a horizontal dimension of stratification, in contrast to the vertical ones of class, status, political power, or whatever. Evidence for persons with inconsistent positions on various dimensions of stratification for countries like the United States pointed toward a stronger support for political

parties in favor of state interventions that redistribute income from the rich to the poor. However, it also was found that persons with inconsistent positions were more likely to be disinterested in politics and to stay at home during polling days. Non-voting was held to add to political stability.

Lipset and Bendix (1959) followed Weber, not so much by giving more flesh to the program of class, status, and power as by raising questions about the degree to which a society's system of stratification is rigid or even closed. They posited that in countries with a strong feudal tradition like those of Europe, social mobility would be less widespread than in countries like the US, where the opposition between capitalists and wage earners was not preceded by that between lords and serfs. Lipset and Bendix came to reject this hypothesis after assembling data for a dozen industrial countries in the 1950s on father–son mobility across the manual/non-manual line. They buttressed this conclusion by bringing in data showing that patterns of intermarriage were pretty much the same in industrial societies too. Since the mid-1960s hypotheses have been proposed and tested about the extent to which parties of the left, either communist or social democratic, increase mobility and decrease income disparities. The mobility data adduced by Lipset and Bendix and other scholars for some time remained limited to men and their fathers. The occupation of men was held to indicate the class of every household member, and the occupation of the father was considered a good gauge of parental influence. In the 1970s, with the onset of a new research program on life chances and resources, the question of women and stratification became a topic in stratification research.

Using election surveys for various industrial countries with universal suffrage, Lipset established that persons from the lower classes were more likely to vote for a left-wing party than persons from the higher classes. Having found that voting depends upon class, the follow-up thesis became that with rising standards of living, class differentials in voting become smaller and the pressure for political change weaker (Lipset 1981 [1960]). However, although differences between the manual and non-manual classes in their support for parties of the right and the old left decreased, new parties emerged in several advanced industrial societies. The Greens cater not to material interests but to post-material ones, like a clean environment and the preservation of animals and plants, and some theories pinpoint highly educated persons working outside the private sector as the prime recruiting ground of these parties (Inglehart 1977). With the emergence of anti-immigrant parties in several European countries, the question arose whether persons with higher chances of unemployment are more likely to vote for the new right.

As indicated, the research program of class, status, and power that dominated the sociology of stratification in the first decades after World War II was somewhat incoherent. The enumeration should have read classes, status groups, and parties, with all three types of groupings amounting to instances of power relations within a society. The program also misleadingly tended to equate class with income. Class is about economic power and means of production. It therefore is about wealth, from which persons of course derive income. The program did recognize that persons who do not own means of production and live from their labor differ in productive skills. It therefore was multidimensional when it came to economic power alone. As has been remarked too, the program of class, status, and power was less than explicit about the effects of economic resources. Perhaps it was taken as a matter of fact that if productive skills are in demand and supply is limited, wages are higher. As conventional wisdom holds, in societies where labor is legally free, unskilled jobs have the lowest wages and the highest unemployment rates, since anybody can perform them. Also, if inventions in the means of production make certain skills obsolete, the chances of unemployment for persons with these skills rise, while their wages drop. Since the consequences of economic resources involve wages and unemployment, multidimensional research is in order here too.

The question of race and stratification has a long standing in US research. However, one exemplar within the program of class, status, and power gave off a wrong signal for answering it (Lipset & Bendix 1959). It is true that the US is a society without a feudal tradition. Yet according to the theory that class is the fundamental dimension of stratification, capitalism was preceded by feudalism and feudalism by slavery. Although slavery had been abolished in 1865 in the US, a century later the legacy of slavery was still visible in the exclusion of African Americans from the polling booth in the areas where most of them lived. According to Wiley (1967), it also showed up in labor market outcomes like lower wages and higher percentages of unemployment, and in market processes for goods and services, such as European American landlords refusing to rent to African Americans, and white-owned restaurants refusing to serve blacks. These European American practices regarding African Americans were liabilities for the latter in the society's distribution processes. For this reason, the late contribution to the program that stratification is multidimensional was also an early contribution to the new program on life chances and resources.

The idea that classes, status groups, and parties are phenomena of the power relationships within a society was called Weberian. Since the end of the 1960s, two other concepts, those of resources and life chances, have become current and have been termed "neo-Weberian." However, the prime contribution of neo-Weberianism is the proposition that the aggregation of the resources of a society's inhabitants into an overall distribution of power determines inequalities in a society's distribution of life chances. Individual resources can be economic, symbolic, and political, with classes, status groups, and parties being aggregate phenomena of the power relationships within a society. Among others, unemployment, wages, and secondary benefits like health insurance are taken as aspects of life chances. In the 1980s, the program of class, status, and power was superseded by that of life chances and resources.

SEE ALSO: Class; Elites; Life Chances and Resources; Mobility, Horizontal and Vertical; Mobility, Intergenerational and Intragenerational; Stratification, Gender and; Stratification and Inequality, Theories of; Stratification, Race/Ethnicity and; Stratification: Technology and Ideology

REFERENCES AND SUGGESTED READINGS

Bendix, R. & Lipset, S. M. (Eds.) (1966 [1953]) *Class, Status, and Power*, 2nd rev. edn. Free Press, Glencoe.

Dahrendorf, R. (1957) *Class and Class Conflict in Industrial Society*. Routledge, London.

Dahrendorf, R. (1979) *Life Chances*. Weidenfeld & Nicolson, London.

Durkheim, É. (1960 [1897]) *Suicide*. Routledge, London.

Inglehart, R. (1977) *The Silent Revolution*. Princeton University Press, Princeton.

Jordan, Z. A. (Ed.) (1971) *Karl Marx: Economy, Class, and Social Revolution*. Nelson, London.

Lenski, G. (1954) Status Crystallization: A Non-Vertical Dimension of Stratification. *American Sociological Review* 19: 405–13.

Lipset, S. M. (1981 [1960]) *Political Man*, expanded and updated edn. Johns Hopkins University Press, Baltimore.

Lipset, S. M. & Bendix, R. (1959) *Social Mobility in Industrial Society*. University of California Press, Berkeley.

Weber, M. (1968 [1922]) *Economy and Society*. Bedminster Press, New York.

Wiley, N. (1967) America's Unique Class Politics: The Interplay of the Labor, Credit, and Commodity Markets. *American Sociological Review* 32: 529–41.

class and voting

Geoffrey Evans

Class voting refers to the tendency for citizens in a particular social class to vote for a given political party or candidate rather than an alternative option when compared with voters in other classes. Though apparently simple, this notion has generated considerable intricacy and ambiguity. The definition of social class has been much debated, as have measures of class position and attempts to summarize statistically the class–vote association. Explanations of patterns of class voting are little in evidence and of uncertain generality. Nevertheless, despite these unresolved disputes concerning measurement and theory, there has at least been a substantial body of research into whether or not levels of class voting have weakened as western democracies have moved from being industrial to post-industrial societies.

Interest in class voting emerged in response in part to the failed agenda of Marxism, for whom electoral politics was an expression of the democratic class struggle that supposedly preceded the expected class-based revolution. This tended to result in a focus on class voting as a dispute between just two classes, the working class and the middle class, and their political representatives, parties of the left and right. Early research also relied on data obtained at the level of electoral constituencies, with the consequent need to make strong assumptions about how voters in different classes actually voted. More recently, studies of class voting have focused on large-scale surveys of voters which have created a vast body of evidence on individual-level class voting.

Possibly the most influential work on the topic is Robert Alford's (1967) analysis of trends in class voting in four Anglo-American democracies (Australia, Britain, Canada, and the US) between 1936 and 1962 using a manual versus nonmanual measure of class position. He also introduced the most commonly used, cited (and criticized) measure of the level of class voting: the "Alford index." The Alford index is the difference between the percentage of manual workers that voted for left-wing parties on the one hand and the percentage of nonmanual workers that voted for these parties on the other. This became the standard instrument in studies that followed, most of which appeared to show that class voting was in decline. As a result, by the 1990s many commentators agreed that class voting in modern industrial societies had all but disappeared. Class was thought to have lost its importance as a determinant of life-chances and political interests because either the working class had become richer, white-collar workers had been "proletarianized," or social mobility between classes had increased. At the same time, post-industrial cleavages such as gender, race, ethnicity, public versus private sector, and various identity groups had emerged and replaced class-based conflict, while new post-material values had supposedly led to the "new left" drawing its support from the middle classes, thus weakening the class basis of left–right divisions. Moreover, rising levels of education had ostensibly produced voters who were calculating and "issue oriented" rather than being driven by collective identities such as class.

All of these accounts assumed that there had indeed been a widespread, secular decline in class voting. However, during the 1980s a movement emerged that questioned the validity of this assumption and argued instead that problems of measurement and analysis seriously undermined the work that had followed Alford's approach. In particular, it was argued that the use of a crude manual/nonmanual distinction obscures variations in the composition of the manual and nonmanual classes (Heath et al. 1985). For example, if skilled manual workers are more right wing than unskilled workers and the number of skilled workers increases, the Alford estimate of difference between manual and nonmanual workers will decline even if the relative political positions of skilled, unskilled, and nonmanual workers remain the same. With this and similar indices the measurement of the class–vote association is thus open to confounding by changes in the shape of the class structure. In other words, this type of index confuses differences in the marginal distributions of the variables with differences in the association it is supposed to measure – a problem also found with the OLS regression techniques used in, among others, Franklin et al.'s (1992) 16-nation study that represents the culmination of this tradition.

In recent years, therefore, the manual/nonmanual representation of class voting has been to a large degree superseded. The most influential class schema used currently was developed by John Goldthorpe and his colleagues (Erikson & Goldthorpe 1992). The main classes identified in this schema are the "petty bourgeoisie" (small employers and self-employed), the "service class" or "salariat" (professional and managerial groups), the "routine nonmanual class" (typically lower-grade clerical "white-collar workers"), and the "working class" (foremen and technicians, skilled, semi-, and unskilled manual workers). The principal distinction underlying the distinction among the employee classes in the schema is between a *service contract* in which employees receive not only salaried rewards but also prospective elements – salary increments,

job security and pension rights, and, most importantly, well-defined career opportunities – and a *labor contract*, in which employees supply discrete amounts of labor, under supervision, in return for wages which are calculated on a "piece" or time basis. As the employment relationship of the service class is relatively advantageous in terms of employment and payment conditions, occupational security, and promotion prospects, its members have a stake in preserving the status quo. In contrast, the disadvantages of the labor contract can explain why the working class provides a basis of support for the redistributive programs of the left.

This shift to greater complexity in the measurement of class has been accompanied by a similar move away from the measurement of political choice as a dichotomy of left versus right (or left versus non-left) to a fuller representation of the voters' spectrum of choice at the ballot box. Apart from its simplicity, the main reason for the use of a dichotomy to represent voter choice seems to have been a desire to make systematic cross-national and over-time comparisons. Unfortunately, the selective nature of what is being compared undermines any true comparability. The problem is analogous to that faced in the analysis of class position. Changes in the composition of composite categories such as "left" or "non-left" may lead to spurious changes in estimates of class voting. The use of dichotomies to represent vote choices and social classes also precludes from observation any processes of class–party realignment. The concept of class realignment in voting implies a change in the pattern of association between class and vote without any change in the overall strength of this association (i.e., without class dealignment or, of course, increase in alignment). But this cannot be discerned if the distinction between realignment and dealignment is obscured by restricting the numbers of parties and classes to two.

The other major innovation of the last two decades is in the statistical measurement of the class–vote association. There has been a move from Alford-type indices to logistic modeling techniques which measure the strength of the relationship between class and vote independently of the general popularity of political parties or changes in the sizes of classes. These techniques also enable the statistical estimation of more complex class and party relationships, thus facilitating greater sophistication in the representation of both class position and party choice.

Research using these advances comes to rather different conclusions than those in the two-class, two-party tradition (for examples, see Evans 1999; Hout et al. 1995). While there is evidence of a linear decline in left versus non-left class voting (most notably in Nieuwbeerta 1995), it is not typical. When examined over the longest available time series, levels of class voting in Britain were found to have *increased* during the 1940s and 1950s before falling back in the 1960s. Similarly, the US, a nation of traditionally low levels of class polarization, may well have seen the growth of new class–vote cleavages – such as between those who vote and those who do not (Hout et al. 1995). And in at least some of the new post-communist democracies the 1990s saw increased levels of class voting as these societies underwent the rigors of marketization (Evans & Whitefield 2006). Only in certain Scandinavian countries is there robust evidence of a decline from an unusually high degree of class voting to levels similar to those in other western democracies.

Despite these methodological and evidential advances, the debate about the decline of class voting remains active, with many authors continuing to claim evidence for a decline (e.g., Oskarsson 2005). By comparison with this extensive literature examining descriptive questions, signs of empirically tested theoretical development are far less noticeable. Most scholars have assumed a sociological, relatively deterministic account of the transition to industrial and post-industrial politics, but there are those who have rejected these in favor of more voluntaristic models. Kitschelt (1994), for example, argues that the electoral fortunes of European social democratic parties are largely determined by their strategic appeals, rather than by secular trends in the class structure – a line of reasoning that echoes Sartori's (1969) influential emphasis on the importance of organization, and especially parties, in the creation of class constituencies. This would suggest that even in post-industrial societies class voting might increase as well as decrease. It also implies that class-relevant policy programs should result in increase in the class basis of party support. Evidence for this in Britain has indeed been provided by Evans et al. (1999), who show a close relationship over a 20-year period between left–right polarization in parties' manifestos and the extent of class voting. Later work by Oskarsson (2005) indicates that this pattern is also found elsewhere in Europe. This is not to say that sociological changes have no impact. Changes in the relative *sizes* of classes have been thought to have implications for party strategy: most importantly, in a change to a "catch-all" strategy by parties on the left in response to the shrinking class basis of support for those parties (Przeworski & Sprague 1986). In some political systems such moves leave open the space for left parties to attract support from marginalized working-class groups; in others, such as first-past-the-post systems, we might expect the start-up costs for electorally viable left parties to be too great. Unfortunately, many of these arguments still await rigorous tests using survey analysis. Research that tries to unravel *why* voters in different classes vote differently is in short supply, though Weakliem and Heath (1994) provide evidence of the role of rational choice and inherited preferences, while Evans (1999) provides evidence that promotion prospects can under certain conditions account for class differences in left-wing versus right-wing party support. A more explicit link between models of class voting and their dependence on advances in theories of voting behavior more generally is an area where further development might still usefully occur.

SEE ALSO: Class; Class Consciousness; Class, Perceptions of; Class, Status, and Power

REFERENCES AND SUGGESTED READINGS

Alford, R. (1967) Class Voting in Anglo-American Political Systems. In: Lipset, S. M. & Rokkan, S. (Eds.), *Party Systems and Voter Alignments: Cross-National Perspectives*. Free Press, New York, pp. 67–94.

Erikson, R. & Goldthorpe, J. H. (1992) *The Constant Flux: A Study of Class Mobility in Industrial Societies*. Clarendon Press, Oxford.

Evans, G. (Ed.) (1999) *The End of Class Politics? Class Voting in Comparative Context*. Oxford University Press, Oxford.

Evans, G. & Whitefield, S. (2006) Explaining the Rise and Persistence of Class Voting in Postcommunist Russia, 1993–2001. *Political Research Quarterly* 59 (March).

Evans, G., Heath, A., & Payne, C. (1999) Class: Labour as a Catch-All Party? In: Evans, G. & Norris, P. (Eds.), *Critical Elections: British Parties and Voters in Long-Term Perspective*. Sage, London, pp. 87–101.

Franklin, M. N., Mackie, T., Valen, H., et al. (1992) *Electoral Change: Responses to Evolving Social and Attitudinal Structures in Western Countries*. Cambridge University Press, Cambridge.

Heath, A. F., Jowell, R., & Curtice, J. (1985) *How Britain Votes*. Pergamon Press, Oxford.

Hout, M., Brooks, C., & Manza, J. (1995) The Democratic Class Struggle in the United States. *American Sociological Review* 60: 805–28.

Kitschelt, H. (1994) *The Transformation of European Social Democracy*. Cambridge University Press, Cambridge.

Lipset, S. M. (1981) *Political Man: The Social Bases of Politics*. Heinemann, London.

Manza, J., Hout, M., & Brooks, C. (1995) Class Voting in Capitalist Democracies Since World War II: Dealignment, Realignment or Trendless Fluctuation? *Annual Review of Sociology* 21: 137–62.

Nieuwbeerta, P. (1995) *The Democratic Class Struggle in Twenty Countries, 1945–1990*. Thesis Publishers, Amsterdam.

Oskarsson, M. (2005) Social Structure and Party Choice. In: Thomassen, J. (Ed.), *The European Voter*. Oxford University Press, Oxford, pp. 84–105.

Przeworski, A. & Sprague, J. (1986) *Paper Stones: A History of Electoral Socialism*. University of Chicago Press, Chicago.

Sartori, G. (1969) From the Sociology of Politics to Political Sociology. In: Lipset, S. M. (Ed.), *Politics and the Social Sciences*. Oxford University Press, Oxford, pp. 65–100.

Weakliem, D. L. & Heath, A. F. (1994) Rational Choice and Class Voting. *Rationality and Society* 6: 243–70.

classification

Roger Burrows

Classification – the process of assigning objects (elements, cases, units, items, and so on) to classes or categories – is fundamental to cognition, language, and the construction of social structures. As such it has long been an important topic for sociological inquiry (Durkheim & Mauss 1963; Bowker & Star 1999; Olsen 2002). At the same time, more formal processes of classification – taxonomies, typologies, the construction of ideal types, and so on – are at the analytic heart of much of the sociological enterprise (Foucault 1970; van Mechelen et al. 1993) and, as such, they are also a central resource for the sociological imagination. Indeed, this distinction between classifications as both a substantive topic of investigation and, simultaneously, as an analytic resource for such investigations, forms the foundation for debates about what has come to be viewed as the issue of the "double hermeneutic" (Giddens 1976) in the discipline. This refers to a central conundrum in sociology in which the concepts and categories drawn upon by lay actors in their everyday practices are "explained" by sets of concepts and categories developed by sociologists that may (or, more likely, may not) be recognized by lay actors themselves. On occasion these sociological concepts and categories are reappropriated by lay actors into everyday language and life (one thinks of "social class" and more recently "social capital," "social networks," "social exclusion," and so on). But on other occasions the challenge is to demonstrate how and why the categories and classifications developed by sociologists are (in any sense) "superior" to those used by lay actors to explain their social actions. Which set of understandings possesses the greatest legitimacy – those provided by social actors in terms of their own lay "vocabularies of motive" or those provided by sociologists in terms of systematically constructed typologies of social action?

This tension between classificatory regimes that are "self-directed" and those that are "externally suggested" or even "externally imposed" is, of course, ubiquitous. It is not just a small band of sociologists who are keen to classify us in ways with which we might not concur. Indeed, some would view the advent of the age of informational capitalism as one in which both the means and the desire to classify populations have undergone a step-change. New and evermore sophisticated systems of social classification underpin a whole assemblage of new technologies of surveillance that involve the creation of what some commentators have termed a "phenetic fix" (Lyon 2002; Phillips & Curry 2002) on society; technologies that capture personal data activated by people as they go about their everyday activities and which then utilize this data in order to construct abstractions to classify people in new social categories (of income, attributes, preferences, offenses, and so on) with the aim of influencing, managing, or even controlling them in one way or another.

Of course, such technologies of classification have long been an endemic feature of modernity, but under conditions of informational capitalism this urge to classify has accelerated (Gandy 1998; Haggerty & Ericson 2000; Staples 2000; Lyon 2002, 2003). Widespread processes of sorting, clustering, and typifying have come to form a central feature of what some would view as *post-panoptic society* (Boyne 2000). Agents of surveillance no longer need to observe concrete individuals. More likely now is the "creation of categories of interest and classes of conduct thought worthy of attention" (Lyon 2002: 3), the data capture necessary for the creation of which is increasingly embedded within many of the mundane social spaces of everyday life (shops, emails, web browsing, post/zipcodes, transportation systems, banks, etc.).

The ability to understand how classification systems are formed, built, implemented, and acted upon is thus likely to become fundamental for understanding how contemporary societies work (Bowker & Star 1999). Classifications, especially those which become "standards," soon sink from sociological view unless we remain alert to their functioning. In particular we are now surrounded – immersed even – by systems of classification, standards, protocols, and so on that we have come to term "software." For Thrift and French (2002) this means that the actual "stuff" that constitutes what we have traditionally thought of as the "social" has "changed decisively"; for them, software now increasingly functions in order to provide what they term a "new and complex form of automated spatiality" which has altered the "world's phenomenality." For Bowker and Star (1999), in their programmatic call for a revitalized sociology of classification, unless we routinely inspect the social construction of the classifications that

have come to dominate our social world we will systematically miss some of the most important elements of the contemporary functioning of power – what Bourdieu (1991) terms the "symbolic power of naming" that (inevitably?) emerges from the quest to classify populations, whether that naming be done by marketing organizations, the criminal justice system, the health care system, or even sociologists.

SEE ALSO: Epistemology; Knowledge; Knowledge, Sociology of; Social Fact

REFERENCES AND SUGGESTED READINGS

Bourdieu, P. (1991) *Language and Symbolic Power*. Harvard University Press, Cambridge, MA.

Bowker, G. & Star, S. (1999) *Sorting Things Out: Classification and its Consequences*. MIT Press, Cambridge, MA.

Boyne, R. (2000) Post-Panopticism. *Economy and Society* 29(2): 285–307.

Durkheim, E. & Mauss, M. (1963 [1903]) *Primitive Classification*. Ed. R. Needham. University of Chicago Press, Chicago.

Foucault, M. (1970 [1966]) *The Order of Things: An Archaeology of the Human Sciences*. Pantheon Books, New York.

Gandy, O. (1998) *The Panoptic Sort: A Political Economy of Personal Information*. Westview Press, Boulder.

Giddens, A. (1976) *New Rules of Sociological Method*. Hutchinson, London.

Haggerty, K. & Ericson, R. (2000) The Surveillant Assemblage. *British Journal of Sociology* 51: 4.

Lyon, D. (2002) Surveillance Studies: Understanding Visibility, Mobility and the Phenetic Fix. *Surveillance and Society* 1(1). Online. www. surveillance-and-society.org.

Lyon, D. (Ed.) (2003) *Surveillance and Social Sorting: Privacy, Risk and Digital Discrimination*. Routledge, London.

Olsen, H. (2002) Classification and Universality: Application and Construction. *Semiotica* 139(1/4): 377–91.

Phillips, D. & Curry, M. (2002) Privacy and the Phenetic Urge: Geodemographics and the Changing Spatiality of Local Practice. In: Lyon, D. (Ed.), *Surveillance as Social Sorting: Privacy, Risk and Digital Discrimination*. Routledge, London.

Staples, W. (2000) *Everyday Surveillance: Vigilance and Visibility in Postmodern Life*. Rowman & Littlefield, Lanham, MD.

Thrift, N. & French, S. (2002) The Automatic Production of Space. *Transactions of the Institute of British Geographers* 27: 4.

van Mechelen, I., Hampton, J., Michalski, R., & Theuns, P. (Eds.) (1993) *Categories and Concepts.* Academic Press, London.

cloning

Matthew David

Claude Lévi-Strauss's *Myth and Meaning* (1978) discusses the cultural significance attached to twins in non-literate societies. Twins are invested with ambivalent feelings, embodying abundance and loss, security and threat, natural and unnatural, good and evil. Twins also challenge the "identity" of being one thing or the other. The spliced-lipped, incipient twin, hare, as messenger/transgressor between binary opposites, is also the mythical carrier of order and mishap. Being born feet first, wanting to move too fast, to get ahead of oneself or one's twin at the expense of mother and nature, is also invested with moral significance.

Mythic thinking is about projecting the desire for social order onto nature. Yesterday's twins are today's clones. Advocates of cloning, and in particular human cloning, are united in the claim that their critics engage in scientifically illiterate mythic thinking, but, as Lévi-Strauss concluded, belief in the inevitability and moral superiority of change, progress, and history also represents a form of "mythic thinking" in modern "scientific" cultures. This entry highlights the mythic constructions of all sides of the cloning debate. It suggests the socially based nature of beliefs in general.

The Collins English Dictionary defines a clone as "a group of organisms or cells of the same genetic constitution that are descended from a common ancestor by asexual reproduction." The Philip's Compact Encyclopaedia extends the definition of asexual reproduction to the use of "artificial means." The wider of these two definitions suggests two forms of cloning, "natural" asexual forms of self-replication and "artificial" replication of a single genetic original by either plant propagation or animal tissue manipulation (i.e., the transfer of the genetic material of one cell into a genetically emptied out egg cell such as was the case in the creation of Dolly the sheep). While plants and many animal species can reproduce asexually, this was not the case in mammals before the advent of scientific cloning techniques.

However, many advocates of scientific cloning research and application argue that the inability of humans (and mammals in general) to reproduce asexually by natural means does not mean that mammalian clones have not always existed. Rather than defining a clone in terms of its being genetically identical to a single parent, such advocates redefine a clone as being any organism that is genetically identical to another organism. By so doing, the definition of a clone can be extended to identical twins, and so it is possible to render the human clone an established part of the natural world.

Whether the difference between being genetically identical to the single individual from whom one's DNA was extracted and being genetically identical to another individual in drawing the same genes at the same time from two genetically distinct individuals is a difference that really makes a difference, marks out a key site in controversy over the social meaning and relations of cloning. In debates over cloning (in mammals generally, but particularly in humans), debates triggered by advances in artificial cloning techniques, the use of the narrower definition leads to the view that mammalian cloning (by nucleic transfer techniques) is an "unnatural" means to an "unnatural" end. Taking the second definition, it could be concluded that such a practice was an "unnatural" means to a "natural" outcome. While critical of the claim that the "unnatural" is necessarily morally inferior to the "natural," advocates of mammalian/human cloning almost invariably also claim the "naturalness" of cloning as part of their justification by including identical twins in their definition. Definitional slippage, the ability to have your cake and eat it, is common practice on all sides of the debate over cloning.

It should also be recalled, as the first definition above notes, that the definition of cloning does not necessarily only refer to reproduction of genetically identical organisms, but may also be extended to include the production of lines of cells with the same DNA as a specific organism. The production of such cell lines in laboratory conditions draws upon embryonic developmental processes to produce cells rather than whole organisms for therapeutic purposes. Some wish to refer to such procedures as cloning, while others prefer to use the phrase "cell nuclear replacement technique" precisely to avoid negative associations with the idea of cloning as the attempt to reproduce identical living organisms (Klotzko 2004: 72). Critics of such therapeutic techniques emphasize the "clone" tag precisely to make this connection. The use or avoidance of such resonant or neutralizing language has become a recurrent theme in public discourse on controversial biotechnology (Turney 1998).

Linguistic slippage occurs also around the boundary between therapeutic and reproductive human cloning. Critics of therapeutic "cloning" can claim that a clone embryo produced artificially for the purpose of harvesting its cells is not different from one produced for reproductive purposes. Critics then seek to show that at no singular moment in the embryonic developmental process can it be said that the embryo objectively ceases to be "just" living and becomes "a life." Many critics conclude that "cloning" human embryos to destroy them for cell harvesting, even at an early stage in their development, is morally wrong. Most critics would also conclude that not destroying these embryos and allowing the birth of a human cloned baby would be equally wrong (Peters 1997; Evans 2002; Habermas 2003).

Advocates of therapeutic cloning seek to diffuse criticism of embryo research by distinguishing an embryonic cluster of cells from an individual organism. If an early set of embryonic cells is divided into two this leads to identical twins, but if these cell clusters are recombined, in time a single organism develops. Can a unique "life" be said to exist through such divisions and recombinations, does "life" begin at the point after which such manipulation ceases to be possible, or is such a line in the sand between living tissue and a living organism a social convention? The establishment of a point after which living cells become taken, in the eyes of the law, as "a life" worthy of some moral status is certainly the product of the balance of social interests and beliefs rather than objective fact (Mulkay 1997).

Critics point out that the techniques enabling therapeutic human cloning are identical to those that would be required to clone a fully formed human. As such, research into the one can only increase the likelihood of the other, even if it does not make it inevitable. Defenders of therapeutic human "cloning" research have suggested that such a "slippery slope" argument is mistaken, as all the necessary data required by a "rogue" scientist bent on producing a cloned human baby are already available from animal research. This defense raises numerous questions. Firstly, if true, why does so much additional human embryonic research need to be done? Secondly, does such a line of argument not further justify the slippery slope view of science? Yesterday's animal cloning research is now said to have made human reproductive cloning possible, and so, given the passage of time, is likely. Is this not the slippery slope writ larger still? Thirdly, if scientists at the time of Dolly's birth assured the public that human reproductive cloning was never their intention, what comfort can we take from similar pronouncements today? Despite reassurances, and irrespective of the inner motivations of Nobel prize winners (Wilmut et al. 2002), we are now told that one outcome of animal cloning research is an increased likelihood of human reproductive cloning. Who should the public believe, trust, and/or follow the advice of? (For accounts of media/public constructions of cloning, expertise, and trust, see Allan 2002; Petersen; 2002; Pilnick 2002.) It may be that unintended consequences make cutting-edge scientists no better futurologists than more skeptical but less scientifically literate citizens. Specific expertise is no guarantee of general authority, either in prediction or in persuasion.

Conceptual slippage and the social relations that play upon ambiguous language are manifested also in debates over whether cloning a human individual by nucleic transfer would be immoral in any case. The inclusion of identical twins within the category of clones has the effect of naturalizing the outcome for some, while critics question the value of such an equation. How does sibling identity relate to parental identity? While religious and many other critics seek to uphold traditional conceptions of family, sexuality, and sexual relations against the threat posed by cloning to such institutions, advocates of human reproductive cloning can claim that such institutions are no less artificial and potentially oppressive as would be the life of a cloned human. Meanwhile, critics of "designer babies" (Ettorre 2002) suggest that reproductive liberty may also be just as oppressive in an age of market-led eugenic pressure.

Advocates of human reproductive cloning can argue that a person genetically identical to their (most likely) socially defined parent is no less an individual than anyone else, except in as far as society might treat them differently. Parents routinely violate a strict reading (or misreading) of Kantian principles regarding the treatment of another as an end in themselves, rather than as a means to an end, so, in this sense, a clone would not be any different. Critics respond in two ways. One is to point out that the desire to have a child cloned from another person already suggests a heightened degree of expectation about the new individual's identity and role. This may impose unacceptable constraints upon the new individual's capacity to develop as an autonomous person (Peters 1997). A second line of criticism would be to suggest that the very defense of a clone's unique individuality, as a moral argument for allowing it, undercuts the practical value of such a technique and vice versa. Any claim that a clone would be valuable to others because of his or her genetic foundation begins to encroach upon their moral status as an individual, but to deny such a benefit would be to make cloning pointless.

Regarding the ethical suspicion surrounding the desire to clone, advocates of human reproductive cloning suggest that clones will not be the mindless zombies of science fiction films such as *Star Wars: Attack of the Clones* (2002) or the *Stepford Wives* (1975, 2004), and so would not offer scope for domination and malign gratification to evil dictators and/or lazy patriarchal men. Advocates suggest such a fear is the result of an irrational splicing of ideas about cloning and genetic modification in the

minds of the scientifically illiterate. Yet, critics point out that it is just such a splicing of cloning techniques and those for genetic modification that has driven genetic research with plants and animals for a generation. The agricultural and pharmaceutical returns and effects of such a fusion far outweigh even the box office potential of science fiction targeted to the socially over anxious. If all the significant information needed to allow "rogue" human cloning is already available in the animal data, what is this research currently aiming to tell us, if not how to fuse cloning with genetic modification? While capacity is not necessity it is not intrinsically irrational to be concerned (Nerlich et al. 1999). For better or worse, cloning challenges the boundary between humans and other species.

Just as some critics of human cloning suggest it is the logical extension of a slippery slope that starts by reducing natural human reproduction to forms of instrumental, mechanistic, and exploitative technique (Rifkin 1998), through such things as contraception, abortion, and *in vitro* fertilization, so some advocates of human reproductive cloning argue that all the above techniques are positive advances in human life for precisely the same reasons. Taking control of reproduction and being able to make choices about the timing and the genetic makeup of one's offspring is seen by such advocates as a logical extension of the liberal principle of reproductive liberty, the right of individuals to make their own reproductive choices, free from the need for permission from any authority that might claim to know better as to how, or when, or with whom they ought to reproduce (Harris 2004). Critics point out the potential eugenic consequences of allowing reproductive cloning, especially if it is combined with forms of genetic modification, while advocates point to the eugenic potential of any attempt to restrict it. Both sides invoke a logical inevitability whereby what might seem innocuous in itself is seen as just the thin edge of a eugenic wedge. Both extremes, and all points in between, can read their own argument into the available evidence, and, mirroring each other's arguments, logic alone cannot determine whether a person should read the world in one way or in another. The supposedly logical "If X, then Y" is still just a rhetorical device in as far as the content of such categories and the relationships between them are always open to reinterpretation.

Cloning (in its many contested aspects) represents a site of conflict between social practices, interests, and beliefs that are irreducible to evidence or logic. Such combinations of practice, interest, and belief are ways of life. The willingness to believe something is always, in part at least, the product of the way of life in which one lives. This is as true for scientists as it is for non-scientists. The meaning of cloning cannot escape from "mythical thinking."

SEE ALSO: Body and Society; Genetic Engineering as a Social Problem; Human Genome and the Science of Life; Medical Sociology and Genetics; Myth; Posthumanism

REFERENCES AND SUGGESTED READINGS

Allan, S. (2002), *Media, Risk and Science*. Open University Press, Buckingham.

Ettorre, E. (2002) *Reproductive Genetics, Gender and the Body*. Routledge, London.

Evans, J. (2002) *Playing God? Human Genetic Engineering and the Rationalization of Public Bioethical Debate*. University of Chicago Press, Chicago.

Habermas, J. (2003) *The Future of Human Nature*. Polity Press, Cambridge.

Harris, J. (2004) *On Cloning*. Routledge, London.

Klotzko, A. K. (2004) *A Clone of Your Own: The Science and Ethics of Cloning*. Oxford University Press, Oxford.

Lévi-Strauss, C. (1978) *Myth and Meaning*. Routledge, London.

Mulkay, M. (1997) *The Embryo Research Debate: Science and the Politics of Reproduction*. Cambridge University Press, Cambridge.

Nerlich, B., Clarke, D. D., & Dingwall, R. (1999) The Influence of Popular Cultural Imagery on Public Attitudes Towards Cloning. *Sociological Research Online* 4(3). Online. www.socresonline.org.uk/socresonline/4/3/nerlich.

Peters, T. (1997) *Playing God? Genetic Determinism and Human Freedom*. Routledge, London.

Petersen, A. (2002) Replicating Our Bodies, Losing Our Selves: News Media Portrayals of Human Cloning in the Wake of Dolly. *Body and Society* 8(4): 71–90.

Pilnick, A. (2002) *Genetics and Society: An Introduction*. Open University Press, Buckingham.

Rifkin, J. (1998) *The Biotech Century: The Coming Age of Genetic Commerce*. Weidenfeld & Nicolson, London.

Turney, J. (1998) *Frankenstein's Footsteps: Science, Genetics and Popular Culture*. Yale University Press, New Haven.

Wilmut, I., Campbell, K., & Tudge, C. (2002) *The Second Creation*. Hardline, London.

cognitive balance theory (Heider)

Paul T. Munroe

Balance theory explains how people tend to maintain consistency in patterns of their liking and disliking of one another and of inanimate objects. When patterns of liking and disliking are balanced, structures are stable. When they are imbalanced, structures are unstable and there is pressure to change in the direction that makes them balanced.

It was the social psychologist Fritz Heider who, in 1946, founded the now widely studied theoretical research program known as balance theory. In balance theory's early statements, for example in "Attitudes and Cognitive Organization" (1946), Heider was interested in the perceptions of a person, p, with respect to another person, o, and an object of mutual interest, x, which could also be a third person. Heider noted that the patterns of perceived relationships among the three entities could be in one of two states: balanced or imbalanced. Imbalanced states produce tension which may be resolved by changing the relations or by distancing oneself from the situation.

Consider three entities: p (person), o (other), and x (an object of interest). Heider identifies three possible relationships among them, L (likes), ~L (dislikes), and U (forms a unit relationship with; i.e., is associated with, owns, or possesses). Accordingly, "p L o" means "p likes o"; "o ~L x" means "o dislikes x"; and "p U x" means "p forms a unit relationship with x," for example, "p owns x" or "p made x." Both L and U are positive relations, while ~L and ~U are negative ones. When considering three entities, a balanced situation exists if there are all

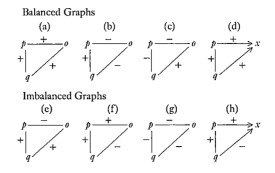

Figure 1   Balanced and imbalanced graphs (Heider's examples using the graph theoretic notation of Cartwright and Harary).

positive relations (e.g., *p* U *x*, *p* L *o*, and *o* L *x*) or when two relations are negative and one positive (e.g., *p* ~L *o*, *o* U *x*, and *p* ~L *x*). When there is one negative relation and two positive (e.g., *p* L *x*, *p* ~L *o*, and *o* U *x*), or when all three relations are negative (e.g., *p* ~L *x*, *p* ~L *o*, and *o* ~L *x*), the situation is imbalanced. Heider's main point was that balanced cognitive structures are stable, while imbalanced structures produce tension, discomfort, and a pressure to change.

The theory was advanced importantly by Dorwin Cartwright and Frank Harary in 1958. They added a graph theoretic nomenclature that allowed for the simultaneous examination of many individuals at once. As a result of this mathematical graph theory, some very interesting theorems were examined, the predictions from which are both powerful and not intuitively obvious.

To understand the graph theory, several definitions are necessary. A "point" represents an individual, such as *p*, *o*, or *q*, or an inanimate object, *x*. A "line" represents a liking, disliking, or unit relation between two points. A directed line or arrow indicates the direction of a relationship, e.g., *p* — + → *o* means "*p* likes *o*." A line with no direction indicates a mutual liking or disliking relationship, e.g., "*p* — + — *o*" means "*p* and *o* like each other." A "path" is a series of lines connecting two or more points, and a "cycle" is a non-intersecting path that begins and ends at the same point. The sign of a path or cycle is the product of the signs of all of the lines in that path or cycle. Consistently with Heider's theory, a graph is balanced if the signs of all of its cycles are positive.

The graphs in Figure 1 show Heider's original balanced and imbalanced structures using the graph theoretic notation of Cartwright and Harary. Graphs (a) through (d) are balanced (all of their cycles are positive), while graphs (e) through (h) are all imbalanced. The graph theoretic version introduces several advantages: it is more efficient because there are fewer statements needed to convey the liking and disliking relationships, there are no limits as to how many entities can be included in a graph, and several properties of mathematics can be used to make predictions about the results of balanced and imbalanced graphs.

When a situation involves imbalance, there is pressure within the system to change the relationships. Several balancing operations have been identified. The simplest to understand, though often the most difficult to enact, is to change one or more of the relationships from disliking to liking, or from liking to disliking. In Figure 1(e), *p* can make overtures to *o* to change the nature of their relationship. If *p* and *o* come to like each other, then the graph will be balanced and equivalent to the graph in (a).

Although one person in the situation can control only his or her own feelings, members of the group may attempt to influence one another. In graph (f), *p* may entice *o* and *q* to like each other. Intriguingly, one such influence attempt uses a principle of reciprocity to induce a positive relationship. Since reciprocated relationships are balanced while non-reciprocated relationships are imbalanced, any non-reciprocated relationship will produce tension. This tension could be resolved by changing to a mutual liking relationship. If p says, "Did you notice the nice thing q did for you, o? q must have positive feelings for you," this may induce just such an asymmetry. Of course, this works two ways; in (e), p may try to convince q to dislike o, and may use the same tactic, as in "Did you hear the nasty thing o said about you, q, last night?"

Other operations may be used to balance a group structure. In graphs (e) through (g), one person may exit the situation, leaving the other two individuals in a balanced structure. Technically, if any of the three individuals leave, the remaining two will be left in a balanced situation. However, as Jordan has shown, people have a preference for positive relationships, so it is more likely that the one who leaves is one who is in a disliking relationship, leaving two persons who like each other behind.

Another balancing operation is known as "partitioning." In this case, one or more group members spend time separately with others who do not like each other. As Johnston and Campbell have shown, joint custody situations are an example of this. With partitioning, only those members who like each other spend time together. However, it is a risk in this situation that the absent other comes up as a topic of conversation (an "x"), reproducing the original imbalanced structure and producing tension in the subsystem.

If no balancing operation is possible (actors cannot leave, and difficult relationships are not repaired), there are ways that actors can restore balance cognitively and reduce their stress. One such operation is to reduce cognitive and/or emotional investment in the situation. Actors may "tune out," decide that the situation is not all that important, and withdraw emotionally. Another stress-reducing operation is to distort reality. Several options are available in our common lexicon for this. Consider p in Figure 1(f). p may convince him/herself that "I think o and q really like each other, they just have a funny way of showing it," or "If they revealed their 'true' selves to one another, they couldn't help but like each other." Parents of embattled siblings can often be heard to say: "They really love each other underneath it all, they are just going through a phase right now." This may ultimately prove true or not true, but at the time only the parent perceives the situation this way. It seems likely that there is some distortion of the current reality.

Cartwright and Harary presented a version of balance theory that used the mathematical theory of linear graphs. As a result, they proposed several theorems that have predictive value for group structure; among them are the completeness theorem and the structure theorem. The completeness theorem claims that previously unacquainted individuals will form relationships that complete a structure in the direction that will achieve balance. People may differentially attend to information about the other person that is consistent with their knowledge of how that person relates to known others. Elliott Aronson and Vernon Cope (1968) have tested this theorem. When people form relationships that are congruent with these predictions, the resulting graphs are balanced.

The structure theorem is also particularly interesting. The theorem states that all balanced structures may be broken down into two subsets, one of which may be empty. Within each subset there are only positive relationships, while between subsets there are only negative ones. This theorem allows one to predict that over time, groups that contain at least one disliking relationship will tend to devolve into two "cliques." Within the cliques, people tend to have positive relationships, but between them, animosity is likely to grow.

Heider's original ideas have proven very fruitful. Many theories of social networks, for example, have their roots in Cartwright and Harary's graph theoretic version of the theory. Festinger's cognitive dissonance theory is another direction focusing mainly on the p, o, x relations, as well as more simple p, x relationships in which there are paths with mixed valences. Heise's affect control theory uses a cognitive consistency argument that builds on Heider's and Festinger's earlier work.

Balance theory predictions and implications are often simple and clear, so much of the research testing balance theory tends to rely on controlled experiments and/or vignette studies. In addition, several applications of balance theory to family and work situations have made important contributions to a number of fields.

SEE ALSO: Affect Control Theory; Attribution Theory; Cognitive Dissonance Theory (Festinger)

REFERENCES AND SUGGESTED READINGS

Aronson, E. & Cope, V. (1968) My Enemy's Enemy is My Friend. *Journal of Personality and Social Psychology* 8(1): 8–12.
Cartwright, D. & Harary, F. (1958) Structural Balance: A Generalization of Heider's Theory. *Psychological Review* 63: 277–93.
Festinger, L. (1957) *A Theory of Cognitive Dissonance*. Stanford University Press, Stanford.
Heider, F. (1944) Social Perception and Phenomenal Causality. *Psychological Review* 51: 358–74.
Heider, F. (1946) Attitudes and Cognitive Organization. *Journal of Psychology* 21: 107–12.
Heider, F. (1958) *The Psychology of Interpersonal Relations*. Wiley, New York.
Heise, D. R. (1979) *Understanding Events: Affect and the Construction of Social Action*. Cambridge University Press, Cambridge.
Johnston, J. R. & Campbell, E. G. (1981) Instability in the Family Network of Divorced and Disputing Parents. *Pacific Sociological Review* 1–23.
Jordan, N. (1958) Behavioral Forces that are a Function of Attitudes and of Cognitive Organization. *Human Relations* 6: 273–87.

cognitive dissonance theory (Festinger)

Monica K. Miller and Alayna Jehle

Cognitive dissonance theory posits that individuals seek to maintain consistency among multiple cognitions (e.g., thoughts, behaviors, attitudes, values, or beliefs). Inconsistent cognitions produce unpleasant arousal that leads individuals to change one of the cognitions to bring it into line with other cognitions.

The theory has its roots in Heider's (1946) balance theory, which states that people strive for balanced relationships between individuals and objects in their environment. Because unstable beliefs are difficult to maintain, people make adjustments in order to regain consistency

and rationality. Festinger (1957) extended balance theory, which focused on perceptions of the external world, to include consistency in self-perception, or one's internal world. Festinger theorized that the driving force behind the need for balance was the aversive arousal caused by inconsistent cognitions. People feel tension if they experience irrational cognitions and will therefore change cognitions to ease the tension and restore balance.

Aronson (1969) later introduced a "self-concept" theory, which posits that an individual is motivated by a threat to the self-concept caused by inconsistent cognitions. When a person has conflicting cognitions such as "I love my wife" and "I was rude to my wife yesterday," he experiences feelings of discomfort that threaten his self-concept. He then takes steps to change or weaken the negative cognition in order to reduce dissonance. For instance, he buys his wife flowers, which bolsters the cognition that he likes his wife and minimizes the dissonant cognition of being rude. This act reduces the threat to self-concept caused by dissonance.

Bem (1965) offered a non-motivational explanation for attitudinal change. His "self-perception theory" stated that people's attitudes are not predetermined, but instead are established by reflecting on one's behavior and then deducing underlying attitudes based on consistency with that behavior. For instance, attitudes are formed or changed when a person thinks "I acted in a certain way, thus my attitudes must be concordant with that behavior." Thus, a change in behavior leads to a change in attitude. This behaviorist explanation assumes that attitudes are formed through a non-motivational assessment of a situation.

Zanna and Cooper (1974) helped bring dissonance theory back to its motivational roots. In an experiment participants wrote counter-attitudinal essays after taking a placebo pill. The authors manipulated having either a high or low choice in writing the essay, as well as telling the participants that the pill made them feel tense, relaxed, or had no side effects (control condition). This research demonstrated that taking a pill allowed participants to blame arousal on the pill, thus reducing the motivation to change the dissonant cognitions. Researchers concluded that arousal caused by internal imbalance (i.e., dissonant cognitions) motivates attitude change, while arousal that is perceived to be caused by external factors (i.e., a pill) will not lead to attitude change.

Another approach was introduced by Steele and Liu (1983), who suggested that attitude change resulting from dissonance is caused by a need for a positive self-image rather than a need for cognitive consistency. Individuals can relieve dissonance-induced arousal simply by reaffirming a valued aspect of the self, even if the aspect is unrelated to the cognitions. For example, if a person who dislikes cherry pie finds herself telling the chef how good the pie is, she experiences dissonance. The dissonance threatens the self-image, leading to arousal. However, the discomfort is relieved when she gives a homeless man money on her way home. This act of self-affirmation relieves dissonance-induced arousal, even though it is unrelated to the cognitions that caused the arousal. Although the dissonant cognitions (i.e., not liking the pie, and saying she liked it) still exist, the arousal has dissipated because she has reaffirmed that she is a caring person by giving the homeless man money. Thus, self-affirmation reduces the need to change one's cognitions in order to restore consistency.

Another perspective, called the "New Look" alternative (Cooper & Fazio 1984), suggests that dissonance occurs when one violates a societal norm. The resulting arousal motivates one to justify this discrepancy through reinterpretation of the outcome (e.g., attitude change) in a more positive direction. Unlike many other dissonance theories, this approach claims that the self and self-esteem are irrelevant.

Through the years, dissonance has been theorized to be caused by inconsistent cognitions, a threatened self-concept, a need to protect one's self-image, and violation of social norms. Thus, it is not surprising that there is some disagreement about the true cause of dissonance-produced attitude change. Some researchers claim that each of these theoretical causes can lead to dissonance in different situations. Additionally, it is difficult to determine which cause leads to dissonance because study results can often be explained by multiple theories. As a result, researchers remain divided in their beliefs about the underlying mechanism that drives dissonance.

Traditional dissonance studies have employed a "forced compliance" paradigm to arouse dissonance. This technique involves convincing participants to do something that they would not usually do, while simultaneously leading the participant to believe that they had freely chosen to complete the behavior. For example, a student is induced to write an essay supporting graduation requirements including a senior thesis. If this behavior is counter to the participant's attitudes, it will create dissonance between the action of writing the essay and the participant's own beliefs.

An alternative dissonance technique called "hypocrisy" gained popularity in the 1990s. Stone and colleagues (1994) theorized that dissonance would result when one gives advice to others but later realize one's own failure to follow the advice. To test this hypothesis, they asked participants in the "hypocrisy" condition to create a speech to be included in a video ostensibly for the purpose of creating an AIDS education video for high school students. Then they asked the participants to list times in their pasts when they had failed to use condoms. Public advocacy of condom use coupled with the realization that they personally had failed to follow their own advice led participants to reduce dissonance by purchasing condoms.

Although forced compliance and hypocrisy studies are among the most noted dissonance studies, other studies have used a variety of techniques to demonstrate the effects of dissonance on decision-making, behavior, attitudes, morals, and learning. For instance, post-decisional dissonance occurs when a person has chosen between two equal choices. To bolster the belief that one has made the right choice, the person will see the chosen alternative more positively than the one not chosen.

Other studies demonstrate that strong commitment to a belief that is later invalidated can lead an individual to attempt to persuade others to support the incorrect belief. Obtaining social consensus then relieves dissonance because the belief and the social support of the belief will be consistent.

Initiation studies demonstrate that individuals report enjoying group membership more if they endure a difficult or painful initiation to join the group. Their liking of the group justifies the high price they paid to be in the group. Similarly, deterrence studies demonstrate that children who obeyed a weak order to avoid playing with a toy reported liking the toy less than children who obeyed a strong order. Because it is reasonable to obey a strong order, but not a weak order, the children rationalized their behavior by thinking they must have avoided the toy because they do not really like it that much.

Just as there is a variety of ways that dissonance is induced, there is also a variety of ways to alleviate dissonance. Festinger suggested that dissonance could be relieved by (1) changing one or more of the cognitions so that all the cognitions would be in agreement; (2) adopting cognitions or behaviors that strengthen the "desirable" cognition and therefore make the "undesirable" cognition less salient; or (3) reducing the importance assigned to the inconsistency. Traditional forced compliance studies typically involve the first method; they measure attitude change in participants who have acted in a counter-attitudinal way. Subsequently, participants adjust their attitudes to be more in favor of the counter-attitudinal position, adjusting their attitude to be more in line with their behavior.

Hypocrisy studies go a step farther and require participants to actually change discrepant behaviors in order to relieve dissonance. Stone and colleagues (1994) found that participants experiencing "hypocrisy" reduced dissonance by purchasing condoms and by stating intentions to use condoms. These behaviors strengthen the desirable cognition ("I practice safe sex") and take the focus off the undesirable cognition ("I have failed to practice safe sex").

The third option for reducing dissonance involves reducing the *importance* of the inconsistency, rather than reducing the inconsistency itself. Such trivialization is likely to occur in circumstances where attitudes are very salient or central to the individual's self-concept and are therefore very resistant to change.

The "hydraulic model" of dissonance reduction suggests that, when several modes of dissonance reduction exist, the easiest mode will be used. Therefore, if changing a central attitude or behavior is difficult, an easier mode of dissonance reduction, such as trivialization, is likely to occur. Dissonance can also be relieved

by other methods such as misattributing the arousal to external elements, creating a positive self-evaluation, receiving ego-enhancing information, reducing the arousal chemically, or by focusing on other valued aspects of the self.

In addition to studying theoretical aspects of how dissonance is aroused and relieved, researchers have also applied dissonance theory to many real-world settings. For instance, recent research has shown that people in some cultures are less likely to experience dissonance. Studies have also demonstrated that people with high self-esteem experience greater dissonance arousal than people with low self-esteem. The social aspects of cognitive dissonance have also been investigated. For instance, researchers have found that social support can reduce dissonance and that people change their attitudes when they witness someone in their group experiencing dissonance.

Researchers in the fields of health and prevention have applied the theory to a variety of behaviors that people carry out even though they know the behavior has negative consequences for their health. For example, recognizing one's dissonant cognitions regarding smoking or body image can lead to a reduction in smoking or bulimic behaviors. In addition, cognitive dissonance theory has been used to study patients suffering from anxiety disorders and depression who experience dissonance as a result of their disorders. Despite extensive evolution, dissonance theory has proved to be a resilient theory useful in many contexts.

Dissonance theory is not without its controversies, however. Early dissonance theory did not offer clearly defined terms, methods, or operational rules. As a result, individual studies confirming the theory were criticized as lucky methodological guesses. Skeptical researchers also questioned whether attitude change (e.g., in the forced compliance paradigm) was a result of dissonance or merely due to the reinforcement effects of the activity. Dissonance theory also challenged established behavioral theories by suggesting that animals had cognitions that could affect learning and behaviors. Finally, methodological techniques, especially deception, gave rise to ethical criticisms. The theory withstood these controversies and has since gained a general acceptance through decades of experiments, which have largely confirmed its basic propositions. Thus, dissonance studies testing the theory itself have declined recently, although researchers continue to test the theory using new operationalizations and new contexts.

SEE ALSO: Attitudes and Behavior; Cognitive Balance Theory (Heider)

REFERENCES AND SUGGESTED READINGS

Aronson, E. (1969) The Theory of Cognitive Dissonance: A Current Perspective. In: Berkowitz, L. (Ed.), *Advances in Experimental Social Psychology*, Vol. 4. Academic Press, New York, pp. 2–34.
Bem, D. (1965) An Experimental Analysis of Self-Persuasion. *Journal of Experimental Social Psychology* 1: 199–218.
Cooper, J. & Fazio, R. H. (1984) A New Look at Dissonance Theory. In: Berkowitz, L. (Ed.), *Advances in Experimental Social Psychology*, Vol. 17. Academic Press, New York, pp. 229–62.
Festinger. L. (1957) *A Theory of Cognitive Dissonance*. Stanford University Press, Stanford.
Heider, F. (1946) The Psychology of Interpersonal Relations. Wiley, New York.
Steele, C. M. & Liu, T. J. (1983) Dissonance Processes as Self-Affirmation. *Journal of Personality and Social Psychology* 45: 5–19.
Stone, J., Aronson, E., Crain, A. L., Winslow, M. P., & Fried, C. B. (1994) Inducing Hypocrisy as a Means of Encouraging Young Adults to Use Condoms. *Personality and Social Psychology Bulletin* 20: 116–28.
Zanna, M. P. & Cooper, J. (1974) Dissonance and the Pill: An Attribution Approach to Studying the Arousal Properties of Dissonance. *Journal of Personality and Social Psychology* 29: 703–9.

cohabitation

Sharon L. Sassler

The past few decades have brought dramatic changes in the residential arrangements of romantically involved unmarried adults. Indeed, as sexual activity has become uncoupled from marriage, growing numbers of young couples have begun sharing a home and a bed without the legal sanction of marriage. Cohabitation, as

this type of living arrangement is commonly known, has become a normative part of the adult life course.

Determining the prevalence of cohabitation is a challenging task. Given the nature of today's dating and mating patterns, measuring trends in cohabitation is a highly subjective undertaking. Legal marriages are officially recorded via state licenses; no such formality is imposed on cohabiting couples. The process of entering into cohabiting unions can be rather indeterminate. Some couples may first spend a night or two together, but then find themselves staying overnight several times a week before ultimately acknowledging that they "live together." During this process, individuals may retain their separate addresses, even if they rarely sleep there, yet remain unwilling to tell family and friends that they cohabit. Other romantic couples proceed quickly and quite consciously into coresidential relationships, but without specific plans to marry. For others, cohabitation is a stepping stone to marriage – a way to test for compatibility or cement their relationship.

The indeterminacy of this process is reflected in how surveys attempt to capture the cohabiting population; there is no consistent definition of what cohabitation entails. Whereas some studies ask if a partner sleeps there most of the time, others rely on a more subjective measure and allow respondents to determine if they are cohabiting. Still other surveys rely on information from a household roster and include partners only if they are there at least half the time or more. The US Census Bureau enabled the identification of household members as "unmarried partner" in the 1990 and 2000 Census. Measures of cohabitation may therefore include those who share a home, along with those who reside together part time, or who are together every night but maintain separate residences. Conflating these definitions is most problematic for minority populations, who are most likely to be part-time cohabitors. The imprecise nature of how cohabitation is defined may therefore exaggerate or understate its prevalence as a living arrangement, or hide variations across groups.

While living together without being married is far from being a new phenomenon, it first drew serious attention in the 1970s and has since been a topic of great interest. It has become increasingly prevalent over the past three decades. In the US, initial estimates from the Current Population Survey (CPS) of 1980 revealed that approximately 1.6 million unmarried couples were cohabiting, more than triple the number that did so in 1970. By 1990 the number of cohabiting couples had grown by another 80 percent, to almost 2.9 million couples. A total of 4.9 million households consisted of heterosexual cohabiting couples in 2000. Despite the dramatic increase in cohabiting couples, at any one point in time the proportion of all co-residential couples who are unmarried is rather small. Cohabitors accounted for only 8.4 percent of all couple households in the 2000 census. Other western countries have also seen rapid growth in the numbers of people cohabiting.

Although cohabitors account for only a small fraction of all households, experience with living together outside of marriage is far more prevalent and has increased dramatically. In fact, cohabitation has become a normative experience. In the late 1980s one-third of all women between the ages of 19 and 44 in the US had ever cohabited in their lives; by 1995, 45 percent of similarly aged women had done so. By 2002 well over half of all women ages 19 to 44 (57 percent) affirmed that they had lived with a romantic partner. Cohabitation remains most common among those in their mid-twenties to mid-thirties. Almost half of all American women aged 30 to 34 (49 percent) in 1995 had lived at some point with a romantic partner without being married, and by 2002 this figure had risen to 62 percent. Living together has also become the modal pathway preceding marriage. Again relying on information from the 1995 NSFG, Raley (2000) found that over half of all women born between 1965 and 1969 (55 percent) had lived with their partner prior to marriage. Marriage records in Great Britain and other European countries also indicate that the large majority of people now cohabit prior to marrying. Furthermore, considerable numbers of adults have cohabited without subsequently marrying their partner.

Despite its increased popularity, cohabitation is still more commonplace among particular subgroups. Living together historically served as the "poor man's" marriage; even today, the least educated continue to lead the growth in cohabitation. In the US over half of women with less than 12 years of schooling had ever lived with a romantic partner as of 1995, compared to about 37 percent among women with at least a Bachelor's degree. Nonetheless, cohabitation has become common even among college graduates. By 2002, 47 percent of women who were college graduates had lived with a partner at some point, compared with 62 percent for women aged 19 to 44 who were high school graduates and 68 percent for those with less than 12 years of schooling. Racial differences in living together have narrowed far more than have educational disparities. Whereas cohabitation used to be more widespread among African Americans, recent increases in the proportion of people cohabiting have been greater among non-Hispanic whites. Both groups were more likely to cohabit than Hispanic women of similar ages in 1995. Nonetheless, given distinctive differences in marriage rates across these racial groups in the US, these results suggest that the role served by cohabitation may increasingly differ by race. Marriage rates are considerably lower among African Americans than for either whites or Hispanics. For blacks, then, living together may serve as a marriage alternative, whereas for whites it is still more likely to be a precursor to marriage. Living together has also been more prevalent among the previously married than the never married. In fact, it is increasingly replacing remarriage, even among those with children.

Cohabitation differs rather dramatically in its prevalence, as well as its role in childbearing, in Canada and Western Europe. In countries that have the highest proportions of cohabiting unions – Sweden, Finland, Denmark, and France – family law often views married and cohabiting couples similarly. In these countries, most non-marital births are to cohabiting couples, in contrast to the US where greater shares of such births are to women living without a partner. But there is considerable variation in the prevalence of cohabitation in Europe, as demonstrated in the research of Kiernan (2004a,b) and Heuveline and Timberlake (2004). Countries such as the UK, Netherlands, Germany, Austria, and Belgium have intermediate levels of cohabitation, and the shares cohabiting in most Catholic countries (Italy, Spain, and Ireland), while substantial, are even lower. The extent to which children are born into cohabiting unions or live with cohabiting parents also fluctuates widely, though in most of the Northern and Western European countries the shares of cohabiting couples living with children are similar to those in the US.

Most cohabiting unions are of relatively short duration, lasting on average only a year or two. A small fraction continue to cohabit indefinitely or represent an alternative to marriage. In the US roughly half of all cohabiting unions end within the first year. In contrast, only about 1 in 10 lasts 5 or more years. Because cohabiting appears to be such a transitory arrangement, many argue that it is not usually an alternative to or a substitute for marriage. Yet the purpose of cohabitation appears to be changing over time. As living together has become more prevalent it has become less likely to serve as a staging ground for marriage. Among those who entered cohabiting unions in the early 1980s, about 60 percent eventually married. The share of those entering cohabiting unions in the 1990s that subsequently married declined to about 53 percent (Bumpass & Lu 2000). Using more recent data from the NLSY for young women for the years 1979 through 2000, Lichter et al. (2006) found that cohabiting unions were more likely to end in dissolution than in marriage.

One possible explanation for this change comes from new evidence that young adults often do not have explicit plans to marry at the time they decide to cohabit. Sassler (2004), in a qualitative study of New York cohabitors, reported that marriage was not discussed seriously prior to entering into shared living arrangements, and in fact was generally not raised in any serious fashion until after a considerable length of time. This finding is being replicated in other qualitative studies conducted on a wider array of social classes in various locations in the US. A growing body of research is reporting that rather than an explicit testing ground for marriage, many cohabitors live together for financial reasons or because it is more convenient. As cohabitation becomes normative, it increasingly appears to serve as an alternative to being single.

Despite common beliefs that living together is a good way to assess compatibility for marriage, couples that lived together prior to marriage have elevated rates of marital dissolution. Cohabitation therefore does not appear to reduce subsequent divorce by winnowing out the least stable couples from marriage. However, the association between cohabitation and relationship disruption has not been firmly established. Using data from the 1987 National Survey of Families and Households, Schoen and Owens (1991) reported finding no connection between premarital cohabitation and subsequent divorce among women born in the early 1960s, though cohabitors from earlier birth cohorts did have a higher likelihood of experiencing a divorce. It remains unclear whether the relationship between cohabitation and divorce has weakened or strengthened among more recent cohorts of cohabiting women. The relation between repeat cohabitation and subsequent union dissolution is more clear cut. Those who have lived with multiple partners in informal living arrangements do experience increased relationship instability.

As mentioned above, those who choose to live together tend to be different from adults who marry without first cohabiting, in that they tend to have lower levels of education, more unstable employment histories, and less traditional orientations towards the family. Another way in which cohabiting couples differ from those who are married is in their divergent backgrounds. For example, cohabiting couples are more likely to consist of partners from different racial backgrounds than are married couples, suggesting that living together is more acceptable than is marriage for interracial partnerships. Cohabitation is also less selective than is marriage with respect to education (Blackwell & Lichter 2000). Finally, several factors increase the likelihood of cohabiting instead of entering into marriage, further differentiating the two groups. Recent work by Qian and colleagues (2005) finds that women who experience non-marital births, for example, are substantially more likely to enter into cohabiting situations than marriage. Less is known about men who enter into cohabiting unions, and how they differ from those who marry, though recent research using data from the Fragile Families study shows that men who have fathered children with multiple partners, and who therefore may have child-support obligations that extend across several families, are less likely to wed their current partner with whom they share a child. In general, cohabiting partners tend to differ more than married couples on a range of dimensions; further research is required to determine the effect that such differences may have on the quality of their match.

Evidence on the domestic labor performed by cohabitors indicates that their patterns are in many ways similar to married couples. Cohabiting men do about as much domestic labor as do married men. While cohabiting women spend far less time on domestic labor than married women, they continue to do more than cohabiting men do (Shelton & John 1993). Furthermore, in a study of transitions in the domestic labor of single adults, Gupta (1999) reports that single women who move into cohabiting unions increase the amount of domestic labor they perform, while cohabiting men do not. These results suggest that cohabiting couples "do gender" in ways that are quite similar to married couples.

A substantial proportion of cohabiting couples reside with children. Some of these children are the result of previous marriages or relationships. But cohabitors are increasingly bearing children without marrying. In the early 1980s in the US, for example, an estimated 29 percent of all births to single mothers were to cohabiting women; by the early 1990s, 39 percent of all non-marital births were to cohabiting women, and estimates from the final years of the twentieth century suggest that births to cohabiting couples accounted for close to half of all births to single women in cities of over 200,000 persons (Bumpass & Lu 2000; Sigle-Rushton & McLanahan 2002). In Britain, some 60 percent of all unmarried mothers are cohabiting at the time of their child's birth. Living together has largely replaced what used to be referred to as "shotgun" weddings, as single women who become pregnant are now just as likely to move in with their partners as they are to marry (Manning 1993; Raley 2001). These developments provide additional fuel to those worried about the effects that the increasing prevalence of cohabitation is having on marital unions.

While an increasing proportion of children are born into cohabiting families, a substantial number of children will spend time in cohabiting families following the divorce or breakup of their parents' relationships. As a result, a rising proportion of cohabitors are residing with children under the age of 15, both biological children and those that might be considered "stepchildren." The proportions have increased from over a quarter of all cohabitors in 1980 to over 40 percent by 2000 (Fields & Casper 2001). Furthermore, children's likelihood of living with a cohabiting parent is even greater. Although estimates vary somewhat, Graefe and Lichter (1999) report, using data from the NLSY, that over a quarter (26 percent) of children born prior to 1992 could expect to live with a cohabiting mother sometime by age 14, while Heuveline and Timberlake (2004) found that about one-third of American children can expect to live with a cohabiting parent.

Since cohabiting unions are less stable than marriages, a growing body of evidence has sought to document how children fare if they spend time with a cohabiting parent (or parents). While we still do not conclusively know whether spending time in a cohabiting family rather than with married parents or an unmarried parent is more or less beneficial to children, cohabiting families do break up more often than do married ones. The preliminary evidence suggests that spending time in cohabiting families can have detrimental effects for children, often because of the transient nature of the relationship. In other words, children who spend time with a cohabiting parent may fare worse developmentally than children raised in stable two-parent families, and even children raised by single-parents who do not cohabit, largely because cohabiting parents tend to experience multiple transitions in and out of relationships. It is these multiple transitions that are detrimental to children (Brown 2004).

The dramatic increase in cohabitation has stimulated a great deal of research exploring who cohabitors are, suggesting what role cohabitation serves in the union formation process, and assessing the impact of cohabitation for the well-being of adults and children. Religious leaders and policymakers are increasingly questioning the impact that living together has on marriage and parenting. The growing acceptance of cohabitation among the general population, in conjunction with its increasing prevalence as a staging ground for parenting, presents new challenges to those concerned about growing inequality across family types. Yet the role cohabitation will play in patterns of family formation in the US and other western countries in the future is still unknown, and will require further study of its impact on individuals and families in differing circumstances and life course stages, how its meaning changes over time, and the impact that living together has on the institution of marriage.

SEE ALSO: Divorce; Family Diversity; Family Structure; Family Structure and Child Outcomes; Family Structure and Poverty; Intimate Union Formation and Dissolution; Love and Commitment; Marriage

REFERENCES AND SUGGESTED READINGS

Blackwell, D. L. & Lichter, D. (2000) Mate Selection Among Married and Cohabiting Couples. *Journal of Family Issues* 21: 275–302.

Brown, S. (2004) Family Structure and Child Well-Being: The Significance of Parental Cohabitation. *Journal of Marriage and the Family* 66: 351–67.

Bumpass, L. & Lu, H.-H.(2000) Trends in Cohabitation and Implications for Children's Family Contexts in the United States. *Population Studies* 54: 29–41.

Fields, J. & Casper, L. (2001) *America's Families and Living Arrangements: Population Characteristics.* Current Population Reports, P20–5327. US Census Bureau, Washington, DC.

Graefe, D. & Lichter, D. (1999) Life Course Transitions of American Children: Parental Cohabitation, Marriage, and Single Motherhood. *Demography* 36: 205–17.

Gupta, S. (1999) The Effects of Transitions in Marital Status on Men's Performance of Housework. *Journal of Marriage and the Family* 61: 700–12.

Heuveline, P. & Timberlake, J. (2004) The Role of Cohabitation in Family Formation: The United States in Comparative Perspective. *Journal of Marriage and the Family* 65: 1214–30.

Kiernan, K. (2004a) Unmarried Cohabitation and Parenthood in Britain and Europe. *Law and Policy* 26: 33–55.

Kiernan, K. (2004b) Redrawing the Boundaries of Marriage. *Journal of Marriage and Family* 66: 980–7.

Lichter, D., Qian, Z., & Mellott, L. (2006) Marriage or Dissolution? Union Transitions among Poor Cohabiting Women. *Demography* 43.

Manning, W. (1993) Marriage and Cohabitation Following Premarital Conception. *Journal of Marriage and the Family* 55: 839–50.

Oppenheimer, V. (2003) Cohabiting and Marriage During Young Men's Career Development Process. *Demography* 40: 127–49.

Qian, Z., Lichter, D., & Mellott, L. (2005) Out-of-Wedlock Childbearing, Marital Prospects, and Mate Selection. *Social Forces* 84: 473–91.

Raley, R. K. (2000) Recent Trends and Differentials in Marriage and Cohabitation: The United States. In: Waite, L. J. (Ed.), *The Ties that Bind: Perspectives on Marriage and Cohabitation.* Aldine de Gruyter, New York, pp. 19–39.

Raley, R. K. (2001) Increasing Fertility in Cohabiting Unions: Evidence for the Second Demographic Transition in the US. *Demography* 38: 59–66.

Sassler, S. (2004) The Process of Entering into Cohabiting Unions. *Journal of Marriage and Family* 66: 491–505.

Schoen, R. & Owens, D. (1991) A Further Look at First Unions and First Marriages. In: South, S. J. & Tolnay, S. (Eds.), *The Changing American Family.* Westview Press, Boulder, pp. 109–17.

Shelton, B. & John, D. (1993) Does Marital Status Make a Difference? Housework Among Married and Cohabiting Men and Women. *Journal of Family Issues* 14: 401–20.

Sigle-Rushton, W. & McLanahan, S. (2002) The Living Arrangements of New Unmarried Mothers. *Demography* 39: 415–33.

Simmons, T. & O' Connell, M. (2003) Married Couple and Unmarried Partner Households: 2000. Online. www.census.gov/prod/2003pubs/censr-5.pdf.

Smock, P. J. (2000) Cohabitation in the United States: An Appraisal of Research Themes, Findings, and Implications. *Annual Review of Sociology* 26: 1–20.

Coleman, James (1926–95)

Peter V. Marsden

James S. Coleman ranks among the most influential sociologists of the twentieth century. Coleman's scholarship pursued several linked lines of inquiry in parallel, but centered on understanding and improving the performance of social systems. He led a study of inequality in educational opportunity (Coleman, Campbell et al. 1966) that had a major impact on US educational policy and served as a model for much subsequent policy research in social science. *Foundations of Social Theory* (1990), his principal theoretical work, outlined an approach to understanding social phenomena resting on interdependent purposive actions. He viewed the rising prominence and power of large organizations ("corporate actors") as the most distinctive feature of contemporary society, and contended that social science and social theory should help to develop new forms of social organization that are more attentive to the interests and welfare of natural persons. Coleman's work has enduring influence on social theory, educational research, organizational analysis, mathematical sociology, and policy research, among other fields.

A native of the Midwestern and Southern United States, Coleman's undergraduate degree was in chemical engineering. He subsequently became interested in the social sciences, earning a doctorate in sociology from Columbia University in 1955. He held academic appointments at Johns Hopkins University (1959–73) and the University of Chicago (1956–9 and 1973–96). He was a member of the US National Academy of Sciences and served as president of the American Sociological Association in 1991–2.

Coleman practiced "middle-range sociology" characteristic of the post-World War II Columbia School (Swedberg 1996), stressing insight into substantive questions about social organization, informed by a close interplay between theory and empirical inquiry. His scholarship reflected the diverse influences of his graduate mentors. He drew theoretical inspiration from Robert K. Merton and an emphasis on macrosocial questions from Seymour Martin Lipset. His studies with Paul F. Lazarsfeld and his background in the sciences oriented Coleman to mathematical models of social processes. His interest in rational choice analysis grew beginning in the 1960s, much influenced by economic analysis and positive political theory.

Coleman's early career works illustrate the breadth of his substantive concerns. He had a penchant for "community" studies focused on structural features and system-level questions (Coleman 1986). He took a quantitative approach to studying social organization that avoided atomization and abstraction away from social context.

Coleman assigned sustained high priority to increasing the responsiveness of social organization. He co-authored *Union Democracy*, which examined political processes within the International Typographical Union (Lipset et al. 1956). The presence of a stable two-party system there avoided the power concentration predicted by Robert Michels's iron law of oligarchy, an outcome attributed to historical and social factors including local autonomy, occupational community among printers, and secret societies providing independent power bases. Legitimate competition among political factions promoted correspondence between union activities and member concerns, mitigating agency problems found in otherwise similar membership organizations dominated by a permanent leadership group. Coleman viewed pluralistic arrangements – legitimate competition among multiple centers of power – as important devices helping to align actions of social organizations with interests of their constituencies.

The Adolescent Society (1961), Coleman's first study to address educational questions, focused on how the social organization of high schools – especially student status hierarchies and value systems – affected their performance. Set against ongoing social changes – increasing specialization, the declining capacity of families to prepare children for economic life, and rising segregation of adults and children – Coleman argued that both formal and informal structures in schools tended to discourage high academic performance. Adolescent cultures prized athletic success and popularity rather than scholastic achievement, and students responded accordingly. Coleman advocated restructuring that would engage students actively and collectively in educational pursuits.

While an associate at the Bureau of Applied Social Research at Columbia, Coleman conducted research on the processes through which physicians came to adopt a new drug. Later published as *Medical Innovation* (Coleman et al. 1966), the study found that both formal communication media and personal contacts (social and professional) influenced adoption decisions. Integration into local social networks alerted physicians to the new drug, but more

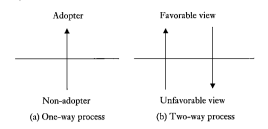

Figure 1 Examples of transition processes.

importantly offered legitimation by resolving uncertainties about its benefits and drawbacks.

Coleman viewed mathematics not as a methodological tool, but instead as a vehicle and formal language for expressing and refining sociological theory. He stressed dynamic modeling of social processes, rather than applications of statistics or static representions of social structure. *Introduction to Mathematical Sociology* (*IMS*; Coleman 1964) outlined an intellectual agenda for mathematical sociology and remains a foundational work in this field.

IMS emphasizes continuous-time, discrete-state stochastic process models, centering attention on transitions from one condition to another. Such transitions can be one-way, e.g., the rate at which physicians move from not prescribing to prescribing a new drug (Fig. 1a) or two-way, e.g., the rates at which adolescent evaluations of the "leading crowd" at school change between favorable and unfavorable (Fig. 1b). Explanatory factors such as network integration or membership in the leading crowd could amplify or dampen transition rates for individuals. Coleman highlighted the equilibrium assumptions required by cross-sectional analyses of such dynamic phenomena, stimulating interest in over-time observation plans. The imagery of distribution of units into states governed by an underlying regime of transition rates subsequently became widespread in sociology, particularly in event history models for longitudinal data analysis.

Beginning in the mid-1960s, Coleman conducted major large-scale research projects that addressed US educational policy issues. The first and best known of these was *Equality of Educational Opportunity* (*EEO*; Coleman, Campbell et al. 1966), a study mandated by the 1964 Civil Rights Act. Examining rural/ urban, regional, and race/ethnic inequalities, *EEO* found only modest differences in "input" school resources such as facilities, textbooks, or teacher salaries – the then conventional standards for gauging equality of opportunity. An important innovation was *EEO*'s attention to disparities in the outcomes of schooling, where substantial race/ethnic differences were evident. The study traced achievement inequalities largely to family background and both peer and teacher characteristics, attributing few to variations in school resources. Results of *EEO* were widely invoked in support of school desegregation policies.

Public and academic debate alike surrounded Coleman's educational policy studies (Ravitch 1993), none more so than a 1970s project that found that court-ordered mandatory school desegregation plans tended to accelerate white residential movement out of central cities. A subsequent study showing that parochial and private school students had higher achievement levels than public school students (Coleman & Hoffer 1987) generated controversy because it implied that policies creating school competition, such as school choice or voucher plans, might improve the performance of public schools. Catholic schools had particularly low dropout rates, and notably high rates of achievement growth among less advantaged students. In accounting for differences across sectors, the public/private school project stressed features of school social organization such as disciplinary climate and the presence of "functional communities" encouraging contact among parents, teachers, and students.

Coleman regarded research projects like *EEO* as a novel genre of social science that provides information about current or prospective policy initiatives, contrasting them with exposés of social problems and basic disciplinary research. He observed that sponsors establish the agenda for policy research projects, and expressed concern that they would exercise undue control over research designs and the dissemination of findings. He advocated a pluralistic framework for the governance of policy research that would engage multiple interested parties in the conception of projects and review of results.

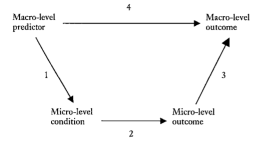

Figure 2 Micro-level translation of macro-level proposition.

Figure 3 Relations between basic elements of Coleman's social system.

Coleman viewed questions about the functioning of social systems as both most difficult and most important for sociology. He advocated multilevel theories that account for systemic phenomena as outcomes of interactions among interdependent micro-level actors (Coleman 1986). An informative theoretical account for relationships between macro-level phenomena would entail linking them to micro-level actions (Fig. 2). To understand a macro–macro (Type 4) proposition, one would show how (1) system-level conditions shape micro-level conditions, (2) micro-level conditions translate into micro-level actions, and (3) micro-level actions combine to produce systemic outcomes. Coleman pointed to micro–macro (Type 3) transitions as the greatest challenge for social science analysis.

Coleman's *Foundations of Social Theory* (*FST*; 1990) develops a rational choice basis for such explanations. Operating within a broadly conceived methodological individualist framework, *FST* aspires toward a transdisciplinary theory of the functioning and performance of social systems. Coleman assumes an economic concept of rational action – use of scarce resources in pursuit of interests – as a model for Type 2 transitions. Economic analysis and the model of the optimizing rational agent appealed to him by offering an approach to making micro–macro transitions, and allowing anticipation of the results of social interventions. He was, however, careful to disavow the assumptions of independent action embodied in many economic models; though interests pursued by actors were often selfish, they could also be influenced by structural features including interdependencies, networks, authority structures, norms, and organizations.

Elementary units in Coleman's framework are actors and resources (also termed events). Actors control resources, which in turn are of interest to actors (Fig. 3). Interdependence exists within this minimal situation by virtue of the interests of actors in resources that others control. Seeking to realize their interests, actors may allocate resources via such means as direct use, compensated transfer, or unilateral transfer. *FST* fashions explanations for dyadic relationships of authority and trust, as well as meso-level structures including exchange, authority, and norms. It develops a mathematical formulation of the exchange model with a structure paralleling that of an open market. This makes micro–macro transitions, showing the implications of distributions of interest and control for power differentials among actors and value variations across resources. Coleman applied this model to understanding collective decisions as well as labor market exchange.

Committed to the view that actions are responsive to the incentives present in social situations, Coleman insisted on explaining rather than assuming the norms that were a staple of mid-twentieth-century sociological analysis. *FST* argued that norms reflected a consensus that "beneficiary" actors legitimately hold rights of control over specified "target" actions of others. Beneficiaries were apt to demand such control when their interests were affected by the actions in question. Effective norms would arise when beneficiaries could not gain control of the target actions via compensated exchanges, and when social organization was sufficient to produce and apply a system of sanctions supporting conformity with a normative prescription.

One of Coleman's most influential works conceptualized social capital as aspects of social structure that facilitate action (Coleman 1988). The term encompasses numerous structural phenomena covered in *FST*, including systems of trust and obligations, networks of information flow, norms backed by sanctioning systems, and centralized structures of authority relations. Social relations often constitute social capital by facilitating the development of trust or serving as a foundation for effective sanctioning systems. Network closure often provides social capital; Coleman's public/private school project attributed some achievement differences to community structures having high student–parent, parent–teacher, and parent–parent contact. These were said to supply sanctions and monitoring that encouraged both continuation in school and academic achievement.

Coleman observed that social capital has a restricted scope of applicability, however; it is a less general ("fungible") resource than economic capital. Features of social structure could result in harmful as well as beneficial consequences. Moreover, a rational choice perspective highlights a public goods dilemma in the production of social capital: benefits of social capital often accrue to actors other than those who produce it, and hence it will typically be underproduced. One important source of social capital is social organization created to pursue one purpose, but subsequently appropriated for another use. Coleman believed that the social capital available to advance the interests of children was in especially short supply, and advocated policy steps to increase incentives for its creation.

Much of *FST* is devoted to "new corporate actors," the feature of contemporary society that Coleman saw as most distinctive. Part of a "Great Transformation" from primordial social organization resting on families as the basic social units to "constructed social organization" in which corporate actors – deliberately designed, special-purpose social structures having a legal standing independent of natural persons – were central features (Coleman 1992).

At base, corporate actors are built on simple authority relations, which arise when one actor grants control over some set of actions to another in exchange for compensation (disjoint authority) or in anticipation of shared benefit (conjoint authority). Their capacity for action and potential complexity grows vastly with the development of complex authority relations, in which a superordinate may delegate the exercise of authority to an agent, and role-based social organization involving relationships among abstract positions rather than persons.

Such innovations expand the range of potentially viable authority configurations, permitting forms in which only a participant's net relationship with the corporate actor, rather than dyadic relationships with each and every other participant, need be profitable. Coleman calls attention to social inventions including the concept of "juristic persons" and limited liability, which offered new means through which individual persons could combine resources in pursuit of interests. Corporate actors could have far greater size, complexity, and longevity than primordial organizational forms; importantly, responsibility for their actions could not be settled on any individual person.

Rational choice analysis sensitized Coleman to principal–agent problems within corporate actors. When possible, self-interested subordinates will pursue their own ends rather than those of the intended beneficiaries of the corporate actor. Likewise, superiors may attempt to expand their control over a subordinate's actions beyond the scope of the latter's grant. Both of these common defects in authority relations lead to suboptimal performance. Coleman suggests that the effectiveness of corporate actors could be enhanced by organizational structures and incentive systems involving short feedback cycles and exchanges among agents in proximate positions, rather than the lengthy loops associated with centralized command-control schemes and extensive oversight on the part of superiors.

The increasing concentration of social power in corporate actors rather than natural persons was of much greater concern to Coleman, however. He was struck by the pervasiveness of corporate actors in contemporary society, and their capacity to pursue specialized purposes relentlessly. Specialization contributed to their efficiency in attaining their ends, but often also predisposed them toward a narrowness of purpose, lack of responsibility due to neglecting collateral effects of their actions, and an unresponsiveness to the interests of natural persons.

Such consequences are especially severe to the extent that the purposes of corporate actors and natural persons diverge. Coleman's major value premise in *FST* is that corporate actors should be judged on the basis of their effects on the interests of persons. Observing that individual welfare is increasingly dependent on

---

affiliations with powerful corporate actors, he raised concern about the fate of unorganized interests and provisions for persons, notably children, who lack such linkages.

Coleman viewed the decline of primordial social organization in favor of constructed social organization as irreversible, and therefore regarded the social control of corporate actors as a prominent item on the agenda for sociology and social policy alike, recommending steps to better align the actions of corporate actors with the interests of persons. He suggested some interventions which would manipulate the environments in which corporate actors operate: changes in tax laws, creation or maintenance of competition within organizational fields (e.g., school choice), the creation of countervailing corporate actors, or audits by external parties. Other steps would alter the internal structures of corporate actors by changing governance structures to increase the influence of affected parties on performance, increasing the incentives for agents to act responsibly, or assigning greater liability for harmful actions to agents.

Skeptical about the capacity of states, themselves large corporate actors, to develop effective remedies, *FST* closed with Coleman's call for a "new social science" oriented to improving the design and performance of organizations and institutions, a process he called the "rational reconstruction of society." Such an enterprise would bridge disciplinary boundaries, resting on basic theory and research, but also entailing major programs of applied social policy research.

SEE ALSO: Educational Inequality; Mathematical Sociology; Merton, Robert K.; Micro–Macro Links; Oligarchy and Organization; Rational Choice Theory (and Economic Sociology); Social Capital and Education

REFERENCES AND SUGGESTED READINGS

Clark, J. (Ed.) (1996) *James S. Coleman*. Falmer, London.
Coleman, J. S. (1961) *The Adolescent Society: The Social Life of the Teenager and Its Impact on Education*. Free Press, New York.
Coleman, J. S. (1964) *Introduction to Mathematical Sociology*. Free Press, New York.
Coleman, J. S. (1986) Social Theory, Social Research, and a Theory of Action. *American Journal of Sociology* 91: 1309–35.
Coleman, J. S. (1988) Social Capital in the Creation of Human Capital. *American Journal of Sociology* 95: S95–S120.
Coleman, J. S. (1990) *Foundations of Social Theory*. Harvard University Press, Cambridge, MA.
Coleman, J. S. (1992) The Rational Reconstruction of Society: 1992 Presidential Address. *American Sociological Review* 58: 1–15.
Coleman, J. S. & Hoffer, T. (1987) *Public and Private Schools: The Impact of Communities*. Basic Books, New York.
Coleman, J. S., Campbell, E. Q., Hobson, C. J., McPartland, J., Mood, A. M., Weinfeld, F. D., & York, R. L. (1966) *Equality of Educational Opportunity*. US Government Printing Office, Washington, DC.
Coleman, J. S., Katz, E., & Menzel, H. (1966) *Medical Innovation: A Diffusion Study*. Bobbs-Merrill, Indianapolis.
Favell, A. (1993) James Coleman: Social Theorist and Moral Philosopher? *American Journal of Sociology* 99: 590–613.
Lindenberg, S. (2000) James Coleman. In: Ritzer, G. (Ed.), *The Blackwell Companion to Major Social Theorists*. Blackwell, Malden, MA, pp. 513–44.
Lipset, S. M., Trow, M., & Coleman, J. S. (1956) *Union Democracy: The Inside Politics of the International Typographical Union*. Free Press, New York.
Marsden, P. V. (2005) The Sociology of James S. Coleman. *Annual Review of Sociology* 31: 1–24.
Ravitch, D. (1993) The Coleman Reports and American Education. In: Sorensen, A. B. & Spilerman, S. (Eds.), *Social Theory and Social Policy: Essays in Honor of James. S. Coleman*. Praeger, Westport, CT, pp. 129–41.
Swedberg, R. (1996) Analyzing the Economy: On the Contribution of James S. Coleman. In: Clark, J. (Ed.), *James S. Coleman*. Falmer, London, pp. 313–28.

collective action

Doug McAdam

The term "collective action" is hopelessly broad. Taken at face value, it could plausibly refer to *all* forms of human social action involving two or more people. Suffice to say,

consideration of such a broadly inclusive category would be well beyond the scope of this
entry. But there is a far narrower subset of
human action to which the term has been
applied and which will be the focus here. For
our purposes, *collective action* refers to *emergent
and minimally coordinated action by two or more
people that is motivated by a desire to change some
aspect of social life or to resist changes proposed by
others*. By "emergent" is meant innovative lines
of action that depart from taken-for-granted
normative routines. "Coordinated" simply
means that the various parties to the emerging
conflict are attuned to one another and acting
in awareness of this fact. Finally, the emphasis
on change and/or resistance to change is
designed to capture the adversarial or potentially conflictual nature of "collective action."

While considerably narrower than the inclusive definition imagined above, even this delimited category of action has been the object of a
great deal of scholarship. In recent years, much
of the relevant work has been done by "social
movement" scholars, principally in sociology
and political science. But there is also a longstanding interest in the dynamics of "collective
action" among some economists and political
scientists intent on understanding the conditions
under which people will engage in emergent
action of this sort. Finally, there is a wealth
of historical scholarship on various instances of
collective action, carried out by historians,
or historically oriented social scientists. While
not claiming to be equally conversant with these
very different and vast literatures, this survey
takes them as its point of departure.

The following three broad animating questions are examined:

- When? Under what conditions can we
  expect collective action to develop?
- Who? What individual-level factors appear
  to predict participation in collective action?
- Impact? What do we know about the outcomes of collective action and the factors that
  may help account for variation in its effects?

WHEN?

In the long history of research and theory
on the topic, no question has received more
attention than that concerning the origins of
emergent collective action. What factors make
for such action in the first place? It is a per-
plexing question. Typically, people's day-to-
day behaviors are governed by predictable,
institutionalized routines. Indeed, most of us
are quite dependent on those routines. So the
interesting question is, under what conditions
will people willingly abandon these routines in
favor of emergent action? There may be no
simple answer. But in the literature one can
discern three main perspectives on the topic.

Strain Theories

The first perspective is not so much a specific
theory as a class of explanations that share the
important assumption that collective action is
typically a response to some form of severe
strain in society. A distinction should be made,
however, between *classic* and more *contemporary*
strain arguments. Classic strain theories suggest
that whatever the underlying structural strain,
the real motive force behind collective action
comes from some identifiable shared *psychological state* or condition. So, for example, for
mass society theorists, the structural condition
that puts a society at "risk" of collective action
is the absence of intermediate groups (political
parties, religious institutions, etc.) by which
citizens are functionally integrated into society.
But the immediate motivation to action stems
from the feelings of *anomie* produced by living
in a "mass society." For classic strain theorists,
then, social movements function principally at
a psychological, rather than a political, level.

This is not true of more contemporary strain
perspectives, such as competition theory or traditional Marxist accounts of revolutionary collective action. The former explains racial or
ethnic conflict as a byproduct of demographic,
economic, and/or political processes that are
perceived as pitting two or more groups against
each other in the search for economic or political power (Olzak 1992). For their part, Marxist scholars continue to attribute revolutionary
collective action to economic dislocations produced by the contradictions inherent in capitalism (Paige 1975). Gone are the mediating
psychological states that play such a central causal role in the classic strain accounts, replaced by

a straightforward link between grievances and action, created by the underlying structural dislocations identified in the theory.

Resource Mobilization

As formulated by McCarthy and Zald (1973), resource mobilization was conceived as an explicit alternative to the then dominant strain perspective. There is always sufficient "strain" or "grievances" in society, they argue, to provide the motivation for emergent collective action. You cannot therefore rely on strain, which is more or less ever present, to account for collective action, which is far more variable. What *does* vary, they argue, is not the motivation to engage in collective action, but the organizational capacity and resources required to do so. So it is not strain per se that produces collective action, but a significant increase in organizational capacity and resources. What produces such an increase? Proponents of the approach have offered two answers to this question. An increase in general societal prosperity is seen as allowing for more collective action, as the "slack resources" needed to support such activity increase as well. The other possibility is for a specific movement to benefit from a significant infusion of funds from one or more external "sponsors."

Political Process Theory

The distinctive contribution of political process theorists has been to reassert the fundamental *political* character and origin of most instances of emergent collective action (Tilly 1978; Tarrow 1998; McAdam 1999). In this conception, society is seen as an elaborate system of power relations that grants some groups routine access to power while denying it to others. In times of political stability, the power disparity between "members" (those who enjoy routine access) and "challengers" (those who don't) is likely to be so great as to virtually preclude the possibility of effective political action by the latter. But no political system, even the most coercive and centralized, is spared periods of instability. It is during such periods that emergent collective action is expected to develop. The main emphasis has been to stress the

catalytic impact of events or processes that weakened established regimes, thereby creating new "opportunities" for successful collective action by challenging groups. Recently, however, proponents of the approach have also sought to incorporate "threat" as well as "opportunity" into the argument (McAdam 1999; Goldstone & Tilly 2001). That is, destabilizing events that come to be perceived as posing serious threats to group interests may also set in motion emergent collective action.

WHO?

If the "when" of collective action has generated the lion's share of research and theory on the topic, the "who" of the matter has not lagged far behind. That is, a great deal of scholarship has been devoted to the question of "differential recruitment." Why does one person come to take part in an episode of collective action while another does not? Answers to this question have tended to fall into two general categories: *individual* and *social structural* accounts of participation.

Individual Explanations

There is a very basic appeal – especially in the West, and the US most of all – to individual accounts of behavior: the idea that to explain behavior one need look no further than the individual. This assumption has given rise to a number of individualistic accounts of participation in collective action, or "activism," to employ the shorthand term. These explanations can be further grouped into three basic types: those that attribute participation to certain psychological characteristics; those that stress rational calculus as the basis for individual activism; and those that see participation as a reflection of a certain attitudinal affinity with the aims of the "movement."

   The oldest accounts of activism identify a particular *psychological state or characteristic* as the root cause of participation. The emphasis is on character traits or states of mind that presumably impel, or at least dispose, an individual to activism. What varies are the specific characteristics or qualities identified as significant in this regard. Even a cursory accounting of the variants of this approach is beyond the scope of this entry. A few examples will have to suffice.

Mass society theory was, for a number of years, an especially influential account of participation in collective action. Proponents of the approach argued that emergent movements serve as "substitute communities" for those alienated, poorly integrated members of society who are disproportionately drawn to activism. An even older psychological tradition – reflected in the work of Adorno and colleagues – identified participation in non-democratic movements with "authoritarian" personality traits. In 1969, Lewis Feuer published an influential account of the student protest movement, arguing that those who were drawn to the movement were apt to be those students, especially males, who saw in it a chance to express unresolved emotional conflicts with their parents. The essence of the approach should be clear: collective action participation stems presumably from the motive force of some characteristic psychological trait or process.

Running very much counter to psychological theories is an important *rationalist* tradition in the study of collective action. Rather than individuals being compelled to participate as a result of specified psychological traits, states of mind, or "needs," activism is held to reflect the same kind of rational cost–benefit calculations that decision theorists assume inform all choice processes. However, the key touchstone text that inspired this important line of work was actually centrally concerned with the seeming irrationality of collective action.

In his classic 1965 book *The Logic of Collective Action*, Mancur Olson posed what he saw as the stark "free-rider problem" that confronted any who would seek to mobilize collective action geared to the provision of a public good. Why, asked Olson, would anyone take part in such an effort when they would receive whatever benefits the group achieved whether they participated or not? From this perspective, individual activism appeared irrational. But Olson was not blind to the fact that, while not normative, there was also no shortage of emergent collective action in the real world. How does one explain this seeming paradox? One option might have been to embrace the then dominant psychological perspective and simply argue that collective action represented a departure from the "normal" rational choice processes thought to structure routine social life.

This was not, however, the tack that Olson took. Instead he went on to explicate two general conditions under which he felt we could expect to see collective action develop. These conditions involve (1) the provision of *selective incentives* to increase the rewards of those engaging in collective action, and (2) the creation of monitoring and sanctioning systems that would effectively deny benefits to those who failed to participate. Since then scholars in this tradition have sought to extend, modify, or refine Olson's rationalist take on individual activism.

The central claim of this third perspective is simple enough: activism grows out of strong *attitudinal support* for the values and goals of the movement in question. This account was especially popular as applied to student activism in the US in the late 1960s and early 1970s. According to the research of Flacks (1971) and others, the actions of student radicals were motivated by values learned from their parents.

To their credit, advocates of this approach rejected the somewhat mechanistic psychological models of participation sketched above in favor of a straightforward behavioral link between a person's values and political attitudes and participation in collective action. Unfortunately, this conceptual advance has not produced any better fit between theory and data. Based on his analysis of 215 studies of the relationship between individual attitudes and riot participation, McPhail (1971) concluded that "individual predispositions are, at best, insufficient to account" for participation in collective action.

Does this mean that attitudes are irrelevant to the study of individual activism? Albeit their importance appears to have been overstated in many accounts of participation, attitudes remain important insofar as they serve as a kind of minimum requirement for involvement in a given instance of collective action. In this sense, a certain attitudinal affinity with the aims of a movement is probably a necessary – but hardly sufficient – condition to account for participation. The question becomes: if attitudes dispose someone to take part in collective action, what additional factors encourage them to act on these dispositions?

Social Structural/Network Explanations

Because of the apparent lack of empirical support for the psychological and attitudinal accounts of participation, attention has turned in recent years to explanations based on an individual's social structural proximity to a given instance of collective action. The argument is that people participate not simply because they are psychologically or attitudinally compelled to, but because their structural/network location in the world puts them "at risk" for participation. But what are the specific structural or network factors that predict variation in individual activism? Twenty-five years of sustained work on this topic have yielded consistent empirical support for two main factors: prior ties to participants and membership in organizations.

The factor that has been shown to bear the strongest relationship to activism is *prior contact with another movement participant*. Several representative studies will help make the point. In a study of all applicants to the 1964 Mississippi Freedom Summer Project, McAdam (1988) found twice as many participants to have "strong ties" to other volunteers than did accepted applicants who withdrew in advance of the campaign. These findings are very much in accord with those reported by Snow et al. (1980) in their groundbreaking survey of the empirical literature on movement recruitment. Of the nine studies reviewed in the article, all but one identified prior interpersonal ties as the most common source of movement recruits.

This consistent empirical finding, however, hardly tells us all we would want to know about the role of prior social ties in recruitment to collective action. First, the finding conveniently skirts the important question of origins. That is, to say that people enter into collective action because they know others who are involved ignores the obvious problem that on the eve of the movement, there are no salient alters already involved to pull ego into participation. Second, this structural account fails to acknowledge conceptually or address empirically the fact that potential recruits invariably possess a multitude of "prior social ties" that are likely to expose them to conflicting behavioral pressures. Here we confront the hoary problem of sampling on the dependent variable.

Overwhelmingly, the studies of recruitment start by surveying activists after their entrance into the action in question. But showing that these activists were linked to the movement by some prior social tie does not prove the causal potency of that tie.

The final lacuna in regard to this issue is theoretical. As Passy (2003: 22) notes: "we are now aware that social ties are important for collective action, but we still need to theorize ... the actual role of networks." Fortunately, scholars of social movements and collective action have begun to move beyond the simple structural relationship between prior ties and participation to theorize and empirically explore the more dynamic social and social psychological processes that appear to account for the effect. The specifics of these efforts are, once again, beyond the scope of this entry. But an article by Gould (2003) illustrates some of the directions in which this work is developing.

The other consistent structural "fact" about the origins of collective action is that the overwhelming majority of emergent movements develop within *established organizations, institutions, or networks*. What this means at the individual level is that, not only are most activists drawn into mature movements through prior ties to other activists, but also that in the early days of a movement, participation tends to overlap substantially with the membership of certain key "mobilizing structures." Either way, the message is the same: throughout the life of a movement, structural connections to other activists or activist organizations appear to shape the chances of participation far more than individual psychological or attitudinal factors.

But, as with the notion of "prior tie," the concept of the "mobilizing structure" has too often been treated as an objective structural facilitator of collective action, rather than a contested site of interaction that can support various lines of action. The point is, existing groups or networks are as apt to constrain as to facilitate collective action. For these settings to become sites of emergent mobilization, they must be culturally conceived and defined as such by a significant subset of the group's members. This process has been termed *social appropriation* by its proponents (McAdam 1999; McAdam et al. 2001).

IMPACT?

If the general topic of collective action is unwieldy, much harder is the assessment of its impact. Nonetheless, since much collective action is motivated by a desire to change aspects of social and political life, understanding something about the effectiveness of such efforts is necessarily an important goal. The most coherent and focused academic take on the issue has come from social movement scholars who, in recent years, have devoted considerable attention to the topic. This attention is in marked contrast to the generalized neglect of the topic evident in earlier periods.

Given the view of social movements that prevailed in sociology and political science well into the 1970s, the failure to consider the issue of impact or consequences is entirely understandable. Both disciplines saw movements as ineffectual. For their part, sociologists grouped social movements together with other unusual/ aberrant social phenomena – crazes, fads, panics, crowds – into a field of study known as "collective behavior." All these forms of behavior were seen as collective responses to rapid social change. They were not, however, *effective* responses to change. They functioned instead at a psychological level as an outlet for the feelings of anxiety and fear which rapid social change inevitably produced. To the extent that movements served any political function whatsoever, it was only in alerting rational policymakers to the strains triggering collective action.

Political scientists paid no more attention to movement outcomes than sociologists, but for a different reason. In considering electoral and policy outcomes, political scientists stressed – indeed, continue to stress – the strategic preference of elected policymakers for broad centrist policies that can attract broad majority support. Down's 1957 work on the "median voter" was both emblematic and influential in this regard.

The turbulence of the 1960s and 1970s undermined the prevailing views of social movements, especially in sociology. Not only did movements appear to be far more political (and consequential) than the collective behavior perspective allowed, but the era also brought scores of younger scholars into sociology who

had themselves been active in those movements and disposed to reshape the field in line with their own experiences. Accordingly, the separate field of social movement studies that emerged in the late 1970s and early 1980s was animated by a very different assumption than the traditional collective behavior perspective. Far from assuming the political/policy irrelevance of social movements, the new generation of sociologists asserted the consequential impact of movements without, however, typically subjecting this assumption to systematic empirical test.

In recent years this has changed, and a discernible literature on "movement outcomes" has emerged in sociology and, to a lesser extent, political science. The earliest works in this area were admittedly quite elementary, seeking simply to assess the impact of this or that movement on some aspect of political or social life. Most of these studies focus specifically on the success of movements in relation to particular policy outcomes (cf. Andrews 1977; Gamson 1990). Others take up the broader and, in some cases, unintended consequences of social movements (McAdam 1988; Katzenstein 1998).

Taken together, then, these studies provide impressive evidence of the potential of social movements to serve, under certain circumstances, as important vehicles of social and political change. That said, researchers are only now turning to the "how" of the question. Having found that movements are capable of producing significant change effects, the more important goal is to identify those factors or processes that account for these outcomes.

To date, three mechanisms have been proposed as keys to the variable impact of movements. These are disruptive protest, signaling, and public opinion shift.

A recurrent debate in the literature concerns the tactical effectiveness of *disruptive protest* versus more moderate forms of collective action. Starting with Lipsky's classic work on "protest as a resource," many analysts have endorsed the general idea that movement success depends on the ability of challenging groups to create "negative inducements" to elite bargaining through the disruption of public order and the threat such disruption poses to the realization of elite interests (Piven & Cloward 1979; McAdam 1999).

Though limited, some empirical evidence can also be cited in support of this particular mechanism (Gamson 1990; McAdam & Su 2002).

Lohmann (1993: 319, emphasis added) proposes a *"signaling* model of information and manipulative political action" in which elected officials use mass political activity to better understand the policy preferences of the electorate. For her, public protest can serve as a kind of mobilized public opinion, providing lawmakers with timely and meaningful information regarding the distribution of policy positions within the general public. The question is, under what conditions will this information prompt lawmakers to shift their own policy behaviors? Lohmann stresses two conditions in particular. The first is the size of the protest. All things equal, lawmakers can be expected to attend to only the largest of movement gatherings. They are also, according to Lohmann, likely to "discount the observed turnout for extremist political action and shift policy [only] if the estimated number of activist moderates exceeds a critical threshold" (p. 319). So, to summarize, movements that are able to organize large, ideologically moderate, public demonstrations are likely to have a demonstrable effect on public policy.

The link between public opinion and policy outcomes has interested political scientists (and, to a lesser extent, economists) for years (Page & Shapiro 1983). Viewing elected officials as rational actors intent on staying in office, these scholars have hypothesized that politicians will generally modify their policy preferences to fit *shifting public opinion* in an effort to retain electoral support. Theory aside, survey articles summarizing the mass of work on the topic find a reasonably strong link between opinion shift and policy change.

All of this suggests another, less direct, link between movement activity, public opinion, and policy change than the one imagined by Lohmann. Here protest does not work directly – as a signal – to change the policy preferences of policymakers, but rather does so only indirectly by first shifting public opinion in the direction of movement goals. Once opinion has shifted in this way, it then acts, in the manner consistent with the aforementioned research, to alter the policy preferences of those public officials who are subject to electoral pressures.

SEE ALSO: Civil Rights Movement; Culture, Social Movements and; Mobilization; Political Opportunities; Political Process Theory; Resource Mobilization Theory; Revolutions; Social Change; Social Movement Organizations; Social Movements; Social Movements, Networks and; Social Movements, Strain and Breakdown Theories of

REFERENCES AND SUGGESTED READINGS

Andrews, K. (1977) The Impact of Social Movements on the Political Process: The Civil Rights Movement and Black Election Politics in Mississippi. *American Sociological Review* 62: 800–19.

Flacks, R. (1971) *Youth and Social Change*. Markham, Chicago.

Gamson, W. (1990) *The Strategy of Social Protest*, 2nd edn. Wadsworth, Belmont, CA.

Goldstone, J. A. & Tilly, C. (2001) Threat (and Opportunity): Popular Action and State Response in the Dynamics of Contentious Action. In: Aminzade, R. et al. (Eds.), *Silence and Voice in the Study of Contentious Politics*. Cambridge University Press, New York, pp. 126–54.

Gould, R. (2003) Why Do Movements Matter? Rationalist and Structuralist Interpretations. In: Diani, M. & McAdam, D. (Eds.), *Social Movements and Networks*. Oxford University Press, Oxford, pp. 233–57.

Katzenstein, M. F. (1998) *Faithful and Fearless: Moving Feminism into the Church and Military*. Princeton University Press, Princeton.

Lohmann, S. (1993) A Signaling Model of Informative and Manipulative Political Action. *American Political Science Review* 87: 319–33.

McAdam, D. (1988) *Freedom Summer*. Oxford University Press, New York.

McAdam, D. (1999) *Political Process and the Development of Black Insurgency, 1930–1970*, 2nd edn. University of Chicago Press, Chicago.

McAdam, D. & Su, Y. (2002) The War at Home: Antiwar Protests and Congressional Voting, 1965–1973. *American Sociological Review* 67: 696–721.

McAdam, D., Tarrow, S., & Tilly, C. (2001) *Dynamics of Contention*. Cambridge University Press, New York and Cambridge.

McCarthy, J. D. & Zald, M. N. (1973) *The Trend of Social Movements in America: Professionalization and Resource Mobilization*. General Learning Corporation, Morristown, NJ.

McPhail, C. (1971) Civil Disorder Participation: A Critical Examination of Recent Research. *American Sociological Review* 36: 1058–73.

Olzak, S. (1992) *The Dynamics of Ethnic Competition and Conflict*. Stanford University Press, Stanford, CA.

Page, B. I. & Shapiro, R. Y. (1983) Effects of Public Opinion on Policy. *American Political Science Review* 77: 175–90.

Paige, J. (1975) *Agrarian Revolution*. Free Press, New York.

Passy, F. (2003) Social Movements Matter. But How? In: Diani, M. & McAdam, D. (Eds.), *Social Movements and Networks*. Oxford University Press, Oxford, pp. 21–48.

Piven, F. F. & Cloward, R. (1979) *Poor People's Movements*. Vintage Books, New York.

Snow, D. A., Zurcher, L. A., & Ekland-Olson, S. (1980) Social Networks and Social Movements: A Microstructural Approach to Movement Recruitment. *American Sociological Review* 45: 787–801.

Tarrow, S. (1998) *Power in Movement*, 2nd edn. Cambridge University Press, New York.

Tilly, C. (1978) *From Mobilization to Revolution*. Addison-Wesley, Reading, MA.

collective consciousness

Susan Wortmann

Two components of Durkheim's project are to establish sociology as a discipline in its own right, distinct from psychology, and to understand and demonstrate the dependence of human beings upon their societies. These come together in Durkheim's *âme collective* (collective mind). This concept, commonly referred to by sociologists as the "collective consciousness" or "conscience collective," exemplifies the crucial role that the social plays in human behavior. While theorists disagree about the ultimate role of the collective consciousness in Durkheim's overall work, the idea of such an entity still provokes discussion, critique, theoretical application, and empirical testing.

Durkheim (1933: 38, 39) defines the collective consciousness as "the totality of beliefs and sentiments common to average members of the same society ... it is an entirely different thing from particular consciences, although it can only be realized through them." Durkheim finds the collective consciousness important enough to be included in his major texts,

The Division of Labor in Society (1933), *Suicide* (1951), *Elementary Forms of Religious Life* (1954), and *The Rules of Sociological Method* (1964). To understand how the collective consciousness functions, one must first understand Durkheim's distinction between what he deems mechanical and organic societies, the people produced in each, and the types of law that govern them.

Durkheim (1933) illustrates the different mechanisms of social order through two societal types. The first type, the *mechanical* society, is a traditional, simpler society composed of economically self-sustaining members who, living in close proximity, are more alike than different. For instance, they live in families or clans, performing similar agrarian tasks. They are unified by language, religious beliefs, values, rituals, and activities common to all and respected by all. Together, these representations comprise the collective consciousness: a real, external, and coercive societal entity that preexists, outlives, is found in, and acts upon all people in the same manner.

In mechanical solidarity the collective consciousness places real and nearly complete force on humans. That is, in a mechanical society, the function of the collective consciousness is to enforce social similarity and to discourage individual variation, which, in such a society, could undermine collective unity. Deviation is likely to be felt strongly by the collectivity, which seeks to prevent it and punish it severely if it occurs. Mechanical solidarity is thus also characterized by repressive law, designed to punish the person who deviates or engages in criminal activity (which is whatever the collective deems offensive to the collective conscience). Durkheim (1972) associates this law with the heart of society, the "center of the common consciousness." Here, violations result in a collective response and swift punishment extending to the person and perhaps to those immediately associated with them, such as spouses, children, and neighbors. This is because, as Durkheim (1933) points out, violation has ultimately been committed against the society itself. Agreement and speed of punishment, therefore, ensure reinforcement of collective rules, continued social unity, integration, and strict control of most, if not all. Indeed, Durkheim (1972) states that repressive law "attaches the particular individual to the conscience collective directly and without mediation; that is the individual to society."

As populations grow, dynamic density increases and people interact more and more intensely. They are also more and more divided by a struggle over scarce resources. Thus, the need for a social division of labor becomes pronounced, leading to a change in societal structure (Harms 1981). This new societal arrangement is marked by the connection of previously separate communities, and by urbanization, industrialization, increased resources, transportation, and communication. Significantly, it is also marked by an increase in occupational specialization: the division of labor. The changed and differentiated division of labor has a paradoxical effect: it creates interdependent individuality. That is, individuals increasingly perform heterogeneous tasks, thus increasing their interdependence on each other and society, but they also perform increasingly specialized tasks, thus increasing their individuality. Their individual consciousnesses are increasingly developed and distinctive from the conscience collective. Durkheim deems such a societal arrangment *organic*. Here, the preeminent law of the land is no longer repressive but restitutive – civil law that, emphasizing individual rights, attempts not to punish or disgrace individuals or their associates, but instead to return a situation to its previous state. Durkheim (1972) describes the collective consciousness in organic solidarity as "feeble" or "nonexistent," saying that it originates not in the heart, like repressive law, but rather "in very marginal regions."

Debated is just what role and content Durkheim leaves to the collective consciousness in organic society. For instance, Talcott Parsons, in *The Structure of Social Action* (1937), argues that Durkheim's own conception of the collective consciousness in organic society is unclear. Parsons believes that Durkheim either discards the notion of the collective consciousness or relegates it to the normative sphere of shared common values (Giddens 1972). Pope (1973), however, critiques Parsons's normative reading of Durkheim, arguing that Parsons sought to promote his own theoretical understandings through Durkheim's foundational work. Giddens (1972) interprets Durkheim as continuing to see the collective consciousness as operational, but changed. For Giddens, Durkheim's

collective consciousness, now generated by the interdependence brought on by the specialized division of labor, is embodied in the state. Whereas the collective consciousness in mechanical society enforced what was necessary for society, in organic solidarity the state, informed by workers' guilds, consciously deliberates and collectively enacts what is best for society.

Durkheim's collective consciousness continues to provoke debate and application. For instance, Lehmann (1994) critiques Durkheim's collective consciousness because it fails to address the social integration or regulation of women. Illustrating that Durkheim's project is influenced by his own sexism, classism, and racism, she points out that Durkheim's "individuals" are men. Women are largely absent from his entire project, relegated to the asocial realm, to home and to reproduction. Thus, to Lehmann, Durkheim's collective consciousness allows for, and explains only, the collective consciousness of men.

Contemporary research applications are diverse. Examples include Greenburg's (1980) test of a collective consciousness as an entity capable of controlling crime rates in Poland; Schindler's (1999) study of the perception of angels as non-judgmental divine forces in the American collective consciousness; Lawson's (1999) exploration of the generative role of religious language among Catholic Charismatics in collective consciousness formation; and Turner and Wainright's (2003) exploration of the collective's power to mediate injury among professional ballet dancers.

The idea of a collective consciousness also seems to appeal to non-academics. The term appears frequently in contemporary public discourse without reference to Durkheim. In this usage it often is associated with what the individual author or speaker perceives to be a normative societal agreement between groups. It has also been used to discuss the existence of a powerful, invisible social force that socially connects and influences individuals. Indeed, it is ironic that the publication *What is Enlightenment?* (2004) contained an article on the collective consciousness that reaches the conclusion, much like Durkheim himself did nearly a century ago in *The Elementary Forms of Religious Life*: beneficial social advance can result from the recognition (and scientific study) of invisible collective forces that co-reside in society and the individual.

SEE ALSO: Anomie; Division of Labor; Durkheim, Émile; Durkheim, Émile and Social Change; Social Change; Social Control; Solidarity, Mechanical and Organic

REFERENCES AND SUGGESTED READINGS

Durkheim, É. (1933 [1893]) *The Division of Labor in Society.* Free Press, New York.
Durkheim, É. (1951 [1897]) *Suicide.* Free Press, New York.
Durkheim, É. (1954 [1912]) *Elementary Forms of the Religious Life.* Free Press, New York.
Durkheim, É. (1964 [1895]) *The Rules of Sociological Method.* University of Chicago Press, Chicago.
Durkheim, É. (1972 [1960]) Restitutive Sanctions and the Relationship Between Mechanical and Organic Solidarity. In: Giddens, A. (Ed.), *Émile Durkheim Selected Writings.* Cambridge University Press, Cambridge, pp. 135–40.
Giddens, A. (1972) *Émile Durkheim Selected Writings.* Cambridge University Press, Cambridge.
Greenburg, D. (1980) Penal Sanctions in Poland: A Test of Alternative Models. *Social Problems* 28(2): 194–204.
Harms, J. B. (1981) Reason and Social Change in Durkheim's Thought: The Changing Relationship Between Individuals and Society. *Pacific Sociological Review* 24(4): 393–410.
Kenny, R. (2004) The Science of Collective Consciousness. *What is Enlightenment?* Online. www.wie.org.
Lawson, M. (1999) The Holy Spirit as Conscience Collective. *Sociology of Religion* 60(4): 341–61.
Lehmann, J. (1993) *Deconstructing Durkheim: A Post-Post Structuralist Critique.* Routledge, London.
Lehmann, J. (1994) *Durkheim and Women.* University of Nebraska Press, Lincoln.
Pope, W. (1973) Classic on Classic: Parsons's Interpretation of Durkheim. *American Sociological Review* 38(4): 399–415.
Ritzer, G. & Goodman, D. (2004) *Classical Sociological Theory.* McGraw Hill, New York.
Schindler, A. (1999) Angels and the AIDS Epidemic: The Resurgent Popularity of Angel Imagery in the United States of America. *Journal of American Culture* 22(3): 49–61.
Turner, B. & Wainright, S. (2003) Corps de Ballet: The Case of the Injured Ballet Dancer. *Sociology of Health and Illness* 25(4): 269–88.

collective deviance

Erich Goode

In *Stigma*, Erving Goffman wrote of the "tribal stigma of race, nation, and religion," these being imputed blemishes of identity that are "transmitted through lineages" which "equally contaminate all members of a family" (1963: 4). For Goffman, tribal stigma makes up one of three major types, the other two being "abominations of the body," namely, "the various physical deformities" such as extreme ugliness and physical disability, and "blemishes of individual character," such as mental disorder, homosexuality, alcoholism, radical political behavior, and dishonesty. With all stigmatized persons, "we" – meaning "normals," persons who do not bear the stigmatizing trait – "exercise varieties of discrimination," we "construct a stigma-theory, an ideology to explain" their inferiority, and we "tend to impute a wide range of imperfections on the basis of the original one" (1963: 5). With tribal stigma, the members of some tribal categories stigmatize *all* the members of another simply on the basis of that membership alone.

Tribal stigma can be referred to as *collective deviance*. Collective deviance is a form of categorical thinking, acting, and reacting that constitutes a typification of *any and all* persons to whom the tribal label applies. Here, deviance is a quality possessed not by an individual but by an entire collectivity. A person is regarded as a deviant because, in certain social circles or categories of humanity, it is stigmatizing to belong to a particular tribal category. One is *tainted* by one's categorical membership and this taint translates into stigmatizing treatment by members of one or more other tribal categories: hostility, censure, condemnation, discrimination, stereotyping, ridicule, scorn, social isolation, and/or punishment.

The term "racism" has been applied to describe collective deviance, but racism is a narrower concept than collective deviance. As it is currently used, racism implies a distinct power differential, a substantial measure of hegemony, and a focus on a category of humanity with genetic, or presumed genetic, characteristics. In contrast, tribal stigma does not necessitate a power dominance of one category over another, does not imply that one category's definitions of reality prevail over the other's, and encompasses race, ethnicity, national background, as well as religious membership (as analytically distinct from religious beliefs per se). It must be emphasized that collective deviance is not a one-sided affair. Indeed, within a particular tribal – that is, racial, ethnic, national, or religious – category, possession of the very trait regarded as normal and acceptable is, outside that category, stigmatizing, and vice versa. This divergent and situationally specific definition of acceptable tribal characteristics implies *mutual deviantization* (Aho 1994: 64), in which members of opposing tribal categories regard members of the other one as deviant.

Hence, among militant Muslims and Arabs, especially militant Palestinians, it is anathema to be an Israeli; among militant Israelis, it is anathema to be a Muslim and an Arab. Among militant, nationalist Indian Hindus, Muslims are considered undesirables; among militant Indian (and Kashmiri) Muslims, Hindus are considered undesirables. Similarly, during periods of violent conflict, in Northern Ireland, Catholics and Protestants; in Rwanda, Hutus and Tutsis; in Bosnia, Catholic Serbs and Muslims, have demonized one another. Collective deviance – and its frequent accompaniment, mutual deviantization – have been significant facts of life in many regions of the world during a major swathe of human history.

Of course, many instances of collective deviance take place in a setting in which the dominant category holds so much power that mutual deviantization cannot take place. For instance, the Jews in Nazi Germany and, during World War II, in most of Europe were stigmatized, demonized, verminized, persecuted, and murdered. But the reverse did not take place; Jews did not persecute non-Jewish Germans. The same applies to African American slaves versus whites prior to the Civil War, and North American Indians versus whites prior to the twentieth century. In these cases, deviantization was entirely, or almost entirely, one-sided. Mutual deviantization takes place only when competing tribal categories are capable of marshaling political, economic, and cultural capital against one another. When such disparities are so lopsided that the less powerful

category cannot inhabit or control deviance-defining contexts, mutual deviantization cannot effectively take place.

Throughout recorded history, members of one racial, ethnic, national, and religious category have stigmatized, deviantized, and demonized members of another category because of the category to which they belonged. To the person applying this evaluation, every person in the collective belongs to an inferiorized category and, hence, deserves to be treated as less than human. Any full and complete exploration of deviance must consider Goffman's "tribal stigma of race, nation, and religion" – in short, *collective* deviance. "Collective" means that one is automatically discredited as a consequence of belonging to a racial, ethnic, national, or religious category of humanity. With respect to the dynamics of stigma, deviance, condemnation, and inferiorization, collective deviance plays as central a role as individual behavior, which has been the almost exclusive focus of research on deviance.

SEE ALSO: Body, Abominations of the; Deviance; Deviance, Constructionist Perspectives; Goffman, Erving; Labeling; Labeling Theory; Race; Race (Racism); Sociocultural Relativism; Stigma

REFERENCES AND SUGGESTED READINGS

Aho, J. (1994) *This Thing of Darkness: A Sociology of the Enemy*. University of Washington Press, Seattle.
Goffman, E. (1963) *Stigma: Notes on the Management of a Spoiled Identity*. Prentice-Hall/Spectrum, Englewood Cliffs, NJ.

collective efficacy and crime

Ruth Triplett

As described by Sampson et al. in 1997, collective efficacy describes a neighborhood-level process that is important to understanding variation in crime rates across neighborhoods.

Collective efficacy involves both the willingness of individuals in a neighborhood to work together toward a common goal, such as crime control, and mutual trust. Since the discussion of collective efficacy in the initial publication in 1997, collective efficacy has been an important new addition to criminology's understanding of the causes of crime across neighborhoods.

Interest in neighborhoods and crime comes from the long recognized fact that there is substantial variation in crime rates across cities and neighborhoods within cities. Explaining this fact was key to the work of early theorists in the Chicago School, in particular Shaw and McKay. Examining crime rates in the city of Chicago, Shaw and McKay found two facts: crime rates vary substantially across areas of the city, and over time crime rates remain stable in areas. Building on the work of Park and Burgess, Shaw and McKay argued that social disorganization is the cause of the variation in neighborhood crime rates. Though not clearly defined by Shaw and McKay, social disorganization was defined by later theorists as revolving around the inability of individuals in a neighborhood to agree upon and work toward a common goal. Social disorganization was theorized to result from neighborhood structural characteristics such as poverty, racial/ethnic heterogeneity, and high rates of mobility. Shaw and McKay then used the idea of cultural transmission to explain the stability of crime rates. Their belief was that the gangs that developed in certain neighborhoods passed down their culture, assuring stability in crime rates.

Until the 1960s, the theory of social disorganization was a dominant one in criminology. Interest waned, however, as theoretical difficulties emerged and tests of the theory became problematic. It was not until the 1980s that new attention to neighborhoods and crime reemerged in a number of works. One particularly important aspect of these new works was the interest in explaining just what it was that led many neighborhoods characterized by poverty, racial/ethnic heterogeneity, and high mobility to have high crime rates.

Perhaps the most innovative of these new works was Sampson et al.'s (1997) ideas on collective efficacy. With collective efficacy, they focused attention on what makes neighborhoods

effective at social control. Sampson and his colleagues ask us to consider three sets of factors important in explaining variation in levels of collective efficacy. The first is the effect of a highly mobile population. As with early social disorganization theorists, Sampson and his colleagues recognize the harm to social ties that occurs when people move in and out of neighborhoods at a rapid rate. A second factor they identify is the pattern of racial and economic segregation by neighborhood that stills persists in the US. Finally, Sampson et al. see as key to understanding levels of collective efficacy the results of this economic and racial segregation, which they identify as alienation, powerlessness, and dependency. The result of all three of these factors is to lower the level of collective efficacy – the trust neighbors have in one another and their willingness to work together as a neighborhood. This has the direct effect of increasing levels of crime.

Since the publication by Sampson et al. in 1997, research on collective efficacy has found support for its importance in understanding neighborhood violent crime rates. In their initial article, Sampson and his colleagues found support for their predictions that neighborhood structural characteristics such as poverty, racial/ethnic makeup, and mobility decrease collective efficacy, and that collective efficacy significantly affects neighborhood crime rates. Others have found a significant relationship between collective efficacy and intimate violence (Browning 2002) and perceptions of collective efficacy and crime.

SEE ALSO: Collective Action; Crime; Criminology; Social Disorganization Theory

REFERENCES AND SUGGESTED READINGS

Browning, C. R. (2002) The Span of Collective Efficacy: Extending Social Disorganization Theory to Partner Violence. *Journal of Marriage and Family* 64: 833–50.
Bursik, R. J., Jr. (1988) Social Disorganization and Theories of Crime and Delinquency: Problems and Prospects. *Criminology* 26: 519–51.
Bursik, R. J., Jr. & Grasmick, H. G. (1993) *Neighborhoods and Crime: The Dimensions of Effective Community Control.* Lexington Books, New York.

Kornhauser, R. R. (1978) *Social Sources of Delinquency*. University of Chicago Press, Chicago.

Sampson, R. J. & Groves, W. B. (1989) Community Structure and Crime: Testing Social Disorganization Theory. *American Journal of Sociology* 94: 774–802.

Sampson, R. J., Raudenbush, S. W., & Earls, F. (1997) Neighborhoods and Violent Crime: A Multilevel Study of Collective Efficacy. *Science* 277: 918–24.

collective identity

Owen Whooley

Within social movement theory, collective identity refers to the shared definition of a group that derives from its members' common interests, experiences, and solidarities. It is the social movement's answer to who we are, locating the movement within a field of political actors. Collective identity is neither fixed nor innate, but rather emerges through struggle as different political actors, including the movement, interact and react to each other. The salience of any given collective identity affects the mobilization, trajectory, and even impacts of social movements. Consequently, collective identity has become a central concept in the study of social movements.

The concept of collective identity emerged in the 1980s in Europe within new social movement (NSM) theory. Most locate its origin in the work of Alberto Melucci (1995). After the 1960s, Europe witnessed an increase in movements espousing post-materialist programs. These "new social movements" focused on questions of identity, originated largely from the middle class, politicized everyday life, and carried out their struggle through cultural and symbolic means. Scholars of new social movements felt that the dominant European paradigms, based on models drawn from materialist movements, offered little conceptual insight into these "new" movements and reoriented the field toward more cultural issues. Believing these differences to be fundamental, European scholars embedded their analysis within a macrohistorical framework that viewed the "new" movements as the paradigmatic movements of the epoch.

While the historical claim of NSM is controversial, it has made an important contribution to social movement theory by opening up new venues of research. The concepts like collective identity derived from NSM now permeate throughout the field of social movement research. Researchers, dissatisfied by what they believed to be the overly structural depiction of social movements offered by the dominant resource mobilization and political process theories, adopted concepts from new social movement theory, like collective identity, to bring the cultural back into the study of social movements. As a concept, collective identity is now widely accepted within social movement research and is used by researchers from a variety of theoretical backgrounds. Researchers acknowledge the relevance of collective identity not only for "new" social movements, but also for a variety of movements, both "old" and "new."

Collective identity is not predetermined. Political actors do not share a de facto identity as a result of their common structural position. Rather, identity emerges through various processes in which movement actors instill it with significance, relevance, and form. The three major processes through which movements construct an identity are (1) the establishment of boundaries, (2) negotiation, and (3) the development of consciousness. In boundary making, social movements create new group values and structures that delineate who they are in relation to other political actors. In negotiation, movements engage with other political actors, continually enacting their shared identity and working to influence symbolic meanings. Finally, the development of consciousness imbues the collective identity with a larger purpose by embedding it within an ideological framework that assigns blame for the injustice against which the movement is mobilized.

Collective identity, therefore, becomes manifest in the day-to-day activities of the social movement. Movements not only have a collective identity, they also act in accordance with that identity. The line between "being" and "doing" is blurred. The various activities in which a movement engages mold and form its collective identity through the enacting of that identity. Identity practices include the making of demands, framing/ideology, culture, leadership, organizational structure, and support resources. A movement's demands reflect its shared identity, for these demands address the grievances of the group as a group. For example, the American Indian Movement made demands in the name of the Native American constituency that it represented. In framing an issue, a social movement defines an injustice, attributes this injustice to its opponents, and defines its collective response to this injustice, establishing the field of relevant actors in a given struggle. A movement's culture also reflects its identity in that activists create a cultural space that resonates with the more general identity of its constituents. The Civil Rights Movement developed an internal movement culture that drew heavily from the black church in order to provide a familiar space for its members. Similarly, a movement chooses its leaders and organizational structures, allocating power and decision-making capacities within the movement in accordance with its collective identity. Finally, the outside resources that the movement solicits give an implicit message as to whom the struggle is for and who its allies are.

Social movement scholars have appealed to the concept of collective identity to bring insight into some of the persistently puzzling issues in social movement theory. A movement's collective identity plays a significant role throughout the course of the movement and, in turn, allows social movement theorists to appeal to it for a variety of explanatory purposes. In explaining the emergence of a movement, identity unites disparate individuals into a cohesive unit by providing a common framework and fostering group solidarity. During recruitment, a strong, salient identity can overcome the free-rider problem by compelling individuals to join the movement even if they could receive its benefits without participating. Identity also informs the choice of tactics, adding more sophistication to the rational choice theoretical models by acknowledging an influence on strategic choices beyond merely pragmatic concerns. Finally, the success or failure of a movement in achieving recognition of identity as legitimate adds further insight into the more general impact of a movement.

The work on collective identity is not without its problems and internal conflicts. Because of its relative novelty, there has been some inconsistency within social movement research as to how the concept of collective identity has been employed. Scholars with a more structural orientation tend to apply it as an add-on to their models, defining it narrowly and relegating it to the periphery of the analysis. Researchers with a more cultural, constructionist orientation define identity widely, attributing nearly every aspect of a movement to its identity. In addition to the different theoretical weight attributed to collective identity, there is also a division between scholars who define identity as constructed, fluid, and dynamic and those who define it in a more reifying and static way. Currently, researchers are attempting to solve these inconsistencies by looking at the relationship between collective identity and other dominant concepts in social movement theory, like opportunities. The most promising direction appears to be finding a middle ground between these various extremes, acknowledging the importance of collective identity without overstating it and recognizing its simultaneously constructed and structurally rooted origins.

Collective identity also faces an empirical challenge from movements that approach the issue of identity in complex and creative ways. While scholars of collective identity have tended to ascribe a single identity to a single movement, many movements face a conflicting set of identities among their members and must attempt to build solidarity *across* these multiple identities. Negotiating these conflicting identities can be a complicated, conflict-ridden process, as exclusion and fracture inevitably are involved in the construction of identity across multiple systems of domination. In addressing these cases, researchers are beginning to draw upon the concept of intersectionality from theories on race. Intersectionality recognizes that various systems of oppression cannot simply be added onto one another, but rather interact in complicated ways. In addition to the complexity of movements with multiple identities, collective identity scholars also need to develop the theoretical sophistication to account for movements that seek to deconstruct identity. There seems to be an implicit assumption within collective identity research that a strong identity has a positive effect on movements by encouraging solidarity. However, some social movements, like the lesbian, gay, bisexual, and transgender (LGBT) movement, attempt to deconstruct oppressive identities and recognize the problematic and often oppressive nature of identities. A dilemma exists within these movements of whether to embrace an identity that has been historically oppressive but could form the basis of cohesion or to deconstruct this identity, possibly risking the mobilizing capacity it brings. Collective identity theory must develop the sophistication to address this issue.

The trend in research on collective identity seems to be moving in three related directions to overcome some of these problems. First, there has been a move to incorporate insights from within social movement theory, such as political opportunity structure and collective action frames, and from outside the field, such as the concept of intersectionality. Bringing together these disparate concepts adds a degree of sophistication to the models of collective identity and possibly synthesis within the field in general. Secondly, social movement scholars are beginning to address the paucity of social movement research that examines the relationship between the individual and the collective. Presently, there are few individual-level analyses of social movements. Collective identity offers a potentially rich solution to this problem by illuminating how individual members come to fuse their identities with that of the collective. Finally, collective identity will increasingly face challenges from movements like LGBT that adopt a creative approach to identity. Researchers must revise their understanding of collective identity to meet the challenges presented by these movements.

SEE ALSO: Culture, Social Movements and; Framing and Social Movements; Identity Politics/Relational Politics; Intersectionality; New Social Movement Theory; Social Movements

REFERENCES AND SUGGESTED READINGS

Gamson, J. (1995) Must Identity Movements Self-Destruct? *Social Problems* 42(3): 390–407.

Hunt, S. A., Benford, R. D., Snow, D. A., et al. (1994) Identity Fields: Framing Processes and the Social Construction of Movement Identities. In: Larana, E., Johnson, H., & Gusfield, J. (Eds.), *New Social Movements: From Ideology to Identity*. Temple University Press, Philadelphia, pp. 185–208.

Kurtz, S. (2002) *Workplace Justice: Organizing Multi-Identity Movements*. University of Minnesota Press, Minneapolis.

Melucci, A. (1995) The Process of Collective Identity. In: Johnson, H. & Klandermas, B. (Eds.), *Social Movements and Culture*. University of Minnesota Press, Minneapolis, pp. 41–63.

Meyer, D. S. (2002) Opportunities and Identities: Bride Building in the Study of Social Movements. In: Meyer, D., Whittier, N., & Robnett, B. (Eds.), *Social Movements: Identity, Culture, and the State*. Oxford University Press, New York, pp. 3–27.

Polletta, F. & Jasper, J. (2001) Collective Identity and Social Movements. *Annual Review of Sociology* 27: 283–305.

Taylor, V. & Whittier, N. (1992) Collective Identity in Social Movement Communities: Lesbian Feminist Mobilization. In: Morris, A. D. & Mueller, C. M. C. (Eds.), *Frontiers in Social Movement Theory*. Yale University Press, New Haven, pp. 104–30.

collective memory

Barry Schwartz

Collective memory refers to the distribution throughout society of beliefs, feelings, moral judgments, and knowledge about the past. Only individuals possess the capacity to contemplate the past, but this does not mean that beliefs originate in the individual alone or can be explained on the basis of his or her unique experience. Individuals do not know the past singly; they know it with and against other individuals situated in conflicting groups, in the context of alienation, and through the knowledge that predecessors and contemporaries transmit to them.

History and commemoration are the vehicles of collective memory. At the formal level, history includes research monographs and textbooks; at the popular level, magazines, newspapers, television, and film; at the informal level, conversations, letters, and diaries.

Commemoration consists of monuments, shrines, relics, statues, paintings, prints, photographs, ritual observances and hagiography (eulogy and ritual oratory). Since historical and commemorative objects are transmissible, cumulative, and interpreted differently from one group to another, they exert influence in ways difficult to understand solely in terms of their producers' convictions and characteristics.

Historians and commemorative agents perform different functions. Historians seek to enlighten by revealing causes and consequences of chronologically ordered events. Commemorative agents seek to define moral significance by marking events and actors that embody collective ideals. Historians describe events in all their complexity and ambiguity; commemorative agents simplify events as they convert them into objects of moral instruction. On the other hand, history and commemoration are interdependent: just as history reflects the values and sentiments that commemoration sustains, commemoration is rooted in historical knowledge.

At the turn of the twentieth century, many scholars wrote about the social context of history and commemoration, but Maurice Halbwachs's pioneering work made it a separate research field. That Halbwachs worked on collective memory while Karl Mannheim wrote his classic essays on the sociology of knowledge is no coincidence. The sociology of memory, like the sociology of knowledge, arose during the era of post-World War I disillusionment and flourishes in societies where cultural values no longer unify, where people have already become alienated from common values, and separate communities regard one another distrustfully. The sociology of memory, like the sociology of knowledge, represents the erosion of dominant symbols.

Between 1945, the year of his execution by the SS, and the early 1980s, sociologists ignored Halbwachs's work. After 1980, however, Halbwachs was cited time and again, even though his two major books, *The Social Frames of Memory* (1925) and *The Legendary Topography of the Gospels in the Holy Land* (1941), had not been translated from their original French. Halbwachs's discoveries did not cause the current wave of collective memory research; they were rather swept into it.

Since the 1980s, collective memory scholars have worked on and debated six sets of basic issues: *history and commemoration* (how historical events furnish the stuff of commemoration and how commemorative symbolism, in turn, defines historical significance); *enterprise and reception* (who produces commemorative symbolism and why their products are sometimes accepted, sometimes rejected); *consensus and conflict* (which beliefs about the past are shared; which beliefs, polarizing); *retrieval and construction* (how historical documentation limits the range of historical constructions); *mirroring and modeling* (the degree to which collective memory shapes and reflects reality); *continuity and change* (how collective memory's malleability is superimposed upon its durable structures). As many scholars addressed these issues in terms of power relations and hegemony, collective memory's traditional articulations of virtue, honor, and heroism began to appear as elite "mystification." Newly favored topics included the commemoration of victims, diversity, unpopular wars, and ignoble events. Holocaust and slavery topics abounded. This pattern accompanied two late twentieth-century trends: multiculturalism, which recognized minorities' dignity and entitlements, and postmodernism, which documented the erosion of tradition and the individual's declining identification with the past. Multicultural and postmodern influence is evident in the continuing debunking of history and a growing body of research on ritual apologies, the "politics of regret," negative commemoration (e.g., museums and monuments for the victims of oppression and atrocity), and discrediting of the great legends and myths that once linked men and women to the dominant symbols of their cultural tradition.

Despite multicultural and postmodern influence, collective memory has remained centered, at the popular level, on traditional (heroic) contents. Also, new perspectives emerged in the late 1990s and early 2000s: (1) appreciation of objective properties that limit what can be done with the past interpretively; (2) a keener sense of the past as a lost source of moral direction, inspiration, and consolation; (3) individual beliefs, once inferred from historical and commemorative materials, are assessed directly within the sociology of cognition, psychology, and, most prominently, through sample survey methods; and (4) models of collective memory are formulated in an increasingly active voice, depicting individuals dialogically reinforcing and modifying the historical texts and commemorative symbols they consume.

The units, trends, and issues of collective memory that show up so clearly in the analyses of communities and nations appear also in the fields of family, organizations, institutions, and communities. Within each field, however, recent claims of collective memory scholarship begin to ring hollow. "Demystifying" the past is a vital program as long as there is something to be mystified, some injustice or atrocity to be concealed. In every culture and in every age we see exclusion and bias, but as the work of civil rights, multiculturalism, and inclusion continues, it becomes more difficult to squeeze out insights from their analysis. How new realities will affect collective memory's program remains for the next generation of scholars to determine.

SEE ALSO: Collective Memory (Social Change); Culture; Halbwachs, Maurice; Knowledge, Sociology of; Tradition

REFERENCES AND SUGGESTED READINGS

Halbwachs, M. (1952 [1925]) *Les Cadres Sociaux de la Mémoire*. Presses Universitaires de France, Paris.
Halbwachs, M. (1980 [1950]) *Collective Memory*. Ed. M. Douglas. Harper & Row, New York.
Merton, R. (1957) The Sociology of Knowledge. In: *Social Theory and Social Structure*. Free Press, Glencoe, IL, pp. 456–88.
Nora, P. (1996) *Realms of Memory*, 3 vols. Columbia University Press, New York.
Olick, J. (1999) Genre Memories and Memory Genres: Continuities and Departures in German Commemoration of May 8th, 1945. *American Sociological Review* 64: 381–402.
Schudson, M. (1992) *Watergate in American Memory*. Basic Books, New York.
Schuman, H. & Scott, J. (1989) Generations and Collective Memories. *American Sociological Review* 54: 359–81.
Zerubavel, E. (2003) *Time Maps: Collective Memory and the Social Shape of the Past*. University of Chicago Press, Chicago.

collective memory (social change)

Bridget Fowler

A group's or nation's collective memory is constituted by its images, concepts, and evaluations of the past. Although memory is only possessed and transmitted by individuals, it is shaped by group relationships. Individuals share their recollections with members of their group and rationally reorganize their stories of the past in accordance with others' understandings of events (Coser 1992: 43).

Collective memory is important because the removal of a group from authority means eradicating its remembered significance within a nation's past activities, not least that nation's most serious or sacred acts (Connerton 1989). Great political dangers lie in such organized forgetting. If the systematic rewriting of history is still largely a dystopian Orwellian future, the active obscuring from historical view of groups such as Tutsis or gypsies has been commonplace. Given privileged access to contemporary media, dominant classes possess unparalleled capacities to marginalize the Other and to redescribe the character of their past.

A familiar dichotomy attributes collective memory to preliterate and traditional societies, while modern societies possess "history." It is certainly true that certain diasporic groups such as the Jews – "the people of memory" – relied almost entirely on oral collective memory to transmit their ethics and their past (Nora 1996–8 I: 3). Yet subordinate classes in capitalist modernity have also possessed their own distinctive collective memory, as in the case of the crafts in the Glasgow Trades Hall. Here, nineteenth-century frescoes portray each collective craft group, while on gold-inscribed walls are recorded successive craft officials, from the medieval city to the present.

Yet if collective memory is the possession of all adults, in modernity it takes a progressively fragmented and weakened form. It is increasingly relegated to those institutional places that Nora has entitled "the realms of memory." In turn, history, the specialized intellectual and critical production of historians, has now become more widespread and more authoritative.

Recent social theory has stressed the importance of consecrated or canonized cultural works and of the active social processes by which a person is attributed with a "name," thus preserving their works for the future. This is another important form of collective memory. Indeed, Bourdieu (1984) has pointed out that the fruits of such social or cultural distinction are not simply symbolic rewards, but that they allow some to have a different relationship to death. The remembrance of the Great through statues, monuments, anthologies, and portraits offers "eternal life." Those who make a mark on posterity have produced the works which sustain collective memory in the future. Cultural memory commonly passes through secular rituals, such as the doctoral induction or the award of state honors. By such means, individuals are selected by an institution, even one which they may themselves reject. Their singular world-vision ceases to appear iconoclastic and becomes part of the communal, sanctified discourse of that society, thus cheating death.

The major architects of the theory of collective memory are Maurice Halbwachs and Walter Benjamin. Halbwachs's interwar writings take up some elements of Bergson's theories, not least his dynamic notion of memory, which functions like an electric circuit or telephone exchange. Bergson, however, still postulated purely individual representations, including memory-images. It was Halbwachs who developed the Durkheimian concept of collective representations for the terrain of memory. In Durkheim's conception, collective representations were distinguished by their obligatory nature, their multiple images of the Great, and by being learnt off by heart. Yet it is important to note that such collective consciousness for Durkheim did not preclude rational representations, including those developed by modern scientific institutions. Halbwachs in this respect did not differ. However, his key point was that we need the social frameworks of time, space, and number for remembering. The absence of such group-supplied frameworks explains the reasons why we do not recall our dreams, for the latter deal with our purely individual needs.

Halbwachs argued that memory is reactivated through encounters with places – hence his interest in the sacred topography that emerged in the Holy Land after Jesus's death, in the form of sites of pilgrimage. In the modern metropolis, too, memory sites are crucial, so that a city like London can be crisscrossed by different groups, each having a past commemorated through different buildings or statues. Here, occupational groups such as painters, novelists, and architects have their own collective memories, directing their gaze through a landscape of monuments. Occupational groups' memories are not, however, restricted to places: they develop their own distinct memory via other techniques, such as musical notation and specialized conversation (Halbwachs 1997: 29). The collective memory of the right performance is also learnt by the body; indeed, the body becomes for Halbwachs – and for Bourdieu – a *pense-bête*, or memory pad.

Halbwachs elaborated on these ideas in relation to various forms of the social, from family traditions, to churches and social classes. He was particularly interested in the regulating processes that created unity within the group, including religious groups' use of dogma to create definitive assessments of the past and the nobility's presupposition that its particular history was identical with the national past. Nor did Halbwachs neglect the division between the dominants and the dominated – as a child he had been given quite different memories of the Paris Commune from his parents and the family servants. Later, he was to write of one other current of the dominated's memory: the collective memory of the cooperative movement, a distinctive invention of the modern working class.

Halbwachs saw memory as dynamic and constantly reconstructed, its peculiar selection of materials being developed in relation to the practical needs of each contemporary group. Yet this theoretical conception has been subsequently disputed, as has his view that history and collective memory are radically differentiated. It is collective memory that carries us "midstream," he argued, while history occurs on "the banks of the river," as the more precise and rigorous assessment of empirical data. This conception of history has been attacked as positivist, while his conception of collective memory has been stigmatized as Romantic and organicist (Osiel 1997).

It is fruitful to consider Walter Benjamin in this light as well. There are three main reasons why he should be understood in this way. First, like Halbwachs, he places major weight on the role of narrative in collective memory, as the preeminent way of recalling to mind the ancestors and defining moments of the group. Unlike Halbwachs, he focuses on the antithesis between the stories told by traditional village tellers of tales and the stories told in newspapers or novels in the capitalist metropolis, which lacked any authentic connection with their readers' perspectives. The ancient, story-telling form of collective memory had, in his view, survived neither the shock of World War I's mass slaughter nor the subsequent loss of money values with the Europe-wide inflation.

For Benjamin, secondly, addressing the "phantasmagoric" consumer cultures of European capitals, such as Berlin or Paris, could attain access to urban collective memory. This requires a practiced technique of social archeology to excavate and reveal the cities' transformations of social relationships. Such archeological methods could highlight the distinctive character of modern society, including the social relations like fashion in which the commodity had been embedded and the charging of commodities themselves with the weight possessed by religious symbols in an earlier period.

Thirdly, Benjamin considers the canon of cultural works – the "bourgeois literary apparatus" – as one form of contemporary collective memory. He is persuasive in identifying the new "magic" of the individual artist's signature and the role of museum curators or critics in the crucial decisions about museum selections and classic editions. Yet he is also attentive to the dangerous narrowness of such a bourgeois canon, not least its dismissal of popular culture, the celebration only of works that were "affirmative," as in Germany after 1933, and the marginalization of anonymous works, such as Chinese pottery.

There are profoundly problematic elements in the theory of collective memory, particularly in the debate around Halbwachs's thought.

For, at the end of his *Social Frameworks of Memory,* Halbwachs noted the increasing anomie of memory within capitalism, a theme which he elaborated in *The Collective Memory* as rival "currents of thought." From the dove-tailed and reinforced collective memories of traditional societies, memories have now become more differentiated and more conflict ridden.

Halbwachs's notion of collective memory as infinitely malleable in relation to present group needs – his "presentism" – has been challenged by studies of American leaders (Schwartz 1990). Even given changing "structures of feeling," Schwartz has shown that not everything is alterable. To take an example, Abraham Lincoln had initially provoked a stereotype of being a "homely man of the people," being characterized at his assassination in 1865 as weak and indecisive. Yet by 1908, divested of this weakness, he had become the visionary leader who fitted the new ethos of a democratic America. Some continuity remained: in 1908, as in 1922, the Lincoln cult honored the collective remembrance that he came from the people, but now subtly omitted the earlier critical censure.

Halbwachs has been accused of retaining a concept of collective memory too close to the dominant class. This is not ultimately persuasive, given his description of the dominated's memory of the Commune, already cited. Nevertheless, following the practices of Foucault and oral historians, it is necessary to differentiate analytically between the dominants' memory, popular memory, and counter-memory. Moreover, in some regions, ideas of the past have been so dangerous and confusing that social memory as a whole has become stunted: "We did not find a common collective memory [about the 1930s famine] in the [Russian] Kuban" concludes one study (Khubova et al. 1992). Contemporary Russia may turn out to be unique, the degree zero of collective memory. Nevertheless, Nora (1996–8) has also pointed to a further form of "alienated memory": the bewildering array of collective memories and histories in the West. He graphically entitles this "era of commemoration" one of "commemorative bulimia."

The main controversy over Halbwachs is whether he was a Burkean or Romantic thinker:

he has been claimed to have a conception of memory that revealed an affinity for organicism or even the regressive reconstructions of a patriarchal *Gemeinschaft*. One such critic, Osiel, arguably fails to sustain his charge. For not only does Halbwachs's notion of collective memory stress the rationality of revising individuals' recollections in the light of others, but Halbwachs himself recognized the increasing differentiation of modern collective memory and hence the diminution of its unifying elements.

Osiel's own contribution to the study of collective memory, building on Halbwachs, is nevertheless outstanding. Using historical studies of "liberal show trials" he critiques those western relativists who deny both the value of witnessing (remembering under oath) and the legal procedures for resolving contests over memory. In post-conflict situations like the trial of Vichy collaborators or the trial of the Generals after the Argentinian dirty war, it is socially unacceptable, Osiel has argued, "to let a thousand ideological flowers bloom." While accepting that there will still be the need for a "Brechtian resolution" of different *private* truths, such trials create a *public consensus* about which witnesses have been more plausible. Collective memory has thus been reestablished, placed on a firmer and more rational foundation.

It is perhaps no coincidence that the phenomenologist Paul Ricoeur has also turned to the Halbwachian/Bourdieusian conception of collective memory in this context. He, too, sees important limits to nihilistic pessimism as to the variability of constructions of the past (Ricoeur 2004). Ricoeur applies the notion of ideology to the vulnerability of collective memory. Thus he suggests that the equivalent of individual blocked memory or manipulated memory is, on the political plane, "memory abusively summonsed." In other words, power elites, with interests in mystification, corrosively distort memory of the past. This can result in the forgetting of a whole dimension of a society's life, such as the institutionalized anti-Semitism and anti-feminism of the Vichy regime in France or the crimes of apartheid in South Africa. Subsequently, history, the alternative to liberal show trials, may regain a crucial role in correcting, disabusing, and extending collective memory within such societies.

SEE ALSO: Art Worlds; Benjamin, Walter; Collective Memory; Collective Trauma; Habitus/Field; Halbwachs, Maurice

REFERENCES AND SUGGESTED READINGS

Bourdieu, P. (1984) *Distinction: A Social Critique of the Judgement of Taste*. Routledge & Kegan Paul, London.

Connerton, P. (1989) *How Societies Remember*. Cambridge University Press, Cambridge.

Coser, L. A. (Ed.) (1992) *Maurice Halbwachs' On Collective Memory*. University of Chicago Press, Chicago.

Eiland, H. & Jennings, M. W. (Eds.) (2002) *Walter Benjamin: Selected Writings*, Vol. 3. Belknap Press of Harvard University Press, Cambridge, MA.

Halbwachs, M. (1997) *La Mémoire collective*. Albin Michel, Paris.

Khubova, D., Ivankiev, A., & Sharova, T. (1992) After Glastnost. In: Passerini, L. (Ed.), *Memory and Totalitarianism*. Oxford University Press, Oxford, pp. 89–101.

Nora, P. et al. (1996–8) *Realms of Memory*, Vols. 1–3. Columbia University Press, Chichester.

Osiel, M. (1997) *Mass Atrocity, Collective Memory and the Law*. Transaction, New Brunswick, NJ.

Ricoeur, P. (2004) *Memory, History, Forgetting*. University of Chicago Press, Chicago.

Schwartz, B. M. (1990) The Reconstruction of Abraham Lincoln. In: Middleton, D. & Edwards, D. (Eds.), *Collective Remembering*. Sage, London, pp. 81–107.

collective trauma

Piotr Sztompka

Social change may have adverse effects, bring shocks and wounds to the social and cultural tissue. This is true even if the changes are beneficial, expected, and defined as a victory by the people. The forerunner of this idea was Durkheim, who coined the famous notion of the "anomie of success."

Traumatogenic change exhibits four traits. First, it is sudden, occurring within a span of time that is relatively short for a given kind of process. For example, a revolution is rapid relative to historical time (even when it takes weeks or months) and a collapse of the market is sudden relative to long-range economic change.

Second, traumatogenic change is usually comprehensive, either in the sense that it touches many aspects of social life or that it affects many actors and many actions. Revolution is a good example of traumatogenic social change because it usually embraces not only the political domain, but also the law, economy, morality, culture, art, even language, and it affects the fate of many groups, if not all the population.

Third, traumatogenic change is marked by specific content, either in the sense that it is radical, deep, and fundamental (i.e., it touches the core aspects of social life or personal fate) or that it affects universal experiences, whether public or private. For example, a shift in dominant values, a transfer of power, or an overturning of prestige hierarchies changes the very constitution of society, whereas a rise in crime, corruption, or pollution degrades the context of everyday life and threatens the immediate lifeworld of every societal member.

Fourth, traumatogenic change is faced with disbelief, as it is unexpected, surprising, shocking. A devaluation of a currency, a collapse of a market, and a *coup d'état* are good examples.

It is important to distinguish mass traumas from truly collective (social) traumas. Mass events produce consequences for a number of people simultaneously – a hurricane leaving thousands homeless, an epidemic affecting large segments of a population, an economic crisis resulting in massive unemployment. When such disasters hit, the victims face them alone at first, as a multitude of private disasters. The trauma is not yet shared; it is suffered side by side with others, but not yet *together* with others.

Truly collective traumas, as distinct from massive traumas, appear only when people start to be aware of a common plight, perceive the similarity of their situation with that of others, and define it as shared. They start to talk about it, exchange observations and experiences, gossip and rumors, formulate diagnoses and myths, identify causes or villains, look for conspiracies, decide to do something about it, envisage

coping methods. They debate and perhaps even quarrel and fight among themselves about all this. Such debates reach the public arena, are taken up by the media, and are expressed in literature, arts, the movies, etc. The whole "meaning industry" is full of rich narratives focusing on giving sense to common and shared occurrences. It is then that the expression of trauma may go beyond the subjective, symbolic, or ideal level and acquire more tangible social forms: intense interaction, outbursts of protest, forming of groups, collective mobilization, and creating social movements, associations, organizations, and political parties. Traumatogenic changes become "societal facts *sui generis*" in the sense given to this term by Durkheim.

There are various domains that can be touched by traumatogenic change. One is the biological substratum of a society, the population. The extreme consequence of a traumatogenic change may be the extermination of societal members. Wars, famines, and epidemics provide numerous tragic examples. Slightly less extreme is a decay of the biological fitness of the population, marked by such indicators as the level of childbirth, death, life expectancy, suicide rates, frequency of diseases, mental disorders, etc. An early example of such a perspective is Pitirim Sorokin's *Sociology of Revolution* (1928), which analyzed in detail the disastrous impact of the Bolshevik revolution on the biological capacity of Russian people.

We reach a truly sociological level of analysis when we turn to structural traumas, affecting social organization: social networks, configurations of groups, associations, and formal organizations, the hierarchies of stratification, class divisions, etc. A forerunner to such a perspective was Ferdinand Toennies's analysis of decaying *Gemeinschaft* (community) and emerging *Gesellschaft* (modern society), followed by rich research on the collapse of communities under the impact of industrialization and urbanization. Another line of research focused on the atomization and individualization of social life, grasped best by David Riesman's memorable term, the "lonely crowd." There is a rich tradition of studies which show the impact of technological inventions on the organization of labor. Recently, much attention has been paid to the destructive effects of autocratic regimes on the organization of civil society.

There is one more domain that can be affected by traumatogenic change. This is culture: the axionormative and symbolic belief systems of a society. The shock of change may reverberate in the area of affirmed values and norms, patterns and rules, expectations and roles, accepted ideas and beliefs, narrative forms and symbolic meanings, definitions of situations, and frames of discourse. The forerunner of this perspective was again Durkheim, with his notion of anomie or normative chaos, rephrased fruitfully by Merton (1996a). Thomas and Znaniecki's (1974) monumental study documented the plight of emigrants who found themselves in a cultural environment entirely at odds with their earlier lifeworld, opposed to deeply ingrained and accustomed habits of thinking and doing.

In the twentieth and twenty-first centuries a large pool of changes has become potentially traumatogenic (i.e., sudden, comprehensive, fundamental, and unexpected). One source of cultural trauma is intensifying intercultural contact and confrontation of diverse cultures, often resulting in tensions and conflict. The most traumatizing situations occur when the imposition and domination of one culture is secured by force. Imperial conquest, colonialism, and religious proselytizing provide prime examples. But even when the spreading of an alien culture is more peaceful (by virtue of economic strength, technological superiority or the psychological attractiveness of cultural products flowing from the core toward the periphery), the result often disrupts the cultural stability, continuity, and identity of indigenous groups. Another source of cultural trauma is the intensifying spatial mobility of people, who as emigrants and refugees, but also as business travelers and tourists, find themselves in an alien culture.

The third source of cultural trauma is a change of fundamental institutions or regimes (e.g., basic political and economic reforms carried out in societies lacking the requisite cultural background, the ingrained competence to deal with new institutions, or even more gravely when new cultural imperatives fitting the reformed institutions run counter to established cultural habits and traditions). Similar effects may be produced by new technological inventions, which require specific skills, care,

and discipline from users, and when all these are absent. Another case is the transformation from rural to urban and a lack of preparedness for the new lifeworld. In all these cases cultural trauma results from the processes of modernization or its components: industrialization, democratization, technological progress, urbanization, new risks, etc. The traumatizing effect is strongest when modernization is imposed, rather than originating from within as an indigenous development. But even when a change of regime originates from below and realizes the aspirations of the people, it inevitably engenders some form of cultural trauma, as it clashes with deeply embedded, thoroughly internalized earlier "habits of the heart" (to use Alexis de Tocqueville's phrase), which create, at least temporarily, "civilizational incompetence" (Sztompka 1993) to follow the cultural imperatives of the new system.

The fourth source of traumatogenic change is located at the level of beliefs, creeds, doctrines, and ideologies. Changes of ideas may take various forms. One is the acquisition of new knowledge, which may shatter established convictions and stereotypes. Thus, news about the Holocaust which emerged fully at the end of World War II produced a traumatic shock accompanied by guilt-feelings among anti-Semitic groups in the US (Alexander et al. 2004). Another instance is the revision of established historical accounts, destroying cherished myths about the past. For example, new perspectives on the French Revolution show it to be much less heroic and much more bloody; the discovery of America is seen as simultaneous with the extermination of its native peoples; the whole history of the USSR is rewritten, revealing terror and extermination rather than a workers' paradise. Still another case is the appearance of new ideas which may raise the sensitiveness or modify perceptions of otherwise well-known facts. For example, the birth of ecological awareness, feminist consciousness, and the concept of universal human rights makes everybody view the conquest of nature, gender oppression, and other inequalities and injustices in a completely new light. In all these cases the clash of old and new beliefs produces at the cultural level a phenomenon akin to cognitive dissonance – the emotional disturbance caused by the incongruence of recently acquired information with deeply held convictions.

Cultural disorganization and accompanying disorientation are necessary but not sufficient conditions for a full-fledged trauma to emerge. At most, they create a raised sensitiveness among people to all adverse experiences or information, facilitating a climate of anxiety and uncertainty. Against this background there must also appear a set of conditions or situations, perceived as pernicious, dangerous, or threatening. It is these that serve as the triggering, precipitating factors for the emergence of trauma. Most often, these conditions or situations are brought about by the same major change that caused cultural disorganization. They may be a direct result of certain policies or reforms undertaken by the government in the aftermath of revolutionary upheaval, for example. Or they may derive from some more general, global tendencies in the wider environment of a society. Some of them are more universal, affecting everybody (e.g., inflation, crime), others are more particular, affecting only some segments of the population (e.g., unemployment, status degradation). Against the background of cultural disorientation – a condition that makes people more sensitive and anxious – such events or situations may engender a traumatic syndrome. But before they do, there is a stage of cultural labeling, framing and redefining.

Trauma, like many other social conditions, is at the same time objective and subjective: it is usually based in actual phenomena, but it does not exist as long as they are not made visible and defined in a particular way. Such defining, framing, and interpretive efforts do not occur in a vacuum: there is always a preexisting pool of available meanings encoded in the shared culture of a given community or society. Individual people do not invent meanings, but rather draw selectively from their surrounding culture and apply them to potentially traumatizing events. Hence, traumatizing conditions or situations are always cultural constructions. There may be traumas which are not rooted in any real traumatizing conditions or situations, but only in the widespread imagining of such events. Moral panics (Thompson 1998) ensue when threats, dangers, or traumas are defined in a highly exaggerated manner. But

the opposite is also possible: events or situations with objectively strong traumatizing potential may not lead to actual trauma because they are explained away, rationalized, or reinterpreted in ways which make them invisible, innocuous, or even benign or beneficial.

Cultural traumas generated by major social change and triggered by traumatizing conditions and situations interpreted as threatening, unjust, or improper are expressed as complex social moods, characterized by a number of collective emotions, orientations, and attitudes. First, there is a general climate of anxiety, insecurity, and uncertainty (Wilkinson 2001). Second, there is a prevailing syndrome of distrust, both toward people and institutions (Sztompka 1999). Third, there is disorientation concerning collective identity. Fourth, there is widespread apathy, passivism, and helplessness. Fifth, there is pessimism concerning the future, matched with nostalgic images of the past. Of course, not all these symptoms accompany every case of trauma, and not all these symptoms are equally manifested by various groups or subgroups within a society. For every traumatogenic change there are some core groups which may experience and perceive it strongly, and peripheral groups for whom it is irrelevant or marginal. Some groups, due to their structural and cultural location, are more insulated and some are more susceptible to the impact of traumatogenic change. One may theorize about the factors responsible for the differences among various groups in their susceptibility to trauma. Crucial variables may include access to various resources – cultural, social, economic, and political capital – helpful in perceiving, defining, and actively facing traumas. On the cultural side, the key factor seems to be education. On the one hand, the higher their level of education, the more perceptive and more sensitive to cultural traumas people become. On the other hand, they are better equipped to express and fight trauma. No wonder that some more subtle and hidden traumas have been perceived, diagnosed, and opposed firstly by intellectuals, philosophers, and social scientists, who have provided ready-made definitions and symbolic frames for other people to pick up. Usually, more educated groups also have better skills for actively coping with cultural trauma. But other kinds of cultural capital, apart from education, may also play a part. For those kinds of trauma that originate in a cultural clash or multiculturalism, a tolerant, relativistic, cosmopolitan orientation – as opposed to ethnocentrism or dogmatism – will allow people to cope better.

In the realm of social capital there is the factor known as social rootedness, or extensive personal contacts. To illustrate, in studies of post-communist societies it was observed that those who have rich social networks of acquaintances, numerous friends, and strong family support are much better prepared to cope with the traumatic reorientation to capitalist entrepreneurship, free markets, and individualistic responsibility. For many kinds of trauma, capital in the literal sense – wealth or power – may provide important cushioning resources, insulating against trauma or providing efficient means to deal with trauma.

Cultural traumas evoke various reactions from people. One may use a typology developed with reference to the classical treatment of anomie and social adaptations to anomic conditions proposed by Merton (1996a). Merton describes four typical adaptations to anomie: innovation, rebellion, ritualism, and retreatism. The first two are active, constructive adaptations; the second two are passive adaptations. This typology may be applied to cultural traumas. Innovation may target culture directly and through socialization or indoctrination redefine a cultural dissonance as less grave, or only temporary; or it may use the opposite strategy by articulating cultural dualism as radical and irreconcilable, idealizing new cultural ways and totally denouncing the old. Such "cultural propaganda," which may be spontanous or purposefully directed, aims at alleviating the incongruence within a culture brought about by traumatogenic change. Another form of innovation targets the resources needed to insulate people against cultural trauma. Efforts at enriching cultural capital (e.g., by obtaining education), social capital (e.g., by entering a network of voluntary associations), or financial capital (e.g., entrepreneurial activities) allow one to locate oneself more securely in a new cultural reality. Rebellion would indicate a more radical effort aimed at the total transformation of culture in order to replace the traumatic

condition with a completely new cultural setup. Counter-cultural movements, anarchic political groups, and some religious sects provide the best illustrations of this adaptation. A passive, ritualistic reaction would mean returning to established traditions and routines and cultivating them as safe hideouts to deflect cultural trauma. Finally, retreatism in this connection would mean ignoring trauma, repressing it, and acting as if it did not exist. This can provide a kind of subjective insulation from the traumatic condition.

Within the incessant flow of social change a cultural trauma may appear in a double capacity: as the consequence or side-effect of some other changes (traumatogenic in character), but also as an instigator of another stream of changes effected by coping actions. Trauma may appear not only as a cost of change, but also as a stimulating and mobilizing factor for human agency. Cultural trauma – in spite of its immediate negative, painful consequences – may show its positive, functional potential as a force of social becoming (Sztompka 1991).

SEE ALSO: Anomie; Civil Society; Collective Memory; Collective Memory (Social Change); Durkheim, Émile; Durkheim, Émile and Social Change; Sorokin, Pitirim A.

REFERENCES AND SUGGESTED READINGS

Alexander, J., Eyerman, R., Giesen, B., Smelser, N., & Sztompka, P. (2004) *Cultural Trauma and Collective Identity*. University of California Press, Berkeley.

Merton, R. K. (1996a [1938]) Social Structure and Anomie. In: Sztompka, P. (Ed.), *Robert K. Merton on Social Structure and Science*. University of Chicago Press, Chicago, pp.132–52.

Merton, R. K. (1996b [1948]) The Self-Fulfilling Prophecy. In: Sztompka, P. (Ed.), *Robert K. Merton on Social Structure and Science*. University of Chicago Press, Chicago, pp. 183–201.

Sorokin, P. (1967 [1928]) *The Sociology of Revolution*. Howard Fertig, New York.

Sztompka, P. (1991) *Society in Action: The Theory of Social Becoming*. Polity Press, Cambridge.

Sztompka, P. (1993) Civilizational Incompetence: The Trap of Post-Communist Societies. *Zeitschrift fur Soziologie* 2 (April): 85–95.

Sztompka, P. (1999) *Trust: A Sociological Theory*. Cambridge University Press, Cambridge.

Thomas, W. I. & Znaniecki, F. (1974 [1927]) *The Polish Peasant in Europe and America*. Octagon Books, New York.

Thompson, K. (1998) *Moral Panics*. Routledge, London.

Wilkinson, I. (2001) *Anxiety in a Risk Society*. Routledge, London.

collectivism

Abdallah M. Badahdah

Collectivism is a cultural pattern that emphasizes the importance of in-group goals, conformity, loyalty, social harmony, and preserving in-group integrity. The concepts of collectivism and individualism have a long history in the social sciences. For example, Ferdinand Tönnies suggested that in a *Gemeinschaft* (community) people have strong personal connections, common values and goals, and a sense of unity and loyalty. In a *Gesellschaft* (society), in contrast, people focus more on their personal interests and gains and less on their sense of belonging. Also, Émile Durkheim contrasted traditional societies with modern ones. In traditional societies, individuals have similar values, conform to the collective's rules and standards, and exhibit little personal uniqueness. In modern societies, conformity to the collective rules and standards is viewed as disadvantageous and personal uniqueness is promoted and expected.

The concepts of collectivism and individualism are widely used by contemporary social scientists, largely as a result of Hofstede's book *Culture's Consequences* (1980). While Hofstede identified four dimensions in his book – power distance, uncertainty avoidance, individualism, and masculinity – individualism and collectivism are the most frequently utilized concepts in studies of cross-cultural differences.

These concepts have been studied at both the cultural and individual levels. At the cultural level, cultures (countries) are used as the unit of analysis, whereas at the individual level, individuals are used as the unit of analysis. The constructs that correspond to individualism and collectivism at the individual level are idiocentrism and allocentrism, respectively. Hofstede's ratings of countries, priming techniques, and the direct assessment of individualism and collectivism are the three commonly used approaches to studying individualism and collectivism. Collectivism has been used to explain differences between cultures, mainly European American and East Asian ones.

Studies have shown that the collectivistic self is an interdependent, flexible, relational, and multiple self that emphasizes the importance of connectedness and maintaining harmonious relationships. Accommodating and adjusting to different situations and taking the roles of others are expected and encouraged, and the resultant inconsistency between attitudes and behavior is tolerated. Collectivistic individuals are good at expressing and experiencing emotions that are other-focused (e.g., shame). Collectivists are sensitive to others' appraisals, susceptible to embarrassment, and concerned about "saving face" and protecting others from embarrassment. Although collectivists consider both internal and external factors when making attributions, they are more perceptive than individualists of social and situational contexts. They use an indirect communication style and prefer to resolve conflicts using means that preserve relationships.

SEE ALSO: Authority and Conformity; Culture; Durkheim, Émile; Individualism; In-Groups and Out-Groups; Self; Tönnies, Ferdinand

REFERENCES AND SUGGESTED READINGS

Ball, R. (2001) Individualism, Collectivism, and Economic Development. *Annals of the American Academy of Political and Social Science* 573: 57–84.

Markus, H. R. & Kitayama, S. (1991) Culture and the Self: Implications for Cognition, Emotion, and Motivation. *Psychological Review* 98: 224–53.

Oyserman, D., Coon, H. M., & Kemmelmeier, M. (2002) Rethinking Individualism and Collectivism: Evaluation of Theoretical Assumptions and Meta-Analysis. *Psychological Bulletin* 128: 3–72.

Triandis, H. C. (1995) *Individualism and Collectivism*. Westview Press, Boulder, CO.

Triandis, H. C. (2001) Individualism–Collectivism and Personality. *Journal of Personality* 69: 907–24.

colleges and universities

Steven Brint

The distant predecessors of colleges and universities go back in the West to the Greek academies of the fourth and fifth centuries BCE. In these academies, young men from the governing classes studied rhetoric and philosophy (and "lesser" subjects) as training for public life (Marrou 1982). In the East, the roots of higher education go back to the training of future government bureaucrats at the feet of masters of Confucian philosophy, poetry, and calligraphy. In both East and West, a tight relationship existed between social class, literate culture, and preparation for public life.

Modern higher education institutions trace a more direct lineage from the medieval *studium generale*. In the first European universities of the twelfth and early thirteenth centuries (notably, Salerno, Bologna, and Paris), students and masters came together to pore over the new knowledge discovered in ancient texts and developed by Arab scholars of Spain. These gatherings of students and teachers were a product of the revival of scholarly inquiry in what has been called the twelfth-century Renaissance. The term university does not, as many believe, refer to the universe of all fields of knowledge. Originally, it meant simply "an aggregate of persons."

The medieval universities have a recognizable similarity to modern higher education in that they were permanent institutions of learning with at least a rudimentary formal organization. Courses of study were formally organized, lectures and examinations were given at scheduled times, administrative officials presided, graduation ceremonies were held, and students lived in lodgings near the university buildings. The *studium generale* were recognized as such because they housed at least one of the "higher faculties" in law, medicine, and theology in addition to faculties of the arts. Courses in the arts, typically with an emphasis on logic and philosophy, were common preparation for study in the three learned professions. Thus, from the beginning, a certain vocational emphasis is evident in the university; degrees awarded on the completion of professional studies certified accomplishments worthy of entry into professional life. However, the spirit of inquiry was equally important; these were places renowned for famous teachers, such as Abelard in Paris and Irnerius in Bologna (Rashdall 1936).

In the seventeenth and eighteenth centuries the fortunes of colleges and universities waned. The causes for decline are numerous. They include the attractiveness of commercial over scholarly careers, the interference (in some places) of religious and political authorities, and the insularity of faculty who jealously guarded their guild privileges but resisted new currents of thought. During this period, colleges and universities became places interested in the transmission of ancient texts, rather than the further advance of knowledge. They were often criticized as little more than pleasant retreats for wealthy students. Professional training moved out of the universities: into Inns of Court, medical colleges, and seminaries. New elites interested in technical and scientific progress established entirely new institutions rather than allying with existing colleges and universities. Napoleon, for example, founded elite professional training institutions, the *grandes écoles*, and the early investigators in the natural sciences created separate societies, such as the British Royal Society, to encourage research and discussion.

The revival of the university is the product of nineteenth-century European reform movements led in the beginning by intellectually oriented aristocrats and eminent philosophers and theologians. The University of Berlin, founded in 1810, was the first reformed university and others shortly followed in its wake. The new university was founded on the "Humboldtian principles" of the unity of teaching and research (meaning that both activities were performed by the professoriate) and the freedom to teach and to learn without fear of outside interference. The development of new academic structures such as the research seminar and the specialized lecture created an environment out of which pathbreaking researchers (e.g., Leopold Ranke in history and Justus von Liebig in chemistry) emerged (McClelland 1980). The German research universities had become by mid-century a model for reformers throughout Europe and from as far away as the

US and Japan. The first research university in the US, Johns Hopkins University, was founded in 1876, explicitly on the model of the German research university.

Higher education's emphasis on training for a wide range of applied fields has been equally important as a source of its current centrality. Here, the US, rather than Germany, has been the decisive innovator. In the US the passage of the Morrill Acts (1862 and 1890) provided land grants to states to establish public universities. These institutions were designed to provide both general education and practical training in agricultural and mechanical arts for all qualified applicants. They encouraged both the democratization of American higher education and a closer connection between universities and emerging markets for educated labor.

The American university's role in society was further enhanced by its willingness to work collaboratively with government, professional associations, and (somewhat later) also with business and community organizations. The Wisconsin Idea encouraged close connection between university experts and government officials during the period before World War I. Universities also cooperated closely with professional associations to raise educational training standards. Connections between university and state were extended, particularly in the sciences, during World War II and the Cold War, when government grants for university-based scientific research became a very large source of support.

These developments encouraged a new view of higher education. In the 1960s, Clark Kerr coined the term multiversity to describe institutions like his own University of California as service-based enterprises specializing in training, research, and advice for all major sectors of society (Kerr 1963). Junior colleges, founded just after the turn of the century, were by the 1960s even more systematically tied than universities to local and regional markets for semi-professional and technical labor. In terms of growth, these two-year colleges are the great success story of twentieth-century higher education and their influence is now evident even in four-year institutions. The utilitarian approach of American educators was resisted for some time in Europe and Asia, where access to

higher education was strictly limited to those students who passed rigorous examinations and where higher degrees had long served as important badges of social status linked to cultural refinement. However, by the last quarter of the twentieth century, the utilitarian approach to higher education had become the dominant model throughout the developed world.

Institutions of higher education rarely shed their earlier identities completely; instead, they incorporate new emphases through reorganization and by adding new units and new role expectations. Much of the nomenclature, hierarchy, and ritual of the medieval university remains and is in full display at graduation ceremonies. Although many new fields have become incorporated into the curriculum, the liberal arts emphasis of the ancient academies remains central in the first two years of undergraduate study (the lower division), at least in countries influenced by the American model. The nineteenth-century emphasis on specialization is evident in the second two years of undergraduate study (the upper division) and in the graduate and professional programs. The nineteenth-century emphasis on research remains an absorbing occupation of faculty and graduate students. The twentieth-century emphases on ancillary training, service, and entertainment activities are typically buffered from the core of teaching and learning (as in the case of university extension, agricultural experiment stations, university-based hospitals, and intercollegiate sports teams).

ACADEMIC ORGANIZATION

Modern institutions of higher education are far from *collegia* in their authority structure, but they also do not fit an ideal-type corporate model of centralized, top-down control. Instead, decision-making structures are based on divided spheres of power and ongoing consultation between two authority structures: one based in knowledge and the other in the allocation of resources. The dual hierarchy of professors and administrators is a structural feature of academic organization with particularly important consequences.

The authority structure of knowledge is constituted by the departments and, within the departments, by the professorial ranks. Advancement in the professorial hierarchy is based in principle on the quality of a faculty member's professional accomplishment (typically involving assessments of research, teaching, and service). Differences in rank are associated with higher levels of professional deference and income. This hierarchy moves from the temporary ranks of lecturer and instructor to the regular ranks of assistant, associate, and full professor. Highly visible full professors may be appointed to named chairs that provide both additional symbolic recognition and a separate budget for research and travel.

The top level of the administrative hierarchy is composed of a president or chancellor, who is responsible for fundraising and interaction with important resource providers as well as overall supervision; a provost or executive vice-chancellor, who is responsible for internal academic matters; and the deans of the colleges and schools. Top administrators are usually drawn from members of the faculty, though an increasing number of lower-tier institutions now hire professional managers at the presidential level. Top administrators make the ultimate decisions about budget allocations, hiring and promotion, and planning for the future. However, the professorate, through its representatives in an academic senate, typically retain a decisive say in all decisions involving curricular organization and instruction. They also retain the predominant say in hiring and promotion decisions, expecting only very rare overrule by administrators.

Universities depend for prestige and resources on the accomplishments of their faculty and, as a general rule, the less distinguished the faculty the more powerful the administration. Professors in non-elite institutions have consequently sometimes chosen to organize in collective bargaining units to control administrative discretion through contractual means. The institution of tenure greatly enhances the influence of faculty. After a 6-year probationary period, assistant professors come up for a decision on promotion to tenure and accompanying advancement in rank. Promotion to tenure, a conventional rather than a legal status, guarantees lifetime employment for those who continue to meet their classes and act within broad bounds of moral acceptability. Together, dual authority and tenure guarantee opposition to any administrative efforts to abandon existing programs or to reduce the work conditions and privileges of the faculty.

SOURCES AND CONSEQUENCES OF GROWTH

Theorists of post-industrial society have suggested that the growth of the knowledge sector in the economy is behind this expansion of higher education (Bell 1973). Estimates vary on the rate of growth of the knowledge sector, depending on the definition used. Industries employing high proportions of professionals are growing faster, by and large, than other industries, but some estimates show the rate of growth slowing over time. No estimate has shown that knowledge industries contribute a dominant share of the national product in the advanced societies, or even the majority of the most dynamic export industries.

While the growth of the knowledge sector may be an important factor in the expansion of graduate and professional education, its importance at the undergraduate level is doubtful. At least three other sources of growth must be given proper emphasis. One is the interest of states in expanding educational opportunities for their citizens. Another is the interest of students, given these opportunities, to differentiate themselves in the labor market. As secondary school completion approaches universality and higher education attendance becomes more feasible, more students have a motive to differentiate themselves by pursuing higher degrees. Finally, and perhaps most important, is the increasing role played by educational credentials as a means of access to desirable jobs in the economy. Credentials are not simply (or in many cases primarily) a guarantee of technical skills. They also signal that their holders are likely to have cultural and personality characteristics sought by employers. These characteristics include middle-class manners, a competitive outlook, literacy and communication skills, and persistence. Colleges both reward and socialize these qualities.

Since the 1960s the trend in the industrialized world has been in the direction of the American model, with an increasing proportion of students entering higher education, but with stratification among institutions and major subjects also increasing. Two quite separate market situations tend to develop: one for largely well-to-do students who can afford an expensive 4-year residential experience and another for largely moderate to lower-income students who desire convenience and flexibility as they juggle school, family, and work. In most countries of Europe, for example, access to higher education is now possible from all secondary school tracks (including vocational tracks) and once-rigorous secondary school-leaving examinations have been relaxed to allow a larger flow of students into higher education. In addition, 3-year degrees have also become normative in many European countries. For these reasons, higher proportions of the age cohort now attend colleges and universities in countries like Australia and Korea than in the US. Over the last quarter century the age of mass higher education has arrived throughout the developed world.

SEE ALSO: Community College; Education and Economy; Educational Attainment; Educational and Occupational Attainment; Institution; Schools, Public; Sport, College; Stratification and Inequality, Theories of

REFERENCES AND SUGGESTED READINGS

Bell, D. (1973) *The Coming of Post-Industrial Society: An Essay in Social Forecasting*. Basic Books, New York.

Kerr, C. (1963) *The Uses of the University*. Harper & Row, New York.

McClelland, C. (1980) *State, Society, and University in Germany, 1700–1914*. Cambridge University Press, Cambridge.

Marrou, H. (1982 [1948]) *A History of Education in Antiquity*. University of Wisconsin Press, Madison.

Rashdall, H. (1936 [1895]) *The Universities of Europe in the Middle Ages*, Vol. 1. Ed. F. M. Powicke & A. B. Emden. Oxford University Press, Oxford.

colonialism (neocolonialism)

Julian Go

Colonialism refers to the direct political control of a society and its people by a foreign ruling state. Essentially it is a political phenomenon. The ruling state monopolizes political power and keeps the subordinated society and its people in a legally inferior position. But colonialism has had significant cultural, social, and economic correlates and ramifications. Neocolonialism is the continued exercise of political or economic influence over a society in the absence of formal political control.

Traditionally, the concept of colonialism has been associated with "colonization," which refers to the transplantation or settlement of peoples from one territory to another. The word colonization is derived from the Latin *colonia*, meaning the settlement of people from home. But popular and scholarly uses of the term later shifted the meaning. Colonialism came to refer to political control with or without settlement. The concept also took on a more explicit ethnic, racial, and geographical component. It increasingly came to refer to the establishment of political control by European or western powers over Asia, Latin America, and Africa. It also signified political control by one "race" over another "race," where the latter is deemed inferior to the former.

Analytically, colonialism is related to but also distinguishable from imperialism. While imperialism also refers to control by one society over another, it does not have to take the form of direct political control. It can also occur through informal political means (such as temporary military occupation), the exercise of economic power (control over finance or imposition of embargoes), or cultural influence (the spread of Hollywood movies around the world). Colonialism, by contrast, is a more specific variant of imperialism, referring to a situation whereby control is exerted directly and for a sustained duration of time. The ruling power officially declares political control over another territory and its people and institutionalizes the control through declarations of law. The colonized country is then a part of the mother country but subordinate to it. In this sense, colonialism can be seen as one particular form of imperialism among others.

Colonialism itself can take various forms and have a number of different correlates. It can involve settlement and the governance of settlers, such as British colonization of the United States, Canada, or Australia. It might also involve economic plunder or the destruction of native inhabitants, as with Spanish colonialism in South America. Colonialism might also involve the establishment of extensive bureaucratic systems designed to control territories by extracting tribute. Furthermore, colonialism can also involve a temporary state of transition from inferior political status to equal political status, whereby the colony becomes fully integrated into the mother country, such as French colonialism in some parts of Africa.

Sociological thought has had varied intellectual relationships with colonialism. On the one hand, Herbert Spencer's social evolutionary theory was sometimes used, implicitly or explicitly, to justify European colonialism in Asia and Africa in the nineteenth and early twentieth centuries. In the United States at the turn of the twentieth century, sociologists such as Franklin Giddens advocated US colonial rule in the Philippines and elsewhere. On the other hand, Karl Marx (1906) criticized colonialism as an economic phenomenon that served the narrow economic needs of the ruling society. In Marx's view, colonialism facilitated the "primitive accumulation" of capital. Marx and Engels (1972) suggested that colonialism further facilitated the spread of capitalist social relations around the world. Other early works tried to specify the particular character of colonial societies. Furnivall's concept, "plural societies," conceived of colonial societies as unique social forms in which people of different cultures, races, and ethnicities mingled.

Later scholarship on colonialism has gone in multiple directions. Some expanded upon Marx's views on colonialism. John Hobson argued that British colonial expansion served as a necessary outlet for overaccumulation; Lenin later expanded this view to theorize colonial expansion as arising from a particular stage of capitalist development, specifically its finance and monopoly stage. A. G. Frank (1969) drew

upon Marx in the 1960s to examine the economic effects of colonialism upon colonized societies. Criticizing modernization theory, Frank argued that Latin American underdevelopment and the economic development of Europe had both been enabled by colonialism. Through colonialism, western powers extracted raw materials and profits from colonial societies to fuel their own industrialization, but that process simultaneously prevented colonial societies from developing.

Other scholarship took the study of colonialism in different directions. Beginning in the 1950s and 1960s, Franz Fanon (1969) and Albert Memmi (1967) examined the forms of racial domination involved in colonialism and their cultural and psychological impact in Africa. In the late 1960s, Robert Blauner (1969) expanded the idea of colonialism to include "internal colonialism" and thereby theorize the difference between the experiences of white immigrants in the United States and those of African Americans and Hispanic immigrants. Later, Edward Said (1979) proposed the concept of "Orientalism" to capture the conceptual and ideological bases of colonialism. In Said, colonialism and associated forms of imperialism depend upon binary concepts revolving around "East" and "West," "Self" and "Other."

The term neocolonialism refers to relations of unequal power between countries despite the formal independence of those countries. The term suggests that, even after colonized societies attain independence, they are kept in a position of political and economic inferiority that reproduces the position they had had when they were formal colonies. In this view, formerly colonized nations remain subject to unequal exchange with western countries, become dependent upon them for capital and technology necessary for their own industrialization, and serve as places for labor exploitation and continued resource extraction by foreign firms. Politically, formerly colonized nations remain subject to various mechanisms of outside control by western powers, either through debt bondage and international institutions like the World Bank or through political pressure or direct military intervention. Consciousness of neocolonialism among formerly colonized peoples was formally declared at the 1955 Bandung conference, when representatives from Asian and African countries met to forge cross-national alliances and express opposition to colonial rule.

SEE ALSO: Decolonization; Dependency and World-Systems Theories; Methods, Postcolonial; Postcolonialism and Sport; Orientalism; Plural Society; Third World and Postcolonial Feminisms/Subaltern

REFERENCES AND SUGGESTED
READINGS

Blauner, R. (1969) Internal Colonialism and Ghetto Revolt. *Social Problems* 16: 393–408.
Brewer, A. (1990) *Marxist Theories of Imperialism: A Critical Survey*. Routledge, London.
Fanon, F. (1969) *The Wretched of the Earth*. Grove Press, New York.
Frank, A. (1969) *Capitalism and Underdevelopment in Latin America*. Monthly Review Press, New York.
Furnivall, J. S. (1944) *Netherlands India: A Study of Plural Economy*. Macmillan, New York.
Hofstadter, R. (1992) *Social Darwinism in American Thought*. Beacon Press, Boston.
Marx, K. (1906) *Capital: A Critique of Political Economy*. Modern Library, New York.
Marx, K. & Engels, F. (1972) *On Colonialism*. International Publishers, New York.
Memmi, A. (1967) *The Colonizer and the Colonized*. Beacon Press, Boston.
Said, E. (1979) *Orientalism*. Vintage, New York.

color line

Earl Wright

In 1903, William Edward Burghardt Du Bois penned the phrase: "The problem of the twentieth century is the problem of the color-line – the relation of the darker to the lighter races of men in Asia and Africa, in America and the islands of the sea" (Du Bois 1994 [1903]: 9). This thunderous statement, appearing in his classic text *The Souls of Black Folk*, served as Du Bois's clarion call for the nation, grappling with tense and volatile relations between blacks and whites, to engage in objective and thorough research on black Americans. Research and propaganda on the color line would be Du Bois's life's work. Some of his book-length treatments of the color line include his Harvard dissertation, *Suppression of the African Slave-Trade to the United States of America, 1638–1870, The Philadelphia Negro*, and *The Souls of Black Folk*. While each of these books, in addition to the many articles he wrote on the subject, are considered classic works in the area of race, arguably, Du Bois's most impressive and influential research on the color line consists of the investigations he spearheaded as the director of research at Atlanta University between 1897 and 1914.

In 1897, W. E. B. Du Bois was chosen to lead the Atlanta Sociological Laboratory, the term used to describe those engaged in sociological activity at Atlanta University between 1896 and 1924, by Atlanta University President Horace Bumstead. Several years prior to Du Bois's appointment, the university institutionalized a program of research into the social, economic, and physical condition of black Americans. Upon completing research for *The Philadelphia Negro*, Du Bois, who quickly became a sought-after scholar, was providentially offered the position of director of research at Atlanta University. President Bumstead's offer to lead the Atlanta Sociological Laboratory coalesced with Du Bois's desire to develop a program of research on the color line. According to Du Bois, "After I finished [*The Philadelphia Negro*], or before I finished it, the question with me was how this kind of study could be carried on and applied to the whole Negro problem in the US" (1961: 3). Du Bois ardently believed, at this point in his life, that the existing racial problems between blacks and whites resulted primarily from a lack of education and knowledge of basic facts concerning the other. Once people were educated and provided with accurate data concerning those on the opposite side of the color line, he believed that relations between blacks and whites would improve. In a 1961 interview, Du Bois discussed his desire to begin a large-scale study of black Americans that would be housed at the member institutions whom we now refer to as the Ivy League. "What we needed was an academic study of the American Negro. I wanted the universities of Pennsylvania, and Harvard and Yale and so forth to go into a sort of partnership by which this kind of study could be forwarded. But of course they didn't do anything at all. But Atlanta University, which was a Negro institution down in Atlanta, Georgia asked me to come down there and teach and take charge of some such study" (1961: 3).

When Du Bois arrived at Atlanta University two studies had already been conducted and a third planned. Of the 20 monographs published by the Atlanta Sociological Laboratory between 1896 and 1917, Du Bois spearheaded the preparation of 16. Notwithstanding his accomplishment prior to and after his tenure at Atlanta University, it can be argued that his most impressive sociological contributions to research on the color line were accomplished during this period. Three of the more significant studies led by Du Bois are highlighted below.

The 1900 study, "The College-Bred Negro," focused on black college graduates. This study is an important examination of the color line given the ideological sparring over the education of black Americans that was taking place between Booker T. Washington and Du Bois. Notwithstanding a more elaborate analysis of the divisions between these giant scholars, Washington believed that black American independence should begin with an entrepreneurial foundation grounded in the vocational and technical, while Du Bois believed it should begin with holistic or liberal arts education. Washington also suggested that it would be very difficult for black college graduates in early twentieth-century America to find gainful employment. Du Bois's main conclusions in this investigation were that black American college graduates were gainfully employed and that there was a demand for college-educated blacks.

The 1906 study, "The Health and Physique of the Negro American," addressed the physical condition of black Americans vis-à-vis whites. During this era it was believed that there were physical and intellectual differences between blacks and whites and that blacks were inferior to whites in both areas. Through a collaborative effort with several black American medical professionals and 1,000 Hampton Institute undergraduate students, the major finding

of this study debunked the widely held belief that there were physical differences between blacks and whites.

Last, the 1911 study, "The Common School and the Negro American," focused on the condition of black public schools. Du Bois discovered that black schools were not receiving their fair share of state and federal funding. For example, one county in Georgia educated 3,165 black students and 1,044 white students. However, the level of state funding for each group was $4,509 and $10,678, respectively. In addition to uncovering disparities in school funding, Du Bois's venture into the color line in education revealed that black teachers were being paid half as much as white teachers.

In summary, while much is known about Du Bois's book-length treatments of the color line, such as the texts mentioned above, few are aware of the dense body of work he conducted on the color line at Atlanta University between 1896 and 1914. An examination of that body of work provides the earliest and most detailed information on the color line in the early twentieth century on topics including education, religion, crime, health, and business.

SEE ALSO: American Sociological Association; Black Feminist Thought; Double Consciousness; Du Bois: "Talented Tenth"; Du Bois, W. E. B.; Park, Robert E. and Burgess, Ernest W.; Race and Ethnic Consciousness

REFERENCES AND SUGGESTED READINGS

Du Bois, W. E. B. (1961) *W. E. B. Du Bois: A Recorded Autobiography*. Folkway Records, New York.

Du Bois, W. E. B. (1994 [1903]) *The Souls of Black Folk*. Dover, New York.

coming out/closets

Chet Meeks

The closet and coming out are key concepts in the sociology of sexualities and in lesbian and gay studies. The closet refers to the systematic repression of homosexuality. The closet exists when the state, science, the media, the criminal justice system, and other social institutions (school, family, etc.) work concertedly to construct homosexuality as a pathological social threat, and to institutionalize heterosexuality as the only "normal" and legitimate sexuality. Coming out refers to the individual and/or collective disclosure of homosexual identity as a way of combating the closet and its effects.

The concept of the closet has become ubiquitous in post-Stonewall gay and lesbian culture. Memoirs and biographies of lesbian and gay people, for example, almost uniformly tell of the evolution of a life from darkness, secrecy, and isolation, to being "out of the closet" (Monette 1992). The American lesbian and gay community has a holiday, National Coming Out Day, to encourage visibility and openness about sexual identity. The closet has been singled out by conservative, liberal, and radical gay activists alike as a penultimate obstacle. Many academics who study sexuality rely on the concept of the closet to discuss all forms – historical and contemporary – of sexual invisibility and disclosure. Sedgwick (1990) argues that western cultures are characterized by a heterosexual/homosexual binary that operates as a master social logic, meaning that this binary informs not only the way sexuality works in our societies, but also the way *all* social institutions operate. This binary works, in part, by organizing all human desires in terms of disclosure or invisibility. The closet, in this view, is not merely a condition that applies to homosexuals as a "sexual minority," but is rather a general social condition that organizes all of social life.

Sociologically, the closet means something very specific, and much attention has been given in recent years to clarifying its meaning. Many have argued recently that prior to the mid-twentieth century, the closet was not an organizing feature of gay life, that especially in America's cities there were high levels of gay and lesbian visibility, and a relative degree of integration of gay life into immigrant and working-class urban culture (Chauncey 1992). It was only during the mid-twentieth century that the social conditions associated with the closet

came into being. It was during this time that homosexuals came to be thought of as moral monsters. The US Congress targeted communists and homosexuals as threats to the integrity and strength of the nation. Police squads in cities across America harassed gay men, lesbians, and transgender people, raiding bars and meeting places, and arresting individuals for sodomy or for not wearing appropriately gendered clothing. Social scientific and psychological knowledge was used to construct homosexuality as a social and personal pathology. The closet, then, refers to a situation in which a sharp cultural distinction is made between homosexuality and heterosexuality, with the former being associated with pollution, suspicion, and danger. All social institutions – the state, the criminal justice system, education, the media, etc. – participate in the making and maintenance of the closet.

The term coming out originally made its debut in gay liberationist discourses as a response to these oppressive mid-century conditions. "Out of the closets and into the streets" was the rallying cry of a social movement against the closet (Jay & Young 1972). It is important to note that, for gay liberationists, coming out meant more than the personal disclosure of one's homosexuality; additionally, it meant taking a collective, political stance against the institutionalized nature of homosexual oppression, as well as the oppression of working-class people, people of the third world, black Americans, and women. Coming out meant coming out *against* "straight" society, announcing allegiance to a collective political movement, and not merely coming out as an individual with homosexual desires.

As symbolic expressions, the closet and coming out have enabled the building of lesbian and gay solidarity and identity because they describe a common, widely shared experience of silence, shame, and isolation. The closet organizes the wide variety of experiences lesbians and gay men have into a single, communally shared narrative (Plummer 1995). Coming out has operated as an extremely efficient mobilizing tool in lesbian and gay politics because it connects political struggle to individual action. Coming out, at least as it was originally articulated, links individual disclosure with broad-scale political action and change.

In recent years, some have suggested that the conditions associated with the closet are weakening. Beginning in the 1990s, European and American societies witnessed an explosion of gay visibility in popular culture. In America, Democratic politicians frequently court the "gay vote." Most recently, the American Supreme Court declared all sodomy laws unconstitutional, perhaps signifying a retreat of the state from the active repression of homosexuality. Although the trend is uneven and incomplete, many lesbians and gay men today do not report feeling a sense of dread or shame attached to homosexuality (Seidman et al. 1999). Many, in fact, report disclosing their sexual identity on a regular basis, making homosexuality a regular, normal feature of their daily lives. If these trends continue, we may indeed be approaching the end of the closet (Seidman 2002). Making sense of how sexuality is regulated and lived in such a world will surely provide social scientists with ripe opportunities for new research.

SEE ALSO: Compulsory Heterosexuality; Gay and Lesbian Movement; Homophobia and Heterosexism; Homosexuality; Identity Politics/ Relational Politics; Patriarchy; Sexual Politics

REFERENCES AND SUGGESTED READINGS

Chauncey, G. (1992) *Gay New York*. Basic Books, New York.
Jay, K. & Young, A. (Eds.) (1972) *Out of the Closets, Into the Streets*. Douglas Books, New York.
Monette, P. (1992) *Becoming a Man*. Harper & Row, New York.
Plummer, K. (1995) *Telling Sexual Stories*. Routledge, London.
Sedgwick, E. K. (1990) *The Epistemology of the Closet*. University of California Press, Berkeley.
Seidman, S. (2002) *Beyond the Closets*. Routledge, New York.
Seidman, S., Meeks, C., & Traschen, F. (1999) Beyond the Closet? The Changing Social Meaning of Homosexuality in the United States. *Sexualities* 2(1): 9–34.

commodities, commodity fetishism, and commodification

Nicholas Sammond

Commodities are things that are useful, or that satisfy human needs. The requirements to which commodities are applied may be fundamental – such as food or shelter – or they may be more ephemeral, such as the desire to appear attractive or successful. The term "commodity" dates back to the late Middle Ages and once carried a variety of meanings, including advantage, convenience, ease, or, in Elizabethan slang, a woman or her genitals. As it is understood today, however, a commodity is a product that is bought and sold. This narrowing of the term came about with the rise of capitalism as the central organizing principle of Euro-American economic and social life.

The pioneering critique of capitalism by the economist and philosopher Karl Marx (1976 [1867]) in the mid-nineteenth century, at the moment when sociology was taking form as a social science, brought the commodity to the fore as a unit of analysis in the study of capitalist social relations. In that work, Marx refined the meaning of the term, suggesting that commodities were not simply objects that fulfilled needs, but that their seeming simple utility served to mask the social and material relations that brought them into existence – particularly the human labor necessary to produce them. For Marx, commodities had a "dual nature," which was comprised of their utility (or use value) and their value in the market (or exchange value). Although a commodity was useful to the person who bought it because it satisfied some need, it was also useful to the person who sold it because its sale yielded value in excess of the cost of the labor and materials necessary to produce it, either in the form of other commodities or in money.

Marx's refinement of the term was in response to the work of economists such as Adam Smith and David Ricardo, who treated commodities as if their value were strictly determined by their utility. This was a fiction, he argued, that caused the social labor that went into the production of commodities to disappear. In particular, it masked the social negotiation of labor in which a producer of a given commodity sold his or her labor to a capitalist, who then sold that commodity at a profit. Another person (another producer of labor) purchasing that commodity would not see that negotiation as a component in the price of the object, but would see its value only as determined by the market. The struggle of a laborer to be paid as much as possible for his or her labor, and of an employer to pay him or her as little as possible, though present in the value of the object, disappeared in the description of commodity value as the result of invisible market forces. The price of food, clothing, or fuel, for example, was seen as set by forces of supply and demand, into which the very social struggle over the price of labor did not figure. Locked in their own struggle to earn a living, and surrounded by the commodities necessary to live, individual laborers were blinded to the social relations they had in common with other workers, seeing commodities as simple objects of utility and not as repositories of those relations.

Marx referred to this epistemological process, by which the designation of commodities as mere objects of utility veiled the other meanings they contained, as *commodity fetishism*. This derisive and sarcastic term was meant to point out that the description of commodities as containing their own value by classical economists, though purporting to be scientific, was actually fantastical and wrong-headed. In using the term "fetishism," Marx was drawing upon emerging anthropological theory, which described primitive religious practices in European colonies in Africa and East Asia as "fetishistic" because adherents of those religions ostensibly believed that their gods or ancestors dwelt in the statues or idols they worshipped. Economists who treated commodities as if they had value in and of themselves – that so much coal was worth so much cloth by virtue merely of what it was, and of its relative availability – were no better than primitive shamans, or worse, hucksters who peddled a demonstrably false religion to unsuspecting followers. Just as the study of the archaic religious practices of their colonial and slave-trade

subjects was revealing to Europeans of the nineteenth century the workings of primitive societies beyond which they had long since evolved, Marx's parodic description of the commodity relation as equally fetishistic was meant to shed scientific light on that relation as not the working of the (super)natural world, but a social process amenable to alteration.

The notion of fetishism as a central element in the organization of primitive societies played an important role in discussions of human social life in the nineteenth century. In making an argument for positive philosophy, Auguste Comte (1855), often considered the founder of modern sociology, argued that fetish worship lay at the root of human social organization. Fetishism, he claimed, marked the beginning of an abstract relationship to the natural world which would eventually evolve into the more highly rational and complexly organized thought and social organization of the modern world in which he and his contemporaries dwelt. This notion was just as widely contested as it was accepted, giving rise to competing theories of primitive social and religious organization, including *animism* (Edward Tylor), *totemism* (John McLennan), and *mana* (Marcel Mauss). At the end of the nineteenth and beginning of the twentieth centuries, even as fetishism was increasingly contested in the rapidly stabilizing disciplines of sociology and anthropology, it gained popularity in studies of psychology and sexuality, most famously by Havelock Ellis and by Sigmund Freud. In this work, the fetish referred to an object of displaced erotic desire – such as a body part or article of clothing – that stood in for the whole person, the desire of whom was, for some cultural or pathological reason, forbidden. For Freud in particular, this definition of the fetish entailed the clear delineation between a natural world in which all objects and creatures obeyed immutable laws, and a cultural world in which the (mis)interpretation of those laws in daily life gave rise to pathological behavior.

The evolution of the concept of fetishism is important to understanding commodity relations, not only because early arguments about fetishism informed Marx's formulation of the commodity fetish, but also because subsequent debate about the fetish's role in mediating between the natural and social worlds would further facilitate the introduction of the notion of commodity fetishism into social theory. At the end of the nineteenth century, even as the role of fetishism in the evolution of human social life was called into question, the centrality of capitalism and commodity exchange in the social organization of the Americas and Europe captured the attention of an emerging sociological discipline. The rapid rise and rationalization of industrial development framed Max Weber's discussion of the relationship of (Christian) religious orientation and capitalist accumulation, and the attendant availability of a wider range of consumer goods informed Thorstein Veblen's analysis of the role of the commodity in bourgeois status hierarchies. What had been for Marx a sarcastic metaphor for the misapprehension of social relations as natural became increasingly a sincere heuristic for examining the role of commodities in the organization of daily social life: like its archaic precursor, the commodity fetish mediated between abstract economic forces and the actions of individuals.

A signal difference between Marx's formulation and those at the turn of the twentieth century was one of intent. Marx's analysis of commodity fetishism was meant to rip away the veil of mystification that kept members of the working class from seeing their common oppression and the common usurpation of their labor power hidden in the notion of the autonomous value of commodities. The ultimate goal of this analysis was to be a revolution by the proletariat and the seizure of the means of production, such as that which ostensibly happened in Russia in 1917. The analysis of social theorists such as Weber and Veblen, however, was at most reformist, suggesting to a largely middle-class audience a means of understanding the alienation and anxiety deriving from rapid changes in its social life, and paving the way for social reforms designed to stave off workers' revolts elsewhere in Europe and in North America.

As industrialization accelerated at the turn of the century, with it came a series of rapid changes in the organization of daily life. Populations shifted from rural to urban settings, and cities grew exponentially. Subsistence production in the home – of clothing, food, toys, furniture, etc. – was replaced by the purchasing of those commodities. First in the middle class and later in the laboring classes, children gradually left the labor market, either in the home or in factories, and attended schools. The advent of movies, radio, and mass publications meant that entertainment, once the province of home or community, became increasingly a mass consumer activity. Toward the middle of the twentieth century, labor movements for a living wage argued for men (as husbands) as the sole wage earners in families, and for the removal of women from the labor market. Both in theory and in practice, this positioned women as the managers of household consumption, a role well established in the middle class and gradually extended to the working class. With these shifts, men and children in particular were seen as either the victims or beneficiaries of commodities, the concrete result of women's purchasing decisions. Commodities were seen as more than simply the bearers of *practical* use value; they also carried in them *social* values, in that they encouraged their users to be passive, consuming members of society rather than active and productive citizens. For example, where families may once have made their own clothing and canned their own foods, by the early twentieth century those activities (which were almost exclusively the province of women) were being replaced by the purchase of readymade clothing and prepackaged foods. Or, if children had once made their own toys from materials at hand, such as sticks, stones, discarded scraps of clothing if they were poor, or had them made by craftspeople if wealthier, they were more likely to have mass-produced toys created by anonymous factories and identical to those held by other children. In popular social theory and criticism, this shift to consumption signaled a loss of productive independence and a more passive relationship to one's environment.

This transition has come to be called the "commodification of everyday life," or the rise of "consumer culture." In the strictest sense, *commodification* refers to the insertion of a product of human labor into a system of exchange such as capitalism. Commodification, then, refers to the removal of an object (or person) from a (theoretical) realm outside the social relations of production and its seemingly forcible incorporation into market relations. Used in the broader sense of the commodification of everyday life, or the commodification of social relations, it suggests the loss of personal and civic autonomy, and is often synonymous with "commercialization." Although this concept of commodification is often deployed as a means of arguing for social life independent of the realm of commerce, in doing so it departs from Marx's observation that imagining an existence independent of commodity relations, or a civil sphere of existence, serves to veil the very notion of commodities as inherently social objects. These two distinct meanings of the term "commodification" derive from different theoretical understandings. The purpose of the Marxist analysis of commodification is to demonstrate to workers their alienation from the products of their labor, to demonstrate the role of political and civic systems in supporting a capitalist system that creates that alienation, and ultimately to end capitalism. A more reformist analysis of commodification has traditionally targeted an audience of consumers in both the middle and working classes, and its purpose has been to alienate them from commodity relations in the service of bolstering the political and civic spheres of social life, rather than to create the intellectual support for revolution.

Much of the impetus for this more moderate approach to the analysis of commodity relations derives from the work of the Frankfurt School of social analysis and its descendants. Although Marxist in its origins and orientation, the analysis of capitalist cultural and social life by theorists such as Max Horkheimer and Theodor Adorno sought to demonstrate how the commodification of daily life in democratic capitalist society naturalized consumption as a form of civic activity, thus weakening a robust and critical civic engagement on the part of its citizens. Similarly, Louis Althusser and György Lukács outlined the means by which commodity relations structured thought and its application in social interaction in capitalist democracies, suggesting (albeit in different ways) that alienation from the social relations of production inherent in the commodity relation extended to the exchange of ideas. In this model, ideology was not external to language but integral to it, and the common discourse of daily interaction was deeply interwoven

with the ideological processes that supported commodification as a natural function of social life. These approaches suggested the possibility of the amendment or gradual epistemological overthrow of consumption and commodity relations as the central organizing principles of social life – primarily through a return to a vigorous analysis of use value and its relationship to exchange value. Arguing against this, however, poststructuralist theorists of political economy such as Jean Baudrillard maintained that the commodity relation was so fundamental to consciousness in a capitalist society that there was no prospect of redemption through alienation. The only possibility for undermining the pervasive presence of consumption in daily life was by undermining the very notion of value itself, whether use or exchange value, a move which would challenge the fundamental structures of social, political, and economic life.

THE STUDY OF THE COMMODITY IN CULTURE

In cultural anthropology, however, there has long been a concern about applying such overly reductive models of value to the complex organization of life in different historical, social, and cultural circumstances. Mauss's preference for the term *mana* over the fetish, for instance, was in part driven by a critique of the projection of European cultural models onto non-western social and cultural groups. These approaches often have proceeded from the assumption that, regardless of cultural context, all objects involved in exchange relations are commodities, and as such embody the social relations of production and consumption for a given culture. This assumption that, in exchange relations in significantly different cultures, things are always *necessarily* commodities may overlay a historically and culturally specific economic model onto a wide range of social interactions. For example, Arjun Appadurai (1986) has argued that anthropologists must model the "social life of things," placing an emphasis not on the *thing* exchanged but on the social processes in a given culture that frame and give meaning to that exchange. In this model, not all exchanges necessarily involve the commodity relation, the value which inheres in an object depends upon the specific social rules through which it is exchanged, and the same object may be a commodity in one set of social circumstances and something else – such as a gift or religious token – in another. Approaches such as Appadurai's permit modeling social and cultural relations such that the commodity relation is only one in a range of possible modes of social interaction in a given culture, and they have called into question the primacy of the commodity as the sole determinant in exchange relations.

Although this suggests a limitation to the heuristic utility of the commodity in anthropology, it has not fundamentally altered the robust critical discussion about the centrality of commodity relations in (primarily) Euro-American social life put forward by the cultural studies school of social analysis, in works by Stuart Hall, John Fiske, Susan Willis, Sut Jhally, Valerie Walkerdine, and others. The rubric of cultural studies is quite broad, encompassing criticism opposed to consumption as a fundamental principle of daily life as well as that which sees consumer society as less clearly inimical to positive social activity. Yet it may broadly be understood as supporting the analysis and critique of consumption as an integral part of social life. This work has included an analysis of how groups subordinated by formations of race, gender, class, or sexuality have found in commodities and their consumption tools for resisting dominant or totalizing ideologies. At the same time, however, arguments for treating the excesses of consumption – such as conspicuous consumption, eating disorders, or addictive reconstructive surgery – not as aberrations in a healthy society but as symptomatic of the alienation inherent in the commodity relation are closer to those of the Frankfurt School.

This very breadth of analytical approaches has laid this school of research open to questions of methodological rigor, and the variety of approaches residing under its aegis to what properly constitute the limits of the approach. Likewise, the emphasis by some practitioners of cultural studies on the empowerment of social groups and individuals has engendered criticism of its analytical detachment. In spite of these hesitations, the insistence by its adherents for an analysis of the use of commodities as tools in the social, economic, and political activities of subordinate groups has gained wide acceptance. With the rise of models of social relations that throw into question nation-based versions of civil society and its relationship to subjectivity, dominant/subordinate cultural relations, and ideology, these approaches have also provided a means for the study of the globalization of social and cultural relations – especially given the expanded global reach of capitalist epistemology in the past 30 years – alternately allowing researchers to model cultural domination and local systems of appropriation and resistance.

If one views the commodity as the embodiment of the social relations of labor, and the acceptance of its autonomy in the marketplace as the mystification of those relations, then the study of commodity relations is more likely one that entails revealing those disappearing social relations of labor. In this sense, "commodity fetishism" – often colloquially understood to mean the elevation of the commodity to the status of a near-deity – is redundant: every commodity is a fetish, and every commodification a fetishistic act. If, however, one sees the commodity as open to unexpected appropriation for use in the distinct symbolic economies resistant to those of the dominant groups, then the commodity may demystify even as it mystifies, and (re)commodification may have the unintended consequence of destabilizing social and material relations between dominant and subordinate groups at a microsocial level, even as it continues to mystify social relations of labor at the macrosocial level. This contradiction between the social and the economic, the danger of the collapse of apparently distinct systems of value into a seamless market-based ethos, make the commodity and its regulation the site of intense scrutiny and debate.

SEE ALSO: Comte, Auguste; Conspicuous Consumption; Consumption, Mass Consumption, and Consumer Culture; Consumption Rituals; Cultural Studies; Gender, Consumption and; Hyperconsumption/Overconsumption; Marx, Karl; Weber, Max

REFERENCES AND SUGGESTED
READINGS

Althusser, L. et al. (1968) *Reading Capital*. Trans. B.
Brewster. Verso, London.
Appadurai, A. (1986) Commodities and the Politics
of Value. In: Appadurai, A. (Ed.), *The Social Life
of Things: Commodities in Cultural Perspective*.
Cambridge University Press, Cambridge.
Comte, A. (1855) *Positive Philosophy*. Trans. H.
Martineau. Calvin Blanchard, New York.
Cook, D. (2004) *The Commodification of Childhood: The
Children's Clothing Industry and the Rise of the Child
Consumer*. Duke University Press, Durham, NC.
Fiske, J. (1996) *Media Matters: Everyday Culture and
Political Change*. University of Minnesota Press,
Minneapolis.
Frank, T. (2002) *New Consensus for Old: Cultural
Studies from Left to Right*. Prickly Paradigm Press,
Chicago.
Horkheimer, M. & Adorno, T. (1975) *Dialectic of
Enlightenment*. HarperCollins, San Francisco.
Jhally, S. (1987) *The Codes of Advertising: Fetishism
and the Political Economy of Meaning in the Con-
sumer Society*. St. Martin's Press, New York.
Lukács, G. (1971) *History and Class Consciousness:
Studies in Marxist Dialectics*. Trans. R. Livingstone.
MIT Press, Cambridge, MA.
Marx, K. (1976 [1867]) *Capital*, vol. 1. Trans. B.
Fowlkes. Penguin, London.
Morley, D. & Chen, K.-H. (Eds.) (1996) *Stuart
Hall: Critical Dialogues in Cultural Studies*. Rou-
tledge, London.
Pietz, W. (1993) Fetishism and Materialism: The
Limits of Theory in Marx. In: Apter, E. & Pietz,
W. (Eds.), *Fetishism as Cultural Discourse*. Cornell
University Press, Ithaca.
Sahlins, M. (1991) *La Pensée Bourgeoise*: Western
Society as Culture. In: Mukerji, C. & Schudson,
M. (Eds.), *Rethinking Popular Culture*. University
of California Press, Berkeley.
Taussig, M. (1980) *The Devil and Commodity Fetishism*.
University of North Carolina Press, Chapel Hill.
Tucker, R. C. (Ed.) (1978) *The Marx–Engels Reader*,
2nd edn. W. W. Norton, New York.
Veblen, T. (1899) *Theory of the Leisure Class: An
Economic Study of the Evolution of Institutions*.
Macmillan, New York.
Walkerdine, V. (1997) *Daddy's Girl: Young Girls and
Popular Culture*. Harvard University Press, Cam-
bridge, MA.
Weber, M. (1930) *The Protestant Ethic and the Spirit
of Capitalism*. Trans. T. Parsons. Scribner, New
York.
Willis, S. (1991) *A Primer for Daily Life*. Routledge,
London.

communism

David W. Lovell

Communism will be examined in its two major
guises: first, as a principle of social organization
that has been advocated since at least the time
of ancient Greece; and second, as a political
movement and system of government that held
power over a substantial part of the earth's
surface during the twentieth century. Though
communism may nowadays be most readily
associated with the works of Marx and his
disciples, Marx grafted a historically specific
project of socialism onto an idea of great antiquity. The core proposition of communism is
that the private ownership of property must
cease because it is the major cause of social
evils, including egoism, excess, and conflict.
The ideal of a communist society substantially
overlaps with utopia. However, the relationship
between the communist ideal and the reality of
communist states, by way of socialism, is not at
all straightforward.

Communism was first systematically examined and advocated in Plato's Socratic dialogue
about the good society – *The Republic* – written
nearly 2,500 years ago. For Socrates, however,
the communal sharing of goods and women was
to be restricted to only one of the three classes
of his ideal society, the Guardians, so that they
would advance the common interest and not
their own. Some ancient communities have,
for certain periods, held their goods in common. This was the case, for example, in some
of the early Christian communities, awaiting
what they believed was the imminent return
of Christ and the creation of the kingdom of
heaven on earth; later, some monasteries
required their clerics to take a vow of poverty
so that they would not be diverted from their
service to God. The idea of communism has
appeared episodically in print across history,
including in works such as Thomas More's
Utopia (1516) and Morelly's *Code of Nature*
(1755), but seems to have been a more persistent
undercurrent in popular discontent against the
wealthy. More believed that communal ownership would abolish the foundations of pride,
envy and greed: "wherever you have private

property, and money is the measure of all things, it is hardly ever possible for a commonwealth to be governed justly or happily ... I am wholly convinced that unless private property is entirely abolished, there can be no fair or just distribution of goods, nor can mankind be happily governed" (More 1989: 38–9). Morelly's agrarian communism envisaged that people would not differ even in dress, so concerned was he about the evil and divisive effects of inequality.

Communism is only one approach to the question of justice and social unity, and has attracted a chorus of critics almost from the beginning. Aristotle, for example, was an early critic of Plato's ideal of communal property and the community of women. As he argued in *The Politics*, "that which is common to the greatest number has the least care bestowed upon it" (Aristotle 1988: 23). Indeed, men who have private property "will make more progress, because everyone will be attending to his own business" (p. 26). Aristotle may have detested "the love of self in excess," but he argued that people would be united and made into a community by education, not by the abolition of private property.

It is probably true to say that most political thinkers have been exercised by the social disorders that are created by the gulf between rich and poor. For most, however, communism is not the solution; indeed, it is seen by them as creating its own set of social problems. Like Aristotle, Jean Bodin (1530–96) argued that social disorder springs not from inequality as such, but from *excessive* wealth and *excessive* poverty. Bodin added that an equality of possessions would not succeed in producing social harmony, for "there is no hatred so bitter, or enmity so deadly as that between equals. Jealousy of equals one of another is the source of unrest, disorder, and civil war" (Bodin 1967: 159). Aristotle, too, had made a similar point: "there is much more quarreling among those who have all things in common" (Aristotle 1988: 27). Many of these critics have also pointed to the practical difficulties raised by equalizing conditions between humans, since it will be immediately upset by human actions, and thus will need constant intervention and even coercion – perhaps by an all-powerful state – to maintain.

Not surprisingly, many discussions of property by social and political thinkers have focused on what gives someone the right to use property to the benefit of one's self and to the exclusion of others. Suffice it to say that these justifications tend to turn either on convention (or possession, with its supporter, legality) or labor (in John Locke's words, property is something a man "hath mixed his *Labour* with") (Locke 1960: 288). Such arguments are met with stiff resistance in the form of accusations that property is theft, or – in Rousseau's celebrated account – that the recognition of property is a type of confidence trick, backed up by the state's laws. As Rousseau put it, "The first man who, having enclosed a piece of ground, bethought himself of saying 'This is mine,' and found people simple enough to believe him, was the real founder of civil society" (Rousseau 1966: 192) with all its crimes, horrors, and misfortunes. The primary modern justification for private ownership, however, is instrumental: that it is conducive to greater exertion in one's own interest and consequently to the greater public benefit (by some mechanism such as Adam Smith's "invisible hand"). Communists, however, continue to insist not just that property has adverse social effects, but also that there is no proper moral foundation for private ownership.

The chief inspiration for the prohibition of private property in communist works is moral: the abandonment of private ownership of goods and property will heighten the sense of community and produce social harmony, as people cease putting their private interest above the collective good. Communist proposals have consequently appeared in many different types of productive system, from simple agrarian and slave-owning societies, through feudal societies, to modern, industrial societies. These proposals have relied not so much on hopes of abundance to satisfy the community, but on the voluntary curbing of appetites and wants to distribute equally what is available.

These moral ideas have sometimes found more practical expression. In addition to the early Christians, a small group of Diggers in seventeenth-century England advocated agrarian communism on the grounds that God had given the earth to humankind in common, but once they tried to cultivate unenclosed common land in 1649 they were crushed by the authorities. More than a century later, however, the French Revolution of 1789–99 ushered in the modern era and, with it, a profound change in approach to political ideas. As the culmination of the Enlightenment, the revolution gave encouragement to the measuring of existing political and social arrangements against ideals. It thereby gave a fillip to many older ideas, including communism, though there was a growing recognition that industry – with its potential to create vast amounts of new wealth – signaled the dawn of a new age. Nevertheless, communism of the traditional variety appeared during the revolution in the form of Gracchus Babeuf and the Society of Equals (1794–7), conspirators who wanted a revolutionary overthrow of authority and the establishment of a community based on equality. Babeuf declared in his *Manifesto of the Equals* (1796) that ownership and inequality were the source of all evil. He advocated that all should work, but that consumption should be modest. The conspiracy was discovered and suppressed by the French authorities, but Babeuf's ideas were passed on to the socialism that emerged in the 1820s and 1830s through the work of a surviving co-conspirator, Filippo Buonarroti.

Socialism and communism are different concepts, but they have overlapped during the last 170 years. Their core differences may be summed up by saying that the abolition of private ownership to produce equal distribution was the central prescription of pre-nineteenth century communism, while conscious and rational organization of economic activity as a basis for abundance is the major prescription of socialism. Durkheim explained the distinction between socialism and communism with great clarity, arguing that communism had appeared throughout recorded history as a moral critique of private consumption, while socialism "was able to appear only at a very advanced moment in social evolution" related to the emergence of industry (Durkheim 1962: 76). Communism therefore is about communal consumption; socialism is an attempt by society to direct its productive activities to the benefit of all. In an important respect, socialism – by assuming the creation of abundance – transcends the key

questions of distribution to which communism was a response.

Diverse systems of socialism emerged in nineteenth-century England, France, and Germany, but they were all concerned with overcoming the disorder and human misery of modern, industrializing, market societies. Socialism was unified not in its prescriptions, but in its concerns. Pierre Leroux put his finger on it when in 1835 he contrasted socialism and individualism. Socialists put *society* at the center of their field of vision and concern. They rebelled against the growing acceptance of economic activity freed from its more limited and instrumental role in managing the household, and becoming an end in itself.

There is a clear affinity between the egalitarian and communitarian themes within pre-socialist communism, and the critique of unrestrained individualism devised by the socialists. But socialism and communism interacted in unexpected ways, more influenced by historical accident than theoretical logic. Socialists were of course keen to claim historical precursors, but the fact that Marx chose to entitle the 1848 *Communist Manifesto* as "communist" rather than "socialist" indicates that he saw it as more radical and more worker-oriented than the schemes of his socialist competitors. Communism thus emerged as the revolutionary and proletarian wing of the socialist movement. Marx's theoretical achievement was to harness modern communism to the emerging industrial working class in a historical story of class struggle that described the growing tensions and inevitable clashes between proletarians and capitalists. As Marx famously declared in the *Communist Manifesto*: "The history of all hitherto existing society is the history of class struggles" (Marx & Engels 1969a: 108). The modern class struggle and the victory of the proletariat, however, would be succeeded by the triumph of the universal human interest, of which the proletariat was the bearer: "The proletarian movement is the self-conscious, independent movement of the immense majority, in the interests of the immense majority" (p. 118).

For Marx, the greatest of the socialist thinkers, the key problem of capitalism was scarcity and its social effects, which he summed up in the concept of alienation. Humans were alienated from their products, from their human essence, from other humans, and from their own society. Communism was about creating a genuinely human society, the details of which were always sketchy and sometimes conflicting, but the precondition of which was material abundance. Humans would move, as Marx put it, from the current realm of necessity to the realm of freedom. According to Marx, the highest development of the productive forces "is an absolutely necessary practical premise [of communism] because without it *want* is merely made general, and with *destitution* the struggle for necessities and all the old filthy business would necessarily be reproduced" (Marx & Engels 1969b: 37). But the principle of distribution in Marx's communism, the end-point of this entire process, would not be egalitarian, but rather: "From each according to his ability, to each according to his needs!" (Marx 1970: 19).

Marx's disciple V. I. Lenin adopted the title "communist" – and his Russian Social Democratic Labor Party (Bolshevik) changed its name to the Russian Communist Party in 1918 – to indicate adherence to "genuine" Marxism and revolutionary social change. The term "communist" was, once again, employed to indicate a divide within the socialist movement. Lenin's communism was distinguished by its stress on leadership of the working class, a commitment to revolution as the forceful overthrow of the bourgeois state, and the creation of a "dictatorship of the proletariat." After the Russian Revolution of November 1917, which ultimately removed Russia from the blood-bath of World War I, communist parties were confirmed as the revolutionary wing of the socialist movement. Communists were fortified by the swingeing attack on war-mongering as the necessary consequence of capitalist monopoly that Lenin launched in his 1917 pamphlet *Imperialism, The Highest Stage of Capitalism*: "The more capitalism is developed, the more strongly the shortage of raw materials is felt, the more intense the competition and the hunt for sources of raw materials throughout the whole world, the more desperate the struggle for the acquisition of colonies" (Lenin 1975: 695) The destruction of capitalism had become vital to the survival of humanity. The

transition to communism, however, was complicated by threats from external enemies and by the discipline required by its major phases, the "dictatorship of the proletariat" and "socialism." Talk of "phases" in the development of communism rightly signaled that the transformation in human relations envisaged by communists would not occur overnight, but it also provided communist leaders with a store of convenient excuses for much of the conflict, misery, and disappointment their citizens had to endure.

Communism held sway in a number of "fraternal" (but ultimately mutually hostile) states during the twentieth century: in the Soviet Union from 1917 to 1991; in Eastern Europe from 1949 to 1989; in China from 1949 onwards; and in some Asian and African states and Cuba from the 1950s. This system was eventually established in at least 14 countries, encompassing perhaps one-third of the world's population at its height. Communists aimed to build a new type of human society, based on solidarity and the fulfilment of people's needs, but most of these states collapsed near the end of the twentieth century under the combined weight of elite disillusionment and popular discontent. The general shape of the communist system was similar across these states, but it owed far more to the practical exigencies of the first communist state, the Russian traditions it inherited, and Lenin's unshakeable belief in the Bolsheviks' duty to take and keep power, than to any theoretical blueprint. The key feature of this system is the directing role of the communist party, and the consequent subordination of all constitutional forms, and all social and economic activity, to the party's rule. Rival parties were not tolerated. National variations modified this tenet only slightly. There were strong links between the party leader's personal style and the behavior and policies of communist governments. Decision-making was conducted chiefly within the party, out of public gaze or control. Rule was maintained by a combination of manufactured "consent" based on ideology and outright coercion. This model of top-down party control meant the centralized control of all key appointments within party and state, strict party discipline, and party supremacy over state institutions.

For all its theoretical stress on the role of vast historical forces, especially social classes, modern communism has been extraordinarily leader-centric. Leaders have been crucial in organizing and maintaining communist parties, in part because of their political skills, and in part because of their (sometimes overstated) theoretical abilities. Leaders' actions have proved decisive in the success or failure of attempts at revolution. And the intellectual, political, and personal styles of their leaders have given a distinctive tone to each of the communist states. Lenin is the acknowledged model of a communist leader, though few others have shared his abilities. Yet even after the shortcomings and crimes of Joseph Stalin were conceded by his successors, emerging leaders such as Mao Zedong, Fidel Castro, and Che Guevara were able in the 1950s and 1960s to give communism a new lease on life by their anti-imperialist rhetoric and their dashing image. Just as Mao in his quest to take power in China had made a revolutionary place for the peasantry in communist theory, so Castro and Guevara gave a fillip to anti-imperialism by promoting the role of guerrilla warfare. In his 1961 manual on *Guerrilla Warfare*, Guevara identified three lessons from the Cuban Revolution: "(1) Popular forces can win a war against the army. (2) It is not necessary to wait until all conditions for making revolution exist; the insurrection can create them. (3) In underdeveloped America the countryside is the basic area for armed fighting" (Guevara 1985: 47). Guevara's death in Bolivia on a guerrilla mission has sustained a romantic view of his life that is no longer enjoyed by either his comrade-in-arms, the aged dictator Castro, or the deeply flawed Mao.

Fundamental to modern communism is state ownership of at least the major means of production, distribution, and exchange, on the grounds that this would end the exploitation that marred previous human affairs, and would produce the abundance which Marx anticipated. Decisions about what to produce, how much, and when, are made politically and administratively, and not by information supplied by a market. This type of economy, which communists attempted to plan, has given rise to numerous problems. As the communist system was established largely in underdeveloped countries, state control was an effective device for industrialization (despite its human costs). Yet the growing complexity of an industrialized economy diminished the ability of planning to control it, and it ultimately proved much less productive and more wasteful than the market.

The communist experiment in state power and central economic planning was disappointing. Despite the enthusiasm with which it began, communism turned out to mean a privileged ruling elite and a subject population; it achieved neither liberty nor equality; and it was unable to innovate or change easily. Many of the achievements of Soviet communism were nevertheless undeniable, including its role in the defeat of Hitler and its rapid rebuilding into a "superpower" after the devastation of World War II.

Not surprisingly, there has been great debate about how far the communist states ever approximated the communist – or socialist – ideal. Those who are disheartened at the inequality, waste, and alienation of capitalist societies have few positive resources from the communist experiment on which to rely for solutions. Leninist communism now has few adherents; but more importantly for this essay, it undermined the belief that common ownership would remove the sources of tyranny and exploitation. And it revealed how difficult it is to replace individual motivation for betterment with a communal motivation.

Socialism introduced the hope that production could be organized in such a way as to deliver abundance, and thus that the issues of distribution that have bedeviled human societies would be overcome. If material abundance could, in fact, be achieved, would this end all the divisions within society? Such an outcome seems implausible. As concern over the conquest of material scarcity declines, demand for socially scarce goods, wherein satisfaction is derived from relative position, increases (Hirsch 1977). Competition does not end, its locus merely shifts. But seriously to anticipate material abundance itself is heroic. It seems much more likely that humans will continue to be confronted by scarcity, as their wants inexorably outstrip the ability to satisfy them, and so questions of distribution will not disappear. Conflicts over the allocation of scarce resources, over the values by which we orient our lives, and over our identities will continue. Politics is one way of acknowledging and managing conflicts in a civilized way. Yet communism has no developed political theory, because the harmony it envisages leaves little room for politics.

The twentieth-century communist movement was distinguished by its stress on revolutionary methods, its reliance on a disciplined revolutionary party and centralized economic planning, its lack of political freedom, and ultimately by its lack of economic success. It is unlikely to make a major resurgence. What will survive, however, is the moral critique of individualism that is at the heart of the communist ideal. If it is ever to be a serious political program, communists must begin to explore the institutional and other consequences of dealing with evil and error in human affairs, not simply expecting that they will disappear with the abolition of private property. But perhaps communism is destined to endure not as a serious model for an alternative social and political system, but as a moral beacon for those frustrated by rampant individualism and disgusted by the increasing commodification of life in market societies.

SEE ALSO: Bourgeoisie and Proletariat; Capitalism; Individualism; Marx, Karl; Socialism

REFERENCES AND SUGGESTED READINGS

Aristotle (1988) *The Politics*. Ed. S. Everson. Cambridge University Press, Cambridge.
Bodin, J. (1967) *Six Books of the Commonwealth*. Trans. M. J.Tooley. Blackwell, Oxford.
Durkheim, E. (1962) *Socialism*. Ed. A. W. Gouldner. Collier Books, New York.
Guevara, C. (1985) *Guerrilla Warfare*. Trans. J. P. Morray. University of Nebraska Press, Lincoln.
Hirsch, F. (1977) *Social Limits to Growth*. Routledge & Kegan Paul, London.
Lenin, V. I. (1975) *Imperialism, The Highest Stage of Capitalism: A Popular Outline*. In: Lenin, V. I., *Selected Works in Three Volumes*, Vol. 1. Progress Publishers, Moscow, pp. 634–731.
Locke, J. (1960) *Two Treatises of Government*. Ed. P. Laslett. Cambridge University Press, Cambridge.
Marx, K. (1970) Critique of the Gotha Programme. In: Marx, K. & Engels, F., *Selected Works*, Vol. 3. Progress Publishers, Moscow, pp. 9–30.
Marx, K. & Engels, F. (1969a) *Manifesto of the Communist Party*. In: Marx, K. & Engels, F.,
Selected Works, Vol. 1. Progress Publishers, Moscow, pp. 98–137.
Marx, K. & Engels, F. (1969b) *The German Ideology*. In: Marx, K. & Engels, F., *Selected Works*, Vol. 1. Progress Publishers, Moscow, pp. 16–80.
More, T. (1989) *Utopia*. Ed. G. M. Logan & R. M. Adams. Cambridge University Press, Cambridge.
Rousseau, J.-J. (1966) *The Social Contract and Discourses*. Trans. G. D. H. Cole. Dent, London.

community

Graham Crow

"Community" is concerned with people having something in common, although there is much debate about precisely what that thing is. The most conventional approach relates to people sharing a geographical area (typically a neighborhood), an idea captured in references to *local* communities. Place is central to such an understanding because of the assumption that people are necessarily brought together by the fact of living in close proximity. This view is contested by those who argue that shared place does not always promote social connections between people. It is an established axiom of urban sociology that modern city spaces can be characterized as anonymous and impersonal, devoid of the collective connectedness associated with the idea of "community." Indeed, the theme of urbanization and increased geographical mobility leading to a loss of traditional patterns of community has been a very powerful one in sociological thought from the very beginning of the discipline. Against this background, the search for the basis of community has led other writers to highlight the importance of people being brought together by common interests or by common identities, neither of which requires co-presence. Occupational communities such as the academic community provide one example of groups of people whose common interests derived from work-based attachments may hold them together despite their being geographically dispersed, while religious communities illustrate the parallel point that a community of identity does not necessitate members being together in the same place. In this vein, Benedict Anderson has described nations as "imagined communities" whose members cannot possibly all have close, face-to-face connections.

Whether the basis of a community is common residence, common interest, common identity, or some combination of these factors, it is necessarily the case that the relationships that are involved will be exclusive to some degree. Put another way, communities operate by distinguishing those who belong ("insiders") from those who do not ("outsiders"). Community is an important dimension of social divisions as well as togetherness because inclusion in community relationships promises benefits (such as access to material resources, social support, or raised social status) that set members apart from others. A strong sense of this difference from non-members, of "us" and "them," is a characteristic of some of the most tightly bonded communities. Conversely, communities to which access is more open are correspondingly looser entities whose members do not have such a marked group identity, loyalty, and solidarity. People's sense of belonging to communities thus varies considerably in its intensity. The same point about variation applies to the degree of commitment that communities require of their members. The contrast between communities that bind members together tightly through similarity and those that have more points of connection with outside groups is captured in the distinction between the two types of social capital, respectively "bonding" and "bridging," that Robert Putnam develops in *Bowling Alone* (2000).

A fourth dimension of communities alongside common residence, interests, and identity is common synchronization of activities, that is, coming together in time. There are several respects in which communities are dynamic phenomena that are marked by variation in people's ability to synchronize their involvement. To begin with, communities are characterized by what Albert Hirschman (1985) calls "shifting involvements." This is most obvious in groups that see the degree of engagement of individual members change as they struggle to combine involvement in that community with their rival commitments to work, to family, and to other communities of which they may also be

a part. Individuals' degrees of involvement vary considerably, both in the short term and over the life course. It is true more generally that communities are engaged in a constant process of recruitment of new participants to replace those who leave. These recruits may need to pass through a period of probation and a ritual of acceptance before they are treated as full members. Ritual events are also an important part of communities' calendars, serving to bring members together both physically and emotionally. The ordinariness of community relationships in people's everyday lives needs to be reinforced periodically by extraordinary gatherings such as carnivals and conferences that celebrate the purpose, achievements, and memory of the community and thereby strengthen members' attachments to the collectivity. Such occasions may also be used to underpin the legitimacy of community leaders, and where necessary to sanction the transfer of power from one cohort of leaders to the next.

The political dimension of community has received a good deal of attention from researchers. Community leaders are not necessarily typical of the constituencies that they claim to represent, notably in terms of social class, age, gender, ethnicity, and disability. Formal political processes are skewed toward favoring those with more resources at their disposal, and in consequence the realm of community politics is typified by contestation over who has most authority to speak for communities. The sphere of community politics also brings to the fore disagreements about strategy concerning the relative merits of following established political procedures compared to community-based direct action. Studies of community involvement in the redevelopment of rundown urban areas that are home to heterogeneous populations highlight the difficulties of seeking to give equal voice to the various groups that have a stake in the process, such as long-established working-class populations, middle-class gentrifiers, ethnic minority in-migrants, and commercial developers. Janet Foster's *Docklands* (1999) is one such study showing that in such settings "community" potentially has more of the character of an arena of conflict than of a body of people with shared interests and identities, although it is the latter perspective of common goals that is emphasized in the rhetoric of community development.

The ideal of community cohesion is one of several powerful forces working toward the creation and reproduction of spatially segregated homogeneous residential communities. The early twentieth-century studies in the Chicago School tradition of research revealed the tendency for migrants to cities to congregate in ethnic enclaves, and segregation along ethnic lines in encapsulated communities remains a marked characteristic of urban settlement patterns. "White flight" from urban centers to suburbia and to rural areas is another manifestation of this phenomenon. Spatial polarization of populations is also the product of economic forces, with many neighborhoods having distinctive social class profiles. People's wish to live among others like themselves also reflects further dimensions of social difference such as age, as occurs in retirement communities. Gated communities are an increasingly common expression of the cultural ideal of community homogeneity and the exclusion of outsiders, although arguably they are better seen as the product of particular planning regimes and property developers' marketing strategies than as the product of spontaneous preferences. In other historical and political contexts urban planners and developers have sought to create "mixed communities" (the British New Towns of the mid-twentieth century are a good example), as part of a deliberate policy of challenging spatial expressions of social divisions.

The pursuit by policymakers of community as an ideal extends far beyond the realm of housing development. A number of policy initiatives in fields as diverse as architecture, the arts, education, health, policing, and the delivery of care services have all been designated types of community work. Such initiatives are underpinned by the assumption of consensus concerning the desirability of promoting "community." This assumption has been challenged by those who see state-sponsored community work as an unwelcome means of extending control over communities that threatens to undermine their autonomy, diversity, and authenticity. An alternative critique highlights the use of community initiatives as a way of reducing welfare state responsibilities for the provision of services, as a result of which community members are required to be more reliant on their own resources. Both of these rival critiques bring into question the view that "community" is always regarded positively. That said, the traditional association of the absence of community with social problems and social exclusion remains a powerful one, as does the idea that the promotion of community can help to solve those problems. Recent debates have sometimes operated with the notions of "civil society" and "social capital" as alternative conceptualizations of "community," but the same points apply whatever terminology is used.

The study of community presents researchers with a number of methodological challenges. The exclusive nature of communities makes it difficult for outsiders to gain ready access, and the processes of negotiating entry and gaining trust can be lengthy. This is one of the reasons why several classic community studies have involved years (and in certain cases decades) of fieldwork. Another reason for community research requiring extensive periods of fieldwork is the ambitiousness of aspiring to research all of the various aspects of "community" and their interconnections. Classic studies such as Robert and Helen Lynd's *Middletown* (1929) have typically sought to report on community members' patterns of work, family relationships and life course transitions, education, leisure activities, religious practices, and political organization; these dimensions of community relationships constitute a substantial research agenda. A further set of difficulties relates to the question of how to compare the findings of different community studies, given that every community is to some extent unique. These are not insuperable problems, however, and community researchers have proved themselves adept at overcoming methodological obstacles. It is possible, for example, for researchers to study communities of which they are already members, or to undertake research as part of a team (although each of these solutions throws up its own problems). It is also possible for rigorous comparative work to be undertaken using the same research instruments in different communities, while re-studies of the same community can also be undertaken to rebut criticism of this type of research as being of limited value in capturing social change.

Arguably the most enduring challenge facing community researchers relates to the definition and operationalization of the concept of "community." The corruption of Ferdinand Tönnies's distinction between *Gemeinschaft* and *Gesellschaft* (translated as "community" and "association") into the idea that a continuum could be identified between strong rural communities and urban social patterns that lacked depth and durability has rightly been criticized for its geographical determinism: people's "community" relationships are not the simple product of their spatial location. It is quite another thing to acknowledge that local context matters to how people live their everyday lives, and ethnography is a favored tool among researchers who seek to capture the nuances of particular community settings. Immersion in a community allows ethnographers to capture the distinctiveness of its culture and to appreciate how belonging to that community is understood by its members. Other approaches focus less on the symbolic meaning of community and more on the mechanics of its operation. Social network analysis has proved particularly illuminating regarding the nature, purpose, and extent of people's connections to others, and it is more open than ethnography is to quantification. Barry Wellman has used this approach to argue convincingly that technological developments in communications (including the development of Internet communities) have freed individuals from dependence on others in their vicinity. Nevertheless, network analysis also reveals that many people's community ties continue to have a strong local component, especially if family and kin members are included in that calculation. Overall, research findings point to the continuing importance of communities of all types, both place-based and others. These findings cast doubt on those general theories of social change that anticipate the demise of community.

SEE ALSO: Chicago School; Civil Society; Community and Economy; Family and Community; Imagined Communities; Networks; New Urbanism; Place; Social Network Theory; Retirement Communities; Social Capital; Solidarity; Tönnies, Ferdinand; Urban Community Studies

REFERENCES AND SUGGESTED READINGS

Anderson, B. (1991) *Imagined Communities: Reflections on the Origin and Spread of Nationalism.* Verso, London.

Foster, J. (1999) *Docklands: Cultures in Conflict, Worlds in Collision.* UCL Press, London.

Hirschman, A. (1985) *Shifting Involvements: Private Interest and Public Action.* Blackwell, Oxford.

Lynd, R. & Lynd, H. (1929) *Middletown.* Harcourt Brace, New York.

Putnam, R. (2000) *Bowling Alone: The Collapse and Revival of American Community.* Simon & Schuster, New York.

Tönnies, F. (1955) *Community and Association.* Routledge & Kegan Paul, London.

Wellman, B. & Berkowitz, S. (Eds.) (1988) *Social Structures: A Network Approach.* Cambridge University Press, Cambridge.

community college

Regina Deil-Amen, Tenisha Tevis, and Jinchun Yu

Although American community colleges (formerly known as junior colleges) have existed since the late nineteenth century, little sociological attention has been paid to these institutions until recently. The conceptual frameworks that do exist highlight the juxtaposition of the community college's function of expanding access to higher education while also limiting opportunity for many students.

In the first two decades of the twentieth century, as secondary school enrollments increased rapidly and the demand for college access grew, university leaders and local school district officials advocated four different models of junior colleges: the junior college, that is, the lower division of a college of liberal arts or a university; normal schools accredited for two years of college work; public high schools extended to include the lower division of college work; and small private colleges limited to two-year college work (Levinson 2005: 51). Presidents of many leading universities tried to emulate the German elite university model that focused on highly specialized professional training and research and to reduce the number of their freshmen and sophomores. They saw the two-year junior college idea both as an upward extension of the high school and as a primary means of responding to the demand from working-class parents and local communities for access to elite higher education. They believed the creation of the junior college system could function as a buffer zone to protect the university by diverting those clamoring for access, leaving the university free to pursue its tasks of research and advanced professional training (Brint & Karabel 1989).

Previously enrolling only about 10 percent of all undergraduates, the community college experienced unprecedented growth in the three decades following World War II. Between 1944 and 1947 community college enrollment doubled as more than 250,000 new students registered for classes. Community colleges grew exponentially in the 1960s and 1970s (Dougherty 1994). Since the 1980s the number of community colleges has stabilized at over 1,100, or over one fourth of all higher education institutions in the US. This level of enrollment accounts for 45 percent of first-time college students and 37 percent of all undergraduates in US colleges and universities.

As a great invention of US higher education in the twentieth century, the community college has made college accessible to those people who may otherwise not be able to attend any college, especially to the working-class and minority populations who were traditionally under-represented in four-year colleges. Because of its open-door admissions policy, low tuition cost, diversity of course offerings, and flexible course schedule, community college is actually accessible to every applicant who may even not finish high school and is touted by its proponents as "democracy's college" or "people's college."

Despite the fact that the low tuition and very low or open admissions policies of community colleges make these institutions a major entryway into college for poor students, racial minorities, lower-achieving, part-time, commuting,

and adult students, surprisingly few sociologists have focused on these institutions and their students. However, several key researchers have illuminated our understanding of the stratifying role that community colleges have played in the expansion of higher education and college access. Lower-class and minority students are still disadvantaged in community colleges in terms of persistence rates and transfer rates. In particular, community colleges are criticized for systematically "cooling out" many of their students' bachelor degree aspirations by channeling them into terminal vocational programs (Clark 1960). The term cooling out is used to describe the process by which community colleges urge students to recognize their academic deficiencies and lower their aspirations (Clark 1960; Karabel 1977). Students are persuaded to lower their original plans for a BA degree and to aim for a one or two-year degree in a vocational or applied program. Colleges accomplish this cooling out by a combination of pre-entrance testing, counseling, orientation classes, notices of unsatisfactory work, further counseling referrals, and probation.

Inspired by Clark's classic idea that community colleges perform the function of cooling out students' bachelor's degree aspirations, Brint and Karabel (1989) challenged the view of community colleges as institutions that democratized higher education by allowing access to those formerly excluded from postsecondary education. The original mission behind the creation of the first community colleges was to offer high school graduates the first two-year college work and then transfer them to four-year colleges for upper division of college work. Most community colleges in the early · years were thus transfer-oriented liberal arts institutions from where students could transfer credits to a four-year college to complete their baccalaureate degree. Although community college advocates in the early years also emphasized vocational education as an essential part of the two-year college curriculum and some early community colleges did offer vocational programs, such semiprofessional training programs were resisted by most students as "dead end" ones and seldom attracted over one third of the total enrollments in any institution.

Brint and Karabel (1989) posit an institutionally based argument in which early community college leaders pushed for the vocationalization of the curriculum in an effort to ensure the legitimacy and survival of an institution that was structurally located at the bottom of the higher education hierarchy and therefore could not compete with the higher status four-year colleges and universities. As a result, community colleges diverted would-be four-year college students toward two-year degrees intended to prepare them for technical and semi-professional occupations rather than transfer to a four-year college.

Dougherty (1994) expands this institutional framework by analyzing the interests and actions of state and government officials in occupationalizing community colleges at the expense of students pursuing transfer goals, who, given their often weak academic preparation, suffer from obstacles that persist due to the institution's inability to perform its contradictory and often competing functions successfully.

Sociologists tend to discuss these dynamics in the context of research that reveals that two-year colleges are associated with a lower educational attainment. A study by Lee and Frank (1990) showed that, four years after graduating from high school, only a quarter of those who enrolled in a community college had transferred to a four-year college, suggesting that attending a community college decreases a student's chances of completing a four-year degree. Dougherty (1994) reports findings from several studies that reveal a sizable gap of 11–19 percent in baccalaureate attainment between community college entrants and comparable four-year college students. Only a handful of sociologists have attempted to identify the institutional mechanisms that lie at the root of this discrepancy. Dougherty suggests that community colleges present an institutional hindrance to those with bachelor's degree aspirations for several reasons, including fewer opportunities for social integration, difficulties obtaining financial aid, and loss of credits for those who do manage to transfer to four-year institutions. He draws upon the research of Weis (1985) and others to suggest that the peer cultures in community colleges discourage academic work, and community college faculty's low expectations and tendency to concentrate on a few promising students while largely giving up on the rest may be partially responsible as well.

The extent to which the institutional disadvantages of community college attendance result from pre- or post-transfer processes has barely been studied at all by sociologists. Some suggest that the minority of community college students who do manage to transfer are no less likely to complete a baccalaureate degree than are "native" students who began at a four-year college. This finding, coupled with the reality of very low community college transfer rates, suggests that the disadvantage does stem from the community college experience. On the other hand, Rosenbaum (2001) explains that part of the reason why some students are not finishing college is that high school counselors view community colleges as providing a second chance for all students, regardless of past effort and achievement. They therefore operate according to a "college-for-all" norm that encourages nearly all students to attend college despite their level of effort, achievement, and preparation. However, this leads to unrealistic educational plans for students who are unprepared for college. In partial contradiction to the community college studies noted above, Deil-Amen and Rosenbaum (2002) find this college-for-all philosophy continuing into the community college setting, where remedial students are encouraged toward their bachelor's degree goals, yet remain uninformed of the gravity of their lack of academic preparation and unaware of their low likelihood of completion. Rather than a diversion toward a lower alternative – a two-year degree in a more vocationally oriented major – most of these students leave college with no degree at all.

Deil-Amen and Rosenbaum (2003) also analyze the differences between community colleges and for-profit and non-profit occupationally oriented colleges and suggest that the minimized bureaucratic hurdles, focused organizational priorities, structured programs, proactive and extensive financial aid counseling, academic advising, and job placement assistance at the occupational colleges can serve as a useful model to enhance retention among similar low-income students at community colleges.

Other recent studies employ a policy oriented perspective and note community colleges' increased focus on workforce preparation, particularly in the form of short-term certificate and contract training programs (Dougherty & Bakia 2000). Shaw and Rab (2003) question this shift and the additional pressures for accountability that face today's community colleges. Their insightful comparative case study reveals the barriers to college access among low-income populations that are created when federal policies encourage community colleges to respond to the needs of the business community as their primary "customer." Others analyze the ways in which ideologies and welfare reform policies have decreased college access and enrollment among recipients of public aid.

Although there is domestic controversy over the future of the US community college, most countries in Europe and Asia have supported creation of two-year colleges similar to American community colleges. In addition to transfer and vocational education, continuing and developmental education, and community education are also critical components of the comprehensive community college curriculum in the US. A new measure taken by community colleges in the 1970s was that "contract" or "customized" training programs tailored to the needs of particular employers were added to community college vocational offerings. Additionally, since the late 1980s, the clear separation between academic and vocational programs has disappeared, and vocational students are now as likely as academic students to transfer to four-year colleges.

SEE ALSO: Colleges and Universities; Educational Attainment; Schooling and Economic Success

REFERENCES AND SUGGESTED READINGS

Adelman, C. (1992) *The Way We Are: The Community College as American Thermometer*. US Government Printing Office, Washington, DC.

Brint, S. & Karabel, J. (1989) *The Diverted Dream: Community Colleges and the Promise of Educational Opportunity in America, 1900–1985*. Oxford University Press, New York.

Clark, B. R. (1960) The "Cooling Out" Function in Higher Education. *American Journal of Sociology* 60(6): 569–76.

Cohen, A. M. & Brawer, F. B. (2003) *The American Community College*, 4th edn. Jossey-Bass, San Francisco.

Deil-Amen, R. & Rosenbaum, J. E. (2002) The Unintended Consequences of Stigma-Free Remediation. *Sociology of Education* 75: 249–68.

Deil-Amen, R. & Rosenbaum, J. E. (2003) The Social Prerequisites of Success: Can College Structure Reduce the Need for Social Know-How? *ANNALS, AAPSS* 586 (March): 120–43.

Diener, T. (1986) *Growth of an American Invention: A Documentary History of the Junior and Community College Movement*. Greenwood Press, New York.

Dougherty, K. J. (1994) *The Contradictory Community College: The Conflicting Origins, Impacts, and Futures of the Community College*. State University of New York Press, Albany.

Dougherty, K. J. & Bakia, M. (2000) Community Colleges and Contract Training: Content, Origins, and Impact. *Teachers College Record* 102 (February): 197–243.

Grubb, N. W. (1996) *Working in the Middle: Strengthening Education and Training for the Mid-Skilled Labor Force*. Jossey-Bass, San Francisco.

Karabel, J. (1977) Community Colleges and Social Stratification: Submerged Class Conflict in American Higher Education. In: Karabel, J. & Halsey, A. H. (Ed.), *Power and Ideology in Education*. Oxford University Press, New York, pp. 232–54.

Lee, V. & Frank, K. A. (1990) Students' Characteristics that Facilitate Transfer from Two-Year to Four-Year Colleges. *Sociology of Education* 63(3): 178–93.

Leigh, D. E. & Gill, A. M. (2004) The Effect of Community Colleges on Changing Students' Educational Aspirations. *Economics of Education Review* 23: 95–102.

Levinson, D. L. (2005) *Community Colleges: A Reference Handbook*. ABC-CLIO, Santa Barbara.

Rosenbaum, J. E. (2001) *Beyond College For All: Career Paths of the Forgotten Half*. Russell Sage Foundation, New York.

Shaw, K. M. & Rab, S. (2003) Market Rhetoric versus Reality in Policy and Practice: The Workforce Investment Act and Access to Community College Education and Training. *Annals of the American Academy of Political and Social Science* 586: 172–93.

Tinto, V. (1993) *Leaving College: Rethinking the Causes and Cures of Student Attrition*, 2nd edn. University of Chicago Press, Chicago.

Weis, L. (1985) *Between Two Worlds: Black Students in an Urban Community College*. Routledge & Kegan Paul, Boston.

community and economy

Amitai Etzioni

Community and economy are two distinct realms of social life. In communities, we largely deal with one another as persons. We value people not only in their own right, but also as neighbors, friends, and those with whom we share a concern for the common good. In the economy, we largely deal with one another as buyers and sellers, as consumers and marketers, and as management and labor. In this realm we often seek to maximize our self-interest. In Martin Buber's (1971) terms, the community is the realm of the I-Thou, the economy that of the I-It. The opposition is not complete. Some people will seek advantage in the realm of community; for example, they may seek to form business connections in the country club. Other people do develop relationships of friendship and loyalty at work. Still, there are basic differences between the two social realms that exist along the lines previously mentioned.

Societies differ according to the relative importance and scope that they accord to community and economy. In earlier historical periods, most if not all societies were more community minded and less economically minded. The terms modernization and industrialization, or the rise of capitalism, are used as markers to indicate when the economy rose in importance and the community declined in importance. In recent decades, societies such as China and India have begun moving in the same direction as other societies did before them. Even today, societies differ significantly in the value that they place on economic achievement versus nurturing various communal goals.

The US is widely regarded as the society most concerned with productivity, profit, efficiency, and other such economic goals. Americans work longer hours (Anderson 2003) and have fewer vacation days (Valenti 2003) than those who live in other industrialized countries.

There are two profoundly different ways of thinking about the relationship between the realm of community and that of the economy.

One treats the economy (sometimes referred to as the market) as self-sustaining and self-regulating. People in the economy are said to seek to increase their well-being. They realize that they can best serve this goal by a division of labor in which each participant specializes in making some product or service and selling it. The division of labor in turn leads to a natural coming together of interests and hence the "market" requires no regulation from outsiders. On the contrary, "interventions" in the market tend to "distort" the market, and make it less efficient. People who subscribe to libertarian and *laissez-faire* conservative social philosophies, as well as many mainstream economists, hold this view.

In contrast, others view the economy as a subsystem of the society; that is, the economy is embedded in society. The society provides a capsule of sorts, which contains the economy, sets goals for it, and guides it through values and political instruments. (This is the main point of an influential book by Parsons and Smelser, 1956.) Government regulations, for instance, limit what the market can do in order to protect workers, children, consumers, and the environment, among other social assets. The government also seeks to affect the economy through its various tax, budgetary, and federal banking policies. The purpose of this is to stimulate the economy to grow faster, to prevent it from overheating (driving prices too high), to smooth out the business cycle, and to increase savings and many other socioeconomic goals. From the second viewpoint the issue is not whether an economy can and should be guided or interfered with, but rather what is the extent to which such interventions are needed and what are the proper interventions. Many liberals, social democrats, and social scientists hold this viewpoint.

The first viewpoint, that of treating the economy as free standing and not as an integral part of society (and community), tends implicitly to assume that the actors are small and hence powerless vis-à-vis the market. It views the economy as composed of many hundreds of thousands of shop keepers, small businesses, and workers. None of them can control the market and the market guides their behavior. Thus if a corporation would set prices above what the market "tolerates," then it is said that such a corporation would be unable to sell its products, and if it set them too low, it would be unable to cover its costs. In either case, those who do not abide by the market will soon be out of business. In contrast, the second view sees the markets as being subject to manipulation by larger corporations that control large segments of the economy. Various antitrust policies have been used over the years to break up such power over the market, although most of these attempts have not been very effective.

To illustrate, George J. Stigler (1968), a Nobel Laureate in economics, argued that the farmers have no say on the price of their products, as each competes with many thousands of others. However, Stigler ignored the rise of agribusiness and larger farming corporations: Oxfam estimates that in the US, 50 percent of all agricultural products come from 2 percent of the farms, 98 percent of poultry comes from large corporations, 80 percent of beef comes from just four firms, and 60 percent of pork comes from four firms (McCauley 2002). Stigler also ignored the fact that farmers use their political power – which they exercise "outside" the economy, in the society – to set prices and improve their returns. This is done through gaining subsidies, obtaining credit below market terms, and limiting entry into their markets (via import quotas).

SOCIOECONOMIC BEHAVIORS

Individuals are, simultaneously, under the influence of two major sets of factors: their pleasure and their moral duty (Etzioni 1988). There are important differences in the extent to which each of these goals drives economic behavior, and which sets of factors are different under different historical and social conditions, and within different personalities under the same conditions. Hence, a study of the dynamics of the forces that shape both kinds of factors and their relative strengths is an essential foundation for a valid theory of behavior and society, including economic behavior (a key subject for the science of socioeconomics).

The independent effects of social values versus prices can be highlighted by the findings of the combined role of information and values in a four-year field experiment with the time-of-day pricing of residential electricity in Wisconsin (Stern & Aronson 1984). Individuals were experimentally assigned to a variety of electricity rate structures. Those individuals who believed that lowered demand in peak periods would be good for the community (e.g., by allowing utilities to shut down inefficient and polluting power plants) and who also believed that households as a group could make a big difference in peak demand, felt a moral obligation to lower electricity use in peak periods (Black n.d.). People who felt an obligation to change their behavior had lower electricity bills than people who felt no moral obligation, but who were charged the same electricity rates.

Another study correlates both income and social/moral attitudes with tax compliance (as measured by the propensity to evade paying taxes that are due). It found that income correlated somewhat more strongly with compliance than did moral attitudes, but only after the study broke rejection of the governing regime, policies, or values into six factors. Even given this procedure, the correlation of compliance with income level was 0.3560, while that with general alienation was 0.3024, followed by a correlation with distrust of 0.2955, with suspicion ("others cheat") of 0.2788, and so on (Song & Yarbrough 1978). Disregarding the question of relative strength, clearly both economic and moral attitudes are at work. Both seem to account for significant chunks of the variance in behavior.

HAPPINESS

There is a considerable deal of social science evidence that shows that human contentment ceases to increase as income grows beyond a fairly modest level. To cite but a few studies of a large body of findings, Andrews and Withey (1976) found that the level of one's socioeconomic status had a limited effect on one's "sense of well-being" and no significant effect on a person's "satisfaction with life-as-a-whole." Freedman (1978) discovered that levels of reported happiness did not vary greatly among the members of different economic classes, with the exception of the very poor, who tended to be less happy than others. Myers and Diener (1995) report that while per capita disposable (after-tax) income in inflation-adjusted dollars almost exactly doubled between 1960 and 1990, 32 percent of Americans reported that they were "very happy" in 1993, almost the same proportion as did in 1957 (35 percent). Myers and Diener also show that although economic growth slowed between the mid-1970s and the early 1990s, Americans' reported happiness was remarkably stable (nearly always between 30 and 35 percent) across both high-growth and low-growth periods. Easterlin's (2001) work found that happiness remains generally constant throughout life cycles. Typically, income and general economic circumstances improve throughout one's life until retirement, but happiness does not experience a comparable level of growth; nor is the leveling off of income during retirement accompanied by a decrease in happiness. In other words, once basic needs are satisfied, the high production/consumption project adds little if anything to human contentment.

SEE ALSO: Community; Economy (Sociological Approach); Management Theory

REFERENCES AND SUGGESTED READINGS

Anderson, G. (2003) Do Americans Work Too Much? Some Social Critics Say Yes – and Point to Europe as a Labor Model. CNN/Money. Online. www.money.cnn.com/2003/10/06/pf/work_less/.
Andrews, F. & Withey, S (1976) *Social Indicators of Well-Being: Americans' Perceptions of Life Quality.* Plenum Press, New York, pp. 254–5.
Black, J. S. (n.d.) Attitudinal, Normative, and Economic Factors in Early Response to an Energy-Use Field Experiment. Unpublished doctoral dissertation, Department of Sociology, University of Wisconsin.
Buber, M. (1971) *I and Thou.* Free Press, New York.
Easterlin, R. (2001) Income and Happiness: Towards a Unified Theory. *Economic Journal* 111: 469–71.
Etzioni, A. (1988) *The Moral Dimension: Toward a New Economics.* Free Press, New York.
Freedman, J. (1978) *Happy People: What Happiness Is, Who Has It, and Why.* Harcourt Brace Jovanovich, New York.

McCauley, M. (2002) Agribusiness Concentration. Oxfam. Online. www.oxfamamerica.org/advocacy/art2563.
Myers, D. & Diener, E. (1995) Who Is Happy? *Psychological Science* 6: 12–14.
Parsons, T. & Smelser, N. (1956) *Economy and Society: A Study in the Integration of Economic and Social Theory.* Free Press, Glencoe.
Song, Y. & Yarbrough, T. (1978) Tax Ethics and Taxpayer Attitudes: A Survey. *Public Administration Review* 447.
Stern, P. & Aronson, E. (Eds.) (1984) *Energy Use: The Human Dimension.* W. H. Freeman, New York.
Stigler, G. (1968) Competition. *International Encyclopedia of Social Science,* Vol. 3. Macmillan, New York.
Valenti, C. (2003) Vacation Deprivation: Americans Get Short-Changed When it Comes to Holiday Time. abcNews.com. Online. www.abcnews.go.com/sections/business/US/vacation_030625.html.

community and media

Simon Cross

"Community" and "media" are independent sociological terms that when combined in the notion of "community media" refer to adaptations of media technology for self-directed use by a given community. They typically involve small-scale media platforms serving the communication and information exchange needs of people who share a bounded geographical location such as a neighborhood, village, town, or even a city. However, since people no longer interpret their community allegiance solely by reference to the geographical place in which they live, this definition can be broadened to include computer-based "communities of interest" where geographically dispersed individuals commune on topics of common interest, although they may never actually meet physically.

Community media practices are grounded in the core principles of public service media – to educate, inform, and entertain – but they also contain a fourth dimension: that of extending citizens' access to and participation in the public sphere. The foregrounding of ordinary people in this way stems from the advocacy by community activists that media should be used to reflect and respond to the lives of the people living in the areas that they serve. It is argued that this can only be achieved when media are used as an expression *of* community rather than *for* the community.

What this means in practice is that media non-professionals participate in both front-stage and back-stage community media activities. In front-stage terms, it means, for example, that community members themselves might present a live radio show dealing with locally relevant topics or personal interests. In back-stage terms it might mean that they are directly involved in planning the stations' future programming possibilities. This helps reinforce accountability for what has been produced within the community.

The normative ideal is that the relevant community-based media resources are owned or managed autonomously from state systems and eschew commercial imperatives. However, some communities receive corporate sponsorship in order to meet expensive startup and training costs. Where the costs of maintaining technology and training lie beyond the financial reach of a community (a special problem in developing countries), media resources are often managed in partnership with non-governmental organizations and community-focused international bodies such as UNESCO.

Community media practice is predicated on a perceived failure by commercial and public service media sectors to ensure pluralism, diversity, and provision of local content. The charge is that mainstream media, usually thought of as homogeneous in form and one-directional in distribution, have muted freedom of expression by failing to provide communities with media content that reflects everyday lives as they are lived in communities. No longer viewed as a fringe cultural activity, the sheer weight of output internationally means that it is now plausible to speak of community media as an important "third sector" of media production.

Because the communicative ethos of community media coheres around people's right to be media producers, i.e., to send as well as to receive, it is often described as a radical form. However, the community media sector per se should not be thought of as necessarily concerned to confront the media establishment, but rather as trying to create a *useful* forum for extending non-exclusive dialogue in local communities.

The notion of citizens "communing" through participatory forms of media expression suggests that it might simply be used to communicate closeness or mutuality ("this is who we are") and which, by definition, calibrates distance from others. It is important to note, however, that community media content nevertheless tends to be outward looking and connected to wider social concerns and issues.

Community media have differing histories according to different national and political contexts. For example, in Latin American countries community radio can be traced back to the 1940s. Political repression led stigmatized, disadvantaged, and repressed communities to participate in community radio broadcasts as a way of maintaining their cultural identity. Since the early 1970s community-based media have also played a key role in social development in Africa and across the Indian subcontinent.

In Europe and North America, the sociopolitical origin of community media is rooted in the 1960s, a time of political upheaval and the emergence of a counterculture. This latter was associated with objections to the societal trend toward large-scale, vertically structured, anonymous institutions. In this context, for example, activists pioneered community television, sustained by the belief that small production units could be more democratically controlled and equipped with less complicated, less expensive equipment for use in local program making. In the United States alone, it has led to more than 1,000 community-access television channels.

In the last two decades, community media initiatives have been closely linked with social development goals. In many of the world's poorest regions, community media not only protect communication and cultural and information rights of indigenous peoples but also facilitate communal forms of decision-making. This is achieved via a range of formats including street theater, video and film production, alternative newspapers, comic books and cartooning, and Internet access. It is, however, radio that continues to flourish as the most important community media platform because of high illiteracy rates and the medium's emphasis on spoken voice.

In deregulated media markets, the release of spectrum and digitalization of communication have created new spaces for ethnic and other minority voices to be heard. Moreover, when we consider that a station serving a small community can potentially reach a national, international, or even a global audience, this serves to dramatize how the conceptual contours of digitized community radio may now be stretched.

The conceptual boundaries of community media have recently been further extended by the notion of virtual "communities of interest" made up of geographically dispersed people with varying degrees of attachment and a complex set of relations to the new geography of cyberspace. The use of computerized media, and ease of access to the Internet and the World Wide Web, have created "virtual communities" extended in time and space and altering geographically bounded conceptions of community media.

The significance of networked communities ("telecommunities") lies in their potential for forging new kinds of links and interconnections between people, and between people and centers of power. This is due to computer-mediated communities being based upon two-way (horizontal) flows of information. Thus, while traditional forms of solidarity are said to be fragmenting and breaking up, it has been claimed that virtual environments offer a way of rebuilding communities (we should add that a growing "digital divide" renders this optimistic prospect neither certain nor universal).

The role of media in building communities is by no means new, however. In Benedict Anderson's (1991) classic definition, the nation-state is an "imagined community," in which a population that could never meet together is bound by a shared language and culture. Anderson argues that the development of what he terms "print capitalism" from the late seventeenth century, based on the spread of literacy and the growing market for publications printed in shared vernacular languages such as English, reinforced demand for reading material by the newly literate. Printers met demand by launching newspapers, which became one of the "mass simultaneous ceremonies" constitutive of nationhood. Thus, the daily ritual of reading the newspaper bound millions of readers together as participants in the construction of a homogeneous national community.

Anderson's concept of a print-based imagined community could be extended to the sphere of broadcasting. In Great Britain, for example, the monarch has, since 1930, used radio first, and subsequently television, to make an annual Christmas message. The broadcast was soon extended to include the 30 or so countries that made up the British Empire (later termed the Commonwealth). The originator of the broadcast, John (later Lord) Reith, the founder of the British Broadcasting Corporation, was in no doubt that radio was a key platform for helping the masses to recognize themselves as members of a cohesive (inter)national community.

Anderson's influential account of imagined community reminds us that there is a fundamental sense in which all communities are fictional creations. In this context, it is important to note that electronic communities do not make either the interaction or the social context less real than communities based on notions of affiliation, ethnicity, and nation. Nevertheless, the formation of virtual communities has given rise to a developing research agenda that coheres around "revival of community" and networked democratic participation, i.e., to investigate whether virtual communities are able to foster long-term responsibility and mutuality as well as participation.

Studies of community media in physical communities currently highlight four areas of research: organization, product, users, and environment. These areas overlap and hence their investigation requires multimethod research designs. Recent studies have developed this multidimensional approach and have also extended empirical lines of enquiry by integrating theoretical perspectives and concepts borrowed from democratic theory (especially Jürgen Habermas's influential concept of the "public sphere"), theories of identity, postmodernism, diaspora studies, community studies, communications policy, human rights, citizenship studies, and communication rights.

The eclectic metatheoretical character of "community media studies" is poised to deliver an abundance of insights about community media activism vis-à-vis the conventional communication role of mainstream media. However, it is also likely that future studies will encounter the thorny problem that the relationship between community media use and participation in a community is not linear but curvilinear. The methodological significance of this point lies in the fact that researchers have yet to develop a theory that accounts for how these two *separate* processes may be related over time; future empirical tests of this relationship will also need to develop longitudinal research designs that will open out this research issue for scrutiny.

The future of community media is likely to be cross-media and multiplatform. It will bring together facilities for sound, video, and multimedia production alongside access to broadband communications, FM and digital radio broadcasting, and digital TV systems. Researchers seeking to understand this multiplatform environment will have to work with and develop a wide range of quantitative and qualitative methods inspired by the multiple disciplines within the social sciences and humanities.

Future studies can be expected to focus on individual community media initiatives that can be used for the comparative analysis of community media resources and ventures. One way around the anecdotal quality of the singular study might be by exploring not an individual community media organization but the umbrella association or network to which most community groups are affiliated. This has the advantage of examining how community media organizations help shape communications policy in relation to their access and participation practices.

Given the seductive appeal associated with the notion of a multimedia future, it is important to avoid romanticizing the transformative possibilities of new kinds of electronic networking. It is by no means certain that every community would wish to replace a bulletin board situated in a local community center with an electronic version. Communities endure because members make their own informed decisions on what are appropriate or relevant media to communicate their sense of belonging and identification.

SEE ALSO: Community; Cyberculture; Diaspora; Digital; Media and Diaspora; Media and Nationalism; Media, Network(s) and; Media and the Public Sphere

REFERENCES AND SUGGESTED READINGS

Anderson, B. (1991) *Imagined Communities: Reflections on the Origins and Spread of Nationalism.* Verso, London.
Berrigan, F. (1977) *Access: Some Western Models of Community Media.* UNESCO, Paris.
Dagron, A. G. (2001) *Making Waves: Stories of Participatory Communication for Social Change.* Rockefeller Foundation, New York. Available at www.rockfound.org/Documents/421/makingwaves.pdf.
Downing, J. (2001) *Radical Media: Rebellious Communication and Social Movements.* Sage, London.
Halleck, D. (2002) *Hand-Held Visions: The Impossible Possibilities of Community Media.* Fordham University Press, New York.
Jankowski, N. W. & Prehn, O. (Eds.) (2002) *Community Media in the Information Age: Perspectives and Prospects.* Hampton Press, Cresskill, NJ.
Jones, S. G. (1995) Understanding Community in the Information Age. In: Jones, S. G. (Ed.), *Cybersociety: Computer-Mediated Communication and Community.* Sage, London, pp. 10–36.
Rheingold, H. (1993) *The Virtual Community: Homesteading on the Electronic Frontier.* Secker & Warburg, London.
Rodriguez, C. (2001) *Fissures in the Mediascape: An International Study of Citizens' Media.* Hampton Press, Cresskill, NJ.
Wasko, J. & Mosco, V. (Eds.) (1992) *Democratic Communications in the Information Age.* Garamond Press, Toronto and Norwood, NJ.

complementary and alternative medicine

Hans A. Baer

Various terms have been bandied around over the past several decades for a wide array of heterodox medical systems, ranging from professionalized to folk medical systems. Within the US context, the term that has become commonplace in various circles is *comple-mentary and alternative medicine*, whereas, for example, in Australia it is simply *complementary medicine*. At any rate, historically, medical sociologists have tended to focus on various aspects of biomedicine, including medical dominance and professionalism, and have tended to ignore alternative medical systems. Exceptions include the work of Walter Wardwell, Lesley Biggs, David Coulter, Ian Coulter, and Evan Willis on chiropractic in the United States, Canada, and Australia. Conversely, medical anthropologists have conducted studies of shamanism and other indigenous and folk medical systems as well as the phenomenon of medical pluralism in complex societies. In modern industrial or post-industrial societies, in addition to biomedicine, the dominant medical subsystem, one finds other medical subsystems, such as homeopathy, osteopathy, chiropractic, naturopathy, religious healing systems, and popular and folk medical systems. Patterns of medical pluralism tend to reflect hierarchical relations in the larger society, including ones based upon class, caste, racial, ethnic, regional, religious, and gender divisions. The medical system of a complex society consists of the totality of medical subsystems that coexist in a generally competitive, but sometimes collaborative or even cooptative, relationship with one another.

Although only a few sociologists, such as Cant and Sharma (1999), have employed the concept of medical pluralism, the growing interest on the part of particularly upper- and upper-middle-class people in alternative medicine in western societies appears to have prompted a growing number of medical sociologists to examine issues such as the sociopolitical relationship between biomedicine and alternative therapies, the holistic health movement, and patient utilization of alternative therapies.

What has come to be termed complementary and alternative medicine (CAM) is an amorphous category that encompasses many medical systems and therapies in various national contexts, but particularly anglophone countries such as the United States, Canada, United Kingdom, Australia, and New Zealand. Whereas alternative practitioners and laypeople have tended to speak of holistic health, CAM and integrative medicine are in large part biomedical constructions.

What started out as the popular holistic health movement in the early 1970s in large part has evolved into the professionalized entity generally referred to as CAM or *integrative medicine*. Alternative medicine generally refers to all medical systems or therapies lying outside the purview of biomedicine that are used in its stead. Complementary medicine refers to medical systems or therapies that are used alongside or as adjuncts to biomedicine. Finally, integrative medicine refers to the effort on the part of conventional physicians to blend biomedical and CAM therapies or to the collaborative efforts between biomedical and CAM practitioners in addressing health-care needs of specific patients.

Scholars have proposed various typologies of CAM therapies. Most typologies of CAM tend to privilege western and Asian therapies over indigenous, folk, and religious therapies. In contrast to most schemes that exclude biomedicine, Nienstedt (1998) presents a "model of complementary medicine and practice" which includes it. Her typology delineates four categories or quadrants: (1) biomedicine which includes MDs, osteopathic physicians, dentists, optometrists, podiatrists, psychologists, pharmacists, nurses, physician assistants, medical technologists, physical therapists, and so on; (2) body-healing alternatives (e.g., chiropractors, homeopaths, medical herbalists, naturopaths, massage therapists, reflexologists); (3) mind/spirit alternatives (e.g., Christian Scientists, faith healers, psychic healers, transcendental meditation); and (4) cross-cultural alternatives (e.g., shamanism, folk medicine, Ayurveda, Chinese medicine, Reiki therapists). Although Nienstedt's scheme includes biomedicine, it does not make any reference to the power difference that exists between it and other therapeutic systems.

The notion of a dominative medical system attempts to recognize the fact that both biomedicine and a wide array of CAM systems coexist within a hierarchical social arrangement. Medical pluralism in the modern world is characterized by a pattern in which biomedicine exerts dominance over alternative medical systems, whether they are professionalized or not. With European expansion, allopathic medicine or what eventually became biomedicine came to supersede in prestige and influence both professionalized indigenous medical systems, such as Ayurveda and Unani in India and Chinese medicine, and a wide array of folk medical systems. The US dominative medical system consists of several levels that tend to reflect class, racial, ethnic, and gender relations in the larger society (Baer 2001). In rank order of prestige, these include (1) biomedicine; (2) osteopathic medicine as a parallel medical system focusing on primary care and incorporative spinal manipulation as an adjunct; (3) professionalized heterodox medical systems (namely, chiropractic, naturopathy, and acupuncture); (4) partially professionalized or lay heterodox medical systems (e.g., homeopathy, herbalism, bodywork, and midwifery); (5) Anglo-American religious healing systems (e.g., Spiritualism, Christian Science, Pentecostalism, and Scientology); and (6) folk medical systems (e.g., Southern Appalachian herbal medicine, African American folk medicine, *curanderismo* among Mexican Americans, and Native American healing systems). With some modification, the model of the dominative medical system can be applied to other modern societies. For the most part, the therapeutic systems that fall under the rubric of CAM tend to be situated under the categories of professionalized, partially professionalized, and lay heterodox medical systems. Within this framework, for example, whereas MDs tend to be white upper- and upper-middle-class males, folk healers tend to be working-class women of color. Alternative medical systems often exhibit counter-hegemonic elements that resist, often in subtle forms, the elitist, hierarchical, and bureaucratic patterns of biomedicine. Conversely, corporate and governmental elites around the world have come to express growing interest in CAM therapies as cost-cutting measures in an era of rising health-care costs.

New medical systems or synthetic ensembles of therapies, such as the hygiene movement in the nineteenth century or the holistic health movement in the late twentieth century, emerge as popular health movements that often undergo a process of professionalization and may in time even be absorbed by biomedicine. The holistic health movement began to emerge on the US West Coast, especially the San Francisco Bay Area, in the early 1970s. It quickly spread to other parts of the United States and also to other, especially Anglophone, countries (Canada, Britain, Australia, and New Zealand), as well as to western European countries such as Germany, the Netherlands, and Denmark. It began as a popular movement or medical revitalization movement that in various ways challenged the bureaucratic, high-tech, and iatrogenic aspects of biomedicine. The holistic health movement was by no means a monolithic phenomenon and varied considerably from society to society where it had emerged. It encompassed numerous alternative medical systems, such as homeopathy, herbalism, naturopathy, and bodywork, with divergent philosophical premises. Although it appeared to have its strongest expression in western societies, it also drew heavily from various eastern healing systems, such as Chinese medicine and Ayurveda. To a large extent, the holistic health movement overlapped with the New Age movement that also became very popular particularly in western societies. Like the holistic health movement, New Ageism focuses upon a balance in the interaction of mind, body, and spirit in its attempts to achieve experiential health and well-being. New Ageism also incorporates many therapeutic techniques and practices, including meditation, guided visualization, channeling, psychic healing, and neoshamanism.

By the late 1970s, an increasing number of biomedical and osteopathic physicians as well as nurses, particularly in the US and UK, began to recognize the limitations of their conventional approach to illness and that they were losing many of their more affluent patients to alternative or heterodox practitioners. A group of MDs and DOs established the American Holistic Medical Association in 1978. Nurses in particular, given their person-orientation, expressed interest in holistic health and formed the American Holistic Nurses' Association in 1981. In time, more and more biomedical schools began to offer courses on alternative medicine – something that is still in process – as it became apparent that the bread-and-butter patients of biomedicine, those with disposable incomes, could afford to pay for alternative therapies out of their own pockets. Although some MDs subscribe to the philosophical underpinnings of various alternative therapies, including their vitalist perspectives, others adopt these techniques without wholeheartedly subscribing to their ideologies or reinterpret them in terms of biomedical concepts or evidence-based medicine.

Ironically, holistic health as a popular movement has by and large been tamed and evolved into a professionalized entity referred to as CAM or integrative medicine. Over the past decade or so, numerous biomedical practitioners have written overviews of CAM and have called for an evidence-based approach (Micozzi 2001). In 1999 the National Institutes of Health's Office of Alternative Medicine (established in 1992 as a result of a Congressional mandate) was renamed the National Center for Complementary and Alternative Medicine. Furthermore, health insurance companies, health maintenance organizations, and hospitals have become increasingly interested in CAM therapies as a way of satisfying patients' demands and curtailing costs. While CAM or integrative medicine often continues to adhere to some notion of holism, in reality it appears to function as a style of health care in which biomedicine treats alternative therapists as subordinates and alternative therapies as adjunct.

Sociologists and anthropologists have addressed a number of issues regarding CAM, including overviews of the holistic health movement (Lyng 1990), social profiles of patients utilizing CAM and their reasons for doing so, social profiles of CAM practitioners or conventional physicians who have incorporated CAM therapies into their practices, the drive for professionalization on the part of specific CAM therapists (including osteopaths in the UK and Australia, chiropractors in the US, Canada, UK, and Australia, naturopaths in the US and Canada, acupuncturists in the US), the transformation of some conventional physicians into holistic healers (Davis-Floyd & St. John 1998), and integrative medical centers (Lowenberg 1989). In part emulating the success stories of chiropractors, naturopaths, and acupuncturists in places such as the US, Canada, and Australia, various other CAM therapists, including homeopaths, bodyworkers, herbalists, and direct-entry midwives, have begun to seek legitimation by creating professional associations, training institutions, and self-regulation as well as lobbying for licensing or certification.

The social scientific study of CAM remains in its infancy. Whereas some scholars posit the existence of a CAM social movement, others point to the growing commercialization of CAM therapies and the emergence of a lucrative CAM industry. One important question that has arisen within this context is whether CAM is a counter-hegemonic force, a hegemonic force, or a bit of both. Some have even argued that biomedicine in various national contexts is being coopted by biomedical institutions, including centers of integrative medicine in which MDs serve as directors, biomedical schools and hospitals, and NIH's National Center for Complementary and Alternative Medicine, which funds efficacy studies of CAM therapies based upon randomized, double-blind methodology (Saks 2003; Baer 2004).

While sociological and anthropological studies of a wide array of alternative medical systems in modern societies have been elucidating much about CAM, most of this research has relied upon archival sources and survey research. What is desperately needed are in-depth studies of CAM practitioners, their educational institutions, associations, conferences, and clinical practices, and the vitalist subcultures within which they and their patients or clients function as well as the increasing number of settings in which biomedical and CAM practitioners interact with one another.

SEE ALSO: Health Care Delivery Systems; Health Maintenance Organization; Medicine, Sociology of; New Age; Professional Dominance in Medicine

REFERENCES AND SUGGESTED READINGS

Baer, H. (2001) *Biomedicine and Alternative Healing Systems in America: Issues of Class, Race, Ethnicity, and Gender.* University of Wisconsin Press, Madison.

Baer, H. (2004) *Towards an Integrative Medicine: From Holistic Health to Complementary and Alternative Medicine.* Altamira Press, Walnut Creek, CA.

Cant, S. & Sharma, U. (1999) *A New Medical Pluralism? Alternative Medicine, Doctors, Patients, and the State*. Taylor & Francis, London.

Davis-Floyd, R. & St. John, G. (1998) *From Doctor to Healer: The Transformative Journey*. Rutgers University Press, New Brunswick, NJ.

Lowenberg, J. S. (1989) *Caring and Responsibility: The Crossroads between Holistic Practice and Traditional Medicine*. University of Pennsylvania Press, Philadelphia.

Lyng, S. (1990) *Holistic Health and Biomedical Medicine: A Countersystem Analysis*. State University of New York Press, Albany.

Micozzi, M. S. (Ed.) (2001) *Fundamentals of Complementary and Alternative Medicine*, 2nd edn. Churchill Livingstone, New York.

Nienstedt, B. C. (1998) The Federal Approach to Alternative Medicine: Coopting, Quackbusting, or Complementing? In: Gordon, R. J. & Nienstedt, B. C. (Eds.), *Alternative Therapies: Expanding Options in Health Care*. Springer, New York, pp. 27–43.

Saks, M. (2003) *Orthodox and Alternative Medicine*. Continuum, New York.

Tovey, P., Easthope, G., & Adams, J. (Eds.) (2004) *The Mainstreaming of Complementary and Alternative Medicine: Studies in Social Context*. Routledge, London.

complexity and emergence

R. Keith Sawyer

Complex phenomena reside between simplicity and randomness. When the laws governing a system are relatively simple, the system's behavior is easy to understand, explain, and predict. At the other extreme, some systems seem to behave randomly. There may be laws governing their behavior, but the system is highly non-linear, such that small variations in the state of the system at one time could result in very large changes to later states of the system. Such systems are often said to be *chaotic*. Complex systems are somewhere in between these two extremes: the system is not easy to explain, but it is not so chaotic that understanding is completely impossible.

An interest in complexity is often accompanied by an interest in *emergence* – the processes whereby the global behavior of a system results from the actions and interactions of agents. There is no central controller or plan. Higher-level order emerges from the interaction of the individual components. Such systems are self-organizing, with control distributed throughout the system. Emergent systems are often complex in that they manifest order at the global system level that is difficult to explain by analyzing the individual components of the system in isolation.

Complex systems that manifest emergence tend to have a large number of units, with each unit connected to a moderate number of other units, and frequent, repeated interactions among the connected units, which occur simultaneously throughout the system. Whereas complex physical systems tend to have simple rules for these interactions, the units in complex social systems are individuals who communicate using the full richness of natural language.

Societies have often been compared to complex systems. Inspired by the rise of science and technology, in the eighteenth century societies were compared to complex artificial mechanisms like clocks. Just after World War II, Talcott Parsons's influential structural functional theory was inspired by cybernetics, a field centrally concerned with developing models of the computational and communication technologies that were emerging in the postwar period. In the 1960s and 1970s, general systems theory continued in this interdisciplinary fashion. It was grounded in the premise that complex systems at all levels of analysis – from the smallest unicellular organisms up to modern industrial societies – could be understood using the same set of theories and methodologies.

Common to all of these metaphors is the basic insight that societies gain their effectiveness and functions from a complex configuration of many people, engaged in overlapping and interlocking patterns of relationship with one another. Some key questions raised by these society-as-system metaphors are: What do these relations and configurations look like? Which systems are most effective, and which are stable and long-lasting? How could a stable complex system ever change and evolve, as societies often do? What is the role of the individual in the system? Such questions have long been central in sociology.

Complexity theory has the potential to provide several new insights into these central sociological questions. Beginning in the mid-1990s, several scientific developments converged to create a qualitatively more advanced approach to complex systems, and complexity theory began to influence a wide range of disciplines, from biology to economics. This influential new approach has begun to filter into sociology. The study of complex dynamical systems can provide new perspectives on important unresolved issues facing the social sciences – the relations between individuals and groups, the emergence of unintended effects from collective action, and the relation between the disciplines of economics and sociology.

Parsons's structural functional theory represented the first wave of systems theories in sociology, drawing on systems concepts from cybernetics to describe human societies as complex self-maintaining systems. The general systems theories of the 1960s and 1970s represented a second wave. General systems theories were always more successful at explaining natural systems than social systems. In spite of the universalist ambitions of such theorists, social scientists generally ignored them. In contrast, the latest work in complexity theory – the *third wave* of systems theory – is particularly well suited to sociological explanation. Third-wave sociological systems theory grew out of developments in computer technology. In the 1990s, computer power advanced to the point where societies could be simulated using a distinct computational agent for every individual in the society, using a computational technique known as *multi-agent systems*. A multi-agent system contains hundreds or thousands of agents, each engaged in communication with at least some of the others. The researcher can use these simulations to create *artificial societies*. The researcher defines and implements a model of the individual agent, creates a communication language for them to interact, and then observes the overall macro behavior of the system that emerges over time.

This new methodology has led complexity theorists in sociology to become increasingly concerned with *emergence*. Examples include traffic jams, the colonies of social insects, and bird flocks. To illustrate, the "V" shape of the bird flock does not result from one bird being selected as the leader, and the other birds lining up behind the leader. Instead, each bird's behavior is based on its position relative to nearby birds. The "V" shape is not planned or centrally determined in "top-down" fashion. Rather, it emerges out of simple pair-interaction rules, i.e., from the "bottom up." The bird flock demonstrates one of the most striking features of emergent phenomena: higher-level regularities are often the result of quite simple rules and local interactions at the lower level.

In the social sciences, a comparable example of an emergent phenomenon is language shift. Historians of language have documented that languages have changed frequently throughout history, with vocabulary and even grammar changing over the centuries. Yet until the rise of the modern nation-state, such changes were not consciously selected by any official body, nor were they imposed by force on a population. Rather, language shift is an emergent phenomenon, arising out of the nearly infinite number of everyday conversations in small groups scattered throughout the society. In this social system, successive conversations among speakers result in the emergence over time of a collective social fact: language as a property of a social group. The study of social emergence requires a focus on multiple levels of analysis – individuals, interactions, and groups – and a dynamic focus on how social group phenomena emerge from communication processes among individual members.

Whether or not a global system property is emergent, and what this means both theoretically and methodologically, has been defined in many different ways. For example, in some accounts, system properties are said to be emergent when they are *unpredictable* even given a complete knowledge of the lower-level description of the system – a complete knowledge of the state of each component and of their interactions. In other accounts, system properties are said to be emergent when they are *irreducible*, in any lawful and regular fashion, to properties of the system components. In yet other accounts, system properties are said to be emergent when they are *novel*, when they are not held by any of the components of the system.

Philosophers of science began debating such properties early in the twentieth century. Social scientists have applied widely different definitions of emergence, resulting in some conceptual confusion.

Complex systems researchers have found that the emergent higher level may have autonomous laws and properties that cannot be easily reduced to lower-level, more basic sciences. Thus the paradigm of complexity is often opposed to the paradigm of reductionism. For example, cognitive scientists generally agree that mental properties may not be easily reduced to neurobiological properties, due to the complex dynamical nature of the brain. In an analogous fashion, several sociological theorists have used complexity theory to argue against attempts to explain societies in terms of individuals, a reductionist approach known as *methodological individualism*. Because many socially emergent phenomena are difficult to explain in terms of the system's components and their interactions, these theorists have claimed that emergentist thinking supports sociological collectivism and realism, and that individualist approaches will have limited success as a potential explanation for many social phenomena.

For example, due to complexity and emergence, there may be potential limitations of individualist methodologies such as neoclassical microeconomics and evolutionary psychology. Complexity theory suggests that both psychology and microeconomics are likely to be severely limited in their ability to explain human behavior in groups. As currently conceived, psychology is the study of system-independent properties of individuals (e.g., variables, traits, mental models, cognitive capacities). Microeconomics is the study of how collective phenomena emerge from aggregations of individual preferences and actions. Both are individualist in that they reject explanations that propose that group properties could lawfully influence individual action. Many contemporary paradigms are based on such reductionist assumptions – evolutionary psychology, cognitive neuroscience, behavioral genetics, and social cognition. Yet an emergentist perspective suggests that many social systems may not be explainable in terms of individuals, and that neither psychology nor microeconomics can

fully explain the socially contextualized nature of human behavior.

Because societies are complex systems, individualists cannot assume that a given social system will be reducible to explanations in terms of individuals. However, anti-individualists cannot assume that a given social system will not be so reducible. Whether or not a social system can be understood solely in terms of its component individuals and their interactions is an empirical question, to be resolved anew with respect to each social system. Theories of emergence from complexity science show why some social properties cannot be explained in terms of individuals. Thus one cannot assume that methodological individualism can exhaustively explain human behavior in social groups. However, not all social systems are irreducibly complex, and some social properties can be explained by identifying their processes of emergence from individuals in interaction. Complexity approaches can help to determine which approach will be most appropriate for which social system.

Studies of social groups must be fundamentally interdisciplinary, because a focus on emergence requires a simultaneous consideration of multiple levels of analysis: the individual, the communication language, and the group. A complete explanation of the most complex social systems may require interdisciplinary teams composed of psychologists, sociologists, communication scholars, and economists.

SEE ALSO: Collective Action; Computational Sociology; Micro–Macro Links; Parsons, Talcott; Structural Functional Theory; System Theories

REFERENCES AND SUGGESTED READINGS

Archer, M. S. (1995) *Realist Social Theory: The Morphogenetic Approach*. Cambridge University Press, New York.
Johnson, S. (2001) *Emergence: The Connected Lives of Ants, Brains, Cities, and Software*. Scribner, New York.
Sawyer, R. K. (2001) Emergence in Sociology: Contemporary Philosophy of Mind and Some Implications for Sociological Theory. *American Journal of Sociology* 107: 551–85.

636 compositional theory of urbanism

636 compositional theory of urbanism

Sawyer, R. K. (2006) *Social Emergence: Societies as Complex Systems.* Cambridge University Press, New York.

Thrift, N. (1999) The Place of Complexity. *Theory, Culture, and Society* 16: 31–69.

Waldrop, M. M. (1992) *Complexity: The Emerging Science at the Edge of Order and Chaos.* Simon & Schuster, New York.

compositional theory of urbanism

Jennifer Schwartz

Compositional theories of urbanism assert that urban unconventionality and urban–rural differences are due mainly to the social characteristics (i.e., class, race/ethnicity, age) of city dwellers. The density and heterogeneity that define the urban environment do not affect how people relate to one another or cause people to deviate. In other words, there are no independent effects of city life on people's behaviors.

Compositional theory developed in the 1960s largely in reaction to determinist models of urbanism that assumed cities had harmful effects on people's well-being. The prevailing ideology of Louis Wirth (1938) and other determinists was that large, dense environments with a mix of different types of people create conditions harmful to people's social and psychological well-being and contribute to the development of social problems, like crime, illegitimacy, and so on. The high concentration of people in an area was thought to overload one's senses, leading urban dwellers to retreat into social isolation as a means of adapting to incessant stimuli (Simmel 1964 [1902]). Further, density or crowding might cause greater friction among people, leading to interpersonal violence, greater withdrawal, and "urban malaise" (i.e., loneliness, depression, and anxiety) (Hall 1966; Galle et al. 1972). The diversity of cities and greater division of labor (i.e., heterogeneity) was believed to heighten competition among interest groups, make moral consensus and a sense of community difficult to achieve, and weaken interpersonal ties and social controls. So, the traditional determinist view was that social conditions of the city undermine social relationships, leading to the adoption of non-traditional values and deviant behaviors.

Proponents of the compositional theory of urbanism, however, argued that even in large, dense, heterogeneous areas, people find their own social worlds that insulate them from the effects of the urban environment. For example, Herbert Gans (1962b: 65–6) suggests that "[the city] population consists mainly of relatively homogeneous groups, with social and cultural moorings that shield it fairly effectively from the suggested consequences of number, density, and heterogeneity." That is, people can achieve a sense of community within their neighborhoods whether they live in large cities or small towns. City dwellers, like others, create and sustain personal networks that lend emotional and social support and provide stakes in conformity. These intimate social circles may be based on kinship, ethnicity, neighborhood, occupation, or lifestyle, but basic group dynamics and the quality and extent of social relationships are unaffected by the urban environment.

Compositional theorists critiqued determinists for failing to recognize the "mosaic of social worlds" that exist in the city and, instead, concentrating on the social problems located in certain segments of the city. By selectively examining highly transient, impoverished (inner-city) areas, determinists mistakenly attributed anemic social bonds among people, higher levels of mental health issues, and social problems to city life when these outcomes are more likely attributable to high population turnover – a feature in some communities that made it difficult to build and sustain social relationships. Transience was responsible for anonymity and detachment from mainstream society and social relationships. In other areas of the city not characterized by such high population mobility, social life was taking place in relatively small groups (e.g., families, neighborhoods) just as in smaller communities across the country.

Early qualitative evidence supports compositionalist claims of the endurance and vitality of social ties in urban settings. In *The Urban*

Villagers, Gans (1962a) presents a picture of organized, cohesive ethnic communities in Boston. In her work *The Urban Neighborhood*, Keller (1968) concludes that urban neighboring exists, but the strength of neighborhood ties varies by the composition of the neighborhood, for example by social class or family structure. Others also demonstrate across various urban contexts that people in cities are not lonely or isolated and have strong family, peer, and neighborhood networks (Suttles 1968; Howell 1973; Fischer et al. 1977). More recent quantitative work has gone beyond documenting the existence of social ties in urban settings and focuses on empirically assessing how the extent/size, type, and use of social networks differ across settings as well as among city dwellers (e.g., by race/ethnicity, life cycle). Further, compositionalist work has provided a basis for the development of more nuanced theoretical approaches to studying social networks in urban (and non-urban) settings, such as Claude Fischer's subcultural theory of urbanism.

Compositional theorists do not deny that there are aggregate-level behavioral differences along the urban–rural continuum. However, they attribute these differences primarily to the different kinds of people found in urban areas compared to suburban and rural areas rather than to effects of urbanism itself. People's characteristics – social class, age/life cycle, family status, race/ethnicity – largely shape their behaviors and define their ways of life. The concentration in urban settings of individuals with certain traits accounts for the greater unconventionality of cities. For example, the effect of being married on the likelihood of engaging in crime is the same in an urban context as in a suburban or rural context. If there is more crime in the city, it is, in good part, due to more crime-prone, unmarried people living in the city than in other types of areas. Further, the city selectively attracts certain kinds of people who are more amenable to non-traditional lifestyles – the young, the deviant, the unmarried – accounting for urban–rural differences. Compositional theorists explain lifestyle differences between urban dwellers and others as being due to demographic differences, not social breakdown. So, they would expect that once demographic differences are taken into account, urban/non-urban differences should disappear.

Urban populations do tend to be younger, less often married, and more heterogeneous in terms of race/ethnicity, religion, and social class. Some studies show that much of the relationship between population density (a measure of how urban a place is) and pathology (e.g., delinquency, welfare, hospitalization for mental illness) disappears once demographic factors are taken into account. For example, higher urban crime rates may be due to greater poverty levels in urban areas: social class affects both living arrangements (i.e., density) and the likelihood of engaging in crime. However, though the relationship is lessened considerably, most empirical research shows that urban/non-urban differences in unconventionality and rates of social problems remain, even after taking into account demographic features of place. It would be an overstatement to conclude that living in an urban environment has *no* effect on people, but compositionalists are likely correct that much of the effects of the urban environment operate through social networks and vary according to social characteristics of residents.

Compositional theorists recognize that demographic characteristics *associated* with urban–rural differences do not *explain* these differences. They emphasize that demographic characteristics shape roles, opportunities, and behavioral expectations, so attention should be directed toward the social, economic, and political forces that shape expectations, opportunities, and roles available to various groups. For example, compositionalists would point to the need to examine how job availability attracts certain kinds of workers to a given place or how housing market practices (including discrimination, but also pricing and lending practices) shape residential "choice" such that certain kinds of people are attracted to certain kinds of neighborhoods. They also emphasize the need to examine the larger social systems in which cities are embedded. Urban economies are shaped by national and international forces; the economic demands placed on cities influence the kind of workers drawn to an area. For example, city economies based on the production of technology (e.g., Silicon Valley) may attract a relatively educated workforce; a labor market rich in construction jobs may attract a greater than average share of men.

At the heart of urban sociology is the question: what are the consequences of urban life? According to compositional theorists, there are no negative consequences of living in dense, urban environments. Social networks are alive and well in cities, if you know where to look. These social networks insulate people from the stress and strains of daily urban living. Compositionalists attribute urban/non-urban differences to the social characteristics of people who live in urban settings, not to the urban environment itself. Though this premise is only partially accurate, compositionalist theory represents one of the first serious statements that ran counter to the popular turn-of-the-century premise that cities were divisive and alienating. The major tenets of the theory have contributed to the development of more sophisticated analytic models that take into account demographic differences across place and self-selection factors. Compositionalist theory has also provided a firm grounding for more current theoretical approaches to understanding urban dynamics and differences across urban and non-urban settings.

SEE ALSO: Urban Ecology; Urban Political Economy; Urban Poverty; Urbanism, Subcultural Theory of

REFERENCES AND SUGGESTED READINGS

Fischer, C. S. (1975) Toward a Subcultural Theory of Urbanism. *American Journal of Sociology* 80: 1319–41.

Fischer, C. S. (1982) *To Dwell Among Friends: Personal Networks in Town and City.* University of Chicago Press, Chicago.

Fischer, C. S. (1984) *The Urban Experience.* Harcourt Brace Jovanovich, New York.

Fischer, C. S., Jackson, R. M., Steuve, C. A., Gerson, K., & Jones, L. M. (1977) *Networks and Places.* Free Press, New York.

Galle, O. R., Gove, W. R., & McPherson, J. M. (1972) Population Density and Pathology: What are the Relations for Man? *Science* 176: 23–30.

Gans, H. J. (1962a) *The Urban Villagers.* Free Press, New York.

Gans, H. J. (1962b) Urbanism and Suburbanism as Ways of Life: A Reevaluation of Definitions. In:

Rose, A. (Ed.), *Human Behavior and Social Processes.* Houghton Mifflin, Boston, pp. 625–48.

Hall, E. (1966) *The Hidden Dimensions.* Doubleday, Garden City, NY, ch. 13.

Howell, J. T. (1973) *Hard Living on Clay Street.* Anchor, Garden City, NY.

Keller, S. (1968) *The Urban Neighborhood.* Random House, New York.

Simmel, G. (1964 [1902]) The Metropolis and Mental Life. In: Wolff, K. (Ed.), *The Sociology of Georg Simmel.* Free Press, New York, pp. 409–24.

Suttles, G. (1968) *The Social Order of the Slum.* University of Chicago Press, Chicago.

Wirth, L. (1938) Urbanism as a Way of Life. *American Journal of Sociology* 44: 1–25.

compulsory heterosexuality

Eric Anderson

Popularized by Rich (1981), compulsory heterosexuality is the cultural assumption that both males and females are biologically predisposed to heterosexuality. The assumption that biology excludes a naturalized explanation of homosexuality limits humans to only heterosexual attraction. Therefore, the operation of compulsory heterosexuality usually involves the hegemonic manner in which heterosexuality is reified and naturalized, while homosexuality is considered the product of either psychological dysfunction or personal deviant choice. From this understanding homosexuality is deviant because it is thought to go against supposed natural inclinations. Hegemonic understandings of heterosexuality have often been supported by the misconception that other animals are also exclusively heterosexual, even though Bagemihl (1999) has shown homosexuality, as temporary sexual behavior and as a form of long-term relationship coupling, exists widely throughout the animal kingdom.

One result of the naturalization of heterosexuality and stigmatization of homosexuality, bisexuality, and transgenderism manifests itself in cultural and institutional inequality for non-heterosexuals. The institutionalization of heterosexuality can be found at all levels of western societies, in which power and privilege are usually dispersed unevenly in the benefit of heterosexuals. Restricting civil marriage to heterosexuals, for example, provides that group of people with significant insurance, taxation, and many other economic and social privileges that are denied to gay and lesbian couples.

Rich goes on to argue that validation of heterosexuals at the expense of non-heterosexuals influences the reproduction of male privilege in a patriarchal society by both political means and social violence. She contends that in a society in which men control most aspects of women's institutional lives, including their right to birth control, abortion, and occupational equality, women are essentially bound to a binary system of oppression. Should they choose not to participate in heterosexual family structure, they are stigmatized and further denied social and institutional support. Rich asserts that the naturalization of heterosexuality is so hegemonic that even feminists have failed to account for the overwhelming effects it has on oppressing women. She even suggests that compulsory heterosexuality promotes a political institution of domestic violence. For example, the naturalization of heterosexuality is thought to excuse men's violence against women because "that's just the way it (biologically) is" (Rich 1981: 154). In some respects, this boys-will-be-boys attitude suggests that men may actually be victims themselves (i.e., victimized by their own biological destiny).

Much of the fervor over Rich's thesis has diminished over the years, which is perhaps attributable to the widespread institutional and cultural gains that gays and lesbians have made since 1981 (Widmer et al. 1998). Whether it is a result of people and societies increasingly viewing homosexuality as the process of natural outcomes or not, gays and lesbians have made substantial progress in securing institutional equality. Consequently, much of the discussion of compulsory heterosexuality has shifted to the examination of heterosexism, which assumes that heterosexuality is and ought to remain culturally and institutionally privileged. Although heterosexism is thought to operate with less overt homophobia than compulsory heterosexuality as well as with more covert mechanisms, Clausell and Fiske (2005) and others have shown that prejudice toward those other than heterosexuals increasingly reflects ambivalence: a combination of both positive and negative attitudes and behaviors. Ambivalence, of course, normally does little to change the status quo, thereby slowing the progress that gays and lesbians make toward full civil and cultural equality.

SEE ALSO: Bisexuality; Heterosexual Imaginary; Heterosexuality; Homophobia; Homophobia and Heterosexism; Homosexuality

REFERENCES AND SUGGESTED READINGS

Bagemihl, B. (1999) *Biological Exuberance: Animal Homosexuality and Natural Diversity*. St. Martin's Press, New York.
Clausell, E. & Fiske, S. T. (2005) When Do Subgroup Parts Add Up to the Stereotype Whole? Mixed Stereotype Content for Gay Male Subgroups. *Social Cognition* 23(2): 161–81.
Rich, A. C. (1981) *Compulsory Heterosexuality and Lesbian Existence*. Only Women Press, London.
Widmer, E., Treas, J., & Newcomb, R. (1998) Attitudes Toward Nonmarital Sex in 24 Countries. *Journal of Sex Research* 35(4): 349–65.

computational sociology

William Sims Bainbridge

A new sociological approach employs computer simulation and artificial intelligence in the development of theories and in empirical research. Much of the early work was carried out in the areas of social exchange and social networks. The initial methodology – variously called *artificial social intelligence, agent-based modeling*, or *multi-agent systems* – employs theory-based computer models of human interaction. Computer and information scientists have recently developed similar techniques for analyzing empirical data, with names like *machine learning, recommender systems*, and *latent semantic analysis*. There is good reason to believe that computational sociology will spread beyond the specialized subfields that first adopted it and become a major approach in all areas of social research.

THEORY CONSTRUCTION

In *The Nature of Social Science* (1967) and *Social Behavior* (1974), George Homans argued sociological theories should be formalized, much in the manner of classical Greek logic and geometry, as hierarchical structures of propositions beginning with axioms and precise definitions of terms. From these, chains of other propositions should be derived by logical inference, down to hypotheses that could be operationalized in rigorous empirical studies. Unfortunately, traditional sociology did not have rigorous methods for carrying out deductions from axioms, or precise definitions of concepts.

This is where computer simulations came in. A computer program is a structure of algorithms, which are formal procedures for achieving particular goals. Typically, an algorithm sets forth a series of unambiguous steps the machine must go through, from an initial set of conditions to the desired result. A mathematical proof is also an algorithm, and computers have begun to play a useful role in sections of mathematical proofs that may be too complex for a human mathematician to handle in a reasonable period of time. Most famously, after a century of effort by human mathematicians, a computer was essential in completing the proof that areas on any flat map can be colored in with only four colors, without there being the same color on both sides of any boundary.

Probably the first example was the computer program Logic Theorist, completed in 1956 by Allen Newell, Herbert Simon, and J. C. Shaw (Crevier 1993). Historians consider it the very first successful artificial intelligence program, and it was able to prove 38 theorems from the influential treatise *Principia Mathematica* by Bertrand Russell and Alfred North Whitehead. Logic Theorist employed simple transformation rules to work from initial axioms to theorems, in the manner of classical deductive logic. Computational sociologists have generally found this particular method too limited, and they have looked for a way to model interaction among human beings more directly. In a review article on computational sociology, Macy and Willer (2002) argue that agent-based modeling is the most promising approach.

An *agent* is a computational entity that can act, somewhat in the manner of an animal or human being, sensing external events and doing things that affect the environment. Autonomous software agents can be either simple or complex, but even the simplest can produce complex effects when many of them interact in a multi-agent system. Agents can be heterogeneous, either following different rules of behavior or possessing different resources and memories that cause them to act in different ways even when following a shared set of rules. As in the real world, interaction in many such programs is a decentralized or distributed process that occurs locally around individuals and small groups, and that builds from the local level to create large-scale social phenomena.

Perhaps the most influential simulation for sociologists was actually carried out by a political scientist, Robert Axelrod, who explored the conditions under which self-interest could bring people to cooperate with each other. Sociologists in some schools of thought had long argued that shared values, religion, or stable cultural institutions are essential to bring people to act cooperatively in their dealings with each other. Axelrod's simulation intentionally left out all these factors, to see if they were really necessary. He challenged social and computer scientists to write algorithms that would compete for resources in a simulated tournament, each representing a strategy that one or more agents would follow in exchanges where each promised to give the other some benefit. One successful algorithm was Tit-for-Tat. It had two simple rules: (1) on the first turn interacting with another agent, cooperate; (2) after the first turn, do whatever the other agent did the previous time. In a population of agents following various rules, Tit-for-Tat outperformed other strategies in terms of allowing the agent to benefit from mutually profitable exchanges, without being exploited frequently by deceitful agents. Axelrod's study does not prove that human cooperation results from entirely self-interested behavior based on a simple strategy, but it does prove that other factors are not logically necessary.

STUDIES IN COMPUTATIONAL SOCIOLOGY

Axelrod's research assumed that individuals have the opportunity to interact repeatedly, and thus to learn how their potential exchange partners habitually behave. Macy and Skvoretz (1998) explored the emergence of cooperation in a population of strangers who interact at random but with three behavioral options: (1) cooperate – give in hopes of a profitable return; (2) cheat – take what the other person offers but give nothing in return; or (3) exit – refuse to give or take. The computer-simulated agents also had the equivalent of visible emotions that might signal their intentions, and some ability to perceive the emotions of others. The study also experimented with how local or distant the exchanges were, effectively dividing relations into neighbors and strangers. The first finding was that the more costly it was to exit exchange relationships, the more likely it was that the agents would cooperate, especially with neighbors. Perhaps most significantly, cooperation between strangers was fragile but could evolve, and the study explores the conditions that permit this to happen. It also illustrates the significance of local groups as the breeding ground for culture, such as implicit norms of trust.

In another research project, Macy (1995) combined computer simulations directly with laboratory experimentation involving real human beings. He was interested in a strategy different from Tit-for-Tat that can also produce cooperation in multi-agent simulations. The PAVLOV algorithm – named for the early twentieth-century Russian psychologist who studied how the behavior of dogs can be conditioned by rewards – has the same first rule as Tit-for-Tat, but its second rule differs: After the first turn, if the previous turn was rewarding repeat that behavior, otherwise switch to the opposite behavior from last turn. After using multi-agent simulations to develop hypotheses about PAVLOV, Macy ran experiments in which a series of volunteer research subjects thought they were playing computer-based exchange games with other people, but those alleged other people were actually a multi-agent simulation.

Many simulations explore factors other than strategies for trading with exchange partners,

notably allowing the agents to gain information from their environments. Takahashi (2000) explored the evolution of general exchange among a group of people, in which individuals would give to other people to the extent they perceived that the other individual behaved fairly in exchanges with others, quite apart from their personal experience of having been rewarded by that individual. Bainbridge (1995a, 1995b) has explored the emergence of both religious faith and ethnic prejudice in societies composed of agents intentionally designed to have limited ability to process information, on the theory that the limitations of the human mind are responsible for some of the key features of culture. Carley (1991) has argued that social organizations can be viewed as mechanisms for processing information. Inspired by Carley's theory, Mark (1998) has used computer simulations of communication interactions to explore how social groups of various sizes become differentiated, on the basis of information shared within subgroups.

Markovsky (1992) has explored the limits of predictability in the behavior of social exchange networks where individual agents may have slightly different structural power. When the networks are small, results tend to be highly regular and predictable. But Markovsky found that larger networks often become highly sensitive to very minor differences in the power of one of the positions. Results can become unpredictable. Thus, complex computer simulations are often chaotic, leading to unexpected outcomes. Markovsky suggests that the behavior of social networks in the real world may be predictable only if they are small and operate for a short period of time. Large-scale social behavior, however, may be chaotic, sometimes fitting into neat patterns, and at other times diverging to quite unanticipated consequences. Carley and Svoboda (1996) have simulated the adaptation of formal organizations such as corporations, finding that the relationship between organizational design and performance is chaotic, with tiny initial differences between organizations sometimes leading to very substantial differences in outcomes.

Similarly, Bainbridge (1997) explored chaotic behavior in the competition between religious movements. Conventional theory holds that religious movements succeed either because they have unusually charismatic leaders or because they serve the status needs of deprived social classes and disadvantaged minorities. Bainbridge experimented with a set of agent-based computer simulations that ignored these factors and simply modeled the spread of competing movements in a social network, following three rules: (1) an individual will convert to a movement if a plurality of his associates already belong to it; (2) an individual will tend to break ties to neighbors who belong to different movements from his own; (3) members of one especially aggressive movement will tend to establish bonds with neighbors regardless of their affiliations, in what sociologists of religion call *outreach*. The first two rules alone produce a quick stalemate, in which a few people are converted before each movement becomes socially isolated and all action halts. The third rule allows a small movement to grow through outreach in an environment consisting of several other denominations, with difficulty but inexorably, if many of its members are initially concentrated in the same neighborhood and therefore can achieve a concentration of forces that gives it a local majority from which it can expand. If the simulation begins with random distribution of movement membership across the social network, the outcome depends very sensitively on whether a critical mass of members of a movement practicing outreach happens to concentrate in one neighborhood.

CHAOS, INDETERMINACY, AND THE LIMITS OF REDUCTIONISM

The frequent appearance of chaotic effects in sociological computer simulations reminds us that chaotic effects have been observed in physical sciences, notably cosmology. No one was watching, perhaps 15 billion years ago, when our current cosmos emerged from an infinitesimal point in the proverbial Big Bang. Both the details and some fundamental principles remain obscure, but the standard cosmological model envisions an expanding mass of subatomic particles, in which the most important for future human life were the free protons and electrons that combined to form hydrogen atoms as the universe cooled. Tiny, random heterogeneities allowed matter to collect

gravitationally into galaxies, stars, and planets. The nuclear reactions inside stars synthesized heavier elements, notably carbon that forms sufficiently complex molecules with itself and with other elements to be the basis of life. Stars of a particular size range exploded and hurled these elements into space where they could collect into planets. On a small fraction of planets – those just the right size at the right distance from a star in a stable solar system – life evolved from inorganic matter, and over time life diversified, including the evolution of very complex life-forms. On at least one planet, but probably on only a vanishingly small fraction of all planets, intelligent social life emerged and founded a science of sociology to study the laws governing its own interactions. From this perspective, the universe is a complex, chaotic system that contains adaptive subsystems, such as biological evolution and human learning.

As George Homans frequently remarked, social process may be either convergent or divergent. In a *convergent* process, random effects are damped out by large numbers of social interactions, so the phenomena are rather lawful and therefore predictable. In a *divergent* process, small changes at one point in time escalate to produce big differences later in time. Divergence is chaotic, but it can lead to situations that stabilize, at least for long periods of time, and thus establish a new, if ultimately temporary, set of sociological laws. For example, the accidental death by disease of Alexander the Great, on June 13, 323 BCE at the age of 32, before he could consolidate his empire, made it possible for Rome to defeat Macedonia a century later, setting the stage for the Roman Empire and such vast cultural developments as the rise of Christianity.

Thus, the chaos arising from the behaviors of individuals in interaction with each other, illustrated by agent-based computer simulations, has an unmeasured but probably great effect on the development of societies and the entire world, at the very least setting some of the cultural characteristics. Some events may set major conditions for future events. In the language of chaos theory, human history is *path dependent*, and the route actually taken to reach the current year constrains what may happen next, even as today's random events may take us on a new course. These observations suggest that sociology and related social sciences must examine the concrete sociocultural conditions that prevail and chart changes as they occur, recognizing that some apparently small but qualitatively different changes may cascade over time to have decisive impacts.

INDUCTIVE THEORY

Since the 1960s, sociologists have been using computers to test theories empirically, chiefly through statistical analysis of quantitative data. In the ideal situation, the theoretical literature provides one or more theories from which the researcher derives one or more testable hypotheses whose key concepts can be operationalized in more-or-less rigorously measured variables. The researcher then either collects new data or finds an existing data set that contains the appropriate variables. The statistical analysis determines whether the hypotheses are supported by the data, taking account of such things as statistical significance and interactions among independent or intervening variables.

This tradition of computer-assisted research has tended to emphasize theory testing rather than scientific discovery, and as computer technology and information resources have improved over the years, this bias has led to an increasing number of lost opportunities. In the 1960s, computers were primarily suited to the testing of well-defined theories, but the Internet-based computational infrastructure of the early years of the twenty-first century is far better suited to discovery, not only of hypotheses that can be tested in subsequent studies following the traditional approach, but also of complex models that transcend twentieth-century notions of what sociological theory fundamentally is.

Data mining is the use of sophisticated statistical and machine learning techniques to discover meaningful patterns in data. It is often associated with *data fusion* and *information integration*, sets of methods for bringing data together from multiple, distributed sources and combining different kinds of information, including multi-modal sources and texts in multiple languages. For decades, sociologists have employed statistical methods like exploratory factor analysis, cluster analysis,

and multi-dimensional scaling to find patterns in raw data, but they have not been especially enterprising in adopting new methods coming out of computer science, notably machine learning techniques in which autonomous software agents hunt for meaningful information.

The World Wide Web has arguably become the chief societal institution that not only transmits but also organizes human culture, and its influence can only grow in the future as most forms of information and culture migrate to it. Like the Roman bureaucracy before it, the Internet provides highways over which long-distance communication takes place, plus the rules that shape the meanings communicated. Consider the *recommender and reputation systems* employed by influential commercial websites like Amazon.com and eBay. The pages on Amazon.com for books by one of the most influential sociologists says: "Customers who bought titles by Max Weber also bought titles by these authors: Émile Durkheim, George Herbert Mead, Erving Goffman, Peter L. Berger." One may then look up each of these other authors, and trace a network of similarities outward until one has a chart of the network of affinities between authors that comprise the cultural territory of sociology. Based on the actual buying behavior of customers, such systems automatically categorize the books, music recordings, and objects sold. Thus, they simultaneously create the cultural ontologies of the future, on the basis of the behavior of the millions of people using the systems, and offer valuable tools for the sociologist who wants to study these phenomena.

New and effective linguistic tools such as Latent Semantic Analysis exist for comparing written texts online, such as political statements or Web home pages. Such methods constitute *computational ethnology*, rigorous techniques for mapping cultures and their processes of change, employing autonomous artificial intelligence agents. For example, one may use the Vivísimo clustering engine to chart relations among websites located by the Lycos search engine, on the basis of the frequencies of words shared by the sites. Searching for "God," in a demonstration limited to fewer than 200 sites, turns up 198 sites that Vivísimo places in ten categories, which it automatically labels: Church (26 sites), Life (17), Ministry (14), Loved (12),

Religious (12), God Exist (9), Children (7), Answers (9), Art (11), and Music (7). Without requiring any judgment by a human researcher, the system has identified ten chief themes surrounding God in our society, which we may further group as follows: religious institutions (Church, Ministry, Religious), personal needs and emotions (Life, Loved, Children), intellectual (God Exist, Answers), and aesthetic (Art, Music).

Websites may also be mapped in terms of the hyperlink connections between them. On June 10, 2004, the Alta Vista search engine was able to find a total of 4,964 websites that had links to the home page of the American Sociological Association. In contrast, it found fully 27,355 websites that linked to the American Psychological Association home page. Such data not only allow one to compare the Web-based popularities of organizations, discovering here that psychology is far more central to American society than sociology, but they can also show connections to specific institutions of society. Only 7.5 percent of the links to the ASA home page are from websites in the .COM domain, compared with 36.4 percent of the sites linking to the APA – strong evidence that psychology is more connected to the commercial sector.

Some of the sociological approaches that made the least use of old-style statistical "number-crunching" – symbolic interactionism, ethnomethodology, and comparative historical analysis – are likely to benefit most from these new forms of computing. What these approaches have in common is a focus on socially constructed realities that cannot easily be captured in discrete variables but consist of a tangle of contested meanings and negotiated roles. With the vast torrent of meaning communicated over the Internet, it is possible to take *grounded theory* (Glaser & Strauss 1967) to an entirely new level of sophistication, allowing us to study the aggregate results of chaotic social processes and thereby discover new theoretical concepts grounded in the socially constructed definitions currently dominant in the society.

This empirical computational sociology can become the input to multi-agent simulations designed to develop formal theoretical systems based on a combination of general laws of interaction with the specific chaos-generated social facts of the current social world. A recent development in computer science is the marriage of realtime empirical research and simulation in dynamic data-driven systems, an approach that apparently has yet to be employed in the social sciences but is being used already in meteorology. Many years of effort will be required to fulfill the vision of computational sociology, as talented sociologists in collaboration with computer and information scientists develop new methods and evangelize for them across the subfields of the discipline.

SEE ALSO: Complexity and Emergence; Computer-Aided/Mediated Analysis; Qualitative Computing; Theory and Methods; Theory Construction

REFERENCES AND SUGGESTED READINGS

Axelrod, R. (1984) *The Evolution of Cooperation*. Basic Books, New York.

Bainbridge, W. S. (1995a) Minimum Intelligent Neural Device: A Tool for Social Simulation. *Mathematical Sociology* 20: 179–92.

Bainbridge, W. S. (1995b) Neural Network Models of Religious Belief. *Sociological Perspectives* 38: 483–95.

Bainbridge, W. S. (1997) Cultural Diffusion. In: Bainbridge, W. S., *The Sociology of Religious Movements*. Routledge, New York, pp. 149–78.

Bainbridge, W. S (Ed.) (2004) *Encyclopedia of Human–Computer Interaction*. Berkshire, Great Barrington, MA.

Bainbridge, W. S., Brent, E. E., Carley, K., Heise, D. R., Macy, M. W., Markovsky, B., & Skvoretz, J. (1994) Artificial Social Intelligence. *Annual Review of Sociology* 20: 407–36.

Carley, K. M. (1991) A Theory of Group Stability. *American Sociological Review* 56: 331–54.

Carley, K. M. & Svoboda, D. M. (1996) Modeling Organizational Adaptation as a Simulated Annealing Process. *Sociological Methods and Research* 25: 138–68.

Crevier, D. (1993) *AI: The Tumultuous History of the Search for Artificial Intelligence*. Basic Books, New York.

Eve, R. A., Horsfall, S., & Lee, M. E. (Eds.) (1997) *Chaos and Complexity in Sociology: Myths, Models and Theory*. Sage, Thousand Oaks, CA.

Glaser, B. G. & Strauss, A. L. (1967) *The Discovery of Grounded Theory*. Aldine, Chicago.

Macy, M. W. (1995) PAVLOV and the Evolution of Cooperation: An Experimental Test. *Social Psychology Quarterly* 58: 74–87.

Macy, M. W. & Skvoretz, J. (1998) The Evolution of Trust and Cooperation between Strangers: A Computational Model. *American Sociological Review* 63: 638–60.

Macy, M. W. & Willer, R. (2002) From Factors to Actors: Computational Sociology and Agent-Based Modeling. *Annual Review of Sociology* 28: 143–66.

Mark, N. (1998) Beyond Individual Differences: Social Differentiation for First Principles. *American Sociological Review* 63: 309–30.

Markovsky, B. (1992) Network Exchange Outcomes: Limits of Predictability. *Social Networks* 14: 267–86.

Takahashi, N. (2000) The Emergence of Generalized Exchange. *American Journal of Sociology* 105: 1105–34.

computer-aided/ mediated analysis

Eben A. Weitzman

One of the key features of qualitative – non-numerical – data is that they are messy and usually voluminous. We wind up with huge piles of texts: transcripts, field notes, documents, questionnaires, pictures, audio, video, and so on, and have to sort our way through them. Add to this the need to find a rigorous approach to the analysis of these large quantities of data, and the researcher faces a daunting task. Researchers from different disciplines and different methodological perspectives will take different approaches to this task, but in most cases, computers can help.

Whether we are looking for what we think are identifiable phenomena that we can cluster together into categories or themes, or some more emergent, holistic sense of the data, we need to be able to organize the data in some way. We need to be able to find our way through it, whether by chronology, narrative structure, topic, case type, theme, or by some other kind of relationship between one piece of text and another. We may need to be able to

pull together all the pieces of text that have to do with a topic. We may need to be able to see each utterance in its original context to know what it means. Or we may need to be able to find support for a proposition or find the data that contradict it. When working with the often enormous piles of text generated in qualitative research, being careful, diligent, and thorough can be a tremendous challenge, both because of the volume of the data and the complexity of the thought required to analyze it. For all of these tasks, computers can be a big help (Weitzman & Miles 1995b; Weitzman 1999, 2003, 2004).

Software for qualitative data analysis (QDA) allows the analyst systematically to index and organize the data and then to retrieve the data reliably and flexibly in many different ways. For example, it can facilitate finding all the data *the analyst has previously identified* as indicating a particular theme or conceptual category, and it can facilitate parsing these data into subgroups based on demographic or other categorical or quantitative variables. It can also find all the cases where a theme was not present, or where combinations of themes are present, and so on. With the use of Boolean operators the analyst can construct queries of arbitrary complexity and execute them nearly instantly. The speed and consistency with which QDA software can carry out such operations already make it far more feasible to regularly carry out the kinds of analyses referred to above (Weitzman 2004).

However, it is critical to remember that software can provide tools to help you analyze qualitative data, but it cannot do the analysis for you – not in the same sense in which a statistical package like SPSS, SAS, or STATA can do, say, multiple regression. Many researchers have had the hope – for others, it is a fear – that the computer could somehow read the text and decide what it all means. That is, generally speaking, not the case. Thus it is particularly important to emphasize that using software cannot be a substitute for learning data analysis methods. The researcher must know what needs to be done and must do it. The software provides some tools to do it with.

An interesting series of empirical studies of research practice by Fielding, Lee, and Mangabeira (Fielding & Lee 1998; Mangabeira et al. 2004) has suggested that QDA software use may not always result in projects being more quickly completed. One important observation is that the work of initial coding of data is not much faster on screen than on paper. Further, on the first attempt at using QDA software, a significant investment of learning time may be required, which may slow things down, particularly at the outset. However, for users who are able to gain proficiency at software use after the initial learning period, the picture may soon change. Considering the sorts of operations described in the paragraph above, and in the discussion of particular types of software below, it is hard to imagine the researcher who can carry out those same functions as quickly by hand. This creates the opportunity for either more rapid production of results by the same methods that would have been employed by hand, or for the use of methods which would be too time consuming without the assistance of software. For a more detailed discussion of hopes and fears, and the limits of what software can do, see Weitzman (2003).

TYPES AND FUNCTIONS OF SOFTWARE FOR QDA

This is a rough sorting of available software into types. There is naturally quite a bit of overlap among categories, with individual programs having functions that would seem to belong to more than one type. However, it is possible to focus on the "heart and soul" of a program: what it mainly is intended for. This categorization scheme was first presented in Weitzman and Miles (1995b). Since then, the landscape has changed somewhat, both in terms of what programs do and in terms of what kinds of programs qualitative researchers are using. Some of the categories, like "code-and-retrieve" software, are virtually empty at this point. Others, like "textbase managers," appear to be rarely used by qualitative researchers. Most of the interest, and virtually all of the recent literature on the use of these programs, has focused on one category, "code-based theory builders." Nonetheless, qualitative researchers often find themselves faced with unique challenges – unusual data sets, novel analytic needs – and a knowledge of the range of

options remains useful. The categories are illustrated with examples of programs that fit them at the time of this writing.

Text Retrievers

Text retrievers specialize in finding all the instances of words and phrases in text, in one or several files. They typically also allow you to search for places where two or more words or phrases coincide within a specified distance (a number of words, sentences, pages, etc.) and allow you to sort the resulting passages into different output files and reports. Free, easy-to-use search programs available on the World Wide Web (e.g., X1 and Google Desktop) do these basic things very well. Many of the programs qualitative researchers typically turn to, on the other hand, may do other things as well, such as content analysis functions like counting, displaying keywords in context, or creating concordances (organized lists of all words and phrases in their contexts), or they may allow you to attach annotations or even variable values (for things like demographics or source information) to points in the text. Examples of text retrievers are Sonar Professional, ZyIN-DEX, and a variety of free (but hard to use) GREP tools available on the World Wide Web.

Textbase Managers

Textbase managers are database programs specialized for storing text in more or less organized fashion. They are good at holding text, together with information about it, and allowing you to organize quickly and sort your data in a variety of ways, and retrieve it according to different criteria. Some are better suited to highly structured data that can be organized into "records" (that is, specific cases) and "fields" (variables – information that appears for each case), while others easily manage "free-form" text. They may allow you to define fields in the fixed manner of a traditional database such as Microsoft Access or FileMaker Pro, or they may allow significantly more flexibility (e.g., allowing different records to have different field structures). Their search operations may be as good as (or sometimes even better than) those of some text retrievers.

Examples of textbase managers are askSam, InfoTree, and TEXTBASE ALPHA.

Code and Retrieve

Code-and-retrieve is the dominant paradigm for qualitative analysis software, but at this point most programs with code-and-retrieve capability have evolved to the more sophisticated code-based theory builder category discussed next. These programs are often developed by qualitative researchers specifically for the purpose of qualitative data analysis. As a baseline, the programs in this category have specialized in allowing the researcher to apply category tags (codes) to passages of text, and later retrieve and display the text according to the researcher's coding. These programs have at least some search capacity, allowing you to search either for codes or words and phrases in the text. They may have a capacity to store memos. Even the weakest of these programs represented a quantum leap forward from the old scissors-and-paper approach, being more systematic, more thorough, less likely to miss things, more flexible, and much, much faster. Examples of code-and-retrieve programs were the earlier versions of The Ethnograph, HyperQual2, Kwalitan, QUALPRO, Martin, and The Data Collector.

Code-Based Theory Builders

Code-based theory builders today appear to attract most of the qualitative researchers who employ software for their analyses. Most of these programs are also based on a code-and-retrieve model, but they go beyond the functions of code-and-retrieve programs. They do not, nor would you want them to, build theory for you. Rather, they have special features or routines that go beyond those of code-and-retrieve programs in supporting your theory-building efforts. For example, they may allow you to represent relations among codes, build higher-order classifications and categories, or formulate and test theoretical propositions about the data. For the most part, these programs allow you to create hierarchical trees of codes, but some (notably Atlas/ti and Hyper-RESEARCH) allow for non-hierarchical networks as well. They may have more powerful memoing features (allowing you, for example, to categorize or code your memos) or more sophisticated search-and-retrieval functions than had the earlier code-and-retrieve programs. They may have extended and sophisticated hyperlinking features, allowing you to link segments of text together, or to create links among segments of text, graphics, photos, video, audio, websites, and more. They may also offer capabilities for "system closure," allowing you to feed results of your analyses (such as search results or memos) back into the system as data. One program, QUALRUS, uses artificial intelligence techniques to suggest coding.

Increasingly, code-based theory builders support the integration of quantitative and qualitative data. It is important to distinguish here between "numbers in" capabilities and "numbers out" capabilities. With regard to numbers in approaches, some programs have strong facilities for applying quantitative or categorical variables to qualitative data sets, allowing the analyst to associate demographics, test scores, or survey results, for example, with the cases in their qualitative data. In the best implementations you can easily import whole spreadsheets of such variables into the qualitative analysis package and flexibly and easily examine subsets of cases based on combinations of these variables. For example, you might want to compare the occurrence of some qualitative theme you have identified in different demographic categories. Numbers out capabilities, on the other hand, allow the analyst to generate quantitative data based on their qualitative work and export it for further analysis in spreadsheets or statistical packages. The best implementations here allow you not only to generate numbers based on frequency of coding, but also to use coding for developing scores, flexibly generate frequencies of co-occurrence of codes either on text passages or within documents, and give you good control over the parameters of the matrices of numbers generated.

Finally, code-based theory builders are supporting teamwork with increasing flexibility. Many programs will now at least allow you to lump together coding work done on different copies of a data set (perhaps by different coders) into one new data set. More sophisticated merge functions allow you to track team members' work: who wrote which memo, who used which code on which passage of text, and so on, allowing not only more control over the merge, but also facilitating collaboration, and particularly discussions of differences in coding. Some programs will allow the generation of statistics assessing consistency of coding, or inter-coder reliability, and it is important to pay attention to the fact that different programs use quite different statistical models for this.

Multimedia capabilities have become for many researchers a significant issue in software choice. There are now several programs in the code-based theory builder category that allow you to use audio and video, as well as text, as data: AFTER, ATLAS/ti, C-I-SAID, Hyper-RESEARCH, InterClipper, TAMS Analyzer, and Transana all allow you to code and annotate audio and/or video files and search and retrieve from them, in ways quite similar to the ways they let you manipulate text. In these programs you can play a media file (audio or video), mark the beginning and ending points of segments, and then treat those segments much like segments of text.

Examples of code-based theory builders are AFTER, AnSWR, AQUAD, ATLAS/ti, C-I-SAID, HyperRESEARCH, MAXqda, NUD•IST, NVivo, QCA, fs/QCA, QUAL-RUS, and The Ethnograph. Three of these programs – AQUAD, QCA, and fs/QCA – support cross-case configural analysis, QCA being dedicated wholly to this method and not having any text-coding capabilities, and fs/QCA supporting Ragin's fuzzy-set extension of this methodology (Ragin 2000).

Conceptual Network Builders

These programs emphasize the creation and analysis of network displays. Some of them are focused on allowing you to create network drawings: graphic representations of the relationships among concepts. Examples of these are Inspiration and Visio. Others are focused on the analysis of cognitive or semantic networks (e.g., the program MECA). Still others offer some combination of the two approaches (e.g., SemNet and Decision Explorer). Finally, ATLAS/ti, a program also listed under code-based theory

builders, also has a fine graphical network builder connected to the analytic work you do with your text and codes, while others, like NVivo, offer an integrated drawing module which does not manipulate underlying relationships.

Summary

In concluding this discussion of the five main software family types, it is important to emphasize that functions often cross type boundaries. For example, askSAM can be used to code and retrieve and has an excellent text search facility. ATLAS/ti, NUD•IST, NVivo, The Ethnograph, and MAXqda graphically represent the relationships among codes, although among these only ATLAS/ti allows you to work with and manipulate the drawing. The first release of NVivo lets you draw diagrams, but any connections you draw are only represented in the diagram – they are not representations of the defined relationships among codes and other objects, as in ATLAS/ti. You see the actual relationships among codes in a hierarchical "explorer" with expandable and collapsible branches, as in NUD•IST, The Ethnograph, and MAXqda. The Ethnograph and MAXqda each have a system for attaching variable values (text, date, numeric, etc.) to text files and/or cases. Sphinx Survey allows you to work with survey data consisting of a mix of qualitative and quantitative data. The implication: do not decide too early which family you want to choose from. Instead, stay focused on the functions you need.

CHOOSING QDA SOFTWARE

There is no one best software program for analyzing qualitative data. Furthermore, there is no one best program for a particular type of research or analytic method. Researchers will sometimes ask "what's the best program for a study of health services?" or "what's the best program for doing grounded theory?" or "what's the best program for analyzing focus groups?" None of these questions has a good answer. Instead, choice needs to be approached based on the structure of the data, the specific things the analyst will want to do as part of the analysis, and the needs of the researcher around issues like ease of use, cost, time available, collaboration, and so on.

Four broad questions, along with two cut-across issues, can be asked that should guide the researcher to such a choice (Weitzman & Miles 1995a, 1995b; Weitzman 2003). These guidelines for choice have seen wide use in practice since their original formulation and have proven to be effective for guiding researchers to appropriate choices. They are presented here only in outline. For fuller discussions of these choice issues, see Weitzman (1999) or Weitzman (2003).

Specifically, there are four key questions to ask and answer as you move toward choosing one or more software packages, and some sub-points to the third and fourth are included here:

1   What kind of computer user am I?
2   Am I choosing for one project or the next few years?
3   What kind of project(s) and database(s) will I be working on?
    Single vs. multiple cases
    Data sources per case: single vs. multiple
    Data types (e.g., text, graphics, audio, video)
    Structured vs. open (e.g., fixed response vs. free text)
    Uniform vs. diverse entries (e.g., all interviews, or a mix of data types)
    Size of DATABASE
4   What kinds of analyses am I planning to do?
    Exploratory vs. confirmatory
    Coding scheme firm at start vs. evolving
    Multiple vs. single coding of passages
    Iterative vs. one pass
    Interest in context of data
    Intentions for displays
    Qualitative only, or numbers included (and numbers in vs. numbers out)
    Collaboration

In addition to these four key questions, there are two cut-across issues to bear in mind: How important is it to you to maintain a sense of "closeness" to your data? What are your financial constraints when buying software and the hardware it needs to run on?

With these basic issues clear (reference to a fuller version of these questions may be necessary), you will be able to look at specific programs in a more active, deliberate way, seeing what does or does not meet your needs. (You may find it helpful to organize your answers to these questions on a worksheet, such as the one proposed in Weitzman (1999), which has rows for each of the questions, and columns for answers, implications/notes, and candidate programs.) For example, if you are working on a complex evaluation study, with a combination of structured interviews, focus groups, and case studies, you will need strong tools for tracking cases through different documents. You might find good support for this in a program's code structures, or through the use of speaker identifiers that track individuals throughout the database.

CONCLUSION

Qualitative data analysis software is not an analysis methodology and it will not automatically analyze data. It provides tools which, in the hands of a competent researcher, can make possible analyses of great depth and rigor. It can facilitate the analyses of data sets of sizes that would not be feasible by hand. (A cautionary note is in order here: there has been an increasing number of projects in recent years in which researchers, believing that software will make it all possible, collect data sets of sizes that make meaningful analyses back-breaking, even with software.) There is a wide range of different software packages of different types available. Investigate what is available at the time you prepare your project. Do not constrain yourself to what the person down the hall or the person you met at the conference raved about (though having colleagues who use what you use can be a boon). QDA software, appropriately matched to a project's needs and thoughtfully applied, can greatly enhance the qualitative research enterprise.

SEE ALSO: Computational Sociology; Content Analysis; Conversation Analysis; Critical Qualitative Research; Documentary Analysis; Ethnography; Qualitative Computing; Text/Hypertext; Validity, Qualitative

REFERENCES AND SUGGESTED
READINGS

Fielding, N. G. & Lee, R. M. (1998) *Computer Ana-lysis and Qualitative Research*. Sage, London.
Mangabeira, W. C., Lee, R. M., & Fielding, N. G. (2004) Computers and Qualitative Research: Adoption, Use, and Representation. *Social Science Computer Review* 22(2): 167–78.
Miles, M. B. & Weitzman, E. A. (1996) The State of Qualitative Analysis Software: What Do We Need? *Current Sociology: Trend Reports* 44(3): 206–24.
Ragin, C. C. (2000) *Fuzzy-Set Social Science*. University of Chicago Press, Chicago.
Weitzman, E. A. (1999) Analyzing Qualitative Data with Computer Software. *Health Services Research* 34(5): 1241–63.
Weitzman, E. A. (2003) Software and Qualitative Research. In: Denzin, N. & Lincoln, Y. (Eds.), *Collecting and Interpreting Qualitative Materials*, 2nd edn. Sage, Thousand Oaks, CA, pp. 310–39.
Weitzman, E. A. (2004) Advancing the Scientific Basis of Qualitative Research. In: Ragin, C. C., Nagel, J., & White, P. (Eds.), *Workshop on the Scientific Foundations of Qualitative Research*. National Science Foundation, Arlington.
Weitzman, E. A. & Miles, M. B. (1995a) *Computer Programs for Qualitative Data Analysis: A Software Sourcebook*. Sage, Thousand Oaks, CA.
Weitzman, E. A. & Miles, M. B. (1995b) Choosing Software for Qualitative Data Analysis: An Overview. *Cultural Anthropology Methods* 7: 1–5.

Comte, Auguste (1798–1857)

David Michael Orenstein

Auguste Comte named sociology and established the French *realist* approach to the subject. He was born Isidore Auguste Marie François-Xavier Comte on January 19, 1798 in the French Mediterranean city of Montpellier during the aftermath of the great French Revolution. In his early teens he rejected the conservative Roman Catholic monarchist views of his parents and declared himself a republican and a free thinker. A prodigy in mathematics, at 15 he passed the nationally competitive entrance exams for the prestigious École Polytechnique, but had to wait a year until he met the minimum age of admission. A charismatic student leader, in April 1816 Comte was expelled from that school and Paris when a student demonstration was used as an excuse to purge anti-monarchist students. Dropping his first name, he returned to Paris as Auguste Comte in July.

Comte supported himself as a private tutor and attended public lectures on an array of scientific topics. At one of these he met the philosopher Henri de Saint-Simon and soon accepted a position as Saint-Simon's secretary and editorial assistant. Their relationship terminated in a bitter falling out in 1824. That year Comte also married Caroline Massine, a former Parisian prostitute. In 1826 Comte initiated work on a series of lectures intended to organize all scientific knowledge into a coherent single system. In the course of writing he suffered a nervous breakdown and was institutionalized. Released as uncured into the care of his wife, he attempted suicide, before completing his lectures. Those lectures provided the foundation for Comte's multivolumed *The Positive Philosophy*.

The Positive Philosophy included Comte's arguments for a science of society detailing its areas of focus, methodological approach, and applied use. In early remarks he called that science *social physics*, but then switched to *sociology*, a term he had previously used in private correspondence. He modified and expanded on his conception of sociology in numerous later writings, the most important of which is the *System of Positive Polity*.

In 1844 Comte met Clotilde de Vaux. He credited her with revealing to him the necessity of altruistic love as a foundation for social harmony. After her death two years later he promoted her to sainthood in the Religion of Humanity that he had founded, surrounded himself with disciples, and rejected those who wanted to develop sociology without embracing his religion. Comte died on September 5, 1857.

SOCIOLOGY, POSITIVISM, AND THE HIERARCHY OF THE SCIENCES

Comte's sociology reflects a rejection of Cartesian rationalism. Social relationships are not to be comprehended by a process of intro-spective doubt and reflection. Rather, sociol-ogy is to be based on empirical observation in order to discover determinate social laws and how these laws can be used to improve social harmony. For Comte, the discovery of such laws constitutes *pure* sociology; dis-covery of how to use those laws in order to engineer a better society constitutes *applied* sociology.

Sociology is conceived by Comte as part of a larger system of knowledge – *the positive philosophy*. This system assumes a series of increasingly complex levels of reality. Each level of reality is governed by a distinct set of determinant laws that cannot be reduced to (i.e., logically deduced from) those of another level. Each level thus requires a separate science to discover its particular laws. These sciences themselves are presented as social evolutionary developments that emerge from pre-scientific explanation. Knowledge originates as *theolo-gical*, becomes *metaphysical*, and culminates as *positive* (or scientific). Theological explana-tions ascribe events to actions of supernatural agencies. Metaphysical explanation assumes that outcomes reflect underlying essences. And positive explanation, according to Comte, relies solely on the objective observation of relationships.

Comte argues that the simpler the subject matter of a science, the sooner it will reach the positive level. In that social reality depends on preexisting physical, chemical, and biologi-cal realities, it is the most complex. Therefore, sociology is the last science to emerge. In Comte's hierarchical arrangement of the sciences, sociology's complexity places it first, followed by biology and so on. There is no science of psychology. The basic unit of the social is not the individual but the family. Indi-viduals obtain their identity in the family and larger social entities evolutionarily emerge from the family.

As the highest and final science to emerge, sociology signifies the completion of transfor-mation from pre-scientific to scientific knowl-edge and allows the reorganization of all of social life on scientific principles. This exalted role of providing the foundation for both per-manent intellectual and social harmony earns it the title of *the Queen Science*.

SOCIAL STATICS AND SOCIAL DYNAMICS

Comte takes a *realist* approach to society. Society is not a mere construct or simply the aggregation of individual activities. It is a real entity that develops over time. For the purposes of study, Comte makes an analytical distinction between *social dynamics* (the study of change) and *social statics* (the study of order). Comte's social dynamics mostly reflects the Enlighten-ment-inspired evolutionism of the Marquis de Condorcet. Social statics is built primarily on the conservative anti-Enlightenment philoso-phy of Joseph de Maistre. In Comte's sociology there is a persistent tension between Enlight-enment and anti-Enlightenment sources. An Enlightenment emphasis on progress, indepen-dent reason, and scientific questioning of dogma coexists with a desire for a return to medieval harmony, religious faith, obligatory moral codes, and traditional gender roles.

Statically, society is presented as an organic system of interdependent parts. Social harmony is dependent on beliefs, values, moral bonds, and altruistic sentiments that obligate indivi-duals to fulfill duties toward one another and the collective good. The greatest danger to social order comes from self-interested *egoism*. Women, who are presumed more socially oriented than men, are essential for reminding men of their social obligations, thereby curbing their tendency toward egoism. Dynamically, society is governed by Comte's famous *law of three stages*. According to this law, society (like each science) evolves from a theological to a metaphysical then to a positive stage. These stages are conceived of mentalistically: that is, all the features of a society are shaped by how the events of the world are understood and explained.

The Theological and Metaphysical Stages

In the *theological stage* events are accounted for by the actions of supernatural agencies. In the earliest period of this stage, *fetishism*, human-like motivations are attributed to non-human entities – the wind, rivers, and animal spirits all have motivations that shape their actions. In that the world is seen as explicable in terms of human-like motivations, fetishism generates little abstract thought to comprehend it and no authoritative priesthood to intercede with greater forces. Accordingly, social progress is slow, technology remains simple, and social organization is marginal with limited coordination of collective undertakings. *Polytheism* replaces fetishism. It personifies the supernatural into deities who control the objects and events of the earth. Contemplation of the deities and the rise of a priesthood with specialized knowledge of how to placate them leads to social advance in intellect and the coordination of collective projects. The evolution of the conception of these deities from simply having differing spheres of control to a hierarchical arrangement ultimately leads to the most advanced form of the theological stage – *monotheism*. ll supernatural powers existing within a single entity. Using exclusively medieval European examples, Comte presents monotheistic society as a stable society in which secular and spiritual powers are divided between national rulers and an international church. The spiritual authority functions to constrain and direct the use of secular power for collective purposes. Although stable and harmonious, monotheism exhausts the evolutionary potential of theological reasoning. Monotheism (and the theological stage as a whole) thus begins a decline that undermines the feudal familial, economic, and political institutions that depend on it.

Metaphysical society is both negative and progressive: negative because it provides no foundation for long-term social harmony, progressive because it paves the way for the *positivism* to follow. Destruction and false starts in creating the new assure it a comparatively short existence full of intellectual discord and violent conflict. The first part of the stage, *Protestantism*, involves a breakup of monotheism's international spiritual and moral unity leading to intellectual and civil conflict. The second part of the stage, *Deism*, is one of failed attempts to recreate social order based on false principles. For example, the metaphysical doctrine of natural rights is seen as leading to egoistic self-aggrandizement and a loss of a sense of obligatory subordination to a greater collective good. Comte views any government and social order intellectually conceived of as a contract based on such supposed rights as a preordained failure.

The Positive Stage and the Religion of Humanity

The *positive stage* requires sociology's emergence so that society can be reorganized on a scientific basis. A republican, but not a democrat, Comte conceives positive society as run on the basis of scientific principles discovered by a meritocratically selected elite. Due to assumed innate gender differences (males having greater rational ability, women having a greater affective role in the maintenance of social harmony by encouraging altruistic behavior), the elite is to be exclusively male. Comte rejects absolute property rights as metaphysical dogma, but he also rejects communism. He envisions privately held but highly regulated industry. Comte began to lose many of his early followers not only when he said that positive society would need a new secular religion to guide it, but when he additionally began to develop that religion, declaring himself its high priest. Positive society in Comte's final works resembles de Maistre's idealized image of medieval society – an organic whole in which all people know their role obligations both to all others and to the societal whole as they live under the watchful eye of a knowledgeable and beneficent international spiritual authority.

Comte's self-anointing as the High Priest of Humanity allowed later generations of sociologists to dismiss him as a mentally unbalanced non-sociologist easily relegated to the field's prehistory. But it is a mistake to understand the Religion of Humanity in purely personal and extra-sociological terms, thereby ignoring its sociohistorical and social theoretical contexts. Comte undeniably had idiosyncrasies, but his use of religion – even an atheological one – to establish a sociomoral order modified an existing approach in French social thought (e.g., Robespierre's Religion of Reason). Moreover, a new religion makes sense in terms of Comte's theory. In Comte's sociology, the theological content justifying subordination to the social was evolutionarily outdated, but not the use of religious symbolism and organization. A positive society did not imply advanced scientific thinking amongst all its members. For the common individual sentiment dominated intellect. Social harmony required collective symbols and rituals to create a sense of obligation and subordination to the collective good. As a transnational entity, the Positivist Church was intended to provide world unity. And as an entity independent of secular political authority, it was also to provide a check on the abuse of political power.

SOCIOLOGICAL METHODOLOGY

Despite an emphasis on empirical observation, Comte insists that systematic theory must precede and guide research: without theory, research would produce inapplicable unintegrated information. Methodologically, Comte maintains that each science resembles most closely those nearest to it on the hierarchy of the sciences. Sociology therefore resembles biology with its emphasis of classification through comparison. Comte's *comparative method* includes three forms of comparison: comparison of human to non-human societies (e.g., insect societies), comparison of societies at the same level of development, and comparison of societies at different levels of development. This third approach forms Comte's *historical method*. st. Following Condorcet, it is based on treating data from different societies around the world and differing historical periods as if they represent data derived from a single society. The historical method is justified by Comte's social dynamics. Society is actually evolving toward a single worldwide positive society. From this inevitable future perspective all humanity is joined together in social evolution.

Unlike later positivists, Comte rejects the use of mathematical formulae, statistical analysis, and causal reasoning in social analysis. Mathematical formulae are deemed appropriate only for sciences lower on the scientific hierarchy. They are insufficient for the complexities of biology and sociology. Statistical probabilistic reasoning is declared incompatible with sociology's focus on discovering definite deterministic lawful relationships. It implies for Comte an uncertainty incompatible with the degree of accuracy necessary for applied ameliorative use of sociological knowledge. And, causal analysis is rejected in terms of Comte's reading of Aristotle, Immanuel Kant, and David Hume.

Aristotle argued that causality implies the existence of some ultimate or first cause. Comte sees this as positing some underlying metaphysical essence extrinsic to scientific observation. Kant locates causes not in reality itself but in the human perception of reality. For Comte, this means a cause describes an intermediary representation and not a feature of social reality itself. And Hume presents a cause as always inferred. It is never the product of empirical observation. Comte thus believes that to say "A" causes "B" involves a metaphysical nonempirical approach that looks at intermediary perceptual phenomena. He proposes instead only to state objective concomitant or sequential relationships (e.g., "A" exists when "B" exists or "A" exists prior to "B"). For Comte, doing so explains social reality without the distortions of metaphysical suppositions.

Comte presents sociological explanation as both absolute and finite: absolute in that it is unmediated, but finite because it is limited by the practical constraints of human observation. A simple example of scientific limitation is found in Comte's discussion of chemistry. Comte assumes that stars are composed of the same chemical compounds found on earth. But their distance from the earth precludes the possibility of ever traveling to the stars to determine their exact makeup. Rather than such limitations humbling Comte, they embolden him. Comte believes that limits to knowledge mean that sociologists can gain almost all the knowledge available to human observation in a relatively short period of time and then quickly move to applying sociological knowledge to usher in the positive stage. Engineers need not know the composition of the stars to design a structurally sound bridge; similarly, sociologists need only finite empirically available knowledge to engineer a structurally sound society.

PROBLEMATIC ELEMENTS IN COMTE'S REASONING

Comte's methodological approach has numerous problems. The acceptance of Condorcet's use of data from diverse societies as if they represented data from a single society at various stages of development is tautological – only if his dynamic theory is correct is using data from non-western societies to describe features of early periods of European ones justified. Comte's exclusive reliance on European illustrations and period names for substages of the metaphysical stage leaves unclear which features of Protestantism and Deism are to be considered universal and which are peculiar to European experience. And Comte's presentation of the features of the final stage are purely speculative. It cannot be grounded in empirical observation in that no fully positivistic societies have ever existed.

Comte attempts to simultaneously declare the coming into existence of sociology and that sociology is sufficiently advanced to prescribe necessary reforms. He can do this only because his theory does not meet the scientific criteria he insists upon! Rather, it is built on what he otherwise describes as pre-scientific metaphysical reasoning. He assumes a necessary and innate universal nature that destines societies to develop in only one particular direction. He then deduces that direction and specifies what the future will and should be.

Comte's *static sociology* is also flawed. It relies not on actual historical analysis of the relationship of institutions but on de Maistre's polemical romanticized representation of medieval Europe as a perfectly harmonious society. It is no more empirical than the image of the noble savage in the writings of Rousseau that Comte detested. Comte never empirically investigates the historical limits of social integration, but instead uses an analogy to biological functioning to assert both past and future near perfect harmony.

Finally, Comte's stated faith in the ability of sociology to achieve pure objective knowledge of the social shows naïveté even for the period in which he is writing. His attempt to get around Kantian relativity of knowledge by avoiding the use of causation is mere semantics. His motto, *prévoir pour pouvoir* (prevision to allow control) implies causal predictive power, even if Comte banishes the terms cause and causality from sociology's vocabulary.

COMTE'S INFLUENCE ON LATER SOCIOLOGY

While Comte was still living, a split developed between those dedicated to the totality of his thought (i.e., who wished to spread his religion) and those solely focused on advancing sociology. Positivistic churches spread to cities in Europe and the Americas. Within sociology, Comte's realist approach soon had both followers and opponents. In his native France, the realists came to be represented by Émile Durkheim and his students. The foremost opponent was Gabriel Tarde. Durkheim, despite other significant influences, always considered Comte to be sociology's founder. Like Comte, Durkheim posited a series of increasingly complex emergent realities, each with its own laws. Though Durkheim did accept the existence of both a psychological reality and the legitimacy of a science of psychology, he argued that the social constituted a reality whose laws and facts could not be reduced to the psychological. The reductionist Tarde rejected this realist image and attempted to construct sociology based on psychological processes of imitation. Durkheim's position at the Sorbonne gave an academic home to his realist view, which also found support from the secular educational liberal ministry of the Third Republic. But French sociology suffered from two world wars. Many Durkheimians perished in the first (including Durkheim's son André), and others (like Maurice Halbwachs) were killed during the Holocaust and the second. Certainly, Comtean realist sociological ideas persisted in later French social thought. But Comte's most persistent influence on sociology is to be found in the reactions against his work in Germany and Italy and in the selective appropriation of his ideas in the English-speaking world.

Reaction to Comte's ideas from German historicists like Wilhelm Dilthey was generally one of hostility. Comte was seen as having gone too far in the wholesale application of natural science reasoning to historical and cultural phenomena. Kantian moral autonomy, individual volition, unique national features, and the impact of genius in shaping the *spirit* of a society were lost in Comte's comparative deterministic focus on universal laws of order and change. But if Comte had exceeded the permissible degree of comparison and generalization in social study, it remained unclear what degree of lawful generalizing was possible in social science. A great late nineteenth-century German discussion ensued. That discussion created the academic environment in which Georg Simmel and Max Weber developed their sociologies. Both Simmel and Weber can each be viewed as defining a middle ground between Comte's positivistic and Dilthey's approach to the social.

Along with Spencer, Comte also serves as a foil used by the neo-Machiavellian Vilfredo Pareto in the development of his sociology. Pareto views Comte's progressive evolutionism as confounding moral wishes with social scientific analysis. Pareto's stark image of the social as non-rational and non-progressive with self-interested elites in the endless pursuit of power for its own sake often reads like a demonic inversion of Comtean sociology. For Pareto, knowledge of social laws has no ameliorative applicability and human irrationality, conflict, and suffering persist unabated forever.

In the English-speaking world the spread of Comte's ideas was greatly assisted by Harriet Martineau's 1853 condensed translation of *The Positive Philosophy*. Praised by Comte himself, its clarity, flow, and focus on core ideas surpassed the original, making Comte's ideas more apprehendable in English than in French. Comte was at first seen as a true social science innovator in British intellectual circles, as evidenced by the early part of his long correspondence with J. S. Mill. For a variety of reasons, though, that correspondence degraded into animosity with Mill rejecting Comte as a social scientist. Herbert Spencer later sought to develop sociology on non-Comtean grounds. Yet Spencer, influenced by Marian Evans (pen-named George Eliot), incorporated the Comtean concept of *altruism* as a necessary mechanism of social solidarity in advanced societies.

In the pre-1920 institutionalizing period of American sociology, Comte was generally accepted as the discipline's founder. Citations to his work were exceeded only by those to Spencer's. Comte was the main influence on Lester Ward, the first president of what is now called the American Sociological Association. Durkheim in this same period was generally dismissed as having a collective image of society incompatible with American views of social action. But in American sociology since World War II Comte is infrequently cited and, when discussed, usually presented only as an anticipator of the field. As Comte's reputation declined, Durkheim's increased, and he is now regarded with Weber (and sometimes Karl Marx) as a true founder of the field. But certain arguments and approaches to sociology still reflect Comtean realism and are remnants of his early influence, or come filtered through the later (albeit selective) appropriation of Durkheimian thought by American sociology. Among these are: the distinction between pure and applied sociology; the analytical separation of the study of developmental social change from the study of social integration and functioning (Comte's statics and dynamics); the view of change as a natural process and not a product of individual genius or rationally connived social contract; the focus on sociology as a holistic field integrating the findings of subfields; the view of social bonds as a product of socialized learning and not rational choice; the emphasis on an empirical research; the insistence that sociology is an independent field and not just the collective subfield of psychology; the widespread use of physical science like determinism in social explanation; and a focus on the family and religious values as central to social order.

Perhaps, though, Comte's greatest influence is to be found not in the particulars of his theory but in the creation of a model of what constitutes theory in sociology. Unlike political science, in which theory denotes the body of work by a particular individual (e.g., Hobbesean, Lockean, or Machiavellian theory), or economics, in which theory often denotes a set of predictive equations, in sociology a theory tends to be a logical deductive system of propositions that includes a model of social structure order and change, a conception of how the individual is related to and internalizes the social, and a related methodology statement on how the social is to be studied. Comte provided that model.

Finally, as we move toward a postmodern future, how terms like postmodern and postmodernity themselves are used may reflect sociology's persistent, but generally unacknowledged, Comtean heritage. Comte, like Durkheim after him, focused on the present as a period of total social transition to an emergent modern social consciousness. To the extent that the postmodern is looked at as a natural worldwide social evolutionary emergent shared social consciousness that impacts on the totality of human thought and action, the term's use appears very Comtean indeed. The view that this transition starts in the West but spreads to all of humanity is also Comtean. And as sociologists construct theories of postmodernity to prevision the direction of that social evolutionary change, guide empirical research, and develop applied programs to improve social harmony, sociology's agenda appears still linked to Comte's image of the academic discipline that he named.

SEE ALSO: Durkheim, Émile; Halbwachs, Maurice; Martineau, Harriet; Positivism; Simmel, Georg; Spencer, Herbert; Theory; Weber, Max

REFERENCES AND SUGGESTED READINGS

Comte, A. (1974) *The Positive Philosophy*. AMS Press, New York.
Comte, A. (1976) *System of Positive Polity*. Burt Franklin, New York.
Heilbron, J. (1995) *The Rise of Social Theory*. University of Minnesota Press, Minneapolis.
Manuel, F. E. (1965) *The Prophets of Paris*. Harper & Row, New York.
Pickering, M. F. (1993) *Auguste Comte: An Intellectual Biography*. Cambridge University Press, Cambridge.
Scharff, R. C. (1995) *Comte After Positivism*. Cambridge University Press, Cambridge.
Wernick, A. (2001) *Auguste Comte and the Religion of Humanity: The Post-Theistic Program of French Theory*. Cambridge University Press, Cambridge.
Wright, T. R. (1986) *The Religion of Humanity: The Impact of Comtean Positivism on Victorian Britain*. Cambridge University Press, Cambridge.

confidence intervals

Geoff Cumming

A confidence interval (CI) is an *interval estimate* of a population parameter. It is a range of values, calculated from data, that is likely to include the true value of the population parameter. When a newspaper reports "support for the government is 43 percent, in a poll with an error margin of 3 percent," the 43 percent is a *point estimate* of the true level of support in the whole population. The CI is 43 ± 3 percent, or (40, 46 percent). The 3 percent is half the width of the CI, and is called the *margin of error*. The endpoints of the CI are the *lower* and *upper limits* or *bounds*.

The *level of confidence*, C, is expressed as a percentage. Most commonly, $C = 95$ is chosen, to give 95 percent CIs, although 99 percent CIs, 90 percent CIs, or CIs with other levels of confidence may be used. Understanding level of confidence is the key to understanding CIs, and will be discussed in the context of an example that also illustrates calculation of a CI in a simple case.

To estimate μ, the mean level of community-mindedness, we administer a measure to a random sample of $n = 30$ people from the population, and calculate mean $M = 59.52$ and standard deviation $s = 32.4$. The margin of error is $w = t_C \times s/\sqrt{n} = 12.11$, where $t_C = 2.045$ is the critical value of t, with $(n - 1) = 29$ degrees of freedom, for confidence level $C = 95$. The 95 percent CI for μ is thus 59.52 ± 12.11, or (47.41, 71.63). There is a link with null hypothesis significance testing (NHST), in that any value outside a 95 percent CI would, given the data, be rejected as a null hypothesis at the .05 level of significance, and any value inside the CI would not be rejected.

Figure 1 shows a simulation of 20 independent random samples of size 30 from a normal population with $\mu = 53$ and standard deviation $\sigma = 30$. The leftmost sample has M and s as stated above. Such a sequence of samples will, in the long run, give CIs that capture μ on C percent of occasions, and this is the correct way to understand level of confidence.

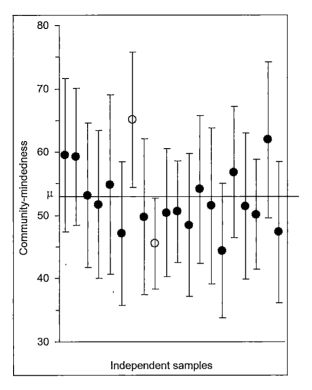

Figure 1 Means and 95 percent confidence intervals (CIs) for 20 independent samples from a population with mean μ = 53, showing sample-to-sample variation. The intervals vary in width because each is based on the standard deviation of that sample. In the long run, 95 percent of CIs are expected to include μ. Here, two CIs (open circles) do not include μ. More generally, *C* percent of CIs will in the long run include μ, where *C* is the level of confidence. Note that μ is more often captured by the central region of a CI than by regions near the upper or lower limits of an interval. In practice, μ is not known and only one sample is taken.

We can say "we are 95 percent confident that our interval (47.41, 71.63) includes μ," but it is misleading to say "the probability is .95 that our interval includes μ" because that suggests μ varies, whereas μ is fixed but unknown. The CI for our sample is just one in an indefinitely long sequence, and we never know whether it does or does not include μ. We know only that 95 percent of all possible CIs will include μ, the population parameter we are estimating.

Each CI in Figure 1 is symmetric about the mean, but CIs for correlations and proportions, for example, are typically asymmetric (Altman et al. 2000). CIs can be difficult to calculate: CIs for some standardized measures of effect size, for example, require use of noncentral distributions and an iterative computer procedure (Cumming & Finch 2001; Smithson 2002).

CIs were introduced by Jerzy Neyman in 1934. They are a key component in *statistical estimation*, part of *statistical inference*. Both CIs and NHST are part of the frequentist approach to probability and statistics. In a quite different approach, Bayesian statistics, an analogous role is played by *credible intervals*, which do permit statements like "the probability is .95 that μ lies in this interval," where the interval has been calculated from the data, after assuming some prior probability distribution for the parameter. Although CIs and credible intervals have entirely different theoretical foundations, in some simple situations, with reasonable assumptions, the 95 percent CI and

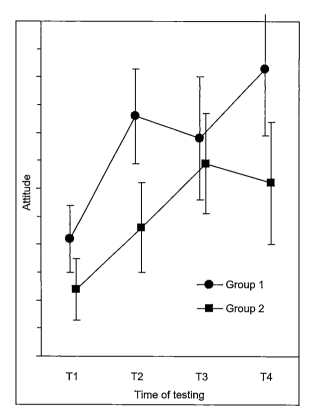

Figure 2   Means and 95 percent CIs for two groups of respondents, each tested on four occasions. Group is a between-subjects factor, and the CIs shown may be used to assess a between-groups comparison, such as Group 1 vs. Group 2, at time T1. Time of testing, however, is a repeated measure, and the CIs may *not* be used to assess a comparison across time, for example T1 vs. T2 for Group 1, because the CIs do not account for the correlation between the measures. In the figure, means at each testing time are slightly offset so CIs can be seen clearly.

the 95 percent credible interval are numerically identical.

During the mid-twentieth century, NHST swept to dominance across the social sciences, although cogent criticisms of it were published. Statistical reformers advocated, among other things, wider use of CIs in addition to or in place of NHST. During the 1980s, medicine largely embraced reform, and it became routine to report CIs. In the social sciences, NHST still dominates, although in psychology reformers have had some success. The influential *Publication Manual* of the American Psychological Association now recommends use of CIs.

Four advantages of CIs are (1) they give point and interval estimates in units that are meaningful in the research context; (2) they help combine evidence over experiments, and thus encourage meta-analysis and meta-analytic thinking; (3) CI width gives information about precision, which may be more useful than a calculation of statistical power; and (4) there is a link with familiar NHST and p values (Cumming & Finch 2001).

However, there is evidence of a widely held misconception about CIs, as there is about NHST. Also, the graphic representing a CI in Figure 1 is ambiguous: it is used also for standard error (SE) bars, which depict an interval

± SE about a mean that is typically about half the total width of the 95 percent CI for the same data. It is unfortunate that the same graphic is used with two such different meanings, and every figure showing error bars must state clearly what they represent.

In Figure 2 the two 95 percent CIs at T1 overlap by about one quarter the length of either interval. For independent means, like them, this amount of overlap corresponds to about $p = .05$ and so the difference between the two means is about at the border of .05 statistical significance (Cumming & Finch 2005). However, for two correlated means, the CIs on the means are *irrelevant* for an assessment of the difference, because the CIs do not reflect the correlation. Therefore, the CIs in Figure 2 may *not* be used to assess comparisons involving a repeated measure, such as T1 with T2 for Group 1. It is a problem that conventional graphics, as in Figure 2, do not distinguish repeated-measure variables from between–subjects variables. CIs have much to offer, but better guidelines are needed for their interpretation, and better graphical conventions that avoid ambiguity and make clear what inferences are justified.

SEE ALSO: Effect Sizes; Experimental Design; Random Sample; Statistical Significance Testing; Variables, Independent

REFERENCES AND SUGGESTED READINGS

Altman, D. G., Machin, D., Bryant, T. N., & Gardner, M. J. (2000) *Statistics With Confidence: Confidence Intervals and Statistical Guidelines*, 2nd edn. British Medical Journal Books, London.
Cumming, G. & Finch, S. (2001) A Primer on the Understanding, Use, and Calculation of Confidence Intervals that are Based on Central and Noncentral Distributions. *Educational and Psychological Measurement* 61: 530–72.
Cumming, G. & Finch, S. (2005) Inference by Eye: Confidence Intervals, and How to Read Pictures of Data. *American Psychologist* 60: 170–80.
Kline, R. B. (2004) *Beyond Significance Testing: Reforming Data Analysis Methods in Behavioral Research*. American Psychological Association Books, Washington, DC.
Smithson, M. (2002) *Confidence Intervals*. Sage, Thousand Oaks, CA.

conflict (racial/ethnic)

John Stone and Polly Rizova

Conflict is a basic process in social life and can be both destructive and cohesive. In some situations, it can be destructive for some groups and act as a cohesive force for others. Racial and ethnic groups may be the source and the result of the two faces of social conflict, acting as a boundary marker between groups that see themselves as distinctive in their interests and values from other such groups. Over the past 50 years, sociologists have grappled with a variety of perspectives on conflict that have emphasized various aspects of the destructive and the integrative nature of the process. Functional theorists have tended to downplay the purely negative forces while conflict theorists have tried to establish the central role of conflict as a means to challenge the status quo and bring about fundamental social change. Several attempts have also been made to refine and integrate the two approaches: pointing to the functions of social conflict or to elements of consensus and equilibrium found in both models.

Much of classical sociological theory analyzed conflict against the backdrop of the industrial and political revolutions of the late eighteenth and early nineteenth centuries in Europe and focused on class, status, and party groups as the principal bases of group struggle. Divisions arising out of racial or ethnic membership tended to be assigned to a peripheral position in the analysis, despite the overwhelming significance of war, colonialism, nationalism, and genocide that formed an equally central part of the historical experience. Some social thinkers did attribute greater importance to race and nation, but these individuals, such as Gobineau or Fitzhugh, were either fully fledged racial theorists or apologists for slavery. W. E. B. Du Bois, whose pioneering sociological studies of race relations at the turn of the century were a notable exception, found his works largely ignored during his lifetime. It was only in the second half of the twentieth century that the catastrophic results of fascism and the expansion of studies of racism, apartheid, and colonialism brought racial and ethnic conflict to the center of sociological analysis.

In the United States, the struggles of the Civil Rights Movement in the 1960s, urban riots, and the violent nature of the confrontation between the forces defending segregation and those demanding racial justice began to make Parsonian theory, the dominant paradigm in the 1950s, look like an increasingly inadequate model to understand current developments. Together with the polarizing force of the Vietnam War, the idea of society viewed as an integrated system of self-regulating subunits became increasingly implausible; somehow, conflict needed to be brought back into the sociological analysis. However, Marxist notions of a bipolar division between bourgeoisie and proletariat, while stressing conflict as a central theme, nevertheless also appeared to ignore, or at best gloss over, the powerful reality of racial, ethnic, and national conflicts. Reformulations of the Marxist tradition, particularly trying to incorporate race and ethnic conflicts into a global – world-systems – approach, seemed to be a better synthesis of class and race.

In South Africa, the implementation of apartheid after 1948 provided a stark example of a society based on racial oppression and naked force exercised by one racially defined group over others. One of the insightful early sociological studies of apartheid was aptly titled *South Africa: A Study in Conflict* (1965), written by a student from Parsons's sociology department at Harvard. Clearly, the reality of racial and ethnic conflict in apartheid South Africa made van den Berghe apply a radically different approach from that advocated by the author of *The Social System*. The decline and fall of apartheid some 30 years later, however, failed to support van den Berghe's conflict-laden predictions of the 1960s, and an understanding of why this relatively peaceful outcome occurred provided some useful lessons in the complex interplay between racial and ethnic divisions. A revolution of rising expecta-

tions, a powerful explanation for fundamental conflicts since its original formulation by Alexis de Tocqueville to interpret the French Revolution, did not escalate into a race war under South African conditions. Whether this was a result of the closely integrated nature of the South African economy, the moderation and wisdom of the ANC leadership, miscalculations by the white elite, or the geopolitical changes produced by the end of the Cold War remain questions that will be the subject of debate for years to come.

Another example of ethnic conflict, but this time one that developed in a much more violent and destructive manner than in South Africa, was the collapse of Yugoslavia in the aftermath of the breakup of the Soviet Union. Unlike South Africa, Yugoslavia appeared to have many favorable preconditions that might have been expected to ameliorate conflict in the runup to the dissolution of the Soviet Empire. Tito's state had been more open to western democratic influences than many of its eastern European neighbors, was more economically advanced, and had a relatively decentralized federal system allowing significant autonomy to its diverse multi-ethnic, territorial units. Of all the satellites of the Soviet Union, this state seemed best positioned to handle the transition from communist rule to democracy without widespread ethnic violence. In reality, the state degenerated rapidly into civil war with a series of secessionist movements that led to the worst examples of ethnic cleansing and genocidal massacres in Europe since the end of World War II. What were the factors that caused this surprising outcome? Most analysts point to the role of geopolitical changes in undermining the legitimacy and rationale of the Yugoslav state. The divergent interests between the Serbian elites and Croatian, Slovenian, and Bosnian leadership produced a new context in which mobilization on an ethnic basis brought about the destruction of the previous federation. Former communist leaders quickly reframed their appeal on nationalist themes and the power vacuum created by the collapse of the Soviet bloc released these forces in a deadly struggle for ethnic autonomy and hegemony.

The examples of South Africa and Yugoslavia suggest the complex dynamics of ethnic and racial conflict in the modern world. Much of the research on ethnicity and racial divisions has shifted toward trying to understand the processes of ethnogenesis, the construction and perpetuation of ethnic boundaries, and the impact of forces like globalization and transnationalism on racial and ethnic conflict. While traditional patterns of international migration continue to play an important role in the generation of racial and ethnic diversity, they have been modified and changed by political and economic factors in complex and unpredictable ways. In the United States, large numbers of Mexican migrants, both legal and unauthorized, have continued the growth of the Latino population into the largest single minority group. In Europe, the relations between immigrants and ethnic minorities – not least the increasing number of Muslim migrants from Turkey and North Africa – will be a major element in determining the conflict and stability of the emerging political structure, no matter whether the European Union becomes a superstate or remains a looser federation.

A central focus of concern among social scientists has been to provide a better understanding of the dynamics of ethnic conflict and racial violence. Inadequate assumptions about the nature of modernization and modernity have been revealed by the increasing salience of such conflicts under capitalism, socialism, and in the developing world. The expectation that modernity would result in a smooth transition from *gemeinschaft* to *gesellschaft*, from community to association, accompanied by the gradual dissolution of ethnic affiliations and racial identities, has proved to be entirely inaccurate. The continuation of persistent racial inequality in the United States, and the stubborn tenacity of ethnic warfare and genocide in societies as diverse and remote from each other as Bosnia and Burundi, suggest that these forms of division have not lost their power to mobilize human groups and to undermine such "rational" considerations as economic profits and losses. Ironically, failure to appreciate the strength of ethnic ties under Marxist regimes was repeated by the advocates of hegemonic global capitalism until the events of September 11, 2001 forced a dramatic reappraisal of the diverse and complex sources of contemporary

identity. Those social scientists who have long argued against a narrow focus on material factors and stressed the fundamental nature of the ethnic bond in explaining the stubborn resilience of nations and nationalism seem to be receiving increasing empirical support from recent developments.

Several different theoretical perspectives can be found supporting contemporary studies of ethnic and racial conflict. Some, like rational choice theory, are methodologically individualistic and apply a cost–benefit formula to account for ethnic preferences and to explain the dynamics of racial and ethnic group formation. These have been criticized on the grounds that they fail to appreciate the collective dynamics of much ethnic behavior and underestimate the irrational side of racial violence. Other common perspectives see ethnicity and racial divisions as a type of social stratification: theories employing neo-Marxist categories stress the economic components underlying much ethnic conflict, while those following in the tradition of scholars like Weber and Furnivall provide a more pluralistic interpretation of the differences in ethnic and racial power. In general, these differences originate from the forces of conquest and migration, and are then perpetuated by the processes of group monopolization once an ethnic or racial boundary has been created. In this way, a hierarchical ordering of racial and ethnic groups is created which will eventually generate conflict as circumstances start to change and disadvantaged groups challenge the status quo. Other theories point to social psychological factors, like prejudice and ethnocentrism, as important explanations for the persistence of ethnic divisions and the ubiquity of racial conflict.

Two highly controversial arguments center on genetic imperatives, which it is claimed operate through the mechanism of kin selection and form part of the application of sociobiological thinking to ethnic and race relations. Neoconservative theories concentrate on cultural factors, which, it is asserted, are disproportionately distributed among certain ethnic and racial groups. Such theories have been vigorously challenged because of their deterministic, if not racist, implications. The heat of the debate reinforces the conclusion that no single theory provides a generally accepted and comprehensive explanation for the complexity of ethnic group formation or the persistence of racial conflict in contemporary society.

As a result of this analytical discord, it is hardly surprising that the proposed solutions to racial and ethnic conflict are equally diverse. Some see these divisions as fundamental to social life and that the search for a final solution to such conflicts is a never-ending task that can be as potentially dangerous as the problem itself. Others propose that it is better to channel and institutionalize diversity in ways that make it less destructive and thereby reduce its enormous potential for violence and bloodshed. Creating cross-cutting cleavages, blurring the boundaries of race and class, decentralizing political power in different forms of federal structures that protect the interest of specific ethnic and racial groups, and trying to ensure that majority rule also respects minority rights are just some of the techniques of social engineering that have been deployed to take the sting out of multi-ethnic political units. Still others claim that the celebration of ethnicity and racial identity will bring about changes in attitudes and behavior that mitigate the dangerous polarization of groups along these types of boundaries. The persistence of ethnic and racial conflicts suggests that the diversity of theoretical interpretations is matched by the range of policy strategies, and that the continuation of ethnic and racial conflicts is likely to be an enduring feature of most societies for the foreseeable future.

SEE ALSO: Burundi and Rwanda (Hutu, Tutsi); Ethnic Cleansing; Genocide; Race; Race (Racism); Racial Hierarchy; Truth and Reconciliation Commissions

REFERENCES AND SUGGESTED READINGS

Horowitz, D. (1985) *Ethnic Groups in Conflict*. California University Press, Berkeley.
Stone, J. (1985) *Racial Conflict in Contemporary Society*. Harvard University Press, Cambridge, MA.
Stone, J. (2004) Scholars and the South African Revolution. In: Conversi, D. (Ed.), *Ethnonationalism in the Contemporary World*. Routledge, London.
Stone, J. & Dennis, R. (Eds.) (2003) *Race and Ethnicity: Comparative and Theoretical Approaches*. Blackwell, Malden, MA.
Van den Berghe, P. (1965) *South Africa: A Study in Conflict*. Wesleyan University Press, Middletown.

conflict theory

Stephen K. Sanderson

The term "conflict theory" came into wide use in sociology during the 1960s, when it was seen as an alternative to and rival of functionalism. Initially, the term seemed merely to identify a more politically neutral Marxian perspective, but for some it meant something much broader. The strongest contemporary advocate of conflict theory is Randall Collins. For him, conflict theory includes not only Marx and the Marxists, but also Weber and a number of other social theorists extending back to earlier times. He sees as early forerunners of modern conflict theory such thinkers as Machiavelli and Pareto. Collins (1974, 1975) has done more than any sociologist to develop a synthesized conflict theory that owes more to Weber than to any other sociologist. Sociologists have often regarded Lewis Coser's *The Functions of Social Conflict* (1956) as a version of conflict theory, but it is more a functionalist analysis of the role of conflict in social life than a use of conflict propositions to explain various social phenomena.

Conflict theory presupposes the following: (1) conflict or struggle between individuals and groups who have opposing interests or who are competing for scarce resources is the essence of social life; (2) competition and conflict occur over many types of resources in many settings, but power and economic resources are the principal sources of conflict and competition; (3) conflict and struggle typically result in some individuals and groups dominating and controlling others, and patterns of domination and subordination tend to be self-perpetuating; (4) dominant social groups have a disproportionate influence on the allocation of resources and on the structure of society.

Marxian conflict theory is the more prominent of two major lines of work. For Marxists, social class is the source of conflict in all societies above the level of primitive egalitarian communities. Class conflict – between masters and slaves or landlords and peasants, for example – pervades history and is the engine of historical change. Marxists have focused most of their attention, though, on the class structure of modern capitalist society. The most prominent feature of capitalist society is the class struggle between capitalists and workers. Marx assumed, and nearly all later Marxists have assumed as well, that to understand the structure, functioning, and evolution of capitalist society you had to start from the fact that capitalists have as their main objective maximizing profits and accumulating capital. They do this by exploiting the working class, i.e., by paying them wages that are less than the full value of the goods they produce. Workers are motivated to resist capitalist exploitation as much as they can, and thus there is an inherent antagonism between capitalists and workers. This class struggle is the foundation of capitalism and the root cause of all other forms of struggle or conflict within capitalism.

In the 1970s some sociologists began to rethink the traditional interpretation of Weber handed down by Talcott Parsons, viewing Weber as offering a kind of conflict theory that was similar to Marxian theory in certain ways, but different in crucial respects (Cohen et al. 1975; Collins 1975, 1986). Collins developed this idea most thoroughly. He argued that Weber was a complex and multidimensional thinker who later in life evolved into a conflict theorist. Like Marx, Weber emphasized the role of conflict, struggle, and discord in social life, viewing them as pervasive features of society and the keys to understanding it.

There are certain crucial differences in the conflict theories of Marx and Weber, and in the conflict theories of their various followers. Four crucial differences can be emphasized:

- *Class and other struggles.* For Marxian theory, class struggle is most fundamental and underlies all other forms. Political, ethnic, religious, and ideological conflicts not only manifest the predominant form of class conflict and the nature of the dominant class, but also in essence would not exist at all were class conflict to be eradicated.

Weberians view this position as excessively "class reductionist." They view class struggle as important in many societies, but often not as the most important form of struggle or as the basis for other forms of struggle. For contemporary Weberian conflict theorists, political, ethnic, and religious struggles are often most important and thus cannot be explained simply by relating them to class struggle. The neo-Weberian theorist Frank Parkin (1979), for example, regards racial conflict as the most crucial type in South African society.

- *Inevitability of conflict, domination, and inequality.* Marxists have held that the capitalist class struggle can be eradicated and, along with it, the other major forms of social conflict that flow from it. Weberians, on the other hand, tend to view at least some degree of conflict as permanent and ineradicable. Attempts to eliminate certain types of conflict are likely to be only partially successful. If more fully successful, then they may very well intensify or create other forms of conflict. Weber, for example, famously argued that attempts to replace capitalism with socialism would intensify the power of the state, and thus would increase the conflict between the state and the citizenry. Weber was a kind of cynical realist (Collins 1986) who saw social life as a continual process of individuals maneuvering for power and control over situations and over each other.

- *Nature and role of the state.* Marx himself, and the majority of Marxists, have tended to view the state as the political agent of the ruling class, although more recently some Marxists have conceded a certain autonomy to state action. Weberians tend to see this type of class reductionism as a great oversimplification. The state is often tied to the ruling class and may do its bidding, but the state has its own interests to pursue, such as maintaining order, enhancing its status, and competing with other states (Collins 1975; Parkin 1979; Skocpol 1979). The autonomous role of states, and the importance of the international states system and geopolitics, are major emphases in Weberian conflict theory but receive little in Marxism.

• *Bureaucratic and organizational power struggles.* Bureaucratic organization was a major focus in Weber's work but almost totally absent from Marx's. For Weber, the alienating consequences of the modern division of labor were produced more by bureaucratic forms of organization than by who owned the means of production. Not only did these forms of organization play a major role in shaping modern social life, but they were also themselves the sites of major power struggles.

Marx's view of the state was that it was "the executive committee of the ruling class." In capitalist society, the main role of the state is to protect the position of the capitalist class and help it to achieve its economic objectives. In the view of such modern Marxists as Miliband (1977) and Szymanski (1978), the modern state in capitalist societies is a *capitalist state*. The state may "govern," but the capitalist class "rules." The state does three primary things to assist the capitalist class. It plays a legitimation role, by which it attempts to promote among the population a consensus regarding the basic moral soundness and appropriateness of capitalism as an economic system. It also engages in repression by preventing people from taking actions that would be harmful to the capitalist class. Finally, it has an accumulation function whereby it enacts and promotes numerous policies, laws, and strategies to aid the capitalist class in its quest for maximizing profits and accumulating capital.

Marxists have also formulated theories of racial antagonism. The so-called orthodox Marxian theory of racial antagonism views it as an attempt to placate the working class and reduce the price of their labor (Reich 1977). Capitalists can take advantage of racial diversity by promoting racial tension among members of the working class, preventing it from achieving its full organizational potential and thus its ability to push for higher wages. Edna Bonacich (1972) has developed an alternative Marxian theory called the *split labor market theory*. This is a more complex and subtle theory that views racial antagonism emerging from a conflict between three groups: capitalists, higher-paid labor, and cheaper labor. When there is a split in the labor market between higher-paid and cheaper labor, capitalists will try to replace the former with the latter as much as possible. If the split in the labor market corresponds to racial divisions, then capitalists may in essence be trying to replace one racial group with another. Higher-paid labor will try to neutralize the threat from cheaper labor by excluding it through racial considerations.

Frank Parkin (1979) has developed a neo-Weberian approach to stratification in modern societies that contrasts sharply with Marxist theory. Parkin accepts the reality of class domination, but adds to it other important forms in his *theory of social closure*. Social closure exists in all societies and involves efforts of individuals to monopolize various resources in order to achieve or maintain a privileged social position. Attempts at closure occur along many lines, including class, gender, race and ethnicity, religion, and educational credentials, and these are to a large extent independent of one another. Closure based on ownership of the means of production is simply one form of closure among several. Parkin's argument is that there are numerous forms of inequality that have little or nothing to do with ownership, and thus they cannot be explained in Marxian terms. In addition to the non-class forms of inequality mentioned above, these include the high incomes and status positions of learned professionals, and the persisting inequalities in the old Soviet Union despite the eradication of all major forms of private property.

Theda Skocpol's (1979, 1994) Weberian work on social revolutions illustrates one of the major differences between Marxian and Weberian conflict theory. She has criticized Marxian theories of revolution for emphasizing class dynamics at the expense of the state, a classical Weberian theme. She asserts that revolutions are not made by revolutionaries, class-based or otherwise, but result from what is happening at the level of the state. All social revolutions have occurred in societies in which the peasantry is the largest social class; however, in her view peasants are almost always discontented and potentially rebellious. Peasant discontent therefore cannot explain why, when, or where revolutions occur. Skocpol argues that revolutions occur when the state is vulnerable to a revolutionary overthrow. Most of the time the state is strong enough to put down revolutionary action, but in certain circumstances it is unable to do so. In the case of the French Revolution, for example, it was a state fiscal crisis, brought on by the draining effects of war, that led to the demise of the old regime. In the case of more recent revolutions, such as the Iranian Revolution of 1979, it was the existence of a regime so brutally repressive of major social groups that it led to a level of popular resistance to the Shah's regime that was strong enough to overcome it.

Conflict theory is alive and well in modern sociology and many sociologists work within that framework, broadly conceived (Lord & Sanderson 1999). It has contributed much to sociological understanding and is being extended in new ways through linkage with perspectives normally thought far removed from it, such as sociobiology (Sanderson 2001) and Durkheimian social theory (Collins 2004).

SEE ALSO: Class Conflict; Conflict Theory and Crime and Delinquency; Critical Theory/Frankfurt School; Dependency and World-Systems Theories; Marx, Karl; Stratification: Functional and Conflict Theories; Stratification and Inequality, Theories of; Weber, Max

REFERENCES AND SUGGESTED READINGS

Bonacich, E. (1972) A Theory of Ethnic Antagonism: The Split Labor Market. *American Sociological Review* 37: 547–59.
Cohen, J., Hazelrigg, L. E., & Pope, W. (1975) De-Parsonizing Weber: A Critique of Parsons's Interpretation of Weber's Sociology. *American Sociological Review* 40: 229–41.
Collins, R. (1974) Reassessments of Sociological History: The Empirical Validity of the Conflict Tradition. *Theory and Society* 1: 147–78.
Collins, R. (1975) *Conflict Sociology: Toward an Explanatory Science*. Academic Press, New York.
Collins, R. (1986) *Max Weber: A Skeleton Key*. Sage, Beverly Hills.
Collins, R. (2004) *Interaction Ritual Chains*. Princeton University Press, Princeton.
Lord, J. T. & Sanderson, S. (1999) Current Theoretical and Political Perspectives of Western Sociological Theorists. *American Sociologist* 30(3): 37–61.
Miliband, R. (1977) *Marxism and Politics*. Oxford University Press, Oxford.
Parkin, F. (1979) *Marxism and Class Theory: A Bourgeois Critique*. Columbia University Press, New York.
Reich, M. (1977) The Economics of Racism. In: Gordon, D. M. (Ed.), *Problems in Political Economy*, 2nd edn. Heath, Lexington.
Skocpol, T. (1979) *States and Social Revolutions*. Cambridge University Press, New York.
Skocpol, T. (1994) *Social Revolutions in the Modern World*. Cambridge University Press, New York.
Sanderson, S. (2001) *The Evolution of Human Sociality*. Rowman & Littlefield, Boulder.
Szymanski, A. (1978) *The Capitalist State and the Politics of Class*. Winthrop, Cambridge.

conflict theory and crime and delinquency

Christopher R. Williams and Bruce A. Arrigo

Much of the sociological and criminological mainstream assumes that society is organized around and characterized by consensus; however, conflict theorists place the process of discord at the center of cultural, institutional, and organizational dynamics. While a number of theoretical variations have emerged from within the general conflict tradition, they share a few basic assumptions. First, conflict theorists assume that in more complex, industrialized societies, values and interests diverge at certain points of social difference. Second, conflict theorists recognize that power and resources are differentially distributed. Consequently, some social groups are in a better position than others to have their own values and interests adopted in a formal capacity and subsequently embedded in the policies and practices of social institutions. Thus, matters of social and cultural significance are points of division and deep struggle rather than points of agreement and commonly shared interest.

Within criminology, the adoption of conflict theory's basic assumptions has led to alternative ways by which to comprehend criminality, lawmaking, and law enforcement. Conflict theorists explain the presence of crime and the enactment of laws in much the same way as they account for other aspects of social life. In short, conflict theorists draw attention to those individuals, groups, or collectives that accumulate the most power and resources sufficient to shape lawmaking and criminal justice policy, consistent with the values and interests of the dominant segment in a given society. Moreover, conflict criminologists assess how these entities influence organizational and institutional dynamics as linked to crime, law, and justice. Finally, conflict criminologists point out these organizations and institutions (including their members) benefit from those who control and shape the agenda when it comes to matters of crime, law, and justice.

Precisely because official definitions of crime are a product of the values and interests of a dominant segment as specified in legal codes and criminal justice practices, individuals or groups with less power, standing, or resources are more likely to have their behavior defined as criminal. In addition, these subordinate groups are subsequently more likely to be labeled and processed as deviant or criminal. Overall, contemporary conflict criminologists are more interested in this process of lawmaking and the dynamics of enforcement than they are in the characteristics or behaviors of individuals who violate the legal order.

For organizational purposes, conflict theories are sometimes grouped under two broad headings: pluralist conflict theories and radical conflict perspectives. Pluralist theories share a concern for the accumulation of social power, arguing that social issues are metaphoric "battlegrounds" within which competing interest groups attempt to exert control and gain ground. Significantly, a plurality of such segments are said to exist for any given issue, including those collectives organized around socioeconomic status, age, gender, race, religion, politics, and many others. As such, there are several competing groups invested in those decisions and actions taken by power brokers in relation to the particular issue under consideration. Consequently, each segment will attempt to exercise influence over those decisions and actions with whatever resources are available to that group. Central to each of these struggles, then, is power or the control of resources that provide a marked advantage in the conflict to achieve greater power, money, or status for the competing collectives.

The intellectual roots of both pluralist and radical conflict perspectives lie with Hegel, Marx, Weber, Simmel, and other classical theorists concerned with various forms of social conflict. Early pluralist conflict criminologists such as Thorstein Sellin and George Vold borrowed liberally from the social theory of both Weber and Simmel, especially when describing theories of crime, law, and justice to which cultural and group-based conflict were central. For example, in one of the earliest efforts to connect criminological concerns with the broader notion of social conflict, Sellin (1938) suggested that there existed a number of "conduct norms" or informal rules of behavior that encouraged people to act in certain ways in particular situations. He argued that these norms were learned through socialization. Moreover, since socialization was subject to cultural and subcultural differences, he noted that people who belonged to different cultural collectives were likely to subscribe to different values and principles of human social interaction. As such, they would behave in accordance with the characteristics of the culture and/or subculture to which they claimed allegiance.

Sellin observed that in less complex, more homogeneous societies there appeared to be consensus surrounding these conduct norms; however, as society became more complex and heterogeneous, the norms were characterized by a plurality of cultural and subcultural groups, each with their own standards for interaction. When the norms of different social segments contradicted one another, conflict ensued. Sellin argued that, given the presence of incompatible norms, the emergence of conflict occurred in one of two ways: when two different cultures were pitted against each other, or when a single culture divided into subcultures. It is no surprise, then, that what is customary within one culture or subculture may be thoroughly deviant from the perspective of another culture. Law and its enforcement represent domains where these conflicts get considerable attention. Specifically, definitions of normalcy and deviance are recognized by and codified into law and public policy (representing the interests of the dominant group), and are simultaneously legitimized and enforced by formal mechanisms of social control.

Twenty years after Sellin's treatise on culture conflict, George Vold articulated the fundamental precepts for what is generally known as group conflict theory. In his work *Theoretical Criminology* (1958), Vold argued that human beings were by nature group-involved, and that our lives were in many ways part and product of these involvements. Vold observed that groups initially form around common needs and interests, serving as "action units." These units more effectively further the segment's shared aspirations. Because groups are many and varied, they inevitably come into conflict with one another, engendering competition or struggle in order to maintain or improve their lot within the greater society. As segments come into conflict with one another, they often solicit the assistance of the state to protect or further their power or resource ambitions. As Vold (1958: 208–9) noted, lawmaking, law breaking, and legal enforcement reflect struggles between competing interest groups to control the police power of the state, with "those who produce legislative majorities win[ning] control over police power and dominat[ing] policies that decide who is likely to be involved in violation of law."

Vold's formulation of group conflict theory was a significant departure from Sellin's for two reasons. First, Vold recognized that interest groups and, consequently, conflict arose not only from cultural and subcultural differences but from other collective needs as well. These other group needs included economic, political, and religious concerns, as well as interests associated with race, gender, and class social divisions. Second, conflict theory was beginning to pose a significant challenge to traditional consensus models of societal analysis. Included among them was functionalist lawmaking. This approach argued that legal provisions developed from societal consensus and, as such, furthered the common interests of the society as a whole. Early work in the pluralist conflict tradition recognized the existence of conflict in these endeavors. Moreover, critical arguments were presented acknowledging that law, policy, and state practices emerged from and were protected by the interests of those dominant segments exercising social, economic, and political power rather than the will of the majority or the isolated needs of cultural collectives.

While the earlier works of Sellin and Vold were among the first to apply the insights of the conflict tradition to criminology, the social and political upheaval of the 1960s and 1970s helped to spawn alternative ways of thinking about the conflict–crime–law relationship. The widespread unrest that characterized the United States during these troubled decades suggested for many that the conventional functionalist consensus paradigm, with its emphasis on harmony and stasis, was wholly inadequate and misguided.

Given these concerns, a more radically inspired conflict criminology emerged. Unlike their predecessors who were rooted largely in the broader social theories of Weber and Simmel, radical conflict theorists such as Chambliss and Seidman (1982) were much more sensitive to the Marxian tradition. As a matter of intellectual history in criminology, part of the radical path pursued by conflict criminologists had already commenced, especially in the work of Richard Quinney (1970). Merging aspects of labeling theory with pluralist conflict insights, Quinney examined the role of societal reaction in the definitions of crime, the enforcement of laws, and the treatment of criminal offenders. At the same time, an increasing "radicalization" of academia was taking place whereby sociologists and criminologists, especially in the United Kingdom and the United States, more generally demonstrated a revived interest in the Marxian tradition of sociology with its emphasis on social class and political economy. Thus, during the decades of the 1970s and the early 1980s, the emergence and development of radical conflict theory reflected a conceptual amalgam of earlier pluralist conflict notions, labeling theory, and the radical insights of Marx and the Marxian sociological tradition.

Radical conflict perspectives are themselves many and varied, though central to most are issues of social class, economic conditions, and the political economy as both the source and product of conflict. Radical criminologists differ from their pluralistic counterparts on the specific causes of struggle and, correspondingly, the nature of crime. Generally speaking, pluralist theories do not identify with great precision the locus of power; instead, they note that different groups possess and exercise different amounts of power and that individuals can voluntarily align themselves with different segments. While radical conflict theorists are sympathetic to this position, they expressly identify structural forces of power and their accumulation as the defining source. For instance, Chambliss and Seidman (1982) argued that the law represents the interests of certain social groups rather than the public at large (a position shared within pluralist models of conflict), and that the groups most likely to have their interests embraced by the legal order are those with higher economic (and, thus, political) standing within society. The greater the economic and political status of an identified group, the more likely it is for that segment to have its interests adopted in an official capacity.

More recent variations of radical conflict theory retain their focus on the political economy and on social class. However, they also incorporate the correlates of race, gender, ethnicity, age, sexual orientation, language, and other features of inequality into a more critical and seamless analysis of lawmaking, criminal behavior, and institutional responses to both. Radical conflict theorists argue that these social divisions are key determinants of social power.

Efforts to develop an integrated conflict theory in criminology also are discernible. Examples of these include Bernard's integrated model, Arrigo's integration of critical criminological theory, and Barak's critical hyperintegration theory. These efforts at conceptual synthesis examine various strains of conflict theory, identifying noteworthy points of theoretical convergence and divergence. The intent here is to develop a more unified theory that explains the presence of conflict in society and then to apply the model to the problems posed by crime and delinquency.

SEE ALSO: Class Conflict; Conflict Theory; Crime; Criminal Justice System; Criminology; Law, Criminal; Marx, Karl; Simmel, Georg; Stratification: Functional and Conflict Theories; Victimization

REFERENCES AND SUGGESTED READINGS

Arrigo, B. A. (Ed.) (1999) *Social Justice/Criminal Justice: The Maturation of Critical Theory in Law, Crime, and Deviance.* Wadsworth, Belmont, CA.

Arrigo, B. A. (2000) Social Justice and Critical Criminology: On Integrating Knowledge. *Contemporary Justice Review* 3(1): 7–37.

Arrigo, B. A. & Bernard, T. J. (1997) Postmodern Criminology in Relation to Conflict and Radical Criminology. *Critical Criminology: An International Journal* 8(2): 39–60.

Barak, G. (1999) *Integrative Criminologies.* Taylor & Francis, Boston.

Bernard, T. J. (1981) The Distinction Between Conflict and Radical Criminology. *Journal of Criminal Law and Criminology* 72(1): 362–79.

Bernard, T. J. (1983) *The Consensus–Conflict Debate: Form and Content in Social Theories.* Columbia University Press, New York.

Chambliss, W. J. & Seidman, R. (1982) *Law, Order, and Power,* 2nd edn. Addison-Wesley, Reading, MA.

Lynch, M., Michalowsk, R., & Groves, W. B. (2000) *The New Primer in Radical Criminology: Critical Perspectives on Crime, Power, and Identity,* 3rd edn. Willow Tree Press, New York.

Quinney, R. (1970) *The Social Reality of Crime.* Little, Brown, Boston.

Sellin, T. (1938) *Culture, Conflict, and Crime.* Social Science Research Council, New York.

Taylor, I., Walton, P., & Yong, J. (1973) *The New Criminology: For a Social Theory of Deviance.* Harper & Row, New York.

Vold, G. (1958) *Theoretical Criminology.* Oxford University Press, New York.

Confucianism

Tan Chee-Beng

It is widely acknowledged that Confucianism has a dominant influence in Chinese culture. But what is religion in the Chinese context? Chinese scholars writing in Chinese generally see Confucianism (*ruxue* or *rujia* thinking) as a school of Chinese philosophy, and the question of whether Confucianism is a religion or not does not arise. Western scholars on religion, however, often regard Confucianism as a religion. Indeed, Weber's famous work on Chinese religion is entitled *The Religion of China: Confucianism and Taoism* (Weber 1951). It is worth noting that, historically, Chinese do not make a clear distinction between moral teaching and the western concept of religious teaching, these being referred to as *jiao* or "teaching." Thus, *sanjiao*, referring to Confucianism, Taoism, and Buddhism, is better translated as "three teachings" rather than as "three religions," for in the Chinese understanding of *jiao*, it is not an important issue whether Confucianism is a religion or not.

Chinese popular religion and its complex of pantheon, rituals, and temples is easily understood as religion. So is Taoist religion (*daojiao*). Once the indigenous institutional religion of China, today its deities and rites can be seen as part of Chinese popular religion. However, anthropologists and sociologists do not see religion as merely an institution that deals with the supernatural, and they seek a more pluralistic definition that can include all religious phenomena. Indeed, it is insufficient to understand the religious life of the Chinese from the perspective of Chinese popular religion only, for their transcendental views of life are guided by the transcendental teaching in Taoism and especially Confucianism. This is particularly obvious in the context of religious dialogue. A dialogue with Muslims about "perfect man" (*al-insân al-kâmil*) will require the Chinese to talk about the Confucian view of *junzi* ("superior man") and relevant ethics, and/or the Taoist view of *zhenren* ("perfect man"). Similarly, the Chinese can invoke the Confucian moral system of the unity of human and heaven when relating to the Muslim and Christian view of the human and God.

Confucianism was developed from the teachings of Confucius (551–479 BCE) and Mencius (371–289? BCE). The most famous Confucian texts are collectively known as *Sishu*, or Four Books: *Daxue* (Great Learning), *Zhongyong* (Doctrine of the Mean), *Lunyu* (Analects), and *Mengzi* (Book of Mencius). Central to Confucian teaching is the idea of *ren*, which Wing-tsit Chan translates as "humanity." Asked about this, Confucius said, "It is to love men" (Chan 1963: 40), and the Confucian moral world involves this transcendental thinking. Through self-cultivation by practicing values that bring about the ultimate value of *ren*, one becomes a Confucian superior person. Of crucial importance is the value of *shu*, or "reciprocity." The most famous teaching about this is: "Do not do to others what you do not want them to do to you" (Chan 1963: 39). This teaching is well known not only to the Chinese but also to the

other East Asian societies that have Confucian influence: Korea, Japan, and Vietnam. But the practice of Confucian love and ultimately *ren* really begins with *xiao* (usually translated as filial piety), a value that emphasizes respect and honor to parents, elders, and ancestors. Mencius said, "To have filial affection for parents is humanity, and to respect elders is righteousness" (Chan 1963: 80). So dominant is this value that, to this day, Chinese generally are guided by the value in their relations with parents and elders, even though its expression changes with time and parents and children may have different standards and expectations.

In fact, *xiao* in Confucian thinking is spiritual. By extending *xiao* beyond the family, one is able to love a wider circle of people. As Mencius said, "In regard to people generally, he (superior person) is humane to them but not affectionate. He is affectionate to his parents and humane to all people. He is humane to all people and feels love for all" (Chan 1963: 81). A related famous saying of Mencius is: "Treat with respect the elders in my family, and then extend that respect to include the elders in other families. Treat with tenderness the young in my own family, and then extend that tenderness to include the young in other families" (Chan 1963: 61). Practicing *xiao* is really the first step in the spiritual journey to attaining humanity (*ren*).

Confucianism developed throughout the centuries, culminating in the neo-Confucianism (*lixue*) of the Song and Ming dynasties. By then, Confucian thinkers had incorporated aspects of Taoist and Buddhist thought into their Confucian teachings. The most famous Confucianist of this period was Zhu Xi (1130–1200), who synthesized various important Confucian ideas, including those of the neo-Confucianists of the Song dynasty. His discussion of the Supreme Ultimate (*taiji*) – the all-embracing ultimate standard in the universe – is so transcendental that it is as religious as it can be.

Since the early twentieth century, especially after the May Fourth Movement of 1919, Confucianism was attacked as upholding feudalism and blamed for China's backwardness. At the same time, Confucian thinkers who were exposed to the West tried to relate it to modern China, giving rise to the modern Confucianism called *xin ruxue* or "New Confucianism."

A well-known founder of this new school was Liang Shumin (1893–1988). Reflection on Confucianism in relation to Christianity and western thought is evident in his writing. He insisted that Confucianism is not religion, which he saw as characterized by superstition. He argued that, in China, moral teaching had taken the place of religion. This of course involves the definition of religion, and it is common to find Chinese intellectuals seeing religion as dealing with the supernatural and with myths. The well-known Chinese philosophy professor Lao Siguang holds this view, too, and considers Confucianism not a religion. However, he points out that Confucianism has religious functions (Lao 1998: 192). A notable exception is Ren Jiyu, who considered Zhu Xi's thought as belonging to the realm of religion although he considered it as not practical. A "third-generation" New Confucianism thinker who is well known in the West is Tu Wei-ming, the Harvard academic who has been active in introducing Confucianism in the West and relating it to modern challenges. He has also been active in participating in interreligious dialogues, speaking about Confucianism.

Overall, Confucianism is important for understanding Chinese religious life, which is much more than just worshipping deities and ancestors, as can be commonly seen being practiced by ordinary Chinese in mainland China, Hong Kong, Macao, Taiwan, Southeast Asia, and elsewhere in the Chinese diaspora among Chinese who still observe indigenous Chinese religious beliefs and practices. Just as not all Christians and Muslims follow the teachings of their religions in daily life, not all Chinese practice Confucian teachings, and few actually read Confucian texts. But Confucianism remains important as a Chinese ideal of spiritual life, and aspects of it, including different expressions of *xiao*, are practiced by ordinary Chinese. Confucius founded a moral and spiritual system that provided the ideal for one to be religious through self-cultivation to be a moral human. Although Confucius and Mencius did not promote belief in the supernatural, the ancient Chinese idea of heaven remained important as the moral absolute, as can be seen in the saying of Mencius: "He who exerts his mind to the utmost knows his nature. He who knows his nature knows Heaven" (Chan 1963: 78).

Confucianism provides the ethical base of Chinese popular religion and various Chinese religious organizations. For example, the *Sanyi Jiao* (Three-in-One Doctrine), *Zhengkong Jiao* (Teaching of True Void), which are "syncretic" Chinese religious organizations based on "three teachings," and *Dejiao*, which is based on "five teachings" incorporating Jesus and the Prophet Mohammed in this "syncretic" Chinese religious organization, have Confucian teaching as an important part of their religious teaching, even though the rites may be more Buddhist or Taoist. As a member of the pantheon of Chinese popular religion, Confucius is a god that blesses educational achievement. Some Chinese parents (such as in Malaysia and Taiwan) still bring children who are entering school for the first time to a temple to worship Confucius, in the hope that they will be blessed to succeed in education. As a member of the Chinese pantheon, Confucius is a minor god among many. As a sage, Confucius is honored by the Chinese in general, and memorial rites are performed in Confucian temples in mainland China and Taiwan and in Confucian associations in Southeast Asia, especially on his birthday anniversary.

There is the rise of "New Confucianism" in the modern Chinese encounter with the West. Toward the end of the Qing dynasty there was also an attempt to make Confucianism the state religion of China, comparable to Christianity in the West. The most prominent leader of this movement in China was Kang Youwei (1858–1927). This Confucian revival movement failed, partly due to the close association of Confucianism with the imperial system, which the Chinese overthrew in 1911. Here it is important to point out that the mandarins in imperial China throughout the centuries had promoted an official Confucianism that served the state and its bureaucracy. This official Confucianism should be distinguished from Confucianism, the ethical and spiritual system.

Nevertheless, the establishment of *Kongjiao Hui*, or Confucian associations, succeeded in promoting the worship of Confucius, especially in Malaya (now Malaysia and Singapore) and Indonesia. In Indonesia, Tiong Hoa Hwee Koan, established in 1900, was the first Chinese association to seriously promote Confucianism. The establishment of Khong Kauw Hwee (i.e., Kongjiao Hui) in Indonesia – the first one was founded in Solo in 1918 (Coppell 1981: 180) – further promoted Confucianism. The formation of a federation of Confucian associations in Jakarta in 1955, the Khong Kauw Tjung Hwee consolidated the promotion of Confucianism and contributed to the formation of an institutional religion that may be called "Confucian Religion" in present-day Indonesia. The growth of Confucianism as an institutional religion was also helped by the official recognition of Confucianism as one of the "six religions" in Indonesia in 1965, alongside Islam, Protestantism, Catholicism, Hindu-Bali, and Buddhism.

Today, the development of Confucianism has been under the organization of MATAKIN (Majelis Tinggi Agama Khonghucu Indonesia – the Supreme Council for the Confucian Religion in Indonesia). Confucian Religion may be considered a new Chinese organization that grew out of the Confucian revival movement. That Confucianism succeeded in forming an institutional Chinese religion in Indonesia is due to the promotion and the politics of religion and identity in Indonesia. The lack of Chinese intelligentsia well versed in Confucianism helped, too, unlike in China, where scholars could not view Confucianism as a religion. The presence and influence of Islam and Christianity were also important. Indeed, the Confucian Religion holds Sunday services, and the Confucian *Four Books* are treated as Holy Scripture. Confucius is referred to as *nabi* (Indonesian for prophet), and *Tian* or Heaven becomes Almighty God.

What is the sociological relevance of Confucianism today? As explained, Chinese religious life cannot be understood without reference to Confucianism or its influence on Chinese life. In fact, Confucianism is not just philosophy articulated by scholars; it is also diffused into Chinese social life. In a way, it resembles a "civil religion" – "a collection of beliefs, symbols, and rituals with respect to sacred things and institutionalized in a collectivity" (Bellah 1967) – of the Chinese. The well educated (in Chinese) can articulate Confucian ideas sophisticatedly, whereas the ordinary masses express Confucianism in their memorial rites and in their rhetoric about filial piety, harmony, and views of life, although often not necessarily conscious of their Confucian origin.

The economic success in East Asia since the 1980s has encouraged scholars to write about Confucianism and modernity. Although Confucianism appears as a common factor in these societies, it is simplistic to attribute economic success and modernity to a religion or an ideological system. Nevertheless, Confucianism is sociologically relevant in its influence on attitudes of life and on social relations. An example of Confucian influence on the Chinese view of life is the idea of fate, which allows humans a dynamic part in determining it (cf. Yang 1970 [1961]: 273). Chan (1963: 79) describes this Confucian doctrine of fate thus: "man should exert his utmost in moral endeavor and leave whatever is beyond our control to fate." This attitude of fate, perhaps more obvious in coping with life than with practicing morality, is commonly held by Chinese in China and in diaspora. It has served them well in striving for higher achievement (such as educational and economic achievement) and coping with difficult life in general. It provides hope for success and a better life.

In social relations, including respect for the elders, the Confucian emphasis continues to be important to the Chinese. Even in mainland China, where Confucianism was condemned during the Maoist period, Confucian ideas of social relations are evident and generally upheld among both the less and better educated Chinese, in relations between parents and children, between teachers and students, between elders and younger people, and between officials and ordinary people. An often debated issue about Chinese society is that of the individual versus the group, and many times a western observer often still assumes that, in Chinese society, individuals are subjected to group interest. In fact, Fei Xiaotong, in his famous small book *Xiangtu Zhongguo* (Earthbound China) (1947), pointed out that Chinese social relationships cannot be described as group-centered or individualistic; they are self-centered or egoistic in a web of relationships (Fei 1992: 65). Indeed, de Bary (2003), discussing this issue in relation to Confucianism, points out that Confucianism does not emphasize the group or community at the expense of the individual. An understanding of Confucian traditions is still important for the sociological understanding of Chinese culture and society as well as Chinese worldview.

672 *conjugal roles and social networks*

Despite western influences, Confucianism remains important for the Chinese and, in fact, for the Japanese and Koreans. For Chinese outside mainland China, Confucian traditions are meaningful to their cultural identity, and Confucius is worshipped as a deity in the popular religion. Because of globalization and the increasing need of interreligious dialogue, the need to turn to Confucianism as an important source of Chinese spiritual traditions will be even more keenly felt. Since 1978, China has been pursuing economic modernization. The collapse of communism as an ideology, and in fact religion, seems to have left a major spiritual vacuum, although giving more room to Chinese popular religion, Buddhism, Christianity, Islam, and other faiths, even new religious experiments such as Falun Gong. Despite all these developments, and although there have been various campaigns against Confucianism since the beginning of the twentieth century, Confucianism is always embraced when the Chinese need to turn to their own spiritual traditions. But what is embraced is not the feudal Official Confucianism that served the imperial regimes but the Spiritual Confucianism that is relevant not only to the Chinese but also to the world community. Globalization and the meeting of civilizations will make this form of Confucianism relevant to China and the Chinese in diaspora. Whatever the development, Confucianism will continue to influence Chinese cultural life, notably in attitudes to life and in social relations. After all, how Chinese can Chinese cultures be without Confucianism?

SEE ALSO: Civil Religion; Family and Community; Globalization, Religion and; Religion; Religion, Sociology of; Taoism

REFERENCES AND SUGGESTED READINGS

Bellah, R. N. (1967) Civil Religion in America. *Daedalus* 96: 1–21.

Chan, W.-T. (Ed.) (1963) *A Source Book in Chinese Philosophy*. Princeton University Press, Princeton.

Coppell, C. (1981) The Origins of Confucianism as an Organized Religion in Java, 1900–1923. *Journal of Southeast Asian Studies* 12(1): 179–96.

De Bary, W. T. (2003) Confucianism and Communitarianism. In: Chen, R. (Ed.), *Ruxue yu Shijie*

Wenming (Confucianism and World Civilizations). Department of Chinese Studies, National University of Singapore, Singapore, pp. 919–32.

Fei, X. (1992) *From the Soil: The Foundations of Chinese Society*. Translation of Fei Xiaotong's *Xiangtu Zhongguo* (1947). Introduction and Epilogue by G. G. Hamilton & W. Zheng. University of California Press, Berkeley.

Lao, S. (1998) *Zhongguo Wenhua Yaoyi Xinbian (Outlines of Chinese Culture: New Edition)*. Chinese University Press, Hong Kong.

Mei, Y. P. (1967) The Basis of Social, Ethical, and Spiritual Values in Chinese Philosophy. In: Moore, C. A. (Ed.), *The Chinese Mind: Essentials of Chinese Philosophy and Culture*. University Press of Hawaii, Honolulu, pp. 149–66.

Weber, M. (1951) *The Religion of China: Confucianism and Taoism*. Free Press, New York.

Whyte, M. K. (2004) Filial Obligations in Chinese Families: Paradoxes of Modernization. In: Ikels, C. (Ed.), *Filial Piety: Practice and Discourse in Contemporary East Asia*. Stanford University Press, Stanford, pp. 106–27.

Yang, C. K. (1970 [1961]) *Religion in Chinese Society: A Study of Contemporary Social Functions of Religion and Some of Their Historical Roots*. University of California Press, Berkeley.

conjugal roles and social networks

Robert M. Milardo

Social networks, or the kin, friends, and other close associates of primary partners (e.g., spouses), can have important influences on the internal character of a marriage or family. Elizabeth Bott (1971) was among the first to recognize this connection in a study conducted in the early 1950s that involved extensive interviews with 20 London families. In a now classic hypothesis, she argued that: "The degree of segregation in the role-relationship of husband and wife varies directly with the connectedness of the family's social network" (p. 60). Spouses with separate networks, where members knew one another (i.e., highly interconnected or dense networks), were thought to have relatively separate conjugal roles, to perform household labor separately, and to engage in separate leisure activities. In contrast, spouses with low-density networks were thought to have relatively joint conjugal roles and leisure activities.

Bott proposed two causal pathways linking network structure with marital outcomes. In the first model, Bott hypothesized that highly interconnected networks would be more apt to share similar values and beliefs regarding conjugal roles relative to loosely connected networks. Consistent norms develop when members of local communities know and interact with one another and are therefore capable of sharing beliefs, conformity, and sanctions. Bott hypothesized a direct path, with network structure determining the strength of normative influence. The specific norm of interest concerned the segregation of conjugal roles. Highly interconnected networks should adopt a consistent gender-based ideology, with husbands and wives having very separate responsibilities for decision-making, household labor, and child-care, as well as separate personal associates and leisure interests. Loosely connected networks are less predictable. Without the coordinated influence of network members, spouses are freer to adopt their own arrangement of roles and responsibilities and accordingly they may adopt separate or joint conjugal roles.

The strength of this first model rests on the recognition that relationship outcomes (e.g., the interactions between spouses and the outcomes of those interactions) are affected by the ties linking network members (i.e., conditions existing apart from spouses' relationship to one another), with the vehicle of influence being a system of normative beliefs. This is an important contribution because it represents the first concrete attempt to define social structure and normative influence in terms of the patterned interconnection of people, and subsequently to quantify the degree of structure in relational terms. It contrasts sharply with traditional conceptualizations of social structure based on categorical memberships like sex, race, or class, conceptualizations from which structure can be only inferred. On the other hand, a sharp limitation of the model is a failure to explain why a network would subscribe to one belief, such as role segregation or patriarchal norms, rather than any other. The underlying model can be usefully restated by simply treating the specific

beliefs, norms, and their attendant sanctions as variable. Whether a particular network shares patriarchal views or egalitarian views is critical to the outcome, but not the structural condition giving rise to the outcome. Greater structural interdependence (e.g., high density) gives rise to more homogeneous attitudes and beliefs on the part of network members, and the potential for coordinated influence. Highly structured networks where members know and interact with one another have greater influence, as Bott initially argued.

Yet another way in which Bott suggested conjugal roles are linked to social networks concerns the exchange of mutual support, including both instrumental supports (e.g., money, direct aid) and symbolic supports (e.g., love, positive regard). Members of dense networks will provide considerable aid to one another, a system of mutual exchange that is possible only to the extent that members know and interact with one another. In dense networks mutual assistance among members is presumed to be high, and as a consequence spouses will have less need for one another's practical aid and companionship, and segregated marital roles emerge. In contrast, in more loosely structured networks, members are less likely to know one another and the network's ability to coordinate mutual aid is limited, so spouses must rely more fully on one another, creating the conditions for joint conjugal roles to emerge.

The Bott hypotheses have engendered considerable research interest, particularly because they offered non-intuitive explanations of marital action located in a social context. A recent review uncovered 14 studies that attempted to examine the link between network structure and the organization of conjugal roles (Milardo & Allan 2000). The original hypothesis has not been widely supported, although no study to date has directly tested the causal models underlying Bott's original hypothesis, and nearly all of these empirical tests have stumbled upon the inherent difficulty in defining a network, identifying its constituency, and quantifying its structure.

Nonetheless, Bott's work influenced several generations of network theory that included refinements in the way networks are defined and measured (Milardo 1992). Substantial advances have also been made in the conceptualization of particular properties of network structure all of which center on the organization of ties linking members to one another. They share the common attribute of describing links between network members apart from their ties to spouses and, as a result, benefit from two distinct advantages. Attributes of network structure are essentially highly refined, quantifiable indices of local social structure that are relationally based. They permit a means to examine the pathways by which basic processes like normative influence and social sanctions, social support, and social interference develop and exert their influence. In the coming decade research will likely explore in greater detail representations of personal networks and their structural features, the potential causal pathways linking network structure with relationship outcomes, and the precise influence of kin, friends, co-workers, and other acquaintances on primary partnerships.

SEE ALSO: Divisions of Household Labor; Kinship; Marriage; Networks

REFERENCES AND SUGGESTED READINGS

Bott, E. (1971) *Family and Social Network*, 2nd edn. Free Press, New York.

Helms, H. M., Crouter, A. C., & McHale, S. M. (2003) Marital Quality and Spouses' Marriage Work With Close Friends and Each Other. *Journal of Marriage and Family* 65: 963–77.

Julien, D., Chartrand, E., & Begin, J. (1999) Social Networks, Structural Interdependence and Conjugal Adjustment in Heterosexual, Gay and Lesbian Couples. *Journal of Marriage and the Family* 61: 516–30.

Milardo, R. M. (1992) Comparative Methods for Delineating Social Networks. *Journal of Social and Personal Relationships* 9: 447–61.

Milardo, R. M. & Allan, G. (2000) Social Networks and Marital Relationships. In: Milardo, R. & Duck, S. (Eds.), *Families as Relationships*. Wiley, London, pp. 117–33.

Schmeeckle, M. & Sprecher, S. (2004) Extended Family and Social Networks. In: Vangelisti, A. L. (Ed.), *Handbook of Family Communication*. Lawrence Erlbaum, Mahwah, NJ, pp. 349–75.

connubium (who marries whom?)

Fabrizio Bernardi

The question "Who marries whom?" refers to patterns of partner choice. The tendency to marry (or enter a long-term relationship such as cohabitation) a person who belongs to the same social group or who is similar with regard to certain characteristics is also known as homogamy. Since Weber argued that connubium (i.e., marriage) is one of the indicators of status group closure, homogamy has become a key object of study in order to highlight properties of the social structure. Sociologists have traditionally been interested in three individual characteristics that can be important in the choice of a partner: race/ethnicity, religion, and socioeconomic resources. Studying patterns of partner choice is important because it allows us to evaluate the degree of openness of the boundaries of different ethnic, religious, and socioeconomic groups. The more frequent marriage between subjects who differ with respect to the characteristics of the group, the more open the group is said to be. Substantively, the likelihood of ethnic intermarriages has been interpreted as an indicator of the level of integration and social cohesion between different ethnic groups. Religious intermarriages reflect the strength of different religions in conditioning individual life choices. Finally, socioeconomic homogamy is related to the openness of the system of social stratification and affects the overall level of social inequality. In fact, in a society with the maximum level of socioeconomic homogamy, all men with a high educational level and occupational class would marry women with a high educational level and occupational class. Conversely, in a society with a minimum level of socioeconomic homogamy, men with a high educational level and occupational class would marry women with a low educational level and occupational class, and the other way around. If one assumes that the social position of a couple results from the combination of both of their resources, then inequality among couples will be highest in the society with a maximum level of homogamy, and lowest in the society with a minimum level.

Theories that aim to explain patterns of partner choice focus on three factors: individual preferences, control over partner choice by third parties (in particular, parents and relatives), and the structural availability of partners with given characteristics. According to modernization theory, for instance, the transformation from agrarian to industrial society also implies a change in the institution of marriage. It is argued that, with the advent of industrial society, the family loses its traditional economic functions and becomes fundamentally an emotional unit that cares for the integration and socialization of new members of the society. The shift to industrial society has also brought about a generalized improvement in standards of living and has been paralleled by the development of a welfare state that protects citizens against health, old age, and income loss risks. Therefore, the parents' need to control their offspring's marriage in order to safeguard the family economic assets and their own well-being when elderly has decreased. Parallel to the transformation in the institution of the family and marriage, other changes such as the diffusion of mass media, the process of urbanization, and geographical and social mobility increase the opportunities for subjects of various social groups and with different socioeconomic resources to come into contact. In sum, modernization theory suggests that control over marriage by third parties (i.e., parents) has diminished, while the opportunities to meet people with characteristics different from one's own have increased. Thus, socioeconomic homogamy should decline over time.

In opposition to this hypothesis drawn from modernization theory, the theory of the educational system as a marriage market argues that increased participation in education segments the marriage market and favors educational homogamy for two reasons. First, by remaining in the education system for a longer time, subjects spend a larger part of their life course in a homogeneous environment with regard to education. Second, a longer amount of time spent in education also implies postponing marriage until school/university is completed. If marriage takes place just after leaving the educational system, it is likely to occur with a partner one met at school/university and, thus, with the same level of education and a similar occupation. In sum, participation in the educational system segments the network of actual and potential acquaintances and limits the opportunities to meet potential partners with different levels of socioeconomic resources.

Other theories have focused on the mechanism underlying the formation of individual preferences for a partner with given characteristics. For instance, it has been argued that the tendency to marry someone from the same ethnic or religious group or with the same level of economic resources reflects individual preferences for cultural similarity. According to this theory, people prefer a partner who shares the same values, opinions, and tastes because this increases the possibility of mutual understanding, reinforces one's worldview, and augments the possibility of spending leisure time together. On the other hand, recent theories about social mobility and educational inequality suggest that in their mobility strategies, with choice of a partner being one of them, individuals aim to avoid downward social mobility. With the increase in the number of dual-earner couples, both partners' social positions have become increasingly important for defining the couple's well-being and social position. Thus, in the search for a partner, people would aim to marry someone who has at least the same level of social resources as they do.

The comparative analysis of ethnic, religious, and socioeconomic homogamy and of its changes over time involves several methodological complications. This is because, independent of individual preferences, the level of homogamy is affected by the marginal distributions of the characteristics under analysis in the populations of potential partners. First of all, the level of homogamy is negatively correlated with the degree of heterogeneity of a population with respect to the characteristic under analysis. For instance, if one considers two religious groups, the number of homogamous couples will tend to be lower in a society where each of the two religions accounts for 50 percent of the population than in a society where a religious group accounts for 90 percent of the population. Moreover, a second difficulty has to do with differences in the distributions of potential partners with respect to the characteristics under analysis. The larger the imbalance in the two distributions, the lower the level of homogamy. For example, educational homogamy will tend to be lower in a society where 30 percent of the women and 10 percent of the men have a university education than in a society where 20 percent of both men and women have a university education. In order to deal with this type of problem associated with the marginal distributions of the characteristics under investigation, empirical research on homogamy has largely borrowed both conceptual distinctions and statistical methods from social mobility studies.

In addition, empirical research on homogamy has traditionally focused only on married couples and has excluded singles from the analysis. In recent years, changes in living arrangements have made this approach increasingly inadequate. There is, therefore, a manifest need to develop more comprehensive theoretical frameworks and analytical models in order to account for the overall process of searching for a partner, which might include the option of remaining single as one of its outcomes. Accordingly, the unit of analysis has shifted from the couple to the individual. Attempts have been made to investigate how individual preferences, third party control, and structural availability of partners with certain characteristics affect an individual's outcome in the marriage market. One should note, however, that by focusing on individuals one gets a one-sided view of the process of partner choice, since it obviously takes two to form a couple. Ideally, one should simultaneously consider the parallel process of searching for a partner in both groups of potential partners.

Although it has long been recognized that patterns of partner choice offer key sociological insights, the mentioned methodological problems have made it difficult to get conclusive results on trends in patterns of partner choice over time and among countries. Still, one might predict that, given the substantive interest in the consequences of ethnic and religious homogamy for social cohesion and of socioeconomic homogamy for income inequality, the question "Who marries whom?" will remain at the core

of the research agenda on social structure in the coming years.

SEE ALSO: Intergenerational Mobility: Methods of Analysis; Marriage; Stratification Systems: Openness

REFERENCES AND SUGGESTED READINGS

Blau, P. & Schwartz, J. (1984) *Crosscutting Social Circles*. Academic Press, New York.
Blossfeld, H.-P. & Timm, A. (Eds.) (2003) *Who Marries Whom? Educational Systems as Marriage Markets in Modern Societies*. Kluwer Academic Publishers, Dordrecht.
Kalmijn, M. (1991) Shifting Boundaries: Trends in Religious and Educational Homogamy. *American Sociological Review* 56: 786–800.
Kalmijn, M. (1998) Intermarriage and Homogamy: Causes, Patterns, Trends. *Annual Review of Sociology* 24: 395–421.
Mare, R. (1991) Five Decades of Educational Assortative Mating. *American Sociological Review* 56: 15–32.
Merton, R. (1941) Intermarriage and Social Structure: Fact and Theory. *Psychiatry* 4: 361–74.
Smiths, J., Ultee, W., & Lammers, J. (1998) Educational Homogamy in 65 Countries: An Explanation of Differences in Openness Using Country-Level Explanatory Variables. *American Sociological Review* 63: 264–85.

consciousness raising

Barbara Ryan

Consciousness raising (CR) was a cornerstone of radical feminist organizing in the late 1960s and early 1970s. Many of the women involved in the anti-war, New Left, and Civil Rights Movements were disillusioned by the end of the 1960s as they found themselves relegated to the role of providing services (including sex) to men, the official leaders of these movements (Evans 1980). In the Civil Rights Movement and in the New Left, many women became unwilling to assume a back seat to men. Instead, they began small consciousness-raising groups to understand what had happened to them in male-defined social movements, and how they could organize on the basis of sex (gender) to form their own movement for women's equality. They spoke of themselves as members of the women's liberation movement, rather than a women's rights movement (Echols 1989).

The term consciousness raising can be traced to other movements for social change, including the New Left where it was called criticism or self-criticism, and earlier as it was practiced in China when Mao sent facilitators into rural villages to raise awareness of the teachings of communism after the 1948 revolution. Mao was particularly interested in raising the consciousness of women to their new role in society under communism – a role of active productivity in the fields and workforce.

The women involved in CR in the US constituted one segment of the contemporary women's movement that can be classified as the small group sector (Ryan 1992), the younger branch (Freeman 1975), or the radical feminist sector (Firestone 1970). As an initial step in their organizing, they met in small groups of 8–15 women and talked about their lives. The recognition that other women were experiencing the same frustrations and blockages in both their professional and personal lives was enlightening and often resulted in a call for action.

Many of these women went on to write classical articles on feminism and, as activists for social change, to use direct action tactics. For instance, Shulamith Firestone and Pam Allen founded New York Radical Women, moving from CR to street theater, civil disobedience, and "zap" strategies that gained media attention. Radical Women are remembered from a statement of principles beginning: "We take the woman's side in everything" (New York Radical Women 1970: 520).

New York Radical Women later splintered into three groups, one of which was Redstockings, co-founded in 1969 by Firestone and Ellen Willis, itself dissolving in 1970. The name Redstockings was taken from two sources: Bluestockings, a term used to describe nineteenth-century feminist writers (revealing regard for historical feminist activism), and Red for revolution. Going further than its origin group,

a Redstockings manifesto stated: "We identify the agents of our oppression as men" (Redstockings 1970: 534).

Identifying themselves as radical feminists, they began a discourse that would later spill over to the larger more generalized movement and society itself. Some of the terminology they placed in popular usage came from the New Left, but most was clearly related to a new emerging lexicon of feminist language that defined meaning and framed debates. Patriarchy, misogyny, oppression, exploitation, traffic in women, hegemony, the personal is political, gender, sexual harassment, and many more movement terms came into vogue during this time. An oft-repeated message coming from this sector was one of hostility to the praxis of progressive movements that spoke for specific sectors of society (e.g., the working class, African Americans, anti-war/anti-draft) but still ignored the constituency of women.

The high energy and "true believer" spirit of the small group sector led to strident encounters both with outside forces and within the groups themselves. Thus, there was increasing disengagement as internal attacks, known as trashing, began to take a toll. Writing under the nomenclature Joreen, Jo Freeman, a founder and activist in the Chicago Women's Liberation Union, details the paralyzing effect of being dismissed from the group you felt provided you with the first understanding you had experienced in your movement activist days (Joreen 1976).

The vitriolic nature of the divisions that arose within this sector of the movement reveals the danger of ideological purity so commonly found in dedicated proponents of social change. The effect was toxic and led to the dissolution of much of the small group sector by the mid-1970s. Other factors contributed to the breakdown of these groups, including those that would lead to serious movement divisions based on race, class, ethnicity, sexual orientation, sexuality, age, and ability. In particular, lesbian and African American women challenged the movement – large and small sectors – to become inclusive of all women or to stop talking about sisterhood (Lorde 1984).

Betty Friedan, a founder of the National Organization for Women (NOW), dismissively called CR navel gazing; but in fact, a CR session is a social process that allows hidden dimensions of women's lives to become transparent. It was the recognition of group subordination that came to be called "the personal is political." Later, this recognition was formulated as the "feminist click" where everyday events, language, and behavior were seen in a new light. The click represented awareness and connectedness for women. Thinking sociologically, rather than psychologically, the spread of feminist thought was the result of interaction. A fruitful analysis of this process is found in the sociological framework of symbolic interactionism (SI), which reveals the interactive process as the foundation of interpretation and meaning (Goffman 1959).

Consciousness raising as a method of "becoming aware" or as an organizing tool no longer played the same role in the women's movement after the 1980s. It became clear that, unless CR groups were representative of all women, the consciousness that was being raised was of the women in that particular group, and most groups that did CR were white middle-class women. In the 1990s international and transnational feminism also called for a widening circle of feminist awareness and increased concern for the differences among women.

Whether the terminology used is consciousness raising, something else, or nothing at all, the process of expanding conceptions to both explore the particular in women's lives as well as to reach out to those women who have been excluded, inclusiveness, transnationalism, and global feminisms are the goals of the women's movement in the twenty-first century.

SEE ALSO: Civil Rights Movement; Feminism; Feminism, First, Second, and Third Waves; Personal is Political; Radical Feminism; Women's Empowerment; Women's Movements

REFERENCES AND SUGGESTED READINGS

Echols, A. (1989) *Daring to Be Bad: Radical Feminism in America, 1967–75.* University of Minnesota Press, Minneapolis.

Evans, S. (1980) *Personal Politics: The Roots of Women's Liberation in the Civil Rights Movement and the New Left.* Vintage Books, New York.

Firestone, S. (1970) *The Dialectic of Sex: The Case for Feminist Revolution.* Bantam Books, New York.

Freeman, J. (1975) *The Politics of Women's Liberation: A Case Study of an Emerging Social Movement and Its Relation to the Policy Process.* Longman, New York.

Goffman, E. (1959) *The Presentation of Self in Everyday Life.* Doubleday, New York.

Joreen (J. Freeman) (1976) Trashing: The Dark Side of Sisterhood. *Ms.* 9(10): 49–98.

Lorde, A. (1984) *Sister Outsider.* The Crossing Press, Trumansburg, NH.

New York Radical Women (1970) Principles. In: Morgan, R. (Ed.), *Sisterhood is Powerful: An Anthology of Writings from the Women's Liberation Movement.* Vintage Books, New York.

Redstockings (1970) Manifesto. In: Morgan, R. (Ed.), *Sisterhood is Powerful: An Anthology of Writings from the Women's Liberation Movement.* Vintage Books, New York.

Ryan, B. (1992) *Feminism and the Women's Movement: Dynamics of Change in Social Movement Ideology and Activism.* Routledge, New York.

conservatism

Andrew Gamble

Conservatism has been one of the principal ideologies of the modern era. It was first articulated in its contemporary form in opposition to liberalism and specifically to the cataclysm of the French Revolution, which challenged the principles and values of the old order, and the authority of monarchs and priests. The deep-seated crisis of the European *ancien régime*, and the sudden appearance of revolutionaries prepared to act out utopian fantasies and inaugurate an entirely new kind of society, prompted a profound intellectual and political response, and laid the foundation for the modern conservative outlook.

Conservatism was part of the more general intellectual movement of the Counter-Enlightenment which challenged many of the ideas of liberalism, in particular its abstract individualism, its universalism, and its demands for equality. Conservatives stressed the importance of history and tradition, the particular and the local. First used as a party label in England in the 1830s, conservatism gradually spread elsewhere, but conservatives tended to regard it not as an overarching doctrine or transnational movement, but as composed of several distinct national traditions, Reflecting this, conservative thinkers have been highly diverse, ranging from Edmund Burke to Joseph de Maistre, and from Michael Oakeshott to Leo Strauss. Because conservatives are so averse to rationalism and to universalism, conservatism has not usually been presented as a universal doctrine in the grand manner of liberalism or socialism, organized around a distinct set of values and principles. It takes the form of a number of separate national traditions, each with its own peculiarities because of its unique national history and the statecraft that is deemed appropriate to conserve it.

Despite frequent attempts to present conservatism as a set of unique national experiences, there are nevertheless – as in all ideologies – common features and common principles. Together, these make up the conservative outlook. Conservatism is a fundamentally defensive doctrine, concerned with the presentation of existing institutions and interests, and with resisting the pressures for reform and change when these are seen to threaten them. Arising from this is a profound skepticism about human reason, human goodness, human knowledge, and human capacity. Conservatives are generally pessimistic about the state of the world and human society, and believe that most schemes of improvement are at best well-meaning and at worse malicious attempts to change society which will end up making it worse. The conservative instinct is always to hang on to what is familiar and known, rather than to risk what is unknown and untried. This attitude towards change is a fundamental human attribute, found in all organizations and all individuals.

Conservatism since its inception has been a long rearguard action against the modern world. As the pace of change has accelerated so a conservative disposition has been increasingly hard to maintain but, its exponents argue, all the more necessary. Most of the original causes which rallied conservatives have all been lost – absolute monarchies, the political power of landed aristocracies, the political authority of the church, slavery, serfdom, the subordination of women. Conservatives have had to accept human rights, democracy, secularism, property taxes, and much more. But this has not invalidated the relevance of the conservative message or the conservative attitude, although it sometimes makes it hard to grasp what it is that conservatives are seeking to conserve.

Conservatism is not just a doctrine about resisting change. It also has its own vision of society and human nature. Conservatives have been strongly critical of individualism and the doctrine of individual rights, because for them society exists before individuals, and the individual is a construction of society, fashioned by its customs, values, and traditions. Individuals do not exist outside society or prior to society, and therefore cannot for conservatives be treated as the yardstick for evaluating politics.

As a political doctrine conservatism is concerned with order, authority, tradition, precedent, and hierarchy. It holds that a secure and stable social order requires that authority be recognized and respected at all levels of the society, from the highest officials of the state, the holders of positions of responsibility in the professions, in companies and public bodies, to the heads of households. Conservatives seek to defend traditions, precedents, and hierarchies because these are the forms which give rise to authority and allow it to be exercised and accepted, the way things have always been done. Most conservatives were extremely hostile to democracy since it promised such a radical change in traditional governing arrangements, substituting the abstract notion of popular sovereignty for the historical sovereignty of the monarch.

As an economic doctrine conservatism has always emphasized property rights, but not as universal individual rights. Instead, property relationships are understood as deeply embedded in the history of particular societies, involving duties as well as rights. During the nineteenth century conservatives were often strong critics of laissez-faire economic individualism, believing that the widening gap between rich and poor, the encouragement of speculation and competition, the growth of cities and the depopulation of the countryside, the loss of national self-sufficiency, the spread of cosmopolitan and anti-national values and traditions, and the leveling down and dumbing down associated with capitalism all represented a huge assault upon the society they sought to conserve. Conservative political economy was highly pragmatic, often directed to protecting and subsidizing particular interests, such as farmers, and the national economy itself. Conservatives therefore often backed protectionist measures, particularly where these were linked to the strengthening of the national capacity for defense. Although conservatives have always tended to be against high levels of taxation, particularly taxes on property, they have not favored a minimal state on the doctrinal grounds professed by liberals, and in certain circumstances conservatives have been enthusiastic supporters of extending the powers of the state to tax and spend. Defense and welfare have both been regarded by conservatives as legitimate areas of state spending. All this has led liberals and some conservatives to question whether conservatism and capitalism are ultimately compatible.

As a cultural doctrine conservatism has been concerned with maintaining the authority of cultural traditions, with resisting the lowering of cultural standards, and bemoaning the decline of moral behavior in the West. This has also been a central concern of conservatives in the Islamic world, fearing the spread of western styles of behavior as well as western attitudes. In the West the spread of permissiveness, the undermining of individual responsibility, the emphasis upon rights rather than duties, the wave of social legislation allowing abortion and divorce, decriminalizing homosexuality, ending capital and corporal punishment have all caused enormous anxiety to conservatives. So too has the decline of education standards and the growth of new media, such as television and the Internet, which threaten traditional cultural standards and achievements. Some of these concerns are new, but cultural conservatism has deep roots, being connected to the desire to protect particular cultural heritages, whether western, Islamic, or Chinese, and the national expressions of those heritages.

Aside from its doctrinal elements conservatism also operates as statecraft. There is not one conservative statecraft, but rather as many statecrafts as there are states. A conservative statecraft is about choosing the best means to conserve the institutions of a particular state

and defend its essential interests. How that is done involves a basic strategic choice: governing by incorporating opposition, making such concessions to them as becomes necessary, or governing in such a way as to make such concessions unnecessary. The latter was the preferred path of Metternich and supporters of the *ancien régime* in Europe, the former being the statecraft of the English Whigs who were to become an essential part of the conservative coalition. Statecraft professed no permanent doctrines or principles, using them as tools in the gaining and holding of power. The substance of this conservatism lay in the institutions of the state which it was seeking to defend, and success was judged by how well that state survived. In the last decades of the Soviet Union the rulers of the Kremlin pursued a thoroughly conservative statecraft. Ultimately, that statecraft failed and the state was dissolved. In England by contrast the conservative statecraft preserved many aspects of the premodern English state throughout the twentieth century, including a monarchy with prerogative powers, a second chamber selected partly on a hereditary basis, and feudal titles and rituals.

Conservatism – whether as statecraft or doctrine – has been forced to adapt because of the huge changes which the modern era has unleashed. It might seek to delay change, but in the end could not resist it. The *ancien régimes* of Europe lasted through the nineteenth century, but most of them perished in the great conflagration of World War I. For conservatives like the Marquess of Salisbury, ensuring "shelter in our time" was as much as conservatives could aspire to. In the twentieth century the upheaval of two world wars and the pace of industrialization and urbanization forced many adjustments. Conservative parties were obliged to compete in the new mass democracies, to organize mass parties, and seek to appeal to a mass electorate. They generally did so by identifying themselves as the party of the nation, rallying national support against foreign enemies and immigrants and all who threatened the national way of life. They were also obliged to come to terms with capitalism and become the defender of capitalist institutions against the threat of Bolshevism.

The twentieth century saw the gradual emergence of conservative capitalism in many states, where conservative rather than liberal parties became the main protectors and defenders of capitalist institutions. This trend accelerated during the Cold War, when the security needs of states brought conservative understanding of national interests to the fore, and made it possible for them to forge coalitions to defend the nation and defend the free market and democracy against threats real or perceived from the left. The identification of the Soviet Union and international communism as the ideological enemy of the West provided a clarity to conservatism by crystallizing the values and the way of life which it was defending. At the same time conservatives found new enemies within, particularly after the emergence of the 1960s counter-culture which rejected cultural and political authority across a broad front, and the tide of social liberalism which questioned traditional values and behavior in respect of sexual orientation, gender roles, and multiculturalism.

Conservatism at the beginning of the 1990s was at war on many fronts, but fairly clear who its enemies were and what it stood for. All this changed with the ending of the Cold War and the disappearance of the Soviet Union – the main rationale for conservative politics in the previous half century. After the Cold War, conservatism struggled to find a clear purpose and a new external enemy, and lost ground in many countries to social democratic and left coalitions. The spread of neoliberal and cosmopolitan ideas was not very conducive to conservative politics, and the proclamations of a new era of peace, prosperity, and steady progress in eliminating social problems seemed to leave little role for a robust conservatism. This particular phase was however abruptly terminated by the security crisis of 9/11, which allowed conservatives in many countries to define a new external enemy and declare a global war on terror. Many of the conservatives active in identifying the need for a new policy initiative to combat global terrorism were dubbed neoconservatives, a label they happily adopted.

Conservatism as a doctrine is wide enough to embrace the tough-minded realism of neoconservatism with the ameliorative and concessionary politics of the Middle Way. In recent decades it has also increasingly converged with certain types of liberalism. The resulting amalgam – liberal conservatism, or free-market conservatism – has become one of the dominant ideological patterns in the western world. It has moved away from certain features of earlier twentieth-century conservatism, particularly the emphasis upon welfare and the extended state and protectionism, and has embraced the market and capitalism, while still remaining confident about the value of the state and the need to use state power in defense of key institutions and interests.

SEE ALSO: Liberalism; Nation-State and Nationalism; Neoconservatism; Tradition

REFERENCES AND SUGGESTED READINGS

Hoover, K. & Plant, R. (1988) *Conservative Capitalism in Britain and the United States*. Routledge, London.

Kirk, R. (1968) *The Conservative Mind: From Burke to Eliot*. Avon Books, New York.

Nisbet, R. (1986) *Conservatism: Dream and Reality*. Open University Press, Milton Keynes.

O' Sullivan, N. (1986) *Conservatism*. Dent, London.

Scruton, R. (1984) *The Meaning of Conservatism*. Macmillan, London.

conspicuous consumption

Juliet B. Schor

The term conspicuous consumption entered the sociological lexicon via Thorstein Veblen's biting analysis of the spending patterns of the rich and *nouveau riches* in the late nineteenth century. *The Theory of the Leisure Class* (1899) is an account of how these groups spent enormous energy and money constructing an ostentatious style of life. They built and decorated ornate homes, adorned their persons with clothing and jewelry, designed elaborate carriages, and employed large numbers of servants dressed in expensive uniforms. Throughout, the principles of waste, luxury, and ornamentation ruled the choices they made. The motive that animated their efforts was the desire for social esteem, which itself was dependent on the possession of wealth. But having money was not enough. It must be put "in evidence," or become conspicuous. Because these are ongoing features of wealth-based status systems, the concept of conspicuousness continues to be important long after the Veblenian era has passed.

THEORY OF CONSPICUOUS CONSUMPTION

The theory of conspicuous consumption is the centerpiece of Veblen's larger analysis of class society and its relation to styles of life and work. Relying on a stylized history of "savage," "barbarian," and "civilized" societies, Veblen argued that the emergence of classes in the barbarian era (roughly synonymous with feudal Europe and Asia) led to the use of wealth as the primary basis of males' social esteem, in contrast to military prowess. Wealth originally reflected booty gained in war, but over time came to be valued for its own sake, even to the extent that inherited wealth was more valued than wealth gained through personal accomplishments. Veblen believed that the desire to attain status, or social esteem, eventually became the dominant motive in individuals' decisions about work and consumption, even eclipsing biological or physical pressures to consume. His account is thus thoroughly sociological.

In a status system based on wealth, the credibility and verifiability of individuals' claims to status become a significant issue. Particularly before the era of paper money, wealth was not easily transportable, and ensuring its safety also militated against public display of money itself. Therefore, proxy measures of wealth-holding developed, chief among them the ability to forego productive labor, and the ability to consume luxuriously, or what Veblen termed *conspicuous leisure* and *conspicuous consumption*. While status accrues in the first instance to the male head of household, wives and servants engaged in vicarious leisure and consumption.

Their idleness and adornment with expensive jewels, furs, and livery are powerful testaments to the pecuniary position of their husbands and masters.

Originally, the ability to forego productive labor was the basis of status. Veblen (1994) argued that labor came to be socially disreputable and associated with inferior groups. Elites' desire to appear "at leisure" led to widespread idleness (e.g., among European nobility), to non-working wives as a symbol of prestige, and even to the employment of servants who did no work. However, the conflict between the prestige value of idleness and what Veblen called the "instinct of workmanship" meant that over time conspicuous consumption, the purchase and display of expensive and luxurious goods, became the dominant status marker. In the modern era, Veblen argued, an affirmative desire to engage in what he called "invidious comparison," or to trump others by amassing more than they have, became less important than a self-protective attempt to keep up. Thus, Veblen believed that consuming conspicuously was as much a defensive as an offensive behavior.

For both leisure and consumption, public visibility is central. In Veblen's day, when the rich gave elaborate dinner parties, they had their menus published in the newspapers. Today, expensive homes are pictured in popular magazines or television shows. This argument explains why furnaces are far less important as status goods than watches, and why some people pay as much for a handbag as a mattress. The need to put spending "in evidence" is because public display solves the informational problems associated with wealth-based status competitions. To operate efficiently such a system needs a method for conveying accurate information about each participant's wealth. Merely telling is not a viable system because of the problem of what social scientists have termed "moral hazard" – the incentive to lie or behave unethically, in this case the possibility of exaggerating one's wealth. Therefore, status claims are verified by the requirement of committing real resources to the game. And a set of complex, unwritten rules for gaining social status have developed (eg., boasting is counter-productive, nonchalance is preferred).

This weeds out pretenders and allows the system to operate in a slightly more oblique and therefore more powerful way. Thus, the role of public visibility, or what Veblen calls conspicuousness, becomes central to the operation of the system.

There are a number of noteworthy features of Veblen's theory of conspicuous consumption, particularly in relation to the contemporary literature on theories of consumption. First, agents are deeply intentional in their spending decisions, making choices for the purpose of maximizing their social status. They are fully informed, in command of their desires, and operate in a well-organized social environment of shared assumptions and values. Consumption is neither personally expressive, nor impulsive. This is similar to conventional economic theories of the rational consumer. In contrast to the dominant economic accounts, however, Veblen's consumer has a pure social orientation. Consumption is valued for what others make of it, rather than for intrinsic product benefits or functions. In this, his approach is similar to anthropological accounts that stress the role of consumption in the construction and reproduction of culture, as for example in Mary Douglas and Baron Isherwood's classic discussion in *The World of Goods* (1979), or sociological accounts that emphasize the importance of symbols and meanings, such as the writings of Jean Baudrillard. Like some of these culturalist accounts, the theory of conspicuous consumption relies on a widely recognized valuation ranking in which all participants covet a set of consensual status symbols.

However, in contrast to standard accounts of consumption as a functional and satisfying cultural expression, in Veblen's account there is a frustrating aspect to spending, because all status is positional and the goal of the game is to *waste*. The dynamic part of his theory involves the "trickle down" of status goods through the layers of the social hierarchy. The rich are the first adopters of new and expensive products. As incomes rise, groups farther down the social hierarchy mimic the spending patterns of those above them. Luxuries turn into necessities with lower status, because everyone owns them, and the rich move on to the next new or more expensive thing. Absolute increases in spending only yield social value when they improve relative position; when increases in standard of living are general, they are like being on a treadmill, merely keeping people from falling behind. (In economics, this approach is called "relative income," following James Duesenberry's appropriation of Veblen's model.) Another classic trickle-down model is found in Georg Simmel's "On Fashion" (*American Sociological Review*, 1957). Simmel argued that fashion trends begin with the wealthy and diffuse throughout the population, and that as styles generalize, the rich abandon them in search of something novel. Thus, fashionability requires novelty.

The theory of conspicuous consumption also explains the pattern of consumer spending. It predicts that people will tend to spend more heavily on socially visible goods, in contrast to products that are used in private. Appearance goods such as dress, footwear, and jewelry have traditionally been central to status competitions. So too have vehicles, from carriages to SUVs and BMWs. The third item in the trio of status display is the home, where ornamentation, size, and materials all figure centrally in the social value of a dwelling. This theory of consumption patterning has been used to predict that people will pay higher status premiums for products that are more socially visible. For example, Angela Chao and Juliet Schor, writing in *the Journal of Economic Psychology* in 1998, showed that women pay higher prices, relative to product quality, for branded lipsticks, which they frequently use in public, than they do for facial cremes, which are used exclusively in the home. A 2004 Princeton doctoral dissertation by economist Ori Heffetz found that the wealthy spend a higher fraction of their income on visible items than do lower-income households. The theory of conspicuous consumption is also central to accounts of branding, and predicts that products that are used in public view will attract more branding resources from advertisers. Similarly, if products follow a trajectory from relatively private to relatively public usage and display, they are likely to become more heavily advertised. Recent examples of newly branded goods which were purely private but are now displayed publicly include undergarments, water, and kitchen appliances.

VEBLEN AND THE SOCIOLOGICAL LITERATURE ON CONSUMPTION

The theory of conspicuous consumption and the broader account of a class-based status-driven consumer system was for decades the dominant approach to consumption in American sociology, and *The Theory of the Leisure Class* was the seminal work. For example, the research of Stuart Chapin, carried out through the 1920s and 1930s, painstakingly recorded the consumption items displayed in the living rooms of households of different social classes and tested subjects' ability to identify the backgrounds of the inhabitants. Classic sociological research such as that carried out by Andrew Warner and the Lynds found that people used consumer goods to signal and solidify status within their communities. The role of visible consumption display was thought to be more important in the US than in Europe because birth-based status claims were weaker and upward mobility based on new money was more accepted. After World War II this approach continued to dominate the field, as considerable empirical research was aimed at describing differences in consumption patterns by social class. The theory of conspicuous consumption got a further boost in the 1950s with the critique of affluence and advertising found in hugely influential books such as John Kenneth Galbraith's *The Affluent Society* and Vance Packard's *The Status Seekers* and *The Hidden Persuaders*. Furthermore, despite some obvious differences, the Frankfurt School critique of mass culture and the 1960s rejection of consumerism in works such as Marcuse's *One-Dimensional Man* also buoyed Veblen's influence. The Frankfurt School and Marcuse took the view that the power of corporations and marketing efforts were primarily responsible for people's consumer behaviors; they saw people as passive, almost powerless victims of a system that required mass consumption, passive leisure, and an uncritical attitude toward capitalism. In Veblen's story people are more active, but there are similarities. People become victims of strong structural forces in both accounts, although not to the same degree. In addition, both approaches take the view that consumer goods are important mainly for their social meanings rather than utilitarian benefits. And perhaps most importantly, both share a deeply critical attitude toward consumption, which differentiates them from mainstream liberal theory as well as postmodernism.

BACKLASH AGAINST VEBLEN

In keeping with the materialist orientation of postwar empirical social science, most of the research in the Veblenian tradition looked at *what* people were purchasing, and ignored direct measures of consumers' intentions as well as how they interpreted consumer goods. The literature called these concepts the "coding" and "decoding" of consumption symbols. In the 1970s, this weakness in the literature was exposed. Two influential articles by Marcus Felson in 1976 and 1978 (published in *Social Indicators Research* and *Public Opinion Quarterly*, respectively) cast doubt on the entire approach on the grounds that consumers did not actually know which goods were more expensive, and in any case, the proliferation of consumer goods had eroded the homogeneity of the status system. While there were weaknesses in Felson's methodology and conclusions, it hardly mattered. The pendulum began to swing away from Veblen. It is not surprising, as his influence had been so profound and had lasted for so many decades, that researchers apparently found it suffocating. Beginning in the 1980s, sociological accounts of consumption contained a ritual denunciation of Veblen and his pernicious influence. While some market researchers did studies in this vein through the 1980s, sociologists and others in the emerging interdisciplinary field of "consumption studies" pursued very different ideas. In his widely cited 1987 *The Romantic Ethic and the Spirit of Modern Consumerism* and elsewhere, Colin Campbell attacked Veblen's theory on the grounds that it was not empirically supported, and failed to sufficiently account for the importance of novelty in "modern" consumer societies. Campbell argued that consumers were driven by an endless cycle of daydreaming–purchase–disappointment. Cultural studies accounts of media consumption emphasized an active viewer making her own meanings, undaunted by the symbolic meanings intended by producers. More generally, research in both sociology and other fields shifted from a critical to an interpretive framework which relied far more on consumers' own interpretations of their actions and what consumption means to them. By contrast, in status-driven systems consumers are not always fully conscious of or willing to admit motives. Evidence of status seeking is largely behavioral.

Postmodern theory also rejected Veblen. Although social differentiation was an essential principle of the consumer system for foundational postmodern consumer theorists such as Baudrillard, as the characterization of postmodernity as an era of fragmentation, pastiche, recombination, and bricolage developed, it became less compatible with the single-minded, consistent, purposive Veblenian status seeker. The "postmodern" consumer is a playful, ironic, novelty-seeking, adventurous individual, putting on and taking off roles like costumes from her eclectic closet. She shuns conventional upscale status aspiration. As Douglas Holt, one proponent of the postmodern markets thesis, has argued, the "good life" is no longer a matter of acquiring a well-defined set of consensual status symbols, but needs to be understood as a project of self-creation. Studies of subcultures also rejected the trickle-down model on the basis of a growing tendency for consumer innovation to come from the social margins. Analysts noted that trends in fashion, music, art, and even language were starting among inner-city youths, rather than wealthy suburbanites.

In the midst of this ferment, Bourdieu's magisterial study *Distinction* was published in French in 1979 and in English in 1984. *Distinction* affirmed the principle of class patterning of consumption, but expanded on the theory of conspicuous consumption by arguing that both "economic capital" (i.e., wealth or purchasing power) and "cultural capital" yield status. Cultural capital is knowledge of elite taste, manners, and habits, and is transmitted through family upbringing and elite educational institutions. Bourdieu's account is far more complex and developed than Veblen's, but *Distinction* has unmistakable Veblenian roots. This may account for some of the negative reception the book received in the American context. An interesting, although limited debate ensued, in which key tenets of the class/consumption approach were explored, such as whether taste

and consumer choice follow class patterns in the US or whether consensual status symbols still exist. The dominant view continues to be that this is an outmoded theory of limited usefulness in explaining consumer behavior. Perhaps not surprisingly, two books in the Veblenian tradition which were published in the late 1990s, Juliet Schor's *The Overspent American* and Robert Frank's *Luxury Fever*, were written by economists rather than sociologists.

CONSPICUOUS CONSUMPTION: OUTMODED OR RELEVANT?

Curiously, as the academy was presiding over the death of conspicuous consumption, consumers embarked on an era of unprecedented luxury spending, much of it patently conspicuous. The dramatic increases in the concentration of income and wealth which began in the 1980s led to booming markets for high-end items, beginning with watches, jewelry, designer clothing, automobiles, and yachts. During the 1990s the competition spread to expensive hotel suites, weddings and other private parties, elaborate mansions, and private airplanes. Analysts also studied the emergence of a "new servant class" of immigrant women, mainly, but also of Europeanstyle butlers, with an unmistakable Veblenian cast. These developments were duly reported on in national newspapers and magazines, as they had been a century earlier. As the corporate financial scandals of the early twenty-first century came to light, so too did the consumption excesses associated with this public looting. It was highly reminiscent of the Gilded Age of the 1890s which had prompted Veblen to write *The Theory of the Leisure Class*. Then, as now, conspicuous consumption was fueled by worsening distributions of income and wealth, a trend which shows no signs of abating, as globalization and conservative policies continue.

What scholarship will eventually make of these developments is hard to say. After 25 years, perhaps it is time for the pendulum to swing back in the direction of the theory of conspicuous consumption, particularly in the wake of a growing grassroots anti-consumerism and "voluntary simplicity" movement. However, that reversal is by no means certain.

Within the academy, consumption continues to be celebrated, and moral or other critiques of consumption remain suspect.

SEE ALSO: Bourdieu, Pierre; Brands and Branding; Consumption; Cultural Capital; Hyperconsumption/Overconsumption; Veblen, Thorstein

REFERENCES AND SUGGESTED READINGS

Bourdieu, P. (1984) *Distinction: A Social Critique of the Judgment of Taste.* Harvard University Press, Cambridge, MA.

Campbell, C. (1994) Conspicuous Confusion? A Critique of Veblen's Theory of Conspicuous Consumption. *Sociological Theory* 12 (2): 34–47.

Dittmar, H. (1992) *The Social Psychology of Material Possessions.* St. Martin's Press, New York.

Frank, R. (1985) *Choosing the Right Pond: Human Behavior and the Quest for Status.* Oxford University Press, New York.

Frank, R. (1999) *Luxury Fever: Why Money Fails to Satisfy in an Era of Excess.* Free Press, New York.

Holt, D. (1997) Distinction in America: Recovering Bourdieu's Theory of Tastes from its Critics. *Poetics* 24: 326–50.

McCracken, G. (1998) Consumer Goods, Gender Construction, and a Rehabilitated Trickle Down Theory. In: McCracken, G., *Culture and Consumption.* University of Indiana Press, Bloomington.

Schor, J. B. (1998) *The Overspent American: Upscaling, Downshifting, and the New Consumer.* Basic Books, New York.

Veblen, T. (1994 [1899]) *The Theory of the Leisure Class.* Penguin, New York.

constructionism

William H. Swatos, Jr.

Preeminently the result of Berger and Luckmann's book *The Social Construction of Reality* (1966), constructionist theory claims that what human beings at any moment hold to be "real" in social experience is itself a social creation, and in that moment is simultaneously a social product and production. Drawing particularly upon the work of Mead and Schütz, they posit a three-moment dialectic using the concepts of *externalization, objectivation,* and *internalization.* Society is a human product. Society is objectively real. "The human" is a social product. These three simple sentences provide a theoretical structure for understanding both in and through time how people relate not only to their external social world, but also to their own identities. Constructionist theory simultaneously incorporates and supersedes role theory inasmuch as it extends beyond roles to both reality and identity. That is, both where I am and who I am socially become both the effect and cause of where I am and who I am socially in and through an unending process of interaction sequences that constitute not merely social experience but also human being itself.

Subtitled "A Treatise in the Sociology of Knowledge," *The Social Construction of Reality* is intended to present a sociological account of how it is that, both collectively and individually, humans "know" the world around them and their place in it. Constructionist theory is empirical in the sense that it begins from an understanding of "society" as a product of human activity. Society does not come into existence apart from the interaction of human beings. Hence, at any point in time, society is being produced by its participants. In the absence of living human beings, there is no society. Yet, as a result of human beings existing through time, society comes to have an objective character (or "facticity") that makes it appear to exist not only potentially over against any specific human being, but also as an object of potentially coercive character against all the human beings who participate in it. What may sometimes be termed the "social system" exists *as if* it is objectively real. And because it is externalized as if it is objectively real, it becomes objectively real to its participants, in the sense that it is both formally and informally transmitted as real both to outsiders and to newborns, hence internalized by them to the extent that they wish to participate in the system. At the same time, however, because humans exist in both natural and technical environments as well as in interaction with multiple social environments, the social world can never be a closed system that reproduces itself unchanged across an extended period of time. Especially with increasing globalization in late modernity, alternative "realities" (or constructions of reality) intersect and force reevaluation of the putatively objective character of the socially constructed reality of any specific situation, giving an ironic postmodern credibility to the Marxist dictum that "all that is solid melts into air," as the "reality" is challenged by a multiplicity of competing realities across cultures.

SEE ALSO: Knowledge, Sociology of; Mead, George Herbert; Role Theory; Schütz, Alfred

REFERENCES AND SUGGESTED READINGS

Berger, P. L. & Kellner, H. (1981) *Sociology Reinterpreted*. Doubleday, Garden City, NY.
Berger, P. L. and Luckmann, T. (1966) *The Social Construction of Reality*. Doubleday, Garden City, NY.
Mead, G. H. (1934) *Mind, Self and Society*. University of Chicago Press, Chicago.
Schütz, A. (1962) *Collected Papers*. Nijhoff, The Hague.

(constructive) technology assessment

Ragna Zeiss

Technology assessment (TA) refers to the study and evaluation of new technologies. The need for technology assessment was first articulated in the late 1960s when growing numbers of people became concerned about the consequences of new technologies and new large technological projects. In this period of environmental, anti-nuclear, and democratization movements, societal problems were regarded as complex and interrelated and could not be solved by simple policy measures. Technology assessment was seen as a way to assess and analyze (adverse) social, economic, legal, political, cultural, and ecological effects of a given technology on society and to give society time to reflect upon these impacts and take appropriate measures.

Societal actors became interested in technology assessment for a variety of reasons. Some were attracted to technology assessment because the combination of scientific analysis and societal involvement seemed to do justice to the complexity of the problems that were faced at the time. The stress on the integration of natural and social sciences and the inter- or multidisciplinarity of teams of independent scientists was popular for similar reasons: these teams might be able to provide society with a complete analysis of the likely consequences of a technology and bring together all facets of the problem. Yet others regarded technology assessment as a way to change anti-technological attitudes; the negative consequences of large technological systems (and their breakdowns) and ideas formulated by influential thinkers such as those from the Frankfurt School will have influenced negative attitudes toward technological developments. The Frankfurt School posed a pessimistic view of technology as a destructive force that was out of control. Companies could use technology assessment to demonstrate to the public that social responsibility was taken seriously. Social movements like the environmental movement saw technology assessment as a legitimate way to ask attention for its requirements and to make them part of the regular policy preparation and decision-making process (see Smits & Leijten 1991).

Despite the fact that societal groups became interested in technology assessment for various reasons, TA remained the generic name for the activity of describing, analyzing, and forecasting the likely effects of technology on all spheres of society. Two aspects are common to the perception of technology assessment by different actors. First, it is a means to analyze the societal consequences of technological developments. Second, technology assessment is considered as a tool to evaluate (technological) developments for policy purposes. The way in which technology assessment is considered and used in specific (national) contexts depends on the political institutions, the political climate, innovation and social policy context, the contemporary pressing issues, and the actors (and their ideas) involved in the process. These issues have also influenced the relation between technology assessment and social studies of technology (or technology studies).

INSTITUTIONALIZATION AND DIVERSIFICATION OF TECHNOLOGY ASSESSMENT

The examples discussed here can be seen as three different prototypes of technology assessment as it originated and became established in three different social, cultural, and political contexts. The first example is the development of technology assessment in the US. The second and third examples focus on, respectively, Denmark and the Netherlands.

The US and the OTA

The US Office of Technology Assessment (OTA) in the United States has long been *the* example of technology assessment. With the establishment of the OTA in 1972, technology assessment was first institutionalized. Apart from seeming an appropriate method for dealing with the (technological) issues raised by social movements, the institutionalization of technology assessment in the OTA was also seen as a way to strengthen the position of the Congress. The OTA was an office of Congress and therefore closely linked to the legislative branch. Its goal was to obtain objective information about the (secondary) effects of technology at an early stage of the technological development. With the help of this information, it could then independently assess the virtues of technological developments and correct the imbalance between legislature and executive. The OTA technology assessment can thus be considered as an "early warning system" that would help decision-makers to avoid unwanted side effects of new technologies. The OTA only became successful after a number of years when the assessment products were extensively reviewed internally and externally and the reports could be regarded as of high scientific quality. It was then that the OTA became seen as an organization providing neutral and objective information. The OTA is sometimes regarded as a prototype of the classic technology assessment model. In the classic model, technology assessment studies the secondary impact of technology and provides decision-makers with objective information on those

impacts. The OTA can then be characterized by its expert orientation and the indirect involvement of interest groups. Others have defined a specific "OTA model" that has developed since its early years (see Eijndhoven 1997). In later years many (societal) actors became disappointed since the high expectations they held of technology assessment had not come true. Technology assessment had not become a major contribution to society; it was realized that the impacts of technology could not be foreseen in their totality; technology assessment had not been the early warning system people had expected it to be (it had been more focused on the short term than on the long term); technology assessment did not provide neutral and objective information; and policymakers and the public had not accepted the results of technology assessment at face value. Technology assessment was then changed from an early warning system to a way to develop policy alternatives. The OTA is here characterized as an organization with much in-house expertise that provided thorough assessments of high scientific quality (through advisory panels, workshops, etc.) that provide options for policy development. In 1995 the OTA was closed. This does not mean that technology assessment no longer exists in the US; people are still concerned about understanding and controlling technical change. Technology assessment has been institutionalized in different places than in the OTA and some see opportunities for different forms of technology assessment, perhaps more similar to those in some European countries (see La Porte 1997).

Europe

The development of technology assessment started in Europe more than a decade later (in the 1980s) and took different forms than the technology assessment that was practiced in the United States. These differences can be explained by a number of things, such as the different political systems, the more limited capacity of especially smaller countries (and thus less in-house expertise), different concerns, and the role of social studies of technology. The early 1980s saw political debates around (new) technologies (nuclear power, microelectronics, biotechnology) and their social, ethical, and economic consequences. It was also a period of economic stagnation during which technological innovation could be seen as a means to overcome crisis. Technology assessment started therefore with (slightly) different assumptions in Europe. There was less attention to the negative consequences of technological developments; one was often more interested in technological developments that could be seen as desirable. The assumptions that technology assessment could turn policy-making into a scientific practice and that the scientific community would be able to predict all possible consequences of technological development, as was thought in the early years of the OTA, were no longer seen as realistic, and the focus turned toward controlling and forming future technological developments. These different assumptions on which some of the technology assessment projects were based were also influenced by the development of social studies of technology.

In many of the smaller countries (Denmark, Finland, Belgium, the Netherlands) social studies of technology are triggered by policy needs and the need to examine the social and environmental consequences of new technologies. This is also true for some larger countries like Germany, although social studies of technology do not have a clear link to technology assessment in Great Britain and France (see Cronberg & Sørensen 1995). Over time, social studies of technology also started to influence technology assessment. New approaches to technology assessment have been created on the basis of insights developed in social studies of technology. These studies emerged partly as a result of a critique on "technological determinism." Technological determinism assumes that technology develops (almost) autonomously; society is not able to change technological developments and their impacts. Social scientists had, in accordance with this determinism, mainly focused on the effects of technology. New perspectives have criticized the line that was drawn between technology on the one hand and the effects of technology on the other. The detailed empirical studies that were carried out by technology studies scholars stressed the mutual shaping of

technology and society. Technology and innovation processes were now understood as integrated in the social, cultural, and political development of society. Rather than focusing on the external effects of technology and on choices between technological options, scholars started concentrating on the internal development of technology. Since technical developments were now understood as being influenced by society, design-related issues and social discussions of the technology and options of technological development were needed. These new insights into the nature of technological change have influenced further development of technology assessment. Technology assessment changed from isolated analyses of social impacts and an early warning system to a constant monitoring of research and development processes. The users and consumers of technologies were no longer regarded as passive; instead they have become very important since what users do results in the consequences of a technology. Technology assessment has thus changed from the way in which it had first been developed in the United States (this is not to say that these changes may not, in their turn, have influenced technology assessment practices in the United States). Yet, there are still differences between technology assessment practices and the ways in which they are institutionalized and carried out in different European countries. Two examples are given below.

Denmark and the Danish Technology Board

In Denmark technology assessment started to become institutionalized in the early 1980s. The Danish Technology Board can be regarded as a prototype of the participatory model or of public technology assessment. Technology assessment in Denmark concentrates on mediating social discussion and fostering public debate about technological developments and their consequences. Whereas in-house expertise was important for the OTA, in Denmark public participation and the involvement of different societal groups in the debate are seen as essential. The Danish Technology Board has developed a standard procedure to achieve debate on the implications of technology in the form of consensus conferences (see below). At the end of the consensus conference a panel of lay people write a consensus document; this document is regarded as an important input for policy.

The Netherlands and the Rathenau Institute: Constructive Technology Assessment

In 1986 the Netherlands Organization for Technology Assessment (NOTA) was established. Since a policy memorandum of 1984, Dutch technology assessment was linked to both decision-making and broader political and societal articulation of opinions on science and technology. The NOTA, which became the Rathenau Institute in 1994, drew on both the model of the Danish consensus conferences to stimulate social debates and a newly emerging form of technology assessment called "constructive technology assessment" (CTA). Consensus conferences in the Netherlands do not have the same importance for policy as they do in Denmark and are therefore often called "public debates." Constructive technology assessment is based on different ideas than consensus conferences. It provided an answer to the critique of technology assessment that its early warning function and ideas about future impacts of technology were elaborated only after the technology had already been developed. It focuses on broadening the design, development, and implementation processes of technologies in all phases of technical change rather than on assessing the impacts of (new) technologies. This is not to say that constructive technology assessment does not attempt to anticipate effects or impacts of new technologies at all. However, where in traditional technology assessment the technology or projects with strong technological components are seen as given, as static, constructive technology assessment concentrates on the dynamics of processes, where the impacts of technologies are building up during the development of the technology. Choices are constantly being made about the form, function, and use of particular technologies and thus the development of these technologies can be steered to a certain extent. Early interaction with (relevant)

actors is therefore seen as a core activity. Constructive technology assessment has thus brought traditional technology assessment, the anticipation and accommodation of social impacts, back to the actual construction of technology. Constructive technology assessment therefore consists of tools and strategies to bring technology assessment activities into the actual construction of technology. It can thus be regarded as a third prototype of technology assessment.

These ideas were influenced and supported by social studies of technology that saw technological development as a function of a complex set of social, economic, technical, and political factors rather than as an autonomous force with its own inner logic. The Rathenau Institute and the social studies of technology scholars mutually supported each other. The Rathenau Institute had an effect on technology studies in terms of funds, and technology studies informed the Rathenau Institute about new analytical techniques and new approaches regarding the development of new technologies.

The task of the Rathenau Institute is still mainly to organize and coordinate large-scale TA studies and to foster public debate. Naturally, other Dutch institutes have also taken up (constructive) technology assessment. Outside the Netherlands many activities take place that can be labeled constructive technology assessment as well, although these activities are often given different names. The core of these activities is always to broaden the design of new technologies, but they may be carried out in different ways to emphasize different aspects and to fit the context in which constructive technology assessment is practiced.

METHODS OF (CONSTRUCTIVE) TECHNOLOGY ASSESSMENT

The above has shown that technology assessment analyzes the possible (long-term and unintended) consequences of particular technologies (often for purposes of policymaking) by means of an interdisciplinary approach. Yet, a number of more specific methods can be and have been identified and used in order to undertake (constructive) technology assessment. These consist of methods such as interviews, brainstorming, literature research, document analysis, expert consultation, case studies, cost-benefit analysis, computer simulations, and scenario development. There are also methods more specific to technology assessment and involvement of the public such as dialogue workshops, social experiments, public debates, consensus conferences, technology forcing programs and platforms, and strategic niche management. Which methods are used for (constructive) technology assessment depends on the type of technology assessment that is practiced and on the wider context in which this form originated and is now used. A distinction can, for instance, be made between project-induced technology assessment (analysis of the possible consequences of one particular project, e.g., highway construction), technology-induced technology assessment (analysis of the impact of a specific technology on society and natural environment), and problem-induced technology assessment (identification of different possible solutions to an existing or future social problem). Another distinction is that between participatory methods based on stakeholder involvement (working groups, scenarios, hearings) and participatory methods that involve the general public (voting conferences, development space, consensus conference). One method more specific to technology assessment is further discussed below.

The consensus conference was developed by the Danish Board of Technology (DBT) to be used in participatory technology assessment. The term "consensus conference" and method were already used in the 1970s by the US health sector where health professionals obtained information from experts and discussed health-related issues. However, the DBT was the first to involve members of the public in decision-making processes; this has been called "the Danish model." Each year one or two consensus conferences are held by the DBT and the method is now used in many other countries as well. A consensus conference often takes place over a number of days during which a dialogue between experts and lay people is established. The conference is open to the public. The experts inform lay people about the technology and its implications and lay people then have the chance to express their (economic, social, legal, and ethical) hopes and concerns about this technology, and their knowledge and experience will be included in the process. An attempt is then made to reach consensus on the issue. In this way, experts and politicians become aware of the attitudes and thoughts of the public about the issue, lay people are actively involved with decisions about technologies, the knowledge and experience of experts and lay people are integrated, and the process adheres to the democratic principle. In cases where the public may be affected by the (new) technology (biotechnology, transport, genetically modified food), the public can be seen as a stakeholder and needs to be involved to act as peer reviewers (see Ravetz & Funtowicz 1996; Fixdal 1997). This method is especially suited for topics that presuppose contributions from experts, are societally relevant, can be limited in scope, and address issues that need clarification of attitudes. The method is used slightly differently in different countries. In the US consensus conferences are, for example, often used to create knowledge rather than to inform the political system and requirements about transparency and accountability therefore differ (see Joss & Durant 1995; Andersen & Jæger 1999).

USE OF (CONSTRUCTIVE)
TECHNOLOGY ASSESSMENT IN
SPECIFIC FIELDS

(Constructive) technology assessment has been used to analyze technological developments in different areas. Biotechnology, energy technology, information technology, nanotechnology, nuclear power technology, and telecommunications are just a few examples. For some areas a specific form of technology assessment that concentrates on just one of these areas has been developed. One can think about environment technology assessment, information technology assessment, and the most substantive and institutionalized of these, health technology assessment (HTA), also called medical technology assessment. HTA is occupied with, for example, coverage decisions, prices for pharmaceuticals, and numbers of services needed in an area. It helps to make policy decisions about priorities and the choice of health interventions by evaluating actual or potential health interventions. By examining short- and long-term consequences of the application of a health technology (or set of technologies) like drugs, devices, and procedures, it aims to help decision-making in policy and practice. Many countries now have health technology assessment offices and centers and also the European Commission supports the forming of national and international networks for health technology assessment. HTA is not new; it started in the 1970s. The Health Program of the US OTA was the first of its kind and was established in 1975. Most European national programs regarding health technology assessment, like other forms of technology assessment, started in the mid-1980s, although earlier projects had already been established in the early 1970s. As with other forms of technology assessment, HTA differs among different countries. Some countries have a public agency for assessment of health technology (Sweden, Spain, France), whereas others make use of health technology assessment with regard to payment for health care through sickness funds and insurance companies (the Netherlands, Switzerland). Yet others have made health technology assessment part of the Department of Health and attempt to bring it into all administrative and clinical decisions (United Kingdom). Likewise, the methods used by different countries also differ.

SEE ALSO: Critical Theory/Frankfurt School; Risk, Risk Society, Risk Behavior, and Social Problems; Science and Public Participation: The Democratization of Science; Science, Social Construction of; Social Movements; Technological Determinism; Technological Innovation; Technology, Science, and Culture

REFERENCES AND SUGGESTED READINGS

Andersen, I. & Jæger, B. (1999) Danish Participatory Models, Scenario Workshops and Consensus Conferences: Towards More Democratic Decision-Making. *Science and Public Policy* 26(5): 331–40.

Banta, D. & Oortwijn, W. (1999) *Health Technology Assessment in Europe: The Challenge of Coordination*. Office for Official Publications of the European Communities, Luxembourg.

Cronberg, T. (1992) *Technology Assessment in the Danish Socio-Political Context*. Technical University of Denmark, Copenhagen.

Cronberg, T. & Sørensen, K. H. (Eds.) (1995) *Similar Concerns, Different Styles? Technology Studies in Western Europe*. Office for Official Publications of the European Communities, Luxembourg.

Cronberg, T. et al. (Eds.) (1991) *Danish Experiments: Social Construction of Technology*. New Social Science Monographs, Copenhagen.

Eijndhoven, J. C. M. (1997) Technology Assessment: Product or Process. *Technological Forecasting and Social Change* 54: 269–86.

Fixdal, J. (1997) Consensus Conferences as Extended Peer Groups. *Science and Public Policy* 24(6): 366–76.

Grin, J., Graaf, H. van de, & Hoppe, R. (1997) *Technology Assessment Through Interaction: A Guide*. Rathenau Institute, The Hague.

Hoo, S. C. de, Smits, R. E. H. M., & Petrella, R. (Eds.) (1987) *Technology Assessment: An Opportunity for Europe*. Government Printing Office, The Hague.

Joss, S. & Durant, J. (1995) *Public Participation in Science: The Role of Consensus Conferences in Europe*. Institute for Social Inventions, London.

La Porte, T. M. (1997) New Opportunities for Technology Assessment in the Post-OTA World. *Technological Forecasting and Social Change* 54: 199–214.

Ouwens, C. D., Hoogstraten, P. van, Jelsma, J., Prakke, F., & Rip, A. (1987) *Constructief Technologisch Aspectenonderzoek, een verkenning (Constructive Technology Assessment: An Exploration)*. Staatsdrukkerij, The Hague.

Rathenau Institute (1996) *De organisatie van Technology Assessment in de gezondheidszorg in Nederland (The Organization of Health Care Technology Assessment in The Netherlands)*. Rathenau Institute, The Hague.

Ravetz, J. & Funtowicz, S. O. (1996) Risk Management, Post-Normal Science, and Extended Peer Communities. In: Hood, C. & Jones, D. K. C. (Eds.), *Accident and Design: Contemporary Debates in Risk Management*. University College London Press, London, pp. 172–81.

Rip, A., Misa, T. J., & Schot, J. W. (Eds.) (1995) *Managing Technology in Society: The Approach of Constructive Technology Assessment*. Pinter, London.

Schot, J. & Rip, A. (1997) The Past and Future of Constructive Technology Assessment. *Technological Forecasting and Social Change* 54: 251–68.

Smits, R. & Leijten, J. (1991) *Technology Assessment: Waakhond of Speurhond. Naar een integraal technologiebeleid (Technology Assessment: Watchdog or Bloodhound: Toward an Integrated Technology Policy)*. Kerkebosch, Zeist.

consumer culture, children's

Daniel Thomas Cook

Children's consumer culture refers to the institutional, material, and symbolic arrangements which organize a young person's involvement in, and movement through, the early life course in terms of commercial interests and values. Children are both subject to and arise as subjects in consumer contexts. The meanings which adhere to commercial goods are at once imposed upon children, childhood, and their social worlds and are taken up by children as resources with which they create selves, identities, and relationships.

Due to longstanding beliefs about childhood "innocence" (Higonnet 1998) and related concerns about children's susceptibility to influence, their involvement in the economic sphere has never been unfettered or come without adult reservations. Moral tensions and considerations comprise the environment of children's consumption because they revolve around determining the kind of social being or "person" a child is. Many observers question the timing of and extent to which children become knowing, reflective beings who have the wherewithal to make informed choices. The evident malleability of children's desires, interests, and pleasures only strengthens the case that a child does not conform to the economist's notion of a rational economic actor. The fear that children's apparent susceptibility to influence invites exploitation on the part of marketers and advertisers is reinforced by a deep-seated cultural uneasiness that arises whenever children and markets commingle (Zelizer 1985; Langer 2002).

Moral concerns undergird children's consumer consumption in another way: children are not involved directly in the material, symbolic, and ideological production of their culture to any great extent. In fact, they are born into it. Children's consumer culture is never merely confined to products made for children's use or to their own use of them, as the term "children's" might imply. It also invariably involves those who produce the goods and make them available – i.e., the manufacturers, designers, advertisers, retailers, and marketers – as well as the regulators of children's consumption – i.e., parents, public advocacy groups, and government – who often make determinations about appropriate or inappropriate goods and activities for children.

EARLY HISTORY

A commercial culture of childhood existed as a social form well before scholars recognized it as something noteworthy to study. Prior to the twentieth century in the US, there were markets for children's books (Kline 1993), toys (Cross 2000), clothing (Cook 2004), and nursery ware which were generally low in volume and sales, had few competitors, and were widely variable in terms of geographical location and concentration. There were, in other words, few goods designated specifically for children's use being manufactured by companies and sold to families. What was available was often sold in local dry goods stores and through mail order catalogues like those published by the Sears company of Chicago.

With the advent of the urban department store in the late 1800s and its rise to prominence in American cities during the first third of the twentieth century, children gained an increasingly visible presence in retail settings. Some stores offered the upper- and middle-class female clientele services in which they could "check" their children at supervised play areas where items available for purchase were also on display. In some cases, the stores offered child-oriented services like barbershops to make the store amenable to both mother and child. As early as 1902, the Marshall Field's store in Chicago sponsored a Children's Day, and by the 1920s the association between children,

Christmas, Santa Claus, and toys was firmly solidified in many people's minds. The now traditional Thanksgiving Day Parade, where the highlight is the appearance of Santa Claus at the end, was inaugurated by George H. Macy to draw shoppers to his New York City store during a normally slow buying season (Leach 1993).

The seasonal attention paid to children at Christmas did not and could not in itself sustain a culture of consumption. More substantively, children began to gain a literal and cultural "space" in retail settings like the department store largely because they began to be seen as having the social right and wherewithal to be desirous of goods and to have their desires attended to by parents and retailers. Sales clerks and store managers in the 1910s and 1920s began to note that mothers increasingly were deferring to young children's requests for toys and to their likes and dislikes regarding clothing.

The institutional response, which took several decades to become widespread, was to begin to create retail spaces specifically designed for children and to merchandise goods with their perspective, not the mother's, foremost in mind. Toys initially had their own shelf, then separate aisle, then entire department. Separate departments for infants' and children's clothing did not exist until the 1910s, but by the late 1930s multiple departments for variously aged children or entire floors for youth clothing from infants through the teen years came into existence. In these departments, age-appropriate iconography on the walls and carpets (such as ducks and bunnies for toddler-aged children), along with child-height mirrors and fixtures gave children the message that the space was theirs, oriented to their perspective. In the 1940s and 1950s, for instance, clothing stores for teen and preteen girls had Coca-Cola dispensing machines, piped-in popular music, and staged fashion shows often featuring the local schoolgirl clientele who served as models (Cook 2004).

Child orientation expanded beyond retail spaces into the realm of specifically child-directed entertainment and media. It made marketing to children and what now is called brand merchandising possible. In the 1920s,

radio shows or segments for children began to be aired which were sponsored by cereal companies. By the 1930s, radio shows and their underwriters had developed the concept of the sponsored children's club. As members, children would receive merchandise or would be cajoled into active participation in a radio program by being made privy to a secret code or inside information. Film stars such as Jackie Coogan and, most famously, Shirley Temple appealed to both adults and children alike. Temple had her own lines of clothing in her own name and image, a doll in her likeness, and gave her name to other merchandise. Mickey Mouse made his debut in the late 1920s and by the mid-1930s was adorning children's wristwatches, drinking cups, and more. These tactics involved children with the company or property by offering them a sense of cultural ownership, of being recognized as legitimate participants in their own world of celebrity and goods.

Until the 1960s, there was no direct marketing per se aimed at children. Much of the understanding of children's perspective, wants, and desires derived from retailers' and manufacturers' own observations and cultural understandings of the nature of children. In the 1930s, some psychological studies of children began to be discussed in advertising and retailing trade journals which addressed, for instance, how differently aged children responded to such things as colors, premiums, and packaging. In the 1950s, Eugene Gilbert became prominent for his approach to the "youth market," focusing mainly on teenage and young adults in their twenties. By the mid-1960s, research on grade school-aged children came into its own as market researchers and marketing professors began to design instruments to elicit consumer-related preferences directly from children (Cook 2000). The significance of this research is not so much in the findings as in the acknowledgment that children can and should be treated as knowing, able consumers.

From the 1960s to the 1970s, a number of noteworthy developments in children's culture made lasting marks. The rise and spread of television increasingly allowed broadcast networks to offer child-directed programs and hence provided advertisers with an increasingly age-circumscribed audience, i.e., target markets. By the early 1960s, the Saturday morning time slot was reserved mainly for children's programming and advertising. A group of concerned mothers formed the political action group Action for Children's Television (ACT) in the latter part of the decade. Spearheaded by Peggy Charren, ACT questioned the social benefits of exposing children to unregulated advertising which, they contended, promoted materialistic values. An early victory for the group was the pressure it brought to bear to eliminate so-called "30-minute commercials" – children's television shows the sole function of which was to spotlight and promote a particular product like Hot Wheels.

CHILDREN'S CONSUMPTION SINCE THE 1980s

Throughout the 1980s and beyond, children's consumer culture has proceeded apace, expanding in market size and in the depth and breadth of its reach. The changing political economy of the household and the increasing centrality of children's voices therein, together with marketers' intensifying efforts to appeal ever more directly to children, contributed to the increasing specificity of the children's market. In the process, childhood itself, in many ways, has become redefined by and equated with market categories and meanings.

Changes in household composition and dynamics helped to facilitate the entrenchment of the kids' market in the everyday lives of families. Mothers entered the paid workforce in greater numbers than in previous decades and, by the late 1990s, a second (i.e., women's) source of income was seen as a necessity by many (Schor 1998). A steady, high rate of divorce and remarriage made *blended families* a common experience for many children. In addition, two prolonged periods of general, relative economic prosperity in the 1980s and 1990s, which were punctuated by only a brief downturn, made conditions favorable for children to become recognized as an economic influence and force by marketers and economists.

Together, these sets of factors also helped chip away at the lingering moral hesitations about the extent to which children could be addressed and targeted as direct consumers aside from the traditional Christmas season and gift-giving occasions such as birthdays. Many observers point to women's absence from the home to work in the labor force as a source of guilt for mothers, who often "compensate" by acquiescing to children's requests for things more than they might have otherwise. Mothers' relative absence has also made for a market of convenience foods which can be easily prepared by the mother or by the children or father. Dining out or ordering food for takeout or delivery have increased dramatically for similar reasons. Marketers began to realize that children consequently were gaining a stronger voice in family purchasing decisions, not only in the area of their own food, toys, and clothes as might be expected, but also in having a say in the choice of such big ticket items as the family car, vacation destination, large appliances, and even the location of the new home (McNeal 1992, 1999; Guber & Berry 1993).

The landscape of children's media and its relation to consumer markets also changed dramatically during this time. Tom Englehardt (1986) coined the term "Shortcake Strategy" to describe the emerging cross-promotion of children's goods that interlaced a number of products with licensed characters and their "back-stories." The doll Strawberry Shortcake began as a greeting card and eventually became a cartoon character and image adorning many kinds of merchandise. Marketers and merchandisers have followed suit and many characters for children are now conceived and planned as the entry point into an entire array of merchandise, promotions, and co-branding efforts with other properties.

The rise and expansion of cable television has produced a number of networks, notably Nickelodeon, Disney, and the Cartoon Channel, that create their own characters and enter into cross-merchandising agreements with clothing manufacturers, makers of Halloween costumes and candies, foods, backpacks, and video games, to name a few. Each major children's product and/or media character undoubtedly has a website where children can "interact" with the characters, play branded games, or communicate with other children via the Internet through the medium of the specific commodity image and form (Kinder 1998).

An increasing ghettoization of children into their own specified worlds, goods, social relations, and media constitutes a strong trajectory of western childhood as it has been elaborated in and through commercial culture over the course of the twentieth and early twenty-first centuries. Media – from cellular communication technology, to web interfaces, to televisual modes of entertainment, to video and digital games – are the keys to children's consumer culture because they act as multinodal portals into a ready-made world of commercial meanings and relationships. This is a culture not initiated by children and not produced by them. It "empowers" them, as marketers like to believe and exhort, by giving children a voice and cultural ownership – a sense of propriety – over the goods and their meanings, but it is a voice articulated in the idiom and vocabulary of corporate-owned and produced branded and licensed characters and products.

Researchers are beginning to address the problems of social inequality that arise in children's lives, such as in school, when some – due to difficult financial circumstances and racial inequities and differences – do not have access to the goods and images which increasingly define a children's culture (Chin 2001; Pugh 2004). Emergent research also delves into how the dynamics of children's engagement with and in commercial, consumer realms becomes articulated through the local understandings of non-western, non-US cultures (Langer 2004; Tobin 2004; Huberman 2005; Peterson 2005). To what extent is the globalization of capitalism enhanced or restrained by the globalization of children's culture? How do family traditionalistic relationships react when confronted with technologies and meaning systems derived from notions of empowered, knowing, and desiring children? What images of childhood, of consumption, and of social life are encoded in the narratives of film, video games, and computer technology? In what way will children come to signify social order? These are some of the questions now being investigated

by researchers who realize that the hand of the market is visible in creating the means through which children come to know themselves as children and that market considerations cannot be separated from the experience of childhood.

SEE ALSO: Childhood; Consumption, Girls' Culture and; Consumption, Provisioning and; Consumption, Youth Culture and; Globalization, Consumption and; Media and Consumer Culture

REFERENCES AND SUGGESTED READINGS

Chin, E. (2001) *Purchasing Power*. University of Minnesota Press, Minneapolis.

Cook, D. T. (2000) The Other "Child Study": Figuring Children as Consumers in Market Research, 1910s–1990s. *Sociological Quarterly* 41, 3 (Summer): 487–507.

Cook, D. T. (2004) *The Commodification of Childhood*. Duke University Press, Durham, NC.

Cross, G. (2000) *An All-Consuming Century*. Columbia University Press, New York.

Englehardt, T. (1986) The Shortcake Strategy. In: Gitlin, T. (Ed.), *Watching Television*. Pantheon, New York, pp. 68–110.

Guber, S. S. & Berry, J. (1993) *Marketing To and Through Kids*. McGraw-Hill, New York.

Higonnet, A. (1998) *Pictures of Innocence*. Thames & Hudson, New York.

Huberman, J. (2005) "Consuming Children": Reading the Impacts of Tourism in the City of Banaras. *Childhood* 12(2): 161–76.

Kenway, J. & Bullen, E. (2001) *Consuming Children*. Open University Press, Buckingham.

Kinder, M. (Ed.) (1998) *Kids' Media Culture*. Duke University Press, Durham, NC.

Kline, S. (1993) *Out of the Garden*. Verso, London.

Langer, B. (2002) Commodified Enchantment: Children and Consumer Capitalism. *Thesis Eleven* 69: 67–81.

Langer, B. (2004) The Business of Branded Enchantment: Ambivalence and Disjuncture in the Global Children's Culture Industry. *Journal of Consumer Culture* 4(2): 251–76.

Leach, W. (1993) *Land of Desire*. Pantheon, New York.

Linn, S. (2004) *Consuming Kids*. New Press, New York.

McNeal, J. U. (1992) *Kids as Consumers*. Lexington Books, New York.

McNeal, J. U. (1999) *The Kids' Market: Myths and Realities*. Paramount Market, Ithaca, NY.

Milner, M., Jr. (2004) *Freaks, Geeks and Cool Kids: American Teenagers, Schools, and the Culture of Consumption*. Routledge, New York.

Peterson, M. (2005) The Jinn and the Computer: Consumption and Identity in Arabic Children's Magazines. *Childhood* 12(2): 177–200.

Pugh, A. (2004) Windfall Child Rearing: Low-Income Care and Consumption. *Journal of Consumer Culture* 4(2): 220–49.

Schor, J. B. (1998) *The Overspent American*. Harper, New York.

Schor, J. B. (2004) *Born to Buy: The Commercialized Child and the New Consumer Culture*. Scribner, New York.

Tobin, J., Jr. (Ed). (2004) *Pikachu's Global Adventure*. Duke University Press, Durham, NC.

Zelizer, V. (1985) *Pricing the Priceless Child*. Princeton University Press, Princeton.

consumer movements

Robert N. Mayer

Consumer movements are the organized actions of individuals in pursuit of greater equality in the relationship between buyers and sellers. While consumer movements rarely resort to revolutionary violence or even civil disobedience in pursuit of their goals, these movements are engaged in life and death issues, like the safety of food, drugs, and automobiles. Consumer movements, once confined to affluent countries like the US and Sweden, are now found in rapidly modernizing countries like China and India, formerly socialist nations like Poland and Russia, and less developed countries like Nigeria and Bangladesh.

The history of consumer movements extends back to the end of the nineteenth century, when middle-class and upper-class women in the US formed local "consumers leagues" to press for better working conditions and greater food safety. In 1899 these leagues coalesced into the National Consumers League, which exists today as the world's oldest consumer organization. After a lull associated with World War I, consumer activism

in the US grew more forceful in the 1920s and 1930s. This era of activism culminated in the creation of Consumers Union, the publisher of *Consumer Reports* magazine and arguably the world's most powerful consumer organization.

Despite more than a half-century of activity, consumer movements were largely unknown by members of the general public until the appearance of Ralph Nader in the mid-1960s. Nader became the first consumer celebrity, garnering ample media coverage for his crusading campaigns and quirky habits. When General Motors was caught illegally spying on Nader, he used the hefty proceeds from an out-of-court settlement to found a network of consumer organizations, most of which persist to this day. Consumer movements began to appear outside the US after World War II, notably in Western Europe; and in 1960, the International Organization of Consumers Unions (later renamed Consumers International) was established to assist consumer organizations around the world.

The earliest scholarship on consumer movements was produced by movement participants. Maud Nathan, the president of the National Consumers League, wrote *The History of an Epoch-Making Movement* in 1926, and Persia Campbell, an economist who later became the consumer counselor to New York Governor Averell Harriman, published *Consumer Representation in the New Deal* in 1940. Scholarship from outside the US consumer movement did not appear until about 1970 (Herrmann 1971; Nadel 1971). Beginning a pattern that has persisted to the present, academic scholarship on consumer movements has been dominated by historians and political scientists, not sociologists (with Robert Mayer (1989) being the main exception).

As research on consumer movements expanded during the later 1970s and 1980s, sociological theory, if not sociologists themselves, began to inform the analysis of consumer movements. The most influential sociological perspective was the resource mobilization approach to social movements. Most closely associated with John D. McCarthy and Mayer N. Zald, this approach is designed to be a counterpoint to more social psychological explanations of collective behavior, with their emphasis on deprivation and widely held beliefs about the need for social change. Resource mobilization theory draws heavily from political science and economics, emphasizing the role of "political entrepreneurs" in summoning the human and financial resources necessary to establish and sustain social movement organizations.

In the study of consumer movements, resource mobilization theory provides an answer to the challenge posed by Mancur Olson, Jr. in his 1965 book, *The Logic of Collective Action*: How can rational individuals be expected to voluntarily bear the costs of a social movement whose benefits go to all citizens? The core of the answer provided by resource mobilization theory is that modern-day social movement leaders benefit in the form of long-term careers as the heads of organizations staffed by additional full-time professionals. These leaders raise funds by selling publications, receiving foundation support and government grants, winning lawsuits, and exploiting other sources of support beyond soliciting dues from consumers.

A number of scholars outside of sociology have drawn on resource mobilization theory to illuminate the dynamics of consumer movements. Legal scholar Joel Handler, in *Social Movements and the Legal System* (1978), was the first to apply the resource mobilization framework to the US consumer movement, focusing on the role of litigation in prompting action from legislators and regulators. Business scholars Paul Bloom and Stephen Greyser were attracted to the obvious business allusions in resource mobilization theory: social movement leaders as *entrepreneurs*, organizations as *competitors* in a social movement *industry*, organizational goals as *products*, adherence to organizations as *demand*, and *advertising* and celebrity *endorsements* as means of appealing to potential constituents. In a 1981 *Harvard Business Review* article, Bloom and Greyser took these allusions literally and divided the US consumer movement into competing *brands*, including "nationals" (reformist organizations that engage in a variety of lobbying and education activities), "corporates" (politically cautious organizations that advise and work with corporations), and "anti-industrialists"

(radicals who are highly distrustful of businesses, government, and technology). Another business scholar, Hayagreeva Rao (1998), used resource mobilization to explain the early history of the product-testing, "consumer-watchdog" organization, Consumers Union. (Rao's article is the only piece on consumer movements to appear in a top-tier sociology journal, the *American Journal of Sociology*.)

The spread of consumer movements from the US and Western Europe to other nations demonstrates the diverse ways in which the social impulse to establish consumer rights is expressed. The Japanese consumer movement, for example, is far less professionalized than that of the US. It relies for its strength on local women's organizations and buying cooperatives (Maclachlan 2002). In contrast, the consumer movement in the People's Republic of China consists of a single, large, government-supported organization – the China Consumers' Association – that focuses primarily on processing hundreds of thousands of consumer complaints rather than on lobbying or litigation. India's consumer movement could not be more different than that of China. India's movement consists of dozens of privately funded regional organizations that reflect the country's tremendous ethnic, religious, and linguistic diversity. As a result, India has more members of Consumers International, the world's umbrella organization for consumer groups, than any other country, including the US.

Consumer movements have appeared in unlikely places. Even before the dissolution of the Soviet Union, Poland and, later, Russia had non-governmental consumer organizations. Today, virtually every country in Central and Eastern Europe has at least one self-sustaining consumer organization (Macgeorge 2000). Consumer movements are also well rooted in countries as diverse as Malaysia, Brazil, and Mali. Regardless of the initial level of economic development, consumer movements appear to flourish wherever economic growth and democratic institutions combine. The many commonalities and differences in the world's consumer movements provide an opportunity for sociologists to test and deepen theories of globalization and development (Buttel & Gould 2004).

Finally, the sociological study of consumer movements dovetails with two closely related areas of research. One of these areas is the study of other modern social movements, especially the environmental movement (Shaiko 1999). Comparsion of consumer movements with other social movements highlights the roles of movement structure, leadership, strategy, and ideology in the success of contemporary social movements. A second area of sociological study that relates to consumer movements is consumer culture. Consumer culture is a variegated field that examines both markets for culture products and the broader process by which the expansion of consumption is expressed in a society's beliefs and values (Cohen 2003). Sociological interest in consumer culture has resulted in the establishment of new journals (e.g., *Journal of Consumer Culture*) and a proposal for a formal section within the American Sociological Association.

SEE ALSO: Advertising; Consumption; Consumption, Green/Sustainable; Consumption, Mass Consumption, and Consumer Culture; Credit Cards; Culture, Social Movements and; Social Movements

REFERENCES AND SUGGESTED READINGS

Brobeck, S. (1997) *Encyclopedia of the Consumer Movement*. ABC-CLIO, Santa Barbara.
Buttel, F. H. & Gould, K. A. (2004) Global Social Movements at the Crossroads: Some Observations on the Trajectory of the Anti-Corporate Globalization Movement. *Journal of World-Systems Research* 10 (Winter): 37–66.
Cohen, L. (2003) *A Consumers' Republic: The Politics of Mass Consumption in Postwar America*. Alfred A. Knopf, New York.
Herrmann, R. O. (1971) The Consumer Movement in Historical Perspective. In: Aaker, D. A. & Day, G. S. (Eds.), *Consumerism: Search for the Consumer Interest*. Free Press, New York, pp. 23–32.
Macgeorge, A. (2000) *Consumer Policy and Consumer Organizations in Central and Eastern Europe*. Consumers International, London.
Maclachlan, P. L. (2002) *Consumer Politics in Postwar Japan: The Institutional Boundaries of Citizen Activism*. Columbia University Press, New York.
Mayer, R. N. (1989) *The Consumer Movement: Guardians of the Marketplace*. Twayne, Boston.
Nadel, M. V. (1971) *The Politics of Consumer Protection*. Bobbs-Merrill, Indianapolis.
Rao, H. (1998) Caveat Emptor: The Construction of Nonprofit Consumer Watchdog Organizations. *American Journal of Sociology* 103(4): 912–61.
Shaiko, R. G. (1999) *Voices and Echoes for the Environment: Public Interest Representation in the 1990s and Beyond*. Columbia University Press, New York.

consumers, flawed

Allison Pugh

Flawed consumers is a term coined by the theorist Zygmunt Bauman to signify prevailing social discourse about poor consumers, or those who, by virtue of their limited means, cannot participate fully in the consumer culture of the contemporary West. While not in extensive usage, the term captures what other scholars have also set out to do: portray and explain how low-income people are pathologized and marginalized as consumer society expands.

Bauman developed this concept in his monograph *Work, Consumerism, and the New Poor* (1998). In the production economies of yore, social acceptance and status rested upon participation and success in the labor force, and the poor were marginalized by claims that they lacked a work ethic. Under this rubric, however, the poor were still nominally useful as a reserve army of labor. But in the elaborated consumer economies of the late twentieth century, the level of production became less dependent on a large labor force in the developed world. Unable to participate fully in contests of consumption with standards set by others far away from poor communities, the poor were now castigated as flawed consumers, with neither social position nor, given the fixity of their predicament, even redeeming potential as some sort of reserve army of consumers-to-be. Bauman argued that social prestige came to be conferred upon the rich, not merely the industrious. The concept of "flawed consumer" depended on the definition of "consumer," emphasizing the relational quality of such notions as "poverty."

The implications of the concept extend to the arenas of family and politics. While the work of quantitative scholars suggests that low-income caregivers spend proportionately more on their children than do the more affluent, this is not necessarily evidence that the notion of "flawed consumers" does not hold sway, but rather implies that the concept influences the buying practices of low-income caregivers. Researchers have found that low-income consumers engage in a sort of "shielding consumption" to ensure their children can participate in peer culture, and to mute the effect of their own poverty on their children's experiences; through consumption, they seek to deflect characterizations of being "flawed consumers" (Pugh 2004a). Low-income caregivers have long been condemned for being unable to provide for their families appropriately. In a context in which consumption forms the bedrock of economic, social, and political activity, low-income people become not just flawed consumers but flawed mothers. Elaine Power's welfare-reliant informants asserted that one of their highest priorities was to ensure their children fit in with their peers, even if they had to sacrifice buying household items, food, or personal items for themselves in order to do so (Power 2003). The low-income women in Edin and Lein's landmark study *Making Ends Meet* also said they felt compelled to spend what it took to make their kids feel normal. At the same time, this priority conflicts with the reality of available resources in many low-income households in the West, not least in the United States, where, according to the US Census, more than 17 percent of children lived in "food insecure homes" in 2001.

In the political sphere, the flawed consumer concept also reverberates. Bauman explored the consequences of this new framing of the poor for social support for the welfare state. Formerly justified as a way to maintain this reserve army of laborers upon whom the economy sometimes depended, welfare benefits which provide (however nominally) for "flawed consumers" can no longer depend on economic

arguments for their rationale. In addition, other scholars have noted the contradictory implications of consumer culture for social patterning. In the American case, the paradox of the consumer culture's promise of a newly egalitarian American society is juxtaposed with its divisive practices of segregating consumers by purchasing power and accentuating what distinguishes them. Those who are economic outcasts by virtue of their inability to consume risk being "flawed citizens" as well, constraining their claim to social personhood (Cross 2000; Cohen 2003).

Aspects of the concept "flawed consumer" remain unsettled. Bauman's definition relied on a fairly narrow definition of consumption as strictly buying, or acquisition; indeed, he also referred to the poor as non-consumers who were unable to buy the goods and services the market offers. Yet as we have seen above, caregivers do stretch budgets to ensure their child has at least some of the commodities of childhood that peer culture deems worthy. In addition, participation in consumer society can also include such practices as fantasy, playing, shoplifting, talking about products, even scavenging dumpsters, as Chin put it in *Purchasing Power* (2001). This wider net catches the poorest members of society within its reach, suggesting that it is not that the poor do not consume that makes them subject to the discourse of "flawed consumers," it is that they cannot consume enough, or that they do not consume regularly (Pugh 2004b), or that they do not consume the right things (Nightingale 1993; Bourgois 1995; Schor 1998).

Bauman relies on broad-brush characterizations of the producer and consumer eras to make his point, but the discourse of "flawed consumers" taps into a scholarly project that transcends his work. Awaiting future research are issues such as the implications of pathologizing low-income consumers for other arenas of social life, such as work, education, and art; the disciplinary effect of this sort of discourse on consumers of greater means; and how such discourse is deployed and experienced in daily life.

SEE ALSO: Consumer Culture, Children's; Consumption, Mass Consumption, and Consumer

Culture; Consumption, Provisioning and; Hyper-consumption/Overconsumption; Poverty

REFERENCES AND SUGGESTED READINGS

Bettie, J. (2004) *Women Without Class*. University of California Press, Berkeley.

Bourgois, P. (1995) *In Search of Respect*. Cambridge University Press, New York.

Cohen, L. (2003) *A Consumer's Republic: The Politics of Mass Consumption in Postwar America*. Knopf, New York.

Cross, G. (2000) *An All-Consuming Century: Why Commercialism Won in Modern America*. Columbia University Press, New York.

Cross, G. (2004) *The Cute and the Cool: Wondrous Innocence and Modern American Children's Culture*. Oxford University Press, New York.

Nightingale, C. (1993) *On the Edge*. Basic Books, New York.

Power, E. (2003) Freedom and Belonging Through Consumption: The Disciplining of Desire in Single Mothers on Welfare. Paper presented to the British Sociological Association annual conference, University of York.

Pugh, A. J. (2004a) "I Want Your Tooth Fairy": Care, Consumption, and Inequality. Paper presented to the Institute for the Study of Social Change, University of California, Berkeley.

Pugh, A. J. (2004b) Windfall Child Rearing: Low-Income Care and Consumption. *Journal of Consumer Culture* 4(2): 229–49.

Schor, J. (1998) *The Overspent American: Upscaling, Downshifting, and the New Consumer*. Basic Books, New York.

consumption

Michael T. Ryan

Consumption has been defined by economists in utilitarian terms as individuals taking care of their needs and maximizing their utilities in market exchanges, with the act of consumption taking place for the most part in private life. Even Marx saw it this way when he conceptualized the production process in four moments: production, distribution, exchange, and consumption. He saw the first three moments as a socialized process determined by the social relations of property and production. While the shares of consumption for individuals were determined by property and production relations, the moment of consumption was a matter for individuals in their private lives. Veblen and Mauss were the first social theorists to detect and conceptualize a social logic of emulation and competition for prestige and power in consumer practices. Competition for prestige was not invented in market economies and societies; it could be found in the gift-giving rituals that Mauss analyzed in tribal cultures. It could also be found in the idle pursuits of nobles in agrarian societies when useful work was considered ignoble and when indolence, warfare, sports, sacred activities, governing, and academic pursuits or devotion to the beaux arts were deemed appropriate because they were thought to have no practical significance, even if they actually did have social significance. So while acts of consumption are the acts of individuals, they also are organized through a social logic of emulation and competition for prestige and power.

In the nineteenth century, capitalist development and the industrial revolution were primarily focused on the capital goods sector and industrial infrastructure (i.e., mining, steel, oil, transportation networks, communications networks, industrial cities, financial centers, etc.). Obviously, agricultural commodities, essential consumer goods, and commercial activities also developed, but not to the same extent as these other sectors. Members of the working class worked for low wages for long hours – as much as 16 hours per day 6 days per week. That did not leave much time or money for consumer activities. Further, capital goods and infrastructure were quite durable and took a long time to be used up. Henry Ford and other enlightened captains of industry understood that mass production presupposed mass consumption. After observing the assembly lines in the meat packing industry, Frederick Winslow Taylor brought his theory of scientific management to the organization of the assembly line in other industries; this unleashed incredible productivity and reduced the costs of all commodities produced on assembly lines. Workers needed higher pay and shorter hours at work to buy and consume the commodities that were produced, while scientific management allowed capitalists to pay higher wages and still raise their profit margins. Ford instituted the first 8-hour work day, 40-hour work week and paid a premium wage of $5 a day during World War I. Consumer goods had a shorter "life expectancy" than producer goods; further, planned obsolescence made for commodities that would disintegrate within a predictable span of time and/or use (e.g., so many miles for a car tire, so many washes for a shirt, so many years for a living room ensemble, etc.). The fashion cycle also accelerated the depreciation of commodities even before they were physically used up. Buying on installment plans or on store credit in the new department stores made it possible to stretch out payments for the more expensive items. Initially, the advertising form informed potential buyers of the qualities and availability of new commodities without manipulating their needs or desires. The consumer society was up and running by World War I, but collapsed after the stock market crash of 1929 and the Great Depression that followed. During the latter era the corporations that had adopted this Fordist strategy returned to lower wages and longer hours. Yet the American labor movement in collaboration with corporations in the core of the American economy reestablished the conditions for this Fordist strategy after 1938, and the consumer society emerged from the ashes of World War II in the US, although it would become a global phenomenon after the reconstruction of Western Europe and Japan.

As Ritzer (1998) pointed out, the profession of sociology in the US has been slow to recognize this social phenomenon as an important topic to which sessions of sociological meetings should be addressed. Lefebvre and his colleagues, Baudrillard and Debord, were the first social theorists in France to take up a critical analysis of these changes in industrial society. Although Weber was not interested in the social logic of consumption per se, he did see status groups as having distinctive styles of life and providing an alternative form of difference to class differences for analyzing power

struggles and social change. Sumptuary laws in medieval societies prescribed distinctive forms of dress for the members of different estates. Institutional economist John K. Galbraith (1969) provided his analysis of these changes in the US. Vance Packard gave the public a more popular account of this new situation in several books (*The Status Seekers*, *The Waste Maker*, *The Hidden Persuaders*). The topic has been addressed by diverse writers in the "cultural studies" areas; conferences bring together philosophers, linguists, historians, anthropologists, sociologists, economists, and English professors beyond their disciplinary boundaries – an amazing outcome given their traditional animosities and turf wars.

Consumption has two levels or forms: individual consumption with its logic of emulation and competition for prestige and power, and collective consumption that corresponds to social needs. The consumer society is a social system that "delivers the goods" according to Herbert Marcuse. This is especially evident in Japan and the nations of Northern and Western Europe, the social democracies, where absolute poverty has been all but eliminated. As Galbraith pointed out in the 1950s, we can still observe "pockets of poverty" in the US, although much of it is relative poverty. Lefebvre notes that modernity is efficient at taking care of individual needs for material products and goods. But there are social needs that are poorly recognized and met: health care, education, childcare, care for the elderly, public spaces for recreation and leisure, love, and community, with community an important foundation for self-actualization. Social goods are different from individual goods; they are not necessarily used up in the same way as a beer or a pair of slacks are used up in individual acts of consumption. Millions of citizens have made use of Central Park in New York City, but they have yet to use it up.

Baudrillard's analysis of consumption begins with a critical analysis of Marx's critique of political economy, especially his analysis of the commodity form as the cellular form of modern society. Marx distinguished the use-value of the commodity from its exchange-value. Commodity logic reduced everything and everyone to exchange-value with the assumption that the exchange-values of the commodites exchanged were always equivalent, but the ideology of fair exchange distorted and made opaque the unequal exchange actually taking place between the working class and the capitalist class when the working class sold its only commodity, its labor power, to the capitalist class. Labor power is a unique commodity because the use of labor power in the labor process produced more value than was returned to the worker in the form of the wage. The working class performed surplus labor for which it was not compensated, and the surplus values produced were appropriated by the capitalist class as profits and were the source of capital formation. Capital is neither a thing nor a person, but a social relation of production that *appears* as the social relation between things. Commodity exchange integrated the members of different classes of modern society, but in a process that produced and reproduced the domination of capital. On the other hand, Marx saw the use-value of commodities as corresponding to needs that were not equivalent and "natural" while recognizing how needs changed over time as well as the ways to satisfy them (e.g., horses, trains, cars, and planes are different modes of transportation corresponding to the human need for transportation). Baudrillard argues that needs are in no way natural and that in our consumer society needs are produced just like the commodities and are just as abstract and equivalent as exchange values. Over the course of the twentieth century we see the creation of a system of needs that completes the system of production. Marx's formula for communism "to each according to his needs" is a formula for the reproduction of the capitalist mode of production, not the way out. In the consumer society, the political economy of the sign has created a new dimension in the commodity form: sign exchange value. Political economy includes the sign form as well as the commodity form. The sign form has a triadic structure: the signified, or meaning; the signifier, or the visual or acoustic image; and the referent, the object. Signifiers tend to become detached from their meanings and referents and exchange or play with each other in similar fashion to the detachment of exchange-values from social labor and their use values. The code of consumption through the medium of the advertising form attaches sign exchange value to all of the commodities. Consumption in its deepest meaning involves the consumption of these differential values which reproduces the code and the mode of production. Consumers are not conscious of this deeper logic, in similar fashion to their lack of consciousness of being exploited in the labor process in the nineteenth century. While workers in modernity are often conscious of being exploited at work, Baudrillard sees this as a more profound form of alienation, since consumers take pleasure or at least satisfaction from their consumer activities.

Lefebvre's analysis of the bureaucratic society of controlled consumption is close to Baudrillard's analysis, but differs in some important respects. Along with Debord, Lefebvre sees class strategy shifting in neo-capitalism to the colonization, or commodification, of everyday life as well as the production, or commodification, of social space. Lefebvre conceptualizes consumption as a total social phenomenon, Mauss's concept, through the sequence: need, work, satisfaction. Everyday life is a residuum, a moment of history; what is left over after working activities are extracted; humble acts that are repeated daily and taken for granted; the positive moment and power of daily life. Everyday life is also the product of modernity, of bureaucratic organization and the programming of private life, "everydayness" as an alienated moment of daily life. Everyday life is a contradictory amalgam of these positive and negative moments. For Lefebvre, everyday life is *the* social structure of modernity, a mediator between particulars and the social totality, a level of the social totality. Further, everyday life is another instance of uneven development, an impoverished sector that had yet to be developed with the available wealth and technologies to the same extent as other sectors like capital goods and the military. As long as people can live their everyday lives, modern society will continue to be reproduced in its present forms and structure. When people can no longer live their everyday lives, the possibilities for change in the forms and social relations become open, concrete. In a more optimistic fashion than Baudrillard, he interrogates modernity to analyze the possible movements

of the concept and the totality, from the pro-
grammed everyday to lived experience, self-
production and generalized self-management
as the revolution in everyday life, self-develop-
ment as a work of art. But he does entertain
the possibility of Terricide, the destruction
of the Earth. The consumer society is to
some extent an American invention, but increasingly it has become a global dream. Will the
carrying capacity of the Earth support a global
consumer society? Both China and India are
rapidly industrializing. Malls are now appearing in China as well as the production of
cars; competition for a declining supply of oil
is heating up international relations as well as
the environment. While the mullahs in Iran
have attempted to protect their traditional Islamic culture, dissident youth have appropriated
hip hop music, drugs, and other western fash-
ions as signs of protest against the mullahs'
theocracy.

Both Lefebvre and Baudrillard go beyond
the mere description of consumer patterns of
different social strata which we can see in the
work of many American researchers. They connect the logic of consumption in everyday life
to the production and reproduction of modern
society as a totality.

Michel de Certeau under the influence of
Lefebvre and other researchers has looked at
how consumers use commodities and the meanings attached to them through the media and
the advertising form. Do consumers submit to
the "terrorism of the code" as Baudrillard
seems to assume? Certeau's research suggests
otherwise, and a good deal of research in the
cultural studies area has similar conclusions.
Gottdiener (2001) finds a struggle over meaning between producers and users of consumer goods. Youth in the 1960s appropriated
working-class clothing like blue jeans and modified them in various ways as a sign of protest
and a sign of proletarianization in the consumer
society. Producers responded and reestablished
the sign exchange value of their goods with
various modifications: stitching, rips, pre-faded
forms, etc. To use a more contemporary example, the hip-hop subculture appropriated the
business casual forms of attire of Tommy
Hilfiger as a sign of their innovative pursuit,
in Merton's terms, of the American dream.

Tommy Hilfiger responded with displeasure
to reestablish the prestige value of his line of
fashion. Gottdiener has also demonstrated how
consumer enterprises like fast food restaurants,
casinos, amusement parks, airports, and malls
compete on the basis of themed environments.
This is a response to the realization problem
which has displaced the valorization problem in
the accumulation of capital. Producers have
solved the problem of producing value through
scientific management and Fordist strategies,
but increasingly they now face the problem of
realizing the values produced through sale of
the commodities in extremely competitive and
saturated markets.

Ritzer (2004) in his research on McDonaldization has demonstrated how Taylor's principles of scientific management and Weber's
ideal type of bureaucracy have been extended
from the labor process to the process of consumption, spreading from McDonald's to the
newspaper *USA Today*, to stand-alone emergency rooms, etc. Like Baudrillard, Lefebvre,
and Gottdiener, he links this process to society
as a totality, although from a different conceptual basis.

Lefebvre has criticized his former colleague
Baudrillard for constructing a social system that
appears to be closed with no further developmental possibilities. Lefebvre sees it as a class
strategy, not an accomplished system. If it were
a system, how would anyone become conscious
of its problematic features? He concedes that
the consumer society takes care of individual
needs, but it does a poor job of recognizing and
taking care of social needs. This helps us
understand why the US, the wealthiest nation
within the bureaucratic society of controlled
consumption, has failed to produce universal
health care, day care for working families, public spaces for recreation and leisure, and a
public life. Lefebvre also argues that the consumer society delivers satisfaction, but what about
pleasure and joy? Consumers are attracted to
malls and festival market places for communion
as well as satisfactions, but these are highly commercialized social environments, pale simulations
of the festivals of agrarian societies or the potlatch
ritual celebrations of tribal cultures. Researchers
in the cultural studies area criticize Baudrillard
for failing to appreciate consumption from the

perspective of the users. His analysis is too aca-demic; he needs to get out of his ivory tower and talk to actual consumers. Ritzer finds too much "commotion" in Baudrillard's theory; he brings together too many different concepts from dia-metrically opposed schools of thought. But the dialectical method of analysis as practiced by Hegel, Marx, and Lefebvre does attempt to bring together what a lot of theorists sepa-rate in their analytical and disciplinary fash-ions. It is unlikely that anyone can theorize modernity, or postmodern society, from a single theoretical approach. Modernity is a complex totality that requires an equally com-plex analysis.

Baudrillard's work is also problematic in terms of his solutions for our modern predica-ment. He suggests that we return to symbolic exchange, but he has little to say about concrete agents of change. He recognizes resistance in the "silent majorities." In contrast, Lefebvre sees some possibilities in an urban revolution, in the struggles for urban rights by differential groups, groups marginalized in modernity: youth, immigrant groups, racial and ethnic minorities, women, intellectuals, and the elderly. He also sees a possibility for the resurgence of the working class in the right economic con-juncture. This class has been somewhat inte-grated in the consumer society, but they may become conscious of their structural power as the producers of wealth when they experience declining standards of living and when they understand how production and property rela-tions are barriers to the production of social goods and services. Lefebvre anticipates that this process could take hundreds of years, but so did the creation of industrial society.

Lefebvre's work is problematic where he remains attached to the revolutionary move-ments in Russia and China. He put far more credence in the Chinese cultural revolution than his colleagues in Debord's Situationist Interna-tional, and he argued that the only barrier to the commodification of space was the strategy of the Soviet bloc. Whatever possibilities that the Russian and Chinese revolutions held out in the past have vanished.

SEE ALSO: Conspicuous Consumption; Consu-mer Culture, Children's; Consumption and the Body; Consumption, Landscapes of; Consump-tion, Masculinities and; Consumption, Mass Consumption, and Consumer Culture; Culture; Economy, Culture and; Lefebvre, Henri; Mass Culture and Mass Society; Popular Culture; Veblen, Thorstein

REFERENCES AND SUGGESTED READINGS

Baudrillard, J. (1975) *The Mirror of Production*. Telos Press, St. Louis.

Baudrillard, J. (1976) *For a Critique of the Political Economy of the Sign*. Telos Press, St. Louis.

Baudrillard, J. (1988) Symbolic Exchange and Death. In: Kellner, D. (Ed.), *Jean Baudrillard*. Stanford University Press, Stanford.

Baudrillard, J. (1998) *The Consumer Society*. Sage, London.

Certeau, M. (1984) *The Practice of Everyday Life*. University of California Press, Berkeley.

Debord, G. (1970) *Society of the Spectacle*. Black & Red, Detroit.

Ewen, S. (1976) *The Captains of Consciousness*. McGraw-Hill, New York.

Fiske, J. (1987) *Television Culture*. Methuen, London.

Galbraith, J. K. (1969) *The Affluent Society*. Mentor, New York.

Gottdiener, M. (2001) *The Theming of America*. Westview Press, Boulder.

Kellner, D. (1988) *Jean Baudrillard*. Stanford University Press, Stanford.

Kellner, D. (1994) *Baudrillard*. Blackwell, Oxford.

Levin, C. (1989) Introduction. In: Jean Baudrillard, *For a Critique of the Political Economy of the Sign*. Telos Press, St. Louis.

Lefebvre, H. (1976) *The Survival of Capitalism*. Allison & Busby, London.

Lefebvre, H. (2002) *Critique of Everyday Life*, Vols. 2–3, 1st edn. Verso, London.

Lefebvre, H. (2003) *The Urban Revolution*. University of Minnesota Press, Minneapolis.

Mauss, M. (1967) *The Gift*. W. W. Norton, New York.

Poster, M. (1975) Introduction. In: *The Mirror of Production*. Telos Press, St. Louis.

Ritzer, G. (1998) Introduction. In: *The Consumer Society*. Sage, London.

Ritzer, G. (2004) *The McDonaldization of Society: Revised New Century Edition*. Pine Forge Press, Thousand Oaks, CA.

Veblen, T. (1953) *Theory of the Leisure Class*. Mentor, New York.

consumption, African Americans

Elizabeth Chin

The topic of African Americans and consumption is fundamentally engaged with slavery, US racial politics, social inequality, and Civil Rights activism. Central questions include the consumption *of* African Americans, and consumption *by* African Americans. Because much theory on consumption implicitly assumes a normative consumer who is white and middle class, consideration of African Americans and consumption has made important challenges to theories claiming to broadly account for all Americans or all consumers. Understood in the context of the structural inequalities of American society, African American consumption is not in and of itself different from normative (white, middle-class) consumption. Rather, it is enacted within constraints, pressures, limits, and opportunities that give that consumption particular form and content. Put another way, it is only partly true that, for instance, a Barbie is a Barbie is a Barbie. The Barbie consumed by the poor African American girl in urban Detroit must be understood differently from that same Barbie, consumed by a well-to-do middle-aged male Caucasian collector in Santa Barbara. The larger social and political context makes consumption and consumers intelligible and meaningful. This point is applicable to all consumption. However, the importance of social, political, and historical context in relation to consumption is powerfully evident in the case of African Americans and consumption.

Under slavery, African Americans were themselves commodities, a history making African American consumption uniquely complex. The material consumption of African American persons during slavery was buttressed by laws and traditions constraining the ability of bondsmen to freely consume time, labor, food, and clothing. Following emancipation, laws aimed at circumscribing African American civil freedoms often focused on restricting access to property – and consumption – of all types. The institutionalization of African Americans as unequal consumers long denied them open access to essential wealth-building commodities, most critically, homes and real estate. It has been argued that one element in the enduring poverty of African Americans can be traced to these policies. In particular the use of restrictive covenants – prohibitions on selling property to people of color – and redlining, the practice of steering African American home buyers to "appropriate" (non-white) neighborhoods, is understood to have shaped African American communities and consumption in enduring ways. The more openly public forms of restricted consumption whose images endure most powerfully – touchstone images such as "whites-only" drinking fountains – are reminders of the restrictions African Americans have faced in even the most mundane forms of consumption.

Consumption is a powerful arena through which the rights of African Americans have been abridged. But with key actions such as the Montgomery bus boycott of 1955–6, the Civil Rights Movement asserted that consumption was an arena through which basic civil rights must be granted. It is no accident that taking a seat at a lunch counter *as a paying customer* was one of the most powerful forms of political action taken by Civil Rights activists in the 1950s. African Americans continue to be especially active in mobilizing their buying power for political causes. A 1990s boycott of Texaco, sparked when executives referred to African Americans as "black jelly beans," resulted in massive corporate change in that company; similar boycotts against Denny's, Mitsubishi, and other corporations forced them to proactively pursue diversity within their ranks as well as their customer base.

The morality of the poor – and the moral implications of their consumption – is a strong theme in the case of African Americans. This topic gained prominence in the 1960s with Caplovitz's examination of the so-called "ghetto marketplace." This work underscored that the poor, and especially African Americans, are a captive market being exploited *because of* their poverty, not despite it. Embedded here was a larger critique of American society whose tolerance for continued inequality, particularly inequality of race coupled with class, belied dominant images of the American dream. Caplovitz also coined the influential term "compensatory consumption" to describe a dynamic through which disenfranchised people buy status items in order to make claims to social equality. He noted that the poor disproportionately consume alcohol, tobacco, or drugs in order to deaden their disappointment and disaffection, a situation exacerbated by aggressive advertising of these items in poverty-stricken neighborhoods. As the term passed into wider usage, it has been used not in the contextual way intended by Caplovitz but rather as a blunt moral criticism, portraying the poor as irrational and impulsive.

By 1990 African Americans had a buying power estimated at over 300 billion dollars. Thanks largely to a rapid expansion of the black middle class, in 2000 that buying power had increased an estimated 86 percent. African Americans were now viewed as an important market segment to be courted rather than problematic populations to be contained, gaining a new consumer legitimacy, but one hardly transcendent of the fundamental dilemmas of race and racism. The 1980s and 1990s also brought the drug wars, film depictions of African American drug lords, and the advent of the $100 sneaker. African American consumption and consumers were nearly always portrayed as both out of control and immoral, a theme with an enduring history rooted in Calvinist doctrine that views material wealth as evidence of God's grace and poverty as evidence of immorality. By this logic, the poor are to blame for their condition, needing discipline and rehabilitation in order to rise up. These notions were actively debated in the 1980s, but whether the intent was to expose the tribulations of poverty or to decry the depravity of the undisciplined poor, consumption gone amok often figured prominently.

Several key works emphasize that the exigencies of poverty are not anti-American but an inevitable outcome of our nation's history and policies. Carl Husemoller Nightingale's melding of history and ethnography in looking at poor African American children in Philadelphia and Kotlowitz's *There are No Children Here* provided influential depictions of the material deprivations of growing up poor while surrounded by images of wealth. Despite the rise of the African American middle class, the continuing dominant image of the African American consumer was as a poor slum dweller. Such images are politically charged. In an analysis of events surrounding the civil uprising in 1992 Los Angeles, John Fiske argued that looting was better understood as "radical shopping," which he interpreted as a form of "loud speech" resorted to in the wake of severe disenfranchisement and oppression. This point of view rejects dominant portrayals of the poor as irrational and insists on recognizing consumption itself as politically powerful.

Images of African Americans produced for mass consumption by dominant interests have illuminated the larger cultural politics of race, advertising, and consumption. Aunt Jemima's transformation from a jolly, round-faced mammy to a professional-looking woman with button earrings and processed hair traces social changes in the images acceptable for use in marketing. (One might wonder, however, why Rasmus, the happy cook on the Cream-of-Wheat box, or Uncle Ben, clearly a servant, have not undergone similar makeovers.) Manring points out in *Slave in a Box* (1988) that depictions of servile/servant African Americans appeal to those for whom the sight of menial African Americans holds a nostalgic warmth. Such images are unlikely to appeal to African American consumers whose nostalgia for doing the serving and the smiling is at best limited. In a testament to the complexity of consumer engagement, rather than seeking to suppress such images, many African Americans work actively to preserve them. Gaining force in the 1980s, collections of racist memorabilia were undertaken by numerous African American institutions and individuals, collections whose purposes are equally political and curatorial. Bringing together items ranging from lawn jockeys, Golliwog dolls, and mammy salt-and-pepper shakers, such collections explicitly challenge viewers, collectors, and sellers to confront the politics of race and racism, and the seemingly innocuous, everyday items that can be harnessed to its purposes.

The continuing use of such images in the consumer sphere has everything to do with African Americans' lack of power in the market, which translates into a lack of image control in that market. There is an old joke that, in the movies, the black guy always dies first. The critique embedded in this joke is that the black guy only dies first in movies made by and for dominant audiences. African American film-makers have directly addressed the linkages between consumption of material goods and consumption of images: US filmmaker Spike Lee's production company is named "40 Acres and a Mule," invoking the failed promise to ensure all African Americans property – and livelihood – after emancipation. Owning property has long ensured rights, including the right to vote, and with the growing power of media and fashion as property realms, African American participation has remained as political and problematic as ever. In the music and fashion industries, "urban" (read African American) style has come to be increasingly powerful as both market force and cultural image. Here, culture and its influence appear not to flow from the dominant to the subordinate but in reverse. While the normative image of the rapper and rap consumer is of the poor, urban black teenager, the largest group buying rap and hip hop music is middle-class whites. It's not only hip, but big business to be urban and cool (and black). Coolhunters stalk the streets of key urban communities, trying to catch the ever changing waves of fashion, manufacturing and selling them in malls throughout the country and the world.

To challenge and/or sidestep the dominant marketplace, African American businesses have long attempted to create an alternative consumer sphere where the needs and desires of African Americans are intimately understood, respected, and catered to; in return, a loyalty to companies by and for African Americans is encouraged. African American entrepreneurs use consumer venues for political and capital forays: the FUBU company, whose acronym stands for For Us By Us, or the toymaker Olmec, whose name refers to Afrocentric theories and worldview. This dynamic keeps money "in the community," and black businesses and black consumers often view their interrelationship in overtly social and political terms. Many of the early successful black-owned businesses sold products for skin and hair, and cosmetics that addressed the intimate needs of African Americans in ways most outsiders could hardly understand or anticipate. Madam C. J. Walker (1867–1919) is perhaps the most well-known entrepreneur in this

mold, becoming the country's first African American woman millionaire with her line of hair care and cosmetic products which were formulated and marketed specifically for African Americans. More recently, toymakers have made inroads by creating and marketing "ethnically correct" dolls for children of color. Much has long been assumed about the ways in which the African American market has historically been constructed by marketers. Recent works rigorously exploring the development of radio advertising to African Americans, for example, are beginning to add nuanced accounts of what for too long has only been a murkily understood aspect of consumer life in the US.

Much work on consumption fails to account for the consumption experiences of persons of color, assuming that because mall and store spaces are themselves increasingly homogeneous, consumption itself is likewise undifferentiated. In recent years, important works that meld personal experience and scholarship have challenged these assumptions, pointing out that African American consumers have long faced inferior service, barriers to shopping where they "don't belong," or outright refusal of entry into stores. These informally practiced slights differ from the formal segregation of Jim Crow, but it is worth noting that consumption remains the battlefield and the encounters remain as damaging and dehumanizing as ever. African American entry into the middle class has provided the foundation for accounts of these personal experiences to be disseminated in mainstream channels. Attainment of positions such as reporter for the *New York Times*, gist has allowed African Americans to describe the complexities of race, class, and consumption while examining the broader implications not only for themselves, but also for the nation.

Many aspects of African Americans and consumption remain poorly documented. Particularly needed is careful empirical work, since so much regarding African Americans and consumption has been based on speculation, conjecture, or opinion. Historical work, newly reinvigorated, promises much regarding African Americans and consumption, from considerations of property and possessions under slavery to the everyday consumer practices throughout the span of the African American past. The middle and upper classes have been especially neglected. The work of Mary Patillo and Monique Taylor breaks new ground by addressing these groups, pointing the way, perhaps, toward more nuanced and embedded understandings of problems which are, undeniably, profoundly – and at times uniquely – American.

SEE ALSO: Brand Culture; Consumption; Consumption, Religion and; Double Consciousness; Race; Taste, Sociology of

REFERENCES AND SUGGESTED READINGS

Austin, R. (1994) "A Nation of Thieves": Securing Black People's Right to Shop and Sell in White America. *Utah Law Review* 1: 147–77.
Cashmore, E. (1997) *The Black Culture Industry*. Routledge, London.
Chin, E. (2001) *Purchasing Power: Black Kids and American Consumer Culture*. University of Minnesota Press, Minneapolis.
Fiske, J. (1994) Radical Shopping in Los Angeles: Race, Media and the Sphere of Consumption. *Media, Culture, and Society* 16: 469–86.
Lipsitz, G. (1998) *The Possessive Investment in Whiteness: How White People Profit from Identity Politics*. Temple University Press, Philadelphia.
Patillo-McCoy, M. (1999) *Black Picket Fences*. University of Chicago Press, Chicago.
Staples, B. (1994) Into the Ivory Tower. *New York Times*, February 6.
Taylor, M. M. (2002) *Harlem [Between Heaven and Hell???]*. University of Minnesota Press, Minneapolis.
Turner, P. A. (1994) *Ceramic Uncles and Celluloid Mammies*. Anchor Books, New York.
Weems, R. E., Jr. (1998) *Desegregating the Dollar: African American Consumerism in the Twentieth Century*. New York University Press, New York.

consumption and the body

Faye Linda Wachs

The relationship between the body and material culture in the post-industrial world is defined through consumption. How one experiences the body, manages corporeal identity, participates in social rituals as an embodied subject is, to a great extent, commodified. Changes in perspectives on the body are intertwined with the advent of consumer culture and the concomitant development of mass media and advertising. The growth of production during the industrial era necessitated a corollary growth in consumption. Markets for the expanding array of goods and services being produced were constructed through the attachment of meaning to consumer goods. The growth of markets driven by advertising profits resulted. The appropriation of meanings for advertising promotes what is termed the "floating signifier" effect (Baudrillard 1975) or the shift in the use value attached to objects such that any meaning or quality can be associated with any object. The body acts as both a carrier of these multiple and shifting meanings and a means for expression as the body becomes what Featherstone (1991) refers to as the "visible carrier of the self."

No longer subject to the dangers of sin so prevalent in nineteenth-century Victorian imagery, the body in twentieth-century consumer culture becomes central to the project of the self as the main focus shifts from the soul to the surface of the body. Burgeoning consumer culture removed ideologies of self-abnegation and replaced them with display imperatives through which social power was demonstrated through consumption, and in particular consumption of recreation and leisure (Veblen 1899). In such forms of display, Victorian preoccupations with health and fitness were retained and commodified. The weight of moral injunction shifts from "health" to the appearance of a healthy body, though what constitutes this appearance reflects current fashion rather than objective standards (Hepworth & Featherstone 1982). While morality had previously been displayed through bodily adornment (appropriate clothing, etc.), the new morality of "body maintenance" demanded that one display an appropriate investment in one's body and, consequently, served to also fetishize the flesh itself. The proliferation of public, visual culture (movies, photographs, and so forth) increased individuals' awareness of and self-consciousness about external appearance and bodily presentation. For example, the burgeoning film industry legitimated and normalized public bodily display and leisure/bodywork activity participation (i.e., sunbathing, weightlifting).

As Featherstone (1982) notes, within consumer culture the "outer" (appearance, movement, and control) and "inner" (functioning, maintenance, and repair) of the body are conjoined. The goal of maintaining the inner body focuses on the improved appearance of the outer body. Hence, the vicissitudes of age came to symbolize moral laxity. The consumer is expected to assume responsibility for appearance, i.e., to engage in bodywork where failing to do so becomes a sign of a host of failures. The proliferation of idealized icons, such as movie stars, provided examples and instruction on how to engage in the "right" kind of (commodified) bodywork. Body maintenance rituals then come to take on the role of virtuous leisuretime activities. Engagement is not only a moral imperative, it also holds out the promise of the rewards that come with enhanced appearance. The appearance of bodily neglect, however, is viewed as an indication of internal failings.

ADVERTISING AND THE MASS MEDIA

Framed as being good to oneself, bodywork has become integral to self-identity and social status. The growth of the mass media provided a way to "educate" consumers about their needs and desires. Throughout the twentieth century advertising increasingly came to act as the guardian of the new consumptive morality, promoting both individualism and expression of the individual self through "conspicuous consumption" (Marchand 1985). Individuals have been taught to self-survey, to eternally turn a critical eye toward their body and bodily displays, rather than toward their soul or moral fiber. Hence, the image the body projects, rather than the body itself, emerges as central to identity (Baudrillard 1975). Moreover, consumption becomes a part of every aspect of social life. A buying imperative comes to dominate how one experiences body, self, and leisure. This imperative is undergirded by institutions such as medical science and discourses that play upon cultural symbols of success and potency.

THE BODY AND THE SOCIAL DISPLAY OF IDENTITY

Scholars like Pierre Bourdieu problematize the interplay between consumption, the body, and social displays of identity. Bourdieu (1984) notes that the body is not simply a surface to be read, but is a three-dimensional expression of social relations that take the form of corporeal or mental schema, referred to as habitus. Through the process of routine symbolic consumption, identity is constructed and embodied. Bourdieu notes through daily practice taste is inscribed upon the body, and therefore taste denotes class status. One's taste serves as a marker of social status and creates a shared experience of class identity. The literal embodiment of class manifests in size, shape, weight, posture, demeanor, tastes, preference, and movement through social space. Other authors have applied similar principles to studying other facets of identity such as gender and/or race. Building on the work of Bourdieu, these scholars note that the politics of cultural legitimation and the cultural capital conferred by one's taste reveal relations of power and privilege. How one's physical abilities, tastes, and proclivities are read and valued by the larger society structures opportunities. Those in dominant groups are much more effective at having their own bodies defined as "superior," "legitimate," "healthy," and/or "normal." Some theorists argue that as culture globalizes, however, global consumer culture and the circulation of "lifestyle" commodities undermine the stability of embodied signifiers. Consumers who occupy different social locations may appropriate the symbols of other groups and thereby use such signifiers as a route to mobility (Featherstone 1991). This debate highlights key trends in body and consumption scholarship.

TRENDS IN BODY AND CONSUMPTION SCHOLARSHIP

Scholarship on bodies and identity is diverse and varied. Two important trends appear as to how the body is viewed in consumer culture: (1) the dominated body and (2) the expressive body. In the first case, many theories have focused on the tyranny of the marketplace and its objectification and alienation of bodies. In the second case, opportunities for bodies to use consumer culture for expressive purposes provide a context for resistance and social change. Finally, many theorists blend approaches.

First, the body is viewed as subject to domination through commodification. Drawing on Marxist perspectives, the fetishization of bodies ultimately leads to the reproduction of socially unequal bodies. The bodies of the privileged are legitimated and idealized through participation in rituals of consumption. "Nondominant" or "othered bodies" are rendered invisible, undesirable, and affixed with markers of stigma. The underrepresentation of and limited roles given to people of color in the mass media demonstrate invisibility, while the common conflation of gay and AIDS provides an example of stigma (Dworkin & Wachs 1998). The individual is then subject to the tyranny of the market regardless of relative position. Through goods, services, and rituals of display, one's body is part of an endless tyranny of marketplace definition. The consumer begins to see his or her body as an alien object that must be constantly managed to preserve position and identity. He or she is not tyrannized by an outsider, but becomes engaged in endless rituals of self-surveillance guided by idealized marketplace images conveyed through the mass media (Bordo 1993). Media forces, in particular advertising, conspire to simultaneously create a culture of lack and an endless array of products to assuage the lack, or at least the stigma of it (Kilbourne 1999). Some theorists note, however, that how one mitigates lack provides an opportunity for expression (Featherstone 1991).

Critiques of the dominated body approach focus on the cultural manufacture of meanings and identities. Baudrillard (1975) notes that individual desires are disguised expressions of social differences in a system of cultural meanings that is produced through commodities. The codes produced by fashion systems are infinitely variable (historically produced) differences attained through consumption. For Baudrillard, the commodified body still acts as a marker of social distinction, but not a permanent one. Altering the physical body can operate to alter one's position in the social order. Of course, one must recognize the limits, and that

some bodies are better able to reposition themselves than others.

This leads to the second way in which bodies are understood as sites of contestable meaning. The expressive body has the ability to participate in what Giddens (1991) terms "reflexive self-fashioning." Through participation in consumer culture, awareness that identity can be self-consciously constructed is generated. Consumers can enact resistance to the tyranny of the marketplace, and market forces can be manipulated to facilitate progressive social change. In this view, the "floating signifier effect" enables consumers to reappropriate symbols to be used in unanticipated ways. The problem is, as gender scholars have pointed out, this reappropriation is not equally accessible to all, and some meanings are more likely to be appropriated for some people than others. In this view, though the signifier may float, it does not float as easily to some meanings as others depending on the visible body possessed.

THE EXAMPLE OF GENDER

Work on gender, consumption, and the body reveals these tendencies, and the ability to consider both positions simultaneously. Scholars such as Lury (1996) note that gender structures one's ability to negotiate embodied identity. Indeed, women often lack the resources necessary to claim ownership of identity, to even be part of an "identity project." Moreover, women's "reflexive project of the self" will reflect historic gendered power relations that impose a specific form of feminine expression that is subordinate. Within feminist studies on bodies and consumption, the aforementioned tendencies emerge in the understanding of women's relationship to consumption. First, women are viewed as essentially passive objects of consumption; and second, women are viewed as active subjects of consumption (Jagger 2002).

In the first case, how consumer culture sexualizes and commodifies women is problematized. Particularly troubling is the normalization of a limited idealized range of images unattainable to most. The few who approach the ideal are subject to a litany of practices designed to stave off inevitable failure (Bartky

1988). Recent research demonstrates that male consumers are also now subject to increasing objectification (Pope et al. 2000). Those who view women as active subjects of consumption argue that this process offers a variety of resources for the construction of the self. The process has both positive and negative implications. While the first group focuses on the tyranny of perfection engendered by idealized images, the second explores how women have become active agents in the construction of self, even if from a limited (but expanding) array of images. This self-construction is viewed as largely democratic and as creating a shared experience of gender in the culture, something that brings women together (Peiss 1999). Further, beauty industries have provided avenues to entrepreneurship for women, especially working-class women and women of color (Peiss 1999).

However, as Lury (1996) notes, the cultural resources available for the construction of the modern self are not equitably distributed. Women's experience of subjecthood through the construction of woman as object engenders a host of conundrums. This type of analysis is now being applied to other facets of identity. Finally, recent research examines the consuming body in the global context. While feminist scholars demonstrate the expansion of women's resources, rights, and opportunities in western culture as demonstrated in consumer imagery (Just Do It), it would be remiss to fail to point out that this expanded access to consumer goods rests on the backs of a global workforce that has little to no access to consumer goods.

SEE ALSO: Advertising; Body and Cultural Sociology; Conspicuous Consumption; Consumption Rituals; Gender, Consumption and; Globalization, Consumption and

REFERENCES AND SUGGESTED READINGS

Bartky, S. L. (1988) Foucault, Femininity, and the Modernization of Patriarchal Power. In: Diamond, I. & Quinby, L. (Eds.), *Feminism and Foucault: Reflections on Resistance*. Northeastern University Press, Boston.
Baudrillard, J. (1975) *The Mirror of Production*. Telos Press, St. Louis.
Baudrillard, J. (1983) *Simulations*. Semiotext(e), New York.
Bordo, S. (1993) *Unbearable Weight: Feminism, Western Culture, and the Body*. University of California Press, Berkeley, CA.
Bourdieu, P. (1984) *Distinction: A Social Critique of the Judgment of Taste*. Harvard University Press, Cambridge, MA.
Dworkin, S. & Wachs, F. L. (1998) "Disciplining the Body": HIV-Positive Male Athletes, Media Surveillance, and the Policing of Sexuality. *Sociology of Sport Journal* 15(1): 1–20.
Featherstone, M. (1982) The Body in Consumer Culture. *Theory, Culture, and Society* 1(2): 18–33.
Featherstone, M. (1991) The Body in Consumer Culture. In: Featherstone, M., Hepworth, M., & Turner, B. S. (Eds.), *The Body: Social Process and Cultural Theory*. Sage, London.
Giddens, A. (1991) *Modernity and Self-Identity: Self and Society in the Late Modern Age*. Polity Press, Cambridge.
Hepworth, M. & Featherstone, M. (1982) *Surviving Middle Age*. Blackwell, Oxford.
Jagger, E. (2002) Consumer Bodies. In: *The Body, Culture, and Society*. Open University Press, Buckingham.
Kilbourne, J. (1999) *How Advertising Changes the Way We Think and Feel*. Touchstone, New York.
Lury, C. (1996) *Consumer Culture*. Polity Press, Cambridge.
Marchand, R. (1985) *Advertising and the American Dream: Making Way for Modernity, 1920–1940*. University of California Press, Berkeley.
Peiss, K. L. (1999) *Hope in a Jar: The Making of America's Beauty Culture*. Metropolitan Books, New York.
Pope, H. G., Phillips, K. A., & Roberto, O. (2000) *The Adonis Complex*. Free Press, New York.
Shilling, C. (1993) *The Body and Social Theory*. Sage, London.
Veblen, T. (1899) *The Theory of the Leisure Class*. Penguin, New York.

consumption, cathedrals of

J. Michael Ryan

George Ritzer has critiqued and built upon Marx's definition of the means of consumption to develop his own definition as "the settings or structures that enable us to consume all sorts of things" (2005: 6). These "new means of consumption" (a term used interchangeably with "cathedrals of consumption" by Ritzer) are more generally related to a wider field of goods and services and tied to production, distribution, advertising, marketing, sales, individual taste, style, and fashion. They are concerned not just with shopping but also relate to the consumer's relationship with entertainment and consumption-oriented settings such as theme parks, casinos, and cruise lines, and other settings including athletic stadiums, universities, hospitals, and museums, the latter of which are surprisingly coming to resemble the more obvious new means of consumption. Examples include shopping centers such as West Edmonton Mall or the Mall of America, themed restaurants such as the Rainforest Café, and "brandscapes" such as Chicago's Nike Town. Such settings are considered important not just for their changing role as consumption settings, but also for the ways in which they are altering consumption more generally and the role many of them play as powerful American icons in the world (Ritzer & Ryan 2004).

Although Ritzer (2005) is the theorist most responsible for popularizing the phrase "cathedrals of consumption," it has been used at least since Kowinski, who stated that "malls are sometimes called cathedrals of consumption, meaning that they are the monuments of a new faith, the consumer religion, which has largely replaced the old" (1985: 218). These geographies are self-contained consumption settings that utilize postmodern techniques such as implosion, the compression of time and space, and simulation to create spectacular locales designed to attract consumers. They can be considered cathedrals because, much like their religious counterparts, they "are seen as fulfilling people's need to connect with each other and with nature, as well as their need to participate in festivals. [They] provide the kind of centeredness traditionally provided by religious temples, and they are constructed to have similar balance, symmetry, and order" (Ritzer 2005: 8). Thus, they are the empyrean form of a consumption setting. Kowinski (1985: 218) also favors this implication that consumption has

replaced religion as the dominant distraction of the masses.

In an ironic reversal, the idea of cathedrals of consumption is reflected in the growing number of religious cathedrals which are turning to consumption in order to maintain a congregation. While some of these churches are locating themselves directly inside consumption settings, others, such as one megachurch in Houston, are working in direct consultation with consumption experts like Disney, and still others are integrating shopping locales such as McDonald's, book stores, food courts, and religious kitsch shops directly into their churches. Many of these churches and megachurches are, according to Leong (2001), "realizing what other institutions – museums, hospitals, airports, schools – are also waking up to: simply, that shopping has penetrated our subconscious to the degree that our participation in it is as natural and effortless as breathing."

SEE ALSO: Consumption, Landscapes of; Consumption, Mass Consumption, and Consumer Culture; Consumption, Spectacles of; Shopping; Shopping Malls

REFERENCES AND SUGGESTED READINGS

Kowinski, W. S. (1985) *The Malling of America: An Inside Look at the Great Consumer Paradise.* William Morrow, New York.

Leong, S. T. (2001) Divine Economy. In: Chuihua, J., Inaba, J., Koolhaas, R., & Leong. S. T. (Eds.), *Harvard Design School Guide to Shopping.* Harvard University Press, Cambridge, MA, pp. 298–303.

Ritzer, G. (2005) *Enchanting a Disenchanted World: Revolutionizing the Means of Consumption,* 2nd edn. Pine Forge Press, Thousand Oaks, CA.

Ritzer, G. & Ryan, J. M. (2004) The Globalization of Nothing. In: Dasgupta, S. (Ed.), *The Changing Face of Globalization.* Sage, Thousand Oaks, CA, pp. 298–317.

Ritzer, G., Ryan, J. M., & Stepnisky, J. (2005) Innovation in Consumer Settings: Landscapes and Beyond. In: Ratneshwar, S. & Mick, C. (Eds.), *Inside Consumption: Frontiers of Research on Consumer Motives, Goals, and Desires.* Routledge, London, pp. 292–308.

consumption and the Chicago tradition

Marc M. Sanford

For the sociologists of the Chicago School, or those formed in that tradition, consumption of goods and services provides a degree of contextuality that locates actors in social and physical space and time. These places and spaces are contextualized through culture, consumption, land values, and myriad other social forces. Consumption adds character to the individual, but also creates external effects in the local neighborhood. For Chicago School sociologists, consumption essentially operates in two ways. First, the location of businesses drives land values that cause a shift in the local population composition. Second, consumption of goods, products, and services characterizes populations according to urban versus rural status, ethnicity, neighborhood, gender, and age. Later theorists in the Chicago mold duly noted the reflexive nature of social networks and local ecology on consumption patterns and identity construction.

CHICAGO SCHOOL OF SOCIOLOGY: A BRIEF VIEW OF A CONCEPTUAL FRAMEWORK

The Chicago School of sociology refers to authors at or affiliated with the University of Chicago sociology department from approximately post-World War I through perhaps the early 1940s. The research conducted at Chicago during this time was largely oriented toward several major themes: urban expansion, community and neighborhood studies, the science of sociology, and symbolic interactionism. The setting for much of the research that came out of Chicago was the city itself.

The major faculty members and PhD recipients at Chicago during this period were Robert Park, Ernest Burgess, W. I. Thomas, Louis Wirth, Morris Janowitz, Harvey Zorbaugh, Nels Anderson, George H. Mead, and others too numerous to list. Their ideas served to create an analytical framework for the study of life within the city. Consumption from

the Chicago perspective must be located within this analytical and research-oriented framework.

The core tenets of research from Chicago sociologists emerge from exploratory analysis, a feel for on-the-ground research, social process, and the unique construction of space, both symbolic and physical, in the growth of the city. The concern over space stems from a focus on neighborhoods, communities, and social actors. Community boundaries exist as situational barriers that affect the people, place, and culture therein. Social actors are often the central "unit of analysis" and situated in a unique physical and temporal setting. In this framework, actors become active participants in constructing both their physical and symbolic surroundings. In short, Chicago scholars argue that social actors and social facts have a degree of contextuality within time and space (both physical and symbolic space) (Abbott 1997).

This exploratory analysis of the city fed into the then-developing fields of urban, neighborhood, and community research, and nascent pursuits in criminology and social psychology. Although it was not the intent of the original Chicago School theorists to study consumption as a central factor of urban expansion, their detailed, one might say intimate, analysis of local neighborhoods in the city of Chicago led them to document a rich array of consumption behaviors as tied to issues of culture, class, race, and neighborhood and community concerns.

CONSUMPTION AND THE CHARACTER OF CITY LIFE

Park and Burgess recognize that the processes of consumption play a significant role in the distribution of populations and cultural groups across the city. Central to their theory of urban expansion, the competition for space by businesses helps to sort population groups into "natural areas." The concentration and location of businesses not only drive land values, but high business concentrations become community centers dominated by spaces of consumption. These spaces of consumption are occupied by various retail businesses including banks, restaurants, and "large and magnificent palaces of amusement." Even as these city centers become dominated by consumption, it is those same goods that allow one to escape local boundaries. Goods such as newspapers, motion pictures, automobiles, and radio "release" the resident from the confines of his or her neighborhood.

Despite this escapism, goods primarily characterize and add concreteness to local community, ethnicity, perceived class status, and other social and symbolic boundaries. Harvey Zorbaugh, Robert Park, and Ernest Burgess suggest that land values tied to retail and other businesses contribute to the solidification of community boundaries. For Gerald Suttles, writing about 1950s and 1960s Chicago, ethnic groups have distinct patterns of consumption of clothing, fashion, food, and entertainment that mark their membership to a particular group and lifestyle and to a particular neighborhood. For example, clothing styles vary according to ethnically derived appearance norms and ethnic identity. Suttles suggests that Italian women wear different styles on the weekdays versus the weekend and that their dress is delineated by age. Almost counter to current trends, Suttles claimed that the males tend to show more differentiation in dress and fashion. For example, the Italian boys occupy a more "avant-garde" fashion, the older African Americans wear more of the standard suits, and the younger African Americans stand out with tight pants, expensive hats, and unique blazers, shirts, and shoes. The Puerto Ricans and Mexicans occupy a more intermediary style position in comparison to other ethnic groups of the time and local area. These clothing styles and other personal belongings clearly mark the person's neighborhood of origin and whether or not he or she belongs in a particular neighborhood at a particular time.

Suttles also shows how the local social ecology impacts neighborhood and community businesses. Ethnically dependent patterns of consumption dominate and determine the makeup of local business and services. For example, Italian barbershops specialize in techniques and styles unique to the Italians and display media publications that contain news and information for people of Italian descent. Local stores carry goods that cater to the local, and often relatively ethnically homogeneous, populations.

Sites of consumption are often intimately tied to the private and networked lives of local residents. Residents of ethnic communities purchase goods in stores where they know the owner and where gossip is traded freely. In this sense, personal networks (often ethnocentric in nature) constrain consumption activities. A rare exception, the food and jukeboxes in the local Italian shops attracted not only Italians, but also younger members of other ethnic groups that bordered the neighborhood. "Ideal" commercial relations existed when ethnic groups conducted their business entirely within ethnocentric stores. Inasmuch as businesses were ethnocentric, they also became gendered consumption spaces. For example, local residents saw local taverns as unfit for a "respectable girl." Often, the success of a business depended on its physical location within the ethnic and symbolic landscape.

In addition to ethnic and geographical demarcation, what one consumes is often critical to forming a sense of identity, belonging, and separation between social and status groups. For example, Elijah Anderson's "Wineheads" consume cheap wine and occupy a lower social status because of what they consume (e.g., Boone's Farm Apple Wine) and where they consume it (on the street). The "Regulars" buy and drink "the expensive good stuff" such as Old Forester, Jim Beam, or Jack Daniels. They also consume "the good stuff" indoors and not in the public view. Park, Burgess, Anderson, and other Chicago theorists recognize the effect that lifestyle, as tied to social status, has in sorting population groups across the urban landscape.

Consumption of goods and services also differentiates the urban versus rural residents. Louis Wirth examines the rate of mass media consumption, the percent of income that goes toward consuming rent, and the amount of time and money the urban dweller spends consuming recreational services and food. According to Wirth, people in cities engage in a different consumptive mode of life. Urban dwellers consume culture, press, radio, theater, hospitals, transportation, and many other services and goods at rates different from their rural counterparts.

The Chicago School of sociology's stance on consumption is certainly not unified due to the fact that consumption was never studied as a phenomenon in and of itself. However, the authors of the Chicago School modality viewed consumption within the framework of urban expansion and embedded in local neighborhood and community contextual factors. Patterns of consumption were constrained by local networks, local culture, race and ethnicity, and urban expansion. At the same time, consumption patterns help to define ethnic and racial boundaries, symbolic boundaries, and neighborhood and community borders.

SEE ALSO: Chicago School; Consumption, Urban/City as Consumerspace; Mead, George Herbert; Park, Robert E. and Burgess, Ernest W.; Urban Ecology

REFERENCES AND SUGGESTED READINGS

Abbott, A. (1997) Of Time and Space: The Contemporary Relevance of the Chicago School. *Social Forces* 75: 1149–82.
Anderson, E. (1976) *A Place on the Corner*. University of Chicago Press, Chicago.
Burgess, E. W. (1925a) The Growth of the City: An Introduction to a Research Project. In: Park, R. E., Burgess, E. W., & McKenzie, R. D. (Eds.), *The City*. University of Chicago Press, Chicago, pp. 47–62.
Burgess, E. W. (1925b) *The Urban Community*. University of Chicago Press, Chicago.
Park, R. E. (1936) Human Ecology. *American Journal of Sociology* 42.
Park, R. E. & Burgess, E. W. (1967) *The City*. University of Chicago Press, Chicago.
Reiss, A. J. (Ed.) (1964) *Louis Wirth On Cities and Social Life*. University of Chicago Press, Chicago.
Suttles, G. (1968) *The Social Order of the Slum*. University of Chicago Press, Chicago.
Suttles, G. (1984) The Cumulative Texture of Local Urban Culture. *American Journal of Sociology* 90: 283–304.
Wirth, L. (1938) Urbanism as a Way of Life. In: Kasinitz, P. (Ed.), *Metropolis: Center and Symbol of Our Times*. New York University Press, New York, pp. 58–82.
Zorbaugh, H. W. (1929) *The Gold Coast and the Slum*. University of Chicago Press, Chicago.
Zorbaugh, H. W. (1961) The Natural Areas of the City. In: Theodorson, G. A. (Ed.), *Studies in Human Ecology*. Harper & Row, New York.

consumption, experiential

Pasi Falk

"Experiential consumption" refers to consumption patterns and practices in which the experiential aspect gains a central role, thus rendering the utilitarian and economic aspects a less significant status as the motivational factors of consumer behavior. The centralization of the experiential aspect implies an emergence of a consumer mentality which is oriented toward the realm of representations rather than mere need satisfaction. Consequently, the rise of experiential consumption is closely linked to the following three historical trends at work in the coming of the (western) consumer society, roughly from mid-nineteenth century onwards.

1　*The expansion of the realms of media publicity, mass culture, and entertainment.* This trend gains strength especially from the late nineteenth century onwards, creating markets for the mass production of (textual and audio-visual-tactile) representations which are consumed primarily in an experiential mode (newspapers, magazines, novels, music halls, spectator sports, cinema, radio, television, amusement parks, theme parks, tourism, and so on). These make up the category of actual experiential goods which are comparable to other "consumables" (versus "durables"; Hirschman 1982) like food where the item is "used up," usually in a single act of consumption. Then again, the actual experiential goods lack the oral materiality of food (which surely can have a high experiential value in addition to its nutritional function): these goods are "incorporated" rather through eyes and ears and "digested" as mental images, evoking a variety of feelings, affects, and emotions.

2　*The rise of modern advertising.* This dimension is entwined with the former and its main effect is the turning of goods into representations to be consumed, first in the mind, and then – as the marketing people expect – realized in the purchase and consumption of the represented (and branded) product, be it a material or immaterial, consumable or durable item. Modern advertising is born with one foot in the world of goods and the other in mass culture. Mass culture transformed experiences into marketable products and advertising turned marketable products into representations. Accordingly, the *consumption of experience* and the *experience of consumption* become more and more indistinguishable (Falk 1994).

3 *The transformation and growth of urban shopping sites.* The evolution of shopping sites proceeds from scattered shops and stores to shopping streets, arcades, and department stores from the late nineteenth century onwards, leading up to the contemporary supermarkets and shopping malls. Contemporary shopping sites – especially the shopping malls – turn the practice of shopping itself into a realm of experience which may or may not involve the actual purchasing of goods. This novel experiential characteristic of shopping is aptly expressed in the double sense of the term: as shopping *for* in distinction to shopping *around*. The former refers primarily to daily or weekly trips to local stores or supermarkets for food and other "necessities" (Bowlby 2000), while the latter has a flavor of entertainment and "spending time" downtown – or more precisely, in the department stores (Leach 1993) and shopping malls (Shields 1992) – without an obligation to spend money, at least in the sense of purchasing necessities.

The centralization of the experiential aspect in consumer behavior, and especially in the practices of shopping, should be recognized as an essential dimension which complements and corrects the one-sidedness of the presentation of self-construction as a process of identity adoption that is guided by the principle of free choice and the aim of social distinction (cf. Bourdieu 1984). The experiential aspect implies a dimension of self-relatedness which locates the experiential (bodily) self and the reflective (cognitive) self on one and the same continuum.

Such a perspective helps in the realization that, in shopping, the interaction with material goods ranges from a variety of sensory experiences to acts of imagination in which the self is mirrored in the potential object of acquisition, with questions that are rarely formulated and hardly ever articulated, such as, "Is that for me?"; "Am I like that?"; "Could that be (part of) me?"; "Could I be like that?"; "Would I like to be like that?" An endless series of questions that are acts of self-formation in themselves, regardless of whether they eventually lead to the realizing phase of purchase or not.

On the other hand, shopping malls bring all the dimensions of experiential consumption into a synthesis. In a larger scale, they are much more than shopping sites: they are, rather, multifunctional hybrids incorporating cinemas, restaurants, art galleries, and even chapels. Actually, they are slightly downscale city centers located downtown or transferred to the outskirts, as artificial copies of originals.

From the commercial point of view of the retailers, all the experiential freeware offered (including the advertisements) should promote the sale of both the experiential goods available to be consumed on the spot and all the goods people buy and carry away. However, another process parallels this promotional pursuit: these places also gain autonomy – in relation to their economic role – as experiential realms in themselves, as places for meeting friends, for walking around and just spending time rather than money. And this is a tendency which is not in any simple way subsumable under the promotional aims: the spatial practices or the "walking rhetorics" (Certeau 1984) of the urbanites – *qua flâneurs qua* shoppers – are largely self-determined, implying a variety of ways in which these places are made "one's own" which ignore, or even oppose, marketing interests (Falk & Campbell 1997).

SEE ALSO: Advertising; Consumption, Urban/City as Consumerspace; *Flânerie*; Lifestyle Consumption; Shopping Malls

REFERENCES AND SUGGESTED READINGS

Bourdieu, P. (1984) *Distinction: A Social Critique of the Judgment of Taste.* Harvard University Press, Cambridge, MA.

Bowlby, R. (2000) *Carried Away*. Faber & Faber, London.

Certeau, M. de (1984) *The Practice of Everyday Life*. University of California Press, Berkeley.

Falk, P. (1994) *The Consuming Body*. Sage/TCS, London.

Falk, P. & Campbell, C. (1997) Introduction. In: Falk, P. & Campbell, C. (Eds.), *The Shopping Experience*. Sage/TCS, London, pp. 1–14.

Goffman, E. (1966) *Behavior in Public Places*. Free Press, New York.

Hirschman, A. O. (1982) *Shifting Involvements*. Princeton University Press, Princeton.

Leach, W. (1993) *Land of Desire*. Pantheon, New York.

Shields, R. (Ed.) (1992) *Lifestyle Shopping*. Routledge, London.

consumption, fashion and

Susan B. Kaiser

Fashion can be understood sociologically as ongoing, processual changes in the "strong norms" (Crane 2000) associated with matters of taste, sensibility, and what it means to be "in the moment." Social institutions ranging from science, media, and cultural politics to products and practices – all of which tap shifts in cultural moods – are susceptible to fashion's processes. Among the most intimate of normative changes, however, are those in which consumers engage as they fashion their bodies in everyday life. One of the most compelling theoretical and empirical questions surrounding fashion is its relation to shifting cultural moods, as well as to just who shapes, and is affected by, these shifts and the strong norms that eventually accompany them in a deeply personal and embodied way. What propels the need for changes in personal appearance styles on an ongoing basis? And how is fashion negotiated socially? That is, how do new ideas about how to look become strong norms within or across social groups? From a sociological point of view, fashion is about more than the latest runway styles presented by celebrity designers; it has to do, instead, with collective ways of

making connections with others and, at the same time, marking differences. This nuanced blend of identification and differentiation is the hallmark of fashion. Fashion requires collective consumer acceptance and, simultaneously, marks differences among consumers.

EARLY SOCIOLOGICAL APPROACHES

Fashion historians point to status competition as an important element in fashion's identity–difference interplay, with some of the initial stirrings of such competition occurring in the proto-capitalist Italian city-states of the Renaissance. These stirrings contributed to a speeding up of style change. During the fifteenth century, the context of Burgundian court life further promoted intense status competition through clothes and accessories.

In general, the growth of fashion has been linked inextricably with western modernity and the associated exigencies of capitalism. Marx's critique of capitalism drew theoretical attention to industrial capitalism and the production of fashionable objects in terms of commodity fetishism. Given Marx's focus on social class as a function of control over the means of production, most sociological explanations of fashion in the late nineteenth and early twentieth centuries centered around class structure and production.

Veblen began to shift the focus toward consumption in *The Theory of the Leisure Class* (1899). He highlighted the interplay among conspicuous leisure, conspicuous consumption, and conspicuous waste in his critique of fashion's hypocrisy and artificiality. He described how fashion functioned to display bourgeois consumer status by revealing the lack of a need to engage in physical labor. He also noted that bourgeois men accomplished this display indirectly – vicariously – through their wives. Since the "masculine renunciation of fashion" associated with the rise of the bourgeois class, over the 100 years previous to Veblen's analysis, men's appearances had become increasingly staid or "unmarked." Gone were the flounces, the laces, the curls, the tights, and the high heels worn by aristocratic men in the seventeenth century. As the spirit of industrial capitalism played out in the restrictive masculine sartorial codes (e.g., the conservative black trouser suit) that represented the managerial class, the corresponding role of bourgeois women was to shop and to throw their energies into the worlds of fashion and beauty. Hence, the consuming fashion subject was gendered (feminized), as Veblen, Simmel, and other sociologists observed at the turn of the century.

Whereas Veblen focused specifically on the leisure (bourgeois) class, Simmel's analysis addressed the consumer motivation for social mobility across the classes. In what has been called the "trickle-down" theory, Simmel explained how the elite are the first to adopt new styles, only to be imitated by those at the next lower class level (in less expensive materials, etc.). Processes of industrialization tended to encourage a simplification (a modern "streamlining") of clothing styles, making such imitation more feasible. In order to maintain their fashion status, as the theory explains, the elite then distance themselves from the lower classes by adopting new styles. And hence, as Simmel (1904) put it, "the game goes merrily on" through a dialectical process of imitation (identification) and differentiation. Although best known for the trickle-down theory, Simmel's contributions to fashion theory are much deeper, broader, and richer, including important work on aesthetics, modern urban life, and the social fabric in general. Further, whereas he focused primarily on social class in his explanation of the dialectical interplay at work in fashion's processes, the fundamental nature of this interplay between imitation (identification) and differentiation has been found to be useful by subsequent fashion scholars in the study of gender and age identity expressions through style – i.e., other identity negotiations that are embedded in power relations (Cook & Kaiser 2004).

NEW CONTEXTS, NEW APPROACHES

Since the 1960s there has been increasing attention to fashion's role in identity politics. The commodification of youth culture and style, coupled with the large baby boom generation, highlighted the importance of age as an identity variable in fashion consumption in the 1960s. The idea of being or looking youthful seemed to be more important than looking rich. Blumer (1969) critiqued Simmel's analysis and argued that fashion should be understood as a process of "collective selection" rather than as a vehicle for class differentiation. Collective selection is the social, negotiated process of working through changing sensibilities and marking what it means to be contemporary, or "in the moment."

Analyses of working-class youth subcultures, especially in the United Kingdom, further fostered a new way of thinking about style innovation and diffusion (Hebdige 1979). Rather than styles "trickling down," it became evident that new looks could emerge from the streets (from youth, minorities, and various subcultural groups – e.g., punk, Rastafarian). Further, the modern western assumption that the consuming fashion subject was white, bourgeois, heterosexual, and female was called into question by the array of stylistic expressions that were in part political, emerging from social movements such as those in the United States: second-wave feminism (initially espousing a rejection of fashion to the extent that it reinforced traditional femininity) and civil rights (for example, the theme of "black is beautiful" and the popularity of Afro hair styles, dashikis, kente cloth). It became evident, however, that styles emerging from grassroots movements could be readily appropriated by the mainstream fashion and beauty industries. Hence, feminist style was appropriated and sold back to women as a "natural" look in makeup and designer jeans (which also alluded to working-class male culture as well as lesbian style). And African American style influenced mainstream fashion, as did gay male culture (e.g., long hair, disco style) and punk style. By the 1970s, interdisciplinary fashion and cultural studies scholars were theorizing style and fashion in ways that asserted the importance of consumer agency and innovation.

At the same time, feminist and poststructuralist theories led to a questioning of some of the major assumptions (e.g., linear progress) and ways of knowing (e.g., binary frameworks) underlying modern western thought. Wilson (1985) argued that ambivalence was a fundamental theme underlying fashion and its relation to capitalism. That is, consumers are likely to both love and hate fashion, just as they both love and hate capitalism. The feminist relationship with fashion could now be seen as one of ambivalence – a more productive (both/and) concept than one of disavowal, because the dichotomous (either/or) choice between being in the fashion system and rejecting it was a false one.

Davis (1992) and others have also used the theme of ambivalence in their fashion theories. Davis described how culturally coded "identity ambivalences" fuel fashion change. Especially prone to an ongoing, ambivalent interplay, he argued, are the "master statuses" of gender, status, and sexuality. Davis made an important distinction, although he noted the "useful confusion" between ambivalence (mixed emotions) and ambiguity (mixed messages).

To the extent that advanced (global) capitalism promotes the use of separates that consumers need to mix and match, identity experimentation through appearance style becomes a key theme in postmodernist explanations of fashion change (e.g., Kaiser et al. 1991). Such experimentation makes the daily connection between ambivalence and ambiguity real and embodied. It points to the fact that identities are not singular, or even binary; rather, they are multiple, partial, complex, and overlapping. In the context of fashion, there is no longer a single "fashionable" look each season; with an increased awareness of what it means to be a multicultural society and global economy, there are multiple looks that can represent "shifting strong norms" within specific groups simultaneously. With a more eclectic array of influences and an ever-increasing frenetic pace of change, coupled with a growing "disconnect" between the production and consumption of fashion (i.e., between the increasingly invisible global assembly line and the hyperbolic visibility of branded fashion in the context of media culture), Blumer's "collective selection" can be reinterpreted and revised in terms of the negotiation of group, rather than societal, norms.

Inevitably, the sociology of fashion (consumption) continues to tap into a range of larger debates that also engage fields ranging from textiles and clothing to cultural studies. Has the fashion system indeed changed from an elitist to a more populist paradigm? Are the days of "modern fashion" really over (i.e., what is new about "postmodern" fashion production and consumption)? Can fashion only be described as a modern western phenomenon, especially in the context of a global economy? How can the "disconnect" between production and consumption be bridged in the context of global capitalism?

The interplay between identification and differentiation continues to be a major theme in contemporary fashion and fashion theory, but there is a heightened emphasis on the intersectionalities among identity variables (i.e., social class, gender, age, sexuality). A reconstruction of masculinity in the last 20 years appears to be blurring, and perhaps broadening, perceptions of how men can look. The commodification of style and the mix-and-match paradigm have undoubtedly been major factors in this reconstruction, as evident in the early twenty-first-century television show, "Queer Eye for the Straight Guy."

Fashion seems to articulate visually that which cannot be readily put into verbal cultural discourse. Perhaps it anticipates shifts in cultural moods, but it does so in a way that inextricably links consumers' everyday looks with social processes of negotiation and change. The sociology of consumption ultimately needs to grapple with the role of visual as well as commodity culture if it is to understand collective selection. Inasmuch as visual culture is intersectional, it sheds light on complex intersections among consumer identities that move beyond binary constructions. Fashion's job is to mix visual metaphors, to tap cultural moods, and to produce and use materials enabling consumers to experiment with identities. In the context of global capitalism, fashion's norms may be a bit looser and more commodified, and it is consumers themselves who are left to their own, subjective and intersubjective, devices to "connect the dots" among goods in the marketplace, media (including celebrity) imagery, innovative and normative appearance styles in everyday life, and (most problematically) the conditions of workers who produce the goods they wear.

SEE ALSO: Blumer, Herbert George; Celebrity Culture; Commodities, Commodity Fetishism, and Commodification; Conspicuous Consumption; Consumption and the Body; Consumption,

Youth Culture and; Globalization, Consumption and; Postmodern Consumption; Simmel, Georg; Veblen, Thorstein

REFERENCES AND SUGGESTED READINGS

Blumer, H. (1969) Fashion: From Class Differentiation to Collective Selection. *Sociological Quarterly* 10: 275–92.
Breward, C. (2003) *Fashion*. Oxford University Press, Oxford.
Cook, D. T. & Kaiser, S. B. (2004) Betwixt and Between: Age Ambiguity and the Sexualization of the Female Consuming Subject. *Journal of Consumer Culture* 4(2): 203–28.
Crane, D. (2000) *Fashion and its Social Agendas: Class, Gender, and Identity in Clothing*. University of Chicago Press, Chicago.
Davis, F. (1992) *Fashion, Culture, and Identity*. University of Chicago Press, Chicago.
Hebdige, D. (1979) *Subculture: The Meaning of Style*. Methuen, London.
Kaiser, S. B. (1997) *The Social Psychology of Clothing: Symbolic Appearances in Context*, 2nd rev. edn. Fairchild, New York.
Kaiser, S. B., Nagasawa, R. H., & Hutton, S. S. (1991) Fashion, Postmodernity, and Personal Appearance: A Symbolic Interactionist Formulation. *Symbolic Interaction* 14: 165–85.
Simmel, G. (1904) Fashion. Reprinted in *American Journal of Sociology* 62 (May 1957): 541–58.
Veblen, T. (1899) *The Theory of the Leisure Class*. Macmillan, New York and London.
Wilson, E. (1985) *Adorned in Dreams: Fashion and Modernity*. Virago, London.

consumption, food and cultural

Grant Blank

Everybody eats to live, but food is more than nutrition. It is a basis for personal identity, a vehicle through which social structure influences individuals, an object that manifests long-term cultural and social trends, and a foundation for social theory. Food is a powerful carrier of cultural meaning.

Food was neglected among most sociological classics. Friedvich Engels describes the awful details of working-class diets in *The Condition of the Working Class in England*, but for his collaborator Karl Marx a "diet" is a German political convention. When Engels and other early sociologists mention food they use it as an illustration of an important social issue, like inequality or stratification, rather than as something to be explained in its own right. Émile Durkheim is the first to give food sustained theoretical attention in his *Elementary Forms of the Religious Life*, where he investigates the question of why in every society certain available and nutritious foods are declared taboo. Thorstein Veblen describes how copious eaters can flaunt high social status via conspicuous consumption.

During the heyday of structuralism in the 1960s and 1970s, food took center stage in the theories of Claude Lévi-Strauss and Mary Douglas. Inspired by structural theories of language, these theories attempted to uncover the underlying rules or "grammar" that governed how people use food. A sufficiently detailed set of rules would derive all the characteristics of a specific culinary system. Lévi-Strauss's famous culinary triangle comparing cooked, raw, and rotten food is the best-known structure. Unlike Lévi-Strauss, Mary Douglas did not seek a universal language encoded in food. Her influential 1972 essay "Deciphering a meal" uses her own experiences and her family's food preferences to describe the rules governing the meaning of meals ranging from Christmas dinner through Sunday dinner to everyday snacks. Structuralist theories declined as their weaknesses became apparent: their lack of historical perspective and their inability to handle change.

Recent theories draw inspiration from Norbert Elias's book *The Civilizing Process* (1994), which argues that there has been a centuries-long trend toward more civilized behavior (though not without reversals). "Civilized" means that a broad range of cultural, political, economic, and social changes have had the effect of reducing the importance of external controls on behavior and increasing reliance on self-control and self-restraint. These theories draw on two primary mechanisms to explain historical change: (1) status seeking, especially when lower-level groups emulate elites, and (2) social arenas where people are thrown into contests for social prestige. The most notable work is by Mennell (1996), who compares France and England to explain the relationship of food and culture since medieval times. Medieval food supplies were unpredictable and often scanty. Elites showed their power and status by feasting in gargantuan excess. Since only wealthy elites could eat enough to gain weight, plump was prestigious. The formation of nation-states, greater internal security, increased trade, and improved transportation all helped to make food supplies increasingly secure, reliable, regular, and varied. Large-scale famines ended by the early eighteenth century. The medieval pattern of elite feasts broke up first in Italian Renaissance city-courts and then in the French court in the seventeenth and eighteenth centuries. In court circles, status competition led to the rapid elaboration of manners and etiquette. By then, large quantities of food were available to most people, so court cuisine distinguished itself from ordinary food by emphasizing quality over quantity. As food became more plentiful and reliable, a hefty physique no longer signaled social prestige. Elites began to distinguish themselves by their slenderness linked to self-restraint in eating; obesity came to be associated with lower-class indulgence. The restraint required to remain slender fit well with the self-control essential for elaborate manners. The contemporary value placed on self-control over appetite, thinness, health, beauty, and related sex-appeal can be traced to these historical patterns of elites.

These theories explain the development of *haute cuisine* as an outgrowth of competitive processes. Within courts, elaboration of cuisine is one form of status competition. Goody (1982) documents virtually identical patterns cross-culturally in court societies in China, India, and the Middle East. Courts are not the only arena where competition leads to elaboration. In nineteenth-century Parisian restaurants competition for status and prestige drove the development of French cuisine. In India, as the ethnic identity of the urban middle class blurs, it is developing a trans-ethnic, pan-Indian national cuisine (Appadurai 1988). Although the Indian urban middle classes do not compete in a single arena, they are

connected via popular cookbooks. Written recipes and extensive commentary about cuisine are vital for the elaboration of high cuisine (Goody 1982). Gastronomic commentary codifies the etiquette of consumption and food service, clarifying and justifying rising standards. In addition, the discourse validates the rising status of cuisine by demonstrating its links to other high status fields.

The shift to a slim ideal body image has created special problems for women. This is signaled by the rise of eating disorders like anorexia nervosa and bulimia nervosa, which affect men too but have been particularly prevalent among women. Feminist research shows that women's deep involvement with food creates multiple cross-pressures (e.g., Charles & Kerr 1986; Bordo 1998). Women are generally responsible for providing healthy, nutritious meals for their partners and children. Women are the primary nurturers and food is an important component of nurturing. Food is a reward and a comfort in times of stress. Women who have been sexually or physically abused frequently turn to food for comfort. However, social competition stresses that women must remain slender in order to be beautiful and sexually attractive. This competitive pressure seems to be increasing. There is evidence that ideal body shapes have become thinner over the past generation. These contradictory demands create a complex relationship between women and food. For women, food is a symbol that is readily available and resonates with many other symbols, enhancing its power. Research shows that as many as 80–90 percent of women monitor their food intake. From this perspective anorexia and bulimia are only extreme manifestations of the tensions that almost all women feel.

In families, food preparation tends to reflect the gendered division of labor. Women usually do the routine day-to-day cooking. Men tend to cook on special occasions or with special tools. A frequent division of responsibilities leaves men cooking only outside on the barbecue, or cooking only special meals.

Food is everywhere much more than the ingestion of nutrients. The study of the cultural meaning of food is becoming more central to sociology. One sign is the fact that food is increasingly seen as a channel used to illustrate theoretical arguments. Bourdieu's (1984) *Distinction* is the preeminent example. His broad argument is that class reproduction is governed in part by the consumption signals that people send, including tastes in food as well as clothing, music, décor, theater, and a host of other areas. Food is linked to class, status, and institutions, and to social reproduction. Unfortunately, Bourdieu's emphasis on reproduction of existing classes gives his work many of the same weaknesses as the structuralist theories: there is little sense of history and mechanisms for change are weak.

The institutional settings where food is served include not only high and low cuisine, but all levels in between, including fast food. There is disagreement about what eating in restaurants means to diners. Finkelstein (1989) attempts to unpack the meanings of restaurant dining. She suggests that public dining is a social act that is strongly influenced by its setting. The ambience, décor, lighting, tableware, personnel, and service in a restaurant create different emotional responses. Pleasurable emotions include a sense of participating in a special occasion as well as a display of the diners' sophisticated taste and wealth. In a restaurant, diners buy entertainment in the form of emotional responses. Finkelstein argues that this indicates how far modern restaurants go to make emotions a commodity that can be bought in a market. Ritzer (2004) restricts his analysis to fast food, and mostly to the production side. Fast food is produced in an environment where service and production are very carefully controlled and rationalized. The goal of what he calls "McDonaldization" is to produce an absolutely uniform experience in every restaurant. Ritzer sees McDonaldization as an extreme form of rationality that controls the diner as well by offering few choices and supporting a narrow range of behaviors. Because of widespread efforts to lower costs and raise profits, Ritzer argues that McDonaldization is characteristic of many areas of modern life.

The ethnographic researchers in Watson's (1997) study argue that the meaning of McDonald's is very different in other cultures. For example, in East Asia, McDonald's has been an impetus for further elaboration of manners and commercial service. It introduced clean bathrooms and much higher standards of service, as well as clean, well-lit dining rooms. The alcohol-free, child-friendly environment is a setting where single, unaccompanied women can interact in public. Watson argues that Asians have localized the meaning of eating at McDonald's. Local owner-operators have introduced localized menu items like the mutton-based Maharaja Mac in India. Instead of being places where diners move in and out quickly, many McDonald's have become places where people linger, more like coffee houses in the US. Diners come to McDonald's for the experience not the product, and they have gradually shaped it so that it is their own experience.

Watson is part of a broader turn away from studies of production toward studies of consumption. One of the lessons of globalization is that producers have little control over the meanings that consumers assign to their products, especially as they are moved far from their origin. Here food is striking. As globalization moves around the world the food available to consumers has become much more diverse. Since many foodstuffs – particularly fruits and vegetables – can be bought year-round, they no longer have a season. Since food can be cheaply transported across the globe, formerly regional foods are available everywhere. As Laudan (2001) points out, this rich environment fosters new social constructions of food. Focusing research on local meanings of food as they are modified by institutional contexts and history is a promising approach for future work.

All people, not just women, have an ambivalent relationship to food. Food is a source of life but also a source of anxiety, whether the anxiety is about obesity, mad cow disease, pesticides, or red meat. Wuthnow points out that people most actively construct culture when they are unsettled. For many people, food is a source of permanent unrest. Their unease leads them energetically to look for and construct the meanings for their food. Food is a rich source of culture, and will richly repay further work.

SEE ALSO: Bourdieu, Pierre; Civilizing Process; Conspicuous Consumption; Consumption and the Body; Distinction; Elias, Norbert; Globalization, Consumption and; McDonaldization

REFERENCES AND SUGGESTED
READINGS

Appadurai, A. (1988) How to Make a National Cui-
sine: Cookbooks in Contemporary India. *Compara-
tive Studies in Society and History* 30 (1): 3–24.
Bordo, S. (1998) Hunger as Ideology. In: Scapp, R.
& Seitz, B. (Eds.), *Eating Culture*. State University
of New York Press, New York, pp. 11–35.
Brumberg, J. J. (1988) *Fasting Girls: The Emergence
of Anorexia Nervosa as a Modern Disease*. Harvard
University Press, Cambridge, MA.
Charles, N. & Kerr, M. (1986) Food for Feminist
Thought. *Sociological Review* 34 (3): 537–72.
Fine, G. A. (1996) *Kitchens: The Culture of Restau-
rant Work*. University of California Press, Berke-
ley.
Finkelstein, J. (1989) *Dining Out: A Sociology of
Modern Manners*. New York University Press,
New York.
Germov, J. & Williams, L. (Eds.) (2003) *A Sociology
of Food and Nutrition: The Social Appetite*, 2nd
edn. Oxford University Press, New York.
Goody, J. (1982) *Cooking, Cuisine, and Class: A Study
in Comparative Sociology*. Cambridge University
Press, New York.
Laudan, R. (2001) A Plea for Culinary Modernism:
Why We Should Love New, Fast, Processed
Food. *Gastronomica* 1: 36–44.
Mennell, S. (1996 [1985]) *All Manners of Food: Eat-
ing and Taste in England and France from the Mid-
dle Ages to the Present*, 2nd edn. University of
Illinois Press, Urbana.
Ritzer, G. (2004) *The McDonaldization of Society*, 4th
edn. Pine Forge Press, Thousand Oaks, CA.
Spang, R. L. (2000) *The Invention of the Restaurant:
Paris and Modern Gastronomic Culture*. Harvard
University Press, Cambridge, MA.
Watson, J. L. (Ed.) (1997) *Golden Arches East:
McDonald's in East Asia*. Stanford University
Press, Stanford.

consumption, girls' culture and

Amy L. Best

Modern girlhood can hardly be understood without attention to the influence of commodities and practices of consumption over modern constructions of self. For a large number of girls in modern America, participating in the consumer realm is a defining feature of life as a girl. Yet, the meaning of girls' consumption has changed considerably over time. The explosion of the Internet, the emergence of segmented marketing as an alternative to mass marketing, the arrival of an organized feminist movement, and demands for external regulation by consumer advocacy groups all come to bear upon the distinct historical relationship between girls and consumption.

The role of the consumer market in girls' lives has sparked much popular debate, often reflecting anxieties about the changing roles of girls in American society. Debates over the perils of excess consumption by girls are hardly new. Girls' participation in the realm of consumption in the last century has generated concern about their appropriate place in society, their sexuality, their self-esteem, and even their likelihood toward delinquency, though rarely calling into question their roles in supporting consumer capitalism itself.

Early studies of youth culture and consumption among sociologists and others failed to examine the distinct relationship between girls and consumption, reflecting an unwillingness to recognize the social significance of girls as cultural consumers and cultural producers. This is hardly the case today. A rich body of scholarship has emerged demonstrating the complex and contradictory connections between girls and consumption. While little mention was made of the ways girls participated in consumer culture or fashioned identities as consumers, feminist cultural scholars, writing since the mid-1980s, have made girls' practices of consumption a primary focus of inquiry, not only investigating the market's bewildering hold over them but also making visible the varied ways girls themselves have engaged in and challenged a consumer culture. Largely interdisciplinary in focus, feminist scholarship has argued that to understand the formation of modern girlhood is to also investigate the emergence and expansion of a commodity culture. Scholars have traced the historical emergence of a consumer culture and girls' relationship to it. Shedding light on the interstices of race, class, and age, cultural scholars have shown how commodity culture operates as a site wherein social inequalities meaningful to girls' lives are both reproduced and confronted.

Marketers have aggressively pursued girls for more than a century, transforming their activities, identities, and social relations. Though a burgeoning market awareness of girls (and boys) as consumers can be traced to the early 1870s, as the popularity of trading cards spread among an emerging middle class, most scholars agree that juvenile markets exploded within the context of post-World War II America, a period of increasing economic prosperity and a dramatic expansion of the middle classes. The growing affluence of families in post-World War II America, combined with a shift in parenting styles toward a more permissive set of practices, handed girls (and boys) of all ages greater economic power than experienced in decades before (Palladino 1996). Increasingly, girls had money of their own to spend and marketers were quick to capitalize on the changing economic and social reality of childhood and adolescence. The market swiftly transformed the leisure activities of girls, the spaces they occupied, and the activities in which they engaged. Advertisers actively courted girls, utilizing a breadth of strategies intended to establish brand loyalty. The now ubiquitous training bra, first marketed by Maidenform in the 1950s, is an exemplary case of marketers' rueful attempts to gain lifelong allegiance among these fledgling consumers (Brumberg 1997). Advertisers actively tapped into and exploited girls' concerns about popularity and appearance, drawing them into a world celebrating a conventional femininity centered on heterosexual romance, beauty, and the body. Entire markets developed around the idea of distinct commodities for the teenage girl; makeup, clothes, music were promised to ensure a particular kind of teen experience for girls, one marked by success in school, in love, and in life. By the late 1940s, girls' lives were largely experienced within the trenches of a commodity culture.

A confluence of forces conspired to cement girls' ties to a consumer market. Girls have long played important consumer roles in families. A century ago as the consumer market was gaining momentum, girls were already tied to work. While many adolescent girls were expected to work with most of their earnings going to household needs, girls also exercised influence over family spending patterns and in this way

first gained the attention of a new suitor – the market (Mitchell 1995).

The growing freedom and independence of girls from family life that followed urban and industrial expansion, increasing school attendance, and entrance into the labor force among youth together played a role in shaping a band of consumer girls. Babysitting, increasingly common in the 1940s, provided older girls with greater disposable income (Innes 1998). Child allowances, a practice that gained in popularity among middle-class parents in the 1920s, provided young girls, not yet eligible for work, the means to consume. Today, the average 16-year-old girl in the US earns $103 weekly from allowance and part-time work according to a Youth Rand Poll.

Youth markets have grown considerably over the last century. Few spaces occupied by girls today have escaped the sway of a consumer market. Even schools have failed to avoid the influence of a commodity culture as public resources for education recede and multinational corporations like Burger King, Coca Cola, and Nike provide funding to schools at an accelerating rate. Drawn into the folds of an ever-expanding culture of consumption shaped by the unassailable pursuit of profit by consumer corporations, girls today are immersed in a dizzying world of beepers and cellular phones, cars and clothes, lip gloss, CDs, DVDs, and more at every turn.

Under consumer capitalism, girls' bodies have become significant commodities of visual display. Today's girls spend upwards of $45 a month on makeup and other beauty aids alone, representing an estimated $9 billion of the cosmetic market. They spend $21.8 billion in clothing and accessories also according to the Youth Rand Poll. One consumer event for teen girls of particular importance is the high school prom (Best 2000). While proms epitomize the expansion of a distinct youth consumer culture and the spending power of youth, much of this market focus on proms is geared toward girls. Popular girls' beauty magazines like *Seventeen* and *Young and Modern* exploit the promise of self-transformation at the prom, securing girls' consent to prevailing feminine forms that concentrate their energies on appearance work, all the while gaining sizable profits. The achievement of femininity for the prom depends on an endless consumption of products: makeup, clothing, hair accessories, shoes, lingerie, handbags, and jewelry, all products readily available in a commodity market and heavily marketed as tools for feminine display and self-reinvention at the prom.

But the teen girl is not alone in this consumer world. As childhood scholars have demonstrated, the pre-adolescent girl is also assailed by a veritable windfall of messages intended to promote consumption of an endless array of consumer goods from bubble gum to Beanie Babies, McDonald's Happy Meals to Groovy Girls (Steinberg & Kincheloe 1997). Barbie, primarily marketed to younger girls and reigning as one of the most popular toys worldwide, has been the subject of much scholarly investigation. Tracing Barbie's cultural importance, feminist scholars have shown how Barbie operates under a veil of whiteness, promotes a narrow construction of the feminine body, and actively normalizes hyperconsumption.

The success of advertising to girls stems from its ability to align consumption with particular social meanings that resonate with girls. Many scholars have demonstrated how marketers have linked consumption with personal empowerment and liberation, even as they promote and uphold rigid and narrow gender prescriptions. This is best illustrated in the much touted though nebulous turn of phrase "girl power," which originated with the London-based pop music group the Spice Girls, intended to inspire groups of girls to exercise their right to consume. Hardly a call to action, "girl power" celebrates a tenuous feminist individualism entirely compatible with consumption. Yet paradoxically, girls have gained power through their participation in the commercial world. The arrival of mass-produced clothing in the 1920s enabled girls to move out from under the yolk of maternal control since mothers no longer made their dresses (Brumberg 1997).

Early scholarship on girls and consumption, emphasizing the pleasures of mass consumption, often overlooked girls' agentic possibilities in the consumer realm. Fueled by a moral protectionism that rested on the enduring notion that girls were especially vulnerable to outside influence, early scholarship cast girls as passive consumers. However, girls' struggles for freedom and independence often take shape within

a consumer realm. Recognizing this, scholarship over the last decade has made visible the new areas of expertise and cultural authority girls have gained as consumers (McRobbie 1991).

Recent scholarship also has highlighted the importance of understanding the material contexts of consumption, arguing that girls' investment in cultural forms is profoundly situational (Roman & Christian-Smith 1988; Harris 2004). Tweens worship hypersexualized pop icon Britney Spears not simply because she embodies an idealized feminine construct but instead because she represents a type of power and autonomy few girls between 8 and 12 experience in their everyday lives. Thus, while girls are consummate consumers of various media, spending countless hours watching television on the WB and UPN and music videos on MTV, listening to CDs of rappers Missy "Misdemeanor" Elliot and Lil' Kim, reading magazines like *Cosmo Girl*, *Seventeen*, and *Sassy* and the popular adolescent book series *Sweet Valley High*, it is the social meanings they generate as they consume that are important to understand. Girls use the objects offered by a consumer market toward their own ends: to construct identities, to express in-group solidarity, to define themselves apart from parents and others. Girls' use of resources provided by a consumer market as they struggle to find their place in a culture that denigrates and dismisses, objectifies and sexualizes girls, sometimes has radical outcomes. Musical and (maga)zine-based movements, most notably Riot Grrrls, have served as important conduits for girls to resist commodification, forge an alternative gender and sexual order, and to articulate a feminist political agenda.

More recently, the attention of scholars has turned to the globalizing forces shaping girls' increasingly complex relationships to consumption in a transnational context, revealing the vast gulf between girls whose sweatshop labor produces these products and those girls, often worlds away, who consume them. A broad range of possible research directions remains open as scholars trace these changes in global and consumer capitalism and the corresponding changes in girlhood.

With this in mind, future research directions are likely to be informed by extended definitions of consumption, greater attention to girls' changing relationship to public life in an ever-changing world economy, and girls' complex and paradoxical engagements with feminism in the consumer realm.

SEE ALSO: Childhood; Consumer Culture, Children's; Consumption and the Body; Consumption, Globalization and; Consumption, Youth Culture and; Culture, Gender and; Gender, Consumption and; Media and Consumer Culture; Riot Grrrls; Socialization, Gender; Youth/Adolescence

REFERENCES AND SUGGESTED READINGS

Best, A. L. (2000) *Prom Night: Youth, Schools, and Popular Culture.* Routledge, New York.

Brumberg, J. J. (1997) *The Body Project: An Intimate History of American Girls.* Random House, New York.

Cook, D. (2004) *The Commodification of Childhood: The Children's Clothing Industry and the Rise of the Child Consumer.* Duke University Press, Durham, NC.

Harris, A. (Ed.) (2004) *All About the Girl: Culture, Power, and Identity.* Routledge, New York.

Innes, S. A. (Ed.) (1998) *Delinquents and Debutantes: Twentieth-Century American Girls' Cultures.* New York University Press, New York.

McRobbie, A. (1991) *Feminism and Youth Culture: From Jackie to Just Seventeen.* Unwin Hyman, Boston.

Mitchell, S. (1995) *The New Girl: Girl's Culture in England, 1880–1915.* Columbia University Press, New York.

Palladino, G. (1996) *Teenagers: An American History.* Basic Books, New York.

Roman, L. G. & Christian-Smith, L. (Eds.) (1988) *Becoming Feminine: The Politics of Popular Culture.* Falmer Press, London.

Steinberg, S. & Kincheloe, J. L. (Eds.) (1997) *Kinder-Culture: The Corporate Construction of Childhood.* Westview Press, Boulder, CO.

consumption, green/sustainable

Joseph D. Rumbo

Green/sustainable consumption refers to various disciplines, discourses, policy initiatives, and practices concerning the design, implementation, and popularization of consumption practices and production innovations that seek to curtail any of the negative environmental and social effects of human economic activity. Moreover, whereas some have linked it to better physical and mental health and an enhanced quality of life, green/sustainable consumption also involves distinctively social psychological aspects (Myers 2003).

Proponents of green/sustainable consumption attempt to raise consumer awareness of oft-latent connections between consumption and production as well as the obscured costs of pursuing a consumer lifestyle. For the former, green/sustainable consumption proponents seek to demystify those upstream and downstream consequences of consumption that have become "distanced" (Princen 2002) for people immersed in consumer society ("upstream" consequences refer to pre-consumption factors involving resource extraction, production, and distribution, while "downstream" consequences involve post-consumption waste and pollution issues). Following the prevailing wisdom of the larger scientific community, the concept of green/sustainable consumption implies that current patterns of resource extraction and usage are unsustainable and, according to more alarmist accounts, will lead to a host of environmental and social crises (Merchant 1989; McKibben 1999). Green/sustainable consumption's guiding global rationale holds that each individual consumer can act to reduce the adverse effects of population pressures and overconsumption on the environment. This may be achieved by consuming goods made using more sustainable production methods, by consuming less, or by engaging in practices such as recycling, conservation, and participation in locally based consumption cooperatives.

ECONOMY AND ECOLOGY

There is considerably less agreement as to what the goals of green/sustainable consumption should be and how public policy should be used to achieve them (Robins & Roberts 1998). Among more hardline "green" advocates, the objective is to identify and promote those consumption practices that can best sustain existing ecosystems while curtailing those practices that are potentially most harmful. Others have oriented themselves toward the more modest goal of maintaining existing systems of consumption and production. Still others wish to implement consumption practices and develop productive technologies that serve the more radical goal of restoring the earth's ecosystems (e.g., Hawken 1993), thereby providing redress to longstanding patterns of environmental degradation.

For ecological economists and environmental scientists operating in the arena of public policy, green/sustainable consumption has become the purview of those concerned with "sustainable development" (World Commission on Environment and Development 1987). These analysts seek to identify ways in which quests for modernization and improved economic standing by developing nations can be achieved in ways that minimize harm to the environment while enhancing life quality. For developed nations, the policy-driven approach of sustainable development aims to (1) provide tax incentives for the development of more efficient and environmentally sound technologies for the production and distribution of consumer goods; - and (2) encourage more environmentally friendly consumption practices through a combination of regulatory incentives and "social marketing" campaigns to stimulate consumer awareness of the negative environmental and social consequences of global consumption and production systems (e.g., global warming/greenhouse effect, deforestation, pollution, waste, ozone depletion, abusive labor conditions, poverty, inequality, etc.) (Organization for Economic Cooperation and Development 1997).

SUSTAINABLE POLICY AND CONSUMER LIFESTYLES

The sustainable development approach has prompted disputes over the role played by institutions and policymakers in regulating consumer demand and encouraging the adoption of sustainable production technologies. Its policy-driven approach has been criticized as a technocratic project based on unrealistic expectations concerning the malleability of presumably passive consumer behaviors through

regulation. The gap between policy and practice is exacerbated by the fact that the unhindered right of individual consumers to pursue comfort and pleasure through free market consumption is considered to be a cornerstone of basic democratic principles. Given this individualistic orientation, those trying to promote green/sustainable consumption and change consumer perceptions have found consumers to be recalcitrant to incentives and awareness campaigns designed to alter their lifestyle practices (e.g., the current popularity of SUVs among outdoor enthusiasts and other lifestyle groups).

In seeking to remedy gaps between formal policy directives and widespread public acceptance of green/sustainable consumption practices, the "ecological modernization" approach of some European environmental sociologists similarly holds that economic growth and resolutions to ecological problems need not be mutually exclusive (Lash, Szerszynski, & Wynne 1996; Spaargaren & van Vliet 2000). Their break with sustainable development adherents hinges on a reconsideration of the view of "the consumer." Whereas, in the sustainable development view, consumers are thought of as passive actors, ecological modernization proponents understand consumers in terms of active – albeit highly rational – choosers. Ecological modernization endeavors to influence consumer choices through a variety of consciousness-raising educational avenues designed to promote green/sustainable consumption as a rational, ethical, and proper way to rein in the aggregate environmental and social damage wrought by consumer lifestyles (Spaargaren & van Vliet 2000; Paavola 2001).

Critics contend that this approach still fails to adequately deal with consumer objections to altering their lifestyle practices to serve needs for environmental sustainability (Hobson 2002). Like sustainable development, ecological modernization has been hard pressed to remedy the inherent difficulties posed by the need to couch green/sustainable consumption in individualistic terms as a "cultural politics" rather than as a movement connected to larger social and environmental justice issues. Accordingly, perhaps the most crucial issue facing green/sustainable consumption advocates involves how best to market and promote socially and/or environmentally beneficial consumption practices to consumers.

UNDERSTANDING GREEN/ SUSTAINABLE CONSUMPTION

Despite the obstacles posed by the individualistic orientation of consumerism, evidence of participation in green/sustainable consumption comes from an assortment of movements at the margins of consumer societies, including downshifters, voluntary simplifiers, anti-globalization groups, local producer cooperatives, consumer banks, "enviropreneurs," and indigenous groups seeking a more direct voice in the governance and control of nearby natural resources. At present there exists a need for more – and more systematic – studies of such movements and the social conditions and personal motivations that give rise to them.

In general, whether the purview of economists, environmental scientists, sociologists, or marketers, there is clearly a lack of applied studies concerning ways to develop, assess, gauge, and modify policies designed to encourage green/sustainable consumption practices. In the future, the need to identify and better understand ways in which such practices can best be implemented is one that must be addressed in greater detail from a variety of disciplinary and empirical angles.

SEE ALSO: Consumer Movements; Ecology and Economy; Economy, Culture and; Environmental Movements; Hyperconsumption/ Overconsumption; Lifestyle Consumption; New Urbanism; Waste, Excess, and Second-Hand Consumption

REFERENCES AND SUGGESTED READINGS

Cohen, M. J. & Murphy, J. (Eds.) (2001) *Exploring Sustainable Consumption: Environmental Policy and the Social Sciences*. Pergamon Press, Oxford.
Hawken, P. (1993) *The Ecology of Commerce: A Declaration of Sustainability*. Harper Collins, New York.
Hobson, K. (2002) Competing Discourses of Sustainable Consumption: Does the "Rationalization of Lifestyles" Make Sense? *Environmental Politics* 11(2): 95–120.

Lash, S., Szerszynski, B., & Wynne, B. (Eds.) (1996) *Risk, Environment and Modernity: Towards a New Ecology*. Sage, London.
McKibben, B. (1999) *The End of Nature*, 2nd edn. Anchor Books, New York.
Merchant, C. (1989) *The Death of Nature: Women, Ecology, and the Scientific Revolution*. Harper & Row, New York.
Myers, D. G. (2003) The Social Psychology of Sustainability. *World Futures* 59: 201–11.
Organization for Economic Cooperation and Development (1997) *Sustainable Consumption and Production*. OECD Publications, Paris.
Paavola, J. (2001) Towards Sustainable Consumption: Economics and Ethical Concerns for the Environment in Consumer Choices. *Review of Social Economy* 59(2): 227–48.
Princen, T. (2002) Distancing: Consumption and the Severing of Feedback. In: Princen, T., Maniates, M., & Conca, K. (Eds.), *Confronting Consumption*. MIT Press, Cambridge, MA, pp. 103–31.
Robins, N. & Roberts, S. (1998) Making Sense of Sustainable Consumption. *Development* 41(1): 28–36.
Spaargaren, G. & van Vliet, B. (2000) Lifestyles, Consumption and the Environment: The Ecological Modernization of Domestic Consumption. *Environmental Politics* 10(1): 50–76.
World Commission on Environment and Development (1987) *Our Common Future*. Oxford University Press, Oxford.

consumption and intellectual property

Kembrew McLeod

The rise of capitalism, the invention of the printing press, and the commodification of literary and artistic domains helped lay the economic, technological, and legal-philosophical groundwork that led to the development of intellectual property laws. There are three major categories of intellectual property law – copyright, trademark, and patent law – though it was copyright law that was the first piece of legislation to arise from the collision of those above-mentioned concepts. In 1710, Britain passed the Statute of Anne, which was akin to modern copyright law, and in 1790 the US

Congress passed a copyright law similar to this British statute.

Copyright law secures protection for all types of original expression, including art, literature, music, songs, choreography, flow charts, software, photography, movies, video games, and videos. Copyright only protects original expression fixed in a medium, and not the underlying concepts and ideas comprising that expression (i.e., you cannot copyright an idea). The differentiation between an idea and the protected *expression* of that idea highlights the way Enlightenment and Romantic notions of originality and authorship are deeply embedded in contemporary copyright law. Trademark law developed from a body of common law that was concerned with protecting commercial marks from being misused and misrepresented by competing companies. Lastly, patent law protects from unauthorized commercial use certain types of inventions.

Intellectual property owners are quite powerful and have at times flexed significant lobbying muscle. For instance, until 1998 the period of copyright protection lasted for the life of the author plus 50 years – unless the creator was a business, in which case the period of protection lasted for 75 years. But, to use one well-known example, many of Disney's copyrights that protected its most lucrative characters were due to lapse near the turn of the century, with Mickey Mouse passing into the public domain in 2003, and Pluto, Goofy, and Donald Duck following in 2009. Disney, along with the Motion Picture Association of America (MPAA) and other content owners, heavily lobbied Congress to pass legislation to extend copyright coverage for an extra 20 years, which Congress did. Named after the late singer-congressman, this piece of legislation was titled the Sonny Bono Copyright Term Extension Act, and it had the effect of preventing any new works from entering the public domain for 20 years after the bill was signed into law.

The intellectual properties sold by lifestyle companies contribute significantly to western economies and consumer culture. By their very nature, these properties – and the copyright, trademark, and patent laws that govern them – exert a powerful influence over social interactions in a consumer society. For instance, Nike is less a shoe company than a conceptual house of cards built around the strength of its trademarks. It is a remarkably sturdy house of cards that is supported by the policing powers of the state. The corporation's marketing philosophy makes it clear that the company is not in the business of manufacturing shoes but in the business of branding – connecting lifestyles to cheap pieces of plastic, leather, and rubber. The growing centrality of corporate identity and corporate "image" requires Nike and others to invest a large percentage of capital on advertising and promotion in order to keep the brand at the center of the popular cultural imagination.

The massive profits generated by Nike and other companies stem not only from outsourcing its factory labor, argues legal and cultural studies scholar Rosemary Coombe, but also from its ability to successfully herd the migration of its trademarked brands into everyday life. Coombe argued in *The Cultural Life of Intellectual Properties* (1998) that companies need to have it both ways, because if they are to remain profitable and relevant, they need to saturate consumers with their logos, brands, and services. Naomi Klein, author of *No Logo* (2000), notes that logos have become the lingua franca of the global village, and these trademarked properties are often used by anti-globalization activists as a site for their protests. Because public spaces, public squares, are disappearing – being replaced by branded environments – activists have come to see logos as a new kind of public square they can occupy.

Popular culture provides social actors with a kind of verbal shorthand. Appropriating words and phrases from mass media, consumer-citizens can convey a wide range of meanings and emotions, sometimes with only one monosyllabic utterance. Religious rites and iconography, many argue, once provided a common reference point for big and little questions, but today mediated, privatized images and meanings have embedded themselves into everyday talk. The average American college student is more likely to recognize a line from the television cartoon *The Simpsons*, for instance, than an allusion to a story from the Old Testament. Referencing pop culture helps shape and define the identity and cultural preferences of social actors, providing a kind of grammar and syntax that structures everyday talk. In face-to-face interactions many ordinary people can still legally refer to these intellectual properties, and we will continue to do so without inhibition. Increasingly, however, personal expression carried out over the World Wide Web, as scholars Siva Vaidhyanathan and Lawrence Lessig have argued, has come under the surveillance and regulation of intellectual property laws which are being enforced by owners through such means as cease-and-desist emails.

In 1999, trademark-owning corporations won a major lobbying victory when the US Congress passed the Anti-Cyber Squatting Consumer Protection Act. Since then, companies have aggressively pursued legal action against those who incorporate their trademarks into domain names. The Act imposes stiff criminal penalties against offenders, though companies can also use an arbitration process to control a domain name they don't like. When so much of culture and language is privately owned, it becomes all the more difficult to play with language, even in non-confrontational ways. For instance, Mike Rowe, a 17-year-old Canadian high school student, discovered the new legalities of personal expression when he registered the domain name MikeRoweSoft.com and soon found himself in legal troubles with Microsoft. Using a now common tactic, the software company offered $10 in order to provoke the teen into a higher counterbid, which then allowed Microsoft to claim that Rowe had filed a "bad faith" registration (i.e., registering a name only for the sake of getting companies to pay him for the rights), and started proceedings to strip him of the domain name. Microsoft backed off its suit slightly after much bad PR, but it still insisted on controlling the domain name.

Regarded by many as vapid and a form of escapism, popular culture does impact the consciousness of consumer-citizens powerfully, which is why it is necessary for social actors to manipulate and transform the language of popular culture that surrounds them. But in recent years, it has been difficult and/or impossible to do so because federal law protects trademarks from being portrayed in an "unwholesome or unsavory context." This provision allows courts to suppress unauthorized uses of famous cultural icons, even when there is no reasonable possibility of confusion in the marketplace. In many ways, the problem is as much with the

way trademark law is interpreted by "brand bullies" as it is with the way it is written.

The interpretation of the law by corporate lawyers requires that these companies go after any and all unauthorized uses, even if they are obviously meant to be "parodic" social commentary – a longstanding exception to the use of copyrighted material. The law is written in such a way that companies are required to zealously police the public, unauthorized uses of their trademark. Failing to do so may result in a "dilution" of the trademark and thus their exclusive right to it. In an era where brand images and icons are virtually equated with a company and its products, it would be almost negligent not to protect the value already invested. This is why lawyers for the Xerox Corporation constantly remind newspapers that its branded name isn't a generic term for photocopying. When a trademarked good loses its specific meaning, its economic value dies, suffering from what is called, fittingly, "genericide."

Another area of culture where intellectual property law and consumption are deeply interconnected is in the practice of product placement in movies, television shows, and more recently video games. Because society is saturated with commodities, advertisers argue, product placements in movies and television shows add "realism" to the production, despite the fact that there's nothing realistic about the way directors place products in the frame or the way products are spoken about in the context of the dramatic narrative.

Video games occupy the imagination of millions of teens and twenty-somethings. These games are important because they seamlessly integrate leisure activity, consumption, everyday life, and branded intellectual properties. Unlike most movies, people play video games multiple times and, by definition, they require the close attention of the viewer. The trademarked and copyrighted goods that appear in the media world typically do so with the explicit permission (and often payment) of the intellectual property owners. This works to shape both the consciousness of social actors and the rules by which they can communicate and interact with each other in media that are regulated by intellectual property laws.

Increasingly, these highly regulated media are becoming the primary ways many people communicate – something that quite literally, under the law, positions branded cultural texts as objects that can only be consumed, not (re) produced or redefined or critiqued. Interestingly, the kind of aggressive tactics employed by intellectual property owners have succeeded in generating a backlash movement against what have been called the "cultural land grabs" of "brand bullies," to use a phrase deployed by author David Bollier. Law professor James Boyle refers to the recent changes in intellectual property law as "the second enclosure movement," referring to the increasing erosion of the "cultural commons" and the privatization of cultural resources.

These laws and the favorable litigious climate they have spawned, together with some high-profile and aggressively pursued suits against alleged violators, threaten to preclude public expression. Few companies or organizations, and fewer individuals, can afford to withstand the kind of legal onslaught that, for instance, Disney can unleash. The sum effect has been a concentration of ownership of public expression, and thus a potential deadening effect on playfulness and creativity at the very moment when new technologies and new modes of communication offer the promise of new horizons.

SEE ALSO: Brands and Branding; Consumption and the Internet; Consumption, Spectacles of; Consumption, Visual; Culture Jamming; Intellectual Property

REFERENCES AND SUGGESTED READINGS

Bettig, R. V. (1996) *Copyrighting Culture: The Political Economy of Intellectual Property.* Westview Press, Boulder, CO.
Coombe, R. (1998) *The Cultural Life of Intellectual Properties: Authorship, Appropriation, and the Law.* Duke University Press, Durham, NC.
Elias, S. (1996) *Patent, Copyright, and Trademark: A Desk Reference to Intellectual Property Law.* Nolo Press, Berkeley, CA.
Klein, N. (2000) *No Logo: Taking Aim at the Brand Bullies.* Picador, New York.
Lessig, L. (2004) *Free Culture: How Big Media Uses Technology and the Law to Lock Down Culture and Control Creativity.* Penguin, New York.
McLeod, K. (2001) *Owning Culture: Authorship, Ownership, and Intellectual Property Law.* Peter Lang, New York.
McLeod, K. (2005) *Freedom of Expression®: Overzealous Copyright Bozos and Other Enemies of Creativity.* Doubleday, New York.
Vaidhyanathan, S. (2001) *Copyrights and Copywrongs: The Rise of Intellectual Property and How it Threatens Creativity.* New York University Press, New York.
Vaidhyanathan, S. (2004) *The Anarchist in the Library: How the Clash Between Freedom and Control is Hacking the Real World and Crashing the System.* Basic Books, New York.

consumption and the Internet

Sonia Livingstone

The study of consumption within the social sciences has a history stretching over a century or more, and has only recently been extended to the study of consumption of and on the Internet. The arrival of the Internet as a mass market technology in the early to mid-1990s throughout western countries and beyond has posed new questions for the multidisciplinary study of consumption and consumer culture, particularly as the Internet seems to facilitate the shift from mass consumption to increasingly specialized, flexible, and geographically dispersed forms of consumption.

Some familiar intellectual debates are now being replayed in this new arena between social researchers who question the power relations inherent in consumption (and its relation to production) and market researchers who approach the study of consumption uncritically as a means of increasing its presence in everyday life. The study of consumption and the Internet has sought to critique the way in which online consumers (and therefore processes of online consumption) are researched within business and marketing schools, whether focusing narrowly on e-commerce or more broadly on the circulation of information in a liberalized market. Studies of consumption and the Internet are particularly concerned to critique accounts of consumer "needs" and "preferences," the decoupling of consumption from production, and economistic agendas that neglect the social and cultural meanings and practices that not merely accompany but also shape consumption.

Specific questions being asked about the Internet and consumption are multiple. First, taking "the Internet" as a "black box," a technology diffusing through the marketplace and into workplaces, homes, schools, and communities, research has asked how the Internet itself is being consumed. Can the spread of the Internet be understood like the spread of any other consumer good – i.e., does it "trickle down" from the wealthy to the masses, and is there a widening or lessening "digital divide" akin to other social inequalities in material goods? Second, opening up the "black box," research is beginning to ask about consumption processes in relation to the many and diverse goods and services increasingly made available through the Internet, where consumption is here understood both narrowly and more broadly. For instance, does e-commerce from business to consumers work in similar ways to high street shopping, or are the conditions of money, trust, pleasure, and practicalities significantly different? Is a consumption perspective helpful in exploring the emerging cultural and social practices by which online content is co-created and co-consumed by its participants, with implications for identity, expression, communicative norms, and social ties?

The better the Internet and its consumers (or "users") are understood, and the more the Internet becomes a complex and plural set of technologies which encompasses information, services, communication, entertainment, work, business, educational, and many other applications, the more these two traditions of early research are converging. Moreover, as "Internet studies" (itself still a contested label) is increasingly attracting the attention of many disciplines across the social sciences and humanities, the more consumption studies must negotiate their contribution to this new interdisciplinary research space. The fundamental intellectual divide between the critical scholars and the more administrative or pluralist scholars persists, while becoming curiously intertwined with the "optimistic"/"pessimistic"

divide that has shaped the early phases of "Internet studies."

Hence, researchers are asking whether the Internet affords new and emancipatory possibilities that can liberate people from well-established and hierarchical practices of material and symbolic consumption "offline." Attention has been focused on the "consumption" of information (as part of the potentially democratizing impact of the Internet, in turn a function of its flexible, heterarchical, even anarchic network structure), on the identity consequences of consumption online (in a domain where anonymity, expressiveness, experimentation, and tolerance supposedly shape the field of consumption), and on the creative potential of new consumption practices (playing with the artistic and innovative possibilities for new "products" – new forms of textual representation, original codes for communication and expressiveness, unexpected or collectively emergent forms of discourse).

More pessimistically, researchers are also asking whether the Internet affords new forms of commercial exploitation or social control, again extending and developing practices of production, distribution, and consumption offline to the online domain. Attention here has centered on the risks attendant on online consumption (risks associated with the commercial or state invasion of privacy, the involuntary collection and exploitation of personal data, the opportunities to monitor and target consumers in vastly greater detail and on a far greater scale than is generally possible offline), on the anxieties and fears of the public, resulting in barriers to online consumption as evident from the considerable reluctance toward e-commerce and other online transactions, and, occupying most research thus far, on the likelihood that this new domain for consumption (both of the technology and of its contents) is adding a further form of inequality (now in relation to digital information, online opportunities, e-learning, etc.), undermining attempts to reduce sources of social exclusion and economic disadvantage.

Research on consumption and the Internet is still in its early stages, the Internet itself only having been widely available since 1995, and even then only in wealthy parts of the world. The field has moved on from the early days of speculative hyperbole toward a solid grounding in empirical research, even if this remains tentative in its preliminary conclusions. It has also moved on from the assumption of a separate domain called "cyberspace" or a clear virtual/real distinction, one that proved unsustainable both theoretically and in terms of everyday consumption practices. And, thirdly, it has moved increasingly away from any simple assertions of technological determinism (asking about the impacts or effects of the Internet on consumption) in favor of either a social determinism (stressing the importance of the offline context in shaping online consumption practices) or a "soft technological determinism" (seeking to understand in a more subtle and careful manner just whether and how consumption online differs from consumption offline, supplementing and diversifying the possibilities and practices of consumption in general).

Empirical studies are beginning to converge on the conclusion that, as is now routinely assumed in (offline) consumption studies, consumption online is integrated into daily life, and is not an activity apart. While the material and symbolic conditions of consumption on the Internet may differ, they are not of a different order from offline consumption and, most important, people move to and fro between these various spaces of, or opportunities for, consumption. Consequently, the social contexts of consumption (on- and offline) represent an increasing focus of research. Online, researchers have been more successful in tracking the (re) emergence of familiar cultural norms, social conventions, and everyday anxieties than they have in documenting radical or alternative forms of consumption, communication, and community building, except perhaps among a highly motivated and generally elite minority of Internet enthusiasts. Online too, the signs are growing that the once free and anarchic or emancipatory potential of the Internet is subject to increasing attempts to privatize, commercialize, control, and profit from the activities of consumers online. Some of these are defended under a "neoliberal" freeing of the market, on- as offline. Others are being hotly contested precisely as incursions into public freedoms, privacy, and rights. There are still many more questions than answers regarding consumption and the Internet. But, it may be fairly suggested, some answers are beginning to emerge.

SEE ALSO: Consumption, Mass Consumption, and Consumer Culture; Cyberculture; Economy, Culture and; Internet; Shopping

REFERENCES AND SUGGESTED READINGS

Lovelock, P. & Ure, J. (2002) The New Economy: Internet, Telecommunications, and Electronic Commerce? In: Lievrouw, L. & Livingstone, S. (Eds.), *Handbook of New Media: Social Shaping and Consequences of ICTs*. Sage, London, pp. 350–68.
Miller, D. & Slater, D. (2000) *The Internet: An Ethnographic Approach*. Berg, London.
Rogers, E. M. (1995) *Diffusion of Innovations*, vol. 4. Free Press, New York.
Warshauer, M. (2003) *Technology and Social Inclusion: Rethinking the Digital Divide*. MIT Press, Cambridge, MA.
Wellman, B. & Haythornthwaite, C. (Eds.) (2002) *The Internet in Everyday Life*. Blackwell, Malden, MA.

consumption, landscapes of

J. Michael Ryan

George Ritzer has built upon his notion of cathedrals of consumption to describe what he terms "landscapes of consumption," or "geographic areas that encompass two, or more, cathedrals of consumption" (2005: 149). This definition can be extended to define landscapes of consumption as *locales that encompass two or more cathedrals of consumption that allow, encourage, and even compel people to consume*. The prototypical example of this would be the Las Vegas strip – an area where multiple cathedrals of consumption exist side by side in the same geographical setting and entice consumers not only through their individual appeal, but also through the techniques made possible by their synergistic proximity.

Elsewhere, Ritzer et al. (2005) have extended the idea of landscapes of consumption with their case study of Easton Town Center in Columbus, Ohio. They argue that Easton serves as a prototype of a consumer setting that is becoming increasingly prevalent – one that seeks to simulate the look and feel of a nostalgic small-town America. By encompassing two or more landscapes of consumption within one setting, Easton is able to expand the spectacle of landscape to a community level (Ryan 2005).

Sharon Zukin (1991) has also contributed much to the idea of landscape. She uses the term landscape to describe a configuration of material geographical surroundings and their related social and symbolic practices. She argues that landscape is the major cultural product of our time and that landscape and power are deeply and intricately connected. Through this, large-scale, bureaucratic, economic structures attempt to impose a new order upon an existing geographical location. Although there is sometimes resistance to these attempts, ultimately capital wins out and landscapes are imposed. Zukin also argues that landscapes, contrary to the assertions of many postmodern social theorists, tend toward "repetition and singularity" and not toward ephemeral aestheticism.

SEE ALSO: Consumption; Consumption, Cathedrals of; Consumption, Mass Consumption, and Consumer Culture; Consumption, Spectacles of; Shopping; Shopping Malls

REFERENCES AND SUGGESTED READINGS

Ritzer, G. (2005) *Enchanting a Disenchanted World: Revolutionizing the Means of Consumption*, 2nd edn. Pine Forge Press, Thousand Oaks, CA.

Ritzer, G., Ryan, J. M., & Stepnisky, J. (2005) Innovation in Consumer Settings: Landscapes and Beyond. In: Ratneshwar, S. & Mick, C. (Eds.), *Inside Consumption: Frontiers of Research on Consumer Motives, Goals, and Desires*. Routledge, London, pp. 292–308.

Ryan, J. M. (2005) Easton: A 21st-Century (R)evolution in Consumption, Community, Urbanism, and Space. MA Thesis. University of Maryland, College Park.

Zukin, S. (1991) *Landscapes of Power: From Detroit to Disney World*. University of California Press, Berkeley.

consumption, masculinities and

Randal Doane

Masculinities and consumption refer to the gendered sense of self constituted through the use of goods and services in the leisure time and spaces of modern life in the West. In markets of goods, hobbies, and sexual practices, individual choice is delimited by the social structure of gender, and these markets provide the symbolic boundaries for the practical embodiment of different masculinities. Masculinities here is offered in the plural, to emphasize how a hegemonic masculinity (Connell 1995: 77) is secured as a temporary solution to problems within a patriarchal order. As a rule, the sexual division of consumption has been dehistoricized, but in the past 30 years, men have embraced a highly commodified, stylized, and androgynous masculinity.

Masculinity is linked with the positive attributes of power and virility, yet depends upon the denigration of femininity as its dialectical Other, and is constituted by antinomies of class, racialization, and sexuality. As a disposition, masculinity is conceptualized as homologous to the penis in a state of arousal: rigid, potent, and virile. This disposition entails a relentless retesting of unprovable ambition (Kimmel 1996: 333), in settings that embrace physical strength, competition, and even violence (Messner 1997). For straights and queers, men and women, to be masculine is to be in control. Representations of the masculine subject at work and play emphasize his concern for the objective results of performance, rather than the subjective yearning of gratification (Bordo 1999: ch. 1). The stoic sovereignty of the audiophile in the Maxell advertisement, for example, derives its meaning from the dialectical implication of both the impotent bureaucrat in his grey flannel suit and the emotional female in the domestic sphere.

The historiography of masculine consumption was largely neglected in modern sociology (1848–1972), and accounts of the male self focused on his role as the laboring provider. Durkheim imagined "cultured men" in their occupations in the public sphere, and "natural women" to be at home in the domestic sphere. Particularly for the middle class, consumption was understood to be a feminine province, and in "Fashion" (1904), Simmel imagined that masculine men were free from such incidental concerns. Masculinity depended upon a circumscribed reflexivity, for to be too self-conscious was to be feminine. Here fashion reflected the articulations of masculinity to power and vigor, and femininity to fragility and docility. In *Theory of the Leisure Class*, Veblen argued that, even in its conspicuous form, men's fashion showed relative constraint compared to the feminine "habitual uselessness" of the high heel, the skirt, and the corset. Men's clothing was more objectively uniform, while women's clothing provoked as it concealed, offering artifice and illusion.

In the mid-1970s, the decline of manual labor and the disappearance of jobs-for-life coincided with the feminist revolution, and gave rise to new models for masculine consumption and its sociological consideration. With the cultural turn in the social sciences, sociologists returned to conflict theory and symbolic interaction, to consider the determinacy of gender and, eventually, the complexity of masculinity. The two were not coincidental, as gender studies valorized women's lives in ways that did not implicate masculine privilege.

The serious consideration of masculinity and consumption in sociology and cultural studies assumed three key subfields: first, the critical synthesis of Marx, Freud, and feminism in cultural studies; second, the Durkheimian legacy of the morality of consumption; and third, the historical studies of masculinity and consumption as key features of industrial modernity. First, research at the Birmingham Center for Cultural Studies on youth and resistance analyzed the intersections of masculinity and consumption, and the privilege of the pub(lic)

over the domestic sphere. Researchers drew on the Marxian legacy of culture as the bulwark against capital, and turned their willful optimism away from the union shop to the street corner, yet neglected to problematize masculinity effectively in initial studies. The "Screen School" of film studies adapted Freud for feminist ends, and focused on ideology and the masculinity of the filmic apparatus (Mulvey 1989).

Second, studies of consumer morality included Goffman's *Gender Advertisements* (1979) and Bourdieu's *Distinction* (1984), which mapped the classificatory schemes of consumption, and analyzed the masculine, whole-mouth ways of eating and speaking. Nixon (1996) and Jackson et al. (2001) extended Goffman's analysis of the commodification of the gendered body, and found a new reflexivity in contemporary variations of masculine consumption. They articulated how men's magazines offer a "constructed certitude" to ease heterosexual men's anxieties brought on by the new visibility of gay masculinities, the delay in marriage, and women's upper hand in educational achievement.

Third, in addition to Kimmel's treatment (1996) of masculinity in general, Ehrenreich (1983) explored hegemonic variations of masculine consumption, and Mort (1996) provided a sharp analysis of leisure and masculine sexuality in London in late modernity.

Sociological theory has had difficulty imagining the positive qualities of masculinity, and has yet to imagine how the emergence of capitalist markets in developing countries might transform traditional forms of masculinity. Likewise, scholarship in consumption has yet to interrogate the genealogy of gender in classic and late modern sociology. Witz and Marshall (2003: 341) offer a critical account of the masculine body as capable, and the feminine body as constrained, in the work of Durkheim and Simmel, respectively, and outline how contemporary sociology of the gendered body might be shaped for future developments in consumption theory.

SEE ALSO: Consumption and the Body; Gender, Consumption and; Femininities/ Masculinities; Lifestyle Consumption; Sexuality, Masculinity and

REFERENCES AND SUGGESTED
READINGS

Bordo, S. (1999) *The Male Body*. Farrar, Strauss, &
   Giroux, New York.
Connell, R. (1995) *Masculinities*. University of Cali-
   fornia Press, Berkeley.
Ehrenreich, B. (1983) *The Hearts of Men: American
   Dreams and the Flight from Commitment*. Anchor,
   Garden City, NY.
Jackson, P., Stevenson, N., & Brooks, K. (2001)
   Making Sense of Men's Magazines. Blackwell, Mal-
   den, MA.
Kimmel, M. S. (1996) *Manhood in America: A Cul-
   tural History*. Free Press, New York.
Messner, M. (1997) *Politics of Masculinities*. Sage,
   Thousand Oaks, CA.
Mort, F. (1996) *Cultures of Consumption: Masculi-
   nities and Social Space in Late Twentieth-Century
   Britain*. Routledge, New York.
Mulvey, L. (1989) *Visual and Other Pleasures*. Indi-
   ana University Press, Bloomington.
Nixon, S. (1996) *Hard Looks: Masculinities, Specta-
   torship, and Contemporary Consumption*. St. Mar-
   tin's Press, New York.
Simmel, G. (1904) Fashion. *International Quarterly*
   10(1): 130–55.
Witz, A. & Marshall, B. (2003) The Quality of
   Manhood: Masculinity and Embodiment in the
   Sociological Tradition. *Sociological Review* 51(3):
   339–56.

consumption, mass consumption, and consumer culture

Russell W. Belk

CONSUMPTION

Consumption, mass consumption, and consumer culture are a growing focus in contemporary life as well as in social science theory and
research. Daniel Miller (1995) even suggests
that consumption is replacing kinship as the
central theme in anthropology. Consumption
is the most basic of these concepts, but not
the least contentious. From the Latin *consu-
mere*, to take up, consumption means to

acquire. But other meanings include using up,
burning, wasting, and decaying. In the first
case consumption adds; in the others it sub-
tracts. In current practice, the term may refer
either to using an object or to both acquiring
and using it. In the broader usage, consumption
also includes such supporting activities as
attending advertising, shopping retail displays,
interacting with salespeople, engaging in word
of mouth, and searching online for a good or
service. This more common view holds that
consumption consists of *activities potentially
leading to and actually following from the acquisition of a good or service by those engaging in such
activities.*

Tangible goods can be acquired and stored
for future consumption, but most services,
including surgery, stage plays, and haircuts,
must be acquired and used simultaneously.
The prototype of current consumption involves
searching for, purchasing, and subsequently
using a branded product. But we can also
acquire goods and services by receiving them
as gifts, borrowing or leasing them, creating
them, finding them, stealing them, or, as with
desks in a classroom, coming to feel they are
ours through habitual use. Consumers are pro-
totypically individuals, although they can also
be couples, families, corporations, or other
groups.

Consumption has come to entail more than is
captured in the preceding definition. *When we
consume an object we also consume its meanings.*
Owning a Mercedes automobile may signify
wealth, appreciating a piece of music may
reflect one's taste, and wearing a certain style
of jeans may signal sexuality to an intended
audience. These meanings are jointly constructed by society, marketing and advertising,
and other cultural meaning makers including
designers, filmmakers, reviewers, newscasters,
copywriters, artists, and musicians. As Charles
Revson, the founder of Revlon, once observed,
"In the factory we make cosmetics, in the store
we sell hope." Meaning elaboration is such an
integral part of the contemporary acquisition
and use of objects that it is difficult to envision
consumption without meanings. Although a
dog might "consume" a bone according to the
previous definition, something is missing that
makes this an awkward construction. That
something is the social meaning. A human

collector of bones (or postage stamps or Beanie Babies) will likely fit them into broader meaning systems understood by other collectors as well as employ collecting rules such as "no-two-alike," "belonging to category X," and "not for everyday use." No matter how much a dog may like bones, it is unlikely to selectively acquire them with such meanings in mind.

One further definitional matter is deciding what, if any, activities are *not* consumption. Since consumption can include non-market means of acquisition, are planting and nourishing a garden forms of consumption? Since we may also consume services, is going to a mosque to pray consumption? What about buying something in the market in order to give it as a gift? Are we consuming when we contribute to a charity? Does an employer consume the services of its employees? As parents, do we consume our children? Is breathing air consuming it? The answers to such questions are by no means fixed. One characteristic of consumer culture is its increasing commodification of the world so that more and more of it can be bought, sold, and consumed. We can now purchase and consume branded bottled water, human sperm, and coffee futures. However, two distinctions commonly limit such conceptual imperialism. One is that production is a separate activity from consumption. An artist painting a commissioned portrait is primarily a producer, even though the activity may involve the consumption of paints and brushes.

Secondly, there exists a shifting and contentious non-commodified sphere of human life. The non-commodity sphere has shrunk in highly marketized economies, but it has not disappeared. As children we are not consuming our parents' services as much as engaging in intimate sharing. Children can, however, consume care from a commercial day-care center. We may consume the services of a prostitute, but we share intimacy in our sexual relations with a love partner. There is a conceptual dividing line between, on the one hand, acquiring and consuming impersonal objects obtained in reciprocal exchange for something else and, on the other hand, giving and receiving personal mementos or services without explicit or implicit reciprocal provisos. A consumable commodity is normally fungible and we may do with it as we please. But an inherited family

heirloom has strings attached that link us to the donor. We cannot give it away or sell it with impunity. Viviana Zelizer (*Pricing the Priceless Child*, 1985) suggests that US child labor prohibitions were an attempt to decommodify the sacralized realm of childhood. Human organs, infants, and stem cells continue to resist commodification despite willing buyers. Those who resist allowing such commodification cling to a distinction between the more impersonal process of consuming and the more intimate process of being. However much we may come to believe that we are what we consume, we nevertheless continue to believe that there is something more to our existence than consumption.

MASS CONSUMPTION

Mass consumption is an evolutionary step from the necessary human act of consumption. Historically, mass consumption, *the consumption of the same objects by a large number of consumers*, emerged with mass production and was soon associated with mass communication, mass media, mass marketing, mass merchandizing, and mass culture. With mass consumption, millions of consumers potentially drive the same cars, eat the same foods from the same restaurant and supermarket chains, wear the same clothing from the same retail chains, watch the same films and television programs, listen to the same music, and fill their homes with the same mass-produced furnishings. The specter of sameness in mass consumption is bothersome in individualistic societies. Even in the absence of strong individualism, massification threatens us with anonymity in an impersonal marketplace where we may as well be consuming machines as people. This is similar to the dehumanizing process that George Ritzer (2004) calls *The McDonaldization of Society*, except that Ritzer focuses more on rationalized massification in delivering services than on consuming them. At the same time that it threatens anonymity, mass consumption allows lower costs of production and results in greater material abundance and affordability for the consumer. Consumption is potentially democratized by having access to the same goods at uniform low prices instead of having to custom order expensive tailor-made consumer goods, as with the carriage trade of prior centuries.

One ironic champion of mass consumption was Andy Warhol. Warhol (1975), who called his supersized atelier The Factory and who lithographed prints of Campbell's soup cans, pop celebrities, and Brillo pads, lauded the identical goods of a mass consumption society. He suggested that the richest consumers buy the same common consumer goods as the poorest. No amount of money can provide a better Coca-Cola than the one a poor person drinks, even if the purchaser is a movie star or the president.

Warhol also said he wanted to be a machine. He aspired to be not only Deleuze and Guattari's (1983) desiring and mass-consuming machine, but a mass-producing machine as well. Nevertheless, behind this populist democratic consumption façade, the gap between rich and poor is growing the world over and there remain many ways to signal one's place on the wealth continuum via consumption. The illusion that we can achieve distinction through mass consumption is sustained by the proliferation of branded consumption choices, market segmentation, and mass customization.

Brands add meaning to goods and services even when the object branded is virtually the same as others. Salt is salt, but Morton Salt with its slogan "When it rains it pours" and its logo of the young girl with the umbrella, spilling salt from a cylindrical blue Morton package, has more meaning than a bag of generic salt. Morton also segments its market, with separate offerings for those who want iodized salt, low-sodium salt, sea salt, road salt, kosher salt, popcorn salt, and so forth. Furthermore, it packages an array of shapes, colors, and sizes from one-serving sachets to picnic-sized shakers to 50-pound industrial-size bags.

Mass customization does not take place with salt, but jeans, automobiles, computers, and bicycles offer so many varieties, options, and components that they can virtually be customized for each individual. At Levi's flagship store in San Francisco, a customer can have his or her measurements input into a computer and subsequently order custom-fit jeans in a variety of cuts, fabrics, colors, and styles. Digital songs can be selectively downloaded from the Internet and mixed, matched, and sequenced in whatever way the consumer desires. In buying a BMW Mini Cooper automobile, the customer has a nearly infinite array of choices through the permutations of interiors, paint jobs, engines, wheels, tires, stereos, and many other available options. After ordering, consumers can watch online as their car is produced to order. Such mass customization has not done away with mass consumption, but for the consumer it does mitigate the specter of sameness.

Considered on a global scale, mass consumption and standardized business practices by multinational consumer goods companies introduce a reverse tendency toward non-segmented and non-customized consumption choices. The general assumptions are that what sells at home will sell abroad, that offering a variety of segmented products may be too risky, and that there are economies of scale to be gained by global advertising and merchandising. Although these assumptions are being challenged as Coca-Cola, McDonald's, MTV, and others begin to tailor their offerings to the culture and local competition, Nike's Air Jordan shoes successfully sold in the same versions worldwide and that was part of their appeal. This is sometimes taken as evidence of cultural imperialism, westernization, or Americanization, but this fails to recognize local adaptations and interpretations of global brands and offerings (e.g., Tamar Liebes and Elihu Katz, *The Export of Meaning*, 1990). At the same time, a part of the meaning of such brands is the consumer's sense of participating in a shared global consumer culture by means of mass consumption.

Even without mass customization, there are ways in which the consumer can decommodify mass-produced consumer goods. Our neighbor's canned beans are fungible and fully equivalent to our canned beans. But an ostensibly identical wedding ring purchased by a neighbor is not. Both by virtue of habituation (like the classroom desk) and by virtue of the symbolic meaning imparted through courtship and wedding rituals, this mass-produced object has been singularized in the eyes of its owner and is no longer fungible. For most people, trading wedding rings would be as unthinkable as trading children.

CONSUMER CULTURE

If consumption involves the purchase of meanings, *consumer culture involves a quest for meaning in life primarily through consumption.* Consumer culture no longer merely refers to a type of emphatic consumption orientation that historically developed in the more affluent capitalist economies of the world. It has also come to mean that consumption and the things we consume *comprise* our culture. Culture has become commoditized to such a degree that we experience it as consumption, by consumption, and through consumption. We are never far away from an advertising message. Most of what we now read, see, and hear via mass media is a message, or a more subtle product placement, for something we can buy. We now speak of things we once actively chose to *do* as things to *consume.* Shopping has become one of our key leisure activities. Travel guides devote more attention to what we can buy in a locale than they do to its natural wonders. Our interpersonal relations are defined increasingly through the mediation of consumer commodities. Our key rituals are now consumption events staged by wedding planners, funeral directors, caterers, and entertainers. With our logo-laden clothing and shopping bags, we are walking billboards for brands as we roam the shopping mall in search of an identity, in search of meaning in life.

Now that promotion has thoroughly colonized mass media, the Internet, email, postal mail, theaters, sports arenas, schools, roads, restrooms, buildings, buses, and busts, it seems that only old-fashioned letter writing and personal conversations are free of commercial messages. But even these forms of intercourse are likely to be liberally sprinkled with mentions of consumption. Children may know only a few varieties of local plants and animals, but they know hundreds of brand names before they start school. What is more, they want to own key brands in order to come of age in a consumer culture. A child who does not know what is showing on television, what music is playing on the radio, and what brands are cool is a disenfranchised child who cannot communicate with peers (Ritson & Elliott 1999). We act no longer so much as citizens as consumers. Our politicians are sold to us in carefully crafted packages with pre-planned sound bites, slick advertising, and celebrity endorsers.

Historically, we came to the present state of global consumer culture through several key developments. Some already mentioned include mass production, mass media, mass consumption, and branding. Others include fashion and rapid innovation (so that there is always something new to want), rapid transportation and multinational corporations (so that we can simultaneously consume the same goods as distant others), affluence (so that we can afford these consumer goods), globalization (so that consumer culture is no longer confined to more affluent nations and more urban areas), and liberated consumption values (so that it is now more sinful, evil, or unpatriotic *not* to consume luxuries than it is to consume them). Although historically in the West the development of the department store, mail order selling, urbanization, industrialization, and the advertising industry was also instrumental in stimulating consumer culture, this is not the case everywhere, especially with the rise of Internet selling.

A good benchmark of global consumer culture is the proliferation, globalization, and commercialization of holidays. Christmas is the most spectacular and successful consumption-dominated holiday. It is now widely celebrated even in such non-Christian nations as China, India, Japan, Thailand, and Turkey. Other western holidays including Mother's Day, Valentine's Day, and Halloween are becoming global as well, just as non-western holidays like Chinese New Year, Diwali, and Ramadan are becoming increasingly commercial and global. In countries where members of the prior generation did not know their dates of birth or who only celebrated name days in conjunction with saints' days, birthday cakes, cards, gifts, and parties are becoming the norm. The spread of these world holidays and the increasing portion of the calendar given over to them have been helped by the promotions of multinational manufacturers, retailers, and industries in such areas as foods, liquors, candies, perfumes, greeting cards, travel, decorations, books, clothing, and many other luxury consumer goods offered as essential for the holiday.

THEORETICAL PERSPECTIVES

Scholars before the 1950s considered only limited aspects of consumption phenomena. Karl Marx in *Capital* (1867) suggested the notion of commodity fetishism, but was more interested in the worker than the consumer. Thorstein Veblen's *The Theory of the Leisure Class* (1899), critiquing late nineteenth-century American *nouveaux riches*, famously introduced the concepts of conspicuous consumption, conspicuous waste, and pecuniary emulation, but avoided emerging mass consumption issues. Werner Sombart (*Luxury and Capitalism*, 1902) critiqued luxury consumption, but also focused on the consumption of the elite rather than the masses. Georg Simmel (*The Philosophy of Money*, 1907) addressed issues involving money and spending, but he too stopped short of addressing the impact of mass consumption. Max Horkheimer and Theodor Adorno (2002 [1944]) as well as Walter Benjamin (1968 [1936]) worried about a debasing of taste and loss of the sacred "aura" of handmade works with the coming of mass reproduction. These were not so much attempts to examine mass consumption as reactions to it.

In the wake of post-World War II American consumer affluence and spending, both critiques such as John Kenneth Galbraith's *The Affluent Society* (1958) and Vance Packard's *Hidden Persuaders* (1957) and defenses such as David Potter's *People of Plenty* (1954) and George Katona's *The Mass Consumption Society* whether rapidly increasing consumption was good for society and character. Galbraith and Packard worried that advertising and other marketing activities create new needs among consumers. In this view, the consumer is the passive victim of marketing.

This view was challenged in Jean Baudrillard's *The Consumer Society* (1970). In this early work, Baudrillard offers a more active view of consumers pursuing the sign value of consumer goods in an effort to communicate and differentiate themselves from others. But he also analyzed consumption as an obligatory moral system that fails to produce pleasure for the individual consumer. In seducing the consumer to want the latest thing, marketing caters to what Baudrillard called the "lowest common culture" by producing gadgets and kitsch objects. This lowest common culture is consumer culture. A part of the seduction of the consumer occurs through the mystification and sacralization of the body, not merely as a site of eroticism but also as a site of fantasy and desire. Advertising, beauty magazines, and fashion models combine first to make us feel uncomfortable with our bodies, and then to offer to sell us signs that promise to make us thin, beautiful, and sexy. This is one of the ways Baudrillard sees advertisers, together with architects, designers, and others, taking on the role of therapists helping a reputedly sick society. Drawing on Daniel Boorstin's *The Image* (1963), Baudrillard saw consumption celebrities who are "known for their well-knownness" replacing production heroes and offering to sell us back a way to be ourselves by dressing, acting, and talking like them. If consumer society has become the dominant discourse, Baudrillard, writing on the heels of the May 1968 French upheaval, also points to a counter-discourse denouncing consumption and keeping it in balance in much the same way that beliefs in God and the Devil kept moral control in medieval society.

In *The World of Goods* (1979), Mary Douglas and Baron Isherwood, like Baudrillard, emphasize the symbolic value of goods. They go beyond the pursuit of consumer goods for the sake of individual differentiation, however, and suggest that these goods also help to separate groups of people by acting as "marker goods," signaling our group belonging. Goods help bind humans together through rituals such as gift-giving, meals, and hospitality. They emphasize that just as one word from a poem has little meaning, one consumer good has little meaning by itself. It is rather the constellation of consumer goods we own that makes meaning in our lives. In their discussion of marker goods, Douglas and Isherwood echo some of the concerns of Pierre Bourdieu's *Distinction*, published (in French) the same year.

Bourdieu revived and extended social class theory by showing how French consumers use systems of taste in consumption, especially regarding their preferences in and knowledge of art, food, music, furnishings, and clothing, as *cultural capital* that establishes and perpetuates their status or *symbolic capital*. These systems of taste are acquired and transmitted through the consumer's *habitus*. Habitus is the family, cultural, and institutional milieu in which we are raised and educated and which structures our ways of examining, thinking about, and acting toward events in the world. Having parents and friends with a certain level of education and certain occupations helps nurture and pass on a certain level of cultural capital. Cultural capital, in turn, may sometimes be converted into *social capital* or *economic capital*. Bourdieu's theory has been more popular in addressing consumption in Europe than in North America and several studies have questioned its relevance in the United States. Holt (2000) has recently demonstrated that by revamping Bourdieu's elements of cultural capital, they can be usefully applied in the US context as well.

If the preceding theories focus on the aggregate and shared meanings of consumption practices, another line of theorizing has focused on the more individual and particular meanings of consumption objects and practices. In *The Meaning of Things* (1981), Mihalyi Csikszentmihalyi and Eugene Rochberg-Halton studied the favorite possessions of three generations of Chicago families. They found that although the younger generation valued consumer goods that helped them do things and that elevated their status, the older generation in the same families valued possessions that represented their experiences and links to family and friends. They distinguished between negative terminal materialism, which values consumer goods as ends in themselves, and positive instrumental materialism, which values favorite possessions for what we can do with them. These themes are extended by Belk in "Materialism" (1985) and "Possessions and the Extended Self" (1988). The former paper finds that materialism, defined as the importance a consumer attaches to worldly possessions, is negatively related to feelings of happiness and well-being. This finding, since replicated, suggests that materialistic beliefs that possessions can bring happiness may be misguided.

In *The Social Life of Things* (1986) edited by Arjun Appadurai, the lead chapter by Appadurai and the following chapter by Igor Kopytoff together offer a theory of consumer commodity value and meaning. They demystify the gift (partly drawing on Bourdieu) and

suggest that this symbolic form of exchange is *not* diametrically opposed to commodity exchange. At the same time, they mystify the commodity as being capable, in practice, of being decommoditized and singularized by the consumer. For example, when the consumer comes to regard a mass-produced purchased commodity as a work of art or as part of a personal collection, it is no longer like the anonymous commodity it was when it was for sale to anyone in the market. The consumer recontextualizes the object in a way that lends it special, extraordinary, and unique meaning. As with the gift, the singular object is no longer fungible and freely exchangeable for another object of similar economic value. Although universal money and mass marketing produce a drive to commoditization and homogeneous value, culture and the individual institute a counter-drive toward sacralization, singularization, and decommoditization. There is a link here to Émile Durkheim's (*The Elementary Forms of Religious Life*, 1915) notion of sacredness that is further developed by Belk et al. (1989). In *Hiding in the Light* (1988), Dick Hebdige discusses another type of sacralizing recontextualization in which British Mods regendered and transformed the meaning of the Italian motor scooter.

In 1987, Colin Campbell published *The Romantic Ethic and the Spirit of Modern Consumerism*. Its title plays off Max Weber's *The Protestant Ethic and the Spirit of Capitalism* (1905), but Campbell focuses on the engines of consumer culture rather than producer capitalism. He ties the origins of consumer culture to the Romantic Movement in late eighteenth- and early nineteenth-century Europe. Specifically, Campbell posits a longing for consumer goods that is bittersweet – a combination of painful longing for the object of our desires coupled with an excited state of anticipation. The consumer imagination is the key to this romantic daydream-like state. This state of imagination has been termed the desire for desire and has been found to be underwritten by a hope for hope. Consumers pursuing this emotional state of desire are quite capable of auto-arousing the focused wish for a consumer good through actively browsing shops, magazines, advertisements, and other sources of new things to want. Far from Galbraith's and Packard's manipulation of consumer needs by marketing sorcerers, in this self-stimulation of consumer desires the consumer acts as an eager sorcerer's apprentice.

In Grant McCracken's *Culture and Consumption* (1988), his concept of *displaced meaning* extends Campbell's arguments. McCracken argues that our hopes, ideals, and values in life are too fragile to stand up to scrutiny in everyday life. In order to sustain our belief in these ideals, we displace them to another place or time. The projection may be either backward in time (e.g., the good old days of our youth) or forward (e.g., when I graduate, get married, retire). In a consumer culture, these displaced meanings often attach to longed-for consumer goods. Consumers may sustain the belief that their ideal existence will emerge in Cinderella-like fashion when they own their dream car, house, stereo, or other special consumption object. McCracken also demonstrates that consumer goods can be a force for either stability or change in our lives. Like the objects of longing to which we displace meanings, he suggests that consumer goods can act as ballast for our sense of identity, as well as allow the possibility or hope for change. This resonates with the arguments of Douglas and Isherwood as well as the findings of Csikszentmihalyi and Rochberg-Halton. It also implicates the notion of continual experiments with and pursuit of lifestyles defined by consumption (Featherstone 1991).

HISTORICAL PERSPECTIVES ON CONSUMPTION AND CONSUMER CULTURE

Campbell and McCracken are also among a growing number of scholars who have addressed the issues of when, where, and how consumer culture first emerged in the world and how it has subsequently evolved. Fernand Braudel (*Capitalism and Material Life, 1400–1800*, 1973) led the way in focusing on everyday material life. McKendrick et al. (1982) examined the origins of consumer culture in eighteenth-century England and concluded that rather than a consumption revolution following from the Industrial Revolution, it may have been the other way around. They also traced

the role of clever merchandising by Josiah Wedgwood and others in stimulating the desire of consumers to have the latest thing. Rosalind Williams in *Dream Worlds* (1982) shows the seductive role of department stores in stimulating consumer culture in late nineteenth-century France. The palatial enticements of the early department store are also explored in consumer culture fiction by Émile Zola (*Au Bonheur des Dames*) and Theodore Dreiser (*Sister Carrie*). Michael Miller's *The Bon Marché* (1981) considers the store that was the inspiration for Zola's tale. Gail Reekie (*Temptations: Sex, Selling, and the Department Store*, 1993) provides an analysis of the role of the department store in stimulating consumer culture in late nineteenth- and early twentieth-century Australia, but she develops a more gendered treatment of the "seduction" of female consumers by the patriarchal store management.

Consumer culture flourished in the United States during the late nineteenth century with the rise of branded packaging (Susan Strasser, *Satisfaction Guaranteed*, 1989), advertising (Roland Marchand, *Advertising and the American Dream*, 1985; Jackson Lears, *Fables of Abundance*, 1994), department stores (Susan Benson, *Counter Culture*, 1986; William Leach, *Land of Desire*, 1993), display (Simon Bronner's edited collection, *Consuming Visions*, 1989), and World's Fairs (Robert Rydell, *All the World's a Fair*, 1984). As Gary Cross (*An All-Consuming Century*, 2000) documents, Puritan opposition, prohibitions, and anti-consumption movements existed simultaneously. But during the twentieth century, consumer culture became the dominant ethos in the US. Religious and secular criticisms of consumption have by no means disappeared (e.g., Robert Wuthnow, *God and Mammon*, 1994; Juliet Schor, *The Overspent American*, 1998). But as Jackson Lears (1984) argues, self-therapy through consumption has largely replaced salvation as the dominant national and personal goal.

Rather than eighteenth-century England or nineteenth-century France, Australia, or America, Chandra Mukerji (*From Graven Images*, 1983) suggests that fifteenth- or sixteenth-century England was the birthplace of consumer culture. She traces global flows of consumer goods such as calicoes, maps, and calendars as indices of developing consumption patterns.

In suggesting instead that the seventeenth-century Dutch were the originators of consumer culture, Simon Schama (*The Embarrassment of Riches*, 1987) also follows global flows of goods from the boom in Dutch shipping and discoveries of objects of desire in the New World and Asia. Analysis of the global flows of consumption is continued in several of the chapters in *Consumption and the World of Goods* (1993), edited by John Brewer and Roy Porter. Rather than trying to fix a time and place that was *the* birthplace of consumer culture, McCracken considers each of these local "orgies of consumption" as an explosion of consumer culture, growing more and more sustained and widespread between the fifteenth and twentieth centuries.

It will be evident from the preceding sources that there is a distinctly western bias in most treatments of the history of consumer culture. Although some recent work has begun to examine consumer culture in Japan (e.g., John Clammer, *Contemporary Urban Japan: A Sociology of Consumption*, 1997), China (e.g., Deborah Davis's edited collection, *The Consumer Revolution in Urban China*, 2000), Russia (e.g., Christoph Neidhart, *Russia's Carnival*, 2003), and India (e.g., William Mazarella, *Shoveling Smoke*, often been that the recent consumer culture in these nations is derivative from and imitative of developments in Europe and North America. There are only a few examinations of early consumer cultures elsewhere. For instance, Craig Clunas (*Superfluous Things*, 1991) examines consumer culture in late Ming China (sixteenth to seventeenth centuries), and Peter Stearns (*Consumerism in World History*, 2001) provides an outline of a global perspective on the history of consumer culture. Contrary to Don Slater's assumptions in *Consumer Culture and Modernity* (1997), it appears that neither advanced capitalism nor widespread wealth is necessary for the development of consumer culture (Belk 1999).

EVALUATION AND DIRECTIONS FOR FUTURE RESEARCH

Consumer research and theory have changed considerably since the critical theory of the Frankfurt School and the elitist criticisms of pop culture by Adorno, Horkheimer, and others. Despite the negative neo-Marxist evaluation of consumer culture and globalism still held by many sociologists (e.g., George Ritzer, *The Globalization of Nothing*, 2004), others, including those in the cultural studies school associated with Birmingham University in the UK, have come to embrace, if not celebrate, consumer culture as liberating. James Twitchell (*Lead Us Into Temptation*, 1999) also has a more favorable evaluation of consumer culture and chides those who see it as evil. Others like Conrad Lodziak (*The Myth of Consumerism*, 2002) condemn such liberatory postmodern takes on consumer culture as failing to discern the compulsory nature of the contemporary consumption system and the relative powerlessness of consumers to transcend their dependencies on illusions promoted by marketers.

It seems clear that there are both pluses and minuses to the advance of mass consumption and consumer culture in much of the world over the past century. Mass production, mass communications, and mass merchandising have made more goods available to more people at more affordable prices. Somewhere between the subjective categories of necessities and luxuries there has arisen a class of goods judged to be decencies (Belk 2004). These standards are becoming global. Soap, clean running water, education, and electricity are now a part of the global "standard package" (David Riesman, *Abundance for What?*, 1964), but perhaps also are cars, cosmetics, sanitary napkins, television, travel, and health care. To the extent that access to these goods is democratized within mass consumption cultures, physical and psychological well-being should increase. The desire to own these consumer goods may have positive motivational consequences as well.

But in a high-level consumer culture there are also often negative consequences. As Lizabeth Cohen (2003) demonstrates in the US, the elderly, ethnic minorities, lower social classes, and women have often not only been left out of consumer culture, but also market segmentation has helped to further marginalize them. These observations are reinforced in work such as Victoria deGrazia's *The Sex of Things* (1996) and Elizabeth Chin's *Purchasing Power* (2001). McCracken revises Simmel's trickle-down theory by suggesting that rather than trickling down the social class ladder, status goods trickle down the gender ladder from males to females, as illustrated by business dress practices. Penny Spark (*As Long As It's Pink*, 1995) argues that in culturally prescribing that design is a male province while aesthetic taste is a female province, women's material culture has been marginalized and trivialized.

The seemingly trivial pursuits of consumption can have profound effects. Too much materialism brings unhappiness. In extreme cases, consumption becomes an obsessive compulsive disorder and leads to unbearable debt and low self-esteem. There are environmental damages from the pursuit of rampant consumerism. Coupled with the policies of the World Bank, the World Trade Organization, and the International Monetary Fund, the gap between rich and poor consumers in the world has grown dramatically since the end of the Cold War. This is true not only between nations but within nations as well. Arguments about the effects of globalism have tended to overlook those who have been left out and left behind in the spread of global consumer culture.

This discussion has only been able to identify some of the major aspects of mass consumption and consumer culture. In the future it should be more useful to think in terms of multiple consumer cultures rather than considering consumer culture to be a uniform phenomenon globally. More attention to consumer cultures in the less affluent world, including places like postcolonial Sub-Saharan Africa, rapidly changing economies like China, India, and Eastern Europe, and among neglected aboriginal and ethnic groups within the more affluent world is clearly needed. Much remains to be discovered about the history of early consumer cultures in China, India, and other ancient civilizations. A great deal of attention has been devoted to advertising and marketplace exchange, but we need to know more about other avenues of consumption including gift-giving, sharing, heirlooms, informal markets, self-production, and barter communities. We need to know more about consumer boycotts, voluntary simplicity consumer lifestyles, and other strategies of resistance. We should consider relationships between religion and consumption, national and ethnic identity reflected in consumption, and virtual and

so-called posthuman consumption. Although it is clear that consumption increasingly permeates nearly every aspect of our lives, we need to better understand the relationships between the existential states that Jean-Paul Sartre (*Being and Nothingness*, 1943) labeled as having, doing, and being.

SEE ALSO: Brands and Branding; Commodities, Commodity Fetishism, and Commodification; Conspicuous Consumption; Consumer Culture, Children's; Consumption; Consumption Rituals; Department Store; Distinction; Globalization, Consumption and; Hyperconsumption/Overconsumption; Latinidad and Consumer Culture; Lifestyle Consumption; Mass Culture and Mass Society; Media and Consumer Culture; Shopping; Shopping Malls

REFERENCES AND SUGGESTED READINGS

Arnould, E. & Thompson, C. (2005) Consumer Culture Theory (CCT): Twenty Years of Research. *Journal of Consumer Research* 31 (March).

Belk, R. (1999) Leaping Luxuries and Transitional Consumers. In: Batra, R. (Ed.), *Marketing Issues in Transitional Economies.* Kluwer, Norwell, MA, pp. 38–54.

Belk, R. (2004) The Human Consequences of Consumer Culture. In: Ekstrom, K. & Brembeck, H. (Eds.), *Elusive Consumption.* Berg, Oxford, pp. 67–85.

Belk, R., Wallendorf, M., & Sherry, J. F., Jr. (1989). The Sacred and the Profane in Consumer Behavior: Theodicy on the Odyssey. *Journal of Consumer Research* 15(1): 1–38.

Benjamin, W. (1968 [1936]) The Work of Art in the Age of Mechanical Reproduction. In: *Illuminations: Essays and Reflections.* Ed. H. Arendt. Trans. H. Zorn. Harcourt, Brace, & World, New York, pp. 59–67.

Cohen, L. (2003) *A Consumers' Republic: The Politics of Mass Consumption in Postwar America.* Alfred Knopf, New York.

Deleuze, G. & Guattari, F. (1983) *Anti-Oedipus: Capitalism and Schizophrenia.* University of Minnesota Press, Minneapolis.

Featherstone, M. (1991) *Consumer Culture and Postmodernism.* Sage, London.

Holt, D. (2000) Does Cultural Capital Structure American Consumption? In: Schor, J. & Holt. D. (Eds.), *The Consumer Society Reader.* New Press, New York, pp. 212–52.

Horkheimer, M. & Adorno, T. (2002 [1944]) *The Dialectic of Enlightenment*. Stanford University Press, Stanford.

Lears, T. J. (1984) From Salvation to Self-Realization: Advertising and the Therapeutic Roots of the Consumer Culture, 1880–1920. In: Fox, R. W. & Lears, T. J. (Eds.), *The Culture of Consumption: Critical Essays in American History, 1880–1980*. Pantheon, New York, pp. 1–38.

McKendrick, N., Brewer, J., & Plumb, J. H. (1982) *The Birth of a Consumer Society: The Commercialization of Eighteenth-Century England*. Indiana University Press, Bloomington.

Miller, D. (1995) Consumption and Commodities. *Annual Review of Anthropology* 24: 141–61.

Ritson, M. & Elliott, R. (1999) The Social Uses of Advertising: An Ethnographic Study of Adolescent Advertising Audiences. *Journal of Consumer Research* 26 (December): 260–77.

Ritzer, G. (2004) *The McDonaldization of Society: Revised New Century Edition*. Pine Forge Press, Thousand Oaks, CA.

Warhol, A. (1975) *The Philosophy of Andy Warhol: From A to B and Back Again*. Harcourt Brace, New York.

consumption of music

Tia DeNora

Music consumption has been a central topic in music sociology over the past three decades. Pursued through quantitative (Bourdieu 1984) and qualitative (DiMaggio 1982) methods, classic work in the area has highlighted music's role as a medium of status distinction. In more recent years, the links between taste and status have been shown to be, in the American context at least, more complex, the highbrow/lowbrow divide modulating into an omnivore–univore model (Peterson & Simkus 1992).

Work produced in the heyday of the Birmingham Cultural Studies tradition shifted the focus from taste and boundary maintenance to social identity construction and to a focus on style, subculture, and self. Most notably, this focus pointed scholarly attention from reception to consumption, from a focus on *what* meanings were found or attributed to musical works, to a focus on the process of meaning making and its role in the constitution of the

life world. In Willis's (1978) work, for example, the investigative lens examined actors themselves as they came to establish connections between music and forms of action and interaction, the links they forged between preferred forms of music and forms of social life and social activity. In this sense, music provided, via its consumption, tools and repertories for action. This shift has been marked by a series of key studies that trace the appropriation and reappropriation within music scholarship and popular culture of key composers and the meanings of their works (Gomart & Hennion 1999), following that process in terms of what, in a performative sense, can be "done" with music reception.

While debates concerning the provenance of meaning continue within some musicological circles, music sociology and the social psychology of music have long-since left this concern behind in favor of music's social functions in natural, everyday life settings (Sloboda & O'Neill 2001). In recent years, the focus on consumption has turned to individual and group listening practices, and to the concept of aesthetic ecology. Gomart and Hennion (1999) and DeNora (2000) have depicted music's use as a technology of self-construction and have explored the minute practices by which actors come to charge music with meaning and power. Gomart and Hennion refer to these practices as "techniques of preparation," procedures of framing music so as to self-induce particular dispositions. They describe, for example, how their interviewees readied themselves for particular emotional responses that they knew, under the right conditions, music would elicit. In this sense, their research highlights the interactive character of music's emotional and social effects, how actors empower music to act "over" them in listening contexts. A related study by Bull (2000) describes how urban residents make use of the personal stereo to render their environments habitable, in particular modulating or cancelling the buffeting and strain of travel on public transport, and unwanted "noise" (including the music of other people, whether in the background, from a boombox, or escaping through headphones).

The history of music consumption has been re-examined in recent years by Maisonneuve (2001), who has considered the role of listening and broadcast technology and its "config-uration" of the listening subject. Like Bull, Maisonneuve has emphasized the vastly increased possibilities for private consumption afforded by recording technology since the early twentieth century. She has focused in particular on the intensification of personal modes of experiencing the "love for music." Maisonneuve finds empiri-cal purchase on these issues with the concept of the listening "set-up" – the conglomerate of technological devices, the material cultural envir-onment in which listening occurs – and the var-ious material and textual artifacts that make up the instruments of listening – liner notes, music reviews, the phonograph or CD player, and so on. The listener is thus conceived as a node within a network of people and artifacts.

This work has highlighted music's role as a resource in self-regulatory strategies and, in turn, the connections between such strategies and institutional requirements, such as the need to engage in emotional work. DeNora (2000), for example, found that respondents described how they used music to relax after a hard day, or to "get in the mood" or "set the scene" for various social tasks and obligations, from attendance at evening meetings, to erotic encounters.

The concept of music consumption has been broadened to include more subtle or tacit fea-tures of "consumption" in an educational con-text where they are pursued ethnographically. There, acts of music performance, instrument choice, and the social distribution of musical activities can be seen to further sexual stereo-typing, providing exemplars of what each sex is like or suited to. Music, in other words, can be seen to provide terms or analogues with which to think about the "differences" between boys and girls. In this way, music "gets into" con-ventional thought patterns; it provides a tem-plate against which to gauge thought and response and a map for the articulation of social and conceptual phenomena.

A further development has been a focus on what music may come to afford, in particular the non-cognitive, embodied dimension of music-as-resource. This perspective has been investi-gated in quasi-public contexts where music is seen to provide a parameter for the production of agency, albeit un- or subconsciously imbibed, as

in the retail sector (North & Hargreaves 1997). It has also been investigated in music therapy, an area too-often mistaken as distant from cultural sociological concerns. One area for further inves-tigation in sociomusical study can be found at the nexus of music, bodily praxis, and bodily phenomena – music's connection to blood pres-sure, heart rate, and pain perception is a classic theme in medical music therapy. Bringing this focus out into the study of social institutions and occasions has the potential to illuminate new micro mechanisms of the interaction order and, perhaps, enrich current debate within sociol-ogy on the mind–body issue by highlighting the material and temporal dimensions of action.

SEE ALSO: Consumption, Youth Culture and; Music; Music and Media; Taste, Sociology of

REFERENCES AND SUGGESTED READINGS

Bourdieu, P. (1984) *Distinction: A Social Critique of the Judgment of Taste*. Trans. R. Nice. Polity Press, Cambridge.
Bull, M. (2000) *Sounding out the City*. Berg, Oxford.
DeNora, T. (2000) *Music in Everyday Life*. Cambridge University Press, Cambridge.
DiMaggio, P. (1982) Cultural Entrepreneurship in Nineteenth-Century Boston: The Creation of an Organizational Base for High Culture in America. *Media, Culture and Society* 4: 35–50, 303–22.
Gomart, E. & Hennion, A. (1999) A Sociology of Attachment: Music Amateurs, Drug Users. In: Law, J. & Hazzart, J. (Eds.), *Actor Network Theory and After*. Blackwell, Oxford.
Maisonneuve, S. (2001) Between History and Com-modity: The Production of a Musical Patrimony Through the Record in the 1920–1930s. *Poetics* 29 (2): 89–108.
North, A. & Hargreaves, D. (1997) Music and Con-sumer Behavior. In: Hargreaves, D. & North, A. (Eds.), *The Social Psychology of Music*. Oxford University Press, Oxford.
Peterson, R. & Simkus, A. (1992) How Musical Tastes Mark Occupational Status Groups. In: Lamont, M. & Fournier, M. (Eds.), *Cultivating Differences: Symbolic Boundaries and the Making of Inequality*. University of Chicago Press, Chi-cago, pp. 152–86.
Sloboda, J. & O' Neill, S. (2001) Emotions in Every-day Listening to Music. In: *Music and Emotion:*

748 *consumption, provisioning and*

Theory and Research. Oxford University Press, Oxford.

Willis, P. (1978) *Profane Culture*. Routledge, London.

consumption, provisioning and

Dale Southerton

Provisioning refers to the social and economic organization of the delivery and consumption of goods and services. Its conceptual application falls within three, not mutually exclusive, areas. First is the relationship between production and consumption, spheres of economic and social life often treated empirically and theoretically as separate from one another. Connections between production and consumption are acknowledged (supply and demand being examples), but their relationship tends to be approached from production- or consumption-led perspectives (Lury 1996). Second, by bringing together production and consumption, provisioning is a concept employed to address socioeconomic change. Third, it draws attention to modes other than economic markets through which goods and services reach consumers.

The concept has its origins in the "new urban sociology" of the 1970s. In *The Urban Question* (1977), Castells represented the city as a site of "collective consumption," an alternative terrain to that of private consumption in commercial markets, highlighting the role of the state in providing for consumers as a public

collective (such as health care and urban infrastructures). Debate emerged surrounding the impact on social relations of shifts between collective and private forms of consumption. Saunders (1986) argued that the principal social cleavage in the UK was no longer class but differential access to consumption – with those reliant on state provisioning (principally in the form of state housing) being distinguished from those with access (through their affluence) to the growing varieties of goods and services provisioned through markets. While not theoretically commensurate, some accounts of consumer society suggest similar divisions. Bauman (1988) distinguished between the "seduced" (into the consumer playground by the market) and the "repressed" (those dependent on the state and subject to its planning and management), while John Galbraith's *The Culture of Contentment* (1992) presented a similar social division.

The "new urban sociology" and theoretical accounts of consumer society placed the term provisioning on the conceptual map, but it has been through its application in critiques of the relationship between production and consumption that it has found clarity. Two quite different approaches have emerged: "mode of provision" and "systems of provision."

Mode of provision is most readily associated with the work of Warde (1992). It builds on Ray Pahl's *Divisions of Labour* (1984), which highlighted the declining centrality of employment (only one form of work) in social and political consciousness, and emphasized the significance of household self-provisioning (producing goods and services for the household often through the use of technologies such as the washing machine and video recorder) as a source of economic productivity and personal satisfaction. Table 1 outlines an ideal-type model of cycles of production and consumption.

Table 1 Cycles of production and consumption

Mode of provision	Access/social relations	Manner of delivery	Experiences of consumption
Market	Price/exchange	Managerial	Customer/consumer
State	Need/right	Professional	Citizen/client
Household	Family/obligation	Family	Self/family/kinship
Communal	Network/reciprocity	Volunteer	Friend/neighbor/acquaintance

Source: Warde (1992).

The links between each mode of provision should be read as tendencies. At the simplest level, the model emphasizes the point that much consumption occurs outside of both market and state modes of provision. Food represents a good example. One might purchase a meal from a restaurant, prepare it oneself, have it provided through the state (such as state-subsidized school meals), prepared by someone else in their household, or eat at the home of a friend. These are ways in which food can be provisioned within society. Each mode involves distinct social rules that govern distribution and access, present different circumstances of delivery, and are located within particular social relations that surround the experience of final consumption. Together, these represent the discrete elements which connect and configure production and consumption.

The systems of provision approach is associated with the work of Fine and Leopold (1993). Criticizing theories of consumption as "horizontal" (i.e., accounts that piece together explanations based on a selection of goods which are then generalized to the consumption of all material goods), they call for a "vertical" approach. First, explanations must be specific to particular commodities or groups of commodities. Second, each commodity must be analyzed according to the interaction between the factors that give rise to it – particularly production, distribution, retailing, consumption, and material culture. Finally, these factors form a differentiated chain of activities for each consumption good – an integral unit termed a system of provision. To illustrate, they provide a detailed analysis of the food and clothing systems of provision, where interconnection of elements across the supply chain (in the case of food, from agricultural regulation to changing relationships between manufacturers, distributors, and retailers, to cultural shifts toward healthier eating) act to configure the system as a whole. Consequently, horizontal explanations (such as consumers demanding variety or convenience) fail to capture the complexities of socioeconomic organization which differentiate between sets of commodities.

One of the difficulties (yet also a strength) of the modes of provision approach is that it fails to instruct where to draw boundaries between different modes and their related cycles of production and consumption. People drive private cars on public roads. State modes of provision have, in many societies, become increasingly marketized (with internal markets in welfare services and public–private finance initiatives). Yet, the framework remains instructive precisely because shifting modes of provision highlight the changing social relations of production and consumption. Questions also emerge as to what constitutes different modes of provision. Can food cooked at home but purchased from a food retailer be regarded as provisioned through the market or the home? Ultimately, the answer would be the market. However, a more nuanced observation is made possible: the combination of mode of provision, access, and manner of delivery affects how that consumption is experienced. In this case, while food might be purchased through the market, it is provisioned through the work that is done in the domestic sphere as part of familial obligations and that transforms ingredients into a meal (DeVault 1991). Thus, consumers are also producers and production is not reduced simply to supply.

The systems of provision approach shares similar empirical and conceptual difficulties. Focusing on commodity chains again raises questions of where to locate the boundaries between sets of commodities. It is also difficult to decipher precisely what key factors influence each link in the system, not least because the harder one looks, the more factors one finds. Systems of provision can also be criticized for being either "linear," with one link having a direct causal effect on the next, or tautological, because any system can only be analyzed within the terms of reference set out by the identification of the boundaries of that system.

Despite such criticisms, both approaches represent important theoretical frameworks for analyzing the changing social and economic relations and organization of production and consumption. They increasingly find salience within critiques of consumer culture and its emphasis on the apparent commodification of ever more aspects of daily life and, through their emphasis on connecting production and consumption, have been employed in debates ranging from environmental sustainability to the construction of "demand."

SEE ALSO: Consumption, Experiential; Consumption, Mass Consumption, and Consumer Culture; Consumption, Urban/City as Consumerspace; Lifestyle Consumption; Markets; Supermarkets; Welfare State

REFERENCES AND SUGGESTED READINGS

Bauman, Z. (1988) *Freedom*. Open University Press, Milton Keynes.
DeVault, M. (1991) *Feeding the Family: The Social Organization of Caring as Gendered Work*. University of Chicago Press, Chicago.
Fine, B. & Leopold, E. (1993) *The World of Consumption*. Routledge, London.
Gershuny, J. (1978) *After Industrial Society? The Emerging Self-Service Economy*. Macmillan, London.
Harvey, M., Quilley, S., & Beynon, H. (2002) *Exploring the Tomato: Transformations of Nature, Economy, and Society*. Edward Elgar, London.
Lury, C. (1996) *Consumer Culture*. Polity Press, Cambridge.
Saunders, P. (1986) *Social Theory and the Urban Question*, 2nd edn. Hutchinson, London.
Southerton, D., Chappells, H., & Van Vliet, B. (Eds.) (2004) *Sustainable Consumption: The Implications of Changing Infrastructures of Provision*. Edward Elgar, London.
Warde, A. (1992) Notes of the Relationship Between Production and Consumption. In: Burrows, R. & Marsh, C. (Eds.), *Consumption and Class: Divisions and Change*. Macmillan, London, pp. 15–31.
Warde, A. & Martens, L. (2000) *Eating Out: Social Differentiation, Consumption, and Pleasure*. Cambridge University Press, Cambridge.

consumption, religion and

Kathleen M. O'Neil

The connection between religion and consumption has been investigated by a wide range of scholars. Topics examining this relationship include: the rise of capitalism and the nature of modern capitalism, competition among religious organizations for religious consumers, the consumption of religious goods and services, as well as consumption as a secular religion.

In *The Protestant Ethic and the Spirit of Capitalism* (1958), Max Weber argued that Puritan religious beliefs, particularly Calvinist doctrine, were among the necessary conditions leading to the development of capitalism. Believing that salvation is predestined but not knowing for certain if they were chosen, Calvinists sought confidence in the fate of their souls through intense engagement in worldly activities. This ethic of hard work was coupled with a belief in the virtue of leading an austere life, including restricting the consumption of luxury goods. Consequently, profits were available for reinvestment in economic enterprise. Thus economic acquisition came to be seen as an end in itself, rather than exclusively as a means of satisfying needs and desires.

Contemporary scholars have questioned whether this process is found only in the West and if religious values identified by Weber are peculiar to Protestant Christianity. Broadening Weber's view, Collins (1997) noted that such beliefs were found in Zen Buddhism in late medieval Japan. Buddhist movements of the time rejected ceremonial religion. Instead, the activities of everyday life became regarded as opportunities for meditative practice. This focus on engagement with the world was also combined with a critique of lavish lifestyles. This combination of religious beliefs facilitated investment in commercial activities, enabling the transition to a market-based economy. Collins also argued that in both the East and the West, religious organizations often contained the first entrepreneurs.

The extent to which the lifestyle of Calvinists and other Protestants involved limits on consumption has also been questioned. Wealthy Dutch Calvinists of the seventeenth century participated in a variety of forms of conspicuous consumption, but their style of consumption reflected an embarrassment with wealth stemming from their religious beliefs (Schama 1987). While the affluent of Italy and France had long preferred ostentatious building facades, Calvinists preferred less ornate exteriors. Interior display, on the other hand, frequently involved luxurious materials: dining tables inlaid with mother-of-pearl and floors constructed of marble were not uncommon.

Paintings became popular among the middle class. In dress Calvinists preferred somber colors, especially black and white, but the materials were first class: black satin or velvet adorned with white collars of linen or lace. Nevertheless, for some seventeenth-century Calvinists income rose even faster than expenditure, and religion, while not limiting consumption, influenced style.

Scholars have also been concerned with the role of the Protestant work ethic in modern capitalism. Some suggest it has fallen away and been replaced by a consumer ethos. Others claim that a culture of hedonism has long existed along with the Protestant ethic. Bell argued that traditional American values of hard work, restraint, and delayed gratification have been replaced by a culture that emphasizes newness of experience and a demand for pleasure and leisure through consumption. Gradually work has become a means of increasing consumption, rather than being viewed as a valued end in itself.

Not denying Weber's claims, Campbell (1987) argued that a romantic ethic promoting a spirit of consumerism developed in parallel with the Protestant ethic and the spirit of capitalism. Arising out of Romanticism at the start of the nineteenth century, hedonism was an important ingredient in the development of consumerism. Pleasure and emotion became a defining feature of life; the search for pleasure led to a desire to consume novel things and an eagerness for new experiences. Campbell argued that consumption played a critical role in the Industrial Revolution and continues to influence the character of modern capitalism.

Sociologists of religion have examined consumption by investigating religion as a marketplace. One theoretical approach conceptualizes religious organizations as marketers of religious products competing with each other for religious consumers (church members). Others have focused empirically on the relationship between contemporary religious practices and consumption.

The theoretical approach of Finke and Stark (1992) was developed to examine the relationship between religious pluralism and religious participation. They argued that an open consumer marketplace for religion, as opposed to a state-dominated monopoly, promotes individual participation in religion. Their proposed mechanism is competition. Religious economies are expected to behave like commercial economies: the more religious organizations there are, the more competition there is for religious consumers. Consequently, the leaders of religious organizations are motivated to produce better religious products, which in turn attract more people to religion. This theoretical argument has been used to explain the relatively high level of religiosity in the United States as compared to most European countries. Competition among religious organizations is expected to be high in the United States, because unlike many European countries the United States lacks a state-sponsored religion (or religious monopoly). A large number of empirical studies have investigated these claims, and the overall findings have been mixed. Many studies of particular times and places have not found that religious pluralism is positively correlated with religious participation (see Chaves & Gorski 2001 for a critical review of this literature).

Analyses of changes in the religious landscape suggest that religious practices have increasingly become connected to consumption. Wuthnow (1998) argued that in the 1950s a "spirituality of dwelling" predominated, where individuals sought the sacred within religious organizations, like churches and synagogues. By the 1960s, a "spirituality of seeking" had increased in popularity. A quest culture led people to look beyond established religious institutions for spiritual direction and insight. Most recently, a "spirituality of practice" has become prominent. Appealing to those uncomfortable within a single religious community but wanting more than endless spiritual seeking, this approach centers on various devotional practices used to connect everyday life to the divine. Both spiritual quests and practice-based spirituality are intertwined with the consumption of particular goods and services.

While interest in spirituality is not new, in the late twentieth century forums for spiritual seekers proliferated. While some forums include less commercial groups like science fiction clubs and self-help meetings, the emphasis on self-understanding and spiritual seeking among the post-World War II generations facilitated the emergence of new spiritual industries. Books, videos, music, psychic services, natural food stores, and retreat centers have become outlets for those seeking a variety of spiritual resources. Suppliers of these goods and services are found both inside and outside of established religion. In particular there has been an increase in the printing and sale of books on spiritual matters. With sections devoted to Buddhism, Native American religion, New Age spirituality, self-help, and religious fiction, bookstores have become the most important centers of spirituality apart from religious congregations. Publishers of print materials have successfully stirred customer interest and tapped into unfulfilled needs, leading some scholars to refer to bookstores as the churches and synagogues of the current period.

Practice-based spirituality often involves efforts to simplify and be more conscious regarding consumption. Ironically, new products and services have emerged to assist in the simplification endeavor: restaurants and stores that provide wholefoods, services such as yoga instruction and guided meditation, and wellness clinics providing holistic healing treatments. In addition, spiritual practices are increasingly structured around specialized niches, such as ecospirituality, feminist spirituality, or combining Christian beliefs and physical fitness. Spiritual entrepreneurs have helped to create those niches. Alternatives and complementary additions to traditional religion are increasingly found in the market.

Religious holidays are increasingly associated with consumption. It has been observed that shopping and gift exchange has replaced the Christian story of the birth of Jesus as the primary meaning associated with Christmas. The purchase of gifts to be exchanged during religious holidays is a major component of the economy of the United States. Many large retail stores conduct 25 percent or more of their business in the weeks preceding Christmas, and American consumers spend $200 billion during the Christmas shopping season or an average of $800 per family (Farrell 2003). In response to the dominance of Christmas and the shopping rituals associated with it, the winter holidays of other religions have been elevated in relative importance.

Examination of the devotion to consumption itself has also been a theme at least since the

writing of Thorstein Veblen. Recently, fast food restaurants, amusement parks, shopping malls, and similar settings have been conceptualized as cathedrals of consumption. Ritzer (2005) argues that such settings drive hyperconsumption. As consumers become disenchanted with rationalized consumption, including the uniformity of available services and products, newer and more magical settings are created to reenchant the experience of shopping. At the same time, the settings themselves are highly rationalized and are being replicated across the world. Shopping malls have become some of the largest and most popular public spaces in urban areas. Others have argued that participation in fashion and shopping involves meaning-making acts. Part of the construction of the perfect self, consumption has been conceptualized as a secular ritual, in part through the efforts of advertising (Twitchell 1999).

SEE ALSO: Asceticism; Conspicuous Consumption; Consumption, Cathedrals of; Consumption, Mass Consumption, and Consumer Culture; Consumption Rituals; Hyperconsumption/Overconsumption; New Age; Religion, Sociology of; Shopping; Shopping Malls

REFERENCES AND SUGGESTED READINGS

Campbell, C. (1987) *The Romantic Ethic and the Spirit of Modern Consumerism.* Blackwell, Oxford.

Chaves, M. & Gorski, P. S. (2001) Religious Pluralism and Religious Participation. *Annual Review of Sociology* 27: 261–81.

Collins, R. (1997) An Asian Route to Capitalism: Religious Economy and the Origins of Self-Transforming Growth in Japan. *American Sociological Review* 62(6): 843–65.

Farrell, J. J. (2003) *One Nation Under Goods: Malls and the Seduction of American Shopping.* Smithsonian Books, Washington, DC.

Finke, R. & Stark, R. (1992) *The Churching of America, 1776–1990: Winners and Losers in Our Religious Economy.* Rutgers University Press, New Brunswick, NJ.

Ritzer, G. (2005) *Enchanting a Disenchanted World: Revolutionizing the Means of Consumption,* 2nd edn. Pine Forge Press, Thousand Oaks, CA.

Roof, W. C. (1999) *Spiritual Marketplace: Baby Boomers and the Remaking of American Religion.* Princeton University Press, Princeton.

Schama, S. (1987) *The Embarrassment of Riches: An Interpretation of Dutch Culture in the Golden Age.* William Collins Sons, London.

Twitchell, J. (1999) *Lead Us Into Temptation: The Triumph of American Materialism.* Columbia University Press, New York.

Wuthnow, R. (1998) *After Heaven: Spirituality in America Since the 1950s.* University of California Press, Berkeley.

consumption rituals

Cele C. Otnes

Consumption rituals can be defined as holidays, special occasions, and other sacred events characterized by the intensive (and sometimes excessive) consumption of goods, services, and experiences. At such events, individuals engage in both consumption and other behaviors with actions that can be characterized as formal, serious, and intense (Rook 1985). Consumption rituals are distinct from other, more mundane types of consumption-laden activities to the extent that they provide opportunities for individual and social transformations which may be temporary or permanent. For example, eating a family dinner might contain some elements of ritualistic behavior (e.g., saying grace at the beginning). In contrast, dinners occurring on Christmas or Thanksgiving are regarded as ritualistic because they commemorate important holidays in the culture, involve gatherings of people not present at "everyday" dinners, and feature special foods and beverages that are reserved and prepared for such occasions.

Consumption rituals also often feature the exchange of gifts. Such exchange can feature reciprocity that is either immediate or delayed. For example, the social norms governing Christmas gift giving require that a giver and recipient typically engage in simultaneous exchange. However, at other social events such as weddings, a giver expects reciprocity when he or she (or a close relative) is married. Because gift giving typically involves imperfect communication between the giver and recipient, researchers have explored the dynamics of this activity across the various gift-giving occasions in many cultures (e.g., Belk & Coon 1993; Ruth et al. 1999; Joy 2001).

Structural and functional elements of consumption rituals can reveal the potency of these occasions. Dennis Rook describes how consumption rituals can be understood in terms of structural elements such as ritual artifacts, ritual scripts, ritual performance roles, and ritual audience. *Ritual artifacts* at a Thanksgiving dinner might include special table decorations, china and silver that are typically kept separate from ordinary cutlery and dishes, and special foods such as a whole turkey which, while plentiful in the American food chain, has maintained a culturally sacred position as a food that should only really be consumed on holidays (Wallendorf & Arnould 1991). *Ritual scripts* are normative guidelines that instruct participants how to consume ritual artifacts. They range from the more formal scripts (e.g., having a Thanksgiving toast), to less formally articulated, but nevertheless influential, rules for behavior (e.g., men should watch football after Thanksgiving dinner while women clear the table).

Ritual performance roles are the sets of behaviors delineated as appropriate (or inappropriate) for each ritual participant. In the ritual script described above, women are assigned the roles of housecleaners, and men the roles of passive spectators. Yet recent shifts in gender roles have resulted in resentment on the part of women, who feel they are constrained by the rules of this ritual, and by many rituals in particular. Moreover, research indicates that "sociological ambivalence," or the mixed emotions that can arise because of role conflict between individuals, can be quite prevalent in ritualistic consumption contexts. For example, brides often wish to have more control over customizing their wedding planning than traditional bridal retailers have allowed (Otnes et al. 1997). As such, brides-to-be often find themselves caught between being grateful for professional assistance with planning such an elaborate and typically unfamiliar ritual and being angry and disappointed with restrictions on their choices regarding the purchase and consumption of artifacts.

Finally, the *ritual audience* involves those consumers who may not be directly involved in a ritual, but who may view it from near or far. While some occasions such as Thanksgiving have few participants who stand on the sidelines, consider the size and composition of the ritual audience who "consumed" the wedding of Prince Charles and Lady Diana Spencer in 1981. While the spectators inside St. Paul's Cathedral consisted of around 1,000 family, friends, politicians, and other wellwishers, the television audience for the wedding was estimated to be 750 million worldwide. Thus, it is quite possible that the audience for a consumption ritual can greatly exceed the number of more immediate participants.

Functionally, consumption rituals can provide us with what Tom Driver (1991) describes as the three "social gifts" of ritual – order, transformation, and "communitas." Order refers to the ability of a ritual to provide structure to our lives and actions, and also to the fact that rituals often possess a fairly fixed sequence of activities within them (e.g., having a special breakfast on Christmas morning, then opening presents afterwards in a particular order within the family). Transformation refers to the ability of a consumption ritual to change the participant in either a slight or significant manner. One woman remarked that when her boyfriend presented her with an engagement ring, she could immediately "see the future, and that I'd have children someday" (Otnes & Pleck 2003). Communitas, a term borrowed from anthropologist Victor Turner, refers to the ability of a consumption ritual to strengthen social bonds with those in the participant's immediate community, and perhaps with those in more peripheral social networks as well.

Research on consumption rituals has its roots in early anthropological studies of such activities as gift giving. Likewise, sociologists have published many studies on gift giving, but typically fewer on the celebration of holidays. Yet the impetus for much of the work on consumption rituals was Rook's seminal article, "The Ritual Dimension of Consumer Behavior," published in 1985. Since that time, scholars in anthropology, consumer behavior, and sociology alike have conducted detailed studies of many holidays and occasions (e.g., Miller 1993), as well as new variants of existing rituals (gift giving in the workplace; Ruth 2003) and even the emergence of new rituals (Sherry & Kozinets 2003). Because of the complex and interdisciplinary nature of the topic, and because rituals are often protracted and involve many members of social networks, qualitative research methods are often employed to provide rich, insightful understandings of these consumption contexts. Future research directions in the area include exploring the ways rituals change meaning over time, the cross-cultural transference of consumption rituals, and the emergence of new rituals with heavy consumption components.

SEE ALSO: Conspicuous Consumption; Consumption, Mass Consumption, and Consumer Culture; Rite/Ritual; Ritual

REFERENCES AND SUGGESTED READINGS

Belk, R. W. & Coon, G. S. (1993) Gift Giving and Agapic Love: An Alternative to the Exchange Paradigm Based on Dating Experiences. *Journal of Consumer Research* 5(20): 393–417.
Driver, T. (1991) *The Magic of Ritual.* HarperCollins, New York.
Joy, A. (2001) Gift Giving in Hong Kong and the Continuum of Social Ties. *Journal of Consumer Research* 28 (September): 239–56.
Miller, D. (1993) *Unwrapping Christmas.* Clarendon, Oxford.
Otnes, C. C. & Pleck, E. H. (2003) *Cinderella Dreams: The Allure of the Lavish Wedding.* University of California Press, Berkeley.
Otnes, C. C., Lowrey, T. M., & Shrum, L. J. (1997) Toward an Understanding of Consumer Ambivalence. *Journal of Consumer Research* 5(24): 80–93.
Rook, D. W. (1985) The Ritual Dimension of Consumer Behavior. *Journal of Consumer Research* 5(12): 252–64.
Ruth, J. A. (2003) Gift Exchange Rituals in the Workplace: A Social Roles Interpretation. In: Otnes, C. C. & Lowrey, T. M. (Eds.), *Contemporary Consumption Rituals.* Erlbaum, Mahwah, NJ, pp. 181–212.
Ruth, J. A., Otnes, C. C., & Brunel, F. F. (1999) Gift Receipt and the Reformulation of Relationships. *Journal of Consumer Research* 5(25): 385–402.
Sherry, J. F., Jr. & Kozinets, R. V. (2003) Sacred Iconography in Secular Space: Altars, Alters, and Alterity at the Burning Man Project. In: Otnes, C. C. & Lowrey, T. M. (Eds.), *Contemporary Consumption Rituals.* Erlbaum, Mahwah, NJ, pp. 291–311.
Wallendorf, M. & Arnould, E. (1991) "We Gather Together": Consumption Rituals of Thanksgiving Day. *Journal of Consumer Research* 5(18): 13–31.

consumption, spectacles of

Sam Binkley

The use of the word "spectacle" in relation to practices of consumption has a specific intellectual genealogy that extends to the radical critiques of a group of French Marxists – the Situationists or the Situationist International – though the term has also come to denote a broader transformation of consumer culture into an expression of visual media. Deriving from Guy Debord's use of the term in the title of his 1967 anti-capitalist screed *The Society of the Spectacle*, to speak of spectacles of consumption is to invoke a critical reading of a fetishized relation to commodities that obscures real social relations, and passifies the spectator-consumer in a synthetic world (Debord 1994). Spectacular consumption, in this sense, asks us to see only the appearance of commodities and not their deeper social character – a misrecognition which alienates us from our personal and social lives while presenting the world of goods as one possessing dynamism and livelihood. While the world of spectacle becomes increasingly vital, so the theory goes, one's own life becomes increasingly empty and thing-like. Yet, in a more modest sense, to speak of consumption as spectacular is to refer to the preponderance of visual symbols, images, and aestheticized surfaces in the design and marketing of goods and services, with no specific claim concerning its wider cultural and political impact (Featherstone 1991). In what follows, the spectacular nature of consumption is discussed with reference to these two distinct meanings: as a general expression of visual culture, and as a uniquely fetishized relation to social life.

VISUAL CULTURE

Commentators from a variety of fields have described the contemporary cultural condition in terms of the ascendance of visual images and representations over other media and forms of social engagement. Whether under the rubric of postmodernity, late capitalism, or post-Fordism, everyday life is believed to be increasingly defined by new ways of looking and seeing that are historically unique to the conditions of advanced capitalist societies (Lash & Urry 1994; Mirzoeff 1999). Under such conditions, the eye is called upon to perform complex cognitive and interpretive tasks necessary for navigating richly symbolic environments and interactions and to take in staggering volumes of information. Through visual media, audiences are demanded to interpret meanings encoded in cryptic and nuanced messages and consider differently the manner in which representations correspond to the purportedly real worlds and social relations outside the image. Such developments, it is argued, impact as powerfully on individual subjectivity as on the character and content of interpersonal behavior and collective forms generally. These assumptions have informed a broad new field of scholarly inquiry loosely dubbed "visual culture," an approach that combines the attention to popular cultural forms, everyday life practices and the micro-politics of identity and cultural life typically identified with cultural studies, with a historically informed reflection on the changing nature of vision in contemporary society. Drawing from psychoanalysis and film theory, an expanded approach to the history of art and a nuanced sense of the interpretive agency of media audiences in their everyday practices, scholars in this interdisciplinary subfield derive a unique warrant for a study of culture and society organized around visual practices of looking, representation, surveillance, and identity formation (Foster 1988). Against the backdrop of a reading of society as spectacle understood as an interconnected set of practices of looking and imaging, a range of social phenomena from sexuality and identity to urban planning, policing, social difference, and cultural change can be read as expressions of changing visual practices. A specifically sociological version of this thesis is evident in the more modest form of a "visual sociology" approach which, while expressing a similar engagement with the visual, is largely limited to methodological assertions of the legitimacy of photography as a research tool (Prosser 1998; Schroeder 2002).

Yet underlying this assumption about the emergence of vision as an evermore hegemonic force in culture and society is a wider account of the expansion of consumption and consumer culture, often read in a negative light. The commodification of social life is read as serving the individualizing ends of the capitalist consumer economy by replacing collective identities with highly individualistic consumer lifestyles, shaped not on concrete engagement with real social worlds, but on imaginary investments in the world of images (Ewen 1988). For scholars in communications and media studies traditions, such visual saturation is traceable to the growth of new media such as television, cinema, photographic reproduction, and more recently digital and electronic media. These developments together foster a unique social disengagement and collapse of civil society through the pacification and atomization of audiences for whom the interpretation of content is reduced to the unthinking reception of retinal, as opposed to discursive, stimuli. For sociologists, the visualization of culture is attributable to the overall weakening of traditional class distinctions and the status hierarchies that expressed them. Such conditions are brought on by the proliferation and inflationary overproduction of status-bestowing commodities and lifestyles in a culture of accelerated consumption. With the democratization of conspicuous forms of consumption once reserved for cultural elites, a general aestheticization of daily life elevates the fleeting, impressionistic appearance over and against other more durable displays of status communication – a quality of social life that is particularly acute in urban contexts (Simmel 1971). For economists, the increasing emphasis on consumption and the maintenance of high levels of consumer demand has brought about an expansion of the visual realm through advertising and product design as the colonization of desire has become more and more the focus of economic growth. And for cultural historians, the expansion of the visual realm is identified with the growing sophistication and semiotic complexity of retail environments and themed spaces, particularly in new postmodern cities and their outlying regions (Leach 1993). While the views of these authors are hardly uniform, they share in common a sense of visual saturation as a cultural trend affecting a broader fragmentation of

personal identity and social life, resulting from the colonization of more and more realms of culture by the consumer market. Perhaps the earliest and most succinct reflection on this process is found in Marx's writings on commodity fetishism, whose assertion of the misrecognition of economic value in the appearance of the commodity form came to influence a century of writings on the spectacular nature of consumption as a more general instance of social misrecognition for political ends. This critique established the groundwork for a general suspicion of consumption based on the presumably dangerous properties of visual images.

FETISHISM OF COMMODITIES

"A commodity appears, at first sight, a very trivial thing," Marx famously wrote in his analysis of the "Fetishism of the Commodity," perhaps the most memorable passage of volume 1 of *Capital* (Marx 1976). But while the ostensible aim of this passage rested with a critique of contemporary nineteenth-century political economy, this goal was far exceeded in a long tradition of twentieth-century cultural Marxism that saw central elements of this analysis applied to fetishization in a broader cultural context. In its original form, Marx's critique was relatively straightforward: political economists, he contended, were flawed in their analysis of the origin of economic value through their narrow adherence to the already constituted objects of value – commodities – whose value was derived not from the kinds of collective efforts put into their manufacture, but from their relation to each other in the marketplace, expressed in their price. Such an approach, Marx wrote, betrayed a fetishistic relation to the commodity. It saw only the appearance of value reflected abstractly in its price, its "exchange value," and not the true origin of such value, which in reality derived from the labor invested in its production. More accurately, such a fetishized view ignored the specifically collective forms such labor took as modern industrial production, with all of its radical and transformative potential. Thus to perceive the commodity only for its "exchange value" was to fall victim to its appearances, its visible manifestation or its spectacle, and to ignore the true social character embodied in what the commodity was in reality – a "use value," whose origins and ultimate ends were not individual but collective. Capitalist relations of exchange, for Marx, reproduced precisely this fetishization, wherein the social character of economic activity was concealed or mystified behind a veil of illusion manifested in the simple appearance of commodities themselves, viewed not as the social and historical product of collective human endeavor, but as things artificially invested with a value they could not, as objects, realistically possess.

Fetishized commodities, in other words, exhibit relations between people as relations between things. Like religious fetishes, they embody falsely externalized powers, projections of power, meaning, and value whose real origins lie not truly in those things themselves, but with the relations that produced them, and with the agency and creativity of the ones who produce and consume them. And, as is well known, such misrecognition of a collective social whole in a falsely individualized fragment served the political instrument of the ruling capitalist class, whose survival and prosperity depended on the suppression of such totalizing apprehensions, and the channeling of all social needs into the market. To fetishize commodities, then, was to live in a state of ideological false consciousness, in which one fails to perceive the social realities concealed behind false appearances.

In the writings of twentieth-century proponents of cultural Marxism, from Georg Lukács to the Frankfurt School theorists, the visual quality of commodities is implicated in the notion of commodity fetishism, expanded to include a far wider range of meanings and cultural values. The individual's relation to herself is subjected to a form of ideological reversal or alienation, in which her own life as a social relation appears more thingish, while the commodity appears to have life – a process Lukács called reification. Spectacular consumption is, in this sense, alienating: because the images of consumption can possess such vitality and meaning, such meaning is drained from the real experiences we have of ourselves

in our social lives, which now appear sadly short of ideal perfection. Through the image, commodities become subjects, while the subjectivity of the viewer and the consumer increasingly appears as a foreign and alien object.

Indeed, consumption, viewed in such a fetishized form, becomes a stand-in not just for community and collective membership, but for the more general experience of modernity itself – a predilection that is not uniformly negative even in the twentieth-century Marxist tradition. Consumption as a metaphor for modernity is embodied optimistically in Walter Benjamin's writings on the flâneur, the euphoric stroller of Parisian arcades and markets described by Baudelaire as emblematic of the ephemeral experience of capitalist modernity itself (Benjamin 1973). Indeed, the uniquely spectacular world unfolded by the commodity serves a potentially radical function for Benjamin as a dream world wherein alternative social horizons are dialectically hatched. But in the words of other critics, most notably Marcuse, Lukács, and the proponents of the Frankfurt School, but also in the French Marxist tradition that included Lefebvre, Barthes, and Debord, such fetishization produced a numbing effect on the individual, forcing an alienating and atomizing culture (Lefebvre 1971).

The linking of these expanded uses of Marx's theory of commodity fetishism with the visual realm came with Debord's *Society of the Spectacle*, which presently enjoys an almost cult status as an underground classic as proto-postmodernist, pre-punk critique. Debord's view was one in which the spontaneity and vitality that constituted real social life was completely absorbed into the cultural fabric of a commodity form whose penetration into the warp and woof of daily experience and subjectivity had been radically enhanced by the arrival of visual media. In the society of the spectacle, not just commodities on display but all of life itself had become misrecognized as a commodity. The process of fetishism has completely encircled the individual as the perception of fabricated appearances has obscured the real social activity underneath, producing a condition of passivity and boredom. In the spirit of the French student movements of May 1968, Debord's tract resonates with an aesthetic vanguardism in its assessment of the possibilities for rupture and transgression.

CONSUMPTION SPECTACLES

The use of Marx's critique of commodity fetishism as a framework for understanding contemporary consumer culture as a visual process finds its most obvious target in the culture of advertising, where values and meanings that are ultimately historical and social in character are routinely transposed onto commodities. A notable application of this approach comes with Roland Barthes's inquiries into the semiotic ordering of culture, and the part played by advertising images in inducing viewers to make associations between ephemeral cultural values and concrete commodities. In *Mythologies* (1972), Barthes argued the ultimately arbitrary nature of the link connecting signifiers (material expressions of meaning) with signifieds (thoughts or ideas communicated by a given sign). For Barthes, the actual fashioning of meaning, the linking of signifiers and signifieds, was a cultural, historical, and deeply social process involving the creative activity of the reader of signs. Yet it was one whose social origins were often concealed, like the social character of Marx's commodities, behind an ideological form which made meanings appear naturally and timelessly to adhere to symbols and expressions. His memorable analysis of a Panzani Past ad in an essay titled "The Rhetoric of the Image" drove home the force with which this process is so effectively accomplished in visual media.

Barthes's semiotic approach to the critique of advertising has inspired volumes of scholarly studies of consumption as a spectacular event, whose net effect it is to engineer a transfer of meanings from a reservoir of cultural and historical sources into commodities themselves (Goldman & Papson 1996). Judith Williamson's *Decoding Advertisements* (1978) stands out as a memorable work in this tradition: combining a Marxist critique of commodity fetishism with Barthes's analysis of the power of images to establish meanings through connotative associations, Williamson studied the various ways advertising images, through a uniquely visual

vocabulary, absorb social meanings into commodity forms. Williamson's classic account of a perfume ad juxtaposes the image of Catherine Deneuve, a person, with a bottle of perfume, a thing, thus orchestrating a semiotic transfer of meaning in which the commodity emerges with a distinctly reified presence.

Such a semiotic critique of consumption as a spectacular process was ultimately taken as the basis for a radical assessment of contemporary culture as postmodern – a direction identified with Jean Baudrillard and his assessment of the collapse of signifying systems generally under the sheer weight of an accelerated visual culture. In the condition of simulacrum, Marx's thesis on commodity fetishism comes to a nihilistic end, as fetishized appearances foreclose any possibility of the social itself (Baudrillard 1981). Adding to Marx's dyad of use and exchange value, Baudrillard speaks of a third morphology of the commodity, into sign value, wherein commodities are valued for their function as signifiers within signifying chains, and all links with the social as a durable referent have been permanently severed. Under such conditions, it is no longer possible to speak of the obfuscation of the social or the alienation of the subject: the social itself has collapsed or imploded under the circulation of disembodied images, while subjectivity itself has become fragmented in an aesthetic hallucination of reality.

Such broad theories of the commodification of social life through spectacle have applications that extend far beyond the narrow culture of advertising and media, into realms such as public space, the body, retail environments, and the proliferation of personal electronic devices from cell phones to laptops – domains of purported social life that are transfigured into visually consumable spectacles. Perhaps most intriguing among these developments has been a growing concern among urban sociologists and historians with the patterns of urban renewal in the years following the crises of the 1970s. With the demise of the manufacturing base, urban centers are increasingly revitalizing themselves as leisure and recreation centers, driven by service and entertainment industries. The postmodern city is driven by a symbolic economy, staffed by cultural specialists and mediators of visual realms, from artists and designers to architects and actors (Zukin 1991). Amid such transformations, historical textures are enhanced or invented altogether, so as to establish visually themed spaces whose allure, while amenable to the commercial interests of retailers, does little to promote public culture or advance genuine historical understanding.

Notable commentaries on the spectacularlization of social space as an implicit obfuscation of the social have been provided by Frederic Jameson in his description of the qualities of the Westin Bonaventure Hotel in Los Angeles, whose disorientingly vertiginous architecture suggested a new experience of postmodern ephemera, and David Harvey's discussion of "time-space compression" in post-Fordist capitalism. George Ritzer has also disclosed the properties of spectacle as directly implicated in the rationalizing tendencies of market economies carried to new and giddy extremes in the current phase of consumer culture. Ritzer, in his uniquely Weberian nomenclature, has written of the "McDonaldization" or the "reenchantment" of environments colonized by the instrumental imperatives of the profit motive. In several cases, most notably several chapters of *Enchanting a Disenchanted World* (2005), Ritzer comments on a variety of sites, including Las Vegas, Mall of America, and TGI Fridays, for their use of spectacle to achieve the ends of profit, and along the way producing a new etherialization of social life. Variously employing Baudrillardian concepts of the implosion of the social, the de-differentiation of institutions, and the compression of time and space, Ritzer uncovers new highly spectacular modes of consumption in the de-differentiation of information and commerce evidenced by the Home Shopping Network, the compression of time and space apparent in the proliferation of historically themed entertainment complexes, and instances of the implosion of social space in Disneyland, which collapses the many traditional distinctions characteristic of modern societies, such as that between education, amusement, art, civil society, and commerce.

Other inquiries into the transformed character of the social under the regime of spectacle have taken on more micro-level investigations into the spectacularization of the body through studies of tattooing and body modification, read not as a simple process of commodification but of subversion and resistance; as well as inquiries into the changing relations of gender, as bodies themselves are called upon to perform more of the signifying functions of identity (Bordo 1999; Pitts 2003).

SEE ALSO: Commodities, Commodity Fetishism, and Commodification; Consumption, Mass Consumption, and Consumer Culture; Consumption, Visual; Debord, Guy; Postmodern Consumption; Situationists

REFERENCES AND SUGGESTED READINGS

Barthes, R. (1972) *Mythologies*. Trans. A. Lavers. Cape, London.

Barthes, R. (1977) Rhetoric of the Image. In: *Image: Music: Text*. Trans. S. Heath. Hill & Wang, New York, pp. 32–51.

Baudrillard, J. (1981) *For a Critique of the Political Economy of the Sign*. Telos Press, St. Louis.

Benjamin, W. (1973) *Charles Baudelaire: A Lyric Poet in the Era of High Capitalism*. New Left Books, London.

Bordo, S. (1999) *The Male Body*. Farrar, Straus & Giroux, New York.

Debord, G. (1994) *The Society of the Spectacle*. Zone Books, New York.

Ewen, S. (1988) *All Consuming Images*. Basic Books, New York.

Featherstone, M. (1991) *Consumer Culture and Postmodernism*. Sage, London.

Foster, H. (1988) *Vision and Visuality*. Bay Press, Seattle.

Goldman, R. & Papson, S. (1996) *Sign Wars: The Cluttered Landscape of Advertising*. Guilford Press, New York.

Jameson, F. (1991) *Postmodernism, or, The Cultural Logic of Late Capitalism*. Duke University Press, Durham, NC.

Lash, S. & Urry, J. (1994) *Economies of Signs and Spaces*. Sage, London.

Leach, W. R. (1993) *Land of Desire: Merchants, Power and the Rise of a New American Culture*. Pantheon Books, New York.

Lefebvre, H. (1971) *Everyday Life in the Modern World*. Trans. S. Rabinovitch. Harper & Row, New York.

Marx, K. (1976) *Capital*, Vol. 1. Penguin, New York.

Mirzoeff, N. (1999) *An Introduction to Visual Culture*. Routledge, London.

Pitts, V. (2003) *In the Flesh*. Palgrave, New York.

Prosser, J. (1998) *Image Based Research*. Taylor & Francis, Philadelphia.

Ritzer, G. (2005) *Enchanting a Disenchanting World: Revolutionizing the Means of Consumption*, 2nd edn. Pine Forge Press, Thousand Oaks, CA.

Schroeder, J. (2002) *Visual Consumption*. Routledge, New York.

Simmel, G. (1971) *On Individuality and Social Forms: Selected Writings*. Trans. D. N. Levine. University of Chicago Press, Chicago.

Williamson, J. (1978) *Decoding Advertisements: Ideology and Meaning in Advertising*. Boyars, London.

Zukin, S. (1991) *Landscapes of Power*. University of California Press, Berkeley.

consumption of sport

Garry Crawford

In most advanced capitalist societies, sport is hard to avoid. Sport-related media shows and channels, magazines, newspapers, Internet sites, films, fictional and non-fictional books, advertising campaigns, video games, and even soap operas saturate our everyday lives. Sport is also a regular conversation topic for many families, friends, and work colleagues, and sport-related goods (often demonstrating sporting allegiances) such as jerseys, scarves, hats, badges, jackets, ties, cups, mouse mats, pennants, etc., are commonplace in our towns, homes, and places of work.

As Coakley (1994) writes: "Throughout history sport has always been used as a form of entertainment. However, sports have never been so heavily packaged, promoted, presented, and played as commercial products as they are today." Giulianotti (2002) suggests that since the late 1980s, sport (and in particular he cites the example of association football) has witnessed a rapid commercialization and what he refers to as "hypercommodification." Giulianotti suggests this hypercommodification has been largely brought about by shifts within late-capitalist society and in particular moves towards "disorganized capitalism" (Lash & Urry 1987), which have led to the contemporary dominance of consumer culture.

However, the question of whether sport audiences can be defined as consumers is a difficult one. Followers of sport are most typically identified as fans, and it is notable that within much of the wider literature on fans (such as that on media fans) that there is a tendency to identify fans as quite distinct from consumers. This is particularly evident in the work of Jenkins (1992), who suggests that fans are different to "ordinary" readers in that fans "actively" engage with the texts they consume. A similar attitude is evident in many studies of sport fan culture, where for instance Wann et al. (2001) construct as series of dichotomies between fans and spectators, direct and indirect sport consumers, and lowly and highly identified sport fans. Though Wann et al. make no value judgments between these "types" of audiences, others, and most notably several key writers on football (soccer) culture such as Taylor (1971) and Redhead (1997), draw value-laden distinctions between what they define as "traditional" fans (often white, male, and working class) and "new" (often middle-class, "family" based) consumers.

However, both Williams (2000) and Crawford (2004) suggest that these categories are often based upon romanticized ideas of "authenticity," which see the celebration of one form of sport support (such as attending live sport events) and the rejection of all that is seen as new (such as following sport via the mass media). Moreover, Crawford (2004: 32) suggests that with regard to the literature on subcultures, "typologies of supporters tend to impose rigid distinctions between 'types' of supporters, which tend towards caricature and force diverse patterns of behavior into restrictive categories. Such typologies and dichotomies do not recognize the fluidity and often temporality of many supporter 'communities.'" It is important to recognize that not all fan activity directly involves acts of consumption. As Crawford (2004: 4) writes: "Much of what makes someone a *fan* is what is located within her or his personal identity, memories, thoughts and social interactions." However, most often these relate (either directly or indirectly) to acts of consumption. For instance, the memories, thoughts, and conversations of sport fans will often relate to events people have attended, games they have seen on television, consumer goods they have bought or seen, and similar acts of consumption.

Consequently, several other authors (e.g., Holt 1995; Sandvoss 2003) suggest that a profitable way forward is to locate discussions of sport fan culture within a wider consideration of consumption, recognizing that sport fans are first and foremost consumers. This approach allows links, both theoretically and empirically, to be formed with wider debates on audiences and consumption, which can inform the understanding and theorization of sport audiences. For instance, Sandvoss (2003) suggests that what constitutes the idea and image of a sport club to its fans is made up of numerous (often diverse) "texts" (such as the stadium, its various players and staff, its history, and various media texts and reading of these), making the club (to a degree) polysemic. That is to say, fans can (within certain boundaries) read into the object of their support a wide variety of different meanings. This (largely) blank canvas, Sandvoss suggests, allows fans to see in the club what they value in themselves. The sport club therefore becomes, like Narcissus' pool, both a self-reflection and the object of their affection. This theorization then provides a useful understanding of the nature of fan affiliations, the diversity of meanings attached to popular cultural texts (such as sport clubs), and, importantly, locates the consideration of sport audiences within wider debates on consumption.

SEE ALSO: Audiences; Consumption; Fans and Fan Culture; Media and Sport; Sport; Sport and Culture; Sport Culture and Subcultures

REFERENCES AND SUGGESTED READINGS

Coakley, J. J. (1994) *Sport in Society: Issues and Controversies*, 5th edn. McGraw Hill, Boston.
Crawford, G. (2004) *Consuming Sport: Sport, Fans and Culture*. Routledge, London.
Giulianotti, R. (2002) Supporters, Followers, Fans, and Flaneurs: A Taxonomy of Spectator Identities in Football. *Journal of Sport and Social Issues* 26(1): 25–46.
Holt, D. B. (1995) How Consumers Consume: A Typology of Consumption Practices. *Journal of Consumer Research* 22: 1–16.
Horne, J. (2006) *Sport in Consumer Culture*. Palgrave, Basingstoke.
Jenkins, H. (1992) *Textual Poachers*. Routledge, London.
Lash, S. & Urry, J. (1987) *The End of Organized Capitalism*. Polity Press, Cambridge.
Redhead, S. (1997) *Post-Fandom and the Millennial Blues: The Transformation of Soccer Culture*. Routledge, London.
Sandvoss, C. (2003) *A Game of Two Halves: Football, Television and Globalization*. Routledge, London.
Taylor, I. (1971) "Football Mad": A Speculative Sociology of Football Hooliganism. In: Dunning, E. (Ed.), *The Sociology of Sport*. Frank Cass, London.
Wann, D. L., Melnick, M. J., Russell, G. W., & Pease, D. G. (2001) *Sport Fans: The Psychology and Social Impact of Spectators*. Routledge, New York.
Williams, J. (2000) The Changing Face of Football: A Case of National Regulation? In: Hamil, S., Michie, J., Oughton, C., & Warby, S. (Eds.), *Football in the Digital Age: Whose Game is it Anyway?* Mainstream, London.

consumption, tourism and

Jennie Germann Molz

Practices of tourism and consumption, and recent sociological interest in the relationship between them, have evolved as part of a broader shift within western societies from production-centered capitalism, with its focus on work and the conditions of labor, to consumer capitalism, with its emphasis on leisure, image, taste, style, and consumption. In fact, many sociologists consider tourism to be emblematic of the contemporary consumer culture that has emerged over the past century in western post-industrial societies.

The development of the seaside resort in early nineteenth-century Britain reflects this shift. During the Industrial Revolution, the rationalization of the labor process resulted in a clear demarcation between work and leisure. For the first time, the working class had the time and the money to pursue leisure activities. At the same time, technological advances in transportation, such as the railway, made travel cheaply and readily available to the masses. Whereas seaside resorts had previously been reserved for the wealthy, the increase in wages, the introduction of paid holidays, and the democratization of transportation meant that even the working classes could holiday at the seaside every year. The era of mass tourism was born.

During this same period, thanks to the increased availability of raw materials and advances in manufacturing technologies, consumer goods were also produced in unprecedented volumes and made available for mass consumption. As consumers enjoyed a greater choice of affordable goods, shopping and consumption took on a social value beyond the mere purchase and utility of commodities. Eventually, goods became valued not just for their usefulness, but rather for what they symbolized. For example, everyday items became associated with abstract qualities such as luxury, quality, youth, or beauty. Consumption practices shifted from an emphasis on use-value or exchange-value to an emphasis on sign-value. Thus, recent studies of consumer culture are often focused on the cultural context of consumption, on the role of material goods as symbols rather than utilities, and on the consumption of intangible items such as services, experiences, images, and fantasies.

As Pierre Bourdieu argues in his influential work *Distinction* (1984), commodities act as symbols and so consumption practices are as much about establishing social hierarchies as they are about satisfying individual needs. In other words, consuming is a means of classification. Within this context, the tourist's choice of destination or style of travel communicates his or her social status. For example, mass tourism is usually associated with the working classes, whereas the middle and upper classes tend to pursue independent travel or luxury tourism that communicates a sense of adventure or exclusivity.

Over the decades, mass tourism and mass consumption have given way to what some sociologists refer to as postmodern or post-Fordist consumption, which is characterized by greater differentiation of products, niche marketing, and customized services. Different sociological approaches to the relationship between tourism and consumption are indicative

of these shifts from a focus on work to a focus on leisure, from an economy of utility and exchange to an economy of signs and symbols, and from mass to post-Fordist consumption.

One way in which theorists have approached the relationship between tourism and consumption is to consider tourism as a form of consumption. However, because tourism is both an industry and a cultural practice, it involves different forms of consumption. The travel and tourism industry is claimed to be the largest industry and one of the largest employers in the world. According to the World Travel and Tourism Council, the world travel industry accounts for over 7 percent of worldwide employment and is worth over 3.5 trillion US dollars. The number of people making international trips each year is equally enormous. The World Tourism Organization reports that the number of international trips grew from 567.3 million per year in 1995 to over 656.9 million in 1999, a number that is expected to reach 1.6 billion by the year 2020. This massive movement of people around the world involves the provision and consumption of material and service commodities such as food, drink, transportation, and accommodation. In this sense, the consumption of tourism can be quantified in terms of airplane trips, hotel beds, meals, and tickets.

Because the movement and accommodation of such vast numbers of tourists involves the consumption of scarce resources such as fuel, water, beachfront property, and local labor, many critics have expressed concern over the environmental impacts of jet travel, the unsustainable use of fresh water, the expansion of tourist resorts in sensitive ecological areas, and the uneven relationships between hosts and guests, especially in developing countries. To counter the damaging effects of mass tourism, various forms of ecotourism have emerged which emphasize sustainable consumption of local resources and even "non-consumptive" forms of tourism.

However, the consumption of material resources is often seen as incidental to the consumption of the intangible qualities and ephemeral experiences that tourists desire. In other words, tourism also operates as an economy of signs, sights, senses, and symbols. The visual appropriation of tourist sights and destinations is a fundamental element of tourist consumption, as evidenced by the popularity of cameras and postcards for capturing and collecting tourist "signs." Starting with Dean MacCannell's analysis of sights and sightseeing in *The Tourist* (1976) and followed by John Urry's *The Tourist Gaze* (1990), the visual aspects of tourism became central to theories of tourist consumption. It is under the gaze of the tourist that cultural rituals and artifacts, local places, sights, and landmarks become packaged as consumable items.

One of the key features of post-Fordist consumer society is that all aspects of social life become commodified, not least of all those aspects that appeal to tourists. In the late 1980s, anthropologists examining the impact of tourism on local communities found that local people objectified their own cultural traditions and artifacts as tourist commodities. In these cases, traditional rituals were performed not for their significance to local people, but rather as spectacles for tourists. Likewise, indigenous artifacts were reproduced as souvenirs with symbolic value for the tourists, but little use-value to the local community. The effects of such cultural commodification are the subject of debate among researchers, with critics arguing that it results in the loss of cultural authenticity. MacCannell, for example, notes that local cultures construct "staged authenticity," a kind of commodified authenticity that inevitably thwarts the modern tourist's search for the authentic. On the other hand, some researchers argue that commodification brings money into impoverished communities and revives traditions that would otherwise die out.

In addition to consuming cultures, tourists also consume places by gazing at their landscapes, moving through them, and spending time in them. In turn, tourist destinations package, brand, and sell themselves to the tourist market. Some critics argue that tourist places become standardized and homogenized through touristic consumption. George Ritzer's (1993) notion of the McDonaldization of society, which identifies a move toward predictability, efficiency, calculability, and control across social institutions in general, manifests in tourist destinations as a form of McDisneyization that provides tourists with familiarity rather than difference. In contrast, other theorists

claim that places are not becoming homogenized, but rather are forced to differentiate themselves even more as they compete on a global stage for tourist interest and investment capital. For example, in order to attract tourists, some places brand themselves as heritage sites where tourists are able to consume the past by gazing upon sights and objects that represent the traditions and history of a specific culture.

In the late 1990s, critics began to challenge the correlation between tourism, consumption, and the gaze. For example, feminist scholars critiqued the disembodied nature of the tourist gaze and sought to reintroduce the body and other senses into analyses of tourism experiences. In addition, they have shown that tourism also often involves the consumption of other bodies, such as the laboring body of the local host or the prostitute's body in sex tourism. In response to such critiques, sociologists have turned to notions of performance to demonstrate the importance of other senses, such as smell, taste, and touch, and other embodied practices, such as walking, shopping, or bungee jumping, in tourism consumption. In these studies, researchers point out that tourists are producers as well as consumers of tourist places and experiences. For example, activities such as building a sandcastle, taking a photograph, or learning a handicraft are productive ways of consuming tourist experiences.

Just as tourism revolves more and more around consumption, consumption is increasingly becoming a form of tourism. Tourism has generally been associated with the purchase of souvenirs, which commemorate tourist experiences. However, the act of shopping itself has become increasingly central to those experiences. In other words, tourists now travel specifically to shop and shopping malls have become significant tourist destinations. The distinction between tourism and consumption becomes blurred in places like shopping malls. Theorists argue that the movement of commodities, the expansion of the global market, the deployment of global icons, and the globalization of products means that consumers do not actually need to travel around the world to consume tourist experiences. The urban consumer in the West can "travel" via the products and images on display in globalized retail outlets such as Benetton and the Body Shop.

Food also becomes a significant vehicle by means of which consumption serves as a form of tourism. Ingredients and recipes, not to mention immigrant restaurateurs, move around the world so the consumer does not have to. The consumer in the West can be a "culinary tourist" in a variety of ethnic restaurants or even in his or her own supermarket where fruits, vegetables, and other foods from other countries converge in a culinary pastiche. This convergence of foods and culinary styles is especially apparent in shopping-mall food courts where kiosks plying Chinese stir-fry, Italian pizza, French crepes, Greek souvlaki, and Japanese sushi serve up the world on a plate.

Whether sociologists approach tourism as a form of consumption or consumption as a form of tourism, it is clear that they consider tourism not as a set of self-contained practices, but rather as deeply embedded in wider consumer society. Thus the shifting roles and practices of the tourist reflect the shifting societal conditions of production and consumption from a Fordist to a post-Fordist economy. The mass tourism that emerged during the nineteenth century resulted from Fordist modes of aggregating consumers into mass markets and offering standardized products. In contrast, post-Fordist production is highly differentiated, allowing consumers to choose from a variety of customized options. In terms of tourism, this means that tourists have the flexibility to choose different styles of travel, from ecotourism to backpacking, or from adventure travel to shopping tourism. The fragmentation of the tourist market and of the tourist product breaks down the distinction between tourism and other activities such as sport or shopping. This has led many researchers to argue that the conflation between tourism and consumption that occurs in places like shopping malls is emblematic of the breakdown between categories such as authentic and inauthentic, exotic and familiar, or home, work, and leisure that characterizes the current social condition in general.

For some social theorists, this breakdown of distinctions between tourism and other forms of daily life such as shopping and consuming signals the "end of tourism" (Urry 1995). This does not mean that people will stop being tourists. On the contrary, it means that we are all already tourists all of the time. As mundane activities such as shopping become more like tourism and daily culture increasingly revolves around touristic features such as spectacle, aesthetics, leisure, and consumption, tourism ceases to provide an escape or counterpoint to the everyday. And yet, scholars find that tourists do continue to uphold the distinctions between the everyday and the extraordinary by performing and producing, as well as consuming, tourist places, senses, sights, and experience.

SEE ALSO: Consumption and the Body; Consumption, Food and Cultural; Consumption, Urban/City as Consumerspace; Cultural Tourism; Fordism/Post-Fordism; McDonaldization; Sex Tourism; Shopping Malls; Status; Urban Tourism

REFERENCES AND SUGGESTED READINGS

Baerenholdt, J. O. et al. (2003) *Performing Tourist Places*. Ashgate, Aldershot.

Germann Molz, J. (2003) Tasting an Imagined Thailand: Authenticity and Culinary Tourism in Thai Restaurants. In: Long, L. (Ed.), *Culinary Tourism: Eating and Otherness*. University of Kentucky Press, Lexington.

MacCannell, D. (1976) *The Tourist: A New Theory of the Leisure Class*. University of California Press, Berkeley.

Meethan, K. (2001) *Tourism in Global Society: Place, Culture, Consumption*. Palgrave, London.

Ritzer, G. (1993) *The McDonaldization of Society*. Pine Forge Press, Thousand Oaks, CA.

Ritzer, G. & Liska, A. (1997) "McDisneyization" and "Post-tourism": Complementary Perspectives on Contemporary Tourism. In: Rojek, C. & Urry, J. (Eds.), *Touring Cultures*. Routledge, London, pp. 96–109.

Sheller, M. (2003) *Consuming the Caribbean*. Routledge, London.

Urry, J. (1990) *The Tourist Gaze*. Sage, London.

Urry, J. (1995) *Consuming Places*. Routledge, London.

Veijola, S. & Jokinen, E. (1994) The Body in Tourism. *Theory, Culture and Society* 11: 125–51.

consumption, urban/city as consumerspace

Daniel Thomas Cook

The term urban consumption describes how the meanings of goods and commercially oriented experiences intermingle with space, place, and social identity in ways made possible by metropolitan life and are thereby specific to it. Urban consumption refers not just to purchases that occur within the confines of a city – as opposed to a suburb, or town or rural area. Rather, there is a character peculiar to the contexts of consumption which is both derived from, and is definitive of, urban culture. Urban life, to put it another way, is enmeshed with urban lifestyle.

MARKETS, PLACES, AND MARKETPLACES

Max Weber points out that cities are marketplaces where inhabitants have been liberated from direct agricultural production and live primarily off commerce and trade. A certain amount of economic versatility distinguishes cities from towns. The relative permanence of residence of many inhabitants makes both cities and towns distinguishable from their predecessors, the bazaar or crossroads market, where merchants and buyers would meet at regular intervals to exchange goods.

As marketplaces, cities combine the specificities and permanence of *place* with the dynamic and generalizing tendencies of *markets*. The great cities of antiquity and modernity – Delhi, Constantinople, Lisbon, Venice, Hong Kong, New York, London, Paris, Tokyo – garnered their character and identity from the dynamism of social and economic intercourse which invites the constant flow and mixing together of peoples, ethnicities, and goods in the form of traders, merchants, laborers, customers, and tourists. Cities, in this way, are portals which acquire and generate their unique culture from an interaction with and integration of many others.

The commercial quality of urban life also figures in the shaping of personal temperament, outlook, and attitude. Georg Simmel understood that the vibrancy of cities fueled what he called the "blasé attitude" of the metropolitan character, whereby urbanites would necessarily come to exhibit an indifference to the liveliness of the streets. In the city, according to Simmel, the dominance of the money economy in conjunction with the proximity of many strangers fosters an individualized kind of freedom which is borne out of the relatively anonymous existence one can lead in urban areas.

CONSUMPTION IN AND OF THE INDUSTRIAL CITY

Large, crowded, and lively cities grew from towns at exponential rates across North America throughout the 1800s. Propelled by the social changes wrought by industrialization and fed with surging immigrant populations from first Western then Eastern and Southern Europe over the 1880–1924 period, a historically unique public culture arose on the streets of the new industrial cities. Inexpensive, public amusements became increasingly available to a growing number of urban inhabitants. Spurred on by technological advances in lighting and electricity, evening performances on the Vaudeville circuit, nickel movie houses known as Nickelodeons, amusement parks like those found at Coney Island in New York City, sports arenas, dance halls, and large, extravagant department stores became some of the most popular and visible of consumer entertainments.

With the increased efficiency and high productivity of mechanized factory production, large varieties and quantities of goods were made available at low prices. When Henry Ford, automobile manufacturer, uniformly raised the wages of his workers to $5 a day and limited them to 8-hour work days in 1914, he was giving concrete recognition that his workers were also consumers who were in need of time and money to participate in the new world of commercial goods and leisure activities. Professional occupations needed to service and coordinate the new economy – secretaries, accountants, lawyers, copywriters, and editors, among others – arose at this time, thereby giving rise to a new middle class with a growing disposable income. In general, increasing numbers of working people found more and more goods within their reach and these new goods were being made in an ever-expanding array of styles and fashions.

The lavish display of many goods in department stores such as Marshall Field's store in Chicago or John Wanamaker's in Philadelphia recalled that of great palaces or cathedrals. They welcomed women to indulge in shopping as a personal pleasure rather than the mere exercise of domestic labor of shopping for the family. Many of the goods on display – silks, perfumes, jewelry – were, in previous times, available only to royalty and the well-to-do. Now they were within the physical, monetary, and social reach of the middle-class woman shopper. Shopping in these stores and among the goods, being able to touch and handle them, evoked images and feelings of abundance and luxury and encouraged fantasy. Many working-class and immigrant women were relegated to another kind of fantasy – window shopping – by viewing the goods separated by the new, large windows that faced the street (Leach 1993).

The new public, urban culture increasingly was experienced as a consumer culture of shopping places, entertainment, and amusements outside of the home. Often understood as having had a "democratizing" influence on social arrangements, the urban cultures of consumption and amusement offered places and activities whereby different people and different kinds of people could come into contact with one another. In these contexts, the varied ways of life brought from different national traditions could be on display for, and mix with, each other. On the other hand, the new forms of public, urban leisure and consumption gave expression to the many social cleavages and social distinctions – such as race, ethnicity, class, and gender – already existing in American life.

The public world of fun and amusement represented a different "culture" than what could be found in the immigrant neighborhoods of working people. In many neighborhoods, Old World sensibilities dominated, particularly regarding the proper arrangement between the sexes. For unmarried women of European descent, the home was often the site

of traditional authority where restrictive social and sexual mores were enforced by immigrant parents. The public world was heterosocial – mixing males and females – and, by its nature, most often took place outside of the surveillance of family and community. Moralists publicly decried the mixing of sexes in the dark movie theaters. The numerous dance halls, spurred by liquor industry interests, were places where "unescorted" women were welcome and where meeting an unknown man would not automatically call the women's "virtue" into question.

"Going out" meant physically and socially to leave one world behind and to enter a new one which was characterized by a sense of freedom. For many unmarried young women, conflicts with their parents were often over how much of their wages they could keep, and thus over their independence and privacy. A girl's dress was also often an issue. Evidence from diaries and subsequent testimonials indicates that some women would hide their "American" clothes somewhere outside their residences to be put on in secret for an evening out and, upon returning home, would don the everyday work clothes or ethnic garb. The "freedom" women experienced in the anonymity of the city and the public nature of amusements also allowed a gay, male world to exist in the interstices of straight culture. In New York in the 1920s and 1930s, for instance, commercialized leisure spaces such as ballrooms, saloons, and cafeterias existed where forms of dress, code words, and other coded signals marked out a discontinuous, half-secret and half-known geography of homosexual association.

Married or unmarried, men or women, gay or straight, those of the working classes spent what meager money they had outside of their small, often crowded rooms mixing with others on city streets. Weekend excursions to amusement places like New York's Coney Island in the early twentieth century gave single women another opportunity to be away from parents and to go on "dates." The new commercial landscape also divided genders, classes, sexualities, and races even as it appeared to have united them. African Americans remained virtually absent from urban public culture, particularly in the industrial cities of the North. Saloons, the haven of working men, were not welcoming to women. The well-to-do created their own exclusive sport clubs in the suburban areas of cities so as to ensure and promote race and class solidarity.

POST-INDUSTRIAL CITIES: THE CITY AS CONSUMERSPACE

Consumption and amusement in the industrial city arose out of commercial and social arrangements that had been based foremost on the structures and cadences defined by the demands of labor. Urban consumption appeared to be derived from and in response to urban production. Commercialized leisure allowed workers to find some sense of self away from the overdetermined environment of the factory, office, or behind the service counter. World's fairs, particularly those in New York City in 1939 and 1964, proffered images of future cities as clean, streamlined machines of efficiency which privileged work over leisure and consumption as the dominant ideal or mode of city life. In contrast, the opening of Disney World in southern California in 1955 offered a vision of community without obvious laborers or labor whereby all activity is centered around touring and consumption.

The transformation from industrial to post-industrial society entails the decline of mass production in favor of flexible forms of production which respond to increasingly specific markets and market fragments. The predominance of part-time labor and the rise of the service sector characterize the trajectory of North American and many western, capitalist economies beginning in the 1970s. The rapid suburbanization of the American landscape in the 1950s and 1960s spawned the growth of shopping centers and eventually shopping malls, which brought together a number of stores in one place under the auspices of a single organization. City populations, particularly that of white European Americans, continued to decline also in response to racial urban unrest in the 1960s in a migration pattern known as white flight. Consequently, by the end of the 1970s, many cities were facing high unemployment, unused factory and office space, and an unflattering image in public culture as places for crime and delinquency.

Urban planners, civic leaders, and real estate developers undertook a variety of efforts over the 1980s and 1990s to "revitalize" city centers by making them attractive places to visit. The key elements of revitalization centered around providing safe, some would say "sanitized," areas where visitors could walk, browse, eat, shop, and be entertained without much worry about personal safety. Disney's fantasy of Main Street USA in many ways has become the prototype for many urban areas and commercial zones in the post-industrial period.

John Hannigan (1998) notes that the formula hit upon by planners and developers was one of a *festival marketplace*, which was distinguished from shopping malls in a number of ways. As opposed to standard shops "anchored" on either end by large retailers, festival marketplaces favored an eclectic mix of stores which emphasized eating and entertainment as much as shopping. Many of these marketplaces were built not in suburbs or outlying areas of the city, but often in downtown areas or old industrial areas of a city, often part of a larger plan at revitalization. Many observers point to Baltimore's Harbor project, San Francisco's Embarcadero, Boston's Faneuil Hall, and Chicago's Navy Pier as quintessential festival marketplaces.

These efforts were spurred by the interest of young urban professionals and artists who, in different ways, saw "inner city" areas as desirable places to live. In the 1970s and 1980s urban artists who were in search of inexpensive living spaces began renting or inhabiting lofts in abandoned or underused factories. Often white and from middle-class, college-educated backgrounds, the artists' presence slowly transformed pockets of poorer areas into spaces where shops and restaurants catered to their tastes and lifestyles. During the same period, many white professionals who grew up in suburban areas but who were employed in cities decided to forego the commuter lifestyle of their parents and live near their workplaces. Some of these *yuppies* were decidedly upper-middle class in taste and lifestyle and they valued the architecture and design sensibilities of earlier periods. Drawn to older homes, many had a penchant for rehabilitating these structures to their original state.

Moving in or near blighted areas with the idea of rehabilitating housing stock is a key component of contemporary *gentrification*. It is also a process fraught with racial and class tensions, in part due to the seemingly inevitable displacement of the often poorer, non-white populations by the gentrifiers, many of whom see themselves as "pioneers" on the urban "frontier." As housing stock improves and as the newcomers (who wield the kind of social and cultural capital necessary to make larger structures like housing authorities and zoning commissions pay attention to them) begin to enact their vision of the community, the area itself begins to transform (Anderson 1990). Restaurants with vegetarian offerings, European-style coffee houses, yoga studios, and second-hand stores which feature expensive or vintage clothing are among the kinds of businesses which mark the class identification of these neighborhoods (Zukin 1991). Eventually, chain retailers such as the Pottery Barn, Z Gallerie, and Whole Foods supermarkets strategically located themselves near their class clientele.

Revitalization and urban consumption have not proven to lift or assist those of racially or economically marginalized groups. As cities have again become places to shop, eat, and seek entertainment, and as more affluent, usually white, populations have come to habitate previously downtrodden areas, some non-European "ethnic" businesses and areas have benefited. Chinatowns, Koreatowns, and Thai restaurants, as well as Mexican eateries and marketplaces, have to varying degrees of success found a niche in the consumer space of the city patronized by increasingly health-conscious or novelty-seeking consumers. Many critics point out that concentrating on upper-income visitors and residents as targets for downtown revitalization ignores the majority of the middle and lower-income populations who have been displaced to the outskirts of cities, "ethnic consumption" notwithstanding.

Sexually marginalized groups such as gay, lesbian, and transgendered people have found a measure of social enfranchisement through urban living and consumption. Stereotyped as affluent, urban, and cultured in taste, some cities have actively courted gay business owners and have provided social sanction in identifying certain neighborhoods as "gay" or gay dominated. Chicago's North Halsted Street corridor is a prime example, where a 20-foot tall street marker painted with the gay rainbow flag announce the area's identity to all.

Urban consumption, in many ways, extends beyond the downtown of the department store or festival marketplace and has come to define the character and identities of populations and neighborhoods with a focus on the particularities of place and population. It is a symbolic activity of identification and social distinction for residents as well as visitors. Spectacular themed environments, stores, and restaurants (e.g., Niketown) have located in high-density urban shopping districts. These combine shopping and entertainment organized around a brand identity and offer visitors an easily accessible set of meanings with which to associate.

The relocating or rebuilding of ballparks in or near city centers has also been part of urban revitalization efforts, particularly in the 1990s. Public–private partnerships between cities and teams position the park as an anchor or main attraction around which shopping, restaurants, new transit hubs, and entertainment districts can arise. The parks themselves have become sites of entertainment beyond that of providing seating to view a sports contest. Often featuring extravaganzas of spectacle and consumption, many of the newer ballparks paradoxically recall a fabled "enchanted" era of non-commercialized sports through their hyper-commercialism (Ritzer & Stillman 2001).

Post-industrial leisure and consumption, much like the case with housing stock and gentrification, finds new markets in old ones. The transformation of former working spaces like the South Street Market in New York, as well as tours of former work spaces like factories, point to the transformation of cities being from primarily places based on production to festival marketplaces based on touring and consumption.

Future research will need to examine the extent to which a group or area will have to market itself as a destination for outsiders in order to maintain economic viability. As many city mayors are required to serve as their city's "brand manager," it will be important to investigate critically the extent to which self-marketing changes the character and identity of cities and neighborhoods and to what extent leveraging small parts of a city as a "destination" harms or helps the large hinterland of non-visitable places where most urban inhabitants live.

SEE ALSO: Consumption, Spectacles of; *Flânerie*; Gender, Consumption and; Lifestyle Consumption; Shopping; Shopping Malls; Urban Tourism

REFERENCES AND SUGGESTED READINGS

Anderson, E. (1990) *StreetWise*. University of Chicago Press, Chicago.
Benson, S. P. (1986) *Counter Cultures: Saleswomen, Managers, and Customers in American Department Stores, 1890–1940*. University of Illinois Press, Champaign.
Chauncey, G. (1997) *Gay New York*. Basic Books, New York.
Chin, E. (2001) *Purchasing Power*. University of Minnesota Press, Minneapolis.
Cohen, L. (1996) From Town Center to Shopping Center: The Reconfiguration of Community Marketplaces in Postwar America. *American Historical Review* 101.
Ewen, E. (1985) *Immigrant Women in the Land of Dollars*. Monthly Review Press, New York.
Hannigan, J. (1998) *Fantasy City*. Routledge, New York.
Harvey, D. (1989) *The Condition of Postmodernity*. Blackwell, Oxford.
Leach, W. (1993) *Land of Desire: Merchants, Power and the Rise of a New American Culture*. Pantheon, New York.
Nasaw, D. (1993) *Going Out: The Rise and Fall of Public Amusements*. Basic Books, New York.
Peiss, K. (1986) *Cheap Amusements*. Temple University Press, Philadelphia.
Penaloza, L. (1994) *Atraves and Fronteras*/Border Crossings: A Critical Ethnographic Exploration of Consumer Acculturation of Mexican Immigrants. *Journal of Consumer Research* 21 (June): 32–54.
Ritzer, G. and Stillman, T. (2001) The Postmodern Ballpark as a Leisure Setting: Enchantment and Simulated De-McDonaldization. *Leisure Sciences* 23(2): 99–113.
Sherry, J. F., Jr. (1998) The Soul of the Company Store: Nike Town Chicago and the Emplaced Brandscape. In: Sherry, J. F., Jr. (Ed.), *Servicescapes*. American Marketing Association, Chicago.
Simmel, G. (1971) The Metropolis and Mental Life. In: Levine, D. N. (Ed.), *On Individuality and Social Forms*. University of Chicago Press, Chicago, pp. 324–39.
Weber, M. (1986) *The City*. Free Press, New York.
Zukin, S. (1982) *Loft Living*. Johns Hopkins University Press, Baltimore.
Zukin, S. (1991) *Landscapes of Power*. University of California Press, Berkeley.

consumption, visual

Jonathan E. Schroeder

Visual consumption characterizes life in the information age. The computer, the Web, and the visual mass media structure twenty-first century lives, commanding time and attention, providing a steady stream of images that appear to bring the world within. Encompassing not only visual-oriented consumer behavior such as watching television, playing video games, bird watching, tourism, museum going, and window shopping, visual consumption also introduces a methodological framework to investigate the interstices of consumption, vision, and culture, including how visual images are handled by consumption studies. Visual consumption constitutes a key attribute of an experience economy organized around attention, in which strategic communication – including advertising, promotion, websites, retail environments, and mass media – incorporates visual images designed to capture attention, build brand names, create mindshare, produce attractive products and services, and persuade citizens, consumers, and voters.

Visual consumption represents an emerging branch of consumption studies, one that relies on interdisciplinary methods, based on a semiotically informed visual genealogy of contemporary images. Approaching visual representation via interpretive stances offers researchers a grounded method for understanding and contextualizing images, as well as the cultural centrality of vision. In connecting images to the external context of consumption, researchers gain a more thorough – yet never complete – understanding of how images function within contemporary society, embodying and expressing cultural values and contradictions.

Visual consumption begins with images, and finds allied approaches within visual sociology and sociology of consumption research (Ekström & Brembeck 2004; Lash & Urry 1994; Schroeder 2002). Acknowledging that products, services, brands, politicians, and ideology are marketed via images, and that consumers consume products symbolically, implies rethinking basic notions of economy, competition, satisfaction, and consumer choice. Visual images exist within a distinctive socio-legal environment – unlike textual or verbal statements, such as product claims or political promises, pictures cannot be held to be true or false. Images elude empirical verification. Thus, images are especially amenable to help strategists avoid being held accountable for false or misleading claims. For example, cigarette manufacturers have learned not to make text-based claims about their products, relying instead on visual imagery such as the lone cowboy.

Researchers have focused on the image and its interpretation as foundational elements of consumption, bringing together theoretical concerns about image and representation to build a multidisciplinary approach to consumption within what has been called the sign economy, the image economy, and the attention economy (Goldman & Papson 1996; Lash & Urry 1994). Images function within culture, and their interpretive meanings shift over time, across cultures, and between consumers. Visual consumption studies' aims are generally interpretive rather than positivistic – to show how images *can* mean, rather than demonstrate *what* they mean. Image interpretation remains elusive – never complete, closed, or contained, to be contested and debated.

Research on visual consumption has gone through several phases. In the first phase, researchers such as Erving Goffman and Howard Becker deployed photographs as data, evidence, and illustrations within research projects and scholarly reports documenting visual aspects of society. In the second phase, visual images came to both reveal and reflect broader sociological issues, such as alienation, anomie, identity, and exclusion, as researchers began to focus on the representational power of images via self-portraits, subject-generated images, and photo elicitation techniques. In the current phase, visual images themselves have assumed central importance, drawing from cultural studies and visual studies disciplines that emerged

to interrogate popular cultural forms, and later visual culture. Within this phase, a typical study might investigate how the television news channel CNN covers a war, emphasizing the visual technologies that structure information and ideology, or bring a sociological perspective to a website art piece, utilizing an interdisciplinary approach beyond the interests of aesthetics or art history.

Each phase contains several streams of research, including those that focus on image interpretation from various perspectives, such as psychoanalysis or semiotics (Hall 1997). Others emphasize image-making as a social psychological act of representing and communicating, drawing on traditional anthropological and sociological theories and methods. Another approach utilizes photographs or other visual artifacts as stimuli for research, for *photo-elicitation*, akin to projective measures within psychology that investigate deeper meanings and associations that people bring to images. An additional related practice concerns visual presentation of research, documentary films, and videos, as well as more filmic treatments of sociological topics such as rituals, subcultures, or tourism.

Visual consumption research rests on a set of assumptions about contemporary consumption in western industrialized societies. First, strategic marketing communication, including advertising, promotion, public relations, and corporate communication – and the mass media that it supports – has emerged as a primary societal institution. For marketing no longer merely communicates information about products, it is an engine of the economy, an important social institution, and a primary player in the political sphere. Marketing communications heavily depend upon photography, which includes still photography, film, and video.

Second, the world's photographability has become the condition under which it is constituted and perceived – every single instant of one's life is touched by the technological reproduction of images. From this perspective, there have been no significant events of the past century that have not been captured by the camera; indeed, photography and film help make things significant.

A third proposition focuses on the intertwined concepts of identity and photography, in which individual and organizational identity remain inconceivable without photography. Personal as well as product identity (already inextricably linked via the market) are constructed largely via information technologies of photography and mass media. The visual aspects of culture have come to dominate our understanding of identity, as well as the institutionalization of identity by societal institutions. Yet photography does not represent the truth; it is not a simple record of some reality (Burgin 1996; Coleman 1998; Slater 1995). Visual consumption research has framed photography as a consumer *behavior* as well as a central information technology. Photography's technical ability to reproduce images makes it a central feature of visual culture.

Fourth, the image is primary for marketing products, services, politicians, and ideas. Products no longer merely reflect images; rather, the image often is created prior to the product, which is then developed to fit the image. Many products and services are designed to fit a specific target market; they conform to an image of consumer demand, exemplifying a seismic economic shift towards experience, towards images, towards attention.

These four propositions create an interdisciplinary matrix for analyzing the roles visual consumption plays in the economy. Specifically, they call attention to photography as an overlooked process within the cultural marketplace of ideas and images. This set of propositions directs our gaze to the cultural and historical framework of images, even as it questions the information that feeds those discourses.

Today's visual information technologies of television, film, and the Internet are directly connected to the visual past (Schroeder 2002). Research on information technology (IT) or information and communication technology (ICT) usually focuses on complex, sophisticated systems such as mass media, the Internet, telecommunications, or digital satellite transmission arrays. These constitute the basic building blocks of the information society, where information is a crucial corporate competitive advantage as well as a fundamental cultural force. The World Wide Web, among its many influences, has put a premium on understanding visual consumption. The Web

mandates visualizing almost every aspect of organizational communication, identity, operations, and strategy. From the consumer perspective, visual experiences dominate the Web, as they navigate through an artificial environment almost entirely dependent upon their sense of sight. Photography remains a key component of many information technologies – digital incorporation of scanned photographic images helped transform the Internet into what it is today. Photography, in turn, was heavily influenced by the older traditions of painting in its commercial and artistic production, reception, and recognition (Osbourne 2000; Slater 1995).

Associating visual consumption with the art historical world helps to position and understand photography as a global representational system. The visual approach to consumption has afforded new perspectives to investigate specific art historical references in contemporary images, such as the gaze, display, and representing identity. In addition, researchers can take advantage of useful tools developed in art history and cultural studies to investigate the poetics and politics of images as a representational system. Finally, art-centered analyses often generate novel concepts and theories for research on issues such as patronage, museum practice, information technology, and marketing communication.

Constructing a visual genealogy of contemporary images helps illuminate how marketing communication works as the *face of capitalism*, harnessing the global flow of images and fueling the image economy. Marketing images often contradict Roland Barthes's influential notion that photography shows "what has been." As consumers, we should know that what is shown in ads has not really been; it is usually a staged construction designed to sell something. Yet, largely due to photography's realism, combined with technological and artistic expertise, marketing images produce realistic, pervasive simulations with persuasive power. Advertising conventions encourage use of a narrow set of expectations to decode and decipher imagery – positive expectations, generally, which promote promising conclusions about the advertised item. Contrary to museum going, for instance, looking at ads seems to require withholding one's cultural knowledge so that ads become spectacles of visual consumption. Furthermore, information technology makes looking at many things possible, but it does not necessarily improve our capacity to *see*, to actively engage our senses in reflective analysis. For most consumers, the growing volume of images works against understanding how they function – they rarely take the time to thoroughly reflect on marketing imagery, its position as something that apparently comes between programs, articles, or websites makes it seem ephemeral or at least peripheral to serious consideration. However, images are vitally connected to the cultural worlds of high art, fashion, and photography on one hand, and media realms of news, entertainment, and celebrity on the other.

A central debate within visual consumption research concerns the polysemy of images. Some approaches suggest that images float in the "postmodern" world – signs disconnected from signifiers – leaving viewers free to generate novel, resistant, and idiosyncratic meaning. Certainly, consumers generate their own meaning, as they bring their own cognitive, social, and cultural lenses to whatever they see. However, researchers generally agree that this does not mean that the historical and political processes that also generate meaning are eliminated – images exist within cultural and historical frameworks that inform their production, reception, circulation, and interpretation.

Methodological issues within visual consumption stem from its interdisciplinary roots. Researchers have debated central concerns such as agency versus structure in image interpretation and influence, the role of the unconscious, and consumer response versus producer intention. One overlooked aspect concerns the role of fellow scholars, particularly those with visual expertise, in doing visual consumption research. Researchers consistently benefit from art historians, artists, and others with specific expertise, yet many scholars rarely make the effort to consult cross-disciplinary colleagues about their visual materials.

Future research must acknowledge the image's representational and rhetorical power both as cultural artifact and as an engaging and deceptive bearer of meaning, reflecting broad societal, cultural, and ideological codes. Research studies focused on the political, social, and economic implications of images, coupled with an understanding of the historical conditions influencing their production and consumption, require cross-disciplinary training and collaboration. To understand images more fully, researchers must investigate the cultural, historical, and representational conventions that limit both encoding and decoding interpretation processes. Greater awareness of the associations between the traditions and conventions of visual history and the production and consumption of images has led to a better understanding of how these representations constitute a discursive space within which a meaningful sense of identity and difference can be maintained. Research that extends previous work on visual representation into historical, ontological, and art historical realms may provide a necessary bridge between visual meaning residing within producer intention or wholly subsumed by individual response, and between aesthetics and ethics. Key questions remain about why certain images are celebrated, ignored, or vilified. Understanding the role that visual consumption plays in identity formation, visual history, and representation signals a step toward understanding how the market structures and subsumes basic sociological concerns of power, desire, and identity.

SEE ALSO: Advertising; Consumption, Spectacles of; Consumption, Tourism and; *Flânerie*; Goffman, Erving; Media and Consumer Culture; Museums; Semiotics; Video Games

REFERENCES AND SUGGESTED READINGS

Burgin, V. (1996) *In/Different Spaces: Place and Memory in Visual Culture*. University of California Press, Berkeley.

Coleman, A. D. (1998) *Depth of Field: Essays on Photography, Mass Media, and Lens Culture*. University of New Mexico Press, Albuquerque.

Ekström, K. & Brembeck, H. (Eds.) (2004) *Elusive Consumption*. Berg, Oxford.

Goffman, E. (1979) *Gender Advertisements: Studies in the Anthropology of Visual Communication*. Harper & Row, New York.

Goldman, R. & Papson, S. (1996) *Sign Wars: The Cluttered Landscape of Advertising*. Guilford Press, New York.

Hall, S. (Ed.) (1997) *Representation: Cultural Repre-sentations and Signifying Practices.* Sage, London.

Lash, S. & Urry, J. (1994) *Economies of Sign and Space.* Sage, London.

Osborne, P. D. (2000) *Travelling Light: Photography, Travel and Visual Culture.* Manchester University Press, Manchester.

Schroeder, J. E. (2002) *Visual Consumption.* Routle-dge, London.

Slater, D. (1995) Photography and Modern Vision: The Spectacle of "Natural Magic." In: Jenks, C. (Ed.), *Visual Culture.* Routledge, London, pp. 218–37.

Van Leeuwen, T. & Jewitt, C. (Eds.) (2001) *Hand-book of Visual Analysis.* Sage, London.

consumption, youth culture and

Murray Milner, Jr.

Youth, especially teenagers, have been closely associated with certain forms of consumption linked to a distinctive youth culture that sets them off from both adults and younger children. This subculture centers on peer relationships – especially one's popularity or status – and the organization of these relationships into an array of cliques and crowds who use various lifestyle symbols to distinguish themselves from one another. Patterns of consumption often serve as key markers of both group identity and indivi-dual membership. August B. Hollingshead's *Elmtown's Youth* in the 1940s and James S. Coleman's *Adolescent Society* in the 1950s were among the first to identify the patterns and characteristics of youth subcultures.

Youth-oriented forms of consumption have nineteenth-century roots in the development of special products for children. Distinctive pat-terns for adolescents grew in intensity in the 1920s and 1930s. The press drew attention to this phenomenon in the early 1940s, when the term teenagers was popularized. Teenagers were portrayed as obsessed with the latest fash-ions in clothes, popular music, and "cool" automobiles. By the 1950s a youth culture, with its particular forms of consumption, was a taken-for-granted feature of adolescence.

A variety of consumer goods and services became common among teenagers, including personal television sets, cell phones, computers, videos, video games, elaborate proms and social events, and vacations to the beach or skiing, as well as more expensive clothes and cars.

Biological and psychological development plays a role in the behaviors characteristic of young people. Puberty involves significant neu-rological, hormonal, bodily, and psychological changes. These are associated with gaining greater autonomy from adults, coming to terms with sexuality, and developing a personal social identity. Dealing with these changes often brings increased levels of psychological and social stress. Such processes take place in all societies and historical periods and do not explain the distinctiveness, influence, and con-tent of contemporary youth culture, which are rooted primarily in the economic, social, and cultural characteristics of advanced industrial societies.

The extended compulsory schooling of developed societies isolates adolescents from adult contact and responsibilities. This is accentuated by parents being employed away from the home and by the increasing time spent commuting by both parents and children. Per-sonal cars and new forms of communication (e.g., mobile phones, email, text messaging, and electronic bulletin boards) increase the rates and frequency of interaction between ado-lescent peers. Links with parents and adults may be further reduced by new forms of enter-tainment such as television, videos, and video games, and by the specialized media content aimed specifically at young people.

A central feature of adolescent culture is a concern about status and popularity. This ten-dency has sometimes been exaggerated in the mass media, but there is little doubt that it is a significant matter for most teenagers. Processes related to psychological development may fos-ter this, but the primary cause is the social and power structure within which adolescents must live. They may have spending money, but they have little economic or political power over the decisions that most shape their lives. They must be in school, cannot change the curricu-lum, cannot hire or fire the teachers. Teenagers do not choose who else will be in the school and often have little influence over where they live or what school they attend. In contrast, people of this age in most historic societies were often married and treated more or less as adults. Modern teenagers do have the power to create their own status systems; adults cannot control whom teenagers admire, emulate, or denigrate. Accordingly, status is the main form of power and autonomy that is available to adolescents.

The key social formations are a type of what Max Weber called status groups. In contemporary US schools these are often referred to as crowds, each with its relatively distinctive lifestyle expressed in clothing, music, argot, and attitudes toward adults. Some of the typical crowds in US schools include preps, jocks, punks, goths, brains, skaters, nerds or geeks, and hicks or cowboys. Crowds are usually subdivided into cliques, which constitute networks of friends who "hang out" together. A key source of status is whom you associate with; associating with higher status people improves one's own status; associating with lower status people lowers one's status. This is especially so for intimate, expressive relationships, as contrasted to instrumental relationships. The status of those one dates and eats with in the lunchroom affects one's status much more than who sits next to whom in class or with whom one works on an assigned project. "Partying," which often involves food and romantic or sexual liaisons, becomes a central social activity for many. There is a strong tendency to avoid intimate associations with those of lower status or those who have significantly different criteria of status, which tends to reduce associations with those from other crowds.

A second source of status is conformity to the norms of the group. This includes displaying distinctive lifestyle symbols through clothes, demeanor, language, etc. This is why teenagers are frequently very concerned to have the "in" or "cool" fashions. Those deemed to be of high status are likely to be emulated in their dress and actions. If you have high status, others are likely to copy what you do and wear. To stay "ahead," high-status people are motivated to constantly change the norms of what is cool. Fashion becomes very dynamic and even ephemeral. "That is so yesterday" is a phrase many contemporary youth use to distance themselves from what they see as outmoded and "not cool." In schools where crowds have

a relatively clear-cut ranking, lower-status groups tend to copy the "popular crowd." In more pluralistic schools where each crowd claims equality or superiority, comparison and emulation tends to be more within these groups.

On the one hand, the centrality of consumption to youth culture is indicated by teens' behavior; for example, they hang out in shopping malls and seek part-time employment to pay for the things they desire. On the other hand, its importance is indicated by the attention businesses have paid to this specialized market. In the early 2000s, it was estimated that US teenagers spent (or influenced their parents to spend) $100–200 billion annually – more than the annual US expenditures on the Iraq War during these years. Since the mid-twentieth century, businesses have created products aimed at the youth and teenage market. Companies invest large amounts in market research and advertising to promote these projects. Some marketing firms specialize in research on teenagers and preteens. Their methodologies range from large sample surveys to seeking out those who are defined as "cool" by their peers and video taping their dress and behavior. This knowledge is used to guide extensive marketing campaigns directed at young people. As teen status structures and styles have become more pluralistic, marketers have had to aim at particular subgroups or niches.

A number of television drama series portray the lives of teenagers and are aimed at marketing products to these groups. Advertisers pay about the same rate for some of these series as some of the most popular adult oriented programming. Popular music is heavily marketed to teenagers. MTV (Music Television) became a major network and a cultural phenomenon by focusing on videos of popular musicians, often including risqué lyrics and sexually suggestive dancing. Hundreds of radio stations (and their advertisers) see young people as their primary audience. Much of Internet-based marketing is aimed at computer and Web-savvy young people. Increasingly, music is sold and distributed over the Internet, and most customers are high school and college students. Publishers have created special teen editions of *Newsweek*, *People*, *Cosmopolitan*, and *Vogue* with advertising aimed at this age group.

Schools have become a site for marketing. Nationally franchised food outlets are available in some schools cafeterias. Schools sell exclusive rights to market particular brands of drinks and snacks, sometimes including the right to advertising on school premises. Some school systems sell advertising space in and on their school buses. Specialized marketing companies sign up school clubs or teams to peddle their products to friends and neighbors, with a percent going to the school or the student organization. Channel One, a national satellite network, provides schools with televisions and related equipment. In return, students are required to watch 12 minutes of Channel One's teen-oriented news programming each day, including two minutes of advertising products that appeal to students. They are also encouraged to visit a related website that includes advertising aimed at teenagers. Another technique, "peer marketing," recruits students to wear or suggest the use of products to their friends without revealing that they are being rewarded with money or gifts.

Some marketing is directed at young people to indirectly shape parents' decisions about major purchases. Car companies, hotels, airlines, cruise lines, banks, credit card companies, insurance companies, and even investment firms advertise in media aimed at young people. In addition to influencing parents, marketers hope to create brand loyalty during adolescence that will shape buying habits well into adulthood.

Younger and older groups have adopted many of the behaviors characteristic of teenagers. Some elementary school girls model themselves after cheerleaders and other popular teenagers, including the use of makeup and clothing that simulates sexuality. Middle school students are often concerned about romance, sexuality, and fashion, and there are specialized media and marketing aimed at this audience. The audiences of television series about teenagers are composed largely of preteen girls. While the intensity of concern about peer popularity declines for post-high school young people, teenage styles influence older age groups. As the age for marriage has increased, the singles' scene draws heavily on the cultural forms of adolescents emphasizing fashion, partying, and casual romance. Accordingly, the forms of consumption resemble teenage life

more than those of the young family of earlier generations. Youth, beauty, and sexuality became key values and status symbols. As the ironic novelist Tom Wolfe remarked: "In the year 2000, [people] prayed, 'Please, God, don't let me look old.' Sexiness was equated with youth, and youth ruled … The social ideal was to look 23 and dress 13."

These developments have made teenage status structures, youth cultures, and the related consumption patterns increasingly important to prosperous societies and their economies. As affluence increases, a higher proportion of consumption is based on acquiring status symbols rather than on technological or physiological requirements. Fashion became relevant not only to an elite, but to most of the population. It is a central source of the consumer demand so crucial to an advanced industrial society. Appropriately, these societies are often referred to as consumer societies. Of course, not all young people are obsessed with their popularity or having the latest cool stuff. In the US, however, teenage status systems play a key role in making a concern with fashion and consumption a taken-for-granted feature of contemporary society.

An extensive sociological literature has developed on both adolescence and consumption, but little on the link and interaction between the two, though several journalistic and cultural studies have appeared. More attention has been paid to children who are seen as more innocent and vulnerable to manipulation. Additional research is needed in many areas. How does the attention to fashion and consumption differ across crowds, schools, and societies and what are the sources of any variations? What are the long-term effects of being preoccupied with these concerns on individuals and collectivities? Does the mass media primarily shape or reflect youth culture? As with consumption in general, scholarly and public opinion remains divided about whether the development of a youth-based culture of consumption is a new form of creativity and freedom, or a new form of manipulation and alienation.

SEE ALSO: Advertising; Age Identity; Childhood; Consumer Culture, Children's; Consumption, Girls' Culture and; School Climate; Socialization, Agents of; Youth/Adolescence

REFERENCES AND SUGGESTED
READINGS

Brown, B. B., Mory, M. S., & Kinney, D. (1994)
Casting Adolescent Crowds in a Relational Per-
spective: Caricature, Channel, and Context. In:
*Advances in Adolescent Development: An Annual
Book Series*, Vol. 6.Sage, Thousand Oaks, CA,
pp. 168–95.
Cook, D. (2004) *The Commodification of Childhood: The
Children's Clothing Industry and the Rise of the Child
Consumer*. Duke University Press, Durham, NC.
Cross, G. (2002) Values of Desire. *Journal of Con-
sumer Research* 29: 441–7.
Danesi, M. (1999) *Cool: The Signs and Meanings of
Adolescence*. University of Toronto Press, Toronto.
Davis, G. & Dickinson, K. (2004) *Teen TV: Genre,
Consumption, Identity*. BFI Publishers, London.
Linn, S. (2004) *Consuming Kids: The Hostile Take-
over of Childhood*. New Press, New York.
Milner, M., Jr. (2004) *Freaks, Geeks, and Cool Kids:
American Teenagers, Schools, and the Culture of
Consumption*. Routledge, New York.
Quart, A. (2003) *Branded: The Buying and Selling of
Teenagers*. Perseus, Cambridge, MA.

content analysis

Kristina Wolff

Content analysis is a method of observation and
analysis that examines cultural artifacts. One of
the most common and frequently cited definitions describes this type of research method as
"any technique for making inferences by systematically and objectively identifying specified
characteristics of messages" (Holsti 1969: 26).
This method emerged in the early twentieth
century when researchers began studying the
texts of speeches, political tracts, and newspapers. It quickly evolved into investigating the
wide array of texts in society, including photographs, movies, diaries and journals, music,
television, film, letters, law cases, manifestos,
and advertisements. Primarily, anything that is
in or can be converted to printed form can be
examined using content analysis. This method
has a long history in sociology as well as many
other disciplines, including political science,
history, law, and policy studies, as well as feminist studies.

Content analysis examines materials using
both quantitative and qualitative techniques as
a means to understand messages within texts as
well as to understand the message's content,
producer, and/or audience. The benefits of this
type of analysis are that it is unobtrusive and
transparent and the material examined provides
an accurate representation of society and various aspects of society, since it is created without the intent of being a subject of a study.
Content analysis is a complement to other
forms of analyses of texts and messages, which
include frame analysis, textual analysis, and
discourse analysis.

Briefly, *frame analysis* may utilize similar
techniques of content analysis, but its approach
varies in that it focuses on examining how
individuals make sense of the world through
studying the ways that people operate within
social structures as well as how events are
framed by these structures. *Textual analysis*
originated in the fields of linguistics and semiotics. Like content analysis, this method looks
for patterns and shifts in rhetoric. One core
difference is the relationship of the reader to
the text. Meaning is produced when the text
is read, not when it is written, a connection
must be made for the text to be "alive,"
whereas for both frame and content analysis,
words, phrases, and documents are considered
complete. Lastly, *discourse analysis* moves
beyond these examinations of what primarily
consists of a message that has been produced,
focusing on the attributes of a specific document or collection of documents. Discourse
analysis follows the language rather than the
document itself. The analysis moves from site
to site rather than focusing on where the discourse resides.

Before a researcher begins the process of
conducting content analysis, they establishe a
specific set of criteria that is used as the framework for examination. Quantitative approaches
select material that relates to the hypothesis of
the study. During this phase, items that do not
apply are eliminated. For example, if someone
were to explore the ways women are portrayed
in newspaper photographs, then one aspect of
the predetermined criteria would be to eliminate all photographs of people containing only
men and boys. Qualitative approaches also utilize a set of criteria, but the rules often are less

narrowly defined and are likely to be limited according to something such as the size or dates of the text being examined. Research questions are still utilized, but nothing from the data is eliminated at this stage. A similar study of images of women would be conducted on the same group of photographs, but the researcher may decide to focus on specific days of the week or types of articles or photographs and then look to see how women are portrayed according to these groupings. While approaches and overall techniques vary, one common element is the need to establish a set of systematic rules for examination before the actual process of analysis begins.

The most essential part of creating the framework for analysis is to clearly determine the unit of analysis to be examined. These can range from focusing on specific words and phrases to large paragraphs, characters, entire works, themes, or concepts that exist in the text. This process of establishing the criteria for analysis, examining the documents, locating, marking, and tallying the unit of analysis is called *coding*. These steps transform the raw data into categories that have been created as part of the established criteria. For example, if a researcher was studying conversations focusing on public opinion about the most recent State of the Union Address by the US President, that were occurring in various blogs on the Internet, the pre-set categories may consist of "positive," "negative," and "mixed." These classifications would then be the actual terms or phrases that appeared in the blogs. Words like "responsible" or "admire" would be counted as "positive," whereas other words such as "insincere" or "unbelievable" would be counted as "negative." These words are tallied and then examined according to frequency of occurrence.

Words or phrases that are obvious in their meaning are called *manifest content*. They are considered the best way to achieve objectivity and reliability due to their ease of identification. Historically, this approach was very time consuming. Gans (1979) utilized quantitative techniques in his content analysis of television news. While he found that he was able to observe recurring patterns in news reporting, he was only able to concentrate on a few themes due to the size of the study and time constraints involved in analyzing the material. The growth of computer software programs designed to perform content analysis allows researchers to perform this type of analysis fairly rapidly. The use of computers also increases reliability and validity of the findings, as it eliminates human error that can occur when counting and categorizing the data. These programs enable researchers to use larger amounts of data and wider time spans, due to the increased efficiency and accuracy, which also provides enough data to analyze the results using quantitative techniques.

Latent content is considered to be words and phrases which are more subjective in their interpretation. This kind of communication consists of phrases, paragraphs, or items that have underlying meanings and/or consist of symbolic messages. If a researcher were looking at the same collection of blogs, they may widen their examination to studying paragraphs. These could then reveal that one posting may use the word "admire" in a sentence, yet the context of the paragraph as a whole reveals that the writer admired the part of the address that focused on health care policy but overall they were disappointed in the president's main message.

Debates about how to use content analysis do exist within sociology and other disciplines. For some, quantitative content analysis is often heralded as *the* preferred or "correct" way to perform this type of analysis. It is the more widely used approach. However, qualitative content analysis is also well established and this approach is often the preferred technique to use when examining latent content or material that requires an interpretive approach. One of the requirements of content analysis is that research is limited to messages that reside within the confines of the document that is being examined. For example, Daniels's (1977) research on documents produced by white supremacist groups was limited to their official publications. Daniels utilized qualitative content analysis techniques; her examination was confined to a predetermined set of publications that covered a specific time period. Anything falling before or after this range in time was not studied. This constraint can be viewed as a strength in that it offers a focused and detailed analysis of the material, but it is also a limit of the method, as one cannot move beyond the predetermined criteria, the list of words or phrases to be used in the study, or the material itself.

Often, the results of content analysis consist primarily of descriptive information. Without looking for patterns that develop over time within the material or using techniques of *triangulation*, then the findings are not generalizable to a large population. Triangulation or "multiple methods" is simply the use of more than one means of data collection and analysis. The combination of qualitative and quantitative techniques or the addition of additional research such as conducting a case study or performing secondary data analysis can complement and clarify the results of the content analysis.

This form of analysis is also reliant on what has been recorded in the cultural artifacts being examined. Scholars using these techniques often focus on what is missing from the messages they are examining, as well as what exists in their documents. For example, if a researcher was studying the police blotter in newspapers, they may focus on counting the number of racial markers that exist in the reporting as a means of understanding how race is understood in that community. Upon reanalyzing the content, they may then look for the absence of racial characteristics to see if any patterns exist; such as by comparing the number of times the label "woman" appears as opposed to the label "black woman."

Through the use of triangulation, a researcher may develop a better understanding about why certain facts, words, or phrases are omitted. Epstein's (1996) examination of the early response to the AIDS epidemic in the US and Cohen's (1999) study on AIDS in African American communities both utilized multiple methods in their research. Each used content analysis to examine their cultural artifacts, which primarily consisted of newspapers. Epstein also utilized discourse analysis and interviews. Cohen included interviews and participant observation and conducted a case study.

Feminist approaches to content analysis also utilize multiple methods. Feminist researchers broaden the depth of investigation to include marginalized groups, particularly women. Cultural artifacts about, produced by, and used by women are examined. Feminist critique of content analysis was one of the first to challenge the claim of the strength of objectivity to this approach. Content analysis begins with preconceived ideas as to what words or phrases best reflect the hypothesis and these ideas are shaped by researchers' biases. Feminist researchers are continually reflexive in their analysis, paying attention to their own biases throughout all phases of research. This is another way to reduce bias throughout the research process.

SEE ALSO: Computer-Aided/Mediated Analysis; Conversation Analysis; Critical Qualitative Research; Documentary Analysis; Methods; Semiotics; Text/Hypertext; Triangulation; Validity, Qualitative

REFERENCES AND SUGGESTED READINGS

Altheide, D. (1996) *Qualitative Media Analysis*. Sage, Newbury Park, CA.

Babbie, E. (2004) *The Practice of Social Research*, 10th edn. Thomson Wadsworth, Belmont, CA.

Bakhtin, M. M. (1986) *Speech Genres and Other Late Essays*. University of Texas Press, Austin.

Berelson, B. (1971) *Content Analysis in Communication Research*. Hafner, New York.

Berg, B. (2004) *Qualitative Research Methods for the Social Sciences*, 5th edn. Pearson, Allyn, & Bacon, Boston.

Bond, D. (2005) Content Analysis. In: Kempf-Leonard, K. (Ed.), *Encyclopedia of Social Measurement*. Elsevier Academic Press, New York, pp. 481–5.

Cohen, C. (1999) *The Boundaries of Blackness: AIDS and the Breakdown of Black Politics*. University of Chicago Press, Chicago.

Daniels, J. (1997) *White Lies: Race, Class, Gender, and Sexuality in White Supremacist Discourse*. Routledge, New York.

Epstein, S. (1996) *Impure Science: AIDS, Activism and the Politics of Knowledge*. University of California Press, Berkeley.

Fields, E. (1988) Qualitative Content Analysis of Television News: Systematic Techniques. *Qualitative Sociology* 11(3): 183.

Foucault, M. (1980) *Power/Knowledge: Selected Interviews and Other Writings 1972–1977*. Pantheon Books, New York.

Frankfort-Nachmias, C. & Nachmias, D. (1996) *Research Methods in the Social Sciences*, 5th edn. St. Martin's Press, New York.

Gans, H. (1979) *Deciding What's News*. Pantheon Books, New York.

Goffman, E. (1974) *Frame Analysis: An Essay on the Organization of Experience*. Harper & Row, New York.

Holsti, O. (1969) *Content Analysis for the Social Sciences and Humanities*. Addison-Wesley, Reading, MA.

Krippendorff, K. (2003) *Content Analysis: An Introduction to Its Methodology*. Sage, Newbury Park, CA.

Manning, P. & Cullum-Swan, B. (1990) Narrative, Content and Semiotic Analysis. In: Denzin, N. & Lincoln, Y. (Eds.), *The Handbook of Qualitative Research*. Sage, Thousand Oaks, CA.

Neuendorf, K. (2001) *The Content Analysis Handbook*. Sage, Newbury Park, , CA.

North, R., Holsti, O., Zaninovich, M. G., & Zinnes, D. (1963) *Content Analysis: A Handbook with Applications for the Study of International Crisis*. Northwestern University Press, Chicago.

Reinharz, S. (1992) *Feminist Methods in Social Research*. Oxford University Press, New York.

Smith, D. (1990) *Texts, Facts and Femininity: Exploring the Relations of Ruling*. Routledge, New York.

Weber, R. P. (1991) *Basic Content Analysis*, 2nd edn. Sage, Newbury Park, CA.

contention, tactical repertoires of

Verta Taylor

Social movement scholars use the concept of tactical repertoires of contention to refer to the strategies used by collective actors to persuade or coerce authorities to support their claims. The tactical repertoires of social movements include conventional strategies of political persuasion such as lobbying, voting, and petitioning; confrontational tactics such as marches, strikes, and public demonstrations that disrupt day-to-day life; violent acts such as bombing, rioting, assassination, and looting that inflict material and economic damage and loss of life; and cultural forms of political expression such as ritual, music, art, theater, street performance, and practices of everyday life that inspire solidarity and oppositional consciousness. If there

is a single feature that distinguishes social movements from routine political actors, it is the strategic use of protest – or novel, dramatic, unorthodox, and non-institutionalized forms of political expression. Because participants in social movements lack access to conventional channels of influence, they often disavow politics through proper channels.

The tactics used by social movements are increasingly examined in terms of their place in a larger repertoire of collective action. The notion of repertoires of contention grows out of the work of Charles Tilly (1978), who introduced the concept to explain historical variations in forms of political contention. Tilly contends that the distinctive forms of claims-making associated with the modern social movement are part of a larger repertoire of contention associated with the growth of national electoral politics and the proliferation of associations as vehicles of collective action. The term "repertoire" implies that the way a set of collective actors makes and receives claims bearing on each other's interests occurs in established and predictable ways. A social movement's tactical repertoire is what a challenging group knows how to do, it is what the larger society expects from it as an aggrieved group, and it accentuates the fact that a group's tactics and strategies are adapted from other challenging groups so that every social movement does not have to reinvent the wheel in each new conflict.

Theorists associated with the contentious politics approach use the repertoires of contention concept as part of a larger framework for analyzing collective claims-making that involves the government as a claimant, target, or mediator. Scholars who adopt this perspective focus on public protest events and link social movements to other forms of contentious politics such as strike waves, revolutions, and nationalism. Critics have objected to the contentious politics approach on the grounds that it is narrowly focused on political action (Goodwin & Jasper 1999). This approach to defining social movements excludes religious and self-help movements not directed at the state, as well as movements that target systems of authority within organizations and institutions, such as the military, medicine, education, and the workplace.

A common theme running through a segment of the literature is the insistence on a broad definition of social movements that recognizes the multiple targets and tactics of social movements. Taylor and her collaborators (Rupp & Taylor 2003; Taylor & Van Dyke 2004) offer a definition of tactical repertoires that encompasses the myriad of strategies used by social movements engaged in challenges to different systems of authority, as well as to the political status quo. They define tactical repertoires as interactive episodes that link social movement actors to each other as well as to opponents and authorities for the intended purpose of challenging or resisting change in identities, groups, organizations, or societies.

TYPES AND DIMENSIONS OF TACTICAL REPERTOIRES

Discussions of social movements invariably differentiate them on the basis of tactical repertoires. Early typologies defined social movements either as instrumental or expressive depending on whether their tactics were directed toward social or personal change. Recently, scholars have distinguished between strategy-oriented and identity-oriented movements on the basis of whether a group's tactics are geared toward policy change or the generation of collective agency and identity. Several scholars question the bifurcation of movements, arguing that most social movements combine both instrumental and expressive action (Bernstein 1997). As a result, current classifications have abandoned dualistic models and draw distinctions between non-confrontational or *insider tactics* (boycotts, lawsuits, leafleting, letter-writing, lobbying, petitions, Internet activism, and press conferences) and confrontational or *outsider tactics* (such as sit-ins, demonstrations, vigils, marches, strikes, symbolic performances, blockades, bombings, assassinations, and other illegal actions). Tarrow introduces violent tactics and offers the following typology of protest: conventional, disruptive, and violent.

Knowledge of social movement tactics derives from "protest event" research, pioneered by Tilly and his colleagues. Protest event research refers to the content coding of newspaper accounts of protest events and other contentious gatherings. This approach uses variation in the number and timing of protest events to assess the level of mobilization of social movements. Some scholars identify problems with using newspapers to collect information on collective action events. Newspaper accounts are biased toward public protest directed at the government. Tactical repertoires that target other institutions and challenge cultural codes in everyday life are best studied through in-depth qualitative and historical methods.

Taylor and her collaborators identify three features of collective action events. First, tactical repertoires are sites of *contestation* in which bodies, symbols, identities, practices, and discourses are used to pursue or prevent changes in institutionalized power relations. The second component is *intentionality*, or the strategic use of collective action to promote or resist change in dominant relations of power. Third, a social movement's tactical repertoires generate oppositional consciousness and *collective identity*.

FACTORS THAT INFLUENCE TACTICAL REPERTOIRES

Tactical repertoires are influenced by external sociopolitical factors and internal movement processes. Theorists of contentious politics link collective action repertoires to modernization, specifically the creation of the nation-state and centralized decision-making, the development of capitalist markets, and the emergence of modern forms of communication. These changes brought shifts in the nature and geographical reach of political authority and gave rise to new forms of political contention expressed in the form of strikes, rallies, public demonstrations and meetings, petitions, marches, sit-ins, boycotts, insurrections, and various forms of civil disobedience. These means of claims-making replaced older direct, local, and patronage-dependent forms of protest with forms that are national in character, autonomous from power-holders, and modular in the sense that similar tactics and strategies can be used by different groups of activists pursuing different targets.

New social movement theory (Touraine 1981; Melucci 1989), a paradigm that competes with the contentious politics approach, links the tactical repertoires of contemporary social movements to the shift from an industrial to a post-industrial economy that brought new forms of social control as a result of the intervention of capitalism and the state into private areas of life, including the self and the body. In western societies, these macrohistorical changes brought about new forms of mainly middle-class activism, such as women's, peace, gay and lesbian, environmental, animal rights, self-help, anti-racist, and other movements. The tactical repertoires of these so-called new social movements are thought to be distinct from earlier forms of class-based activism because activists are concerned with issues of identity and quality of life rather than economic redistribution. Although the new social movement approach has brought attention to cultural repertoires, evidence for the hypothesis that contemporary movements are a product of the post-industrial society is questionable. Scholars also take issue with the notion of "newness," arguing that some presumably new movements, such as the women's movement, date to the nineteenth century.

Sidney Tarrow advances the notion of protest cycles to understand how macrohistorical factors influence social movement tactics. Protest tends to follow a recurrent cycle or wave in which collective mobilizations increase and decrease in frequency, intensity, and formation. The ebb and flow that characterize protest cycles influence the tactics adopted by different movements in the cycle. In the early stages, disruptive tactics predominate, and, as a protest wave develops, interaction between protestors and authorities stimulates the institutionalization of moderate tactical repertoires and the radicalization of others as routine tactics become less effective. Paul Almeida's research on protest waves in El Salvador between 1962 and 1981 illustrates the role that threat and state repression play in this process. He shows how, over time, protest shifted from reformist contention based on non-violent strategies to a radicalized movement reliant on violent protest.

The preponderance of empirical research on the way internal characteristics of social movements influence social movement tactics has focused on the relationship between a movement's form of organization and its capacity to engage in disruptive and confrontational protest. William Gamson (1990) provides powerful evidence that social movement organizations

facilitate disruptive protest, although Frances Fox Piven and Richard Cloward (1979) take issue with this based on their study of US poor people's movements, which demonstrates that the involvement of social movement organizations channels energy away from mass defiance into institutional forms of action. Research on Islamic activism in the Arab world demonstrates that organizational form remains important for understanding tactical repertoires.

Frequently, collective actors adopt strategies and tactics not because they have been shown to be effective, but because they resonate with the cultural frames of meaning participants use to legitimate collective action. Finally, the structural position of protestors influences a group's tactical repertoires. Several studies, including research on the mobilization of contention to support Muslim causes, report that economically and socially marginal actors who lack access to political and economic power are more likely to engage in disruptive and even violent forms of protest. A body of research also finds that inequalities of gender, race and ethnicity, class, and sexuality influence tactical choices (McCammon et al. 2001).

THE RELATIONSHIP BETWEEN TACTICS AND MOVEMENT OUTCOMES

Tactical repertoires have implications for movement success. Researchers interested in whether and how social movements produce social and political change identify several characteristics of protest that relate to effectiveness. Novelty, or the use of innovative tactics, is more likely to lead to success because innovative protest catches authorities off guard and increases the likelihood that the protest event will be covered by the media (McAdam 1983). William Gamson presents convincing evidence that disruptive tactics are more successful than conventional strategies. Aldon Morris's (1993) study of the 1963 Birmingham, Alabama, campaign against racial segregation suggests that using a variety of tactics yields favorable results. Size, or the ability to mobilize large numbers of participants, is another ingredient in a campaign's success because large demonstrations capture media attention, demonstrate public support, and increase disruptive potential. Cultural resonance – or public displays of protest that tap into prevailing beliefs and identities – also increases the likelihood of positive outcomes.

Repertoires and tactics of protest are the theoretical building blocks of all theories formulated to understand social movements. There is need for continuing research to address ongoing debates over the impact of sociopolitical factors and social movement organization on tactical repertoires and the relative effectiveness of militant versus non-militant tactics. The question of how the unorthodox tactics used by social movements influence the cultural fabric of societies remains unexamined. Because social movements in western democracies have received most of the scholarly attention, it is also reasonable to wonder how thinking about social movement tactics might change by closer attention both to social movements in non-democratic states and to transnational activism.

SEE ALSO: Collective Action; Collective Identity; Culture, Social Movements and; New Social Movement Theory; Political Process Theory; Political Sociology; Protest, Diffusion of; Social Change; Social Movement Organizations

REFERENCES AND SUGGESTED READINGS

Almeida, P. D. (2003) Opportunity Organizations and Threat-Induced Contention: Protest Waves in Authoritarian Settings. *American Journal of Sociology* 109: 345–400.

Bernstein, M. (1997) Celebration and Suppression: Strategic Uses of Identity by the Lesbian and Gay Movement. *American Journal of Sociology* 103: 531–65.

Gamson, W. A. (1990) *The Strategy of Social Protest*, 2nd edn. Wadsworth, Belmont, CA.

Goodwin, J. & Jasper, J. (1999) Caught in a Winding, Snarling Vine: The Structural Bias of Political Process Theory. *Sociological Forum* 14: 27–54.

McAdam, D. (1983) Tactical Innovation and the Pace of Insurgency. *American Sociological Review* 48: 735–54.

McAdam, D., Tarrow, S., & Tilly, C. (1996) To Map Contentious Politics. *Mobilization* 1: 17–34.

McCammon, H. J., Campbell, K. E., Granberg, E. M., & Mowry, C. (2001) How Movements Win: Gendered Opportunity Structures and US

Women's Suffrage Movements, 1866–1919. *American Sociological Review* 66: 49–70.

Melucci, A. (1989) *Nomads of the Present: Social Movements and Individual Needs in Contemporary Society*. Temple University Press, Philadelphia.

Morris, A. (1993) Birmingham Confrontation Reconsidered: An Analysis of the Dynamics and Tactics of Mobilization. *American Sociological Review* 58: 621–36.

Piven, F. F. & Cloward, R. (1979) *Poor People's Movements*, 2nd edn. Vintage, New York.

Rupp, L. J. & Taylor, V. (2003) *Drag Queens at the 801 Cabaret*. University of Chicago Press, Chicago.

Taylor, V. & Van Dyke, N. (2004) Tactical Repertoires of Social Movements. In: Snow, D. A., Soule, S.A., & Kriesi, H. (Eds.), *The Blackwell Companion to Social Movements*. Blackwell, Oxford, pp. 262–93.

Tilly, C. (1978) *From Mobilization to Revolution*. Random House, New York.

Touraine, A. (1981) *The Voice and the Eye: An Analysis of Social Movements*. Cambridge University Press, New York.

control balance theory

Charles R. Tittle

Control balance is a general, integrated theory to explain deviant behavior by individuals or organizations, although it explains conformity and submission as well. Deviant behavior consists of acts disapproved by the majority of a group or that typically bring about negative social reactions. Since criminal behavior is usually deviant, the theory also explains most crime.

Theoretically, the likelihood of deviance in some form is predictable from a control imbalance and a motivation-producing provocation. A control imbalance exists when the control a social entity (individual or organization) can exercise over things, circumstances, or individuals is greater or less than the control to which the social entity is subject. Relative amounts of total control are registered as control ratios, which can show balance, deficits, or surpluses. With a given control imbalance and a motivating provocation, specific deviance is chosen from acts within a restricted range of control balance desirability (CBD). Since the degree of CBD varies among acts, all misbehaviors can be arrayed over a continuum of CBD. The range of the CBD continuum from which an act is chosen is related to a person's control ratio, opportunity, possible counter-control the act will likely attract, and the person's self-control. Choosing a particular deviant act is called control balancing – weighing perceived gain in control from possible deviant behavior against the counter-control that it may produce.

Being rooted in social statuses, personal characteristics, and organizational affiliations, control ratios are global and situational. All people are assumed to want to gain more control, no matter how much or little they have, and actors are assumed to rely principally on deviant behavior in trying to overcome control imbalances. However, preexisting desire to extend control does not produce deviance unless it is brought into awareness by situational circumstances and other conditions exist. Actors become motivated toward deviance when sharply reminded of their control imbalances, especially if reminders involve denigration or humiliation, and they perceive that deviance can help. Motivation may lead to deviance if the behavior is possible in the situation (opportunity) and potential counter-controls do not outweigh (or are not perceived as outweighing) potential gain in control to be realized from misbehavior. Because opportunities for deviance of some kind are omnipresent and the chances of controlling reactions are highly variable, some kinds of deviance always provide favorable balances. As a result, the strength of motivation predicts the chances of deviance in some form. If researchers measure the chances of subjects' committing each of a large number of deviant acts, along with their control ratios and motivation, they should find those with control imbalances who are motivated to be much more likely to commit one or more of the acts than are those with balanced controls. The control ratio and motivation, however, are not sufficient to predict the exact act to be committed.

Because serious deviant acts have the greatest potential for increasing one's control, a motivated person first contemplates committing one or more of them. But serious acts also imply great potential counter-control. Therefore, only those

with small control deficits or any degree of control surplus can realistically resort to serious misbehavior. As a result, deviantly motivated people cognitively slide over a continuum of CBD to find an "appropriate" deviant act. Those with balanced control ratios are more conformist because they are less likely to become motivated toward deviance and they face greater potential counter-control. By contrast, overwhelming control deficits reduce the ability to imagine alternatives, leading to submission.

Those with control deficiencies are frequently motivated by reminders of their relative helplessness, while those with surpluses are often motivated by not receiving the deference they expect. The specific act of deviance resulting from a convergence of a control imbalance, provocation and motivation, opportunity, and control balancing reflects its CBD, which is composed of two elements: (1) the act's likely long-range effectiveness in altering a control imbalance, and (2) the extent to which the act requires direct and personal involvement of the perpetrator with a victim or an object affected by the deviance. When the theory's theoretical causal variables converge for a given individual, that person chooses from among deviant acts with similar scores on the CBD continuum.

An actor with a control ratio between the second and third quartiles of a continuum from maximum deficit to maximum surplus (excluding the balanced zone) is liable for acts somewhere between the second and third quartiles of CBD, provided that the actor has sufficient self-control to avoid "unrealistic" action, there is opportunity to do them, and the risk of counter-control does not outweigh the gain from the deviant act. The choice of deviant act is also influenced by such things as moral commitments, intelligence, habits, and personality.

Thus, an unbalanced control ratio, in combination with deviant motivation, will lead to a choice of a specific deviant act within a restricted range of the CBD continuum. The zone from which the deviant act is chosen narrows with increasing inclusion of the theoretical variables. Taking all of the theoretical variables into account allows the range of likely deviant acts to be quite narrow, though it may still contain a large number of different acts with similar CBD. Thus, the theory cannot predict choice of a specific deviant act, such as stealing an object or assaulting a spouse.

The validity of the theory currently rests mainly on argument. The original statement (Tittle 1995) was quickly recognized as worthy of attention, but only limited tests were conducted. The research that was conducted, though challenging some aspects of the theory, nevertheless suggests that control imbalances are important predictors of deviance. Those empirical challenges and logical critiques led to a major revision (Tittle 2004a). That refined version has not yet been tested, so whether the theory fulfills its theoretical promise remains to be seen.

SEE ALSO: Crime, Life Course Theory of; Crime, Social Control Theory of; Deviance; Deviance, Crime and; Deviance, Theories of; Identity, Deviant; Juvenile Delinquency; Organizational Deviance; Rational Choice Theory: A Crime-Related Perspective; Self-Control Theory

REFERENCES AND SUGGESTED READINGS

Tittle, C. R. (1995) *Control Balance: Toward a General Theory of Deviance*. Westview Press, Boulder.
Tittle, C. R. (2001) Control Balance. In: Paternoster, R. & Bachman, R. (Eds.), *Contemporary Theories*. Roxbury, Los Angeles, pp. 315–34.
Tittle, C. R. (2004a) Refining Control Balance Theory. *Theoretical Criminology 8*.
Tittle, C. R. (2004b) Control Balance and Violence. In: Brownstein, H., Zahn, M. A., & Jackson, S. L. (Eds.), *Violence: From Theory to Research*. Anderson, Cincinnati.

controversy studies

Chandra Mukerji

Controversy studies have been an important part of the sociology of science since the late 1970s when Merton's more institutional approach to the field began to be displaced by the sociology of scientific knowledge (SSK). Inspired by Kuhn (1970), the new sociologists

of science were determined to show empirically what Kuhn had suggested conceptually: that knowledge-making was a social process. Controversy studies were important to this project because they focused on moments of change between more stable regimes of knowledge. Kuhn had argued that researchers during most historical periods engaged in "normal science" based on a shared paradigm. This kind of collective practice was particularly productive of new knowledge because researchers worked with recognized techniques on puzzles of common interest. They could learn from and build on what others were doing and collaborate more easily because they shared many assumptions about their research. But paradigms had limits that became increasingly visible over time. In moments of revolutionary change, new paradigms were developed to make sense of these anomalies, displacing the old regime of normal practice. In the transition period, scientists engaged in controversies about elements of the paradigm.

Scholars in SSK became interested in controversies to understand the processes of scientific change. Kuhn was vague in his theory about the character of the conflict before and during a revolution. Shifts in scientific models and practices seemed to have complex, emergent properties that seemed better studied ethnographically. Once in the laboratory, sociologists of science found a rich social life among scientists that included collective struggles for authority over fields (Barnes 1977; Knorr-Cetina 1981; Barnes & Bloor 1982; Latour 1988; Lynch 1990).

Contests of knowledge in moments of controversy, when studied empirically, turned out to be deeply social processes. The truth of ideas was tested less with logical analysis of a philosophical sort than with debates about validity that had sometimes modest, sometimes epic proportions. The scientists involved in controversies were hardly dispassionate. They looked for ways to advance their ideas, enroll allies in their movements, and promote their schools of thought. At the same time, their critics and competitors looked for fallacies in their arguments, flaws in their data, and reasons to doubt their approaches to problems. Opponents and advocates alike vetted the work. Criticisms appeared in many different venues: universities during personnel decisions, journals when articles were reviewed, and conferences when new papers were presented. Communities of practitioners worked to make their perspectives powerful in their fields (Latour 1988; Epstein 1996).

These wars over the nature of things were in part wars of words. As most epistemologists assumed, these struggles entailed some assessments of truth statements. What sociologists pointed out was that this linguistic and logical vetting was the work of scientists, not philosophers. Scientists were not just bench practitioners and mathematicians, but also writers. Their verbal assertions were matters of professional attention. Ethnographers of science followed the linguistic practices of scientific knowledge-making both in the laboratory and the literature to see the social patterns of epistemic work (Latour & Woolgar 1979; Knorr-Cetina 1981).

Controversy studies in SSK were historically not simply a reaction to Mertonian sociology of science, but also part of a more general shift in sociology that occurred during the 1970s and 1980s as the hegemony of functionalism dwindled. Radical critiques by structuralists and constructivists alike started to reshape much of the field. On the micro side, ethno-methodologists argued against traditional ethnography that used analytic categories from sociology instead of research subjects' understandings of things. They argued that meaning-making was a local and emergent practice of ordinary people, not something that needed to be or should be imposed from above. On the macro side, Marxists confined their analyses to the structural properties of historical change – exactly what ethnomethodologists denied or decried. Structuralists wanted to specify the contradictions in regimes that drove history, and argued that the meaning-making studied by ethnographers was epiphenomenal and not necessary to sociological explanations.

In spite of their opposed theoretical commitments, both groups of sociologists studied revolutions and purified their research practices in ways that targeted and excluded functionalist sociology. Few sociologists of science admitted that science was important to study because of its hegemonic properties and role in the Cold War, since this required asking scientists about their relationship to the government, not their

epistemic practices (Mukerji 1977). Still, the Cold War helped give salience to SSK. A contest of knowledge systems of grand proportions was shaping history at that time and gave intuitive salience to this work.

The collective commitment in SSK to studying social epistemology using ethnographic methods kept scholars in science studies focused on knowledge-in-the-making. Science was studied mainly through the lens of ethno-methodology as a local group accomplishment, disconnected from institutional constraints. Truth was a product of identifiable social interactions that fieldwork made visible and studies of language made understandable (Knorr-Cetina 1981; Lynch 1990).

The "strong program" in SSK provided a research strategy for approaching scientific controversies: methodological symmetry. Barnes and Bloor (1982) argued that sociologists should treat accepted and rejected forms of knowledge symmetrically, not attempting to explain what was good about accepted science and bad about rejected knowledge. The point was not to privilege successful claims to truth and to naturalize the boundaries around "real" science. The effect was to privilege knowledge and internalist accounts of it in the sociology of science. Methodological symmetry technically made SSK agnostic about scientific knowledge and respectful of scientists' words and work. But by systematically denying the authority of scientific knowledge, methodological symmetry helped to foster antipathy toward this kind of sociology of science among both positivist sociologists and some scientists.

Nonetheless, the elegance of the strong program and methodological symmetry was appealing to many young scholars. They liked addressing philosophical issues with sociological tools and they made controversy studies in the SSK tradition the center of the new sociology of science. If the adjudication of controversies was social, then things like tests of fit, logic, and research methods were tools of social struggle. Determining the truth was less a matter of logic than a test of social strength (Latour 1988). Paradigms had allies and advocates. Ideas were associated with groups of people. And controversies pitted groups against one another for dominance of a field. Labs were described as centers of calculation through which resources and knowledge flowed. The exercise of scientific skepticism was recharacterized as part of an agonistic system for allocating power and fame (Latour 1988; Epstein 1996). The ideas with the greatest numbers of powerful advocates were the ones accepted as established knowledge. According to Shapin and Schaffer (1985), the processes involved in the determination of scientific truths paralleled the ones governing public life. Solutions to problems of knowledge were necessarily also solutions to problems of politics – ways to gain social authority. The scientific experiment was an exercise in proper governance. It was a way to produce trust as well as knowledge by modeling the systematic and successful exercise of human will on the natural world.

Callon (1986) and Latour (1988) argued that the groups that were victorious in scientific controversies had to contain not only social actors (researchers), but also non-human actants (experimental objects and quasi-objects). Successful experiments were ways to make parts of the natural world testify on behalf of theoretical assertions. Things could *show* that scientists were right and make their ideas more than simply a matter of opinion and refined argumentation. Reproducible tests of scientific truths – played out in the actions of things – took some of the burden of proof off linguistic assertions or truth claims. Scientific knowledge was based on witnessing of events as well as language practices. Things helped to make people trustworthy (Latour 1988; Shapin & Schaffer 1985).

In labs, the connections between objects of scientific study and technical language were invented through "shop talk" (Knorr-Cetina 1981; Lynch 1990) and promoted through "literary practices" (Shapin & Schaffer 1985). Inscription devices (Latour & Woolgar 1979) such as print-outs or images made with laboratory instruments provided researchers with common objects of discussion. They could determine from them how to analyze or supplement the data, adding new layers of social cognition to the process. Printed journal articles also allowed those without direct access to laboratory tests virtual means for witnessing them (Shapin & Schaffer 1985). Experiments circulated through these inscription devices allowed scientists to share a common "experience" of natural phenomena even at a distance.

In the 1990s the interest in controversy studies declined in the sociology of science along with the authority of SSK. Studies of knowledge without attention to its power began to seem limited as a new generation of scholars came to the field after reading Foucault about power/knowledge. Controversy studies lost their Kuhnian significance, too, once fieldwork revealed that these struggles were part of the routine operation of normal science, and were rarely openings for fundamental change such as a paradigm shift. Conflict no longer had the caché of revolutionary potential, either. Sociologists were generally not so interested in revolution – even in historical sociology.

Sociologists drawn to science through poststructuralism wanted to know how classification systems worked as political tools, shaping social life. Like ethnomethodologists and epistemologists, they were interested in language, but did not share the assumption that close technical readings of statements could capture meaning. Language was a tool for power, but one accessible to ordinary people and flexible in its uses. Meaning was a site of contest, not a route to a determined truth. These "cultural" scholars in science studies started to question the primacy of epistemological issues in SSK, wondering why philosophical debates were allowed to set research agendas for sociologists. Methodological symmetry still had appeal to postmodernists, feminists, and cultural analysts who were entering the field because the principle seemed useful for revealing the political aspects of drawing boundaries between science and nonscience. But many of these scholars eschewed the commitment to ethnography and relativism in SSK. They wanted to follow Foucault, using history to study the power of knowledge (Haraway 1989; Epstein 1996).

If knowledge defined the reality upon which political regimes founded their authority, it was not benign, but rather a means of gaining or stabilizing advantages. Epistemological issues were not technical questions, but rather tools for managing social forms of consciousness. SSK with its emphasis on knowledge practices could help scholars see the social foundations of truth claims, but it did not help analyze who was being advantaged or disadvantaged by the changing realities woven with scientific facts. The idea that solutions to problems of knowledge were also solutions to problems of politics (Shapin & Schaffer 1985) linked power and knowledge, but not in the same way as Foucault. SSK was built on the assumption that there *could be* solutions to problems of knowledge. With Foucault, there was no such assurance or prospect of real stability. Knowledge, including social knowledge, was a means for exercising and justifying acts of domination. The controversies in SSK could be about nuclear weapons without the military significance of the work really requiring analytic attention. The new work in science studies had to consider how science and technology were used (Latour 2004).

Although the SSK version of controversy studies declined in intellectual importance, many elements of this early work continued into the 1990s. Scholars paid ongoing attention to instrumentation, for example (Clarke & Fujimura 1992). The techniques of research that Kuhn had described as fundamental to normal science and SSK researchers had noted as important to labs (Barnes 1977; Latour & Woolgar 1979; Knorr-Cetina 1981) were now a free-standing matters of research set between science and technology (Clarke & Fujimura 1992).

The patterns of trust that held allies together and helped to make regimes of truth both powerful and useful were also pursued in new ways. Porter (1995) looked at the role of mathematics in establishing bonds of trust both in social science and social policy circles. Controversy studies had been turned on their head. Now the question was explaining how cooperation and mutual understanding were possible within and across highly contested social worlds of science (Martin 1991; Epstein 1996).

The science/nonscience boundary was also approached in new ways by scholars interested in how scientific facts met ordinary life (Epstein 1996). Now sociologists of science wanted to consider expertise, how it was authorized, and in what ways it was used (Martin 1991; Porter 1995; Collins 2002; Latour 2004). Scientific controversies were now part of public debates about policy, law, and natural resources.

Most importantly, sociologists started to question the notion of closure in scientific debates. Oreskes (1999) showed that the complete rejection of continental drift as a theory of geology early in the twentieth century did not prevent the revival of this theory after World War II. Similarly, Simon (2002) showed that research on cold fusion continued after this idea was discredited. Controversies seemed to be so common in science in part because some never did reach closure, and ideas that seemed beyond the pale could still find allies. Knorr-Cetina (1999) even showed that different science had different epistemic cultures. There was no single test of truth that research findings could satisfy for all fields. What was called scientific was not monolithic.

Now many sociologists of science are interested in the role of science in political controversies (Latour 2004) and the contest of scientific ideas against other kinds of expert and lay knowledge. The interest in scientific controversies has been transformed. Sociologists are less concerned with the social processes determining what is legitimate science and more with the importance of science in the public sphere (Collins 2002). There has been a retreat from the relativism and methodological symmetry that were central to controversy studies in SSK. Some sociologists of science (Collins 2002) have become allies of scientists, championing their ways of knowing and arguing for its importance to social policy. In the face of the growing power of religion in public life, science has been redefined as a cornerstone of rationality that may be fallible and contested, but still remains vital as both a human collective activity and tool for shaping public life.

SEE ALSO: Epistemology; Ethnomethodology; Expertise, "Scientification," and the Authority of Science; Feminism and Science, Feminist Epistemology; Foucault, Michel; Knowledge, Sociology of; Kuhn, Thomas and Scientific Paradigms; Merton, Robert K.; Military Research and Science and War; Poststructuralism; Technology, Science, and Culture; Trustworthiness

REFERENCES AND SUGGESTED READINGS

Barnes, B. (1977) *Interests and the Growth of Knowledge*. Routledge & Kegan Paul, London.
Barnes, B. & Bloor, D. (1982) Relativism, Rationalism and the Sociology of Knowledge. In: Hollis,

M. & Lukes, S. (Eds.), *Rationality and Relativism*. Blackwell, Oxford, pp. 21–47.

Callon, M. (1986) Some Elements of a Sociology of Translation: Domestication of the Scallops and the Fishermen of St. Brieuc Bay. In: Law, J. (Ed.), *Power, Action and Belief*. Routledge & Kegan Paul, London, pp. 196–233.

Clarke, A. & Fujimura, J. (1992) *The Right Tool for the Job: At Work in Twentieth Century Life Sciences*. Princeton University Press, Princeton.

Collins, H. M. (2002) The Third Wave of Science Studies: Studies of Expertise and Experience. *Social Studies of Science* 32(2): 235–96.

Epstein, S. (1996) *Impure Science: AIDS, Activism, and the Politics of Knowledge*. University of California Press, Berkeley.

Haraway, D. (1989) *Primate Visions: Gender, Race and Nature in the World of Modern Science*. Routledge, New York.

Knorr-Cetina, K. (1981) *The Manufacture of Knowledge: An Essay on the Constructivist and Contextual Nature of Science*. Pergamon Press, Oxford.

Knorr-Cetina, K. (1999) *Epistemic Cultures: How the Sciences Make Knowledge*. Harvard University Press, Cambridge, MA.

Kuhn, T. (1970 [1962]) *The Structure of Scientific Revolutions*, 2nd edn. University of Chicago Press, Chicago.

Latour, B. (1988) *The Pasteurization of France*. Trans. A. Sheridon & J. Law. Harvard University Press, Cambridge, MA.

Latour, B. (2004) Why Has Critique Run Out of Steam? From Matters of Fact to Matters of Concern. *Critical Inquiry* 30(2): 25–48.

Latour, B. & Woolgar, S. (1979) *Laboratory Life: The (Social) Construction of Scientific Fact*. Sage, Beverly Hills.

Lynch, M. (1990) *Art and Artifact in Laboratory Science: A Study of Shop Work and Shop Talk in a Research Laboratory*. Routledge & Keagan Paul, London.

Martin, B. (1991) *Scientific Knowledge in Controversy: The Social Dynamics of the Fluoridation Debate*. State University of New York Press, Albany.

Mukerji, C. (1977) *A Fragile Power: Science and the State*. Princeton University Press, Princeton.

Oreskes, N. (1999) *The Rejection of Continental Drift*. Oxford University Press, New York.

Porter, T. (1995) *Trust in Numbers*. Princeton University Press, Princeton.

Shapin, S. & Schaffer, S. (1985) *Leviathan and the Air-Pump: Hobbes, Boyle, and the Experimental Life*. Princeton University Press, Princeton.

Simon, B. (2002) *Undead Science: Science Studies and the Afterlife of Cold Fusion*. Rutgers University Press, New Brunswick, NJ.

convenience sample

Clifford E. Lunneborg

Convenience samples are best described as what they are not. They are non-probability samples. That is, no attempt is made in their construction to sample randomly from any well-defined population. Random sampling is almost always difficult and expensive, often prohibitively so. Convenience samples, as the name implies, are more easily obtained. They may be self-selected respondents to a mail-out survey. Or they may be readily to hand, patrons of a local gay bar who agree to be interviewed.

The non-randomness of the convenience sample militates against straightforward inference from sample to population. The percentage of those who call in to a local talk show host and voice opposition to the proposed location of a halfway house for parolees cannot be taken as an unbiased estimate of the proportion opposed, for any population that a researcher might define. Berk and Freedman (2003) amply describe the mismatch between classical statistical inference and convenience sample data. In particular, they point to the difficult task of trying to link the social processes that lead to the convenience sample data and the assumptions underlying statistical inference.

Non-randomness severely limits, but does not completely preclude, the possibility of gaining scientific knowledge from data contributed by a convenience sample. As a prime exhibit, the "gold standard" in medical research, the randomized clinical trial, almost always rests on a convenience sample, those patients who volunteer (or consent when asked) to participate. The key here is the randomization. The volunteer patients are randomly assigned either to a "standard treatment" group or to a "new treatment" group and their progress is studied following the administration of the corresponding treatment.

The randomization serves two important purposes. First, it serves to level the playing field; it is unlikely that the two treatment groups will differ on any characteristic that might influence their response to treatment, other than the actual differences in treatment. Second, the randomization creates two random samples, albeit samples from a very limited, local population, the convenience sample itself. Nonetheless, the random samples facilitate statistical inference. We can draw inferences about the local population from the responses of the samples. And, owing to the randomization, those inferences have a causal implication, the differences in treatment causing the differences in response to treatment. The role of randomization in attributing causation is developed in Rubin (1991) and the use of randomization as a basis for statistical inference, originally proposed by Pitman (1937), is well described in Edgington (1995), Lunneborg (2000), and Ludbrook (2005).

Of course, the linkage of treatment and response, even a causal one, might be thought to be of little importance as it is established only for this convenience sample of patients. The importance of the linkage can be generalized, though, in either of two ways. First, the medical community may be in agreement that the patients in this local population are broadly like similarly diagnosed patients seen in other clinics. What was demonstrated here ought to hold true, they are willing to conclude, for other patients seen by other practitioners in other clinics. This form of generalization speaks to the distinction drawn by MacKay and Oldford (2001) between statistical inference directed at the population actually sampled and scientific inference (or generalization) directed at some larger target population. Having statistically established a (causal) linkage over the local population, we might propose to our scientific colleagues that the results generalize to a larger target population.

The second form of generalization is what Mook (2001) refers to as theoretical. If the linkage reliably established for the convenience sample via randomization and randomization-based inference is grounded in a particular, explicit theory, then the results generalize the support for that theory. Or, of course, the convenience sample data could weaken the support for that theory if the results were to contradict theoretical predictions.

Random allocation among "treatments," though providing the strongest support for both causal and statistical inference from convenience sample studies, is not always possible. Rosenbaum and Rubin (1983) propose the use of propensity scores as a surrogate for active randomization. Consider a convenience sample of active non-monogamous male homosexuals, the members of which can be characterized as either "committed" or "uncommitted" to the use of condoms. The men were not randomized between the two orientations. Assume, though, that for the sample there is a relationship between the choice of condom behavior and certain characteristics of the men, e.g., their ages, years of education, employment stability, residential stability, length of "outage." This relationship can be used to assign to each man a propensity score, the modeled probability that he will be committed to the use of condoms. By restricting attention to those pairs of men, one committed and one not committed, who can be closely matched on their propensity scores, one can carry out as-if-randomized analyses. These provide a more reliable comparison of the behaviors of the two groups than would a raw between-groups comparison. Rubin (1991) describes the conduct of one such study in great detail.

Convenience samples can be useful even where formal statistical inference would be inappropriate. They are suitable for pilot studies. Will respondents be able to understand the questions in this survey? Can we get volunteers for the proposed study who are of the target age? Further, it might be considered unwise to commit to a more critical (and expensive) study unless a postulated relationship were not first observed in a convenience sample.

Berk and Freedman (2003) stress the importance of replication and replicability in interpreting convenience sample studies. Is what we observe in this convenience sample consistent with what we have seen in other samples? Can we successfully predict from this sample what we will see in a second sample?

The convenience sample, intentionally neither random nor representative, may lack homogeneity as well. Our description of the sample data, then, may lack stability, as it may be strongly influenced by a small fraction of the sample. Berk and Freedman (2003) advocate the routine use of sensitivity analyses to guard against mistakenly describing the outcome of the convenience sample study. Lunneborg (2000) describes the use of subsamples of the non-random sample to this end.

SEE ALSO: Chance and Probability; Random Sample; Replicability Analyses

REFERENCES AND SUGGESTED READINGS

Berk, R. A. & Freedman, D. A. (2003) Statistical Assumptions as Empirical Commitments. In: Blomberg, T. & Cohen, S. (Eds.), *Law, Punishment, and Social Control: Essays in Honor of Sheldon Messinger*, 2nd edn. Aldine de Gruyter, New York.

Edgington, E. S. (1995) *Randomization Tests*, 3rd edn. Dekker, New York.

Ludbrook, J. (2005) Randomization-Based Tests. In: Everitt, B. S. & Howell, D. C. (Eds.), *Encyclopedia of Statistics in Behavioral Science*, Vol. 3. Wiley, Chichester, pp. 1548–50.

Lunneborg, C. E. (2000) *Data Analysis by Resampling: Concepts and Applications*. Duxbury, Pacific Grove, CA.

MacKay, R. J. & Oldford, R. W. (2001) Scientific Method, Statistical Method and the Speed of Light. *Statistical Science* 15: 254–78.

Mook, D. G. (2001) *Psychological Research: The Ideas Behind the Methods*. Norton, New York.

Pitman, E. J. G. (1937) Significance Tests Which May Be Applied to Samples From Any Population. *Royal Statistical Society Supplement* 4: 119–30.

Rosenbaum, P. R. & Rubin, D. R. (1983) The Central Role of the Propensity Score in Observational Studies for Causal Effects. *Biometrika* 70: 41–55.

Rubin, D. R. (1991) Practical Implications of Modes of Statistical Inference for Causal Effects and the Critical Role of the Assignment Mechanism. *Biometrics* 47: 1213–34.

conversation

Dan E. Miller

A conversation is an exchange of thoughts and ideas between two or more people. An instance of focused interaction, a conversation occurs when people cooperate with each other in order to introduce and sustain a single focus of attention by taking turns talking with each other. Conversations are the most natural, most frequent, and most universal of all forms of spoken language. Generally restricted to small groups, conversations involving larger groups tend to divide into several conversational groups. For example, even groups as small as four people tend to separate into two dyadic units.

The significance of conversations cannot be overstated. Much of day-to-day life is organized and carried out through conversations – from institutional conversations (as between supervisor and worker, physician and patient, or between representatives of labor and management) to more casual conversations (as between a couple getting to know each other or two friends being sociable over lunch). Conversely, when social relationships break down, conversations are the primary source of remediation. Through conversation conflicts are resolved, friendships are rekindled, and labor contracts negotiated.

The study of conversations has its roots in several academic subdisciplines. They are: symbolic interaction, sociolinguistics, ethnomethodology, and conversation analysis. Although concepts employed and methods of analysis vary, throughout each approach one finds an underlying concern for pragmatic questions – how conversations are constructed, how conversational openings and closings are accomplished, conversational difficulties between men and women, and how conversations can be repaired. By focusing their study on the microsocial worlds of naturally occurring conversations, analysts have uncovered a rich source of data pertaining to how the interaction and social order is constructed and maintained.

To become native speakers, children must learn words, pronunciation, and grammar. They also learn how to construct different forms of conversation. These include gossip, sociability, bargaining, negotiation, critical deliberation, playful repartee, argument, interviewing and interrogation, persuasion, reciprocal self-disclosure, and coquetry. Each of these forms involves distinct interaction patterns and relationships between actors. For example, sociability is a form of interaction wherein the participants, as equals, move from one topic to the next, each expressing her views, demonstrating her knowledge, and introducing new topics as the conversation proceeds. On the other hand, an interrogation is asymmetrical, wherein one participant controls the situation by asking questions, interrupting, forcing topics, making threats, and calling for accounts.

Also, conversations can range from the highly ordered to the seemingly chaotic. In some situations, conversations are constructed with orderly turn-taking sequences wherein one speaks while the other listens. However, the politeness of this conversational form may not be present in other situations. Among family members or in groups of close friends a more raucous form of conversation may be constructed in which those involved are more passionate, employing interruptions, simultaneous talk, and friendly argumentative banter.

Conversations are not restricted to face-to-face situations; they may be conducted via telephones, two-way radios, the Internet, or with the exchange of letters. The technological limitations of these media require a strict adherence to the polite turn-taking rule – one speaks or writes while the other listens or waits. In these situations simultaneous talking or writing destroys the topical continuity and interaction reciprocity that form the basis of all conversation.

SEE ALSO: Conversation Analysis; Discourse; Ethnomethodology; Interaction; Sociolinguistics; Symbolic Interaction

REFERENCES AND SUGGESTED READINGS

Goffman, E. (1963) *Behavior in Public Places*. Free Press, New York.
Goffman, E. (1983) The Interaction Order. *American Sociological Review* 48: 1–17.
Hintz, R. A. & Miller, D. E. (1995) Openings Revisited: The Foundation of Social Interaction. *Symbolic Interaction* 18(3): 355–69.
Maynard, D. W. & Clayman, S. E. (2003) Ethnomethodology and Conversation Analysis. In: Reynolds, L. T. & Herman-Kinney, N. J. (Eds.), *Handbook of Symbolic Interactionism*. AltaMira Press, Walnut Creek, CA, pp. 173–202.
Sacks, H. (1992) *Lectures on Conversation*. Blackwell, Oxford.
Schegloff, E. A. (1968) Sequencing in Conversational Openings. *American Anthropologist* 70: 1075–95.
Simmel, G. (1971) Sociability. In: *On Individuality and Social Forms*. University of Chicago Press, Chicago, pp. 127–40.
Tannen, D. (1990) *You Just Don't Understand: Women and Men in Conversation*. William Morrow, New York.

conversation analysis

Anssi Peräkylä

Conversation analysis (CA) is a method for investigating the structure and process of social interaction between humans. It focuses primarily on talk, but integrates also the nonverbal aspects of interaction in its research design. As their data, CA studies use video or audio recordings made from naturally occurring interaction. As their results, CA studies yield descriptions of recurrent structures and practices of social interaction. Some of these, such as turn taking or sequence structure, are involved in all interaction, whereas others are more specific and have to do with particular actions, such as asking questions or delivering and receiving news, assessments, or complaints. CA studies can focus either on ordinary conversations taking place between acquaintances or family members, or on institutional encounters where the participants accomplish their institutional tasks through their interaction. CA elucidates basic aspects of human sociality that reside in talk, and it examines the ways in which specific social institutions are invoked in, and operate through, talk.

CA was started by Harvey Sacks and his co-workers – most importantly Emanuel Schegloff and Gail Jefferson – at the University of California in the 1960s. The initial formation of Sacks's ideas is documented in his lectures from 1964 to 1972 (Sacks 1992a, 1992b). CA was developed in an intellectual environment shaped by Goffman's work on the moral underpinnings of social interaction and Garfinkel's ethnomethodology focusing on the interpretive procedures underlying social action. Sacks started to study the real-time sequential ordering of actions: the rules, patterns, and structures in the relations between actions. Thereby, he made a radical shift in the perspective of social scientific inquiry into social interaction: instead of treating social interaction as a screen upon which other processes (moral, inferential, or others) were projected, Sacks started to study the very structures of the interaction itself (Schegloff 1992a: xviii).

MAJOR DIMENSIONS

There are perhaps three basic features shared by CA studies: (1) they focus on *action*, (2) the *structures* of which they seek to explicate, and thereby (3) they investigate the achievement of *intersubjective understanding*. As general research topics, these three would be shared by many "schools" of social science. The uniqueness of CA, however, is in the way in which it shows how "action," "structure," and "intersubjectivity" are practically achieved and managed in talk and interaction.

Action

Some CA studies have as their topics the organization of actions that are recognizable as distinct actions even from a vernacular point of view. These include, for example, openings and closings of conversations, assessments, storytelling, and complaints. Many CA studies have as their topic actions that are typical in some institutional environment. Examples include questioning and answering practices in cross-examinations, news interviews and press conferences, and diagnosis and advice in medical and pedagogical settings. Finally – but perhaps most importantly – many conversation analytical studies focus on fundamental aspects of conversational organization that make any action possible. These include turn-taking, repair (i.e., the ways of dealing with problems of hearing, speaking, or understanding), the general ways in which sequences of action are built, and the ways in which the participants of interaction manage their relation to the utterances through gaze and body posture.

Structure

In the CA view, human social action is thoroughly structured and organized. In pursuing their goals, the actors have to orient themselves

to rules and structures that make their actions possible.

Sacks et al. (1974) outlined the rules of turn taking in conversation. A current speaker is initially entitled to one *turn constructional unit* (smallest amount of talk that in its sequential context counts as a turn). The participants in interaction orient to the completion of such a unit as a *transition-relevance place* where the speaker change may occur. A current speaker may select the next; if she does not do that, any participant can self-select at the transition-relevance place; and if even that does not happen, the current speaker may (but need not) continue. The explication of these simple rules has massive consequences for the analysis of social interaction, because virtually all spoken actions are produced and received in the matrix provided by them. Many institutional settings involve specific applications of these rules (Drew & Heritage 1992).

Single acts are parts of larger, structurally organized entities. These entities can be called *sequences* (Schegloff 2006). The most basic and the most important sequence is called *adjacency pair* (Schegloff & Sacks 1973), consisting of two actions in which the first action ("first pair part"), performed by one interactant, invites a particular type of second action ("second pair part"), to be performed by another interactant. Typical examples of adjacency pairs include question–answer, greeting–greeting, request-grant/refusal, and invitation-acceptance/declination. The relation between the first and the second pair parts is strict and normative: if the second pair part does not come forth, the first speaker can for example repeat the first action, or seek explanations for the fact that second is missing.

Adjacency pairs serve often as a core, around which even larger sequences are built (Schegloff 2006). So, a *pre-expansion* can precede an adjacency pair; an *insert expansion* involves actions that occur between the first and the second pair parts and make possible the production of the latter; and in a *post-expansion*, the speakers produce actions that follow from the basic adjacency pair.

Intersubjectivity

In CA studies, talk and interaction are examined as a site where intersubjective understanding concerning the participants' intentions, their state of knowledge, their relation, and their stance towards the talked-about objects is created, maintained, and negotiated (Heritage & Atkinson 1984: 11).

The most fundamental level of intersubjective understanding – one that constitutes the basis for any other type of intersubjective understanding – concerns the understanding of the preceding turn displayed by the current speaker. Just like any turn at talk is produced in the context shaped by the previous turn, it also displays its speaker's understanding of that previous turn (Sacks et al. 1974). Thus, in simple cases, producing a turn at talk that is hearable as an answer, the speaker also shows that she understood the preceding turn as a question. Especially in longer utterances, the recipient's understanding of, and stance towards, the co-participants' action can be displayed through vocal and nonvocal means during the production of that action, and this displayed understanding can inform the further unfolding of that action. In cases where the first speaker considers the understanding concerning his talk, displayed in the second speaker's utterance, as problematic, the first speaker has an opportunity for correcting this understanding in his or her subsequent talk (Schegloff 1992b).

An important aspect of intersubjective understanding concerns the *context* of the talk. This is particularly salient in institutional interaction where the participants' understanding of the institutional context of their talk is documented in their actions (Drew & Heritage 1992). If the "institutional context" is relevant for interaction, it can be observed in the details of the participants' actions; for example, in their ways of giving and receiving information and asking and answering questions.

Research Process

As their data, conversation analytical studies use video or audio recordings of naturally occurring social interaction. Video and audio recordings give the researcher direct access to the details of social action, and they make it possible to scrutinize the data over and over again. The focus on naturally occurring data entails that the researcher investigates specimens rather than

representations of the actual social action that he wants to understand. The video or audio recordings are transcribed using a detailed notation. The notation of audio data was developed by Gail Jefferson and it includes symbols for a wide variety of vocal and interactional phenomena. The transcription of visual data is less standardized, except for a widely used notation for gaze direction developed by Goodwin (1981). The transcript is not a substitute for the audio and video recordings: researchers recurrently return to the original recordings.

The analysis of the data proceeds from case-by-case examination of data, through creation of collections of phenomena that become objects of study, towards the explication of the structural features of the phenomena. In this process, a careful examination of *deviant cases* is of greatest importance.

Example

The conversation analytical transcription and some of its analytical concepts are exemplified in the following segment taken from Pomerantz (1980).

```
01 B: Hello::,
02 A: HI:::.
03 B: Oh:hi:: 'ow are you Agne::s,
04 A: Fi:ne. Yer line's been busy.
05 B: Yeuh my fu (hh) .hh my father's wife
      called me.
```

CA notation used in this segment includes:

.	Period indicating falling intonation at the end of an utterance
,	Comma indicating flat intonation at the end of an utterance
:	Colon indicating prolongation of sound
a̲	Underlining indicating emphasis
hh	Row of h's indicating aspiration
.hh	Row of h's preceded by a dot indicating inhalation
A	Capital letters indicating louder volume than surrounding talk

As Schegloff (1986) has shown, the openings of telephone conversations, as the one above, usually consist of four short sequences: (1) Summons (telephone ringing, not shown in the transcript) and answer (line 1); (2) identification/recognition (accomplished in lines 1–3);

(3) greetings (lines 2–3); (4) and "howareyou" sequence (lines 3–4). In a very dense form, these sequences establish the setting for the interaction and reinvoke the social relation between the participants.

B's answer to the "howareyou" is, in line 4, followed by her assertion that A's line has been busy. The assertion is about an event that the co-participant (A) has a privileged access to (as it was her line). Pomerantz shows how assertions of this kind serve as "fishing devices" which cast their recipient in a position where it becomes relevant for him or her to speak about the referred-to event. However, fishing takes place without the subject directly asking for information: the recipient, if he or she will speak about the event, will *volunteer* the information. That is what B does in line 5, where she tells who she was talking with. Pomerantz identified and explicated a particular form of social action that is recurrently resorted to in ordinary conversation. Subsequent studies have shown how this generic sequence can be made use of in eliciting clients' talk in institutional encounters in psychiatric and counseling settings.

CURRENT AREAS OF EXPANSION

Since the early 1990s the study of institutional interaction has proliferated. Medical interactions and interactions in the media are currently among the most intensively researched settings; the study of technological working environments (Heath & Luff 2000) has also been strongly influenced by the CA method. Another area of intensive study is the interface between grammar and social interaction (Ochs et al. 1996), focusing on questions such as the construction of turns and repair. Yet another area of expansion involves the exploration of the uses of prosody (Couper-Kuhlen & Selting 1996) and gesture (Goodwin 2000) in social interaction. There is also an ongoing debate concerning the applicability of quantitative techniques, along with qualitative ones, in CA studies.

SEE ALSO: Conversation; Discourse; Ethnomethodology; Goffman, Erving; Quantitative Methods; Sacks, Harvey; Sociolinguistics; Symbolic Interaction

REFERENCES AND SUGGESTED READINGS

Couper-Kuhlen, E. & Selting, M. (Eds.) (1996) *Prosody in Conversation*. Cambridge University Press, Cambridge.

Drew, P. & Heritage, J. (1992) Analyzing Talk at Work: An Introduction. In: Drew, P. & Heritage, J. (Eds.), *Talk at Work: Interaction in Institutional Settings*. Cambridge University Press, Cambridge, pp. 3–65.

Goodwin, C. (1981) *Conversational Organization: Interaction between Speakers and Hearers*. Academic Press, New York.

Goodwin, C. (2000) Gesture, Aphasia, and Interaction. In: McNeill, D. (Ed.), *Language and Gesture*. Cambridge University Press, Cambridge, pp. 84–98.

Heath, C. & Luff, P. (2000) *Technology in Action*. Cambridge University Press, Cambridge.

Heritage, J. (1984) *Garfinkel and Ethnomethodology*. Polity Press, Cambridge.

Heritage, J. & Atkinson, J. M. (1984) Introduction. In: Atkinson, J. M. & Heritage, J. (Eds.), *Structures of Social Action*. Cambridge University Press, Cambridge, pp. 1–15.

Maynard, D. (2003) *Bad News, Good News: Conversational Order in Everyday Talk and Clinical Settings*. University of Chicago Press, Chicago.

Ochs, E., Schegloff, E. A., & Thompson, S. A. (Eds.) (1996) *Interaction and Grammar*. Cambridge University Press, Cambridge.

Pomerantz, A. M. (1980) Telling My Side: "Limited Access" as a "Fishing Device." *Sociological Inquiry* 50: 186–98.

Sacks, H. (1992a) *Lectures on Conversation*, Vol. 1. Blackwell, Oxford.

Sacks, H. (1992b) *Lectures on Conversation*, Vol. 2. Blackwell, Oxford.

Sacks, H., Schegloff, E. A., & Jefferson, G. (1974) A Simplest Systematics for the Organization of Turn-Taking for Conversation. *Language* 50: 696–735.

Schegloff, E. A. (1986) The Routine as Achievement. *Human Studies* 9: 111–51.

Schegloff, E. A. (1992a). Introduction. In: Jefferson, G. (Ed.), *Harvey Sacks: Lectures on Conversation*, Vol. 1. Blackwell, Oxford.

Schegloff, E. A. (1992b) Repair After Next Turn: The Last Structurally Provided Defense of Intersubjectivity in Conversation. *American Journal of Sociology* 98: 1295–345.

Schegloff, E. A. (2006) *Sequence Organization in Interaction*. Cambridge University Press, Cambridge.

Schegloff, E. A. & Sacks, H. (1973) Opening Up Closings. *Semiotica* 8: 289–327.

convivium (who is friends with whom?)

Beate Volker

The degree to which people from different social strands have relations with each other indicates social cohesion. Therefore, the question of who is friends with whom is nontrivial. Compared to marriage, friendship is a non-institutionalized relationship: there is no formal start of a friendship and one can break off or change a friendship without notifying any third parties.

A generally accepted principle is that people prefer being friends with others who are like themselves. Interactions with similar others are rewarding (Homans 1984: 158). Seminal research has been done by Lazarsfeld and Merton (1954), who discuss value and status homophily affecting the selection of friends. Yet explanatory mechanisms differ among theories: *demand*-side theories focus on individual preferences, while *supply*side theories are directed to the distribution of meeting chances in society. Important demand-side perspectives are balance theory (Heider 1946) and the theory of social capital (on a micro-level, Flap 2004). Important supply-side perspectives are (macro-) structuralism (Blau 1977) and focus theory (Feld 1981). An integration of both perspectives is the choice-constraint approach (Fischer et al. 1977).

With regard to demand-side perspectives, balance theory states that a friendship between two actors depends on their relationship with a third party. If two actors have a positive relation to a third party, they are likely to also form a positive relationship with each other. Yet if one actor has a positive and the other a negative relationship to a third party, the positive relationship is less likely. The theory assumes that imbalance in relationships produces a strain, which people reduce by changing or breaking off relationships. Importantly, balance theory takes existing friendships into account when it comes to the decision to create a new one. Further, social capital theory states that people become friends if they face a common future, if they are in one or another way dependent on

each other, or if they have invested in the relationship formerly.

The most prominent supply-side theory is Blau's (1977) structural approach, which abandons a pure micro-level exchange perspective and takes macro-structures into account. Patterns of homophily are dependent on relative group sizes in the population. Interestingly, if different individual attributes are not closely correlated, intergroup associations can result despite the preference for ingroup associations. Related to the importance of numerical distribution is the argument on geographical proximity. Proximity reduces costs of interaction and facilitates the emergence of mutual trust. Furthermore, focus theory generalizes from numbers and places and assumes that individuals who share foci of activity have higher chances for meeting, and therefore greater chances for becoming friends (Feld 1981).

Lastly, the choice-constraint approach emphasizes that relationships are the result of individual choices made under social constraints (Fischer et al. 1977). People choose to construct and maintain social exchanges with some of those whom they encounter and they make this choice on the basis of weighing rewards and costs.

Like marriage, friendship is a relationship that occurs among those who are similar in relevant social dimensions, like age, education, class, ethnicity, and religion (Laumann 1973; Fischer et al. 1977). Yet, unlike marriages, cross-sex friendships are a rare phenomenon. With regard to age, Fischer et al. (1977) found that 38 percent of respondents' close friends were within 2 years of their age. Friendships are class-sensitive in general, yet similarity is highest within higher classes. With regard to ethnicity, friends are also remarkably similar in ethnicity. Esser (1989) found that even second-generation immigrants in Germany had friendship networks that were largely in their own group. Cohen (1977) showed that Jewish and black people have the highest tendency for ingroup association and Scottish people the lowest. Further, Protestants are somewhat more ingroup-oriented than Catholics. Little research has been done on the question of whether similarity in one social dimension is associated with similarity in another. An exception is the study by Jackson (1977), which shows that friends who work in the same economic sector also have a higher chance to be similar in education, age, and ethnicity.

A number of studies focus on the question "who has friends" rather than on who is a friend to whom. Interesting findings have been provided, showing that structural characteristics strongly influence people's associations. For example, married people have fewer friends than unmarried people and higher-educated and richer people have more friends. With increasing age, the number of friends first increases, but then decreases. Lastly, numbers of friends also differ between people from different countries.

Tests of balance theory largely corroborate the "friends of friends are friends" proposition. Yet the difference between cognitive balance (indicating a state of mind) versus structural balance (indicating the structure of personal networks) should be taken more seriously in research.

Research into friendship and social capital mainly studies what friends can do for each other in order to achieve important individual goals. It has been shown that strong ties are not important in attaining things like a job (Granovetter 1995). Weaker ties are more important for these kinds of achievements. Fischer (1982) showed, in addition, that friends are not important for monetary transactions or any other material exchanges. Furthermore, while friendships are important for all kinds of social activities, they are not that important for matters of serious advice.

Blau's macro-structural theory has been tested by Blum (1985) for socializing relationships and with regard to ethnic and religious heterogeneity. Blum demonstrated that while there are preferences for ingroup association, structural conditions exert substantial constraints. Heterogeneous populations promote intergroup relationships. McPherson and Smith Lovin (1987) also provide a test of Blau's theory and find evidence for the higher importance of group composition compared to individual preferences.

Concerning the social settings from which friends are drawn, Feld (1981) found that 68 percent of the relationships of the respondents in his study were formed in a shared setting with roughly a third in work or voluntary associations (see also Marsden 1990). Social settings differ in the degree to which they enhance friendship formation. Friends drawn from childhood are most similar in age, friends drawn from the work setting are most similar in occupational level, and friends drawn from a kin setting are above all similar in ethnicity (Jackson 1977). Furthermore, the importance of settings for recruiting friends differs between classes and life stages and also between countries.

Friends are remarkably similar to each other in various dimensions, and the tendency to associate with similar others differs according to age, education, class, ethnicity, and religion. The degree to which similarity in one dimension is associated with similarity in another is rarely investigated. Furthermore, friendships are drawn from different sources and the dimension on which friends are similar partially depends on the source from which the friends are recruited.

Both perspectives, demand as well as supply side, have been corroborated in research, and although there is some evidence that the supply side might be even more important, it is not clear what the relative importance of preferences and constraints in friendship choice would be. It is furthermore noteworthy that systematic empirical accounts on "convivium" are somewhat dated and restricted to the US. Future research has the task to overcome these shortcomings. In addition, the assumption that everybody needs and has friends might not be true. Lastly, most research concentrates on friendship dyads and not on networks, thereby disregarding the fact that friendship relationships are not exclusive relationships, but are embedded in social networks.

SEE ALSO: Connubium (Who Marries Whom?); Friendship: Structure and Context; Friendships of Children; Social Change

REFERENCES AND SUGGESTED READINGS

Blau, P. (1977) *Inequality and Heterogeneity*. Free Press, New York.

Blum, T. (1985) Structural Constraints on Interpersonal Relations: A Test of Blau's Macrosociological Theory. *American Journal of Sociology* 91(3): 511–21.

Cohen, S. M. (1977) Socioeconomic Determinants of Intraethnic Marriage and Friendship. *Social Forces* 55(4): 997–1010.

Esser, H. (1989) The Integration of the Second Generation: Toward an Explanation of Cultural Differences. *Zeitschrift für Soziologie* 18(6): 426–43.

Feld, S. L. (1981) The Focused Organization of Social Ties. *American Journal of Sociology* 86: 1015–35.

Fischer, C. S. (1982) *To Dwell Among Friends.* University of Chicago Press, Chicago.

Fischer, C. S. et al. (Eds.) (1977) *Networks and Places: Social Relations in the Urban Setting.* Free Press, New York.

Flap, H. (2004) Creation and Returns of Social Capital: A New Research Program. In: Flap, H. & Volker, B. (Eds.), *Creation and Returns of Social Capital: A New Research Program.* Routledge, London, pp. 3–23.

Granovetter, M. (1995 [1974]) *Getting a Job.* Cambridge University Press, Cambridge.

Hallinan, M. (1990) The Formation of Intransitive Friendships. *Social Forces* 69(2): 505–19.

Heider, F. (1946) Attitudes and Cognitive Organization. *Journal of Psychology* 21: 107–12.

Homans, G. C. (1984) *The Human Group.* Harcourt, New York.

Jackson, R. M. (1977) Social Structure and Process in Friendship Choice. In: Fischer, C. S. et al. (Eds.), *Networks and Places: Social Relations in the Urban Setting.* Free Press, New York, pp. 59–78.

Laumann, E. O. (1973) *Bonds of Pluralism: The Form and Substance of Urban Social Networks.* Wiley Series in Urban Research. Wiley & Sons, New York.

Lazarsfeld, P. & Merton, R. K. (1954) Friendship as a Social Process: A Substantive and Methodological Analysis. In: Berger, M., Abel, T., & Page, C. H. (Eds.), *Freedom and Control in Modern Society.* D. Van Nostrand, Toronto, pp. 18–66.

McPherson, M. & Smith Lovin, L. (1987) Homophily in Voluntary Organizations: Status Distance and the Composition of Face-To Face Groups. *American Sociological Review* 52(3): 370–9.

Marsden, P. (1990) Network Diversity, Substructures and Opportunities for Contacts. In: Calhoun, C., Meyer, M. W., & Scott, W. R. (Eds.), *Structures of Power and Constraints.* Cambridge University Press, Cambridge, pp. 397–410.

cool

Ellis Cashmore

Cool emerged in indifferent response to the great surge of optimism that followed World War II. It was driven by the rhythms of the bebop music of Miles Davis and Charlie Parker, a rebellious, musical counterpart to the abstract expressionism of De Kooning, Jackson Pollock, and Franz Kline.

Vincent (1995) approaches cool as a style, an attitude, and an approach to music (and, we might add, art in general) that reflected the temperament of groups of African Americans including John Coltrane, Miles Davis, and other musicians who identified with cool. They literally turned their back on audiences, as if to signify their defiance and intentions not to become entertainers, at least not entertainers in the way of the earlier minstrels, who pandered to whites' conceptions of blacks.

The cool ethic informed a self-conscious turning away from playing or performing simply for the delectation of whites – which is what the minstrels had done. Cool jazz musicians did not want to extend this tradition: they played for themselves and for each other, and if whites were willing to pay to watch, so be it. There was no concession; there was no acting up to stereotypes. Being cool implied a rejection of the values that ensured the subjugation of blacks, politically and culturally. Cool conveyed a covert anger, which, if ever made overt, would draw retribution from white society. Instead, musicians detached themselves from their audiences and created a manner, a posture, a "look," and even an argot, all recognizable to those who shared their orientation yet invisible and inaccessible to outsiders, known as squares.

Heroin became integral to the aura of cool. Its users included many jazz musicians who coalesced into a junkie subculture and so reinforced the sense of isolation from mainstream society, while promoting an in-group of users and dealers. Sidran (1995) argues that the drug was well suited to cool musicians as it suppressed emotional excesses and allayed anxieties.

Charlie Parker had used heroin since he was 12 years old and was one of countless jazz players and aficionados who became dependent on and were ultimately destroyed by the drug. "These musicians were less secular stars than quasi-religious figures and their fans often referred to them with godly reverence," wrote Nelson George in his *The Death of Rhythm and Blues* (1988: 25).

If artists wishing to break into the mainstream were playing the whites' game, cool musicians decided the game was not worth playing. They remained almost arrogantly outside the musical establishment, attracting little interest from record corporations.

Like most gestures of defiance that start life among a circle of like-minded rebels, cool became appropriated by both blacks and whites who were fascinated perhaps not by the politics of cool so much as by the external appearance, its image. To look unflappable in the face of turmoil, to prefix and suffix sentences with "man" or "baby," to talk with a hip-sounding slur that made you sound as if you were on heroin, to wear apparel with a certain looseness, to walk with a distinct swagger: all these were features of cool that were soon seized by what Norman Mailer once called the "white Negro" and were eventually dissipated. Jack Kerouac and the beat generation of which he was part embraced many of the idioms and some of the values inherent in cool; a critical pulse of scornful, mocking contempt for orthodoxy ran through both.

Even today, we use the term without reflecting on its source in African American culture and on its eventual ramification. Sidran concludes that the disaffection behind the cool movement was much the same as that behind the much more overt expressions of the 1960s (e.g., race riots).

SEE ALSO: Cultural Resistance; Culture Industries; Identity, Deviant; Music and Media; Popular Culture Forms (Hip-Hop; Jazz; Rock 'n' Roll); Popular Culture Icons (Hendrix, Jimi; Marley, Bob); Subculture

REFERENCES AND SUGGESTED READINGS

George, N. (1988) *The Death of Rhythm and Blues.* Pantheon, New York.

Pountain, D. & Robins, D. (2001) *Cool Rules.* Reaktion, London.

Sidran, B. (1995) *Black Talk.* Payback Press, Edinburgh.

Vincent, T. (1995) *Keep Cool: The Black Activists Who Built the Jazz Age.* Pluto, London.

Cooley, Charles Horton (1864–1929)

Hans-Joachim Schubert

Charles Horton Cooley was a prominent member of the founding generation of American sociologists. Named a full professor of sociology at the University of Michigan in 1907, he was then elected president of the American Sociological Association in 1918. It was his aim and achievement to apply the ideas of pragmatism to the development of a sociological theory of social action, social order, and social change, which he ultimately accomplished with his trilogy (Cooley 1963, 1964, 1966).

Cooley achieved the transition from the philosophy of the mind to a pragmatistic theory of action and communication in the course of his criticism of Descartes's proposition *cogito ergo sum*. For Descartes, only "a self-absorbed philosopher" isolated from other people (Cooley 1963: 6) can discover through spiritual contemplation or introspection (*cogito*) the meaning of the objective, social or subjective world (*sum*). According to Cooley, this position is not self-evident (*ergo*). Rather, the meaning or value of objects is defined by actors in situations of symbolic mediated interaction (Cooley 1966: 284). Cooley argued that Descartes should have said *cogitamus* rather than *cogito*. The prerequisite for the generalization of meaning or social order is that individuals be able to coordinate actions using significant or "standard symbols" (Cooley 1963: 63). For Cooley, "communication" is the deciding "mechanism through which human relations exist" (Cooley 1969a: 61). Due to the "plasticity" of human nature (Cooley 1964: 19), neither the identity of the self nor the social order of society is instinctive. Individuation can only take place through socialization (and vice versa) (i.e., in interaction

with the social environment; more specifically, through "mutual understanding"). Thus,
the discussion on Darwinism regarding the
mechanism that enables human beings to deal
with environmental change played a central role
in the foundation and historical development of
sociology. In that debate, Cooley veered away
from the philosophy of the mind, but without
pursuing approaches such as instinct psychology (McDougall), psychology of crowds (Le
Bon), imitation or suggestion theory (Tarde,
Ross). Cooley recognized that social macro-
structures, as well as structures of communities
and individuals, develop through communicative interaction. The central "thesis" – his
"organic view" – that he conceptualized at the
end of the 1900s and later completed in his
trilogy, is that sociability and individual autonomy are two sides of the interaction and communication process. "Communication" was his
"first real conquest" he has been "working out
ever since" (Cooley 1969b: 8).

In the first part of his trilogy, *Human Nature
and Social Order*, he examines the "distributive
aspect" (Cooley 1964: 37) of intersubjective
relationships from a social psychological perspective; namely, the development of the self
through symbolically mediated interaction.
Cooley reconstructed three progressive phases
of the evolving self: (1) the "sense of appropriation," which is the expression of a biologically manifested spontaneity and activity; (2)
the "social self," which is developed by taking
in the attitude of others; and (3) the famous
"looking-glass self" (Cooley 1998: 155–75),
which describes neither an "over-socialized
self" characterized by passive internalization
of given habits and values, nor an "unencum-
bered self" freed from all social constraints.
The metaphor "looking-glass self," as Cooley
explicitly declared, means not a "mere mechanical reflection of ourselves," but it represents an
open and distinctive self-image, created through
the imagination and interpretation of the world
we inhabit. A looking-glass self, according to
Cooley, has three "principal elements": first,
the imagination of our appearance to the other
person; second, the imagination of his judgment
of that appearance; and third, some sort of
self-feeling, such as "pride or mortification"
(Cooley 1964: 184). Like William James and

James Mark Baldwin, Cooley considered the
development of the self to be a process of
interaction between the self and the surrounding world. But unlike James, who saw this
process as an "appropriation" of the world,
and unlike Baldwin, who held the methods
of "ejection," "accommodation," and "imitation" responsible for the constitution of the
self, Cooley described the mechanisms that
mediate between self and society as "communication" and "understanding." With this, he
rejected utilitarian approaches on the one
hand, which assume a given autonomy of the
self without taking anthropological and societal preconditions into consideration, and on
the other hand rejected culturalistic and structural deterministic approaches, which can only
reconstruct subjectivity within the framework
of social norms and cultural values.

In the second part of his trilogy, *Social Organization*, Cooley avoids the dualism of "utilitarianism" and "normativism" as well, when he
defines the sociological or "collective aspects"
of social action (primary group, public opinion,
democracy, social classes and institutions). His
term *primary group* contains the first response
to the question of social order. Primary groups
are "face-to-face associations" such as "the
family, the play-group of children, and the
neighborhood or community group of elders."
They are "primary" because the "social nature"
and the "ideals of the individual" develop in
these interactive relationships. On the one hand,
primary groups are "not independent of the
larger society"; their normative rules are influenced through "special traditions" of the respective society, and on the other hand, primary
groups are also marked by "universal" communicative structures (Cooley 1963: 27). Parent–
child communicative relationships, for example,
are beyond cultural differences because the
adoption of social roles and the development
of personality can only occur when children
are able to participate in reciprocal forms of
social action. The mechanism of learning is
communication and understanding and not
conditioning. The specific harmony of communities, customs, and traditions develops
through the universal mechanism of "mutual
understanding." Cooley does not define the
term "primary group" or "community"

(*Gemeinschaft*) as Tönnies does (whose concept Weber and Durkheim adopted), with the help of a normativistic or even ontological concept of human action (*Wesenwille*); much less does he identify society (*Gesellschaft*) with a purely rational concept of human action (*Kürwille*), since communal norms and traditions, as well as societal interests and institutions, are the result of communicative and creative human actions. Contrary to Tönnies, Cooley saw that individuals experience solidarity, equality, and freedom as characteristics of the communication process, directly in communities. With this reformulation of the premises of enlightenment, based on a theory of human action, Cooley wants to avoid reducing the establishment of values to Natural Law and procedural theory. Democracy is, therefore, for him, not only a form of government, but also a way of living that is grounded in primary group experiences. In primary groups, individuals acquire the social competence and normative ideals that are the prerequisites for societal democratization. Democracy is endangered if, in primary groups, democratic options are masked by undemocratic cultural traditions. A further "primary aspect" of social organization is the "mind of the group." The development of a "social consciousness" leads Cooley neither mentalistically nor metaphysically back to transcendental structures of the mind, nor does he define the collective consciousness positivistically as a "social fact" (Durkheim). Cooley shows, in contrast, based on communications theory, that "public consciousness," as with all forms of social order, comes about through "interaction" and "mutual influence," if not expressly through "agreement" (Cooley 1963: 10–11). "Public impressions" emerge when actors formulate demands in the public sphere because they are affected by social problems. Cooley does speak of *public opinion*, but only when the negative consequences of actions are evaluated and dealt with in public discourse. Unlike proponents of utilitarianism, Cooley does not reduce democracy to a consensual balance between fractional interests, nor, like Rousseau, to a "common will" (*volonté générale*). Democracy consists of deliberations through which the identities of the participants, their social bonds, as well as the organizational and institutional structures of

the society, are constantly changing. An important "collective aspect" of democracy is that of *social classes*, which enable actors confronted with structural inequalities to generate consciousness and political power. In the confrontation between classes, the deliberations are not only about economic, but also about cultural capital, which the "leisure class" uses to secure its hegemony (Veblen, in Cooley 1963: 119). Social classes are part of democracy, which is only endangered when classes close socially and refuse public discussion. Classes, like all institutions, are "a definite and established phase of the public mind" or "a mature, specialized and comparatively rigid part of the social structure." *Institutions* are, over time and space, expanded structures of action such as "enduring sentiments, beliefs, customs" and large organizations such as "the government, the church and laws," but also microsocietal "apperceptive systems" and individual "habits of mind and of action." Institutions unburden actions and cultivate the "permanent needs of human nature." As "organized attitudes," they provide important options for individuals and, simultaneously, they also limit their activities. "The individual," according to Cooley, "is always cause as well as effect of the institution" (Cooley 1963: 313–19). Due to ongoing environmental changes, institutions must constantly be recreated. Social "disorganization" arises when actors cannot solve problems of action because institutional change is blocked.

Cooley set up his conception of social change as a creative search and experiment process in the third part of his trilogy, *Social Process*. In it, Cooley discusses terms such as intelligence, reconstruction, anticipation, and creativity. Because the theory of social change, in tandem with a critique of ontological and teleological theories of action, is at the core of pragmatism, these terms have central importance for all pragmatists. Individual actions have their origin, according to Cooley, in "suggestions" and "habits" of the social world. Nevertheless, generalized meanings never provide complete answers to specific situations and concrete action problems; they must therefore be reconstructed in experiments and tentative trial phases. Drawing on past experience, actors continuously create ideas and hypotheses they can test as new habits. Most significant in the sequence of action (habit, conflict, experiment, and new habit) is the experimental phase of "imaginative reconstruction" (Cooley 1966: 358). According to Cooley, the rationality of human action is not based on the context of justification, but on the context of discovery, on the invention of new ideas through "creative synthesis" derived from experiences: the "test of intelligence is the power to act successfully in new situations" (Cooley 1966: 351–3). Tentative and creative action is not only the mechanism of social change, but also of social order. The pivotal point is that social order is guaranteed neither through the pressure of inner or outer nature (behaviorism and empiricism), nor through the internalization of social norms (normativism). Nor is it warranted through a metaphysical mind (idealism), nor reflected in a balance or aggregation of rational individual action (utilitarianism); rather, social order is a constant interpretation and reconstruction of generalized meaning (pragmatism). Social order or "life itself" is not a "state" but a "process." Thus, we cannot "expect anything final," but we can "discover in the movement itself sufficient matter for reason and faith" (Cooley 1966: 377). For Cooley, social action is not limited either to the rational pursuit of clear goals or to the execution of social norms. With his pragmatistic social theory Cooley avoids the *homo oeconomicus* and *homo sociologicus*, showing that neither subjective ends (individuum) nor generalized behavioral expectations (society) are a given; they are instead constituted and stabilized through creative action. Therefore, for him, open questions and conflicts are basic motivations for actions, not, as in utilitarianism, the maximization of given ends and also not, as in normativism, internalized social facts (Cooley 1966: 241–54). Social order is consequently not a state of balanced individual interests and not an autonomous normative structure determining the boundaries of action, but rather a process of permanent "imaginative reconstruction" of social, subjective, and objective meanings.

With his trilogy, Cooley established a general pragmatistic sociology, elaborating a theory of social action, social order, and social change. This integrated approach is unique, and was not achieved either by his contemporary George Herbert Mead or by members of the Chicago School of sociology and symbolic interactionism who followed the Cooley–Mead approach.

SEE ALSO: Chicago School; Looking-Glass Self; Mead, George Herbert; Pragmatism; Primary Groups; Social Order; Social Change; Symbolic Interaction

REFERENCES AND SUGGESTED READINGS

Cooley, C. H. (1963 [1909]) *Social Organization: A Study of the Larger Mind.* Schocken, New York.
Cooley, C. H. (1964 [1902]) *Human Nature and the Social Order.* Schocken, New York.
Cooley, C. H. (1966 [1918]) *Social Process.* Southern Illinois Press, Carbondale.
Cooley, C. H. (1969a [1894]) The Theory of Transportation. In: Angell, R. C. (Ed.), *Sociological Theory and Social Research: Selected Papers of Charles Horton Cooley.* Kelley, New York, pp. 17–118.
Cooley, C. H. (1969b [1928]) The Development of Sociology at Michigan. In: Angell, R. C. (Ed.), *Sociological Theory and Social Research: Selected Papers of Charles Horton Cooley.* Kelley, New York, pp. 3–14.
Cooley, C. H. (1998) *On Self and Social Organization.* Ed. H.-J. Schubert. University of Chicago Press, Chicago.
Mead, G. H. (1930) Cooley's Contribution to American Social Thought. *American Journal of Sociology* 35: 693–706.
Schubert, H.-J. (2006) The Foundation of Pragmatistic Sociology: George Herbert Mead and Charles Horton Cooley. *Journal of Classical Sociology* 6: 1.
Schubert, H.-J. (1995) *Demokratische Identität: Der soziologische Pragmatismus von Charles Horton Cooley.* Suhrkamp, Frankfurt am Main.

corrections

Melvina Sumter

Corrections is the subsystem of the criminal justice system responsible for the care, custody, and control of juveniles and adults who have been accused of committing a criminal offense and offenders who have been convicted of committing a crime. As such, the apparatus of corrections, through either institutional confinement or non-institutional alternatives, consists of a variety of agencies, institutions, programs, and services necessary to manage accused suspects and convicted offenders who are remanded to their care.

HISTORY

Historically, offenders were punished through the use of various forms of torture, corporal punishment, capital punishment, banishment, or fines. In colonial America, prisons as we know them did not exist; instead, prisons were used as holding cells for the purpose of eliciting a confession. In order to extract a confession, oftentimes brutal torture was administered, which was then followed by the penalty of a fine, but more often capital punishment or banishment. During this period, there were few written laws or prescribed codes for law violations, very harsh and brutal torture and corporal punishment, and extensive use of public executions.

In response to these autocracies, a wing at the Walnut Street Jail in Philadelphia was expanded from a typical jail that held debtors and those awaiting punishment into a wing called the "penitentiary house" of 16 separate cells designed for solitary confinement (Friedman 1993). Inspired by the work of the Quakers who believed that offenders could be reformed if they were placed in solitary confinement, where they could reflect on their criminal wrongdoings and thereby repent, this system of prison discipline became the first penitentiary used exclusively for the correction of convicted offenders in the United States (Stinchcomb & Fox 1999). As such, the main element of this system called for the reform of the offenders through hard labor and solitary confinement at night to prevent external communication, limited low-tone conversation prior to bedtime, and silence enforced in the shops and at meals (Inciardi 1987; Friedman 1993).

The Walnut Street Jail served as the model for what became known as the Auburn and Eastern penitentiary systems. Influenced by many of the principles of the Walnut Street Jail, the Auburn Penitentiary was opened in New York in 1817 and erected a portion of the new facility on that model (Stinchcomb & Fox 1999). However, as a result of reports of high rates of insanity and suicides, the concept of complete solitary confinement proved to be a failure. This concept was therefore discontinued and replaced by a system that became known as the congregate system (Mays & Winfree 2002). The congregate system allowed offenders to work together in workshops during the day while forbidding any type of communication and imposing sleep in isolation at night. Later, in 1829, a complete system of solitary confinement was adopted at Eastern State Penitentiary in Philadelphia where the offenders were only removed from their cells when they were sick or released from prison; as such, they ate, slept, received moral instruction, and worked in their cells (Clear & Cole 2003).

RATIONALE FOR PUNISHMENT

Throughout the history of corrections four major justifications have dominated the field at different times, to explain why offenders are punished.

Retribution is the oldest justification for punishment. Dating back to biblical times, it refers to revenge or retaliation for a harm or wrong done to another individual where the wrongful act is repaid by a punishment that is as severe as the wrongful act (Newman 1985). The theoretical premise of retribution is that punishment is inflicted on a law violator who deserves to be punished as repayment in proportion to the severity of the offense or the extent to which others have been made to suffer (Clear & Cole 2003).

Deterrence is a penal philosophy which states that the aim of punishment is to prevent future offenses by example to both the offenders (specific deterrence) and individuals who may be contemplating committing an offense (general deterrence) (Newman 1985). The theoretical premise of deterrence is that if the threat of punishment is severe enough, people will be dissuaded from committing a criminal offense.

Rehabilitation is the penal philosophy which maintains that the aim of punishment is to bring about reform and change in offenders, thereby helping them attain or regain a proper concern for law and become law-abiding productive citizens (Duff 1995). The theoretical premise of rehabilitation is that offenders can be reformed by providing vocational, educational, or treatment programs (Clear & Cole 2003).

Incapacitation is the penal philosophy which states that the purpose of punishment is to reduce the likelihood of crime by physically restricting an offender's ability to commit an offense. The theoretical premise underlying incapacitation is that if offenders are locked up, it will curtail their ability to commit additional crimes (Stinchcomb & Fox 1999).

COMPONENTS OF CORRECTIONS

While prisons and jails are the most visible components of corrections, a significant part of corrections is unrelated to the imprisonment of the offender. A vast part of corrections is carried out in the community setting (Stinchcomb & Fox 1999). As such, corrections is divided into custodial institutions which are used to incarcerate accused suspects and convicted offenders and non-custodial, community-based alternatives which are designed to carry out the sentence imposed by the court in the community. The custodial institutions include jails and prisons and the community-based alternatives include probation, intermediate sanctions, and parole.

Jails are considered to be the gateway to the criminal justice system. They are typically administered by the county; however, in some localities, jails are administered by a regional, state, or federal law enforcement agency. The primary functions of jails are to hold suspects who are apprehended as well as suspects who are not released on bail (Stinchcomb & Fox 1999). Jails also house offenders who are convicted of crimes and sentenced to a year or less, who are sentenced to more than one year and are awaiting transfer to a federal or state prison, probation and parole violators, and bail absconders.

Probation is a conditional sentence imposed by the court in lieu of incarceration, which allows a convicted offender to serve the sanction in the community under the supervision of a probation officer. As such, probation generally replaces a term in an institution and is a contract between the court and the offender in which the former agrees to a prison term if the terms of probation are not met. Since probation is a conditional sentence, offenders sentenced under this option are required to meet a number of conditions which can be revoked at any time should the provisions be violated. Probation revocation may occur if there is a new arrest or conviction or a technical violation in which the probationer fails to abide by the rules and conditions of probation. If the offender successfully completes the terms of probation, he or she is discharged at the expiration of the sentence.

Intermediate sanctions are a range of punishment options that fall on a continuum between traditional probation and incarceration, which vary in intrusiveness and control over the offender. These sanctions are imposed on offenders who are perceived to require more rigorous supervision than traditional probation services provide, but less restrictive supervision than imprisonment (Clear & Cole 2003). As such, intermediate sanctions include a wide variety of penalties that allow a judge to match the severity of the punishment with the severity of the offense, such as community service, electronic monitoring and house arrest, restitution and fines, day reporting centers, house arrest and electronic monitoring, halfway houses, drug courts, boot camps, and intensive supervision probation (ISP).

Prisons, also called correctional facilities or penitentiaries, house offenders with sentences that range from one year to life. These facilities are designed to receive, house, and care for offenders as well as provide the programs and services necessary to prevent escapes, maintain a secure and safe environment, and promote the efficient functioning of the overall institution (Stinchcomb & Fox 1999). In order to accomplish these goals, prisons operate at varying levels of security classification which are maximum, medium, and minimum depending on the offenders' perceived level of dangerousness, offense committed, sentence length, and escape risk.

Parole is the conditional release of an offender from prison before the expiration of the sentence, after a portion of the sentence has been served, where the offender remains under the continued supervision of the state or federal government. Since parole is a form of conditional release, like probation, it can be revoked for failure to maintain the conditions upon which it was granted or if there is a new arrest or conviction.

CORRECTIONS TODAY

The apparatus of corrections changed drastically during the latter part of the twentieth century.

The United States moved from an emphasis on rehabilitation back to a form of retribution, known as "Just Deserts." As such, the current trend is to have tougher criminal justice legislation and provide more punitive penalties. These policies are designed to provide offenders with longer sentences and keep them in prison longer. For example, sentence enhancement statutes such as determinate sentencing, mandatory minimums, and three strikes authorize judges to impose longer sentences. Likewise, legislation such as truth in sentencing which usually requires that offenders serve at least 85 percent of the maximum sentence imposed by the court and the abolition of parole have contributed to their remaining in prison longer. In addition, there has been an influx of waiver transfer of juveniles to adult prisons and the expanded use of capital punishment. As such, since the 1970s there has been an unprecedented growth in individuals under some form of correctional supervision.

The rate of increase in the US prison population was not the only astounding feature of the imprisonment binge (Blomberg & Lucken 2000). The change in the composition of the prison population was equally dramatic. The current get tough legislation and changes in drug laws have resulted in an escalation in the number of African Americans, females, juveniles, geriatric, and mentally ill offenders (Blomberg & Lucken 2000). These populations are intricately tangled with social disadvantages, such as poverty, unemployment, low levels of education, and deficit cognitive skills (Currie 1998; Blomberg & Lucken 2000). They are mainly non-violent, with incarceration for drug offenses constituting the largest component of the increase of offenders under some

form of correctional supervision (Currie 1998; Blomberg & Lucken 2000; Austin & Irwin 2001; Robinson 2002).

In addition to the diverse population, correctional administrators face several significant challenges to include an increase in probation and parole caseloads which makes it difficult to manage case files, offer the necessary services, and provide the required level of supervision. As well, correctional administrators are faced with prison and jail overcrowding which makes it difficult to manage and maintain a safe and secure correctional facility. It also increases the propensity for violence among offenders, therefore posing safety risks for the offenders and staff. Another challenge is the increased medical and health care costs due to the rise in the special needs population and offenders with HIV/AIDS. Although correctional budgets have increased dramatically, these funds are used primarily for operational expenses.

SEE ALSO: Crime; Criminal Justice System; Prisons

REFERENCES AND SUGGESTED READINGS

Austin, J. & Irwin, J. (2001) *It's About Time: America's Imprisonment Binge*. Wadsworth, Belmont, CA.

Blomberg, T. G. & Lucken, K. (2000) *American Penology: A History of Control*. Aldine de Gruyter, New York.

Clear, T. R. & Cole, G. F. (2003) *American Corrections*, 5th edn. Wadsworth, Belmont, CA.

Currie, E. (1998) *Crime and Punishment in America*. Henry Holt, New York.

Duff, A. (1995) Expression, Penance, and Reform. In: Murphy, J. G. (Ed.), *Punishment and Rehabilitation*, 3rd edn. Wadsworth, Belmont, CA, pp. 169–209.

Friedman, L. M. (1993) *Crime and Punishment in American History*. Basic Books, New York.

Inciardi, J. A. (1987) *Criminal Justice*, 2nd edn. Harcourt Brace Jovanovich, San Diego.

Mays, G. L. & Winfree, L. T. (2002) *Contemporary Corrections*. Wadsworth, Belmont, CA.

Newman, G. (1985) *The Punishment Response*. Harrow & Heston, New York.

Robinson, M. B. (2002) *Blind Justice*. Prentice-Hall, Upper Saddle River, NJ.

Stinchcomb, J. B. & Fox, V. B. (1999) *Introduction to Corrections*, 5th edn. Prentice-Hall, Upper Saddle River, NJ.

correlation

Robin K. Henson

Correlation refers to the relationship between two or more variables. Many different forms of correlation exist, but they all reflect a quantitative, statistical means for describing relationships. There are many so-called univariate (i.e., one variable) statistics which are useful for describing single distributions of scores, including the mean, median, variance, and standard deviation. In contrast, a correlation statistic, as a measure of relationship, is inherently at least *bivariate* (i.e., two variables) in nature.

The most common manifestation of bivariate correlation is the Pearson product-moment correlation coefficient, which was named after the British scientist Karl Pearson (1857–1936), who popularized the statistic originally introduced by Sir Francis Galton (1822–1911). The statistic is more commonly known as Pearson *r* or just *r*. Pearson *r* represents a very important development in the field of statistics because a large section of statistical work can be traced to the simple correlation coefficient.

Statistical relationship for two variables, or correlation, speaks to whether or not the variables are systematically related in some predictable fashion. For example, assuming no irrigational intervention, annual rainfall is likely related to growth in agricultural crops, such that crops receiving more rain likely will be more productive. Of course, this relationship probably varies somewhat depending on the type of crop, amount of sunlight, and many other variables.

Similarly, the hypothetical data in Table 1 reflect a relationship between annual family income and the average number of times family members use public transportation in a week. Here, however, there is an inverse relationship, such that there tends to be increased utilization of public transportation as annual income decreases.

The relationship between the two variables in Table 1 can be graphically displayed in a *scatterplot*. Scatterplots are often used to display the relationship between variables, where each axis represents one of the variables and the entries reflect the paired data for each observation. Figure 1 is a scatterplot for the above data, and allows for a visual inspection of the inverse relationship.

It seems clear from Figure 1 that there is a tendency for public transportation use to decrease as familial income increases. Of course, it is also clear that this relationship is not perfect, because in a few cases families with more income used public transportation with greater frequency than families with lower income levels.

Correlation, then, is interpreted in terms of the strength and directionality of the relationship. The *correlation coefficient* is the statistical summary of the relationship under study. This coefficient normally ranges from +1 to −1, inclusive. Within this range, a coefficient of 0 would represent no relationship. At one extreme, a coefficient of +1 would represent a perfect, positive (i.e., direct) relationship. At the other extreme, a coefficient of −1 would represent a perfect, negative (i.e., indirect, inverse) relationship. Therefore, the absolute value of the coefficient speaks to the strength of the relationship, such that coefficients closer

Table 1   Annual family income and utilization of public transportation (average number of uses per week)

Family	*Income ($)*	*Public transportation use*
Smith	80,000	0
Washington	30,000	6
Jones	90,500	2
Wilson	60,500	4
Allen	60,000	3
Roberts	20,500	7
Thompson	50,000	2

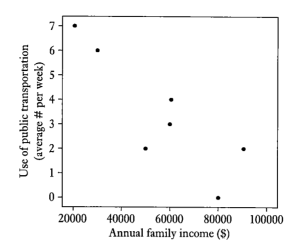

Figure 1 Scatterplot of hypothetical data for annual family income with public transportation utilization ($n = 7$).

to 0 reflect weaker relationships than coefficients nearer the extremes. The sign of the coefficient indicates the directionality of the relationship, either positive or negative.

As noted, there are many different types of correlation coefficients, and r is the most common. Pearson r can be used when both variables are continuous in nature, or intervally scaled, which indicates that the observations of measurement are based on meaningful differences between the scores (e.g., $60,000 is twice as much income as $30,000). For the Figure 1 example, the $r = -.86$, which indicates a relatively strong, inverse relationship between the two variables.

Not all variables are continuously scaled, and therefore r would not be the appropriate correlation coefficient in such cases. When at least one of the variables represents ranked data, such as places in a graduating class, then the Spearman's rho correlation would be appropriate. Spearman's rho is often symbolized with r_s or ρ. Kendall's tau (τ) also can be computed for ranked data, but tau is generally thought to better handle data sets where there are tied ranks (Huck 2004).

In some data situations one of the variables might represent a dichotomy, which indicates two mutually exclusive categories of observations. Gender is an example of a naturally occurring dichotomy (male and female) that

might be coded with 0's and 1's in a data set. In medicine, the presence or absence of a particular disease would also represent a dichotomy. In situations where one variable is a dichotomy and the other is continuous in nature, then the point biserial correlation (r_{pb}) could be computed.

In some cases, however, one of the variables might represent an artificial dichotomy, where some type of cut-off is applied to a continuous variable to create two groups. The biserial correlation (r_{bis}) applies to the relationship between an artificial dichotomy and a continous variable.

Finally, when both variables are dichotomous, the phi coefficient (ϕ) could be computed. If both variables are artificial dichotomies, a tetrachoric correlation would be appropriate. There are other correlation coefficients to deal with other types of data, but these are the most common.

Although correlations do statistically describe the relationship between two variables, it is very important to note that the presence of correlation does not necessarily imply that the variables are somehow causally related. The issues of cause and effect are much more complicated than the computation of a simple correlation coefficient, and they depend on other factors in a research study. It is true that the presence of correlation between two variables is a necessary condition for establishing causality, but it is not a sufficient condition.

For example, the relationship between incidences of violent crime and the number of houses of worship across a variety of communities is positive and fairly strong. This indicates that communities with more houses of worship also tend to have more incidences of violent crime. This relationship is not causal, however, because a third variable, population density, actually influences both original variables and accounts for their relationship.

The correlation coefficient nevertheless is a key element to most classical statistical analyses, which belong to a family of analyses within the general linear model (GLM). Within the GLM, all classical analyses attempt to maximize shared variance, or relationship, between two or more variables. Because of this, all GLM techniques are correlational in nature and therefore yield r^2-type effect sizes. An r^2 effect size, also called the coefficient of determination, is simply the square of a Pearson r. This statistic informs the proportion of variance in one variable that can be explained by the variance of the second variable. For example, if $r = .50$ between X and Y, then $r^2 = .25$, and 25 percent of the variance in X can be explained by the variance in Y. This effect size is important because it informs the amount of variance that both variables share.

The bivariate correlation should be distinguished from other forms of correlation that involve more than two variables, such as part correlation, partial correlation, and multivariate correlation. At times, bivariate relationships are called zero-order correlations so as to differentiate them from other more complex forms of statistical relationship.

SEE ALSO: Descriptive Statistics; Effect Sizes; General Linear Model; Quantitative Methods; Statistical Significance Testing

REFERENCES AND SUGGESTED READINGS

Cohen, J. & Cohen, P. (1983) *Applied Multiple Regression/Correlation Analysis for the Behavioral Sciences*. Erlbaum, Hillsdale, NJ.

Henson, R. K. (2000) Demystifying Parametric Analyses: Illustrating Canonical Correlation as the Multivariate General Linear Model. *Multiple Linear Regression Viewpoints* 26(1): 11–19.

Hinkle, D. E., Wiersma, W., & Jurs, S. G. (2003) *Applied Statistics for the Behavioral Sciences*, 5th edn. Houghton Mifflin, Boston.

Huck, S. W. (2004) *Reading Statistics and Research*, 4th edn. Allyn & Bacon, Boston.

Roberts, J. K. & Henson, R. K. (2002) Correction for Bias in Estimating Effect Sizes. *Educational and Psychological Measurement* 62: 241–53.

Sherry, A. & Henson, R. K. (2005) Conducting and Interpreting Canonical Correlation Analysis in Personality Research: A User-Friendly Primer. *Journal of Personality Assessment* 84: 37–48.

corruption

Barry Hindess

The most general meaning of corruption is that of impurity, infection, or decay. Corruption can happen to anything – a piece of fruit, a sporting event, a religious community, or a university – but the term is now most commonly used to suggest that there is something rotten in the government of the state. Thus, as conceptions of the naturally sound condition of government change, so too does the focus of concern regarding its corruption. In the social thought of western classical antiquity and early modern Europe, for example, corruption was seen as a disease of the body politic. It was a destructive social condition whose effects included improper behavior on the part of many individuals. During the modern period, however, politics has come to be seen in individualistic and economistic terms, with the result that corruption now tends to refer to the improper behavior itself, and especially to conduct which involves the use of public office for the purposes of illicit private gain. Some commentators (e.g., Euben 1989) deplore this change in usage, seeing it as reflecting the triumph of liberal individualism and a corresponding loss of concern with the public good.

In fact, it is far from clear that this more restricted usage of the term necessarily reflects any lessening of this concern. While they may not appeal to the older meaning of corruption, for example, public choice theory in economics and political science, and the "classical" liberalism of Friedrich Hayek, are very much concerned with minimizing what would once have been called corruption of the body politic. Or again, the early arguments in favor of representative government clearly saw it as a means of keeping in check the corruption of government by factions drawing on the short-term interests of the poor and poorly educated majority. Much of the subsequent history of western political thought can be seen as focusing on the new sources of corruption created by the institutions of representative government and the opportunities they provide for politicians, public servants, and business interests to pursue their own private advantage. The older usage of the term corruption may have been abandoned, but many of the earlier concerns with the health of the body politic have continued, albeit now pursued under rather different headings.

Following initiatives taken by the World Bank and international development agencies, empirical research on corruption has grown enormously since the late 1980s. It concentrates largely on the public sector, and especially on areas in which the improper conduct of public officials seems likely to have damaging economic effects. Development agencies are particularly concerned with the impact of corruption on economic growth. Thus, while recognizing that corruption poses problems in all societies, they tend to see these problems as being especially serious in the non-western world. This developmental perspective on corruption is particularly concerned with what it sees as the limitations of non-western cultures and ways of life, and especially with cases in which conduct that was once regarded as acceptable "no longer fits modern conditions" (Rose-Ackerman 1999: 5). Not surprisingly, perhaps, this perspective also suggests that an important part of the corruption on which it focuses is likely to involve the conduct of western businesses operating in these societies.

In practice, the precise incidence of corruption is difficult to determine, in part because many of those involved in corrupt conduct have an interest in secrecy. Yet there will also be cases in which corrupt individuals prefer to advertise the fact. Indeed, if corruption is an abuse of public office, then the flaunting of corruption might be seen as an affirmation of one's power, of one's ability to get away with such behavior. It might also be seen, somewhat more positively, as evidence of one's capacity to get things done in spite of the obstacles which the law and the rules of proper procedure seem to put in the way. Even in such cases, however, while the fact of corruption will be only too clear, many of its details are likely to remain hidden. Public regulatory bodies have been established in many societies to deal with entrenched corruption in the public and private sectors, but their ability to deal with those who are powerful in the sense just noted is likely to require considerable support from their political masters. The findings of such bodies must therefore be interpreted with some caution. Even in the best of cases, they present us with the tip of an iceberg whose true dimensions always remain obscure.

It is partly because the incidence of corruption is so difficult to establish that indirect measures have proved so attractive to many observers. The most influential of these is the Corruption Perceptions Index (CPI) published annually by Transparency International, an international NGO devoted exclusively to combating corruption. The CPI purports to rank countries in terms of the perceived incidence of corruption by bringing together a number of polls and surveys carried out primarily among professional risk analysts and business people. Like many such indices, its methodological failings are widely acknowledged and equally widely ignored. Its rankings are routinely reported in the national and international media, and they can have a real political and economic impact. Nevertheless, because they reflect perceptions rather than actual behavior, these rankings must always be taken with a pinch of salt. They reflect the perceived impact of corruption on the investment decisions of private business, which is not necessarily the area of greatest popular concern. Indeed, Transparency International's own Global Corruption Barometer shows that, in three countries out of four, the kind of corruption that people are most concerned about is that which occurs in political parties.

SEE ALSO: Authority and Legitimacy; Crime; Deviance; Transparency and Global Change

REFERENCES AND SUGGESTED READINGS

Euben, J. P. (1989) Corruption. In: Ball, T. et al. (Eds.), *Political Innovation and Conceptual Change.* Cambridge University Press, Cambridge.

Philp, M. (1997) Defining Political Corruption. In: Heywood, P. (Ed.), *Political Corruption.* Blackwell, Oxford, pp. 20–46.

Rose-Ackerman, S. (1999) *Corruption and Government: Causes, Consequences and Reform.* Cambridge University Press, Cambridge.

Transparency International (2003) Corruption Perceptions Index 2003. Online. www.transparency.org/cpi/2003/cpi2003.en.html.

Transparency International (2004) *Global Corruption Report.* Transparency International, Berlin; Pluto Press, London.

counterculture

Sam Binkley

Similar in meaning to the more inclusive term "subculture," counterculture designates a group whose norms, values, symbolic references, and styles of life deviate from those of the dominant culture. Indeed, sociological commentary on the counterculture of the 1960s is so deeply informed by the rubric of subculture as to render the terms inseparable in many respects. Initially applied to the study of youth cultures in the sociology of deviance, subculture research drew heavily on the contributions of the Chicago School sociologists Robert Park and later Howard Becker, but also on the Durkheimian sociology of Robert Merton, whose formulation of Durkheim's concept of anomie provided the basis for delinquency and deviance. Subcultures were viewed as alternative moral formations in which the blocked status aspirations of disadvantaged working-class youth were realized through appropriations and inversions of dominant moral codes. Whether criminal or retreatist, such groups were considered as aspirational, if innovative,

in their aims. This largely American analysis of subculture received a more political interpretation in the works of the British Birmingham School of Cultural Studies, where blocked avenues of class agitation were expressed through styles of life in which symbols were appropriated and modified in their meanings (Hebdige 1979).

Yet while subculture is the generic term typically applied to a range of such groups, from post-war British youth cultures to inner-city African American youth cultures, counterculture is typically invoked with specific reference to the youth movements that swept American and Western European societies in the late to mid-1970s. First introduced by Roszak (1968), the term came to refer to a diffuse movement of students, youth, and other marginalia whose mobilizing strategies rejected that of traditional social movements, and appealed to diffuse concepts of anti-technological sentiment to achieve spontaneous and widespread reforms. The counterculture, in Roszaks's formulation, is a specific case of subculture. It had an alternative strategy of political agitation to that of other subcultures. The appeal was more to a presumed mentalist, spiritual, and lifestyle development which, members of the counterculture argued, would serve as a basis for overturning hierarchical structures implicit within advanced technological societies.

The counterculture of the 1960s is typically traced to early reactions to the conformity and mediocrity associated with the years of the post-war economic expansion. Beatniks and others drew on African American expressive traditions to fashion a vanguard sensibility in music, drugs, philosophy, literature, and poetry. Amid accelerating popular opposition to the war in Vietnam and an emerging student left, together with the growth of hippie enclaves and the increasing thematization of drug experiences in music, film, and media, a distinctly oppositional culture formed around what was termed a new "consciousness." Rejecting not only the values of the mainstream middle class from which it emerged, but also the class-based political traditions of an older generation of leftist opposition, the counterculture advocated an immediate and practical approach to social reform, beginning with the individual reform of personal relationships and daily habits, and the adoption of utopian egalitarianism in one's everyday style of life. Sociological inquiries into the counterculture examined its religious and mystical aspirations (Tipton 1982), its historical origins (Gitlin 1993), its ongoing dialogue with consumer culture (Frank 1997), and ultimately its incorporation into the mainstream of American society in the form of a distinct demographic, variously termed yuppies or Bobo's (Brooks 2000).

The phrase counterculture still circulates in popular and sociological discussions, though its use has largely been elided with that of its more inclusive and richly conceptualized parent term, subculture.

SEE ALSO: Birmingham School; Cultural Studies; Deviance; Lifestyle; Social Movements; Subculture

REFERENCES AND SUGGESTED READINGS

Brooks, D. (2000) *Bobo's in Paradise: The New Upper Class and How They Got There*. Simon & Schuster, New York.
Frank, T. (1997) *The Conquest of Cool: Business Culture, Counterculture and the Rise of Hip Consumerism*. University of Chicago Press, Chicago.
Gitlin, T. (1993) *The Sixties: Years of Hope, Days of Rage*. Bantam, New York.
Hebdige, D. (1979) *Subculture: The Meaning of Style*. Routledge, New York.
Roszak, T. (1968) *The Making of a Counterculture*. University of California Press, Berkeley.
Tipton, S. (1982) *Getting Saved from the Sixties*. University of California Press, Berkeley.

couples living apart together

Mary Holmes

Living apart together (LAT) broadly refers to couples, heterosexual or homosexual, who have an ongoing self-defined couple relationship without cohabiting. Some couples keep separate residences, even though they both live within the same locale. Levin (2004) has suggested that the dual-residence aspect of LAT couples distinguishes them from a *commuter marriage* where there is one main household and just a second apartment for when one partner is away. However, with many commuter couples it is difficult to say which might be the "main" household. Distance perhaps better demarcates LATs from commuter marriages. LAT couples may live near each other, or far apart. Typically, those in commuter couples have residences at some distance and spend time apart in order for both partners to pursue professional careers. Such arrangements now encompass not just heterosexual and married couples, and for that reason Holmes (2004) uses the term *distance relationship*. LAT can serve as an umbrella term for all couples with dual residences. What the terms LAT, commuter marriage, and distance relationship have in common is that they refer to situations in which the woman partner/s has some independent existence, in ways not seen in the past.

Historically, there have always been couples who have had to endure separation, mostly when the husband's work took them away from home regularly. Such separations continue, but the husband's periodic absences from the family home are usually spent in temporary and/or institutional accommodation, as with sailing, fishing, military service, or incarceration. LAT relationships differ in that partners visit each other, but each returns to their own residence. These new arrangements have emerged as a result of women's increasing entry into the workforce, especially the professions, and the associated financial and social independence this allows. Yet the extent of living apart together is difficult to judge.

One major methodological problem with LAT couples is measuring their numbers. Many large data sets use households as the unit of measurement and therefore do not capture couples living apart. There have been recent efforts to correct this, but estimates vary depending on different definitions of the target population. Ermisch and Kiernan's respective analyses of the British Household Panel Survey and the European Family and Fertility Survey suggest that as many as one third of those in Europe not married or cohabiting may be having a relationship with someone in another household (Holmes 2004: 187). It is not known, however, how many of these may realistically be defined as living apart together, nor how far apart such couples live. However, Levin (2004: 228–9) has collected some quantitative data for Norway and Sweden which suggests that 8–14 percent of those who are not married or cohabiting are in a LAT relationship. This probably constitutes up to 4 percent of those populations, but may be a conservative estimate given Levin's rather strict definition. She notes that French and German scholars suggest slightly higher figures in their own nations, but based on broader definitions. As regards distance relationships, the American psychologist Gregory Guldner, in his book *Long Distance Relationships: The Complete Guide* (2003), states that one quarter of non-married people in the US live in a long-distance relationship (LDR). But work in this area has so far been almost wholly qualitative.

Sociological attention to couples living apart in new ways emerged in the late 1970s in the context of investigating the rise of dual-career couples. Farris reported the findings from her Masters thesis on commuting in the Rapoports' 1978 collection on *Working Couples*. Kirschner and Walum discussed "two-location families" in the first volume of *Alternative Lifestyles* published the same year. The focus was on commuter marriage – perhaps because unmarried couples who lived apart would not have been visible at the time (Levin 2004). The key issues have been to compare the satisfaction of such lifestyles in relation to cohabitation (Bunker et al. 1992) and to assess living apart as an attempt to achieve some balance between work and family demands. The latter is central to the first comprehensive sociological study of commuting couples by Gerstel and Gross (1984), who merged the qualitative data from their independent studies in the 1970s to give them a sample of 121 respondents, half of which had children. They looked at the costs and benefits of commuter marriage and argued such marriages illustrated that the demand of the economic system for mobile workers does not fit well with traditional family patterns of shared residence. This challenges the usual functionalist and Marxist arguments that the nuclear

family suits capitalism's needs. There are a few superficial inquiries into commuting in the early 1990s that mostly confirm Gerstel and Gross's findings. It is not until the end of the century that a shift in focus within the sociology of family, intimacy, and relationships prompts new, more substantial work.

Although interest in work–family "balance" continues, a focus on changes in intimate life is now driving much theoretical and empirical work on couples who live apart. These changes are being discussed in terms of how they relate to processes of individualization and the supposed impacts on traditional family, community bonds, and relations of care. Theoretical musings on these issues by the likes of Bauman and Giddens have begun to be questioned with the aid of empirical information. The issue of *Current Sociology* in which Irene Levin's article appears is a useful example of contemporary work in this line. The examination of couples living apart together, in all their forms, plays a crucial part in providing information about to what extent traditional or "conventional" ways of relating have become less dominant in the face of new conditions of social life prevailing at the beginning of the twenty-first century. In particular it is arguably becoming less taken for granted that cohabitation, or indeed proximity, is necessary for intimate relationships. There is still much to be done, however, in terms of exploring the complex relationships between individualization, geographical mobility, sexuality, and the ways in which people love and care for each other.

Individualization has not extended equally to all groups of people. As with other "non-conventional" forms of relating, research on LATs can help assess the effects of a supposedly greater social focus on autonomy. However, research so far indicates that even relationships seemingly based on high levels of independence may involve inequalities and interdependence. In order to better illuminate these issues further research on distance relationships needs to pay more attention to work being done on migration and globalization. Who you can love, how and where, is likely to be heavily influenced by discourses and practices relating to "race"/ethnicity, religion, security, home, and care. In addition, the sociology of the body and of emotions has a part to play in making sense of forms of "everyday migration" involved in maintaining relationships without frequent proximity. Physically and emotionally, long-term pursuit of such relationships may be sometimes exhausting and sometimes exhilarating. What might contribute to tired bodies and frayed nerves, rather than well-being, requires investigation. Access to economic resources, gendered practices, flexibility at work, and transport and communication networks are likely to be crucial. Other factors that might determine whether such arrangements will grow in popularity will include the numbers and status of women in the workforce, the operation of global and local labor markets, and changing ideas about intimacy, gender, sexuality, and relationships. Already sociologists exploring sexuality have made a considerable contribution to illustrating that (hetero)sexual cohabitational relationships are not the only, or indeed necessarily best, way to live love. It would be extremely useful to have more quantitative data on the extent of non-cohabitational relationships in order to establish just how non-conventional such arrangements are. This would help provide a context for further qualitative research which locates LATs not just in relation to "traditional" relationships, but within broad social and global processes which might offer new possibilities as well as new problems for loving.

SEE ALSO: Cohabitation; Households; Intimacy; Lesbian and Gay Families; Marriage

REFERENCES AND SUGGESTED READINGS

Bunker, B. B., Zubek, J., Vanderslice, V. J., & Rice, R. W. (1992) Quality of Life in Dual-Career Families: Commuting versus Single-Residence Couples. *Journal of Marriage and the Family* 54: 399–407.
Gerstel, N. & Gross, H. (1984) *Commuter Marriage.* Guilford Press, New York.
Holmes, M. (2004) An Equal Distance? Individualization, Gender and Intimacy in Distance Relationships. *Sociological Review* 52: 180–200.
Levin, I. (2004) Living Apart Together: A New Family Form. *Current Sociology* 52: 223–40.

courts

Yenli Yeh

Courts cover broad perspectives (Gifis 1998). First, the court is a part of the judicial branch of the government consisting of a judge or a few judges responsible for adjudging disputes under the laws. Second, the court represents a judge or judges on the judicial bench. Third, the court is a legislative assembly that interprets laws. Fourth, the court stands for a legal system or process.

There is variation and diversity in respect to courts globally. This entry focuses on the court system of the US, which has a dual court system which includes the federal and state courts. There was a major debate between anti-federalists and federalists after the American Revolution concerning whether it was necessary to have a federal court system separate from the state systems. As a result of compromise, the federalists finally were able to have the federal courts with a minimal supervision system along with the state court systems (Neubauer 1984). Rapid population growth and industrialization after the Civil War resulted in the increased volume of litigations on the local and state levels. Many states expanded their state and local courts, and this kind of expansion created a very complex American legal system.

In general, the federal courts have the authority to decide controversial cases related to the US Constitution, and disputes between citizens of different states as well as between a state and citizens of another state (Lectric Law Library 2002). The federal court system includes the US Supreme Court, Courts of Appeals, Courts of Appeals for the Federal Circuit, District Courts, and Magistrate's Courts. The US Supreme is the highest court, consisting of nine justices appointed for life by the president, with the approval of the Senate. The role of the Supreme Court is to maintain the order of the US Constitution, resolve disputes between states, and guarantee the uniform enforcement of all federal laws (Freund 1961). The Supreme Court hears appeals from US circuit courts and state supreme courts which involve questions of the Constitution and violations of federal laws. A *writ of certiorari* will be processed to the Supreme Court. Then justices will determine whether the laws were applied appropriately. The US Supreme Court is the court of last resort.

The next level of the federal court system is US courts of appeals, also referred to as circuit courts. There are 12 courts of appeals consisting of 11 circuits and the District of Columbia. Generally, each circuit court includes three or more states. Judges of courts of appeals are also appointed for life by the president with the consent of the Senate. Courts of appeals have the jurisdiction to review the appeals from district courts. The US Court of Appeals for the Federal Circuit was created by the merging of the US Court of Claims and the US Court of Customs as well as Patent Appeals in 1982 (Lectric Law Library 2002). Court of Appeals for the Federal Circuit has the specialized jurisdiction over appeals from specific federal agencies, which includes the US Court of International Trade, the US Court of Veterans Appeals, the US Court of Federal Claims, the US Tax Court, the Patent and Trademark Office, the Board of Contract Appeals, and the US Courts of Military Appeals (Lectric Law Library 2002).

Historically, under the courts of appeals are district courts which are trial courts of the federal court system. Most federal criminal and civil cases are tried and adjudicated in the district courts. Each state at least has one district court, while New York, California, and Texas have the exceptions of four district courts each. Currently, there are 94 district courts in 50 states, the District of Columbia, the Commonwealth of Puerto Rico, the Territories of Guam, the US Virgin Island, and the Northern Mariana Islands. Judges of district courts are nominated by the president and confirmed by the Senate. Federal district courts have jurisdiction over civil cases involving more than $10,000 and criminal cases dealing with federal agencies. Each district court has a bankruptcy court that hears bankruptcy petitions of individuals and business.

The purpose of magistrate judges is to assist district court judges. Magistrate judges are authorized to hear civil cases of less than $10,000. Felony charges will only be heard by district courts judges. However, magistrate judges deal with pretrial work in many district courts, such as bail and counsel appointment.

State courts handle the vast majority of cases and have a more complex structure than the federal courts. Some states, such as Texas and New York, have numerous levels of lower courts. Although no two state courts are alike, there are four basic levels of state courts: lower court, superior court, intermediate court of appeals, and supreme court. Lower court, also referred to as inferior court, is the first level of the state court system. It has limited jurisdiction. There are more than 13,500 lower courts and they constitute more than 75 percent of the judicial courts in the US (Neubauer 1984; Abadinsky 2003). Lower courts include various types of courts: city court, county court, justice of the peace court, magistrate court, municipal court, city magistrate, justice court, traffic court, and probate court. Generally, lower courts only handle traffic violations, misdemeanor criminal cases, and civil disputes under $5,000. Due to the limited jurisdiction, lower courts are responsible for criminal preliminary hearings, such as arraignments, setting bail, and appointing public counsels. Lower courts are generally authorized to impose a maximum fine of $1,000 and no more than one year in prison. Appeals from lower courts will be heard in state superior courts.

The next level of the state court system is the state superior court, sometimes referred to as trial court, district court, circuit court, and court of common pleas. Superior court is a major trial court with authorization to hear all types of criminal and civil cases. Typically, superior court handles civil cases and criminal cases at the felony level as well as criminal and civil appeals from lower courts. Some superior courts also hear misdemeanor cases if joint jurisdiction existed with lower courts. There are multi-divisions existing in some superior courts, including criminal, civil, family, and juvenile cases.

Intermediate courts of appeals are also known as courts of appeals, district courts of appeals, or appeal courts. A few states separate courts of appeals for civil and criminal cases, such as Alabama, Oklahoma, Tennessee, and Texas. All cases are typically heard by panels of three judges in intermediate courts of appeals. Although the lower and superior courts hear the largest volume of cases, intermediate courts of appeals also handle a large volume of cases. Some states, because of small populations, do not have courts of appeal. These states are Maine, New Hampshire, North and South Dakota, Vermont, and Wyoming.

The court of last resort in the state court structure is the state supreme court. The number of supreme court judges per state varies from five to nine. State supreme courts handle limited cases of appeals and cases involving interpretations of state constitutions as well as state laws. Capital punishment cases are automatically appealed to state supreme courts. *Briefs* or *petitions*, written documents with legal arguments, will be sent to state supreme courts. Then, *oral arguments* are held before the final written statements are produced. Only appeals from state supreme courts involving the US Constitution and violations of federal laws will go on to the US Supreme Court.

According to the nature of courts, courts generally can be divided into criminal court, civil court, and juvenile court. The rule of *nullum crimen sine lege*, no crime without a law, is applied in the criminal process. It means courts have no jurisdiction to hear criminal cases unless a law has been broken. A defendant is entitled to have a series of due process rights that are guaranteed by the US Constitution. These guarantees include right to remain silent, right to counsel, right to bail, right to speedy and public trial, right to confront witness, and double jeopardy prohibition. Most misdemeanor cases begin and end in the lower courts in a process of *rough justice* (Abadinsky 2003). Due process is not the major focus in the process of rough justice due to the very large volume of misdemeanor cases handled by lower courts. Most defendants quickly plead guilty to avoid trial or incarceration. The flow of felony cases in criminal trial courts is very complex. It includes initial appearance (counsel, charges, and bail are addressed), preliminary hearings (probable cause and bail are reviewed), arraignment (plea bargaining and bail are decided), trial (pretrial motions and hearing, open statements, cross-examinations of evidence and witnesses, trial motions, and closing statements as well as deliberations are included), and sentencing (Abadinsky 2003). Jury trial is indicated in the Sixth Amendment of the Constitution. However, only a small amount of criminal cases go through jury trial. Each state has its own standards and applications of a jury trial. The US Supreme Court ruled that jury trial is required in cases of capital crime. The burden of proving criminal conviction is *beyond a reasonable doubt*.

While the prosecutor charges the defendant in a state criminal court, an individual could file a civil action against another private party in a civil court. Civil court serves the purpose of adjudicating personal disputes. Cases handled by civil courts include disputes involving torts, personal properties, contracts, succession, family relations, and civil rights (Abadinsky 2003). A trial is not the major goal of civil courts. Most civil cases are settled in an informal setting when the plaintiffs are willing to accept settlements. The flow of a civil case includes filing a complaint from the plaintiff, filing a response by the defendant, pretrial activities (motions, discovery, and conferences are arranged), trial hearing (trial motions, opening statements, examinations of witnesses and evidence, and summations and deliberations are included), and judgment/verdict either for the plaintiff or the defendant (Abadinsky 2003). Small claim courts are designed to resolve civil cases that involve small amounts of money (less than $5,000) in a quick and inexpensive process. Only a small fee is required when a private party files a complaint in small claim courts. In addition, there is no attorney practice in small claim courts. Most civil cases are determined by bench trial instead of jury trial, just as in the criminal courts. The burden of proving civil liability is *preponderance of evidence*.

The first juvenile court in the US was established in Cook County, Illinois in 1899. The purpose of Cook County Juvenile Courts was designed to assist juveniles instead of punishing them. The nature of juvenile court has not changed over the years. Although the definitions of juvenile and the juvenile court process are different from state to state, the juvenile courts basically handle cases of juvenile delinquency, status offense, child neglect and abuse, and dependency. For the purpose of preventing labeling, juveniles enter the juvenile courts as the last resort after failing efforts from police, schools, families, and social agencies. The juvenile court process includes intake, petition, preliminary hearings (the waiver decision will be made if it is necessary to transfer delinquent juveniles to criminal courts), adjudication hearing and dispositional decision.

Currently, almost all states allow juveniles to be tried as adults in criminal courts. This means laws allow juveniles to be waived/transferred to criminal courts because of the severity of crimes committed by juveniles and prosecutorial discretion. Delinquent juveniles will more likely receive harsher punishment in criminal courts than by remaining in juvenile courts.

SEE ALSO: Corrections; Criminal Justice System; Juvenile Delinquency; Race and the Criminal Justice System

REFERENCES AND SUGGESTED READINGS

Abadinsky, H. (2003) *Law and Justice: An Introduction to the Legal System.* Prentice-Hall, Englewood Cliffs, NJ.
Freund, P. (1961) The Supreme Court. In: Berman, H. (Ed.), *Talk on American.* Vintage Books, New York.
Garner, B. (2001) *A Handbook of Family Law Terms.* West Group, St. Paul, MN.
Gifis, S. (1998) *Dictionary of Legal Terms.* Barron's Educational Series, New York.
Lectric Law Library (2002). Online. www.lectlaw.com.
National Center for State Courts. Online. www.ncsconline.org.
Neubauer, D. (1984) *America's Court and the Criminal Justice System.* Brooks/Cole Publishing, Pacific Grove, CA.

credit cards

Lloyd Klein

Credit cards are a popularized economic instrument enabling the consumer acquisition of goods or services in exchange for assured merchant or provider payment through financial institutions. The resulting transfer of funds was enabled through a change in the cultural view of thrift and systematic savings. Much of the pattern was driven by a transformation from ideological values associated with savings into a culture focused on consumer acquisition. Max Weber's view of social change stressed an intensified neutralization of the "Protestant Ethic" into a more vigorous consumer orientation. In Weber's analysis, credit was viewed as more culturally acceptable beginning early in the twentieth century. This trend gave way to the "democratization of credit" and the increasing acceptance of consumer credit in the form of credit cards and other financial mechanisms.

The utility of credit cards was enhanced as consumers shifted from the "future orientation" of saving for planned purchases into a "present orientation" of buying now and paying for the goods or services at a later point. According to at least one industry insider, the original credit cards began as paper cards authorizing the acquisition of restaurant meals and eventually evolved into plastic strips facilitating the purchase of virtually any good or service.

The term credit card became culturally and economically significant as financial credit became associated with the use of financial instruments or bank cards issued by businesses. Banks and other financial institutions joined with the Interbank Organization (Mastercard) and eventually Visa, American Express, and Discover in working with merchants and national businesses. The credit card companies would license their name to the specific bank or company in exchange for a fee charged in permitting the use of their product.

Over time, some credit cards were transformed into affinity cards. These affinity cards focused on organizations such as the American Sociological Association, major league sports teams, and other special interest groups. A percentage of the generated consumer or member charges would be returned to the original sponsoring organization as a direct payment.

Credit cards are much more than just financial instruments enabling economic transactions. The cultural ramifications of credit cards include changes in consumer behavior and a significant revision in the definition of social class. The "present" orientation enabled by credit card purchasing was driven by consumer desire for commodity acquisition as much as changes in the business community. In the matter of consumers driving this important economic transformation, Thorstein Veblen discusses the idea of conspicuous consumption wherein individuals compete with each other for social status. The game of "keeping up with the Joneses" is further referred to by Veblen as invidious emulation. Credit cards facilitate consumer desire to spend funds one may not immediately possess for the purpose of maintaining appearances. The ultimate effect is a greater emphasis on acquiring material goods (e.g., appliances, automobiles, clothing, etc.) or products with symbolic capital (travel experiences, knowledge acquired in universities or educational programs such as the Learning Exchange wherein entrepreneurs and entertainers share their unique talents or skills).

The development of credit cards can be expressed as a juxtaposition between entertainment and lifestyle vehicles and more sophisticated "all purpose" plastic cards enabling the consumption of everyday wants or needs associated with everyday acquisition of necessary goods and services. The entertainment lifestyle associated with the Stork Club and an ability to charge expensive restaurant meals was transformed by the ascendancy of Master Charge and American Express. Master Charge became Mastercard and Visa entered the fray in challenges to American Express. The all-purpose cards were embraced by businesses and service providers throughout the world. Travel, restaurant meals, college tuition, and even fast food were immediately attainable with the application with preapproved plastic cards linked with vast computerized authorization systems.

Department stores had much earlier entered into the business with issuance of their own credit cards. Bloomingdale's, Macy's, Nordstrom's, and other retailers issue their own credit cards with higher rates than the already existent bank cards. The selling point for these cards was associated with an extra discount on merchandise purchased at the retail establishment with the given store credit instrument.

One must examine the marketing of consumer credit in order to understand the full impact of these socioeconomic changes. Early advertising associated with credit cards emphasized the class status of women during the emerging women's liberation movement. "Mastercard and Me – We Can Do It All" was targeted at professional women seeking recognition through the acquisition of suitable goods and services facilitating their emerging careers. Other Mastercard and Visa advertising formulated during the 1980s focused on the applicability of credit cards in arranging vacations and life-changing moments (such as weddings). American Express jumped into the fray emphasizing the Amex card for protecting one's vacation with specified travel services (replacing a lost card, covering emergency expenses while traveling, etc.). The Discover Card was launched during an early 1980s Super Bowl ad depicting everyday people marching into a better life and "discovering the potential" that can be obtained with consumer credit.

Not all these developments were smoothly navigated by the credit card companies and merchants. An overheated economy in 1977 led to President Jimmy Carter's call to consumers to go easy on credit card spending. The banks, credit card companies, and retailers were busy promoting consumerism for the sake of consumer spending. However, the debt margin on credit cards kept rising and consumers found themselves hit with a downturn in the economy. Jobs were lost in a stagflation period featuring inflation and recessionary difficulties with economic growth. Credit card spending flagged somewhat during this time while the marketing of consumer credit and credit cards began stressing personal consumer responsibility in monitoring debt levels.

Collateralized credit cards became more acceptable during this time. Individuals with a poor credit history or young people seeking to establish credit were offered a card with set spending limits based on a bank deposit. This device gave individuals the convenience of credit card spending without worrying about the repercussions of future consumer debt. Looked at from another way, it allowed people to borrow their own money at high interest.

The pressures of the 1970s gave way to more pronounced credit card spending during the economic boom of the 1980s. The stock market was up, employment was more plentiful, and consumer confidence in the economy built steadily upward. Credit cards were more socially acceptable as "Generation X" (the new group of young people) went out and embraced consumer spending. Credit card companies became emboldened and marketed their product to anyone and everyone. More merchants and companies affiliated themselves with the cards produced by American Express, Mastercard, and Visa. Merchants sought out the help of credit reporting companies in seeking lists of good credit risks. Unfortunately, the seeking out of qualified applicants for preapproved credit cards reached a frenzied level. As pointed out by Bankrate.com, merchants were grabbing at every name perceived as a viable consumer risk. Cats, dogs, and even children whose names were obtained from merchandise ordering lists were sent solicitations for credit cards. The resultant publicity led to more careful screening.

The connection between credit cards and bankruptcy is an important contemporary subject. A 2005 revamped bankruptcy law makes it harder for consumers to dissolve their debts through filing for systematic relief. The reason for this legislation, which was lobbied strongly by the financial community, was the rise in consumer bankruptcy filings. As Caplovitz pointed out many years ago, and a trend that continues today, consumers utilized credit cards and often found themselves in ever-increasing debt. Curiously enough, credit card companies still persisted in sending their consumer credit products to individuals deeply in debt or those struggling with declared bankruptcy. The battle to secure spending overwhelmed common sense in screening out these questionable credit risks.

SEE ALSO: Bankruptcy; Consumer Movements; Consumption; Consumption, Mass Consumption, and Consumer Culture; Money; Money Management in Families

REFERENCES AND SUGGESTED READINGS

Evans, D. S. & Schmalensee, R. (2005) *Paying with Plastic: The Digital Revolution in Buying and Borrowing*, 2nd edn. MIT Press, Cambridge, MA.
Manning, R. D. (2001) *Credit Card Nation: The Consequences of America's Addiction to Credit*. Basic Books, New York.
Ritzer, G. (1995) *Expressing America: A Critique of the Global Credit Card Society*. Pine Forge Press, Newbury Park, CA.

creolization

Robin Cohen

The words Creole and creolization have been used in many different contexts and generally in an inconsistent way. "Creole" was possibly derived from the Latin *creara* ("created originally"). The most common historical use was the Spanish *criollo*, which described the children of Spanish colonizers born in the Caribbean. The French transformed the word to *créole*. However, the racially exclusive definition, which confined the term to whites in colonial societies, had already been challenged in the early eighteenth century and referred also to indigenous people and other immigrants who had acquired metropolitan manners, cultures, and sensibilities.

The major form of acculturation was to adapt the language of the superordinate group – principally the French, Spanish, English, Dutch, and Portuguese. Using a European acrolect and an African or indigenous basilect generated many Creole languages. These are different from pidgins (simple contact languages) in that they have an elaborated lexicon and become mother tongues. "Creole" has adjectivally been applied to music (especially jazz), dancing, cuisine, clothing, architecture, literature, and art; there are even creole fish, flowers, and pigs. More recently sociologists, anthropologists, and cultural studies theorists have seen that creolization can be used in a much richer sense, alluding to all kinds of cross-fertilization that take place between different cultures when they interact. When creolizing, participants select particular elements from incoming or inherited cultures, endow these with meanings different from those they possessed in the original culture, and then creatively merge these to create totally new varieties that supersede the prior forms.

Creolization can easily be distinguished from *indigenization*, where global threats reauthenticate local cultural forms, from *homogenization*, where dominant cultural forces flatten everything in their path, and from *multiculturalism*, where the component cultural segments remain viable even if there is some dialogue between them. It is somewhat more complex to separate the contemporary understanding of creolization from cognate terms like hybridity, syncretism, cosmopolitanism, transnationalism, and interculturality. But creolization does have a distinctive emphasis on cultural creativity, sharing, transcendence, and invention.

Contemporary understandings of creolization have been signaled in the work· of the Martinican writer and cultural theorist Edouard Glissant, who asks whether we should favor "An identity that would not be the projection of a unique and sectarian root, but of what we call a rhizome, a root with a multiplicity of extensions in all directions? Not killing what is around it, as a unique root would, but establishing communication and relation?" Equally important is the work of the Swedish social and cultural anthropologist Ulf Hannerz. In his work on the evolution of a "global ecumene," he suggests that the "world is in creolization." Hannerz continues: "Creolization also increasingly allows the periphery to talk back. As it creates a greater affinity between the cultures of the center and the periphery ... some of its new cultural commodities become increasingly attractive on a global market."

Attention to the "creolizing world" has considerable social scientific potential as a suggestive, instructive, and subtle means of describing our complex world and the diverse societies in which we all now live.

SEE ALSO: Acculturation; Hybridity; Multiculturalism; Race; Race and Ethnic Consciousness; Race (Racism)

REFERENCES AND SUGGESTED READINGS

Glissant, E. (n.d.) Creolization du monde. In: Ruano-Borbalon (Ed.), *L'Identite, le groupe, la societe*. Sciences Humaines Editions, Auxerre.

Hannerz, U. (1987) The World in Creolization. *Africa* 57: 546–59.

Hannerz, U. (1996) *Cultural Complexity: Studies in the Social Organization of Meaning*. Columbia University Press, New York.

crime

John T. Whitehead

Criminologists differ on how they define crime. One definition is a legal definition: crime is a violation of the criminal law. Criminologists Edwin Sutherland and Donald Cressey call this the conventional definition of crime because it is the commonly used definition. They add that it is typical to distinguish a crime from a tort. A crime is a violation against the state whereas a tort is a violation against an individual and the civil law. Hence in criminal law the charge reads *The State of* ____ v. *John Doe* while in civil court it is *Mary Smith* v. *John Doe*. A dramatic example of crime versus tort occurred in one of the most well-known crimes of the twentieth century, the O. J. Simpson matter. In criminal court he was acquitted of the crime of murder but he was found civilly liable for wrongful death in civil court. Two such trials do not violate the constitutional protection against double jeopardy (being tried twice for the same crime), because criminal and civil court are considered two completely distinct systems and civil court carries no stigma of a criminal conviction.

Within the framework of the legal definition of crime, crime is distinguished from delinquency by the age of the offender. In most states an offender has to be 18 to be arrested and prosecuted as a criminal. Under 18 the youth is processed as a delinquent in a separate juvenile or family court and legally there is not a criminal conviction. A few states set 16 or 17 as the age for the beginning of criminal court jurisdiction.

Some other points to note about this conventional definition of crime are that not everyone who violates the criminal law is apprehended and that crime can vary from jurisdiction to jurisdiction. For example, only about 20 to 30 percent of burglaries and robberies are cleared or solved. Also, if state X defines felony shoplifting to be theft of merchandise valued at over $25 and state Y defines the limit to be $100, a theft could be a felony (a serious crime) in one state and only a misdemeanor (a less serious crime) in another state. A felon can go to prison and loses important rights such as the right to vote. A misdemeanant can only go to a county jail or prison for a sentence of less than one year and does not lose such important rights as the right to vote.

Sociologist Émile Durkheim argued that crime is normal. By this he meant that even a society of saints would have persons with faults that the society would judge and punish. In other words, each society has a collective conscience that notices and punishes faults so as to reinforce the common values that most members should be striving to emulate and show allegiance to. In fact, Durkheim notes, the absence of crime might be a problem. It might mean that a society is overly repressive and does not allow enough room for dissent and innovation. So no society should congratulate itself for completely eliminating crime.

Building on this notion of the societal reaction to crime, some criminologists argue that crime and other types of deviance do not have unique elements in themselves that define them but that the criminal or the deviant "is one to whom that label has successfully been applied; deviant behavior is behavior that people so label" (Becker 1963: 9). This labeling perspective does not have as much popularity as it once did but the perspective still reminds us that societal reaction is critical in any definition of crime.

On the other hand, noted criminologists Michael Gottfredson and Travis Hirschi define crimes as "acts of force or fraud undertaken in pursuit of self-interest" (1990: 15). So contrary to Sutherland, they see much crime as ordinary and mundane. In fact, they see crime stemming from human nature which focuses on pursuing pleasure and avoiding pain. And they see commonalities in crime, deviance, sin, and accident rather than conceptualizing them as distinct phenomena. For example, they argue that sin and crime are often the same actions, such as stealing someone else's property. The difference is that religion (a church) sanctions sin while the government (a court) sanctions crime.

Herman and Julia Schwendinger suggest still another definition of crime. They defined crime as acts against human rights. If they were writing today instead of 40 years ago, they might well include either terrorism or unjust wars as part of what they defined as criminal. For example, using their definition, some could argue that various national leaders are criminals if they are violating human rights, even though as president or leader of their countries they are arguably acting under color of law.

A recent perspective, but one with an ancient history, the restorative justice perspective focuses on harms instead of "crimes." Contrary to the legal definition of crime noted above, restorative justice proponents disagree that the "state" is the aggrieved party. Restorative justice proponents argue that this conceptualization of crime dates back to the end of the Dark Ages when crime was seen as a felony against the king. So restorative justice theorists and practitioners argue that they are going back to the true definition of crime as a harm, injury, or wrong done to another individual. The response of society should be first to acknowledge the hurt and injury that has occurred. Then there should be attention to the needs of the victim. And there also should be attention to the needs of the person who has inflicted the harm, the offender. Thus a crime is seen not simply as an occasion for the state to inflict punishment, but as an opportunity for the community to intervene and help both the victim and the offender. Even more idealistically than this, peacemaking criminologist Richard Quinney (going beyond the critical criminology he once espoused) argues that crime is an opportunity for all of us to work on "the transformation of our human being" (2000: 188) and create a good society. To achieve such goals, some restorative justice proponents argue that community groups or religious groups, not government agencies like probation, should operate restorative justice programs as the emphasis is on a forgiving justice process rather than a bureaucratic punishing process.

Perspectives such as that of the Schwendingers and the restorative justice perspective, which some call radical, see the usual emphasis on crime and criminal justice as too narrow. Such criminologists think that the criminal justice system puts too much emphasis on street crime and not enough emphasis on the crimes of the powerful. These criminologists contend that corporations or even the government can and do perpetrate "crimes" or injuries. For example, Jeffrey Reiman argues that while the FBI focuses on homicide, many more Americans are dying from occupational hazards at work or from malpractice in the hospital operating room. But because our capitalist system protects both corporations and doctors, there is considerably less attention to and enforcement of statutes pertaining to workplace crime. The result is that "the rich get richer and the poor get prison" (the title of his book). In the words of criminologist Richard Quinney: "It is through a critical criminology that we can understand how American law preserves the existing social and economic order. Criminal law is used in the capitalist state to secure the survival of the capitalist system and its ruling class" (2000: 90).

Building on this type of thinking but tying it in with some of the most recent economic trends, John Hagan argues that the new globalized economy has resulted in disinvestment in many communities, which has made job prospects very bleak. In other words, many transnational companies are exporting jobs to countries such as China or India where wages are much lower. Blocked out of high-paying factory jobs, residents in low-income areas turn to crime, especially drug dealing, as a way to earn a living. Thus Hagan argues that social inequality and capital disinvestment cause such crime as drug dealing in poverty-stricken areas. So crime "has become a short-term adaptive form of recapitalization for youth" (1994: 87).

Hagan also emphasizes that crime and our conceptions of crime are changeable. One specific and clear example of the changeable aspect of crime is Prohibition. Approximately 80 years ago the United States defined the manufacture, distribution, and sale of alcohol as criminal. Today alcohol production and consumption is a vital part of our economy, as advertising demonstrates. Instead of pursuing bootleggers, contemporary police are pursuing drug dealers. So whereas ethnic group members in low-income neighborhoods once supplied their own neighborhoods with bootleg beer, today ethnic group members are selling drugs to neighborhood residents and to consumers from other areas in what contemporary social scientists call deviance service centers.

Despite the existence of varying emphases by criminologists, two common ways of measuring crime that follow the legal definition to varying degrees are arrest statistics typically reported in the FBI Uniform Crime Reports and victimization studies such as the National Crime Victimization Survey. The FBI Uniform Crime Reports frame the discussion of crime in the United States by reporting the numbers of offenses reported to the police and the numbers of arrests. The FBI Crime Index is composed of violent and property offenses. Murder, rape, robbery, and aggravated assault make up the Violent Crime Index. Larceny-theft, burglary, and arson compose the Property Crime Index. In 2002 there were over 11.8 million offenses reported to the police for an Index Crime rate of 4,118.8 offenses per 100,000 residents in the United States. This rate was down 1.1 percent from 2001 and down almost 25 percent from 1993. Larceny-theft crimes account for about 60 percent of Index crimes in the United States. Murder and robbery, two crimes that citizens fear and television crime shows emphasize, account for one tenth of 1 percent and 3.5 percent of Index offenses, respectively.

Criminologist Edwin Sutherland noted that both criminologists and ordinary citizens, in accord with the FBI emphasis on Index crimes, often overemphasize street crime and underemphasize white-collar crime. Writing over 60 years ago yet bearing uncanny relevance to the current rash of corporate and executive wrongdoing, Sutherland noted that examples of white-collar crime "are found in abundance in the business world" (in Jacoby 1979: 17).

Victimization studies such as the National Crime Victimization Survey (NCVS) read descriptions of personal and property crimes to survey respondents who answer whether they have been a victim of such incidents in the past 6 months. The interviewers and the questions frame the implicit definitions of criminal acts (based on legal definitions) but to some extent the respondent defines acts as victimizations or not. If a respondent actually experienced such a victimization but thinks it is not a crime and does not tell it to the survey interviewer, then that action is not counted as a victimization. Or if a victimization was quite trivial and would not have ended in an arrest, the respondent may still report it as a victimization. Victimization studies have helped criminologists study crime because they allow for the analysis of crimes that do not get reported to the police, what some call the dark figure of crime. The NCVS also transcends state-to-state variation in the criminal law; the survey uses the same descriptions of victimizations in every state.

In 2002 US residents aged 12 or older experienced approximately 23 million violent and property victimizations. The overall violent victimization and property crime rates were the lowest recorded since the start of the NCVS in 1973. The rate of violent victimization decreased 21 percent from the period 1999–2000 to 2001–2. Concerning property crime, from 1993 through 2002, the household burglary rate fell 52 percent; the auto theft rate decreased 53 percent; and the rate of theft declined 49 percent.

Marcus Felson points out that there are many fallacies in the general understanding of crime in the United States even when we use the legal definition of crime. As noted in the discussion of the FBI Crime Index above, minor property offenses vastly outnumber murders, especially dramatized murders such as gangland killings and sniper attacks. Related to this, most crime goes unreported and does not result in an arrest. Further, contrary to what many think, most crime is not organized and prosperity may actually increase crime by making more goods available for theft.

As noted above, the FBI rate of Index Crime in 2002 was down 1.1 percent from 2001 and down almost 25 percent from 1993. Newspapers and others attributed this decline to less reporting of crime to the police, more effective use of policing, increased incarceration, changes in demand for illegal drugs, especially crack cocaine, decreased use or availability of guns, improvement in the economy, and changes in youth attitudes. Criminologist John Conklin has done a thorough analysis of the dramatic crime decline in the 1990s. He concludes that the increased use of imprisonment was the major factor in the crime decline, followed by changes in the crack market and a switch to marijuana. Careful analyses such as this are important because politicians often make claims that are not based on evidence. In New York City, for example, politicians claimed that changes in policing produced the crime reductions when the evidence does not clearly support such a claim.

A related issue is the comparison of the extent of crime in the United States to the extent in other countries. Despite recent decreases in US crime rates, criminologists Steven Messner and Richard Rosenfeld argue that crime is more prevalent in the United States than in other advanced societies. To demonstrate the preeminence of the United States in crime, they note that in 1997 the US had a robbery rate of 186.1 robberies per 100,000 residents. The next closest country was France with a rate of under 140 robberies per 100,000 residents. The US rate was more than two and one-half times above the average rate for the 15 other countries in the comparison group. Similarly, the US homicide rate for 1993–5 was 8.2 homicides per 100,000 population. This was about six and one-half times higher than the average rate of the other countries in the sample. American culture may be one reason for this. Messner and Rosenfeld argue that the American Dream – our emphasis on monetary success via competition – helps many of us to reach our own success goals but that it also contributes to the high level of crime in the United States compared to other nations. Their suggestion for reducing crime in the United States is to focus more attention on goals other than monetary success and to put some restraints on the individual achievement of material success instead of family and community interests.

In summary, police, prosecutors, and correctional officials act on the assumption that the conventional definition of crime, any violation of the criminal law, is both generally accepted and valid. Criminologists often do the same. But there are other definitions of crime, especially the definitions proposed by critical criminologists and restorative justice theoreticians, that raise important questions about our understanding of crime and our reaction to it.

SEE ALSO: Age and Crime; Alcohol and Crime; Class and Crime; Collective Efficacy and Crime; Conflict Theory and Crime and Delinquency; Crime, Biosocial Theories of; Crime, Broken Windows Theory of; Crime, Corporate; Crime, Hot Spots; Crime, Life Course Theory of; Crime, Organized; Crime, Political; Crime, Psychological Theories of; Crime, Radical/Marxist Theories of; Crime, Schools and; Crime, Social Control Theory of; Crime, Social Learning Theories of; Crime, White-Collar; Criminal Justice System; Criminology; Deviance, Crime and; Environmental Criminology; Index Crime; Juvenile Delinquency; Law, Criminal; Measuring Crime; Property Crime; Public Order Crime; Race and Crime; Sex and Crime; Social Support and Crime; Victimization; Violent Crime

REFERENCES AND SUGGESTED READINGS

Becker, H. S. (1963) *Outsiders: Studies in the Sociology of Deviance*. Free Press, New York.
Braithwaite, J. (2002) *Restorative Justice and Responsive Regulation*. Oxford University Press, Oxford.
Conklin, J. (2003) *Why the Crime Rates Fell*. Allyn & Bacon, Boston.
FBI (2003) *Uniform Crime Reports: Crime in the United States*. Online. www.fbi.gov/ucr/.
Felson, M. (2002) *Crime and Everyday Life*, 3rd edn. Sage, Thousand Oaks, CA.
Gottfredson, M. R. & Hirschi, T. (1990) *A General Theory of Crime*. Stanford University Press, Stanford, CA.
Hagan, J. (1994) *Crime and Disrepute*. Pine Forge Press, Thousand Oaks, CA.
Jacoby, J. E. (1979) *Classics of Criminology*. Moore Publishing, Oak Park, IL.
Messner, S. F. & Rosenfeld, R. (2001) *Crime and the American Dream*, 3rd edn. Wadsworth/Thomson Learning, Belmont, CA.
Quinney, R. (2000) *Bearing Witness to Crime and Social Justice*. State University of New York Press, Albany.
Reiman, J. H. (2001) *The Rich Get Richer and the Poor Get Prison*, 6th edn. Allyn & Bacon, Boston.
Rennison, C. M. & Rand, M. R. (2003) *Criminal Victimization, 2002*. US Department of Justice, Washington, DC.
Sullivan, D. & Tifft, L. (2001) *Restorative Justice: Healing the Foundations of Our Everyday Lives*. Willow Tree Press, Monsey, NY.
Sutherland, E. H. & Cressey, D. R. (1960) *Principles of Criminology*, 6th edn. J. B. Lippincott, Chicago.

crime, biosocial theories of

Lee Ellis

Most sociologists do not believe that biological factors play a significant role in causing crime, instead attributing it almost entirely to social learning. Sociologists and criminologists generally share this strict environmental perspective, and thereby keep biology at arm's length. A recent survey of criminologists indicated that only about 15 percent believe biology is important for understanding criminality. They are known as *biosocial criminologists*.

It is interesting to note that when criminology began to form about a century and a half ago, it exhibited a fairly strong biological emphasis. At that time, a physician named Cesare Lombroso argued among other things that the most persistent and vicious criminals were *atavistic*. By this term, Lombroso meant that hardened criminals were "throwbacks" to more barbaric stages in human evolution. He went so far as to propose that one could even identify such individuals by their exhibiting a number of relatively "primitive" physical characteristics.

By the early twentieth century, most criminologists had largely dismissed Lombroso's ideas and turned their attention to strictly environmental explanations of criminal behavior based on various principles of social learning. However, beginning in the 1970s, several criminologists began to give renewed attention to biology as providing significant explanatory power. None of them denied that learning and social influences were involved, but they suggested that biological forces could also be at work in the sense of affecting people's propensities to be more readily influenced by some social learning factors more than others. For example, persons who were biologically predisposed toward being risk-takers might be more easily drawn into various types of crime than those who rarely took risks.

The biosocial perspective in sociology and criminology has two distinguishable but complementary traditions. One focuses on identifying evolutionary forces that may underlie criminal behavior. The other tradition is mainly interested in linking criminality to specific biological processes such as those involving hormones and brain-functioning patterns. Examples from each of these two traditions are summarized below.

Since the 1980s, several evolutionary theories of criminal behavior have been published. Among the least technical of these proposals was one articulated by Linda Mealey (1995). She put forth a theory of why criminal behavior in all cultures is committed primarily by males, particularly during their early reproductive years.

Mealey's evolutionary reasoning went as follows. Because they do not gestate offspring, males have more options than females do regarding how they will allocate their "reproductive effort." As a result, males in many species have evolved a variety of "creative" ways to augment the minimal time they have to devote to reproduction. Along these lines, biologists have documented in quite a number of species what are called *alternative reproductive strategies*, all of which are found only in males. For example, in a common freshwater fish known as the *bluegill*, most adult males jealously defend a little territory near the bottom of the pond where they spend most of their time. In the midst of their territory, each male hollows out a "nest" in the sediment. If a receptive female swims by and finds the male's territory attractive, she descends for a closer inspection. Sometimes, her visit is followed by the couple performing a synchronous courtship dance. He then ushers her to his nest, nuzzles her belly, and prompts her to lay several dozen eggs. This is followed by the male depositing a cloud of sperm over the clutch of eggs in order to fertilize them.

The scenario just presented is often more complicated due to the fact that not all male bluegill reproduce in this way. A second type of male bluegill has evolved called a *sneaker*. Sneakers do not defend territories or build nests, and females never seem to choose them as mating partners. Even so, sneakers manage to pass their genes on generation after generation, thus maintaining a representation in bluegill populations. Here is how they do it. Sneakers stealthily wait in the vicinity of a courting couple, usually without detection. Then, after

the female deposits her eggs, a sneaker will dart between the courting couple and spew out his own sperm cloud over the freshly deposited eggs. This is done literally in the blink of an eye to avoid being bitten by the mating pair, and therefore the number of eggs a sneaker can fertilize is usually limited to about 20 percent. Bluegill sneakers are an illustration of an evolved alternative reproductive strategy.

Humans are obviously not bluegill, but Mealey argued that males of our species may have also evolved an alternative reproductive strategy. She suggested that males who are clinically known as *psychopaths* (i.e., those suffering from what psychologists and psychiatrists call the *antisocial personality syndrome*) often pass their genes on to future generations by engaging in unusually manipulative and deceptive behavior. They often misrepresent their intentions to prospective mates, as well as intimidate and assault rival males and steal property with which to attract as many potential mates as possible. Mealey proposed that true psychopaths are genetically prone to engage in their lawless acts throughout their reproductive careers, but she also suggested that an even larger proportion of males (and even some females) merely learn similarly deceptive reproductive strategies. These individuals, she believed, will adopt more socially acceptable strategies by the time they become full adults. Mealey's theory is one of several recent attempts to apply modern evolutionary concepts to the study of criminal behavior.

The second tradition among biosocial criminologists focuses on specific biological processes, especially those having to do with the brain. The theories that have emerged out of this tradition are known as *neurologically specific theories*.

One of the very first neurologically specific theories to be proposed is called *arousal theory* or *suboptimal arousal theory*, and it usually focuses on the *reticular formation*, a diffuse area of the brain located primarily at the top of the brain stem. The reticular formation essentially monitors the environment and helps to regulate attention and the sleep–wake cycle. According to proponents of arousal theory, some people have reticular formations that are unusually insensitive to incoming stimuli. As a result, these individuals often feel bored unless they are in the midst of unusually intense and novel environmental stimuli. In childhood, they will frequently exhibit hyperactivity and inattention. By the time they reach adolescence, these suboptimally aroused individuals will gravitate toward all sorts of intense and novel activities, quite a few of which will be illegal. Theoretically, besides stealing and fighting, suboptimally aroused adolescents and adults should be attracted to mind-altering drugs and irresponsible sexual activities.

Another neurologically specific theory concentrates on the two hemispheres of the neocortex, which is the outermost layer of the brain and is largely responsible for language ability and other forms of "higher thought." Studies have shown that the two hemispheres of the neocortex tend to function differently. In general, the left hemisphere thinks in linguistic terms, which usually involves stringing ideas into logical sequences. The right hemisphere, in contrast, thinks more intuitively, often by organizing experiences and thoughts in three-dimensional space, and then it envisions solutions to obstacles (Ellis 2005). Furthermore, studies have indicated that the left hemisphere tends to be more "social" and "friendly" than the right hemisphere (reviewed in Ellis 2005).

The above evidence has led to what is known as *hemispheric functioning theory*. This theory asserts that persons who are most likely to repeatedly engage in crime have a less dominant left hemisphere than do people in general, a phenomenon called a *rightward shift in neocortical functioning*. Among the predictions of the hemispheric functioning theory is that offenders will do poorly in school, at least when it comes to subject areas with strong language components, although they may excel in other areas such as mathematics. Many studies have provided support for this prediction (Ellis 2005).

A novel prediction of hemispheric functioning theory is that criminality will be more prevalent among left- and mixed-handers than right-handers. This is because the right hemisphere tends to control the left side of the body, while the left hemisphere controls the right side. Evidence is fairly consistent with this prediction, although differences are not pronounced.

Ellis (2005) has suggested how the evolutionary and neurologically specific traditions in biosocial criminology can be combined into a "synthesized theory" – called the *evolutionary neuroandrogenic (ENA) theory*. Central to this theory is the idea that testosterone (the main so-called male hormone) has evolved ways of altering the brain so as to make males more competitive and victimizing toward others than are females. One consequence of this "hormonal wiring" of the brain is that males are more involved in most victimful crimes (as opposed to victimless crimes).

To explain why males have evolutionarily favored competitive/victimizing behavior, the theory contends that females generally prefer to mate with males who are reliable provisioners of resources rather than with males who are not. In order to become a reliable provisioner, a male must be overtly competitive, often to the point of injuring rivals and stealing or damaging property.

Regarding its neurologically specific features, ENA theory maintains that exposing the brain to testosterone, both prior to birth and following the onset of puberty, facilitates competitive/victimizing behavior. Among the brain regions most affected are the reticular formation and the neocortex. Regarding the first, exposing the brain to testosterone subdues the reticular formation's responsiveness to incoming stimuli, thereby causing the brain to require more intense environmental stimulation than a brain exposed to little testosterone. In the case of the neocortex, testosterone appears to shift functioning away from the left hemisphere toward the right. This tends to increase spatial reasoning and retard language development.

The end result, according to ENA theory, is individuals who are willing to compete for resources with which to attract sex partners, even if doing so victimizes others. Sometimes, sex partners themselves can be the objects of victimization, such as in the case of rapes and spousal assaults.

ENA theory still envisions learning as playing an important causal role in criminality, although the nature of that role differs somewhat from more traditional criminological theories. According to ENA theory, people's brains vary, and as a result they are inclined to learn some things more readily than other things even when it comes to various forms of criminality.

Many new and exciting ideas have been proposed by biosocial theorists in sociology, criminology, and other social sciences in the past couple of decades. Much of their work is being inspired by the advances still being made in understanding evolution, the brain, and other biological phenomena.

SEE ALSO: Biosociological Theories; Crime, Life Course Theory of; Evolution; Lombroso, Cesare; Neurosociology

REFERENCES AND SUGGESTED READINGS

Agnew, R. (2005) *Why Do Criminals Offend? A General Theory of Crime and Delinquency.* Roxbury, Los Angeles.

Ellis, L. (2005) Theoretically Explaining Biological Correlates of Criminality. *European Journal of Criminology* 2: 287–314.

Ellis, L. & Walsh, A. (1997) Gene-Based Evolutionary Theories in Criminology. *Criminology* 35: 229–76.

Lanier, M. M. & Henry, S. (2004) *Essential Criminology.* Westview Press, Boulder, CO.

Mealey, L. (1995) The Sociobiology of Sociopathy: An Integrated Evolutionary Model. *Behavioral and Brain Sciences* 18: 523–99.

Raine, A., Brennan, P., Farrington, D. P., & Mednick, S. A. (Eds.) (1997) *Biosocial Bases of Violence.* Plenum, New York.

Robinson, M. (2004) *Why Crime: An Integrated Systems Theory of Antisocial Behavior.* Prentice-Hall, Upper Saddle River, NJ.

Walsh, A. (2002) *Biosocial Criminology: Introduction and Integration.* Anderson, Cincinnati, OH.

Walsh, A. & Ellis, A. (Eds.) (2004) *Biosocial Criminology: Challenging Environmentalism's Supremacy.* Nova, New York.

crime, broken windows theory of

Doris Chu

Social psychologists use the term broken windows to signify the characteristics of neighborhood deterioration. They argue that if a broken window in a building or in a car is left untended, other signs of disorder will increase. Wilson and Kelling (1982) suggest that an unrepaired broken window is a signal that no one cares for the neighborhood. They argued further that if the window is left broken, it can lead to more serious crime problems.

Phillip Zimbardo (1969), a psychologist, tested the broken window theory with some experiments. He arranged that a car without a license plate be parked in a Bronx neighborhood and one comparable car be parked in Palo Alto, California. The car in the Bronx was destroyed within ten minutes, while the car in Palo Alto was left untouched for more than a week. After Zimbado smashed the car in Palo Alto, passersby started to vandalize the car. In both cases, once the car was damaged and looked abandoned, destruction, vandalism, and even theft soon followed.

Signs of neighborhood deterioration or disorder, such as broken windows, can lead to the breakdown of social controls. In stable neighborhoods, residents tend to watch out and care more for their property, children, and public safety. Residents in these neighborhoods are more attached to their neighborhood and more likely to consider their neighborhood as their home. Thus, any broken windows or other signs of disorder in these stable neighborhoods will soon be addressed and fixed. In these stable neighborhoods, more informal social controls are exercised by residents, the result being that crime is less likely to invade such areas. On the other hand, when a neighborhood can no longer regulate signs of public disorder, such as broken windows, more deterioration and even serious crime can result (Wilson and Kelling 1982).

Former New York City Mayor Rudy Giuliani implemented zero tolerance policing across New York City (NYC). Zero tolerance policing, primarily based on the philosophy of broken windows theory, is an approach of rigid enforcement of minor offenses and disorderly behavior such as jaywalking, panhandling, public drunkenness, and graffiti. Zero tolerance policing claims that if little things such as broken windows or graffiti are left untended, it can encourage more disorderly behavior or more crime. Thus, it is argued that the enforcement of laws governing minor offenses, especially public order offenses, can further prevent more serious crime from occurring and ultimately lead to a decline in crime rates. During the period of the implementation of zero tolerance policing in NYC, the violent crime rate was found to decline dramatically (Bratton 1997). However, whether the precipitous decline in violent crime in New York City in the 1990s can be attributed to the broken windows philosophy is still debated. Harcourt (2002) argues that the crackdown on quality of life offenses and disorderly behavior has little impact on the decline of crime rate. He further states that no one has ever shown a direct connection between neighborhood disorder and crime rate. Comparing crime rates in New York City with those of four other large American cities (Chicago, San Diego, Washington, DC, and Los Angeles), Brereton (1999) found that reductions in crime rates in the mid-1990s occurred in cities with very different policing approaches from those operating in New York. The corresponding decline in crime rates in other cities without New York's zero tolerance approach strongly suggests that other factors may be involved.

Kelling et al. (2001) used the precinct-level arrests for misdemeanors in NYC as the measure of broken windows enforcement. They found that the increased misdemeanor arrests in NYC reduced the violent crime rates. However, since one of the main features of the broken windows theory is the presence of existing disorders in a given neighborhood, a measure of misdemeanor arrests does not fully capture the construct of broken windows, as the reduction in violent crime may be attributed to the increased police surveillance and police presence. Research with more sophisticated measurement is needed to disentangle whether there is a direct or indirect relationship between broken windows and crime rates in a given neighborhood. For example, the crime rate of neighborhoods with the features of public disorders can be compared to neighborhoods with renewal projects to further examine whether fixing broken windows can reduce the crime rates. Factors that may mediate the relationship between broken windows and crime – such as neighborhood characteristics and unemployment rate – should also be taken into consideration.

SEE ALSO: Crime; Social Disorganization Theory; Zimbardo Prison Experiment

REFERENCES AND SUGGESTED READINGS

Bratton, J. (1997) Crime is Down in New York City: Blame the Police. In: Dennis, N. (Ed.), *Zero Tolerance: Policing a Free Society*. Institute of Economic Affairs, London, pp. 29–42.

Brereton, D. (1999) Zero Tolerance and the NYPD: Has It Worked There and Will It Work Here? Paper presented to the Australian Institute of Criminology Conference "Mapping the Boundaries of Australia's Criminal Justice System." Canberra, March 22–23.

Dean, J. (1997) Can Zero Tolerance and Problem Oriented Policing Be Part of the Same Philosophy? *Police Journal* (October): 345–7.

Harcourt, B. (2002) Policing Disorder: Can We Reduce Serious Crime by Punishing Petty Offenses? *Boston Review* (April/May).

Harris, B. (2001) A Key to Lancaster Renaissance: Fix the "Little Things"; New Quality of Life Task Force Targets Graffiti, Trash, Junked Cars. *Lancaster New Era* (June 19).

Kelling, G. L., Sousa, J., & William, H. (2001) Do Police Matter? An Analysis of the Impact of New York City's Police Reforms. Center for Civic Innovation at the Manhattan Institution, New York.

Sampson, R. & Raudenbush, S. (1999) Systematic Social Observation of Public Spaces: A New Look at Disorder in Urban Neighborhoods. *American Journal of Sociology* 105 (3): 603–51.

Sampson, R., Raudenbush, S., & Earls, F. (1997) Neighborhoods and Violent Crime: A Multilevel Study of Collective Efficacy. *Science, New Series* 277 (5328): 918–24.

Skogan, W. (1997) Fixing Broken Windows: Restoring Order and Reducing Crime in Our Communities. Review. *American Journal of Sociology* 103 (2): 510–12.

Wilson, J. Q. & Kelling, G. (1982) Broken Windows: The Police and Neighborhood Safety. *Atlantic Monthly* (March): 29–38.

Zimbardo, P. G. (1969) *The Cognitive Control of Motivation*. Scott, Foresman, Glenview, IL.

Zimbardo, P. G. & Ebbesen, E. B. (1969) *Influencing Attitudes and Changing Behavior*. Addison Wesley, Cambridge, MA.

crime, corporate

Gilbert Geis

Corporate crime involves organizational wrongdoing, such as anti-trust violations, false earnings statements, and misleading advertising.

The doctrine of corporate crime permits the justice system to deal with an organization as if it were a real person, despite the fact that, unlike humanity itself, a corporation can have an indefinite life span and possesses no corporeal substance that can be hauled before a court. In the early 2000s, corporate lawbreaking captured media headlines when scandals erupted that involved Enron, Adelphia, WorldCom, Arthur Andersen, and a number of other Fortune 500 businesses, though the invasion of Iraq soon thereafter relegated these cases to a secondary status in public consciousness.

Punishing corporate bodies was not allowed in early British and American law. One difficulty in punishing corporate bodies is that the web of decision-making within a large institution often makes it exceedingly difficult to pinpoint culpable individual miscreants. Gradually, however, the doctrine of corporate crime won jurisprudential favor, primarily as a means to control the damaging misdeeds of an ever-increasing number of very powerful businesses. In addition, corporations possess deep pockets that can be made to disgorge monies to compensate those they have injured.

The doctrine of corporate criminal liability rests on a distinction that can confound logic. Why should a corporation be vulnerable to criminal prosecution when other organizational entities are exempt from such actions? If the father of the Oliver family, for example, burglarizes a neighbor's house, no criminal charge of *State* v. *The Olivers* follows. When war criminals are indicted by the victors (it is invariably the victors who are able to punish the loser's war criminals) it is individuals who are named, not nations. In the end, it was pragmatism that prevailed, however: corporations need to be and can be reined in, at least somewhat, though it would seem unfair to prosecute families and futile to try to criminalize the entire population of a nation.

Until recently, the assumption was that fines against corporations, however large, could be passed along to customers by raising prices or, if that was not possible because of competition, could be written off as a routine part of the expense of doing business. But the government's 2002 prosecution of the Arthur Andersen accounting firm, a large limited liability partnership, demonstrated that when an organization depends on the trust of its customers, its revealed wrongdoing can force it out of business.

Corporate criminal liability finds support in philosophical observations that portray a corporate entity as something other than an accumulation of its component human parts. A group decision is said to represent an amalgam of inputs that often lead to actions that no individual in the group would have carried out alone. Others maintain that the doctrine anthropomorphizes corporations and that the law should have paused and created a separate set of rules for dealing with organizations rather than relying on preexisting statutes and judicial decisions that were tailored to handle criminal offenses by individuals.

Countries in Europe and Asia initially refused to follow the English and American path, insisting that criminal punishment could not be inflicted upon a corporation because it did not possess the requisite *mens rea*, the guilty mind essential to the assignment of responsibility for a criminal act. Increasingly, however, particularly in regard to environmental offenses, many of the world's countries are beginning to enact statutes that permit corporate bodies to be sanctioned criminally.

The major stamp of approval of the criminal culpability of corporations in the US was set forth in the 1908 ruling by the Supreme Court in *New York Central & Hudson Railroad Co.* v. *United States* regarding illegal rebates paid by the American Sugar Refining Company to preferred companies. The company primarily relied on the argument that its punishment fell upon innocent shareholders who were unable to defend themselves against the government's action. The Supreme Court, rejecting this argument, declared that if authorities could not punish the company there would be no effective way to deal with a harmful and illegal way of doing business.

For sociologists, the most provocative writing on the subject of corporate crime is found in an interchange between Donald Cressey and a pair of Australian scholars, John Braithwaite and Brent Fisse. Cressey maintained that it is impossible to formulate a social-psychological theory of corporate crime. Braithwaite and Fisse insisted that sound scientific theories can be based on an analysis of corporate behavior and that some theories of individual action can fruitfully be applied to corporate activities. Such work could be based, for example, on decisions by boards of directors and a review of the overarching corporate ethos.

SEE ALSO: Class and Crime; Crime, Social Learning Theory of; Crime, White-Collar; Law, Economy and; Organizational Deviance; Sutherland, Edwin H.

REFERENCES AND SUGGESTED READINGS

Blankenship. M. B. (Ed.) (1993) *Understanding Corporate Criminality*. Garland, New York.

Braithwaite, J. (1984) *Corporate Crime in the Pharmaceutical Industry*. Routledge & Kegan Paul, London.

Braithwaite, J. & Fisse, B. (1990) On the Plausibility of Corporate Crime Control. *Advances in Criminological Theory* 2: 15–37.

Clinard, M. B. & Yeager, P. C. (1980) *Corporate Crime*. Free Press, New York.

Coffee, J. C., Jr. (1981). "No soul to damn, no body to kick": An Unscandalized Inquiry into the Problem of Corporate Punishment. *Michigan Law Review* 79: 386–459.

Cressey, D. R. (1988) Poverty of Theory in Corporate Crime Research. *Advances in Criminological Theory* 1: 31–56.

DiMento, J. F., Geis, G., & Gelfand, J. M. (2001) Corporate Criminal Liability: A Bibliograhy. *Western State University Law Review* 2000: 255–75.

Geis, G. & Di Mento, J. F. C. (2002) Empirical Evidence and the Legal Doctrine of Corporate Criminal Liability. *American Journal of Criminal Law* 20: 342–75.

Glasbeek, H. (2002) *Wealth by Stealth: Corporate Crime, Corporate Law, and the Perversion of Democracy*. Between the Lines, Toronto.

Pearce, F. & Snider, L. (Eds.) (1995) *Corporate Crime: Contemporary Debates*. University of Toronto Press, Toronto.

Simpson, S. S. (2002) *Corporate Crime, Law, and Social Control*. Cambridge University Press, New York.

crime, hot spots

Lorraine Mazerolle

Hot spots of crime are defined as "small places in which the occurrence of crime is so frequent that it is highly predictable, at least over a one

year period" (Sherman 1995: 36). Hot spots are places like street corners, malls, apartment blocks, subway stations, and public parks that generate a large number of complaints to police. Research shows that about 3 percent of all places generate over half of all citizen complaints about crime and disorder to the police.

Researchers from a number of disciplines (including geography, architecture, environmental planning, sociology, social psychology, political science, and criminology) have studied hot spots of crime. The "crime and place" perspective that informs today's hot spots of crime research has a long history dating back to late nineteenth-century researchers in France (e.g., Andre-Michel Guerry and Adolphe Quetelet) and early twentieth-century researchers in Chicago (e.g., Clifford Shaw and Henry McKay). Recent hot spots of crime research straddles a number of theoretical perspectives, such as ecology of crime, environmental criminology, routine activities theory, crime pattern theory, defensible space, crime prevention through environmental design, and situational crime prevention. All of these perspectives contribute to our understanding of why crime clusters into hot spots and argue that crime is not random, but rather the result of environmental factors. These environmental (and situational) factors create opportunities for crime in some places and prevent crime from occurring in other places.

Sherman (1995) proposes six primary dimensions that help to define and distinguish one hot spot of crime from another:

1 *Onset*: This dimension deals with the factors that make a place become "bad." Such factors might include some form of distinctive character (e.g., a bar or parking lot), a change in the routine activities of a neighborhood, or mere chance.

2 *Recurrence*: This dimension deals with the point at which a place is labeled a hot spot. As an example, when a place experiences 3 robberies during a 1-year period, that place has a 58 percent chance of recurrence. Recurrence encourages us to ask if that is the threshold of activity that would define a place as a hot spot.

3 *Frequency*: This dimension deals with the number of times per year crime occurs in a given space.

4 *Intermittency*: This dimension deals with two issues. The first is the amount of time *between* criminal events. The second is what explains intermittency. Such factors as (a) criminal habits of the occupants, (b) economic difficulties of place owners, and (c) changes in traffic flow that impacts the flow of targets and offenders have been considered.

5 *Career length and desistence*: The fifth dimension is concerned with the desistence of crime problems in a particular space. Places desist from having crime problems for five reasons: death (e.g., a hot spot bar is torn down); vigilante behavior (e.g., omnipresence patrol by police, patrol by citizens); incapacitation (e.g., civil remedies, boarding up buildings); blocking opportunities (e.g., re-routing a bus); building insulators (e.g., community cohesion, problem solving).

6 *Crime types*: This dimension describes the fact that places tend to have crime specialization because the place characteristics limit the types of crimes possible (e.g., drug dealing).

Most research into hot spots of crime requires the use of sophisticated spatial analysis using geographic information systems to understand the distribution of crime and pinpoint the locations of crime hot spots. Many techniques have been used to empirically and conceptually describe the clustering of crime into hot spots and new, innovative techniques often developed in the physical sciences are used to understand the non-random distributions of crime.

A recent line of inquiry in the crime and place tradition has been the application of trajectory research, traditionally used to describe individual offending patterns over the lifecourse (Weisburd et al. 2004). The use of trajectory analysis enables researchers to view crime trends at places over long periods of time and use group-based statistical techniques to uncover distinctive developmental trends and identify long-term patterns of offending in crime hot spots.

The concentration of crime in hot spots suggests significant crime prevention potential for law enforcement strategies such as directed patrols and problem-oriented policing (Braga 2001). These types of police strategies focus crime prevention resources at micro-places with large numbers of crime events. Recent research agrees with this "hot spots policing" approach, but finds that police need to distinguish between short-lived concentrations of crime in hot spots versus those hot spots that have long histories (Weisburd et al. 2004). Indeed, Weisburd and his colleagues suggest that if hot spots of crime shift rapidly from place to place it makes little sense to focus crime control resources at such locations. By contrast, the police would be most effective by identifying and targeting resources at those hot spots with long histories of crime.

SEE ALSO: Crime; Drugs, Drug Abuse, and Drug Policy; Experimental Design; Methods, Visual; Police; Public Order Crime; Routine Activity Theory

REFERENCES AND SUGGESTED READINGS

Braga, A. A. (2001) The Effects of Hot Spots Policing on Crime. *Annals of the American Academy of Political and Social Science* 578: 104–25.

Eck, J. & Weisburd, D. (1995) Crime Places in Crime Theory. In: Eck, J. & Weisburd, D. (Eds.), *Crime and Place: Crime Prevention Studies*, Vol. 4. Criminal Justice Press and Police Executive Research Forum, pp. 1–33.

Sherman, L. (1995) Hotspots of Crime and Criminal Careers of Places. In: Eck, J. & Weisburd, D. (Eds.), *Crime and Place: Crime Prevention Studies*, Vol 4. Criminal Justice Press and Police Executive Research Forum, pp. 35–52.

Taylor, R. (1998) Crime and Small-Scale Places: What We Know, What We Can Prevent and What Else We Need to Know. *Crime and Place: Plenary Papers of the 1997 Conference on Criminal Justice Research and Evaluation*. National Institute of Justice, Washington, DC.

Weisburd, D., Bushway, S., Lum, C., & Yang, S. (2004) Trajectories of Crime at Places: A Longitudinal Study of Street Segments in the City of Seattle. *Criminology* 42(2): 283–322.

crime, life course theory of

Alex R. Piquero and Zenta Gomez-Smith

The life course perspective emphasizes the importance of time, social context, and process in both theory and analysis by taking into account historical events and changes as well as individual lives. The two central concepts in the life course perspective are trajectories and transitions. Trajectories are the long-term patterns and sequences in an individual's life. These are pathways such as marriage, parenthood, careers, and criminal or non-criminal behaviors. Transitions, on the other hand, occur within trajectories and are single events that are often age-graded, such as changes in societal roles or status. They can include graduation, divorce, retiring, an arrest, and so on. These specific life events can be so abrupt and influential that they transform life trajectories. Therefore, there is a sequence of life trajectories, transitions, and adaptations during the life course.

This interlocked nature of trajectories and transitions leads to the broadly accepted viewpoint of the life course perspective that an individual's childhood is connected to adulthood experiences. The life course focus on the full life span, from birth to death, thus posits that transitions occurring early in life or childhood can have consequences and shape events later in life. In addition, the life course perspective examines the social meaning of age throughout the life span, how social patterns are transmitted from generation to generation, and the effects of social historical events such as wars and tragedies, structural locations, and personal life histories. In short, the essence of the life course perspective is its concern with the duration, timing, and ordering of transition events and their effects on long-term development and trajectories. Nowhere has this perspective been so central to thinking than criminological theory in general, and explanations for the longitudinal patterning of criminal activity in particular.

THE LIFE COURSE AND CRIMINOLOGICAL THEORY

Over the past dozen years, criminological theory has paid close attention to the longitudinal patterning of criminal activity. Much of this focus can be attributed to the important criminal career studies carried out in the early 1970s, 1980s, and 1990s in the United States, Canada, Puerto Rico, England, Sweden, Finland, Denmark, China, and Australia/New Zealand, as well as the review of the criminal career literature published by the National Academy of Sciences (Blumstein et al. 1986). This literature, aided by important theoretical models developed to better understand criminal activity over the life course, has grown tremendously since the late 1980s (Piquero et al. 2003).

Four main components underlie the study of criminal careers, and also underlie several life course-influenced criminological theories: participation, frequency, seriousness, and career length. *Participation* separates those who have a criminal career from those who do not; *frequency* indicates the rate of criminal activity among active offenders; *seriousness* describes the severity of the offenses committed by an individual; and *career length* describes the length of time between an individual's last and first crimes.

A number of criminological theories have made exclusive use of this line of research and directly speak to the longitudinal patterning of crime over the life course. From this an entire subfield of criminological theory, developmental criminology, has emerged. In particular, developmental criminology focuses on two areas: (1) the study of the development and dynamics of offending with age; and (2) the identification of causal factors that predate or co-occur with the behavioral development and have an effect on its course.

As an exemplar, we focus on three of these theoretical models: Moffitt's (1993) developmental taxonomy, Loeber and Hay's (1994) multiple pathways model, and Sampson and Laub's (1993) age-graded informal social control theory.

Moffitt's theory begins with the classic aggregate age–crime curve, which exhibits a peak in late adolescence followed by a precipitous decline throughout early and middle adulthood, reaching virtually zero in later adulthood. Moffitt claims that the aggregate age–crime curve hides two distinct groups of offenders, one characterized by highly active, short-term participation during the adolescent years, and another characterized by a very small subset of individuals who engage in criminal activity at fairly frequent rates throughout most of the life course. The former group of offenders, "adolescence-limiteds," begin offending during the adolescent time period largely as a result of the peer social context that emerges in adolescence and the maturity gap, or the recognition that adolescents look and feel like adults but are not allowed access to adult-like activities. As a result of this maturity gap, similarly situated adolescents seek the aid and comfort of one another and engage in acts that seek to relieve them of their situation, such as vandalism, alcohol and drug use, sexual activity, and minor theft. With adulthood they tend to leave their dabbling in antisocial activity and function as normal adults with careers, relationships, and so forth. Only among a small number of adolescence-limiteds does criminal activity continue into adulthood. The causal forces underlying their persistence include snares that encapsulate individuals, such as a criminal record, teenage childbearing, and so on.

The second group of offenders, "life course persistents," begin their involvement in antisocial and criminal activity early in the life course, offending at fairly stable yet high rates throughout adolescence, and continue into adulthood. Unlike the situated maturity gap and peer social context which adolescence-limiteds find themselves subjected to, life course-persistent offending is a function of neuropsychological/cognitive problems that are formed early in the life course. Such problems typically go undetected and uncorrected, in part because children suffering from these problems oftentimes are reared in disadvantaged familial and socioeconomic contexts. Also, unlike their adolescence-limited counterparts, life course-persistent offenders engage in all sorts of antisocial and criminal activity including theft, drug use, and violence. The prospects for desistence from crime in adulthood are bleak for life course-persistent offenders because the neuropsychological deficits influence all facets of their lives, including employment, relationships, and overall decision-making patterns. Thus, while desistence for adolescence-limiteds is the norm, persistence is the norm for life course-persistent offenders (though see Sampson & Laub 2003).

Loeber and his colleagues formulated a three-pathway model to delineate developmental sequences in three domains: overt behavior problems, covert behavior problems, and problems with authority figures. The overt pathway starts with minor aggression (bullying), followed by physical fighting, and then by violence (rape, strongarm). The covert pathway consists of a sequence of minor covert behaviors (shoplifting, lying), followed by property damage (vandalism), and moderate to serious forms of delinquency (fraud, burglary). The authority conflict pathway (prior to age 12) consists of a sequence of stubborn behavior, defiance, and authority avoidance (running away, truancy). According to this three-pathway model, individuals begin at a lower order (less serious behavior) and then proceed through the hypothesized sequences. It is also possible that individuals' development can take place on more than one pathway, with some youths progressing on all three pathways. The most frequent offenders are overrepresented among individuals in multiple pathways, especially those displaying both overt and covert behavior problems.

Unlike the typological models presented by Moffitt and Loeber, Sampson and Laub (1993) propose a single-pathway model (there is only one group of offenders) that takes both childhood and adulthood factors into account in understanding the longitudinal patterning of criminal activity. Specifically, these scholars develop an age-graded theory of informal social control that has three distinct components: (1) the structural context mediated by informal family and school social controls explains delinquency in childhood and adolescence; (2) there is continuity in antisocial behavior from childhood through adulthood in a variety of life domains; and (3) informal social bonds in adulthood to employment and family explain changes in criminality over the life course despite early childhood factors. Thus, for

Sampson and Laub, there is both continuity and change.

WHAT DO WE KNOW?

Research on life course criminology has generated a number of important "facts," many of which have been controversial (Farrington 2003). Some of these facts, directly emerging from the studies outlined above, include: (1) the prevalence of offending peaks between ages 15 and 19; (2) the peak age of onset of offending is between 8 and 14, while the peak age of desistence from offending is between 20 and 29; (3) an early age of onset predicts a relatively long criminal career duration and the commission of relatively many offenses; (4) there is marked continuity in offending and antisocial behavior from childhood to the teenage years and to adulthood; (5) a small fraction of the population ("chronic offenders") commits a large fraction of all crimes; chronic offenders tend to have an early onset, a high individual offending frequency, and a long criminal career; (6) offending is versatile rather than specialized; violent offenders in particular appear to be indistinguishable from frequent offenders; (7) the types of acts defined as offenses are elements of a larger syndrome of antisocial behavior that include heavy drinking, reckless driving, and so forth; (8) most offenses up to the late teenage years are committed with others, whereas most offenses from age 20 onwards are committed alone; (9) the reasons given for offending up to the late teenage years are quite variable, including utilitarian ones, for excitement/enjoyment, out of boredom, and/or emotional ones; from age 20 onwards, utilitarian motives become increasingly dominant; and (10) different types of offenses tend to be first committed at distinctively different ages. This sort of progression is such that shoplifting tends to be committed before burglary, burglary before robbery, and so forth. In general, diversification increases up to age 20, but after age 20, diversification decreases and specialization increases.

WHAT DON'T WE KNOW?

Still, there exist some contentious life course criminology issues that have been ill studied and/or have generated discrepant results. Seven issues in particular are identified here. (1) While it is clear that the prevalence of offending peaks in the late teenage years, it is less clear how the individual offending frequency varies with age. (2) It is not clear whether the seriousness of offending escalates up to a certain age and then de-escalates, or whether it does not change with age. (3) It is clear that early onset of offending predicts a long career and many offenses, but it is far less clear whether early onset predicts a high individual offending frequency or a high average seriousness of offending. Nor is it clear whether early-onset offenders differ in degree or in kind from later-onset offenders, whether onset age relates to offense seriousness over time, or how much there are distinctly different behavioral trajectories. (4) Although chronic offenders commit more offenses than others, it is not clear whether their offenses are more serious on average or whether chronic offenders differ in degree or in kind from non-chronic offenders. (5) While it is clear that certain offenses occur on average before other types and that onset sequences can be identified, it is not clear whether these onset sequences are merely age-appropriate behavioral manifestations of some underlying theoretical construct or if the onset of one type of behavior facilitates or acts as a stepping stone toward the onset of another. (6) Although there appears to be some research indicating that offenders are more versatile than specialized, these findings have been produced largely by research using official records through age 18. Very little information has been provided about how specialization/versatility varies with age into adulthood, and even less attention has been paid to the extent to which specialization/versatility varies in official and/or self-report records. (7) While there has been much attention paid to the topic of desistence, little attention has been paid to developing estimates of career length or duration as well as residual career length. Such information bears directly on policy issues regarding sentence lengths. Smaller residual careers would be indicative of shorter and not longer sentences.

SEE ALSO: Crime; Deviance, Crime and; Juvenile Delinquency; Life Course Perspective; Race and Crime; Social Psychology; Theory

REFERENCES AND SUGGESTED READINGS

Blumstein, A., Cohen, J., Roth, J. A., & Visher, C. A. (Eds.) (1986) *Criminal Careers and "Career Criminals."* 2 vols. National Academy Press, Washington, DC.

Elder, G. H., Jr. (1985) Perspectives on the Life Course. In: Elder, G. H., Jr. (Ed.), *Life Course Dynamics: Trajectories and Transitions, 1968–1980.* Cornell University Press, Ithaca, NY.

Farrington, D. P. (2003) Developmental and Life Course Criminology: Key Theoretical and Empirical Issues. The 2002 Sutherland Award Address. *Criminology* 41: 221–56.

Laub, J. H. & Sampson, R. J. (2003) *Shared Beginnings, Divergent Lives: Delinquent Boys to Age 70.* Harvard University Press, Cambridge, MA.

Le Blanc, M. & Loeber, R. (1998) Developmental Criminology Updated. In: Tonry, M. (Ed.), *Crime and Justice: A Review of Research,* Vol. 23. University of Chicago Press, Chicago.

Loeber, R. & Hay, D. F. (1994) Developmental Approaches to Aggression and Conduct Problems. In: Rutter, M. & Hay, D. F. (Eds.), *Development Through Life: A Handbook for Clinicians.* Oxford, Blackwell, pp. 488–516.

Loeber, R. & Le Blanc, M. (1990) Toward a Developmental Criminology. In: Tonry, M. & Morris, N. (Eds.), *Crime and Justice: A Review of Research,* Vol. 12. University of Chicago Press, Chicago.

Moffitt, T. E. (1993) "Life Course-Persistent" and "Adolescence-Limited" Antisocial Behavior: A Developmental Taxonomy. *Psychological Review* 100: 674–701.

Piquero, A. R., Farrington, D. P., & Blumstein, A. (2003) The Criminal Career Paradigm. In: Tonry, M. (Ed.), *Crime and Justice: A Review of Research,* Vol. 30. University of Chicago Press, Chicago.

Sampson, R. J. & Laub, J. H. (1993) *Crime in the Making: Pathways and Turning Points through Life.* Harvard University Press, Cambridge, MA.

Sampson, R. J. & Laub, J. H. (2003) Life Course Desisters? Trajectories of Crime Among Delinquent Boys Followed to Age 70. *Criminology* 41: 555–92.

crime, organized

Sean Patrick Griffin

Though the study of organized crime is primarily a sociological pursuit, the phenomenon is a subject of study in numerous other disciplines, including anthropology, economics, history, and political science. Despite, if not because of, this broad and varied inquiry into the topic, there is little consensus on what constitutes "organized crime."

Perhaps the broadest interpretation of organized crime is offered by sociologist Joseph Albini (1971). His analysis identified four types of organized crime: political social (e.g., Ku Klux Klan), mercenary (predatory/theft-oriented), ingroup (gangs), and syndicated (offers goods and services, and infiltrates legitimate businesses). Many scholars, for reasons that have inspired considerable debate within this research area, have opted to narrowly focus on syndicated organized crime as described by Albini (1971).

Albini argued for identifying the common characteristics among syndicated groups. This approach has been replicated numerous times. Four characteristics are most frequently cited in the academic literature when defining syndicated organized crime: a continuing enterprise, using rational means, profiting through illegal activities utilizing the corruption of officials. Several other authors have argued that groups must also use (or threaten) violence, and be involved in multiple criminal enterprises, to merit inclusion in the organized crime discussion.

While these "defining characteristics" are commonly cited among scholars, this should not be interpreted as settling the issue. For instance, there is no consensus regarding what constitutes "continuity." Is it continuity of a group, of a conspiracy, or of a crime pattern? What duration of time constitutes continuity, regardless of which factor is chosen? Similarly, there are questions regarding "multiple enterprises." How many are required and how would this be operationally defined? For example, an organization may be grounded on narcotics trafficking while by necessity evading taxes and laundering money. Furthermore, it can be argued that violence and corruption are merely "management tools" and that criminal enterprises may indeed thrive without the necessity of these tools (e.g., if law enforcement is ignorant of the problem).

There are other ongoing debates in the study of organized crime, and three stand out. Researchers continue to discuss such issues as the distinctions between organized crime and "white-collar" crime, and between organized crime and gangs. The other dispute concerns the degree of organization or sophistication exhibited by syndicates.

White-collar crime is most commonly defined as "crimes committed by persons of high social status and respectability in the course of his occupation" (Sutherland 1983 [1949]: 7). However, if one focuses on the activities as opposed to the individuals involved in the activities, numerous white-collar conspiracies quite easily fit the criteria listed above (i.e., continuity, corruption, multiple enterprises). For instance, several studies have demonstrated that securities frauds are often enduring and complex, requiring the use of financial "fronts," money laundering, and the artful skills of accountants, financiers, and lawyers, the corruption of public and regulatory officials, and/or violence and so on. These studies have thus demonstrated that without an emphasis on the economic and social standing of the offender, these offenses would be considered organized crimes.

Today, numerous gangs engage exclusively in narcotics trafficking. Some scholars thus argue such organizations do not meet widely held characteristics of organized crime (i.e., these groups do not engage in multiple enterprises). There is no consensus in the academic literature on this matter, however. Some gang researchers delineate between gangs and "drug gangs," with the latter obviously focusing on the drug trade and monopolizing sales market territories instead of residential territories, among other differences. Other researchers argue some gangs have become so sophisticated they are in fact organized crime groups. One example is Chicago's Gangsters Disciples (Decker et al. 1998).

The most fundamental and contentious issue concerns the extent to which organized crime is, in fact, organized. Early studies stressed bureaucracy, adherence to protocols and rules, and what was essentially a business model for illicit endeavors. Later studies emphasized more informal relationships that were often fleeting and predicated on patron–client networks. The distinction can be viewed through the prism of two different models of research, each identified by a variety of terms. The more bureaucratic

interpretation of organized crime was characterized as the governmental/law enforcement/traditional view, whereas the other perspective was considered the informal structural functional system/developmental association model. Earlier studies emphasizing bureaucracy eventually gave way to the latter subset of models that now dominate the literature. Though membership in an organized crime group provides access to networking channels and increases the predictability of illegal venture, economic conditions tend against rigid structure in the "underworld." As economist R. T. Naylor (1997) argues, there are three risks associated with the illegality of organized crime: underworld contracts are not legally enforceable; the entrepreneur might be arrested; and criminal assets might be seized. Thus, the key contradiction of organized crime is that there is a need to provide substantial information to prospective customers but this process places the conspiracy in jeopardy because of fears of detection (by authorities and competitors).

SEE ALSO: Crime, Corporate; Crime, White-Collar; Drugs and the Law; Gangs, Delinquent

REFERENCES AND SUGGESTED READINGS

Albanese, J. S. (2004) *Organized Crime in Our Times*, 4th edn. Anderson Publishing, Cincinnati.

Albini, J. L. (1971) *The American Mafia: Genesis of a Legend*. Appleton-Century-Crofts, New York.

Calavita, K. & Pontell, H. N. (1993) Savings and Loan Fraud as Organized Crime. *Criminology* 31: 519–48.

Decker, S. H., Bynum, T., & Weisel, D. (1998) A Tale of Two Cities: Gangs as Organized Crime Groups. *Justice Quarterly* 15: 395–425.

Griffin, S. P. (2002) Actors or Activities? On the Social Construction of "White-Collar" Crime in the United States. *Crime, Law, and Social Change* 37: 245–76.

Hagan, F. (1983) The Organized Crime Continuum: A Further Specification of a New Conceptual Model. *Criminal Justice Review* 8: 52–7.

Naylor, R. T. (1997) Mafias, Myths and Markets: On the Theory and Practice of Enterprise Crime. *Transnational Organized Crime* 3: 1–45.

Sutherland, E. (1983 [1949]) *White-Collar Crime: The Uncut Version*. Yale University Press, New Haven.

crime, political

Kenneth D. Tunnell

Political crime is an illegal offense against the state with the intention of affecting its political or economic policies, or an illegal domestic or international offense by the state and its agents. Political crime is conceptualized as individual, occupational, and organizational. Individual political crimes benefit individuals. Occupational crimes, occurring within the context of agents' legitimate occupations, also benefit individuals. Organizational political crimes benefit the organization as a whole rather than specific individuals.

Offenses against the state are treated as oppositional crimes committed by single individuals or organized groups. A lone individual hacking into government computers or selling classified government documents is an example of the former; groups of domestic and international terrorists planting bombs are an example of the latter.

Offenses by the state and its agents include organizational crimes such as unlawful surveillance of its citizens or, on the international front, destabilizing democratically elected governments or assassinating foreign leaders. These operations are systemic and benefit the state and its preferred economic and political order. On the other hand, political crimes by the state can also be individually based when, for example, state agents, operating within the legitimate authority and power of their political occupations, engage in crime for their own personal gain or to prevent loss. Political corruption within the office of elected officials, extortion among police officers, and cover-ups within the executive branch constitute individual political crime when each is intended to benefit the office holder rather than the state (Turk 1982).

As egregious as political crime typically is, it has received only scant coverage in most criminology and criminal justice textbooks. As a result, this important crime type is often omitted from survey classes, and students in the sociology of crime often have little exposure to the vagaries of political crime and its consequences. Nonetheless, there are a few publications in the area of political crime that comprise the bulk of the body of knowledge.

Early writings on political crime most often were case studies. Some focused on individuals or groups committing oppositional crimes against the state (e.g., revolutionary actions intended to disrupt normal activities and effect change). Others focused on the state and its agents committing crimes against its citizens and peoples of other countries (e.g., the unlawful opening of mail, spying on citizens' groups, circumventing democratic elections and their outcomes) (Churchill & Vander Wall 1988; Davis 1992; Ermann & Lundman 2001).

Some early (and recent) writings encouraged a broader definition of crime by suggesting that all crime is politically constructed in the arenas of politics and public opinion. Rather than accepting the state's politicized definitions of crime (which conveniently exclude the state and its behaviors), they suggest using social harm as a definition of crime. After all, evidence suggests that across human history, the actions with the most egregious results – physically, economically, environmentally, and in terms of human rights violations – have been carried out by the state and its agents, who generally are free from the application of the rule of law. Thus, the state's unethical but currently legal behaviors, under a broader political definition, would be subject to the criminal label (Bohm 1993). More recently, the literature has encouraged using human rights violations as a starting point for defining crime and particularly for political crimes of the state, especially within a global context and a world economy (Barak 1993).

The state and its violations have received greater attention in recent years and to such an extent that the term state crime has emerged. This term better articulates state actions and better delineates it from other types of political crime (Ross 2000). Within this growing body of literature, the term state-corporate crime has emerged. A concept that focuses especially on the political activities of the state in conjunction with industry or specific corporations, it has proven especially useful for teasing out details of harmful actions often concealed within public and private sector bureaucracies (Friedrichs 1996). Case studies, such as that of the explosion of the US space shuttle *Challenger* in 1986 and the loss of its 7 crew members, reveal the politicized and organizational antecedents for such disasters (Vaughn 1996).

There is no widely accepted theoretical explanation for political crime, nor method for studying it. Rather, a wide variety of classical and contemporary sociological theories (both social and social psychological) have been applied to it. Research methods used to study political crime mainly have been those central to case studies (viz., interviews and document research). Researching political crime undoubtedly has been and remains difficult; the various agents involved in any given political crime are secretive and documents typically are unavailable to researchers. Given these impediments, most research relies on secondary rather than primary data. Theoretical specificity and research strategies that are more imaginative are perhaps those areas within the study of political crime that most need improvement and that scholars more than likely will address in coming years.

SEE ALSO: Collective Action; Crime; Crime, White Collar; Organizations; Political Leadership; Political Sociology; Politics; Praxis; Social Change; Social Movements; State

REFERENCES AND SUGGESTED READINGS

Barak, G. (1993) Crime, Criminology and Human Rights: Toward an Understanding of State Criminality. In: Tunnell, K. D. (Ed.), *Political Crime in Contemporary America*. Garland, New York, pp. 207–30.
Bohm, R. M. (1993) Social Relationships That Arguably Should Be Criminal Although They Are Not: On the Political Economy of Crime. In: Tunnell, K. D. (Ed.), *Political Crime in Contemporary America*. Garland, New York, pp. 3–29.
Churchill, W. & Vander Wall, J. (1990) *The COINTELPRO Papers*. South End Press, Boston.
Davis, J. K. (1992) *Spying on America*. Praeger, New York.
Ermann, M. D. & Lundman, R. J. (2001) *Corporate and Governmental Deviance*. Oxford University Press, New York.
Friedrichs, D. (1996) *Trusted Criminals*. Wadsworth, New York.
Ross, J. I. (2000) *Varieties of State Crime and Its Control*. Criminal Justice Press, Monsey, NY.
Ross, J. I. (2003) *The Dynamics of Political Crime*. Sage, Thousand Oaks, CA.
Tunnell, K. D. (Ed.) (1993) *Political Crime in Contemporary America*. Garland, New York.
Turk, A. (1982) *Political Criminality*. Sage, Newbury Park, CA.
Vaughn, D. (1996) *The Challenger Launch Decision*. University of Chicago Press, Chicago.

crime, psychological theories of

J. C. Oleson

Psychological theories of crime suggest that some offenses may be caused by mental factors or conflicts. Like biological theories, psychological theories of crime deal with causes at the individual level, but instead of associating crime with observable phenomena like brain abnormalities, psychological theories associate crime with abstractions like mental illness, intelligence, or personality.

For centuries, psychology has been essential to understanding criminal responsibility. Under criminal law, defendants who do not possess the requisite criminal intent (*mens rea*) are not guilty of a crime, even if they committed the criminal act (*actus reus*). This is why, for example, some offenders are found not guilty by reason of insanity. Mental states also regularly help distinguish varying levels of criminal responsibility, such as deciding between murder and manslaughter, or between first- and second-degree murder. Yet while legal evaluations of mental states extend back to ancient law, the search for the psychological origins of crime is only 150 or 200 years old.

Nineteenth-century researchers, like Philippe Pinel and Benjamin Rush, claimed that criminal behavior was closely linked to forms of insanity. Henry Maudsley went even further, claiming that crime and madness were equivalents: criminals would go mad if they did not offend, and they do not go mad because they are criminals. More contemporary efforts havefocused upon several psychological explanations for crime: psychodynamic conflicts, cognitive deficits, traits or personality, and various forms of mental illness.

The psychodynamic psychology developed by Sigmund Freud has been used to explain criminal behavior. In *Wayward Youth* (1935), August Aichorn applied psychoanalytic theory to the causes of crime and delinquency. He claimed that crime is caused by "latent delinquency" that is partly biological, and partly shaped by one's early relationships. If the process of socialization goes astray, individuals become "dissocial." They seek immediate gratification, consider their needs more important than dealing with others, and guiltlessly pursue their urges without weighing right and wrong.

Other psychoanalysts interested in psychodynamic conflict have explained crime by focusing on components of the personality. Freud believed that the personality consists of three parts: the id, the ego, and the superego. The id represents the primitive unconscious drives for food, sex, and other biological necessities. Following the "pleasure principle," the irrational id seeks instant gratification and has no regard for other people. The ego, guided by the "reality principle," seeks to satisfy the demands of the id while simultaneously adapting to social conventions and norms. The superego, consisting of the conscience and the ego ideal, incorporates the moral values that have been socialized in the individual. When one fails to live up to moral standards, the conscience induces feelings of guilt; when one satisfies these standards, the ego ideal creates feelings of pride. Psychoanalysts believe that criminals are id-dominated individuals, with underdeveloped egos and superegos, who cannot regulate their pleasure-seeking drives. Criminals have failed to progress from the pleasure principle to the reality principle.

Researchers focusing on cognitive deficits have linked crime to moral reasoning, intelligence, and information processing. Lawrence Kohlberg suggests that crime may be related to the way people organize their thinking about moral decisions. He posits six stages of moral judgment, moving from concrete thinking in the lower stages to abstract reasoning in higher stages. Pre-moral reasoning (stages one and two) defines right as obedience to authority and the avoidance of punishment, and as looking after one's own needs and leaving others to

themselves. Conventional reasoning (stages three and four) defines right as having good motives and earning social approval, and as maintaining social order for its own sake. Postconventional reasoning (stages five and six) defines right as recognition of a social contract conferring individual rights, and as an understanding of universal ethical principles such as justice, equality, and the value of human life. Kohlberg (1969) suggests that criminals are more likely to engage in concrete, pre-moral reasoning and that non-criminals are more likely to engage in conventional or post-conventional reasoning.

Some researchers who focus on cognitive deficits claim that crime is linked to low intelligence. In *The English Convict* (1913), Charles Goring concluded that it was not physical differences that distinguished British prisoners from non-prisoners but their defective intelligence. Others have supported Goring's claim. Psychologists Henry Herbert Goddard and Lewis Terman both argued that feeblemindedness and crime were inextricably linked. While early criminologists like Edwin Sutherland and Carl Murchison questioned the IQ-crime relationship, many criminologists currently accept low IQ as a robust correlate of delinquency and crime. In their review of the literature, Travis Hirschi and Michael Hindelang (1977) concluded that while the average IQ score is 100, offenders have average IQ scores of about 92, or half a standard deviation below the population average. In *Crime and Human Nature* (1985), James Q. Wilson and Richard Herrnstein confirmed the low IQ-crime relationship, but suggested a deficit of ten – not eight – points.

Other researchers interested in cognitive deficits claim that impaired information processing causes crime. While rational choice theorists believe that criminals conduct cost-benefit analyses and offend because it is in their interest to do so, psychologists have demonstrated that individuals often fail to analyze information in an accurate or efficient manner. For example, Wilson and Herrnstein noted that because of time discounting, the immediate rewards associated with crime may seem especially attractive, even given the risk of punishment, simply because of the immediacy of the payoff. Some individuals are able to delay gratification and to work for distant goals while others seem incapable of this, and are therefore more likely to commit crimes. In volume one of *The Criminal Personality* (1976), Yochelson and Samenow identified dozens of thinking patterns that underlie criminal behavior, including irresponsible decision-making, lack of empathy, concrete thinking, and seeing themselves as victims. Other criminologists have emphasized the role of mental "scripts" in making interpersonal judgments. Criminals may use fewer informational cues than most people, thereby misperceiving the intentions of others as hostile or malicious, and thus resort to familiar scripts of violent or criminal behavior.

Some criminologists have linked crime to personality traits. Sheldon and Eleanor Glueck (1950) identified a number of traits associated with antisocial behavior in young people, including ambivalence, defiance, destructiveness, distrust of authority, extraversion, impulsiveness, inadequate social skills, mental instability, narcissism, sadism, self-assertiveness, and suspicion. Traits of aggressiveness, hostility, and impulsivity have been particularly implicated in studies of personality and crime. In their general theory of crime, Michael Gottfredson and Travis Hirschi (1990) suggest that impulsivity is essential to understanding crime. In their view, people with low self-control are impulsive risk-takers, are non-verbal, are physical rather than mental, lack empathy and shame, and are oriented to the here and now. They do not work toward distant goals, and lack discipline and persistence. Their careers and relationships are unstable, and they are more likely to engage in behaviors like smoking, drinking, speeding, and promiscuous sex. Those with low self-control are also far more likely to commit crimes.

Hans Eysenck (1977) suggested that personality could be measured on three dimensions: psychoticism (P) (where high scores signify tough-mindedness and disregard for others), extraversion (E) (where high scores indicate impulsivity and sensation seeking), and neuroticism (N) (where high scores signify anxiety and emotional volatility). Eysenck believed that high E and N scores impede social conditioning. People with high E and N scores are less likely to be effectively socialized, and are therefore more likely to become criminals.

Individuals who score high on all three dimensions are especially at risk, particularly for crimes involving the victimization of others.

In many ways, Eysenck's measure of tough-minded psychoticism resembles another frequently invoked explanation for crime: antisocial personality disorder. Antisocial personality disorder is also interchangeably called psychopathy or sociopathy. Whatever term is used, the individuals with this condition lack feelings of guilt, remorse, or anxiety, and persistently violate the rights of others. They are often intelligent and superficially charming individuals, wearing "masks of sanity" (Cleckley 1976), concealing fundamentally damaged personalities that prevent them from forming meaningful relationships and that repeatedly lead them into risky behavior, crime, substance abuse, and violence. Analyzing the 16 characteristics proposed by Hervey Cleckley, Robert Hare (1980) identified five factors that describe psychopaths: inability to develop empathic relationships, unstable lifestyle, inability to accept responsibility for their antisocial behavior, absence of other intellectual or psychiatric problems, and weak behavioral control. Antisocial personality disorder is strongly associated with crime, and with chronic offending. Although psychopaths constitute only 4 percent of the male population and less than 1 percent of the female population, they are responsible for half of the serious felonies committed annually.

Research linking other forms of mental disorder to crime is equivocal. Building on the nineteenth-century theories that linked crime to madness, early research found a robust relationship between offending and mental illness. As diagnostic criteria have evolved and as research methodologies have improved, however, the relationship has grown less clear. While individuals who have been diagnosed mentally ill are arrested at disproportionate rates, research suggests that the mentally ill are more likely to harm themselves than to hurt others.

Research typically shows that rates of mental disorder in prison populations are higher than in the general population, especially for psychopathy, schizophrenia, and depression. These studies, however, do not prove that mental illness causes crime. Several explanations are possible: mentally ill offenders may be less successful at committing crimes, and more easily detected; police may be more likely to arrest mentally ill offenders; guilty pleas may be easier to obtain from mentally ill offenders; or the deprivations of prison might *cause* the mental illness. Research indicates that rates of offending in psychiatric hospital populations are generally higher than in the general population. Again, this finding does not in itself prove that mental illness *causes* crime. Early research actually suggested that psychiatric populations committed crimes at the same rate as the general population; the more recent research indicating that rates of robbery (and possibly rape) are higher among psychiatric populations may say more about who is institutionalized in psychiatric facilities than about rates of crime. In the future, careful research design may disaggregate the concepts of mental illness, crime, and institutionalization, and allow scientists to separate cause from correlation, but the relationship between mental illness and crime currently remains equivocal.

The psychological causes of crime remain a rich area of investigation. Contemporary research is already exploring the neurological bases of psychological phenomena such as psychopathy, intelligence, and personality. As biological and psychological explanations converge, the mechanisms of the individual-level causes of crime may become clear. Psychological criminologists also may bridge individual-level and interpersonal explanations to explain, for example, how personality traits contribute to the social bonds that underlie social control theory or how intelligence contributes to the trajectory of a criminal life course.

SEE ALSO: Crime, Biosocial Theories of; Crime, Social Learning Theory of; Freud, Sigmund; Law, Criminal; Rational Choice Theory: A Crime-Related Perspective; Self-Control Theory; Sutherland, Edwin H.

REFERENCES AND SUGGESTED READINGS

Cleckley, H. J. (1976) *The Mask of Sanity*, 5th edn. C. V. Mosby, St. Louis, MO.
Eysenck, H. J. (1977) *Crime and Personality*, 3rd edn. Routledge & Kegan Paul, London.
Glueck, S. & Glueck, E. (1950) *Unraveling Juvenile Delinquency*. Harper & Row, New York.
Gottfredson, M. & Hirschi, T. (1990) *A General Theory of Crime*. Stanford University Press, Stanford.
Hare, R. D. (1980) A Research Scale for the Assessment of Psychopathy in Criminal Populations. *Personality and Individual Differences* 1: 111–19.
Hirschi, T. & Hindelang, M. J. (1977) Intelligence and Delinquency: A Revisionist Review. *American Sociological Review* 42: 571–87.
Kohlberg, L. (1969) *Stages in the Development of Moral Thought and Action*. Holt, Rinehart, & Winston, New York.

crime, radical/Marxist theories of

Barbara Sims

Marxist criminological theory asserts that crime is the result of structural inequalities that are inherently associated with capitalist economic systems. Although Marx himself wrote very little about crime, theorists have relied on his economic theory to provide a foundation for a *critical* theory of criminal behavior. Marx believed that throughout history, human societies have consisted of two classes: those who have the power to create the rules under which everyone must live, and those who have neither the resources nor the political clout to have a say in just what those rules will be. Examples of these economic or political systems are master versus slave, lord versus serf, and, under modern-day capitalism, capitalist versus proletariat. The capitalists are those who own the means of production, and the proletariats are those who work for them.

Marx used a base structure metaphor to describe the role of social institutions, with the economic mode of production providing the base of that structure. For Marx, the mode of production determines the characteristics of other social institutions, e.g., the social, political, and spiritual institutions.

Marxist criminologists argue that a society where some people, because of their place in the capitalist system, are able to accrue a great deal of wealth and material goods, and some are not, is setting itself up for criminal behavior. Such behavior results from a lack of attention by those in power to the growing tensions among the working classes, who see a great divide between what the culture teaches them they can, and should, achieve, and the actual opportunities that could assist them in such achievement.

Intellectually, critical theorists rely on Marx's notion of exploitation of the working class by the capitalists to further explain growing frustrations by the former and rebellion, some of which could be criminal in nature. The capitalist class is able to earn extraordinary rates of surplus value, the profit produced by the workers for the capitalists, made possible through the labor of the worker. The workers are paid a subsistence living wage, barely enough to feed, clothe, and shelter themselves and, when relevant, their families.

At the time Marx was writing, the Industrial Revolution was underway with untold accounts of workers being injured or killed in the factories because of unsafe working conditions. Further, men, women, and children were being worked long hours in the factories of the capitalists, and in some cases suffered the lash of their supervisors should their work be deemed not to be of sufficient quality. The growing working class was increasingly viewed by Marx as exploited and, arguably, a powder keg about to explode.

Modern-day Marxist theorists argue that although much has changed in the world since Marx's writings, there is still room for improvement when it comes to the working class. Neo-Marxists, for example, suggest that although a revolution and the overthrow of the capitalist economy is not an appropriate solution to the problem of worker exploitation and gross inequalities of opportunity, there is much that could be done to reduce the boiling tensions and frustrations of the have-nots in society. The minimum wage could be increased to an amount established by leading economists, factoring in the costs of food, clothing, and shelter in today's economy. Job creation and training programs could be established in local communities hit hard by the outsourcing of manufacturing sector employment to foreign markets. Assistance to families could take many forms. For one, subsidized and quality day care for the children of the working class could alleviate the stress of worrying about who will take care of the children while the parents are at work. Medical leave with pay for workers who become unable to work or who have a family member in need of assistance could reduce the stress of worrying about missed wages or losing one's job because of an unexpected turn of events. Government-sponsored health care programs that provide quality health care to the working class could also relieve much of the stress associated with worries over how to take care of oneself or one's family should illnesses or injuries occur.

On another level, Marxist criminologists argue that the criminal justice system, the system through which people who break the law are processed, should become more equitable. There should be an expectation that all individuals who come in contact with the system will be treated justly and equitably, with the rich receiving the same treatment as the poor. A system where "the rich get richer and the poor get prison" (Reiman 2001) should be abolished once and for all. Corporate fraud, or suite crime, that bilks retirement funds from longtime and loyal employees should be punishable by hard prison time no less than crimes of the street. When differences exist between the haves and the have-nots when it comes to the meting out of justice, it becomes clear that the system is, in fact, unjust. Increasingly, members of the lower class, sometimes referred to as the truly disadvantaged, view the system as broken, and act out in ways that are hurtful to society.

One area that has always interested Marxist criminologists is the relationship between economic inequality and crime. Beginning with Willem Bonger (1969), Marxist theorists have attempted to demonstrate the relationship between economic inequality and crime. For Bonger, egoism is the result of the inherent ruthlessness of capitalism and its underlying competitiveness to get ahead by any means necessary. Members of the working class are forced to live in sometimes brutal conditions, and, at the same time, have the ruling class inculcating the culture with images of materialistic success. In this type of environment, the good of the whole is not considered, and altruism that would lead to prosocial attitudes and behaviors cannot take root. Richard Quinney, while agreeing with Bonger that capitalism causes crime, also pointed attention toward the crimes of the ruling class. Those crimes are price fixing, political corruption, police brutality, violation of citizens' civil rights, and so on. According to Quinney, the ruling class must engage in actions of this sort in order to maintain the existing system.

In the 1980s and the 1990s, critical theorists, relying heavily on Marxist notions, continued to look at the relationship between structural inequalities and crime, and continued to examine more closely the crimes of the powerful. In an effort to demonstrate the importance of structural variables on individual interactions within the existing culture, Colvin and Pauly created an integrated structural–Marxist theory of delinquency. They argued, and were able to demonstrate through an empirical test of their theoretical model, that parents discipline their children along the same lines as they themselves are treated within the workplace by their employers. Those who are supervised by employers who use coercive methods to obtain conformity in their workers use coercive methods in the household, as opposed to egalitarian means, to obtain conformity in their children.

Sims (1997) has argued that a well-received theoretical model developed by Messner and Rosenfeld (1997) does not go far enough in explaining the role that social institutions play in the production of violent crime in America. The sociological paradigm developed by Messner and Rosenfeld does include strain theory and social disorganization theory, with a discussion of how inequality in opportunity within social institutions that are in disarray creates a society ripe for crime. What is left out, however, is the inclusion of Marxist criminology that can explain how social institutions are formed and function within the capitalist society. Sims (1997) argues that the economic foundation sets the stage for both the cultural messages received by the populace and the environment in which social interaction takes place. Marxist concepts can be used to add the missing link to Messner and Rosenfeld's model of crime.

Since the early 1960s, Marxist theories of crime have spawned several new theories, each bringing forth new ideas about the problem of crime. Left realism addresses the increasingly repressive control of the state over individuals who engage in lawbreaking, and calls for a closer look at the toll that crime takes on individuals and communities. Feminist theory asserts that women continue to take a backseat to males in a patriarchal system, calling for studies that consider gender constructs in research designs. This approach would be one that goes beyond simply adding the variable *gender* to studies of crime and deviance and that demonstrates a clear understanding of the role that culture and social conditions contribute to society's views of and attitudes toward women. Peacemaking criminology attacks the militaristic approach to crime control, agitating for a system that looks toward an end to the "war on crime" and/or the "war on drugs" and the ushering in of a system in which all sides can live in peaceful coexistence with one another.

At the core of all of these theoretical perspectives, however, are basic Marxist principles. In sum, the economic mode of production dictates how the other social institutions will function. Although they may shift and do have some degree of autonomy, the economic foundation does not allow for too great a deviation from the base structure. The economy, then, takes a front seat to such institutions as the family, schools, the polity, and the spiritual. Under capitalism, a two-class system emerges with a heavy emphasis on materialism and extreme competitiveness. The ruling class, those who own the means of production, are able to exploit the working class, and those who are most likely to suffer under this type of system are the poor, minorities, women, and children. At the same time, the ruling class is able to focus society's attention on the crimes of the lower classes while engaging in behavior that is corrupt, but that allows them to stay in power.

While some suggest that Marxist theories are somewhat utopian, other theorists see the importance of the contribution of the concepts of Marx to a more comprehensive examination of crime and delinquency. They argue continually that to ignore the more proximate (e.g., macro or structural) variables in any theoretical model of crime, in light of the fact that it is the more distal variables (e.g., micro or individual) that seemingly explain more in a multivariate (predictive) statistical model, is to miss the point. It is the way society is structured that determines the form that the social institutions take and the culture that arises out of interactions with individuals within those institutions.

SEE ALSO: Capitalism; Feminist Criminology; Marx, Karl; New Left Realism; Peacemaking; Stratification and Inequality

REFERENCES AND SUGGESTED READINGS

Bonger, W. (1969) *Criminality and Economic Conditions*. Indiana University Press, Indiana.

Caringella-MacDonald, S. (1997) Taking Back the Critical: Reflections on the Division of Critical Criminology in Light of Left Realism, Feminism, Postmodernism, and Anarchism. *Critical Criminologist* 7(2/3): 22–4.

Cohen, L. E. & Felson, M. (1979) Social Change and Crime Rate Trends: A Routine Activity Approach. *American Sociological Review* 44: 588–608.

Grose, G. & Groves, W. B. (1988) Crime and Human Nature: A Marxist Perspective. *Contemporary Crises* 12: 145–71.

Groves, W. B. & Sampson, R. J. (1987) Traditional Contributions to Radical Criminology. *Journal of Research in Crime and Delinquency* 24(3): 181–214.

Lynch, M. & Groves, W. B. (1989) *A Primer in Radical Criminology*, 2nd edn. Harrow & Heston, New York.

Messner, S. F. & Rosenfeld, R. (1997) *Crime and the American Dream*, 2nd edn. Wadsworth, Belmont, CA.

Reiman, J. (2001) *The Rich Get Richer and the Poor Get Prison*. Allyn & Bacon, Boston.

Sims, B. (1997) Crime, Punishment, and the American Dream: Toward a Marxist Integration. *Journal of Research in Crime and Delinquency* 34(1): 5–24.

Taylor, I., Walton, P., & Young, J. (1973) *The New Criminology: For a Social Theory of Deviance*. Harper & Row, New York.

Weiner, R. R. (1981) *Cultural Marxism and Political Sociology*. Sage, Beverly Hills, CA.

Wilson, W. J. (1988) *The Truly Disadvantaged: The Inner City, the Underclass, and Public Policy*. University of Chicago Press, Chicago.

Wolff, R. (1984) *Understanding Marx: A Reconstruction and Critique of Capital*. Blackwell, Oxford.

crime, schools and

Thomas W. Brewer and Daniel J. Flannery

The majority of schools in America are safe places. A comparison of national data from 1995 and 2001 shows the percentage of students who reported being victims of crime at school decreased by 4 percent (DeVoe et al. 2003). In 1999 the US Departments of Education and Justice reported that almost 90 percent of all in-school student injuries that required medical treatment were accidental, rather than the result of intentional acts of physical violence. Schools see fewer homicides and nonfatal injuries than homes or neighborhoods. From 1992 to 2000, school-aged youth were 70 times more likely to be murdered outside of school than in school (US Department of Education 2001). The violence that does occur in schools, however, has changed. Serious violent acts are now more common than in the past. In the 1940s, school discipline problems generally involved running in the halls, chewing gum, talking out of turn, and other unruly behavior. In the 1970s, discipline problems progressed to dress code violations; in the 1980s, fighting became a concern. By the 1990s, school problems were defined as weapons possession, drug and alcohol abuse, gang activity, truancy, and violent assaults against students and teachers.

In schools, violence occurs along an age-graded continuum. With younger children, violence is manifest as aggressive behavior such as kicking, hitting, or name-calling. As children grow older, however, violent behavior becomes more serious and is characterized by assaults against other students and teachers, sexual harassment, gang activity, or carrying a weapon.

Students are not the only victims of violence at school; teachers can be targets as well. Between 1997 and 2001, on average, 21 out of every 1,000 teachers were victims of violent school crime; however, only 2 out of 1,000 teachers were likely to be victims of serious violent offenses such as robbery, aggravated assault, or sexual assault. Teachers in urban schools were more likely to be victims of violent crime than teachers in suburban or rural districts (DeVoe et al. 2003).

To minimize violence at school, it is important to understand the risk factors for violent behavior, so that effective school-based prevention and intervention programs can be implemented. This is no easy task, however, as risk factors are complex and multidimensional, and may change over time. In addition, factors associated with the potential for violence in school occur at both the individual and group level, and effective prevention programs must include a consideration of an individual school's design and operation.

Although violence is a learned behavior, other factors can influence an individual's propensity to behave violently. Two such factors are prenatal risk and a child's temperament. For example, birth complications such as oxygen deprivation can result in brain dysfunction and neurological and learning deficits that predispose an individual to violent behavior. Impulsive children and children with difficult personalities are also at risk for aggressive and violent behavior. Low cognitive abilities, especially verbal skills, and lack of school achievement constitute another set of risk factors for violent and aggressive behavior. Aggressive and violent youths tend to interpret neutral cues in their environment as hostile; thereby increasing the likelihood that they will react aggressively to a particular situation; such misattribution may cause a student to escalate an accidental bump in the hallway into a more serious altercation.

Aggressive behavior tends to be a pattern that persists over time, especially for children who are "early starters." One consistent finding in the research literature is a link between aggressive and violent behavior in adolescence, and negative, aggressive behavior in kindergarten and first grade. The pattern is one of early conduct problems leading to poor academic achievement, dropping out of school, and rejection by peers, all of which are factors associated with delinquent behavior.

Any effective strategy for reducing and preventing school violence needs to include parents, children, school staff, media, police officers, community members, and community-based organizations. The most effective programs go beyond a concentration on individual children and singular risk factors, and attempt to change the climate or culture of the entire school. It is clear that a change in individual behavior cannot be sustained unless the social environment is also changed. Ensuring that basic safety needs are met is an essential first step in providing a school environment that is conducive to learning and proper socialization. An effective school safety program is essential to prevent the onset of school violence, including a protocol for responding to crises, acts of violence, and even minor conflicts. Popular elements of school safety programs include the use of metal detectors, a zero tolerance policy for weapons, and using police officers as security guards.

There is a trend toward treating violent incidents as criminal acts to be handled by law enforcement officials and the courts, and the creation of alternative schools or programs for youths deemed too unruly for the regular school setting. School safety, however, is not just about "hardening the target" – using security cameras or metal detectors to deter unusual activity. Less punitive approaches include conflict resolution programs to settle disputes peaceably, mentoring programs to provide at-risk students with supportive adult role models, new curricula to build character and develop moral reasoning, special-skill-building programs, and partnerships between schools and social service and mental health agencies. Other program components include structured playgrounds, closely supervising student behavior, and rewarding positive conduct. Schools are also implementing proactive programs designed to prevent aggressive acts by students, and to refer students to appropriate intervention services in the event that violence does occur. Many of these programs strive to increase student social skills while also working to reduce aggressive behavior. Fostering positive relationships between students and staff also creates a more caring school climate.

Despite the increase in the intensity of school violence in recent years, there are some encouraging signs that it can be prevented or at least reduced. School personnel and community members need to work together to create a positive environment that promotes social skills and high performance expectations, as well as a safe and caring climate where students are free to devote their time and energy to learning and developing the skills necessary to become successful and productive members of the community. Safe school strategies should focus on targeting goals that sustain expectations for acceptable behavior, and provide a disincentive for negative behavior, such as bullying, threats, vandalism, fighting, and theft. Understanding the relationship between risk, prevention, intervention, and policy is also essential in implementing safe school policies and procedures. The key is to implement programs that have been shown to be effective in preventing violence or intervening when violence occurs.

SEE ALSO: Age and Crime; Crime; Criminology; Juvenile Delinquency; Scapegoating; School Discipline; Victimization; Violence; Violent Crime

REFERENCES AND SUGGESTED READINGS

De Voe, J. F., Peter, K., Kaufman, P., Ruddy, S. A., Miller, A. K., Planty, M., Snyder, T. D., and Rand, M. R. (2003) *Indicators of School Crime and Safety: 2003*. NCES 2004–004/NCJ 201257. US Departments of Education and Justice, Washington, DC.

Embry, D. & Flannery, D. (1999) Two Sides of the Coin: Multi-level Prevention and Intervention to Reduce Youth Violent Behavior. In: D. Flannery & C. R. Huff (Eds.), *Youth Violence: Prevention, Intervention, and Social Policy*. American Psychiatric Press, Washington, DC, pp. 47–72.

Flannery, D. (1997). *School Violence, Risk, Preventive Intervention and Policy*. Monograph for the Institute of Urban and Minority Education, Columbia University, and the ERIC Clearinghouse for Education, Urban Diversity Series No. 109 (ED 416–272).

Flannery, D. & Huff, C. R. (Eds.) (1999) *Youth Violence: Prevention, Intervention, and Social Policy*. American Psychiatric Press, Washington, DC.

Flannery, D. & Williams, L. (1999) Effective Youth Violence Prevention. In: T. Gullotta & S. McElhaney (Eds.), *Violence in Homes and Communities: Prevention, Intervention, and Treatment*. National Mental Health Association/Sage, Thousand Oaks, CA, pp. 207–44.

Flannery, D., Singer, M., & Wester, K. (2001) Violence Exposure, Psychological Trauma, and Suicide Risk in a Community Sample of Dangerously Violent Adolescents. *Journal of the American Academy of Child and Adolescent Psychiatry* 40: 435–42.

Flannery, D., Hussey, D., Biebelhausen, L., & Wester, K. (2003) Crime, Delinquency and Youth Gangs. In G. Adams & M. Berzonsky (Eds.), *The Blackwell Handbook of Adolescence*. Blackwell, Oxford, pp. 502–22.

Flannery, D., Vazsonyi, A., Liau, A., Guo, S., Powell, K., Atha, H., Vesterdal, W., & Embry, D. (2003) Initial Behavior Outcomes for

Peacebuilders Universal School-Based Violence Prevention Program. *Developmental Psychology* 39: 292–308.

Singer, M., Anglin, T., Li yu Song et al. (1995) Adolescents' Exposure to Violence and Associated Symptoms of Psychological Trauma. *Journal of the American Medical Association* 273: 477–82.

Singer, M., Miller, D., Guo, S. et al. (1999) Contributors to Violent Behavior among Elementary and Middle School Children. *Pediatrics* 104: 878–84.

US Department of Education (2001) *Youth Violence: A Report of the Surgeon General*. Department of Justice, Office of Justice Programs, Washington, DC.

crime, social control theory of

James D. Orcutt

The social control theory of crime is fundamentally a theory of conformity. Instead of theorizing about the motivations for criminal behavior, control theorists ask, "Why do people conform?" Their answers to this question stress the importance of strong group relationships, active institutional participation, and conventional moral values in constraining and regulating individual behavior. When these controlling influences are weak or rendered ineffective, people are freer to deviate from legal and moral norms. Thus, in explaining conformity, control theorists highlight the conditions under which crime and delinquency become possible, if not likely, outcomes. Following this lead, a large body of criminological research inspired by social control theory has focused on how variations in the strength of individuals' bonds to family, community, school, and other conventional groups and institutions relate to patterns of self-reported and officially recorded deviant behavior.

Social control theory has origins in the early works of the moral and utilitarian philosophers, the nineteenth-century writings of Émile Durkheim, and the early twentieth-century research of the Chicago School of sociology. It is now counted among the leading sociological perspectives on crime and juvenile delinquency, largely because of the influence of Travis Hirschi's formulation and evaluation of control theory in his book *Causes of Delinquency* (1969). Hirschi not only contributed a systematic theoretical analysis of the social bonds that account for conformity to legal and moral standards. He also assessed the explanatory power of his theory with a well-designed survey of self-reported delinquency among male adolescents. Most of the subsequent research and critical debate in the social control tradition has been addressed specifically to Hirschi's theoretical framework, which is often referred to as social bonding theory.

Hirschi explicitly grounds his version of control theory on Durkheim's classic analysis of suicide. Durkheim (1951) proposed that a lack of social integration — "the relaxation of social bonds" between individuals and society — was a source of high rates of "egoistic suicide" in certain societies. Hirschi (1969: 16) begins his theoretical statement by quoting Durkheim's characterization of how weak or ruptured social bonds to the family, community, or other groups create a condition of excessive individualism in which individuals depend only on themselves and recognize "no other rules of conduct than what are founded on [their] private interests." Hirschi goes on to identify four conceptually distinct "elements" of the social bond that, when strong and viable, work against individualizing tendencies and maintain conformity to conventional rules of conduct.

First, Hirschi's concept of attachment, the *emotional element* of the social bond, comes closest to Durkheim's conception of the integrative influences of strong family and group relationships. Clearly, when individuals lack close emotional ties with others and do not care about other people's feelings or opinions, they are freer to deviate. Second, the *rational element* of the social bond, commitment, is based on individuals' calculation of the cost of deviance: the potential risk to their investments in conventional lines of action such as educational or occupational careers, if they were to be caught in an act of crime. In short, individuals who lack a commitment to school or a career have less to lose by committing crime. Third, involvement constitutes a *temporal element* of the social bond. People who are heavily engaged

in conventional activities have less free time to deviate than do those individuals with lots of "time on their hands." Fourth, Hirschi's concept of belief, a *moral element* of the social bond, assumes that there is a common set of moral values that is shared, more or less, by all members of modern societies. However, the strength of belief varies across individuals, and those who are more weakly bonded to conventional morality will feel freer to violate the laws and norms of this common value system.

Hirschi (1969) treats these four elements theoretically as an interrelated network of variables: "In general, the more closely a person is tied to conventional society in any of these ways, the more closely [he or she] is likely to be tied in the other ways" (p. 27). However, he appears to assign causal priority to the emotional element of attachment by focusing on how close family ties subsequently affect the development of educational and career commitments and conventional beliefs in the moral validity of rules. Thus, Hirschi, like many other control theorists, implies that failure of the family to provide a strong and enduring emotional bond to the conventional social order is a basic source of criminality and other forms of disorderly conduct. A more controversial implication of social bonding theory is that attachment to any primary group, including delinquent friends, will strengthen the individual's bond to conventional society. Here, Hirschi's formulation runs counter to a central proposition of differential association and social learning theories, as well as to a large body of empirical evidence showing a positive relationship between social ties to deviant companions and delinquent or criminal behavior. Indeed, in light of similar findings in his own research on self-reported delinquency, Hirschi concludes that his theoretical statement underestimates the importance of delinquent friends as a cause of law-violating behavior. In most other respects, Hirschi's research and the results of numerous other investigations of delinquency and crime provide at least modest support for the argument that strong bonds to the family, school, work, and other conventional institutions discourage deviant behavior.

Hirschi's *relational* focus on the strength of the social bond distinguishes his theory from previous versions of control theory that employed a *dualistic* conception of internal or personal controls versus external or social controls. For instance, following in the footsteps of W. I. Thomas and Florian Znaniecki's early work on *The Polish Peasant in Europe and America*, sociologists at the University of Chicago during the 1920s portrayed crime and delinquency as a joint product of *social disorganization* – the weakening of community control over group and individual behavior – and *personal disorganization* that left some individuals more vulnerable than others to the demoralizing or unconventional influences of urban life. Later renditions of control theory by two sociologists trained at Chicago, Albert J. Reiss and Walter C. Reckless, provide particularly clear examples of the dualistic approach.

Reiss (1951) presented the first systematic statement and empirical assessment of control theory based on his dissertation research on recidivism of juvenile offenders. His broad conception of social controls in the adolescent's environment included *primary group controls* (e.g., family structure, parents' "moral ideals" and techniques of control) and *community and institutional controls* (e.g., neighborhood quality and delinquency rate, school attendance, and compliance with authority). However, his psychoanalytic view of personal controls, which included "ego strength" and "super-ego controls," created a sharp conceptual separation between the external social world and the internal state of the adolescent's personality. As a result, Reiss gives license to the reductionistic argument that psychopathology – the failure or inadequacy of personal controls – may be a sufficient cause of delinquency irrespective of the strength of the individual's bonds to conventional groups and institutions.

A decade later, Reckless (1961) proposed his version of control theory, which he labeled containment theory. He explicitly characterized his theory as an explanation of conforming behavior as well as of a wide range of criminal and delinquent behaviors, with the exception of deviance that is attributable to personality disorders or criminal cultures (like the infamous "criminal tribes of India"). Similar to Reiss, he drew a clear conceptual boundary between the "internal control system" of the self and the "external control system" of the family and other conventional institutional supports in the individual's immediate social environment. In his commentary and research on this dualistic notion of containment, Reckless placed special emphasis on the importance of a "good self-concept" as an inner "buffer" or "insulator" against environmental "pulls" or "pressures" toward delinquency. This rather mechanistic approach, which tends to rest much of its explanatory force on vaguely conceptualized psychological factors, has been widely criticized and was largely superseded by Hirschi's social bonding theory in the late 1960s.

Whereas Reiss, Reckless, and other early theorists such as Ivan Nye and Jackson Toby conceptualized external and internal controls as relatively stable, deterministic constraints on behavior, some control theorists have treated the interplay of control and deviation as a stochastic situational process. For example, Briar and Piliavin (1965) argue that the probability that individuals will act on short-run "situational inducements" to deviate is contingent on the current strength of their "commitment to conformity." In the same vein, David Matza's (1964) analysis of *Delinquency and Drift* portrays delinquent behavior as a situational choice – an act of "will" – that becomes possible when adolescents are temporarily freed from moral constraints and "drift between criminal and conventional action." The ideas of these processual theorists have been difficult to examine empirically, but these works underscore a key assumption of contemporary versions of social control theory: crime is better understood as an exercise of freedom from constraint than as a product of deviant motives, environmental pressures, and other deterministic forces.

Since Hirschi's (1969) statement of social bonding theory, theoretical work on the relationship between social control and crime has moved in three different directions that are generally beyond the scope of this entry. First, a number of sociologists and criminologists have offered various forms of "integrated theory," which blend concepts and propositions from control theory with other theoretical explanations of deviant behavior. Most often, integrated theories add motivational components such as differential association with deviant peers or cultural or psychological "strain" to Hirschi's framework, thereby altering its distinctively agnostic stance regarding the motives for deviant behavior.

Second, as anticipated by Kornhauser's (1978) comprehensive discussion of the origins of control theory in early work on social disorganization, a large body of recent theory and research has focused on ecological variations in forms and patterns of social control and rates of crime in urban neighborhoods. By conceptualizing informal control as a systemic property of communities, new disorganization theorists have revitalized links between contemporary research on social control and its roots in the macro-level analyses of Durkheim and the Chicago sociologists.

Third, Hirschi, in collaboration with Michael R. Gottfredson, has taken a sharp turn toward micro-level analysis of individual differences in deviance and control in the influential work *A General Theory of Crime*. Gottfredson and Hirschi (1990) argue *low self-control* is the basic source of crime, which they define as "acts of force or fraud undertaken in pursuit of self-interest" (p. 15). In advancing this argument, they abandon the relational focus of Hirschi's previous theory of the social bond in favor of a psychological explanation that is more in line with Reiss and Reckless's notions of internal or personal control. Relationships to family, friends, and other external sources of control virtually vanish from the general theory once the individual's capacity for self-control is fixed at a particular level during childhood socialization.

SEE ALSO: Anomie; Authority and conformity; Control Balance Theory; Durkheim, Émile; Self-Control Theory; Social Control; Social Disorganization Theory

REFERENCES AND SUGGESTED READINGS

Briar, S. & Piliavin, I. (1965) Delinquency, Situational Inducements, and Commitment to Conformity. *Social Problems* 13: 35–45.

Durkheim, E. (1951) *Suicide: A Study in Sociology*. Trans. J. A. Spaulding & G. Simpson. Free Press, New York.

Gottfredson, M. R. & Hirschi, T. (1990) *A General Theory of Crime*. Stanford University Press, Stanford.

Hirschi, T. (1969) *Causes of Delinquency*. University of California Press, Berkeley.

Kornhauser, R. R. (1978) *Social Sources of Delinquency: An Appraisal of Analytical Models*. University of Chicago Press, Chicago.

Matza, D. (1964) *Delinquency and Drift*. Wiley, New York.

Reckless, W. C. (1961) A New Theory of Delinquency and Crime. *Federal Probation* 25: 42–6.

Reiss, A. J., Jr. (1951) Delinquency as the Failure of Personal and Social Controls. *American Sociological Review* 16: 196–207.

crime, social learning theory of

Ruth Triplett

The social learning theory of crime basically argues that some people learn to commit crimes through the same process through which others learn to conform. The theory assumes that people are "blank slates" at birth, having neither a motivation to commit crime nor to conform. The theory then asks two questions. First, at the micro-level, it asks why an individual commits crimes. The answer to this question stresses the process of learning, which involves the interaction between thought or cognition, behavior and environment. Second, at the macro-level, social learning theory asks why some groups have higher crime rates than others. The answer to this question involves the concepts of culture conflict, differential social organization, and social structure.

Social learning theory is rooted in the work of the Chicago School theorists of the early twentieth century. At the individual level, social learning theory draws on the idea of symbolic interactionism found in the work of Chicago School theorist W. I. Thomas, Cooley, and Mead. Symbolic interactionism is a social psychological theory that is based on the idea that all human behavior can be understood in terms of the way that individuals communicate through social symbols. People communicate through symbols that are social in origins. These symbols give meaning to the world. Symbolic interactionism then sees human behavior as social in origin and as something that can only be understood when we understand how the individual interprets the symbols. At the group or societal level, social learning theories are based on the ecological work of Park and Burgess, the ideas of social disorganization found in Shaw and McKay, and Sellin's idea of culture conflict.

Along with social control theory, social learning theory is now considered one of – if not *the* – dominant theory of crime and deviance today. Its dominance is largely due to the work of two theorists, Edwin Sutherland (1939, 1947) and Ronald Akers (1985, 1998). In 1939, Sutherland published the first version of his theory of social learning in his textbook *Principles of Criminology*, with the final version published first in 1947. With this theory, he presented criminology with a purely sociological theory of crime that addressed his concerns about the biological and psychological theories of crime that were dominant at the time. Akers (Burgess & Akers 1966; Akers 1985, 1998) later revised Sutherland's theory of differential association, rewriting it in the language of modern learning theory and expanding on it to make it more comprehensive. Besides his theoretical contributions, Akers has also been a leader in empirically testing social learning theory across a variety of groups and crimes.

Sutherland's (1939, 1947) social learning theory is called the theory of differential association. Differential association, which is the central concept in the theory, refers to the idea that people come into contact with different types of people with different ideas about the acceptability of crime. Written in nine basic propositions, the theory starts with the idea that criminal behavior is learned largely through a process of interaction in small groups. When individuals learn criminal behavior they learn both the techniques (the how) and the motivations (the why) for committing crimes. The motivations, which Sutherland refers to in terms of attitudes, drives, and definitions, are critical to the learning process. Sutherland argued that one becomes criminal, not through association with criminals, but when definitions favorable to the violation of the law outweigh definitions unfavorable to the violation of the law.

If individuals become criminal through a process of learning both the how and the why of committing a crime, why does one group have higher crime rates than another? Compared to his ideas on why an individual commits crime, Sutherland addressed this question only briefly. In answering this question, he came to disagree with an idea that is closely identified with the work of Chicago School theorists Shaw and McKay. They theorized that variation in crime rates across neighborhoods was due to social disorganization, an inability of a group of people to agree upon and work toward a common goal such as crime control. Sutherland came to argue that high crime rate areas were not disorganized, but were organized differently. Building on the work of Sellin in culture conflict, Sutherland then referred to differential social organization across groups and areas. Some areas have higher crime rates than others, then, because they are organized around principles that differ from the principles of those that have been embodied in the law.

Despite the recognition of its importance and its continuing dominance as a theory of crime, Sutherland's theory of differential association was not without its critics. It was in large part as a response to one of the most important criticisms that Akers came to develop his social learning theory. Written prior to the development of modern learning theories, Sutherland said little in his theory of learning about the process through which individuals actually learn.

A number of theorists worked to demonstrate the usefulness of Sutherland's theory and to expand on it by linking it with a modern learning theory. Included among these theorists are DeFleur and Quinney (1966), who demonstrated how differential association is logical and capable of producing testable propositions. They rewrote the theory in axiomatic form. Another theorist, C. Ray Jeffrey (1965), was the first to actually link differential association with operant conditioning, a modern learning theory that proposes that individuals learn based on the consequences of their behavior. In 1966, Burgess and Akers rewrote differential association in the language of operant conditioning. In doing so they explained more fully than did Sutherland how people learn and developed what Akers considers a more general theory of human behavior. The work of Burgess and Akers is perhaps of most importance among these revisions and expansions, in large part because of the continued efforts, both theoretical and empirical, of Akers on the behalf of social learning theory.

Since his initial work with Burgess in 1966, Akers has continued to develop social learning theory both theoretically and through his empirical testing of the theory. Today, he has what he now calls his own social learning theory. Akers' theory currently centers around four major concepts: differential association, definitions, differential reinforcement, and imitation. *Differential association* refers, as it did for Sutherland, to the varying pattern of associations with which individuals may have contact. Like Sutherland, Akers recognizes that few people would have contact with exclusively criminal patterns or exclusively non-criminal patterns of associations. Most individuals associate with a variety of people, some of whom will define criminal behavior as acceptable and some of whom will not. *Definitions* refer to the cognitive part of the process or the "why" someone would commit a crime. This includes all the items Sutherland mentioned, such as attitudes and drives, as well as rationalizations.

Both differential association and definitions are central concepts in Sutherland's as well as Akers' theories. It is with the concepts of differential reinforcement and imitation that Akers expands on Sutherland's ideas to explain more fully how it is that individuals learn. *Differential reinforcement* refers to "the balance of anticipated or actual rewards and punishments that follow or are consequences of behavior" (Akers 1998: 67). Akers recognizes that rewards and punishments can be both social and non-social, but it is those rewards and punishments which are social that he stresses as most important. In fact, he argues that much of what may initially look like non-social rewards are actually social. For example, money, which may be categorized by some as a non-social reward for a crime, is argued by Akers to be in fact a social reward. This is because the meaning of money comes from the social. Money gets its importance to individuals as a reward because it can give us status and power, each of which is a particularly social reward. Akers then defines social rewards and punishments very broadly. Non-social rewards are defined narrowly by Akers to include largely the psychological and physiological effects of drugs. Finally, *imitation* refers to the existence of models for observation. Akers expands Sutherland's ideas then to include the idea that one need not be in "interaction" with others to learn from them.

Basically, Akers' social learning theory argues that criminal behavior is more likely when the effects of all four of these central concepts combine to strengthen criminal behavior over conformity. Thus, criminal behavior is more likely when someone has contact with patterns of association that support criminal behavior by defining it as favorable, provide rewards for it, and model it.

In his initial work with Burgess, the emphasis was on rewriting differential association; thus their work, as well as much of Akers' own work, has focused on the individual level. Akers has however had a long-term interest in the question of why certain groups have higher crime rates than others. Akers (1998) outlined a theory linking social structure and social learning. His social structure-social learning (SSSL) theory of crime argues that four social structural variables – social correlates, sociodemographic/socioeconomic, theoretically defined structural variables, and differential social location – affect group or area crime rates through the influence they have on the process of learning that individuals go through. With *social correlates*, Akers recognizes Sutherland's idea that societies, communities, and cultures, for example, are organized differently. *Sociodemographic/socioeconomic* refers to the location individuals have in the social structure because of characteristics such as class position, gender, race, and/or ethnicity. Akers argues social learning theory can by integrated with existing social structural theories. Thus included in *theoretically defined structural variables* are variables found in structural theories such as social disorganization, culture conflict, and anomie. Finally, *differential social location* refers to the place individuals have in relation to primary, secondary, and reference groups. This refers to the place of individuals in more intimate groups such as family and friendship networks.

SEE ALSO: Crime, Social Control Theory of; Criminology; Social Disorganization Theory; Social Support; Sutherland, Edwin H.; Symbolic Interaction

REFERENCES AND SUGGESTED
READINGS

Akers, R. (1985) *Deviant Behavior: A Social Learning Approach*, 3rd edn. Wadsworth, Belmont, CA.
Akers, R. (1998) *Social Learning and Social Structure: A General Theory of Crime and Deviance*. Northeastern University Press, Boston.
Burgess, R. & Akers, R. (1966) A Differential Association-Reinforcement Theory of Criminal Behavior. *Social Problems* 14: 128–47.
DeFleur, M. & Quinney, R. (1966) A Reformulation of Sutherland's Differential Association Theory and a Strategy for Empirical Verification. *Journal of Research in Crime and Delinquency* 3: 1–22.
Glaser, D. (1956) Criminality Theories and Behavioral Images. *American Journal of Sociology* 61: 433–44.
Glaser, D. (1960) Differential Association and Criminological Prediction. *Social Problems* 8: 6–14.
Jeffrey, C. R. (1965) Criminal Behavior and Learning Theory. *Journal of Criminal Law, Criminology and Police Science* 56: 294–300.
Sutherland, E. (1939) *Principles of Criminology*, 3rd edn. J. B. Lippincott, Philadelphia.
Sutherland, E. (1947) *Principles of Criminology*, 4th edn. J. B. Lippincott, Philadelphia.

crime, white-collar

Gilbert Geis

The term white-collar crime is not found in any statute book. It was coined by Edwin H. Sutherland in his 1939 presidential address to the American Sociological Society. Sutherland stated that his focus was on crime in the upper or white-collar class, composed of respectable or at least respected business and professional men. A decade later, in his book *White Collar Crime*, he declared that white-collar crime may be defined approximately as a crime committed by a person of responsibility and high social status in the course of his occupation. Corporate executives who murdered a spouse were not to be regarded as white-collar criminals, but those who traded on insider information would meet the definition. In the same vein, a striking employee who assaulted a member of the corporate management team would not be considered a white-collar criminal by

Sutherland, but the vice president who maimed a striker would fall within the definition's embrace.

A major aim of Sutherland's formulation was to overthrow explanations of crime common at the time, such as feeblemindedness, Oedipal complexes, and racial identification, traits which were not characteristic of the majority of upperworld offenders. Sutherland maintained that all crime could be interpreted by a single theoretical postulate, which probably explains his indifference to a precise definition of white-collar crime. Later, others would argue that particular forms of white-collar crime, such as anti-trust violations, insider trading, and securities frauds, could be analyzed only by interpretive schemes tailored to ingredients of the offenses.

A white-collar crime definition contrary to Sutherland's was advanced later by a Yale Law School research team that emphasized the nature of the offense rather than the position of the lawbreaker. Their study sample was derived from a survey of federal prosecutors concerning their understanding of what statutory violations might properly be regarded as white-collar crimes. The Yale focus undercut Sutherland's spotlight on abuses of power, but paved the way for sophisticated analyses of persons who violated specified statutes. Critics noted that a not inconsiderable number of the Yale subjects were unemployed and had engaged in relatively tame lawbreaking, such as passing checks with insufficient funds behind them.

Legal scholars also have taken issue with Sutherland's formulation, declaring that it promiscuously labels as "criminal" persons who violated only administrative laws or were charged civilly. Some insisted that Sutherland fouled the legal nest by running riot over such sacred concepts as criminal intent and presumption of innocence. For his part, Sutherland responded that social scientists should not be bound by legal definitions of crime, which often are the product of partisan actions by powerful elites to protect and advance their own interests. He believed that white-collar researchers should examine the details of each case and determine for themselves whether it ought to be classified as a white-collar crime.

Many white-collar offenders, Sutherland maintained, escape criminal convictions only because they come from the same social classes as judges, have gone to the same schools, and live in the same neighborhoods. In addition, prosecutors often are disinclined to pursue an offender charged with violating a complex statute in which the sometimes-elusive existence of criminal intent has to be proven beyond a reasonable doubt. White-collar offenders also have the wherewithal to hire astute attorneys. Prosecutors further realize that they may have to face a jury that might be swayed by the social skills and respectable appearance of the alleged perpetrator.

Relying on the Yale group's definition of white-collar crime, Michael Gottfredson and Travis Hirschi maintained that the phenomenon was the result of an absence of self-control among perpetrators, but their position has been repudiated by a number of scholars who insist that, at least in regard to the offenders Sutherland was concerned with, white-collar criminals rank high on any reasonable measure of self-control, and that it usually was personal discipline that enabled them to obtain the power necessary for their lawbreaking.

White-collar crime has always been something of an outlier in the sociological domain, in part because it tends to be resistant to quantification. Besides, an understanding of the dynamics of white-collar crime often requires a working knowledge of economics, jurisprudence, and regulatory practice, among other matters. White-collar offenders, unlike, say, juvenile gang members, also are not likely to be accessible for fieldwork research. At the same time, the extraordinary outbreak of high-profile white-collar crime cases at the beginning of the current century that involved executives at Enron, WorldCom, Tyco, Adelphia, and other corporations highlighted the behavior, though research support for the topic from federal agencies remains sparse. Part of that indifference to funding white-collar research is believed to inhere in the vulnerability of political administrations to possible findings of wrongdoing by their supporters whose donations are essential to survival in elective office.

SEE ALSO: Class and Crime; Corruption; Crime, Corporate; Crime, Political; Crime, Psychological Theories of; Crime, Social Learning Theory of; Law, Economy and; Sutherland, Edwin H.

REFERENCES AND SUGGESTED READINGS

Calavita, K., Pontell, H. N., & Tillman, R. (1997) *The Money Game: Fraud and Politics in the Savings and Loan Crisis.* University of California Press, Berkeley.

Friedrichs, D. O. (2004) *Trusted Criminals: White Collar Crime in Contemporary Society,* 2nd edn. Thomson/Wadsworth, Belmont, CA.

Mann, K. (1985) *Defending White Collar Crime: A Portrait of Attorneys at Work.* Yale University Press, New Haven.

Rosoff, S. M., Pontell, H. N., & Tilliman, R. H. (2004) *Profit Without Honor: White-Collar Crime and the Looting of America,* 3rd edn. Pearson/Prentice-Hall, Upper Saddle River, NJ.

Schlegel, K. & Weisburd, D. (Eds.) (1992) *White Collar Crime Reconsidered.* Northeastern University Press, Boston.

Segal, L. G. (2004) *Battling Corruption in America's Public Schools.* Northeastern University Press, Boston.

Sutherland, E. H. (1983 [1949]) *White Collar Crime: The Uncut Version.* Yale University Press, New Haven.

Toombs, S. & Whyte, D. (Eds.) (2003) *Unmasking the Crimes of the Powerful: Scrutinizing States and Corporatons.* Peter Lang, New York.

Weisburd, D., Waring, E., & Chayet, E. F. (2001) *White-Collar Crime and Criminal Careers.* Cambridge University Press, New York.

Weisburd, D., Wheeler, S., Waring, E. J., & Bode, N. (1991) *Crimes of the Middle Classes.* Yale University Press, New Haven.

criminal justice system

Leigh Culver

The American criminal justice system is a network of government agencies and individuals whose purpose is to apprehend, prosecute, and punish criminal offenders, maintain societal order, prevent and control crime, and ensure public safety. Most criminal justice agencies and organizations that are responsible for these functions can be classified under three primary groups: law enforcement, courts, and corrections.

The term "system" implies that each group within the criminal justice network collaborates with one another to achieve a common goal. Although this is true in many respects, the criminal justice system resembles more of a loosely connected chain of individual entities that have separate and, at times, competing roles. For example, one of the responsibilities of law enforcement is to apprehend and arrest offenders, a function that operates on the crime control, or reduction of crime, model. Courts in the criminal justice system, however, operate under the due process model, which emphasizes fair application of the law and protection of individual rights. Individual entities within the system also frequently make significant decisions without consideration of how their decisions will impact the larger system. An aggressive driving while intoxicated law enforcement strategy, for example, can result in a high number of arrests. This decision can significantly affect the resources and case management capability at both the court and corrections stages of the system. Finally, the structure and organization of the criminal justice system vary widely among federal, state, county, and local jurisdictions. Acts which are classified as criminal violations in some jurisdictions may not be violations in others. A city prosecutor may endorse particular criminal justice policies that are not equally supported by the county prosecutor. In short, given the lack of coordination and consistency among individual entities, the criminal justice system is often referred to as a *non-system*.

A common thread woven throughout the criminal justice system is the use of discretion, or individual professional judgment, to guide decision-making. Not all persons who commit a crime can be arrested and processed through each stage of the criminal justice system. Therefore, criminal justice personnel in all levels routinely use discretion to make decisions on whether or how criminal offenders should proceed through the system. Law enforcement officers use discretion in deciding whether to issue a verbal warning or a ticket for a speeding violation. Prosecutors make discretionary decisions as to what cases to file with the court. The decision to release an inmate to parole is up to the discretion of the parole board members. While there is the potential for abuse (i.e., cases are disproportionately filed against a segment of the community, arbitrary application of the

law), the system relies on discretion to operate efficiently.

LAW ENFORCEMENT

Law enforcement serves several functions in the criminal justice system: preventing, detecting, and investigating crime, enforcing the law, protecting the public and property, apprehending and arresting offenders, and community service. Media images often depict law enforcement personnel as crime-fighters who are regularly involved in high-speed police pursuits, make large numbers of arrests, and routinely handle crisis situations. Contrary to these images, however, law enforcement officers spend most of their time gathering information for investigations and reports, maintaining order, establishing ties with community members, and providing services. Nationwide there are approximately 18,000 federal, state, county, and municipal law enforcement organizations. This estimate includes specialized law enforcement agencies such as university and college police, port authority police, and railroad police. In light of the increase in private security forces, many of which have some form of law enforcement powers, it is difficult to determine the exact number of organizations. Adding to the problem is the fact that there is little consistency among law enforcement agencies in terms of roles and responsibilities. Agencies can vary from one another according to mission, geographical area, community size, and community expectations. For example, a state highway patrol agency that focuses on enforcing motor vehicle laws plays a much different role in law enforcement than a sheriff's department that is responsible for the county jail and local court security.

Entry into the criminal justice system begins when law enforcement officers make an arrest for a crime. Law enforcement officers rarely observe crimes in progress. Reports from victims, witnesses, or other citizens, or information from an investigation, are the main sources of crime reporting. Therefore, law enforcement officers rely heavily on their relationship with the public to perform their job. Law enforcement officers cannot arrest all citizens for all criminal violations, so they routinely use discretion to decide the best outcome for each situation. This outcome may involve handling criminal violations informally (e.g., verbal warning) or exercising other options besides arrest (e.g., transporting a homeless person to a shelter rather than making an arrest for loitering). Given their authority to decide who enters the criminal justice system, law enforcement officers are often called *gatekeepers* of the system.

After a law enforcement officer makes an arrest the case is presented to the prosecutor, who decides to either file formal charges against the defendant or not file charges and release the defendant. This action marks the transition into the courts stage of the criminal justice system. Law enforcement officers may additionally be called upon to participate in this stage by gathering more evidence for the prosecution's case and/or testifying if the case goes to trial.

COURTS

Many of the most significant decisions in the criminal justice system are made in the criminal courts. After an offender is arrested, the courts assume the responsibility of bail issues and proceedings, preliminary hearings, arraignments, pre-trial motions, and plea bargains. At the same time, court personnel (prosecutors, defense attorneys, judges) make determinations as to whether a case proceeds through the criminal justice system, is removed from the system, or is referred to services outside of the system (e.g., treatment). Later phases in the court process establish the guilt or innocence of the accused, and the type of punishment, if any, a convicted offender should receive.

Courts in the United States operate under a *dual court system*, which encompasses both federal and state courts. Federal courts hear cases that fall within the federal government's authority such as counterfeiting, money laundering, mail fraud, and kidnapping. In addition to one federal court structure, each state operates its own court system which differs by organization, procedural steps, rules, and constitution. In general, most states have three levels of courts in their judicial system: lower courts, trial courts, and appellate courts.

At the lowest level are courts of limited jurisdiction or *lower courts*. These courts typically hear cases on minor or misdemeanor offenses such as trespassing, theft, assault, and violation of city codes. Some jurisdictions have specific courts for traffic violations, family and probate issues (divorce, wills, child support), and small-claims courts. Preliminary hearings for major civil suits and felony criminal cases may also be conducted in the lower courts. Cases generally move through the lower courts quickly and no detailed record of the proceedings is kept.

At the next highest level are the trial courts. Also called *courts of general jurisdiction*, criminal trial courts hear cases ranging from minor offenses to serious felonies. The purpose of the trial courts is to decide on matters of fact and evidence. Most courts of general jurisdiction also hear cases on appeal from the lower courts and have the authority to grant a *trial de novo*, or new trial. Under a trial de novo, the trial courts retry cases as if they have never been heard before. Although much of the media and public perception of what occurs in court proceedings is based on the trial court, most cases do not go to trial. Instead, the majority of cases are handled informally through bargaining between the primary court actors: the judge, prosecutor, and defense attorney.

The highest level of courts in each state is called the appellate court, supreme court, or *court of last resort*. Some states have intermediate courts of appeal which review cases to be sent to the state's supreme court. After a verdict has been reached in a trial court, either the defense or prosecution can appeal the case to the appellate courts. Unlike trial courts, however, appellate courts do not decide on facts and evidence. Rather, they review the written transcript from the trial courts to ensure the proceedings were fair and carried out in compliance with the state law. The highest federal appellate court is the US Supreme Court. Comprised of eight justices and a chief justice, the US Supreme Court hears a select number of cases on matters related to the federal statutes and the US Constitution.

Courts are also responsible for sentencing convicted offenders. Sentences can come in many forms including imprisonment, fines, restitution, community service, probation, and, in some cases, death. Several factors are taken into account in the sentencing phase. The pre-sentence report (investigation conducted on an offender's background to aid in sentencing decisions), for example, may reveal both miti-gating and aggravating circumstances which impact the severity of punishment. Mitigating circumstances, or factors that may help reduce the offender's degree of blame, can include a defendant's admission of guilt for the crime, a defendant's strong employment record, volun-teer service to the community, and the will-ingness to compensate a victim. On the other hand, aggravating circumstances, or factors that increase the offender's blameworthiness, are generally a previous criminal record, use of a weapon to commit the crime, cruelty to the victim, heinousness of the crime, and lack of remorse. Many states have some form of struc-tured sentencing, mandatory minimum senten-cing laws, or sentencing guidelines in which the judges' discretion on how to sentence an offender varies. Sentences, like convictions, can be appealed to a higher court; most death sen-tences undergo an automatic review by the appellate courts.

Like many areas of the criminal justice system, the courts are overburdened. Conse-quently, given the high volume of cases pre-sented to the system, courts are often unable to process cases in a timely manner. Suggestions to minimize the clogged courts consist of hiring more court administrators and personnel, sche-duling night courts, alternative courts for spe-cific offenses (i.e., gun courts, drug courts), and court-ordered mediation, a form of alternative dispute resolution.

CORRECTIONS

The corrections component of the criminal jus-tice system is responsible for managing both defendants in pre-trial detention and convicted offenders who have been sentenced by the courts. This includes maintaining secure facil-ities such as jails and prisons, as well as non-institutional community-based corrections such as probation and intermediate sanctions. Finally, corrections personnel monitor inmates who are released from prisons out onto parole.

Incarceration

Jails and prisons are the most common forms of incarceration in the United States. They are predominantly used for detaining offenders temporarily before trial and for housing inmates convicted of serious crimes who present too great a risk to be placed on probation. Although both jails and prisons house offenders, they differ in several respects. Jails are operated locally by municipal or county governments, and lodge inmates who have received short-term sentences, generally a year or less, for misdemeanor offenses. Jails also serve as tem-porary holding facilities for inmates awaiting bond, trial, or transfer to prison. Community-based corrections including day reporting and electronic monitoring may also operate from jail facilities. Prisons, on the other hand, are oper-ated by state or federal governments and house inmates convicted of felonies. Offenders can serve prison sentences ranging from longer than a year to life. Depending on the seriousness of the offense and risk to public safety, prisoners will be sent to facilities ranging in security levels from minimum, medium, to maximum.

While the organization and structure of jail and prison systems vary among federal, state, and local levels, all share the problem of inmate overcrowding. Prison overcrowding can result in ineffective prison management, behavioral problems among inmates, limited resources, and a reduction in rehabilitative pro-gram opportunities. Constructing more pris-ons, releasing inmates early, diverting less serious cases to intensive supervision probation, and contracting with privately owned prisons have been suggested to alleviate overcrowding. In addition to the problems associated with overcrowding, there are other concerns about special populations housed within correctional facilities. Inmates with sexually transmitted diseases and HIV/AIDS, female prisoners, mentally ill, inmates with substance abuse issues, and the growing elderly population all create unique challenges to an already over-loaded correctional system.

Probation

Most offenders convicted of less serious crimes are sentenced to some form of probation, which is the supervised conditional release of offenders into the community. Under probation, offenders must follow specific court-ordered regulations or conditions which can require them to complete a substance abuse treatment program, obey curfews, meet regularly with a probation officer, and not associate with particular people (e.g., convicted felons). Probation can be revoked if an offender violates any conditions specified by the courts, is arrested, or convicted of a new crime. This means that, depending on the violation, offenders may be subject to further restrictive probation conditions, or possibly incarceration, for the completion of their sentence. Probation as a form of community-based corrections is a viable alternative to correctional confinement in jails and prisons. It emphasizes keeping offenders in their communities and with their families, without experiencing the emotional and physical costs of incarceration.

Intermediate sanctions, which extend beyond simple probation, can be ordered for more serious offenders and can consist of intensive supervision (strictly supervised probation), day reporting centers, home confinement, and electronic monitoring. Community service, boot camps, fines, and restitution are also commonly used intermediate sanctions.

Parole

The supervised early release of an inmate from incarceration is called parole. Most states have parole boards that hold discretionary power to grant parole to offenders who have not served their entire prison sentence. In some jurisdictions, parole boards also have the authority to define conditions of release and revoke parole if appropriate. Factors for consideration in granting parole may consist of an inmate's good behavior/disciplinary problems while incarcerated, seriousness of current offense, prior offenses, and acceptance of responsibility for actions.

Parole functions, in part, to transition inmates from an institutional environment back into society. Therefore, conditions of release may consist of working with a parole officer to find housing, enrolling in treatment centers, securing stable employment, and pursuing

educational opportunities. Offenders who violate the conditions of release may have their parole revoked and be returned to prison to serve the remainder of their sentence.

JUVENILE JUSTICE

Entry into the criminal justice system for both adult and juvenile offenders in many respects is very similar. An adult arrest or juvenile detainment initiates the system's attention. Once in the system, however, juveniles are handled distinctly differently from adults. Unlike the punitive (punishment) approach in the adult system, the attitude toward youth in the juvenile justice system is rehabilitation (treatment).

The primary concern in the juvenile justice system is the well-being of a child. Juvenile courts operate under the philosophy of *parens patriae*, which gives the state the power to exercise authority as a parent on the behalf of a child who may need protection. Further, in a juvenile court proceeding, judges consider both legal (e.g., seriousness of offense) and extralegal factors such as the situation of a child's home life, school performance, potential mental health, and/or substance abuse issues in deciding the outcome of a case. Another contrast to the adult system is the prosecution of juveniles for *status offenses*, acts that are considered law violations only when committed by minors (juveniles). For example, truancy, curfew violations, running away from home, and disobeying parents are status offenses. Juvenile courts also hear cases on other matters specifically related to juveniles, such as neglect and abuse, adoption, and parental rights of children who are in the custody of the state.

A final distinction between the adult and juvenile system is the informal handling of most juvenile cases before reaching a formal adjudication (trial) hearing. At the intake or screening process in the juvenile courts, intake officers frequently refer youth to social service agencies or impose restitution, fines, or community service rather than move their cases to the court phase. Diversion, the redirection of juveniles from the court system to treatment and community services, is often implemented at this stage. The goal of diversion is to keep youths from entering juvenile court yet ensure that they remain accountable for their actions. Generally used for first-time offenders who have committed minor offenses, diversion programs utilize a variety of options tailored for individual youth. Substance abuse treatment, counseling, restitution, letters of apology, community service, life skill development classes, and school attendance requirements are popular diversion program requirements.

Juveniles who receive a disposition (sentence) by the court may be required to live in non-secure facilities such as foster homes, group homes, and halfway houses, or be sent to secure facilities such as reform or training schools. Juvenile offenders can also be assigned to community-based corrections such as in-home placement with intensive supervision, residential treatment programs, and probation.

SEE ALSO: Corrections; Courts; Crime; Juvenile Delinquency; Law, Criminal; Police; Prisons

REFERENCES AND SUGGESTED READINGS

Champion, D. J. (2003) *The Juvenile Justice System: Delinquency, Processing, and the Law*, 4th edn. Prentice-Hall, Upper Saddle River, NJ.

Cole, G. F. & Smith, C. E. (2004) *The American System of Criminal Justice*, 10th edn. Wadsworth, Belmont, CA.

Cromwell, P. F., Alarid, L. F., & del Carmen, R. V. (2004) *Community-Based Corrections*, 6th edn. Wadsworth, Belmont, CA.

Hunter, R. D., Barker, T., & Mayhall, P. D. (2004) *Police–Community Relations and the Administration of Justice*, 6th edn. Prentice-Hall, Upper Saddle River, NJ.

Neubauer, D. W. (2005) *America's Courts and the Criminal Justice System*, 8th edn. Wadsworth, Belmont, CA.

Schmalleger, F. (2005) *Criminal Justice Today: An Introductory Text for the 21st Century*, 8th edn. Prentice-Hall, Upper Saddle River, NJ.

Senna, J. J. & Siegel, L. J. (2002) *Introduction to Criminal Justice*, 9th edn. Wadsworth, Belmont, CA.

Seiter, R. P. (2005) *Corrections: An Introduction*. Prentice-Hall, Upper Saddle River, NJ.

Smith, C. E. (2003) *Courts and Trials: A Reference Handbook*. ABC-CLIO, Santa Barbara, CA.

Walker, S. & Katz, C. (2005) *The Police in America: An Introduction*, 5th edn. McGraw-Hill, New York.

Whitehead, J. T & Lab, S. P. (2003) *Juvenile Justice: An Introduction*, 4th edn. Anderson, Ohio.

criminology

Stephen E. Brown

Criminology is the study of crime and related phenomena. A common starting point in defining criminology is to cite Edwin Sutherland's (1883–1950) tripartite definition of it as an examination of the process of creating laws, violation of laws, and reacting to those violations. While this is a relatively broad definition, it is not all encompassing. Moreover, while Sutherland's status in the field of criminology was enormous, his definition of the bounds of criminology intentionally excluded a litany of perspectives. This controversy over the parameters of criminology has always plagued the discipline. To appreciate the challenge of defining criminology to the satisfaction of a highly diverse population of scholars of crime and related phenomena, it is essential to identify a multitude of issues that divide criminologists into various camps.

At the heart of divisiveness regarding the parameters of criminology lies ideological conflict. It is ideological identities that have created a vast range of criminological perspectives and even staunch disagreement regarding definition of the term itself. Ideology strongly influences definitions of crime, the subject matter of criminological scrutiny. Disagreement over the definition of crime is a reflection of its relativity, also deeply rooted in ideological predispositions. What the law criminalizes at any given location in time and space is a product of prevailing ideologies. Moreover, the question of whether or not criminology should seek to explain behaviors that are not criminalized at a given time and place has been debated. Thus, defining criminology is deeply embedded in the polemical concepts of ideology and the relativity of crime. Defining criminology devoid of an appreciation of these concepts inevitably excludes some criminological perspectives, while inherently favoring others. Therefore, objectively defining criminology to incorporate its full breadth requires acknowledgment of the ideological differences that underlie distinct paradigms.

The study of crime and related matters has not always been dubbed criminology. Likewise, definitions of both crime and criminology have evolved, and sometimes been revolutionized, across time and space. Aristotle and Plato were debating the essence of justice long before any specific scholarly identity, criminology or otherwise, emerged for assessing obligations of humans to conform to the needs or desires of others. Much later, Enlightenment philosophers such as Voltaire, Montesquieu, and Rousseau were planting the ideological seeds of what came to be classical criminology. The so-called classical school of criminology that is extended much attention in most basic criminology texts was actually a vast, ideologically driven humanitarian reform movement. Paradigmatic differences in the field notwithstanding, this movement is widely considered to be the beginning of modern-day criminology.

A broad understanding of criminology necessitates a historical perspective to identify the social contexts of paradigm shifts and the penchant for history to repeat itself. Classical criminology, for example, was a political/ideological reaction to the cruel and arbitrary social controls in place during the European Holy Inquisition. Thus the movement focused not on the criminal, but rather on the reaction of the state and church to various behaviors construed as criminal.

The philosophical rationale, developed by philosopher-reformers such as Cesare Beccaria and Jeremy Bentham, was that behaviors could be controlled via appropriate state reactions to rational, free-willed, and hedonistic human beings. Given those underlying assumptions regarding human nature, it was argued that behaviors stand to be deterred by punishments characterized by sufficient certainty, severity, and celerity. Consequently, the classical school of criminology led to reforms in the late eighteenth century that provided the framework for modern criminal justice systems. These classical ideas reemerged in the rational choice paradigm that evolved in the closing decades of the twentieth century, although emanating from a different social context, and remain popular today.

Positivists were the first to actually use the label of criminology to denote the scholarly study of crime. Cesare Lombroso, in fact, is often called the "father of criminology," based on the impact of *The Criminal Man*, published in 1876. While he viewed himself as a criminal anthropologist, followers such as Raffaele Garofalo were among the first to call it the field of criminology. The intellectual shift from classicism to positivism represented a marked schism in the conceptualization of the crime problem, moving away from the search for appropriate punishments to deter potential offenders to a search for the origins of defects in criminals. The new paradigm redefined the field by focusing on the presumably defective criminal rather than the formal social controls thought necessary to regulate the behavior of naturally hedonistic people. Given that the new positivistic paradigm dominated scholarly examination of lawbreaking for roughly the next century, it is understandable how the prevailing definitions of criminology incorporated a distinct positivistic bias that carries over to a degree even today.

At the heart of positive criminology are two central theses, both antithetical to classical conceptions of crime. First is the assumption that criminal behavior is determined by forces not under the control of the offender. These deterministic forces or causes of criminal behavior were initially considered to be biological in origin, but later came to include psychological factors and finally were dominated by social factors for most of the twentieth century within the United States. The second essential component of positive criminology insists that criminals be studied by application of the scientific method. Empiricism supplanted the philosophical reasoning of the classicists. As positivism came to dominate twentieth-century criminology, the archetypical definition of the field gravitated toward "the scientific study of the causes of crime." Definitions along these lines continue to be the modal depiction of criminology, as is evident in a review of both lay dictionaries and basic criminology textbooks. While such a positivistic-biased explication includes a broad array of biological, psychological, and social forces impinging upon offenders, they clearly exclude both classical criminology and perhaps much of its contemporary counterpart in the form of a rational choice paradigm.

Also at odds with the typical definition of criminology as the scientific study of the causes of crime are numerous paradigms or perspectives that have emerged more recently. Labeling theory, for example, rooted in the works of symbolic interactionists such as George Herbert Mead and Charles Horton Cooley, came to the American criminological forefront in the 1960s and 1970s. This perspective incorporated the relativity of criminal law, asserting that there are ultimately no forms of conduct that are inherently deviant. Instead, deviant status is a function of the reactions of others to particular behaviors. Therefore, this perspective shifted focus away from both crime (the classical interest) and criminals (the positivistic concern) in favor of scrutinizing social reactions to persons or their behaviors. The essence of this perspective is that the relative reactions of others play a more significant role in shaping the self than do either positive forces or rational decision-making. Consequently, the importance of studying prior influences on the offender or the dynamics of their choices is overshadowed by the need to examine the contribution of social reactions to their behavior. The centrality of social reactions takes two relatively distinct forms. First, hostile reactions to initial behavior may trap the offender in a downward social spiral of lowered self-image, isolation from conforming others, increased associations with similarly labeled persons and production of a deviant identity, ultimately committing the actor to a career of secondary deviance. Secondly, an individual's deviant status may be literally created by affixing the deviant label to behaviors heretofore not categorized as deviant. In the latter case, the behavior is deviant only because reaction to it has changed.

Social reaction theories such as labeling are ideologically distinct from both classicism and positivism. Social reaction theories do not presume, as do classicism and positivism, that the laws enacted by the state serve the interests of all, but rather see any given set of laws as the outcome of conflict among competing groups. Therefore, they allow that the problem may not be so much in law violation as in the creation and enforcement of the law, thus shifting focus from crime and criminals to the social reactions of others. Labeling theory, in fact, depicts the law and criminal justice system as doing more harm than good. In sum, a third major paradigm requires a definition of criminology that

concentrates on matters neglected by the earlier dominant perspectives.

Critical criminology similarly rejects the assumption that there is agreement on the law, but many variations of critical thought also strongly critique the empirical methods of positivists. Marxism in particular, and many conflict theorists in general, are unreceptive to or skeptical of the scientific method as a path to accumulate knowledge. Many conflict theorists fault the scientific pursuit of value-free knowledge as impossible and see science itself as biased in favor of the elite. Marxism proper calls for historical eclecticism as a means of analyzing the dominance of the bourgeoisie over the masses. Similarly, some variations of radical feminism envision empiricism as a male tool for interpreting and constructing the world to reflect the interest of males.

Postmodern thinking has also made its way into the bounds of criminology, rejecting the premise that rationalism and/or empiricism are essential to the accumulation of truth or knowledge. At the center of postmodernism is a rejection of the notion that truth itself can be objectively pursued, or that there even is any singular truth. Instead it is believed that many truths may exist simultaneously and that no one version of truth or method of arriving at that knowledge should be considered superior. Postmodernists view all "experts" with a suspicious eye, believing that their claims to special expertise extend them special privilege in the pursuit of knowledge and invalidate the experiences of those lacking that expertise. Thus the empirical skills of the social scientist or the legal knowledge of the lawyer, for example, are not viewed as providing more valid insight into crime than the experiences of anyone else. Of particular concern to postmodernists is the control that specialists or experts gain over the language of a given realm. Relating to the definition of criminology, the postmodern critique would be that the rational and scientific jargon of the trained criminologist excludes the experiences of many victims, offenders, community residents, and others from contributing to our understanding of crime and related phenomena. The solution is to engage in a discourse analysis that gives equal weight to all persons' stories about crime, whatever mode of expression they choose for communicating. However, since experts have so dominated the accumulation of criminological knowledge, deconstruction of existing knowledge is advocated to return the pursuit of truth to a fair playing field. More conventional criminologists, of course, regard this as nihilistic.

Emergence of criminology as peacemaking over the last two decades is another branch of critical criminology that summons a far broader definition of criminology. Leaders on this front such as Richard Quinney and Harold Pepinsky have been frustrated by the level of dividends yielded by more conventional approaches to understanding crime. Their call is for a humanistic approach, with a faith that only compassion can ultimately relieve the suffering associated with crime. Peacemaking, then, also is a splinter group from within the criminological community that has grown skeptical of the traditional methods for studying crime and related phenomena.

Disagreement also thrives regarding the pragmatic role of criminology. While there is wide agreement that criminology should generate knowledge about crime and criminals, there is less accord regarding the purpose of pursuing that knowledge. Some argue that the primary purpose of accruing explanatory power lies in the application of that knowledge to alleviate the problems associated with crime and criminals. Others believe that we should pursue knowledge for its own sake rather than for practical value. Perhaps most criminologists take a middle road, seeing knowledge as worthwhile for a variety of reasons, including the enhancement of understanding ourselves, our larger social world, and deviance. Most probably see a variety of ways for criminology to contribute to improvement of the human condition, but do not limit the pragmatic value of criminology to the control of those designated as deviants.

That diversity characterizes the field of criminology should be quite evident.

Besides conflict over ideological differences, criminologists are often divided along lines of "parent disciplines." Edwin Sutherland, for example, was quite successful in bringing sociology to dominance in the mid-twentieth century. Many of those who identify with a psychological perspective still feel alienated from the larger criminological community, as often evidenced by their commentaries in introducing psychologically informed criminology texts. Similarly, biologically rooted criminology suffered from a long period of intellectual ostracism as a consequence of ideological clashes in the mid-twentieth century. Finally, a lack of agreement regarding the practical implications of the field separates criminologists. At one extreme are the staunch conservatives who see criminology as a storehouse of information for control of defective persons or decisions. These criminologists feel comfortable pursuing a range of typically unpleasant control measures to impose on people. At the other extreme, advocating praxis, are criminologists who focus on advocacy of policies that would enhance the playing field for persons whose existence is more likely to be labeled deviant by the state. In short, these criminologists feel comfortable arguing that the world should be transformed into a more just place for the existence of those who are designated criminal.

With such a lack of consensus among professional criminologists, the question is how we can define criminology in an inclusive manner. If we fail to do so, we are at risk of excluding from its bounds the contributions of a portion of serious scholars who devote their careers to pursuit of knowledge about crime and related phenomena. On the other hand, an overly broad definition of criminology risks diluting the subject matter and methods of its study to a level that obfuscates the knowledge that the field ought to produce. With such a cautious balance in mind, it might be proposed that criminology is the study of crime, criminals, and related phenomena within the context of their cultural environment, seeking to contribute to a body of explanatory theory through application of a range of scholarly perspectives and methods of analysis.

This definition is considerably more detailed than those typically offered, as it seeks to find a place for most of the paradigms and perspectives reviewed above. It incorporates scrutiny of both crime and criminals, as well as related phenomena. Examples of the related phenomena would include criminological focus on victims, police, or correctional settings as primary forces in the criminal environment. Including the cultural environment allows for consideration of criminogenic factors such as gender, race, or social stratification. This expanded definition also allows incorporation of ideologically opposed perspectives and diverse methods of study that lie at the heart of criminological diversity. What remains essential in delineating the bounds of criminology, however, is a body of theory derived from a scholarly approach to understanding crime, criminals, and related phenomena. Omitted from criminology owing to a lack of such explanatory theory would be bodies of knowledge or skills related solely to the processing of crime or criminals such as the practice of law, crime investigation, evidence examination, counseling of offenders, and the like. Similarly excluded as atheoretical would be the investigative efforts of reporters to describe crime and the activist efforts of social reformers insofar as those efforts are distinct from the development of theoretical explanations of crime-related phenomena. While these non-theoretical endeavors may inform or be informed by criminology, they are not oriented toward the essential goal of scholarly development of a body of theory to explain crime, criminals, and related phenomena.

Although the practice of criminal justice does not fall within the domain of criminology, the scholarly examination of criminal justice is closely related. Arguably, the development that has most impacted evolution of the parameters of criminology over the past three decades or so has been the emergence of criminal justice as a scholarly discipline. Even Sutherland's widely cited but more narrow mid-twentieth-century definition of criminology included what later emerged as the academic discipline of criminal justice by virtue of his reference to reactions to law violation. With the proliferation of doctoral studies in criminology and criminal justice in recent decades, the distinction between the two has grown even more narrow. Increasingly, American doctoral-level studies of crime and criminals have shifted from sociological emphases to criminal justice, criminology, or some combination of the two. Consequently the training of criminologists has come to draw less distinction between criminology and criminal justice. In the context of the proposed broad definition of criminology, it is a matter of emphases, with one sector focusing on the criminal, while the other (criminal justice scholarship) tends to concentrate on crime or

related phenomena such as the roles of law enforcement and corrections in crime and criminality. A considerable portion of criminal justice study, however, primarily below the doctoral level, continues to fall outside the bounds of criminology by focusing on knowledge and skills relevant only to the processing of the accused and not on a body of theory to further understanding of crime and related phenomena.

Essential to conceptualizing criminology is balancing the need to include study of crime from a full range of ideological perspectives, while demanding rudimentary scholarly criteria. The former is necessary to capture the dynamic and relative nature of crime, while the latter is necessary for criminology to offer insight that can withstand critical scrutiny. Criminological perspectives have changed dramatically across time and will undoubtedly continue to do so. A vibrant criminology will continue to contribute to our understanding of the most critical cornerstone of all cultures, the control of fellow beings.

SEE ALSO: Beccaria, Cesare; Crime; Crime, Radical/Marxist Theories of; Criminology: Research Methods; Deviance, Positivist Theories of; Feminist Criminology; Labeling; Labeling Theory; Lombroso, Cesare; Peacemaking; Postmodernism; Rational Choice Theory: A Crime-Related Perspective; Sutherland, Edwin H.

REFERENCES AND SUGGESTED READINGS

Beccaria, C. (1963 [1764]) *On Crimes and Punishments*. Trans. H. Paolucci. Bobbs-Merrill, Indianapolis.
Becker, H. S. (1963) *Outsiders: Studies in the Sociology of Deviance*. Free Press, New York.
Hirschi, T. (1969) *Causes of Delinquency*. University of California Press, Berkeley.
Lombroso-Ferrero, G. (1972 [1911]) *The Criminal Man*. Patterson Smith, Patterson, NJ.
Merton, R. K. (1938) Social Structure and Anomie. *American Sociological Review* 3: 672–82.
Quinney, R. (1970) *The Social Reality of Crime*. Little, Brown, Boston.
Sutherland, E. H., Cressey, D. R., & Luckenbill, D. F. (1992) *Principles of Criminology*, 11th edn. General Hall, Dix Hills, NY.

criminology: research methods

John Wooldredge

Research methods are procedures for obtaining information on individual and/or aggregate phenomena for the purpose of (1) creating a general explanation or *theory* to explain a phenomenon; (2) testing the applicability of an existing theory to a subgroup of the population; or (3) testing the effectiveness of an existing social policy or program. Topics (1) and (2) are critical to the dialectic of scholarly knowledge in criminology and criminal justice. Somewhat unique to the field of criminal justice, however, is a heavier emphasis on (3) as a product of research. The phenomena of primary interest to criminologists include juvenile delinquency, adult criminality, and victimization, at both the individual and aggregate levels. The interests of criminal justice researchers appear more eclectic, only a few of which include police practices and effectiveness, the dynamics of criminal case processing, sentencing discrimination, inmate violence, and correctional program effectiveness.

The methods employed in criminological and criminal justice research are identical to those in the behavioral and social sciences in general. A critical assumption underlying the use of these procedures involves the belief in an objective reality, or a world that different people perceive in similar fashion. Related to this assumption is that such a reality can be studied objectively. The perspective that individual and social processes can be studied dispassionately or scientifically is referred to as positivism.

Not all criminologists share the positivist perspective. For example, any effort to derive a social psychological theory of criminality relies on the idea that social processes operate uniformly across most (if not all) individuals. One might argue, however, that such uniformity does not exist, due to individual differences in perceptions of these processes. Ethnomethodology involves the perspective that all "realities" are socially constructed. From this perspective, individuals perceive their world in terms of how it makes sense to

them, thus introducing different perceptions of reality that may not be reconcilable.

The pieces of information that are gathered and examined during the course of research are referred to as data, which may be either qualitative or quantitative in form. Both forms of information may be gathered through observations of the phenomena under study, and quantitative information may also be compiled through survey research or a review of archival data. Qualitative observations are recorded by researchers as verbal statements that describe particular processes and outcomes, whereas quantitative observations consist of pieces of information recorded in numerical form. Both qualitative and quantitative methods are useful for theory development and testing, although a heavier emphasis in criminology and criminal justice appears to be placed on qualitative research for theory development versus quantitative research for theory/hypothesis testing and program evaluation. Many investigators use both approaches in a single study, however, because findings from each serve as a check on the other.

Ethnography is used to refer to a qualitative study of a social group or (sub)culture in which a researcher compiles a detailed description of processes and outcomes related to the phenomenon of interest. An example of ethnography would be a study of prison inmate social systems and adaptation to incarceration in a particular prison (such as the classic studies conducted by Clemmer, Sykes, Carroll, Jacobs, and Irwin). A penologist might make observations about the types of inmates that exist in that prison and how they interact with each other in order to understand, for example, why some inmates adapt to incarceration more easily than others. This information could then be used to create a general theory of inmate behavior that extends beyond the specific prison to all similar inmate populations. Critical to the success of such an endeavor is the researcher's objectivity in making and recording his or her observations regarding inmate behaviors.

In contrast to qualitative research, a quantitative study involves gathering information and attaching numerical values to each piece. Some types of information already have numbers attached to them (e.g., a person's age in years), whereas other types are assigned numerical values by the researcher (e.g., the sex of an individual, where every male in a sample is coded as "0" and every female in the sample is coded as "1"). When a researcher attaches his or her own numerical values, these values are determined by the researcher and must be defined for someone who is trying to understand the study. These scales or variables are then analyzed with statistics in order to make sense of the information for subsequent interpretation. Statistics, therefore, are also pieces of information, the difference being that the statistical information is a more general summary of the information gathered by a researcher. Numbers are assigned to pieces of information only when a researcher intends to apply statistics in order to produce new information that cannot be obtained through verbiage.

Unlike qualitative research, where a researcher remains "open" to new information, the types of information gathered from a quantitative study are determined before data collection begins. This is one reason why quantitative research is used primarily for theory/hypothesis testing, because such research involves collecting information that has already been described in a specifically worded hypothesis derived from a testable theory. Quantitative research can be used for theory development when the theory of interest focuses on the causal order of events and behaviors rather than the substance of those events/behaviors. Even then, however, the application is usually limited to reducing the number of possible orders rather than pinpointing the exact causal model.

More steps are typically involved in quantitative research designed to test a theory/hypothesis compared to qualitative exploratory research for the purpose of theory construction. The research design of such a quantitative study always falls into one of three broad types: experimental, quasi-experimental, and non-experimental or correlational. These groupings reflect differences in methodological rigor, or the ability of a study to establish the causal order of events (which is relatively rare in criminological and criminal justice research). The specific steps involved in this application of quantitative research include the following:

1   Begin with a theoretical model (paradigm) of interest, which, in criminology, often involves a general perspective of a social, political, and/or economic process. For example, a "conflict paradigm" involves the perspective that many social problems such as discrimination, poverty, environmental pollution, and crime in a capitalist society are consequences of economic (and thus power) "conflicts" between groups.

2   The theoretical paradigm selected at step 1 is applied to a particular aspect of society. For example, a conflict criminologist is only concerned with the part of the conflict perspective that explains crime in a capitalist society.

3   Theories involve theoretical, or abstract, concepts (e.g., "economic power" and "crime"). In order to test a theory, one must be able to transform the theoretical concepts into operational definitions that are directly observable and measurable (e.g., "economic power" may be operationalized as gross annual household income). These definitions are then placed into a hypothesis, or a proposition that describes the predicted (hypothesized) relationship between the variables (e.g., persons with lower household incomes are more likely to be arrested). Any test of a theory actually involves a test of a specific hypothesis stemming from a general theory, and so the specific nature of any hypothesis means that a theory can never be tested directly. It is always possible that the measures tested do not accurately reflect the "true" theoretical concept. This is why such measures are constantly being refined.

4   A researcher then plans the data collection that is required for the hypothesis test(s), involving the determination/selection of the (a) target population, or the population to which the results will be generalized, (b) units of analysis reflected in each hypothesis (individuals, organizations, cities, counties, etc.), (c) time dimension to be reflected in the data (e.g., one point in time versus two or more points in time), (d) research design (based on the hypothesis and the level of rigor desired, such as matched pairs, factorial, pretest-posttest, time series, etc.), (e) sample that represents the target

population (using one of a number of probability sampling techniques such as simple random sampling, systematic random sampling, sampling proportionate to size, etc.), (f) data collection instrument for compiling and coding the information (such as with a survey questionnaire), and (g) procedures for gathering information (telephone, mail, face-to-face, reviewing archival data, etc.).

5 The data collection phase consists of completing/obtaining completed instruments for all cases in the sample.

6 With the data compiled, the information should be checked for accuracy during the recording procedures. Computers are used for the purpose of data cleaning.

7 The data are examined in order to test each research hypothesis. This step involves the computation of statistics that help to summarize large quantities of data in order to test the hypotheses of interest and to describe the empirical relationships involved. Like the data collected for a study, statistics are also pieces of information, although they are designed to help make sense out of the data collected. It is up to the investigators, however, to apply and to interpret these statistics correctly in order to derive accurate conclusions regarding their data.

The use of quantitative methods for criminological and criminal justice research has steadily increased since the 1940s, due in part to the growing number of techniques, the availability of technology which facilitates data collection and analysis, and the proliferation of graduate programs and methods courses in the field. Ethnography remains a more powerful tool for theory construction, however, and many scholars place a high priority on combining the qualitative and quantitative.

The growing popularity of quantitative research has been met with resistance on the part of some qualitative researchers. Some individuals believe that the inability to numerically measure and evaluate many of the key concepts and processes that are critical to the field will produce misleading information regarding the validity of these ideas. When faced with having to operationalize highly abstract theoretical concepts, researchers can only measure observable proxies for the concepts of interest.

These proxies may not capture the full essence of the original idea, as when researchers use structural attributes such as the poverty rate or the unemployment rate to proxy the more complex process of structurally induced strain. This problem is exaggerated when a researcher does not fully understand the theoretical concepts and/or the procedures and limitations of complicated statistical techniques used in order to examine the data. The current state of graduate education in criminology and criminal justice programs contributes further to concerns over knowledge destruction, since these programs are often void of courses in theory construction and offer a very limited number of courses in research methodologies.

Some of the more common problems in extant criminological research include a lack of objectivity in theory construction (e.g., "convict criminology"), model misspecification (often due to poor conceptualization of the relevant theories), poor operationalization of concepts (e.g., unidimensional measures of multidimensional concepts such as low self-control or social capital), inappropriate units of analysis (e.g., testing neighborhood level theories with county or state level data), inappropriate samples for the target populations (e.g., testing routine activities theory with college freshmen enrolled in a criminology class), and misapplications of statistical techniques (such as meta-analyses of quasi- and non-experimental findings, multi-level analyses with insufficient samples, and over-corrections for spatially correlated error).

SEE ALSO: Criminal Justice System; Criminology; Ethnography; Measuring Crime; Positivism

REFERENCES AND SUGGESTED READINGS

Blalock, H., Jr. (1969) *Theory Construction: From Verbal to Mathematical Formulations.* Prentice-Hall, Englewood Cliffs, NJ.

Campbell, D. & Stanley, J. (1963) *Experimental and Quasi-Experimental Designs for Research.* Rand McNally, Chicago.

Farrington, D. P. (1983) Randomized Experiments in Crime and Justice. In: Tonry, M. & Morris, N. (Eds.), *Crime and Justice: An Annual Review of*

Research, Vol. 4. University of Chicago Press, Chicago, pp. 257–308.

Lofland, J. (1984) *Analyzing Social Settings*. Wadsworth, Belmont, CA.

Luckman, T. (Ed.) (1978) *Phenomenology and Sociology*. Penguin, New York.

Moser, C. A. & Kalton, G. (1972) *Survey Methods in Social Investigation*, 2nd edn. Basic Books, New York.

Popper, K. R. (1959) *The Logic of Scientific Discovery*. Basic Books, New York.

critical pedagogy

Rachel A. Dowty

Critical pedagogy challenges both students and teachers to channel their experiences of oppression into educating and empowering marginalized peoples. Critical pedagogues approach education as a process of social, cultural, political, and individual transformation, where social equity can be nourished or social inequity perpetuated. According to critical pedagogues, notions defining rational classification of people into categories that diminish their social affect and importance keep them oppressed. Oppressed peoples thus require not only awareness of inequities they suffer but also an understanding of ways that oppressive social mechanisms and beliefs endure, and of resistance strategies. Reflection on one's own experiences of oppression and the feelings of frustration, shame, guilt, and rage that accompany those experiences help shape practices of critical pedagogy. Critical pedagogues redirect these feelings that can incite violent acts, submission, and/or ongoing repression into dynamic dialogue that defines literacy in terms of participatory citizenship.

Methods of critical pedagogy are as diverse as the people who practice them. However, some common elements and general themes include reworking roles of student and teacher, questioning economic categories of worth and success, and ongoing engagement with the social, cultural, and political interactions that perpetuate disenfranchised and marginalized identities. In a traditional educational environment, students listen to a lecturing teacher, who controls the flow of questions and answers. Part of the traditional student–teacher relationship is that students consume decontextualized knowledge produced by the teacher (and those who dictate what the teacher teaches). This arrangement, according to critical approaches to pedagogy, disenfranchises people by removing their control over experiential reflection, and by neglecting to address emotionally charged daily experiences through which cultural symbols gain greater meaning.

Critical pedagogy incites critique of social values based on economic measures of worth and identity. When economic value defines products and peoples who can or cannot afford them, participation in community governance pits those who have against those who have not, and freedoms may only be afforded by people with enough money to buy them. Critical pedagogues teach people how to effectively participate in community governance (voting, legislating, finding alternative resources), thereby empowering people who are in no position to challenge oppressive economic systems and values based on economic leverage. Many scholars attribute the beginning of critical pedagogy to Karl Marx's writings on commodity fetishism and the social stratification that accompanies economic classification of people and resources, and to John Dewey's writings on educational theory and progressive schooling. More frequently, however, the beginnings of critical pedagogy are traced back to a school of thought, referred to as the Frankfurt School, that applied Marx's writings and critiques of capitalism to academic inquiries.

THE FRANKFURT SCHOOL

The Frankfurt School identifies a school of thought originating at the Institute for Social Research (Institut für Sozialforschung) established at Frankfurt University in 1923. As such, its members, many Jewish radicals and all various Marxist scholars, observed first hand the German fascists' rise to power. Austrian economist and historian Carl Grünberg became the first director of the Institute. Under Grünberg's charge, the Institute's research followed an orthodox Marxist avenue to investigate the economic structures of bourgeois society and problems with the European working-class movement. Institute staff during its first six years included economist Henryk Grossman, who worked on crisis theory, and Orientalist Karl Wittfogel, then an active member of the German Communist Party (KPD).

After Grünberg suffered a stroke, Max Horkheimer became director in 1930. With this change of directorship came changes in the Institute's general approaches to studying capitalism and socialism. In addition to Horkheimer, some notable Frankfurt School figures from this period include Erich Fromm (psychologist and philosopher), Theodor W. Adorno (philosopher, sociologist, and musicologist), Herbert Marcuse (philosopher), and Walter Benjamin (essayist and literary critic). Changes in the way Institute members approached capitalism and socialism included distancing academic study from activism while nurturing inquiry into how cultural systems, Marx's historical materialism, and Freud's psychoanalysis help explain dynamics of working-class political struggles. Later in the 1950s and 1960s, former Hitler Youth member Jürgen Habermas and others steered the Frankfurt School back toward left-wing student activist stances, which required ongoing intellectual disagreement amongst Institute members.

By this time the Russian Revolution had transformed Marxism as a subject of intellectual inquiry into the state ideology of Marxism-Leninism. This transformation, together with Adolf Hitler's accession to power in Germany in 1933, the abolition of the Austrian workers' movement in 1934, and Francisco Franco's seizure of power through the Spanish Civil War (1936–9), represented a decade of defeat for the ideals and freedom of inquiry sought by Institute members, who fled Germany in exile.

Because of these developments, the Institute began referring to its brand of Marxism as "critical theory," thereby distancing its work from overt ties to subversive ideals without abandoning them. In his 1937 paper "Philosophie und Kritische Theorie" (Traditional and Critical Theory), Horkheimer wrote: "The Marxist categories of class, exploitation, surplus value, profit, impoverishment, and collapse are moments of a conceptual whole whose meaning is to be sought, not in the reproduction of the present society, but in its transformation to a correct society." Themes developed by different Institute members in Horkheimer and Adorno's *Dialectic of Enlightenment* (1944) include the mass culture industry, Enlightenment philosophy, postpositivism, rationality, anti-Semitism, fascism, authoritarianism, and psychoanalysis. Later, critical pedagogues developed these ideas into educational approaches for steering social transformations toward using more equitable categories.

CRITICAL THEORY, PEDAGOGY, AND CONSCIOUSNESS

After Frankfurt School exiles developed critical theory as their brand of Marxism, Paulo Freire spread his brand of Marxism as a form of empowering education during his exile from Brazil. Brazilian voting laws in the 1950s and 1960s dictated that only functionally literate people were allowed to vote. Because sharecroppers and peasants were not given access to educational opportunities, these laws maintained a hegemonic power structure that kept the lower economic classes from having a voice in their governance. Freire spearheaded successful educational programs for these Brazilians, teaching them not only to read and write, but also how their constructive reflection and discussion of their experiences could sow literacy and participation in morally and ethically responsible community decision-making. After President Joao Belchior Goulart invited Freire to implement a literacy program that aimed to teach reading, writing, and political understanding to 5 million illiterate Brazilians in the first year, a coup d'état plunged Brazil into over 20 years of military rule under which Freire was arrested twice and spent two months in prison before beginning his 16 years in exile.

Freire traveled extensively during those 16 years, a time in the United States marked by student activism and challenging capitalistic values. He defined the term "praxis" as a continual and balanced process of reflection and action, emphasizing that action arises from critical perception of lived experiences that can challenge oppressive social arrangements, so long as reflection does not dominate action or vice versa. Praxis at both the individual and collective level involves coming to what Freire described as a "critical consciousness," engaging in an ongoing process ("conscientization") of theoretical application, evaluation, reflection, and further theorizing. Freire and many others who furthered the concepts of praxis and critical consciousness helped not only to develop critical pedagogy but also to pave the road to studies of postcolonialism and postmodernism.

The Civil Rights Movement in the United States at that time significantly fueled the development of critical pedagogy. Septima Poinsette Clark, who taught both children and illiterate adults in South Carolina and Tennessee (with Myles Horton at the Highlander Folk School), related problems these people faced in everyday life to English, math, and political concepts. She founded "citizenship schools" on these principles, and worked with judges and community groups to get equal pay for black and white schoolteachers. As a young black woman in the Southern, rural United States, bell hooks identified with the marginalized peasants she read about in Freire's work. Yet hooks challenged the language Freire used as one that marginalized women, and subsequently became a figure in the feminist movement, educating and writing on topics that encouraged people to use education as a means of practicing freedom.

Ivan Illich's *Deschooling Society* (1970) described this in terms of how traditional school systems make all students powerless and directly model capitalist social arrangements that critical pedagogies aim to transform. Paul Willis presents his notable ethnographic work on how schools ensure that working-class students get working-class jobs in his book *Learning to Labor* (1977). Ira Shor, another leading proponent of critical pedagogy, joined forces with Freire and emphasized that traditional capitalist definitions of literacy and education not only oppress lower social classes, but also perpetuate inequality through middle and upper social class strata as well. Because social transformation arises from praxis at the collective level, critical pedagogues maintain that education for critical consciousness must take place at all levels of society and among all categories of people to instigate necessary social change.

The democratic school and free school movement grew from these and many others' works. These schools focus on participatory democracy by allowing student-teachers and teacher-students the power to choose what they learn and teach, with minimal class or activity requirements. By so doing, participation in democratic school activities helps people question the mass culture industry that perpetuates inequalities. The mass culture industry commodifies education just like any other good or service, but critical pedagogues aim to spread informed dissidence that breaches the boundaries set by capitalist categories of people and of knowledge.

When corporations superficially adopt principles of critical pedagogy to sell products, they introduce elements of confusion to those new to the concepts of critical pedagogy. For example, "praxis" became the name of a standardized test used to evaluate teachers in training. A main goal of critical pedagogy challenges people to think and act against forces of commodification and the stratified categories that perpetuate social injustices. Such categories inherently define most, if not all, standardized tests, and place pressure on critical pedagogues to conform instead of transform.

Henry Giroux, another noted critical pedagogue, chose to leave the more culturally credentialed Penn State University, after 10 years, for McMaster University in Canada, because he observed increased alliances among corporate values and interests in the United States' university system. Giroux's move exemplifies problems faced by critical pedagogues. On one hand, they draw emotional and material support for their ideas and their communities from people raised according to capitalistic values. On the other hand, the principles they live and learn by inherently reject capitalistic values and ways they find support (such as commodification of educational services and concepts). Concepts drawn from social constructivism address these issues through exploration of how people "socially construct" their society, culture, and realities through enactment of recurring stratified interactions.

SEE ALSO: Civil Rights Movement; Commodities, Commodity Fetishism, and Commodification; Critical Theory/Frankfurt School;

Feminist Pedagogy; Foucault, Michel; Knowledge, Sociology of; Postmodernism; Praxis

REFERENCES AND SUGGESTED READINGS

Dewey, J. (1997 [1938]) *Experience and Education.* Simon & Schuster, New York.

Freire, P. (1994) *Pedagogy of Hope: Reliving Pedagogy of the Oppressed.* Continuum, New York.

Gatto, J. T. (2002) *A Different Kind of Teacher: Solving the Crisis of American Schooling.* Berkeley Hills Books, California.

Giroux, H. & Giroux, S. S. (2004) *Take Back Higher Education: Race, Youth, and the Crisis of Democracy in the Post-Civil Rights Era.* Palgrave Macmillan, New York.

Holt, J. (1970) *What Do I Do Monday?* Dell, New York.

Horkheimer, M. (1975) *Critical Theory: Selected Essays.* Continuum, New York.

Kohn, A. (1999) *The Schools Our Children Deserve.* Houghton Mifflin, Boston.

McLaren, P. (2002) *Life in Schools: An Introduction to Critical Pedagogy in the Foundations of Education.* Allyn & Bacon, Boston.

Morais, A., Neves, I., Davies, B., et al. (Eds.) (2001) *Toward a Sociology of Pedagogy: The Contribution of Basil Bernstein to Research.* Peter Lang, New York.

critical qualitative research

Gaile S. Cannella

In the first edition of *The Handbook of Qualitative Research* (Denzin & Lincoln 1994), Kincheloe and McLaren (1994) begin by describing research and theory that could be labeled criticalist. Such work assumes socially and historically embedded power relations, "facts" as ideologically inscripted, language as both constructing and limiting consciousness, oppressions as multiple and interconnected, and research as producing and reconstituting (however unintended) systems of power.

Further, criticalist research assumes the need for emancipatory actions that lead to increased social justice and social transformation.

These assumptions would, at first, appear to construct new "critical truths" for a postmodern age, and have done so when dominated by an unrelenting focus on the victimization of those who have been oppressed (whether socioeconomically, sexually, racially, or otherwise). This is certainly a focal point that is warranted within the confines of patriarchy and racist, economic imperialism. However, recognizing that the practice of research has often itself resulted in the production and reproduction of power for researchers, along with an increasing awareness of diverse forms of resistance, critical qualitative researchers attempt to challenge even the construction of critical truths. Therefore, various forms of critical qualitative research are embedded within a self-conscious criticism that requires that the researcher continually challenge her "will to conduct research" as well as the "will to define and impose equity and justice." The researcher's ideological and epistemological biases are referenced from the beginning, are politically self-conscious, and are open to revision. This critical self-consciousness even challenges "master narratives" that would "lead to emancipation" while at the same time maintaining as major purposes the elimination of oppression and the construction of an emancipatory social transformation that would be recognized as tentative and shifting.

These criticalist, self-conscious assumptions have led to reconceptualizations of research in ways that affirm diverse knowledges and ideologies. These reconceptualizations challenge truth-oriented belief structures that are not even considered questionable from within forms of science that function as if ahistorical and apolitical. Critical qualitative research even deconstructs and blurs the boundaries of traditional disciplines. The following are examples of critical research questions that can provide the reader with a feel for the range of possibilities for exploration, research, and critique from within and across disciplinary boundaries:

• How did the creation of the "Orient" benefit European cultural strength and identity?

- How have androcentric orientations influenced the selection of problems identified as important for human cultural research?
- Does/how does the culture of caring in secondary schools create privilege for some students and serve as a form of erasure and exclusion for others?
- What are contemporary ways of speaking/acting within academic communities that are used to discredit forms of research that are not positivist and/or experimental in nature?
- How have particular forms of knowledge (and resultant knowledge bases) used in educational practices privileged particular groups of people and disqualified others?

Although the term *critical* most often evokes thoughts of neo-Marxist "critical theory," critical qualitative research is actually a hybrid and emergent form of inquiry. Calls for a critical social science (Popkewitz 1990), a postimperialist science (Lather 1998), and indigenous research agendas (Tuhiwai Smith 2001) are attended to as research is constructed that would uncover the ways that social relations are shaped by ideology and such research explores how these relations can be altered. This type of research is embedded within the history of qualitative research that has resulted in a scholarly environment in which diverse voices and ways of living in the world have been heard and respected. Additionally, critical qualitative research draws from the range of theoretical perspectives that have challenged notions of universalist truth, have acknowledged the political and power orientations of human knowledge(s), and have fostered emergent, activist orientations.

THE LEGACY OF QUALITATIVE RESEARCH

Qualitative research, as conceptualized from within ontological and epistemological perspectives that acknowledge the connections between knower and known (e.g., naturalistic, phenomenological), is foundational to the construction and contemporary acceptance of critical qualitative research. While specific "qualitative" methods may be used by truth-oriented

scholars, the field of qualitative research overall has fostered a paradigm dialogue that challenges deterministic notions like generalizability and validity, as well as deconstructed the "will to truth" found in dominant constructions of science. Qualitative research in general has created a scholarly environment in which diverse research questions and methodologies are encouraged and fostered with the recognition that change, emergence, and new constructions (even as related to research questions and data collection methods) are necessary. This intellectual environment is necessary for a critical science that would unveil societal power relations, while at the same time engaging in self-conscious examination of assumptions and biases even within the specific research that is being conducted.

Further, the various strengths of qualitative research as the avenue for diverse paradigmatic perspectives is directly related to and applied in critical scholarship. First, objectivist approaches have been discredited as not humanly possible, a position that can result in disciplinary boundary crossing, the acknowledgment of ideological embeddedness, and increased contextual awareness. Second, the acceptance of human subjectivity within qualitative research practices ensures an advanced rigor that attempts to make assumptions and biases clear up front. The various forms of qualitative research have attempted to document "lived experience," often as played out in the lives of those who have suffered societal injustices and those whose voices have not usually been heard, or even acknowledged. Third, some forms of qualitative research have been implicitly critical in nature as research purposes and collaborations have dealt directly with the imbalance of power in society. Examples include research that addresses women's/gender issues, ethnic/linguistic minority issues, race, and various practices of marginalization (Lincoln & Cannella 2004).

HYBRID AND DYNAMIC THEORETICAL ORIENTATIONS

A range of theoretical positions has challenged modernist truth orientations while at the same time introducing diverse explanations for the construction (and imposition) of power within social relations. These various theoretical and even anti-theoretical lenses have been/are being combined and reconfigured as needed in the practice of critical qualitative research. Perspectives that are employed include critical theory, poststructuralism, a range of feminist forms of critique that challenge patriarchy and sexism, queer theory, cultural studies, and postcolonial critique. These hybrid combinations result in "unthought of" ways of understanding the world and vantage points from which to examine rhizomes, tentacles, and sites of power and oppression. These previously unthought interpretations and contingencies foster border understandings, unrecognized possibilities, and the celebration of diverse and shifting identities.

When the term *critical* is used regarding scholarship, most scholars immediately think of the work in critical theory conducted at the Frankfurt School in Germany. Certainly, the neo-Marxist work of Horkheimer, Adorno, and Marcuse while living in the US generated a site from which power could be explored while at the same time creating avenues for resistance, hope, and democratic possibility. However, a range of scholars who represent various power-oriented traditions influence critical qualitative research. Continental theorists like Foucault and Derrida, Latino scholars like Friere and Fals-Borda, and feminists like Kristeva and Irigaray would be included. Work in cultural studies and the various forms of tricontinental scholarship most often labeled postcolonial critique also represent perspectives that recognize power while avoiding its construction as a new truth. Perhaps more importantly, no theoretical view is treated as pure; each is increasingly emergent and hybrid. Feminism has reconceptualized cultural studies – poststructuralism and feminism have reconceptualized critical theory – postcolonialism has reconceptualized poststructualism, and on and on. Critical qualitative research uses these hybrid constructions and even combines and revises them as needed to address particular social questions and problems.

Critical qualitative research methods of data collection and analyses include the range of qualitative techniques such as ethnographic interviews, participant observation, focus group discussions, and document analyses that can be structured or emergent as needed. However, power-oriented theoretical perspectives have made possible an expanded group of methods that include archeology, genealogy, deconstruction, and juxtaposition. As researchers attempt to gather data that would address issues like the construction of dominant discourses/knowledges, regulations/rules regarding who is authorized to speak, and the ways that subjects are constructed and positioned, new methods are often needed, chosen, and even designed. For example, a researcher may find, upon attempting to determine the impact of welfare reform on individuals, that money has been redeployed away from welfare services to programs that attempt to promote heterosexual marriage for the poor; the study, although begun using predominantly ethnographic interviews, may be revised to collect quantitative data as to the location and use of allocated funds in various state government locations. Finally, even though critical qualitative research methods appear to privilege language and various forms of discourse analyses (in a broad sense), the methodologies are not considered bounded by such perspectives and are open to emergent designs and diverse data orientations.

Depending on the actual theory/practice used in the particular research, critical qualitative scholarship has faced a range of criticisms. As examples, work with poststructural leanings tends to appear rationalist and "stereotypically" masculine; scholarship that uses postcolonial critique is judged as reinscribing power within the academic community; as discussed previously, the research faces the same criticisms leveled at qualitative research in general as being without rigor or objectivity. However, if the underlying assumptions of critical qualitative research are consciously placed at the forefront – especially the recognition that research is conceptually a power-oriented construct or that theories can be used to reconceptualize each other but do not create new truths – then the criticisms become strengths.

EMERGENT, ACTIVIST ORIENTATIONS

Criticalist research is not simply hybrid and emergent, but, perhaps most importantly, strives for actions that would increase the possibilities for social justice-oriented societal transformation. The research questions that are implied are especially useful contemporarily when qualitative paradigms that challenge dominant truth orientations are coming under fire. Further, the discourse of research is currently being used to reinforce dualistic thinking that legitimates power for some and discredits and labels others as immoral, evil, not patriotic, socialist, or incompetent. Words like *accountability, profits, experimental or clinical trials*, and *evidenced-based* are being used. Critical qualitative research demonstrates that research is never apolitical, is always complex and even ambiguous, requiring a critique of the underlying assumptions. In this contemporary postmodern time, critical qualitative research generates questions such as:

- How are children being "used" to perpetuate specific political agendas? How are they helped and harmed through such discourses?
- What is hidden or ignored related to the implementation of research results (e.g., in the field of education) in the contemporary labeling of decades of scholarship as "poor quality"?

The most activist possibility for critical qualitative research is to contribute to a critical social science that constructs public imaginaries (and continuous discussions) that embrace the complexities and ambiguities of research, yet at the same time recognizes its usefulness. These public discourses would place resistance to research at the center even as research is conducted to address contemporary societal problems; construct research collaborations with the public while at the same time avoiding the denial of difference; explore ways to challenge our positions of privilege (including those of researchers); question "knowing" as the very purpose of research; challenge public discourses that privilege forms of legitimation that reinscribe oppressive power(s); reconceptualize forms of representation that avoid oppressive results and interpretations; construct a critical public research dialogue; and create nonimpositional forms of critical transformative actions.

SEE ALSO: Critical Pedagogy; Critical Realism; Critical Theory/Frankfurt School

REFERENCES AND SUGGESTED READINGS

Denzin, N. K. & Lincoln, Y. S. (Eds.) (1994) *Handbook of Qualitative Research*. Sage, Thousand Oaks, CA.

Kincheloe, J. & McLaren, P. (1994) Rethinking Critical Theory and Qualitative Research. In: Denzin, N. K. & Lincoln, Y. S. (Eds.), *Handbook of Qualitative Research*. Sage, Thousand Oaks, CA, pp. 138–57.

Lather, P. (1998) Validity, Ethics, and Positionality in Qualitative Research: Wrestling with the Angels. Paper presented at the Bergamo Conference on Curriculum Theorizing, Bloomington.

Lincoln, Y. S. & Cannella, G. S. (2004) Qualitative Research, Power, and the Radical Right. *Qualitative Inquiry* 10(2): 175–201.

Popkewitz, T. (1990) Whose Future? Whose Past? Notes on Critical Theory and Methodology. In: Guba, E. (Ed.), *The Paradigm Dialog*. Sage, Newbury Park, CA, pp. 46–66.

Tuhiwai Smith, L. (2001) *Decolonizing Methodologies: Research and Indigenous Peoples*. Zed Books, London.

critical realism

Jamie Morgan

Critical realism in its contemporary usage emerged out of debates in the philosophy of science in the 1970s (e.g., Harré & Madden 1975; Bhaskar 1997). It focused on what could be argued from the relative success of laboratory experiment to create artificial closed systems where causal relationships could be isolated and explored. It was argued that such closed systems of regular causal relations were rare outside the laboratory and that non-social reality consisted of complex and stratified structures in open or variable and changing systems. The purpose of natural science method was to explain the powers of these structures as tendencies to act in particular ways. Because, in the ordinary course of things, regular outcomes were rare outside the laboratory it was then inferred that reality could be analytically distinguished into structures, the outcome of their complex interplay, and human experience, perception, or interpretation of those outcomes. It was then argued that this distinction could make sense of the difference between theory and the rest of reality in quite a different way than the philosophies of idealism or materialist empiricism (Morgan 2006). Idealism argues that reality is mind-dependent, while materialist empiricism argues that reality consists of a series of external objects of sense perception that are the basis of causal laws. Critical realism argued that neither actually accounts for natural science method. Idealism could not account for how laboratory experiment, methods, and theories could also fail as well as succeed. Empiricism could not account for why laboratory experiment was necessary at all if reality could be reduced to sense perception of causal regularities. Accordingly, it was argued that reality was mind-practice affected in a continuing interplay of theoretical research programs of *depth reality*. This approach, as part of a broader movement termed scientific naturalism, had major implications in the philosophy of science in terms of mediating between the important insights of different responses to the failure of logical empiricism and positivism, particularly by acknowledging Kuhn and Lakatos's focus on the sociological conditions of scientific method and theoretical development (Sayer 1992).

At first sight critical realism does not seem particularly relevant to social science. However, it has been a growing influence within social theory and sociology, especially in the UK and Scandinavia, but also in the US via the *Journal for the Theory of Social Behavior*, initially for two reasons. First, it provides a philosophical argument for why positivism may be inappropriate as an account and method within natural science and, as such, undermines the universal science project that underpins the application of positivism to social science, especially the mathematical aspects of economics and behavioristic sociology which rely heavily on statistical methods, prediction, and closed-system modeling. Second, it provides an alternative to forms of strong relativism in some

kinds of constructivism and postmodernist social theory that also reject positivism in social theory. The basis of this alternative was to adapt the natural science depth realist argument to societies. The conceptual problem was that humans, unlike electrons, think. The complexity and variability of society could not therefore be of the same kind as the rest of reality because change clearly has a different significance for a critical language-using entity than it does for a weather system. The methodological problem was that there is also no obvious analogue to the laboratory on which to base any argument. The critical realist solution that developed through the early 1980s (Bhaskar 1998) was to revive the agency-structure debate. Others, particularly Anthony Giddens, W. G. Runciman, Charles Tilly, and Pierre Bourdieu, were also pursuing this line of inquiry.

Both Giddens and Bhaskar explore and reject theories of methodological individualism and structuralism. Methodological individualism is rejected on the basis that although human action is central to social reality there are problems with reducing that reality solely to the beliefs and actions of the individual because it then becomes impossible to account for where beliefs come from, how actions and their goals are constrained, enabled, and conditioned, how goals sometimes fail, and why there may be unintended consequences (for the actor and for society at large) from the action, or lack thereof. Structuralism is rejected on the basis that although it is plausible to argue that every action must have a condition, it is implausible to translate that condition into a strong sense of conditioning because if structure is deterministic there is no sense that things can be otherwise and the characteristics of a critical language-using entity are lost. The solution favored was to argue for a kind of analytical dualism where agency and structure are distinct but mutually dependent. Put another way, structure is the ever-present condition and continuous outcome of human activity and, though human activity is conditioned by structures, no individual's activity is simply the interplay of structural forces. Giddens refers to this as structuration and Bhaskar as the transformational model of social activity. For Bhaskar and for critical realists, structures are real, with real causal powers. However, those powers are practically and conceptually dependent in a different way than is the case for the objects of natural science. Most importantly, they are powers in the sense that they provide a relational authority and rules for particular actions for individuals, which also set in motion consequences and outcomes for those individuals and others. A banking system exists only insofar as there is a concept of banking and a practice of banking within a society. The act of banking reproduces the banking system, the act relies on a relation and its characteristics (one's status as a customer with a given credit rating, etc.) but is personalized by individual goals (applying for a mortgage to buy a particular house), and is also depersonalized in terms of indiscriminate effects for the individual (changes in the recycling of the dollar by China can affect the availability and interest rates for mortgages in the US).

What critical realists generally take from the agency-structure problem is that a form of depth realism does apply to society. Society is a relatively enduring set of structures in complex stratified relations that are continually reproduced, inadvertently changed, and sometimes consciously and critically appraised and transformed by the humans whose activity sustains them. The powers and characteristics of structures and agents provide the background to each interaction of agents and structures from which particular events arise that cannot be reduced solely to how the agent perceives or experiences that event or interaction. Methodologically, in the absence of any analogue to the laboratory, social science can investigate the characteristics of structures and the effects on the socialization of agents to explore tendencies in the possibilities of action. As such the sociologist might focus on the interpretations of the individuals and thus seek to understand their motives and goals in a personal way, but can also link this to broader themes of how they fit into tendencies to act and provide explanations of that in terms of relatively enduring structures. Critical realism therefore accepts that the traditional explaining–understanding distinction refers to different methods, but rejects that the former is applicable to nature and the latter to society (Sayer 1992). As such, critical realism is a form of philosophical naturalism.

By the mid-1990s critical realism had become a vibrant multidisciplinary research community in the social sciences. At least three main strands of debate have emerged as significant to sociology and social theory. First, concerning the degree to which sociology does or does not benefit from or even require basic philosophical argument about the metaphysics of social reality and its significance for social science (Callinicos 2004), arguments vary from discussions of the applicability of naturalism to social science to debates concerning the relative merits of different meta-theories, such as pragmatism versus realism (Kivinen & Piiroinen 2004), Marxism and critical realism (Brown et al. 2002), and – particularly in terms of later systematic developments by Bhaskar (1993) – to debates concerning the degree to which one can make substantive philosophical claims about reality and what this means for the appropriate relationship between science and social theory and philosophy (Morgan 2004). Second, there is a broad debate between realists on what kinds of research methods are compatible with social science (Carter & New 2005). Since critical realism rejects theorizations of society that are based on closed-system assumptions, it also rejects research approaches that model or seek to do no more than identify particular regular relations between variables as accounts of events (e.g., age and suicide). This raises the issue of what value there might be in particular tools or methods such as analytical statistics. Critical realists tend to be split over this issue (Olsen & Morgan 2005). Third, there is a continuing debate focused on the agency-structure problem itself. Margaret Archer has been the prime mover within critical realism in developing a distinctive approach to the agency-structure problem. Her particular contribution has been a close critique of Giddens, arguing that his form of dualism collapses agency and structure together and that it is more plausible to separate them out on the temporal basis that structure always precedes an act of agency (Archer 1995). If one does not maintain this distinction it not only becomes impossible to explore the way in which agency uses and elaborates upon structures, but it also becomes impossible to differentiate how the agent is more than simply a product of and reducible to structures (Archer 2000, 2003).

Stones (2005) has replied directly to this critique, defending structuration on the basis that it is compatible with the "objectivity" of structure.

Others have contributed different lines of development and critique of the concept of structure in particular. Porpora (1998) defends an account of structure as systems of human relations among social positions. The philosopher Rom Harré, an early progenitor of what has become critical realism, has developed a critique of causal powers inherent in structures on the basis that only agents have particular powers to act (Valera and Harré 1996). Lewis (2000), following Porpora, has responded by differentiating the concept along Aristotelian lines. Structures may be material causes in the sense that they are the materials from which events are brought about, but are not themselves the means by which, or efficient causes by which, events are brought about. Finally, the social philosopher Ruth Groff (2004) has developed this position in terms of the overall coherence of the metaphysics of critical realist argument. The work of all these academics points to the current diversity of opinion and positions within and regarding critical realism.

SEE ALSO: Agency (and Intention); Bourdieu, Pierre; Critical Qualitative Research; Paradigms; Positivism; Scientific Knowledge, Sociology of; Stratification Systems: Openness; Structuralism

REFERENCES AND SUGGESTED READINGS

Archer, M. (1995) *Realist Social Theory: The Morphogenetic Approach*. Cambridge University Press, Cambridge.
Archer, M. (2000) *Being Human: The Problem of Agency*. Cambridge University Press, Cambridge.
Archer, M. (2003) *Structure, Agency and the Internal Conversation*. Cambridge University Press, Cambridge.
Bhaskar, R. (1993) *Dialectic: The Pulse of Freedom*. Verso, London.
Bhaskar, R. (1997 [1976]) *A Realist Theory of Science*. Verso, London.
Bhaskar, R. (1998 [1979]) *The Possibility of Naturalism: A Philosophical Critique of the Contemporary Human Sciences*. Routledge, London.

Brown, A., Fleetwood, S., & Roberts, J. (2002) *Critical Realism and Marxism*. Routledge, London.
Callinicos, A. (2004) *Making History: Agency, Structure and Change in Social Theory*. Brill, Leiden.
Carter, B. & New, C. (Eds.) (2005) *Making Realism Work*. Routledge, London.
Groff, R. (2004) *Critical Realism: Post-Positivism and the Possibility of Knowledge*. Routledge, London.
Harré, R. & Madden, E. (1975) *Causal Powers: A Theory of Natural Necessity*. Blackwell, Oxford.
Kivinen, O. & Piiroinen, T. (2004) The Relevance of Ontological Commitments in Social Science: Realist and Pragmatist Viewpoints. *Journal for the Theory of Social Behavior* 34(3): 231–50.
Lewis, P. (2000) Realism, Causality and the Problem of Social Structure. *Journal for the Theory of Social Behavior* 30(3): 249–68.
Morgan, J. (2004) The Nature of a Transcendental Argument: Towards a Critique of Dialectic: The Pulse of Freedom. *Journal of Critical Realism* 3(2): 305–40.
Morgan, J. (2006) "Idealism" and "Empiricism." Entries in: Hartwig, M. (Ed.), *A Dictionary of Critical Realism*. Routledge, London.
Olsen, W. & Morgan, J. (2005) Towards a Critical Epistemology of Analytical Statistics: Realism in Mathematical Method. *Journal for the Theory of Social Behavior* 35(3).
Porpora, D. (1998) Four Concepts of Social Structure. In: Archer, M., Bhaskar, R., Collier, A., Lawson, T., & Norrie, A. (Eds.), *Critical Realism: Essential Readings*. Routledge, London, pp. 339–55.
Sayer, A. (1992 [1984]) *Method in Social Science*. Routledge, London.
Stones, R. (2005) *Structuration Theory*. Palgrave Macmillan, Basingstoke.
Varela, C. & Harré, R. (1996) Conflicting Varieties of Realism: Causal Powers and the Problems of Social Structure. *Journal for the Theory of Social Behavior* 26(3): 313–25.

critical theory/Frankfurt School

Lauren Langman

Critical theory, the legacy of the Institute for Social Research at the University of Frankfurt, is rooted in the philosophies of Kant and Hegel, and in Marx's critique of capitalism which claimed that it exploited and alienated workers, while its ideologies of reason, freedom, and democracy disguised its actual operations. "Critical theorists" integrated Weber's notions of rationality and Freud's theories of character and desire into a theory of capitalism and its culture. They looked at sociology, political science, philosophy, art, literature, and cultural studies, including film theory and popular culture, to fashion a multidisciplinary, multidimensional, dialectical social theory largely concerned with the alienation, domination, and commodification and dehumanization in modern societies (Kellner 1989). Critical theory thus embraced the notion of *totality*: society was an outcome of a number of not always harmonious parts and levels; contradictions and tensions are seen as inherent. It is *critical* in the sense of critique as explicating what is not empirically given but apprehended through critical reason. Thus, unlike most social theories, it is very concerned with epistemology. Nor does it attempt "objectivity" because this is assumed both to promote and to hide domination. Rather, as an *emancipatory theory*, it seeks to foster the freedom, equality, and fraternity promised by the Enlightenment thinkers, these qualities being incompatible with late capitalism and hence undercut by technological logic, consumerism, and mass culture. It promotes a society where people may create democratic communities and realize their creative, unique human potentials.

To comprehend the rise of critical theory we need to consider at least two factors: the then state of Marxist theory and the social conditions of Germany following World War I. Marxist theory, as embraced by the Communist International, had become an "official orthodoxy" of economically determined laws of history as the progression of class conflict. But many academics, loyal to Marx's visions, such as Korsch and Lukács, began to reexamine consciousness and ideology after capitalist societies had entered a new phase with major economic, social, and technological changes. Finance had become as important as manufacturing and sales, while the welfare state and Keynesian economics were embraced. Nationalism had become a major social force and consumerism was beginning to grow. New and unprecedented technologies of mass production, rapid transportation, electronic communication, and even

warfare had transformed the early twentieth century. Yet while they focused on culture and ideology, they maintained the Marxian notion of immanent critique of capitalism, its alienation and reification, its mode of producing value through exploitation, and ideologies that disguised its actual operations.

World War I was an industrial war in which modern weapons such as battleships, machine guns, tanks, and even planes led to millions of deaths. Empires had fallen. The progressive Weimar government of post-war Germany was relatively weak and little able to both forge a new democratic society and at the same time pay huge reparations imposed by the Versailles Treaty. The mood of the times, its angst and ennui, was captured in the existential philosophy of Heidegger, the novels of Kafka and Mann, the art of Grosz, and the music of Schoenberg. But these same conditions fostered the rise of fascism.

It was in this context that a uniquely talented collection of scholars came together in the mid-1920s to establish the Institute for Social Research, loosely affiliated with the University of Frankfurt. The best known of these men, whose work is influential to this day, were the philosophers Horkheimer, Adorno, and Marcuse, and sociologist turned psychoanalyst Erich Fromm. The goal of the group was to retain Hegel's notion of the movement and promise of reason, to rethink the Marxian critique of capital and the categories of its analyses in view of the social and technological changes of the age, and to develop an interdisciplinary theory that would go beyond the boundaries of economics, philosophy, sociology, and even psychoanalysis.

Their first task was to revive the tradition of Kant's critiques of reason as actively engaging and constructing the world. But with Hegel, they agreed that reason was historically determined, yet that unfolding of history promised human freedom and joyous consciousness. Weber, however, argued that rationality, i.e., *instrumental reason*, led to capitalist prosperity and technologies of domination over nature. Yet that same logic dehumanized people and led to their entrapment into "iron cages."

Inspired by the discovery of Marx's writings on alienation and Lukács's analysis of the reification of consciousness, the critical theorists looked at the consequences of various epistemologies. More specifically, the logic of the physical sciences, when applied to the human sciences, served the goals of domination by reducing people to objects or reified entities, much as did capitalism. The logic of scientific objectivity and rationality fostered passivity and sustained the domination of capital. When Erich Fromm introduced Freud to the group, depth psychology – specifically, the theory of the superego as internalized authority – became part of a larger critique of domination.

In Germany in the 1920s, given a worldwide depression and growing unemployment, there were frequent conflicts between the left and right, and often bloody fights in the streets. In 1933, aided by the votes of many workers, the Nazi Party gained political power. The world would soon face the most massive war and unprecedented genocide in its history. In this latter context, the Frankfurt School began to investigate how and why such atavistic barbarism could surface in what had been one of the most culturally advanced societies in the world. They soon began a large-scale study of the patterns of authority found in the families of modern society. This research revealed how a certain character type – the sadomasochistic authoritarian – when beset by economic hardships and social uncertainty, was disposed to follow a powerful leader who would forge new kinds of communities, promise a restoration of a former greatness that would provide the people with pride and dignity. Meanwhile, there were scapegoats to blame for adversity. The Jews had long served that role. The appeal of fascism and reception to its propaganda depended on (1) the psychological gratifications it gave to the individual; (2) a reactionary ideology that provided meaning in an increasingly heartless world; and (3) rituals and social organizations that offered a sense of community. Moreover, the Nazis brilliantly refined and exploited the new mass media, film and radio, for the purposes of propaganda and mobilizing an entire population, and the ruling classes supported Hitler as the bulwark against Bolshevism.

Fearing Hitler, the Frankfurt scholars moved to France and eventually the United States. After the war, Horkheimer and Adorno returned while Marcuse and Fromm chose to remain. By then Fromm had both drifted away and faced exclusion. Nevertheless, the basic insights of the earlier period were developed and refined, as in large-scale studies of authoritarianism in the US (Adorno et al. 1950). Following the concern with fascist political propaganda, they noted how the "culture industry" – the producers of books, films, music, and television, including advertising the "good life" – served political functions by fostering deception and escapism, paving the way for celebrity politicians like Reagan or Schwartzenegger.

During the 1960s, between a protest movement against the war in Vietnam and a growing counterculture that comprised the vanguard of the sexual revolution, Marcuse became a folk hero to progressive youth involved in what was called the "movement." Marcuse's trenchant *One-Dimensional Man* (1964) argued that "one-dimensional, rational thought" sustained an "administered society" while the mass media inculcated "false needs" that were gratified in consumer behavior that integrated the person into the society, yet coopted his or her agency to erode the possibilities that critical thought and resistance would overcome the status quo. Although capitalism had once required "surplus repression" of desire, with affluence and consumerism, "repressive desublimation" (sexual freedom) made people feel free while being entrapped.

Critical theory diverged from orthodox Marxism by not regarding class conflict as the basis of social change. The working classes, coopted by bourgeois ideologies and enthralled by consumer goods, were no longer seen as the agents of progressive social change. Finally, socialist revolution was not seen as inevitable nor even desirable, given the despotism and gulags of the USSR. Theorists eventually became pessimistic about the possibilities of progressive social transformation. Many ultimately retreated to the high culture of the educated German bourgeoisie where they found freedom in aesthetics as a realm still free of commodification.

By the late 1960s, a new generation of critical theorists had emerged. Jürgen Habermas (1984) often is considered the most important philosopher of the late twentieth century. His critical social theory attempted to incorporate

Weberian rationality, Schutz's concern with life world, Parsons's structural functionalism, and Mead's symbolic interactionism. In his attempt to resurrect the "uncompleted project of modernity," Habermas was concerned with the nature of communication, about which Marx said little. He showed how the rise of print media enabled a bourgeois "public sphere" where people could debate and argue various truth claims to arrive at certain social understandings and eventually overthrow monarchies. But eventually, in view of media commercialization, the critical aspects of media would wane. In his work on epistemology, he clearly differentiated rational/technical interests in *controlling* the world, practical/hermeneutic interests in *understanding* the world and other people, and emancipatory/critical interests in *overcoming domination*. He would later argue that the colonization of the life world – the realm of practical interests taken over by rational technical interests – secured domination through both passivity and marginalizing alternative forms of the social as "unpractical." His work also examined the nature of crises, student protest in the 1960s, and so on. Much like his teachers, there was little interest in the worker, perhaps because workers had become part of the forces conserving and protecting the society.

In his best-known and most debated work, Habermas (1984) argued that communication was not well analyzed by Marx. Building upon ordinary language philosophy (Searle, Austin) and the developmental theory of Piaget and Kolberg, he argues that speech acts have a goal of mutual understanding. But for various reasons, with the evolution of modernity, instrumental rationality has come to dominate all spheres of life, leading to distorted communication. Rejecting the Freudian theories of character, desire, and repression, but following Freud's model of therapeutic interpretation and understanding, he has argued that capitalist markets, the modern state, and bureaucratic organizations embracing instrumental reason and technological thought colonize the life world and attenuate communicative competence. His more recent work has become concerned with questions of justice and constitutionalism.

Today we might note what has been considered a third generation of critical theorists. Scholars such as Douglas Kellner, Andrew Feenberg, and Timothy Luke have been at the forefront of the critiques of technology as having both liberating and dominating moments. Kellner, attempting to incorporate certain aspects of postmodernism, has written a number of scathing critiques of media and popular culture/current events including the first Gulf War, the O. J. Simpson trial, the theft of the 2000 US presidential election, and the corruption of the Bush dynasty. We might also note the work of Axel Honneth, who has been concerned with the need for recognition often lacking today, and Nancy Fraser's critiques of the meanings of "needs."

Other critical theory scholars worth noting might include Moishe Postone, who has rekindled the concerns with Marx's value theory, Harry Dahms, who has been rethinking alienation and globalization, Robert Antonio, who has been interested in globalization, David Smith, who has noted relations of current authoritarianism and genocide, and Lauren Langman, for whom psychoanalysis still provides trenchant insights into such diverse realms as consumerism, nationalism, Islamic fundamentalism, aspects of popular culture, and the alternative globalization movements. Moreover, there has been a resurgence of interest in some of the other Frankfurt School scholars such as Benjamin and Bloch.

To illustrate the value of critical theory for today, recall the central question of why German workers were attracted to Hitler and fascism, which proved to be contrary not only to their class interests but also to their very lives. Moreover, how could they commit the barbarities of the camps and "willingly" execute Jews? Many contemporary critical theorists can remember when the US was fighting an imperialist war against communism in Vietnam. Incidents such as My Lai or Operation Phoenix sanctioned the torture and deaths of many peasants. The hatred and dehumanization of the Vietnamese enemy "Other," much like the Nazis toward the Jews, could easily sanction torture, rape, and murder on a large scale.

Many blue-collar voters supported that war and voted for Nixon, who continued a failed policy. More recently, workers gave G. W. Bush their votes and early support for the premeditated invasion of Iraq. Why do people support the policies of such leaders? Critical theory suggests at least two reasons. First, the ideologies that shape consciousness emanating from the "culture industry," from Rambo movies in the 1980s to Fox News of today, much like the propaganda of the Nazis, present damning worldviews, values, and depictions of Others that are not subjected to critical reason and democratic debate. Moreover, the conservative Christian segments of society see geopolitics in terms of a good Us and evil Others. Second, there is a large number of authoritarian personalities with sadomasochistic tendencies who, in face of economic threats, seek a strong, powerful, tough "father figure" who will use violence to protect his frightened followers. Given the anxieties and uncertainties of job security in these days of globalization, automation, and outsourcing, such men, and now even women, support "tough guys" or "strong men."

Critical theory can be considered a product of capitalist domination that inspires intellectual, social, and political critique. Critical theory, with its multidisciplinary, dialectical analysis and critique of advanced capitalist society, its shallow consumerism and its suppression of human freedom, is not, nor can it really be, one of the dominant schools of social thought. But at the same time, the power of its logic, its capacities to reveal and clarify what might otherwise be obscured, mean that it will remain an enduring part of social theory and retain an influence that extends far and wide, even to those who would question its premises and conclusions. As long as social systems breed alienation, oppression, and domination, critical theory will seek to understand and to alleviate these problems.

SEE ALSO: Adorno, Theodor W.; Advertising; Alienation; Capitalism; Commodities, Commodity Fetishism, and Commodification; Consumption, Mass Consumption, and Consumer Culture; Cultural Critique; Culture Industries; Freud, Sigmund; Fromm, Erich; Horkheimer, Max; Marcuse, Herbert; Marx, Karl; Psychoanalysis; Weber, Max

REFERENCES AND SUGGESTED READINGS

Adorno, T. et al. (1950) *The Authoritarian Personality*. Harper, New York.

Best, S. & Kellner, D. (1991) *Postmodern Theory: Critical Investigations*. Guilford Press, New York.

Fromm, E. (1941) *Escape from Freedom*. Holt Rinehart, New York.

Habermas, J. (1984) *Theory of Communicative Action*, 2 vols. Beacon Press, London.

Jay, M. (1973) *The Dialectical Imagination*. Little, Brown, Boston.

Kellner, D. (1989) *Critical Theory, Marxism, and Modernity*. Johns Hopkins University Press, Baltimore.

Marcuse, H. (1964) *One-Dimensional Man*. Beacon Press, Boston.

Wiggerhaus, R. (1995) *The Frankfurt School: Its History, Theories, and Political Significance*. MIT Press, Cambridge, MA.

cross-sex friendship

Michael Monsour

Friendships between males and females, hereafter referred to as cross-sex friendships, are non-romantic (but not necessarily non-sexual), voluntary, non-familial relationships in which both individuals label their association as a friendship. The distinguishing characteristic of a cross-sex friendship is that the friends are of different biological sexes. Similar to other kinds of friendships, such as same-sex friendships, interracial friendships, and friendships of sexual minorities, cross-sex friendships are characterized by generic benefits in the form of mutual trust, loyalty, fun, enjoyment, and social support which manifests itself as aid, affect, and affirmation. From a symbolic interactionist perspective, however, cross-sex friends also offer one another the unique benefit of providing an insider's perspective on how members of the other sex think, feel, and behave. The bestowing of insider perspectives between cross-sex friends enables males and females of all ages to take the role of the other sex, thereby increasing their understanding of their friend and the gender their friend represents.

Cross-sex friendships have a protean nature, meaning that their form and function change as they appear in different stages of the life cycle. Consequently, a thorough understanding of cross-sex friendships requires taking a life cycle approach to those relationships. A life cycle approach focuses on how cross-sex friendship experiences in earlier stages of life influence cross-sex friendship experiences in subsequent stages of life. Those experiences encompass everything from the micro-level formation of cross-sex friendship schemas and communicative practices to macro-level societal and group norms concerning the appropriateness of such relationships and how they should be initiated and maintained. The transition from one stage of life to another is often marked by dramatic events and processes such as puberty, getting married or staying single, divorce, having children, entering the workplace, and retirement. These transitional events and processes have an impact on how cross-sex friendships are initiated, maintained, and sometimes discontinued.

Friendship historians agree that cross-sex friendships were exceedingly rare in the United States until the 1970s. Scholarly analysis of the friendships between men and women can be traced back to 1974, with the publication of the landmark article "Cross-Sex Friendship" by Booth and Hess in the *Journal of Marriage and the Family*. There has been a steady increase in the number of published investigations of cross-sex friendships since 1974, but the numbers pale in comparison to the research conducted on same-sex friendships and other-sex romantic relationships. Researchers investigating cross-sex friendships use a fairly wide range of methodological tools and strategies. The most common of these methods are surveys, observational analysis (most often of children in day-care centers, preschool, and elementary school), and qualitative interviewing. With a few exceptions in which investigators observe children over the course of three or four months, there has been very little longitudinal research (but see Griffin & Sparks 1990).

Investigations of cross-sex friendships have uncovered important findings when viewed from a life cycle perspective. Two significant life cycle milestones to recognize and study are when individuals have their first opportunity to mingle with members of the other sex (typically a family member), though they do not realize they are doing so, and when they have their first opportunity to interact with members of the other sex and know that they are doing so. Life cycle experts generally agree that children are able to differentiate between the sexes around the age of 2 or 3 years. At that point, developing gender schemas guide how they think and behave in reference to members of the other sex (Martin 1994). Research has established that some 1-year-olds form cross-sex friendships (Howes 1996), though a more typical developmental age for those friendships is 3 or 4 years when the word "friend" actually becomes part of their working vocabulary (Bukowski et al. 1996). Cross-sex friendships between toddlers and preschoolers are not the same as cross-sex friendships in middle school, where participants have entered puberty and are contending with sexual identity issues and societal messages about appropriate gender behavior. Adolescent friendships between heterosexual boys and girls are quite different than the ones formed in earlier life because puberty introduces romantic and sexual tensions. Those friendships are also invariably affected by social network factors such as clique and crowd formations. Friendships in young and middle adulthood are similarly beset by romantic and sexual challenges. If an individual gets married and has children, his or her cross-sex friendships change in that married individuals tend to form couple friendships with other married individuals rather than pursuing individual friendships with members of the other sex. Cross-sex friendships of older Americans are affected by factors not as salient as they were in earlier stages of the life cycle, e.g., mobility, health issues, and the death of a spouse (Adams & Blieszner 1989). Despite the differences in cross-sex friendships in stages of the life cycle, there are also similarities in that in each stage of life, cross-sex friends support one another and enjoy each other's company.

From a structural perspective, there are a number of social and structural facilitators and barriers to cross-sex friendship. The most obvious structural barriers to cross-sex friendships are sex segregation in schools and many work environments, social network structures in elementary and middle school such as crowd and clique affiliations, and mobility issues in old age. There are also, however, structural facilitators of cross-sex friendship formation.

Just as the workplace and school settings can inhibit the formation of cross-sex friendships, they can also encourage and even require cross-sex interaction, which creates the potential for friendships to develop. Structural facilitators and barriers to cross-sex friendships are interrelated and must be studied as such. Researchers need to examine as many structural characteristics as methodologically possible if they want to understand the structural inhibitors and accentuators of cross-sex friendship.

In every stage of the life cycle, social barriers to the initiation and maintenance of cross-sex friendships originate from third parties or the cross-sex friends themselves. Most commonly, social barriers are obstacles created by individuals in a person's social network that discourage the formation of friendships between men and women and boys and girls. Parents may discourage their elementary age children from having sleepovers that involve members of the other sex, even at the innocent age of 5 or 6. A man's or woman's jealousy over the cross-sex friendship of their spouse or lover jeopardizes many cross-sex friendships. The friends themselves may also present social barriers to their friendship, for example if one friend has a hidden agenda and secretly wants the relationship to be romantic in nature. Social barriers to cross-sex friendship also reflect normative relational constraints, which are societal norms that place constraints on where, when, and how cross-sex friendships may be initiated, developed, and maintained.

The significance of cross-sex friendships to society and the individuals who constitute that society is largely unexplored terrain. An essay of this length cannot begin to cover the complexities of friendships between females and males. Indeed, even entire books are woefully inadequate. Unfortunately, cross-sex friendships have been marginalized in the sense that relationship scholars pay them relatively little attention, and heterosexual laypersons often believe that the paradigmatic or ideal relationship between a male and a female should be a romantic one. Research has established one thing, however; males and females of all ages can be friends, and the benefits of those friendships are often qualitatively different than the

friendships formed between members of the same sex and even romantic relationships.

SEE ALSO: Friendship During the Later Years; Friendship: Interpersonal Aspects; Friendship, Social Inequality, and Social Change; Friendship: Structure and Context; Friendships of Adolescence; Friendships of Children; Friendships of Gay, Lesbian, and Bisexual People; Gender, Friendship and; Race/Ethnicity and Friendship

REFERENCES AND SUGGESTED READINGS

Adams, R. G. & Blieszner, R. (1989) *Older Adult Friendships: Structure and Process.* Sage, Newbury Park, CA.

Blieszner, R. & Adams, R. G. (1992) *Adult Friendship.* Sage, Newbury Park, CA.

Bukowski, W. M., Newcomb, A. F., & Hartup, W. W. (1996) Friendship and its Significance in Childhood and Adolescence: Introduction and Comment. In: Bukowski, W. M., Newcomb, A. F., & Hartup, W. W. (Eds.), *Friendship in Childhood and Adolescence.* Cambridge University Press, New York, pp. 1–15.

Griffin, E. & Sparks, G. G. (1990) Friends Forever: A Longitudinal Exploration of Same-Sex and Platonic Pairs. *Journal of Social and Personal Relationships* 7: 29–46.

Howes, C. (1996) The Earliest Friendships. In: Bukowski, W. M., Newcomb, A. F., & Hartup, W. W. (Eds.), *Friendship in Childhood and Adolescence.* Cambridge University Press, New York, pp. 66–86.

Martin, C. (1994) Cognitive Influences on the Development and Maintenance of Gender Segregation. In: Leaper, C. (Ed.), *New Directions for Child Development. Childhood Gender Segregation: Causes and Consequences,* Vol. 65. Jossey-Bass, San Francisco, pp. 35–50.

Monsour, M. (2002) *Women and Men as Friends: Relationships Across the Life Span in the 21st Century.* Lawrence Erlbaum, Mahwah, NJ.

O'Meara, D. (1989) Cross-Sex Friendships: Four Basic Challenges of an Ignored Relationship. *Sex Roles* 21: 525–43.

Rawlins, W. K. (1992) *Friendship Matters: Communication, Dialectics, and the Life Course.* Walter de Gruyter, New York.

Rubin, L. (1985) *Just Friends: The Role of Friendships in Our Lives.* Harper & Row, New York.

crowd behavior

Clark McPhail

Herbert Blumer was the most influential crowd sociologist of the twentieth century. To his credit, he recognized in mid-career that "sociologists had done a rather miserable job in studying the crowd systematically because they had done little to assemble empirical accounts" (Blumer 1957). He attributed this to the lack of "a well thought out analytic scheme which would provide fruitful hypotheses and lead to more incisive observations." But systematic study of "the crowd" proves to be impossible precisely because that concept, despite considerable cachet, is not a useful tool for investigating the phenomenon to which it purportedly refers. "The crowd" implies a homogeneity of actors and motives and, consequently, continuous and mutually inclusive action. Scholars who have taken a slightly different tack have produced extensive empirical evidence that refutes both those implications and their consequences.

Over the past two decades sociologists working at different levels of analysis have adopted "the gathering" as a more neutral and useful concept for referring to a temporary collection of at least two persons in a common location in space and time without regard to their actions or motives. All temporary gatherings have a *life course* consisting of three phases. An assembling process forms the gathering by bringing two or more persons together in a common location. A dispersing process terminates the gathering by vacating that location. The gathering is a kaleidoscopic mix of elementary forms of collective action by two or more of its members alternating or concurrent with their various individual actions. These three phases of temporary gatherings are not independent, but do divide a hitherto complex phenomenon into more manageable pieces for research and lend themselves to different and appropriate research methods that have produced the evidence summarized here.

Temporary gatherings of human beings are ubiquitous. Multitudes, crowds, and mobs have preoccupied preachers, politicians, and police for centuries because of their concerns with persuading, producing, or controlling the behavior of the members of such gatherings. Most scholarly concerns have been with political gatherings that challenge the status quo. Late nineteenth-century and early twentieth-century scholars were critical of those gatherings and the allegedly disreputable and irrational character of the actors and actions that composed them. Contemporary scholars have been more concerned with describing and explaining than with discrediting political gatherings. Many collective action scholars have systematically coded newspaper archives to create databases with which to plot the rise and fall in the frequency of protest events, campaigns, and waves as measures of the life course of social movements.

Other scholars have been more concerned with describing and explaining the actions that compose the political gatherings of which protest events, campaigns, and waves are composed (Wright 1978; McPhail & Wohlstein 1983). Some have extended those concerns to similarities and differences across prosaic, religious, sport, and political gatherings. While both description and explanation of these units of analysis are equally worthwhile, far more attention has been given to the latter than to the former. Consequently, explanations have often been advanced for phenomena that are rare if not apocryphal. It is useful to provide a broad description of the phenomena to be explained before briefly reviewing the relevance of existing explanations for collective phenomena.

Some temporary gatherings assemble periodically, ranging from national independence days and inaugurations to daily prosaic gatherings on street corners. Ad hoc gatherings are assembled non-periodically but are announced and mobilized well in advance (e.g., sport events, political and religious rallies); still others assemble in impromptu fashion (e.g., at the scene of fires or auto accidents, or for upset-victory celebrations). Extensive surveys of participants (and sometimes non-participants) in political gatherings and riots, in religious rallies, periodic holiday celebrations, and sport victory celebrations establish three noteworthy facts. First, individual attributes and attitudes do not predict who will or will not participate. Second, participation is a function of (1) *solicitations* from friends, family, or acquaintances with whom the solicited are connected in social networks (Oliver & Marwell 1992) and (2) the *availability* to assemble when and (3) *means of access* to where the gathering in question occurs (McPhail & Miller 1973). Third, most people assemble for most gatherings with one or more friends, family, or acquaintances, remain together, and eventually disperse with those companions. Thus, most gatherings are composed of some singles but predominantly of small groups of companions. Those companions act alone; they interact with one another; and they occasionally act together with other singles and small groups in more inclusive collective actions. This contributes to the dynamic mix of alternating and varied individual and collective actions across the duration of most temporary gatherings.

Efforts to characterize entire gatherings by one or another prevailing attribute (e.g., "active crowd" versus "expressive crowds") have not proved effective because entire gatherings are never exclusively one or the other. The emotional expressions of cheering and applauding in religious, sport, and political gatherings, or the weeping and wailing at religious funeral gatherings, are themselves expressive actions. But it is rare for any collective action (or expression) to include the entire gathering and when that occurs it is of brief duration.

McPhail (1991) defines collective action as any activity that two or more individuals take with or in relation to one another. He inductively generated a taxonomy of elementary forms of collective action from on-site observation records of hundreds of prosaic, religious, sport, and political gatherings over a period of three decades. Schweingruber and McPhail (1999) reported that the most characteristic feature in a periodic political gathering was alternation between and variation in the proportion of people engaged in different elementary forms of collective action. McPhail et al. (2006) further documented that feature in a systematic quantitative description of the proportion of people participating in various "directions of facing," "body positions or movements," "types of voicing," and "types of manipulation" in a large religious gathering over the course of a 9-hour period. Their evidence further refuted the classic stereotype of

"the crowd's" continuous and uniform action throughout the rally phase of the gathering and provided new evidence on the distinctive "milling" phase that precedes (and often follows) religious, sport, and political rallies. This study also established several similarities in the elementary forms of collective action in this religious gathering (e.g., cheering and clapping) that have been reported in quantitative studies of sport and political gatherings.

It is not surprising that violence against person or property was not observed in this religious gathering, but it is important to note that violence is the exception rather than the rule in most gatherings. Extensive examination of videotape records of the 1990 Poll Tax Riot in London and the 1992 South Central Los Angeles riot indicates that there were far more onlookers than participants in violence, and the latter participated intermittently rather than continuously. This reflects at the micro level what is now well established in archival studies of thousands of political gatherings in Europe from 1830 to 1930 (Tilly et al. 1975) and in the US during the twentieth-century Civil Rights Movement: violence against person or property occurred in less than 10 percent of those political gatherings.

Routine dispersals have rarely been investigated, although there are numerous opportunities to do so. Sport stadiums and arenas containing tens of thousands of spectators routinely empty in 10–15 minutes after the contests' conclusion. University lecture halls filled with hundreds of students are routinely vacated in 5 minutes after the scheduled end of the class period. Movie theaters offer another venue for investigation, as do periodic worship services of all faiths.

Coerced dispersals traditionally involved police or military agents of social control escalating the level of force necessary to compel gathering members to "cease, desist, and disperse." These actions stemmed from the agents' assumptions that "crowd" members were incapable of controlling themselves, derived in large measure from traditional sociological stereotypes of the crowd. More recently in democratic nations in Europe and North America, police agencies that routinely deal with political protest gatherings have gradually moved toward regulating dispersal by negotiating in advance with protest organizers the time, place, and manner that political gatherings commence, continue, and conclude (Della Porta & Reiter 1998).

Emergency dispersal has been extensively investigated by students of disaster planning and management as well as by fire and safety engineers. The most consistent and important finding for students of temporary gatherings is that incapacitating fear and/or irrational actions (a.k.a. panic) are rare phenomena. Rather than losing control when faced with life-threatening problems, most individuals are creative problem solvers. Research consistently establishes that individuals are more likely to act altruistically than egoistically to assess the welfare of their companions and to assist in their safe evacuation (e.g., Johnson et al. 1994).

The preceding describes some of the phenomena to be explained; viz., what people do collectively in the formation, development, and termination of temporary gatherings. Any general theory of collective action should address all three phases; the majority of extant collective action theories fail to do so. Transformation (a.k.a. contagion or deindividuation) theories offer no explanation for the formation of "the crowd." They claim that individuals within "the crowd" lose control of their cognitive processes, mindlessly comply with the suggestions of charismatic leaders, and unwittingly imitate the actions of those around them. One alleged consequence of this "deindividuation" is mutually inclusive collective behavior. The same irrational mindlessness allegedly produces "panic" in emergency dispersals. However, neither on-site observation records nor ex post facto interviews of participants provides any support for either of those claims. There is no mutually inclusive behavior; there is no evidence of lost cognitive control. Further, Postmes and Spears's (1998) meta-analysis of 60 experimental studies of the deindividuation phenomenon established no support for the claim of impaired cognitive processes . Finally, the absence of individual cognitive control postulated by these theories simply does not fit and cannot explain the dynamic alternation and variation in what individuals do alone and together over the course of most gatherings.

Predisposition (a.k.a. convergence) theories claim that crowds form because two or more individuals with the same innate or acquired predispositions to behave – attitudes, personality types, and grievances – converge on the same location for the same reasons. The urban riots, civil rights, and anti-war demonstrations of the 1960s provided repeated opportunities to empirically examine those claims and yielded virtually no support. The mutually inclusive behavior that should occur within a gathering after similarly predisposed persons have assembled does not occur. Finally, theories based on similar predispositions cannot account for the alternating and varied individual and collective actions constituting the phenomena to be explained.

Emergent norm theories claim that mutually inclusive behavior is an illusion. Its adherents claim instead that crowds are composed of individuals with diverse predispositions that lead them to participate in different ways; this includes the interaction among individuals attempting to determine what they should do in ambiguous and uncertain situations. That interaction is said to yield an emergent norm that constrains most people to behave collectively consistent with that norm and that restrains others from behaving inconsistently. Some critics charge that emergent norm theories imply compromised or crippled cognitive processes under the conditions of ambiguity and uncertainty. Without question, interaction among companions in the situation is the source of some decisions about what to do with or in relation to one another; however, all collective action in all gatherings does not stem from such interaction. Some derives from repertoires shared by many if not most members of a gathering enabling them to independently generate collective action (e.g., cheering or applause) without consultation with companions or solicitation from a third party; and, other collective action (e.g., civil disobedience) is planned and rehearsed well in advance of the gathering in which it is launched.

Rational choice theories acknowledge diversity in the phenomena to be explained. They recognize the influence of interaction upon individuals while deciding the costs and benefits of alternative courses of collective action. Rational choice theories are a step in the right direction because they place individuals in control of their own behavior. However, they are flawed in several ways: they do not explain how alternative courses of action are initially formulated; they offer but one criterion – the minimax calculus – in terms of which a course of action is selected; they fail to accommodate errors and unanticipated consequences and the necessary adjustments required in the face of such negative feedback; and, last but not least, they fail to embody the behavioral choice that was rationally made. In short, they do not connect cognition to action.

Complexity and control systems theories begin with the recognition that the phenomena to be explained are variable and dynamic. These theories argue that the varied and dynamic yet coordinated actions to be explained can only be understood by assuming that the individual actors who participate in those actions are autonomous, heuristic, interdependent, and adaptive agents. McPhail et al. (2006) use a negative-feedback, control-system model of such actors to make sense of the three most common ways in which collective action has been observed to develop in many gatherings. These purposive actors adjust their actions in order to realize their goals or to display their approval (or disapproval) of others or their own words and deeds that realize or are consistent with those goals. Collective action by two or more individuals requires similar goals; these can be established independently, interdependently, or by adopting them from a third party. Thus, some collective actions (e.g., *cheering* and *applause* and the alternation between *sitting* and *standing*) were independently generated by the actors without consulting their companions or third-party solicitation. Other collective actions (e.g., *conversing within convergent facing clusters* and milling *pedestrian clusters* in the pre-rally and post-rally period) were interdependently generated within the small companion groups that assembled, remained, and dispersed together in this as in most temporary gatherings. Still other collective actions (e.g., the distinctive prayer prostrations and huddles during the religious rally) resulted from voluntary compliance with the solicitations of a third party. That compliance was not collectively mindless obedience to the suggestions of charismatic speakers as hypothesized by traditional explanations because the observed proportion complying never approached unanimity.

Thus, complexity explanations recognize that some collective actions result from autonomous, self-directing actors who can independently generate and pursue similar goals and independently participate in collective evaluations of the outcomes. Most of these actors are also embedded in small groups of companions who can interdependently generate their own goals, interdependently pursue their own collective actions, and evaluate the outcomes. Intermittently, these same individuals, acting alone or in consultation with their companions, can adopt the goals proposed by third parties, resulting in still other forms of collective actions by larger proportions of the gathering. These three means of generating collective action can occur separately at different times or concurrently in different sections of large gatherings. This may explain why the kaleidoscopic collective actions that occur across the duration of temporary gatherings are purposive but are neither mutually inclusive nor continuous.

SEE ALSO: Blumer, Herbert George; Collective Action; Complexity and Emergence; Emergent Norm Theory; Identity Control Theory; Rational Choice Theories; Riots

REFERENCES AND SUGGESTED READINGS

Blumer, H. (1957) Collective Behavior. In: Gittler, J. (Ed.), *Review of Sociology: Analysis of a Decade.* Wiley, New York.
Della Porta, D. & Reiter, H. (Eds.) (1998) *Policing Protest: The Control of Mass Demonstrations in Western Democracies.* University of Minnesota Press, Minneapolis.
Johnson, N., Feinberg, W., & Johnston, D. (1994) Microstructure and Panic: The Impact of Social Bonds on Individual Action in Collective Flight from Fire. In: Dynes, R. & Tierney, K. (Eds.), *Disaster, Collective Behavior and Social Organization.* University of Delaware Press, Newark.
McPhail, C. (1991) The *Myth of the Madding Crowd.* Aldine, New York.
McPhail, C. & Miller, D. (1973) The Assembling Process. *American Sociological Review* 38: 721–35.
McPhail, C. & Wohlstein, R. T. (1983) Individual and Collective Behaviors in Gatherings, Demonstrations and Riots. *Annual Review of Sociology* 9: 579–600.

McPhail, C., Schweingruber, D. S., & Ceobanu, A. (2006) Describing and Explaining Collective Action. In: McClelland, K. & Farraro, T. (Eds.), *Purpose, Meaning, and Action: Control Systems Theories in Sociology*. Palgrave–MacMillan, New York.

Oliver, P. & Marwell, G. (1992) Mobilizing Technologies for Collective Action. In: Morris, A. & Mueller, C. (Eds.), *Frontiers of Social Movement Theory*. Yale University Press, New Haven.

Postmes, T. & Spears, R. (1998) Deindividuation and Anti-Normative Behavior: A Meta-Analysis. *Psychological Bulletin* 123: 238–59.

Schweingruber, D. S. & McPhail, C. (1999) A Method for Systematically Observing and Recording Collective Action. *Sociological Methods and Research* 27: 451–98.

Tilly, C., Tilly, L., & Tilly, R. (1975) *The Rebellious Century, 1830–1930*. Harvard University Presss, Cambridge, MA.

Wright, S. (1978) *Crowds and Riots: A Study in Social Organization*. Sage, Beverly Hills.

cults: social psychological aspects

Gary Shepherd

The term cult has become, since the latter part of the twentieth century, one of the most controversial concepts in the social sciences. The term was originally employed by scholars of religion to signify a system of activities centering on an object of worship, but the concept has been gradually changed by sociologists to identify a particular residual type of religious group that fell outside the boundaries of recognized religious organization. Subsequently, scholarly attempts to redefine or specify the dimensions and implications of cult groups have proliferated, while at the same time the term cult has been appropriated for polemical purposes by opponents of unconventional religious organizations who characterize such organizations under the cult label as dangerous to both individuals and the larger society. The mass media in modern nations have largely adopted and disseminated these morally charged, negative definitions, and thus pejorative notions of the term cult and of the many groups to which it is uncritically attached have become virtually universal among the general public. Many scholars of contemporary religions, especially sociologists, have now chosen to drop the term cult as a descriptor of a type of religious group, concluding that it is a conceptually polluted concept, and replaced it with a morally neutral term, such as new religious movement or alternative religious group. Others have argued that the term cult has a scientifically useful conceptual function and should be retained even though there is not yet a social science consensus on its essential definitional characteristics.

Both Durkheim, in *The Elementary Forms of Religious Life* (1915), and Weber, in *The Sociology of Religion* (1922), employed a classical conception of cult as designating a ritual system of worship activities. Durkheim focused attention on what he saw as the essential function of cultic activity within a community, namely to periodically renew, through participation in sacred rites, a collective sense of social unity and moral force around a set of shared values that constitute the community itself. Weber emphasized the rationalizing tendencies of cultic organization over time, particularly through the emergence of priestly roles to articulate, elaborate, coordinate, officiate, defend, propagate, and otherwise administer the system of religious practices and doctrines centered on the worship of a god or gods or other supernatural entities.

The rationalizing tendencies of religious organization noted by Weber were further elaborated by Ernst Troeltsch's attempt to specify the characteristics of Weber's two types of religious community organization: the church (a socially inclusive, less restrictive membership group embracing and embraced by the larger society) and the sect (an exclusive, particularistic, and restrictive membership group that by its strict requirements sets itself apart from and at odds with both the parent religious body and the larger society). In *The Social Teachings of the Christian Churches* (1931) Troeltsch placed the categories of Christian sects and churches along a dynamic, cyclical continuum in which sects were seen as typically breaking away from established churches to reclaim a perceived lost purity of belief or practice, only to gradually accommodate worldly pressures in order to flourish, thereby acquiring church-like characteristics that in turn generate a new schismatic cycle. He recognized, however, that even within Christianity not all organized religious expressions fit comfortably within the church–sect continuum, notably religious associations that give priority emphasis to achieving personal, non-rational experiences. Troeltsch assigned such expressions to a residual category called mysticism, which was conceptually only vaguely connected to the church–sect continuum.

Howard Becker, in *Systematic Sociology* (1932), exchanged the term cult for mysticism, resulting in an influential shift in the sociological designation of cult as a particular type of religious group rather than referring only to the structuring of worship activities within all religions. Becker's definition of a cult included the characteristics of loosely structured, non-demanding, non-exclusive, and transient associations between individuals in urban settings who share interest in a limited set of esoteric spiritual beliefs typically propounded by a charismatic but not necessarily authoritarian teacher-leader. Variations on the defining characteristics of cults as a type of religious group have subsequently proliferated. The greatest stimulus to reconceptualization and study of groups identified as cults occurred in the mid-1960s through mid-1970s as a consequence of certain elements within the hippie-oriented youth counterculture (e.g., the Jesus Movement, the New Age Movement, the Communitarian Movement, etc.) and especially the increasing visibility and proselytizing activities of foreign and non-Christian religious groups within western nations generally and the US in particular (e.g., the Unification Church, or "Moonies," the Divine Light Mission, the International Society for Krishna Consciousness, or "Hare Krishnas," etc.).

Although some sociologists argued that these contemporary, radically different groups were best seen as extreme variations of religious sects, most concluded that it was useful to expand the cult concept in a way that would account for more dynamic, structured, innovative, and purposive new religious movements that seemed to be more than just dissenting splinter groups from an already established religious tradition. Both Geoffrey Nelson's

Sociological Review article on "The Concept of Cult" (1968) and Milton Yinger's *The Scientific Study of Religion* (1970) emphasized the radical break from established religious worldviews characteristic of cults and the potential for cult groups to grow, increase their organizational complexity, and elaborate their own coherent, innovative worldview. From such developments over time, new religious traditions are formed that may, depending on a complex of social and historical conditions (and parallel to the institutional path of some sects), even ascend to the status of institutionalized "church" in the Weberian sense.

This line of thinking on cults was most clearly extended and articulated by Rodney Stark and William Bainbridge in their article "Of Churches, Sects, and Cults: Preliminary Concepts for a Theory of Religious Movements" (1979) and in their more comprehensive book, *The Future of Religion: Secularization, Renewal, and Cult Formation* (1985). Stark and Bainbridge distinguish cults as religious novelties that are not the product of schism from the established religions within a particular host society. Cults may originate in one of two ways: either from borrowing or "importing" their essential elements from an alien cultural tradition (i.e., from outside of the host society), or through the religious innovations of charismatic leaders who assert a new order of belief and practice that is substantially independent of established religious traditions. An example of the former would be the International Society of Krishna Consciousness (the "Hare Krishnas") in America (but not in India, where ISKON would be a sect of Hinduism); an example of the latter would be primitive Christianity in ancient Judea and adjacent areas of the Roman Empire. A contemporary cult may be present itself as the kind of amorphous, esoteric, and low-commitment social enterprise identified by Becker in either of the two forms. The first form, according to Stark and Bainbridge, is the audience cult – a mystical or spiritually centered set of topics and ideas that are promoted through various media means. Adherents or advocates of these ideas are fundamentally consumers of the occult rather than members of a concrete religious organization. The second form is the client cult, which revolves around a kind of patient–therapist relationship in which adherents seek personal assistance, guidance, or reassurance (psychological, physical, or spiritual) directly from agents who claim access to various supernatural powers. Neither of these forms creates a strong social identity for participants, and both are seen as focused on magical manipulations of non-empirical forces to achieve desired empirical ends. However, cults may also coalesce into much more distinct membership groups with strict requirements, organizational hierarchies, broadly conceived ideologies, and long-term aspirations for growth and influence. Stark and Bainbridge refer to this development as a cult movement and see such movements, in rare cases, as having the potential eventually to become transformed into new religious traditions. Even though the vast majority of cult movements do not succeed in achieving this outcome, cult movements are still seen as significant religious responses within secularized segments of modern society in which the appeal of established faiths has considerably weakened.

Sociological understanding of cults, however, has had little impact on public perceptions. From the 1960s onwards, the apparent proliferation of non-conventional or alien religious groups in western societies, which were primarily successful in recruiting young people coming from conventional backgrounds, was deeply disturbing to many parents, mainstream Christian clergy, and various secular groups. From this public consternation emerged new, pejorative, polemical, and non-scholarly definitions of cults. For many in the Christian clergy, a cult essentially came to be understood as any religious group that deviates from what are defined as orthodox Christian beliefs and practices – a "fake" religion that tempts people away from "true" religion. Such faith-based, ethnocentric definitions considerably widen the category of groups labeled as cults, prominently including such well-known American-born religious organizations as the Church of Jesus Christ of Latter Day Saints (the "Mormons"), the Church of Christ, Scientist (Christian Science), and the Jehovah's Witnesses.

Secular opponents of various unconventional religious groups (including some academic sociologists but mostly clinical psychologists, a variety of different types of therapists,

entrepreneurial and self-styled "cult experts," and several different anti-cult organizations), beginning in the early 1970s, emphasized the dangers that cult groups were presumed to pose for both individuals who were snared by them and to the larger society that harbored them. Lists of identifying cult characteristics included (and currently still do) notions of "brainwashing" or mind-control tactics employed as recruitment and retention devices; fraudulent motives and totalitarian methods of charismatic leaders; exploitation or abuse of duped or cowed members for the benefit of leaders; secrecy and isolation from the outside world; a potential if not an actual tendency toward the use of violence; and so on.

This understanding of cults as dangerous or destructive groups engaging in fraudulent or even illegal activities was (and remains) largely adopted and disseminated by the mass media. Several spectacular and tragic episodes involving unconventional religious groups since the late 1970s have garnered massive media attention (e.g., the People's Temple slayings and mass suicide in Jonestown, Guyana; the Rajneeshpuram takeover of a small Oregon community; the prolonged siege and fiery deaths of the Branch Davidians in Waco, Texas; the subway poison gas attacks by Aum Shinrikyo in Japan; and the mass suicides among followers of the Solar Temple in Switzerland and Heaven's Gate in California). Other highly publicized, controversial groups whose reported activities continue to reinforce the widespread perception of cults as dangerous threats that need to be exposed and suppressed include the Church of Scientology (throughout Europe particularly) and the Falun Gong/Daffa movement (in mainland China).

Anti-cult organizations such as the Cult-Awareness Network (now defunct) and the American Family Federation have long advanced the claim that cults "brainwash" their members to such an extent that individuals within the group are significantly impeded in exercising full free agency and are thus largely helpless to avoid the abuse to which they are presumably subjected. This claim was bolstered from non-random interview samples of ex-group members and became the basis for involuntary removal of members from groups labeled as destructive cults by hired "deprogrammers" until the American Psychological Association officially declared "brainwashing" to be an unscientific concept in the late 1980s, and American courts began convicting deprogrammers on charges related to kidnapping.

In contrast, most sociologists of religion continue to advocate a more detached, objective, and analytical understanding of cults and their relationships to conditions in both mainstream religions and society generally. Of the hundreds of groups that can reliably be identified as cult movements, only a very small fraction have or are likely to have violent confrontations with outsiders. Sociologists who specialize in the study of cult movements through field research or direct observations typically find that most groups they investigate, while espousing beliefs or practices that may seem outlandish, restrictive, or otherwise unappealing to outsiders, generally develop a core of sincere and committed followers whose right of religious choice ought not be trammeled by indiscriminate negative labeling. The term new religious movement (NRM) has been widely adopted as a substitute for cult by many sociologists in order to neutralize the negative connotations that have accumulated around the term cult and to emphasize the need to examine every group on its own observable merits rather than simply stigmatizing unconventional religious organizations on the basis of a pejorative stereotype. Nevertheless, controversy over the nature of cults, how cults ought to be studied, whether the term itself ought to be discarded, and what kinds of policies, if any, ought to be adopted toward religiously deviant groups by secular authorities, continues.

SEE ALSO: Charisma; New Religious Movements; Religious Cults; Sect; Social Psychology

REFERENCES AND SUGGESTED READINGS

Barker, E. (1989) *New Religious Movements: A Practical Introduction.* HMSO, London.
Bromley, D. G. & Melton, J. G. (2002) *Cults, Religion, and Violence.* Cambridge University Press, Cambridge.
Bromley, D. G. & Shupe, A. D. (1982) *Strange Gods.* Beacon Press, Boston.
Dawson, L. L. (1998) *Comprehending Cults: The Sociology of New Religious Movements.* Oxford University Press, New York.
Elwood, R. (1986) The Several Meanings of Cult. *Thought* 61: 212–24.
Galanter, M. (1999) *Cults: Faith, Healing, and Coercion.* Oxford University Press, New York.
Melton, J. G. (1992) *Encyclopedia Handbook of Cults in America.* Garland, New York.
Richardson, J. T. (1993) Definitions of Cult: From Sociological-Technical to Popular-Negative. *Review of Religious Research* 34(4): 348–56.
Saliba, J. A. (2003) *Understanding New Religious Movements.* Alta Mira Press, Walnut Creek, CA.
Zablocki, B. & Robbins, T. (Eds.) (2001) *Misunderstanding Cults.* University of Toronto Press, Toronto.

cultural capital

Elliot B. Weininger and Annette Lareau

The French sociologist Pierre Bourdieu, working with various colleagues, developed the concept of cultural capital in the early 1960s in order to help address a particular empirical problem – namely, the fact that "economic obstacles are not sufficient to explain" disparities in the educational attainment of children from different social classes (Bourdieu & Passeron 1979 [1964]: 8). Bourdieu argued that, above and beyond economic factors, "cultural habits and … dispositions inherited from" the family are fundamentally important to school success (Bourdieu & Passeron 1979 [1964]: 14). In doing so, he broke sharply with traditional sociological conceptions of culture, which tended to view it primarily as a source of shared norms and values, or as a vehicle of collective expression. Instead, Bourdieu maintained that culture shares many of the properties that are characteristic of economic capital. In particular, he asserted that cultural "habits and dispositions" comprise a *resource* capable of generating "profits" that are potentially subject to *monopolization* by individuals and groups; and, under appropriate conditions, that can be *transmitted* from one generation to the next (Lareau & Weininger 2003).

As the originator of the concept of cultural capital, Bourdieu was notoriously disinclined to elaborate the meaning and significance of concepts outside of the concrete context offered by empirical research. At the most general level, however, he emphasized that any "competence" becomes a capital insofar as it facilitates appropriation of a society's "cultural heritage" but is unequally distributed, thereby creating opportunities for "exclusive advantages." In societies characterized by a highly differentiated social structure and a system of formal education, Bourdieu further asserted, these "advantages" largely stem from the institutionalization of "criteria of evaluation" in schools – that is, standards of assessment – which are favorable to children from a particular class or classes (Bourdieu 1977).

Bourdieu (1986) further argued that cultural capital exists in three distinct forms. In its "embodied" form, cultural capital is a "competence" or skill that cannot be separated from its "bearer" (i.e., the person who "holds" it). As such, the acquisition of cultural capital necessarily presupposes the investment of time devoted to learning and/or training. For example, a college student who studies art history has gained a competence which, because it is highly valued in some institutional settings, becomes an embodied form of cultural capital. Additionally, Bourdieu suggests that the objects themselves may function as a form of cultural capital, insofar as their use or consumption presupposes a certain amount of embodied cultural capital. For example, a philosophy text is an "objectified" form of cultural capital since it requires prior training in philosophy to understand. Finally, in societies with a system of formal education, cultural capital exists in an "institutionalized" form. This is to say that when the school certifies individuals' competencies and skills by issuing credentials, their embodied cultural capital takes on an objective value. Thus, for example, since persons with the same credentials have a roughly equivalent worth on the labor market, educational degrees can be seen to be a distinct form of cultural capital. Because they render individuals interchangeable in this fashion, Bourdieu suggests that institutionalization performs a function for cultural capital analogous to that performed by money in the case of economic capital.

Nevertheless, despite the similarities between cultural and economic capital, Bourdieu also

recognized that they differ from one another in important respects. In particular, he noted that the legitimation of inequality in cultural capital occurs in a manner that is highly distinct from the legitimation of economic inequality. Despite the fact that cultural capital is acquired in the home and the school via exposure to a given set of cultural practices – and therefore has a social origin – it is liable to be perceived as inborn "talent," and its holder "gifted," as a result of the fact that it is embodied in particular individuals. Moreover, because the school system transforms "inherited" cultural capital into "scholastic" cultural capital, the latter is predisposed to appear as an individual "achievement." For example, scholars have demonstrated that middle-class parents typically talk more to infants and young children than do working-class or poor parents. As a result, middle-class children often have larger vocabularies when they enter school, and subsequently score more highly on standardized tests measuring verbal skills (Lareau 2003). Nevertheless, teachers, parents, and students themselves are likely to interpret the differences in test scores as a matter of natural talent or individual effort.

Bourdieu's arguments concerning cultural capital were notable because they vociferously challenged the widespread view of modern schooling as a mobility engine that promotes or demotes people through the class structure simply on the basis of their talents and efforts. Indeed, from Bourdieu's highly critical vantage point, modern systems of schooling are far more adept at validating and augmenting cultural capital inherited from the family than they are at instilling it in children who enter the institution with few or none of the requisite dispositions and skills. Consequently, he maintained, the educational systems of modern societies tend to channel individuals toward class destinations that largely (but not wholly) mirror their class origins. Moreover, they tend to elicit acceptance of this outcome (i.e., legitimation), both from those who are most privileged by it and from those who are disfavored by it (Bourdieu & Passeron 1977 [1970]).

The concept of cultural capital also had tremendous impact in sociology because it placed culture at the core of stratification research. Bourdieu's subsequent work used the notion of cultural capital to further reinforce the premise that culture is directly implicated in social inequality. This is especially apparent in the thoroughgoing reconceptualization of social class that he presented in *Distinction* (1984 [1979]; Weininger 2005). For Bourdieu, classes are differentiated from one another in terms of the overall *volume of capital* (economic plus cultural) controlled by individuals or families. Within classes, "class fractions" are differentiated from one another by the *composition* of the capital controlled – or in other words, by the ratio of economic capital to cultural capital. Using this reconceptualization, *Distinction* analyzed the aesthetic practices and preferences of classes and class fractions located across the French social structure, focusing, in particular, on the taste or distaste for "highbrow" art forms (painting, music, literature, drama, etc.). Bourdieu's data indicated that each class (and class fraction) exhibited a relatively unique pattern of tastes, one consistent with its particular mix of cultural and economic capital. Thus, for example, professors and artistic producers – one fraction of the dominant class – utilized their superior endowment of cultural capital to appreciate the most avant-garde forms of art. By contrast, employers, the fraction of the dominant class richest in economic capital, tended to prefer less intellectually demanding forms of art, and especially those which conformed to traditional conceptions of beauty, and which connoted a sense of luxury. These differences of taste, Bourdieu argued, should be viewed as claims for the prestige constitutive of status, in Weber's sense of "social honor," which Bourdieu termed "symbolic capital." As such, these differences were said to play an integral role in the legitimation of class stratification.

Within English-language sociology, the concept of cultural capital began to make its way into the literature starting in the late 1970s with the translation of *Reproduction* (Bourdieu & Passeron 1977 [1970]). Given its genesis in Bourdieu's study of the French educational system, it has unsurprisingly been in the field of educational research that the notion of cultural capital has triggered the greatest amount of empirical research and theoretical reflection, and the greatest contention. However, the concept has proven fruitful in a number of other research areas. For example, proceeding from Bourdieu's interest in the way that different forms of capital are implicated in complex patterns of stratification, Eyal et al.'s (1998) examination of the class structure of post-communist societies in Central Europe focuses on cultural capital. Contrary to many predictions, they argue, members of the bureaucratic *nomenklatura* did not successfully exploit their authority under communism to appropriate large amounts of state property during the privatization process that marked the transition to capitalism. Nor have the small-scale entrepreneurs who were tolerated in the final decades of state socialism managed to leverage their "head start" and become a full-blown capitalist class in the post-1989 period. Rather, in countries such as the Czech Republic, Hungary, and Poland, a stratification system has emerged which can be characterized as a type of "capitalism without capitalists." In this system, cultural capital stands as the most important basis of power and privilege. Thus, the dominant class in these societies can be described as a "cultural bourgeoisie" rather than an economic bourgeoisie. This cultural bourgeoisie, which is a diverse group that includes former technocrats and dissident intellectuals, has largely monopolized the skills, know-how, and credentials (i.e., cultural capital) that have become critical to occupational success. The authors demonstrate that possession of cultural capital makes possible access to leading positions in the economy and the state and, conversely, that lack of cultural capital is a substantial barrier.

The concept of cultural capital has also proven highly productive in the study of aesthetic tastes and preferences. In this context, sociologists have evaluated the association between social position and taste, concentrating on the upper-class predilection for exclusively "highbrow" aesthetic forms at the heart of *Distinction*. The evidence for this proposition strongly indicates that in the contemporary United States, for example, the relation is different from that charted by Bourdieu. Thus, Peterson and colleagues (Peterson & Kern 1996; Peterson & Simkus 1992) report that in matters of cultural taste, "elites" in the US are more accurately characterized as "omnivores" than "snobs": status claims now tend to hinge on familiarity with a wide variety of genres within each cultural form (music, literature, film, etc.) – genres that range from the high-brow (e.g., classical music and opera) to the middlebrow (e.g., Broadway show tunes) and the lowbrow (e.g., country music and rock). Those claiming status are expected to be able to distinguish laudable examples of each genre according to standards of judgment that are unique to it. Despite the fact that it differs substantially from the form of aesthetic compe-tence delineated in Bourdieu's account of French lifestyles, this "cosmopolitan" orienta-tion is clearly conditional upon indicators of social class such as education, and therefore prone to function as a form of cultural capital. Indeed, Bryson (1996) goes so far as to dub it "multi-cultural capital."

At the same time that it has been incorpo-rated into various areas of English-language sociology, the concept of cultural capital has also been the object of considerable criticism. Giroux (1983) has argued, for example, that when culture is viewed primarily as a form of capital, it becomes impossible to acknowledge the role it plays in enabling those in subordi-nate positions to resist domination. Similarly, Lamont (1992) asserts that conceptualizing cul-ture in this manner prevents sociologists from recognizing that it contains repertoires which actors use to evaluate the moral quality of their own experiences and those of others – reper-toires that do not necessarily have the character of a resource implicated in stratification pro-cesses. These debates are sure to intensify as scholars continue to interrogate the relation between culture and inequality. Regardless of the shape that they take, Bourdieu's concept of cultural capital, with its distinctive focus on the social value of cultural habits, dispositions, and skills, is likely to be an important part of the discussions in theories of inequality, the sociol-ogy of culture, and the sociology of education in the future.

SEE ALSO: Bourdieu, Pierre; Capital: Eco-nomic, Cultural, and Social; Class, Percep-tions of; Cultural Capital; Cultural Capital in Schools; Distinction; Life Chances and Resources; Stratification, Distinction and; Stra-tification and Inequality, Theories of; Symbolic Classification

REFERENCES AND SUGGESTED READINGS

Bourdieu, P. (1977) Cultural Reproduction and Social Reproduction. In: Karabel, J. & Halsey, A. H. (Eds.), *Power and Ideology in Education*. Oxford University Press, New York, pp. 487–511.

Bourdieu, P. (1984 [1979]) *Distinction: A Social Cri-tique of the Judgment of Taste*. Trans. R. Nice. Harvard University Press, Cambridge, MA.

Bourdieu, P. (1986) The Forms of Capital. In: Richardson, J. G. (Ed.), *Handbook of Theory and Research for the Sociology of Education*. Greenwood Press, New York, pp. 241–58.

Bourdieu, P. & Passeron, J.-C. (1977 [1970]) *Repro-duction in Education, Society and Culture*. Trans. R. Nice. Sage, London.

Bourdieu, P. & Passeron, J.-C. (1979 [1964]) *The Inheritors: French Students and their Relations to Culture*. University of Chicago Press, Chicago.

Bryson, B. (1996) "Anything But Heavy Metal": Symbolic Exclusion and Cultural Dislikes. *Amer-ican Sociological Review* 61: 884–99.

DiMaggio, P. (1982) Cultural Capital and School Success: The Impact of Status Culture Participa-tion on the Grades of US High School Students. *American Sociological Review* 47: 189–201.

Eyal, G., Szelényi, I, & Townsley, E. (1998) *Making Capitalism without Capitalists: The New Ruling Elites in Eastern Europe*. Verso, London and New York.

Giroux, H. (1983) *Theory and Resistance in Educa-tion: A Pedagogy for the Opposition*. Bergin & Gar-vey, South Hadley, MA.

Hart, B. & Risley, T. R. (1995) *Meaningful Differ-ences in the Everyday Experiences of Young Amer-ican Children*. Brookes, Baltimore.

Lamont, M. (1992) *Money, Morals, and Manners: The Culture of the French and the American Upper-Middle Class*. University of Chicago Press, Chicago.

Lareau, A. (2003) *Unequal Childhoods: Class, Race, and Family Life*. University of California Press, Berkeley, CA.

Lareau, A. & Weininger, E. B. (2003) Cultural Capital in Educational Research: A Critical Assessment. *Theory and Society*: 567–606.

Peterson, R. A. & Kern, R. M. (1996) Changing Highbrow Taste: From Snob to Omnivore. *Amer-ican Sociological Review* 61: 900–7.

Peterson, R. & Simkus, A. (1992) How Musical Taste Groups Mark Occupational Status Groups. In: Lamont, M. & Fournier, M. (Eds.), *Cultivat-ing Differences: Symbolic Boundaries and the Mak-ing of Inequality*. University of Chicago Press, Chicago.

Weininger, E. B. (2005) Foundations of Pierre Bourdieu's Class Analysis. In: Wright, E. O. (Ed.),
Approaches to Class Analysis. Cambridge University Press, Cambridge.

cultural capital in schools

Elliot B. Weininger and Annette Lareau

One of the central goals of sociological studies
of education has been to understand the role of
schools in society. Do schools promote equal
opportunity? Do schools help to recreate social
stratification? In American society, where the
ideology of meritocracy has taken root, American social science researchers have been preoccupied with issues of mobility and status
attainment. The concept of cultural capital
offers an alternative to the classic view of
schools as the "great equalizer" which assesses
students based on their raw talent or merit.
Instead, the concept of cultural capital suggests
that students' performance in schools draws on
students' cultural resources where the habits,
dispositions, and skills that children learn in
the home are unequally valued by educators.
For example, in this perspective children who
learn classical music or other highly valued
cultural practices at home may have an advantage in the educational setting compared to
children who learn hip hop music or other
cultural practices that are accorded lower social
value. The profit yielded by cultural capital is
linked to the value accorded to particular skills,
dispositions, and habits by educators and other
people in positions of power in dominant institutions. The concept of cultural capital plays a
large role in arguments concerning social reproduction, in which schools are posited to play a
key role in channeling individuals toward class
destinations that reflect their class origins, and
in legitimating inequality.

The concept of cultural capital grew out of
the work of the French social thinker Pierre
Bourdieu and his broader theory of social life.
As Lamont and Lareau (1988) note, Bourdieu
offers differing definitions at various points
in his numerous writings. Bourdieu's most
influential discussions of cultural capital in

education can be found in an early co-authored
work (Bourdieu & Passeron 1977) and in an
article (Bourdieu 1977). Bourdieu's (1986) article offers the most direct discussion of the
topic.

As with many core sociological concepts, the
notion of cultural capital has been subject to a
profusion of definitions in the literature. There
has also been a profusion of indicators used to
measure it. DiMaggio (1982), in a highly influential article, focused on students' attitudes,
activities, and information regarding art, music,
and literature. The assumption made by DiMaggio (and those who have followed him) is that
proficiency with highbrow aesthetic culture of
this sort enables students to carry out "status
displays" which teachers, in turn, are inclined
to reward. Lamont and Lareau (1988) defined
cultural capital as "institutionalized, i.e. widely
shared, high-status cultural signals (attitudes,
preferences, formal knowledge, behaviors,
goods, and credentials) used for social and cultural exclusion." In doing so, however, they
argued that in order for a given set of attitudes
or preferences to be declared "cultural capital,"
this institutionalization must first be empirically documented. This argument was widely
ignored. Instead, in part as a result of the constraints of representative survey data, empirical
research has largely followed the work of
DiMaggio and settled for indicators of cultural
capital that hinge on knowledge of or facility
with "highbrow" aesthetics (e.g., attendance at
art museums, theater, or plays). While some
studies have established a relationship between
this type of "high-status cultural consumption"
and educational experiences, others (De Graaf
et al. 2000) have found that parents' language use
in the home, particularly in the form of reading,
is more influential.

Some scholars, such as Kingston (2001), have
declared the concept and the literature it has
spawned to be of little or no value. Lareau and
Weininger (2003), in a comprehensive review,
criticize the English-language literature for
unnecessarily narrowing the concept by focusing on "highbrow" aesthetic culture. They also
object to the partitioning of effects attributable
to cultural capital from those attributable to
"human capital" or "technical ability." They
call for a broader conception of cultural capital
which stresses the micro-interactional strategies

through which children and their parents gain advantages in schools. For educational research, they stress the value of Bourdieu's definition of cultural capital as "the educational norms of those social classes capable of imposing the ... criteria of evaluation which are the most favorable to their children." Although abstract, this definition implies the need to look critically at the standards which determine success in school and at the strategies that families pursue in relation to these standards. For example, child-rearing practices that emphasize language development or parent involvement in schooling offer cultural capital to family members (Lareau 2000).

In sum, while pursuing different empirical approaches, researchers using the concept of cultural capital generally challenge the view of schools as adhering to objective and socially neutral standards of success. Instead, the concept of cultural capital stresses the ways in which the standards for success are drenched in family cultural practices. Advantaged families transmit an advantage to their children because educators proclaim the cultural practices in these families to be more valuable. From this vantage point, the role of schools in society – despite the well-intentioned beliefs of educators – too often offers an advantage to children from the dominant class as they approach school with a set of powerful, albeit largely invisible, cultural advantages which they draw on to comply with standards for school success.

SEE ALSO: Bourdieu, Pierre; Capital: Economic, Cultural, and Social; Cultural Capital; Educational Inequality; Educational and Occupational Attainment

REFERENCES AND SUGGESTED READINGS

Bernstein, B. (1970) *Class, Codes, and Control*, Vol. 1: *Theoretical Studies Towards a Sociology of Language*. Routledge & Kegan Paul, London.

Bourdieu, P. (1977) Cultural Reproduction and Social Reproduction. In: Karabel, J. & Halsey, A. H. (Eds.), *Power and Ideology in Education*. Oxford University Press, New York, pp. 487–511.

Bourdieu, P. (1986) The Forms of Capital. In: Richardson, J. G. (Ed.), *Handbook of Theory and*

Research for the Sociology of Education. Greenwood Press, New York, pp. 241–58.

Bourdieu, P. & Passeron, J.-C. (1977 [1970]) *Reproduction in Education, Society and Culture*. Trans. R. Nice. Sage, London.

Bourdieu, P. & Passeron, J.-C. (1979) *The Inheritors: French Students and their Relations to Culture*. University of Chicago Press, Chicago.

De Graaf, N. D., De Graaf, P. M., & Kraaykamp, G. (2000) Parental Cultural Capital and Educational Attainment in the Netherlands: A Refinement of the Cultural Capital Perspective. *Sociology of Education* 73: 92–111.

DiMaggio, P. (1982) Cultural Capital and School Success: The Impact of Status Culture Participation on the Grades of US High School Students. *American Sociological Review* 47: 189–201.

Kingston, P. (2001) The Unfulfilled Promise of Cultural Capital Theory. *Sociology of Education* (Extra Issue): 88–99.

Lamont, M. & Lareau, A. (1988) Cultural Capital: Allusions, Gaps and Glissandos in Recent Theoretical Developments. *Sociological Theory* 6: 153–168.

Lareau, A. (2000) *Home Advantage: Social Class and Parental Intervention in Elementary Education*, 2nd edn. Rowman & Littlefield, Lanham, MD.

Lareau, A. & Weininger, E. B. (2003) Cultural Capital in Educational Research: A Critical Assessment. *Theory and Society* 32: 576–606.

cultural criminology

Jeff Ferrell

Cultural criminology explores the many ways in which cultural dynamics intertwine with the practices of crime and crime control in contemporary society; put differently, cultural criminology emphasizes the centrality of meaning and representation in the construction of crime as momentary event, subcultural endeavor, and social issue. From this view, the appropriate subject matter of criminology transcends traditional notions of crime and crime causation to include images of illicit behavior and symbolic displays of law enforcement; popular culture constructions of crime and criminal action; and the shared emotions that animate criminal events, perceptions of criminal threat, and public efforts at crime control. This wider cultural focus, cultural criminologists argue, allows scholars and the public alike to better understand crime as meaningful human activity, and to penetrate more deeply the contested politics of crime control.

At a fundamental level cultural criminology in this way integrates the insights of sociological criminology with the orientations toward image and style offered by the field of cultural studies. Within this broad confluence of the criminological and the cultural, though, cultural criminology has emerged from a rather more complex co-evolution of sociology, criminology, and cultural analysis. A fundamental starting point in this emergence is the work of scholars associated with the Birmingham School of Cultural Studies, the National Deviancy Conference, and the "new criminology" in Great Britain during the 1970s. Reconceptualizing the nature of contemporary power, these scholars explored the cultural and ideological dimensions of social class, examined leisure worlds and illicit subcultures as sites of stylized resistance and alternative meaning, and investigated the mediated ideologies driving social and legal control. Around this same time, American sociology provided a second starting point for what was to become cultural criminology: the symbolic interactionist approach to crime and deviance. As conceptualized in labeling theory and embodied in the naturalistic case study, this interactionist model likewise highlighted the contested construction of meaning around issues of crime and deviance, and in this sense explored the situated politics of even the most common of crimes.

As these two orientations co-evolved – with American interactionists and ethnographers providing phenomenological inspiration for British scholars, and British cultural theorists and "new criminologists" offering American scholars sophisticated critiques of legal and ideological control – the transatlantic foundations for today's cultural criminology were laid. With the rapid growth of punitive criminal justice systems in the US and Great Britain during subsequent decades, and the concomitant ascendance of an administrative "criminal justice" in place of a critical sociological criminology, however, little was immediately built from these foundations. It was not until the mid-1990s that a distinct cultural criminology began to emerge (e.g., Ferrell and Sander's *Cultural Criminology*). While drawing on earlier British and American conceptualizations, cultural criminologists now began to integrate into their work the sensibilities of postmodernism and deconstruction as well; elaborating on the "symbolic" in symbolic interaction, they began to explore the looping circulation of images, the representational hall of mirrors, that increasingly define the reality of crime and justice. In an echo of earlier transatlantic conversations, contemporary cultural criminology by intention also emerged as an integration of scholarly work from Great Britain, the US, and beyond.

Cultural criminologists' transatlantic analysis of contemporary urban graffiti exemplifies the depth and complexity of this approach. Hip-hop graffiti, the most pervasive form of contemporary urban graffiti, emerged out of the US hip-hop movement of the 1970s as a stylized medium for displaying artistic ability and negotiating subcultural status. The practice of this illegal street graffiti also embodied what its practitioners called the "adrenalin rush": the vivid, intoxicating experience of executing alternative artistry in situations of extreme physical and legal risk. As an increasingly prominent form of illicit public display, hip-hop graffiti quickly attracted the attention of legal authorities who saw it as violating their own aesthetics of legal control. In response, authorities launched high-profile media campaigns designed to define such graffiti exclusively as vandalism and threat, and aggressively enforced new anti-graffiti ordinances, all of which accelerated graffiti's experiential adrenalin rush, pushed the graffiti underground from subculture to counterculture, and helped construct hip-hop graffiti over the next two decades as a global phenomenon. As hip-hop graffiti has continued to develop in the new millennium, cultural criminologists note, so has this ironic spiral of culture and crime. Hip-hop graffiti artists now maintain their own websites, art galleries, and magazines, and surreptitiously hang their paintings in the Louvre, the Museum of Modern Art, and the Tate Museum. Legal and political authorities counter by continuing to orchestrate media campaigns meant, above all, to poison the public perception of urban graffiti. US shoe companies in turn sell "SuperStar Graffiti" sneakers, US fashion designers stage graffiti demonstrations and promote hip-hop graffiti video games, British advertisers employ graffiti artists to paint corporate logos in city streets and appropriate existing hip-hop graffiti for CD covers and ad campaigns – and graffiti practitioners continue to be arrested and incarcerated on charges of graffiti vandalism and destruction of private property (Ferrell 1996; Alvelos 2004).

In the same way that cultural criminology's analytic approach to contemporary crime issues embodies these sorts of interlocking cultural, critical, and interactionist frames, its methods emerge from its roots in naturalistic case study. While cultural criminology incorporates a variety of methods – among them textual, semiotic, and visual analysis – some of the more prominent work in cultural criminology has been characterized by forms of extreme ethnography. Immersing themselves in illicit subcultures, attempting at times to "become the subject matter," constructing at other times auto-ethnographies of their own lives, cultural criminologists have embraced ethnographic method as an avenue into the situated meaning and subtle symbolism constructed within criminal subcultures and events. In part this approach has been underpinned by cultural criminology's conceptualization of illicit subcultures like that of hip-hop graffiti as collectivities of shared meaning and perception, linked by elaborate symbolic codes as much as by calculated criminal endeavor. Yet it has also been founded in a particular etiology of crime that points, at least in part, to crime's origins inside the immediacy of the criminal event, and to the shared experiences and emotions that develop within moments of criminality and crime control (Katz 1988; Lyng 1990). For cultural criminologists, the primacy of criminal subcultures, criminal events, and the meanings and emotions they spawn confirms the importance of methods that can move criminologists inside them; in the same way this focus reconfirms the value of a Weberian, *verstehen*-oriented criminology and sociology.

Such experiences and emotions have also come into focus as part of cultural criminology's emphasis on everyday existence as an essential arena of criminality and control. Cultural criminology highlights the currents of carnivalesque excitement, pleasure, and risk-taking that animate everyday life, but equally so the many capillaries of daily control designed to contain and commodify these experiential currents (Presdee 2000). In fact, cultural criminologists argue, it is this very tension that accounts for various contemporary confluences of crime and culture: the aggressive policing of alternative subcultures and their styles; the mediated consumption of crime as commodified titillation and entertainment; and the shifting and always contested boundaries between art and pornography, music and political provocation, entertainment and aggression, crime and resistance. In all of these cases, cultural criminologists attempt to account for the political economy of crime by locating it inside the dynamics of the everyday, amid the ambiguities of day-to-day transgression and control.

While exploring the everyday meanings of crime and control, cultural criminologists have in this way also endeavored to fix these situated meanings within larger historical patterns. In a contemporary world shaped by the endless circulation of images and symbols, for example, conventional dualities of the "real" and the "representational" seem to make less and less sense – and so cultural criminology emphasizes the permeability of images as they flow between the mass media, criminal subcultures, and crime control agencies, and likewise the essential role of image and ideology in constructing crime control policies and practices. Following this line of analysis, cultural criminology suggests that everyday criminal justice has now become in many ways a matter of orchestrated public display, and an ongoing policing of public perceptions regarding issues of crime and threat. Shifts such as this are in turn seen to reflect still other dimensions of contemporary life, among them the emergence of a globalized economy of image and consumption, the tension between late modern patterns of social inclusion and exclusion, and the uncertain dynamics of personal and cultural identity within these arrangements (Young 2003). In this context cultural criminologists highlight especially the importance of the global city to the understanding of crime and crime control. With its contested cultural spaces of consumption and display, its amalgam of illicit subcultural dynamics, and its spatial and symbolic practices of everyday policing, the city seems an essential embodiment of contemporary social and cultural trends.

Throughout this range of substantive and theoretical work, cultural criminologists have quite explicitly challenged the conventional practices of criminology and criminal justice on two fronts. A first challenge has been issued in the area of style. Turning their cultural critique to the practice of contemporary criminology and criminal justice, cultural criminologists have noted there a style of writing wanting in elegance and engagement, and a social science culture of detached obfuscation operating so as to maintain a facade of objective neutrality. In response, cultural criminologists have noted the slippery politics of such representational codes – codes that have functioned, in both the historical emergence of criminology and the contemporary ascendance of criminal justice, as cultural displays masking intellectual alliances with political and economic power. Relatedly, cultural criminologists have noted the role of this arid criminological culture in sanitizing what would otherwise seem among the most engaging of subject matters: crime, violence, guilt, and transgression. In this context, cultural criminologists have sought to revitalize the enterprise of criminology, and to restore something of its humanistic orientation, through styles of research and presentation designed for engagement and effect. Along with the texture and nuance offered by ethnographic research, these have included the development of biographical and autobiographical writing styles, the incorporation of evocative vignettes drawn from popular culture, and the inclusion of visual materials and visual analysis. While better communicating the everyday importance of crime and crime control, cultural criminologists argue, such styles also offer a more honest accounting of criminologists' involvement with the politics of crime and crime control.

Cultural criminology's second challenge has occurred in the realms of theory and method. Cultural criminologists argue that survey research methods and quantitative data analysis – dominant modes of research within the objectivist culture of criminology and criminal justice – remain dominant not because of their innate scholarly merit, but due in large part to their utility in generating the sort of distilled data necessary for the administration of the criminal justice system. In fact, cultural criminologists contend, such modes of research

remain useful in this context precisely because they are meaningless: that is, because they drain from crime its situated meaning and seductive symbolism, leaving behind only the residues of statistical analysis. Likewise, rational choice theory and similar criminological theories founded on assumptions of instrumental rationality miss, from the view of cultural criminology, the very essence of much everyday criminality: pleasure, excitement, anger, and risk. As with other reductionist approaches, such theories may buttress calls for individual responsibility and punitive justice, and in this sense may find a home within the current practice of criminal justice, but they can hardly account for the inherent sensuality, ambiguity, and irrationality of crime itself.

Emerging from the alternative and critical criminologies of the 1970s, cultural criminology in these ways provides, by practice and intention, a contemporary alternative criminology, and a cultural critique of contemporary crime control arrangements. With its interdisciplinary foundations and emphasis on meaning, mediated representation, and style, it may also hold out the possibility of significantly expanding the analytic range and substantive scope of future criminological scholarship.

SEE ALSO: Birmingham School; Conflict Theory and Crime and Delinquency; Cultural Studies, British; Culture; Deviance, the Media and; Labeling Theory; Subcultures, Deviant; Symbolic Interaction

REFERENCES AND SUGGESTED READINGS

Alvelos, H. (2004) The Desert of Imagination in the City of Signs: Cultural Implications of Sponsored Transgression and Branded Graffiti. In: Ferrell, J., Hayward, K., Morrison, W., & Presdee, M. (Eds.), *Cultural Criminology Unleashed*. Cavendish/Glasshouse, London, pp. 181–91.
Ferrell, J. (1996) *Crimes of Style: Urban Graffiti and the Politics of Criminality*. Northeastern University Press, Boston.
Ferrell, J. (1999) Cultural Criminology. *Annual Review of Sociology* 25: 395–418.
Ferrell, J. & Sanders, C. R. (Eds.) (1995) *Cultural Criminology*. Northeastern University Press, Boston.

Ferrell, J., Hayward, K., Morrison, W., & Presdee, M. (Eds.) (2004) *Cultural Criminology Unleashed.* Cavendish/Glasshouse, London.

Hayward, K. & Young, J. (2004) Cultural Criminology: Some Notes on the Script. *Theoretical Criminology* 8(3): 259–73.

Katz, J. (1988) *Seductions of Crime.* Basic Books, New York.

Lyng, S. (1990) Edgework: A Social Psychological Analysis of Voluntary Risk Taking. *American Journal of Sociology* 95: 851–86.

Presdee, M. (2000) *Cultural Criminology and the Carnival of Crime.* Routledge, London.

Theoretical Criminology (2004) Special Issue: Cultural Criminology. *Theoretical Criminology* 8(3).

Young, J. (2003) Merton with Energy, Katz with Structure: The Sociology of Vindictiveness and the Criminology of Transgression. *Theoretical Criminology* 7(3): 389–414.

cultural critique

Douglas Kellner and Tyson E. Lewis

Cultural critique is a broad field of study that employs many different theoretical traditions to analyze and critique cultural formations. Because culture is always historically and contextually determined, each era has had to develop its own methods of cultural analysis in order to respond to new technological innovations, new modes of social organization, new economic formations, and novel forms of oppression, exploitation, and subjugation.

The modern European tradition of cultural critique can be traced back to Immanuel Kant's (1724–1804) seminal essay entitled "What is Enlightenment?" Here, Kant opposed theocratic and authoritarian forms of culture with a liberal, progressive, and humanist culture of science, reason, and critique. By organizing society under the guiding principles of critical reason, Kant believed that pre-Enlightenment superstition and ignorance would be replaced by both individual liberty and universal peace.

Friedrich Nietzsche (1844–1900) historicized Kant's version of critique through a technique called genealogy. Nietzsche argued that Kant's necessary universals are born from historical struggles between competing interests.

Compared to Greek culture, Nietzsche saw contemporary Germany as degenerate. Prominent figures such as David Strauss and Friedrich Schiller represented "cultural philistines" who promoted cultural conformity to a massified, standardized, and superficial culture. Thus contemporary culture blocked the revitalization of a strong, creative, and vital society of healthy geniuses. Here Nietzsche rested his faith not in universal categories of reason but rather in the aristocratic will to power to combat the "herd mentality" of German mass culture.

Like Nietzsche, Karl Marx (1818–83) also rejected universal and necessary truths outside of history. Using historical materialism as his major critical tool, Marx argued that the dominant culture legitimated current exploitative economic relations. In short, the class that controls the economic base also controls the production of cultural and political ideas. Whereas Nietzsche traced central forms of mass culture back to the hidden source of power animating them, Marx traced cultural manifestations back to their economic determinates. Here culture is derived from antagonistic social relations conditioned by capitalism, which distorts both the content and the form of ideas. Thus for Marx, cultural critique is essentially ideological critique exposing the interests of the ruling class within its seemingly natural and universal norms.

Whereas Kant defined the proper uses of reason for the creation of a rational social order, Sigmund Freud (1856–1939) argued that the liberal humanist tradition failed to actualize its ideal because it did not take into account the eternal and unavoidable conflict between culture and the psychological unconscious. Freud argued that the complexity of current society has both positive and negative psychological implications. On the one hand, individuals have a certain degree of security and stability afforded to them by society. Yet at the same time, this society demands repression of aggressive instincts, which turn inward and direct themselves toward the ego. This internalization of aggression results in an overpowering superego and attending neurotic symptoms and pathologies. For Freud, such a conflict is not the result of economic determination (as we saw with Marx), but rather is a struggle fundamental to the social contract and is increasingly exacerbated by the social demand for conformity, utility, and productivity.

With the Frankfurt School of social theory, cultural critique attempted to synthesize the most politically progressive and theoretically innovative strands of the former cultural theories. Max Horkheimer (1895–1971), Theodor Adorno (1903–69), and Herbert Marcuse (1898–1979) are three of the central members of the Frankfurt School who utilized a transdisciplinary method that incorporated elements of critical reason, genealogy, historical materialism, sociology, and psychoanalysis to analyze culture. While heavily rooted in Marxism, the members of the Frankfurt School increasingly distanced themselves from Marx's conception of the centrality of economic relations, focusing instead on cultural and political methods of social control produced through new media technologies and a burgeoning culture industry. In the classic text *Dialectic of Enlightenment* (1948), Horkheimer and Adorno demonstrate that Kant's reliance on reason has not resulted in universal peace but rather increasing oppression, culminating in fascism. Here reason becomes a new form of dogmatism, its own mythology predicated on both external domination of nature and internal domination of psychological drives. This dialectic of Enlightenment reason reveals itself in the rise of the American culture industry whose sole purpose is to produce docile, passive, and submissive workers. Marcuse argued along similar lines, proposing that the American "one-dimensional" culture has effectively destroyed the capacity for critical and oppositional thinking. Thus many members of the Frankfurt School (Adorno in particular) adopted a highly pessimistic attitude toward "mass culture," and, like Nietzsche, took refuge in "high" culture.

While the Frankfurt School articulated cultural conditions in a stage of monopoly capitalism and fascist tendencies, British cultural studies emerged in the 1960s when, first, there was widespread global resistance to consumer capitalism and an upsurge of revolutionary movements. British cultural studies originally was developed by Richard Hoggart, Raymond Williams, and E. P. Thompson to preserve working-class culture against colonization by the culture industry. Thus both British cultural

studies and the Frankfurt School recognized the central role of new consumer and media culture in the erosion of working-class resistance to capitalist hegemony. Yet there are distinct differences between British cultural studies and proponents of Frankfurt School critical theory. Whereas the Frankfurt School turned toward the modernist avant-garde as a form of resistance to instrumental reason and capitalist culture, British cultural studies turned toward the oppositional potentials within youth subcultures. As such, British cultural studies was able to recognize the ambiguity of media culture as a contested terrain rather than a monolithic and one-dimensional product of the capitalist social relations of production.

Currently, cultural critique is attempting to respond to a new era of global capitalism, hybridized cultural forms, and increasing control of information by a handful of media conglomerates. As a response to these economic, social, and political trends, cultural critique has expanded its theoretical repertoire to include multicultural, postcolonial, and feminist critiques of culture. African American feminist theorist bell hooks is an exemplary representative of new cultural studies who analyzes the interconnected nature of gender, race, and class oppressions operating in imperialist, white supremacist, capitalist patriarchy. Scholars of color such as hooks and Cornell West critique not only ongoing forms of exclusion, marginalization, and fetishization of the "other" within media culture, but also the classical tools of cultural criticism. Through insights generated by these scholars, cultural criticism is reevaluating its own internal complicity with racism, sexism, colonialism, and homophobia and in the process gaining a new level of self-reflexivity that enables it to become an increasingly powerful tool for social emancipation.

SEE ALSO: Cultural Studies, British; Critical Theory/Frankfurt School; Ideology, Economy and; Marxism and Sociology; Nietzsche, Friedrich; Psychoanalysis; Racialized Gender

REFERENCES AND SUGGESTED READINGS

Durham, M. G. & Kellner, D. (2001) *Media and Cultural Studies*. Blackwell, Malden, MA.

Freud, S. (1930) *Civilization and its Discontents.* J. Cape & H. Smith, New York.

Kant, I. (1992) *Cambridge Edition of the Works of Immanuel Kant.* Ed. P. Guyer & A. Wood. Cambridge University Press, Cambridge.

Kellner, D. (1989) *Critical Theory, Marxism, and Modernity.* Johns Hopkins University Press, Baltimore.

Nietzsche, F. (1989) *On the Genealogy of Morals and Ecce Homo.* Vintage, New York.

Tucker, R. (Ed.) (1978) *The Marx–Engels Reader.* Norton, New York.

cultural diversity and aging: ethnicity, minorities, and subcultures

Peggye Dilworth-Anderson and Gracie Boswell

Current US Census population projections (2004) clearly show a growing number of diverse racial, ethnic, and cultural groups in American society. Parallel to this increase in diversity, the number of older adults in America is increasing. Older adult members of society are increasing at a faster rate than any other subgroup in America, and among this aging population, the percentage of the population who are members of minority groups will grow, between 2000 and 2050, at an even faster rate than the white majority. In 2002 (US Census 2002), the older population numbered 35.6 million; this was an increase of 3.3 million or 10.2 percent since 1992. Minority populations are projected to represent 26.4 percent of the elderly population in 2030, up from 17.2 percent in 2002. Between 2000 and 2030, the white population 65 and older is projected to increase by 77 percent compared with 223 percent for older minorities, including Hispanics (342 percent), African Americans (164 percent), American Indians, Eskimos, and Aleuts (207 percent), and Asians and Pacific Islanders (302 percent). Accompanying this tremendous boom in population growth and ethnic makeup will be economic problems as well as promises of diversity. These economic problems and promises will be directly associated with living arrangements and health care needs of increasingly frail members of the population as well as the satisfaction of the supply and demand requirements for diversified goods and services of a vibrantly aging population (Angel & Hogan 2004).

In light of the demographic changes noted above, the need to understand diversity beyond racial categories and changes in the numbers of group members is a major challenge for researchers and other scholars of the twenty-first century. Of great importance is to understand the range of factors that represent cultural diversity in a society. Central to this understanding is how best to define cultural diversity to reflect the changing and emerging identities of diverse groups. The biggest challenge in this definition is rooted in the term culture. Half a century ago, one study identified 150 definitions of culture (Kroeber & Kluckhohn 1952). Goodenough's (1999) definition of culture is a set of shared symbols, beliefs, and customs that shape individual and group behavior. He also suggested that culture provides guidelines for speaking, doing, interpreting, and evaluating one's actions and reactions in life. Goodenough's (1981) concept of cultural frame provides further insight into how individual characteristics and experiences, such as gender and age, can influence cultural beliefs and values. He suggested that cultural frame allows us to understand how an individual's culture is developed through the incorporation of the totality of one's experiences, interactions, and thoughts with the norms and expectations one perceives as being held by other group members. Therefore, due to differences in individual cultural frames, people can simultaneously be cultural group members and hold cultural beliefs that are not shared by some members of the group (Goodenough 1981).

At the expense of compounding the complexity inherent in the term culture, an understanding of what diversity means in the twenty-first century is also important. Today the term diversity represents a more inclusive concept than in the past. It is used to model current dialogue and ideologies about inequality and social structures that are used to help resolve problems of social and professional interactions in a pluralistic society. Although it is under the rubric of multiculturalism that culture, ethnicity, and race have been the usual variables of research interest, diversity is a multilevel and multidimensional concept that addresses more than culture, ethnicity, and race.

Representing the concerns of many interest groups, many variables may be used to bracket a linkage with diversity. Here, age is pulled into the diversity equation along with culture, ethnicity, and race. The inclusion of age is of paramount importance in social, economic, and legal institutions. In order to better appreciate the raison d'être for including age as a factor in the dialogue on diversity, we must move beyond mere awareness of negative attitudes toward the elderly to the cold hard facts supported by the social demographics of aging.

The discourse on cultural diversity and aging in social science research speaks to examining the theoretical and conceptual frameworks and perspectives that allow for capturing the cultural–historical background (values, beliefs, identities, and meanings assigned to experiences) and sociopolitical conditions (economic status and access to goods and services) of diverse groups. When culturally relevant, these frameworks and perspectives should also allow for defining and giving meaning to certain concepts from a cultural frame of reference. However, since theories of aging evolved out of a traditional Eurocentric social and cultural milieu, they have not proven effective in explaining aging in a culturally diverse context. In *Multiculturalism and Intergroup Relations* (1989), Ujimoto posited that traditional theories of aging (i.e., disengagement and activity) were not adequate to theorize about the Japanese ethnic population in Canada, because of the history of discriminatory practices endured by this group in relation to the majority Caucasian population. Similarly, this assertion is supported for some racial or ethnic minority groups in America, who were once thought to merge into a "melting pot" with Americanism as the central identifying group characteristic. Contemporary perspectives on diversity are centered on multiculturalism and cultural competence that take into account larger societal values and beliefs, and diverse cultural beliefs as well.

Multiculturalism became the buzzword of the 1990s in order to address the cultural pluralism caused by the interrelationships between many racial and ethnic groups in America. Acknowledging individual differences, multiculturalism seemed to imply a commitment to a greater good for the whole society. However, in order to make this claim, something must be at stake for the various racial or ethnic groups that make up the society. Therefore, the central premise underlying multiculturalism was to recognize and respect the cultural heritages of various minority groups, while not creating alienation of one from the other. Otherwise, the result would be nothing more than the old pre-Brown "separate but equal" ideology which was a dismal failure for already marginal members of society. By moving beyond the "melting pot" perspective, multiculturalism was a concept that embodied tolerance and less ethnocentrism. However, cultural bias was already pervasive due to cultural pluralism.

In order to assure that the various institutions in society were equitable for all members of the various groups, a system had to be in place that encouraged and facilitated culturally sensitive interactions between various interest groups. This recognition, along with the reality of widespread inequities, has moved contemporary discourse forward to what is referred to as a need for more "cultural competence." At any rate, cultural competence is not believed to be a state of being; instead, it is thought to be "a process of becoming over time," as suggested by Campinha-Bacote in *The Process of Cultural Competence in the Delivery of Healthcare Services* (2003). This has been especially true with regards to interactions between aging individuals in the health care setting. In the context of the health care setting, cultural competence was described in the Commonwealth Fund field report (Betancourt et al. 2002) as being able to provide care to patients with diverse values, beliefs, and behaviors. This includes tailoring delivery to meet patients' social, cultural, and linguistic needs. Cultural competence was also described as both a vehicle to increase access to quality care for all patient populations and a business strategy to attract new patients and market share.

Betancourt et al.'s definition of cultural competence is steeped in humanistic terminology as well as a political economy perspective, whereby the idea of a moral economy is invoked by acknowledging that cultural factors impact social institutions and change along with political and economic processes. Building upon the concept of multiculturalism and moving toward the dynamism represented by cultural competence, there are orientations which members of various interest groups and races or ethnicities might adopt or at least come to terms with. The three orientations are what Martin (1997) describes as diversity orientations, based on the interactions of different cultures, ethnicities, and races. The cultural orientation assumes that individuals abandon their ethnocentrism and learn rules guiding the behaviors of people from other cultures. The ethnic orientation assumes that individuals of different ethnic identities deserve equal respect. The oppression orientation, with regards to race, assumes dignity and power are restored to the oppressed minority. With this power, healing should take place in the psychological, economic, and political domains regarding interrelationships of the members of society. There is no clear evidence in American society that shows that these assumptions of diversity orientations have been realized. For this reason, diversity is the unfinished business of the twenty-first century for social scientists to ponder.

As we move forward to address issues surrounding culture, ethnicity, or race, other social constructs will be called into question in the search for greater tolerance for individual differences and the need to dispel social inequalities. Research questions with other social constructs (i.e., age, gender, sexual orientation, disability, social class, language barriers, and religious and spiritual orientations) require examining the multiple concerns of multiple interest groups. This level of investigation beyond culture, race, and ethnicity embodies the new discourse on diversity that specifically includes age.

Although growing old has been thought to have marginalizing influences, many other factors weigh in to create an even more complex set of circumstances and individual differences that are demanding attention. Overshadowing the new demands on social structures will be the various factions representing racial subgroups and interest groups, not only stratified by age and race or ethnicity, but also impacted by gender, sexual orientation, religious or spiritual tradition as well as other unnamed constructs. These competing interests of subgroups, stratified by various constructs of interest, signify the non-monolithic nature of diversifying variables (i.e., age and gender) and recapitulate the notion that diversity is a multilevel and multidimensional concept that addresses more than culture, ethnicity, and race. However, of the three constructs, cultural diversity in the context of an aging society is of more paramount concern. Mindful of a rapidly aging society, social interactions need to place high priority on social changes in a variety of institutions, including the workplace, the health care arena, faith-based organizations, communication networks, educational as well as leisure pursuits, and many other unlisted institutions.

Although the research terminology is new, cultural diversity is an outgrowth of the racial inequality debates of the past 50 years. Due to these past unresolved issues and changes in demography, current research on aging is challenged by many new methodological concerns. Consequently, aging is just one of the many social structures that is so dynamic that it begs to be addressed in the context of cultural diversity. The differences between the health outcomes of elderly whites and blacks have been well documented over the past 30 odd years. In some cases this research has informed the need for new policies, but in other cases it has simply raised more questions about the role of structure and agency and debates about social causation or social selection in studies of life stress. Furthermore, Williams (2004) has pointed out that inherent in the use of race to study health differences between groups of individuals is a tendency to mask problems associated with racism. By merely controlling for race of individuals or even stratifying by age, the richness of social and cultural contexts may be lost (Dilworth–Anderson et al. 2002). While research that merely emphasized racial differences in outcomes might have been the necessary foundation for current theorizing, it did not go far enough.

Taking the context of cultural diversity into consideration, many contemporary methodological challenges are disclosed in the social science of aging. One of the main areas of investigation for diversity research is "inclusion." The science of inclusion goes beyond racial and ethnic differences to address gender and poverty as well as language barriers that impact health differentials. These may be just a few of the factors forming the building blocks of diversity, which have been dictated by policy and that now affect what Curry and Jackson (2003) refer to as a science of inclusion. Among the main challenges embedded in this science of inclusion are the means of recruiting and retaining individuals from diverse backgrounds in health research. The idea of cultural competency becomes an important consideration in these recruitment and retention efforts, as the need to establish credibility becomes so essential in minority communities (Curry & Jackson 2003; Levkoff & Sanchez 2003). Additionally, training of investigators for diverse groups and research topics must become a priority as the scientific community grapples with issues of aging and associated disabilities.

Other methodological concerns include addressing the appropriateness of measures (i.e., are CES-D scales useful for blacks?). Cross-disciplinary methods (i.e., combining sociology and medical anthropology) as well as mixed methodologies (i.e., using qualitative to inform quantitative) are also important tools to use in investigating older adults and understanding the cultural contexts where they are found. Simultaneously, there is a need to display the qualities necessary for recruitment and retention of participants among diverse older adult populations (Yeo 2003).

As we look toward the future of research on aging and cultural diversity, theories and methods that are appropriate for inclusive scientific research should be a priority. Those theories and methods must be appropriate for research questions that address cultural complexity (i.e., aging of the gay and lesbian community, cultural heterogeneity of Latino and Asian Americans, spirituality and religiosity in health care). In other words, racial and ethnic groups should not be investigated as if they were monolithic entities. They each have their complex sets of problems and circumstances that need to be recognized as unique. For example, there are no typical persons of color (i.e., all persons with Afrocentric genetics in America are not African Americans), Asian, or Latino etc.

It is also important to not study aging in a vacuum. Older adults have a history. This history encourages the use of the life course perspective as a useful methodological tool in the future. However, there must be ways to safeguard individuals with specific genetic predispositions from culturally biased or ethnically insensitive research that drives health policy.

New approaches to studying death and dying need to be addressed for an aging and culturally complex society. In order to prepare for this, more effort needs to be made in order to understand the health beliefs and attitudes as well as spiritual and religious beliefs and orientations of diverse cultural groups of older adults.

Finally, research in our pluralistic society is appropriate for cross-national investigation. Jackson (2002) posits that the cultural complexity of the United States provides excellent models for research on aging that advances the field beyond investigating separate national and cultural perspectives. This would further advance understanding aging and cultural diversity in a global societal context.

SEE ALSO: Aging, Demography of; Aging and Health Policy; Aging and Social Policy; Aging, Sociology of; Culture; Diversity; Race; Race (Racism); Social Integration and Inclusion; Subculture

REFERENCES AND SUGGESTED READINGS

Angel, J. L. & Hogan, D. P. (2004) Population Aging and Diversity in a New Era. In: Whitfield, K. E. (Ed.), *Closing the Gap*. Gerontological Society of America, Washington, DC, pp. 1–12.

Betancourt, J. R., Green, A. R., & Carrillo, E. J. (2002) Cultural Competence in Health Care: Emerging Frameworks and Practical Approaches. Commonwealth Fund No. 576. Online. www.cmwf.org.

Curry, L. & Jackson, J. (2003) Recruitment and Retention of Diverse Ethnic and Racial Groups in Health Research: An Evolving Science. In: Curry, L. & Jackson, J. (Eds.), *The Science of Inclusion: Recruiting and Retaining Racial and Ethnic Elders in Health Research*. Gerontological Society of America, Washington, DC, pp. 1–7.

Dilworth-Anderson, P., Williams, I. C., & Gibson, B. E. (2002) Issues of Race, Ethnicity, and Culture in Caregiving Research: A 20-Year Review (1980–2000). *Gerontologist* 42(2): 237–72.

Goodenough, W. H. (1981) *Culture, Language, and Society*. Benjamin-Cummings, Menlo Park, CA.

Goodenough, W. H. (1999) Outline of a Framework for a Theory of Cultural Evolution. *Cross-Cultural Research* 33: 84–107.

Jackson, J. S. (2002) Conceptual and Methodological Linkages in Cross-Cultural Groups and Cross-National Aging Research. *Journal of Social Issues* 58(4): 825.

Kelty, M. E., Hoffman III, R. R., Ory, M. G., & Harden, T. J. (2000) Behavioral and Sociocultural Aspects of Aging, Ethnicity, and Health. In: Eisler, R. M. & Hersen, M. (Eds.), *Handbook of Gender, Culture, and Health*. Erlbaum, Mahwah, NJ, pp. 139–58.

Kroeber, A. L. & Kluckhohn, C. (1952) *Culture: A Critical Review of Concepts and Definitions*. Vintage, New York.

Leavitt, R. L. (Ed.) (1999) *Cross-Cultural Rehabilitation: An International Perspective*. W. B. Saunders, Philadelphia, PA.

Levkoff, S. & Sanchez, H. (2003) Lessons Learned About Minority Recruitment and Retention from the Centers on Minority Aging and Health Promotion. *Gerontologist* 43: 18–26.

Martin, K. P. (1997) Diversity Orientations: Culture, Ethnicity, and Race. In: Naylor, L. L. (Ed.), *Cultural Diversity in the United States*. Bergin & Garvey, Westport, CT, pp. 75–88.

US Census Bureau (2002) The 65 and Over Population: 2000. *Census 2000 Brief*. Online. www.census.gov/prod/2001pubs/c2kbr01–10.pdf.

US Census Bureau (2004) US Interim Projections by Age, Sex, Race, and Hispanic Origin. Online. www.census.gov/ipc/www/usinterimproj/.

Williams, D. R. (2004) Racism and Health. In: Whitfield, K. E. (Ed.), *Closing the Gap*. Gerontological Society of America, Washington, DC, pp. 69–80.

Yeo, G. (2003) How Should Investigators Be Trained for Effective Research in Minority Aging and Ethnogeriatrics? In: Curry, L. & Jackson, J. (Eds.), *The Science of Inclusion: Recruiting and Retaining Racial and Ethnic Elders in Health Research*. Gerontological Society of America, Washington, DC, pp. 90–4.

cultural feminism

Kristina Wolff

Cultural feminism seeks to understand women's social locations in society by concentrating on gender differences between women and men. This type of feminism focuses on the liberation of women through individual change, the recognition and creation of "women-centered" culture, and the redefinition of femininity and masculinity. Cultural feminism utilizes essentialist understandings of male and female differences as the foundation of women's subordination in society.

Early cultural feminists sought to reclaim and redefine definitions of femininity and masculinity through recognizing and celebrating women's unique characteristics. Cultural feminists believe that women are inherently nurturing, kind, gentle, egalitarian, and nonviolent. These tenets can be traced back to the *first wave* of feminism. During this time, scholars such as Jane Addams and Charlotte Perkins Gilman stressed the superiority of women's values, particularly compassion and pacifism, believing that these would conquer masculine qualities of selfishness, violence, and lack of self-control in relation to sexual behavior. This was also a means to challenge the dominant cultural discourse that women were inferior and subservient to men. Efforts at fighting women's subordination included working for women's suffrage, women's right to free expression, and women's culture as well as outreach to poor and working-class women. The decline of this early stage of cultural feminism has been attributed to World War I and societal reaction to these early feminists' opposition to the war.

Cultural feminism returned during the *second wave* of feminism in the early 1970s, when it reemerged out of the radical feminist movement. *Radical feminism* directly challenges biological definitions of male and female while actively working toward eliminating women's oppression. One aspect of this type of feminism was the minimization of gender differences and advocation of androgyny. Within the movement, lesbians seeking to achieve recognition for their efforts, as well as visibility, created another body of feminism, *lesbian feminism*. Lesbian feminism focuses on unique issues that homosexual women face within feminism and throughout society, as well as examining the ways in which sexuality is socially constructed. Included in both lesbian and cultural feminism is the practice of separatism, the creation of spaces, groups, and communities that are separate from men. Cultural feminists employed some of the practices of both radical and lesbian feminism but diverged from them due to its central focus. Cultural feminism emphasizes a need to highlight women's uniqueness and feminine qualities as positive attributes rather than erasing the differences between men and women, as stressed in radical feminism. It also modified lesbian feminism to create a feminism that appealed to a wider audience, while retaining a women-centered focus. Cultural feminism is bounded by the practice of concentrating on the differences between genders as its foundation, while placing "woman" at the center. While there is great variety within this body of feminism, the main areas of scholarship focus on individual change, the development of women's culture, the redefinition of femininity and masculinity, and examinations of sexuality.

Foundationally, cultural feminism is the reclaiming and redefinition of female identity. Women's liberation occurs through the rejection of society's conception of "woman" since this is based on a male model of understanding. During a time period when some other branches of feminism were rejecting traditional values of womanhood, challenging and/or erasing what was understood as inherently female, cultural feminists sought to revalidate the essence of what it means to be "female" by embracing and reappropriating female attributes. This practice focuses on honoring one's femaleness through challenging traditional definitions of "woman" as well as the expected gender roles as defined by men. At the same time, traits that are attributed to women, such as the natural ability to nurture, are viewed as positive attributes that should be honored.

The early process of redefining and reclaiming femaleness took shape in a variety of forms and largely concentrated on changing personal behavior and attitudes and on creating a cultural transformation. This included the recognition and development of women's culture to counter women's invisibility, subordination, and often isolation from one another. Women's experience is the foundation of a "sisterhood," based on the belief that all women share a commonality due to gender. Women sought to establish "safe" places, free from male dominance, where they could build community. Often these events or spaces did not allow men to participate, thus giving women freedom

from men and men's subordination. Some defined this process of creating strong relationships and women-centered spaces as "female bonding." This label sought to capture the inherent essence in women, one that naturally ties them together. Its purpose is to demonstrate the importance of placing "woman" at the center of their lives. The term also clashes with lesbians, as cultural feminists primarily defined "female bonding" as a non-sexual, emotional connection. The result was that lesbianism quickly became subsumed under the label and, once again, left on the margins. Culturally, there was a surge in women's scholarship, art, and literature which focused on issues specifically related to and about women. Throughout the United States, women-centered events and spaces were established. This included, but was not limited to, music festivals, businesses and organizations, women's centers, domestic violence shelters and rape crisis centers, and numerous community groups. Additionally, Take Back the Night marches were established to draw attention to rape, domestic violence, and abuse of women.

Central to this cultural shift is the development of an alternative consciousness, one that rejects what is "male" and how society is defined through a male lens. Cultural feminists view essentialist definitions of female and the qualities attached to understandings of femininity as powerful assets for women. Socially conditioned aspects of femininity, which include characteristics such as passivity and submissiveness, are redefined and revalidated as exemplifying women's innate ability to be nurturing, loving, non-violent, cooperative, and egalitarian in nature. Men and masculinity are viewed as inherently violent, aggressive, and competitive. Men are seen as the "enemy" by virtue of their biological maleness. Women are subordinated due to men's nature. Women are also secondary because contemporary western society and western thought do not value women's virtues. Instead, male thought and ideas of hierarchy, domination, and independence are held in the highest esteem. Cultural feminism challenges these male values, seeking to change society and methods of governing through emphasizing women's natural ability to solve conflict through cooperation, pacifism, and non-violence.

These changes in viewpoint, in placing women at the center, created a shift and dramatic growth in feminist scholarship. Cultural institutions that were often viewed as secondary in importance in society, such as women's roles, primary modes of employment, and motherhood, were now examined through a female lens. For example, Adrienne Rich and Nancy Chodorow examined the richness of women's experiences and roles as mothers, and Carol Gilligan joined Chodorow in utilizing psychological theories to further understand gender differences, thus helping to establish *psychoanalytic feminism*. Deborah Tannen's scholarship explores gender differences in the way men and women communicate with one another. Mary Daly, who also is influential in radical feminism, critiques and creates new languages as well as a feminist theology, both of which place women as central to her development of these new meanings. Ingrained in all of these "new" forms of scholarship is the inherent belief that women have certain innate qualities that should finally be recognized and honored by society, rather than remaining invisible or denigrated.

Included in these critiques and new scholarship was the development of standpoint theory and feminist epistemology. Both recognize that women have a unique perspective based on their experiences as women and that this should be valued, explored, and learned from. Both directly challenge traditional approaches to knowledge and understanding, recognizing these as grounded in and stemming from elite males in society. *Standpoint theory* posits that women's understanding of the world is different from men's, even if it is shaped by men's definitions. This difference is based on women's experiences and knowledge, both formal and informal. Women's perspectives vary in ways that are visible and invisible and affect the ways in which people understand and also approach the social world. Sandra Harding's development of a *feminist epistemology* centers on critiquing society's understanding and creation of knowledge, thus shaping the ways in which science and the quest for knowledge occur. Harding analyzes traditional approaches to expanding knowledge in society from a woman's standpoint to illustrate how women's "ways of knowing" differ from men's. This

ever expanding scholarship assisted in providing a foundation for the establishment of women's studies as a discipline, as well as in the development of many other concentrations and changes in focus of numerous disciplines. In sociology, for example, it provides a foundation for the sociology of sex and gender, feminist sociology, and feminist methods within sociology.

Inherent in the focus on differences between genders is the issue of sexuality and sexual practices. Approaches to sexuality vary. Some cultural feminists embrace women's ability to reproduce and promote it as "the" source of female power. They believe that men are afraid and/or jealous of women and their ability to reproduce and thus they try to control reproduction through a variety of means, including policy and technology. One direct result of this belief was the development of women's resources for health care and reproduction, including the publication in 1970 of *Our Bodies, Ourselves* by the Boston Women's Health Book Collective, which was the first publication dedicated to women's health written by and for women. Other cultural feminists seek to reclaim the power of positive sexual practices and desires through exploring women's fantasies, desires around intimacy, and ability to be open to and want emotional experiences. Addressing the focus of sexual behavior on the pleasures of women links directly back into radical feminism, which sought to highlight the importance of women enjoying sex. This included a reformulation of heterosexual practices that sought to concentrate on women's satisfaction instead of men's.

Some also focus on men's sexual behavior as a specific practice of male domination over women. Female sexuality is believed to naturally concentrate on relationships and intimacy. The focus is on reciprocity and caring rather than solely engaged on physical ecstasy. Sexuality for men is believed to primarily be focused on the merger of power and orgasm. Men naturally concentrate on their own physical desire, seeking to maintain power over women. Men want to be intimate with women in order to satisfy their own needs. In this respect, men and women are viewed as complete opposites.

Some cultural feminists advocate that women embrace their femininity as well as their sexuality by rejecting sexual activity with men, viewing male penetration as domination. Many of these early feminists were also part of the radical feminism movement. Some of these women also apply the term "female bonding" here to illustrate the conscious focus on surrounding oneself with other women and having them fulfill every need, including as sexual partners. This approach to sexuality led to the creation of the anti-pornography movement and also created a split among cultural feminists, particularly those who do not view sexual behavior as a source of men's domination.

One of the accomplishments of cultural feminism was the emergence of the anti-pornography movement. This movement materialized out of the establishment of women's groups and organizations, particularly those that focused on issues of domestic violence, abuse, and rape. One of the beliefs of the movement is that men are unable to control themselves, that their desire to dominate women is due to their biological makeup. Women are then responsible for curtailing and controlling their behavior. This approach is very similar to the first wave of feminism, including those women involved in the temperance movement. Pornography is believed to perpetuate our culture's misogyny and also causes violence against women, often because it depicts women being subjected to acts of violence. Some claimed that rape was simply due to men's male essence, and others proclaimed that "porn is the theory, rape is the practice" (see, e.g., Brownmiller 1975; Dworkin 1979). It is believed that pornography also affects women negatively, compelling them to accept the negative images of women. The movement has had a varied history of success, resulting in the creation of anti-pornography legislation and increased regulation, particularly around issues of age of participants and the elimination of highly violent images. It also continues to critique the role of pornography in society and has developed another area of feminist scholarship surrounding law, media, and sexuality studies. While many communities adopted strict anti-pornography laws, many of these have been overturned on constitutional grounds.

Cultural feminism continues to influence current feminisms as well as other disciplines, including sociology, in particular concerning issues of women and work, mothering, sexuality, and women's role as "caretaker." Cultural feminism is one of the most successful and influential types of feminism. However, it is not without critics. One of the most common critiques concerns its reliance on applying biological definitions of "woman." The use of essentialist conceptions of "woman" reifies the societal beliefs it seeks to redefine. This key premise tends to invoke a universal conception of what "woman" is, failing to offer a response to traditional patriarchal beliefs of women and men. By embracing socially constructed ideas of femininity and masculinity, there is an implication that women cannot escape their destinies as females. Also embedded within these biological assumptions is the premise that women's duty is to control men because they cannot control themselves due to their inherent essence. By relying on women to change their behaviors and seek to control men, cultural feminism leaves unchallenged the overarching system of patriarchy, which shapes societal understandings and practices of gender. Some early cultural feminists such as Adrienne Rich, Andrea Dworkin, and Susan Brownmiller have also offered critiques, but these are largely based on the application of essentialist definitions of "woman" rather than the belief itself. For some, the application is not complete without female scientists researching women's natural traits from their own perspective, thus countering male biases.

By seeking to unite all women under a banner of a "global sisterhood," many argue that differences based on race, class, nation, status, age, and other complexities in women's lives are erased. In many ways, cultural feminists have broadened their focus and depth of analysis to include other elements of culture. This includes the unique history and practices of women of color in the United States as well as women's experiences in other nations. However, the criticism remains that through maintaining a singular focus on "woman," even with this expansion, these other factors remain in a secondary position. Additionally, many of the feminists who do utilize a wider definition of cultural feminism, one that includes race, class, age, and so on, resist using an essentialist foundation of gender and instead focus on the complexities of all of these differences.

Another strong critique of cultural feminism is that it resulted in establishing "rules" as to "who" could be a feminist. Women were expected to embrace the concept of being "woman-centered" or "woman-identified." This often resulted in an expectation that women would decrease their involvement with and reliance on men. This practice did not last long, nor was it widely embraced by all cultural feminists. Additionally, men were discouraged from being part of this type of feminism no matter how "liberated" they might have been. Women were expected to change their ideas and behaviors in order to liberate themselves, yet many women felt judged as not being "feminist enough" or "women-centered enough," and that only true feminists were in a position to determine who or what "woman" meant. This created and encouraged an elitist attitude within cultural feminism. Additionally, by not challenging patriarchal systems that create and perpetuate the ideology that women are inferior to men, this type of feminism fails to address larger systemic issues and relies on meeting needs within the status quo rather than critiquing the status quo.

SEE ALSO: Addams, Jane; Femininities/Masculinities; Feminism; Feminism, First, Second, and Third Waves; Feminism and Science, Feminist Epistemology; Feminist Activism in Latin America; Feminist Methodology; Feminist Standpoint Theory; Gender Ideology and Gender Role Ideology; Lesbian Feminism; Liberal Feminism; Materialist Feminisms; Multiracial Feminism; Patriarchy; Postmodern Feminism; Psychoanalytic Feminism; Radical Feminism; Third World and Postcolonial Feminisms/Subaltern; Transnational and Global Feminisms

REFERENCES AND SUGGESTED READINGS

Addams, J. (1960) *Jane Addams: A Centennial Reader*. Macmillan, New York.
Alcoff, L. (1988) Cultural Feminism Versus Post-Structuralism: The Identity Crisis in Feminist Theory. *Signs: A Journal of Women in Culture and Society* 13: 405–36.
Brownmiller, S. (1975) *Against Our Will: Men, Women, and Rape*. Simon & Schuster, New York.
Daly, M. (1978) *Gyn/Ecology, the Metaethics of Radical Feminism*. Beacon Press, Boston.
Daly, M. (1985) *Beyond God the Father: Toward a Philosophy of Women's Liberation*. Beacon Press, Boston.
Donovan, J. (1985) *Feminist Theory: The Intellectual Traditions of American Feminism*. F. Ungar, New York.
Dworkin, A. (1979) *Pornography: Men Possessing Women*. E. P. Dutton, New York.
Echols, A. (1983) The New Feminism of Yin and Yang. In: Snitow, A., Stansell, C., & Thompson, S. (Eds.), *Powers of Desire: The Politics of Sexuality*. Monthly Review Press, New York, pp. 439–59.
Griffin, S. (1981) *Pornography and Silence: Culture's Revenge Against Nature*. Harper & Row, New York.
Irigaray, L. (1994) Equal to Whom. In: Schor, N. & Weed, E. (Eds.), *The Essential Difference*. Indiana University Press, Bloomington, pp. 63–81.
Morgan, R. (1977) *Going Too Far: The Personal Chronicle of a Feminist*. Random House, New York.
Rich, A. (1977) *Of Woman Born*. Bantam, New York.
Tannen, D. (1990) *You Just Don't Understand: Women and Men in Conversation*. William Morrow, New York.

cultural imperialism

Kristina Wolff

Cultural imperialism is the process and practice of promoting one culture over another. Often this occurs during colonization, where one nation overpowers another country, typically one that is economically disadvantaged and/or militarily weaker. The dominant country then forces its cultural beliefs and practices onto the conquered nation. This has happened since nations have been warring, beginning with the Greek and Roman empires to the French and British empires, the American Revolution and the rise of communist governments in China and the Soviet Union to present-day changes in governments around the world.

Culture can be imposed in a variety of ways, such as through creating new laws and policies concerning what specific types of education, religion, art, and language are to be used. For example, when Native North American tribes were forced onto reservations, the United States government dictated that children attend

Christian-based boarding schools, they were taught to read and write English, and the use of their native language was discouraged and/or forbidden.

As a result of this, people find alternative ways of maintaining their culture; sometimes groups are forced into exile and their cultural practices are outlawed. Language or music is adapted as a means to continue the culture. For example, stories can be hidden within song lyrics and rhythms from their traditional music are merged with the new dominant forms as a means of maintaining parts of their culture. As with the Native North Americans, other populations have also been forced to change their style of dress, religion, language, and customs. This is common through the suppression of religion and has happened in various countries including China, Cuba, Germany, the Soviet Union, and Afghanistan.

Cultural imperialism differs from cultural diffusion primarily due to the mechanisms used to change culture and the roles that power plays in the process. Cultural diffusion occurs "naturally" when people and groups from other cultures interact with each other. It does not result in the purposeful reduction or elimination of various cultural aspects.

Cultural imperialism also occurs through programs designed to assist other nations, particularly developing nations. This can range from the ways in which small groups from western nations help out communities and villages to the impact of large international organizations' efforts at creating positive change. It is not uncommon for organizations such as the United Nations or World Bank to place conditions on loans or grants they provide to nations. Often monies are designated for specific projects such as building roads where these groups believe it is most beneficial for the nation, as well as constructing schools or health clinics. Complications arise through this process, such as when curricula are being developed for the schools. By teaching students English, in the belief they are being better prepared for opportunities outside of their native country, this practice, along with the ways in which students are being instructed, reinforces western ideals and behaviors, often to the detriment of their existing culture.

Globalization has created a new vehicle by which cultural imperialism can occur, often

with minimal resistance or acknowledgment that it is happening. Supporters of the expansion of "free markets" argue that cultures are fluid and therefore cultural imperialism is a "natural" part of the growth of trade. If western practices and ideas are the most successful, then it is believed that cultural practices associated with them are better than other cultures. Some of the main challenges to this thinking include investigating what exactly is being transferred or imposed onto other nations, what group benefits from the cultural shifts, and what cultural aspects become lost. Research focuses on examining changes in images and content of art, music, fashion and clothing, sports and recreational activities as well as changes in consumerism, due to the influences of globalization.

Critiques of the effects of globalization often concentrate on "what" is being imposed on other nations. For example, many argue the spread of McDonald's, Kentucky Fried Chicken, and Wal-Mart represents positive change as they bring jobs and relatively inexpensive goods to other nations. However, the rapid expansion of these types of restaurants or stores also reflects a specific kind of American culture that is shaped and dictated by corporations. Many ask whether these kinds of businesses reflect US culture or whether they are simply an expansion of US capitalism.

Those who are actively challenging and resisting the spread of western practices and the effects of globalization often reside in places where they are experiencing this "new" wave of cultural imperialism. Scholars are examining the impact of cultural imperialism and larger issues connected to colonialism as a means to retain culture that is in danger of disappearing as well as to develop deeper understandings of the impact of outside forces on their nation and to expose the effects of these practices. Many citizens are openly challenging the oppressive nature of western expansion, creating coalitions and organizations aimed at maintaining cultural traditions and practices. Some nations have created protectionist policies in an effort to slow down the pace of western nations purchasing their land and other natural resources.

SEE ALSO: Colonialism (Neocolonialism); Cultural Studies; Ethnocentrism; Globalization; Imperialism; McDonaldization

REFERENCES AND SUGGESTED
READINGS

Alexander, M. J. & Mohanty, C. (1997) *Feminist Genealogies, Colonial Legacies, Democratic Futures.* Routledge, New York.

Alhassan, A. (2005) Market Valorization in Broadcasting Policy in Ghana: Abandoning the Quest for Media Democratization. *Media, Culture, and Society* 27(2): 211.

Antonazzo, M. (2003) Problems with Criminalizing Female Genital Cutting. *Peace Review* 15(4): 471.

Bhabha, H. (1994) *The Location of Culture.* Routledge, New York.

Busia, A. (1993) Performance, Transcription, and the Languages of the Self: Interrogating Identity as a "Post-Colonial" Poet. In: James, S. & Busia, A. (Eds.), *Theorizing Black Feminisms: The Visionary Pragmatism of Black Women.* Routledge, New York.

Churchill, W. (1997) *A Little Matter of Genocide: Holocaust and the Denial in the Americas, 1492 to Present.* City Lights Books, San Francisco.

Ferguson, R., Gever, M., Minh-ha, T., & West, C. (1990) *Out There: Marginalization and Contemporary Cultures.* MIT Press, Cambridge, MA.

Minh-ha, T. (1989) *Woman Native Other.* Indiana University Press, Bloomington.

Ritzer, G. & Ryan, M. (2002) The Globalization of Nothing. *Social Thought and Research* 25(1–2): 51.

Rothkopf, D. (1997) In Praise of Cultural Imperialism? *Foreign Policy* 107: 38.

Said, E. (1978) *Orientalism.* Vintage, New York.

Shohat, E. (1998) *Talking Visions: Multicultural Feminism in a Transnational Age.* MIT Press, Cambridge, MA.

UNESCO (1980) *Sociological Theories: Race and Colonialism.* United Nations Educational, Scientific, and Cultural Organization, Poole.

Vaidhyanathan, S. (2005) Remote Control: The Rise of Electronic Cultural Policy. *Annals of the American Academy of Political and Social Science* 597: 122.

cultural relativism

Bernd Weiler

Cultural relativism, a highly complex doctrine surrounded by various epistemological, political, and ethical controversies, can be broadly defined as the view that culture is the key variable to explain human diversity and that an individual's behavior, thought, emotion, perception, and sensation are relative to and bound by the culture of the group he or she belongs to. Within this frame of thought, culture is usually conceptualized as a holistic, historically grown entity with distinctive features and clear-cut boundaries. The period of enculturation during early childhood is regarded as crucial. The autonomy of the individual is seen as more or less negligible, intragroup differences are usually minimized, and intergroup differences maximized. In the history of ideas, the emphasis on the cultural diversity, the cultural relativity, and boundedness of human experience has often been linked to and, at times, conflated with normative relativism, holding that all cultures are of the same "worth" and that an individual's ethical behavior ought to be judged in terms of the values of his or her culture (cf. Spiro 1986). Cultural relativist arguments have also often been employed to support moral skepticism and to criticize the values of one's own culture. Michel de Montaigne's (1533–92) famous essay "Of Cannibals" might serve as a famous example of the argumentative intertwining of the descriptive and the moral aspect of cultural relativism.

The cultural relativist stance is opposed to the universalist position according to which the cultural context is irrelevant to the concepts of truth, beauty, goodness, justice, and so on. It is also opposed to other forms of relativism, such as biological or racial relativism, which holds that differences between groups are due to differences in innate endowments. Analytically, the various forms of cultural relativist arguments can be distinguished along the two dimensions of extent and intensity. In its broadest form, cultural relativism extends to all manifestations of human existence. In this context even truth is regarded as a local and culture-bound phenomenon, a position known as epistemological or cognitive relativism. In its narrow form, cultural relativists argue that culture is relevant only to certain aspects of human life (e.g., aesthetics and ethics) and irrelevant to others (e.g., knowledge). With regard to the dimension of intensity, one can distinguish between those cultural relativists who argue that culture is the sole *explanans* versus those who hold that culture is a significant *explanans* of human thought, emotion, volition, and so on. In its broadest and most intense version, radical cultural relativism, a position favored today by some postmodernist thinkers, can be seen as a form of group solipsism beset with the various methodological difficulties and inconsistencies associated by R. K. Merton with the doctrine of insiderism (cf. Merton 1972).

Cultural relativist patterns of argumentation have been a constant feature of social analysis and criticism in the intellectual history of the West since the days of the "founding fathers" of ethnography, Hecataeus of Miletus and Herodotus of Halicarnassus. Modern-day cultural relativism, an intellectual twin of historicism, can be traced back to the eighteenth-century critical appraisal and partial rejection of the Enlightenment's over-rationalistic and atomistic picture of the human being and its progressivist conception of history. Opposing the stage theories of civilizational development, the thinkers of the so-called Counter-Enlightenment, most notably Vico, Möser, and Herder, argued that every historical period and every culture has to be understood as an end in itself and as intrinsically valuable. The German American cultural anthropologist Franz Boas and his students (e.g., A. L. Kroeber, R. H. Lowie, E. Sapir, R. Benedict, M. Herskovits, and M. Mead), the scholars most often associated with the doctrine of cultural relativism in the twentieth century, can be seen as the heirs to this Counter-Enlightenment's emphasis on the uniqueness of each culture. By criticizing simultaneously unilineal theories of social evolutionism, racial relativist explanations of cultural differences, and the axiological relativism à la Lévy-Bruhl's prelogical mentality, Boas and his school contributed decisively to the contemporary relativistic and pluralistic concept of culture (cf. Stocking 1982 [1968]). The epistemological and moral issues associated with cultural relativism have been hotly debated within and without anthropology throughout the twentieth century. Identifying a number of human universals, critics argued that there existed a "common denominator of cultures" and that the diversity of cultural forms was limited by the psycho-physical constitution of humans (e.g., B. Malinowski), the external environmental constraints (e.g., M. Harris), and/or the possible number of

functional relations and logical combinations of society's subsystems (e.g., G. P. Murdock). With regard to the moral questions, it was above all the human rights movement, arising in the aftermath of World War II, that severely challenged and undermined cultural relativist thinking. If one contextualizes the cultural relativism of the early twentieth century, however, it is important to note that to the first generation of professional anthropologists cultural relativism was not so much a codified doctrine and an epistemological position as part of the attitudinal tool kit when working in the field. As such, it amounted to a liberal-minded plea for tolerance, implying the postulate to rid oneself of one's own cultural prejudices, to suspend moral judgments, and to approach "strange" cultural values as "objectively" as possible. This legacy still deserves attention as even today a certain dose of cultural relativism might be a good, if not the best, medicine against the universal disease of ethnocentrism.

SEE ALSO: Boas, Franz; Ethnocentrism; Eurocentrism; Progress, Idea of; Sumner, William G.

REFERENCES AND SUGGESTED READINGS

Benedict, R. (1989 [1934]) *Patterns of Culture.* Houghton-Mifflin, Boston.

Boas, F. (1963 [1938]) *The Mind of Primitive Man,* rev. edn with a new foreword by M. J. Herskovits. Free Press, New York.

Geertz, C. (1984) Distinguished Lecture: Anti Anti-Relativism. *American Anthropologist* n.s. 86: 263–78.

Herskovits, M. J. (1948) *Man and His Works: The Science of Cultural Anthropology.* Knopf, New York.

Herskovits, M. J. (1972) *Cultural Relativism: Perspectives in Cultural Pluralism.* Random House, New York.

Hollis, M. & Lukes, S. (Eds.) (1982) *Rationality and Relativism.* Blackwell, Oxford.

Lévy-Bruhl, L. (1984 [1926]) *How Natives Think.* George Allen & Unwin, London.

Merton, R. (1972) Insiders and Outsiders: A Chapter in the Sociology of Knowledge. *American Journal of Sociology* 78(1): 9–47.

Murdock, G. P. (1945) The Common Denominator of Cultures. In: Linton, R. (Ed.), *The Science of*

Man in the World Crisis. Columbia University Press, New York.

Rudolf, W. (1968) *Der kulturelle Relativismus: kritische Analyse einer Grundsatzfragen-Diskussion in der amerikanischen Ethnologie.* Duncker & Humblot, Berlin.

Spiro, M. E. (1986) Cultural Relativism and the Future of Anthropology. *Cultural Anthropology* 1 (3): 259–86.

Stocking, G. W., Jr. (1982 [1968]) Franz Boas and the Culture Concept in Historical Perspective. In: Stocking, G. W., Jr. (Ed.), *Race, Culture, and Evolution: Essays in the History of Anthropology.* University of Chicago Press, Chicago, pp. 195–233.

Sumner, W. G. (1906) *Folkways: A Study of the Sociological Importance of Usages, Manners, Customs, Mores, and Morals.* Ginn, Boston.

Tilley, J. J. (2000) Cultural Relativism. *Human Rights Quarterly* 22: 501–47.

Winch, P. (1988 [1958]) *The Idea of a Social Science and its Relation to Philosophy.* Routledge, London.

cultural reproduction

Adrian Franklin

Cultural reproduction is frequently considered to describe how cultural forms (e.g., social inequality, privilege, elite status, ethnicity) and cultures themselves are transmitted intact, from one generation to another. This idea emanates strongly from original work by Pierre Bourdieu in the 1970s on the role of the education process in reproducing class inequality and from such ethnographic classics as Paul Willis's *Learning to Labour* (1977) that showed how inequality could be reproduced culturally despite the best efforts of a benevolent education system. However, subsequent work on the concept of culture suggests that a concentration on class reproduction implies a very restricted sense of the term "reproduction," and that more significant dimensions of reproduction inhere in the idea of culture itself (Jenks 1993). Indeed, Jenks shows how cultural reproduction lies at the heart of more traditions of sociology than Marxism and neo-Marxism.

The word culture derives from the notion of growth and development and does not imply stasis or repetition. Williams (1981) shows how by the eighteenth and nineteenth centuries the word had itself grown to mean not only husbandry but also human development, specifically the cultivation of aptitude and understanding or, in other words, cultural capital or *change*. Critically, it remained only a *verb* until the nineteenth century. Another way of looking at this is suggested by Jenks, who argues that the idea of culture emerged from the noun *process*, in the sense of nurture, growth, and bringing into being – in fact to cultivate in an agricultural or horticultural sense. "Culture as process is emergent, it is forthcoming, it is continuous in the way of reproducing and as in all social processes it provides the grounds and parallel context of social action itself" (Jenks 1993: 1).

Drawing on definitions of culture from anthropologists, Jenks suggests that culture embodies the idea of accumulated resources (material and immaterial) that a community might employ, *change*, and pass on. Essentially it is the socially learned behavior and the shared symbolism of a community: it reveals and structures, empowers and constrains. The problem with cultural reproduction as Jenks sees it also concerns a restricted sense of the term reproduction. The tendency within Marxist traditions of sociology has been to see reproduction phenotypically. In this, reproduction is restricted negatively to repetition, to the copy or, in a weaker sense, to "imitation" or "likeness." As replication it implies a metaphor of restraint or the restriction on choice, and here of course is where ideology, state apparatuses, and symbolic violence are deployed in Marxian terms.

However, reproduction also has the *genotypical* sense of excitement, positivity, and vibrancy – as is implied in the newness of sexual and biological reproduction. Here the image changes to one of generation rather than repetition, of change and new combinations, innovation and creativity.

Jenks argues that in several traditions of sociology there is an implicit sense of a more positive form of cultural reproduction. In Durkheim's work the challenge of cultural reproduction was "to search for the appropriate collective credo that will ensure the reproduction of solidarity in the face of change" (Jenks 1993: 8). In other words, for Durkheim, it is a defining feature of cultures that forms of solidarity will be produced in changed circumstances. The churning nature of modernization undermined mechanical forms of solidarity based on traditional societies, but new organic forms appeared among the newly individualized cultures of the city. As Jenks argues, "the Durkheimian tradition views reproduction with an optimism, indeed a positivism; its metaphors are consensual rather than divisive and its motivation is integrative" (1993: 8).

Equally, for ethnomethodologists there is a strong sense of creative cultural reproduction emanating from ordinary conversation and interaction. According to this view an inarticulate consensus must exist between competent social actors in order for interaction to work at all. And it is within the contexts of conversations and interactions that the business of cultural reproduction, whether of restraint and replication or innovation, is carried out/ negotiated.

Cultural reproduction as a process must therefore be tracked and watched over time in methodological terms, and Willis's ethnographic work on the working-class "lads" in a Midlands school remains the archetype. In this study it was shown that the lads were not failed by an educational system geared solely to reproduce the privilege of the elite but by their own culture whose appeal proved stronger than the alien culture of education-based social mobility. Willis shows how the cultural richness of working-class culture competed with that offered by the school and how the lads embodied this culture and used it against the school and its teachers. However, this study took place in the context of a vibrant and secure labor market for blue-collar workers. A later (1990s) study was completed when that labor market had all but evaporated (Mac an Ghaill 1994) and this showed how new circumstances engendered new forms of cultural response. Mac an Ghaill did find a group corresponding to the lads, but unlike the superconfident 1970s group, they were undergoing a crisis of masculinity as the economic base of their culture had disappeared. Meanwhile, the new circumstances had produced a more fragmented masculine culture at the school with far more reaching out for the cultural capital that the school could offer.

Blasko's work in Hungary also found that schools offering cultural capital had been used effectively by working-class parents and children to achieve social mobility and by the upper classes to maintain their existing positions (Blasko 2003: 5).

SEE ALSO: Bourdieu, Pierre; Cultural Capital; Cultural Capital in Schools; Educational and Occupational Attainment; Ethnography; Habitus/Field; Inequality, Wealth; Occupations

REFERENCES AND SUGGESTED
READINGS

Blasko, Z. (2003) Cultural Reproduction or Cultural Mobility? *Review of Sociology* 9(1): 5–26.
Bourdieu, P. (1973) Cultural Reproduction and Social Reproduction. In: Brown, R. (Ed.), *Knowledge, Education, and Cultural Change*. Willmer Brothers, London.
Bourdieu, P. (1990) *In Other Words: Essays Towards a Reflexive Sociology*. Trans. M. Adamson. Polity Press, Cambridge.
Jenks, C. (1993) *Cultural Reproduction*. Routledge, London.
Mac an Ghaill, M. (1994) *The Making of Men: Masculinities, Sexualities, and Schooling*. Open University Press, Buckingham.
Williams, R. (1981) *Culture*. Fontana, London.
Willis, P. (1977) *Learning to Labour*. Gower, London.

cultural resistance

Stephen Duncombe

Cultural resistance is the practice of using meanings and symbols, that is, culture, to contest and combat a dominant power, often constructing a different vision of the world in the process. The practice is as old as history. The Hebrew Scriptures, for example, were a cultural means with which to create Jewish identity and then hold on to that identity in the face of Roman oppression. The stories of Jesus and Mohammed served similar functions. The modern theory of cultural resistance, however, was first articulated in the mid-nineteenth century by Matthew Arnold.

Arnold wrote his famous essay *Culture and Anarchy* at a time when his England was undergoing massive change: industrialization, urbanization, and an extension of the franchise to the working classes. Whereas some considered this progress, Arnold saw only chaos. But culture, as "the best which has been thought and said" (1990 [1869]: 4), offered a solution. It was a way to resist and rise above the politics and commerce and machinery of the day, providing a universal standard upon which to base "a principle of authority, to counteract the tendency to anarchy which seems to be threatening us" (p. 82). Culture was a Platonic platform where "total perfection" could be cultivated, eventually returning to the messy material world – if at all – in the form of an ideal state to guide society.

Arnold may have been the first modern voice to articulate a strategy of cultural resistance, but it is an intellectual and activist on the opposite side of the political spectrum, the Italian communist Antonio Gramsci, who framed its contemporary use. Gramsci, writing from prison in the late 1920s and 1930s, reflected on why the revolutions he fought for in the West had so far failed. Part of the reason, he concluded, was a serious underestimation of culture and civil society. Power resides not only in institutions, but also in the ways people make sense of their world; hegemony is a political *and* cultural process. Armed with culture instead of guns, one fights a different type of battle. Whereas traditional battles were "wars of maneuver," frontal assaults which seized the state, cultural battles were "wars of position," flanking maneuvers, commando raids and infiltrations, staking out positions from which to attack and then reassemble civil society (1971: 229–39). Thus, part of the revolutionary project was to create counterhegemonic culture behind enemy lines. But if this culture was to have real power, and communist integrity, it could not, as Arnold believed, be imposed from above; it must come out of the experiences and consciousness of people. Thus, the revolutionary must discover the progressive potentialities that reside within popular consciousness and from this fashion a culture of resistance. Gramsci's theories of cultural resistance can be glimpsed in the practice

of Mahatma Gandhi's invocation of *satyagraha* and Indian tradition to resist British colonialism, and, more recently, in the culture-heavy tactics of the rebel Zapatista army in Mexico and the magical realist communiqués of their Subcommandante Marcos.

In the academy, Gramsci's ideas shaped the mission of the Center for Contemporary Cultural Studies (CCCS) at the University of Birmingham in the 1970s. The CCCS is best known for its subcultural studies, and it was within these mainly working-class subcultures that researchers found an inchoate politics of resistance. Dick Hebdige, for example, writes about how punk rockers performed the decline of post-war Britain with ripped-up clothes, songs mocking the queen, and lyrics that warned: "We're your future, no future." Through culture young people contested and rearranged the ideological constructions – the systems of meaning – handed down to them by the powers that be. Cultural resistance, however, was recognized as a double-edged sword by CCCS director Stuart Hall and his colleagues. Subcultures opened up spaces where dominant ideology was challenged and counterhegemonic culture created, but these contestations and symbolic victories often remained imprisoned in culture, never stepping outside to confront material power. These were "magical resolutions," as Stanley Cohen explains, to real-world problems.

Cultural studies continues to be concerned with cultural resistance. Readers "re-read" romance novels against the grain, and music fans claim ownership of the bands they love through zine writing. Even shopping is championed by John Fiske as an act of resistance: "a sense of freedom, however irrational, from the work involved in working and loving under patriarchy" (1989: 42). But Gramsci's question of how this cultural resistance translates into a revolutionary strategy, or even the less ambitious question of how these cultural practices translate into material changes, is less often posed. Given the left-of-center politics of many in the cultural studies camp, it is ironic that culture is often celebrated as an escape – cultural resistance as the conservative Matthew Arnold understood and appreciated it.

Critics have also questioned the efficacy of cultural resistance within a consumer capitalist economy that needs constant innovation to survive. Within this context, the drive to create an oppositional culture merely serves to create a new market for new products. As Frankfurt School critic Theodor Adorno snidely remarked about the jazz music fan as far back as 1938: "He pictures himself as the individualist who whistles at the world. But what he whistles is its melody" (2002 [1938]: 298). (Adorno did, however, maintain that the patently unpopular atonal music of Schoenberg held out resistant possibilities.)

Today, there is a renewed understanding – by activists, if not yet all academics – that cultural resistance is a necessary, but not sufficient, means of resistance. Using culture as a political tool is absolutely critical in a media-saturated society linked by a global communications network. But in a world where the image of Che Guevara sells Swatch watches, cultural resistance, by itself, is not enough.

SEE ALSO: Adorno, Theodor W.; Birmingham School; Cultural Studies; Culture Jamming; Culture, Social Movements and; Gramsci, Antonio; Subculture

REFERENCES AND SUGGESTED READINGS

Adorno, T. (2002 [1938]) On the Fetish-Character in Music and the Regression of Listening. In: Duncombe, S. (Ed.), *Cultural Resistance Reader*. Verso, New York, pp. 276–303.

Arnold, M. 1990 [1869]) *Culture and Anarchy*. Cambridge University Press, Cambridge.

Cohen, S. (1973) *Folk Devils and Moral Panics*. Paladin, London.

Duncombe, S. (1997) *Notes from Underground: Zines and the Politics of Alternative Culture*. Verso, New York.

Duncombe, S. (Ed.) (2002) *Cultural Resistance Reader*. Verso, New York.

Fiske, J. (1989) *Reading the Popular*. Unwin Hyman, Boston.

Frank, T. (1997) *The Conquest of Cool*. University of Chicago Press, Chicago.

Gramsci, A. (1971) *Prison Notebooks*. Ed. Q. Hoare & G. Nowell Smith. International, New York.

Hall, S. & Jefferson, T. (Eds.) (1976) *Resistance through Rituals*. Unwin Hyman, London.

Hebdige, D. (1979) *Subculture*. Methuen, London.

Radway, J. (1984) *Reading the Romance*. University of North Carolina, Chapel Hill.

cultural studies

Elizabeth Long

Cultural studies is an interdisciplinary field that explores the linkages between society, politics, identity (or the person), and the full range of what is called "culture," from high culture and the popular arts or mass entertainment, to beliefs, discourses, and communicative practices. Cultural studies has drawn on different national traditions of inquiry into these connections – from the Frankfurt School's studies of the mass culture industry, and of the psychological processes that undercut democracy in liberal and affluent societies, to French structuralist and poststructuralist critiques of ideology, constraining categorical frames, and a monadic and unified concept of the self. The branch of cultural studies that early drew the most attention from sociologists was that articulated by the Birmingham Centre for Contemporary Cultural Studies, perhaps in part because Birmingham scholars were inspired by some aspects of American sociology, especially the Chicago School tradition, which gave their work a recognizably social dimension.

Taking Birmingham as an example is instructive in pointing out some characteristics of cultural studies as a field. Conventionalized intellectual genealogies often begin with the work of Raymond Williams (1958, 1961), Richard Hoggart (1957), and E. P. Thompson (1963). All three challenged dominant traditions in the humanities in post-war England. Hoggart and Williams argued first that literary or "high" culture is just one expression of culture, in the more anthropological sense – the broad range of meanings and interactions that make up social life. Second, they argued that cultural expressions could only be understood in a broader social context of "institutions, power relations, and history" (Seidman 1997). This led Williams (1961) to analyze, for example, the rise of the novel in modern England as part of the gradual evolution of a broad-based reading culture, and to discuss the shifting meanings and (sometimes ideological) images that clustered around "city" and "country" as agriculture, industry, and urbanization changed the landscape of England

(Williams 1973). In *The Uses of Literacy*, Hoggart examined the changing culture of the working class through analysis of neighborhoods, pubs, and family interaction as well as popular music and literature in a book that combined personal reflection with historical sociology (Hoggart 1957). E. P. Thompson's *The Making of the English Working Class*, addressing similar problems of historical change in the early nineteenth century, showed that both Marxist conceptions of class and the discipline of history could be fruitfully broadened if culture – whether Methodism or the literary-minded corresponding societies developed by skilled craftsmen – were taken into account in analyzing working-class English politics (Thompson 1963).

This first generation of British cultural studies scholars were all "men of the left," confronting the failures of communism, the idiosyncrasies of English working-class politics, and the peculiarities of democratization under the sign of commercial culture. All were, in other words, *critical* analysts of what they liked to call "lived experience," that very term indicating how thoroughly this version of cultural studies integrated cultural expressions with social life. They also were all seriously involved with alternative sites of mainly working-class education, whether Workers' Education Association classes or University Extension courses (Goodwin & Wolff 1997), a commitment that led to the rather unusual institutionalization of cultural studies at Birmingham. And for all three, the scholarly moves they made were from the humanities and its traditional categories of analysis and evaluation into a more fully articulated sense of cultural and social reality.

When cultural studies became institutionalized under Hoggart as one subgroup of literary studies at the University of Birmingham in 1964 as the Centre for Contemporary Cultural Studies (CCCS), it retained some distinctive features from its prehistory. For example, staff and student groups cooperated in administering the center, and a Centre General Meeting of administrative and intellectual groups formulated policy. Most innovative, perhaps, were the self-governing "subgroups" of researchers (often students) and teachers. Richard Johnson (1997) mentions that in 1974, for example,

there were groups on Art and Politics, Cultural History, Media, Subcultures, Women's Studies, Cultures of Work, and two Marxist Reading Groups. These groups produced most CCCS books and journals, and the "collective book" remained typical of Birmingham scholarship into the 1990s. So, too, did a relatively interdisciplinary and activist approach to scholarly careers, which may have contributed to the precarious institutionalization of cultural studies in Britain and its common location in academic sites that were themselves interdisciplinary.

As a younger generation of scholars moved to the fore in British cultural studies, they brought with them concerns from the student movement (Johnson 1997), and also training in sociology. Seidman, for example, mentions Stuart Hall, David Morley, Dorothy Hobson, Paul Willis, Phil Cohen, Dick Hebdige, Ian Chambers, and Angela McRobbie in this regard (Seidman 1997; Hall 1980b). They turned from the earlier thinkers' humanism to take up insights from sociological studies of deviance, subcultures, and popular culture, and at the same time turned towards strands of European Marxism – notably Althusser and Gramsci – as a corrective to what they characterized as the earlier generation's a-theoretical "Englishness."

Concerned about the new ways social domination operated in a post-war world that was, at least for many in Europe, both relatively affluent and at peace, these scholars investigated the culture/society connection as a promising location for understanding this process. Post-war shifts in the social organization of cultural and communications media also gave popular forms of culture immense social power. This was particularly true of cultural forms and technologies developing in and exported from the US, which was becoming a global force because of television, Coca-Cola, and rock and roll – and later, MTV, the shopping mall, music videos, and theme parks – as well as more traditional forms of economic and military power. This shift also required new ways of thinking that linked culture, as it was linked in people's lives, more closely to society and politics, especially in relation to critical questions about democracy and equality.

Birmingham scholars often used a processual view of Gramsci's ideas about hegemony and resistance in their analyses of popular cultural forms and usages. Subcultures became a particularly interesting object of study because members of subcultures formed collective and often countercultural identities around styles they fashioned from cultural commodities (Willis 1977; McRobbie, 1984). Birmingham appropriations of both Gramsci and Althusser also emphasized the contingent nature of ideological formations and their relative autonomy – from class determinism, in particular. This foregrounded history and human activity, which Birmingham scholars often discussed as "practice," as well as opening up consideration of other forms and sites of domination, such as gender, race, or region (Bennett et al. 1986; Hall 1980a, 1991).

The problematic that informed scholars at Birmingham also influenced research arising from different national traditions. So in France, for example, structuralist semioticians like Roland Barthes (1972) drew on a long French preoccupation with language and linguistic culture to investigate how language-like cultural forms encoded social domination in popular cultural "mythologies." Somewhat later, post-structuralist thinkers like Michel Foucault (1977, 1978, 1980) moved beyond purely linguistic discourses to understand how power and knowledge shape subjectivity, and Pierre Bourdieu (1977, 1984, 1991), drawing on both anthropology and sociology, considered the way culture, and legitimate culture in particular, influenced both social stratification and personal "dispositions."

At roughly the same time in Germany, Jürgen Habermas drew on the Frankfurt tradition of critical social thought to examine the failure of formal politics to address new configurations of social domination. His influential response turned toward an analysis of the public sphere – conceived as a "realm" outside of the marketplace and the state, yet not reducible to private life. His formulation was itself profoundly cultural, first, because of its insistence that communication was an aspect of social reality irreducible to economic interests. Second, he discussed the evolution of the public sphere in Europe historically, locating different sites (e.g., the coffee house) and media (the newspaper) of communication that enabled conversation based on reasoned arguments about

fundamental social and political assumptions to take place. In his view, this was a necessary precondition for democracy. Although his conviction that both state and market were eroding the public sphere made Habermas pessimistic about the prospects for genuine democracy in the present, he argued nonetheless for a basic human capacity to engage in the rational discussion it would require (Habermas 1971, 1979, 1984–7, 1989).

Habermas's work remains at a high level of abstraction, and has filtered into American scholarship mainly as the point of departure for more concrete – and often historical – examinations of "the public sphere" and for critical appraisals of the concept itself (Fraser 1989; Calhoun 1992a, 1992b; Schudson 1998). This kind of interdisciplinary, international borrowing is quite typical of cultural studies, and may partially explain why cultural studies scholarship has been more easily integrated into multidisciplinary fields, subfields, or programs than into more rigidly bounded disciplines. Similarly, the fact that several strands of cultural studies work (as was the case in Birmingham) originated as critical reformulations of the humanities, and have maintained a close connection to interpretive methodologies and to culture itself (however broadly defined), may explain why US cultural studies has been largely institutionalized in humanities rather than in the social sciences, with the exception of anthropology, some culturally inflected areas of sociology, and some aspects of political theory.

Nonetheless, broad questions about how contemporary culture relates to an emerging geopolitical order featuring new constellations of technology and capital and new configurations of collective organization – from regional religious fundamentalisms to transnational corporations and political unions – have continued to bring many scholars into the interdisciplinary arena of cultural studies. Since the academy is itself experiencing the same kind of dislocations, dispersals, and reconcentrations of power that scholars are attempting to understand in the environing social world, the enterprise of cultural studies has generated a broad array of such theoretical and empirical lines of inquiry. For example, urbanists have noted (like Hoggart in the 1950s) that the communities that provided roots for ethnic or class solidarity have been dispersed by urban renewal, deindustrialization, and other developments effacing an older sense of place in contemporary cities. But more recently, gentrification, global hip-hop culture, planned communities, and theme parks have begun to provide other material for thinking through the connections between "community" and identity. So critical geographers have turned to work by Jameson (1991), Lyotard (1984), and other postmodernists to understand how these new urban forms might structure people's experiences and possibilities for collective action (Harvey 1989; Zukin 1991, 1992; Gregory 1994). At the same time, changes in the social organization of sexuality and medical science have led other scholars to take up thinking by Foucault (1978) that examines how discursive formations linking textual knowledge, technical capabilities, and institutional developments have worked to structure contemporary sexual subjectivities and their emergence as socially recognized "identities" (see Butler 1993; Weston 1998; Sedgewick 2003; Seidman 2003; Eribon 2004).

Some of this reinvention involves the disappearance of traditional grounds for disciplinary activity. For example, high cultural texts no longer have the privileged place they enjoyed in early twentieth-century public education. This has led critical literary scholars to become self-conscious about the historical roots of national literary studies and the sociopolitical dimension of canonization. In turn, this has engendered an examination of the institutions (literary criticism, the discipline of English, the Book-of-the-Month Club) that work to define what we call literature and to assign criteria of literary value (Radway 1997), as well as a broad-ranging analysis of popular cultural "texts" and their uses in the social world. Similarly, small-scale low-technology societies are either vanishing or negotiating their induction into global networks of technology, labor, and consumption. These geopolitical developments have led anthropologists to rethink the relationship between ethnographer and subject, to search at home as well as among traditional Others for ethnographic opportunities, and to recognize affinities between their signature methodology and that of tourists, state department officials, and world music entrepreneurs (Marcus 1999).

Yet, similar opportunities for cultural studies scholarship appear as new disciplinary formations emerge in response to social change. Social studies of science, for instance, have grown up in tandem with the enormous growth of "big science" in the recent past, and their critical take on science comes as much from public questions about an endeavor that has brought us nuclear weapons and environmental devastation alongside space flight and the Salk vaccine, as from purely academic developments. Other new areas of investigation that are attracting cultural studies scholars include visual studies, cybercultures and communities (this has also spawned Internet-based research methodologies), new technologies of embodiment and possibilities for identity construction, and globalization, which has affected the whole range of what are sometimes called the human sciences.

While this scholarship has spurred some significant departmental or program-level institutionalization in American universities, it is most obviously present as a major paradigm in existing interdisciplinary programs, such as American studies, ethnic and women's studies, urban studies, and science and technology studies, and is an important intellectual force in publishers' offerings and conferences both in the Anglophone world and beyond. It is also what one scholar calls an "accent" in more entrenched academic fields, perhaps more welcome in traditionally interpretive disciplines or traditions of inquiry than in those underwritten by positivist epistemology. For this reason, much of sociology has seen cultural studies as a threat rather than an opportunity, yet one can clearly see openings toward cultural studies in cultural sociology, sociology of religion, gender/sexuality, and race/ethnicity, urban sociology, qualitative sociology, and some branches of social theory.

SEE ALSO: Birmingham School; Critical Theory/Frankfurt School; Cultural Studies, British; Culture; Gramsci, Antonio; Popular Culture

REFERENCES AND SUGGESTED READINGS

Barthes, R. (1972) *Mythologies*. Trans. A. Lavers. Cape, London.

Bennett, T., Mercer, C., & Woollacott, J. (Eds.) (1986) *Popular Culture and Social Relations*. Open University Press, Philadelphia.

Bourdieu, P. (1977) *Outline of a Theory of Practice*. Trans. R. Nice. Cambridge University Press, Cambridge.

Bourdieu, P. (1984) *Distinction: A Social Critique of the Judgement of Taste*. Trans. R. Nice. Harvard University Press, Cambridge, MA.

Bourdieu, P. (1991) *Language and Symbolic Power*. Trans. G. Raymond & M. Adamson. Polity Press, Cambridge.

Butler, J. (1993) *Bodies that Matter: On the Discursive Limits of "Sex."* Routledge, New York.

Calhoun, C. (Ed.) (1992a) *Habermas and the Public Sphere*. MIT Press, Cambridge, MA.

Calhoun, C. (1992b) Sociology, Other Disciplines, and the Project of a General Understanding of Social Life. In: Halliday, T. C. & Janowitz, M. (Eds.), *Sociology and its Publics: The Forms and Fates of Disciplinary Organization*. University of Chicago Press, Chicago, pp. 137–95.

Eribon, D. (2004) *Insult and the Making of the Gay Self*. Trans. M. Lucey. Duke Universitiy Press, Durham, NC.

Foucault, M. (1977) *Discipline and Punish: The Birth of the Prison*. Trans. A. Sheridan. Pantheon Books, New York.

Foucault, M. (1978) *History of Sexuality*. Trans. R. Hurley. Pantheon Books, New York.

Foucault, M. (1980) *Power/Knowledge: Selected Interviews and Other Writings, 1972–1977*. Trans. C. Gordon. Harvester Press, Brighton.

Fraser, N. (1989) What's Critical about Critical Theory: The Case of Habermas and Gender. In: *Unruly Practices: Power, Discourse, and Gender in Contemporary Social Theory*. University of Minnesota Press, MN, pp. 113–43.

Goodwin, A. & Wolff, J. (1997) Conserving Cultural Studies. In: Long, E. (Ed.), *From Sociology to Cultural Studies: New Perspectives*. Blackwell, Oxford, pp. 123–49.

Gregory, D. (1994) *Geographical Imaginations*. Blackwell, Oxford.

Habermas, J. (1971) *Knowledge and Human Interests*. Beacon Press, Boston.

Habermas, J. (1979) *Communication and the Evolution of Society*. Beacon Press, Boston.

Habermas, J. (1984–7) *Theory of Communicaive Action*. Beacon Press, Boston.

Habermas, J. (1989) *The Structural Transformation of the Public Sphere: An Inquiry into a Category of Bourgeois Society*. MIT Press, Cambridge, MA.

Hall, S. (1980a) Cultural Studies: Two Paradigms. *Media, Culture and Society* 2: 57–72.

Hall, S. (1980b) Cultural Studies and the Centre: Some Problematics and Problems. In: Hall, S. et al. (Eds.), *Culture, Media, Language*. Hutchinson, London.

Hall, S. (1991) Signification, Representation, Ideology: Althusser and the Post-structuralist Debates. In: Avery, R. K. & Eason, D. (Eds.), *Critical Perspectives on Media and Society*. Guilford Press, New York, pp. 88–113.

Harvey, D. (1989) *The Condition of Postmodernity*. Blackwell, Oxford.

Hoggart, R. (1957) *The Uses of Literacy*. Chatto & Windus, London.

Jameson, F. (1991) *Postmodernism or, the Cultural Logic of Late Capitalism*. Duke University Press, Durham, NC.

Johnson, R. (1997) Reinventing Cultural Studies: Remembering for the Best Version. In: Long, E. (Ed.), *From Sociology to Cultural Studies: New Perspectives*. Blackwell, Oxford, pp. 452–88.

Lyotard, J. (1984 [1974]) *The Postmodern Condition: A Report on Knowledge*. University of Minnesota Press, Minneapolis.

McRobbie, A. (1984) Dance and Social Fantasy. In Mc Robbie, A. & Nava, M. (Eds.), *Gender and Generation*. Macmillan, London, pp. 130–61.

Marcus, G. (Ed.) (1999) *Critical Anthropology Now: Unexpected Contexts, Shifting Constituencies, Changing Agendas*. School of American Research Press, Santa Fe.

Radway, J. (1997) *A Feeling for Books: The Book-of-the-Month Club, Literary Taste, and Middle-Class Desire*. University of North Carolina Press, Chapel Hill.

Schudson, M. (1998) *The Good Citizen: A History of American Civic Life*. Martin Kessler Books, New York.

Sedgwick, E. K. (2003) *Touching Feeling: Affect, Pedagogy, Performativity*. Duke University Press, Durham, NC.

Seidman, S. (1997) Relativizing Sociology: The Challenge of Cultural Studies. In: Long, E. (Ed.), *From Sociology to Cultural Studies: New Perspectives*. Blackwell, Oxford, pp. 37–61.

Seidman, S. (2003) *The Social Construction of Sexuality*. Norton, New York.

Thompson, E. P. (1963) *The Making of the English Working Class*. Victor Gollancz, London.

Weston, K. (1998) *Long Slow Burn: Sexuality and Social Science*. Routledge, London.

Williams, R. (1958) *Culture and Society 1780–1950*. Penguin, London.

Williams, R. (1961) *The Long Revolution*. Chatto & Windus, London.

Williams, R. (1973) *The Country and the City*. Chatto & Windus, London.

Willis, P. (1977) *Learning to Labour: How Working Class Kids Get Working Class Jobs*. Saxon House, Farnborough.

Zukin, S. (1991) *Landscapes of Power: From Detroit to Disney World*. University of California Press, Berkeley.

Zukin, S. (1992) Postmodern Urban Landscapes: Mapping Culture and Power. In: Lash, S. & Friedman, J. (Eds.), *Modernity and Identity*. Blackwell, Oxford, pp. 221–47.

cultural studies, British

John Storey

British cultural studies works with an inclusive definition of culture. That is, it is a "democratic" project in the sense that rather than study only what Matthew Arnold called "the best which has been thought and said" (*Culture and Anarchy*, 1867), British cultural studies is committed to examining *all* that has been thought and said. To put it simply, culture is how we live nature (including our own biology); it is the shared meanings we make and encounter in our everyday lives. Culture is not something essential, embodied in particular "texts" (that is, any commodity, object, or event that can be made to signify); it is the practices and processes of making meanings with and from the texts we encounter in our everyday lives. In this way, then, cultures are made from the production, circulation, and consumption of meanings.

Cultures, therefore, do not so much consist of, say, books, but are the shifting networks of signification in which, say, books are *made* to exist as meaningful objects. For example, if I pass a business card to someone in China, the polite way to do it is with two hands. If I pass it with one hand I may cause offense. This is clearly a matter of culture. However, the "culture" is not so much in the gesture, it is in the "meaning" of the gesture. In other words, there is nothing essentially polite about using two hands; using two hands has been made to signify politeness. Nevertheless, signification has become embodied in a material practice, which can, in turn, produce material.

This is not to reduce everything "upwards" to culture as a signifying system, but it is to insist that culture defined in this way should be understood "as essentially involved in *all* forms of social activity" (Williams 1981: 13). While there is more to life than signifying systems, it is nevertheless the case that "it would ... be wrong to suppose that we can ever usefully discuss a social system without including, as a central part of its practice, its signifying systems, on which, as a system, it fundamentally depends" (p. 207).

According to British cultural studies, then, to share a culture is to interpret the world – make it meaningful and experience it – in recognizably similar ways. So-called "culture shock" happens when we encounter a radically different network of meanings; when our "natural" or "common sense" is confronted by someone else's "natural" or "common sense." However, cultures are never simply shifting networks of shared meanings. On the contrary, cultures are always both shared and contested networks of meanings. That is, culture is where we share and contest meanings of ourselves, of each other, and of the social worlds in which we live.

British cultural studies draws two conclusions from this way of thinking about culture. First, although the world exists in all its enabling and constraining materiality outside culture, it is only in culture that the world can be *made to mean*. In other words, culture constructs the realities it appears only to describe. Second, because different meanings can be ascribed to the same "text" (anything that can be made to signify), meaning-making (i.e., the making of culture) is always a potential site of struggle and negotiation. The making of meaning is always entangled in what Volosinov (1973) would call the politics of "multi-accentuality." Rather than being inscribed with a single meaning, a "text" can be articulated with different "accents." That is, it can be *made to mean* different things; in different contexts, with different effects of power. A text is not the issuing source of meaning, but a site where the articulation of meaning – variable meaning(s) – can be produced in specific contexts. We implicitly recognize this when ever we refer to, for example, a feminist reading, a Marxist reading, a queer reading, a postcolonial reading. In each instance, the intertextuality of the text is confronted by the intertextuality of the reader. In this way, then, the symbolic work of "production in use" is never a simple repetition of the semiotic certainties of the lecture theater or the seminar room. For example, masculinity has real material conditions of existence, but there are different ways of representing masculinity in culture and different ways of being "masculine." Therefore, although masculinity seems to be fixed by its biological conditions of existence, what it *means*, and the struggle over what it means, always takes place *in* culture. This is not simply an issue of semantic difference, a simple question of interpreting the world differently; it is about relations of culture and power; about who can claim the power and authority to define social reality; to *make the world (and the things in it) mean* in particular ways.

Meanings (i.e., cultures) have a "material" existence in that they help organize practice; they help establish norms of behavior. My examples of different masculinities and the passing of business cards in China are both instances of where signification organizes practice. Those with power often seek to regulate the impact of meanings on practice. In other words, dominant ways of making the world meaningful, produced by those with the power to make their meanings circulate in the world, can generate "hegemonic truths," which may come to assume an authority over the ways in which we see, think, communicate, and act in the world: that is, become the "common sense" which organizes our actions (Gramsci 1971). Culture and power, therefore, are the primary object of study in British cultural studies.

SEE ALSO: Audiences; Birmingham School; Cultural Studies; Culture; Culture, Gender and; Hegemony and the Media; Popular Culture

REFERENCES AND SUGGESTED READINGS

Gramsci, A. (1971) *Selections from Prison Notebooks*. Lawrence & Wishart, London.

Morley, D. & Kuan-Hsing, C. (Eds.) (1996) *Stuart Hall: Critical Dialogues in Cultural Studies*. Routledge, London.

Storey, J. (Ed.) (1996) *What is Cultural Studies*. Arnold, London.

Storey, J. (2003a) *Cultural Studies and the Study of Popular Culture*, 2nd edn. Edinburgh University Press, Edinburgh.

Storey, J. (2003b) *Inventing Popular Culture*. Blackwell, Oxford.

Turner, G. (2002) *British Cultural Studies*. Routledge, London.

Volosinov, V. N. (1973) *Marxism and the Philosophy of Language*. Seminar Press, New York.

Williams, R. (1981) *Culture*. Fontana, London.

cultural tourism

Melanie Smith

"Cultural tourism" could be defined as tourism that focuses on cultural attractions and activities as a primary motivating factor for travel. Notwithstanding the broad definitions of culture that abound within postmodern and populist writings, parameters need to be drawn around what is defined as "culture" in this context. It is therefore useful to break the concept of cultural tourism down into a number of subsets. As argued by Smith (2003: 29), "cultural tourism can no longer be considered as a special interest or niche sector, but instead as an umbrella term for a range of tourism typologies and diverse activities which have a cultural focus."

Richards (2001: 7) suggests that cultural tourism covers the consumption not just of "the cultural products of the past," but also of contemporary culture or the "way of life" of a people or region. Hughes (1996, 2000) differentiates between "universal," "wide," "narrow," and "sectorized" cultural tourism. These definitions correspond broadly to perceiving culture as a whole way of life; to engaging with specific ethnic or indigenous groups; to experiencing the "artistic and intellectual" activities of a society; to visiting specific heritage attractions or arts venues. Cultural tourism encompasses heritage (both tangible and intangible), the arts (including festivals and events), and contemporary culture insofar as it relates to the lifestyles and traditions of a people or place. Cultural tourism is not simply about the passive consumption of heritage attractions or attendance of festivals, it can also involve a high degree of interaction with local people, as well as the pursuit of creative activities (e.g., painting, photography, dance). Indeed, Richards and Raymond (2000) suggest that creative tourism is becoming a growth subsector within cultural tourism.

As the demand for tourism increases, so apparently does the demand for cultural tourism, which appears to have grown exponentially in recent years. For example, McKercher and Cros (2002) estimate that as many as 240 million international journeys annually involve some element of cultural tourism. This may have something to do with broadening definitions of culture, as well as the apparent diversification of tourist interests (Sigala & Leslie 2005). The cultural tourist could be described as a tourist who is better educated than average (Richards 1996), and generally concerned with knowledge-seeking and self-improvement, thus the inner journey is likely to be as important as the outer journey. Cultural tourists actively seek difference and authentic and spontaneous (rather than "staged" or contrived) interaction with local people and places (Smith 2003). Tourism may often be described as "travel" whereby the cultural tourist elevates him/herself to the level of an adventurer or explorer. This is particularly the case in the context of indigenous and ethnic tourism. For this reason, cultural tourism has become increasingly politicized, and has sometimes been accused of being imperialistic, Eurocentric, or voyeuristic (Smith & Robinson 2006). However, cultural tourists are by no means homogeneous, neither in terms of motivations nor profiles. For example, McKercher and Cros (2002) differentiate between tourists for whom culture is a primary motivating factor ("purposeful") and those who are "serendipitous" or "incidental."

Cultural tourism can be subdivided into a number of typologies for the sake of greater definitional clarity, the facilitation of research, and product development.

HERITAGE TOURISM

Heritage tourism focuses on tangible artifacts from the past, including historical monuments, archaeological sites, religious sites, and museums. This includes World Heritage Sites, of which there are now over 750 (including the Taj Mahal in India and the Pyramids in Egypt). Intangible heritage is also an important resource (e.g., the traditions, lifestyles, arts and crafts of local people). The interpretation and representation of heritage can be complex and contentious (e.g., concentration camps such as Auschwitz in Poland; Robben Island in post-apartheid South Africa). Many heritage sites suffer from over-visitation (e.g., Stonehenge in the UK; Ephesus in Turkey), therefore conservation and visitor management issues are of primary concern for this form of cultural tourism.

ARTS TOURISM

Arts tourism focuses on the visual arts (e.g., galleries) as well as performance (e.g., theaters, concerts) and other experiential forms of activity (e.g., festivals and events). There are some concerns that tourism can dilute or "trivialize" the arts. Many ethnic and indigenous art forms (e.g., Caribbean carnivals, Asian Mela festivals, Aboriginal arts and crafts, Andalucian flamenco dancing) are becoming more popular on a global scale, so care needs to be taken to ensure that they are not overcommodified.

CREATIVE TOURISM

Creative tourism involves tourists undertaking creative activities such as painting, pottery making, glass blowing, weaving, photography, and wood carving, either under the guidance of or independently of local people (e.g., with a tour operator). In many cases, creative tourism may be a subsidiary activity rather than a primary motivating factor, although growing numbers of tour operators are now offering special interest tours focused on creative activities (e.g., salsa holidays in Cuba, watercolor painting in Provence, cookery in Tuscany).

URBAN CULTURAL TOURISM

Urban cultural tourism focuses on city activities, which may include certain forms of heritage or arts tourism. Historic cities (e.g.,

Venice, Prague, Oxford) attract large numbers of international tourists. However, increasingly, cultural tourists are being drawn to deindustrialized cities that are being regenerated (e.g., Glasgow, Bilbao, Rotterdam). They may experience cultural mega-events (e.g., expos) or visit "flagship" museums (e.g., the Guggenheim in Bilbao) or whole new cultural quarters or waterfronts (e.g., Barcelona, Cardiff).

RURAL CULTURAL TOURISM

Rural cultural tourism may incorporate aspects of indigenous or ethnic tourism, or creative activities. In some cases attractions have been purpose-built to help develop tourism (e.g., ecomuseums in France and Scandinavia; holistic centers in Ireland, Greece, and Spain). In others, former industrial sites such as coal mines have been regenerated and turned into attractions. For example, Blaenavon in Wales, Ironbridge in the English Midlands, and the Wieliczka salt mines in Poland have all been designated World Heritage Sites. Spinoffs from agro- or farm tourism include gastronomic tourism, arts and crafts tourism, not to mention wine tourism (e.g., in the Douro Valley in Portugal; Stellenbosch in South Africa).

INDIGENOUS CULTURAL TOURISM

In this type of tourism, tourists visit indigenous peoples in their own habitat, although in many cases land has been taken from such peoples and they are forced to live in reservations (e.g., North American Indians) or to integrate into mainstream society (e.g., Australian Aborigines, Canadian Inuits). Tourists are generally interested in the lifestyles and traditions of indigenous groups, and may stay with families in their village (e.g., in Indonesian jungles or the Tunisian desert). Trekking and staying with tribal groups is popular in countries like Thailand or the countries of Central and South America. The environmental and sociocultural impacts can be significant, although cultural tourism can also help to raise the profile of indigenous groups and contribute to the renewal of traditions and cultural pride.

POPULAR CULTURAL TOURISM

This form of tourism focuses on some of the more "populist" forms of culture, such as attending sporting events or pop concerts, and visiting shopping malls and theme parks. It may also include visits to film or television locations or studios. In many regenerated former industrial cities, such attractions are proliferating and are often combined with more traditional forms of cultural tourism (e.g., art galleries, architectural features, museums).

The boundaries of cultural tourism are clearly being pushed further and further toward more global and contemporary forms of culture. Although a recognition of definitional and conceptual boundaries is important, the postmodern dedifferentiation of tourism, culture, leisure, and lifestyles can render this a somewhat elusive task.

SEE ALSO: Consumption, Tourism and; Culture; Culture Industries; Leisure; Leisure, Popular Culture and; Museums; Postmodern Culture; Urban Tourism

REFERENCES AND SUGGESTED READINGS

Hughes, H. (1996) Redefining Cultural Tourism. *Annals of Tourism Research* 23(3): 707–9.

Hughes, H. (2000) *Arts, Entertainment, and Tourism.* Butterworth-Heinemann, Oxford.

McKercher, B. & Cros, H. (2002) *Cultural Tourism: The Partnership Between Tourism and Cultural Heritage Management.* Haworth Press, New York.

Richards, G. (1996) *Cultural Tourism in Europe.* CABI, Wallingford.

Richards, G. (2001) Cultural Tourists or a Culture of Tourism? The European Cultural Tourism Market. In: Butcher, J. (Ed.), *Innovations in Cultural Tourism.* ATLAS, Tilburg.

Richards, G. & Raymond, C. (2000) Creative Tourism. *ATLAS News* 23: 16–20.

Sigala, M. & Leslie, D. (Eds.) (2005) *International Cultural Tourism: Management, Implications, and Cases.* Butterworth-Heinemann, Oxford.

Smith, M. K. (2003) *Issues in Cultural Tourism Studies.* Routledge, London.

Smith, M. K. & Robinson, M. (Eds.) (2006) *Cultural Tourism in a Changing World: (Re)presentation, Participation, and Politics.* Channel View, Clevedon.

culture

Lyn Spillman

Although the idea of culture seems commonplace and indispensable for thinking about human groups and human action, the term has resonated for more than a century with a variety of sometimes dissonant connotations (Kroeber & Kluckhohn 1963; Williams 1976; Smelser 1992). In vernacular usage, it may refer either to all the symbols, meanings, and values shared by members of a group, by contrast to other groups; or else to a specialized realm of expressive activities and artifacts contrasted with other institutional realms, like politics or the economy. Cultural sociologists now encompass both commonsense meanings of the term by treating as "culture" all socially located forms and processes of human *meaning-making*, in specialized institutions, and whether or not they are confined to one clearly bounded group.

Cultural sociology is an area of social inquiry into meaning-making, defined by its analytic perspective, rather than a particular empirical topic or institutional domain. Cultural sociologists investigate how meaning-making happens, why meanings vary, how meanings influence human action, and the ways meaning-making is important in generating solidarity and conflict. This analytic perspective applies to a wide range of substantive topics and social domains, contributing to the understanding of key sociological topics such as stratification, political institutions, social movements, and economic action, as well as to specialized domains of cultural production such as the arts, media, science, and religion. As a perspective, cultural sociology contrasts with sociological perspectives which focus on analyzing social structures regardless of the meanings attached to them, and with investigations which, although they might include information about norms, attitudes, and values, do not examine the contingent processes of their formation and change.

Sociological research on culture demonstrated significant intellectual and institutional growth as a well-recognized area of inquiry only in the last decades of the twentieth century. As a result, cultural sociologists work with and weave together theoretical perspectives, concepts, and methodologies drawn not only from classical sociology and its subsequent twentieth-century developments, but also from a wide range of other disciplinary sources in anthropology and the humanities. Many significant contributions to the field, as well as its productive issues and tensions, derive their importance and their productivity from new syntheses of a variety of scholarly approaches (Friedland & Mohr 2004; Jacobs & Hanrahan 2005).

The sense in which "culture" refers to a clearly bounded group, by contrast to other groups, emerged in comparative reflection about differences among human populations which was prompted by European exploration and conquest across the globe (Stocking 1968). In this view, the entire way of life of a bounded group is thought to be embedded in, and expressed by, its "culture," and evident in anything from weapons to religious myths. This idea of culture was central to the formation of cultural anthropology as a discipline (Kuper 1999). In the nineteenth century different cultures were often understood as hierarchically arranged according to western ideas of progress, but these evaluative connotations were pluralized and relativized in the course of the twentieth century, from the work of Boas through to the influence of postmodern and postcolonial theorists more recently. By the mid-twentieth century, anthropological approaches had influenced common beliefs about culture, especially (1) that human societies cannot be explained simply by natural environment or human biology; (2) that cultural possibilities are innumerable; (3) that cultures are diverse; (4) that different elements within a culture are patterned and interconnected; and (5) that elements of culture must be understood by placing them in their context, rather than by treating them in isolation. It is indicative of the central importance of anthropology in the development of the idea of culture that sociological dictionaries, textbooks, and encyclopedias referred mostly to anthropology for their explanations of the term until the 1980s. Since then, sociological and anthropological approaches to culture have diverged, with anthropological research influenced more by postmodernism and postcolonial theory than research on culture in sociology. Anthropologists who were particularly influential in the formation of cultural sociology are Clifford Geertz, especially for the strong rationale he provided for interpretive methods, and Mary Douglas and Victor Turner, for their Durkheimian analyses of cultural categories and of ritual, respectively. Questions canvassed in debates about culture in anthropology in the first half of the twentieth century – such as whether culture should be treated as patterned and emergent or as a collection of discrete traits, how to specify the relation between social structure and culture, how to understand persistence and change in cultural patterns, and how much analytic emphasis to place on "carriers" of culture, such as networks or cultural producers – have reappeared in contemporary sociological work on the topic (Singer 1968).

The sense in which "culture" refers to a specialized realm of expressive activities and artifacts also emerged in the nineteenth century, but it marked an increasingly strong contrast *within* western societies between expressive activities and other realms of social life (Williams 1976; Eagleton 2000). In the social differentiation and conflict of the transition to capitalism, industrialization, urbanization, revolution, and democracy, art and morality were thought to express higher human capacities and ideals than could be seen in economic and political life – though, for the same reasons, they could also be dismissed as unimportant for understanding the core dynamics of modern societies. The classification and evaluation of particular ideas and activities as "cultural" made the realm of culture a basis for critical judgment, as, for instance, for the Romantic writers of the nineteenth century or for critics of mass media in the mid-twentieth century. This sense of "culture" became the core of scholarship in the humanities, as in the study of literature or art. It is in this sense that scholars have contrasted "high," "popular," "mass," and "folk" culture, echoing in different ways the implication that culture should be a purer realm of human activity than the mundane realms of economic and political action, though the specific moral valuation attached to each term has often been the focus of extended scholarly debate. Within sociology the study of the arts

and mass culture developed a long tradition, but until recently was mostly considered peripheral to the discipline's concern with the core dynamics of modern societies. More recently, theoretical approaches and methodologies drawn from the humanities, such as semiotics and narrative theory, have been important in the development of cultural sociology, enabling sociologists to conceptualize and analyze culture as an independent object of inquiry in new ways.

Influential classical social theorists – especially Marx, Durkheim, Weber, Simmel, and Mead – were writing at a time when the multiple senses in which culture might be understood were in flux. Against the background of issues generated by changes in European societies, culture did not become a central concept in sociological theory in the way it did in anthropology (Kroeber & Parsons 1958). Nevertheless, important ideas of each classical theorist seeded the study of culture in subsequent sociological investigation, and continue to do so (Alexander 1990). Marx's linking of culture and power in the theory of ideology, and his critique of idealist theories, were refined and developed in the work of important twentieth-century theorists such as Gramsci, Adorno, and Williams and the related work of the Frankfurt School and the Birmingham School. Weber's historicist and hermeneutic emphases on understanding the implications of particular sets of ideas – such as those of the Protestant Reformation – as well as his theorization of cultural stratification by status, and of rationalization in modernity, added, for sociologists, an important theory of the historical significance of meaning-making processes which remained in productive dialogue with Marx's theory of ideology. Durkheim's work on collective conscience, collective representations, cognitive categories, and ritual theorizes cultural processes as essential and constitutive social forces, though this work only had strong impact in sociology towards the end of the twentieth century. Like the other classical theorists, Simmel analyzed in depth the cultural impact of increasing complexity in modern societies, with special attention to issues of the changing nature of individuality and to increasing dominance of "objective" cultural products over autonomously generated "subjective" culture. In contrast to these European theorists, the work of Mead, and more generally the American pragmatist tradition, influenced later work on culture by providing a basis for examining meaning-making processes at the microsociological level, in interaction and in subcultures (Long 1997).

Nevertheless, "culture" remained a residual category in sociology, and cultural sociologists now find precedents for their studies of collective meaning-making under many different labels – for instance, in mid-twentieth studies of the arts and of mass culture, in ethnographic studies of mostly deviant or powerless subcultures, in constructivist studies of social problems, and in the sociology of knowledge. Important studies of meaning-making were also generated in the mid-twentieth century by two major but opposing theoretical approaches: critical theories of ideology and structural-functionalist theories of attitudes, values, and norms. However, the productivity of these theories for studies of culture ultimately ran aground on a theoretical impasse (Spillman 1995). Both generated important insights, but they took contradictory positions on the relative significance of domination and solidarity, or conflict and consensus. Both also tended to over-generalize about culture, seeing it as a "reflection" of society, oversimplifying internal complexity, active cultural production, and the independent effects of meaning-making processes themselves. These issues became the central focus for later sociological research on culture, which drew new theoretical energy from the work of theorists such as Foucault and Bourdieu on cultural power.

From the 1970s there were increasingly frequent calls for new sociological approaches to culture which avoided over-generalized assumptions about consensus or ideology, which avoided both idealism and reductionism, and which did not confine themselves either to the study of subcultures or to the study of expressive artifacts like art. Cultural theorists working from a variety of different starting points (Geertz 1973; Bourdieu 1977; Hall 1978; Peterson 1979; Archer 1985; Swidler 1986; Wuthnow & Witten 1988; Alexander 1990) all rejected the contrasting alternatives which had previously shaped sociological approaches to culture, and introduced a variety

of conceptual innovations which generated more particular accounts of meaning-making processes. These developments loosened old assumptions and shifted old debates, encouraging an unprecedented growth in sociological analyses of meaning-making processes and the institutionalization of cultural sociology (Crane 1994; Smith 1998; Spillman 2002).

Three mid-range reconceptualizations of "culture" then emerged in cultural sociology, although different approaches were often productively combined. First, drawing on the sociology of organizations, and on the sociology of knowledge, some scholars argued for a focus on specific contexts of cultural production, an examination of the ways particular meanings, values, and artifacts are generated in particular organizations, institutions, and networks, and how those social contexts influence emergent meanings (Peterson 1976; Crane 1992; Peterson & Anand 2004). This approach challenged over-generalizations about cultural "reflection" of societies as wholes, drawing on theoretical resources from the sociology of knowledge and the sociology of organizations. Although many "production of culture" studies focused on specialized realms of mass media, the arts, and sciences, attention to particular institutional circumstances and constraints affecting meaning-making processes is also crucial for the study of more diffuse cultural phenomena such as national identity, social movements, collective memory, or religion.

Another mid-range approach to culture, influenced sometimes by pragmatism and sometimes by practice theory, focused attention on how interactions and social practices are themselves meaning-making processes, and on the context-dependent ways in which individuals and groups endow actions with meanings (Certeau 1984; Becker & McCall 1990; Fine & Sandstrom 1993; Swidler 2001; Eliasoph & Lichterman 2003). Like production-of-culture approaches, this focus on meaning-making in action and interaction challenged overly general reflection models of the relation between culture and society; it also relaxed the assumption that meanings and values are entirely shared, coherent, or consistent for a given group or even an individual, providing a better understanding of diverse interpretations of common norms, values, and cognitive frames and analyzing how individuals and groups draw fluidly on different elements in symbolic repertoires ("toolkits") according to context. Culture, here, is a contingent and variable element of the ways action is framed. Applicable to understanding any sites of action and interaction, this approach has been applied to such diverse topics as corporate culture, the formation of racial and class identities, audience interpretations of mass media and artistic forms, and everyday engagement with politics.

Third, other sociologists, building on Durkheimian insights, have emphasized the importance of the deep formal structure of discourses for meaning-making. Analyses of culture-structures have built on two distinct traditions. First, discourse analysts have drawn on theories and concepts of textual structure derived from work in the humanities to analyze meaning-making (Alexander 1989; Wuthnow 1992; Mohr 1994; Jacobs & Smith 1997; Franzosi 1998; Alexander 2004). They investigate the deep internal structure of discourses in terms of their categories, codes, genre, and narrative, showing how signifiers derive meaning from their relations in systems of signs. Such analyses of culture as structured discourse introduce to sociology a previously neglected set of influences in processes of meaning-making, which provide a basis for constituting culture as a distinct object of inquiry that is analytically independent of, and sometimes causally efficacious for, both institutional and interactional dimensions of meaning-making. Second, other cultural sociologists explore links between meaning-making and social psychological processes of cognition, especially categorization (Schwartz 1981; DiMaggio 1997; Zerubavel 1997; Cerulo 2002). Analysts of cultural structures in sociology have investigated such topics as political discourse, media texts, and gender, but this approach may be adopted whenever the *underlying* cultural forms which are contingently mobilized in organized cultural production and informal interaction are of interest.

Understanding institutionalized cultural production, practices, and interaction, and "culture-structures" as analytically distinct dimensions of meaning-making, each worthy of investigation in its own right, has helped cultural sociology specify earlier vague and overarching assumptions about culture, and the ways it might "reflect" social structures and generate social action. These specifications have also meant that culture is no longer considered to be the "whole way of life" of a clearly bounded group, nor confined to a domain of expressive artifacts and activities distinct from politics or economics. Thus, cultural sociologists investigate specific dimensions of meaning-making, but in a wide range of empirical sites. Of course, while many investigations focus primarily on one dimension of meaning-making – cultural production, culture in interaction, or culture as text – a full understanding of any particular topic involves all three levels, and many studies touch on all three with different degrees of emphasis. So, for instance, a study of the codes and categories structuring a political ideology may also extend to related processes of institutional production, and a study of variant audience interpretations of television will also include analysis of important features of the textual structure of programming.

At the same time, fundamental disagreements and debates have also emerged between cultural sociologists prioritizing one approach to culture over others. Those who emphasize institutionalized cultural production would view an overemphasis on textual structure as idealist, detached from the political and organizational dynamics of the social contexts in which texts are embedded. Production-of-culture perspectives also suggest that analyzing meaning in practices and interaction misses the central significance of organized institutional processes for the possibilities available for meaning-making in complex societies. Against this, those committed to the "thick description" of meaning-making in practice argue that the production-of-culture perspective elides meaning in favor of organizational dynamics. Practice theorists of various types also suggest that focusing on "culture-structures" or cognitive categories underestimates the importance of the many, varied ways in which people interpret cultural codes in different contexts. In the third camp, analysts of "culture-structures" argue, like practice theorists, that the production-of-culture perspective elides the more hermeneutic analysis of meaning-making. Against practice theorists, though, they suggest that focusing on variant contextual uses of meanings, values, and symbols in particular practices inevitably misses the larger cultural framework which constrains and enables particular instances of meaning-making.

Such disagreements about emphasizing institutions, emphasizing practices, or emphasizing textual or cognitive structure are fundamental faultlines in cultural sociology, and constitute points of view for mutual critique of particular studies of culture. Tensions between "culture-structure" theories (whether textual or cognitive) and "practice" theories are particularly evident in contemporary cultural sociology, but other lines of tension outlined above also continue to regenerate debate. However, such disagreements also generate productive research programs, and some of the richest contributions to contemporary understandings of culture carefully combine analysis of production, interaction, and formal structure while preserving the analytical distinctions between the different cultural dynamics.

Distinctions between the different cultural dynamics have also created new approaches to long-lasting tensions in sociology – tensions between interpretation and explanation, between microsocial and macrosocial analysis, between structure and agency, and between an emphasis on consensus and solidarity, on the one hand, and on conflict, domination, and resistance, on the other. Cultural sociology has made significant recent contributions to understanding these issues and bridging these divides. Analyzing meaning-making processes along the three dimensions outlined above has encouraged sociologists writing on a wide range of topics to combine interpretive and explanatory strategies; to link micro settings with macro processes in their research designs; to show how the limits and possibilities of meaning-making mediate the obdurateness of social structures with their intermittent possibilities of agentic change; and to open to investigation the ways solidarity and conflict are empirically mixed.

Important topics which have engaged the sustained attention of cultural sociologists include the construction and reconstruction of class, gender, race, national, ethnic, sexual, and other axes of social identity, distinction, and dispute; the role of meaning-making processes in generating and sustaining political engagement in social movements and in civil society; the discourses and issues generated in political, legal, religious, scientific, and professional institutions; collective memory and historical amnesia; mass media production, texts, and audiences; and artistic products, practices, and institutions (Spillman 2002; Friedland & Mohr 2004; Jacobs & Hanrahan 2005; Jacobs & Spillman 2005).

Important sets of empirical questions receiving increasing attention concern meaning-making processes which operate at transnational or global levels (e.g., among immigrants or social movements); meaning-making in economic action and industries; how newer communications technologies influence social identities and interactions; and the relation between embodiment, materiality, and the discourses which constitute the significance of that materiality.

Some emerging theoretical and methodological issues in the sociological analysis of culture may change the terms in which the relations between cultural production, practices, and structures are understood. One question receiving renewed attention is the historical impact of specialized arenas of cultural production – such as art, literature, and science – on broader political and economic change. Another issue is the relation between generic psychological and biological capacities for cognition and emotion, and their particular expressions in socially situated meaning-making process. Third, theories of meaning-making as performance are offering new ways of analyzing links between production, text, and action at both macro-historical and micro-situational levels. Fourth, there is renewed attention to the ways in which meanings and values have specific causal consequences for social action and for institutional change.

Pressing questions contemporary cultural sociologists are raising or revisiting thus include: What is the best way of combining analyses of culture-structures and of practices? When do specialized cultural products and meaning-making processes influence broader social change? How should the relation between generic cognitive and emotional processes and meaning-making be understood? How does culture link structure and action in moments of performative contingency? How can the causal impact of meaning-making processes be specified while preserving the central importance of interpretation?

The idea of culture has long been both capacious and ambiguous, due to its complex historical origins and intellectual development, and cultural analysis was not generally considered central to sociological inquiry for much of the twentieth century. However, sociologists now think of culture as human processes of meaning-making generating artifacts, categories, norms, values, practices, rituals, symbols, worldviews, ideas, ideologies, and discourses. They currently identify and analyze three different types of influence on meaning-making: institutional production, interactional process, and textual structure, emphasizing each dimension to different degrees according to empirical topic and theoretical perspective, and often debating their relative importance. These analytic tools have helped avoid over-generalization about cultural processes – for instance, about consensus or conflict, about idealism or materialism, about macro or micro levels of analysis, or about structure and agency. In turn, this has encouraged an efflorescence of sociological studies of culture on such topics as identity and difference, group boundaries, political institutions and practices, and the mass media and arts and their audiences. Cultural perspectives are also frequently integrated into research on such standard sociological issues as stratification, religion, immigration, and social movements. Since new empirical topics and theoretical issues in the sociological study of meaning-making continue to emerge rapidly, the likelihood is that culture will become much more central to sociological analysis.

SEE ALSO: Adorno, Theodor W.; Art Worlds; Bourdieu, Pierre; Critical Theory/Frankfurt School; Cultural Capital; Cultural Critique; Cultural Studies; Cultural Studies, British; Culture: Conceptual Clarifications; Culture Industries; Culture, Production of; Discourse; Distinction; Emotion: Cultural Aspects; Foucault, Michel; Gramsci, Antonio; Hermeneutics; Ideology; Narrative; Norms; Parsons, Talcott; Practice; Pragmatism; Semiotics; Structuralism; Symbolic Classification; Values; Williams, Raymond

REFERENCES AND SUGGESTED READINGS

Alexander, J. (1989) *Structure and Meaning: Relinking Classical Sociology.* Columbia University Press, New York.
Alexander, J. (1990) Analytic Debates: Understanding the Relative Autonomy of Culture. In: Alexander, J. & Seidman, S. (Eds.), *Culture and Society: Contemporary Debates.* Cambridge University Press, Cambridge, pp. 1–27.
Alexander, J. (2004) *The Meanings of Social Life.* Oxford University Press, New York.
Archer, M. (1985) The Myth of Cultural Integration. *British Journal of Sociology* 36: 333–53.
Becker, H. & McCall, M. (1990) *Symbolic Interaction and Cultural Studies.* University of Chicago Press, Chicago.
Bourdieu, P. (1977) *Outline of a Theory of Practice.* Trans. R. Nice. Cambridge University Press, New York.
Certeau, M. de (1984) *The Practice of Everyday Life.* Trans. S. Rendall. University of California Press, Berkeley.
Cerulo, K. (Ed.) (2002) *Culture in Mind: Towards a Sociology of Culture and Cognition.* Routledge, New York.
Crane, D. (1992) *The Production of Culture: Media and the Urban Arts.* Sage, Newbury Park, CA.
Crane, D. (Ed.) (1994) *The Sociology of Culture.* Blackwell, Oxford.
DiMaggio, P. (1997) Culture and Cognition. *Annual Review of Sociology* 23: 263–87.
Eagleton, T. (2000) *The Idea of Culture.* Blackwell, Oxford.
Eliasoph, N. & Lichterman, P. (2003) Culture in Interaction. *American Journal of Sociology* 108: 735–94.
Fine, G. & Sandstrom, K. (1993) Ideology in Interaction: A Pragmatic Approach to a Contested Concept. *Sociological Theory* 11: 21–37.
Franzosi, R. (1998) Narrative Analysis – or Why (and how) Sociologists Should Be Interested in Narrative. *Annual Review of Sociology* 24: 517–54.
Friedland, R. & Mohr, J. (Eds.) (2004) *Matters of Culture: Cultural Sociology in Practice.* Cambridge University Press, New York.
Geertz, C. (1973) *The Interpretation of Cultures.* Basic Books, New York.
Hall, S. (1978) The Hinterland of Science: Ideology and "the Sociology Of Knowledge." In: Birmingham Centre for Contemporary Cultural Studies (Ed.), *On Ideology.* Hutchinson, London, pp. 9–32.
Jacobs, M. D. & Hanrahan, N. W. (Eds.) (2005) *The Blackwell Companion to the Sociology of Culture.* Blackwell, Oxford.

Jacobs, M. D. & Spillman, L. (2005) Cultural Sociology at the Crossroads of the Discipline. *Poetics* 33: 1–14.

Jacobs, R. & Smith, P. (1997) Romance, Irony, and Solidarity. *Sociological Theory*: 60–80.

Kroeber, A. L. & Kluckhohn, C. (1963 [1952]) *Culture: A Critical Review of Concepts and Definitions*. Vintage, New York.

Kroeber, A. L. & Parsons, T. (1958) The Concepts of Culture and of Social System. *American Sociological Review* 23: 582–3.

Kuper, A. (1999) *Culture: The Anthropologists' Account*. Harvard University Press, Cambridge, MA.

Long, E. (1997) Engaging Sociology and Cultural Studies: Disciplinarity and Social Change. In: Long, E. (Ed.), *From Sociology to Cultural Studies*. Blackwell, Oxford, pp. 1–32.

Mohr, J. (1994) Soldiers, Mothers, Tramps and Others: Discourse Roles in the 1907 New York City Charity Directory. *Poetics* 22: 327–57.

Peterson, R. (Ed.) (1976) *The Production of Culture*. Sage, Beverley Hills.

Peterson, R. (1979) Revitalizing the Culture Concept. *Annual Review of Sociology* 5: 137–66.

Peterson, R. & Anand, N. (2004) The Production of Culture Perspective. *Annual Review of Sociology* 30: 311–34.

Schwartz, B. (1981) *Vertical Classification: A Study in Structuralism and the Sociology of Knowledge*. University of Chicago Press, Chicago.

Singer, M. (1968) The Concept of Culture. In: Sills, D. L. (Ed.), *International Encyclopedia of the Social Sciences*, Vol. 3. Crowell Collier & Macmillan, New York, pp. 527–43.

Smelser, N. (1992) Culture: Coherent or Incoherent. In: Munch, R. & Smelser, N. (Eds.), *Theory of Culture*. University of California Press, Berkeley, pp. 3–20.

Smith, P. (Ed.) (1998) *The New American Cultural Sociology*. Cambridge University Press, Cambridge.

Spillman, L. (1995) Culture, Social Structure, and Discursive Fields. *Current Perspectives in Social Theory* 15: 129–54.

Spillman, L. (Ed.) (2002) *Cultural Sociology*. Blackwell, Oxford.

Stocking, G. W. (1968) *Race, Culture, and Evolution*. Free Press, New York.

Swidler, A. (1986) Culture in Action: Symbols and Strategies. *American Sociological Review* 51: 273–86.

Swidler, A. (2001) *Talk of Love*. University of Chicago Press, Chicago.

Williams, R. (1976) Culture. In: William, R., *Keywords: A Vocabulary of Culture and Society*. Oxford University Press, New York, pp. 76–82.

Wuthnow, R. (Ed.) (1992) *Vocabularies of Public Life: Empirical Essays in Symbolic Structure*. Routledge, London.

Wuthnow, R. & Witten, M. (1988) New Directions in the Study of Culture. *Annual Review of Sociology* 14: 49–77.

Zerubavel, E. (1997) *Social Mindscapes: An Invitation to Cognitive Sociology*. Harvard University Press, Cambridge, MA.

culture: conceptual clarifications

Chris Jenks

Raymond Williams (1976) informs us that "culture is one of the two or three most complicated words in the English language," which is a good place to begin. Despite the contemporary upsurge of interest in the idea – what Chaney (1994) refers to as the "cultural turn" in the humanities and social sciences – culture is a concept with a history. One compelling account is that the idea of culture emerged in the late eighteenth century and on into the nineteenth century as part of (and largely as a reaction to) the massive changes that were occurring in the structure and quality of social life – what we might also refer to as the advance of modernity. These changes at the social, political, and personal levels were both confusing and disorienting, and at least controversial. Such changes, through industrialization and technology, were unprecedented in human experience: they were wildly expansionist, and horizons were simply consumed; they were grossly productive, for good and ill; and they were both understood and legitimated through an ideology of progress. The social structure was politically volatile, being increasingly and visibly divisive. This was a situation brought about through the new forms of social ranking and hierarchy that accompanied the proliferating division of labor, being combined with the density and proximity of populations, through urbanization, and the improved system of communications. In one sense the overall aesthetic quality of life, compared with the previously supposed rural idyll, was threatened by the machine-like excesses of industrial society. There was an increasing gap between the creative and the productive, formulated for materialism by Marx as "alienation," and for the Romantic-idealist tradition by Carlyle as a loss of the folk purity of a past era. The machine was viewed as consuming the natural character of humankind, a call to be later echoed in the work of the Frankfurt School, Benjamin's "Age of Mechanical Reproduction," even Marcuse's sense of one-dimensionality, and finally the *cri de coeur* of Baudrillard's evocation of postmodernism with its horror of simulacra. Whereas we began with "culture" mediating between humankind and Nature, it can now be seen to mediate between humankind and Machine. This provides us with several available "meanings" of culture.

Another account looks back to classical society. *Civilization*, deriving from the Latin *civis*, is a term descriptive of a state of belonging to a collectivity that embodied certain qualities, albeit self-appointed, which distinguished it from the "mass" or more lowly state of being typified as that of the "barbarian." Such was the ancient Greek and Roman sense of identification with nation and state.

In this context the idea of culture is not so much descriptive as metaphoric, and derives philologically from the agricultural or horticultural processes of cultivating the soil and bringing fauna and flora into being through growth. Whereas the former concept, "civilization," is descriptive of a kind of stasis, a membership, a belonging, indeed a status once achieved not to be relinquished, the latter, "culture," is resonant with other ideas of emergence and change, perhaps even transformation. Thus we move to ideas of socialization as "cultivating" the person, education as "cultivating" the mind, and colonialization as "cultivating" the natives. All of these uses of culture, as process, imply not just a transition but also a goal in the form of "culture" itself; it is here that hierarchical notions begin to emerge, such as the "cultured person" or "cultivated groups or individuals" and even the idea of a "high culture," all of which reduce the metaphoricity of process and begin to coalesce with the original notion of a descriptive state of being not essentially unlike the formative idea of civilization itself.

Just as in many forms of discourse *culture* and *civilization* are used interchangeably, so in others *culture, society,* and *social structure* are conflated, though not necessarily confused. The idea of culture as a theory of social structure has given rise to the major division between "social" and "cultural" anthropologies, the former stressing universality and constraint and the latter emphasizing relativism and difference between societies. In contemporary cultural studies some would argue that the concept of social structure has been abandoned altogether and that culture has become the sole source of causal explanation.

Social theories that are based on a materialist interpretation of reality, such as the variety of Marxisms, see culture as essentially an ideological set of understandings that arise from the sometimes calculated but more often simply distorted representations of the basic set of power and economic relationships at the heart of the society. Here we would include such thinkers as Marx himself, but also Gramsci, Althusser, Lukàcs, Goldmann, Benjamin, Adorno, Horkheimer, and Williams. Of course, this group remains varied and subtle in their range of explanations, but all argue essentially for the primacy of the material world and thus produce culture as an epiphenomenon. Contrasting with this body of thought are the interpretive social theorists whose ideas derive more from the philosophies of Kant and Hegel. Within such an idealist tradition culture is realized far more as an autonomous and self-sustaining realm of social experience: a repertoire and a fund of symbolic forms that although related to their time are nevertheless both generative and self-reproducing in a way that escapes the constraints of materiality. Here culture is liberating rather than constraining; here creativity exceeds replication as a causal force. In the context of interpretive theory we would be addressing the sociologies of Weber, Simmel, Schütz, Geertz, and even Parsons.

Sociologists and anthropologists have come to account for the concept of culture in a variety of ways. In its most general and pervasive sense it directs us to a consideration of all that which is symbolic: the learned, ideational aspects of human society. In an early sense culture was precisely the collective noun used to define that realm of human being which marked off its ontology from the sphere of the merely natural. To speak of the cultural was to reaffirm a philosophical commitment to the difference, particularity, and supposed plasticity that is "humankind." Human beings inevitably transform their world into, and by way of, a series of symbolic representations. The symbolic then satisfies and absorbs the projections of human beings into objects and states of affairs that are different, and it also acts as a mediator between these two provinces. We no longer confront the natural as if we were continuous with it. We now meet with the natural and, indeed, experience it as preformed, through our vocabulary of symbols which are primarily linguistic but increasingly elaborate out into other forms like custom, convention, habit, and even artifact. The symbolic representations that constitute human knowing are, in their various groupings, classifications, and manifestations, the *cultural*. The very idea of culture therefore generates a concept which, at one level, provides a principle of unification for the peoples of the world, including those who once have and also those who continue to populate the world through time and across space. We can see here the origins of structuralism espoused primarily by Lévi-Strauss, but then by Piaget, Chomsky, and others with great impact across a range of social and human sciences.

Culture, for early anthropology, was the common domain of the human; it distinguished our behavior from that of other creatures and it provided a conceptual break with the dominant explanatory resource of biological and, latterly, genetic determinism. From this happy state of egalitarian oneness through the aegis of culture – the very inspiration for cultural anthropology – the story takes a different turn and we move into accounts of diffusion, stratification, hierarchy, and relativism, still clinging to the unrevised central concept of culture. The dominant European linguistic convention equates "culture" largely with the idea of "civilization": they are regarded as synonymous. Both ideas may be used interchangeably with integrity in opposition to notions of that which is vulgar, backward, ignorant, or retrogressive. Within the German intellectual tradition, a different and particular sense of culture emerged that was to assume a dominant place in our

everyday understandings. This was the romantic, elitist view, that culture specified the pinnacle of human achievement. Culture, in this sense, came to specify that which is remarkable in human creative achievement. Rather than encapsulating all human symbolic representation, German *Kultur* pointed us exclusively to levels of excellence in fine art, literature, music, and individual personal perfection. The main body, or in this formulation the residue of what we have previously meant as culture, was to be understood in terms of the concept of *Zivilisation*. This distinction, by no means fine, in many ways reflected the dichotomy provided by Kantian philosophy between the realms of "value" and "fact," and was generative of two different ways of understanding and relating to the world. This divide also informs the distinction between philosophical idealism and materialism and informs discussions over cultural stratification. We might here note that such distinctions also gave rise to the belief that the human spirit (perhaps the *Geist* itself) came under successive threat with the advent and advance of modernity and the inexorable process of material development which, it was supposed, gave rise to an increasingly anonymous and amorphous urban mass society. The impersonal, yet negative, forces of standardization, industrialization, and technologies of mass production became the analytic target for the romantic neo-Marxist criticism of the Frankfurt School within their theories of aesthetics, mass communication, and mass society, and also in the early sociology of culture propounded by Norbet Elias with his ideas of the "civilizing process."

Within the confines of British and American social theory the concept of culture has been understood in a far more pluralist sense and applied, until relatively recently, on a far more sparing basis. Although culture is a familiar term within our tradition and can be employed to summon up holistic appraisals of the ways of life of a people and their beliefs, rituals, and customs, it is not most common. We social scientists are rather more accustomed to mobilizing such batteries of understanding into "action sets." That is, we tend to use more specific concepts like, for example, "value systems" (even "central value systems"), "patterns of belief," "value-orientations," or more critical notions like "ideologies." Culture to British and American social theorists tends to have been most usefully applied as a concept of differentiation within a collectivity rather than a way of gathering. That is to say that the concept has become artfully employed in, for example, the sociology of knowledge that Karl Mannheim recommended, and also in the spectrum of perspectives on the sociology of deviance – ranging from Parsonian theory through to symbolic interactionism – in the manner of "subculture." A subculture is the way of defining and honoring the particular specification and demarcation of special or different interests of a group of people within a larger collectivity. So just as classical sociology in the form of Tönnies or Durkheim, or indeed Comte, had recognized that the composition of the overall collective life emerged through the advance of the division of labor – by dint of the fragile integration through interdependence of a whole series of smaller, internally cohesive, social units – so also does modern social theory by articulating the specific mores of these minor groups, albeit often as "non-normative" or even "deviant." This dispersion of subcultures is at the base of what we might mean by a "pluralist" view of culture; it is modern and democratic and shies away from all of the excesses of a grand systems theory with all of its incumbent conservative tendencies and its implicit "oversocialized conception of man" (Wrong 1961). Such thinking succumbs, however, to the problem of order. Without a coherent, overall theory of culture (which still, in many senses, eludes us) it is hard to conceive of how consensus is maintained within a modern society. In response to precisely this problem, contemporary Marxism has generated the "dominant ideology thesis" which supposes that varieties of hegemonic strategies of mass media and political propaganda create a distorted illusion of shared concerns in the face of the real and contentious divisions that exist between classes, genders, ethnic groups, geographical regions, and age groups. Such a thesis is by no means universally accepted within the social sciences and in many ways the more recent explosion of interest in and dedication to the schizophrenic prognosis of postmodernisms (and even complexity theory) positively accelerates the centrifugal tendencies of the cultural particles.

We can summarize some of the above accounts of the genesis of our concept "culture" through a four-fold typology. First, culture is a cerebral, or certainly a cognitive, category. Culture becomes intelligible as a general state of mind. It carries with it the idea of perfection, a goal or an aspiration of individual human achievement or emancipation. At one level this might be a reflection of a highly individualist philosophy and at another level an instance of a philosophical commitment to the particularity and difference, even the "chosenness" or superiority, of humankind. This links into themes of redemption in later writings, from Marx's false consciousness to the melancholy science of the Frankfurt School. In origin we will see it mostly in the work of the Romantic literary and cultural criticism of William Coleridge and Thomas Carlyle and latterly Matthew Arnold.

Second, culture is a more embodied and collective category. Culture invokes a state of intellectual and/or moral development in society. This is a position linking culture with the idea of civilization and one that is informed by the evolutionary theories of Darwin and informative of that group of social theorists now known as the early evolutionists who pioneered anthropology, with their competitive views on "degeneration" and "progress," and linking the endeavor with nineteenth-century imperialism. This notion nevertheless takes the idea of culture into the province of the collective life, rather than the individual consciousness.

Third, culture is a descriptive and concrete category: culture viewed as the collective body of arts and intellectual work within any one society. This is very much an everyday language usage of the term culture and carries along with it senses of particularity, exclusivity, elitism, specialist knowledge, and training or socialization. It includes a firmly established notion of culture as the realm of the produced and sedimented symbolic, albeit the esoteric symbolism of a society.

Fourth, culture is a social category: culture regarded as the whole way of life of a people. This is the pluralist and potentially democratic sense of the concept that has come to be the zone of concern within sociology and anthropology and latterly, within a more localized sense, cultural studies.

SEE ALSO: Benjamin, Walter; Cultural Critique; Cultural Reproduction; Culture; Gramsci, Antonio; Williams, Raymond

REFERENCES AND SUGGESTED READINGS

Adorno, T. (1976) *The Positivist Dispute in German Sociology*. Heinmann, London.

Althusser, L. (1971) Ideological and Repressive State Apparatuses. In: *Lenin and Philosophy and Other Essays*. New Left Books, London.

Baudrillard, J. (1983) *Simulations*. Semiotext(e), Paris.

Benjamin, W. (1970) *Illuminations*. Cape, London.

Chaney, D. (1994) *The Cultural Turn: Scene-Setting Essays on Contemporary Social History*. Routledge, London.

Chomsky, N. (1965) *Aspects of a Theory of Syntax*. MIT Press, Cambridge, MA.

Elias, N. (1939) *The Civilizing Process*. Blackwell, Oxford.

Geertz, C. (1975) *The Interpretation of Cultures*. Hutchinson, London.

Goldmann, L. (1964) *The Hidden God*. Routledge, London.

Gramsci, A. (1973) *Selections from the Prison Notebooks*. Lawrence & Wishart, London.

Lévi-Strauss, C. (1964) *Triste topique*. Atheneum, London.

Lukàcs, G. (1963) *The Meaning of Contemporary Realism*. Merlin, London.

Marcuse, H. (1972) *One Dimensional Man*. Abacus, London.

Marx, K. (1970) *The German Ideology*. Lawrence & Wishart, London.

Parsons, T. (1951) *The Social System*. Routledge & Kegan Paul, London.

Piaget, J. (1972) *Psychology and Epistemology*. Penguin, London.

Simmel, G. (1950) *The Sociology of Georg Simmel*, ed. K. Wolff. Free Press, New York.

Weber, M. (1965) *The Protestant Ethic and the Spirit of Capitalism*. Free Press, New York.

Williams, R. (1976) *Keywords*. Fontana, London.

Wrong, D. (1961) The Oversocialized Conception of Man in Modern Sociology. *American Sociological Review* 26 (April): 205–16.

culture, economy and

Marion Fourcade-Gourinchas

In traditional academic discourse, culture and economy have long been regarded as separate analytical spheres: on the one hand, the realm of shared cognitions, norms, and symbols, studied by anthropologists; on the other hand, the realm of self-interest, where economists reign supreme. Though the two disciplines overlap occasionally (in economic anthropology mainly), radical differences in the conceptual and methodological routes each field followed during the twentieth century have prevented any sort of meaningful interaction.

By contrast, the interaction between culture and the economy has always been a central component of sociological analysis. All the founding fathers of sociology were, one way or another, interested in the relationship between people's economic conditions and their moral universe. In his famous presentation in the *Preface to a Contribution to the Critique of Political Economy*, for instance, Marx described "forms of social consciousness" essentially as an epiphenomenon of material relations. Later interpretations, however, have suggested that even for Marx and Engels the relationships between "material base" and "superstructure" were far from deterministic. The "western" Marxist traditions that developed in Europe after World War I proposed a somewhat more sophisticated analysis that emphasized the integration of culture into the apparatus of domination – either because the hegemony exerted by bourgeois culture induces the masses into implicitly consenting to their own economic oppression (Gramsci 1971), or because the incorporation of culture into the commercial nexus of capitalism leads to uniformity of spirit and behavior and the absence of critical thinking (Adorno & Horkheimer 2002). Still, in these formulations culture remains wedded to its material origins in capitalist relations of production.

Partly reacting against what they perceived to be a one-sided understanding of the relationships between base and superstructure in Marxist writings, Weber and Durkheim both sought to demonstrate the greater autonomy of the cultural realm, albeit in quite different ways. Both insisted that people's behavior is always infused with a meaning that is not reducible to their material positions. Weber (2002), more than anyone else, demonstrated the influence of preexisting ideas and, in particular, religious worldviews on the economic conduct of individuals. For instance, even though their actions may look rational from the outside, the behavior of early Protestant capitalists was quite illogical from the inside: anxiety about salvation, rather than self-interest, motivated them to accumulate. In other words, their search for profit was not based on instrumental rationality, but it made psychological sense given the religious (cultural) universe in which they lived. In fact, Weber considered that all religions condition individual attitudes toward the world and therefore influence involvement in practical affairs – but, of course, they all do it differently, so that the "economic ethics" of individuals varies substantially across social contexts.

It is Durkheim, however, who best articulated the *collective* basis of our meaning-making orientation: groups of individuals share certain understandings that they come to take for granted in their routine dealings with each other. Hence how people behave, including in economic settings, is not a priori reducible to a set of predetermined individual preferences and the interests they support. Rather, most of people's actions are motivated by habit and routine; and preferences, as well as the institutions they support, are informed by cultural norms (Meyer & Rowan 1977). In each society, then, culture and institutions act in tandem to shape individual consciousness and thereby representations of what is understood to be "rational." This is what DiMaggio (1994) calls the "constitutive effect" of culture. Because these mental maps are widely shared, they have much greater efficacy than others that would be out of place, or misunderstood, in the same context.

CULTURAL SHAPING OF ECONOMIC INSTITUTIONS

As a system of representations that exists separately and independently of individuals, culture may shape economic behavior in many different ways. It may be more or less institutionalized. Corporate cultures, for instance, are often highly formalized, even bureaucratized, but the rules that underlie bazaar interactions, though obviously codified, remain very informal (Geertz 2001). Second, the effect of culture may be more or less profound. Meyer and

Rowan (1977), for instance, have famously suggested that many organizational rules are adopted in a purely ceremonial way, but have little impact on actual practice – a claim that has been notably supported by research on educational institutions and hospitals. On the other hand, substantial evidence has come out of cross-national studies of a deep patterning not only of economic values and norms (Hofstede 1980), but also of economic institutions and organizations (Dore 1973; Hamilton & Woolsey-Biggart 1989). The critical question, then, is whether the two are related, and how.

One possible answer has been provided by Dobbin's (1994) suggestion of the existence of an elective affinity between economic and political culture (see also Beckert 2004). In his comparative analysis of the development of the railway sector in the nineteenth century, Dobbin shows that public officials in three countries sought to achieve economic growth in very different ways, and were influenced in doing so by their cultural perceptions about the nature and sources of the political order in their own nation. In the US, they strove primarily to protect community self-determination; in France they oriented themselves towards centralized planning by the state in an effort to avoid logistical chaos; and in the UK they were mainly concerned with protecting the individual sovereignty of firms. Ultimately, then, the economy of each country ended up "reflecting" the polity it originated from.

Some sociologists, however, would argue that there is no such inherent consistency to national cultures. Biernacki (1995), for instance, finds that the process of their formation is eminently fragile, almost serendipitous. In his comparative study of textile mills at the onset of the industrialization process, he finds that the concept of labor had a substantially different meaning in Britain and Germany, but that these differences originated in on-the-ground practices by workers and employers rather than in some preexisting mental categories. These practical conceptions, derived from the material context of industrialization in each country, tended then to crystallize into full-fledged meaning-making systems, which became eventually codified in writing by political economists and other intellectuals. Through this process they acquired a great cultural depth, and ended up shaping a whole set of outcomes in the development pathways of the two countries, such as the wage calculation system, disciplinary techniques within factories, forms of workers' collective action, and even industrial architecture. Yet, even then, the systems remained vulnerable to a change in practices (which eventually took place in the early twentieth century).

EMERGENCE OF CULTURE WITHIN THE ECONOMY

Biernacki's study illustrates particularly well the fact that we should think about the role of culture primarily through its inscription in *practices*. Economic settings, therefore, do not simply display, or reflect, preexisting cultural understandings, but should be regarded as places where distinctive local cultures are formed and carried out. There are two main ways in which this point has been articulated in the sociological literature. The first emphasizes the social meanings people produce (whether voluntarily or involuntarily) through their use of economic settings and economic objects, and is best illustrated by consumption studies. The second suggests that some form of social order (i.e., regulating norms and practices) emerges out of the interpersonal interactions that take place within economic settings, particularly formal organizations and markets.

The first set of questions goes back to Veblen's (1994) and Simmel's analyses of consumption, and was most noticeably extended by Bourdieu (1984). The fundamental idea here is that consumption is not about individual parameters (preferences, income), but is profoundly *relational*. Consumption practices are the site of a competitive struggle whereby individuals seek to position themselves vis-à-vis other individuals in the social space. For Veblen (1994), it is essentially about vertical hierarchy – leisurely elites seek to demarcate themselves from those below them by wasting money and time on perfectly useless purchases and activities. For Bourdieu, the structure of the social "space" is more complex: education and socialization into high culture (or not) play as much a part as money in determining taste, and beyond,

consumption practices. What structures consumption practices (as all forms of action), then, is what Bourdieu calls *habitus* – a system of dispositions that is formed through the individual's trajectory in the social space (understood, again, in a relational manner vis-à-vis other individuals).

The study of consumption practices thus provides an extraordinarily rich terrain for analyzing how people relate to one another, both structurally and cognitively. In a creative variation on this theme, Zelizer (1985, 1994) has shown that these relational meanings are not only expressed through *what* people purchase, but often in *how* they pay for it – cash, gift certificates, checks, food stamps. People, in fact, constantly personalize, differentiate, and earmark money in ways that can be understood as metaphors about social relations and identity. (Whether the *how*, like the *what*, is also subject to the logic of habitus, remains to be studied systematically.)

The second question – the cultural universe produced within and by economic institutions – has also given rise to a diverse and extremely rich literature. We may illustrate this point with three examples: anti-trust law, financial markets, and the McDonald's corporation. Fligstein (1992), most prominently, has studied the way in which the legal environment shapes the formation of distinctive economic cultures. Corporate managers, he argues, act on the basis of "conceptions of control" – shared understandings about how a particular market works. These conceptions evolve in close connection with changes in the legal regulation of corporate competition, which tip the balance of power toward management groups with certain organizational cultures at the expense of others. In the course of the twentieth century, for instance, the American corporation was a contested and historically evolving cultural terrain, where conceptions of control shifted from production to sales and marketing, and finally finance and shareholder value. In this case, organizational culture fundamentally emerges out of a combination of institutional forces and power struggles.

Of course, such tacit understandings and patterned practices may emerge in a more decentralized way, out of interpersonal interactions in corporations, factories, workshops, and markets, including the most "rational" ones. Sociologists, for instance, have revealed the existence of all kinds of rituals, beliefs, customs, and informal control structures that regulate social life in the financial markets – the very heart, supposedly, of instrumental action. In fact, the economic potential of culture has not been lost on corporations, many of which try actively to "engineer" predictable behaviors and commitments on the part of their employees through the use of quasi-religious rituals and the enforcement of strict codes regulating social interactions.

The organizational innovations introduced by the McDonald's corporation are probably among the most potent examples of the cultural effects of corporate logics. As Ritzer (2004) has shown, they had a dramatic effect on human experience and social organization well beyond the boundaries of the firm of origin, helping spread the values and practices of efficiency, calculability, predictability, and control to various organizations and social institutions (education, medicine, and the criminal justice system), both in the US and abroad. The sheer success of this model is thus a precious reminder that instrumental rationality – as Weber worried – is also a very powerful "culture" in and of itself.

ECONOMY AS THE CULTURE OF MODERNITY?

The example of McDonald's suggests a broader point, then: the constitution of economic categories themselves is through and through a social process. Consequently, what gets incorporated (or not) into the sphere of the marketplace reveals much about how we understand ourselves, about our "culture." As Polanyi (2001) argued long ago, the hallmark of post-eighteenth century modernity was the emergence of a distinctive social order dominated by market relations. Following nineteenth-century critics (among them Marx, Weber, and Simmel), Polanyi articulated the dehumanizing effect of modern capitalism and calculative rationality on personality and human relations, whereby individuals come to be seen as commodities and means to an end rather than as ends in themselves.

Empirically, however, there is quite a bit of debate about whether such effects really exist: recent economic experiments in small-scale societies, for instance, have suggested that market integration is *positively* correlated with human cooperation (Henrich et al. 2004), thereby vindicating earlier commentaries about the civilizing (Hirschman 1977) and socially integrating effects of commerce. It is also unclear whether the penetration of markets has been as universal and far-reaching as some skeptics believe. Modernity certainly does not mean that everything has been engulfed into the sphere of the marketplace; for instance, the study of the conditions under which boundary "objects" such as children, death, organs, or art are subject to economic exchange has revealed a quite varied landscape. Hence, as sources of economic benefit, children were *removed* from labor markets around the turn of the twentieth century in the US (and countries that continue to authorize such practices today face grave political and economic pressures). On the other hand, as sources of emotional and social benefit, they were commodified in ways that were not foreseen in the nineteenth century, mainly through the adoption, insurance, and consumption markets (Zelizer 1985).

The intellectual challenge, then, is twofold: to specify the distinctive nature of the moral order capitalism relies upon, and to understand how it is produced. Perhaps this challenge is nowhere as obvious as in the current emergence of a new and eclectic vocabulary that seeks to overcome the conceptual divide between culture and economy, and focuses instead on the always inextricably moral dimensions of economic discourses and practices (Amin & Thrift 2004). Particularly noticeable is the work on logics of moral justification, which identifies the recent appearance of the discursive figure of "connectivity" as a new regime of justification conceived in and for the post-industrial capitalist economy (Boltanski & Chiapello 2005). Dezalay and Garth (2002) explore another exciting avenue in their analysis of the mutually reinforcing, profoundly entangled discourses of economic and political individualism (e.g., human rights and the market) and their worldwide diffusion under US hegemony. Finally, Callon (1998) and others have investigated the *performative* nature of the knowledge forms that sustain the development of capitalism, mainly economics and accounting. They have shown that through their language, techniques, and representations, these disciplines produce a world of "calculative agencies" and create a host of new institutions in which these agencies may exercise their calculative power — thereby formatting, little by little, our cultural selves onto the model fiction of *homo economicus*. This outburst of work seems to signal that sociology is finally ready for a real engagement with economics that will demystify it as a cultural form, as the discursive rationalization and active formatting, by capitalism, of itself and for itself — not merely the science of how the economy "works."

SEE ALSO: Civilization and Economy; Culture; Economy (Sociological Approach); Moral Economy

REFERENCES AND SUGGESTED READINGS

Adorno, T. & Horkheimer, M. (2002) *Dialectic of Enlightenment*. Stanford University Press, Stanford.

Amin, A. & Thrift, N. (Eds.) (2004) *The Cultural Economy Reader*. Blackwell, Oxford.

Beckert, J. (2004) *Unverdientes Vermögen. Soziologie des Erbrechts*. Campus, Frankfurt am Main.

Biernacki, R. (1995) *The Fabrication of Labor: Germany and Britain 1640–1914*. University of California Press, Berkeley.

Boltanski, L. & Chiapello, E. (2005) *The New Spirit of Capitalism*. Verso, London.

Bourdieu, P. (1984) *Distinction*. Harvard University Press, Cambridge, MA.

Callon, M. (1998) The Embeddedness of Economic Markets in Economics. In: Callon, M. (Ed.), *The Laws of the Markets*. Blackwell, Oxford.

Dezalay, Y. & Garth, B. G. (2002) *The Internationalization of Palace Wars: Lawyers, Economists, and the Contest to Transform Latin American States*. University of Chicago Press, Chicago.

DiMaggio, P. (1994) Culture and Economy. In: Smelser, N. & Swedberg, R. (Eds.), *The Handbook of Economic Sociology*. Princeton University Press, Princeton, pp. 27–57.

Dobbin, F. (1994) *Forging Industrial Policy*. Cambridge University Press, Cambridge.

Dore, R. (1973) *British Factory, Japanese Factory: The Origins of National Diversity in Industrial Relations*. Allen & Unwin, London.

Fligstein, N. (1992) *The Transformation of Corporate Control*. Harvard University Press, Cambridge, MA.

Geertz, C. (2001) The Bazaar Economy: Information and Search in Peasant Marketing. In: Granovetter, M. & Swedberg, R. (Eds.), *The Sociology of Economic Life*. Westview Press, Boulder.

Gramsci, A. (1971) *Selections form the Prison Notebooks*. Lawrence & Wishart, London.

Hamilton, G. & Woolsey-Biggart, N. (1988) Market, Culture, and Authority: A Comparative Analysis of Management and Organization in the Far East. *American Journal of Sociology* 94: 52–94.

Henrich, J. et al. (2004) *Foundations of Human Sociality: Economic Experiments and Ethnographic Evidence from Fifteen Small-Scale Societies*. Oxford University Press, Oxford.

Hirschman, A. (1977) *The Passions and the Interests*. Princeton University Press, Princeton.

Hofstede, G. (1980) *Culture's Consequences: International Differences in Work-Related Values*. Sage, Newbury Park, CA.

Meyer, J. & Rowan, B. (1977) Institutionalized Organizations: Formal Structure as Myth and Ceremony. *American Journal of Sociology* 83(2): 340–63.

Polanyi, K. (2001 [1944]) *The Great Transformation*. Beacon Press, Boston.

Ritzer, G. (2004) *The McDonaldization of Society*. Pine Forge Press, Thousand Oaks, CA.

Smith, C. (1990) *Auctions: The Social Construction of Value*. University of California Press, Berkeley.

Veblen, T. (1994 [1899]) *The Theory of the Leisure Class*. Penguin, New York.

Weber, M. (2002) *The Protestant Ethic and the Spirit of Capitalism*. Routledge, New York.

Zelizer, V. (1985) *Pricing the Priceless Child*. Princeton University Press, Princeton.

Zelizer, V. (1994) *The Social Meaning of Money*. Princeton University Press, Princeton.

culture, gender and

Andrea Press

The reproduction of our society's sex-gender system has been a continuing puzzle for sociologists of gender. The history of western writings on gender has long included ruminations on the role of culture in constituting gender difference and privilege (Wollstonecraft 1978; Mill 2003; and especially de Beauvoir 1993). Yet during the last 40 years of the sociology of gender, material characteristics – in particular, women's position as paid and unpaid laborers – have received more attention than cultural factors (Hartmann 1980; Blum 1991). These findings have revealed large differences in the paid and unpaid work lives of men and women in our society, and they have led to a number of political reform movements and initiatives – Title IX, the comparable worth movement, lawsuits demanding equal pay for equal work – that have resulted in somewhat more equality in the workplace.

There seem to be limits to these efforts toward workplace equality between the genders, both at the highest levels, where the prototypical "glass ceiling" seems to prevent women from achieving the same levels of leadership afforded to men, and at the lower levels, where women continually seem to function as a "reserve" labor force, dropping in and out of full-time paid labor according to the demands of their families (Callaghan & Hartmann 1991). Even a cursory examination of the beliefs and plans of current American college student women indicates that they expect to spend varying degrees of time out of the paid labor force caring for their children (Douglas 2004), a plan which demonstrably contributes to their continuing inequality in the workplace. Hays (1996) documents that a large portion of so-called "stay-at-home moms" actually plan to head back into the labor force as soon as they are able.

These limits have led to a cultural turn of sorts in the field of the sociology of gender. Second wave feminism, influenced by Marxist materialist theory, has challenged the necessity and desirability of gendered social arrangements in both family and workplace. Despite the social movements the second wave has inspired, which have challenged these arrangements, and despite the fact that there is some evidence that they may be slowly changing, their overall persistence is indisputable and is one of the paradoxes of modern social science. In fact, some argue that there is a backlash against feminism which is stronger and more persistent than was second wave feminism

itself. Sociologists of gender, long rooted in a materialist tradition that privileged phenomena related to occupational statuses and earning levels, have turned to culture to explain the persistence of gendered social arrangements in family and workplace.

This turn to culture is partly a result of the influence of new intellectual currents more generally in the social sciences. Poststructuralism, identified with the works of Derrida, Foucault, Lacan, and others, led many in the social sciences and humanities to reflect deeply on the impact of discourse and categories of thought on our analyses of social life. Feminism has been integrally engaged with poststructuralism at a theoretical level. As Barrett describes it:

> Feminist theory has been able to take up a number of issues outside the classically "materialist" perspective ... Poststructuralist theories, notably Derridian deconstructive readings, Lacanian psychoanalysis, and Foucault's emphasis on the material body and the discourses of power have proved very important in this. Feminists have appropriated these theories rather than others for good reasons: these theories address the issues of sexuality, subjectivity and textuality that feminists have put at the top of the agenda. (Cited in Brooks 1997: 6)

Postmodernism has extended the critiques of poststructuralism to challenge some of our most fundamental notions, such as the individual self, linear time, and the concept of space. Feminism's engagement with postmodernism has also been fundamental and complex. As Brooks notes, "the relationship between feminism, poststructuralism, and postmodernism has been both dynamic and productive for feminism and social theory more generally" (p. 6). Some note the conceptual equivalence between postmodern feminism and postfeminism (McLennan, cited in Brooks 1997: 6). While sociologists have often been slowest among social scientists in acknowledging the importance and influence of both the poststructuralist and postmodernist intellectual movements, it is often through the impact of feminist and cultural sociology, both of which are fundamentally interdisciplinary, that these traditions have entered the field and been accorded full consideration.

In light of these observations, what can the variable of culture offer to the study of gender in sociology? First, like the term gender, the term culture carries with it a long, interdisciplinary, multi-perspectival heritage that transcends the limits of the field of sociology. In the discipline of anthropology the concept of culture has long been an organizing term that structures discussion of the object, as well as more recently the "medium," of analysis for the field (Ortner 1999). In this sense, culture is very broadly conceived in Tylor's famous definition as a "way of life" (Williams 1981) to be looked at through a series of academic practices that themselves constitute another way of life (Geertz 1973; Clifford 1986). Analysis in the field of anthropology has become extremely self-reflexive, while retaining its core interest in the analysis of culture generally as an object of study.

SOCIOLOGY OF GENDER AND THE CULTURAL TURN

Where the sociology of culture has been important in gender studies has been in its attempt to define the use of the concept of culture in sociology. Various and competing definitions have been proffered. Some of these display an affinity with anthropological definitions of culture, descending from Tylor (1958), wherein culture is defined as a set of practices and beliefs that characterize particular societies, subgroups, and groups of societies. Other definitions focus more on the analysis of cultural products, their production, meanings, and uses. Sociologists tend to move back and forth quite easily between these different senses of the term culture and so there is no easy way to characterize the sociological consensus on its use, even as the subfield of the sociology of culture has continued to develop and grow.

Sociology as a discipline began in the US by employing a culturalist definition of culture, adapted from the Tylorian definition of culture as a "complex whole" produced by people's historical experience, including knowledge, belief, art, morals, law, and custom. This concept was challenged by Radcliffe-Brown (1958) and his followers, who proposed in contrast a "structuralist" theory asserting the primary importance of social structure in determining the important facets of social life. After an

initial series of debates, American anthropology became primarily a culturalist discipline in which the Tylorian definition of culture has been prominent. Nevertheless in American sociology the notion that structural issues are of primary importance has of course been prominent. However, of late we have witnessed a cultural turn throughout the social sciences which has affected many of the primary subfields of sociology, including the sociology of gender. This has meant that the importance of culture has been widely recognized throughout the discipline.

Nowhere has this been more primary than with the rise of the sociology of culture, which has now risen to be one of the most popular affiliations elected by members of the ASA. In this group the definition of culture includes both those who use the term in its more amorphous, Tylorian sense to mean patterns of life and ways of living, and those who define the study of culture as focused on the artifacts of recorded culture such as books, media, music, museums, photographs, etc. At the same time, the concept of culture has gained relevance in many other areas of the discipline, including the sociology of gender. This can be seen in recent works by Adams et al. (2005), in addition to areas outside the field of sociology altogether, like the rapidly expanding interdisciplinary field of cultural studies (Grossberg et al. 1992).

When cultural categories are applied to thoughts about gender the concept of culture offers a way to conceptualize those dimensions of our gendered beliefs and practices that cannot be reduced to social structural or biological features alone. With regard to the paradox of gender difference, culture has proved to be an important variable. Sociologists have turned to culture to explain a variety of findings about gender that persist even as consciousness about structural discrimination and inequality has been raised and discussed. Indeed, there appears to be a core aspect of gender which is culturally, rather than biologically or structurally, determined.

The issue of mothering serves as a key example of this explanatory dynamic wherein the concepts of gender and culture intertwine. While biological explanations account for the fact that women give birth, sociologists of gender realized early on in the discipline that recourse to the mothering "instinct" was inadequate as an explanation of why women performed so much more of the labor involved in mothering than did fathers or male caretakers (Hartmann 1980; Rich 1986). Yet an initial turn by gender sociologists to labor market explanations left gaps as well: gender sociologists became adept at explaining what labors women performed in the paid labor force, ways they were inadequately compensated for this work, and how women performed the vast majority of unpaid labor in the home – mothering included. But such discussions fell far short of offering adequate explanations for how this state of affairs came about. That women perform unpaid labor does not explain how this situation came about, nor why it persists. It is to this explanatory level that cultural explanations of mothering are directed. They fall into different categories, depending on the approach to culture which is used.

"Women mother" begins one paradigmatic feminist work on mothering (Chodorow 1978). This book posed the question of why it is that women do the work of mothering virtually universally across cultures and throughout history. This question has been answered in many different ways by those who analyze the intersection of gender and culture in the institution of motherhood. Psychoanalysis has long provided a key set of terms used in cultural analysis, although of course psychoanalytic theory employs only one particular set of cultural tools. These focus on the penetration of culture into the reproduction of our personality processes. Chodorow draws on psychoanalytic categories as they are structured by our cultural arrangements. She argues that a nuclear family, in which it is almost exclusively women who do the work of mothering, reproduces the capacity to mother in daughters, but not in sons, who are treated more distantly because of their anatomical difference from the mother. The psychoanalytic theory Chodorow uses is itself dependent on a series of cultural arrangements and conditions for the truth of its insights. While her basic insights revolve around the psychoanalytic preoccupation with the reproduction of psychological relationships between people in the family, these relationships themselves are embedded in a series of culturally determined patterns which structure the family and its interpersonal matrix.

Other gender sociologists have drawn from psychoanalysis as well to explain phenomena as disparate as gender identity in the military (Williams 1989), women's relationships to their bodies (Martin 1987), and our culture's patriarchal thrust more generally (Dinnerstein 1976). Newer works by Chodorow (1999) summarize the importance of psychoanalytic theory for gender and other areas of sociology.

While Chodorow and others turn to psychoanalytic categories, other sociologists turn to more explicitly historical and ideological – but equally cultural – reasons why women perform the role of mothering. Those examining American society often cite the role of American cultural traditions (Hays 1996) or American mass media culture (Douglas 2004) in maintaining and reproducing the "custom" of female labor in the family and home. These cultural explanations have been important because they fill in where other types of explanations fall short of explaining the persistence and ubiquity of gender inequality.

Cultural explanations account for not only why women consent to perform unpaid labor in the family, but also explain why women resist other types of explanations, and criticisms of their actions – such as those offered by the women's movement or feminist academics, which label this extra labor as oppressive or exploitative. Women's own explanations for their lives often reject such accounts, substituting instead the idea that they perform family labors out of love and devotion. Larger cultural factors like their belief in religious ideas about women's familial role, or their adherence to certain secular notions about the importance of traditional family values, can be invoked to help make sense of why women consent to a gendered division of labor that analysts find oppressive.

Hays (1996) and Douglas (2004) interrogate the history and development of current cultural ideas and policies about motherhood in our society, each in turn exposing the different ways these ideas and policies disadvantage women as a social and cultural group. Douglas relies in part for her evidence of the development and reproduction of social attitudes on a variety of popular media like film and television that indicate how our society makes, and has historically made, contradictory demands on mothers. For example, the vast majority of mothers work, and for an increasing number of hours, yet particularly over the last 10 years the growth of the ideology of "intensive mothering" has demanded that an increasing number of hours be devoted to the tasks of childrearing. Many pages of popular culture lore are devoted to increasing guilt among those mothers who work for their inability to meet the demands of this mothering "speed up." Her book is a prime example of works which combine cultural analysis with other types of analysis and evidence. Together, these forms of analysis enable one to develop a critical perspective on an aspect of social activity in which women's work plays the major role. It is an extremely politically informed commentary on many aspects of our "culture of motherhood" in the contemporary US. Douglas supplements her cultural history with a running account of all the policy decisions affecting mothers that have been made by the US government over the last four decades – what she has dubbed the backlash era against feminism. Douglas's work stands as an interesting methodological example among books discussing the gendered aspects of our culture in that it addresses not only gender and culture, but the political issues and related policy debates that highlight their importance for our everyday lives.

Hays (1996) is similarly cultural in her level of explanation, yet is both more specific and even more historically framed. Hays interrogates our widespread cultural assumption that what she calls intensive mothering is necessary or even beneficial for children. Marshaling historical evidence, Hays examines the historical growth of this assumption and analyzes its relationship to our society's varying use of women as a reserve labor force, as women are pulled in to work when needed and pushed out with cries of child neglect when they are not. The argument is cultural throughout in that it challenges those who assert that women's biology accounts for their desire to mother according to the intensive style she describes. The cultural evidence Hays uses, then, is both historical and socioeconomic in nature.

Yet another cultural take on the study of mothering focuses on the representation of mothering as a gendered practice in a series of cultural artifacts like film, television, books, newspapers, etc. There has been much work on the intersection of gender and culture focused on the topic of mothering from this perspective. Kaplan (1992), for example, focuses on the representation of mothers in popular Hollywood film, identifying several prototypes typical of Hollywood's images and classifying a plethora of Hollywood works according to these prototypes. Many others have commented on various aspects of motherhood's filmic representation and its potential impact on women viewers, and on our cultural ideas about mothering generally (Geraghty 1991).

Press (1991) and Press and Cole (1999) and others discuss some aspects of the representation of mothering in television, and its impact on the viewers they researched. Press (1991) focuses generally on analyzing the representation of women and families in prime-time television, and in particular discusses women's reactions to and interpretations of these representations. Many women interviewed for the study mentioned their reactions to the mothers and families depicted in the television they had watched. Some even described their own mothering styles, current or planned, in relation to these images. Press and Cole (1999) again discuss issues surrounding motherhood with women, this time in the context of broader dialogues on and off television about abortion. Discussion took place in groups and preceded or followed viewing of various prime-time television treatments of the issue. While mothering itself was not the actual focus of the discussions, the topic was central to the abortion opinions expressed by many of the women in the study.

Many works (e.g., Walters 2001) discuss multiple types of cultural artifacts more directly, including films, entertainment, television, books, and news media, all from the perspective of how motherhood is represented in different ways and with what impact on society. These works all support the importance of cultural representations of gender in contributing to the reproduction of our gendered system and the inequalities inherent in it.

CONCLUSION

This brief discussion illustrates that the study of gender is intertwined with cultural concepts and factors. The definition of culture itself is difficult to pin down, and ranges from an amorphous notion encompassing many aspects of social existence, to one more specifically based on cultural artifacts and products. The sociology of gender cannot be imagined without a strong notion of the importance of culture and the ubiquity of cultural factors.

As the interdisciplinary study of gender has developed in a distinctive way, it has in turn influenced the sociology of gender to move in a more cultural direction. The recent influx of studies focusing on the gendered aspects of culture is a good example of the impact this has had on the sociology of gender. Press (2000) details three axes for recent work in the field of communication focusing on gender issues: technology, the body, and the public sphere. All of these topics have been taken up in recent work on the sociology of gender. The increasing tendency of the field to assimilate influences from interdisciplinary studies which have transformed the very nature of the field itself is good evidence that the cultural bent in gendered sociology is here to stay.

SEE ALSO: Culture; Doing Gender; Gender Ideology and Gender Role Ideology; Hegemonic Masculinity; Psychoanalytic Feminism

REFERENCES AND SUGGESTED READINGS

Adams, J., Clemens, E. S., & and Orloff, A. S. (2005) Introduction: Social Theory, Modernity, and the Three Waves of Historical Sociology. In: Adams, J., Clemens, E. S., & and Orloff, A. S. (Eds.), *Remaking Modernity: Politics, History and Sociology*. Duke University Press, Durham, NC, pp. 1–72.

Baxter, J. & Wright, E. O. (2000) The Glass Ceiling Hypothesis: A Comparative Study of the United States, Sweden, and Australia. *Gender and Society* 14(2): 275–94.

Beauvoir, S. de (1993) *The Second Sex*. Trans. H. M. Parshley. Alfred A. Knopf, New York.

Blum, L. (1991) *Between Feminism and Labor: The Significance of the Comparable Worth Movement*. University of California Press, Berkeley.

Blum, L. (1999) *At the Breast: Ideologies of Breast-feeding and Motherhood in the Contemporary United States*. Beacon Press, Boston.

Brooks, A. (1997) *Postfeminisms: Feminism, Cultural Theory and Cultural Forms*. Routledge, New York.

Callaghan, P. & Hartmann, H. (1991) *Contingent Work: A Chart Book on Part-Time and Temporary Employment*. Economic Policy Institute, Washington, DC.

Chodorow, N. (1978) *The Reproduction of Mothering: Psychoanalysis and the Sociology of Gender*. University of California Press, Berkeley.

Chodorow, N. (1989) *Feminism and Psychoanalytic Theory*. Yale University Press, New Haven.

Chodorow, N. (1999) *The Power of Feelings: Personal Meaning in Psychoanalysis, Gender, and Culture*. Yale University Press, New Haven.

Clifford, J. (1986) *Writing Culture: The Poetics of Ethnography. A School of American Research Advanced Seminar*. University of California Press, Berkeley.

Dinnerstein, D. (1976) *The Mermaid and the Minotaur: Sexual Arrangements and Human Malaise*. Harper & Row, New York.

Dirks, N. B., Eley, G., & Ortner, S. B. (Eds.) (1994) *Culture/Power/History: A Reader in Contemporary Social History*. Princeton University Press, Princeton.

Douglas, S. J. (2004) *The Mommy Myth: The Idealization of Motherhood and How It Has Undermined Women*. Free Press, New York.

Geertz, C. (1973) *The Interpretation of Cultures; Selected Essays*. Basic Books, New York.

Geraghty, C. (1991) *Women and Soap Opera: A Study of Prime Time Soaps*. Polity Press, Cambridge.

Grossberg, L., Nelson, C., & Treichler, P. A. (Eds.) (1992) *Cultural Studies*. Routledge, New York.

Hartmann, H. (1980) The Family as the Locus of Gender, Class, and Political Struggle: The Example of Housework. *Signs* 6(3).

Hays, S. (1996) *The Cultural Contradictions of Motherhood*. Yale University Press, New Haven.

Hays, S. (2003) *Flat Broke with Children: Women in the Age of Welfare Reform*. Oxford University Press, New York.

Kaplan, E. A. (1992) *Motherhood and Representation: The Mother in Popular Culture and Melodrama*. Routledge, New York.

McLennan, G. (1994) Feminism, Epistemology and Postmodernism: Reflections on Current Ambivalence. *Signs* 29 (Autumn): 98–124.

Martin, E. (1987) *The Woman in the Body*. Beacon Press, Boston.

Mill, J. S. (2003) *On Liberty*. Ed. D. Bromwich & G. Kateb. Yale University Press, New Haven.

Mitchell, J. & Rose, J. (Eds.) (1982) *Feminine Sexuality: Jacques Lacan and the École Freudienne*. Macmillan, London.

Ortner, S. B. (Ed.) (1999) *The Fate of "Culture": Geertz and Beyond*. University of California Press, Berkeley.

Press, A. L. (1990) Class, Gender, and the Female Viewer: Women's Responses to Dynasty. In: Brown, M. E. (Ed.), *Television and Women's Culture*. Sage, Newbury Park, CA, pp. 158–72.

Press, A. L. (1991) *Women Watching Television: Gender, Class and Generation in the American Television Experience*. University of Pennsylvania Press, Philadelphia.

Press, A. L. (2000) Recent Developments in Feminist Communication Theory: Difference, Public Sphere, Body and Technology. In: Curran, J. & Gurevitch, M. (Eds.), *Mass Media and Society*. Routledge, New York, pp. 27–44.

Press, A. L. & Cole, E. R. (1999) *Speaking of Abortion: Television and Authority in the Lives of Women*. University of Chicago Press, Chicago.

Radcliffe-Brown, A. R. (1958) *Method in Social Anthropology: Selected Essays*. Ed. M. N. Srinivas. University of Chicago Press, Chicago.

Rich, A. C. (1980) *Compulsory Heterosexuality and Lesbian Existence*. Antelope, Denver.

Rich, A. C. (1986) *Of Woman Born: Motherhood as Experience and Institution*. Norton, New York.

Tylor, E. B. (1958) *Primitive Culture*. Harper, New York.

Walters, S. D. (1992) *Lives Together/Worlds Apart: Mothers and Daughters in Popular Culture*. University of California Press, Berkeley.

Williams, C. L. (1989) *Gender Differences at Work: Men and Women in Nontraditional Occupations*. University of California Press, Berkeley.

Williams, L. (1990) Something Else Besides a Mother: *Stella Dallas* and Maternal Melodrama. In: Erens, P. (Ed.), *Issues in Feminist Film Criticism*. Indiana University Press, Bloomington, pp. 137–62.

Williams, R. (1981) *Culture*. Fontana, London.

Wollstonecraft, M. (1978) *Posthumous Works of the Author of a Vindication of the Rights of Women*. J. Johnson, London.p

culture industries

Nicholas Garnham

Culture industries is a term which performs both a descriptive and conceptual function. It also has a history. Since the term was coined by Horkheimer and Adorno in their 1947 essay "The Culture Industry: Enlightenment as Mass Deception," both what the term designates and its theoretical implications have undergone a number of shifts.

In its original Frankfurt School usage the term was a polemical intervention into the mass society/mass culture debate and a development of the Marxist theory of Ideology. On the one hand, the term culture referred to the superstructure – the social realm of meaning construction and circulation where symbolic forms of all types were produced and distributed – and to the German Idealist tradition of culture (or art) as a realm of freedom from material constraint and interests. Its linkage to the term industry (in the singular), on the other hand, was intended polemically to indicate the destruction of the relative autonomy of the superstructure and of the emancipatory possibilities of art by the economic dynamics of the base. The culture industry thus primarily referred to the industrialization and commodification of the process of symbolic production and circulation *in toto*. For Horkheimer and Adorno, the ideological domination of capitalism, and thus the suppression of revolutionary possibilities, was effected not by the overt content of cultural production, but by the deep structure of the cultural forms and the alienated relations between both producer (artist) and cultural work and between producers and audiences that the system of capitalist industrial cultural production produced. In this period this approach was counterposed to the widespread sociopolitical concern with propaganda as a key element in the construction and maintenance of authoritarian regimes (fascism and Stalinism).

The use of the term industry referred (drawing on Marx) to the domination of the cultural realm by competitive and increasingly monopolistic corporations driven by the search for profit through the exchange of cultural commodities, thus necessarily alienating. It also referred (drawing on Weber) to a process of organizational rationalization, whereby cultural production and consumption were increasingly planned, thus suppressing cultural and political alternatives. Importantly, this approach placed the analysis of advertising and marketing at the center of a general process the purpose and effect of which was to hold the audience in thrall (the new opiate of the people).

This rationalization took place not just within the process of production, but within the cultural form. Cultural products were standardized and produced "pseudo-individuality" in consumption.

Importantly, this vision and theoretical analysis were starkly opposed to Walter Benjamin's (1970) view of media technologies as emancipatory advances which shifted the relation between audience and art work from one of worship ("aura") to one of education and rational inquiry.

Through the 1950s and 1960s the term culture industry and its accompanying theoretical approach was largely forgotten in favor of a pluralist analysis of the mass media and their power (or lack of it). It was dismissed as the nostalgic and elitist response of exiled German intellectuals to US popular culture. The term reappeared, more usually in the form of cultural industries, in the late 1960s with the revival of theoretical Marxism and the New Left. It now drew on three developments: (1) the revival of a political economy of communications which returned to a serious analysis of the economics of the mass media in contrast to the ideological analysis of media content; (2) the turn to cultural studies, which shifted the emphasis in the wider analysis of and opposition to capitalist consumerist hegemony from economic to cultural structures and processes; (3) the revival of the Frankfurt School analysis of capitalism and its social and cultural effects in the form of a utopian, countercultural, anti-consumerist critique of capitalism as the society of the spectacle (deBord 1995) symbolized by the May 1968 events in France and by Marcuse's role as a guru of the US New Left (Marcuse 1991).

Now the use of the term signaled a shift away from a focus on the mass media, understood as the print publishing and broadcasting industries, and the overwhelming focus on the direct political effects of those media, to a focus on popular entertainment and, in particular, linked to a heightened sociological interest in youth culture, to a concern with the music and film industries.

It is important to note that in this new usage the cultural industries were no longer assumed to be alienated and repressive. On the contrary, the term could now be used positively in a critique of the elitist implications of established public policies for the support of art and media (Garnham 1990). It was thus associated with a widespread positive evaluation, both within economics and cultural studies, of consumerism, and the discovery of the "empowered" consumer and audience.

At the same time the use of the term signaled a refusal to follow the "cultural turn" in rejecting economic determination. Those analyzing the cultural industries now drew not only on Marxist economics, but on developments in mainstream industrial and information economics, to make much more detailed and nuanced analyses of the economic structure and dynamics of the cultural industries than that of the Frankfurt School. The cultural industries were now analyzed in terms of the special nature of their products and markets. Indeed, the term industries in the plural was now used to indicate the existence of important economic differences between these industries. Stress was now placed on the particular nature of symbolic or immaterial products and services and the difficulties in commodifying them. Rejecting Frankfurt School notions of rationalization and planning, this new analysis emphasized the exceptionally risky and irrational nature of the production and distribution process stemming from the need for constant product innovation and the inherent uncertainty of demand. This created a "hit and flop" economy where a few super-profitable, but inherently unpredictable, hits paid for the high percentage of losers. A distinction was drawn between the high sunk costs of production (so-called first copy costs and more akin to R&D in classical material goods-producing industries) and the low costs of reproduction and distribution which resulted in increased returns to scale and thus a powerful drive towards audience maximization and both sectoral and cross-sectoral concentration of ownership and control. The structure and dynamics of the cultural sector were explained as the response of management under conditions of intercapitalist competition to these problems of realization.

On this basis the French school (Miege 1989; Flichy 1991) distinguished subsectors of the cultural industries (*les industries de l'imaginaire*) nature of their products, their relations of production, their relation to their markets, and their relation to the underlying technologies of distribution and appropriation. These subsectors were, first, *editorial* (of which book publishing and records were the classic cases) where control over a catalog of products – and thus the ability to spread the investment risk – was strategically crucial. Here, production of the cultural products remained artisanal, was outsourced, and the key workforce was managed and subordinated through contract and intellectual property rights. The second subsector regarded *flow* (i.e., broadcasting in its various forms) where customer loyalty to a constantly replenished service and series of channels required control over distribution and the centralized planning of content production – and thus also the employment of content producers as wage workers in large industrial organizations. Here the commodity being sold was audiences to advertisers and a major share of value added was extracted not by the content producers but by the producers of consumer electronics (e.g., TV and radio sets, video recorders, DVD players, etc).

The cultural industries approach now developed in three distinct although not necessarily incompatible directions, and in so doing largely lost its original link to Marxism. First, the focus on distribution and the industries' links with the consumer electronics sector led to a focus on the impact of developments in ICTs (information and communication technologies) and related policy issues. Here the central argument was over the extent to which developments in the communication and cultural sectors were technologically determined and whether technological development was or was not broadly emancipatory (de Sola Pool 1984).

Secondly, the focus on the industrial economics of information led to a merger with the broader post-Fordist analysis of the development of the capitalist economy, which saw the economy in general satisfying immaterial (and therefore cultural), rather than material, needs (Lash & Urry 1994). Here the distinction between cultural industries and other economic sectors is increasingly brought into question. These two developments have led to the absorption of the cultural industries analysis into a broader information sector, information economy, information society analysis.

Thirdly, the term cultural industries has given way to a range of terms such as entertainment industry, information sector, knowledge industries and, in particular, creative industries. Here, linked to a more general analysis of the knowledge economy (Castells 1999), itself a development of the concepts of the post-industrial and service economies, the center of analysis is immateriality, the percentage of value added attributable to "knowledge," the dependency on intellectual property. In particular, the role and formation of "knowledge" or "creative" workers becomes a matter of central concern. This development is largely policy driven. On the one hand, it is based on an argument that the cultural sector is a key growth sector globally and thus, as a response to deindustrialization, nations need to foster their "creative industries" in order to get a share of this market and the profits and export earnings that flow from it. On the other hand, "knowledge" creation generally is a condition for success in the new information economy and thus comparative advantage stems from creating conditions – educational, legal, and fiscal – to foster this creativity.

Analysis of and debates surrounding the cultural industries relate to two other important topics: the public sphere and intellectuals. Habermas's original formulation of his public sphere thesis stems directly from Adorno's analysis of the culture industries. It is the creation of the culture industries that destroys the public sphere as an arena for free discussion and deliberation upon which democracy is founded. Thus an analysis of the structure and dynamics of these industries is central to an understanding of the history and future possibilities of the public sphere.

Central to the culture industries tradition has been a concern with the socioeconomic position and role of cultural workers and the extent to which, as intellectuals, they can continue to exercise an autonomous and critical role in the development of knowledge and culture. The shift to a focus on creative industries and the information society places this concern with the relations of cultural production center stage.

SEE ALSO: Adorno, Theodor W.; Benjamin, Walter; Commodities, Commodity Fetishism and Commodification; Critical Theory/Frankfurt

School; Culture, Production of; Ideology; Information Society; Mass Culture and Mass Society; Media Monopoly; Political Economy

REFERENCES AND SUGGESTED READINGS

Adorno, T. & Horkheimer, M. (1997) *Dialectic of Enlightenment*. Verso, London.
Benjamin, W. (1970) The Work of Art in the Age of Mechanical Reproduction. In: *Illuminations*. Fontana, London.
Castells, M. (1999) *The Rise of Network Society*. Blackwell, Oxford.
DeBord, G. (1995) *The Society of the Spectacle*. Zone Books, New York.
De Sola Pool, I. (1984) *Technologies of Freedom*. Harvard University Press, Cambridge, MA.
Flichy, P. (1991). *Les Industries de l'imaginaire*. PUG, Grenoble.
Garnham, N. (1990) *Capitalism and Communication*. Sage, London.
Lash, S. & Urry, J. (1994) *Economies of Signs and Space*. Sage, London.
Marcuse, H. (1991 [1965]) *One Dimensional Man*. Beacon Press, Boston.
Miege, B. (1989) *The Capitalization of Cultural Production*. International General, New York.

culture jamming

Jay M. Handelman and Robert V. Kozinets

Culture jamming refers to an organized, social activist effort that aims to counter the bombardment of consumption-oriented messages in the mass media. For Habermas (1985), an ideal speech situation is one in which all participants within a public space are empowered to reach consensus on issues of mutual importance through engagement in symmetrical discourse. Culture jammers see contemporary public space as filled with distorted communications, and seek to right the situation. These activists see fair and accessible public discourse as eroded by a mass media controlled by corporations, whose sponsored advertising has become the primary propagandist supporting the social logic of consumption culture. Culture jamming, then, is consumer culture jamming. The activists seek to break through the wall of corporate controlled, distorted, asymmetrical public discourse, awakening people from the hegemonic culture where the logic of consumption permeates all aspects of their lived experience (Rumbo 2002).

The rationale for culture jamming is found in the writings of Frankfurt School theorists, perhaps most powerfully espoused by Horkheimer and Adorno (1996). The Frankfurt School's conceptual framework critiques social structures constructed under the guise of a capitalist ideology that come to define a culture of consumption. Here, corporations act as "cultural engineers" (Holt 2002) that define a limited set of socially acceptable human activities and identities, inherently limiting human potential and freedom. By controlling and permeating virtually all public spaces, corporations and their capitalist ideology serve as the groundwork for a hegemonic cultural logic of consumption. Ontologically, while this culture of consumption is socially constructed, it becomes reified as a "natural" social order, appearing concrete, objective, and void of competing worldviews and any alternative possibility for human expression.

Consistent with the underlying philosophy of the Frankfurt School, culture jamming involves at least three steps in its effort to break through this oppressive framework of social meaning. First, culture jamming tries to identify the contradictions buried beneath the apparently seamless barrage of capitalist messages. Advertising, the communication carrier of the capitalist cultural code, naturalizes consumption by interweaving consumer goods and the very fabric of social life (Leiss et al. 1990). Through advertising, consumption of consumer goods appears as the sole route to solving life's problems and achieving individual happiness. Culture jamming's first step is to unveil the economic, social, and environmental misery that hides beneath this happy exterior.

The second step in culture jamming involves achieving a type of reflexive resistance whereby consumers (i.e., the general public) become aware of the hidden contradictions underlying the cultural ideology of consumption. By revealing these otherwise hidden contradictions, culture jamming empowers consumers by enabling them not only to see the discrepancies lurking beneath capitalism's glossy and seductive messages, but also to examine critically how the dominant capitalist ideology imposes constraints on human freedom. In achieving this, culture jamming sets the stage for the third step, which is emancipation. Here, consumers are changed – which is the culture jammers' ultimate objective. They are able to envision and act upon other cultural logics and alternative possibilities for social expression and individual happiness.

Culture jamming's perspective of omnipotent consumer culture that can only be broken by organized activists who heroically emancipate consumers has come under considerable scrutiny. At the axiological level, the culture jamming project inherently assumes that consumers are cultural dupes who have been hoodwinked by clever capitalists and are in dire need of emancipation by enlightened activists. Cultural studies of consumers have found that individual consumers can, on their own, be well aware of the contradictions that permeate a culture of consumption. These consumers come to see the contradictions in culture jamming itself as an attempt by yet another set of cultural elitists (social activists) to control the social agenda (Kozinets & Handelman 2004).

Ontologically, postmodern researchers view the erosion of a culture of consumption as occurring not through top-down activist attempts at culture jamming, but via fragmented and self-produced consumption whereby individual consumers produce their own system of cultural meanings (Holt 2002). With this type of resistance, consumers come to form their own patterns of social interaction and cultural meaning, which are organically produced not through consumption of mass-produced products but by alternative methods of exchange, such as gift giving and sacrificial practices (Kozinets 2002).

Empirical research in this area lends itself best to interpretive (qualitative) techniques. As the issue of culture jamming is intricately tied with issues of cultural meaning, social movements, ideology, and the like, examining culture jamming and other forms of consumer resistance is best achieved by studying these activities embedded in their cultural context. Ongoing research in the area of culture jamming will grapple with the alternative axiological and ontological perspectives mentioned

above. On the one hand is the idea of consumer resistance such as culture jamming as occurring in the form of an organized, top-down social activist attempt to break consumers free from a hegemonic capitalist ideology that sustains materialism as a central cultural value. On the other hand is a postmodern conceptualization of consumer resistance that advocates self-directed agency towards consumer sovereignty (Thompson 2004).

SEE ALSO: Advertising; Consumption; Cultural Resistance; Culture; Culture, Social Movements and; Ideology

REFERENCES AND SUGGESTED READINGS

Habermas, J. (1985) *The Theory of Communicative Action.* Beacon Press, Boston.
Holt, D. B. (2002) Why Do Brands Cause Trouble? A Dialectical Theory of Consumer Culture and Branding. *Journal of Consumer Research* 29(2): 70–90.
Horkheimer, M. & Adorno, T. W.(1996 [1944]). *Dialectic of Enlightenment.* Continuum, New York.
Kozinets, R. V. (2002) Can Consumers Escape the Market? Emancipatory Illuminations from Burning Man. *Journal of Consumer Research* 29(1): 20–38.
Kozinets, R. V. & Handelman, J. M. (2004) Adversaries of Consumption: Consumer Movements, Activism, and Ideology. *Journal of Consumer Research* 31: 4.
Leiss, W., Klein, S., & Jhally, S. (1990) *Social Communication in Advertising: Persons, Products and Images of Well-Being.* Routledge, London.
Rumbo, J. D. (2002) Consumer Resistance in a World of Advertising Clutter: The Case of Adbuster. *Psychology and Marketing* 19(2): 127–48.
Thompson, C. J. (2004) Marketplace Mythology and Discourses of Power. *Journal of Consumer Research* 31(2): 162–80.

culture, nature and

Chandra Mukerji

There is a movement among sociologists and social critics to include the built environment and physical bodies in social analysis, and to think seriously about the ways that locations and creatures (including people) matter to group life. Part of this comes from anthropological leanings in sociology, and the tradition of thick description that includes discussions of chickens and back streets as well as group life. Part of it is motivated by feminist theory, and the determination to keep bodies and gender cultures in social analysis. Not only the settings for social life but also the human form itself is a cultural artifact made from natural materials. Part of the interest in cultures of nature also comes from Foucault. It is clear that power founded in the built environment provides an almost unnoticed but consequential regulatory mechanism.

Sociologists have had a long-term interest in describing the physical forms and social effects of cultural relations to the natural world. While relatively few ethnographic sociologists have paid serious attention to the physical settings for social life, those who have done community studies have sometimes illustrated the centrality of cultures of nature to collective life. Kai Erikson in *Everything in its Path* (1976) describes the social devastation of the Buffalo Creek flood, and how the mining industry, in disposing of its wastes, set up the conditions for the flood. He makes clear that the physical locations where social relations play out matter, and that these are shaped through human hands as well as by natural forces. The book by John Walton (2001) about Carmel, California, again looks at history, environment, and community, showing the enduring value of community studies that focus on cultures of nature and the forms of life they sustain.

Urban sociologists have also written about nature, too – the persistence of natural forces in artificial worlds. Sharon Zukin (1995) describes cities as quasi-natures of living creatures and supposedly inanimate structures that nonetheless settle and move. The city may seem to be the opposite of nature, but it is better understood as a culture of nature that seeks its control. Patrick Joyce (2003) looks at the meaning and forms of material control in two British cities, showing how political liberalism developed in the context of highly regulated material life. The compact between liberal, self-governing individuals and the regimes of power they inhabit is partly written on the ground in the places they inhabit.

Ecofeminists write quite differently about cultural relations to nature, bringing gender critique to the patterns of seeing and using the physical world. They argue that gender domination has been both symbolically and practically played out on the earth. Carolyn Merchant (1980) describes the masculine gaze in science. She argues that longstanding popular respect for female deities or Mother Nature was undermined by the promotion of objectivity in modern science. The power that was gained this way and through the culture of stewardship helped to erode the quality of human life in spite of the rhetoric of improvement. Donna Haraway (2002), in quite a different move, looks at the companion species that live with human beings, sometimes known as pets, to meditate on domination of nature and the possibility of friendships with non-human beings. She asks whether cross-species companionship can be a model for human relations to the natural world.

Sociologists of science, after focusing most of their attention for years on epistemological issues, are now asking about cultural formations of nature, their connections to science, and their implications for power. Chandra Mukerji (1997) looks at the role of territoriality in state formation in France, asking not simply about land claims but also about the territorial engineering used to define and defend them. Patrick Carroll (2001) writes about the role of "engine science" or engineering in the British control of Ireland. Like Patrick Joyce (2003), he identifies the exercise of power with control of the built environment. But Carroll sees Ireland as a laboratory for the British to experiment with tools of colonial control that were exported to other parts of the empire.

Prakash (1999) documents some of the results of these British efforts at material domination. In *Another Reason*, he follows the tools of engineering from Britain to India. There western science confronted local intellectual elites, who tried to find ways to engage it. Some picked up western intellectual styles, and saw the colonial railroad and other engineering projects as ways to modernize India. Others tried to find ways to build intellectual links between traditional forms of Indian culture and the imported ones. British colonial government established its hegemony through the environment, and brought face to face a utilitarian western reason and an indigenous one more deeply rooted in the subcontinent.

What makes work in this subfield so engaging is that it still takes materialism seriously even in this period when Marxist materialism has shown its intellectual failings. Human life remains embedded in the earth, and the landscapes people shape and inhabit. They regulate their bodies through material means, controlling diet, health, and habitations. In this period of globalization, when there are massive efforts to restructure relations to the natural world, this kind of social analysis has continued practical salience. And with the need to define a new materialism for the social sciences, studying the meeting places of nature and culture is intellectually vital as well.

SEE ALSO: Body and Cultural Sociology; Built Environment; Collective Identity; Consumption, Food and Cultural; Culture, the State and; Ecofeminism; Ecology; Environment, Sociology of the; Environment and Urbanization; Foucault, Michel; Human–Non-Human Interaction; Materialism; Nature; Technology, Science, and Culture

REFERENCES AND SUGGESTED READINGS

Carroll, P. (2001) Tools, Instruments, and Engines. *Social Studies of Science* 31(4): 593–625.
Erikson, K. (1976) *Everything in its Path*. Simon & Schuster, New York.
Haraway, D. (2002) *The Companion Species Manifesto*. Prickly Paradigm, Chicago.
Joyce, P. (2003) *The Rule of Freedom*. Verso, London.
Merchant, C. (1980) *The Death of Nature*. Harper & Row, New York.
Mukerji, C. (1997) *Territorial Ambitions and the Gardens of Versailles*. Cambridge University Press, Cambridge.
Prakash, G. (1999) *Another Reason*. Princeton University Press, Princeton.
Walton, J. (2001) *Stories Land*. University of California Press, Berkeley.
Zukin, S. (1995) *The Culture of Cities*. Blackwell, Cambridge, MA.

culture, organizations and

Andrew Chan

Culture in organizations refers to the values, norms, and patterns of action that characterize the social relationships within formal organizations. Jaques (1951) first described the changing culture of a factory, defining it as the customary or traditional ways of doing things, which are shared to a greater or lesser extent by all members of the organization and which new members must learn and at least partially accept in order to be accepted into the service of the firm.

Turner (1971) defines culture and its importance for organizing. According to Turner, part of the effectiveness of organizations lies in the way in which they are able to bring together large numbers of people and imbue them for a sufficient time with a sufficient similarity of approach, outlook, and priorities to enable them to achieve collective, sustained responses which would be impossible if a group of unorganized individuals were to face the same problem. However, this very property also brings with it the dangers of a collective blindness that some vital factors may be left outside the bounds of organizational perception. Culture is the source of blind spots because sharedness in values, norms, and perceptions results in a similarity of approach, shared expectations among members of the group to bring certain assumptions to the task of decision-making within the organization, and to operate with similar views of rationality. Culture is therefore a double-edged sword.

INTELLECTUAL AND SOCIAL CONTEXT

Culture was primarily a central concern for anthropologists and sociologists throughout the twentieth century. Only more recently, in the 1980s, did it catch the attention of the structural contingency school of organization theorists and economists, as a result of a number of popular texts that advocated an optimistic, even democratic view of the capacities of ordinary employees: *In Search of Excellence* (1982), *The Art of Japanese Management* (1982), *Theory Z* (1982), *The Winning Streak* (1984), and *Corporate Cultures* (1988) are some examples. These popular books reiterated and consolidated the insights of the human relations approach of industrial relations. These books also prefigured alternative management theories, ones that capitalized on culture as a precursor of more effective production and less hierarchical arrangements. Rediscovering culture seemed to be a way of responding to economic recessions at that time, and especially the challenges coming from Japanese companies. Organizational culture became seen as a variable in the firm's success equation and ultimate performance. As Chan and Clegg (2002) observe, one consequence of these enthusiasms has been to reduce the culture concept to an effect, constituted as a (metaphorical) object of inquiry. In the realm of organizational research, culture therefore very often only refers to "organizational culture" – a term that came to the fore in a series of British and American popular management texts of the 1980s. However, research did not stop with this popular consensus. Existing chasms between functionalist and pluralist paradigms, modern and postmodern approaches, and science and contra-science were reiterated in much of the research on organizational culture. Authors argued differences openly in a number of publications. A major axis of difference centered upon the definition of the construct per se (ontology), and upon the paradigms and methodologies used to apprehend it and to generate knowledge about it (epistemology).

MAJOR DIMENSIONS OF CULTURE

One dimension of culture was depicted by organizational anthropologists who pointed out that the organizational literature hijacked culture and used familiar concepts related to it (i.e., rituals, myths, taboos, and symbols) in disconcertingly unrecognizable ways (Marcus 1998). The displacement or transfer of the terms from anthropology to organization studies was inadequate and far from satisfying. Anthropologically and sociologically informed researchers considered that culture was not as

pliable as practitioners and managers seemed to think it should be (Meek 1988). For the latter, culture, as broadly construed by the organization and management literature, embodied consultant-driven reform initiatives for corporations, as well as managers' own attempts to gain control of their organizations through influencing the value premises on which organizational members' behavior was based. With this dimension of organization culture, clearly the least deeply conceived, widespread interest and enthusiasm extolled its perceived potency; culture assumed the character of a panacea, one that, potentially, could solve many organizational ailments. The business community had no qualms about the seductiveness of cultural management techniques as they infiltrated management circles. The panacea attributes of culture became widely identified with and internalized by the practitioner and managerial community throughout the 1980s and 1990s, even while more fundamental research continued. Willmott (1993) provided a comprehensive review of this "corporate culturalism" phenomenon over that decade.

METHODOLOGICAL ISSUES

Martin (2002) used the metaphor of "culture war games" to describe the paradigm dissensus and struggle for intellectual dominance within culture research communities throughout the 1980s and 1990s. From the outset, the culture movement represented a promising alternative and even a counter-initiative to functionalist and quantitative approaches in organization studies. The interest in culture in the 1980s gathered momentum amid a general discontent with quantitative approaches and structural contingency theories of organization that had already evolved from the systematic critique of normal organization science developed in the 1970s.

Administrative studies of culture favored quantitative techniques to provide functionalist accounts that lent themselves to the development of empirically based generalizations. Chatman (1991) and O'Reilley et al. (1991) were good examples. On the other hand, more pluralistic researchers had good reason to employ qualitative methodology and other multi-paradigmatic methodologies in developing context-specific explanations of culture. Qualitative research on culture allowed multi-perspective ethnographic methodologies to acquire legitimacy, representing an opportunity to break with the constraints of dominant quantitative and positivistic approaches.

The underpinnings of the two broad camps may be classified using Martin's (2002) "differentiation" perspective and its opposite, the "integrationist" genre of culture research. Research following a differentiation perspective, according to Martin, acknowledges inconsistencies in attitude. It sees consensus as occurring only within subcultural boundaries. It acknowledges conflicts of interest, for example, between top management and other employees, and within the top management team. These studies describe the inconsistencies and subcultural differences they find, so that inconsistency, subcultural consensus, and subcultural clarity become seen as the characteristic hallmarks of differentiation research.

The integrationist perspective drew from the managerially oriented and popular culture writings. Many quantitative studies depicted culture as an internally consistent package that fostered organization-wide consensus, usually around some set of shared values. Aspects of change and reform in organizations were seen as an embodiment of organization-wide cultural transformation, whereby either an old unity could be replaced (it was hoped by a new one) or unity forged out of difference. Some of the major themes that directed work undertaken in the integrationist framework were concerned with the management of meaning and various practices and devices through which managers attempt to bring off acceptable definitions of organizational reality as a basis for collective action, such as, for example, specific adoption of language, ritual, myth, story, legend, and narrative, etc., that were organizationally approved.

On one hand, the integrationist genre sees pragmatism, certainty, rationality, homogeneity, harmony, and a unified culture as an order of things that are both to be striven for and are achievable. Research in the integrationist genre conceptualized culture as a benign panacea, with properties that lent themselves to being pliable, at will, by managers. By contrast, the differentiation perspective criticized integrationist social engineering and value management treatments of culture. The differentiation perspective developed a critical assortment of theories of organizations that opposed a seemingly scientific, variable-based cultural theory of organization.

The bifurcation of cultural research into differentiation and integrationist camps was a result of resistance to the dominant integrationist and positivist approaches to organization theory and culture. The differentiation perspective argued that the existence of dissent and ambiguities, conflicts, and confusion in organizations, and the nature of the workers' passionate engagement in work, are glossed and rendered mute by the mainstream integrationist literature.

FUTURE DIRECTIONS

Between 1990 and 2001 three major handbooks were published: *Organizational Climate and Culture* (1990), *Handbook of Organizational Culture and Climate* (2000), and the *International Handbook of Organizational Culture and Climate* (2001). Additionally, economists such as Hermalin (2001) provided a comprehensive review of the relationship between economics and corporate culture. Administrative study of culture continues to thrive, emphasizing employee and company culture fit. Culture audit and organizational culture diagnosis tools continue to be refined mainly in in-company organizational development and applied settings that make use of such survey tools. More classically, future research in the differentiation tradition is likely to develop in the broad direction of studies of the hermeneutics of sense-making and exploration of process philosophy views of culture.

The first view considers that material aspects of organizations are made real only by being given meaning. We make sense of the realities of our everyday world by invoking and bringing to bear prior experience and assumptions. When we observe culture, whether in an organization or in society at large, we are observing an evolved form of social practice that has been influenced by many complex interactions between people, events, situations, actions, and general circumstances. The hermeneutic perspective is based on culture being constructed and accounted for through meaning-giving and sensemaking.

The process philosophical perspective treats culture not as entity-like structures but as instances that give meanings to actions and behaviors (Chia 2002). Culture is treated as a process of reality construction enabling people to understand certain events, action, things, and situations in distinctive ways. The treatment of culture as a fixed, unitary, bounded entity gives way to a sense of fluidity and permeability. It requires also that explanation of cultural forms be situated in a larger environment and a wider arena of different forces.

Future research on culture is likely to become more fruitful by returning to analysis of the social interactive processes through which actors create their world, via interpretive schemes. Deterministic models of culture are likely to give way to a reconsideration of culture as an inference-making process, except perhaps where culture is conceived of as the subject of managerial tools and techniques.

SEE ALSO: Culture; Labor–Management Relations; Organizational Contingencies; Organizations as Social Structures

REFERENCES AND SUGGESTED READINGS

Chan, A. & Clegg, S. (2002) History, Culture and Organization Studies. *Culture and Organization* 8(4): 259–73.

Chatman, J. (1991) Matching People and Organizations: Selection and Socialization in Public Accounting Firms. *Administrative Science Quarterly* 36(3): 459–84.

Chia, R. (2002) Time, Duration and Simultaneity: Rethinking Process and Change in Organizational Analysis. *Organization Studies* 23(6): 863–8.

Hermalin, B. (2001) Economics and Corporate Culture. In: Cooper, C. et al. (Eds.), *International Handbook of Organizational Culture and Climate.* Wiley, Chichester.

Jaques, E. (1951) *The Changing Culture of a Factory: A Study of Authority and Participation in an Industrial Setting.* Tavistock, London.

Marcus, G. (Ed.) (1998) *Corporate Futures: The Diffusion of the Culturally Sensitive Corporate Form.* University of Chicago Press, Chicago.

Martin, J. (2002) *Organizational Culture: Mapping the Terrain.* Sage, London.

Meek, V. (1988) Organizational Culture: Origins and Weaknesses. *Organization Studies* 9(4): 453–73.

O'Reilley, C., Chatman, J., & Caldwell, D. (1991) People and Organizational Culture: A Profile Comparison Approach to Assessing Person–Organization Fit. *Academy of Management Journal* 34(3): 487–516.

Turner, B. (1971) *Exploring the Industrial Subculture.* Macmillan, London.

Willmott, H. (1993) Strength is Ignorance, Slavery is Freedom: Managing Culture in Modern Organizations. *Journal of Management Studies* 30(4): 512–52.

culture of poverty

Kristina Wolff

The phrase culture of poverty was coined by Oscar Lewis (1965) to describe the combination of factors that perpetuate patterns of inequality and poverty in society. By focusing on the experiences of Puerto Ricans, Lewis illustrated how difficult it was for people to escape poverty due to the influence of cultural beliefs that support behaviors that contribute to people remaining in poverty. He described how the poor feel alienated in society. Because of their frustrations with their inability to transcend poverty, a culture develops which supports behaviors providing short-term gratification and other conditions of poverty as "normal." This is largely due to the conviction that it is impossible to improve their lives. These beliefs and behaviors are then instilled from one generation to the next, which eventually develops into a culture of poverty.

This concept has been used as a rationale to both increase and decrease government support for the poor, ranging from individuals within the US to debates about developing nations and the amount of aid they "deserve" from industrialized nations. A liberal approach utilizes this theory as a means to examine the structural impediments that create barriers for people to move out of poverty. These include absence of jobs, poor transportation, and limited access to adequate education and health care. Conservative interpretations of poverty use Lewis's concept as an illustration of the lack of motivation of individual poor people. Often drawing on stereotypes within popular culture, that people on welfare are "lazy," "hedonistic," or possessing questionable morals, a culture of poverty represents an individual's choice to remain dependent on the government instead of seeking gainful employment.

Sociologists have explored the relationships of ethnicity, race, and gender with various interpretations of the culture of poverty. By using this concept as a means to illustrate groups as having a "defective" culture, it becomes politically justifiable to limit support for the poor. For example, when the US restructured welfare programs in the 1990s, many argued in support of forced birth control or caps on the number of children women on public assistance could have and still receive government funds. Women and children constitute a large segment of the impoverished and proportionally more women of color are in poverty or are part of the working poor in US society. By focusing on individuals or specific populations as responsible for their impoverished state, social structures and practices that create barriers to success escape accountability.

SEE ALSO: Feminization of Poverty; Poverty; Poverty and Disrepute; Race; Race (Racism)

REFERENCES AND SUGGESTED READINGS

Edin, K. & Lein, L. (1997) *Making Ends Meet: How Single Mothers Survive Welfare and Low Wage Work*. Russell Sage Foundation, New York.
Gans, H. (1995) *The War Against the Poor: The Underclass and Antipoverty Policy*. Basic Books, New York.
Lawson, B. (1992) *The Underclass Question*. Temple University Press, Philadelphia.
Lewis, O. (1965) *La Vida: A Puerto Rican Family in the Culture of Poverty – San Juan and New York*. Random House, New York.
Moynihan, D. (1968) *On Understanding Poverty: Perspectives from the Social Sciences*. Basic Books, New York.
Wilson, W. (1996) *When Work Disappears: The World of the New Urban Poor*. Vintage Books, New York.

culture, production of

Richard A. Peterson

The production of culture perspective focuses on the ways in which the content of symbolic elements of culture are significantly shaped by the systems within which they are created, distributed, evaluated, taught, and preserved. The initial focus was on the production of expressive symbols such as art works, scientific research reports, popular culture, religious practices, legal judgments, journalism, and other parts of the culture industries. Now the perspective is also applied to many situations where the manipulation of symbols is a byproduct rather than the purpose of the collective activity (Peterson 1976; Crane 1992, Peterson & Anand 2004).

In the 1970s, when the production of culture emerged as a self-conscious perspective, it challenged the then-dominant idea that culture values and social structure mirror each other, a view held by most Marxists and functionalists – among them Talcott Parsons. Breaking from the mirror view, the production perspective sees culture and social structure as elements in an ever-changing patchwork (Peterson 1979). Research in the perspective draws freely on theories and methods developed in other branches of sociology. It is, however, distinctive in focusing on the consequences of social activities for the symbolic elements of culture (DiMaggio 2000).

Cultural production systems change slowly, but occasionally there is rapid change altering the aesthetic expression of a cultural expression. Such change is illustrated by the study that helped inspire the production perspective in culture, Howard and Cynthia White's 1965 study *Canvases and Careers*. It showed the transformation of the nineteenth-century French art world and the consequent emergence of Impressionist art. Six production factors are identified as making possible rapid cultural change. These include changes in law and regulation, technology, industrial structure, organizational structure, occupational careers, and the consumer market. The workings of these facets should be considered together as part of an interdependent production network (Peterson & Anand 2004).

Technology provides the tools with which people and institutions augment their abilities to communicate, while changes in communication technology profoundly destabilize and create new opportunities in art and culture. Technological innovations including radio, phonograph records, movies, television, and digitalized communication transformed art and popular culture in the twentieth century. At the micro-level, the electronic manipulation of guitar sounds transformed pop music, and digital communication media have facilitated the rapid globalization of culture (Waksman 1999; Goodall 2000).

Law and regulation create the ground-rules which shape the ways in which creative fields develop. Changes in copyright law have influenced the kinds of fiction that gets published, and restrictive notions of intellectual property continue to inhibit cultural expressions. Censorship of the culture industries has shaped what can be produced, and federal restrictions on multiple ownership of newspapers, and TV and radio deregulation, have led to less diversity in points of view being expressed.

Industrial fields and *organizational structures* in creative industries tend to be structured in one of three ways. There may be many small competing firms producing a diversity of products, a few vertically integrated oligarchical firms that mass produce a few standardized products, or a more open system of oligarches with niche-market-targeted divisions plus a large number of small specialty service and market-development firms, where the former produce the most lucrative products, while the latter produce the most innovative (Negus 1999; Caves 2000).

Occupational careers develop in each cultural field. The distribution of creative, craft, functionary, and entrepreneurial occupations is determined largely by a field's structure, which in turn helps determine the symbolic output. Careers tend to be chaotic and foster cultural innovation, as creative people build careers by starting from the margins of existing professions and conventions (Becker 1982; Grazian 2003).

Markets are constructed by producers to render the welter of consumer tastes comprehensible. Once consumer tastes are reified as a market, those in the field tailor their actions

to create cultural goods like those currently most popular as measured with tools devised by producers (Turow 1992; Caves 2000).

The production perspective has proved a useful model for organizing ideas and research in five areas where the production of culture is itself not consciously sought. First, it has spawned the *culture industries* model in academic management research and become the prime model of post-bureaucratic organization. Second, studies of the *autoproduction* of culture show that people produce identities and lifestyles for themselves from elements of traditional and mass-mediated symbols. Third, studies show that *cultural omnivorousness* is replacing highbrow snobbery as people show their high status by consuming not only the fine arts but also appreciating many, if not all, forms of popular culture. Fourth, studies focused on *resistance and appropriation* show how young people take the products tendered to them by the culture industries and recombine them in unique ways to show their resistance to the dominant culture and to give expression to their own identities. Fifth, much of what is taken to be subcultural resistance is actually *fabricated* by the *consumer industry*. The contrast between the artifice of manufacture and the fan's experience of authenticity is arguably the most important unresolved paradox of cultural sociology (Negus 1999; Peterson & Anand 2004).

SEE ALSO: Art Worlds; Culture; Culture Industries; Popular Culture

REFERENCES AND SUGGESTED READINGS

Becker, H. S. (1982) *Art Worlds*. University of California Press, Berkeley.

Caves, R. E. (2000) *Creative Industries*. Harvard University Press, Cambridge, MA.

Crane, D. (1992) *The Production of Culture*. Sage, Newbury Park, CA.

DiMaggio, P. (2000) The Production of Scientific Change. *Poetics* 28: 107–36.

Goodall, H. (2000) *Big Bangs: Five Discoveries that Changed Musical History*. Chatto & Windus, London.

Grazian, D. (2003) *Blue Chicago: Authenticity in Blues Clubs*. University of Chicago Press, Chicago.

Negus, K. (1999) *Music Genres and Corporate Structures*. Routledge, London.

Peterson, R. A. (Ed.) (1976) *The Production of Culture*. Sage, Beverly Hills, CA.

Peterson, R. A. (1979) Revitalizing the Culture Concept. *Annual Review of Sociology* 5: 137–66.

Peterson, R. A. & Anand, N. (2004) The Production of Culture Perspective. *Annual Review of Sociology* 30: 311–34.

Turow, J. (1992) *Media Systems in Society*. Longman, White Plains, NY.

Waksman, S. (1999) *Instruments of Desire: The Electric Guitar and the Shaping of Musical Experience*. Harvard University Press Cambridge, MA.

culture, social movements and

Rhys H. Williams

Culture is the symbolic and expressive dimensions of social life. This includes sets of symbols such as language, intangible, abstract "mental products" such as ideas, beliefs, values, and identity, and the meanings given to material objects such as clothing, decorations, art objects, buildings, and the like.

Social movements are sustained, more or less organized attempts at change. They may try to change individuals, group behaviors, government policies, or society's cultural understandings. Social movements are generally thought to last longer and be more organized than a mob or a crowd, but are not as established or institutionalized as a political party or lobbying group.

Sociologists have studied culture and social movements with three basic sets of questions. First, many accounts of social movement emergence posit their basic causes as cultural. Second, when studying the processes and dynamics that allow social movements to function and maintain themselves, analysts have focused on cultural factors such as collective identity, ideological claims, emotions, and internal group norms, rituals, and practices. Third, scholars who study the impact that movements have on society have often focused on the cultural changes that are their goals for action (cf. Johnston & Klandermans 1995).

MOVEMENT EMERGENCE

Most of the sociological study of social movements since the end of World War II has sought to ascertain why social movements emerge. One way to categorize the answers is whether they put the basic cause of movement emergence in the social structural dimensions of society or in societal and group culture. Social structural causes include changing economic fortunes of particular classes, the formal political systems of society, or the resources (such as money, members, and organizations) that a group can mobilize in order to mount collective action. Cultural answers to the question of movement emergence have generally fallen within one of two categories: changes in the national or societal culture or changes in group subculture among those people involved in a social movement.

For example, both Gurr (1970) and Melucci (1989) basically claim that movements develop because large-scale social and cultural changes result in a collective social psychological anomie or alienation among people experiencing these changes. Various types of cultural "strain" lead to breakdowns in normal routines and result in disruptive and innovative collective actions. European-based "new social movements" of the 1970s and 1980s, such as the Greens, were theorized as the cultural response to late capitalism's elevation of "lifestyle" concerns over redistributive economic politics (Scott 1990). Middle-class cultural movements replaced labor as central collective actors. A more specific analysis of the role of group culture was Gusfield's (1986) thesis that the US Prohibition Movement was led by people concerned about their declining social status. Their movement was a "symbolic crusade" to restore their cultural prestige.

At a more micro-level perspective, scholars have focused on the language and "framing" work done by movement leaders. Analysts argue that many groups have the potential for collective action, but it takes the articulation of an ideology and a sense of collective identity for this potential to turn into an actual movement. Movements are thus "constructed" by the frames of movement leaders, who convince people to engage in collective action. Collective action frames interpret people's life situations, including such emotions as the anger and fear they may feel, by articulating them as grievances against an unjust system or enemy. Frames also tell people how they might change such situations, and try to convince them their own involvement will make a difference (see Benford & Snow 2000).

In all of these examples, it is something in culture – changes in the culture of a particular group, changes in the larger culture, or the use of cultural objects such as rhetoric, ideology, and identity – that is responsible for causing a social movement to emerge.

MOVEMENT DYNAMICS

Once a social movement has emerged, it needs to sustain collective action through mobilizing people repeatedly to action. This involves both cultural objects and processes that work cognitively, emotionally, and morally. Movement ideology is composed of language and non-textual symbols directed at both movement members and the society the movement is trying to persuade. Other dimensions of culture, such as collective identity, group practices, and shared emotions and narratives, help people who are mobilized stay committed to their movement and their cause.

Social movements use ideological claims and symbolic messages to make their case for social change (Williams 1996; Platt & Williams 2002). Sometimes ideology is a straightforward articulation of the ideas that motivate the movement and include the visions of how society might be different. For example, Students for a Democratic Society drafted the *Port Huron Statement* that gave their rationale for action; similarly, Marx and Engel's *Communist Manifesto* was the ideological base for the international communist movement's plans for social change.

Movements experience some limitations in the ideological claims they can make (Williams 1995). While activists are free to formulate any argument they choose, many claims will not be effective in particular contexts. There is a "cultural repertoire" that puts boundaries on what a given society or historical period will consider legitimate ideas. These repertoires develop through the interaction of challenger claims and the reigning hegemonic ideology (Steinberg 1995). Movements face the challenge of articulating innovative calls for change, while using ideological claims and symbolic messages that are largely within the boundaries of the legitimate.

Movements' ideological messages are often reduced to easily remembered slogans, such as "Make Love, Not War," "God is Pro-Life," or "No Blood for Oil." These slogans are a shorthand that is only effective when the movement's fuller ideology is well enough known that audiences can fill in the potential ambiguity in content (e.g., a San Francisco bumper sticker, "I own a dog and I vote," only makes sense if one understands current land-use issues in the Bay Area).

Another method of communicating the content of movement claims is to reduce them further to pictures or non-textual figures. The pro-choice movement consistently uses a drawing of a coat hanger with a line through it to symbolize the dangers of illegal abortions. Christian right organizations distribute bumper stickers with the word "vote" in which the "t" is elongated into a cross. Communist movements have used red stars historically, while white supremacist groups in the US and Europe resurrect the Nazi swastika. Non-textual symbols provide even less information about specific issues, and yet make even broader political and social claims. They are often ambiguous enough that multiple groups use them, as in the Vietnam War era in the US when counterculture protesters stitched American flags on to the backs of their blue-jean jackets at the same time that pro-war blue-collar workers were putting American flag decals on their hard hats. In such cases, the ideological message was not readable directly from the symbol used, but could only be understood within the context of a general presentation of self.

Movements must create and sustain a collective identity (e.g., Polletta & Jasper 2001). That is, people must feel that they share important characteristics with others in the movement, and that this identity is important enough to promote or protect through action. So, while slogans and non-textual symbols articulate a social movement's ideas, the individuals and groups who display them are also making a statement about their personal and social identity. Symbolic displays mark those using them as part of a particular movement, and encapsulate their basic attitudes and values.

The creation and nurturance of a shared collective identity produces a sense of "we-ness," in such a way that it can become the basis for action. People may identify themselves as the victims of an injustice, experience anger or determination as a result of this, and organize to combat the injustice. Other times, the "we" becomes people who hold a certain set of values or interests (such as preserving wilderness areas) and feel both motivated and obligated to act. Sometimes the "we" seems obvious, as when it is built on a longstanding ethnic or religious identity.

Collective identity helps mobilize and sustain a movement (Fantasia 1988; Nepstad 2004). People must be willing to continue to contribute time and energy, and perhaps withstand risk, through both victories and setbacks. Spirits must be kept up, shared identities must be reaffirmed, and group solidarity must be cultivated. Songs, slogans, a particularized vocabulary, items of clothing or grooming, flags or pennants, all can contribute to this process – letting fellow movement members know who one is, and distinguishing movement "members" from others. Narratives and stories allow group members to frame a shared history and align their experiences, motives, emotions, and identities (Davis 2002).

Another dimension of movement culture is the discourse and practices used among movement members in the processes of internal debate, decision-making, and interpersonal interaction. "Backstage" arguments among movement members are connected to the public ideology movements articulate, but they are often not identical (Kubal 1998). They may be dress rehearsals for later public positions, they may be quarrels among factions vying for control of the group's message (Benford 1993), and they may be jokes, rationales, or beliefs purposely kept from public view. Movement members develop norms of etiquette (Polletta 2002) or styles of discourse (Hart 2001) that govern what types of arguments are allowed within group meetings, what types of relationships are considered the model for action, and what types of people movement members should want to try to be. These are cultural rules of action that help shape movement ideological

claims, group strategic decisions, and public collective identity.

MOVEMENT IMPACT

Almost all social movements have a variety of goals. Many want to change laws, or enact policy changes within institutions such as schools, churches, or hospitals. But many movements also seek changes in their wider societal culture (Epstein 1991; D'Anjou 1996). For example, the gay and lesbian liberation movement wants policy changes that will end discrimination against gays and lesbians, but it also wants to change the cultural values associated with homosexual orientations. Similarly, the women's movement in the US and globally has worked at combating stereotypes about women (Naples & Desai 2002), while the vegetarian movement has tried to change people's ideas (as well as habits) about food and non-human animals (Maurer 2002). The Christian Right has sometimes been interested almost exclusively in symbolic change, as when it advocates putting the 10 Commandments in government buildings. Movement groups are often particularly interested in creating "activists"; that is, the change in which they are most interested is in the set of personal and collective identities found within groups of people (Lichterman 1996). Helping to transform individuals and groups into people who continue to agitate for sociocultural change is itself a form of cultural impact.

SEE ALSO: Collective Identity; Culture; Framing and Social Movements; Ideology; New Social Movement Theory; Social Change; Social Movements; Social Movements, Strain and Breakdown Theories of

REFERENCES AND SUGGESTED READINGS

Benford, R. D. (1993) Frame Disputes Within the Nuclear Disarmament Movement. *Social Forces* 71: 677–701.

Benford, R. D. & Snow, D. A. (2000) Framing Process and Social Movements: An Overview and Assessment. *Annual Review of Sociology* 26: 611–39.

D' Anjou, L. (1996) *Social Movements and Cultural Change*. Aldine de Gruyter, New York.

Davis, J. E. (Ed.) (2002) *Stories of Change: Narrative and Social Movements*. SUNY Press, Albany, NY.

Epstein, B. (1991) *Political Protest and Cultural Revolution: Nonviolent Direct Action in the 1970s and 1980s*. University of California Press, Berkeley.

Fantasia, R. (1988) *Cultures of Solidarity: Consciousness, Action, and Contemporary American Workers*. University of California Press, Berkeley.

Gurr, T. (1970) *Why Men Rebel*. Princeton University Press, Princeton.

Gusfield, J. (1986) *Symbolic Crusade*, 2nd edn. University of Illinois Press, Urbana.

Hart, S. (2001) *The Cultural Dilemmas of Progressive Politics*. University of Chicago Press, Chicago.

Johnston, H. & Klandermans, B. (Eds.) (1995) *Social Movements and Culture*. University of Minnesota Press, Minneapolis.

Kubal, T. J. (1998) The Presentation of the Political Self: Culture, Mobilization, and the Construction of Collective Action Frames. *Sociological Quarterly* 39: 539–54.

Lichterman, P. (1996) *The Search for Political Community*. Cambridge University Press, New York.

Maurer, D. (2002) *Vegetarianism: Movement or Moment?* Temple University Press, Philadelphia.

Melucci, A. (1989) *Nomads of the Present*. Temple University Press, Philadelphia.

Naples, N. & Desai, M. (Eds.) (2002) *Women's Activism and Globalization*. Routledge, New York.

Nepstad, S. E. (2004) *Convictions of the Soul*. Oxford University Press, New York.

Platt, G. M. & Williams, R. H. (2002) Ideological Language and Social Movement Mobilization: A Sociolinguistic Analysis of Segregationists' Ideologies. *Sociological Theory* 20: 328–59.

Polletta, F. (2002) *Freedom is an Endless Meeting*. University of Chicago Press, Chicago.

Polletta, F. & Jasper, J. M. (2001) Collective Identity and Social Movements. *Annual Review of Sociology* 27: 283–305.

Scott, A. (1990) *Ideology and the New Social Movements*. Unwin Hyman, London.

Steinberg, M. (1995) The Roar of the Crowd: Repertoires of Discourse and Collective Action Among the Spitalfield Silk Weavers in 19th-Century London. In: Traugott, M. (Ed.), *Repertoires and Cycles of Collective Action*. Duke University Press, Durham, NC, pp. 57–88.

Williams, R. H. (1995) Constructing the Public Good: Social Movements and Cultural Resources. *Social Problems* 42: 124–44.

Williams, R. H. (1996) Religion as Political Resource: Culture or Ideology? *Journal for the Scientific Study of Religion* 35: 368–78.

culture, the state and

Chandra Mukerji

Studies of culture and the state focus on a range of relationships between modern political regimes and patterns of symbolic and material life. They reveal the diverse ways that power works through culture, and provide means for a better understanding of how power is accumulated, organized, and deployed in or around state systems.

Much work in this subfield takes nationalism to be the fundamental culture of states, but most scholars working in this tradition do not make the mistake of treating national cultures as natural kinds. They try instead to understand how the processes involved in developing and shaping state power since the nineteenth century have generated distinctive national forms of political culture. Sociologists studying nationalism and its development have revealed the cultural techniques used in the creation of nationalist movements and identities. They have investigated the use of propaganda, the arts, gender relations, sexuality, storytelling, engineering, dress, and the media to establish taken-for-granted connections between populations and their governments.

Other scholars interested in culture and states have examined political processes like voting, policymaking, public advocacy, court procedures, and the use of violence, considering these activities as cultural performances or narrative devices, and following the complex rituals by which power is both exercised and legitimated. Among the students of American culture, there has also been broad interest in the moral dimensions of political participation and the practices of political activists. And Europeans have written with insight and precision about the cultures of bureaucracies, economic institutions, and educational systems that have helped to shape state-based political life and national identities.

Studies of culture and the state in the US surprisingly had methodological roots in urban sociology, particularly work of the Chicago School with its fundamental interest in political culture. Fieldwork studies of urban political life and social movements made their cultural forms evident. Scholars schooled in this tradition but caught up in the social activism and analytical Marxism of the 1960s and 1970s began to broaden the area of political concern, asking questions not only about cities but also about states and how they gain or lose authority. They were given tools for their analyses of politics by European sociologists such as members of the British School of Cultural Studies, and the French scholars working with Pierre Bourdieu. These analysts showed how seemingly innocent cultural practices, particularly education and popular culture, had effects on stratification and national identity. Unfortunately, scholars working in these schools generalized about "culture" from their own national traditions, as though there were no cultural differences or different uses of culture among states. This lack of attention to states and culture was criticized by Michele Lamont, and led to her work with Laurent Thevenot to compare class cultures in France and the US (Lamont & Thevenot 2000).

While techniques for analyzing political culture were developing among sociologists of culture in the mid-twentieth century, theories of the state became a major area of sociological concern. This was motivated by some of the same historical conditions: the social activism of the 1960s and 1970s. By doing comparative research across countries and historical periods, students of the state hoped to see when and why political regimes failed or endured. Most of the work in the field was strictly structuralist, and explicitly so. Guided by the traditional Marxist theory of history, these scholars assumed that the political fates of regimes would be a consequence of structural processes, and dismissed culture and ideology as objects of analysis. Methodologically, they used the extant historical accounts of states and empires to compare their trajectories of power. Where they found states (as they often did) to be "semi-autonomous," they could have asked questions about culture, but did not. Only in the last decade has there been a turn toward culture by theorists of the state. The results have been impressive, if different in method and implication. Tilly's (2003) elegant analysis of violence has revealed the unclear border between legitimate and illegitimate forms of collective violence. Charrad's (2001) award-winning study

of the political cultures of gender in North African countries has shown how differently a common religion could be portrayed and used in political processes of state building.

Given the fundamental differences in theoretical orientation and methodology between macrosociology of state systems and microsociology of culture, it seemed unlikely between 1960 and 1990 that sociologists would have considered seriously cultural studies of states. But outside sociology, there were shifts in intellectual culture that pushed sociologists in this direction. One was strong interest in comparative cultural studies of states among anthropologists and historians who wrote influential pieces about the political cultures of these systems. Their empirical work made sense to sociologists working with similar methods and interested in comparable concerns. The other influence was more powerful and disconcerting to sociologists: the rapidly growing interdisciplinary interest in cultural studies and the writings of Foucault. Foucault argued that power did not primarily reside in institutions like the state, but rather in the processes of social classification that simultaneously organized knowledge and social relations.

Structural analyses like those developed by historical sociologists of the state, from this perspective, were fundamentally misguided. Even power (as legitimate violence) was not a monopoly of armies and police systems, but was a part of the discursive terrain that aligned power with knowledge. Cultural studies begged the question of whether there were any distinctive kinds of powers that states could wield to their advantage. It was a good question, so rather than destroying all efforts to study states, poststructuralism simply sent sociologists back to the historical record to see what could be learned about the cultural powers of states.

Foucault's early work on hospitals, clinics, and prisons had been easily folded into the sociology of deviance. But later poststructuralists' mantra-like invocation of class, gender, and race and treatment of complex cultures as texts were more grating to sociologists. They seemed to provide humanists with prefabricated versions of social analysis, making even constructivist sociologists weary of this approach to culture. Some scholars in the field shared Foucault's interest in the politics of language and labeling, but even these often remained advocates of fieldwork methods and more local ways of understanding stratification and power.

Studying culture, then, seemed more important than before, but the question was how to improve sociological analysis. Many sociologists simply did fieldwork to address questions raised by poststructuralists. But a substantial number of new works in historical sociology appeared, using subjects in political culture to address the workings of power itself. They rejected Foucault's aversion to traditional politics as an object of study, but embraced his project of seeking out neglected cultural practices of power. Michael Schudson (1992) and Barry Schwartz (2000) considered the powers of collective memory, while Joseph Gusfield (1981) and Robin Wagner-Pacifici (1986) wrote on the performative aspects of political events. Meanwhile, Chandra Mukerji (1997) focused on material culture and the built environment, the ways that state power could be stabilized and materialized in maps, styles of dress, and places themselves.

In the 1990s, perhaps in response to the Reagan years in American politics, many new works on culture and the state appeared, focusing on nationalism, fascism, and the Holocaust. The question of why fascism gained power in the mid-twentieth century had dominated critical theory and neo-Marxism, bringing cultural issues to the heart of Marxist thought. Now the subject was being reexamined, using the tools of cultural sociology to explain the seductions of political imagery and identities that supported genocide (Berezin 1997; Falasca-Zamponi 1997).

In the face of theoretical challenges from cultural studies and methodological ones from anthropology and history, sociologists interested in culture and the state have become better scholars. The push to produce a more richly nuanced cultural history of states has made it harder simply to skim off the secondary literature. At the same time, sociological understandings of states have matured, too. They are not automatically reduced to apparatuses (as structures) or nations (as a natural counterpart to states). They are analyzed as places of power, engineered to be politically identifiable

and materially managed territories, and sites of performances of power, linking people to places. States in the new sociology of culture are simultaneously imagined communities, narratively organized sets of social relations, socially sanctioned ways of using the land, and elements in webs of violence and control. They exist as social institutions but exercise power not as some passive apparatus, but rather through politically nuanced and intentional practices of cultural domination through design.

SEE ALSO: Bourdieu, Pierre; Built Environment; Collective Memory; Critical Theory/ Frankfurt School; Cultural Reproduction; Cultural Studies; Cultural Studies, British; Diaspora; Foucault, Michel; Ideological Hegemony; Media and Nationalism

REFERENCES AND SUGGESTED READINGS

Berezin, M. (1997) *Making of the Fascist Self.* Cornell University Press, Ithaca.
Charrad, M. (2001) *States and Women's Rights in the Making of Postcolonial Tunisia, Algeria, and Morocco.* University of California Press, Berkeley and Los Angeles.
Falasca-Zamponi, S. (1997) *Fascist Spectacle: The Aesthetics of Power in Mussolini's Italy.* University of California Press, Berkeley.
Gusfield, J. (1981) *The Culture of Public Problems.* University of Chicago Press, Chicago.
Lamont, M. & Thevenot, L. (2000) *Rethinking Comparative Cultural Sociology.* Cambridge University Press, Cambridge.
Mukerji, C. (1997) *Territorial Ambitions and the Gardens of Versailles.* Cambridge University Press, Cambridge.
Patterson, O. (1998) *Rituals of Blood.* Civitas, Washington, DC.
Schudson, M. (1992) *Watergate in American Memory.* Basic Books, New York.
Schwartz, B. (2000) *Abraham Lincoln and the Forge of National Memory.* University of Chicago Press, Chicago.
Tilly, C. (2003) *The Politics of Collective Violence.* Cambridge University Press, Cambridge.
Wagner-Pacifici, R. (1986) *Moro Morality Play: Terrorism as Social Drama.* University of Chicago Press, Chicago.

cybercrime

Samuel Nunn

Cybercrime refers to the commission of criminal acts that target computers, use computers as an instrumentality to traditional crimes, or transmit illegal information using computer networks. One continuing form of cybercrime targets computers. So-called hackers and crackers, through various means, gain access to closed computer networks in order to vandalize or otherwise damage databases or network software by introducing computer viruses or "denial of service" attacks. Denial of service refers to computer viruses or worms that create an overabundance of computer transactions, to the extent that entire systems will slow significantly or shut down completely.

Cybercrime comes in many guises. The objective of many early cybercrimes involving computer intrusions was to destroy data or interrupt the flow of computerized services. As the cybercrime concept evolved, it began to include similar break-ins to protected computer networks, but instead of mischievous vandalism, theft and material gain were the motivation. Common cybercrimes now include the theft and subsequent sale or counterfeiting of debit and credit card numbers from the protected databases of private financial firms, as well as larceny involving intellectual property such as computer software, movies, digital videos, recorded music, or other items. The commission and camouflage of other traditional crimes such as child pornography are considered cybercrimes because of the widespread use of computer networks, digital photography, electronic mail, and encryption techniques to support the operation of globalized schemes. "Cyberstalking" involves the use of electronic communications to transmit threats of personal violence or kidnapping. The increasing creativity of terrorist attacks during the 1993–2004 period created the term "cyberterrorism" to describe criminal acts involving interference with the computer networks and automated operations of federally defined critical infrastructure such as banking, aviation, finance, power, gas, petroleum, transportation, and water networks.

As with other offenses, cybercrime involves the three traditional elements of crime: *actus reus*, *mens rea*, and concurrence. The *actus reus* usually involves the illegal entrance into protected computer systems and subsequent actions taken against or in pursuit of electronic properties. The *mens rea* of cybercrime is more complex. Destructive, larcenous, and other criminal acts using computerized resources are typically accompanied by varied motivations including power, greed, dominance, revenge, or satisfaction of prurient interest. Concurrence is also a complicated aspect of cybercrime. Many cybercrimes, such as computer break-ins and intellectual property theft, might not be detected for long periods of time. Computer-assisted identity theft might go on for months before victims become aware a crime has occurred.

The most common forms of cybercrime are credit or bank card fraud, child pornography, unauthorized access to a computer, identity theft, and cyberstalking. In the US, many cybercrimes are federal offenses because they involve use of computer networks that cross interstate boundaries. By 2004, the US criminal code included approximately two dozen chapters devoted to aspects of cybercrime. It is common for major law enforcement agencies to form computer forensics and other specialized squads to investigate cybercrime. Similar organizational strategies have been followed by international police agencies such as Interpol and Europol.

Criminal justice agencies face several challenges in their fight against cybercrime. Because computer networks are globalized, many cybercrimes raise questions regarding which jurisdictions have responsibility for investigation. Further, many cybercrimes are perpetrated by single individuals or small groups that nonetheless affect the computers or electronic property of hundreds or thousands of persons or organizations located in many different locales across the globe. For any single victim, the costs of these cybercrimes are often too low to warrant reporting formally, but taken in sum the costs of the crimes for all victims can be massive. Effective enforcement and adjudication of cybercrime law often requires interjurisdictional task forces, including cross-national teams to conduct simultaneous investigations and arrests in different countries across many different time zones.

SEE ALSO: Consumption and the Internet; Crime; Crime, White-Collar; Criminal Justice System; Internet; Measuring Crime

REFERENCES AND SUGGESTED READINGS

Casey, E. (2000) *Digital Evidence and Computer Crime: Forensic Science, Computers, and the Internet.* Academic Press, San Diego.
Denning, D. (1999) *Information Warfare and Security.* Addison-Wesley, Reading, MA.
Drucker, S. J. & Gumpert, G. (2000) Cybercrime and Punishment. *Critical Studies in Media Communications* 17(2): 133–58.
Wall, D. S. (2005) The Internet as a Conduit for Criminal Activity. In: Pattavina, A. (Ed.), *Information Technology and the Criminal Justice System.* Sage, Thousand Oaks, CA.

cyberculture

David Bell

A neologism derived from a neologism, cyberculture welds together the "cyber-" from cyberspace with "culture." It is important to understand what happens when cyber- and culture are brought together, and in order to work toward that understanding we need to begin by saying a few words about cyberspace (and some related things). The term cyberspace was famously coined by cyberpunk novelist William Gibson in his 1984 novel *Neuromancer*, to describe the imaginary "datascape" which his characters entered by "jacking in" – connecting their consciousness directly to networked computers. The well-known and often-quoted formulation in *Neuromancer* runs like this:

> Cyberspace. A consensual hallucination experienced daily by millions of legitimate operators. ... A graphic representation of data abstracted from the banks of every computer in the human system. Unthinkable complexity. Lines of light ranged in the nonspace of the mind, clusters and constellations of data. Like city lights, receding. (Gibson 1984: 67)

This vivid description offered a powerful fictional portent for the future, a future of unthinkable complexity and constellations of data. However, the computing science realities of what was then emerging as cyberspace were little known to Gibson; nevertheless, the term and the way cyberspace was depicted in *Neuromancer* have had a profound influence upon its development and its representation – an influence Gibson did not foresee when he cobbled the word together. As he put it:

> Assembled word *cyberspace* from small and readily available components of language. Neologic spasm: the primal act of pop poetics. Preceded any concept whatever. Slick and hollow – awaiting received meaning. All I did: folded words as taught. Now other words accrete in the interstices. (Gibson 1991: 27)

Other words have indeed accreted in the interstices of Gibson's cyberspace – including cyberculture. Moreover, cyberspace came to be the preferred term for scholars writing about particular configurations of media and communications technologies, most especially the Internet (though others prefer an expanded definition that encompasses other realms of digital technology and digital culture; see Bell 2001). Cyberspace became a hot topic across a range of academic disciplines in the 1990s, as more and more researchers turned their attention to the many ways that the Internet was transforming ever greater parts of people's lives. Through the course of the 1990s, research and writing on cyberspace began to branch and specialize, and there was something of a publishing boom. Aside from computer science research, a large body of work emerged which focused on the social and cultural aspects of cyberspace. These "cyberspace studies" have morphed over time, particularly as scholars have brought ideas and theories from other disciplines – psychology, sociology, cultural studies, or geography, for instance – into contact with the Internet and related technologies.

In terms of the subject area we might call "cyberculture studies," David Silver (2000) has tracked the development of cyberculture as a field of study across the 1990s, identifying three distinct phases. His typology offers a useful way of introducing the trajectory of these diverse studies in this important decade, during which the foundations of cyberculture studies were solidified. Silver names the first substantive phase "popular cyberculture," characterized by journalistic writing, personal accounts of being online, popular history publications about the development of the Internet, and large numbers of "how to" books helping people make use of computers and networks. Accounts from this phase tend to be descriptive, often experiential, but are split in terms of how their authors view the impacts that the Internet is having on people's lives. At the most extreme ends of this divide are what Silver calls techno-futurist writings, which tend to be overwhelmingly optimistic, even utopian, about the promises of online life. Journalists writing in new US magazines like *Wired* or *Mondo 2000* typify technofuturism for Silver, as do writers describing cyberspace as a new frontier ripe for pioneers to colonize (see, e.g., Rheingold 1993). Writing from a polar-opposite, profoundly dystopian, perspective are the "Neo-Luddites," who see in cyberspace multiple threats to human existence (see, e.g., Sale 1995). Of course, most writing during this phase falls somewhere in between these "dystopian rants or utopian raves" (Silver 2000: 20). Nevertheless, this fundamental binary divide – is cyberspace good or bad? – continues to structure many scholars' thinking; indeed, later periods in the development of cyberculture studies revisit this in their own terms, and rants and raves continue to appear from both sides. However, as the field of study has evolved, it has refined both the theoretical and methodological tools brought to analyze the Internet, as well as focusing in on more specific domains and effects of cyberspace.

The second phase of cyberculture scholarship is called by Silver simply "cyberculture studies," in recognition of a shift away from populist accounts (though these continue to be published) toward a more scholarly approach to understanding the Internet. Crucially, two major focuses were brought center-stage in this phase, both of which are concerned with the relationship between online and offline life: studies of community and studies of identity. Here we see one way in which cyber- and culture are brought together: by exploring how some of the key concerns of cultural studies (such as identity or community) are transformed in cyberspace. Silver rightly identifies

the *ur-texts* here as Rheingold's *The Virtual Community* (1993) and Turkle's *Life on the Screen* (1995) – these are the "twin pillars" of second-phase cyberculture studies (Silver 2000: 23), hugely influential books whose impact can be felt to this day. Turkle's book is an important illustration of the second way that cyber- and culture are brought together in this phase: the use of cultural theory to think about cyberspace. In her exploration of online identity, Turkle draws heavily on psychoanalytic, poststructuralist, and postmodern theories of self-identity, which help her to understand how online identities are fractured and multiple. Other scholars also began to bring their own favorite theories and theorists into cyberspace, leading to a productive period in which cyberculture studies diversified: sociologists brought social network approaches to understanding online communities, for example, while geographers brought theories of space and place into contact with cyberspace and feminist scholars introduced ideas of cyberfeminism (see, e.g., Plant 1997; Crang et al. 1999; Smith & Kollock 1999). At the same time, there was also a diversification in terms of research methods used to study cyberculture, as researchers brought their own methodological traditions and innovations into cyberspace: qualitative and quantitative methods, linguistic and textual techniques, and so on.

Silver notes that studies produced in this phase tend to be more positive and optimistic about cyberspace, seeing productive new possibilities for identity and community online. However, many accounts rest on a problematic separation of online and offline (sometimes called "real life" or "real world") experiences – another dualism which continues to haunt many studies of cyberculture to this day. Nevertheless, this second phase marks a consolidation of academic cyberculture studies marked by diverse theories and methods, intersections with diverse disciplines, and a gathering momentum in terms of both volume and growing sophistication of published material. We could say that this phase marks the beginning of something of a discipline of cyberculture studies itself, in fact, as degree courses, conferences, and networks blossomed in academia.

In the latter part of the 1990s, a third phase is identified by Silver. This he labels "critical cyberculture studies." Marked by continuing growth and diversification, Silver tracks four themes which rose to dominance in this period (for an overview of the breadth of this phase, see Bell & Kennedy 2000). The first is in part a counter to the problematic online/offline split of phase two, and is concerned with contextualizing cyberspace and cyberculture, in terms of how economic, social, and cultural interactions occur simultaneously in cyberspace and in "real life." Empirical work bridging online and offline field sites – such as Miller and Slater's (2000) ethnographic study of Internet use in Trinidad – has been particularly important in bringing back together the two worlds split apart in earlier studies. Detailed empirical work has also performed a valuable hype-busting function, replacing the rants and raves of earlier phases with more balanced, empirically grounded studies.

The second theme of critical cyberculture studies picked out by Silver focuses on discursive constructions of cyberspace – the stories we tell about it. This means unpacking the ways that cyberspace is imagined and represented across a wide range of cultural texts, from cyberpunk novels and movies to Internet service providers' adverts or pop songs (see Bell 2001). It also involves exploring the dominant discourses via which the Internet is talked about, whether the frontier mythology mentioned earlier or the "gold rush" discourse that provoked and sustained the dot.com explosion. Thirdly, Silver notes an increasing emphasis on questions of access and inequality – another valuable dose of hype-busting, since it replaces the discourse of information freedom and the Internet's democratic "worldwideness" with studies highlighting patterns of uneven development, issues of marginalization, and barriers to access to technology at all levels, from the global to the individual. Access questions bring into focus the extent to which axes of social identity such as race, class, gender, and sexuality are either reproduced or challenged in cyberspace, with studies concluding both that cyberspace reinforces existing divides as well as bringing in new ones, and that it can provide space for new and productive kinds of identity work to take place (see, e.g., Nakamura 2002).

Finally, Silver notes an increase in studies exploring design and visual culture aspects of cyberspace, particularly around the idea of the interface: how cyberspace is represented to us on the screens of our computers – a neat return to Gibson's originary formulation. Work on interfaces has also returned to themes introduced in earlier phases, such as the role of web pages in expressing self-identity, and the role of participatory design in facilitating online communities. Crucially for Silver, critical cyberculture studies finally acknowledges the messy commingling of online and offline life and experience: "cyberculture is best comprehended as a series of negotiations that take place both online and off. … In the new millennium, it is the task of cyberculture scholars to acknowledge, reveal and critique these negotiations to better understand what takes place within the wires" (Silver 2000: 30).

Having described Silver's useful brief history of cyberculture studies, attention can now be turned to an essay which attempts to define a program for cultural studies of the Internet, Jonathan Sterne's "Thinking the Internet: Cultural Studies versus the Millennium" (1999). This is an important article in that it attempts to lay out a specifically cultural studies approach to cyberspace, therefore productively exemplifying Silver's critical cyberculture phase. It provides a road map of what cultural studies as a discipline uniquely brings to analysis of cyberspace, urging scholars to "move beyond the commonplaces and clichés of Internet scholarship and [to] reconceptualize it in intellectually challenging and politically vital terms" (Sterne 1999: 260). It is, perhaps, in the last part of that statement – about being politically vital – that Sterne's essay is most insightful; he reminds scholars of the deep political commitment at the heart of the cultural studies project, arguing that if it is (or should be) about anything, then cultural studies is about culture and power. Any critical study of the Internet should therefore have at its heart an analysis of culture and power since, as Poster (2001: 2) suggests, "without a concept of culture, the study of new media incorporates by default the culture of the dominant institutions in society" – the state and the market.

To advance his argument, Sterne places emphasis on the need to understand and critically analyze the politics of knowledge production (asking what is at stake in studying the

Internet, and how new knowledge of cyberspace can advance emancipatory politics), the need to be acutely aware of context (the manifold relationships between people, place, practices, and things), and the need to produce a theory of articulation (how things are connected together). Such a theory would have as its central concerns "(a) *what counts* in a cultural study of the Internet and (b) *how to think about* and represent the Internet" (Sterne 1999: 263, emphasis in original). Finally, and echoing points made earlier, Sterne reinforces the necessity of a commitment to theory as a way of finding new and more effective ways to describe and analyze cyberspace and cyberculture.

Making a point resonant with Silver's discussion of critical cyberculture studies, Sterne calls for a move beyond the simplistic online/offline (or virtual/real) split which has for so long impaired analyses of cyberspace, toward a conceptualization that emphasizes understanding the place of the Internet in everyday life. Equally importantly, Sterne argues for the need to reconnect the Internet to other media, and to techniques of analyzing other media. This is particularly crucial in the current period, given the increasing convergence of new (and old) media. As new digital devices such as MP3 players and palm pilots become more and more ubiquitous, and as existing media are repurposed for the digital age (mobile phones, for example), so the idea of separating out the Internet as an object of study becomes redundant. At the same time, the uses to which we may now put our computers – from listening to the radio to editing home movies to shopping – calls for a broader rethinking of what it is we are studying when we are studying cyberculture.

This last point is worth exploring in a bit more detail. Some researchers have suggested that we need to track the myriad sites where we encounter digital culture beyond the narrow emphasis on the computer screen: cyberspace exists in all kinds of places, from CGI-heavy movies to imaging technologies used in biomedicine (see Bell 2001). Moreover, the kinds of contact that we have with these new technologies is equally varied: we may be transformed into data and lodged in databases thanks to the manifold technologies of data collection that monitor our habits and routines (from our shopping practices to our workplace productivity);

equally, we may have particularly intimate relationships with devices that become part of our everyday lives, even part of our bodies – leading some scholars to theorize the body–technology interface by using ideas of the cyborg or the post-human (see Gray 1995; Badmington 2000).

Cyberculture must be about critically analyzing all of these sites, and the discourses and representations that surround them. In part that means attending to the mundane interactions we have with technologies such as word processors or console games; but it also requires an awareness of the cutting edge of new and future technologies, such as nanotechnology, artificial life, and artificial intelligence. To fully encompass all that cyberculture means is no easy task, therefore. While some scholars have called for junking the term cyberculture studies in favor of newer, more inclusive terms like web studies or new media studies (or even new media cultures; see Marshall 2004), others continue to see valuable mileage in working with and through cyberculture as a "contested and evolving discourse [whose] discussants include activists, politicians, computer geeks, social scientists, science fiction writers, digital artists, etc., all of whom are involved in the creation of new concepts and ideas" (Bell et al. 2004: xiii). To that end, the concept is still very much alive, indeed teeming with life, and we need the open, even promiscuous, approach to theory and method, as well as the political commitment, of critical cyberculture studies to continue to engage creatively and critically with the past, present, and future of cyberculture.

SEE ALSO: Consumption and the Internet; Cybercrime; Cybersexualities and Virtual Sexuality; Digital; Information Technology; Internet; Simulation and Virtuality

REFERENCES AND SUGGESTED READINGS

Badmington, N. (Ed.) (2000) *Posthumanism*. Palgrave, Basingstoke.

Bell, D. (2001) *An Introduction to Cybercultures*. Routledge, London.

Bell, D. & Kennedy, B. (Eds.) (2000) *The Cybercultures Reader*. Routledge, London.

Bell, D., Loader, B., Pleace, N., & Schular, D. (2004) *Cyberculture: The Key Concepts*. Routledge, London.

Crang, M., Crang, P., & May, J. (Eds.) (1999) *Virtual Geographies: Bodies, Space and Relations*. Routledge, London.

Gibson, W. (1984) *Neuromancer*. Grafton, London.

Gibson, W. (1991) Academy Leader. In: Benedikt, M. (Ed.), *Cyberspace: First Steps*. MIT Press, Cambridge, MA, pp. 27–30.

Gray, C. (Ed.) (1995) *The Cyborg Handbook*. Routledge, London.

Marshall, P. D. (2004) *New Media Cultures*. Arnold, London.

Miller, D. & Slater, D. (2000) *The Internet: An Ethnographic Approach*. Berg, Oxford.

Nakamura, L. (2002) *Cybertypes: Race, Ethnicity, and Identity on the Internet*. Routledge, London.

Plant, S. (1997) *Zeros + Ones: Digital Women + the New Technoculture*. 4th Estate, London.

Poster, M. (2001) *What's the Matter with the Internet?* University of Minnesota Press, Minneapolis.

Rheingold, H. (1993) *The Virtual Community: Homesteading on the Electronic Frontier*. Addison-Wesley, Reading, MA.

Sale, K. (1995) *Rebels Against the Future: The Luddites and their War on the Industrial Revolution – Lessons for the Computer Age*. Addison-Wesley, Reading, MA.

Silver, D. (2000) Looking Backwards, Looking Forwards: Cyberculture Studies, 1990–2000. In: Gauntlett, D. (Ed.), *Web.Studies: Rewiring Media Studies for the Digital Age*. Arnold, London, pp. 19–30.

Smith, M. & Kollock, P. (Eds.) (1999) *Communities in Cyberspace*. Routledge, London.

Sterne, J. (1999) Thinking the Internet: Cultural Studies versus the Millennium. In: Jones, S. (Ed.), *Doing Internet Research: Critical Issues and Methods for Examining the Net*. Sage, London, pp. 257–87.

Turkle, S. (1995) *Life on the Screen: Identity in the Age of the Internet*. Touchstone, New York.

cybersexualities and virtual sexuality

Ken Plummer

Just as when photography and film were first introduced they generated the pornographic photograph and film, so as soon as the newer information technologies appeared, an erotic world of cybersex and intimacy appeared alongside and embedded within it. New information technologies are used in ways that can facilitate new patterns of sexualities and intimacies. And this is no small world. Surfing the Internet gives access to a medium full of intimate words and images: from guidance pages on infertility (over a million sites on sperm banks), to sites engaged in bride-mail ordering; from images of the most "extreme" sexual fetishes ("Extreme" is indeed the name given to one such site), to access to potentially endless partners on email. The sheer range, number, and intense flow of unregulated intimacy and erotica of all kinds that becomes available at the press of a button could never have happened before in history.

These new technologies have generated multiple new forms of intimacy: sex messaging, sex chat rooms, sex news groups and bulletin boards, email discussion groups, camcorder sex, new forms of porn, access to relationships of all kinds, new social movement campaigns around sexuality, even so-called cyborg sex, teledildonics, virtual sex, and new approaches to the body and emergent "techno- identities" and "techno-cultures." Along with this a new language has emerged that mirrors new forms of sexualities: cyberporn, cyberqueer, cyberstalking, cyberrape, cybervictim, cybersex. Although such new forms can result in people meeting in real space for "real sex," there is also a great deal of masturbatory sex being generated through these media, as well as virtual sex taking place in these virtual spaces.

What this means is that in recent years many new sexual practices have unfolded along with an array of new issues. Sociologists are starting to provide critical ethnographic materials on their day-to-day workings, and are developing innovative theorizations of the whole field, clarifying and criticizing links to postmodern social theory and connecting these globally. Thus, Dennis Waskful in *Self Games and Body Play: Personhood in Online Chat and Cybersex* (2003) applies the theoretical work of Erving Goffman on self-management and the presentation of self in sexual communications online. Aaron Ben-Ze'ev has examined *Love Online* (2004), providing detailed accounts of how people meet online. Others have documented some of the pitfalls of cybersex – how it can generate infidelity, the growth and routinization of pornography, the development of sexual harassment online, and the growth of "sexual addiction" on the Internet (e.g., Maheu and Subotnik's *Infidelity on the Internet*, 2001, and Patrick Carnes's *In the Shadow of the Net*, 2001). On a wider level, sociologists have suggested that moral panics and hysteria gather around such sexualities. Most prominently, there is the concern with pedophilia on the net, and the ways in which young people can be misled, "groomed," and ultimately seduced and abused (see Philip Jenkin's *Beyond Tolerance: Child Porn Online*, 2001).

Cybsersexualities, then, are becoming increasingly an important means of sexual communication in the twenty-first century. And they have both positive and negative impacts. They reveal changing spaces and boundaries for new forms of sexualities and suggest key shifts in public/private dimensions. Through both webcams and the global nature of communications the old boundaries in sexual relations break down. The body starts to change its contours – no longer simply fixed and corporeal, but fluid, boundary-less and "virtual" (as with ideas of changing gender identity online raised by transgender activist Sandy Stone, 1995). Some have suggested that much of this leads to "posthumanism," a marker for the end of the human being as such and the discovery of tools for articulating the embodied human with intelligent machines (Hayles 1999; Hables Gray 2002). A new form of being – the cyborg – may be in the making. Yet we must be careful. Even though there are already new worlds of cybsersex, the posthuman, and the cyborg, and even though these will probably grow and develop, talk of cyberworlds still makes little sense to large populations that do not yet even have access to basic water, medication, shelter, phone lines, or computers, let alone the Internet.

Cybersex opens up political and moral questions that are emerging around the control and regulation of such sites. Hamelink (2000)

suggests a wide array of ethical issues in web issues. For instance, how decent it is it to post a picture of your ex-partner on the web? How far is it infidelity to find partners on the web while concealing this from one's "real" partner? Should children's access to cyberspace be guarded? What dangers threaten your children when they surf the Internet? What should we do if we want free speech in cyberspace but also want to rid the Internet of child pornography and racism? Do we need a new morality for virtual reality?

Cybersex is a new phenomenon raising many new questions. At the start of the twenty-first century, there are signs that sociologists are taking significant interest in it.

SEE ALSO: Body and Culture Sociology; Body and Sexuality; Consumption and the Internet; Internet; Posthumanism

REFERENCES AND SUGGESTED READINGS

Ben-Ze'Ev, A. (2004) *Love Online: Emotions on the Internet*. Cambridge University Press, Cambridge.

Calder, M. C. (Ed.) (2004) *Child Sexual Abuse and the Internet: Tackling the New Frontier*. Russell House, Lyme Regis.

Ellison, L. (2004) Cyberstalking. In: Wall, D. S. (Ed.), *Crime and the Internet*. Routledge, London.

Hables Gray, C. (2002) *Cyborg Citizen: Politics in the Posthuman Age*. Routledge, London.

Hamelink, C. (2000) *The Ethics of Cyberspace*. Sage, London.

Hayles, N. K. (1999) *How We Became Posthuman*. University of Chicago Press, Chicago.

Stone, S. (1995) *The War of Desire and Technology at the Close of the Mechanical Age*. MIT Press, Cambridge, MA.

Turkle, S. (2005) *Life on the Screen*. Simon & Schuster, New York.

Waskful, D. D. (Ed.) (2004) Net.SeXXX: Readings on Sex, Pornography and the Internet. *Digital Formations* 23.